Safe Boating, Travel, and Adventure

As we embark on another exciting year of delivering the 2025 editions of Waterway Guide into your hands and on your boat, I am reminded of the responsibility and privilege we share as stewards of these incredible resources. To continue to do our part for as long as we have (78 years), our mission has always been clear: promote safe boating, travel, and adventure on our waterways.

Boating is about more than just getting from point A to point B—it's about discovering the unique destinations that lie along the way. From bustling marinas to quiet, untouched coves, each stop is an opportunity to connect with new communities, experience local cultures, and uncover hidden gems. Whether it's the charm of a historic coastal town or the serenity of a secluded anchorage, every journey is enriched by the destinations you encounter. At Waterway Guide, we're committed to helping you find those special places that turn a routine trip into an unforgettable adventure.

We understand that every boater has their own way of accessing information, which is why we offer our content across a variety of platforms to suit your needs. Whether you prefer planning with the online Waterway Explorer, using the Waterway Guide App, or relying on our popular and cockpit-enhancing printed guides, we have you covered. You can also access extensive details on marinas, anchorages and points of interest through our presence on third-party navigation apps and chart plotters, ensuring that you have the information you need, wherever and whenever you need it.

As we look to the future, our dedication to this mission only grows stronger. We are committed to expanding our resources, enhancing our coverage, and leveraging the latest technology to continuously improve and deliver the content we provide. Whether through digital platforms, navigation apps, or chart plotters, we aim to deliver the highest standards of quality and reliability. Your safety, enjoyment, and the preservation of our waterways will always be at the forefront of everything we do.

Thank you for being a part of the Waterway Guide community. I encourage you to visit us and join the community at waterwayguide.com and look at everything we have available for you to plan, contribute, and connect with others. Together, we can continue to explore, protect, and celebrate the incredible waterways that connect us all.

Safe travels and happy boating!

Sincerely,
Graham Jones

Publisher, Waterway Guide

WATERWAY GUIDE MEDIA, LLC

P.O. Box 419, Midlothian, VA 23113

Phone: 800-233-3359
Fax: 888-951-7890
www.waterwayguide.com

BOOK SALES

waterwayguide.com/shipstore
Phone: 800-233-3359
Support@waterwayguide.com

Waterway Guide is published in the following editions—Bahamas, Southern, Florida Keys, Gulf Coast, Mid-Atlantic, Chesapeake Bay, Northern, Great Lakes Vol. 1, Great Lakes Vol. 2 and Cuba—by Waterway Guide Media, LLC © 2024. All rights reserved. Reproduction in whole or part or use of any data compilation without written permission from the publisher is prohibited. The title Waterway Guide is a registered trademark. ISBN Number: 979-8-9903530-7-7 for the Northern 2025 Edition. Purchase and use of Waterway Guide constitutes acceptance of the restrictions set forth herein.

Waterway Guide Media, LLC , the publisher of Waterway Guide (Guide), makes reasonable efforts to ensure the accuracy of the information in this Guide. However, Waterway Guide must rely on others over which it has no control for certain information. In addition, no book or guide is a substitute for good judgment, experience and firsthand knowledge. Therefore, Waterway Guide hereby gives notice that the charts, descriptions, and illustrations in this Guide are not to be used for navigation. The use of any navigational reference or description contained in the Guide is at the user's own risk. Inclusion in the Waterway Guide of marine facilities, services, restaurants and other information is for informational purposes only; no guarantee is provided as to the accuracy or current status of this information, nor does Waterway Guide Media, LLC endorse any of the facilities or services described herein.

Because Waterway Guide Media, LLC cannot and does not guarantee or warrant that the information in the Guide is complete or current, Waterway Guide Media, LLC disclaims all warranties, express or implied, relating to the information in any manner, including, without limitation, implied warranties of merchantability and fitness for a particular purpose.

Waterway Guide Media, LLC shall not be liable to the purchaser or any third party for any loss or injury allegedly caused, in whole or in part, by Waterway Guide Media , LLC and/or Waterway Guide (or the information contained therein) or for consequential, exemplary, incidental or special damages. Furthermore, in any event, Waterway Guide Media, LLC's liability, if any, shall never exceed the amount paid by the original purchaser for the directory.

To provide the most complete and accurate information, all facilities have been contacted within the past year. Although facility operators supplied this data, we cannot guarantee accuracy or assume responsibility for errors. Entrance and dockside soundings tend to fluctuate. Always approach marinas carefully. Reference numbers on spotting charts indicate marina locations. Aerial photos are for general overview only and are not to be used for navigation.

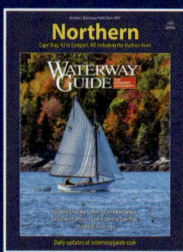

About the Cover:
Autumn cruising the east side of Damariscotta River. Photograph by Tabor Chichakly

F O U N D E D   I N   1 9 4 7

Publisher	**JEFF JONES** jjones@waterwayguide.com
President	**GRAHAM JONES** graham@waterwayguide.com
Editor-in-Chief	**ED TILLETT** etillett@waterwayguide.com
Operations Manager	**HEATHER SADEG** heather@waterwayguide.com
Managing Editor	**JANI PARKER** jparker@waterwayguide.com
Art Director/ Production Manager	**SCOTT MCCONNELL** scott@waterwayguide.com
Customer Success Manager	**KARLA LOCKE** karla@waterwayguide.com
Marketing/News Editor	**WHITNEY LAW** whitney@waterwayguide.com
Customer Support Specialists	**LINDA JERNIGAN** linda@waterwayguide.com
	ANNE EMERSON anne@waterwayguide.com
Data Support Specialist	**RILEY VAUGHN** riley@waterwayguide.com
Senior Advisor/ Skipper Bob Editor	**TED STEHLE** tstehle@waterwayguide.com
Software Engineer	**MIKE SCHWEFLER**
National Sales	**GRAHAM JONES** graham@waterwayguide.com
Sales & Marketing Manager	**KELLY CROCKETT** kelly@waterwayguide.com
Regional Account Executives	**KIM EATON** kim@waterwayguide.com
	MARLÈNE CROCKETT marlene@waterwayguide.com
	BOB BOWER bobby@waterwayguide.com

REGIONAL CRUISING EDITORS

SCOTT RICHARD BERG

MATT & LUCY CLAIBORNE

GINA L. CICOTELLO

EMILY KIZER

BOB SHERER (CONTRIBUTING EDITOR)

ONNE VAN DER WAL (CONTRIBUTING EDITOR)

CUBA CRUISING EDITORS

ADDISON CHAN

NIGEL CALDER (CONTRIBUTING EDITOR)

PRINTED IN CANADA

@Waterway Guide   @Waterway_Guide

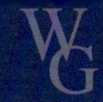

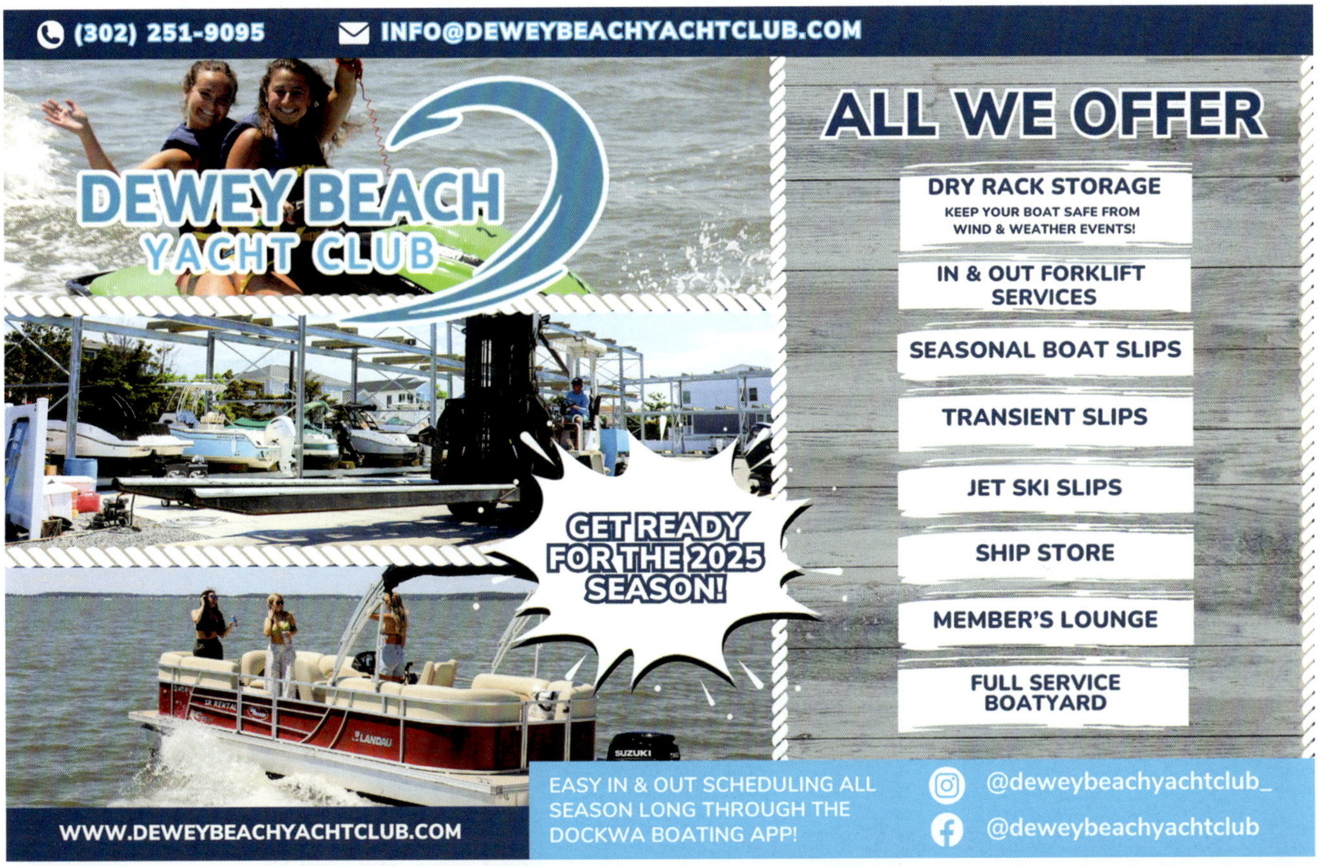
(302) 251-9095
INFO@DEWEYBEACHYACHTCLUB.COM
DEWEY BEACH
YACHT CLUB
ALL WE OFFER
DRY RACK STORAGE
KEEP YOUR BOAT SAFE FROM WIND & WEATHER EVENTS!
IN & OUT FORKLIFT SERVICES
SEASONAL BOAT SLIPS
TRANSIENT SLIPS
JET SKI SLIPS
SHIP STORE
MEMBER'S LOUNGE
FULL SERVICE BOATYARD
GET READY FOR THE 2025 SEASON!
WWW.DEWEYBEACHYACHTCLUB.COM
EASY IN & OUT SCHEDULING ALL SEASON LONG THROUGH THE DOCKWA BOATING APP!
@deweybeachyachtclub_
@deweybeachyachtclub

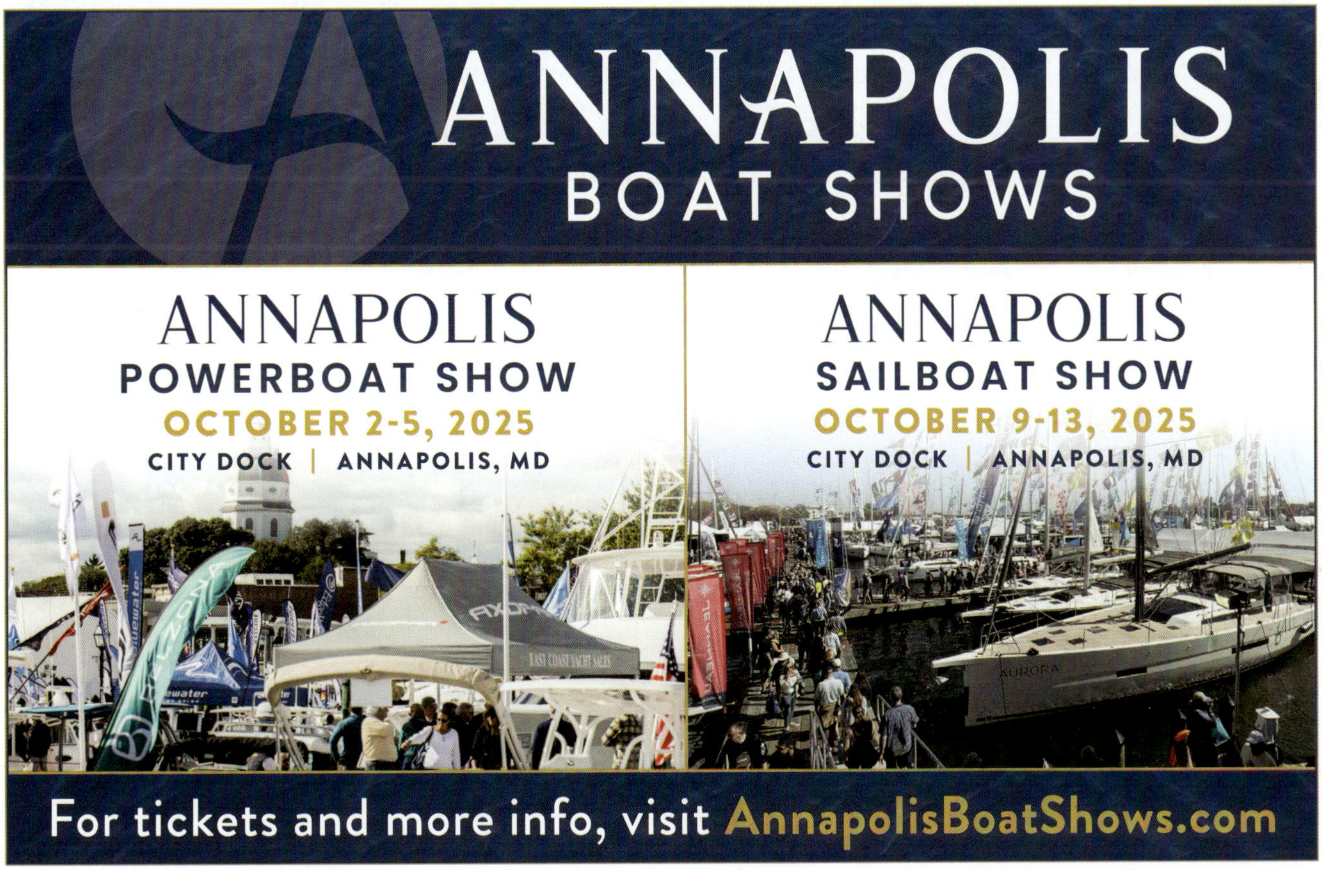
ANNAPOLIS
BOAT SHOWS
ANNAPOLIS
POWERBOAT SHOW
OCTOBER 2-5, 2025
CITY DOCK | ANNAPOLIS, MD
ANNAPOLIS
SAILBOAT SHOW
OCTOBER 9-13, 2025
CITY DOCK | ANNAPOLIS, MD
For tickets and more info, visit AnnapolisBoatShows.com

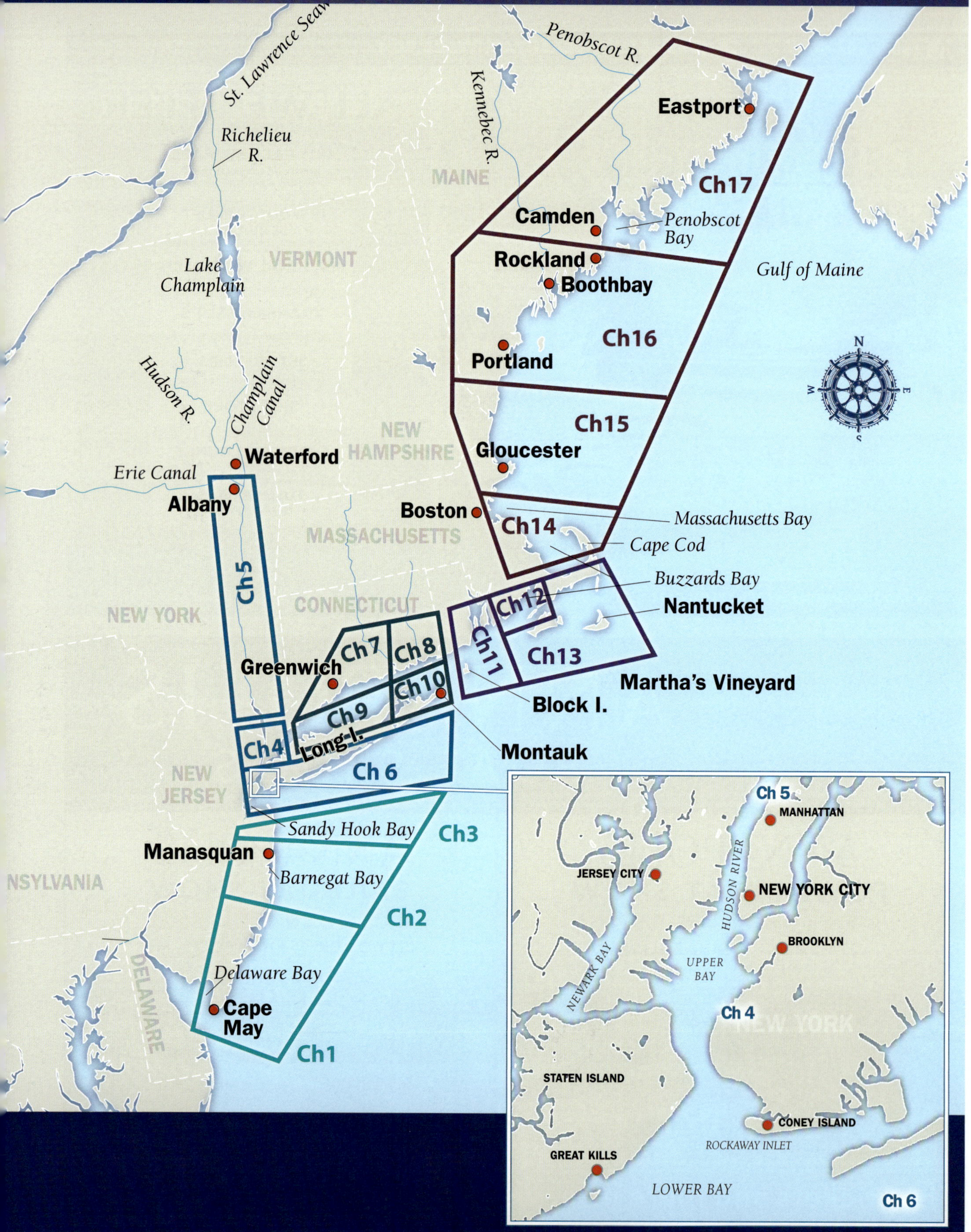

St. Lawrence Seaway

Richelieu R.

Penobscot R.

Kennebec R.

MAINE

Eastport

Ch17

Penobscot Bay

Camden

Rockland

Boothbay

Gulf of Maine

VERMONT

Lake Champlain

Ch16

Hudson R.

Champlain Canal

Ch15

Portland

NEW HAMPSHIRE

Waterford

Erie Canal

Gloucester

Albany

MASSACHUSETTS

Boston

Ch14

Massachusetts Bay

Cape Cod

Ch 5

Buzzards Bay

Ch12

Nantucket

CONNECTICUT

Ch7

Ch8

Ch11

Ch13

Greenwich

NEW YORK

Ch10

Martha's Vineyard

Ch9

Block I.

Ch4

Long I.

Montauk

Ch 6

NEW JERSEY

Sandy Hook Bay

Ch3

Manasquan

Barnegat Bay

NSYLVANIA

Ch2

Delaware Bay

DELAWARE

Cape May

Ch1

Ch 5

MANHATTAN

HUDSON RIVER

JERSEY CITY

NEW YORK CITY

NEWARK BAY

BROOKLYN

UPPER BAY

Ch 4

NEW YORK

STATEN ISLAND

CONEY ISLAND

ROCKAWAY INLET

GREAT KILLS

LOWER BAY

Ch 6

Table of Contents 2025 Northern Edition

Table of Contents 2024 Northern Edition

New Jersey offers the mariner a diverse mix of both open water and protected cruising grounds. The Jersey coast, while open ocean, offers all-weather inlets spaced close enough to be convenient for even slower craft seeking protection, with full amenities just inside the jetties. In comparison, the New Jersey Intracoastal Waterway is protected and offers a plethora of intriguing and convenient ports to visit for those able to navigate its shallow depths.

At Sandy Hook, the skipper can turn the helm in any direction and head for a wide choice of destinations. To the west across Raritan Bay are the sheltered industrial canals of Arthur Kill and Perth Amboy, seldom visited by yachts going north or south. To the east lies Long Island, Rockaway Inlet and the entrance to the inside passage along the South Shore.

Long Island Sound, a popular inland sea, lies between New York City and Block Island, RI. It is 90 nautical miles long, up to 20 miles wide and narrower at both ends. "The Sound," as it is commonly called, is a major commercial artery, an important fishing and lobstering ground and one of the great cruising areas in the United States. Many mariners based on Long Island Sound never leave the Sound, even though they cruise all season long, year after year. Crisscrossing between Connecticut's rocky shore and Long Island's sandy beaches, they cruise the summer away, anchoring in isolated coves, visiting luxurious marina cities, racing under sail, fishing, taking long side trips up navigable rivers and exploring big bays.

After exiting Long Island Sound through the current-washed Race, mariners enter the varied cruising grounds of southern New England-Block Island Sound, the Atlantic coast of Rhode Island and the justly famous waters of Narragansett Bay, including Newport. The big, crooked arm of Cape Cod and its island neighbors represent some of the most famous and beloved summer communities in the United States. Much of the charm of the whole area–bound by Buzzards Bay on the west, Vineyard and Nantucket sounds on the south, the Atlantic Ocean on the east and Cape Cod Bay on the north–comes from the dominating influence of the Atlantic Ocean, always nearby in one form or another.

The passage through or around the crooked elbow of Cape Cod marks a major step for most coastal cruising plans and the entrance into an endless mariner's paradise. Waterway Guide covers the waters from Cape Cod Bay to Eastern Maine in the final chapters of this edition.

INDEXES

*Sponsors are listed in **BOLD** and are <mark>highlighted in yellow</mark> in marina tables.

Perkins Cove, ME

Waterway Guide's on-the-water Cruising Editors bring us firsthand information about the navigation, news and trends along the waterways we cover. In addition to contributing to the annual guide, they provide daily updates on the Waterway Explorer at www.waterwayguide.com. We are pleased to introduce you to our crew.

Scott Richard Berg has been sailing, racing and cruising for the past 50 years and has experience on a range of power and sailing vessels from an El Toro Pram to a 135' Baltic Trader. Scott is an experienced delivery and commercial captain and the owner of Chardonnay Boatworks, a full service marine repair and consulting company focusing on the repair and re-engineering of sail and motor yachts. He frequently lectures on marine electrical systems, communication, electronics, and yacht systems for off shore cruising. Scott holds multiple certifications from the ABYC and NMEA. He is the co-founder of the SSCA HF Radio Network (KPK), holds both commercial and amateur radio licenses, and represents recreational boaters as member of the USCG's Global Maritime Distress & Safety System(GMDSS) Task Force. Scott is a member of the Capital Yacht Club, the Ocean Cruising Club and the Seven Seas Cruising Association (Past President). He holds a USCG 100T Masters license and currently lives on his 60-foot Seaton Ketch, *CHARDONNAY.*

Addison Chan is an experienced software entrepreneur, a world traveler and a committed sailing cruiser. He is the founder of Land and Sea Software Corp., which has engineered a revolutionary platform to produce mobile friendly, piracy-resistant, interactive content for traditional publishers. Waterwayguide Media is using the platform to provide its users with an enhanced digital experience that always delivers the most currently available information to mobile devices. Addison and his wife, Pat, have traveled extensively through Cuba, Mexico and the Bahamas on their 42-foot Catalina sailboat, acquiring deep local knowledge over the years. The depth of his local knowledge and understanding of local culture is evident in his work as the coauthor of *Waterway Guide Cuba,* which is the gold standard of cruising guides for Cuba. His latest project has the working title of "A Handbook for Comfortable Cruising in The Bahamas" which will be representative of a new breed of interactive cruising guides. He is active within the cruising community and maintains the popular Cuba, Land and Sea and Bahamas Land and Sea groups on Facebook.

Capts. Matt & Lucy Claiborne are full-time cruising sailors and storytellers. After college, Matt and Lucy lived on a 32-foot sailboat in the Florida Keys. Even while working in the "real-world" as professors at a university, they continued cruising and camping with a trailerable 21-foot cuddy cabin. In 2014, they cast off on a full-time sailing adventure on a 38-foot Lagoon catamaran. Both Matt and Lucy have USCG Master and FAA pilot licenses. They are full-time digital nomads who work from their boat. Their favorite offices are quiet anchorages; their favorite coworkers are dolphins and pelicans. Matt and Lucy are passionate about education and helping new boaters fulfill their cruising dreams. In 2019, they purchased their "forever dream boat"–a Cabo Rico 38 named *Dulcinea.* After a year outfitting for off-the-grid living and long-distance cruising, you'll now find them cruising Chesapeake Bay, the ICW, Bahamas and beyond with their adventure dog, Chelsea.

Gina L. Cicotello and Peter Henry share an irrational love of old wooden boats. Together they became caretakers of a 1958 Laurent Giles Vertue. *Ariel* didn't need a full restoration, but her new owners find endless opportunities to practice their skills in woodworking, old school rigging, and proper techniques for varnishing. Once they had a boat, Gina's next challenge was learning to sail. She started with classes sailing Flying Scots around the Anacostia River, and they've been cruising around the Chesapeake Bay ever since. Someday *Ariel* and her crew will broaden their adventures beyond the estuary. Gina lives in Arlington, VA. She's had a long career working for various publishers, which culminated in a dream job with National Geographic that lasted 14 years. She managed technology systems while collaborating with the cartographers, explorers and storytellers. After easing out of the corporate world she started freelancing and became her own boss, which means spending more time on the boat.

Emily Kizer and her husband, Lucas, are currently cruising the US East Coast. Emily has spent the past 10 years building a career in communications with a focus on infrastructure communications. In 2018, a random Reddit post sparked a dream of cruising full-time on a sailboat. Over the next five years, Emily and Lucas saved money, learned how to sail and fixed up their 1986 Solum 43 sailboat, *Alaya*. They left their land life in 2023, moving on board *Alaya* full-time after quitting their jobs and selling their house. Originally from Southeast Michigan, the Kizers have sailed for the past four years on the Great Lakes, mostly in Lake Erie. They did a 700-mile shakedown sail traveling from Lake Erie to Lake Michigan before turning back around and traversing the Erie Canal and Hudson River on their way east. Future cruising dreams include exploring the Bahamas and Caribbean islands.

Bob & Ann Sherer started sailing in 1985 with charters in Maine, Florida and the Caribbean followed by their first sailboat in 1986, which then lead to a 38-foot Ericson, followed by their present boat, a 42-foot Beneteau 423 in 2004. They started their yearly cruises on the ICW from New York to Key West in 2010 and Bob became known as Bob423, the person to follow for advice navigating through the many shoals of the ICW. He published his first *ICW Cruising Guide* in 2015 and has published an updated edition every year. The guide not only includes charts to avoid groundings but also tips learned from years of boating and a review of basic and advanced topics covering the ICW. In 2018, Bob started the ICW Cruising Guide Facebook page, which has grown to 13,500 members. His most recent efforts include the publishing of Bob423 Tracks in GPX format for free downloading, which follow the deep-water path around the shoals of the ICW to enable a less stressful cruise in staying out of the mud. He is routinely consulted by NOAA, the USACE, and the Coast Guard on matters affecting the boating public. Bob and Ann reside 9 months of the year aboard their latest boat, a 42-foot Beneteau 423 sailboat, with their fearless dog, Hoolie, a Brittany.

Onne van der Wal is one of the most prolific and talented marine photographers in the world of sailing. Before he learned to walk, he learned to sail aboard his grandfather's boat, and after progressing through youth sailing training programs he discovered his passion for ocean racing. As the bowman and engineer aboard the Dutch maxi-boat *Flyer II*, Onne won all four legs of the 1981-82 Whitbread Round the World Race. Along the way, he took his camera everywhere to document the experience, even to the top of the mast and the end of the spinnaker pole. Many admirers of Onne's work believe that his background as a world-class sailor informed the artistic choices he made as a world-class artist. In addition to editorial work, Onne has shot for blue chip commercial clients, including the likes of Hinckley Yachts, J Boats, Sperry, Patagonia, North Sails, and Harken. Despite all of the accolades and accomplishments over a career that has covered more than three decades and all seven seas, Onne is always looking forward to the next assignment.

Other Contributors: Waterway Guide gathers information and photos from a variety of sources, including boaters, marinas, communities and tourism divisions. We thank everyone who has contributed to our updates through their comments, reviews, and email. Your efforts are most appreciated.

The end of the National Oceanic and Atmospheric Administration's (NOAA) updates to paper charts has arrived. When sunsetting of the paper charts was first announced in 2019, concern for how the transition would come about was palpable among many veteran skippers who had grown up using all manner of NOAA printed charts in various formats and from a multitude of vendors. Common denominators across all charts were nomenclature, design and a unique reference number that identified geographical coverage areas.

NAVIGATION: Use NOAA Charts 12358 and 13209. Just north of Long Beach Point, Orient Harbor is open to the southwest. The village of Orient is located on its northeastern shore. Do not cut between flashing

Waterway Guide used the chart numbers to provide cross-references for locating specific areas we covered. Now that the charts and numbers have been replaced with a new digital methodology Waterway Guide is removing chart numbers from our publications.

For those who have printed charts in their collections and want to maintain knowledge and access to the traditional library, NOAA has created a repository of every printed (raster) chart produced by the agency. *The Historical Chart & Map Collection* is located online at www.historicalcharts.noaa.gov from the Office of Coast Survey. The portal offers search options and displays original printed charts from different eras and sources.

You may feel a little overwhelmed initially attempting to get to specific charts but remain vigilant. There is a wealth of information alongside valuable historical charts and maps in the portal, including guidance from NOAA on how to locate what you want.

As this transition to digital vector-based or Electronic Nautical Charts (ENCs) continues, the ways in which we use various media and sources to access them are also evolving. Chart plotters, mobile navigation applications, chart viewers via the internet and data distribution across different delivery platforms provide choices for improving safe navigation as never before. The transition, though, is not without complications.

Information from years of drawings on paper charts has not all been converted and stored in the databases. And errors and omissions are sometimes obvious when cross-referencing legacy paper charts against digital versions of the same region, whether using NOAA's online ENC chart viewer or other sources such as Navionics, Raymarine, Garmin or other ENC offerings. But the work continues, and NOAA and other members of the International Hydrographic Organization (IHO) are committed to accuracy and coverage.

As Waterway Guide develops solutions to the changing landscape of charts and charting, our most recent response has been to publish chart extracts from the cartographers at Aqua Map who use NOAA data in their nautical charts for the U.S. The Aqua Map mobile app is a respected source and effective tool for navigation when employed as part of an overall plan of course-plotting and routing. The chart extract images we provide from Aqua Map in our guidebooks are designed for situational awareness and to show the locations of marinas and harbors at appropriate scale and detail.

Source: Aqua Map and NOAA data

Depths in Feet

Legacy NOAA chart numbers are no longer relevant to a subjective view of a geographical area, which is how NOAA's data is now provided in their online ENC viewers and custom chart portal, where you can now design your own charts, save, and print them. Borders and scale are not necessary when employing a screen that allows you to zoom and slide to reveal what you want.

Removing chart numbers from Waterway Guide's publications is our response to a changing environment. NOAA's chart numbers, an integral reference tool for navigators for many years, no longer serve the purpose for which they were intended originally. The sun has set.

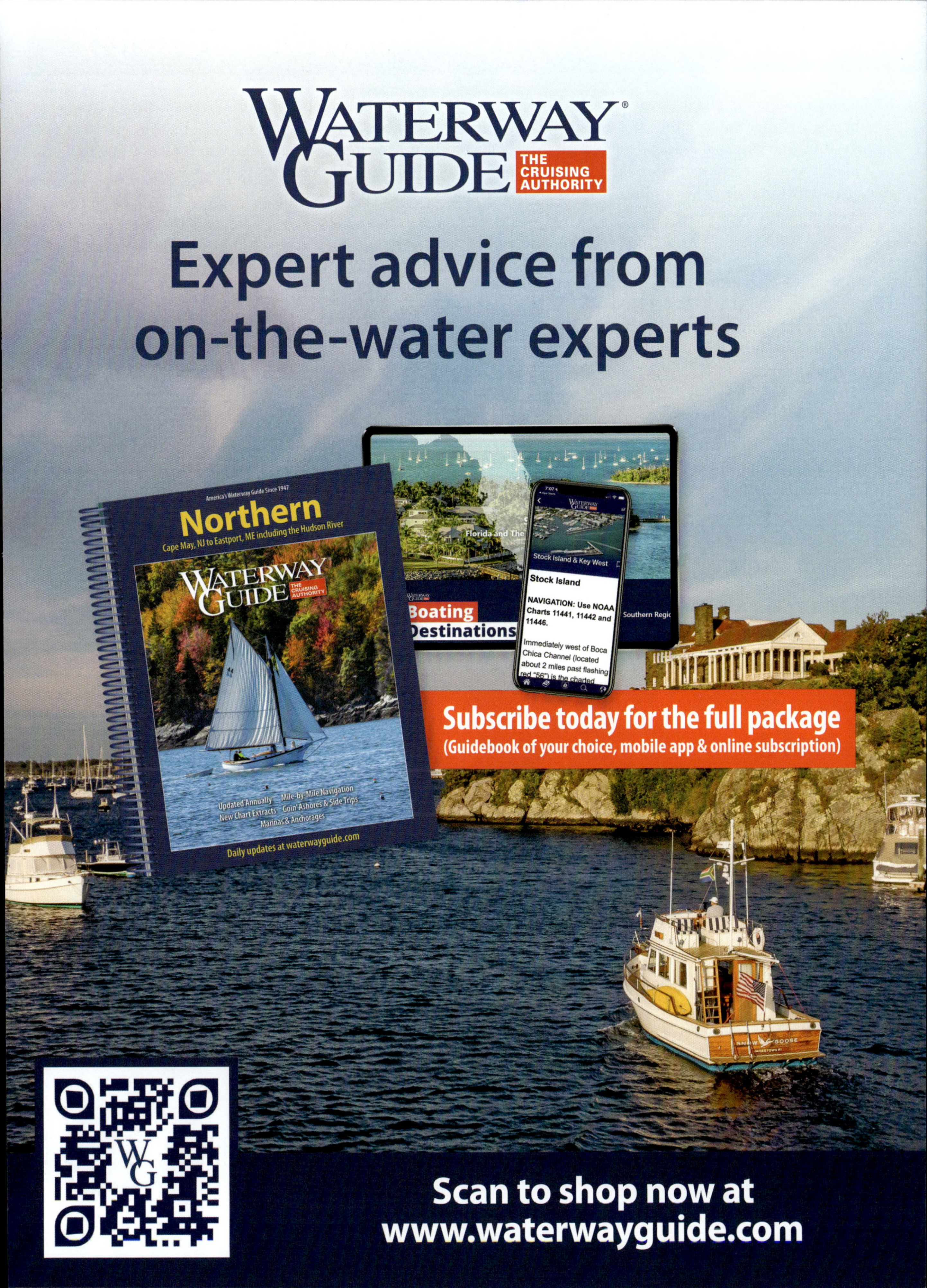
WATERWAY GUIDE
THE CRUISING AUTHORITY
Expert advice from on-the-water experts
America's Waterway Guide Since 1947
Northern
Cape May, NJ to Eastport, ME including the Hudson River
WATERWAY GUIDE THE CRUISING AUTHORITY
Updated Annually
Mile-by-Mile Navigation
New Chart Extracts
Goin' Ashores & Side Trips
Marinas & Anchorages
Daily updates at waterwayguide.com
Boating Destinations
Stock Island & Key West
Stock Island
NAVIGATION: Use NOAA Charts 11441, 11442 and 11446.
Immediately west of Boca Chica Channel (located about 2 miles past flashing
Subscribe today for the full package
(Guidebook of your choice, mobile app & online subscription)
Scan to shop now at
www.waterwayguide.com

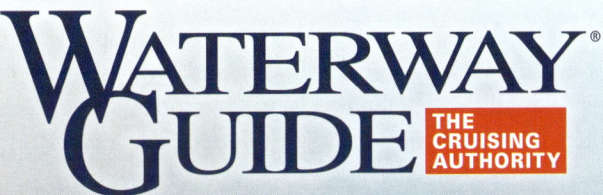

While a hunter or angler may not think of themselves as a boater, any time you're on the water, a life jacket should be part of your essential gear and worn at all times. Often a hunter or angler will set out on their trip alone, and neglect to wear a life jacket or file a float plan with the details of their trip.

A person who falls into the water experiences increased danger with water temperature that is below normal body temperature (98.6 degrees F). You have one minute to adjust to the cold shock of being in the water, 10 minutes of meaningful movement to get help and get out of the water, and one hour before he/she becomes unconscious from hypothermia.

Here are some tips to keep in mind before you go cold weather boating this winter and early spring.

• Do make sure everyone is wearing a life jacket. Even experienced swimmers can experience shock within one minute in the frigid water and may lose muscle control within 10 minutes.

• Do file a float plan with someone you trust that includes details about the trip, boat, passengers, towing or trailer vehicle, communication equipment, and emergency contacts. Download a free float plan template at www.FloatPlanCentral.org.

• Do dress properly for the weather, always wearing layers, and bring an extra set of clothes in case you get wet. Remember, dress for the water temperature, not the air temperature.

• Do catch your breath. A sudden unexpected fall into cold water causes an involuntary gasp (or torso) reflex. It takes less than ½ cup of water in your lungs to drown. If you remain calm, you have a greater chance of self-rescue.

• Do look for ways to increase your buoyancy. If you're in the water with others, huddle together with everyone facing inwards to help everyone stay afloat and keep warm.

• Don't panic if you fall into the water. Stay afloat with the help of your life jacket, regain control of your breathing, and keep your head above water in vision of rescuers. Stay with the boat if possible.

• Don't apply heat to extremities like arms and legs of a rescued victim. This sudden change in temperature may cause cardiac arrest.

Recreational water activities during the cold months are a lot of fun, but always remember safety first....You never know when wearing your life jacket will save your life.

Source: The National Boating Safety Council (www.safeboatingcampaign.com)

America's Great Loop Cruisers' Association ™

The adventure of a lifetime
America's Great Loop

2+ Countries • 14+ States and Provinces • 100+ Locks • 5,250+ Miles...
... all aboard your own boat!

Are you ready for a journey that is both high-adventure and low-risk?

Join our group of likeminded boaters exploring the 6,000-mile waterway known as the Great Loop. There's no better way to travel extensively while remaining socially distant than aboard your own vessel! Whether you're brand new to the idea of the Great Loop, actively planning your trip, or ready to drop the dock lines and head out, we offer something for you!

**Visit us at
www.greatloop.org
or call 877-GR8-LOOP**

Membership in America's Great Loop Cruisers' Association includes:

- Access to hundreds of harbor hosts to assist you with local knowledge around the route
- Participation in our discussion forum that offers a deep-dive into Great Loop-related questions and topics
- Webinars exclusively for members
- Discounts on dockage, fuel, equipment, and more
- Monthly digital magazines and newsletters
- Access to our distinctive AGLCA burgee
- Members-only events

and so much more!

Scan the QR code
to start your adventure

Preferred Destinations from

WATERWAY GUIDE MEDIA

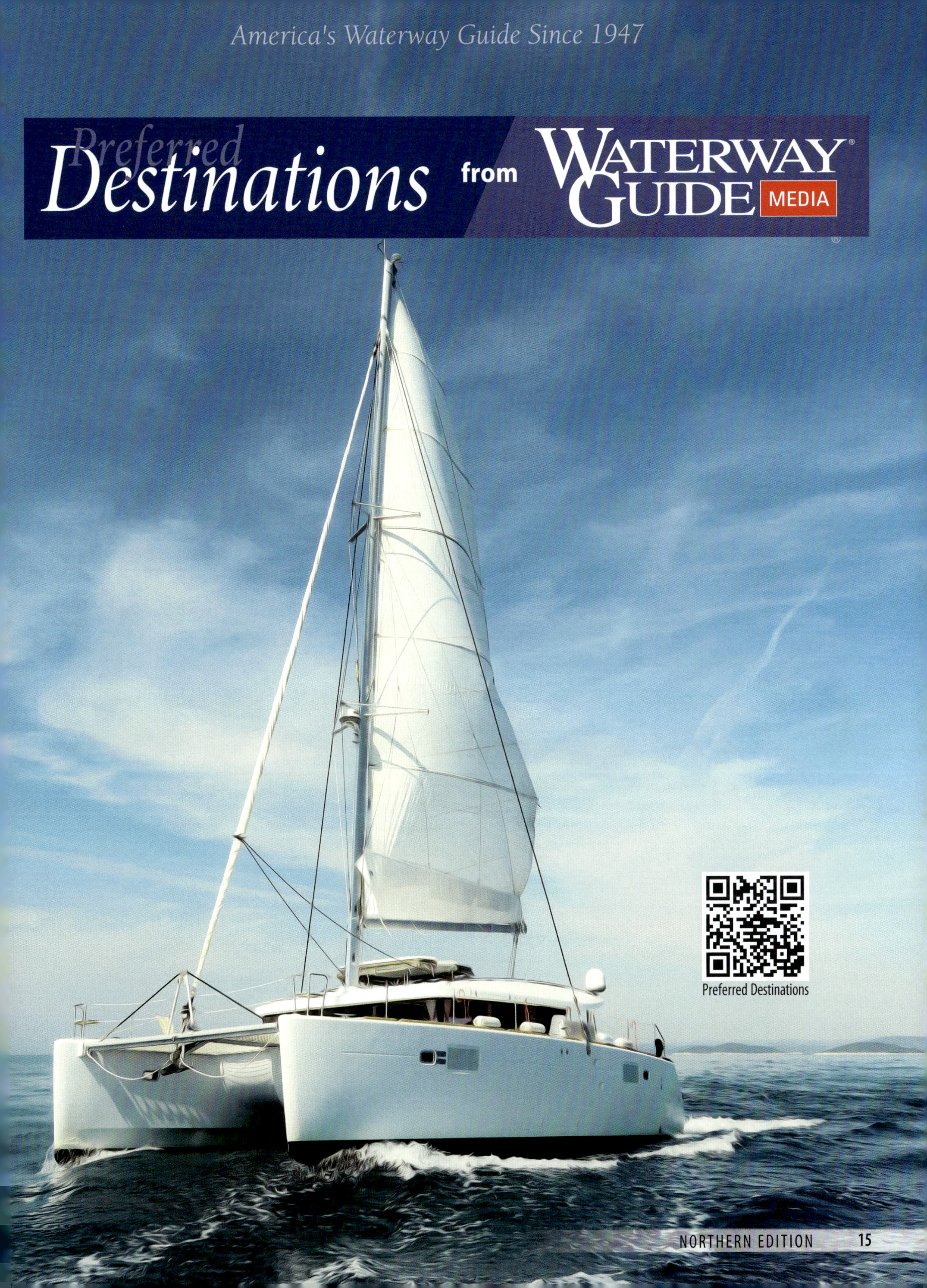

Preferred Destinations

Onancock, VA

A Little Slice of Nowhere Else

Onancock, Virginia, offers a unique slice of maritime charm nestled between the bay and the sea on Virginia's picturesque Eastern Shore. This quaint town, enriched by over four centuries of history, continues to captivate visitors much like it did when Captain John Smith first explored the area.

Onancock, established in 1680, is steeped in history as a deep-water port. Its strategic location made it a vital hub for trade via the Chesapeake Bay. Today, Onancock maintains its historical significance while embracing modernity, making it a perfect destination for boaters and history enthusiasts alike.

ONANCOCK
1680
VIRGINIA'S EASTERN SHORE

With its deep roots and welcoming community, Onancock serves as more than just a stopover; it's a gateway to the rich cultural and natural landscapes of the Eastern Shore. Whether you're mooring your boat at the well-equipped marina or just passing through, Onancock offers a blend of history, hospitality, and beauty that makes it a standout destination on the Chesapeake Bay.

Dining Delights

Onancock's dining options reflect its coastal heritage and agricultural bounty. From the historic Mallards at the Wharf, situated in a converted 1842 store offering views of Onancock Creek, to Bizzotto's Gallery Caffe, where diners can indulge in both international cuisine and local Eastern Shore specialties like soft-shell crabs, there's a plate for every palate. The Blarney Stone Pub provides a traditional Irish pub experience with classic dishes like shepherd's pie and fish & chips, served in a friendly, welcoming atmosphere. For those with a sweet tooth, the family-run Corner Bakery offers freshly made donuts and pastries, perfect for a morning treat or an afternoon snack.

I

n Onancock, every visit offers a blend of indulgence, exploration, and relaxation, making it a perfect escape on Virginia's Eastern Shore. Whether you're docking for a weekend getaway or just passing through, Onancock provides a rich, engaging experience that invites visitors to return time and again.

Learn more about this Preferred Destination at www.experienceonancock.com

Things To Do Ashore

Onancock is not just a haven for foodies but also an adventurer's delight and a cultural hotspot. Launch a kayak or canoe at Onancock Wharf and explore the intricate waterways or take a guided tour with local experts like Mary and Bill Burnham to learn about the area's ecosystems. History buffs will appreciate the self-guided walking tours through the Historic District of Onancock, where each turn reveals buildings steeped in centuries-old stories.

For more exploration, visit the Roseland Theatre for Onancock International Films series or catch a live performance at the North Street Playhouse, showcasing the area's artistic talents. Outdoor enthusiasts can venture along the nature trails at the Historic Onancock School, offering serene walks and ample bird-watching opportunities against the backdrop of Onancock Creek.

The town also serves as a starting point for the Tangier Ferry, providing access to the secluded Tangier Island, a unique day trip to see one of the Chesapeake's most isolated and charming communities.

Lancaster County, Virginia
A Boater's Haven

In the heart of Virginia's River Realm, Lancaster County stands out as a premier destination for boaters, history enthusiasts, and nature lovers. The county's ongoing commitment to enhancing its maritime facilities while preserving the natural charm of the Chesapeake Bay area makes it a top choice for those seeking a serene getaway. Among the standout developments is the transformation of Windmill Point into a comprehensive maritime campus.

Windmill Point Maritime Campus
Rappahannock River, White Stone, Virginia

Windmill Point is undergoing an ambitious transformation that promises to enrich Lancaster County's appeal. The initial phase of development includes constructing offshore breakwaters, beach expansion, and dune restoration, enhancing the site's natural defenses and beauty. The vision extends to adding comprehensive public amenities such as a new parking lot, a fishing pier, restrooms, and scenic landscaping, creating a beachfront campus that will be the pride of Northern Neck.

Currently, Windmill Point Marina offers 94 slips with modern facilities in a protected basin just off the Rappahannock River, complete with a pool and a lively Tiki Bar. Future visitors to the campus can look forward to an expanded beach and a 450-foot fishing pier and observation deck, making it a hub for both leisure and fishing enthusiasts.

Lancaster County offers an abundance of maritime services across several other marinas. In addition to ample dockage Lancaster is also home to specialized service yards such as Ampro Shipyard & Diesel and Custom Yacht Service ensuring comprehensive care and expert handling for all types of vessels. The county's "No Boat Tax" policy further enhances its appeal, drawing boaters with the promise of cost-effective docking and maintenance.

Virginia's RIVER REALM
VIRGINIA IS FOR LOVERS

Tides Inn Resort & Marina
Carter Creek, Irvington, Virginia

The Tides Inn Resort & Marina blends the serenity of a secluded harbor with the luxury of a top-tier vacation destination. With 24 all-transient slips, boaters enjoy access to an array of premier amenities including a beachside pool, tennis courts, a renowned golf course, and a full-service spa. The marina is a perfect spot for those looking to indulge in upscale dining, with options ranging from casual bites by the sand to elegant meals accompanied by stunning waterfront views.

Carters Cove Marina
Carter Creek, Irvington, Virginia

Carter Cove Marina in Irvington, Virginia, nestled along the peaceful waters of Carter Creek, provides a serene docking experience for boaters exploring the Northern Neck. This quaint, family-owned marina, situated on historic land granted by King Charles II in 1642, offers a few well-equipped transient spaces alongside essential amenities for a comfortable stay.

Yankee Point Marina
Corrotoman River, Lancaster, Virginia

This full-service marina accommodates both long-term and transient guests with amenities tailored to enhance the boating experience. Boaters can take advantage of the 12-foot depth at mean low water, ample space on the 85-foot fuel dock, and the convenience of fenders on each piling. Yankee Point Marina stands out with its ability to haul catamarans using a 25-ton yard trailer, showcasing their commitment to servicing a diverse range of vessels.

Chesapeake Boat Basin
Fleets Bay, Kilmarnock, Virginia

Chesapeake Boat Basin, located just off the Chesapeake Bay in Kilmarnock, Virginia, is a haven for cruising boaters seeking both convenience and charm. This well-established marina features well-sheltered, fixed and state-of-the-art floating docks, with lighted power pedestals at each slip, ensuring all the comforts needed for a pleasant stay.

Greenvale Marina
Greenvale Creek, Lancaster, Virginia

On a sheltered creek just a quarter mile from the Rappahannock River, Greenvale Marina offers a range of boating and recreational amenities. The marina features a variety of covered and open slips equipped with fresh water and electric service. Large power vessels and deep draft sailboats should call ahead to confirm whether access to Greenvale Marina is possible.

Plan your trip today — By River or By Road

virginiasriverrealm.com/by-river-or-by-road/

Urbanna, Virginia

Where History Meets Harbor

Whether you're docking for a weekend or seeking a picturesque escape, Urbanna, Virginia, invites you to experience its colonial charm, vibrant community events, and rich maritime heritage. It's a place where history can be learned and lived, making every visit a memorable journey into the heart of Virginia's colonial past.

Founded in 1680 and named for Queen Anne of England, it was originally intended as a trade hub and was one of America's original colonial ports, with deep draft ships loading tobacco from area plantations. Urbanna retains its historical allure with architecture dating back to the 18th century, including one of Virginia's surviving colonial courthouse; a delightful, hospitable, and walkable town.

EXPLORE
Middlesex Co.
Virginia

VIRGINIA IS FOR LOVERS

Enhance Your Urbanna Experience with the Explore Middlesex App!

Watermen Heritage

In the 1930s, Urbanna experienced significant growth when it became a refuge for 14 families from Tangier Island following the catastrophic "August Storm" that inundated their homes. The Tangier families were already familiar with Urbanna, or "Banna" as they called it, due to their seasonal work in the oyster beds when the State of Virginia's Public Oyster Hand Tong season opened each October. By the 21st century, the town became known for its oyster packing plants and as a charming, waterside destination.

Home to the Urbanna Oyster Festival

The Urbanna Oyster Festival, established in 1958 as "Urbanna Days," has grown into a major annual event that draws over 50,000 visitors from Virginia and beyond. As the official oyster festival of the Commonwealth, it honors the rich oyster culture of the region. The festival features numerous highlight events, including an almost deafening display of sirens and lights during the Fireman's Parade and the Virginia State Oyster Shucking Competition, where winners advance to compete in the National Shucking Competition in Maryland.

Dock the Boat and Explore

Urbanna has two main marinas. Urbanna Boat Yard and Marina (URBBY) offers 160 slips with facilities for vessels up to 100ft. The Urbanna Town Marina anchors the northern section of the waterfront offering 15 transient slips for vessels up to 65 ft. Both are a short jaunt up the hill into town.

Just steps from the Urbanna Town Marina, visitors can immerse themselves in history at the Friends of Urbanna Museum and James Mills Scottish Factor Store, home to the John Mitchell Map. You can also take to the streets with Urbanna's Museum in the Streets—a self-guided walking tour with QR-coded markers narrated by historian Larry Chowning. For paddling enthusiasts, the Urbanna Creek Kayak Trail offers a trip through history, accessible from the town marina.

Urbanna for All Seasons

Throughout the year, the town offers abundant dining options. The Town of Urbanna is more notably a seafood lover's delight with local aquaculture ensuring fresh oysters are available year round and local watermen's daily catch of Chesapeake Bay blue crabs throughout the summer.

The monthly Urbanna Farmers Market and Second Saturdays feature local produce, handmade goods, live music, and wine tasting with a festive atmosphere that celebrates the best of local culture.

Visit a Place Where Adventures are as Vast as the Sea

Hampton, VA.

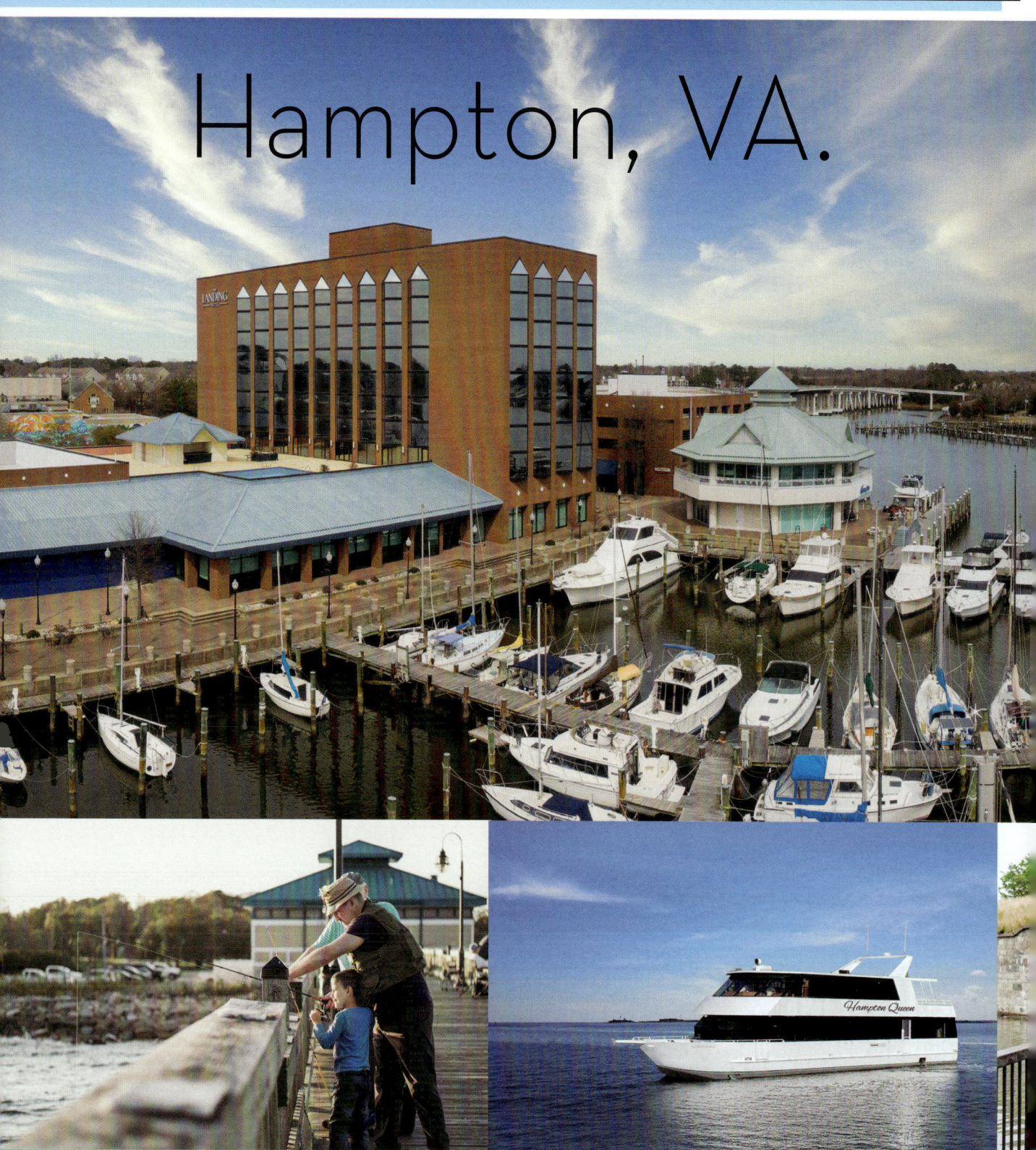

We're home to a vibrant boating, fishing and ocean-faring culture that dates back centuries. Tour the Chesapeake Bay and cast your line for an incredible time on the James T. Wilson Fishing Pier. Soak up the sun and the fun at Buckroe beach where you can fulfill your thrill with watersports, jet skiing, kayaking and paddle-boarding. Savor the moment, and the flavors, with waterfront dining and fresh, delicious seafood.

Looking for something more personal? Charter a boat for a private tour, and savor fresh seafood straight from the Atlantic, with the world's greatest natural harbor as your backdrop. Starting this Spring, climb aboard the all-new Hampton Queen and see the sea!

Need an adventure outside the water? Experience our attractions, history and culture. Hampton's numerous world-class attractions, including Fort Monroe National Monument, the Virginia Air & Space Science Center, and the Hampton University Museum, have been inspiring visitors for decades. See history and adventure come alive in Hampton.

Get Inspired at VisitHampton.com

VISIT
HAMPTON
VIRGINIA

Unveiling the Charms of
Washington, NC

Nestled on the picturesque banks of the Pamlico River, Washington, North Carolina, holds a special allure for boating enthusiasts in search of a coastal adventure. With its rich historical significance, scenic waterfront, and abundant natural beauty, Washington, NC presents an enticing destination for boaters of all levels of expertise.

First called Forks of the Tar, the city name was changed in 1776 in honor of Gen. George Washington. Because it was America's first city to be named for Gen. Washington, it is sometimes referred to as "The Original Washington" or "Little Washington" to avoid confusion. "Little" does not, however, describe the amenities here.

Whether you're an experienced captain or a novice sailor eager to dip your toes into new waters, Washington, NC promises tranquility, scenic beauty, and a warm hospitality that will make your boating experience truly memorable.

Curious Foodies Welcome

Washington, NC, beckons curious foodies to embark on a culinary adventure, where they can indulge in a wide array of flavors and delights. The town boasts several noteworthy eateries that showcase the region's culinary treasures. Among the must-visit establishments, Bill's Hot Dogs stands as a true local institution since 1928. Renowned for their mouthwatering classic hot dogs topped with their signature, original-recipe chili and an array of fixings, Bill's Hot Dogs guarantees a taste of tradition.

To help wash things down, a visit to Pitt Street Brewing on the Pamlico is in order. Housed in a converted waterfront craft brewery that was once a rowing club, Pitt Street Brewing invites patrons to enjoy the gentle breezes of the Pamlico while sipping on a refreshing selection of lagers, ales, and stouts. The brewery offers a perfect setting to relax and savor the craft beer experience.

Things To Do Ashore

For boaters venturing ashore in Washington, NC, an array of enjoyable activities awaits, showcasing the town's natural beauty, cultural exploration, and historical charm. Goose Creek State Park, a hidden gem, provides an idyllic escape into nature. With its tranquil waterways, lush forests, and scenic trails, the park beckons outdoor enthusiasts for hiking, boating, fishing, and wildlife spotting.

Continue your journey of discovery at the North Carolina Estuarium, where the fascinating world of estuaries comes to life. Explore interactive exhibits, aquariums, and educational displays that highlight the unique ecosystems of the Pamlico River and its surrounding estuarine environments. Dive into the diverse marine life, ecological importance, and conservation efforts of this captivating coastal region.

To further immerse yourself in the town's history and architecture, embark on self-guided audio tours of Washington's Historic Districts. Wander through the charming streets and listen to informative narratives that bring the town's rich heritage to life. From well-preserved homes to significant landmarks, these tours offer a glimpse into Washington's storied past and its contributions to North Carolina's history.

Discover the allure of Washington, NC—an enchanting blend of natural beauty, rich history, and warm hospitality. From serene waters to captivating museums, this coastal gem offers a truly unforgettable experience.

Discovering Timeless Treasures In
Beaufort & Port Royal
South Carolina

Welcome to the picturesque haven of Beaufort and Port Royal, South Carolina, where a delightful blend of southern hospitality, rich culture, and tantalizing cuisine awaits your discovery. Nestled between the Beaufort River and Battery Creek, these enchanting twin cities are loved by history enthusiasts, nature lovers, and those yearning for a peaceful escape.

Founded in 1562, Port Royal Island has been a beacon of attraction for explorers throughout its rich history. Upon your arrival, you'll be transported to a bygone era, where exquisitely preserved pre-Civil War architecture graces every corner. Wander through the historic downtown, a designated district that offers a glimpse into the past, and lose yourself in the splendor of the south's most extraordinary bed and breakfasts, restaurants, and hotels.

Where To Dine

This area boasts a wide array of restaurants, catering to every preference, from laid-back coastal cuisine to elegant fine dining.

When it comes to seafood, the Beaufort & Port Royal area is a reigning champion, and your visit here would be incomplete without savoring the culinary delights offered by its many local eateries, where seafood dishes take center stage on the menus. Witness the docks of Battery Creek bustling with activity as a vibrant fleet of trawlers sets sail daily, ensuring a continuous supply of the freshest catches. Prepare to revel in a delightful assortment of oysters, shrimp, crab, and freshly caught fish, all sourced from the local waters.

For an authentic taste of Lowcountry living, head over to Fishcamp on 11th Street – a beloved spot cherished by locals and visitors alike. The menu here is a true treasure trove, featuring mouthwatering seafood delicacies alongside succulent steaks, catering to the diverse preferences of every palate.

If you're looking for a fine dining experience, head to the Ribaut Social Club, a fine dining and social space for Beaufort locals and visitors to mingle over cocktails and impeccable regional cuisine. The concise menu presents imaginative interpretations of meats, seafood, and fresh vegetables. Be sure to secure reservations ahead of time, as this culinary haven is in high demand and promises an unforgettable dining experience.

Local Events & Festivals

Throughout the year, Beaufort, South Carolina, is a bustling hub of annual festivals and events, ensuring there is never a dull moment for both locals and visitors. Mark your calendars and embrace the opportunity to partake in these local events.

Take a Journey into Gullah Culture

Delve into the rich heritage of the Gullah people, African Americans who have made their home in the Lowcountry region of South Carolina and Georgia, including the coastal plains and Beaufort Sea Islands. Immerse yourself in the culture and history of the Gullah community with a guided tour by native experts from St. Helena, courtesy of Gullah-N-Geechie Mahn Tours. The Gullah culture is a source of immense pride and has inspired documentary films, children's books, and popular novels that celebrate its unique traditions and contributions.

Travel Back in Time

Exploring the local history of Beaufort and Port Royal is like stepping into a living time capsule, where every street corner and historic landmark reveals fascinating stories from the past. Beaufort and Port Royal, both deeply intertwined with the nation's history, boast an exquisitely preserved charm that takes visitors on a captivating journey through time.

Founded in 1711, Beaufort holds a significant place in history as the second oldest city in South Carolina, only trailing behind Charleston. With its roots intertwined with early European explorations, this charming city thrived as one of the economic hubs of the Lowcountry throughout the 1800s.

To truly immerse oneself in the past, a visit to the numerous cultural sites scattered across historic Beaufort is a must. Step back in time and witness the echoes of bygone eras as you explore the rich heritage that has shaped this captivating city.

Discover a haven that effortlessly transforms overnight anchorages into week-long retreats, and visitors into locals captivated by the enchanting allure of this coastal gem. Learn more about the Beaufort and Port Royal area at https://www.beaufortsc.org/

Florida's Forgotten Coast

is a Boater's Paradise

Florida's Forgotten Coast, along the North Florida Gulf Coast, is a boater's paradise with hundreds of miles of freshwater creeks, sloughs and rivers that empty into nutrient-rich bays and out to the Gulf of Mexico.

Getting out on the water is easy here. The area features more than 40 boat ramps stretching from Alligator Point to Apalachicola. Bring your boat and tie up at one of the area's 10 commercial marinas.

APALACHICOLA

The downtown historic district of Apalachicola stretches three blocks deep from where the historic Apalachicola River meets the oyster-famous Apalachicola Bay. Everything is walkable here - stroll along the wide tree-lined streets with historic homes or hole up along the waterfront and enjoy the music scene in pubs and local eateries just blocks from the waterfront. Apalachicola's commercial marina facilities include the Scipio Creek, Water Street and Apalachicola Marina with services and available at Scipio Creek.

EASTPOINT

Across the bay from Apalachicola, Eastpoint features rustic seafood houses, weather-worn docks and fresh seafood markets run by families four generations deep. There are RV parks here, two boat ramps, a full-service bait and tackle shop, fresh seafood restaurants, causal fare and even a waterfront brewery!

ST. GEORGE ISLAND

Just offshore, St. George Island is a 22- mile barrier island that hosts some of Florida's most beautiful and serene beaches. There is a protected anchorage spot on the bayside of St. George Island. Don't expect to walk to amenities from this anchorage but it's not far from the Julian G. Bruce St. George Island State Park which boasts some of the best camping facilities in the region. Elsewhere on the island, accommodations range from quaint beach cottages to luxurious beach homes and can be reserved with any of the island's vacation rental companies. The historic St. George Island Lighthouse is located at the St. George Island public beach park.

CARRABELLE

Carrabelle is about 30 nautical miles from Apalachicola and it's a must stop spot for boaters and fishermen. Carrabelle features three public commercial marinas along the Carrabelle River and all are located within walking distance of restaurants, a grocery and all three offers either fuel or service facilities. There is public dockage along the river and a private boat club nearby on Timber Island.

Carrabelle is considered ground zero for fishing enthusiasts because of its easy access to offshore fishing and boating. The town features a natural deep-water harbor plus a nearby renowned golf resort. The nearby Crooked River Lighthouse reminds you of the town's maritime importance and features monthly full moon climbs.

To learn more about Franklin County boating, fishing charters, restaurants, and accomodations, visit Floridasforgottencoast.com/FCboat

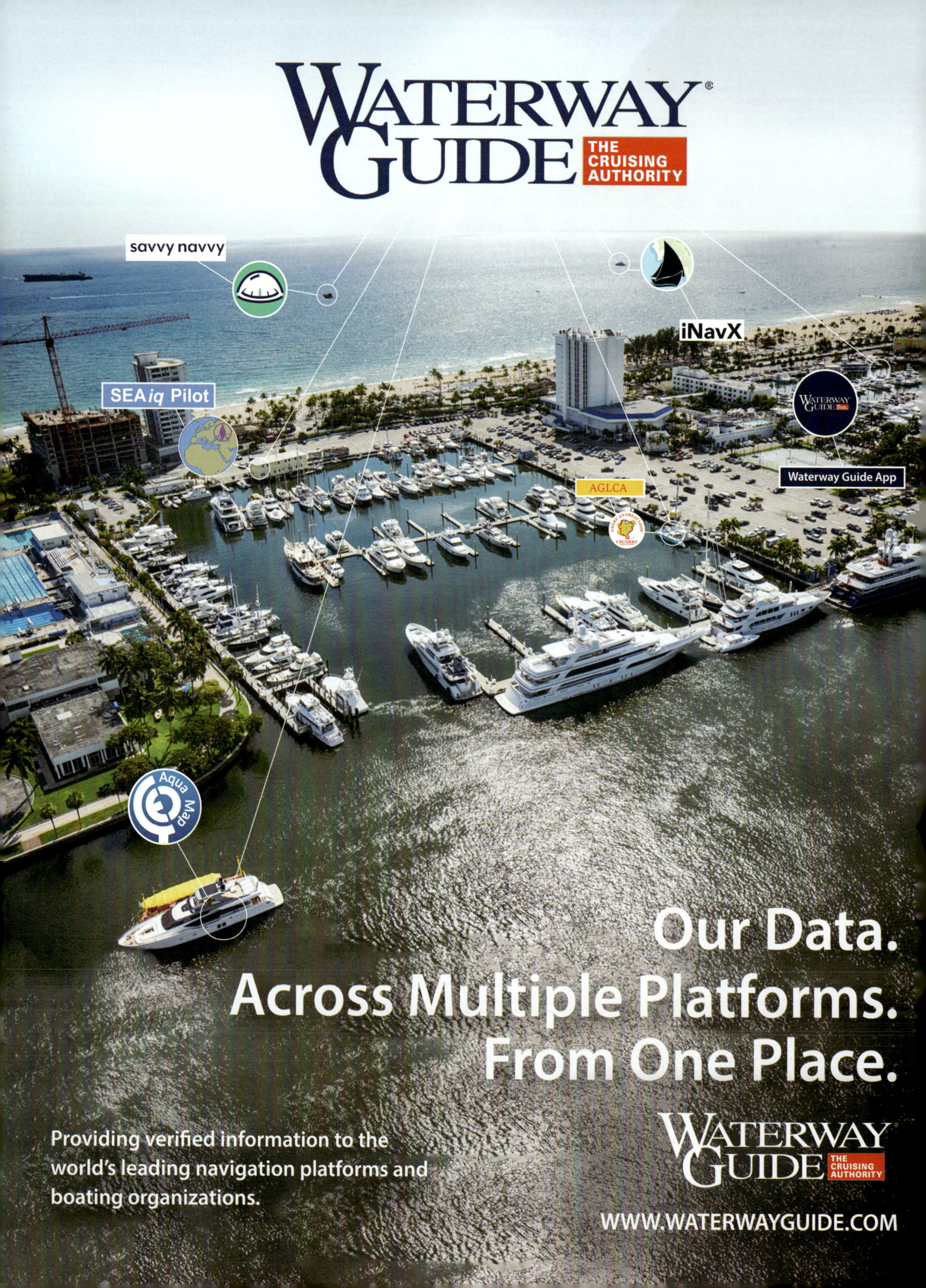
WATERWAY GUIDE
THE CRUISING AUTHORITY
savvy navvy
iNavX
SEAiq Pilot
Waterway Guide App
AGLCA
Aqua Map
Our Data.
Across Multiple Platforms.
From One Place.
Providing verified information to the world's leading navigation platforms and boating organizations.
WATERWAY GUIDE
THE CRUISING AUTHORITY
WWW.WATERWAYGUIDE.COM

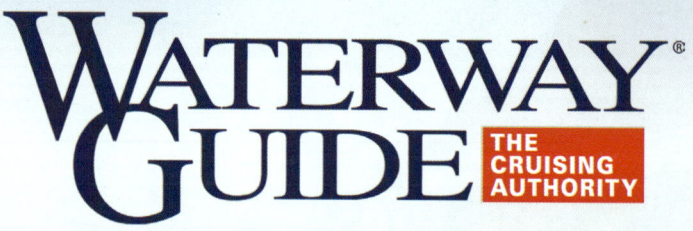

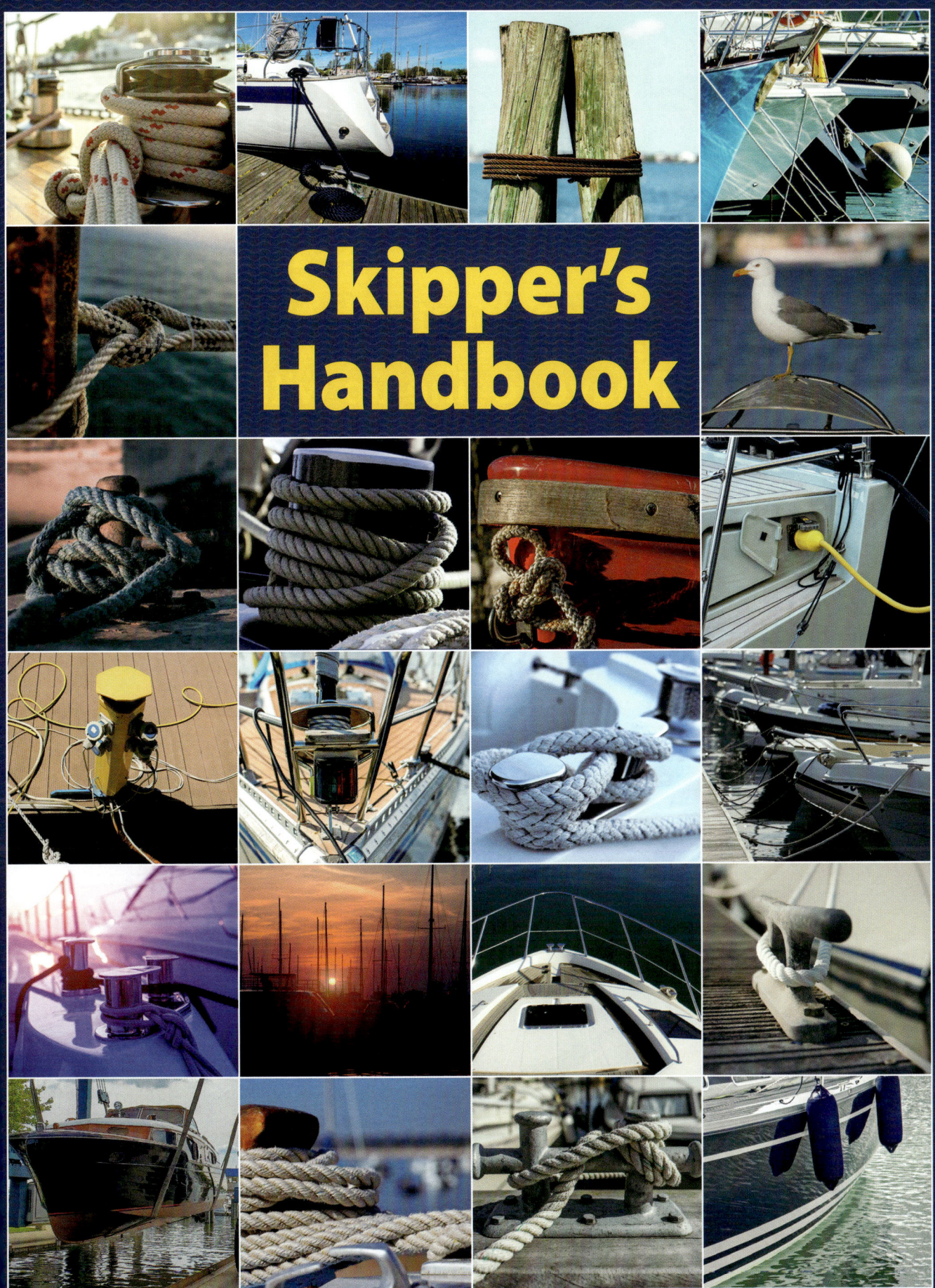

Skipper's Handbook

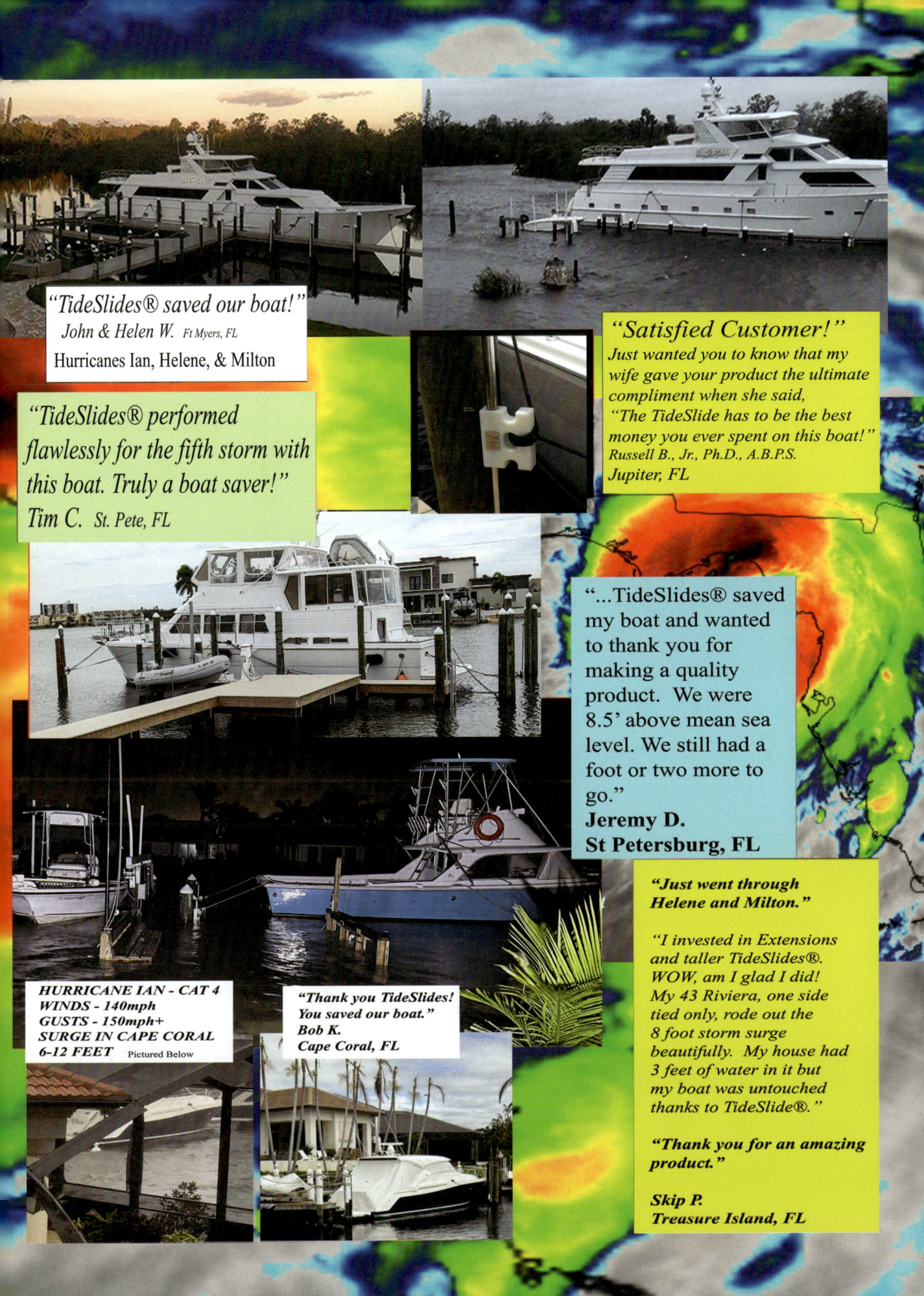

"TideSlides® saved our boat!"
John & Helen W. Ft Myers, FL
Hurricanes Ian, Helene, & Milton

"TideSlides® performed flawlessly for the fifth storm with this boat. Truly a boat saver!"
Tim C. St. Pete, FL

"Satisfied Customer!"
Just wanted you to know that my wife gave your product the ultimate compliment when she said, "The TideSlide has to be the best money you ever spent on this boat!"
Russell B., Jr., Ph.D., A.B.P.S.
Jupiter, FL

"...TideSlides® saved my boat and wanted to thank you for making a quality product. We were 8.5' above mean sea level. We still had a foot or two more to go."
**Jeremy D.
St Petersburg, FL**

"Just went through Helene and Milton."

"I invested in Extensions and taller TideSlides®. WOW, am I glad I did! My 43 Riviera, one side tied only, rode out the 8 foot storm surge beautifully. My house had 3 feet of water in it but my boat was untouched thanks to TideSlide®."

"Thank you for an amazing product."

*Skip P.
Treasure Island, FL*

**HURRICANE IAN - CAT 4
WINDS - 140mph
GUSTS - 150mph+
SURGE IN CAPE CORAL
6-12 FEET** Pictured Below

"Thank you TideSlides! You saved our boat."
Bob K.
Cape Coral, FL

Port Security

The U.S. Coast Guard and Customs and Border Patrol–both components of the Department of Homeland Security–handle port security in the United States. Local law enforcement agencies and the FBI also have a role in port security at the local and regional level. Each year more than 11 million maritime containers arrive at our seaports. At land borders, another 11 million arrive by truck and 2.7 million by rail. Homeland Security is responsible for knowing what is inside those containers, whether it poses a risk to the American people and ensuring that all proper revenues are collected.

As an example, one in five food items is now imported. American consumers demand fresh limes and blueberries all year round and, as a result, during the winter months in the U.S. nearly 80 percent of the fresh fruits and vegetables on our tables come from other countries. With the ever-increasing amount of trade, the agricultural risks to the United States grow. The threat to crops and livestock is real.

In response to this threat and others, the U.S. Coast Guard has established "protection zones" around all U.S. Navy vessels, tank vessels and large-capacity cruise vessels, even when underway. U.S. Navy bases, U.S. Coast Guard bases and some shoreside facilities such as nuclear power plants are also in protection zones. Non-military vessels (this means YOU) are not allowed within 100 yards of these protection zones. To do so can rack up serious civil penalties and even imprisonment.

These protection zones vary from port to port and from facility to facility but ignorance of the protection zones is not a viable excuse. Having said that, law-abiding boaters sometimes find themselves unable to comply with the letter of the law without hitting a jetty, for example. In such cases, common sense and good communication should prevail.

America's Waterway Watch Program

Government officials view the recreational boating community as an ally. We can do our part (and perhaps stave off more stringent regulations and surveillance measures) by becoming familiar with the Coast Guard's America's Waterway Watch program. Think of it as a neighborhood watch program for the waterways.

It is not the intent of America's Waterway Watch to spread paranoia or to encourage spying on one another and it is not a surveillance program; it is instead a simple deterrent to potential terrorist activity. The purpose of the program is to allow boaters and others who spend time along the water to help the authorities counter crime and terrorism. To report suspicious behavior, call the National Response Center at 877-249-2824 (877-24WATCH). For immediate danger to life or property, call 911 or contact the U.S. Coast Guard on Marine VHF Channel 16.

Staying safe and responsible requires a little forethought and vigilance on your part. Following the steps outlined below will help ensure a trouble-free journey and keep you and your crew out of the headlines.

Be Prepared

■ Before you leave, check the current charts for the area in which you will be traveling and identify any security areas. Security zones are highlighted and outlined in magenta with special notes regarding the specific regulations pertaining to that area.

■ Check the latest *Local Notice to Mariners* (available online at www.navcen.uscg and posted at some marinas) and identify any potential security areas that may not be shown on the chart.

■ Prior to your departure, listen to VHF Channel 16 for any Sécurité alerts from the Coast Guard (departing cruise ships, U.S. Navy vessels, fuel tankers, etc.) for the area you will be cruising.

■ Talk to other boaters in your anchorage or marina about the areas where you will be traveling. They may have tips and suggestions on potential security zones or special areas they may have encountered along the way.

Stay Alert While Underway

■ Mind the outlined magenta security areas noted on your charts.

■ Look for vessels with blue or red warning lights in port areas and, if approached, listen carefully and strictly obey all instructions given to you.

■ Keep your VHF radio switched to VHF Channel 16 and keep your ears tuned for bulletins, updates and possible requests for communication.

■ Avoid commercial port operation areas, especially those that involve military, cruise line or petroleum facilities. Observe and avoid other restricted areas near power plants, national monuments, etc.

■ If you need to pass within 100 yards of a U.S. Navy vessel for safe passage, you must contact the U.S. Navy vessel or the Coast Guard escort vessel on VHF Channel 16 to let them know your intentions.

■ We advise that if government security or the U.S. Coast Guard hails you, do exactly what they say, regardless of whether or not you feel their instructions have merit.

Additional Resources
Atlantic Intracoastal Waterway Association: www.atlanticintracoastal.org.
America's Waterway Watch: www.americaswaterwaywatch.org
Department of Homeland Security: www.dhs.gov
U.S. Customs and Border Protection: www.cbp.gov

Customs Reporting Procedures

Operators of small pleasure vessels, arriving in the U.S. from a foreign port are required to report their arrival to Customs and Border Patrol (CBP) immediately. The master of the vessel reports their arrival at the nearest Customs facility or other designated location. These reports are tracked in the Pleasure Boat Reporting System. An application to lawfully enter the U.S. must be made in person to a CBP officer at a U.S. port-of-entry when the port is open for inspection.

CBP has designated specific reporting locations within the Field Offices that are staffed during boating season for pleasure boats to report their arrival and be inspected by CBP. The master of the boat must report to CBP telephonically and be directed to the nearest Port of Entry to satisfy the face-to-face requirement, or report to the nearest designated reporting location, along with the boat's passengers for inspection.

You may be required to rent a car or take a cab to the nearest airport or federal office several miles away for the inspection. These offices are often closed on weekends. If your arrival is after working hours, you are required to stay on board and clear in the next morning. You must, however, clear in within 24 hours of your arrival. Everyone on board, regardless of nationality, has to report in person. U.S. nationals must take their passports or passport cards. All non-U.S. Nationals should take their passports with valid visas and a Green Card, if held. Take your boat papers, either U.S. documentation or state registration with state decal number. You should also present a list of firearms and ammunition on board.

Clearing In with the ROAM App

Travelers arriving by boat into many popular U.S. ports can check into the country on their phones or tablets. The Reporting Offsite Arrival–Mobile (ROAM) app is the official replacement for the Local Boater Option (LBO) and Small Vessel Reporting System (SVRS) programs that have been used over the years. These programs required an initial interview to get in but usually resulted in a quick phone call instead of a face-to-face meeting to re-enter the U.S.

If you have a www.Login.gov account, you can log into the app immediately. If you need a password, the app directs you to the website. Then it walks you through the steps, including entering the specifics for each person on board and for your vessel. Once you've entered all of the details and submitted it for a review, an officer may initiate a video call to discuss the trip or to ask any necessary questions. All of this happens directly inside the app. Of course, there are still instances where in-person reporting is required. If you require an I-94, need to pay customs fees or duties, or need to obtain a cruising permit, you will still need to check in in-person. Boaters are still required to have a current fee decal onboard.

Now that the app has been implemented on a larger scale, travelers entering by boat in the Great Lakes; most of the East Coast (Delaware to Florida); Texas and San Diego, CA; and the U.S. territories in the Caribbean can use the app. New locations are continually being added, and because the program is new, it's probably a good idea to call your port of arrival to ensure they are using the ROAM app.

To download the ROAM app, just search the Apple App Store or the Google Play Store on your device. For more information, visit the CBP website or contact the CBP office at your port of arrival.

Additional Resources

U.S. Customs and Border Control:
www.cbp.gov/travel/pleasure-boats-private-flyers

Float Plan   BoatU.S.

1. Phone Numbers

Coast Guard:_____

Marine Police:_____

Local TowBoatU.S. Company:_____

2. Description of the Boat

Boat Name:_____Hailing Port:_____

Type:_____Model Year:_____

Make:_____Length:_____Beam:_____Draft:_____

Color, Hull:_____Cabin:_____Deck:_____Trim:_____Dodger:_____

Other Colors:_____# of Masts:_____

Distinguishing Features:_____

Registration No:_____Sail No:_____

Engine(s) Type:_____Horsepower:_____Cruising Speed:_____

Fuel Capacity, Gallons:_____Cruising Range:_____

Electronics/Safety Equipment Aboard

VHF Radio:_____Cell Phone:_____CB:_____SSB:_____

Frequency Monitored:_____Loran:_____SatNav:_____

Depth Sounder:_____Radar:_____GPS:_____

Raft:_____Dinghy:_____EPIRB:_____A/B/C/406M
(Indicate Type)

3. Trip Details

Owner/Skipper (Filing Report):_____

Phone:_____Age:_____

Address:_____

Additional Persons Aboard, Total:_____

Name:_____Age:_____

Address:_____Phone:_____

Boating Experience:_____

Name:_____Age:_____

Address:_____Phone:_____

Boating Experience:_____

Name:_____Age:_____

Address:_____Phone:_____

Boating Experience:_____

Name:_____Age:_____

Address:_____Phone:_____

Boating Experience:_____

Name:_____Age:_____

Address:_____Phone:_____

Boating Experience:_____

Departure Date/Time:_____Return No Later Than:_____

Depart From:_____

Marina (Home Port):_____Phone:_____

Auto Parked At:_____

Model/color:_____Lic. #_____

Destination Port: _____

_____ETA:_____No Later Than:_____

Phone:_____

Anticipated Stopover Ports:_____

_____ETA:_____No Later Than:_____

Phone:_____

_____ETA:_____No Later Than:_____

Phone:_____

_____ETA:_____No Later Than:_____

Phone:_____

_____ETA:_____No Later Than:_____

Phone:_____

_____ETA:_____No Later Than:_____

Phone:_____

Plan Filed With:_____

Name:_____Phone:_____

Get in the habit of filing a Float Plan. It can assure quicker rescue in the event of a breakdown, stranding or weather delay. Fill out the permanent data in Sections 1 and 2. Then, make enough copies to last for the season. If you file a Float Plan with someone not at your home, such as a harbormaster or boating friend, be sure to notify them as soon as you return. Don't burden friends or authorities with unnecessary worry and responsibility if you are safe.

Check your *BoatU.S. Towing Guide*. Some listed companies will accept a verbal Float Plan via telephone or VHF.

VHF Communications

Skippers traveling the U.S. inland waterways use their VHF radios almost every day to contact other vessels and bridgetenders, make reservations at marinas, arrange to pass other vessels safely and conduct other business. Waterway Guide has put together the following information to help remove any confusion as to what frequency should be dialed in to call bridges, marinas, commercial ships or your friend anchored down the creek.

Remember to use low power (1 watt) for your radio transmission whenever possible. If you are within a couple of miles of the responding station (bridge, marina or other craft), there is no need to broadcast at 25 watts and disturb the transmissions of others 25 miles away.

Channel Usage Tips

■ VHF Channel 16 (156.8 MHz) is by far the most important frequency on the VHF-FM band. VHF Channel 16 is the international distress, safety and calling frequency.

■ If you have a VHF radio on your boat, Federal Communications Commission (FCC) regulations require that you maintain a watch on either VHF Channel 09 or 16 whenever you are underway and the radio is not being used to communicate on another channel. Since the Coast Guard does not have the capability of announcing an urgent marine information broadcast or weather warning on VHF Channel 09, it recommends that boaters remain tuned to and use VHF Channel 16.

■ Recreational craft typically communicate on VHF Channels 68, 69, 71, 72 or 78A. Whenever possible, avoid calling on VHF Channel 16 altogether by prearranging initial contact directly on one of these channels. No transmissions should last longer than 3 minutes.

■ The Coast Guard's main working VHF Channel is 22A and both emergency and non-emergency calls generally are switched there to keep VHF Channel 16 clear. Calling the Coast Guard for a radio check on VHF Channel 16 is prohibited.

■ Radio-equipped bridges on the Atlantic ICW use VHF Channel 09 with a few exceptions.

■ The Bridge-to-Bridge Radio Telephone Act requires many commercial vessels, including dredges and tugboats, to monitor VHF Channel 13. VHF Channel 13 is also the frequency used by bridges in several states.

Distress Calls

MAYDAY: The distress signal "MAYDAY" is used to indicate that a vessel is threatened by grave and imminent danger and requests immediate assistance.

PAN PAN: The urgency signal "PAN PAN" is used when the safety of the ship or person is in jeopardy.

SÉCURITÉ: The safety signal "SÉCURITÉ" is used for messages about the safety of navigation or important weather warnings.

VHF Channel 16 is the distress call frequency. The codeword "MAYDAY" is the international alert signal of a life-threatening situation at sea. After a MAYDAY message is broadcast, VHF Channel 16 must be kept free of all traffic, other than those directly involved in the rescue situation, until the rescue has been completed.

If you hear a MAYDAY message and no one else is responding, it is your duty to step in to answer the call, relay it to the nearest rescue organization and get to the scene to help. Remember, a MAYDAY distress call can only be used when life is threatened. For example, if you have run on the rocks but no one is going to lose their life, that is NOT a MAYDAY situation.

> Note: The Coast Guard has asked the FCC to eliminate provisions for using VHF Channel 09 as an alternative calling frequency to VHF Channel 16 when it eliminates watch-keeping on VHF Channel 16 by compulsory-equipped vessels. Stay tuned for updates.

How to Make a Distress Call

MAYDAY! MAYDAY! MAYDAY!

This is: Give your vessel name and call sign.

Our position is: Read it off the GPS or give it as something like "2 miles southwest of Royal Island." (Your rescuers must be able to find you!)

We are: Describe what's happening (e.g., on fire/hit a reef/sinking).

We have: Report how many people are on board.

At this time we are: Say what you're doing about the crisis (e.g., standing by/abandoning ship).

For identification we are: Describe your boat type, length, color, etc. (so your rescuers can more readily identify you).

We have: List safety equipment you have (e.g., flares/smoke/ocean dye markers/EPIRB).

We will keep watch on Channel 16 as long as we can.

VHF Channels	
09	Used for radio checks and hailing other stations (boats, shoreside operations). Also used to communicate with drawbridges in Florida.
13	Used to contact and communicate with commercial vessels, military ships and drawbridges. Bridges in several states monitor VHF Channel 13.
16	**Emergency use only.** May be used to hail other vessels, but once contact is made, conversation should be immediately switched to a working (68, 69, 71, 72, 78A) VHF channel.
22	Used for U.S. Coast Guard safety, navigation and Sécurité communications.
68 69 71 72 78A	Used primarily for recreational ship-to-ship and ship-to-shore communications.

Rules of the Road

Anyone planning to cruise U.S. waterways should be familiar with the rules of the road. *Chapman Piloting: Seamanship and Small Boat Handling* and *The Annapolis Book of Seamanship* are both excellent on-the-water references with plentiful information on navigation rules. For those with a penchant for the exact regulatory language, the U.S. Coast Guard publication *Navigation Rules: International–Inland* covers both international and U.S. inland rules. (Boats over 39.4 feet are required to carry a copy of the U.S. Inland Rules at all times.)

Following is a list of common situations you may likely encounter on the waterways. Make yourself familiar with them, and if there is ever a question as to which of you has the right-of-way, let the other vessel go first.

Sailors need to remember that a boat under sail with its engine running is considered a motorboat.

Passing or Being Passed:

■ If you intend to pass a slower vessel, try to hail them on your VHF radio to let them know you are coming.

■ In close quarters, BOTH vessels should slow down, which normally allows the faster vessel to pass quickly without throwing a large wake onto the slower boat.

■ A boat passing another is the "give-way" vessel and is required to keep clear of the slower "stand-on" vessel until past and well clear of it.

■ Sound signals when overtaking (both vessels heading the same way):
"See you on the one (whistle)" = overtake on his starboard (your port)
"See you on the two (whistle)" = overtake on his port (your starboard)

Additional Resources

U.S. Coast Guard Boating Safety Division:
www.uscgboating.org

U.S. Coast Guard Navigation Center:
www.navcen.uscg.gov

■ Sound signals when passing (vessels going in opposite directions):
"See you on the one (whistle)" = pass port to port
"See you on the two (whistle)" = pass starboard to starboard

■ As you pass a slower boat, take a look back to see how they were affected by your wake. Remember: YOU are responsible for your wake. It is the law to slow down and it is common courtesy.

At Opening Bridges:

■ During an opening, boats traveling with the current go first and generally have the right-of-way.

■ Boats constrained by their draft, size or maneuverability (e.g., dredges, tugs and barges) take priority.

■ Standard rules of the road apply while circling or waiting for a bridge opening.

Tugs, Freighters, Dredges & Naval Vessels:

■ These vessels are usually constrained by draft or their inability to easily maneuver. For this reason, you will almost always need to give them the right-of-way and keep out of their path.

■ You must keep at least 100 yards away from any Navy vessel. If you cannot safely navigate without coming closer than this, you must notify the ship of your intentions over VHF Channel 16.

■ Keep a close watch for freighters, tugs with tows and other large vessels while offshore or in crowded ports. They often come up very quickly, despite their large size.

■ It is always a good practice to radio larger vessels (VHF Channel 13 or 16) to notify them of your location and your intentions. The skippers of these boats are generally appreciative of efforts to communicate with them. This is especially true with dredge boats on all the waterways.

In a Crossing Situation:

- When two vessels under power are crossing and a risk of collision exists, the vessel that has the other on her starboard side must keep clear and avoid crossing ahead of the other vessel.

- When a vessel under sail and a vessel under power are crossing, the boat under power is usually burdened and must keep clear. The same exceptions apply as per head-on meetings.

- On the Great Lakes and western rivers (e.g., the Mississippi River system), a power-driven vessel crossing a river shall keep clear of a power-driven vessel ascending or descending the river.

Power Vessels Meeting Any Other Vessel:

- When two vessels under power (either sailboats or powerboats) meet "head-to-head," both are obliged to alter course to starboard.

- Generally, when a vessel under power meets a vessel under sail (i.e., not using any mechanical power), the powered vessel must alter course accordingly.

- Exceptions are vessels not under command, vessels restricted in ability to maneuver, vessels engaged in commercial fishing or those under International Rules such as a vessel constrained by draft.

Two sailboats meeting under sail:

- When each has the wind on a different side, the boat with the wind on the port side must keep clear of the boat with the wind on the starboard side.

- When both have the wind on the same side, the vessel closest to the wind (windward) will keep clear of the leeward boat.

- A vessel with wind to port that sees a vessel to windward but cannot determine whether the windward vessel has wind to port or starboard will assume that windward vessel is on starboard tack and keep clear.

Keep Watch for Crab Pots!

While crab pots with marker buoys are not intentionally placed inside navigational channels, they sometimes break loose and find their way there. The terms "pot" refers to the enclosed traps (usually a framework of wire) used to catch crabs in shallow waters. The attached retrieval markers can range from colorful buoys to empty milk jugs (or anything else that floats). Most buoys are painted in a color that contrasts the water surface but some are black or even dark blue, which are especially difficult to see in the best of conditions. You do NOT want to get a line wrapped around your prop so it is advisable to have a spotter on the foredeck when traversing fields of pots.

Coast Guard Requirements

The U.S. Coast Guard stands watch at all times to aid vessels of all sizes and the persons on board. In some areas, you can quickly reach the Coast Guard by dialing *CG on a cellular phone. If you have a question of a non-emergency nature, the Coast Guard prefers that you telephone the nearest station. As always, if there is an emergency, initiate a "MAYDAY" call on VHF Channel 16.

In addition to aiding boaters in distress, the Coast Guard also enforces maritime law and conducts safety inspections. While a Coast Guard boarding can be unnerving, if you are responsible and prepared, it will only take 15 to 30 minutes and will be a non-event. First, have your boat in order. This includes having your vessel documentation, registration and insurance documents on hand, as well as your passport. Organize this in a binder and keep it in the nav station so you don't have to fumble around looking for documents and paperwork. You will need to acknowledge the location of any weapons on board and show a permit (when required by state law). The officers will likely focus on areas with the largest safety concerns including the following.

Note that state and local requirements are also considered. If there is a minor violation, they may give you a written warning explaining what needs to be fixed to be in compliance. If you are found with a small violation and correct it quickly, then this will merely be a chance to interact with those whose goal is to keep you as safe as possible on the water.

Life Jackets: One Type I, II, II or V per person plus one Type IV throwable device is required. PFDs must be U.S. Coast Guard-approved, wearable by the intended user and readily accessible. The Type IV throwable device must be located so that it is immediately available.

Visual Distress Signals: All vessels 16 feet and over must be equipped with minimum of 3 day-use and 3 night-use or 3 day/night combination pyrotechnic devices. Non-pyrotechnic substitutes are orange flag (for day use) and electric S-O-S signal light (for night use). Flares must be up to date (e.g., not expired).

Sound Producing Devices: A whistle, horn, siren, etc. capable of a 4-second blast audible for 0.5 mile must be on board for use during periods of reduced visibility. Boats 65 feet and over must have a bell and one whistle or horn required to signal intentions.

Navigation Lights: All powered vessels under 12 meters (39.4 feet) must have working navigational lights and an independent all-around anchor light. Sailboats under power are considered powerboats and must follow "power" rules.

Fire Extinguisher: U.S. Coast Guard-approved, marine-type fire extinguishers are required on any boat with enclosed fuel or engine spaces, enclosed living spaces or permanent (not movable by one person) fuel tanks. They must be in good working condition and readily accessible. (Number of units required depends on vessel length.)

Ventilation: Boats built after August 1, 1980, with enclosed gasoline engines must have a powered ventilation system with one or more exhaust blowers.

Backfire Flame Arrester: All gasoline-powered inboard/outboard or inboard motor boats must be equipped with an approved backfire flame arrester.

Pollution Placard: It is illegal to discharge oil or oily waste into any navigable waters of the U.S. Boats over 26 feet must display a durable oily waste pollution placard of at least 5 by 8 inches in a prominent location.

MARPOL Trash Placard: It is illegal to dump plastic trash anywhere in the ocean or navigable waters of the U.S. Boats over 26 feet must display a durable trash placard at least 4 by 9 inches in a prominent location.

Navigation Rules: Boats 39.4 feet and over must have a copy of current Navigation Rules on board. You can download a copy at www.uscgboating org.

Marine Sanitation Devices: The discharge of treated sewage is allowed within 3 nm of shore except in designated "No Discharge Zone" areas. The Coast Guard will check that overboard discharge outlets can be sealed (and remain sealed if within 3 nm of shore).

Reference Materials

U.S. Coast Guard *Local Notice to Mariners*

The U.S. Coast Guard provides timely marine safety information for the correction of all U.S. Government navigation charts and publications from a wide variety of sources, both foreign and domestic via the *Local Notice to Mariners*. These are divided by district, updated weekly and available as a PDF at www.navcen.uscg.gov. (Select LNMs tab at top of page.)

Cruising Guides

- *ICW Cruising Guide (by Bob423)*, Robert A. Sherer
- *Skipper Bob Cruising Guides*, Ted Stehle (editor)

Navigation

- *A Boater's Guide to Federal Requirements for Recreational Boaters.* Covers equipment requirements, navigation rules and aids to navigation, a sample float plan and safety and survival tips. Can be downloaded as a PDF at www.uscgboating.org/images/420.PDF.

- *NAVIGATION RULES, INTERNATIONAL—INLAND*, U.S. Dept. of Homeland Security. The U.S. Coast Guard requires all vessels over 39 feet carry this book of the national and international rules of the road. Can be downloaded as a PDF at www.navcen.uscg.gov.

- *U.S. Coast Pilot (1-5)*, NOAA. Includes piloting information for coasts, bays, creeks and harbors. Also includes tide tables and highlights restricted areas. Updated weekly and can be downloaded as a PDF at www.nauticalcharts.noaa.gov/publications/coast-pilot/index.html.

- *U.S. Chart No 1. (Chart Symbols)*. Describes the symbols, abbreviations and terms used on NOAA nautical charts. Available online at www.nauticalcharts.noaa.gov/publications/us-chart-1.html.

- *U.S. Aids to Navigation System* is a downloadable guide from the U.S. Coast Guard with basic information on the recognition of U.S. Aids to Navigation System (ATONS). Find it at www.uscgboating.org/images/486.PDF.

Maintenance

- *Boatowner's Mechanical & Electrical Manual* (4th Edition), Nigel Calder
- *Boatowner's Illustrated Electrical Handbook*, Charlie Wing
- *Boat Mechanical Systems Handbook*, David Gerr

Seamanship

- *Anchoring: A Ground Tackler's Apprentice*, Rudy and Jill Sechez
- *Boater's Pocket Reference*, Thomas McEwen
- *Chapman Piloting & Seamanship* (68th Edition), Charles B. Husick
- *Eldridge Tide and Pilot Book* (Annual), Robert E. and Linda White
- *Heavy Weather Sailing* (7th Edition), Peter Bruce
- *Nigel Calder's Cruising Handbook*, Nigel Calder
- *Offshore Cruising Encyclopedia*, Steve & Linda Dashew
- *The Annapolis Book of Seamanship* (4th Edition), John Rousmaniere
- *The Art of Seamanship*, Ralph Naranjo
- *World Cruising Essentials*, Jimmy Cornell

First Aid & Medical

- *Advanced First Aid Afloat* (5th Edition), Dr. Peter F. Eastman
- *DAN Pocket Guide to First Aid for Scuba Diving*, Dan Orr & Bill Clendenden
- *First Aid at Sea*, Douglas Justin and Colin Berry
- *Marine Medicine: A Comprehensive Guide* (2nd Edition), Eric Weiss and Michael Jacobs
- *On-Board Medical Emergency Handbook: First Aid at Sea*, Spike Briggs and Campbell Mackenzie

About the Weather

Every day on the water can't have balmy breezes, abundant sunshine and consistently warm weather; however, staying out of bad weather is relatively easy if you plan ahead. The National Weather Service (NWS) provides mariners with continuous broadcasts of weather warnings, forecasts, radar reports and buoy reports over VHF-FM and Single Side Band (SSB) radio. There are almost no areas on the Atlantic ICW where a good quality, fixed-mount VHF cannot pick up one or more coastal VHF broadcasts. Also, there is no substitute for simply looking at the sky, and either stay put or seek shelter if you don't like what you see.

Reading the Skies

Water and metal are excellent conductors of electricity, making boating in a thunderstorm a risky prospect. While the odds of a given boat being hit are small, the consequences are severe and deadly. Do not try and play the odds! The best advice if you are out on the water and skies are threatening is get back to land and seek safe shelter, but that's not always practical for cruisers who live aboard or are not near land.

Thunderstorms occur when air masses of different temperatures meet over inland or coastal waters. An example of this would be when air with a high humidity that is warm near the ground rises and meets cooler air, which condenses and creates water droplets. This releases energy, which charges the atmosphere and creates lightning. This is why thunderstorms are a daily occurrence between March and October near southern waterways.

A tell-tale sign of a thunderstorm is cumulonimbus clouds: those tall clouds with an anvil-shaped (flat) top. Thunderstorms can also precede even a minor cold front. Keep in mind that thunderstorms generally move in an easterly direction so if you see a storm to the south or southwest of you, start preparing.

Don't Wait Until It's Too Late!

Almost all lightning will occur within 10 miles of its parent thunderstorm, but it can strike much farther than that. Also, the current from a single flash will easily travel for long distances. Because of this, if you see lightning or hear thunder, you CAN get struck!

Weather Apps (Free)
Boat Weather
Buoycast: NOAA Marine Forecast
National Hurricane Center Tracker
NOAA Marine Weather Radar
NOAA Weather
PredictWind
Wind Alert
Windfinder
Windy

Weather Online
Accuweather (www.accuweather.com)
BoatUS Hurricane Tracking & Resource Center (www.boatus.com/hurricanes/tracking)
Buoy Weather (www.buoyweather.com)
Coastal Marine Forecast (www.weather.gov/marine)
National Hurricane Center (www.nhc.noaa.gov)
National Weather Service (www.weather.gov)
Passage Weather (www.passageweather.com)
Predict Wind (www.predictwind.com)
Sailflow (www.sailflow.com)
The Weather Channel (www.weather.com)
Windfinder (www.windfinder.com)

The ability to see lightning will depend on the time of day, weather conditions and obstructions, but on a clear night it is possible to see a strike more than 10 miles away. Thunder can also be heard for about 10 miles, provided there is no background noise such as traffic, wind or rain.

If you see lightning, you can determine the distance by timing how long it takes before you hear thunder. The old rule that every 5 seconds of time equals 1 mile of distance works well. So if it takes 20 seconds to hear thunder after you see lighting, then the storm is 4 miles away. Time to drop anchor and "hunker down"!

Lightning Safety Tips

Lightning tends to strike the tallest object and boats on the open water fit this profile. The lightning will try to take the most direct path to the water, which is usually down the mast on a sailboat or the VHF antenna on a powerboat. However, both sailboats and powerboats with cabins–especially those with lightning protection systems properly installed–are relatively safe, provided you keep a few things in mind:

■ Before the storm strikes, lower, remove or tie down all antennas, fishing rods and flag poles.

■ Stay down below and in the center of the cabin. Avoid keel-stepped masts and chain plates (on sailboats) and large metal appliances such as microwaves or TVs. Remove any metal jewelry.

■ Disconnect the power and antenna leads to all electronics including radios. Do not use the VHF radio unless absolutely necessary.

■ If you are stuck on deck, stay away from metal railings, the wheel, the mast and stays (on sailboats) or other metal fittings. Do not stand between the mast and stays as lightning can "side-flash" from one to the other.

■ Stay out of the water and don't fish or dangle your feet overboard. Salt water conducts electricity, which means that it can easily travel through the water toward you.

■ Don't think rubber-soled deck shoes will save you; while rubber is an electric insulator, it's only effective to a certain point. The average lightning bolt carries about 30,000 amps of charge, has 100 million volts of electric potential and is about 50,000°F.

If You Are Struck:

1. **Check people first.** Many individuals struck by lightning or exposed to excessive electrical current can be saved with prompt and proper cardiopulmonary resuscitation (CPR). Contrary to popular belief, there is no danger in touching persons after they have been struck by lightning.

2. **Check the bilge** as strikes can rupture through-hull fittings and punch holes in hulls. Props and rudders are natural exit points on boats.

3. **Check electronics and the compasses.** Typically everything in the path of the lightning is destroyed on the way down to the water including instruments, computers and stereos.

4. **Consider a short haul** to check the bottom thoroughly. Lightning strikes sometimes leave traces of damage that may only be seen when the boat is out of the water.

Don't Rush Back Out

Because electrical charges can linger in clouds after a thunderstorm has passed, experts agree that you should wait at least 30 minutes after a storm before resuming activities. And remember: If you can hear thunder, you can still be struck by lightning!

Natural Seasickness Remedies

■ *Take slow, deep breaths.* This helps soothe upset stomach and dizziness.

■ *Focus on the horizon.* Keep your body still and head facing forward and watch a stationary object. Taking the helm always helps.

■ *Ginger can help.* Eat ginger snaps, drink ginger tea or ginger ale or digest in capsule form ahead of time.

■ *Peppermint works too.* Sucking on a peppermint candy, drinking peppermint tea or breathing in peppermint oil dabbed on a cloth can help with stomach issues.

■ *Try acupuncture wristbands.* Apply pressure to specific points on your wrist to reduce nausea.

Tropical Weather & Hurricanes

While all coastal areas of the country are vulnerable to the effects of a hurricane (especially from June through November), the Gulf Coast, Southern and Mid-Atlantic states typically have been the hardest hit. But northern locales aren't immune; several destructive hurricanes have dealt a blow to areas in New England over the last 100 years including Hurricane Sandy in 2012 and Matthew in 2016. While hurricanes can create vast swaths of devastation, ample preparation can help increase your boat's chances of surviving the storm.

According to the National Weather Service, a mature hurricane may be 10 miles high with a great spiral several hundred miles in diameter. Winds are often well above the 74 mph required to classify as hurricane strength, especially during gusts. Hurricane damage is produced by four elements: tidal surge, wind, wave action and rain.

Distance from Eye	Force Level	Wind Speed
150 miles	Force 8	34–40 knots
100 miles	Force 11	56–63 knots
75 miles	Force 12	over 64 knots

■ Tidal surge is an increase in ocean depth prior to the storm. This effect, amplified in coastal areas, may cause tidal heights in excess of 15 to 20 feet above normal. Additionally, hurricanes can produce a significant negative tidal effect as water rushes out of the waterways after a storm.

■ Wind gusts can exceed reported sustained winds by 25 to 50 percent. For example, a storm with winds of 150 mph might have gusts of more than 200 mph, according to the National Weather Service.

■ Wave action is usually the most damaging element of a hurricane for boaters. The wind speed, water depth and the amount of open water determine the amount of wave action created. Storm surges can transform narrow bodies of water into larger, deeper waters capable of generating extreme wave action.

■ Rainfall varies but hurricanes can generate anywhere from 5 to 20 inches or more of rain.

Hurricane Categorization

CATEGORY	PRESSURE	WIND SPEED	SURGE
1	Above 980 mb (Above 28.91 in.)	64–82 knots (74–95 mph)	4–5 ft. (1–1.5 m)
Visibility much reduced. Maneuvering under engines just possible. Open anchorages untenable. Danger of poorly secured boats torn loose in protected anchorages.			
2	965–979 mb (28.50–28.91 in.)	83–95 knots (96–110 mph)	6–8 ft. (1.5–2.5 m)
Visibility close to zero. Boats in protected anchorages at risk, particularly from boats torn loose. Severe damage to unprotected boats and boats poorly secured and prepared.			
3	945–964 mb (27.91–28.50 in.)	96–113 knots (111–130 mph)	9–12 ft. (2.5–3.5 m)
Deck fittings at risk and may tear loose, anchor links can fail and unprotected lines will chafe through. Extensive severe damage.			
4	920–944 mb (27.17–27.91 in.)	114–135 knots (131–155 mph)	13–18 ft. (3.5–5.4 m)
Very severe damage and loss of life.			
5	Below 920 mb (Below 27.17 in.)	Above 135 knots (131–155 mph)	Above 18 ft. (Above 5.4 m)
Catastrophic conditions with catastrophic damage.			

If your boat is in a slip, you have three options: Leave it where it is (if it is in a safe place); move it to a refuge area; or haul it and put it on a trailer or cradle. Some marinas require mandatory evacuations during hurricane alerts. Check your lease agreement and talk to your dockmaster before a hurricane if you are uncertain. Keep in mind that many municipalities close public mooring fields in advance of the storm. In some localities, boaters may be held liable for any damage that their boat inflicts to marina piers or property; check locally for details. Because of this, rivers, canals, coves and other areas away from large stretches of open water are best selected as refuges.

Consult your insurance agent if you have questions about coverage. Many insurance agencies have restricted or canceled policies for boats that travel or are berthed in certain hurricane-prone areas. Review your policy and check your coverage as many insurance companies will not cover boats in hurricane-prone areas during the June through November hurricane season. Riders for this type of coverage are notoriously expensive.

Preparing Your Boat

- Have a hurricane plan made up ahead of time to maximize what you can get done in the amount of time you will have to prepare (no more than 12 hours in some cases). Plan how to tie up the boat or where to anchor before a hurricane is barreling down on you. Make these decisions in advance!

- Buy hurricane gear well in advance. When word of a hurricane spreads, local ship stores run out of storm supplies (anchors and line, especially) very quickly.

- Strip everything that isn't bolted down off the deck of the boat (e.g., canvas, sails, antennas, bimini tops, dodgers, dinghies, dinghy motors, cushions, unneeded control lines on sailboats) as this will help reduce windage and damage to your boat. Remove electronics and valuables and move them ashore.

- Any potentially leaky ports or hatches should be taped up. Dorades (cowls) should be removed and sealed with deck caps.

- Make sure all systems on board are in tip-top shape in case you have to move quickly. Fuel and water tanks should be filled, bilge pumps should be in top operating condition and batteries should be fully charged.

- You will need many lengths of line to secure the boat; make certain it is good stretchy nylon (not Dacron). It is not unusual to string 600 to 800 feet of dock line on a 40-foot-long boat in preparation for a hurricane. If you can, double up your lines (two for each cleat) as lines can break during a strong storm. Have fenders and fender boards out and make sure all of your lines are protected from chafing.

- If you are anchored out, use multiple large anchors; there is no such thing as an anchor that is too large. If you can, tie to trees with a good root system such as mangroves or live oaks. Mangroves are particularly good because their canopy can have a cushioning effect. Be sure mooring lines include ample scope to compensate for tides 10 to 20 feet above normal.

- Lastly, do not stay aboard to weather out the storm. Many people have been seriously injured (or worse) trying to save their boats during a hurricane. Take photos of the condition in which you left your boat and take your insurance papers with you.

Returning Safely After the Storm

- Before hitting the road, make sure the roads back to your boat are open and safe for travel. Beware of dangling wires, weakened docks, bulkheads, bridges and other structures.

- Check your boat thoroughly before attempting to move it. If returning to your home slip, watch the waters for debris and obstructions. Navigate carefully as markers may be misplaced or missing.

- If your boat should sink, arrange for engine repairs before floating it but only if it is not impeding traffic. Otherwise, you will need to remove it immediately. Contact your insurance company right away to make a claim.

Additional Resources

National Hurricane Center: www.nhc.noaa.gov

BoatUS Hurricane Tracking & Resource Center: www.boatus.com/hurricanes

 **WINTERIZING CHECKLIST**

Boat's Name: _____ Length: _____ Model: _____

Name: _____

Address: _____

City:_____ State: _____ Zip: _____

Phone: _____ Email: _____

ENGINE ROOM

ENGINE(S)

- ☐ Fill fuel tanks and add stabilizer to gasoline
- ☐ Change oil and filter
- ☐ Change fuel filters/separators in engine(s)
- ☐ Check coolant level in freshwater-cooling system and add coolant if necessary
- ☐ Run antifreeze through raw-water-cooling system
- ☐ Make sure water strainers are filled with antifreeze
- ☐ Fog cylinders in gasoline engines
- ☐ Top up battery electrolyte level and put batteries on marine charger

INSTALLED GENERATOR

- ☐ Change oil and filter
- ☐ Change fuel filters/separators
- ☐ Check coolant level in freshwater-cooling system and add coolant if necessary
- ☐ Run antifreeze through raw-water-cooling system
- ☐ Make sure water strainers are filled with antifreeze

OTHER SYSTEMS

- ☐ Flush and fill air conditioning system with antifreeze
- ☐ Run antifreeze through watermaker and pickle as per owner's manual

OUTBOARDS

- ☐ Fill installed fuel tanks and add stabilizer
- ☐ Turn off fuel supply and fog while running
- ☐ Drain gear case and add fresh lubricant
- ☐ Flush engine with muffs and fresh water
- ☐ Store unit in lowest position
- ☐ Inspect/replace anodes
- ☐ Empty fuel from portable tanks into car tank and take them home for storage

 **WINTERIZING CHECKLIST**

OUTDRIVES

- ☐ If water intake is in lower unit, flush and run antifreeze through using muffs
- ☐ Drain gear oil and add fresh lubricant
- ☐ Inspect/replace anodes

BELOWDECKS

- ☐ Pump out holding tank and add antifreeze to head
- ☐ Drain water heater and bypass it
- ☐ Drain freshwater system and run antifreeze through it
- ☐ Run antifreeze through refrigeration, deck washdown pump, etc., per owner's manual
- ☐ Drain shower sump and other places where water pools
- ☐ Remove food
- ☐ Open lockers to air
- ☐ Take home cushions or store on their sides
- ☐ Take home portable electronics
- ☐ Close propane valves and take home portable canisters
- ☐ Verify bilge pump and switch operate properly
- ☐ Clean and dry bilges
- ☐ Secure all ports and hatches
- ☐ Turn off all circuit breakers

IN THE WATER

- ☐ Close all seacocks except for cockpit drains
- ☐ Plug exhaust ports
- ☐ Check docklines and chafe guards – center boat in slip
- ☐ Add or adjust fenders for proper placement

BEFORE YOU GO

- ☐ Tie off tiller/steering wheel
- ☐ Cover/shrinkwrap boat
- ☐ Lock cabin and leave spare key with marina manager

Picking an Anchorage (excerpt)

We all know that unless it is an emergency, in addition to being verboten, it's just plain common sense and courteous to avoid encroaching on or anchoring in a marked channel, or in a location that inhibits a boat's access to or from a slip, mooring, boatyard, or marina, or that interferes with another anchored vessel. Otherwise, just about any other location is fair game, but there are a few prerequisites that should be met in order to qualify it as an acceptable anchorage.

First, there's a minimum acceptable depth of water, which is determined by your boat's draft, plus any additional distance the tide will drop, plus another foot or two–just in case. In dam controlled waterways, the height of the water level above normal pool should also be considered, as the elevated pool level can be lowered back to normal pool without notice, often quickly–think hours.

Also, the wind, depending on its direction can blow water out, anywhere from a few feet in gale force conditions, to ten feet or more in storms or hurricane force winds. Water levels can also become lower than normal when: the moon is in perigee, or during seiches, spring tides, and winter solstice. Neglecting these influences could leave the boat bottoming out, aground, or with too little water to get over a bar.

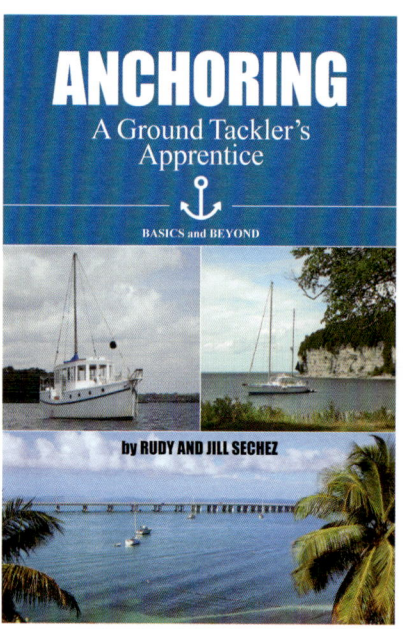

The amount of rode that you can deploy establishes the maximum depth in which you can anchor. If you're anchoring to 5:1 scope, then one fifth the length of your rode is the maximum depth where you can set your anchor; however, in demanding conditions you may need to use 10:1 scope; if so, one tenth the length of your rode would be the maximum depth where you'd want to set your anchor.

Fetch–the distance that the wind can blow over the water without obstruction–can also be a factor when choosing an anchorage, as it can affect comfort. The greater the fetch, the bigger the seas or waves, the more uncomfortable the boat's motion. Our goal is to try to anchor where the fetch is less than a few hundred yards, as beyond this, wave action becomes livelier.

It's prudent to enter unfamiliar anchorages slowly, remaining alert to potential hazards, not just below the surface, but overhead, too–you want enough clearance to prevent snagging bridges, tree limbs, or other dangers, and with power lines, to prevent arcing.

If obstructions are a concern or soundings reveal questionable depths, not only where the boat will initially be anchored, but later where the boat might swing if wind or current shifts direction or strength, then relocate the anchor, or set out an additional anchor or two in a manner that would keep the boat away from any danger.

And keep in mind that your anchor must be compatible with the type of seabed in which you will be anchoring, as well as sized for the wind speed and seas that you will encounter.

Cruising guides are a great resource for identifying anchorages, but if you keep the above guidelines in mind, you just might discover many others, perhaps some that are picturesque, others offering solitude… maybe both.

Rudy and Jill Sechez are the authors of "ANCHORING–A Ground Tackler's Apprentice." To read more, order a copy at www.waterwayguide.com or call 800-233-3359. Rudy and Jill are Trawler Training and Anchoring Consultants, providing one-on-one onboard sessions, consultations, and group seminars. They are also available to talk to groups and clubs. To arrange to have them speak to your organization, contact them at rudyandjill@yahoo.com.

Overview of a Mooring System

A mooring refers to any permanent structure to which a vessel may be secured. A "mooring system" refers to the various components–an anchor, a rode (typically a rope, chain, or cable), a buoy and a pennant. An anchor is used to fix a vessel to a point on the bottom of the seafloor without connecting it to land.

There are four basic types of anchors used in moorings: deadweight anchors, mushroom anchors, pyramid anchors and helix anchors. The table below describes the types of anchors and their characteristics.

Anchor Summary Table

	HOLDING POWER	ADVANTAGES	DISADVANTAGES	NOTES
DEADWEIGHT	An 8,000-lb. concrete mooring has approximately 4,000 lb. of holding power	• Simple design • Good for most bottom types • Holds position even if dragged during storm	• Heavy and bulky • Requires assistance for installation	• Better suited for rock bottoms • Deadweight moorings made from concrete can lose over one-half of their weight when submerged in water • Deadweight moorings made from granite can lose over one-third of their weight when submerged in water • Fault lines in stone anchors can crack when putting in staples
MUSHROOM	A 500-lb. mushroom anchor has approximately 1,200 lb. of holding power	• High holding power-to-weight ratio	• Limited success in rocky areas • Prone to spin-out and chain wrap	• Better suited for muddy bottom conditions • Weight of mushroom anchors generally would be 10 to 20 lbs per foot of boat in mud bottom • Proper installation is important to assure it is buried
PYRAMID	A 650-lb. pyramid anchor has approximately 6,500 lb. of holding power	• High holding power-to-weight ratio • Simple design	• Limited success in rocky areas • Higher cost	• Better suited for muddy bottom conditions • Size and shape help penetrate the bottom more rapidly • Weight of pyramid anchors generally would be 10 to 20 lbs per foot of boat in mud bottom
HELIX	A 10-inch screw Helix anchor has approximately 10,000 lb. of holding power	• High holding power-to-weight ratio • Small size • Longevity • More environmentally sensitive	• Heavy and bulky • Requires specialized installer • Difficult in rock • More difficult to move	• Better suited for softer bottom conditions • Don't perform as well in rocky bottoms • Type of helix used might differ with condition of bottom • Requires diver to set and maintain

Source: *A Preliminary Guide to Mooring Systems, Mooring Choices and Mooring Selection.* Maine Coastal Program (www.maine.gov/dmr/mcp/downloads/access/moorings.pdf. For other helpful publications visit www.maine.gov/dmr/mcp/publications/index.html).

America's Waterway Guide Since 1947

Southern

Chesapeake Bay

Great Lakes Vol. 1

Great Lakes Vol. 2

Northern

Mid-Atlantic

Bahamas

Florida Keys

Gulf Coast

Cuba

Skipper Bob Publications

Bahamas Bound

Anchorages
Along the Intracoastal Waterway

Cruising the
New York Canal System

Cruising the
Gulf Coast

Cruising America's
Great Loop

Cruising the
Rideau & Richelieu Canals

Marinas
Along the Intracoastal Waterway

Cruising the
Trent-Severn Waterway,
Georgian Bay and North Channel

Cruising from
Chicago to Mobile

The Mobile App from Waterway Guide

To St. Augustine

The beach regions running south from Jacksonville are collectively referred to as the "First Coast" because this is the location of Florida's first European settlements. It vigorously competes with the Gold Coast, the Sun Coast and the Treasure Coast for developer and tourist dollars. The area begins a parade of shoreside communities

Download on the **App Store**

GET IT ON **Google Play**

No Signal? No Problem!
DOWNLOAD CONTENT

Boating Destinations

Boating Destinations in the Chesapeake Bay Region

Destinations · Destinations · Destinations

The Explorer web app
waterwayguide.com

WATERWAY GUIDE® MEDIA

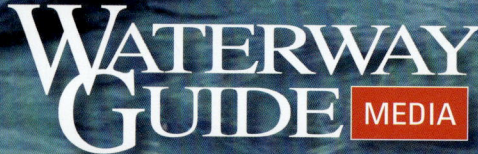

Ditch Bag Checklist

Rescue Items

- [ ] Functioning, registered EPIRB
- [ ] Handheld VHF radio (waterproof or in sealed pouch with extra batteries)
- [ ] Sea anchor, drogue and line
- [ ] Manual inflation pump
- [ ] Selection of flares (parachute and handheld) and smoke signals
- [ ] Strobe light (may be present in inflatable PFD)
- [ ] Flashlight & batteries (headlamp is ideal)
- [ ] Whistle (may be present in inflatable PFD)
- [ ] Signal mirror
- [ ] Handheld GPS or compass (for position)
- [ ] Small pair of binoculars (to confirm a boat or plane spotting before using flares)

Survival Items

- [ ] Sponges and bailer (with handle)
- [ ] Patch kit for inflatable dinghy or life raft (or emergency clamps)
- [ ] Water (individually sealed or in collapsible containers)–at least 2 gallons per person
- [ ] Emergency food rations and can opener (if needed)
- [ ] Power Bars
- [ ] Prescription medications
- [ ] Seasickness medications/remedies
- [ ] First aid kit
- [ ] Multipurpose tool or sailor's knife
- [ ] Waterproof matches

Other Items

- [ ] Solar blanket
- [ ] Heavy-duty coated gloves
- [ ] Duct tape
- [ ] Sewing kit
- [ ] Simple fishing gear (line, jigs, hooks, etc.)
- [ ] Polypropylene line
- [ ] Waterproof sunscreen and zinc oxide
- [ ] Bug repellent
- [ ] Ziploc bags (gallon size)
- [ ] Paper and pen in Ziploc bag
- [ ] Spare prescription glasses and sunglasses (polarized to reduce glare)
- [ ] Laminated copies of passports or license
- [ ] Cash ($50 in small bills)
- [ ] Copy of the yacht's papers (including insurance)

Dealing With Onboard Waste

Up until the late 1980s, many boaters simply discharged their untreated sewage overboard into the water. After a revision to the Clean Water Act was passed in 1987, the discharge of untreated sewage into U.S. waters within the 3-mile limit was prohibited. Shortly thereafter, pump-out stations became a regular feature at marinas and fuel docks throughout the U.S. waterways.

Simply stated, if you have a marine head installed on your vessel and are operating in coastal waters within the U.S. 3-mile limit (basically all of the waters covered in the guide you are now holding), you need to have a holding tank and you will obviously need to arrange to have that tank pumped out from time to time.

Government regulation aside, properly disposing of your waste is good environmental stewardship. While your overboard contribution to the waterways may seem small in the grand scheme of things, similar attitudes among fellow boaters can quickly produce unsavory conditions in anchorages and small creeks. The widespread availability of holding tank gear and shoreside pump-out facilities leaves few excuses for not doing the right thing.

No-Discharge Zones

- No-Discharge means exactly what the name suggests: No waste, even waste treated by an onboard Type I marine sanitation device (MSD), may be discharged overboard. All waste must be collected in a holding tank and pumped out at an appropriate facility.

- Keep in mind that there are some areas that forbid overboard discharge of any waste including gray water from showers or sinks. Familiarize yourself with local regulations before entering new areas to ensure you don't get hit with a fine.

The Law

- If you have a marine head onboard and are operating on coastal waters within the U.S. 3-mile limit (basically all of the waters covered in this guide), you need to have an approved holding tank or Type I MSD. In a No-Discharge area even a Type I MSD system must have a holding tank.

- All valves connected to your holding tank or marine head that lead to the outside (both Y-valves AND seacocks) must be wire-tied, padlocked or absent of the valve handle and in the closed position. Simply having them closed without the (non-releasable) wire ties will not save you from a fine if you are boarded.

- You may discharge waste overboard from a Type I MSD in all areas except those designated as No-Discharge Zones. A Type I MSD treats waste by reducing bacteria and visible solids to an acceptable level before discharge overboard.

- While small and inconvenient for most cruisers, "Port-A-Potties" meet all the requirements for a Type III MSD as the holding tank is incorporated into the toilet itself.

Pump-Out and Holding Tank Basics

- Some marinas are equipped with pump-out facilities, normally located at the marina's fuel dock. Note that some marinas charge a fee for the service.

- Several municipalities and local governments have purchased and staffed pump-out boats that are equipped to visit boats on request, especially those at anchor. Radio the local harbormaster to see if this service is available in the area you are visiting. There is normally a small fee involved.

- You will want to keep an eye out on your holding tank level while you are cruising, especially if you are getting ready to enter an area where you many not have access to proper pump-out services for a few days. Plan a fuel stop or marina stay to top off the fuel and water tanks and empty the other tank before you set out into the wild.

Marine Sanitation Devices

- Type I MSD: Treats sewage before discharging it into the water using maceration. The treated discharge must not show any visible floating

solids and must meet specified standards for bacteria content. Raritan's Electro Scan and Groco's Thermopure systems are examples of Type I MSDs. Not permitted in No-Discharge Zones.

■ Type II MSD: Type II MSDs provide a higher level of waste treatment than Type I units and are larger as a result. They employ biological treatment and disinfection. These units are usually found on larger vessels due to their higher power requirements. These may not be discharged in No-Discharge Zones.

■ Type III MSD: Regular holding tanks store sewage until the holding tank can either be pumped out to an onshore facility or at sea beyond the U.S. boundary waters (i.e., 3 miles offshore).

Composting Heads

Composting heads are essentially Type III MSDs but rather than simply storing sewage, composters separate liquid and solid waste, which speeds up decomposition and reduces odors. This "dry" system promotes decomposition through controlled composting in which the solid portion is converted into an

easy-to-handle, safe, non-odorous humus. There is no need for plumbing, valves, pump or thru-hull and no components to break down, clog up or leak. Other advantages include no pump-outs, uses no water, reduces onboard weight and opens up storage space.

Penalties and Fines

■ Misuse or failure to equip a vessel with a Marine Sanitation Device may result in a non-criminal infraction with a $56 penalty.

■ Illegal dumping/discharge of a Marine Sanitation Device may result in a non-criminal infraction with a $250 penalty.

Additional Resources

BoatU.S. Guide to Overboard Discharge:
www.boatus.com/foundation/guide/environment_7.html

EPA Listing of No-Discharge Zones:
www.epa.gov/vessels-marinas-and-ports/no-discharge-zones-ndzs-state

GPS Waypoints

The following list provides selected waypoints for the waters covered in this book. The latitude/longitude readings are taken from government light lists and must be checked against the appropriate chart and light list for accuracy. Some waypoints listed here are lighthouses and should not be approached too closely as they may be on land, in shallow water or on top of a reef. Many buoys must be approached with caution, as they are often located near shallows or obstructions. The positions of every aid to navigation should be updated using the Coast Guard's *Local Notice to Mariners* (www.navcen.uscg.gov/lnm).

The U.S. Coast Guard will continue to provide Differential GPS (DGPS) correction signals for those who need accuracy of 10 meters or less, even though most GPS receivers now come with an internal capability for receiving differential signals.

Prudent mariners will not rely solely on these waypoints to navigate. Every available navigational tool should be used at all times to determine your vessel's position.

C&D Canal to Cape May

LOCATION	LATITUDE	LONGITUDE
Junction Lighted Bell Buoy CD	N 39°33.867'	W 075°33.300'
Ship John Shoal Light (on shoal)	N 39°18.317'	W 075°22.600'
Elbow of Cross Ledge Light	N 39°10.933'	W 075°16.100'
Miah Maull Shoal Light (on shoal)	N 39°07.600'	W 075°12.600'
Fourteen Foot Bank Light	N 39°02.900'	W 075°10.933'
Brandywine Shoal Light (on shoal)	N 38°59.167'	W 075°06.783'
Brown Shoal Light	N 38°55.333'	W 075°06.050'
Cape May Canal W. Ent. S. Jetty Light 10	N 38°57.967'	W 074°58.033'

Cape May to Sandy Hook

LOCATION	LATITUDE	LONGITUDE
Cape May Inlet West Jetty Light 5	N°38 56.200'	W 074°51.917'
Great Egg Harbor Inlet Otr. Lgtd. Whst. B. GE	N°39 16.233'	W 074°31.933'
Absecon Inlet Breakwater Light 7	N°39 21.833'	W 074°24.433'
Little Egg Inlet Outer Lighted Whistle B. LE	N°39 26.800'	W 074°17.367'
Barnegat Lighted Whistle Buoy B1	N°39 44.483'	W 074°03.850'
Manasquan Inlet Light 3	N°40 00.170'	W 074°01.917'

New York Harbor

LOCATION	LATITUDE	LONGITUDE
Ambrose Light	N 40°27.000'	W 073°48.000'
Junction Lighted Buoy TC	N 40°28.400'	W 074°02.300'
Atlantic Highlands Breakwater Light	N 40°25.117'	W 074°01.167'
Great Kills Light	N 40°31.300'	W 074°07.900'
Coney Island Light	N 40°34.600'	W 074°00.700'
Romer Shoal Light	N 40°30.800'	W 074°00.800'

South Shore of Long Island

LOCATION	LATITUDE	LONGITUDE
Rockaway Inlet Lighted Bell Buoy 2	N 40°31.767'	W 073°56.383'
Jones Inlet Light	N 40°34.383'	W 073°34.533'
Fire Island Light	N 40°37.950'	W 073°13.117'
Moriches Inlet Approach Breakwater Light 2	N 40°45.800'	W 072°45.183'
Shinnecock Inlet Approach Lgtd. Whst. B. SH	N 40°49.000'	W 072°28.600'
Montauk Point Lighted Whistle Buoy MP	N 41°01.800'	W 071°45.700'

Long Island Sound, North Shore

LOCATION	LATITUDE	LONGITUDE
Chimney Sweeps Lighted Buoy 1	N 40°51.750'	W 073°46.783'
Hen and Chickens South Lighted Buoy 2	N 40°54.200'	W 073°44.400'
Great Captain Rocks Lighted Buoy 2	N 40°58.950'	W 073°39.067'
Great Captain Island Light	N 40°58.900'	W 073°37.400'
Twenty-Six Foot Spot Lighted Bell Buoy 32A	N 40°58.100'	W 073°32.800'
Stamford Harbor West Breakwater Light 3	N 41°00.900'	W 073°32.800'
Greens Ledge Light 4	N 44°17.417'	W 068°49.700'
Cable and Anchor Reef Lighted Bell B. 28C	N 41°00.550'	W 073°25.133'
Bridgeport Harbor Ch. Appr. Lgtd. Whst. B. BH	N 41°06.233'	W 073°11.733'
Middle Ground Light	N 41°03.583'	W 073°06.083'
Stratford Point Light	N 41°09.117'	W 073°06.200'
New Haven Harbor Lighted Whistle B. NH	N 41°12.100'	W 072°53.800'
Branford Reef Light	N 41°13.300'	W 072°48.300'
Goose Island Lighted Bell Buoy 10GI	N 41°12.100'	W 072°40.500'
Guilford Harbor Lighted Bell Buoy 4	N 41°15.000'	W 072°39.200'
Long Sand Shoal W. End Ltd. Gong B. W	N 41°13.583'	W 072°27.600'
Saybrook Breakwater Light	N 41°15.800'	W 072°20.567'
Long Sand Shoal East End Buoy E	N 41°15.800'	W 072°19.350'
Bartlett Reef Light	N 41°16.467'	W 072°08.233'
New London Channel Lighted Buoy 1	N 41°17.600'	W 072°04.800'
Seaflower Reef Light	N 41°17.767'	W 072°01.983'
North Dumpling Light	N 41°17.300'	W 072°01.200'
Latimer Reef Light	N 41°18.300'	W 071°56.000'
Inner Reef North Buoy 5	N 41°14.533'	W 072°46.050'

Long Island Sound, South Shore

LOCATION	LATITUDE	LONGITUDE
Stepping Stones Light	N 40°49.467'	W 073°46.483'
Hart Island Light 46	N 40°50.700'	W 073°46.000'
Plum Point Lighted Buoy 1	N 40°49.933'	W 073°43.717'
Gangway Rock Light 27A	N 40°51.483'	W 073°44.750'
Execution Rocks Light	N 40°52.683'	W 073°44.267'
Glen Cove Breakwater Light 5	N 40°51.700'	W 073°39.600'
Cold Spring Harbor Light	N 40°54.800'	W 073°29.600
Eaton's Neck Light	N 40°57.233'	W 073°23.717'
Port Jefferson Appr. Lighted Whistle Buoy PJ	N 40°59.300'	W 073°06.400'
Mattituck Inlet Breakwater Light MI	N 41°00.917'	W 072°33.667'
Orient Point Light	N 41°09.800'	W 072°13.400'
Valiant Rock Lighted Whistle Buoy 11	N 41°13.767'	W 072°04.000'
Race Rock Light	N 41°14.617'	W 072°02.817'
Gardiners Island Lighted Gong Buoy 1GI	N 41°09.000'	W 072°08.900'
Gardiners Bay S. Ent. Lighted Bell Buoy S	N 41°02.200'	W 072°03.100'
Threemile Harbor Ent. Lighted Bell Buoy TM	N 41°02.700'	W 072°11.300'
Montauk Harbor Ent. Lighted Bell Buoy M	N 41°05.100'	W 071°56.400'

Rhode Island

LOCATION	LATITUDE	LONGITUDE
Watch Hill Lighted Bell Buoy 2	N 41°17.983'	W 071°51.667'
Great Salt Pond Entrance Bell Buoy 2	N 41°12.100'	W 071°35.700'
Block Island N. Reef Lighted Bell Buoy 1BI	N 41°15.500'	W 071°34.600'
Point Judith Lighted Whistle Buoy 2	N 41°18.500'	W 071°28.300'
Narragansett Bay Ent. Lighted Whistle B. NB	N 41°23.000'	W 071°23.400'
Beavertail Light	N 41°26.967'	W 071°23.983'
Brenton Point Lighted Whistle Buoy 2	N 41°25.900'	W 071°21.800'
Sakonnet River Ent. Lighted Whistle B. SR	N 41°25.700'	W 071°13.400'

Buzzards Bay

LOCATION	LATITUDE	LONGITUDE
Buzzards Bay Entrance Light	N 41°23.800'	W 071°02.017'
Westport Harbor Entrance Light 7	N 41°30.400'	W 071°05.300'
Padanaram Breakwater Light 8	N 41°34.450'	W 070°56.350'
Phinney Rock Lighted Buoy DP	N 41°33.100'	W 070°53.000'
Butler Flats Light	N 41°36.200'	W 070°53.700'
New Bedford West Barrier Light	N 41°37.617'	W 070°54.367'
Dumpling Rocks Light 7	N 41°32.300'	W 070°55.283'
Ned Point Light	N 41°39.050'	W 070°47.733'
Sippican Harbor Lighted Buoy 2	N 41°39.700'	W 070°43.600'
Cleveland East Ledge Light	N 41°37.850'	W 070°41.650'
Quisset Harbor Entrance Lighted Buoy 2	N 41°32.600'	W 070°40.000'
Lone Rock Lighted Buoy	N 41°27.650'	W 070°51.150'
Cuttyhunk East Ent. Lighted Bell Buoy CH	N 41°26.600'	W 070°53.400'
Cuttyhunk West Entrance Buoy 1W	N 41°26.700'	W 070°55.500'

Cape Cod's South Shore, Vineyard Sound, Nantucket Sound

LOCATION	LATITUDE	LONGITUDE
Coffin Rock Lighted Buoy 1	N 41°30.700'	W 070°39.700'
Falmouth Inner Harbor Light 1	N 41°32.517'	W 070°36.500'
Hyannis Harbor Appr. Lighted Bell Buoy HH	N 41°36.000'	W 070°17.200'
4. Chatham Roads Bell Buoy 3	N 41°38.300'	W 070°02.900'
Vineyard Sound Ent. Ltd. Whistle Buoy 32	N 41°22.100'	W 070°57.400'
Quicks Hole Entrance Ltd. Bell Buoy 1	N 41°25.800'	W 070°50.400'
Tarpaulin Cove Light	N 41°28.133'	W 070°45.450'
West Chop Light	N 41°28.850'	W 070°35.983'
East Chop Light	N 41°28.217'	W 070°34.050'
Edgartown Light	N 41°23.450'	W 070°30.183'
Cape Poge Light	N 41°25.167'	W 070°27.133'
Nantucket Bar Lighted Bell Buoy NB	N 41°19.000'	W 070°06.200'
Brant Point Light	N 41°17.400'	W 070°05.417'

Cape Cod Bay to Boston

LOCATION	LATITUDE	LONGITUDE
Cape Cod Canal Appr. Lighted Bell Buoy CC	N 41°48.900'	W 070°27.600'
Billingsgate Shoal Lighted Bell Buoy 1	N 41°48.800'	W 070°05.417'
Long Point Shoal Lighted Bell Buoy 3	N 42°02.000'	W 070°09.700'
Plymouth Bay Channel Lighted Buoy 3	N 41°59.700'	W 070°36.100'
Scituate Approach Lighted Gong Buoy SA	N 42°12.100'	W 070°41.900'
Nantasket Roads Channel Lighted Bell B. 3	N 42°19.100'	W 070°52.800'
Boston Lighted Whistle Buoy B	N 42°22.700'	W 070°47.000'
Boston South Channel Entrance Buoy 1	N 42°21.900'	W 070°53.800'
Boston North Chan. Ent. Lighted Whistle B. NC	N 42°22.500'	W 070°54.300'

Massachusetts Bay to Portsmouth

LOCATION	LATITUDE	LONGITUDE
Tinkers Rock Gong Buoy TR	N 42°28.900'	W 070°48.900'
Marblehead Harbor Buoy 1MH	N 42°30.500'	W 070°50.000'
Salem Channel Buoy 3	N 42°31.100'	W 070°45.100'
Eastern Point Lighted Whistle Buoy 2	N 42°34.200'	W 070°39.800'
Annisquam River Ent. Lighted Bell Buoy AR	N 42°40.400'	W 070°41.000'
Essex Bay Entrance Lighted Bell Buoy 1	N 42°40.800'	W 070°42.300'
Merrimack River Ent. Lighted Whistle B. MR	N 42°48.600'	W 070°47.100'
Rye Harbor Ent. Lighted Whistle Buoy RH	N 42°59.633'	W 070°43.750'
Wood Island Lighted Buoy 2	N 43°27.400'	W 070°19.700'
Isles of Shoals Bell Buoy IS	N 42°58.867'	W 070°37.267'

Kittery to Portland

LOCATION	LATITUDE	LONGITUDE
York Harbor Lighted Bell Buoy YH	N 43°07.800'	W 070°37.000'
Perkins Cove Lighted Bell Buoy PC	N 43°14.400'	W 070°34.200'
Cape Porpoise Lighted Whistle Buoy CP	N 43°20.300'	W 070°23.600'
Wood Island Light	N 43°27.400'	W 070°19.700'
Portland Lighted Horn Buoy P	N 43°31.600'	W 070°05.500'
Portland Head Light	N 43°37.400'	W 070°12.500'

Casco Bay to Penobscot Bay

LOCATION	LATITUDE	LONGITUDE
Halfway Rock Light	N 43°39.350'	W 070°02.200'
Little Mark Island Monument Light	N 43°42.533'	W 070°01.867
Fuller Rock Light	N 43°41.750'	W 069°50.017'
Pond Island Light	N 43°44.400'	W 069°46.200'
Sheepscot River Ent. Lighted Bell Buoy 2SR	N 43°45.600'	W 069°41.200'
Seguin Light	N 43°42.500'	W 069°45.500'
Burnt Island Light	N 43°49.500'	W 069°38.400'
The Cuckolds Light	N 43°46.800'	W 069°39.000'
Ram Island Light	N 43°48.233'	W 069°35.950'
Manana Island Lighted Whistle Buoy 14M	N 43°45.300'	W 069°22.500'
Pemaquid Point Light	N 43°50.200'	W 069°30.350'
Marshall Point Lighted Whistle Buoy MP	N 43°55.300'	W 069°10.900'
Two Bush Ledge Lighted Bell Buoy 5TB	N 43°56.783'	W 069°04.917'
Tenants Harbor App. Lighted Bell Buoy 1	N 43°57.700'	W 069°10.900'
Whitehead Light	N 43°58.717'	W 069°07.450'
W. Penobscot Bay Ent. Lighted Gong B. PA	N 44°01.100'	W 069°00.300'
Matinicus Island Lighted Bell Buoy 9MI	N 43°53.100'	W 068°52.867'

Penobscot Bay to West Quoddy Head

LOCATION	LATITUDE	LONGITUDE
Brown Cow Ledge Whistle Buoy 2BC	N 44°06.733'	W 068°43.850'
Isle Au Haut Light	N 44°03.900'	W 068°39.100'
Saddleback Ledge Light	N 44°00.900'	W 068°43.600'
Burnt Coat Harbor Ent. Whistle Buoy BC	N 44°05.017'	W 068°26.233'
Long Island Lighted Gong Buoy LI	N 44°08.300'	W 068°20.500'
Long Ledge Lighted Gong Buoy 1	N 44°13.267'	W 068°17.783'
Frenchman Bay S. App. Lighted Whistle B. FBS	N 44°09.600'	W 068°08.800'
Great Duck Island Light	N 44°08.500'	W 068°14.700'
Mount Desert Rock Light	N 43°58.100'	W 068°07.700'
Schoodic Lighted Bell Buoy 2S	N 44°19.100'	W 068°02.100'
Southeast Rock Lighted Whistle Buoy 6A	N 44°19.800'	W 067°48.600'
Seahorse Lighted Bell Buoy 2SR	N 44°25.700'	W 067°38.500'
Moose Peak Light	N 44°28.500'	W 067°31.900'
Libby Island Light	N 44°34.100'	W 067°22.000'
Little River Daybeacon 1	N 44°39.050'	W 067°11.533'
West Quoddy Head Bell Buoy WQ	N 44°48.900'	W 066°57.000'

Distance: Outside (Coastwise) Route–Nantucket Shoals to Chesapeake Bay Entrance

	Chesapeake Bay Entrance	Chincoteague, VA	Ocean City, MD	Indian River Inlet, DE	Trenton, NJ	Former U.S. Steel Basin, PA	Philadelphia, PA	Chester, PA	Marcus Hook, PA	Wilmington, DE	C & D Canal, East Entrance	Harbor of Refuge, DE	Delaware Bay Entrance	Cape May Harbor, NJ	Atlantic City, NJ	Barnegat Inlet, NJ	Manasquan Inlet, NJ	New York, NY	Montauk Point, NY	Nantucket Shoals
Nantucket Shoals 40°30.0'N., 69°25.0'W.	381	328	295	285	400	395	372	356	353	347	336	285	285	271	242	221	212	223	113	-
Montauk Point, NY 41°01.7'N., 71°47.3'W.	322	262	227	209	327	322	299	283	280	274	263	212	212	192	157	131	117	122	-	
New York, NY 40°42.0'N., 74°01.0'W.	267	201	161	145	268	263	240	224	221	215	204	153	153	128	94	63	40	-		
Manasquan Inlet, NJ 40°06.9'N., 72°30.3'W.	291	161	121	105	212	207	184	169	165	159	148	98	97	85	52	22	-			
Barnegat Inlet, NJ 39°46.0'N., 74°06.3'W.	199	141	101	86	193	188	165	150	146	140	129	79	78	65	32	-				
Atlantic City, NJ 39°22.6'N., 74°24.9'W.	171	113	73	57	164	159	136	121	117	111	100	50	49	37	-					
Cape May Harbor, NJ 38°57.1'N., 74°52.6'W.	141	80	40	24	131	126	103	88	84	78	67	17	16	-						
Delaware Bay Entrance 38°50.5'N., 75°03.3'W.	136	72	32	15	115	110	87	72	68	62	51	2	-							
Harbor of Refuge, DE 38°49.0'N., 75°05.2'W.	136	71	31	14	116	111	88	73	69	63	52	-								
C & D Canal, East Entrance 39°33.8'N., 75°32.8'W.	206	123	83	66	64	59	36	21	17	11	-									
Wilmington, DE 39°43.2'N., 75°31.5'W.	218	134	95	77	54	49	26	11	8	-										
Marcus Hook, PA 39°48.2'N., 75°25.2'W.	224	140	101	83	46	41	18	3	-											
Chester, PA 39°50.0'N., 75°22.0'W.	227	144	104	86	43	38	15	-												
Philadelphia, PA 39°56.8'N., 75°08.3'W.	242	159	119	101	28	23	-													
Former U.S. Steel Basin, PA 40°08.2'N., 74°45.3'W.	265	182	142	124	5	-														
Trenton, NJ 40°37.6'N., 73°34.9'W.	270	187	147	129	-															
Indian River Inlet, DE 38°36.5'N., 75°03.6'W.	118	60	20	-																
Ocean City, MD 38°19.6'N., 75°05.6'W.	100	41	-																	
Chincoteague, VA 37°56.1'N., 75°22.8'W.	69	-																		
Chesapeake Bay Entrance 36°56.3'N., 75°58.6'W.	-																			

Five Fathom Bank Lighted Buoy F (38°46.8'N., 74°34.5'W.) to Philadelphia, 111 miles
Delaware Lighted Buoy D (38°27.3'N., 74°41.8'W.) to Philadelphia, 116 miles
Chesapeake Light (36°54.3'N., 75°42.8'W.) to Norfolk, 42 miles; to Baltimore, 165 miles

Distances: Hudson River–New York (The Battery) to Troy Lock, NY

	Troy Lock	Watervliet	Troy	Rensselaer	Albany	Coeymans	Coxsackie	Athens	Hudson	Catskill	Saugerties	Kingston	Hyde Park	Poughkeepsie	Newburgh	West Point	Peekskill	Haverstraw	Ossining	Nyak	Tarrytown	Yonkers	New York (The Battery)
New York (The Battery) 40°42.0'N., 74°01.0'W.	134	132	132	126	126	115	108	102	102	99	89	80	71	66	53	45	38	33	29	25	24	16	-
Yonkers 40°56.1'N., 73°54.3'W.	118	116	116	110	110	100	93	86	86	83	74	64	55	50	37	29	23	18	14	10	9	-	
Tarrytown 41°04.7'N., 73°52.2'W.	110	108	108	102	102	92	85	78	78	75	66	56	47	42	29	21	15	9	6	2	-		
Nyack 41°05.4'N., 73°54.9'W.	110	108	108	102	102	92	85	78	78	75	66	57	48	43	29	22	15	10	6	-			
Ossining 41°09.6'N., 73°52.3'W.	106	104	104	98	98	88	80	74	74	71	62	52	43	38	25	17	11	5	-				
Haverstraw 41°11.8'N., 73°57.5'W.	102	100	100	94	94	84	76	70	70	67	58	48	39	34	21	13	6	-					
Peekskill 41°17.3'N., 73°56.0'W.	96	94	94	88	88	78	71	64	64	61	52	43	34	29	15	8	-						
West Point 41°23.1'N., 73°57.3'W	89	87	87	81	81	70	63	57	57	54	45	35	26	21	8	-							
Newburgh 41°30.1'N., 74°00.3'W.	81	79	79	73	73	62	55	49	49	46	37	27	18	13	-								
Poughkeepsie 41°42.3'N., 73°56.5'W.	68	66	66	60	60	49	42	36	36	33	24	14	5	-									
Hyde Park 41°47.3'N., 73°56.9'W.	63	61	61	55	55	44	37	31	31	28	19	9	-										
Kingston 41°55.1'N., 73°59.0'W.	56	54	54	48	48	38	30	24	24	21	12	-											
Saugerties 42°04.4'N., 73°56.7'W.	46	44	44	38	38	28	21	14	14	11	-												
Catskill 42°13.0'N., 73°52.1'W.	37	35	35	29	29	19	11	5	5	-													
Hudson 42°15.3'N., 73°48.1'W.	32	30	30	24	24	14	7	1	-														
Athens 42°15.6'N., 73°48.5'W.	32	30	30	24	24	14	6	-															
Coxsackie 42°21.0'N., 73°47.6'W.	26	24	24	18	18	7	-																
Coeymans 42°28.5'N., 73°47.4'W.	18	16	16	10	10	-																	
Albany 42°37.9'N., 73°45.3'W.	8	6	6	0	-																		
Rensselaer 42°37.9'N., 73°45.1'W.	8	6	6	-																			
Troy 42°43.7'N., 73°41.8'W.	2	0	-																				
Watervliet 42°43.7'N., 73°41.9'W.	2	-																					
Troy Lock 41°45.1'N., 73°41.1'W.	-																						

Distance: Inside (NJ ICW) Route–New York (The Battery) to C&D Canal (east entrance)

	C & D Canal (east entrance)	Cape May Canal (west entrance)	Cape May Harbor	Wildwood	Stone Harbor	Avalon	Sea Isle City	Ocean City	Mays Landing	Atlantic City	Beach Haven	Barnegat Inlet	Forked River (town)	Seaside Park	Toms River (town)	Mantoloking	Bay Head	Manasquan Inlet	Shark River Inlet*	New York, NY (The Battery)
New York, NY (The Battery) 40°42.0'N., 74°01.0'W.	190	142	138	133	128	123	119	108	124	97	79	66	63	54	58	46	44	40	34	-
Shark River Inlet* 40°11.2'N., 74°00.5'W.	156	108	103	99	94	89	85	74	90	62	45	32	29	20	23	11	9	6	-	
Manasquan Inlet 40°06.1'N., 74°01.9'W.	150	102	98	93	88	83	79	68	84	57	39	26	23	14	18	6	4	-		
Bay Head 40°03.8'N., 74°03.1'W.	146	98	94	89	85	79	76	64	80	53	35	22	19	10	14	2	-			
Mantoloking 40°02.2'N., 74°03.4'W.	144	96	92	88	83	77	74	63	79	51	33	20	17	9	12	-				
Toms River (town) 39°56.9'N., 74°11.8'W.	142	94	90	86	81	75	72	60	77	49	31	18	15	7	-					
Seaside Park 39°55.3'N., 74°05.0'W.	137	89	85	80	75	70	66	55	71	44	26	13	10	-						
Forked River (town) 39°50.1'N., 74°11.7'W.	132	84	80	75	70	65	61	50	66	39	21	8	-							
Barnegat Inlet 39°46.0'N., 74°06.3'W.	131	83	79	74	69	64	60	49	65	38	20	-								
Beach Haven 39°34.0'N., 74°14.8'W.	111	63	59	54	49	44	40	29	45	18	-									
Atlantic City 39°22.6'N., 74°24.9'W.	95	47	43	39	34	28	25	13	30	-										
Mays Landing 39°26.9'N., 74°43.4'W.	100	52	47	43	38	33	29	18	-											
Ocean City 39°17.3'N., 74°34.4'W.	82	34	30	25	20	15	11	-												
Sea Isle City 39°09.4'N., 74°42.0'W.	71	23	18	14	9	4	-													
Avalon 39°06.6'N., 74°44.0'W.	67	19	15	10	5	-														
Stone Harbor 39°03.4'N., 74°46.0'W.	62	14	9	5	-															
Wildwood 39°00.5'N., 74°49.8'W.	57	9	5	-																
Cape May Harbor 38°57.1'N., 74°52.6'W.	52	4	-																	
Cape May Canal (west entrance) 38°58.0'N., 74°58.0'W.	48	-																		
C & D Canal (east entrance) 39°33.8'N., 75°32.8'W.	-																			

*Outside distances between New York and Manesquan Inlet

Distances: Long Island Sound–Greenport, NY to Manasquan Inlet, NJ

	* Manasquan Inlet, NJ	* New York (The Battery)	* Rockaway Point	East Rockaway Inlet	Long Beach	Freeport	Jones Inlet	Jones Beach	Amityville	Babylon	Fire Island Inlet	Bay Shore	Patchogue	Bellport	Moriches Inlet	Westhampton Beach	Shinnecock Inlet	Shinnecock Canal (north end)	Riverside	Sag Harbor	Greenport
Greenport 41°06.0'N., 72°21.5'W.	116	107	94	85	80	77	76	72	66	61	62	57	48	42	34	28	21	16	21	11	-
Sag Harbor 41°00.2'N., 72°17.7'W.	117	108	95	86	81	78	77	73	67	62	63	58	49	43	35	29	22	17	22	-	
Riverside 40°55.0'N., 72°39.4'W.	108	99	86	77	72	69	68	64	58	53	54	49	40	34	26	20	13	8	-		
Shinnecock Canal 40°53.9'N., 72°30.3'W.	100	91	78	69	64	61	60	56	50	45	46	41	32	26	18	12	5	-			
Shinnecock Inlet 40°50.3'N., 72°28.6'W.	97	88	75	66	61	58	58	54	47	42	44	39	29	23	15	9	-				
Westhampton Beach 40°48.2'N., 72°38.4'W.	89	80	67	58	53	49	49	45	39	34	35	30	21	15	7	-					
Moriches Inlet 40°45.8'N., 72°45.3'W.	85	76	63	54	49	46	45	42	35	30	32	27	17	11	-						
Bellport 40°45.1'N., 72°56.0'W	75	66	53	44	38	35	35	31	24	19	21	16	6	-							
Patchogue 40°45.5'N., 73°01.2'W.	72	63	50	41	36	32	32	28	22	17	18	13	-								
Bay Shore 40°42.8'N., 73°14.2'W.	60	51	38	29	24	21	21	17	10	5	9	-									
Fire Island Inlet 40°37.8'N., 73°18.6'W.	60	51	38	29	24	21	20	16	12	8	-										
Babylon 40°41.2'N., 73°18.9'W.	57	48	35	26	21	18	17	13	6	-											
Amityville 40°39.6'N., 73°24.8'W.	51	42	29	20	15	12	11	7	-												
Jones Beach 40°36.2'N., 73°30.8'W.	44	35	22	13	8	4	4	-													
Jones Inlet 40°34.4'N., 73°34.9'W.	41	32	19	10	5	4	-														
Freeport 40°37.6'N., 73°34.9'W.	42	33	20	11	6	-															
Long Beach 40°35.7'N., 73°39.4'W.	36	27	14	5	-																
East Rockaway 40°34.9'N., 73°45.4'W.	31	22	9	-																	
* Rockaway Point 40°32.4'N., 73°56.5'W.	27	13	-																		
* New York (The Battery) 40°42.0'N., 74°01.0'W.	40	-																			
* Manasquan Inlet, New Jersey 40°06.1'N., 74°01.9'W.	-																				

* Outside distances westward of East Rockaway Inlet

Distances: Outside (Coastwise) Route– Cape Cod Canal (East Entrance) to Port Newark, NJ

	Port Newark, NJ	Elizabethport, NJ	Perth Amboy, NJ	New York City, NY	Montauk Point, NY	Port Jefferson, NY	Greenport, NY	Sag Harbor, NY	Montauk, NY	Stamford, CT	South Norwalk, CT	Bridgeport, CT	Stratford, CT	New Haven, CT	Hartford, CT	New London, CT	Stonington, CT	Great Salt Pond, RI	Providence, RI	Fall River, MA	Newport, RI	New Bedford, MA	Woods Hole, MA	Vineyard Haven, MA	Nantucket, MA	Nantucket Shoals, MA	Cape Cod Canal (E. Ent.)
Cape Cod Canal (E. Ent.) 41°46.8'N., 70°29.0'W.	193	191	202	182	76	134	99	100	85	152	151	138	132	127	140	89	77	66	74	69	54	31	22	43	69	144	-
Nantucket Shoals, MA 40°30.0'N., 69°25.0'W.	227	225	223	223	113	178	142	143	127	196	195	182	176	171	187	136	126	114	131	126	111	111	92	88	85	-	
Nantucket, MA 41°17.2'N., 70°05.7'W.	208	206	216	196	89	149	113	114	99	167	166	153	147	140	155	103	92	80	91	77	71	53	33	29	-		
Vineyard Haven, MA 41°27.3'N., 70°35.8'W.	183	181	191	171	63	123	87	88	74	141	140	127	121	114	129	77	67	54	65	51	45	28	7	-			
Woods Hole, MA 41°31.4'N., 70°40.4'W.	178	176	186	166	59	118	82	83	69	136	135	123	117	109	125	72	61	50	57	44	38	15	-				
New Bedford, MA 41°38.1'N., 70°55.1'W.	178	176	186	166	60	118	80	81	66	136	135	122	113	111	124	74	58	48	58	54	38	-					
Newport, RI 41°29.8'N., 71°19.8'W.	151	149	159	139	35	91	56	57	42	109	108	95	90	84	98	48	34	23	21	16	-						
Fall River, MA 41°42.4'N., 71°09.8'W.	166	164	174	154	51	107	71	72	58	125	124	110	105	100	113	63	49	38	21	-							
Providence, RI 41°48.5'N., 71°24.0'W.	171	169	179	159	56	112	76	77	63	130	129	115	110	105	118	68	55	43	-								
Great Salt Pond, RI 41°11.1'N., 71°34.9'W.	133	131	141	121	15	74	37	39	23	92	91	78	72	65	80	29	19	-									
Stonington, CT 41°19.9'N., 71°54.6'W.	121	119	129	109	19	61	28	29	18	79	77	64	59	52	66	12	-										
New London, CT 41°21.4'N., 72°05.4'W.	116	114	124	104	28	56	25	27	20	74	73	60	54	49	62	-											
Hartford, CT 41°45.0'N., 72°39.0'W.	143	141	151	131	75	84	62	64	66	102	101	86	81	74	-												
New Haven, CT 41°17.4'N., 72°54.5'W.	80	78	88	68	62	23	47	49	51	37	36	25	15	-													
Stratford, CT 41°11.3'N., 73°07.3'W.	69	67	77	57	65	15	52	54	56	27	26	10	-														
Bridgeport, CT 41°10.3'N., 73°10.8'W.	64	62	72	52	74	15	58	60	62	22	21	-															
South Norwalk, CT 41°05.7'N., 73°24.7'W.	52	50	60	40	84	23	71	73	75	11	-																
Stamford, CT 41°01.8'N., 73°32.3'W.	45	43	53	33	85	24	72	74	76	-																	
Montauk, NY 41°02.8'N., 71°57.5'W.	117	115	125	105	16	58	22	21	-																		
Sag Harbor, NY 41°00.2'N., 72°17.7'W.	115	113	123	103	32	56	11	-																			
Greenport, NY 41°06.0'N., 72°21.5'W.	114	112	122	102	30	54	-																				
Port Jefferson, NY 40°57.0'N., 73°04.5'W.	64	62	72	52	68	-																					
Montauk Point, NY 41°01.7'N., 71°47.3'W.	126	124	123	20	-																						
New York City, NY 40°42.0'N., 74°01.0'W.	12	10	20	-																							
Perth Amboy, NJ 40°30.3'N., 74°15.7'W.	15	10	-																								
Elizabethport, NJ 40°38.8'N., 74°11.2'W.	5	-																									
Port Newark, NJ 40°41.8'N., 74°09.0'W.	-																										

Distances: Gulf of Maine–Calais, ME to Nantucket Shoals

	Nantucket Shoals	Provincetown, MA	Cape Cod Canal	Plymouth, MA	Scituate, MA	Boston, MA	Lynn, MA	Marblehead, MA	Salem, MA	Gloucester, MA	Rockport, MA	Newburyport, MA	Portsmouth, NH	York Harbor, ME	Portland, ME	Augusta, ME	Bath, ME	Wiscasset, ME	Boothbay Harbor, ME	Bangor, ME	Bucksport, ME	Searsport, ME	Rockland, ME	Stonington, ME	Buck Harbor, ME	Bar Harbor, ME	Jonesport, ME	Machiasport, ME	Lubec, ME	Eastport, ME	Calais, ME
Calais, ME 45°11.4'N., 67°16.7'W	312	258	270	268	259	265	261	251	252	245	236	241	230	222	198	214	187	189	168	176	159	152	145	118	125	98	66	61	26	24	-
Eastport, ME 44°54.3'N., 66°59.0'W.	297	243	255	253	244	250	246	236	237	230	221	226	216	208	183	200	173	175	153	162	145	137	130	102	109	83	42	46	3	-	
Lubec, ME 44°51.7'N., 66°59.0'W.	286	232	244	242	233	239	235	225	226	219	210	215	204	196	172	188	161	162	142	150	133	126	118	91	98	72	40	35	-		
Machiasport, ME 44°41.9'N., 67°23.6'W.	271	214	226	224	215	221	217	207	208	200	192	197	186	178	153	169	142	144	123	132	115	107	100	73	80	52	20	-			
Jonesport, ME 44°31.6'N., 67°37.0'W.	257	197	209	206	196	203	198	188	189	182	173	178	167	159	135	149	122	124	105	113	96	89	82	53	60	34	-				
Bar Harbor, ME 44°23.5'N., 68°12.0'W.	243	179	190	188	177	184	179	169	170	163	154	159	148	140	115	130	103	105	86	94	77	70	62	33	39	-					
Buck Harbor, ME 44°20.3'N., 68°44.2'W.	237	165	176	174	159	162	157	148	149	138	131	137	123	114	85	94	67	68	57	39	22	16	22	16	-						
Stonington, ME 44°09.2'N., 68°39.8'W.	226	155	165	163	155	158	153	143	145	133	126	132	119	109	81	90	63	64	53	47	30	24	20	-							
Rockland, ME 44°06.0'N., 69°05.5'W.	223	148	160	155	142	147	142	132	133	126	115	118	107	99	71	86	59	62	42	50	33	23	-								
Searsport, ME 44°27.0'N., 68°54.0'W.	242	166	178	174	161	166	161	151	152	145	134	137	127	118	90	105	78	80	61	30	13	-									
Bucksport, ME 44°34.3'N., 68°48.0'W.	250	175	187	182	169	174	169	159	160	153	143	145	135	126	98	113	86	89	70	17	-										
Bangor, ME 44°47.7'N., 68°46.3'W.	267	192	204	199	186	191	186	176	177	170	160	162	151	144	115	131	104	106	87	-											
Boothbay Harbor, ME 43°51.0'N., 69°37.6'W.	207	119	130	125	112	115	110	101	102	95	84	86	74	64	36	50	23	21	-												
Wiscasset, ME 43°59.5'N., 69°40.1'W.	217	127	139	133	120	123	118	109	110	103	92	94	82	72	44	57	30	-													
Bath, ME 43°54.5'N., 69°48.7'W.	213	123	137	129	115	119	114	104	105	98	88	89	78	67	40	27	-														
Augusta, ME 44°18.9'N., 69°46.4'W.	240	150	164	156	142	146	141	131	132	125	115	116	104	94	66	-															
Portland, ME 43°39.4'N., 70°14.7'W.	203	107	118	112	97	100	95	86	87	79	66	67	56	43	-																
York Harbor, ME 43°07.9'N., 70°38.6'W.	182	75	83	75	60	63	58	48	49	42	29	25	11	-																	
Portsmouth, NH 43°04.6'N., 70°44.5'W.	180	73	81	73	58	61	56	46	47	40	27	22	-																		
Newburyport, MA 42°48.8'N., 70°52.4'W.	171	63	72	64	48	51	47	37	38	31	16	-																			
Rockport, MA 42°40.0'N., 70°36.5'W.	157	49	58	50	34	37	33	23	24	17	-																				
Gloucester, MA 42°36.6'N., 70°39.6'W.	155	45	52	43	26	26	22	11	12	-																					
Salem, MA 42°31.3'N., 70°52.5'W.	159	49	53	45	24	27	18	5	-																						
Marblehead, MA 42°30.2'N., 70°50.7'W.	156	45	48	39	22	19	14	-																							
Lynn, MA 42°27.3'N., 70°56.6'W.	159	47	48	40	22	13	-																								
Boston, MA 42°22.0'N., 71°03.0'W.	163	49	52	40	21	-																									
Scituate, MA 42°11.9'N., 70°43.5'W.	143	29	29	20	-																										
Plymouth, MA 41°57.6'N., 70°39.8'W.	144	26	20	-																											
Cape Cod Canal 41°46.8'N., 70°29.0'W.	144	22	-																												
Provincetown, MA 42°02.5'N., 70°10.0'W.	132	-																													
Nantucket Shoals 40°30.0'N., 69°25.0'W.	-																														

Each distance is by the shortest route that safe navigation permits between the two ports concerned. Vessels standing along the coast must make their own adjustments for non-direct routes. For example the table shows a distance of 214 miles by direct route from Machiasport to Provincetown; the distance via Matinicus Rock and Cape Ann is 235 miles. Distances from Eastport to Machiasport and other ports southward are via the deep Head Harbour Passage, which is 8 miles farther than via the shallower Lubec Channel.

Bridge Basics

Bridges have to be factored in when planning a trip. Depending on where you cruise, you may be dependent on bridge openings; a particular bridge's schedule can often decide where you tie up for the evening or when you wake up and get underway the next day. While many are high (over 65 feet) and some usually remain open (such as railroad bridges), others are restricted for different hours in specific months, closed during rush hours and/or open on the quarter-hour, half-hour or even at 20 minutes and 40 minutes past the hour.

To add to the confusion, the restrictions are constantly changing. Just because a bridge opened on a certain schedule last season does not mean it is still on that same schedule. Changes are posted in the Coast Guard's *Local Notice to Mariners* reports, which can be found online at www.navcen.uscg.gov/lnm. It is also a good idea to check locally to verify bridge schedules before your transit.

Measuring Vertical Clearance

Most bridges carry a tide board to register vertical clearance at "low steel" or the lowest point on the bridge. (Note that in the State of Florida waters the tide board figure–and the one noted on the chart–is generally for a point that is 5 feet toward the channel from the bridge fender.) In the case of arched bridges, center channel clearance is frequently higher than the tide gauge registers. Some bridges bear signs noting extra height at center in feet.

Calling a Bridge

Most bridges monitor VHF Channel 13, designated by the Federal Communications Commission as the "bridgetender channel" until you get to South Carolina (southbound), where it changes to VHF Channel 09. (The exception is the locks on the Okeechobee Waterway, which respond to VHF Channel 13).

In any waters, it is a good idea to monitor both the bridge channel and VHF Channel 16–one on your ship's radio and one on a handheld radio, if your main set doesn't have a dual-watch capability–to monitor oncoming commercial traffic and communications with the bridgetender.

Swing bridges have an opening section that pivots horizontally on a central hub, allowing boats to pass on one side or the other when it is open.

Lift bridges normally have two towers on each end of the opening section that are equipped with cables that lift the road or railway vertically into the air.

When using VHF, always call bridges by name and identify your vessel by name and type (such as sailing vessel or trawler) and whether you are traveling north or south. If you are unable to raise the bridge using VHF radio, use a horn signal.

Note that some bridges are not required to open in high winds. If you encounter a bridge that won't open (for whatever reason), it is prudent to drop the hook in a safe spot until the situation is resolved.

Pontoon bridges consists of an opening section that must be floated out of the way with a cable to allow boats to pass. Do not proceed until the cables have had time to sink to the bottom.

Bascule bridges are the most common type of opening bridge you will encounter. The opening section has one or two leaves that tilt vertically on a hinge, like doors being opened skyward.

Bridge Procedures:

- First, decide if it is necessary to have the drawbridge opened. You will need to know your boat's clearance height above the waterline before you start. Drawbridges have "clearance gauges" that show the closed vertical clearance with changing water level but a bascule bridge typically has 3 to 5 feet more clearance than what is indicated on the gauge at the center of its arch at mean low tide. Bridge clearances are also shown on NOAA charts.

- Contact the bridgetender well in advance (even if you can't see the bridge around the bend) by VHF radio or phone. Alternatively, the proper horn signal for a bridge opening is one prolonged blast (four to six seconds) and one short blast (approximately one second). Bridge operators sound this signal when ready to open the bridge, and then usually the danger signal–five short blasts–when they are closing the bridge. The operator of each vessel is required by law to signal the bridgetender for an opening, even if another vessel has already signaled. Tugs with tows and U.S. government vessels may go through bridges at any time, usually signaling with five short blasts. A restricted bridge may open in an emergency with the same signal. Keep in mind bridgetenders will not know your intentions unless you tell them.

- If two or more vessels are in sight of one another, the bridgetender may elect to delay opening the bridge until all boats can go through together.

- Approach at slow speed and be prepared to wait as the bridge cannot open until the traffic gates are closed. Many ICW bridges, for example, are more than 40 years old and the aged machinery functions slowly.

- Once the bridge is open, proceed at no-wake speed. Keep a safe distance between you and other craft as currents and turbulence around bridge supports can be tricky.

- There is technically no legal right-of-way (except on the Mississippi and some other inland rivers) but boats running with the current should always be given the right-of-way out of courtesy. As always, if you are not sure, let the other boat go first.

- When making the same opening as a commercial craft, it is a good idea to contact the vessel's captain (usually on VHF Channel 13), ascertain his intentions and state yours to avoid any misunderstanding in tight quarters.

- After passing through the bridge, maintain a no-wake speed until you are well clear and then resume normal speed.

Bridge Schedules

KEY:

Statute Mile Marker
Vertical Clearance

Drawbridge clearances are vertical, in feet, when closed and at mean high water in tidal areas. Bridge schedules are subject to schedule changes due to repairs, maintenance, events, etc. Check Waterway Explorer at www.waterwayguide.com for the latest shedules or call ahead.

NEW JERSEY BRIDGES MONITOR (VHF) CHANNEL 13

New Jersey ICW

112.2 / 23'
Two Mile Bridge: Opens on signal except: (1) From 9:15 a.m. to 10:30 a.m. on the fourth Sunday in March of every year, when the draw need not open for vessels. If the fourth Sunday falls on a religious holiday, the draw need not open for vessels from 9:15 a.m. to 10:30 a.m. on the third Sunday of March of every year. (2) From 10:30 p.m. on December 24 until 10:30 p.m. on December 26, the draw need open only if at least two-hour notice is given.

108.9 / 25'
Wildwood (Rio Grande/NJ 47) Bridge: Opens on signal.

105.2 / 55'
North Wildwood Blvd. (NJ 147) Bridge: Fixed

102.0 / 10'
Stone Harbor Blvd. Bridge: Opens on signal except: (1) From October 1 through March 31 from 10:00 p.m. to 6:00 a.m., when the draw need only open if at least eight-hour notice is given. (2) From Memorial Day through Labor Day from 6:00 a.m. to 6:00 p.m. on Saturdays, Sundays and Federal holidays, the draw need open only on the hour, 20 minutes after the hour, and 20 minutes before the hour. (3) From 10:00 p.m. on December 24 until 6:00 a.m. on December 26, the draw need open only if at least two-hour notice is given.

98.5 / 35'
Avalon Blvd. (601) Bridge: Fixed

96.0 / 23'
Townsend Inlet Bridge (exit to ocean): Opens on signal except: (1) From 9:15 a.m. to 2:30 p.m. on the fourth Sunday in March of every year, when the draw need not open for vessels. If the fourth Sunday falls on a religious holiday, the draw need not open from 9:15 a.m. to 2:30 p.m. on the third Sunday of March of every year. (2) From 11:00 p.m. on December 24 until 11:00 p.m. on December 25, the draw need open only if at least two-hour notice is given.

93.2 / 35'
Sea Isle Blvd. (625) Bridge: Fixed

84.5 / 35'
34th St. (Roosevelt Blvd.) Bridge: Fixed

80.1 / 55'
Stainton Memorial (NJ 52) Bridge: Fixed

77.0 / 65'
Ocean City-Longport Bridge (exit to ocean): Fixed

76.0 / 56'
NJ 152 Bridge: Fixed

75.0 / 25'
JFK Memorial Bridge (exit to ocean): Fixed

74.0 / 14'
Margate City Bridge: Opens on signal

71.2 / 9'
Dorset Ave. Bridge: Opens on signal except from June 1 through September 30 from 9:15 a.m. to 9:15 p.m., when the draw need only open at 15 and 45 minutes after the hour.

70.0 / 10'
Albany Ave. Bridge: Opens on signal except: (1) Year-round, from 11:00 p.m. to 7:00 a.m.; and from November 1 through March 31 from 3:00 p.m. to 11:00 p.m., when the draw need only open if at least four-hour notice is given. (2) From June 1 through September 30 from 9:00 a.m. to 4:00 p.m. and from 6:00 p.m. to 9:00 p.m., when the draw need only open on the hour and half hour; and from 4:00 p.m. to 6:00 p.m., when the draw need not open. Opening schedule can vary with annual events. Call ahead.

69.0 / 35'
Atlantic City Expressway Bridge: Fixed

68.9 / 5'
AMTRAK Bridge: Usually open unless a train is approaching.

67.2 / 20'
Absecon Blvd. (U.S. 30) Bridge: Opens on signal if at least four hours of notice is given by calling 609-441-3174, except from April 1 through October 31 from 7:00 a.m. to 11:00 p.m., when the draw need only open on the hour. Opening schedule can vary with annual events. Call ahead.

65.1 / 60'
Brigantine Blvd. Bridge (exit to ocean): Fixed

37.0 / 60'
Manahawkin Bay (NJ 72) Bridge: Fixed

NEW JERSEY BRIDGES MONITOR (VHF) CHANNEL 13

14.1 **30'** **Thomas A. Mathis (NJ 37) Bridge:** Opens on signal except (1) From December 1 through March 31, when the draw need only open if at least four-hour notice is given. (2) From April 1 through November 30 from 11:00 p.m. to 8:00 a.m., when the draw need only open if at least four-hour notice is given. (3) From Memorial Day through Labor Day from 8:00 a.m. to 8:00 p.m., the draw need only open on the hour and half hour.

14.0 **60'** **J. Stanley Tunney Bridge:** Fixed

6.3 **30'** **Mantoloking Bridge:** Opens on signal except from Memorial Day through Labor Day on Saturdays, Sundays and Federal holidays from 9:00 a.m. to 6:00 p.m., when the draw need only open on the hour, 20 minutes after the hour, and 40 minutes after the hour.

3.6 **30'** **Rt 632 (Bridge Ave.) Bridge:** Opens on signal. Note: Vertical clearance of 65 feet when open.

3.0 **31'** **Point Pleasant Bridge:** Opens on signal. Note: Vertical clearance of 66 feet when open.

1.1 **30'** **NJ 35 Bridge:** Opens on signal except (1) From May 15 through September 30 on Saturdays, Sundays and Federal holidays from 8:00 a.m. to 10:00 p.m., when the draw need only open 15 minutes before the hour and 15 minutes after the hour; on Mondays to Thursdays from 4:00 p.m. to 7:00 p.m., and on Fridays, except Federal holidays, from 12:00 p.m. to 7:00 p.m., the draw need only open 15 minutes before the hour and 15 minutes after the hour. (2) Year-round from 11:00 p.m. to 8:00 a.m., the draw need only open if at least four-hour notice is given.

0.9 **3'** **Brielle Railroad Bridge (exit to ocean):** Open unless train approaching. Note: Draw is at 45-degree angle in open position so favor north side of channel.

Shark River Inlet, NJ

0.0 **15'** **Shark River Inlet (Ocean Ave.) Bridge (exit to ocean):** Opens on signal.

0.8 **13'** **Main St. (NJ 71) Bridge:** Use South Channel. Operates as one unit with Shark River Railroad Bridge. Opens on signal except from May 15 through September 30 from 4:00 p.m. to 7:00 p.m. Monday through Friday except Federal holidays and from 9:00 a.m. to 9:00 p.m. Saturdays, Sundays, and holidays, when the draw need only open on the hour and half hour if a vessel is waiting to pass.

0.9 **8'** **Shark River Railroad Bridge:** Operates as one unit with Main St. Bridge. (Same schedule)

0.9 **50'** **NJ 35 Bridge:** Fixed

Sandy Hook, NJ

65' **Highlands Bridge:** Fixed

22' **Oceanic Bridge:** Opens on signal except from December 1 through March 31, when the draw need only open if at least a 24-hour notice is given by calling the number posted at the bridge.

20' **Sea Bright Bridge:** Opens on signal except from the Friday before Memorial Day through Labor Day, on Friday, Saturday, Sunday and holidays, between 9:00 a.m. and 7:00.pm., when the draw need only open on the hour. Note: The draw need not be opened at any time for a sailboat unless it is operating under auxiliary power or is being towed by a powered vessel.

Alternate Route: Arthur Kill, NY/NJ

143' **Outerbridge Crossing Bridge:** Fixed

140' **Goethals Bridge:** Fixed

31' **Arthur Kill Railroad Bridge:** Open unless train approaching.

150' **Bayonne Bridge:** Fixed

The Narrrows, NY

215' **Jamestown-Verrazzano Bridge:** Fixed

East River, NY

127' **Brooklyn Bridge:** Fixed

134' **Manhattan Bridge:** Fixed

133' **Williamsburg Bridge:** Fixed

NEW YORK BRIDGES MONITOR (VHF) CHANNEL 13

131'   **Queensboro Bridge:** Fixed

40'   **Roosevelt Island Bridge:** Opens on signal if at least two-hour notice is given to the New York Department of Transportation (NYCDOT) Radio Hotline (311) or NYCDOT Bridge Operations Office. Openings may be delayed up to one-half hour.

138'   **Robert F. Kennedy (Triborough) Bridge:** Fixed

134'   **Hell Gate Railroad Bridge:** Fixed

130'   **Bronx-Whitestone Bridge:** Fixed

152'   **Throgs Neck Bridge:** Fixed

Side Trip: Harlem River, NY

25'-55' All Harlem River non-fixed bridges from **Wards Island Foot Bridge** to **Henry Hudson Bridge** open on signal if at least 4-hour advance notice is given to the New York Department of Transportation (NYCDOT) Radio Hotline (311) and the Triborough Bridge and Tunnel Authority (TBTA). The draws need not open from 6:00 a.m. to 9:00 a.m. and 5:00 p.m. to 7:00 p.m., Monday through Friday except federal holidays. (Note the **Broadway Bridge** has a different schedule as detailed below.) Also, the draws of the **Willis Avenue Bridge**, **Third Avenue Bridge** and the **Madison Avenue Bridge** need not open at various times between 8:00 a.m. and 5:00 p.m. on the first Sunday in May and November. The exact time and date of each bridge closure will be published in the *Local Notice to Mariners* several weeks prior to each closure.

25'   **Metro North (Park Ave.) Bridge:** Opens on signal if at least 4-hour advance notice is given to the New York Department of Transportation (NYCDOT) Radio Hotline (311) and the Triborough Bridge and Tunnel Authority (TBTA). The draw need not open from 5:00 a.m. to 10:00 a.m. and 4:00 p.m. to 8:00 p.m., Monday through Friday, except Federal holidays. The draw of the railroad bridge may remain in the closed position from the time a train scheduled to cross the bridge is within five minutes from the bridge until that train has fully crossed the bridge. The maximum time permitted for delay shall not exceed 10 minutes.

24'   **Broadway Bridge:** Open on signal if at least 4-hour advance notice is given to the New York Department of Transportation (NYCDOT) Radio Hotline (311) and the Triborough Bridge and Tunnel Authority (TBTA). The draws need not open from 7:00 a.m. to 10:00 a.m. and 4:00 p.m. to 7:00 p.m., Monday through Friday except federal holidays.

5'   **Spuyten Duyvil Railroad Bridge:** Opens on signal.

Side Trip: Hudson River, NY

213'   **George Washington Bridge:** Fixed

139'   **Tappan Zee Bridge:** Fixed

155'   **Bear Mountain Bridge:** Fixed

172'   **Newburgh-Beacon Bridges:** Fixed

134'   **Mid-Hudson Suspension Bridge:** Fixed

167'   **Walkway Over the Hudson Bridge:** Fixed

135'   **Kingston-Rhinecliff Bridge:** Fixed

142'   **Rip Van Winkle Bridge:** Fixed

139'   **Alfred H. Smith Railroad Bridge:** Fixed

135'   **Castleton-on-Hudson Bridge:** Fixed

60'   **Dunn Memorial Bridge:** Fixed

25'   **CSX Transportation Railroad Bridge:** Swing bridge that opens on signal, except from Dec. 16 through Mar. 31, when the draw opens on signal if at least 24-hour notice is given.

60'   **Patroon Island Bridge:** Fixed

61'   **Troy-Menandes Bridge:** Fixed

55'   **Congress St. Bridge:** Fixed

NEW YORK BRIDGES MONITOR ((VHF)) CHANNEL 13

29' **Federal St. Bridge:** Opens on signal from Apr. 1 through Dec. 15 if at least 24-hour advance notice is given. From Dec. 16 through Mar. 31, the draw need not open.

61' **Collar City (NY 7) Bridge:** Fixed

150' **Troy Federal Lock & Dam:** Schedule varies with season. Monitors VHF Channel 13. Operational hours in 2019 were from 7:00 a.m. to 5:00 p.m., May 17 to Oct. 16. Vessels are required to arrive at a lock at least 15 minutes prior to closing to ensure being locked through, and at a bridge at least 5 minutes prior to ensure an opening. Refer to the Waterway Explorer at waterwayguide.com for the most up-to-date schedule.

Long Island South Shore, NY

30' **Atlantic Beach Bridge (exit to ocean):** Opens on signal (1) From October 1 through May 14. (2) Opens on signal from May 15 through September 30 except from 4:00 p.m. to 7:00 p.m. on weekdays and from 11:00 a.m. to 9:00 p.m. on Saturdays, Sundays, Memorial Day, Independence Day, and Labor Day, when it need only open on the hour and half-hour. (3) From May 15 through September 30 it need only open from two hours before to one hour after predicted high tide. (Predicted high tide occurs 10 minutes earlier than that predicted for Sandy Hook, as given in the tide table published by the National Oceanic and Atmospheric Administration.)

14' **Reynolds Channel Railroad Bridge:** Opens on signal.

20' **Long Beach Twin Bridges:** Opens on signal, except (1) From midnight to 8:00 a.m. year-round, when at least four-hour notice is given. (2) From 3:00 p.m. to 8:00 p.m. on Saturdays, Sundays, and holidays from May 15 through September 30, when the draw need only open on the hour and half hour. (3) From 10:00 p.m. to midnight on July 3 each year, the draw need not open for the passage of vessel traffic.

20' **Loop Parkway Bridge (West):** Fixed

21' **Loop Parkway-Long Creek Bridge:** Opens on signal every other hour on the even hour, except from April 1 through October 31 on Saturday, Sunday and federal holidays, when the draw opens on signal every three hours from 3:00 a.m.

20' **Loop Parkway Bridge (East):** Fixed

21' **Meadowbrook State Parkway Bridge:** Opens on signal if at least a one-half hour notice is given to the New York State Department of Transportation, as follows: (1) Every other hour on the even hour. (2) From April 1 through October 31, on Saturdays, Sundays, and Federal holidays, every three hours beginning at 1:30 a.m. Notice may be given from the telephone located at the moorings on each side of the bridge or by marine radio. (3) From 9:00 p.m. to midnight on the Fourth of July the bridge need not open.

20' **Wantagh State Parkway (Sloop Channel) Bridge:** Opens on signal after at least a one-half hour advance notice is given by calling the number posted at the bridge. From 6:30 a.m. through 12 noon and from 12:15 p.m. through 4:00 p.m., Monday through Friday, one bascule lift span may remain in the closed position. A full two-lift span opening will be given between 12 noon and 12:15 p.m. if at least a one-hour advance notice is given by calling the number posted at the bridge. From 7:30 a.m. through 8:30 p.m. on Saturday, Sunday and Federal holidays, the draw will open on the hour and half-hour if at least a half-hour notice is given by calling the number posted at the bridge.

24' **Alternate: Wantagh State Parkway (Goose Creek Channel) Bridge:** Fixed

60' **Robert Moses Causeway Bridge:** Fixed.

29' **Alternate: Captree State Parkway Bridge:** Opens on signal if at least a one-half hour notice is given by calling the number posted at the bridge, as follows: (1) Every other hour on the even hour. (2) From April 1 through October 31, on Saturday, Sunday, and Federal holidays, every three hours beginning at 3:00 a.m.

65' **Robert Moses Bridge (exit to ocean):** Fixed

18' **Smith Point Bridge:** Opens on signal from October 1 through April 30 from 8:00 a.m. to 4:00 p.m. and from May 1 through September 30 from 6:00 a.m. to 10:00 p.m. At all other times during these periods, the draws will open as soon as possible but no more than one hour after a request to open is received.

NEW YORK & MASSACHUSETTS BRIDGES MONITOR VHF CHANNEL 13

10' **West Bay Bridge:** Opens on signal from October 1 through April 30 from 8:00 a.m. to 4:00 p.m. and from May 1 through September 30 from 6:00 a.m. to 10:00 p.m. At all other times during these periods, the draw will open as soon as possible but no more than one hour after a request to open is received.

14' **Beach Lane Bridge:** Opens on signal from October 1 through April 30 from 8:00 a.m. to 4:00 p.m. and from May 1 through September 30 from 6:00 a.m. to 10:00 p.m. At all other times during these periods, the draw will open as soon as possible but no more than one hour after a request to open is received.

15' **Quogue (Post Lane) Bridge:** Opens on signal from October 1 through April 30 from 8:00 a.m. to 4:00 p.m. and from May 1 through September 30 from 6:00 a.m. to 10:00 p.m. At all other times during these periods, the draw will open as soon as possible but no more than one hour after a request to open is received.

55' **Ponquogue Bridge:** Fixed

Shinnecock Canal, NY

25' **CR 80 Bridge:** Fixed

22' **Shinnecock Canal Railroad Bridge:** Fixed

Shinnecock Lock: Open unleoss train approaching. Operates 24 hours a day. Opens on signal (three short blasts on the horn or whistle).

23' **Sunrise Highway (NY 27) Bridge:** Fixed

Cape Cod Canal, MA

0.7 **7'** **ConRail Railroad Bridge:** Usually open, except for the passage of trains or for maintenance. If the draw is not in the fully open position, the opening signal is one prolonged and one short blast.

2.0 **135'** **Bourne Bridge:** Fixed

4.5 **135'** **Sagamore Bridge:** Fixed

Cape Cod

Section 1: Cape May to Raritan Bay, NJ

Chapter 1: Cape May to Little Egg Harbor, NJ   **Chapter 2:** Barnegat Bay to Shark River Inlet, NJ

Chapter 3: Sandy Hook & Raritan Bay, NJ

Perth Amboy

Kill Van Kull

Raritan Bay

Sandy Hook

Twin Rivers

Chapter 3: Page 123

Shark River Inlet

PENNSYLVANIA

Manasquan

Point Pleasant

Chapter 2: Page 101

Mantoloking

Toms River

Barnegat Bay

Barnegat Inlet

NEW JERSEY

Little Egg Harbor

Chapter 1: Page 74

Atlantic City

Great Egg Harbor Inlet

Ocean City

DELAWARE

Delaware Bay

Atlantic Ocean

Stone Harbor

Cape May

Pages 97-100

Little Egg Harbor

Great Bay

NEW JERSEY

Pages 87-97

Absecon Inlet

Atlantic City

Great Egg Harbor Inlet

Ocean City

Atlantic Ocean

Delaware Bay

Stone Harbor

Pages 77-87

Wildwood

Cape May

■ NAVIGATION NOTES

The New Jersey Intracoastal Waterway (NJ ICW) provides something for every taste, beginning with serious birdwatching in Cape May and including the amazing estuaries and pinelands.

The south Jersey shore towns along the NJ ICW offer fresh seafood, beautiful sunrises and sunsets, deep water inlets, fishing opportunities galore, kayaking, swimming and dockage at marinas along the way.

Cape May, Atlantic City, Atlantic Highlands, and Highlands are the more well-known stops along this route, but Ocean City, Toms River, Point Pleasant/Brielle and Manasquan are also noteworthy stops.

On the ocean route from Manasquan Inlet, it is just 24 nm to Sandy Hook, which opens up to an enclosed, single body of water that comprises three separately charted bays: Sandy Hook Bay to the southeast, Raritan Bay to the west and Lower Bay to the north, which is largest of the three and sometimes referred to as Lower New York Harbor.

At Sandy Hook you can set a course in almost any direction and head for any one of many destinations. To the south on the ocean side are the beaches and inlets of the New Jersey coast, while to the south on the inside of Sandy Hook is the popular harbor of Atlantic Highlands and two rivers: Shrewsbury and Navesink. To the west through Raritan Bay are the harbors of Keyport, NJ; Perth Amboy, NJ; and Great Kills, NY. To the north you will find New York City and Jersey City.

Cruising Conditions

The NJ ICW follows the same marking as the Atlantic Intracoastal Waterway (ICW) with red markers inland and green markers seaward. Where inlet channels cross the NJ ICW marker colors will reverse sides. Boaters are encouraged to pay very careful attention at all times and are advised to generally follow the outside radius of curves; however, do honor the markers because the navigation channel itself is very narrow.

> NOTE: Wind dictates the water levels in the NJ ICW and supersedes tidal considerations.

The NJ ICW can be challenging for a couple of reasons: First, the channel has not been dredged in many years and as a result there is shoaling along the route, some of which is severe especially between Cape May and Atlantic City. Second, the NJ ICW is one of the most congested waterways in the country so it is not uncommon, especially on weekends, to find fishing boats blocking the channel.

The entire length of the NJ ICW from Cape May to Manasquan Inlet is subject to rapid change. Channels deepen and shoals form without warning. In general, cruising boaters report a clear passage for the entire 118-mile statute mile (102.3-nm) length of the NJ ICW with depths typically ranging anywhere from 4 to 6 feet MLW on the route. Depths of 3.5 feet MLW (and sometimes less)

Cape May

Buck Landing

Cape Island Creek

Where's the Buoy?

Aids to Navigation (ATONs) along New Jersey ICW and its associated waterways are made of two types: (1) USACE ATONs and (2) state and private ATONs. The USACE ATONs, with the possible exception of nuns and cans, usually remain in place year-round. State and private ATONs are usually pulled at the end of summer (Labor Day) and not replaced until late May (Memorial Day). Navigation before all of the ATONs are in position, with the exception of the year-round USACE ATONs, relies on local knowledge.

Boaters traveling in early spring or late fall should not assume that all charted aids to navigation will be present. Some of the floating aids to navigation between Cape May Inlet and Manasquan Inlet are removed each fall to avoid damage from ice during winter months. Coast Guard Group Cape May (609-898-6900, ext. 8) attempts to service and reestablish all aids to navigation by Memorial Day each spring. Also, the Coast Guard frequently moves floating aids to mark the best channel; therefore, your charts may not agree with the aids you see. Be advised that many facilities remove their floating docks after Labor Day and replace them around Memorial Day.

do exist; therefore, cruisers should seek local knowledge to get the latest on current channel conditions whenever possible. You can review the Coast Guard's *Local Notice to Mariners* (District 5) for the latest conditions on the NJ ICW (www.navcen.uscg.gov).

The following are some suggestions for safely traveling the NJ ICW:

- Do not travel on weekends when the traffic on the waterway can be overwhelming.

- Pay strict attention to the state of the tide if you draw more than 3 feet.

- Boats drawing between 3 and 3.5 feet should leave Cape May 2 to 3 hours after low tide in Cape May Harbor to ensure sufficient water to Atlantic City.

- Boats drawing more than 3.5 feet should consider the ocean route to Atlantic City.

- Between Cape May and Atlantic City (Mile 65), the controlling vertical clearance on the waterway is 35 feet.

Navigation

Aids to Navigation (ATONs) along New Jersey ICW and its associated waterways are made of two types: (1) USACE ATONs and (2) state and private ATONs. The USACE ATONs, with the possible exception of nuns and cans, usually remain in place year-round. State and private ATONs are usually pulled at the end of summer (Labor Day) and not replaced until late May (Memorial Day). Navigation before all of the ATONs are in position, with the exception of the year-round USACE ATONs, relies on local knowledge.

Boaters traveling in early spring or late fall should not assume that all charted aids to navigation will be present. Some of the floating aids to navigation between Cape May Inlet and Manasquan Inlet are removed each fall to avoid damage from ice during winter months. Coast Guard Group Cape May (609-898-6900, ext. 8) attempts to service and reestablish all aids to navigation by Memorial Day each spring.

Also, the Coast Guard frequently moves floating aids to mark the best channel; therefore, your charts may not agree with the aids you see. Be advised that many facilities remove their floating docks after Labor Day and replace them around Memorial Day.

South Jersey Marina

Utsch's Marina

Cape May Inlet

Two Mile Bridge

Thorofare Island

■ CAPE MAY TO STONE HARBOR

Cape May Inlet

Cape May is a safe, all-weather entrance from the Atlantic Ocean into Cape May Harbor at the southern terminus of the NJ ICW (Mile 114). The well-protected harbor makes it a popular layover for skippers waiting out bad weather before heading north along the New Jersey coast or for those headed to the Delaware Bay or the C&D Canal farther north.

NAVIGATION: One of the best-marked inlets on the East Coast, Cape May Inlet is deep and visibly protected by substantial rock jetties on either side. A strong north or south wind that has built up large waves parallel to the shoreline creates the only condition in which the approach may be dangerous as it will require turning broadside to the waves at the entrance and judging the waves as they break and curl around the windward jetty.

Approaching Cape May Inlet from either the NJ ICW or the Atlantic Ocean, distinct landmarks orient you to the area. A charted 641-foot tall LORAN tower located on the east side of the inlet is topped by a flashing red light. The 165-foot tall Cape May Lighthouse at the southwestern tip of the Cape has a flashing white light.

Additionally, an onshore Ferris wheel, which is located at Wildwood Amusement Park on the oceanside beach north of Cape May is easily seen up to 5 miles offshore.

Cape May Inlet is deep and visibly protected by substantial rock jetties on either side, making it one of the safest and best-marked inlets on the East Coast. The inlet is extremely busy and you can expect to meet every type of vessel at every speed imaginable. The inlet is popular with sportfishing vessels and the mouth is often congested with small recreational fishing boats. The commercial fishing fleet generally has its outriggers extended while traversing the inlet, making them very beamy. The outriggers are not lighted and can be very difficult to see in poor light.

> NOTE: During periods of reduced visibility, you can activate the Mariner Radio Activated Sound Signal (MRASS) at Cape May Canal West Entrance North Jetty Light 11 (LLNR 1675). Use VHF-FM Channel 83A/157.175MHz and key the microphone five times when within a range of 1 nm of the light. Following activation, the MRASS will provide a sound signal for approximately 30 minutes and then automatically secure.

Cape May

Cape May was settled by whalers and fishermen in colonial times and is reputed to be "the nation's oldest seashore resort." Its heritage dates from at least 1812, peaking architecturally in the late 19th century. The entire town has been proclaimed a National Historic Landmark. Cape May's beaches are legendary, its dunes are still nearly pristine and the harbor is a secure storm anchorage.

NAVIGATION: Entering Cape May Harbor is straightforward. You can access the harbor from Delaware Bay through the jettied entrance to the Cape May Canal, from the NJ ICW itself on the north or through Cape May Inlet on the east. (Note access restrictions to the canal due to 55-foot vertical clearance bridges along the canal.) Ebb tides run east, both in the canal and in the inlet. Waterway Explorer will be helpful in sorting out the buoys and depths for all three approaches.

During the peak travel season when the weather and tide turn favorable, you can expect an armada of yachts to pour out of Cape May Harbor in both directions to take advantage of an opportunity for a smooth passage. On the other hand it is also not uncommon to see yachts–even high-powered ones–return to Cape May after taking a pounding from the elements at work in both Delaware

Bay and the Atlantic Ocean. Any attempt to challenge the opposition of both wind and tide along the axis of the bay is not recommended.

Dockage: Cape May has many large, accommodating marinas with transient slips but most cater to sportfishing vessels and space may be severely limited during fishing tournaments. Corinthian Yacht Club of Cape May (CYCCM) is the first facility on the south side of the harbor, west of the Coast Guard station. CYCCM enjoys a reputation for world-class sailing and instructional programs and offers reciprocity with recognized yacht clubs around the world. Dock facilities include seasonal water and hot showers.

The full-service South Jersey Marina is just inside the mouth of Schellenger Creek and is reached by continuing on a straight-ahead course into the creek between green daybeacon "1" and red daybeacon "2" (instead of turning northwest toward Cape May Canal at flashing red "14"). Turning room is at a premium here but there is plenty of depth. The well-respected marina provides in-slip fueling and has a clean restroom and shower complex and on-site laundry. Vessels up to 140 feet long and requiring depths up to 10 feet can be accommodated. Services include the coordination of boat repairs through their sister facility, Canyon Club Resort Marina. This is a popular location; call ahead.

Near the west end of Cape May Harbor the 350-slip Utsch's Marina offers all the usual amenities plus a well-stocked marine store and good restaurants nearby. They fuel boats at a pair of floating-dock slips, one for gas and one for diesel. They have factory-trained mechanics on site. This popular marina has been family-owned and -operated since 1951. There is plenty of transient space but it is best to call ahead for slip availability (and approach directions). Across Lafayette St. is SeaGear Marine Supply with a full complement of supplies for cruising or commercial boats (609-884-2711).

To reach the facilities on Spicer Creek Canal you must backtrack to the **NJ 109 Bridge** (55-foot fixed vertical clearance) over Cape May Canal. Access to these facilities directly from Cape May Harbor is limited by **Lafayette Street Bridge** (4-foot fixed vertical clearance).

Miss Chris Marina has limited space and few amenities but offers paddleboard and kayak rentals for bird watching and is home to several charter boats. The 210-slip Cape May Marina, LLC is located on Cape Island Creek and caters to transients in an attractive environment.

Just east of the Cape May Canal entrance in Cape May Harbor, Canyon Club Resort Marina's wide docks are canopied by hundreds of outriggers, extending from the hulls of sportfishing boats dedicated to searching off-shore canyons. There is usually ample transient space on floating concrete docks with in-slip fueling. There is also a large infinity pool in a well-landscaped setting, a complete repair and service department and a well-stocked ship store.

Snug Harbor Marina is in the protected Cedar Creek off the channel. Call ahead for slip availability, approach depths and directions. To reach Port Marina Cape May (formerly Harbor View Marina) and Bree-Zee-Lee Yacht Basin turn to the north (starboard) just after flashing green "7" adjacent to the Coast Guard's northernmost docks. Head straight in the narrow channel for Bree-Zee-Lee. For Port Marina Cape May head toward the middle entrance of the seawall and then travel adjacent to the wall to the westernmost entrance toward the fuel docks. Like many facilities in this area both facilities cater to sportfishing vessels. Call ahead for approach depths and slip availability.

Hinch Marina is north of the Two Mile Bridge over Middle Thorofare. The marina is home to Cape May Outboard and has slips to just 35 feet. The draw of Two Mile Bridge opens on signal with a few exceptions. Farther east on Lower Thorofare is Two Mile Landing Marina, which is on site at a popular restaurant and has limited space.

Anchorage: Although marina slips are usually available (even during the peak of fall migration), all bets are off during Cape May's frequent fishing tournaments. Fortunately, considerable anchorage space is available along the south side of the harbor east of the U.S. Coast Guard station. Shoal-draft vessels can anchor west of the station outside the mooring field.

Anchor at least 100 yards off the Coast Guard pier in Cape May Harbor or you may be told to move. This is a shoal-draft anchorage only. Expect good holding but some boat wakes from commercial fishing vessels. You may experience early-morning reveilles and cadence calls as new recruits go through their paces at the station. When the anchorage is crowded, particularly during the passage of cold fronts during fall and spring, coordinating with other boaters to deploy two anchors could increase security without having to go short on scope. No launch service is available and the facilities and restaurants to the west are a long row away. Utsch's Marina offers a courtesy dinghy dock for those at anchor as do some of the shoreside restaurants.

GOIN' ASHORE
CAPE MAY, NJ

ATTRACTIONS

1. Cape May Welcome Center
Located within walking distance to the Washington Street Mall with maps and local information, restrooms and a bicycle rack at 609 Lafayette St. (609-884-5508).

2. Cape May Trolley Tours
Purchase tickets online or at the Washington Street Mall Information Booth at Ocean St. where most tours start (unless otherwise noted). Call 609-884-5404 for details.

3. Emlen Physick Estate
Victorian-era home that provides a portal to the past via exhibits depicting daily life in 1879 at 1048 Washington St. (609-884-5404).

4. Colonial House Museum
Originally a tavern and the family house of Revolutionary War Patriot Memucan Hughes (c. 1730). Open seasonally (June 15 to September 15) on Wednesdays through Saturdays (1:00 p.m. to 4:00 p.m.) at 653 1/2 Washington St. (609-884-9100).

5. Washington Street Mall
Pedestrian mall lined with over 75 establishments including specialty boutiques, eateries and dessert shops at 401 Washington St. Serves as Cape May's town square.

SERVICES

6. Cape May County Library
110 Ocean St. (609-884-9568)

7. Cape May Post Office
700 Washington St. (609-884-3578)

8. Cape Regional Urgent Care
406 W. Rio Grande Ave. (609-465-6364)

9. SeaGear Marine Supply
Offers a full complement of supplies for cruising or commercial boats at 1144 Rt. 109 (609-884-2711).

10. The Laundry Dude
1430 B, Texas Ave. (215-617-3751)

MARINAS

11. Canyon Club Resort Marina
900 Ocean Dr. (844-384-6353)

12. Cape May Marina LLC
124 Rosemans Ln. (609-435-5757)

13. Corinthian Yacht Club of Cape May-PRIVATE
1819 Delaware Ave. (609-884-8000)

14. Miss Chris Marina
1212 Wilson Dr. (609-884-3351)

15. South Jersey Marina
1231 Route 109 (800-754-0622)

16. Snug Harbor Marina
926 Ocean Dr. (609-884-4217)

17. Utsch's Marina
1121 Rt. 109 Schellengers' Landing (609-884-2051)

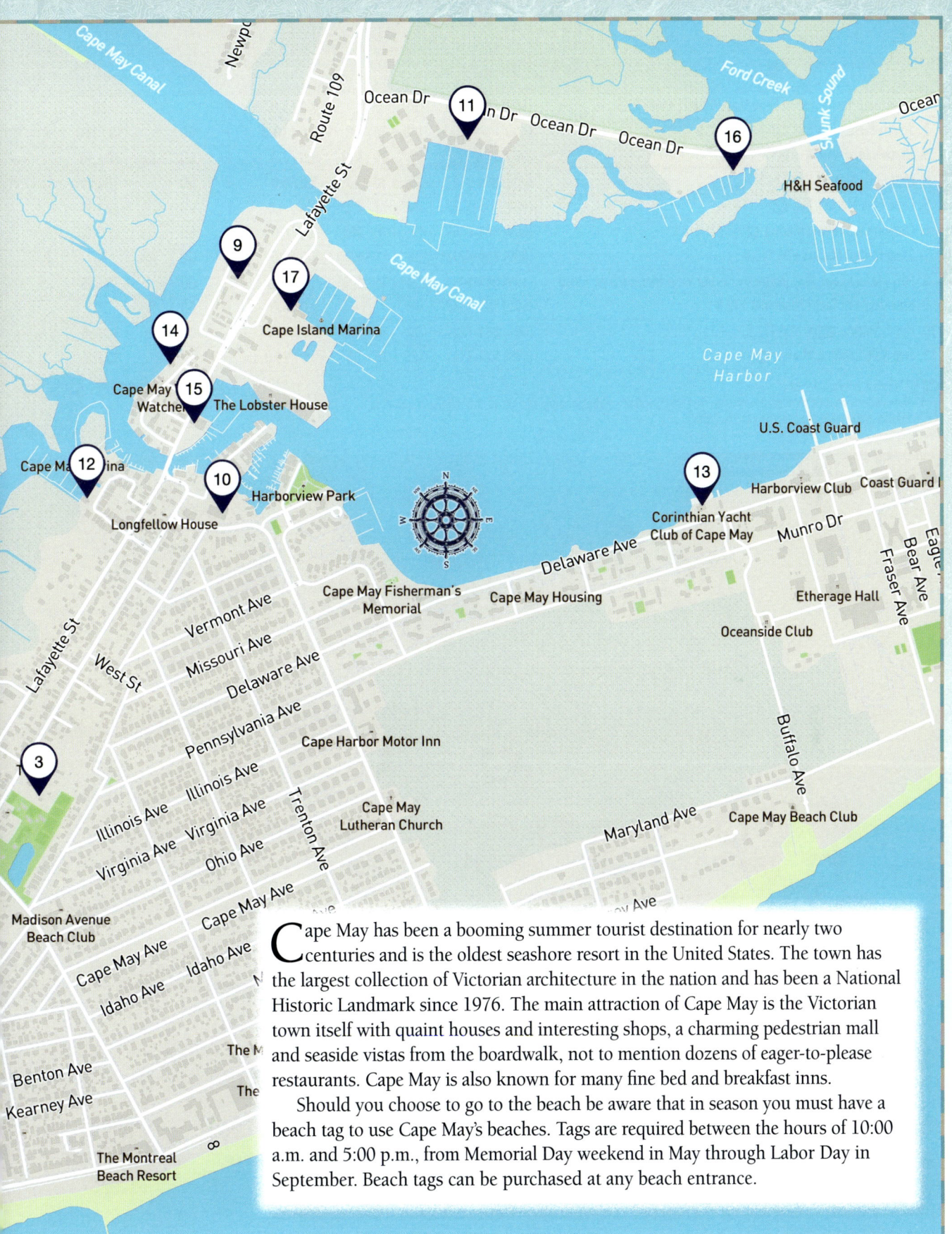

Cape May Canal

Newpo

Route 109

Ocean Dr **11** n Dr Ocean Dr Ocean Dr

Lafayette St

Ford Creek

Skunk Sound

Ocean

16

H&H Seafood

9

Cape May Canal

17

Cape Island Marina

14

Cape May
Harbor

Cape May
Watcher **15** The Lobster House

Cape Ma ina **12**

10 Harborview Park

Longfellow House

N
W   E
S

U.S. Coast Guard

13

Harborview Club Coast Guard

Corinthian Yacht
Club of Cape May Munro Dr

Delaware Ave

Cape May Fisherman's
Memorial Cape May Housing

Etherage Hall

Oceanside Club

Vermont Ave

Missouri Ave

West St

Delaware Ave

Pennsylvania Ave

Lafayette St

3

Cape Harbor Motor Inn

Illinois Ave

Illinois Ave

Virginia Ave

Virginia Ave

Ohio Ave

Trenton Ave

Cape May
Lutheran Church

Buffalo Ave

Maryland Ave

Cape May Beach Club

Eagle
Bear Ave
Fraser Ave

Madison Avenue
Beach Club

Cape May Ave

Cape May Ave

Idaho Ave

Idaho Ave

The M

The

Benton Ave

Kearney Ave

The Montreal
Beach Resort

Cape May has been a booming summer tourist destination for nearly two centuries and is the oldest seashore resort in the United States. The town has the largest collection of Victorian architecture in the nation and has been a National Historic Landmark since 1976. The main attraction of Cape May is the Victorian town itself with quaint houses and interesting shops, a charming pedestrian mall and seaside vistas from the boardwalk, not to mention dozens of eager-to-please restaurants. Cape May is also known for many fine bed and breakfast inns.

Should you choose to go to the beach be aware that in season you must have a beach tag to use Cape May's beaches. Tags are required between the hours of 10:00 a.m. and 5:00 p.m., from Memorial Day weekend in May through Labor Day in September. Beach tags can be purchased at any beach entrance.

Cape May, NJ

CAPE MAY HARBOR AREA		Largest Vessel	VHF	Total Slips	Approach/ Dockside Depth	Floating Docks	Gas/ Diesel	Repairs/ Haulout	Min/Max Amps	Pump-Out Station
1. Corinthian Yacht Club of Cape May-PRIVATE MM 113.5	(609) 884-8000	50			7.0 / 5.0	F			30	
2. South Jersey Marina WiFi MM 114.0	(800) 754-0622	140	16	70	10.0 / 10.0	F	GD		30 / 100	P
3. Utsch's Marina WiFi MM 114.0	(609) 884-2051	75	16	350	8.0 / 7.0	F	GD	RH	30 / 50	
4. Miss Chris Marina MM 114.5	(609) 884-3351	100	16	13	8.0 / 6.0	F	GD		30 / 50	
5. Cape May Marina, LLC WiFi 114.5	(609) 435-5757	70	73	210	10.0 / 4.0	F	GD	H	30 / 50	P
6. Canyon Club Resort Marina WiFi MM 114.0	(609) 884-0199	125	16	260	8.0 / 6.0	F	GD	RH	30 / 100	P
7. Snug Harbor Marina MM 113.0	(609) 884-4217	32		124	5.0 / 5.0	F	GD	RH	30	P
8. Port Marina Cape May (formerly Harbor View Marina) MM 113.0	(609) 884-5444	50	16	200	7.0 / 20.0	F	GD		30 / 50	P
9. Bree-Zee-Lee Yacht Basin MM 112.8	(609) 884-4849	46		1100	4.0 / 6.0	F	GD	RH	30	
10. Hinch Marina WiFi MM 112.5	(609) 884-7289	33	16	116	10.0 / 5.0	F		H	30 / 50	
11. Two Mile Landing Marina WiFi 112.5	(609) 522-1341	125	16	60	20.0 / 20.0	F			30 / 50	

WiFi Wireless Internet Access
Visit www.waterwayguide.com for current rates, fuel prices, website addresses and other up-to-the-minute information.
(Information in the table is provided by the facilities.)

Scan here for more details:

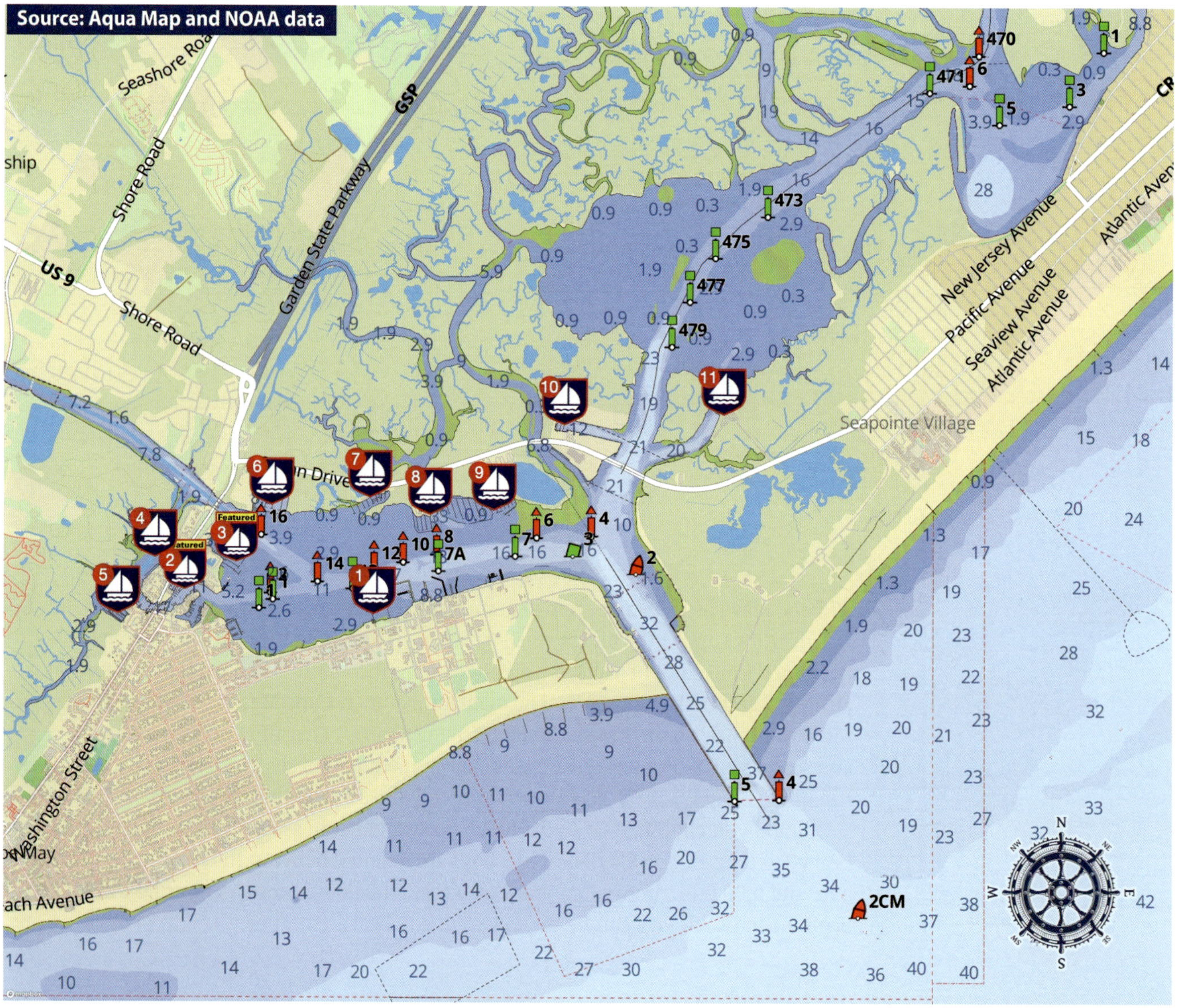

Source: Aqua Map and NOAA data

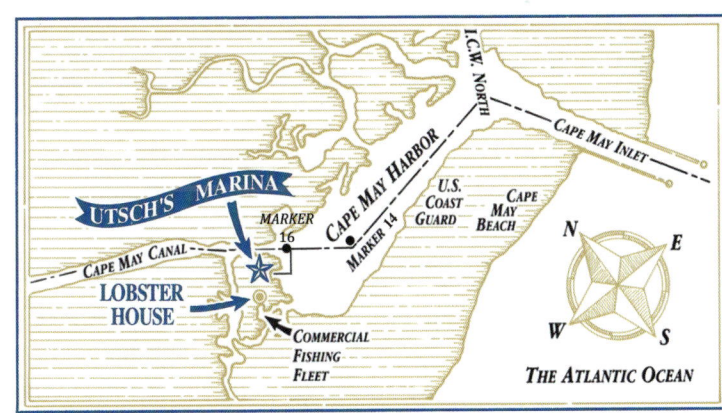

Wildwood Boardwalk

You can drop the hook west of the Coast Guard station, outside (or even in) the mooring field, where there is ample space for shallow-draft vessels. Again, expect some boat wakes. It is also possible to anchor in thick mud in Lower Thorofare (near Two Mile Landing Marina) but the depths are reportedly less than shown on the charts. Proceed with caution.

Wildwood–NJ ICW Mile 110

The NJ ICW route is easily followed to Wildwood, a beachfront resort town with a variety of attractions including a beach boardwalk and several amusement parks. The Wildwood boardwalk is 2 miles long and 5 blocks from the marinas. There are beautiful, wide, white sandy beaches a little farther on. With over 2 miles of arcade games, carousels, water parks and restaurants, Wildwood is a great family destination. There is a tram service that runs along the boardwalk from sunrise to sunset during the summer and several trolley companies conduct tours that run all year through different routes around town. Visit www.wildwoodsnj.com for a monthly calendar of events.

NAVIGATION: Heading north up the NJ ICW (inside route) you will pass the Coast Guard installation to starboard then Sewell Point, where the Cape May (Cold Spring) Inlet channel branches off to starboard and the NJ ICW heads to port. From this point, the 641-foot LORAN tower with flashing red light should be quite obvious.

> ⚠️
> *CAUTION:* Shoaling has been reported in the NJ ICW between Cape May Inlet and Manasquan Inlet. Mariners are advised to use extreme caution when transiting any parts of the inner passage due to shoaling.

New Jersey ICW, NJ

WILDWOOD		Largest Vessel	VHF	Total Slips	Approach/ Dockside Depth	Floating Docks	Gas/ Diesel	Repairs/ Haulout	Min/Max Amps	Pump-Out Station
1. Schooner Island Marina  **WiFi** MM 109.0	(609) 729-8900	110	16	320	12.0 / 8.0	F	GD	RH	30 / 50	P
2. Lighthouse Pointe Marina **WiFi** 109.0	(609) 729-2229	40	16	160	12.0 / 7.0	F			30 / 50	P
3. Grassy Sound Marina MM 105.5	(609) 846-1400	40		90	16.0 / 6.0	F	G	RH	30 / 100	P
STONE HARBOR										
4. Camp Marine Services MM 101.0	(609) 368-1777	45		30	4.0 / 8.0	F		RH		P

WiFi Wireless Internet Access
Visit www.waterwayguide.com for current rates, fuel prices, website addresses and other up-to-the-minute information.
(Information in the table is provided by the facilities.)

Scan here for more details:

Source: Aqua Map and NOAA data

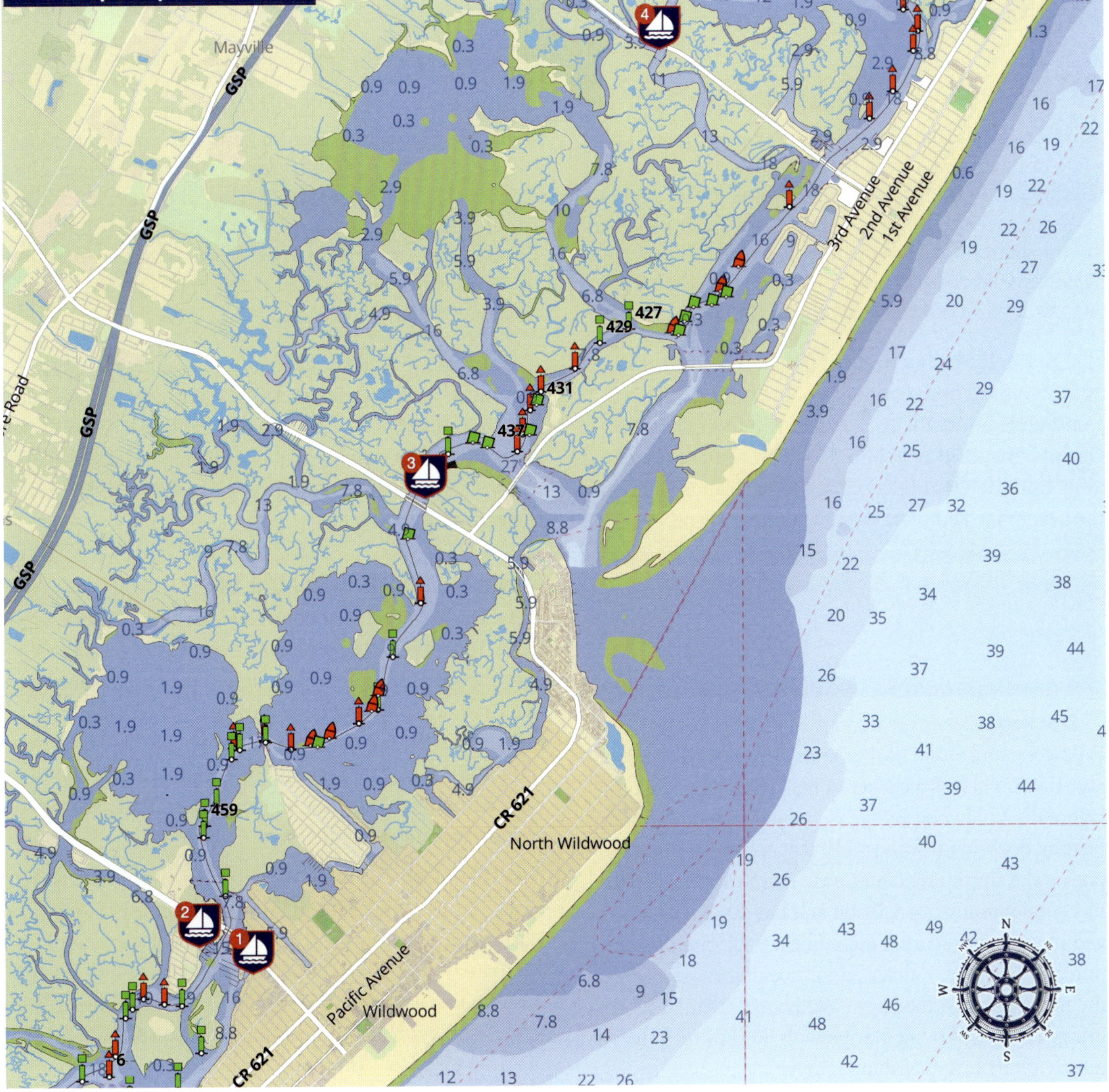

The first bridge you will encounter upon leaving Cape May is **Two Mile Bridge** across Middle Thorofare in Wildwood Crest (Mile 112.2). The bascule bridge has a closed vertical clearance of 23 feet and opens on signal with exceptions for Easter and Christmas. See details at Waterway Explorer (www.waterwayguide.com). In case of an emergency call 609-368-4591.

The next bridge when northbound is the **Wildwood (Rio Grande/NJ 47) Bridge** at Mile 108.9 in Stone Harbor. The bascule bridge has a 25-foot vertical clearance and opens on signal. At Mile 107.1 you will pass an old railroad bridge of which the center span has been removed.

> *CAUTION:* Shoaling has been observed on the south side of the channel from flashing green "453" to flashing green "449" and from flashing green "441" to flashing green "439." Shoaling has also been observed in the main navigation channel between flashing green "399" the old railroad bridge, even though the chart shows 5- to 7-foot MLW depths in this area.

The **North Wildwood Blvd (NJ 147) Bridge** at Mile 105.2 is a fixed bridge with 55-foot vertical clearance. Continuing north, the ICW passes within sight of the **Ocean Drive Bridge** at Mile 104. The NJ ICW then heads away from Hereford Inlet (closed to navigation) and into the Great Flat Thorofare west of Nummy Island.

> NOTE: Do not attempt to travel from this bridge to the Atlantic Ocean through Hereford Inlet. Despite dredging in 2020, Hereford Inlet remains closed and all aids to navigation have been removed. At low tide a sandbar known locally as "Champagne Island" has formed across the inlet.

Dockage: There are numerous marinas in the Wildwood and Stone Harbor areas between Miles 108 and 109.5. There is a cluster of marine facilities just before the Wildwood Bridge. Schooner Island Marina has floating docks with slips to 110 feet, a large swimming pool and a ship store. Lighthouse Pointe Marina is part of a condominium association and has 40-foot slips and numerous amenities including a pool, laundry and pump-out service. Call ahead for docking assistance. To the north just past the North Wildwood Blvd (NJ 147) Bridge is Grassy Sound Marina with 90 slips to 40 feet that mostly caters to sportfishing vessels.

Anchorage: Sunset Lake (Mile 110) carries 5-foot MLW depths at the entrance and depths inside are much less than charted (as low as 4 feet MLW). Keep in mind the tidal range in this area is 5 feet during normal tidal cycles and plan accordingly. Enter Sunset Lake from the ICW by turning between flashing red "470" and flashing green "471" and following the NJ channel markers. The first set of NJ markers are flashing red "6"and flashing green "5." (Leave the green on the right and the red on the left as you exit the ICW.) Turn right (south) to enter Sunset Lake. Anchor in thick mud with all-around protection.

> *CAUTION:* Local (i.e., non-USACE) buoys are removed in the off season in Sunset Lake. If unfamiliar with this anchorage, this makes navigating around this shallow basin challenging. Staying in the center of the south entrance channel (green marker "471") until inside where more than 4 feet of water can be difficult to find during MLW. (Tidal range in this area is 5 feet during normal tidal cycles.)

There are several "head boat" docks along the city's edge, and visiting yachts should not infringe on their path from or to their dock. This can prove difficult when these boats are not present in their slips. While heavily used, the well-protected anchorage affords privacy and easy access to nearby ocean beaches.

Stone Harbor–NJ ICW Mile 102

Stone Harbor has its own bird sanctuary and the only heron rookery located within a city. Both herons and egrets nest here, and bird watchers come in late summer and early fall to watch these and other species that stop off during their migrations. The nearby Wetlands Institute (609-368-1211) features exhibits on local marine life in their natural habitat, dune walks and kayaking. See more at www.wetlandsinstitute.org.

NAVIGATION: The NJ ICW route runs behind the barrier beach of this popular resort area. The depths at Stone Harbor are generally good and cruising boat amenities are more than adequate. The **Stone Harbor Blvd. Bridge** (also known as the 96th St. Bridge) at Mile 102 has a 10-foot closed vertical clearance and opens on signal except (1) from October 1 through March 31 from 10:00 p.m. to

Stone Harbor

6:00 a.m. when the draw need only open if at least 8 hours notice is given; (2) from Memorial Day through Labor Day from 6:00 a.m. to 6:00 p.m. on Saturdays, Sundays and federal holidays, when the draw need open only on the hour, 20 minutes after the hour and 20 minutes before the hour; and (3) from 10:00 p.m. on December 24 until 6:00 a.m. on December 26, when the draw need open only if at least 2 hours notice is given. The bridge is subject to temporary closures and changes in schedule due to repairs and maintenance, and can be very slow to operate, so use caution as you pass. Bridges in this area monitor VHF Channel 13.

Dockage: Camp Marine Services at the southern base of the Stone Harbor Bridge on Scotch Bonnet Creek has a few transient slips and an on-site marina supply store. Most of the boating facilities just north of the bridge offer services only (no slips) but might be able to accommodate you in a pinch.

Anchorage: You can anchor south of the Stone Harbor Blvd. Bridge at Mile 102.1 in Shelter Haven with at least 15 feet MLW. The entrance carries at least 6 feet at mid-tide. Restaurants and dinghy docks are nearby. The next place to drop the hook is about 10 miles north at Whale Creek at Corson Inlet (before the lift bridge).

◼ GULL ISLAND THOROFARE TO ATLANTIC CITY

To Great Egg Harbor Inlet–NJ Mile 102 to Mile 77

The NJ ICW route swings away from the barrier beach through Gull Island Thorofare (beginning at Mile 101) and then crosses Great Sound and wiggles its way through Ingram Thorofare.

The resort town of Ocean City is set between the Atlantic Ocean, Great Egg Harbor Inlet and Great Egg Harbor Bay with elegant homes and a splendid beach. Docks run side-by-side along the NJ ICW route on the city waterfront and also across the harbor in Somers Point. Ocean City is a good take-off point for one of the NJ ICW's most attractive side cruises.

The route runs along an unspoiled wilderness river that is unknown even to many resident mariners. Meandering west from Great Egg Harbor Bay, Great Egg Harbor River is safe and well-marked with deep cedar-stained waters and marshy pine-lined banks that offer a glimpse of the unspoiled New Jersey of old.

Great Egg Harbor Area, NJ

AVALON				Largest Vessel	VHF	Total Slips	Approach/ Dockside Depth	Floating Docks	Gas/ Diesel	Repairs/ Haulout	Min/Max Amps	Pump-Out Station
1. Commodore Bay Marina WiFi MM 96.5		(609) 967-4448		105	16	110	6.0 / 10.0	F			30 / 100	

WiFi Wireless Internet Access
Visit www.waterwayguide.com for current rates, fuel prices, website addresses and other up-to-the-minute information. (Information in the table is provided by the facilities.)

Scan here for more details:

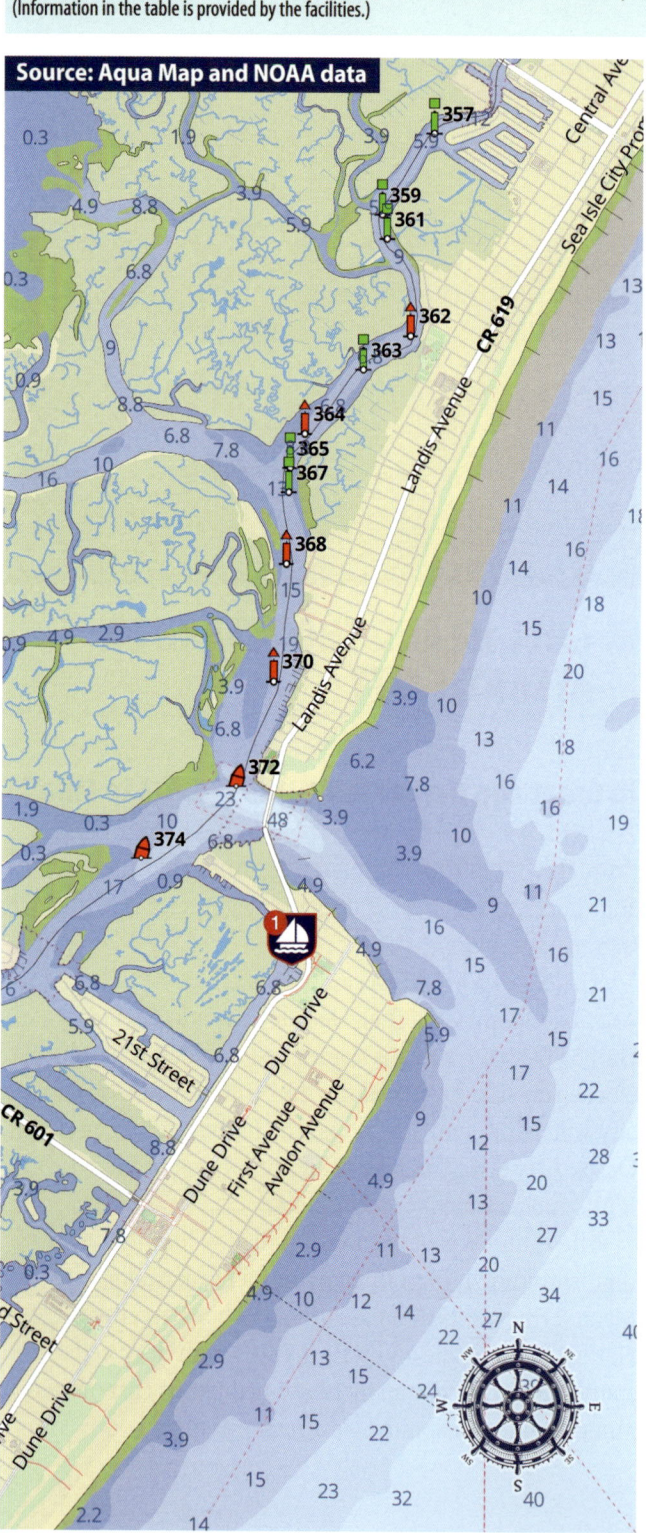

Source: Aqua Map and NOAA data

NAVIGATION: The fixed **Avalon Blvd. (601) Bridge** (35-foot fixed vertical clearance) crosses the channel at Mile 98.5. Exit to the ocean is via the Townsend Inlet Bridge (23-foot vertical clearance) at Mile 97. The bridge opens on signal except at Easter and Christmas. (See the restricted schedule at www. waterwayguide.com.) If staying on the NJ ICW, continue north.

After passing Townsend Inlet, the inland route runs through twists and turns before crossing Ludlam Bay. At Mile 93.5 is the fixed **Sea Isle Blvd. (625) Bridge** (35-foot vertical clearance). Note that Great Sound and Ludlam Bay are extremely shallow outside the narrow channel, especially on a falling tide.

The **34th Street (Roosevelt Blvd.) Bridge** has 35-foot fixed vertical clearance and is at Mile 84.5 south of Peck Bay. A narrow channel carries you through Peck Bay and along Beach Thorofare to the fixed **Stainton Memorial (NJ 52) Bridge** (55-foot vertical clearance).

⚠️ *CAUTION:* Shoal areas deserving increased attention include Peck Bay (Mile 83.5) between daybeacon "282" and daybeacon "272" and Beach Thorofare near daybeacon "262" (Mile 81.3), which has reported depths near 5 feet MLW. Be sure to proceed on a rising tide and use caution in these areas. It is best to check the NOAA charts online for the latest updates before transiting this area, as well as the Local Notice to Mariners (www.navcen.uscg.gov).

Dockage: The Avalon Yacht Club (609-967-4444) also offers courtesy dockage to members of reciprocal yacht clubs. Sunrise Marina (formerly The Marina at Avalon Anchorage) is located in an upscale neighborhood and 31 slips to 65 feet.

Great Egg Harbor Area, NJ

OCEAN CITY AREA		Largest Vessel	VHF	Total Slips	Approach/ Dockside Depth	Floating Docks	Gas/ Diesel	Repairs/ Haulout	Min/Max Amps	Pump-Out Station
1. All Seasons Marina 84.5	(609) 390-1850	50	16	300	12.0 / 5.0	F	GD	RH	30 / 50	
2. 10th St. Wharf WiFi	(609) 398-0424	85		25	20.0 / 6.0	F	GD		30 / 50	
3. Somers Point Marina 1.0 mi. NW of MM 79.0	(609) 927-5900	28	16	80	18.0 / 4.0	F		R		
4. Harbour Cove Marina 1.0 mi. NW of MM 79.0	(609) 927-9600	55		420	4.0 / 4.0	F	GD	RH	30 / 50	P

WiFi Wireless Internet Access
Visit www.waterwayguide.com for current rates, fuel prices, website addresses and other up-to-the-minute information.
(Information in the table is provided by the facilities.)

Scan here for more details: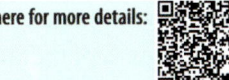

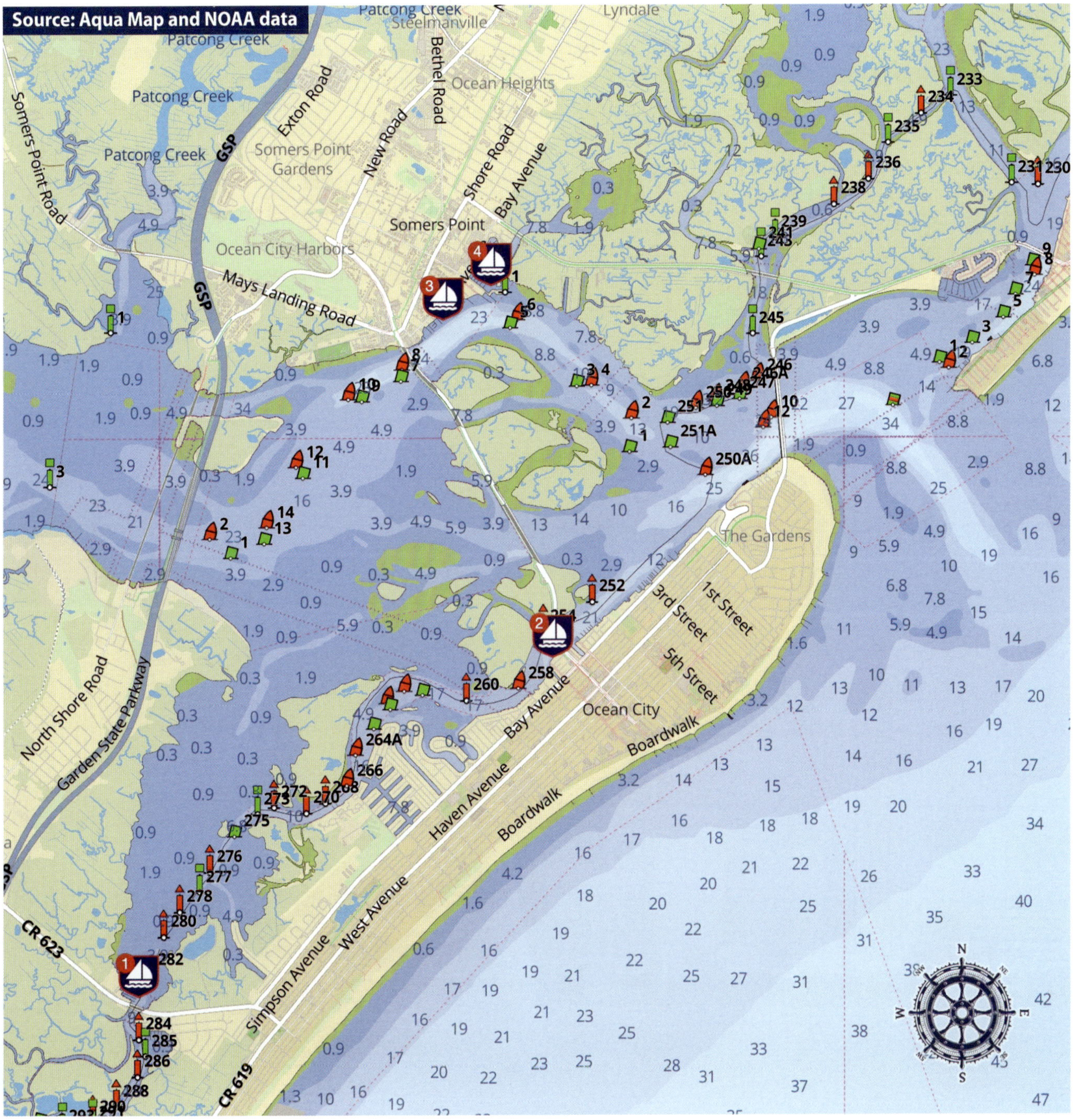

Source: Aqua Map and NOAA data

Commodore Bay Marina is located in a quiet, protected lagoon off Cornell Harbor at red nun buoy "374" south of the **Townsends Inlet Bridge**. They have slips to 105 feet with full amenities and concierge service.

Several marinas are located just north of the 34th Street Bridge at Mile 84.5, which spans the lower end of Peck Bay at Crook Horn Creek. All Seasons Marina has slips to 50 feet and storage options. They also offer some services.

Just south of the Stainton Memorial Bridge (55-foot vertical clearance) is 10th St. Wharf, which can accommodate vessels to 85 feet.

Numerous marinas are located to the north of the fixed **Ship Channel Bridge** (with 60-foot vertical clearance) just 1 nm northwest of Mile 79 of the NJ ICW. Picturesque Somers Point Marina offers an on-site brokerage, engine sales and service, a parts department, boat storage and slips (to 30 feet). The 420-slip Harbour Cove Marina to the north has a floating fuel dock, on-site restaurant, and a long list of services and amenities and is well worth the side trip.

Anchorage: There is room to anchor on Main Channel in Whale Creek at Mile 89.8 before the **Corson Inlet Bridge**. While somewhat exposed to the east, there is excellent holding here in 7- to 14-foot MLW depths with a mud and sand bottom.

The Rainbow Channel anchorage at Ocean City (Mile 80) has 6-foot to 15-foot MLW depths with excellent holding in mud and sand. It is, however, exposed to the northeast and west. Be aware there is a jet ski rental place that uses the open area here.

To Atlantic City: Outside Passage

In pleasant weather, most skippers prefer to run outside from Ocean City to its companion resort, Atlantic City. It is only 8 nm between sea buoys and Ocean City's Great Egg Harbor Inlet is generally safe for passage in reasonable weather.

NAVIGATION: Depths in Great Egg Harbor Inlet shift frequently and buoys are moved accordingly so reliable local information is a must if you plan to try the inlet. The **Ocean City-Longport Bridge** (65-foot charted fixed vertical clearance) crosses to the southwest of the inlet at Ocean City. When taking Great Egg Harbor Inlet to the ocean, the best approach is to follow the red-and-white center-channel buoys to green-red flashing (2+1)

Atlantic City

buoy "GH." Breakers may be prevalent due to frequent shoaling near "GH." Proceed following numbered buoys through the inlet.

The ocean approach through Absecon Inlet at Atlantic City is easy, although it can be a rollicking ride when a southerly wind is up. Hundreds of boats make the passage daily in all but the worst conditions and weekends are especially busy. Enter from the sea buoys (green "1" and red "2") located 2 nm offshore and honor the approach buoys to stay clear of the bar reaching toward the ocean along the northerly side of the channel. Channel depths are well maintained to provide easy access to all but the largest commercial vessels.

Follow the seaward buoy line into the very wide channel. As with all inlets, the buoys and markers are moved often to reflect changing conditions making an up-to-date NOAA Chart and *Local Notice to Mariners* (www.navcen.uscg.gov) navigation alerts a must when entering any of the inlets along the New Jersey coast.

To Atlantic City: Inside Passage– NJ ICW Mile 77 to Mile 67

Protected from gales and free of the small-boat fishing fleets, the inside passage to Atlantic City is the preferred route to take in heavy weather.

NOTE: If you stop in Margate City, check out Lucy the Elephant, a local landmark with a colorful past. The 65-foot-high structure was built in 1881 as a tavern and inn. Today, the huge belly of the elephant houses a museum of local memorabilia.

NAVIGATION: Easterly winds in the summer raise tides for better channel depths, but spring and fall northwesterlies blow the water out to sea, making the NJ ICW channel even more shallow.

CAUTION: Attempt this passage only on a rising tide and try to get local advice as depths as low as 4 feet MLW have been reported in some spots.

The **Margate City Bridge** (14-foot closed vertical clearance) at Mile 74 opens on signal. The channel between Margate and Ventnor is generally deep and

clear but mind the strong currents that flow in this area between Great Egg Harbor and Absecon Inlets.

Turn south into the West Canal at Ventnor City, being sure to honor the three green buoys ("217," "215" and "213") that lead you around the south point at the canal entrance. There is no water inside those buoys! Our Cruising Editor has observed less than 6 feet at three-quarter tide near the **Dorset Ave. Bridge**, which crosses the channel at Mile 71.2 at Ventnor City. The 9-foot vertical clearance bascule bridge opens on signal except from June 1 through September 30, from 9:15 a.m. to 9:15 p.m., when the draw need only open at 15 and 45 minutes after the hour.

The next bridge (**Albany Ave. Bridge**) crosses at Mile 70 and has a 10-foot vertical clearance and a seasonal schedule. The bridge opens on signal except: (1) year-round from 11:00 p.m. to 7:00 a.m., and from November 1 through March 31 from 3:00 p.m. to 11:00 p.m. when the draw need only open unless at least a 4-hour notice is given; and (2) from June 1 through September 30 from 9:00 a.m. to 4:00 p.m. and from 6:00 p.m. to 9:00 p.m. when the draw need only open on the hour and half hour (from 4:00 p.m. to 6:00 p.m. the draw need not open). The schedule of annual events also affects bridge openings. Call ahead or see detail at Waterway Explorer.

At Mile 68 on Great Thorofare, the fixed **Atlantic City Expressway Bridge** (35-foot vertical clearance) is followed immediately by an **AMTRAK Bridge**, a swing bridge with 5-foot closed vertical clearance. The railroad bridge operates remotely will open on signal from 11:00 p.m. to 6:00 a.m. At all other times, the draw will open on signal from 20 minutes to 30 minutes after each hour and remain open for all waiting vessels. When the draw is opening and closing or is closed, yellow flashing lights located on the ends of the center piers are displayed continuously until the bridge is returned to the fully open position.

Anchorage: The Margate City anchorage at Mile 74.2 is a nice place to stop. Pick your spot carefully if you draw more than 3.5 feet. There is a 4-foot tide here. At Mile 71.5 boaters can anchor in the Ventnor City Basin in 6 to 8 feet MLW with good all-around protection and excellent holding in mud and sand.

Atlantic City–NJ ICW Mile 65

Atlantic City is renowned for its classic boardwalk, wide sandy beaches, imposing piers, elegant beach front hotels and gambling casinos; however, the city should also be known for its all-weather inlet from the Atlantic Ocean and its secure harbor along a considerable and relatively uninterrupted stretch of New Jersey coastline.

NAVIGATION: Atlantic City is easily approached from either the NJ ICW or the Atlantic Ocean via Absecon Inlet. From the south, the NJ ICW passes under the 20-foot vertical clearance **Absecon Blvd. (U.S. 30) Bridge** at Mile 67.2. This bascule bridge opens on signal on the hour and half hour from April 1 through October 31, from 7:00 a.m. to 11:00 p.m. At all other times, a 4-hour notice is required. The bridge is subject to temporary closures and changes in schedule due to repairs and maintenance or annual events; call ahead on VHF Channel 13.

To reach most of the local marinas, repair yards and other marine facilities, you must head toward the ocean under the fixed **Brigantine Blvd. Bridge** (60-foot vertical clearance), then enter Clam Creek in front of the U.S. Coast Guard Station. Favor the ocean side of the channel as you make your way through the entrance, especially rounding red nun Clam Creek Buoy "2," which marks a 5-foot (or less) shoal.

CAUTION: There are several small buoys between the jetty and red nun "2" that are very hard to see in waves. Keep your eyes open. There is a fair amount of deep water, but you don't want to go too far to the north.

If approaching from the ocean, the lights of Atlantic City are visible for 20 miles north or south on an offshore approach. Pay attention to the position of the entrance buoys if approaching in the dark as they can be obscured in the background lighting of the casinos.

NOTE: As an interesting side note, the lighted backdrop of the city proved to be particularly hazardous to commercial shipping during World War II. German U-Boats would lay offshore at night and fire torpedoes at freighter traffic, which was conveniently (and fatally) silhouetted against the bright shoreline.

GOIN' ASHORE

ATLANTIC CITY, NJ

Atlantic City is one of the best cruising destinations on the New Jersey coast. Its blazing skyline has become the east coast's most impressive all-night beacon for offshore cruisers. Whether you are planning a several-day stop or you need a place to get out of the weather, look no farther than this robust port with some of the most beautiful beaches on the New Jersey coast. The original 7-mile-long Atlantic City Boardwalk, built in 1870, was the first of its kind in the world and was the inspiration for the board game Monopoly. Today's boardwalk, which has been rebuilt over the years, stretches from Absecon Inlet southwest along 4 miles of spectacular beach and is the longest in the world.

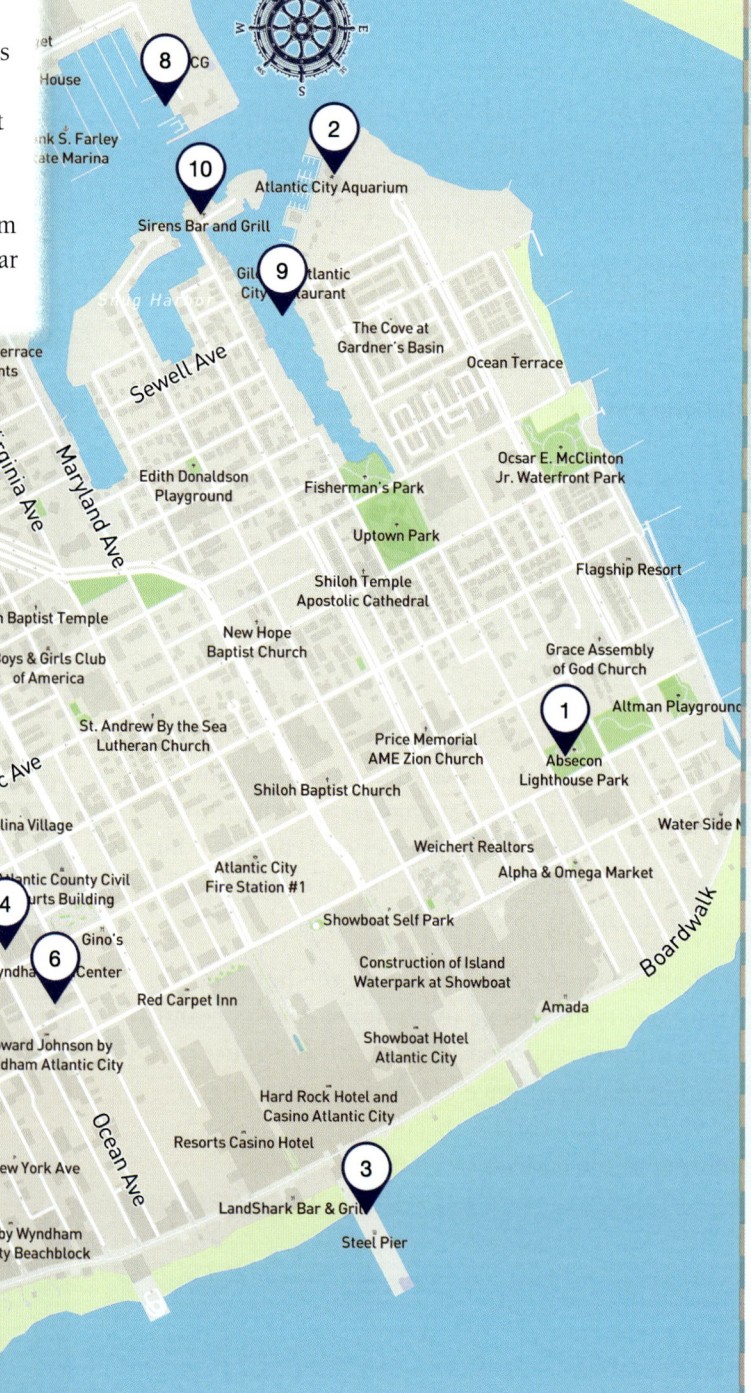

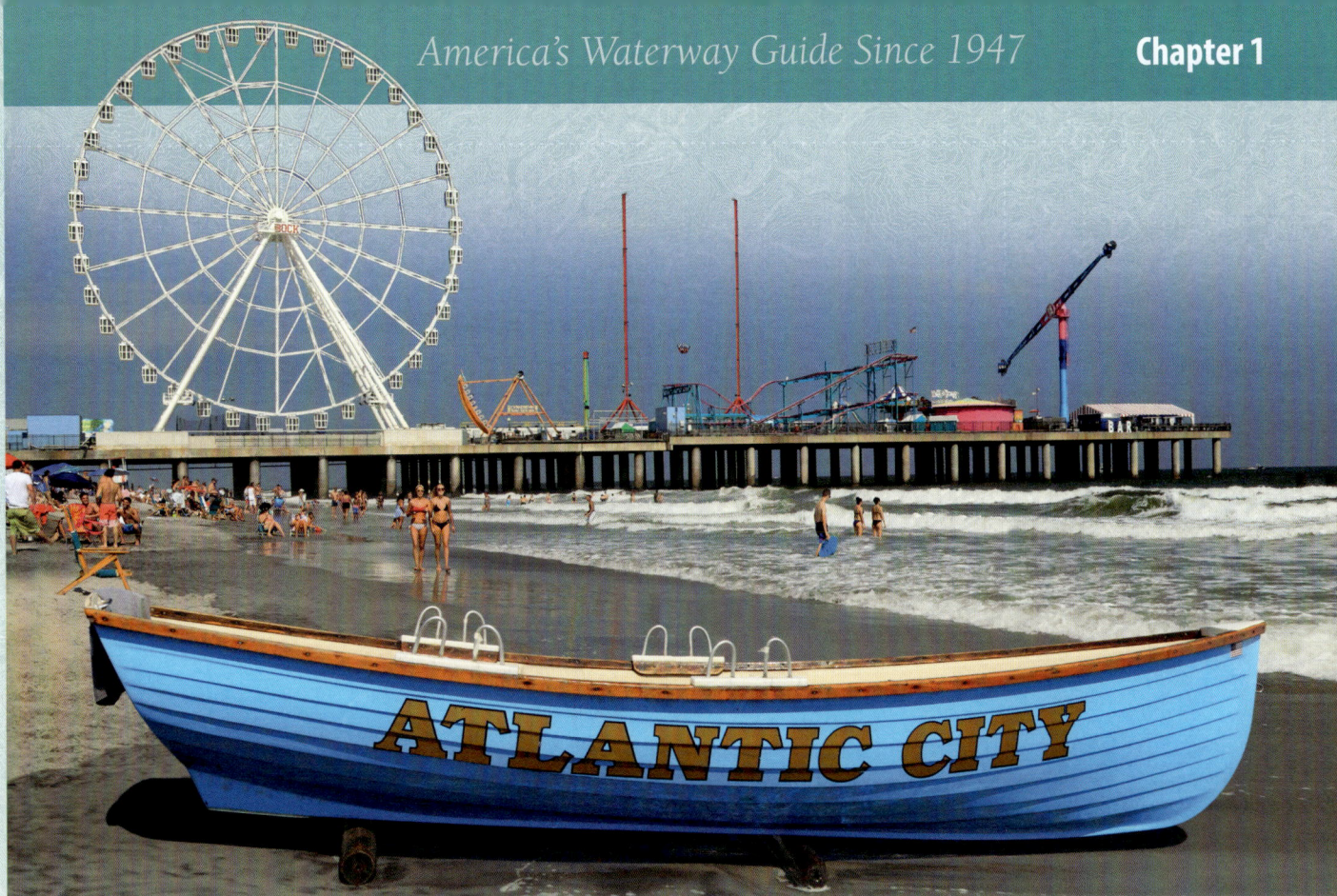

ATTRACTIONS

1. Absecon Lighthouse
History museum and state's tallest lighthouse open for climbing with sweeping views of Atlantic City at 31 S. Rhode Island Ave. (609-449-1360).

2. Atlantic City Aquarium
Large aquarium featuring underwater exhibits plus an exotic animal show and other rotating events. Open daily 10:00 a.m. to 5:00 p.m. at Historic Gardner's Basin (800 N. New Hampshire Ave., 609-348-2880).

3. Steel Pier
Amusement park located on an ocean pier with rides, a midway and food vendors. Home to a 227-foot-tall ferris wheel (The Wheel) with 40 temperature-controlled gondolas (1000 Boardwalk).

SERVICES

4. Atlantic City Free Public Library
1 N. Tennessee Ave. (609-345-2269)

5. Atlantic City Post Office
1801 Atlantic Ave., Ste. 101 (609-348-2940)

6. HealthMed Urgent Care
24 S. South Carolina Ave. (609-345-8000)

7. Scrub A Dub Laundromat
1401 McKinley Ave. (609-344-8940)

MARINAS

8. Farley State Marina at Golden Nugget Casino & Hotel
600 Huron Ave. (800-876-4386)

9. Historic Gardner's Basin
800 N. New Hampshire Ave. (609-348-2880)

10. Kammerman's Marina
447 Carson Ave. (609-348-8418)

Atlantic City, NJ

CLAM CREEK		Largest Vessel	VHF	Total Slips	Approach/ Dockside Depth	Floating Docks	Gas/ Diesel	Repairs/ Haulout	Min/Max Amps	Pump-Out Station
1. Historic Gardner's Basin (WiFi) 1.0 mi. S of MM 65.0	(609) 348-2880	50	9	35	12.0 / 4.5	F			30	
2. Kammerman's Marina (WiFi) 1.0 mi. S of MM 65.0	(609) 348-8418	200	16	50	12.0 / 10.0	F	GD		30 / 200+	
3. Farley State Marina at Golden Nugget Casino & Hotel (WiFi)	(609) 441-8487	300	65	640	12.0 / 8.0	F	GD		30 / 100	P

(WiFi) Wireless Internet Access
Visit www.waterwayguide.com for current rates, fuel prices, website addresses and other up-to-the-minute information.
(Information in the table is provided by the facilities.)

Scan here for more details:

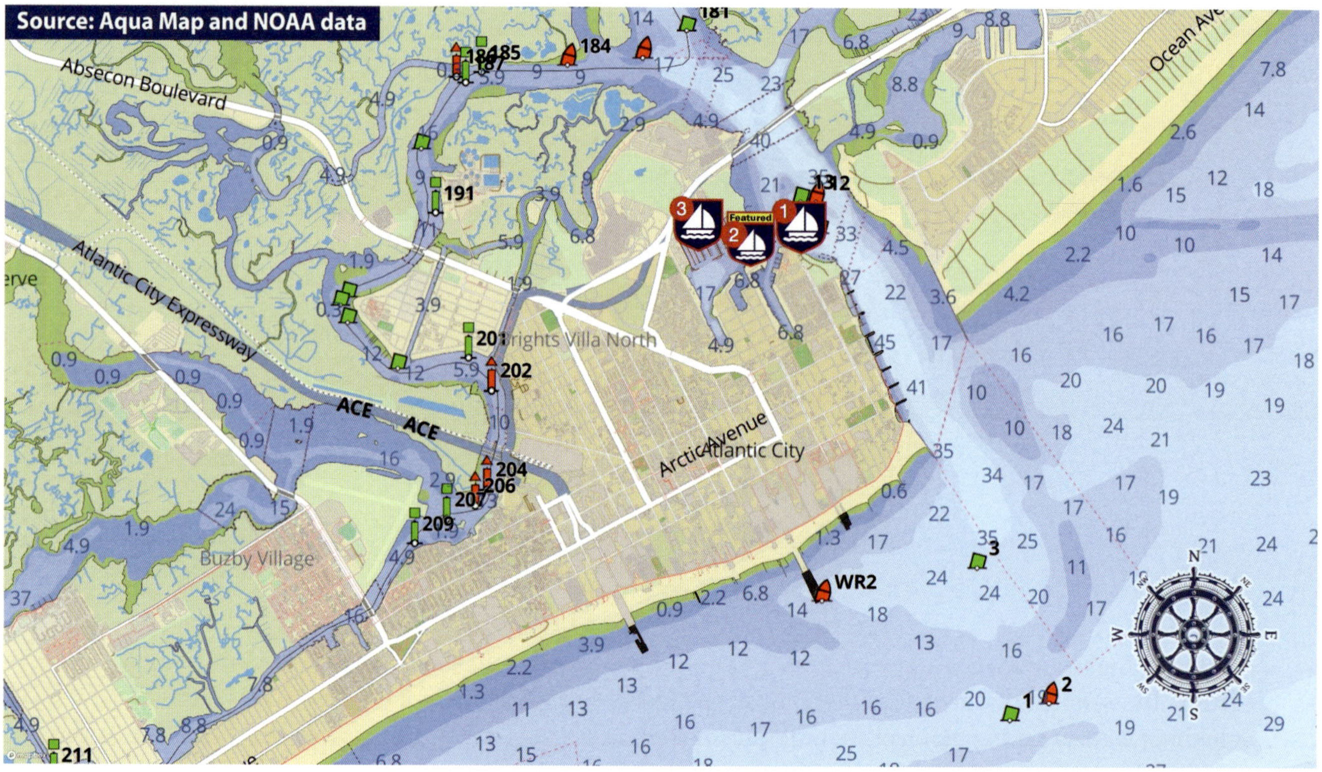

Source: Aqua Map and NOAA data

Dockage: Cruisers arriving in Atlantic City have several marina choices. Historic Gardner's Basin is situated on the easterly side of Clam Creek Basin and is essentially an aquarium that is home to some serious commercial fishing boats. The restrooms are public (without locks) and WiFi only reaches the porch of the aquarium. On the plus side there are nearby restaurants and it is bicycling distance to the boardwalk.

Kammerman's Marina is at the entrance to the second inlet from Clam Creek Basin across from the Coast Guard station. Family-owned and -operated since 1961, they offer fair fuel prices, bulk fuel pricing, transient and seasonal dockage, marine mechanics on call, a helpful staff and all the expected amenities. Kammerman's has the largest fuel dock in the city (180-foot fuel docks with 8 ultra-high speed dispensers). The facility is expanding and has 500 feet of new bulkhead, all new floating docks and has increased the transient dockage to 50 slips. The area has also been dredged to 12 feet.

The largest marina in the area is the 640-slip Farley State Marina at Golden Nugget Casino & Hotel situated on the west side of Clam Creek Basin adjacent to the Golden Nugget Casino. This is a full-service marina with dockage for a variety of crafts up to 300 feet in length. Spend a day on the water, then head on over to enjoy the award-winning restaurants, shows, casino games and nightlife at Golden Nugget. Reservations are a good idea as the marina is often busy.

Should you need them, Mid Coast Marine Repair offers mobile electrical and mechanical service all over New Jersey as well as in Delaware and Pennsylvania. Their licensed technicians will come to you for marine repair services so you spend more time having fun on your boat.

Nearby Offshore Bait & Tackle sells some marine supplies at 433 N. Maryland Ave. (609-345-9099).

Anchorage: The Coast Guard does not permit anchoring in Clam Creek Basin; however, there is a substantial anchorage area in Atlantic City near the marinas in 8- to 22-foot MLW depths with good holding in sand. Take care to honor flashing green "CC" at the mouth to Clam Creek Basin as there is a shoal to the west of the line joining them. Expect challenging currents and a 5-foot tidal range in calculating appropriate scope. You will share this space with scores of local boats on weekends as well as traffic, noise and loads of lights from land. From here, it will be a dinghy ride of about 0.5 mile to the basin where a dinghy landing is available at Historic Gardner's Basin. There is a 4-hour time limit on the public dock.

There is also a popular anchorage at Rum Point Basin (Mile 65.1) on the opposite side of the inlet with excellent holding and all-around protection in 6- to 15-foot MLW depths. Follow the "stakes" (placed by locals) when navigating the entrance. Hug the port side to avoid a sandbar that extends from the sandy beach. The anchorage opens up with 8 feet MLW depth once you pass the last marker. Be careful when the current is running, as it will push you and you will need to power in and out of the mouth to maintain control. Expect lots of traffic during the day.

■ ABSECON INLET TO LITTLE EGG HARBOR

To Little Egg Inlet –NJ ICW Mile 65 to Mile 51

NAVIGATION: A 7-mile alternate route for shoal-draft boats parallels the barrier beach at Brigantine at Mile 64 then rejoins the ICW at Mile 60. The NJ ICW shoals easily in the stretch between Absecon Inlet and Great Bay, and you may see birds strolling on the sandbars building out into the channel.

CAUTION: Shoaling has been reported between green daybeacon 159 and red daybeacon 160 at Mile 59.7. The area is impassable at low tide.

Many daybeacons along this route have been replaced by buoys, which may not be indicated on the chart. If you draw more than 4 feet, be sure to go through on a rising tide (half tide or better). Also, sections of the NJ ICW can be very narrow here with a strong current that is strong and sets across the channel. If the magenta line goes on the wrong side of a buoy, do honor the buoy since the shoals are close on both sides.

NOTE: The NJ ICW runs through the middle of the Brigantine National Wildlife Refuge. The best way to observe the amazing variety of bird life in the refuge is by taking a small boat or dinghy to explore the creeks and passages away from the ICW. The fall migrations are spectacular but it can be extremely buggy in this area during the summer months.

As a potential side trip, the deep, winding Mullica River to the north snakes its way west into the Pine Barrens at the northwest corner of Great Bay. Three miles up the Mullica River, 14-foot-deep Blood Ditch Cut bypasses a nearly 2.5-mile-long loop in the river. Just beyond is the entrance to the deep Bass River, which leads north and is navigable to the town of New Gretna, home of many marinas and marine services and a good hurricane hole with lots of anchorages.

Stick dead on course when crossing Great Bay, which is extremely shallow. The bottom builds up every spring from the continuous sweep of inlet waters so you should try to run this area on a rising tide. This stretch of the NJ ICW will always suffer from shifting sands and uncertain depths.

CAUTION: There is no magenta line on the chart between green can "125" and green-red buoy "LEI." Underpowered auxiliaries with deep drafts should transit this area on a rising tide.

Prudence must prevail where the New Jersey ICW route crosses the twin inlets, Beach Haven and Little Egg, between Mile 55 and Mile 50. The ocean swells carry inside to break on shoal spots, but with care you can make the crossing in all but the worst weather conditions. Although occasionally dredged, the Little Egg inlet buoys are not charted and it should only be transited with local knowledge.

Little Egg Harbor, NJ

TUCKERTON		Largest Vessel	VHF	Total Slips	Approach/ Dockside Depth	Floating Docks	Gas/ Diesel	Repairs/ Haulout	Min/Max Amps	Pump-Out Station
1. Sheltered Cove Marina 📶 MM 126.0	(609) 296-9400	50	9	250	5.0 / 8.0	F	GD	RH	15 / 50	P
2. Tuckerton Marine	(609) 296-1820	40	16	60	5.0 / 8.0	F		R	30	
3. Keeney's Marina LLC	(609) 709-5267			25	6.0 / 6.0	F		R		

📶 Wireless Internet Access
Visit www.waterwayguide.com for current rates, fuel prices, website addresses and other up-to-the-minute information.
(Information in the table is provided by the facilities.)

Scan here for more details:

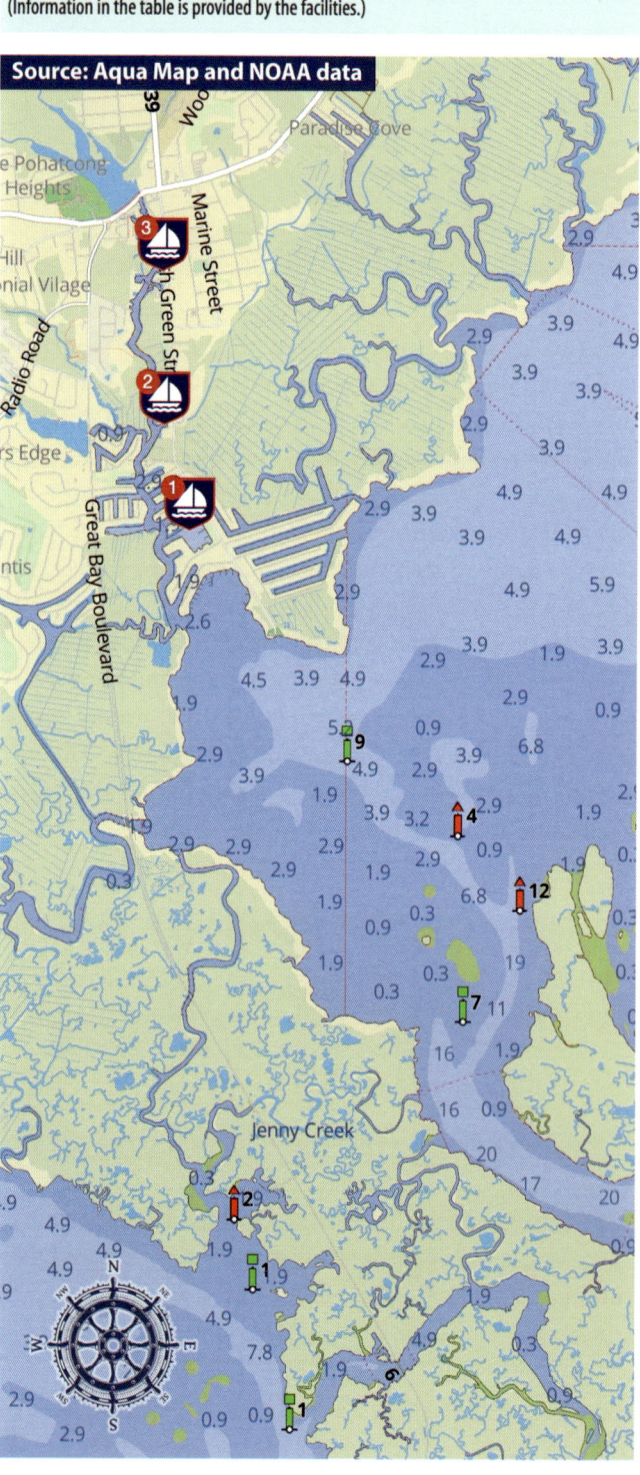
Source: Aqua Map and NOAA data

Prepare in advance to sort out the confusion of inlet and side-channel markers near Mile 50. The buoyed Marshelder Channel at Mile 50 which leads into Little Egg Harbor, can easily be mistaken for the NJ ICW. Check the buoy numbers before committing to a course. Buoy numbering will generally conform to an up-to-date NOAA chart but the location might be quite different, as the Coast Guard is constantly moving buoys to keep up with the changing conditions.

Anchorage: Storm waves and day-to-day currents along the shore and through the inlets make and unmake anchorages, and those you knew previously should be approached carefully before trying them again. Shoal-draft boats will find good holding and shelter from southerly and westerly winds in Great Bay at Landing Creek at Mile 55.5 with 4- to 12-foot MLW depths with holding in thick mud.

The old Coast Guard station in Shooting Thorofare (charted as cupola) at Mile 52 is a safe refuge when weather is rough around the inlets, but note that the sill to the basin has built up. Low-tide depths are minimal so it is best to go in at high tide.

Side Trip: Tuckerton

NAVIGATION: Just after Mile 50, the well-marked Marshelder Channel heads off to the northwest in Little Egg Harbor toward the village of Tuckerton, a natural hurricane hole. The Tuckerton Seaport & Baymen's Museum at 120 West Main St. is open daily (609-296-8868).

Dockage: The 250-slip Sheltered Cove Marina welcomes transients (to 50 feet) on their floating docks with reported 5-foot approach depths. They have an easy-access fuel dock and offer discounted fuel for slip rental customers. Tuckerton Marine is a marine service center and yacht brokerage with seasonal slip rentals. Farther upriver is Keeney's Marina, offering haulout, storage, sales, slips and service.

Little Egg Harbor, NJ

BEACH HAVEN AREA		Largest Vessel	VHF	Total Slips	Approach/ Dockside Depth	Floating Docks	Gas/ Diesel	Repairs/ Haulout	Min/Max Amps	Pump-Out Station
1. Little Egg Harbor Yacht Club–PRIVATE MM 45.5	(609) 492-2529	40			8.0 / 4.0				30	
2. Beach Haven Yacht Club Marina (WiFi) 45.5	(609) 492-9101	80	16	55	8.0 / 8.0		GD		30 / 50	P
3. Queen City Marina (WiFi) 45.4	(609) 492-2150	60		136	5.0 / 5.0	F	GD	RH	30 / 50	P
4. Shelter Harbor Marina (WiFi) MM 44.8	(609) 492-8645	55	16	206	5.0 / 5.0	F		R	30 / 50	P

(WiFi) Wireless Internet Access
Visit www.waterwayguide.com for current rates, fuel prices, website addresses and other up-to-the-minute information.
(Information in the table is provided by the facilities.)

Scan here for more details:

Source: Aqua Map and NOAA data

⫸⫸⫸ ⚠ ⫸⫸⫸

CAUTION: A cofferdam has been installed in Little Egg Harbor approximately one mile northwest of Ham Island at Mile 43. The structure extends approximately 10 feet above the water line and is surrounded by yellow painted pilings. Six of these pilings have white lights placed on top of them. Mariners are advised to exercise caution when transiting the area.

Just before Mile 40 at flashing red "78," a channel branches off to starboard from the NJ ICW. Boats with less than the 18 feet overhead clearance needed for the fixed bridge can leave the NJ ICW here and follow this shorter channel along Long Beach Island, rejoining the NJ ICW at quick flashing red "62."

Boat traffic from this point north on the NJ ICW is heavy, even during mid-week. If you can, avoid traveling this stretch on weekends or holidays. The channel is extremely narrow in the vicinity of the **Manahawkin Bay (NJ 72) Bridge** at Mile 37 (60-foot fixed vertical clearance) with depths outside the channel of only 1 to 2 feet MLW.

Dockage: All the marinas here are close to the beach, market, shops

Long Beach–NJ ICW Mile 51 to Mile 37

North of Little Egg Inlet, the NJ ICW passes behind aptly-named Long Beach. You can bypass Little Egg Harbor by sticking to the NJ ICW channel running close along Long Beach. Beach Haven, Spray Beach, Ship Bottom and Surf City are a few of the communities you pass in this section, all with marinas and hundreds of boats.

NAVIGATION: At Mile 51 watch very carefully for the next pair of daybeacons and favor the red side due to shoaling from Tuckers Island to the east. Be especially vigilant at flashing red "116" where the magenta line denoting the NJ ICW leads directly across a shoal area. Depths here can be as low as 3 to 4 feet MLW.

Little Egg Harbor, NJ

BRANT BEACH AREA		Largest Vessel	VHF	Total Slips	Approach/ Dockside Depth	Floating Docks	Gas/ Diesel	Repairs/ Haulout	Min/Max Amps	Pump-Out Station
1. Hagler's Marina MM 40.0	(609) 494-4509	30		66	3.0 / 4.0	F	G	R	30	
2. Duck Cove Marina MM 40.0	(609) 361-1400	50	67	100	4.0 / 4.0		GD	RH	30	P
3. Hochstrasser's Marina	(609) 494-5340	30		65	17.0 / 10.0			RH	20	

WiFi Wireless Internet Access
Visit www.waterwayguide.com for current rates, fuel prices, website addresses and other up-to-the-minute information.
(Information in the table is provided by the facilities.)

Scan here for more details:

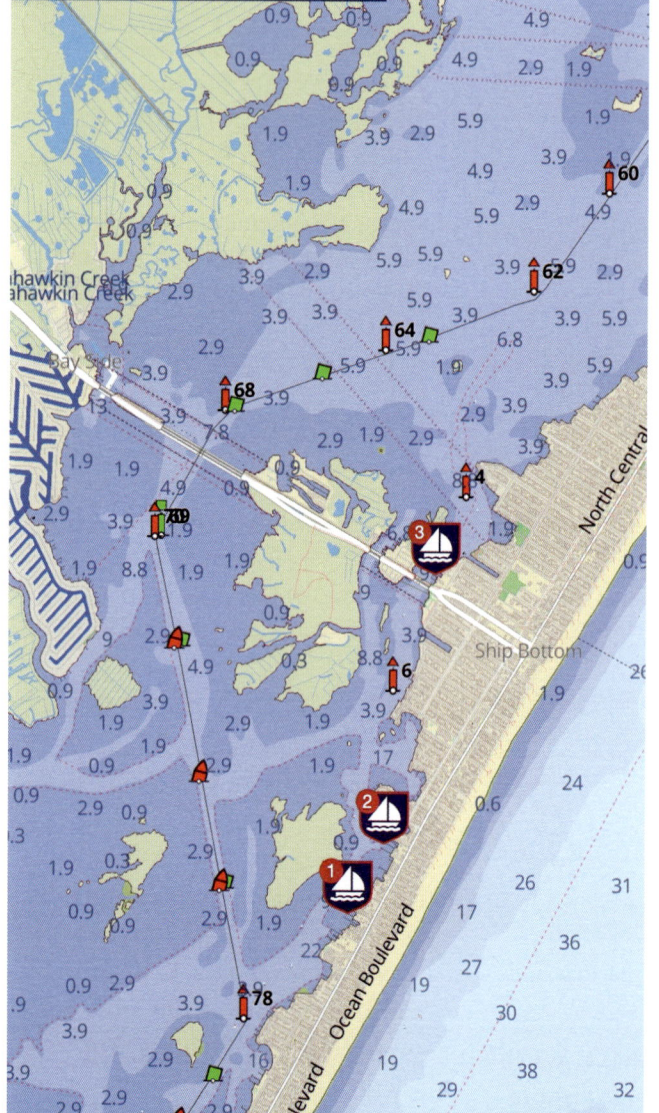

Source: Aqua Map and NOAA data

and fine restaurants. Several facilities in this area are filled with seasonal slip rentals but may be able to make room for you. The first cluster of facilities can be found starting at NJ ICW Mile 45.5 in the heart of Beach Haven. Little Egg Harbor Yacht Club is private but may recognize reciprocity from other clubs. Call ahead. Family-owned Beach Haven Yacht Club Marina offers a relaxing atmosphere with professional, friendly service. Transient visitors can borrow beach tags and enjoy the beautiful Beach Haven area.

Just to the north Queen City Marina welcomes transients (to 60 feet) and has a well-stocked ship store. Shelter Harbor Marina at Mile 44.8 welcomes vessels to 55 feet with full amenities.

Anchorage: There is an anchorage behind Mordecai Island at Liberty Thorofare (Mile 46) with 5 to 9 feet MLW with good holding in sand and mud. It is exposed to the north.

Side Trip: Brant Beach

Just before Mile 40 at flashing red "78," a channel branches off to the northeast from the NJ ICW. Boats with less than the 15 feet overhead clearance needed for the fixed bridge, noted as "under construction" on the NOAA chart, can leave the NJ ICW here and follow this shorter channel along Long Beach Island, rejoining the NJ ICW at quick flashing red "62."

Dockage: Marinas at Brant Beach include the small boat facilities (to 30 feet) at Hagler's Marina and Duck Cove Marina (to 50 feet). To the north of the Manahawkin Bay Bridge is Hochstrasser's Marina, which can accommodate vessels to 30 feet. Approach and dockside depths are reportedly shoal here (3 to 4 feet) so call ahead for directions in. The Boatyard is a seasonal dock and dine made up of two food trailers and a wrap-around bar plus a marina store.

Anchorage: There is a cove just south of the marinas at Mile 40 with charted depths of 12 to 25 feet MLW with room for four to six cruising boats.

Pages 116-122

Shark River Inlet

Manasquan
River

● **Manasquan**

Manasquan Inlet

Metadeconk River

● **Point Pleasant**

● **Mantoloking**

Pages 113-116

Toms River ● Toms River

Atlantic Ocean

Pages 102-112

Forked River

Barnegat Bay

● **Island Beach**

NEW JERSEY

Barnegat Inlet

NAVIGATION NOTES

Barnegat Bay is very popular with both power boaters and sailors. The Bay was designated as a national estuary with lovely scenery, superb beaches, plenty of shoreside attractions and inviting sailing conditions.

When cruising this magnificent body of water, you will find a number of resorts preserving either the grand socialite splendor of an earlier day or a more modest and casual flavor. Piney rivers make excellent hurricane holes and historical New Jersey water traditions survive in many of the mainland towns.

Cruising Conditions

The entire length of the NJ ICW in Barnegat Bay is safe and sheltered with little more than a stiff chop during strong winds that normally occur in the afternoon. In the spring and early summer when a front of warm, humid air moves up from the south, be prepared for dense advection fogs when transiting the NJ ICW along the bay.

The tidal range of the entire bay is less than 6 inches; however, strong southwest winds can increase height of the tide and, conversely, strong northeasts can lower it. This is especially true in the northern bay.

North of Toms River, Barnegat Bay is shoal but well marked with depths ranging from 6 to 8 feet MLW. Make certain to follow the markers with the familiar yellow logo of the ICW as you transit the bay. Do not be misled by side-channel markers and entrances to rivers that do not show the yellow logo of the ICW.

The southern portion of the bay ranges from 8 to 10 feet MLW in the channel and dependable winds help make it one of the coast's most popular sailing centers. The diurnal wind pattern in this part of Barnegat Bay is for the sea breeze to begin at about 11:00 a.m. and then increase by mid-afternoon to a velocity usually greater than that predicted. A windless day on Barnegat Bay is rare.

A good rule to remember when cruising Barnegat Bay is that the deepest water is to the west near the mainland, while the shallowest is on the east next to the barrier island. Although crab trap buoys and eel trap buoys are often scattered throughout the bay, few are near the channel.

BARNEGAT BEACH TO TOMS RIVER

Barnegat Beach & Waretown– NJ ICW Mile 30

On the west side of Barnegat Bay, across from the town of Barnegat Light, well-marked channels lead into Barnegat Beach and Waretown where marine services and repairs are available.

Barnegat Inlet

Barnegat Bay, NJ

WARETOWN		Largest Vessel	VHF	Total Slips	Approach/ Dockside Depth	Floating Docks	Gas/ Diesel	Repairs/ Haulout	Min/Max Amps	Pump-Out Station
1. Mariner's Marina MM 28.0	(609) 698-1222	40		200	6.0 / 6.0	F		RH	30	
2. Double Creek Marina	(609) 698-8581	34		18	6.0 / 6.0				15 / 50	
3. Key Harbor Marina (WiFi) 27.8	**(609) 693-9355**	65		260	6.0 / 6.0		GD	RH	30 / 50	P
4. Leamings Marina	(609) 971-1514	26		76	/ 8.0	F	G	RH		
5. Long Key Marina MM 26.0	(609) 693-9444	45	16	142	6.0 / 6.0	F	GD	RH	30	P
6. Spencer's Bayside Marina (WiFi) MM 26.0	(609) 693-0100	55	16	22	5.0 / 6.0	F		RH	30 / 100	P
7. Holiday Harbor Marina (WiFi) 25.8	(609) 693-2217	65		200	6.0 / 6.0	F	GD	RH	30 / 50	P

(WiFi) Wireless Internet Access
Visit www.waterwayguide.com for current rates, fuel prices, website addresses and other up-to-the-minute information.
(Information in the table is provided by the facilities.)

Scan here for more details:

NAVIGATION:

⚠️ **CAUTION:** Shoaling has been reported in the NJ ICW between Manasquan Inlet and Cape May Inlet. Mariners are advised to use extreme caution.

Dockage: The 200-slip Mariner's Marina is located west of Conklin Island on Double Creek. The family-owned and -operated marina caters to both sailboats and power boats to 40 feet and advertises comprehensive service offerings. Double Creek Marina specializes in boating, fishing and crabbing. They have a marina store and tackle shop and offer repairs. Both of these have limited slip space so call ahead.

To the north, Key Harbor Marina at Waretown has 260 slips that can accommodate boats up to 65 feet. In a basin just to the north is Leamings Marina, which may have space for smaller vessels (to 26 feet) but call ahead.

The intimate (22 slips total) and private Spencer's Bayside Marina on Waretown Creek in Barnegat has an extensive parts inventory with engine parts, general boating and safety supplies, electronics and anchors. They may be able to provide you a berth in a pinch. Family-owned Long Key Marina has 142 slips (to 45 feet) and offers extensive services.

North in a protected harbor is Holiday Harbor Marina, a deep-water facility that caters to sportfishing vessels to 65 feet.

Anchorage: Just off the mainland town of Barnegat Beach, anchor just north of Conklin Island for protection from the prevailing south and southwest winds in 4 to 8 feet MLW with good holding in soft mud. This is exposed from the north through the east. At Pebble Beach to the north, nudge in close to shore and clear of the private channel markers for 6 feet MLW.

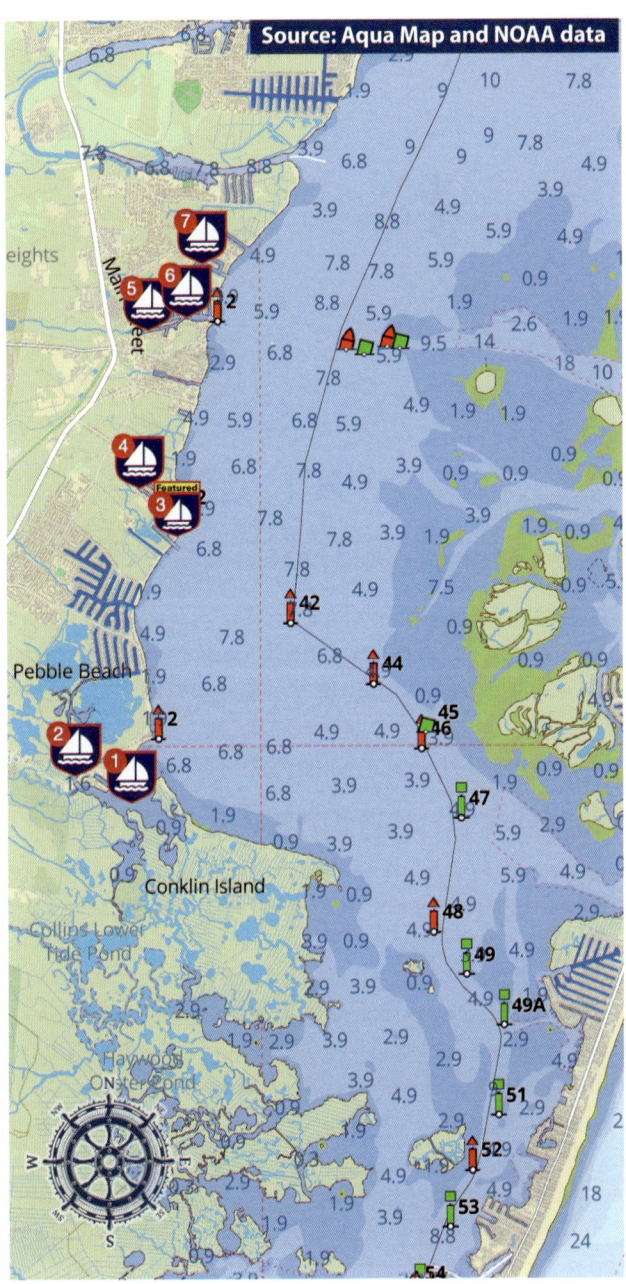

Source: Aqua Map and NOAA data

Barnegat Bay, NJ

BARNEGAT LIGHT	Largest Vessel	VHF	Total Slips	Approach/ Dockside Depth	Floating Docks	Gas/ Diesel	Repairs/ Haulout	Min/Max Amps	Pump-Out Station
1. Lighthouse Marina MM 26.0 (609) 494-2305	70	16	50	7.0 / 8.0		GD	H	30	
2. Bayview Harbor (WiFi) MM 26.0 (609) 494-7450	125	68	150	7.0 / 8.0	F	GD	RH	30 / 100	P

(WiFi) Wireless Internet Access
Visit www.waterwayguide.com for current rates, fuel prices, website addresses and other up-to-the-minute information.
(Information in the table is provided by the facilities.)

Scan here for more details:

Source: Aqua Map and NOAA data

To Barnegat Inlet

At the northern tip of Long Beach Island next to Barnegat Inlet is Barnegat Lighthouse, which is located in the town of Barnegat Light. With fair weather and seas, the town of Barnegat Light can be a fine overnight stop for those traveling the coastline.

Because it is about halfway between New York City and Cape May, a boat capable of 6-knot speeds can make the trip down the entire New Jersey coast in two daytime hops. (The three-day alternative for slower boats consists of overnight stops at Manasquan and Atlantic City.)

The familiar 163-foot red and white tower was commissioned into service in 1859 and served faithfully until 1944 when it was decommissioned. The light was relit on January 1, 2009, and now flashes a white light every 10 seconds. A private group maintains the lighthouse, which is open daily from 10:00 a.m. to 4:30 p.m. (weather permitting). Barnegat Lighthouse State Park is open for fishing, hiking, birding and picnicking.

NAVIGATION: Three channels branch off next to the Coast Guard Station at Barnegat Inlet. The channel to the south enters the harbor at Barnegat Light. To the north is Oyster Creek Channel, which leads to the NJ ICW on the west side of Barnegat Bay. Be sure not to bear southeast off the main channel into Double Creek Channel, which is closed periodically due to shoaling and in the best conditions has just 3-foot MLW depths in portions of the channel. It eventually leads back to the NJ ICW but seek local knowledge before attempting to enter.

Barnegat Inlet is straightforward and easy to navigate; however, there can be large waves and breakers if there is an outgoing tide that is opposed by a strong easterly wind. An inquiry on VHF Channel 16 will usually bring a response of good local knowledge of the inlet conditions. Call for advice and also trust your own prudence and judgment.

The south jetty of Barnegat Inlet is marked with a 35-foot-high tower made of black steel, which is 8 feet in diameter and topped with a green light and horn. Look for the square green "7" daybeacon portion during daylight hours. The north jetty is marked with a 40-foot-high tower topped with a red light and a triangular red "6" daybeacon. It is best to favor this (red "6") daybeacon when coming in and going out of the inlet.

CAUTION: Potentially dangerous shoals continually develop just outside the mouth of Barnegat Inlet. Shoaling on the ocean side of the inlet is most treacherous with a strong northeast wind and an outgoing tide, which can build 6-foot to 8-foot breaking seas capable of dropping you on the bottom in the troughs. These are extreme conditions but prudence suggests that you consider an alternative entrance in such conditions. Also be aware that the first 0.10 mile of the jetty behind red daybeacon "6" submerges at high tide so use caution transiting this inlet.

Dredges work on Barnegat Inlet three times a year for a month at a time. During these periods, transiting the narrow passage past the dredge equipment can be difficult.

Dockage: Located south of the inlet entrance at Barnegat Harbor is Lighthouse Marina with a commercial dock that can be a bit bouncy but they have a well-stocked ship store and there are grocery stores and restaurants nearby.

Bayview Harbor Marina is in a protected harbor just south of the inlet and includes two adjacent marina basins with 150 floating docks. It is within walking distance of restaurants, a grocery store, shops and the town beach. The marina serves boats from 25 to 125 feet and offers fuel, pump-out and repair/haul-out services. The marina also operates an inn, The SandCastle, for boaters needing overnight accommodations.

Anchorage: Coming from the inlet, bear south as you pass the lighthouse toward the town of Barnegat Light and anchor west of the Coast Guard building at Barnegat Harbor A or near Bayview Harbor South Basin in Barnegat Harbor B. Anchor well away from the channel; large commercial fishing boats are berthed at the end of the harbor. There is a small dinghy dock at the boat ramp.

To Oyster Creek Channel Junction–NJ ICW Mile 26

NAVIGATION: West of the Barnegat Lighthouse, Oyster Creek Channel joins Barnegat Inlet with Barnegat Bay. Oyster Creek Channel is subject to continual change due to severe shoaling. The numbered buoys marking this channel are shifted frequently to mark the best water and therefore are not charted. This passage should never be attempted at night by a newcomer. Even in daylight, sharp doglegs of nearly 90° can be easily overlooked and wide scans for the next set of buoys are mandatory since missing a set will probably put you aground.

The channel can be very congested on summer weekends with fishing boats drifting in the channel and blocking your views of the navigational markers. Boats with a draft of 5 feet or more should only attempt to transit the Oyster Creek Channel on a rising tide. Shoals do shift frequently so caution is advised. Flashing red-and-white 17-foot Morse (A) light "BI" marks the junction of Oyster Creek Channel and the NJ ICW on Barnegat Bay. This aid to navigation has a white light, which flashes Morse (A) (one short, one long).

If heading to Forked River or other destinations to the north, do not cut this buoy! Leave it well to starboard before turning north. There is extensive shoaling inside the buoy off the Sedge Islands to the east.

Forked River

Forked River–NJ ICW Mile 24

NAVIGATION: Flashing red "2" just west of Morse (A) marker "BB" at Mile 24 marks the entrance to the Forked River. Stay in the channel when navigating the river as shoaling is present on both sides. Three branches of the river run back into the mainland. The two south forks are residential, while the north branch has all the facilities of interest to the cruiser including numerous boatyards and marinas, waterfront restaurants and easy access to grocery stores, drugstores and bus service to New York and Atlantic City.

Dockage: Transient dockage can be found at Marina at Southwinds, the first marina to starboard on the river. This is a full-service marina that can accommodate boats to 58 feet. The marina also has top-notch marine mechanics. Next is Townsend's Marina with slips to 50 feet and ample parts and services. The adjacent Captain's Inn offers dockage (white pilings) to diners for a modest fee and has ample slip space.

Continuing upriver are boat sales, storage and repair yards (but few transient slips). The Tide's End Marina has just two reserved transient slips to 44 feet plus offers services, maintenance and repair.

Barnegat Bay, NJ

FORKED RIVER		Largest Vessel	VHF	Total Slips	Approach/ Dockside Depth	Floating Docks	Gas/ Diesel	Repairs/ Haulout	Min/Max Amps	Pump-Out Station
1. Marina at Southwinds WiFi MM 23.5	(609) 693-6288	60	17	174	8.0 / 6.0		GD	RH	30 / 50	P
2. Captain's Inn MM 23.5	(609) 693-3351	70		45	7.0 / 6.0				30	
3. Townsend's Marina WiFi MM 23.5	(609) 693-6100	50		96	6.0 / 6.0	F		RH	30	
4. North Branch Yachting Center MM 23.5	(609) 693-2134	60		76	10.0 / 10.0			RH	30 / 50	P
5. Tide's End Marina MM 23.5	(609) 693-9423	44		35	10.0 / 6.0	F	G	RH	30	P
6. The Marina at Tall Oaks MM 23.5	(609) 693-2145	65		125	8.0 / 6.0		GD	RH	30 / 50	P
7. Silver Cloud Harbor Marina MM 23.5	**(609) 693-2145**	**75**		**300**	**10.0 / 9.0**		**GD**	**RH**	**30 / 50**	**P**
8. Wilbert's Marina WiFi MM 23.5	(609) 693-2145	65	16	17	8.0 / 6.0		GD	RH	30 / 50	P
9. Forked River State Marina MM 23.5	(609) 693-5045	50	16	125	6.0 / 6.0				30	P

WiFi Wireless Internet Access
Visit www.waterwayguide.com for current rates, fuel prices, website addresses and other up-to-the-minute information.
(Information in the table is provided by the facilities.)

Scan here for more details:

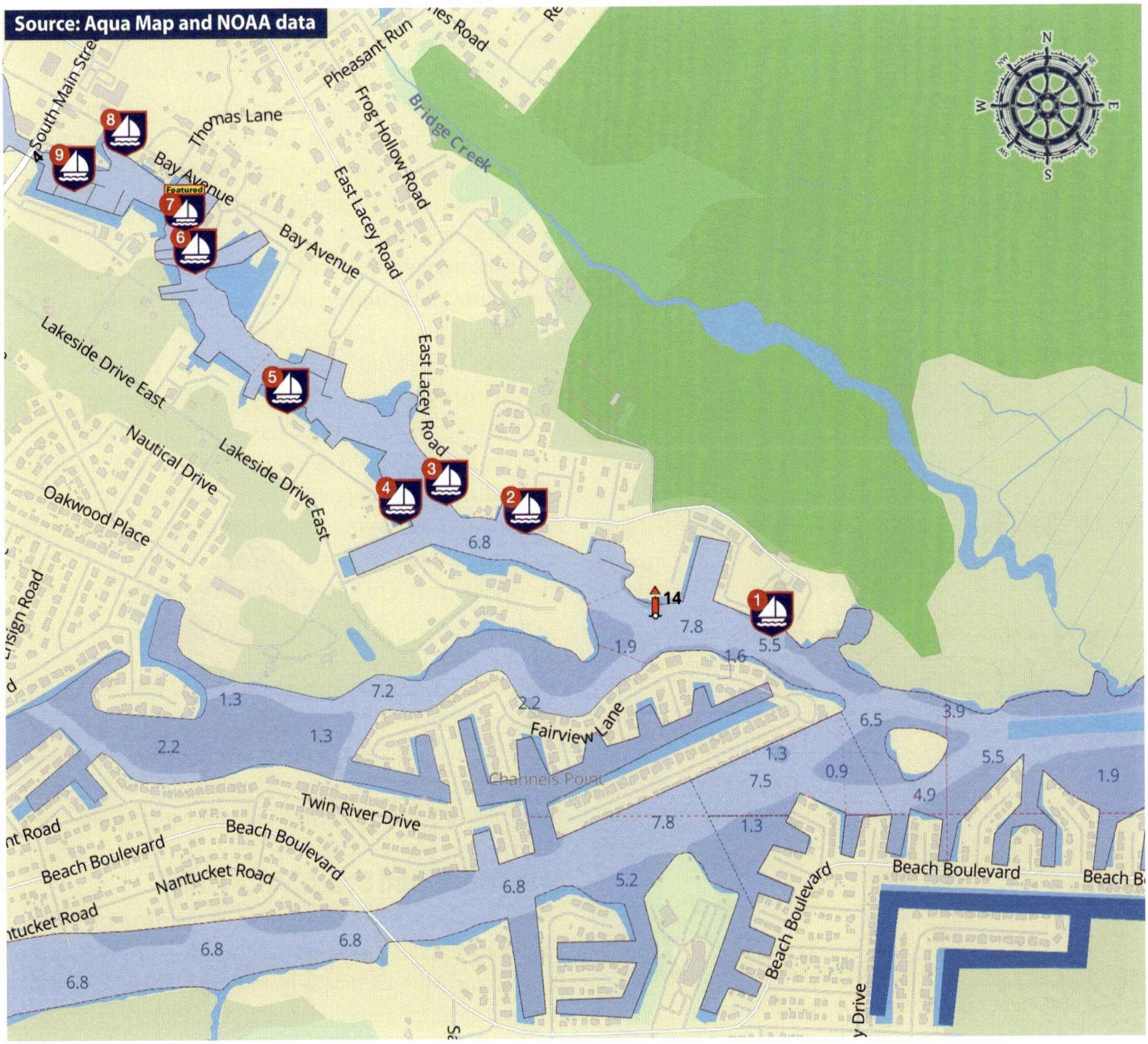

Source: Aqua Map and NOAA data

Barnegat Bay, NJ

			Largest Vessel	VHF	Total Slips	Approach/ Dockside Depth	Floating Docks	Gas/ Diesel	Repairs/ Haulout	Min/Max Amps	Pump-Out Station
LAUREL HARBOR											
1. Laurel Harbor Marina and Yacht Club (WiFi) MM 20.5	(609) 693-6112		50		156	4.0 / 4.0		G	RH	30	P
CEDAR CREEK											
2. Ocean Beach Marine Center MM 20.0	(609) 242-2200		40	68	110	5.0 / 5.0		GD	RH	50	P
3. Lanoka Harbor Marina MM 20.0	(609) 693-2674		60		200	5.0 / 5.0		GD	RH	30 / 50	P
4. Cedar Creek Sailing Center/Marina (WiFi) MM 20.0	(732) 269-1351		45	78	60	6.0 / 5.5			RH	30	P
GLEN COVE											
5. Berkeley Island Marine	(732) 269-1186		30			/		G	RH		

(WiFi) Wireless Internet Access
Visit www.waterwayguide.com for current rates, fuel prices, website addresses and other up-to-the-minute information.
(Information in the table is provided by the facilities.)

Scan here for more details:

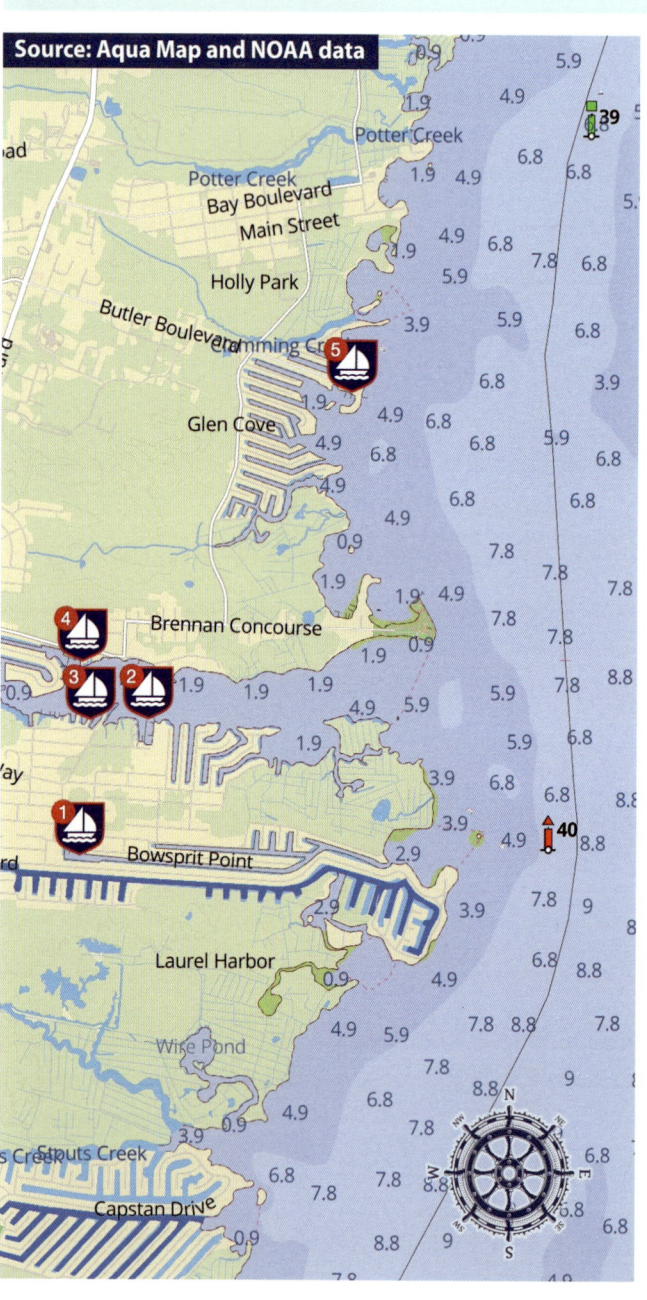

Source: Aqua Map and NOAA data

The large complex of Silver Cloud Harbor Marina features 300 seasonal slips and some reserved transient space. Amenities include a ship store, fuel dock, pool with cabanas, picnic areas and all types of services and repairs (including emergency repairs). Their sister facilities are The Marina at Tall Oaks, Wilbert's Marina and North Branch Yachting Center (formerly Rick's Marina) with deep-water slips (to 60 feet) for those who need marine services.

At the head of the river is the 125-slip Forked River State Marina with limited transient space and full amenities. Other yards may be able to make room for you but these are working boatyards with few amenities.

Anchorage: Forked River is one of the best hurricane holes on the coast. It has proven nearly impervious to even the worst blows. The charted bight on the south side of the channel at the mouth of Forked River (commonly called Sissy Cove) is popular for swimming and overnight anchoring. Although exposed from the northeast through the east, there is 4 to 8 feet MLW with good holding in mud. If the weather turns, move farther up the river to the South Branch for more protection.

Another good anchorage area is in the North Branch where you can drop the hook close to shore in 5- to 8-foot MLW depths with protection from winds in the western semicircle. This is next to a wetlands and is farther from the wakes of boats using the Forked River channel.

Side Trip: Island Beach State Park

Island Beach State Park, a 10-mile-long strip of pristine barrier island, lies on the east side of the NJ ICW between Mile 27 and Mile 15, across from Forked River. To this day it is undeveloped and preserved in its natural condition.

About 200 yards after passing flashing white Morse (A) "BB" at NJ ICW Mile 22, you may see boats anchored close to shore at Island Beach State Park. This area is known as Tices Shoal. You can anchor here in 4-to 10-foot MLW depths with a hard sand bottom and dinghy to shore to explore.

There is a small sandy beach on the bay side and a stairway and walking path through the rolling dunes to the ocean beach about 0.25 mile across the barrier island. A small fee ($3.00) is collected from those boaters who dinghy ashore here to visit the ocean beach, which is a popular spot for local boaters on summer weekends. Expect lots of loud music and partying.

Cedar Creek–NJ ICW Mile 20

NAVIGATION: North of Forked River, the west side of Barnegat Bay shows evidence of a dredge and developer with most of the channels leading to residential subdivisions. Cedar Creek, however, retains the "Down-Jersey" pine-and-cedar appeal and has emerged as a sailing center that is worth a visit. Pay close attention to channel markers as shoaling is present on both sides of the channel.

Dockage: The family-owned Laurel Harbor Marina and Yacht Club is up a protected channel with 156 slips to 50 feet as well as a dry storage yard. On Cedar Creek to the north, co-owned Ocean Beach Marine Center-Lavalette and Lanoka Harbor Marina may have slip space but call ahead. Cedar Creek Sailing Center/Marina caters to sailboats with a sailmaker/rigger on site. They are also the home of Barnegat Bay Sailing School and Charters. They

only have two reserved transient slips so call ahead.

One mile north between green daybeacon "39" and red daybeacon "40" (Mile 21) is Berkeley Island Marine. The marina is tucked away from the harsh northeast winds and waves and accommodates vessels to 30 feet.

Toms River–NJ ICW Mile 15

This picturesque river lined with houses and high banks opens to the west and a number of its attractive coves provide excellent anchorages and delightful possibilities for exploring. Several marinas accept transients including a few of complete resorts with swimming pools, on-site restaurants and shore accommodations.

The City of Toms River is an historic port dating to 1624 at the head of the river. The Toms River Yacht Club, founded in 1871, is the second oldest in the country. Traditional captains' houses line the street, and the town is working to preserve its maritime history. The Toms River Seaport Society has acquired several historic boats and other artifacts for its maritime museum and waterfront display and there is an annual Wooden Boat festival, usually during July. Call the Society at 732-349-9209 for details.

NAVIGATION: Shoaling has been reported in the NJ ICW near red daybeacon "38." When entering Toms River, stand off of Goodluck Point to avoid shoaling. There is also shoaling off Long Point so do not cut inside flashing red "10" on the Tom's River.

Heading north from Toms River, heed all marks since there is shoaling on both sides of the NJ

ICW, especially just beyond the two bridges at about Mile 14 that cross from the mainland to the resort town of Seaside Heights on the barrier beach. At Seaside Heights, a 1-mile-long boardwalk with an amusement park is worth a stop, especially if you have young (or young at heart) ones aboard.

The northernmost of the twin bridges, **J. Stanley Tunney Bridge,** is fixed with a 60-foot vertical clearance. **Thomas A. Mathis (NJ 37) Bridge** (30-foot closed vertical clearance) will open on signal from Memorial Day through Labor Day except from 8:00 a.m. to 8:00 p.m., when the draw need only open on the hour and half hour. From April 1 through November 30 from 11:00 p.m. to 8:00 a.m. and at all times from December 1 through March 31, the draw need only open if at least four hours notice is given.

Be careful as you approach the bridges from the south. The channel is well marked but outside the channel there are charted submerged objects and light pilings leveled by winter ice. They constitute a hazard until they are removed when new pilings are set out (usually in June). Just north of the bridges pay close attention to the daybeacons because shallow flats crowd in on both sides and sandbars often move into the edges of the channel. Deep water is to the west with shallow flats to the east throughout the rest of this section.

Dockage/Moorings: There are many boat yards, marinas and yacht clubs on the Toms River. Near the mouth of the river around Goodluck Point is the full-service Ocean Gate Yacht Basin, which welcomes transients to 45 feet.

Barnegat Bay, NJ

TOMS RIVER		Largest Vessel	VHF	Total Slips	Approach/ Dockside Depth	Floating Docks	Gas/ Diesel	Repairs/ Haulout	Min/Max Amps	Pump-Out Station
1. Ocean Gate Yacht Basin MM 15.0	(732) 269-2565	45		180	6.0 / 6.0		GD	RH	50	P
2. Shore Point Marina & Yacht Sales WiFi MM 15.0	(732) 244-2106	57		205	6.0 / 6.0	F	GD	RH	30 / 50	P
3. Lighthouse Point Marina MM 15.0	(732) 341-1105	75		248	6.0 / 5.0			RH	30 / 100	P
4. Tom's River Yacht Club-PRIVATE WiFi	(732) 929-0888			90	/					P
5. Island Heights Yacht Club-PRIVATE MM 15.0	(732) 929-9813				/					
6. Nelson Marine Basin WiFi MM 15.0	(732) 270-0022	40	79	100	5.0 / 5.0			RH	30 / 50	P
7. Cozy Cove Marina MM 15.0	(732) 929-1171	40		85	6.0 / 6.0		G	RH	30	
8. Dillon's Creek Marina WiFi MM 15.0	(732) 270-8541	46		210	6.0 / 6.0			RH	30 / 50	P
9. Pier One Motel & Marina WiFi MM 14.0	(732) 270-9090	45	9	65	7.0 / 7.0				30 / 50	

WiFi Wireless Internet Access
Visit www.waterwayguide.com for current rates, fuel prices, website addresses and other up-to-the-minute information.
(Information in the table is provided by the facilities.)

Scan here for more details:

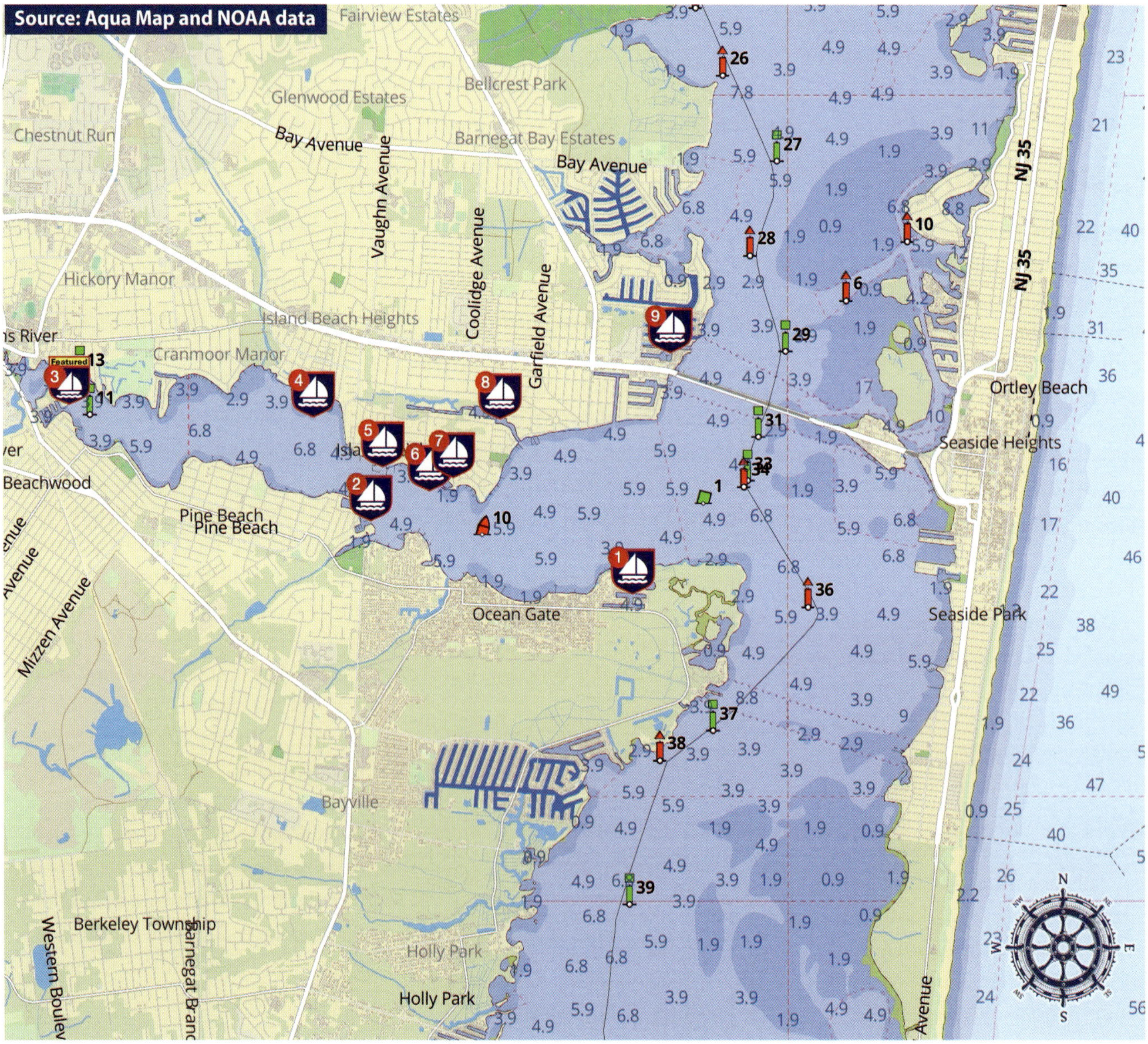

Source: Aqua Map and NOAA data

Shore Point Marina & Yacht Sales is located in an enclosed, well-protected basin at the mouth of Mill Creek on the south side of the Toms River. They maintain transient slips to 57 feet and offer mechanical and yard services.

The friendly Lighthouse Point Marina and Yacht Club is set on 14 acres at the head of the Toms River with amenities that include deep-water slips to 75 feet, a pool and an array of services.

Marinas on the north side of the river include the private Toms River Yacht Club (the second oldest club in America) and Island Heights Yacht Club. Both offer courtesy dockage for members of reciprocal yacht clubs. Call ahead.

Nelson Marine Basin has slips and moorings (to 40 feet) and is home to Nelson Sailing Center. They also offer restoration and engine/mechanical services. Cozy Cove Marina is snug to enter because it is so protected and has just two reserved transient slips to 40 feet. Call ahead.

The well-regarded Dillon's Creek Marina has just two reserved transient slips (to 45 feet) and offers mechanical and other services.

Pier One Motel & Marina just north of the twin bridges has slips to 45 feet and is a good opportunity to host friends or get off the boat for a night or two.

Anchorage: Quiet and protected overnight anchorage can be found anywhere along the shores of Toms River but Cocktail Cove (south of Mill Creek) is particularly popular with 5 to 8 feet MLW and holding in mud with open exposure to the north.

There is a nice, protected anchorage at Mill Creek. Drop anchor in 6 to 8 feet MLW. Good protection from all directions but east-northeast. Expect some wakes during the day but quiets down at night.

Another popular anchorage is just east of Money Island on the north side of the river with good holding in 5 to 6 feet MLW with open exposure to the south.

The Pine Beach anchorage to the west on the Toms River (south shore) is the most protected with excellent holding and wind protection.

Barnegat Lighthouse

Barnegat Bay

Barnegat Bay, NJ

ISLAND BEACH		Largest Vessel	VHF	Total Slips	Approach/ Dockside Depth	Floating Docks	Gas/ Diesel	Repairs/ Haulout	Min/Max Amps	Pump-Out Station
1. Seaside Park Yacht Club-PRIVATE MM 15.5	(732) 793-9611	60		41	/					
2. Lavallette Yacht Club-PRIVATE 1.5 mi. SE of MM 10.0	(732) 793-8747				/					
3. Ocean Beach Marina - Lavallette 1.5 mi. SE of MM 10.0	(732) 793-7460	45		170	5.0 / 7.0		G	RH	30	P
4. Chadwick Island Marina (WiFi)	(732) 965-8563	42		202	/		G	RH	30 / 50	P

WiFi Wireless Internet Access
Visit www.waterwayguide.com for current rates, fuel prices, website addresses and other up-to-the-minute information.
(Information in the table is provided by the facilities.)

Scan here for more details: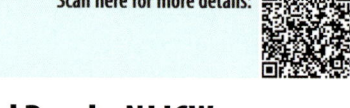

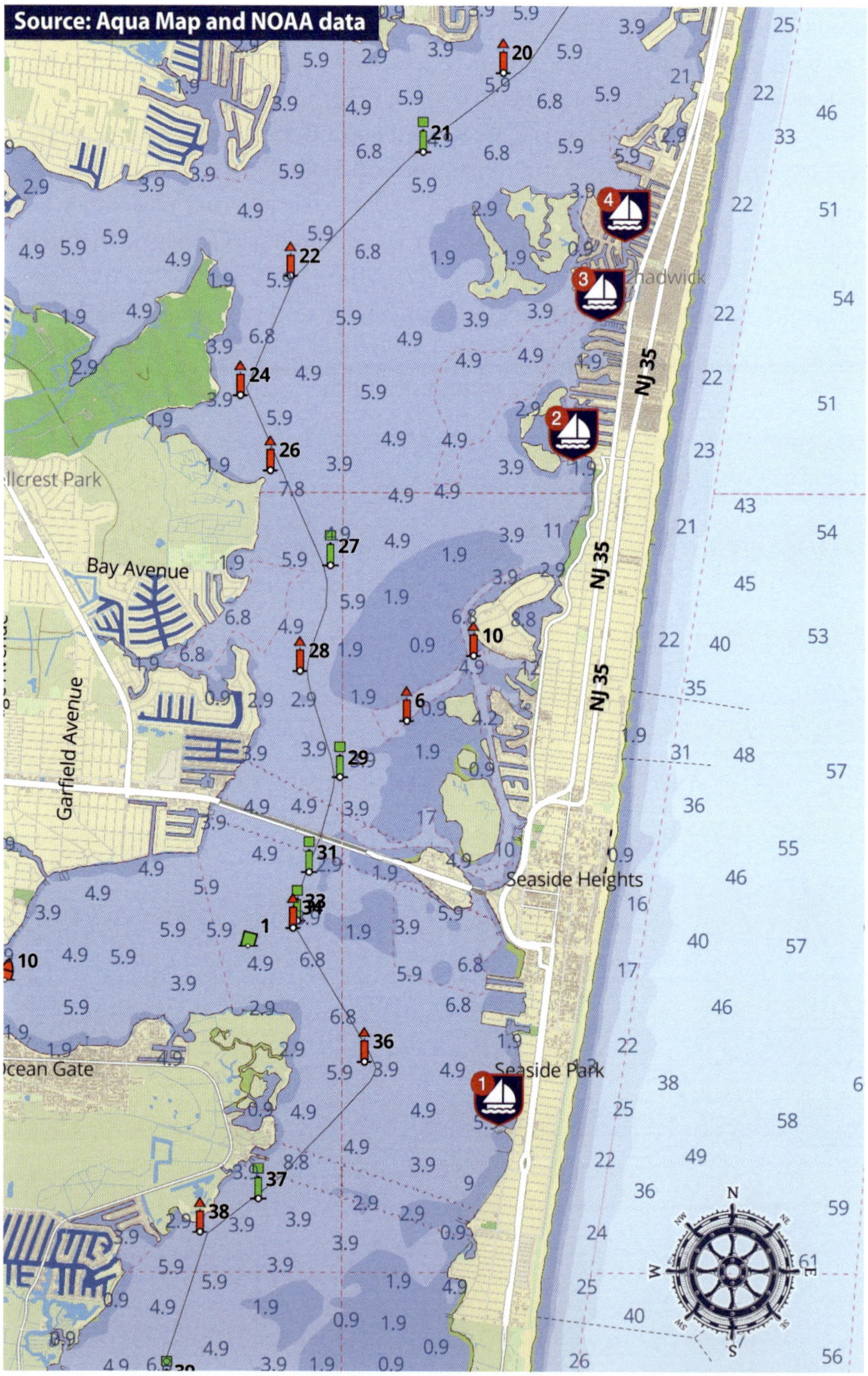

Source: Aqua Map and NOAA data

Island Beach–NJ ICW Mile 15 to Mile 10

The towns of Seaside Heights, Lavallette and Normandy Beach string along the east side of the NJ ICW route and all have marinas that can be reached through marked channels across the flats.

Dockage: Both Seaside Park Yacht Club (south of the bridges at Mile 15.5) and Lavallette Yacht Club (north of the bridges) are private but offer limited courtesy dockage for members of reciprocal yacht clubs.

Ocean Beach Marine Center (Lavallette) has a full-time staff of certified marine technicians as well as a full-time dockmaster and 250 slips to 45 feet. Chadwick Island Marina is a small, full-service marina with 202 slips for boats between 16 and 42 feet (as well as jet ski ports, which are fairly common along this stretch).

Anchorage: At Seaside Park (Mile 15.8), there is an anchorage with excellent holding in sand with 4 to 5 feet MLW. It is exposed to the west and south. A public dock is near the Seaside Park Yacht Club for dinghy landings.

Barnegat Bay, NJ

MANTOLOKING		Largest Vessel	VHF	Total Slips	Approach/Dockside Depth	Floating Docks	Gas/Diesel	Repairs/Haulout	Min/Max Amps	Pump-Out Station
1. Baywood Marina **WiFi** MM 8.0	(732) 477-3322	40		200	4.0 / 4.0		G	RH	30	P
2. David Beaton & Sons, Inc. Boatyard MM 6.0	(732) 477-0259	42	68	65	4.0 / 4.0			RH	30	P
3. Barnegat Bay Marina **WiFi** 6.3	(732) 477-7700	65	16	110	6.0 / 6.5		GD	RH	30 / 50	P
4. Mantoloking Yacht Club–PRIVATE 6.3	(732) 892-6281			52	4.0 / 4.0				30	
5. Traders Cove Marina 6.2	(732) 644-7618			120	6.0 / 6.0	F			15 / 30	P

WiFi Wireless Internet Access
Visit www.waterwayguide.com for current rates, fuel prices, website addresses and other up-to-the-minute information.
(Information in the table is provided by the facilities.)

Scan here for more details:

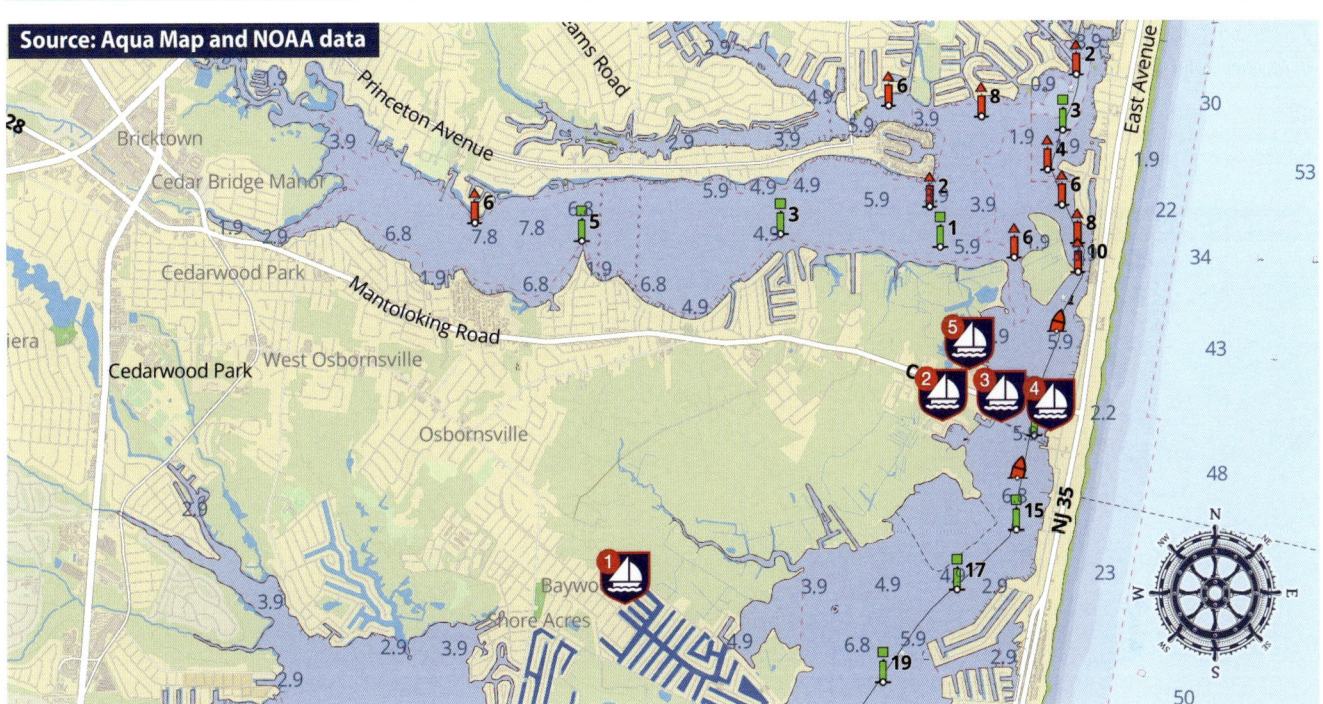

Source: Aqua Map and NOAA data

MANTOLOKING TO POINT PLEASANT CANAL

Mantoloking—NJ ICW Mile 6

NAVIGATION: At Mile 6.3 the NJ ICW is crossed by the **Mantoloking Bridge** (30-foot closed vertical clearance) and leaves Barnegat Bay as it swings east to run close inside of the barrier beach. The bridge opens on signal except Memorial Day through Labor Day when on Saturdays, Sundays and federal holidays from 9:00 a.m. to 6:00 p.m. the draw need only open on the hour, 20 minutes after the hour, and 40 minutes after the hour.

Dockage: Yacht amenities are located on both the mainland and beach on the NJ ICW in the Mantoloking area. Most marinas will accommodate cruising yachts and several offer a full range of services, along with restaurants and shore accommodations.

To the south of Mantoloking and on the western shore of the NJ ICW the 200-slip Baywood Marina is in a protected channel near Havens Point. This is primarily a yacht brokerage with slips to 40 feet. They also have a marina store.

To the south of the Mantoloking Bridge is the venerable David Beaton & Sons, Inc. Boatyard, which mostly caters to smaller, local boats. Next is Barnegat Bay Marina with 110 deep-water slips for boats to 65 feet with full amenities. They also have fully certified mechanics on staff. The private Mantoloking Yacht Club is across the waterway and extends the courtesies and limited privileges of the club to fellow BBYRA clubs.

Barnegat Bay, NJ

METEDECONK RIVER		Largest Vessel	VHF	Total Slips	Approach/ Dockside Depth	Floating Docks	Gas/ Diesel	Repairs/ Haulout	Min/Max Amps	Pump-Out Station
1. Metedeconk River Yacht Club-PRIVATE	(732) 477-9781	36		64	4.0 / 4.0				30	
2. The Marina at Beacon 70 (formerly Forge Landing Marina) **WiFi**	(732) 477-0404	65		200	6.0 / 6.0		G	RH	30	P
3. Brennan Boat Company & Marina **WiFi**	(732) 840-1100	50	16	80	4.0 / 4.0	F		RH	30	P
4. Jersey Shore Marina	(732) 840-9530	50		175	4.0 / 5.0		G	RH	30	P
5. Green Cove Marina **WiFi**	(732) 840-9090	46		210	5.0 / 3.5		GD	RH	30 / 50	P
6. Wehrlen Bros Marina	(732) 899-3505	57		200	5.0 / 4.0			RH	30	P
7. Pier 281 Marina **WiFi**	(732) 714-2061	75		100	/			RH		P
BEAVERDAM CREEK										
8. Comstock Yacht Sales & Marina	(732) 899-2500	65	9	71	6.0 / 5.0		GD	RH	30 / 50	P
9. Arnold's Yacht Basin **WiFi**	(732) 892-3000	45		190	6.0 / 5.0	F		RH	15 / 50	P

WiFi Wireless Internet Access
Visit www.waterwayguide.com for current rates, fuel prices, website addresses and other up-to-the-minute information.
(Information in the table is provided by the facilities.)

Scan here for more details:

Source: Aqua Map and NOAA data

The municipal Traders Cove Marina can accommodate boats up to 60 feet in length. Customers have access to the transient boaters lounge and laundry facilities in the Traders Cove Resource Building.

Anchorage: There are communities on Silver Bay on the west side of Barnegat Bay near Mile 10. This is a prime anchorage area but it is often crowded during the summer. Drop the hook anywhere along the south shore of Silver Bay. If you go far enough off the bank, you can catch the southerly breeze and be free of pesky insects. Charted depths are only 5 to 6 feet MLW in Silver Bay, but it has good holding in mud.

It is also possible to drop the hook in Kettle Creek (Mile 9.5) with good holding in mud but charted depths are only 4 to 5 feet MLW and it is somewhat exposed to the southeast.

Metedeconk River—NJ ICW Mile 5

West along the Metedeconk River, marinas and docks line the shore all the way to the town of Brick. It is deep and well marked and carries 5-foot MLW depths well up the left-hand branch offering a calm, pleasant side trip past pine-lined shores with summer homes nestled beneath the trees. A fall cruise on the Metedeconk River is especially enjoyable.

Dockage: The first facility on the Metedeconk River (south shore) is the private Metedeconk River Yacht Club with courtesy dockage for members of reciprocal yacht clubs.

At the head of the river on the south shore is The Marina at Beacon 70 (formerly Forge Landing Marina) offering over 200 deep water slips and has a self-serve fuel dock that is open 24 hours for your convenience. They also boast an on-site marina with casual fine dining. It is followed by Brennan Boat Company & Marina (with full amenities); community-oriented Jersey Shore Marina, located on 9 acres; and nestled in a protective cove just to the south, the family-friendly Green Cove Marina.

Continuing south on the north shore, Wehrlen Bros Marina has 200 slips, a pool and some services. Call ahead for slip availability. Next is Pier 281 Marina with more than 100 slips that can accommodate vessels to 75 feet including sailboats. This is home to a well-respected sailing school and a pirate boat, as well as a nice boater lounge.

Anchorage: The entire Metedeconk River makes a fine anchorage, although seaweed can be a bother at times. The holding is excellent in mud with depths from 5 feet MLW. A particularly popular spot is in the (unnamed) south fork in 4 to 6 feet MLW. Dinghy to the American Legion dock or to Mermaid's Cove Marina and ask to tie up. One mile west is a large mall with a supermarket, restaurants, specialty shops and a West Marine (732-864-8140).

Point Pleasant Area—NJ ICW Mile 4.5

Clustered around the southern end of the Point Pleasant Canal are some of the boatyards that made New Jersey famous as a boatbuilding center. Many of these yards have consolidated and, while still building custom boats, now offer transient slips and complete marina services.

The lovely seaside area of Bay Head marks the northern entrance to (or exit from) Barnegat Bay. Often called "A Country Village by the Sea," this has been a popular vacation spot since Victorian times and still treasures its culture and heritage. It is a great place to take a break and explore for a few days. (Note that the Bay Head beaches, while not considered private, can be difficult to access.)

NAVIGATION: When transiting the area through Bay Head to the Point Pleasant Canal, be aware that the NJ ICW runs through a complex of marinas and boatyards with rigid speed regulations and the entire area is actively policed. Note that shoaling has been reported in this area so proceed with caution.

On the west side of Barnegat Bay, the long, narrow Wardells Neck separates the Metedeconk River and Beaverdam Creek. The river and the creek are entered from the northwest side of Herring Island. Turn west between green "3" and red "2" to avoid mud flats. Only boats drawing less than 4 feet should attempt to enter from the southwest side of Herring Island as depths are reported as between 2 and 3 feet MLW.

Dockage: This boating area is extremely popular as evidenced by the number of yacht clubs and marinas with a concentration at Bay Head and along Beaverdam Creek. On the north side of Wardells Neck (western shore of bay) beyond the **Beaver Dam Road Bascule Bridge** (14-foot vertical clearance) is Comstock Yacht Sales & Marina, a yacht brokerage with a ship store/parts department that welcomes transients in deep-water slips.

Nearby Arnold's Yacht Basin has on-site boat mechanics, a fiberglass shop, canvas shop and vinyl craft shop as well as slips to 45 feet. Call ahead to these facilities for bridge clearance and schedule.

Anchorage: Bay Head Harbor has at least 4- to 6-foot MLW depths with excellent holding in mud and sand. It is somewhat exposed from the south and to boat wakes along the NJ ICW.

Point Pleasant Canal

The only way out of the bay on the northeast end is to transit the Point Pleasant Canal to the Manasquan Inlet via the Manasquan River. The 2-mile-long canal connects Bay Head with the Manasquan River.

NAVIGATION:

CAUTION: There is a swift current through the Point Pleasant Canal approaching 4 knots on the ebb and flood. If you require the bridges to open, make arrangements with the bridgetender before you enter the canal. The canal is very narrow and there is little room to maneuver if the bridge is not open when you arrive. Do not follow another boat too closely, particularly around the bridges, and allow adequate time for the bridges to open completely before moving through the opening.

Two lift bridges cross the canal: the **NJ 632 (Bridge Ave.) Bridge** with a closed vertical clearance of 30 feet (65 feet when open) and **SR88 (Veterans Memorial) Bridge**, which has a 31-foot closed vertical clearance (66-foot open vertical clearance). Both bridges open on signal. Before entering the canal, it is possible

to make detailed checks with the bridgetender at the SR88 (Veterans Memorial) Bridge regarding the condition of the current. (Contact the tender on VHF Channel 13 and be sure to refer to this specific bridge.)

If you are without adequate power, the trip can be challenging because of the great difference between the 4-foot tidal range at Manasquan Inlet and that of less than 1 foot at the Barnegat Bay end of the canal. Try to plan your transit through the canal to coincide with slack water. Underpowered sailboats (those able to make no more than 4 or 5 knots at full throttle) should limit themselves to an hour on either side of slack water.

Predicted slack water in Point Pleasant Canal is 2 to 3 hours after high or low tides in the Atlantic Ocean, and this time can vary greatly, depending on the direction, strength and duration of the wind. The safest time to make the passage is at slack high water when current is at a minimum. (Slack low water averages 0.2 knot faster.) See up-to-date tide tables at NOAA Tides and Currents (www.tidesandcurrents.noaa.gov).

The entire canal is a "No Wake" zone. Take extra care on the weekends and holidays when canal traffic is heaviest.

The channel between the north end of Point Pleasant Canal and flashing red "6" is extremely narrow with shoaling on both sides. Make sure that the current does not sweep you out of the channel. If you must go through with the current during heavy traffic times, be aware that not all of the vessels going through the canal will be able to give way in the case of problems.

◼ MANASQUAN RIVER TO SHARK RIVER INLET

To Manasquan Inlet– NJ ICW Mile 0

The towns of Point Pleasant and Brielle face each other across the Manasquan River at Mile 0 on the NJ ICW and the resort towns of Point Pleasant Beach and Manasquan face each other at the Manasquan Inlet.

The waters in this area form one of the busiest ports on the NJ ICW with hundreds of berths, restaurants, chandleries, marinas, boat builders, repair yards and boat brokerages. Droves of charter captains are ready to take you deep-sea fishing and reservations are a must, especially on summer weekends. Boat traffic can be extremely congested on summer weekends in both the inlet and the river.

The splendid beach at Point Pleasant is privately owned but you can pay a fee to access it. The 1-mile-long boardwalk at Point Pleasant (with the usual arcades, rides, and bars) terminates at the mouth of Manasquan Inlet. Manasquan Inlet is said to be one of the widest and safest inlets on the New Jersey coast due to well-maintained jetties and depths.

NAVIGATION: After passing through the Point Pleasant Canal, you can turn west into the Manasquan River or east towards the inlet. (There is no inside route north from here.) Severe shoaling lines both sides of the Manasquan River so make certain you stay within the channel.

If headed towards the inlet, the opening under the **NJ 35 Bridge** is only 47 feet wide and the current can be challenging at times. Traffic

can be extremely heavy, particularly on weekends after the Brielle Railroad Bridge has been closed for a while. Choose your time carefully through the railroad bridge. When approaching the NJ 35 Bridge, use enough power to control your boat as the current tries to push you towards the sides of the opening. The wind going against the tide dictates extreme caution.

The **NJ 35 Bridge** (30-foot closed vertical clearance) crosses the Manasquan River at Mile 1.1. The draw will open on signal, except (1) from 8:00 a.m. to 10:00 p.m. between May 15 and September 30 on Saturdays, Sundays and federal holidays, when the draw need only open 15 minutes before the hour and 15 minutes after the hour; and (2) from 4:00 p.m. to 7:00 p.m. on Mondays through Thursdays and from 12:00 p.m. to 7:00 p.m. on Fridays (except federal holidays), when the draw need only open 15 minutes before the hour and 15 minutes after the hour. Year-round from 11:00 p.m. to 8:00 a.m. the draw need only open if at least a 4-hour notice is given.

The **Brielle Railroad Bridge** follows at Mile 0.9 and is kept open except when a train is coming, which is several times each hour. When in the open position, the draw is at a 45-degree angle so favor the north side of the channel.

CAUTION: The opening under the Brielle Railroad Bridge is very narrow (approximately 40 feet) and there is a very strong current that does not follow the direction of the bridge opening. Also, the opening is not in line with the channel leading to the bridge opening. We recommend that before entering, you line up the opening so you can see through it to be sure another boat isn't coming towards you. Proceed carefully; should the railroad bridge close, you do not want to become caught in the current between it and the NJ 35 Bridge.

Channel depths in the Manasquan Inlet vary greatly. If you must enter the inlet under adverse conditions and your boat is fast, synchronize your speed with the speed of the seas and ride through on the back of a wave, keeping well aft of the crest. In a slow boat, throttle way down so that the waves will pass under your boat.

If you are cruising in a moderate-sized sailboat and the wind is against the tide, turning around after committing to either enter or exit the inlet will probably not be an option. Be prepared for a bit of discomfort and very slow

Barnegat Bay, NJ

MANASQUAN INLET		Largest Vessel	VHF	Total Slips	Approach/Dockside Depth	Floating Docks	Gas/Diesel	Repairs/Haulout	Min/Max Amps	Pump-Out Station
1. Captain Bill's Landing	(848) 232-2880	110	15		/ 6.0		GD		50	
2. Hoffman's Marina (WiFi) 0.9	(732) 528-6200	130	16	175	14.0 / 16.0	F	GD	RH	30 / 100	P
3. Brielle Yacht Club Marina (WiFi) 1.0	(732) 528-6250	100	16	125	8.0 / 6.0	F	GD	R	30 / 50	
MANASQUAN RIVER										
4. Clarks Landing Marina (WiFi) MM 2.0	(732) 899-5559	65	5	105	5.0 / 6.0		GD	RH	30 / 50	
5. Safe Harbor Crystal Point 1.0 mi. NW of MM 2.5	(732) 892-2300	90		200	8.0 / 8.0	F	GD		30 / 50	P
6. Safe Harbor Manasquan River	(732) 840-0300			200	/	F			30	P

(WiFi) Wireless Internet Access
Visit www.waterwayguide.com for current rates, fuel prices, website addresses and other up-to-the-minute information.
(Information in the table is provided by the facilities.)

Scan here for more details:

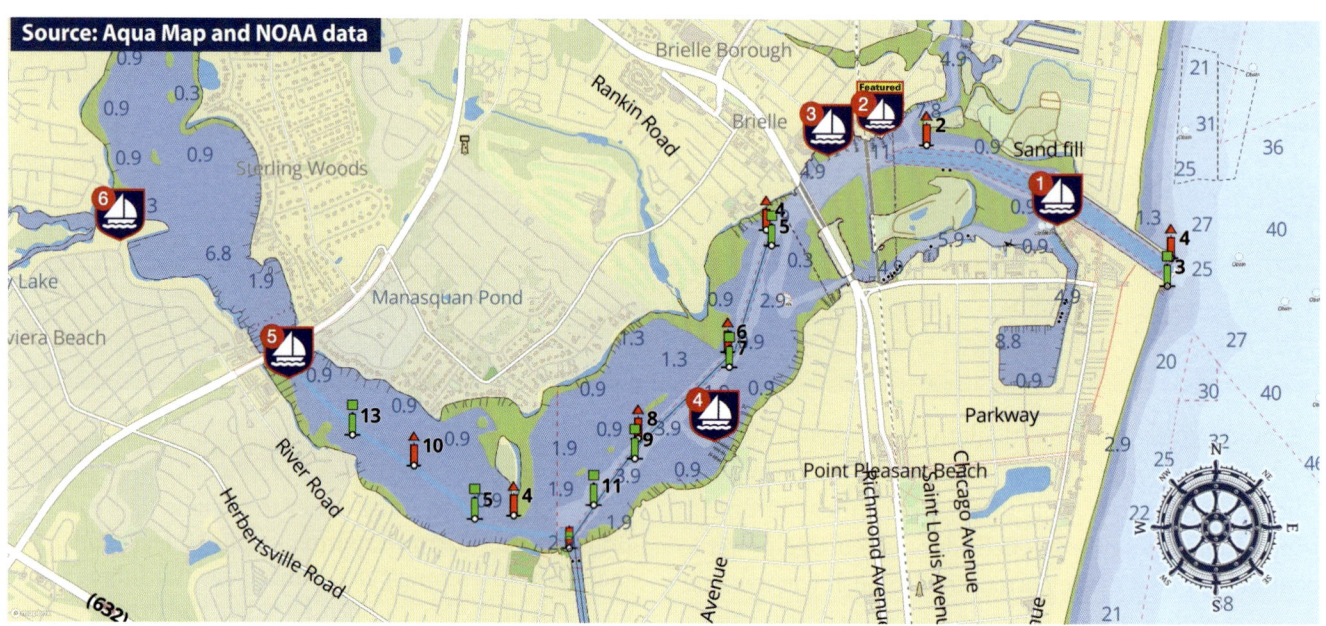

Source: Aqua Map and NOAA data

progress if you attempt to navigate the inlet when the directions of wind and tide are in opposition.

Proceed slowly in the inlet. An incredible amount of commercial, charter and recreational boat traffic goes in and out of Manasquan Inlet. Exercise caution, be sure to control your speed and wake and remember that you are responsible for any damage caused by your wake. The Coast Guard monitors inlet traffic closely and enforces safe boating practices.

Dockage: You will find dockage all along the Manasquan River including at several good restaurants along the river. To access marine facilities on the west end of the river, you must be able to negotiate the NJ 70 Bridge with 25-foot fixed vertical clearance.

The well-regarded Captain Bill's Landing offers transient slips with easy in and out at the inlet. Expect some wakes and there is no power on the dock but it is

super convenient to restaurants and the boardwalk and has great fuel prices.

Hoffman's Marina has transient slips to 130 feet with resort amenities including an infinity pool, private showers, a laundry room and access to several on-site restaurants. It is a short walk to shopping in Brielle from either of these marinas.

The Brielle Yacht Club Marina has 10 transient slips to 100 feet and is home to the popular Pig & Parrot Restaurant. Clarks Landing Marina in Point Pleasant provides seasonal and transient slip rental (to 70 feet) with full amenities. Marine provisions and groceries are just a short car ride from the waterfront in Brielle on the north side of the river.

On the west end of the river just north of the **NJ 70 Bridge** is Safe Harbor Crystal Point in a setting of riverfront mansions and magnificent sunrises and sunsets

Shark River Inlet

and amenities include an automated 24/7 fuel dock. Nearby River Rock Restaurant & Marina Bar has slips to 26 feet for diners.

North of the bridge is Safe Harbor Manasquan River with full amenities (including a pool). Call ahead for slip availability.

Anchorage: Manasquan anchorages are severely limited because space is lacking and the heavy boat traffic creates considerable wake. On the west end of the river there's space to anchor Some boaters anchor in the Manasquan River north of the bridge and across from the marinas. Holding is fair in mud with 4 to 8 feet MLW.

The Glimmer Glass on Crabtown Creek for all-around protection in and good holding in 5-to 7-foot MLW depths. At red daybeacon "2," turn north into Crabtown Creek and follow the well-marked private channel through **The Glimmer Glass (Brielle Rd) Bridge** (9-foot vertical clearance), which opens on signal on the hour and half-hour from 7:00 a.m. to 8:00 p.m. from Memorial to Labor Day. This bridge is a close fit for sailboats even when open, as it does not open straight up. Bear to port just past green day mark into protected basin. Stay close to northern shore and only 20 feet off the boats in slips. Anchor near the moorings in 6 feet

MLW. Deep water extends about 15 feet past the mooring buoys to the south. This is a narrow anchorage in a quiet, residential area.

Shark River Inlet

After exiting the Manasquan Inlet, Shark River Inlet is just 5 miles north (no inside route). Don't rely on the landmarks named on the chart for fixing your position on the trip north or south. Multi-story buildings, which obscure the charted landmarks, are strung along the Jersey shore.

NAVIGATION: You can count on the Shark River Inlet as a storm haven along the stretch of coast between Manasquan and Sandy Hook. It has 12-foot MLW depths and is considered safe for even those not familiar with the area and is a worthwhile cruising stop. You will find ample accommodations, a busy charter fleet and fine beaches.

Shark River Inlet (Ocean Avenue) Bridge (15-foot closed vertical clearance) crosses Shark River Inlet near its opening to the ocean. The bridge opens on request. On an incoming tide, do not enter the channel between the breakwaters until you are sure the bridge is going to open! Maneuvering room is very limited and a strong flood tide can sweep you down into it quickly.

Shark River, NJ

SHARK RIVER AREA		Largest Vessel	VHF	Total Slips	Approach/ Dockside Depth	Floating Docks	Gas/ Diesel	Repairs/ Haulout	Min/Max Amps	Pump-Out Station
1. Belmar Manutti Municipal Marina **WiFi**	(732) 681-2266	100	16	294	7.0 / 7.0	F	GD		30 / 50	P
2. Shark River Municipal Marina **WiFi**	(732) 775-7400	40		155	6.0 / 6.0	F		H	30 / 50	
3. Shark River Yacht Club Inc.	(732) 502-0094	65		160	6.0 / 6.0	F		RH	30 / 50	P

WiFi Wireless Internet Access
Visit www.waterwayguide.com for current rates, fuel prices, website addresses and other up-to-the-minute information.
(Information in the table is provided by the facilities.)

Scan here for more details:

Source: Aqua Map and NOAA data

Local fishing party boats know to wait outside in all conditions until the bridge opens. Even in benign conditions, do not commit to passage until the span rises. Bridgetenders, who are aware of the hazard, are quick to open but heavy auto traffic sometimes causes delays, especially on summer weekends.

Three bridges cross the main (south) channel of the Shark River: Main St. (NJ 71) Bridge (South Channel) (13-foot closed vertical clearance), Shark River Railroad Bridge (8-foot closed vertical clearance) and the NJ 35 Bridge (50-foot fixed vertical clearance). The two bascule bridges operate as one unit and open on signal, except from May 15 through September 30 from 4:00 p.m. to 7:00 p.m., Monday through Friday, and from 9:00 a.m. to 9:00 p.m., Saturdays, Sundays and holidays, when the draw need only open on the hour and half hour if a vessel is waiting to pass.

Dockage: The municipal Belmar Manutti Municipal Marina is less than 0.5 mile from the ocean with concrete floating docks with ample transient space to 100 feet, full security and marine services. They cater to sportfishers. Shark River Municipal Marina on the northwest side of the Shark River is at the Neptune township and has transient slips to 40 feet on floating docks.

On the north side of Shark River Island is the well-maintained Shark River Yacht Club Inc. with slips to 65 feet and ample amenities. Fine dining, café-style restaurants and water taxi service are all available in the marina area.

Anchorage: It is possible to anchor in Shark River in the charted 6-foot area east of the Shark River Municipal Marina. Here you will find at least 6 feet MLW with good holding and protection from all but southerly winds.

Pages 135-138

Pages 124-130

Pages 131-134

Arthur Kill

Perth Amboy

Raritan Bay

Sandy Hook

Sandy Hook Bay

Atlantic Highlands

Highlands

Atlantic Ocean

Navesink River

Shrewsbury River

SANDY HOOK AREA

To Sandy Hook

Sandy Hook opens up to an enclosed, single body of water that comprises three separately charted bays: Sandy Hook Bay to the southeast, Raritan Bay to the west and Lower Bay to the north, which is the largest of the three and referred to as Lower New York Harbor.

NAVIGATION: The Atlantic Ocean is the only navigable route to Sandy Hook, which is 17 miles north of the Shark River Inlet. There is no inside route. Except in heavy weather, you can stay fairly close to shore (keeping far enough off to clear rocks along the beach).

> ⚠️
>
> *CAUTION:* Steer clear of the shallowing water here in any kind of swell as the seas will sharpen and rise in response to the changing water depth. If headed north, do not turn to NW until Sandy Hook Channel.

The preferred passage to follow is the main Sandy Hook Channel, which is well offshore. Start at the Scotland Lighted Whistle Buoy "S" (red and white stripes with red spherical top mark and flashing white 8s light). This well-marked channel is dredged and maintained.

Recent USACE surveys show depths of 40-plus feet the entire way.

Do not attempt to follow the former False Hook Channel, shown on older charts running close to the beach, as severe shoaling can occur. Unpredictable changes in depth can also create confused seas and uncomfortable conditions.

Seas break on the long bar eastward from the point on Sandy Hook. This bar sets up the famed "Sandy Hook rip," in which the turbulent, tide-tumbled waters produce some of the best fishing (striped bass and bluefish) found anywhere on the Atlantic coast.

Inside of Sandy Hook and south beyond the fixed-span **Highlands Bridge** (61-foot vertical clearance over the Shrewsbury River), the Navesink and Shrewsbury Rivers lace the northeastern corner of New Jersey with well-protected cruising waters. These lovely cruising grounds are complete with excellent beaches, deep sea fishing opportunities and convenient dockage near ferry transportation into New York City.

The current runs swiftly here so watch for turbulence under the bridge at full current. The rivers pass high, green banks, marshy islands and attractive residential areas. Yacht clubs, marinas and boatyards, waterfront restaurants with docks, scenic anchorages and old, established communities line the shores. In many places the Atlantic Ocean is only a short walk away across the barrier strip.

Sandy Hook Bay

NOTE: Pump-out service in Sandy Hook Bay is available by calling the Baykeeper Pump-Out Boat at 732-888-9870 or on VHF Channel 9.

Sandy Hook Bay

Sandy Hook, NJ, a 9-mile, 1,665-acre barrier peninsula, is part of the National Gateway Recreation Area that includes ocean and bay beaches, excellent surf fishing, miles of bike and nature trails, a spectacular holly forest, Fort Hancock (a former military base) and Sandy Hook Lighthouse, the oldest working lighthouse in the country, which is now a National Historic Landmark.

The active Sandy Hook Coast Guard complex dominates the narrow peninsula inside the northern tip of the hook. From there the sandy dunes stretch several miles south before rejoining the mainland in Sea Bright, NJ.

If you have access to a car or bike, be sure to stop at the Sandy Hook Visitors Center (732-872-5970) at the former Spermaceti Cove Lifesaving Station near the entrance to Sandy Hook State Park (about 3.5 miles south-southeast of Sandy Hook Point Light). They have maps and brochures for a self-guided tour.

Sandy Hook is a protected wildlife preserve and many areas of the dunes are closed to foot traffic to protect several species of birds. When entering Sandy Hook by car, there is a per-vehicle daily charge from Memorial Day to Labor Day. Note that the parking lots on Sandy Hook fill up early on weekends, at which time the gates are closed.

> NOTE: You can dinghy ashore and explore ruins of World War II bunkers north of the cove or walk the boardwalk into the marshes to view the protected species of birds. You can walk to the beach on the island's eastern shore from here as well. Drums for garbage and recyclables are near the footbridge at the north end of Horseshoe Cove.

NAVIGATION: Sandy Hook Bay is easily approached by well-buoyed thoroughfares–Sandy Hook Channel from the Atlantic Ocean, Chapel Hill Channel from New York Harbor and Raritan Bay East Reach from Raritan Bay–but multiple navigational aids on the intersecting channels and side channels can be confusing, especially in poor light.

If approaching Sandy Hook from the Atlantic Ocean, follow the Sandy Hook Channel around the hook into Sandy Hook Bay. If heading into Sandy Hook Bay, note that inside the tip of the "hook" green can buoys mark the shallows near shore; otherwise, depths of 15 to 20 feet MLW prevail on the route south to Atlantic Highlands. Keep a sharp lookout for the fish weirs (stakes) in this area, particularly when visibility is poor. They are rarely lighted and hard to see, even in daylight.

Also be sure to avoid Naval Weapons Station Earle, the very long trident-shaped pier in Sandy Hook Bay, restricted by white flashing buoys.

> ⚠️
> *CAUTION:* A vigorously enforced security zone exists in the waters surrounding the pier at the Naval Weapons Station Earle about 1.25 nm southwest of Sandy Hook Point Light. Military Police patrol the area, and you will be stopped if you venture within the security area that is clearly marked by white buoys. Hefty fines are levied for the first offense. Any boater who finds it impossible to stay clear should immediately contact the U.S. Coast Guard by VHF radio or some other means.

If continuing north into New York Harbor, deviate from the Sandy Hook Channel into the Swash Channel, which runs parallel to the Ambrose channel but stays south of Romer Shoal, and then join the Chapel Hill Channel at red and green nun buoy "CH." This route allows smaller vessels to avoid traveling in the Ambrose Channel, which usually has a significant amount of large ship traffic. The Swash Channel is simple to navigate by following a course from Sandy Hook Channel (starting at the lighted front and back range markers for the eastbound channel) and then leaving the 54-foot-high flashing white "2" Romer Shoal Horn to starboard.

Anchorage: In settled weather or during an east wind, there is decent anchorage to the north off the charted Coast Guard station behind Sandy Hook with at least 7-foot MLW depths at low tide. This anchorage offers excellent holding but is exposed northwest through south. Don't forget that you must stay at least 500 feet away from all Coast Guard vessels. There are lots of wakes here from all types of vessels.

About 2 nm south inside the Sandy Hook northern tip is the pretty and always-popular anchorage at Horseshoe Cove, where you will find deep water (10 feet MLW) fairly close to shore. This area is more shoal than charts indicate so use caution. Unfortunately, severe winter storms over the past decade have also submerged the once-visible sand spit that protected the cove and you will be subject to passing wakes from ferries; nevertheless, Horseshoe Cove remains a desirable anchorage.

Atlantic Highlands & Highlands

South of Sandy Hook and east of Leonardo, the very hospitable Atlantic Highlands harbor is an excellent storm haven and a great place to stop for a couple of days. Atlantic Highlands offers a great alternative to New York City dockage with the SeaStreak high-speed ferry running several times daily to Manhattan and back from the Atlantic Highlands harbor. (See the full schedule for the 1-hour ride at www.seastreak.com.) You can stay here and still enjoy the sights of New York City, and if you must wait for better weather before continuing north, east, or south, this is a perfect port.

The Twin Lights, situated 200 feet above sea level atop the Navesink Highlands, overlook the Shrewsbury River, Sandy Hook, Raritan Bay, the New York skyline and the Atlantic Ocean. The Two Lights, a pair of beacons built in 1862 and dedicated by President Lincoln, are the latest in a long line of lighthouses built on this promontory, which is one of the highest points of land on the Atlantic coast. The first light on this spot was erected by New York merchants in 1765 and a light has shone here continuously ever since.

Today a state-maintained occulting white light shines from the north tower during the boating season. The Twin Lights now house a state-run nautical museum displaying marine artifacts and the original building of the old Life Saving Service (732-872-1814).

Be aware that during severe storms from the north, incoming waves build to considerable heights over the long fetch across the bay from the NY side. Some waves even make their way over the town's substantial breakwater.

NAVIGATION: The protected harbor of Atlantic Highlands is situated 3 miles south of green can buoy "1," which marks the western end of Sandy Hook Point. The 33-foot-high flashing white Atlantic Highlands Breakwater Light at the eastern end marks the 0.75-mile-long breakwater across Atlantic Highlands harbor. Both the light and the eastern end of the breakwater are sometimes difficult to spot from a distance so set a waypoint or compass course for an efficient passage across Sandy Hook Bay. Commercial vessels also regularly enter the harbor at the western end of the breakwater, but this is not recommended without local knowledge.

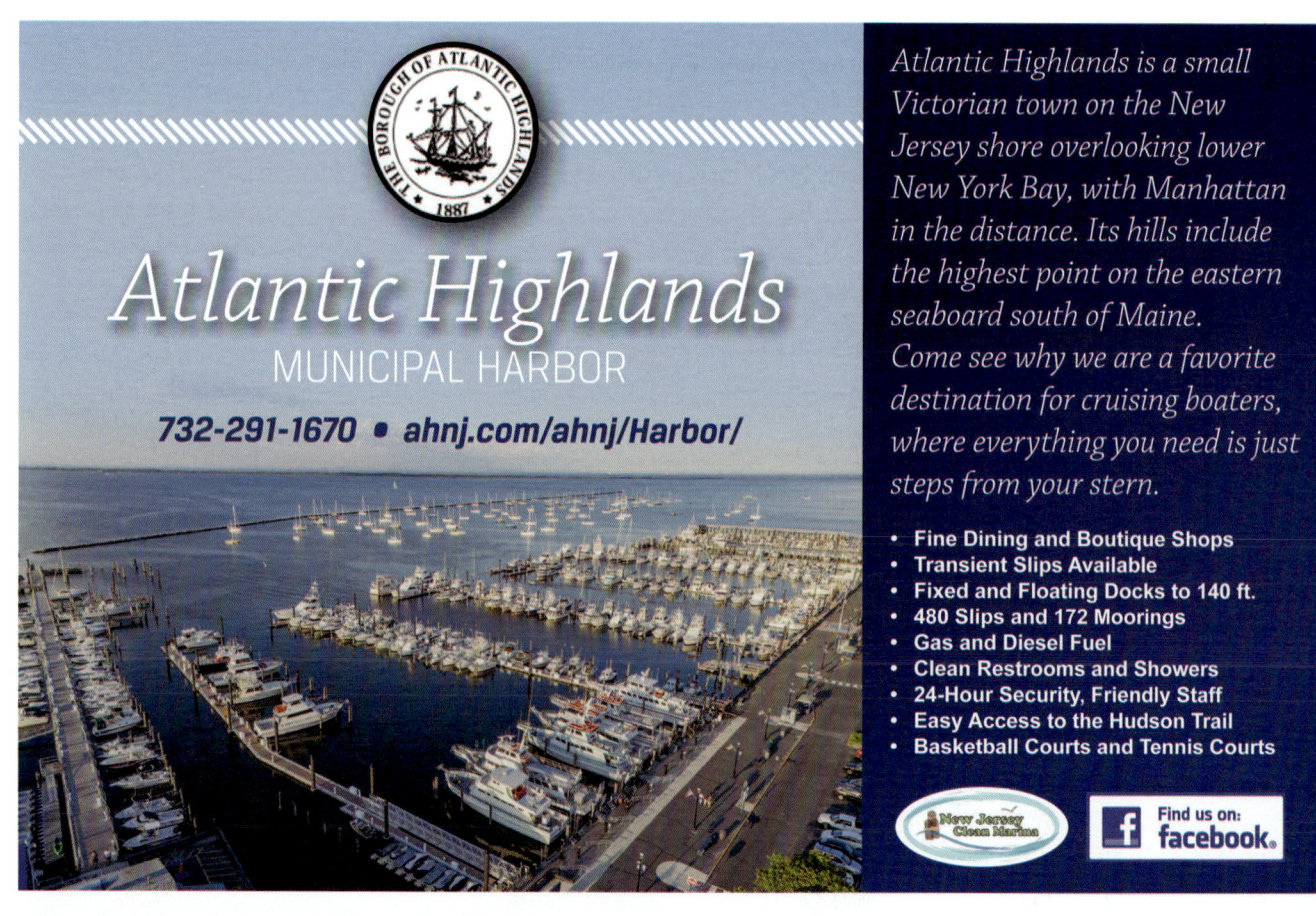

Sandy Hook Bay, NJ

LEONARDO		Largest Vessel	VHF	Total Slips	Approach/ Dockside Depth	Floating Docks	Gas/ Diesel	Repairs/ Haulout	Min/Max Amps	Pump-Out Station
1. Leonardo State Marina	(732) 291-1333	50	16	176	3.0 / 6.0	F			30	P
ATLANTIC HIGHLANDS										
2. Atlantic Highlands Yacht Club-PRIVATE	(732) 291-1118	130	9		10.0 / 10.0	F	GD		30 / 50	P
3. Atlantic Highlands Municipal Harbor **WiFi**	(732) 291-1670	140	9	480	10.0 / 6.0	F	GD	H	30 / 50	P
HIGHLANDS										
4. Sandy Hook Bay Marina	(732) 872-1511	60	7	130	8.0 / 6.0	F			30 / 100	
5. Captains Cove Marina	(732) 290-1000	38	13	92	15.0 / 6.0	F			30	
6. Bakers Marina on the Bay **WiFi**	(732) 872-9300	50		150	12.0 / 10.0	F		RH	30	
7. Twin Lights Marina	(732) 872-7200	45		18	/	F	GD	R	30 / 50	P
8. Bahrs Landing Marina **WiFi**	(732) 291-9554	130	9	30	18.0 / 12.0	F	GD		30	

WiFi Wireless Internet Access
Visit www.waterwayguide.com for current rates, fuel prices, website addresses and other up-to-the-minute information.
(Information in the table is provided by the facilities.)

Scan here for more details:

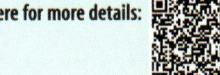

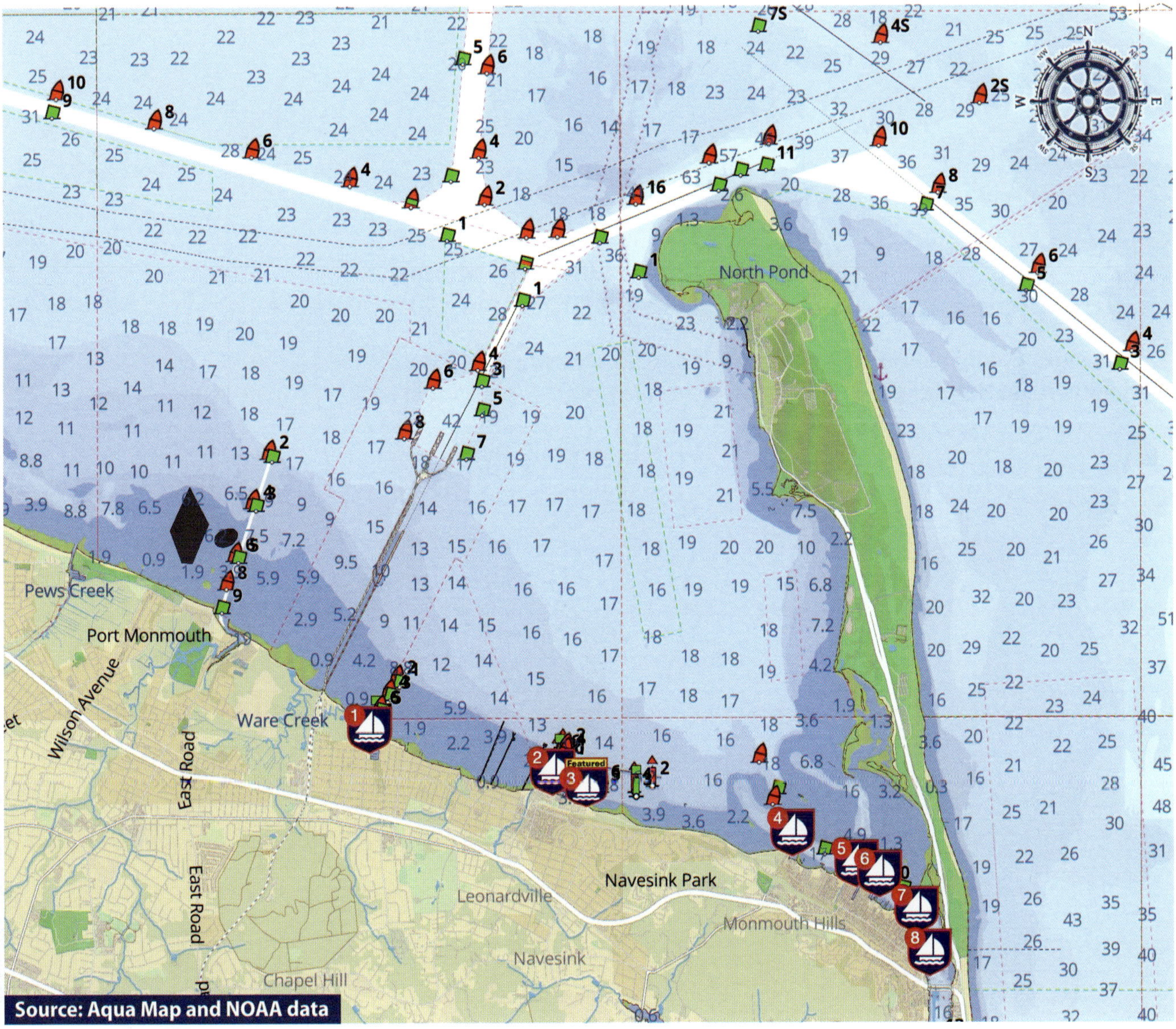

Source: Aqua Map and NOAA data

GOIN' ASHORE

ATLANTIC HIGHLANDS & HIGHLANDS, NJ

ATTRACTIONS

1. Mount Michill Scenic Overlook
Highest point on the Atlantic seaboard offering views of Sandy Hook, Raritan Bay, New York Harbor, New York City and Long Island. Includes 9/11 memorial with timeline of events. Located at 460 Ocean Blvd. in Atlantic Highlands.

2. Twin Lights State Historic Site
Self-guided and guided tours are available of the former lighthouse featuring two beacons with tower climbs, exhibits and panoramic ocean and harbor views. Operated by the Twin Lights Historical Society at 2 Lighthouse Rd. (732-872-1814).

SERVICES

3. Atlantic Highlands Animal Hospital
77 Memorial Pkwy. (732-291-4400)

4. Monmouth County Library - Atlantic Highlands Branch
100 First Ave. (732-291-1956).

5. Highlands Post Office
170 Bay Ave. (732-872-0622)

6. SeaStreak Ferry
326 Shore Dr. (800-262-8743)

7. Shoreside Veterinary Care
182 Bay Ave. #1624 (732-204-2318)

MARINAS

8. Atlantic Highlands Municipal Harbor
2 Simon Lake Dr. (732-291-1670)

9. Atlantic Highlands Yacht Club
6 Simon Lake Dr. (732-291-1118)

10. Bahrs Landing Marina
2 Bay Ave. (732-872-1245)

11. Bakers Marina on the Bay
1 Marina Bay Ct. (732-872-9300)

12. Captain's Cove Marina
2 Washington Ave. (732-872-1479)

13. Gateway Marina
34 Bay Ave. (732-291-4440)

14. Sandy Hook Bay Marina
1 Willow St. (732-872-1511)

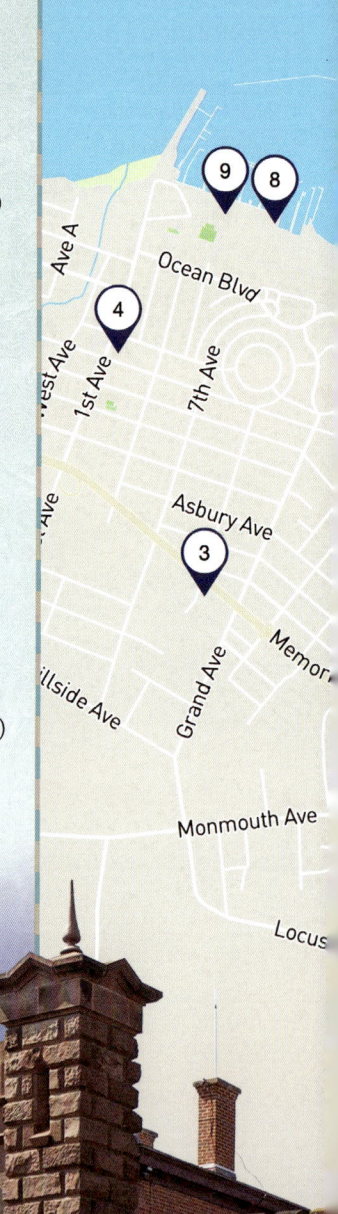

The side-by-side villages of Atlantic Highlands and Highlands are two distinct boroughs in Monmouth County. Both are equally attractive to cruisers and offer many amenities from services to attractions and top-notch marine facilities. The charming and unpretentious village of Atlantic Highlands is a great stop for cruisers transiting the coast and looking for a safe harbor to spend a night, a few days or even longer. The shoreside town has everything one might want or need in the way of dockage, anchorage, fuel, provisions, transportation and restaurants within a short walk from the harbor. Be sure to visit the Strauss Mansion built in 1893 by a wealthy New York merchant. The 21-room, Victorian-era, Queen Anne-style "cottage" offers stunning views from the third floor Tower Room. Open for free self-guided tours on Sunday afternoons (seasonal) at 27 Prospect Cir. (732-291-1861).

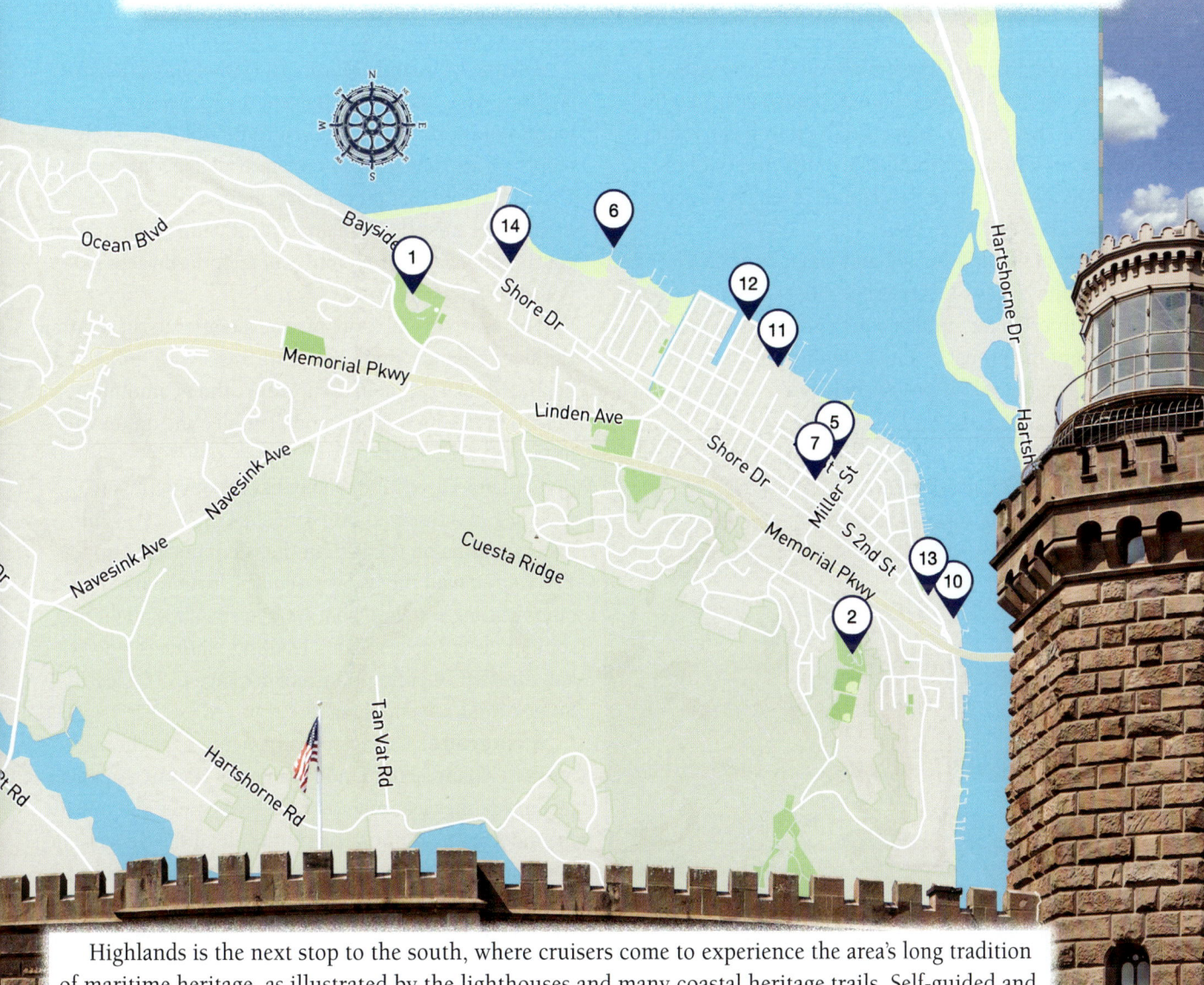

Highlands is the next stop to the south, where cruisers come to experience the area's long tradition of maritime heritage, as illustrated by the lighthouses and many coastal heritage trails. Self-guided and guided tours are available of the Twin Lights, a former lighthouse featuring two beacons with tower climbs, exhibits and panoramic ocean and harbor views 2 Lighthouse Rd. (732-872-1814).

Plan to spend several days exploring these waterfront retreats with sweeping views of the Atlantic Ocean and New York City skyline. Better yet, take the SeaStreak Ferry directly to New York City. Runs daily from Atlantic Highlands and Highlands waterfronts (800-262-8743).

Between Atlantic Highlands and Sandy Hook at the town of Highlands, pick up flashing red buoy "2" marking the shared entrance of the Navesink and Shrewsbury Rivers (also known as the Twin Rivers), which is charted as the Shrewsbury River. Because the low intensity light can be lost among shore lights at night, a daylight approach is strongly recommended. Obtain the latest information on depths before heading in since navigation on ebb tides can be tricky.

Many marinas line this 1-mile-plus stretch to the mouth of the Navesink River, which bears off westward to the town of Red Bank, NJ. Whether you turn into the Navesink River or stay straight on the Shrewsbury River, be careful of three (charted) orange-striped white can buoys that mark a submerged rock wall extending northeasterly from the south side of the mouth of the Navesink River. Stick to the channel, even if you see a local boat head over the line.

Note that the flashing red-and-green buoy "NS" marking the Navesink/Shrewsbury River junction appears to be all red until you are close by. This makes sorting out the proper channels confusing. Once the mid-channel marker is positively identified, the approach becomes straightforward. To continue to the Twin Rivers, proceed under the fixed Highlands Bridge (65-foot vertical clearance).

Dockage/Moorings: Leonardo has an almost landlocked harbor that—while extremely protected—can get hot in summer. A 5-foot-deep MLW channel leads to a basin with 7-foot MLW depths. The municipal Leonardo State Marina has some slips reserved for transients (to 50 feet). Maneuvering room is very tight here and no anchoring space is available. The marina reports 3-foot MLW approach depths so a call ahead concerning depths and other conditions would be warranted.

Atlantic Highlands Municipal Harbor has extensive facilities, diesel and gas, transient docks, services, tennis courts and a recreation area for children. Daily moorings and launch services are available May through October. (Note that power boats are not permitted on the moorings.) Atlantic Highlands Yacht Club (with limited courtesy dockage for members of reciprocal yacht clubs) is also located here.

There are several more marine facilities to the south in Highlands. Sandy Hook Bay Marina is a wave-protected floating dock marina in an upscale condo community with full amenities including a pool, laundry and an upscale restaurant next door.

Captains Cove Marina may have room with you with just two reserved transient slips to 38 feet, while Bakers Marina on the Bay has transient dockage up to 110 feet with all the usual amenities. Twin Lights Marina offers marine services, boat storage and slips, including some transient space. Bahrs Landing Marina is a dock and dine with floating transient dockage to 130 feet. Reservations are encouraged.

Anchorage: There is usually plenty of anchorage room in Atlantic Highlands Municipal Harbor. Anchor just inside the eastern end of the breakwater and outside the mooring field or on the south side of the eastern end of the mooring field along the shore. Depths are 8 to 10 feet MLW but shoals to 4 to 5 feet MLW closer to shore. Holding is good in mud and the breakwater protects the harbor from all except east-northeast to east winds.

It is quite a distance to get to shoreside facilities but there are ample dinghy landings. A dock is located immediately to the east of the harbormaster's office and floats are at the head of each aisle past the fuel dock.

Navesink River, NJ

NAVESINK RIVER AREA		Largest Vessel	VHF	Total Slips	Approach/ Dockside Depth	Floating Docks	Gas/ Diesel	Repairs/ Haulout	Min/Max Amps	Pump-Out Station
1. Oceanic Marina	(732) 842-1194	50		85	6.0 / 5.0	F		RH	30	P
2. Shrewsbury River Yacht Club-PRIVATE	(732) 747-9873	50	9	60	8.0 / 6.0	F			30	
3. Fair Haven Yacht Works (WiFi)	(732) 747-3010	55	9	80	6.0 / 6.0	F		RH	30 / 50	P
4. Irwin Marine Center (WiFi)	(732) 741-0003	70		145	8.0 / 6.0	F		RH	30 / 50	P
5. Molly Pitcher Inn/Marina (WiFi)	(732) 747-2500	65	9	76	6.0 / 6.0	F			30 / 50	P
6. The Oyster Point Hotel & Marina (WiFi)	(732) 747-2500	60	9	34	5.0 / 4.0	F			30	P

(WiFi) Wireless Internet Access
Visit www.waterwayguide.com for current rates, fuel prices, website addresses and other up-to-the-minute information.
(Information in the table is provided by the facilities.)

Scan here for more details:

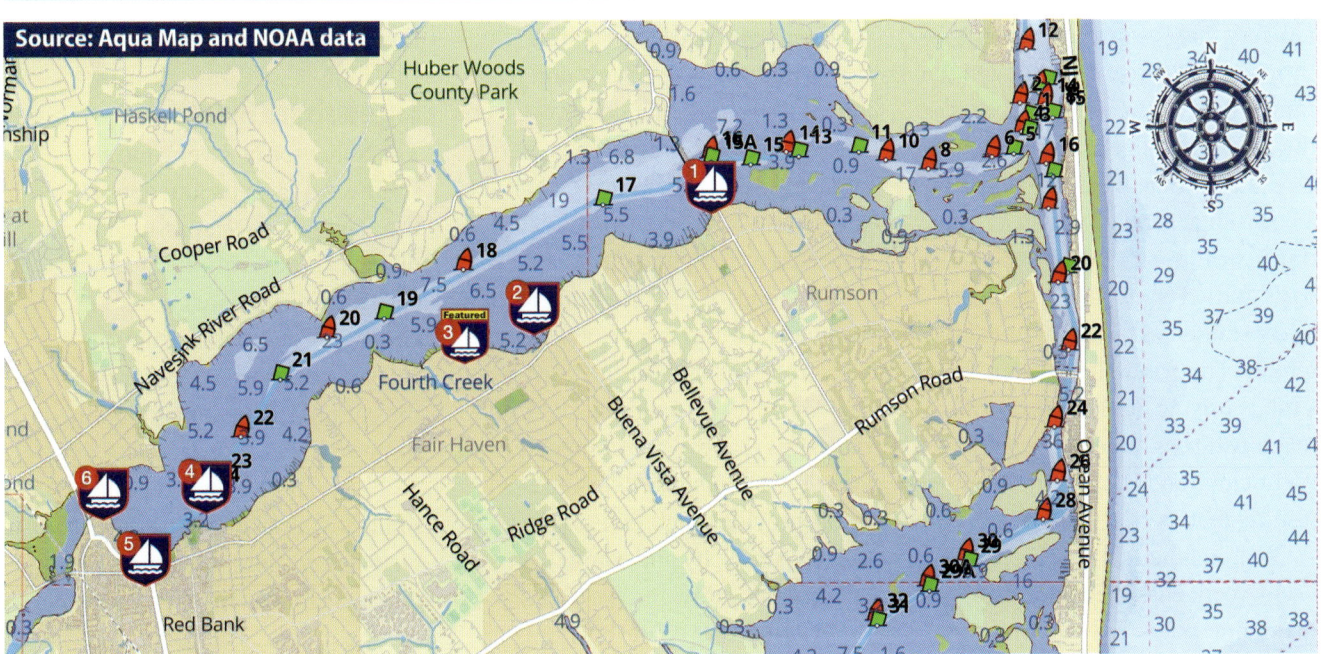

Source: Aqua Map and NOAA data

SIDE TRIP: THE TWIN RIVERS

Navesink River

The historic harborside town of Red Bank, NJ, is at the head of navigation on the Navesink River. It is named for the color of its riverbanks. In the 1800s Red Bank was a thriving shipping center and popular Victorian resort. Even though it is still a commercial center, it retains its rural beauty and Victorian charm.

Red Bank offers many restaurants, full-service marinas, shopping and a main-line train station all within walking distance of any dockage or anchorage. Over the past decade, Red Bank has grown in popularity with gourmet diners and those seeking a lively environment.

NAVIGATION: Transiting the Navesink River can be tricky and local knowledge can be helpful. Pay close attention to depths. There are rocky ledges to the north and shoals on both sides of the narrow channel. The area between the junction of the Twin Rivers and the Oceanic Bridge is very tricky. USACE surveys show shallow areas south of red nun "2" at the opening to the Navesink River. To avoid them, first pass outside red and green junction buoy "NS" then turn into the river and pass close to green can "1." Continue to follow the curving channel past red nun buoys "4" and "6," particularly watching for shoaling in the vicinity of red nun buoy "6."

About 1 mile upriver from the mouth of the Navesink River, Barley Point Reach passes between sandbars that are bare at low tide. Controlling depth is only 2.5 feet MLW so be sure to stay in mid-channel well past the **Oceanic Bridge** (22-foot closed vertical clearance). The bridge opens on signal at all times except from the Friday before Memorial Day through Labor Day, on Friday, Saturday, Sunday and holidays, between 9:00 a.m. and 7:00 p.m., when the draw need only open on the hour. The draw need not open at any time for a sailboat unless it is operating under auxiliary power or is being towed by a powered vessel.

Dockage/Moorings: There are several marine facilities here but not very many reserved transient slips so be sure to call ahead. On the south shore of the river just below the Oceanic Bridge at Locust Pt. is Oceanic Marina, which is primarily a boat rental service with just two transient slips (to 50 feet), plus parts and services. The marina also offers skiff, kayak and pontoon boat rentals. The Shrewsbury River Yacht Club is private but has reciprocal relationships with most accredited yacht clubs and is happy to host their visiting members.

Well-maintained Fair Haven Yacht Works has meticulously maintained slips and moorings that can accommodate power boats and sailboats up to 65 feet. They also offer full mechanical, electronic, fiberglass and woodwork repairs. It is a short walk from here to a hardware store, coffee shop and other amenities.

Closer to Red Bank is the family-owned Irwin Marine. They offer summer dockage, summer and winter land storage and winter storage inside. This is a great location close to town with a helpful staff.

The well-respected Molly Pitcher Inn/Marina has ample transient space on their state-of-the-art floating docks for vessels to 65 feet and resort amenities including a swimming pool and pool bar. The Inn, rich in history and elegance, is a charming boutique waterfront hotel and a great place to house crew and guests.

The modern Oyster Point Hotel/Marina is a full-service hotel facility with transient slips on floating docks. They have 34 overnight or dock and dine slips that can accommodate vessels up to 60 feet. Buses and trains provide quick transportation to New York City and a large hospital is nearby.

Anchorage: A fine anchorage is 1 mile upriver at Upper Rocky Point. Just past the point, turn to starboard and head back east up the old channel of the Navesink River. Make the turn well to the west of red nun buoy "10" to clear the shoal and then favor the north shore. You can anchor in 4- to 10-foot MLW depths under a high bluff. Be sure to give yourself swing room for tide changes. A small island protects you from wakes without stopping the breeze. If you plan to swim, trail a line overboard as the current is strong at maximum flood and ebb.

Shrewsbury River

The Shrewsbury River continues southward from its junction with the Navesink River, passing low and marshy shores with the channel cutting through shoal water on either side. Ashore on Rumson Neck (between the two rivers), the countryside still maintains a somewhat rural appearance.

As in days past when Long Branch was the queen resort of the New Jersey shore, swimming in the area remains the great summer attraction here. The commuter railroad to Bay Head is still called the New York and Long Branch,

Sea Bright Bridge

Shrewsbury River

Shrewsbury River, NJ

SEA BRIGHT		Largest Vessel	VHF	Total Slips	Approach/ Dockside Depth	Floating Docks	Gas/ Diesel	Repairs/ Haulout	Min/Max Amps	Pump-Out Station
1. Carriage House Marina WiFi	(732) 741-8113	50		37	10.0 / 10.0			RH	30	P
2. Cove Sail Marina	(732) 842-5319	50		46	10.0 / 13.0			RH	30	P
3. Surfside Marina	(732) 842-0844	60		52	6.0 / 4.0	F		RH	30	
4. Navesink Marina WiFi	(732) 842-3700	80	16	115	15.0 / 8.0	F		RH	30 / 50	P
MONMOUTH BEACH										
5. Atlantis Yacht Club-PRIVATE WiFi	(732) 222-9693	70	69	55	6.0 / 6.0				30 / 50	P
6. Channel Club Marina WiFi	(732) 222-7717	100	9	144	8.0 / 6.0	F	GD	RH	30 / 50	P
LONG BRANCH REACH										
7. Patten Point Yacht Club-PRIVATE WiFi	(201) 314-5171	50		63	5.0 / 3.5	F			15 / 50	P
8. Kelly's Landing Marina	(732) 544-1243	55		86	4.0 / 4.0	F			30	P
9. Pleasure Bay Yacht Basin	(732) 222-8563	50		70	5.0 / 4.0			RH	30	
10. Oceanport Landing	(732) 229-4466	60		85	6.0 / 5.0	F		RH	30 / 50	P

WiFi Wireless Internet Access
Visit www.waterwayguide.com for current rates, fuel prices, website addresses and other up-to-the-minute information.
(Information in the table is provided by the facilities.)

Scan here for more details:

and the once-fashionable Jockey Club with its gambling casino and race track is now lush Monmouth Park where thoroughbreds race (June to August) within 1 mile of the Oceanport Landing.

NAVIGATION: Sea Bright Bridge (20-foot closed vertical clearance) at Mile 4 opens on signal at all times, except from the Friday before Memorial Day through Labor Day on Friday, Saturday, Sunday and holidays, between 9:00 a.m. and 7:00 p.m., when the draw need only open on the hour. Note: The draw need not open at any time for a sailboat unless it is operating under auxiliary power or is being towed by a powered vessel.

Strong currents and congestion on the approach channel to the bridge make this an area for caution and requires a firm grip on the helm. The bridge is under reconstruction with an undetermined completion date. Use caution transiting this area.

Beyond Sea Bright, the main channel turns to the west between Gunning and Sedge Islands. The route continues west along Long Branch Reach and the narrow paths crook through shoals. After rounding Raccoon Island, the channel leads to Pleasure Bay where you can find marinas and other amenities.

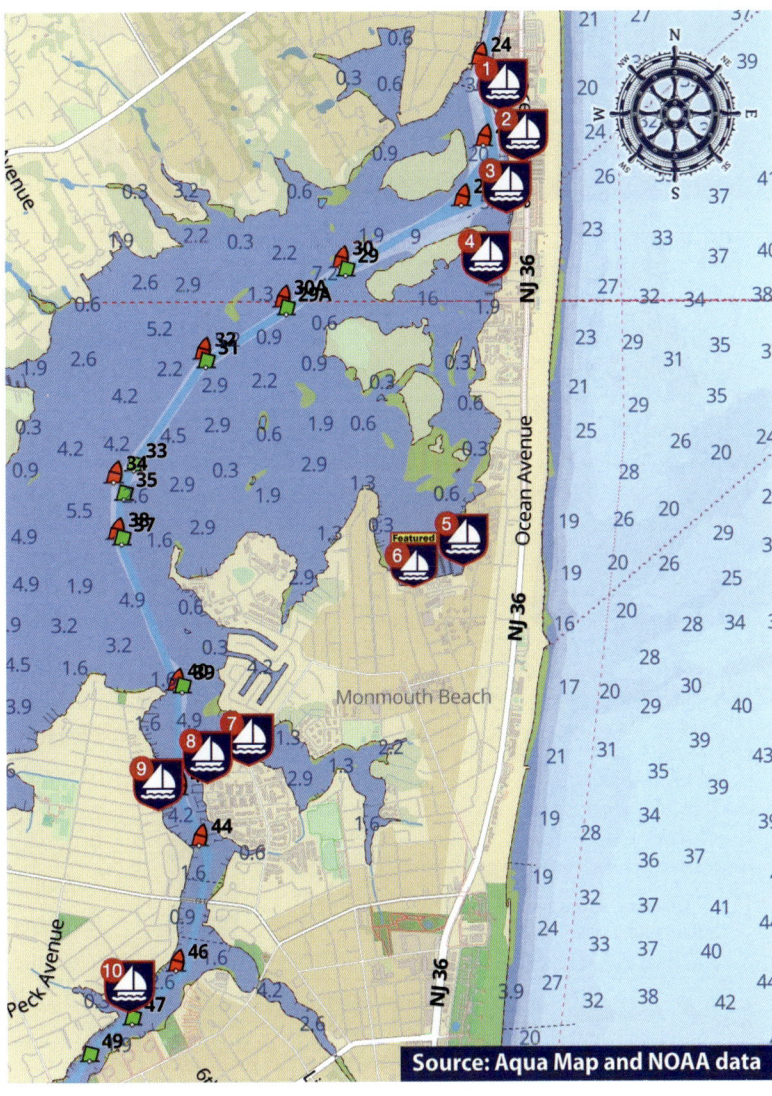

Source: Aqua Map and NOAA data

A historic side passage created as a turnaround channel for big steam-powered boats once lead southward from Sea Bright to Galilee, then swung northwest to rejoin the main channel west of Sedge Island. Unlit buoys may still exist today marking this route, but be warned that it could be too shallow to navigate safely.

The rest of the Shrewsbury River is shallow but there are several creeks to explore. The fixed **Gooseneck (Parkers Creek) Bridge** has a 24-foot vertical clearance, which will mark the end of the journey for many vessels.

Dockage: North on the Shrewsbury River in the Sea Bright area just past the Sea Bright Bridge are several facilities with transient dockage. Carriage House Marina offers easy in and out and is very accommodating to cruisers. This is a family-owned and -operated facility offering slips and a wide range of services.

Cove Sail Marina has slips to 50 feet, while Surfside Marina has limited transient space to 60 feet. The full-service Navesink Marina welcome transients, offers repairs and has an on-site tiki bar and restaurant. Call ahead.

In the area of Galilee, the residential shore is sealed from the Atlantic Ocean by a massive sea wall. Numerous marinas and boatyards can be found here including the private Atlantis Yacht Club (which recognizes reciprocity) and the 144-slip Channel Club Marina, which can accommodate vessels to 100 feet and has an on-site heated pool and numerous other amenities. This 4-acre property is within walking distance of the beach.

The private Patten Point Yacht Club on Manahassett Creek at North Long Point may have space on their floating docks for members of reciprocal yacht clubs. The facility is located before a low fixed bridge with a 6-foot fixed vertical clearance.

On Branchport Creek are the full-service Kelly's Landing Marina (east shore) and Pleasure Bay Yacht Basin (west shore). Both have slips to 50 feet and offer repairs. Pleasure Bay offers a great family destination with all types of water recreation including kayaking, paddleboarding, water skiing, tubing, crabbing and fishing right from their docks.

Boats that can clear the **Hwy. 33 (Pleasure Bay) Bridge** (25-foot fixed vertical clearance) can find dockage (to 60 feet) in deep-water slips and repairs at family-friendly Oceanport Landing.

RARITAN BAY

After rounding Sandy Hook, NJ, you can access Arthur Kill and Kill Van Kull (an alternate route around Staten Island to New York Harbor) from Raritan Bay. A number of harbors that sit along the south shore of Raritan Bay provide protection for cruising mariners. To the north through The Narrows lies New York Harbor, where a skipper can head north up the Hudson River or east through the East River to Long Island Sound.

Keansburg & Keyport Harbor

NAVIGATION: West of Point Comfort at Keansburg, the marina is on Waackaack Creek, which is protected by tidal gates. There are no channel markers on entry and there is shoaling and a 32-foot overhead cable crossing the entrance.

You can also continue west to Keyport Harbor, which is easily entered through a well-marked, deep water channel into Matawan Creek. To access the marinas you must navigate the **West Front St. Bridge** with 12-foot fixed vertical clearance, and there is shoaling on both sides of the channel on entry so be sure to stay in the channel.

Dockage/Moorings: The 125-slip Lentze Marina Inc. at West Keansburg has transient dockage to 45 feet and has a complete marine service shop. At Keyport to the southwest, Keyport Marine Basin has slips to 32 feet. While there, take a peek to see what's going on at Hans Pedersen & Sons Marina, which has been located in Keyport since 1934. They offer boat repairs and restoration with a specialty in wooden boats.

Cheesequake (Morgan) Creek

NAVIGATION: Farther west on Raritan Bay is Cheesequake Creek (also known as Morgan Creek). It is entered through jetties, although the east jetty might be submerged at high water. Flashing green "1" and flashing red "2" mark the entrance. There are no channel markers inside the creek.

The **NJ 35 (Cheesequake Creek) Bridge** (25-foot closed vertical clearance) and the adjacent **NJ Transit Rail Operations Bridge** (3-foot closed vertical clearance) have restricted hours: (1) From April 1 through November 30 from 7:00 a.m. to 8:00 p.m., the draw need only open on the hour. From 8:00 p.m. to 11:00 p.m. the draw will open on signal. From 11:00 p.m. to 7:00 a.m. the draw will only open after at least a two-hour advance notice is given by calling the number posted at the bridge. (2) From December 1 through March 31, the draw opens on signal after at least a two-hour advance notice is given by calling the number posted at the bridge.

When leaving Cheesequake (Morgan) Creek, make sure to be inside the NJ Transit Rail Operations Bridge before it closes or you may stand the chance of missing the hourly opening of the NJ 35 (Cheesequake Creek) Bridge. Both bridges monitor VHF Channel 13.

Dockage: Raritan Marina is located in Stump Creek on the port side immediately after you enter Cheesequake Creek. The well-respected facility provides gated security, is family (and pet) friendly and has transient slips to 75 feet on floating docks and offers repairs. They are known for quick turnaround on all services, even emergency situations.

When traveling up Cheesequake Creek, favor the west side to avoid mud flats and transit on a rising tide. There are several full-service marinas in the creek including the family-owned Lockwood Boat Works, which services powerboats and sailboats and can accommodate vessels up to 50 feet on floating docks. Their ship store provides an exceptionally well-stocked line of marine hardware, engine parts, painting and repair supplies as well as a host of other items for all types of boats.

In addition to summer slips and winter storage, Morgan Marina offers a complete line of services and a wide array of amenities for boaters plus slips to 45 feet.

Perth Amboy

The historic town of Perth Amboy is located at the intersection of the Raritan River, Arthur Kill and Raritan Bay. Recreational boaters rarely transit the Raritan River north from Perth Amboy as facilities are limited.

NAVIGATION: Pay attention to all channel markers in this area to avoid shipping traffic, which must remain in the channels. There is plenty of water for pleasure craft outside of the channels, except off of Ward Point at the tip of Staten Island where it is not advisable to cut inside the red aids to navigation.

Should you choose to explore upriver, **NJ Transit Railroad Bridge** (8-foot closed vertical clearance) between Perth Amboy and South Amboy carries heavy commuter traffic. It opens on signal, except from

Raritan Bay, NJ

		Largest Vessel	VHF	Total Slips	Approach/ Dockside Depth	Floating Docks	Gas/ Diesel	Repairs/ Haulout	Min/Max Amps	Pump-Out Station
KEANSBURG										
1. Lentze Marina Inc.	(732) 787-2139	45	16	125	7.0 / 7.0	F		RH	30 / 50	P
KEYPORT HARBOR										
2. Keyport Marine Basin WiFi	(732) 264-9421	32		275	6.0 / 5.0	F	G	RH	30	P
CHEESEQUAKE CREEK										
3. Raritan Marina WiFi	(732) 566-5961	75	69	210	6.5 / 6.5	F	GD	RH	30 / 100	P
4. Lockwood Boat Works	(732) 721-1605	50	72	185	5.0 / 5.0	F	GD	RH	30 / 50	P
5. Morgan Marina WiFi	(732) 727-2289	45		280	15.0 / 10.0	F	GD	RH	30 / 50	P
PERTH AMBOY										
6. Raritan Yacht Club-PRIVATE WiFi	(732) 826-2277	55	9		/					P
7. Perth Amboy Harborside Marina	(732) 442-1596	40		137	/	F			30	P

WiFi Wireless Internet Access
Visit www.waterwayguide.com for current rates, fuel prices, website addresses and other up-to-the-minute information.
(Information in the table is provided by the facilities.)

Scan here for more details:

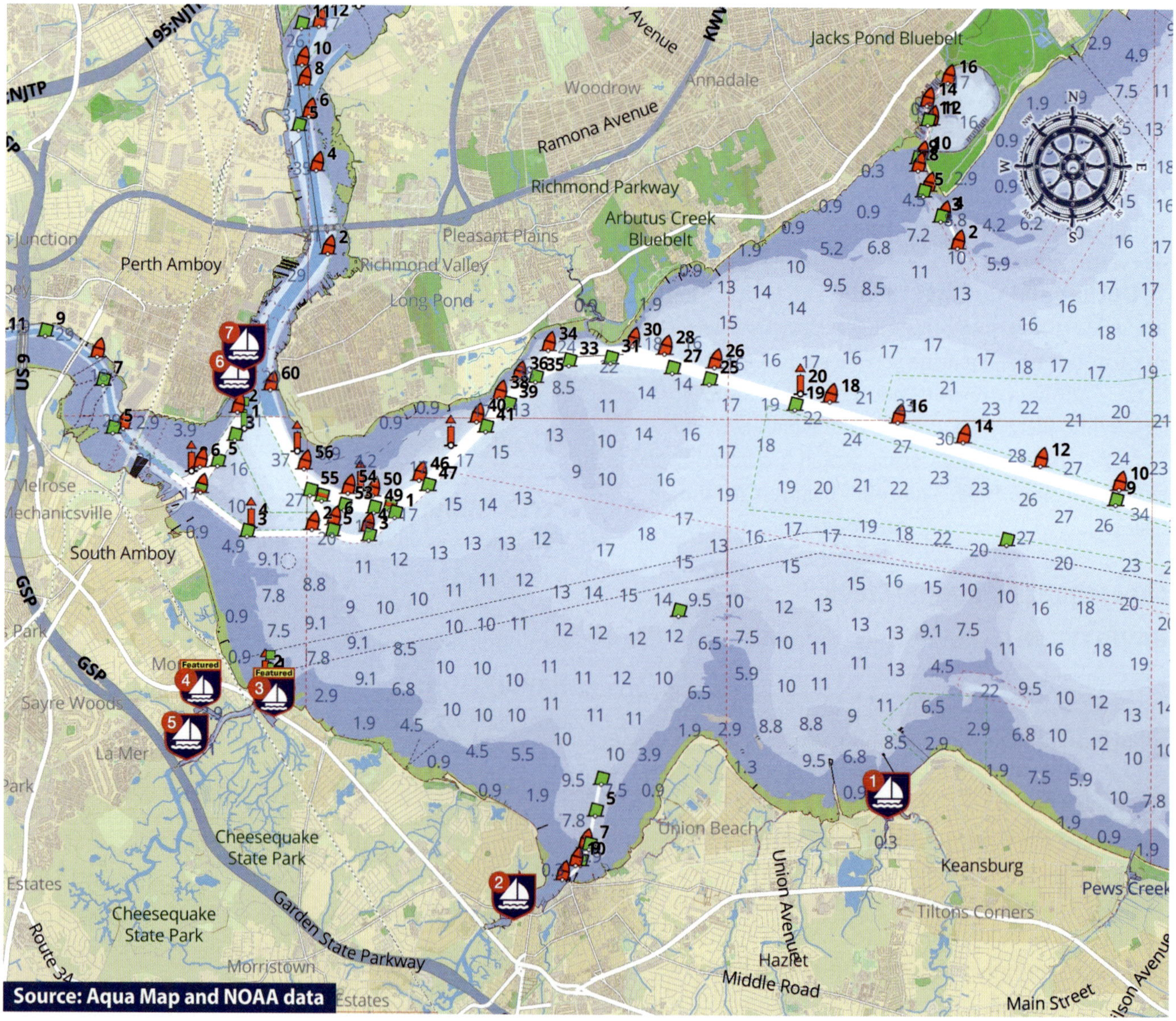

Source: Aqua Map and NOAA data

6:00 a.m. to 9:30 a.m. and from 4:30 p.m. to 7:30 p.m., Monday through Friday (except Federal holidays), when the lift need not open.

The **Victory Bridge**, just beyond the railroad bascule, has a fixed vertical clearance of 110 feet. The highway bridges farther upriver are the **Edison (U.S. 9) Bridges** and the **Garden State Parkway Bridge** with 110- and 134-foot fixed vertical clearances, respectively.

From the bridges, the Raritan River is navigable 11 miles upriver to New Brunswick through a crooked but well-marked channel and carries a fair amount of industrial traffic and flotsam through the salt marshes. Depths diminish to about 4 feet MLW in its upper reaches.

About 6 miles north of the bridges, the South River curves off to port. The Raritan River continues to starboard with shallow depths and limited facilities. Beyond the **I-95/NJ Turnpike bridge** (45-foot fixed vertical clearance) you

come to New Brunswick, the head of navigation for the river and the home of Rutgers University.

Depths abruptly shoal from 10 to 4 feet MLW at the remains of the entrance to the Delaware and Raritan Canal, which closed in 1933. This canal once linked New Brunswick to Trenton on the Delaware River and is now part of a state park.

Dockage: Perth Amboy is home to the friendly Raritan Yacht Club, which is private, but offers guest moorings to reciprocal yacht club members. The yacht club launch can be hailed on VHF Channel 9. Also located here is the municipal Perth Amboy Harborside Marina with 137 slips on concrete floating docks, which can accommodate boats to 40 feet plus has a 300-foot berth for larger vessels. Note that there is no fuel available in Perth Amboy.

NOTE: Pump-out services can be obtained by calling the Baykeeper Pump-Out Boat at 732-832-1499 or on VHF Channel 9.

Provisions are only a short walk up the street to the town of Perth Amboy. The North Jersey Coast train station is an easy 0.5-mile walk from the harbor up Market Street.

Alternate Route to Upper Bay: Arthur Kill & Kill Van Kull

If you have traveled the normal route to New York Harbor more than once and are looking for something different or, if the weather is deteriorating and a trip through the Narrows does not seem inviting, think about using the protected waters of Arthur Kill to the west of Staten Island as a new route.

Although the trip is twice as long, the channel is well marked, there are no bridge delays and depths are excellent.

Perth Amboy

Kill Van Kull Area, NJ

ARTHUR KILL		Largest Vessel	VHF	Total Slips	Approach/ Dockside Depth	Floating Docks	Gas/ Diesel	Repairs/ Haulout	Min/Max Amps	Pump-Out Station
1. The Municipal Marina at Carteret Waterfront Park	(732) 541-3800	85	73	185	20.0 / 17.0	F	GD		30 / 100	P
2. Elizabeth Marina	(908) 820-4297	40		38	/		GD		30 / 50	P

WiFi Wireless Internet Access
Visit www.waterwayguide.com for current rates, fuel prices, website addresses and other up-to-the-minute information.
(Information in the table is provided by the facilities.)

Scan here for more details:

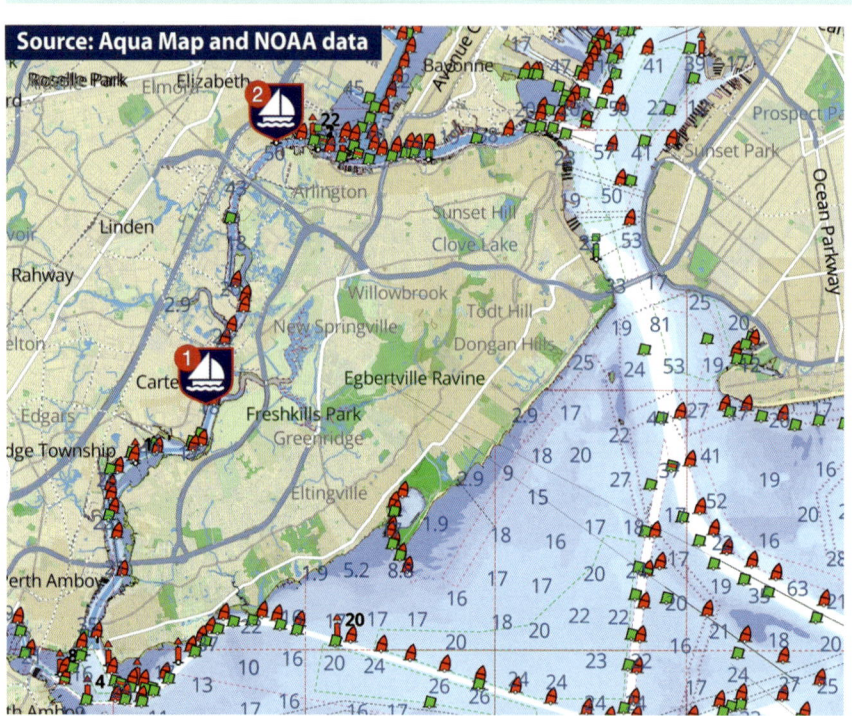

Source: Aqua Map and NOAA data

Arthur Kill to the west and north and Kill Van Kull to the north join to separate Staten Island from New Jersey. There is no room for anchoring in the waterway proper but along this route are a myriad of kills, rivers, streams and bays that are seldom on the itinerary of recreational boaters (but should be).

> NOTE: "Kill" comes from the Dutch settlers and refers to a channel, stream, creek or river.

NAVIGATION: Near the south end of the Arthur Kill, expensive homes line the shoreline on Staten Island to the east, Perth Amboy to the west and South Amboy to the south on the New Jersey side. Keep in the channel when rounding Ward Point at the southerly tip of Staten Island.

On the Staten Island shore, just below the cantilevered **Outerbridge Crossing Bridge** (143-foot fixed vertical clearance) are small marinas offering some dockage and restaurants.

CAUTION: The actual velocities and directions of tidal currents in Arthur Kill may deviate significantly from those shown in tidal current tables.

Arthur Kill leads north around Staten Island in a well-marked, protected channel. Proceed north in the channel keeping west of Pralls

Island (a protected bird sanctuary) to Goethals Bridge. The fixed high-rise bridge with a 140-foot vertical clearance is followed by the 31-foot vertical clearance Arthur Kill Railroad Bridge (usually open).

Just past Shooters Island, a wildlife sanctuary between Shooters Reach north and south branches, a large channel branches off to the north. Charted as Newark Bay South Reach, this is the route for container ships bound for Port Elizabeth and Port Newark. Straight ahead on the charted Bergen Pt. West Reach is the 215-foot fixed vertical clearance **Bayonne Bridge**.

Note that if you are entering Kill Van Kull from New York Harbor (i.e., headed south), you will be heading inland and buoys would be "red-right-returning" as expected but when you head out under the **Goethals Bridge** (leading to Bayway on the New Jersey side and Gulfport on the Staten Island side), you are technically heading out to sea and the buoys are suddenly reversed (red to port and green to starboard).

Dockage: There are a few facilities on Arthur Kill above the Outerbridge Crossing Bridge with dockage. Newly renovated The Municipal Marina at Carteret Waterfront Park has excellent depths, wide concrete docks and transient slips are available. This location has excellent security, as the marina is co-located with the state police marine station.

The municipal Elizabeth Marina, north of the Goethals Bridge, has transient docks with slips to 40 feet, a concrete boat ramp and restrooms.

Section 2: New York Waters

Chapter 4: New York Harbor & The East River

Chapter 5: Side Trip: The Hudson River to Troy Lock   Chapter 6: Side Trip: The South Shore of Long Island

Inset #1

Troy Lock

Troy

Inset #2

Shinnecock Canal

Shinnecock Inlet

Nyack

To Troy Lock
See Inset #1

Chapter 5: Page 157

Tarrytown

NEW YORK

Hudson River

Yonkers

Englewood

George Washington Bridge

Bronx

Harlem River

Throgs Neck

Flushing

Manhatten

East River

NEW YORK

Chapter 4: Page 140

Newark Bay

Governors Island

Kill Van Kull

Upper Bay

Brooklyn

Jamaica Bay

Verrazano Narrows

Staten Island

Coney Island

Shinnecock Inlet & Canal
See Inset #2

Rockaway Inlet

Chapter 6: Page 185

Lower Bay

Great Kills Harbor

Atlantic Ocean

Pages 147-150

George Washington Bridge

Harlem River

Throgs Neck

Wards Island

Rikers Island

East River

Flushing Bay

Hudson River

NEW JERSEY

Hell Gate

Pages 151-15

Manhatten

Roosevelt Island

East River

New York City

NEW YORK

Newark Bay

Upper Bay

Brooklyn

Jamaica Bay

Staten Island

Verrazano Narrows

Pages 143-147

Gravesend Bay

Coney Island

Rockaway Beach

Lower Bay

Rockaway Inlet

Atlantic Ocean

■ NAVIGATION NOTES

North through The Narrows into New York Harbor–one of the world's finest natural harbors–is the great city of New York with five boroughs and 8.5 million residents. Many superlatives apply to New York City and it is not lacking in boating amenities.

While there are a few possibilities in Manhattan, most of the marinas are found on the New Jersey side of New York Harbor in Jersey City, Weehawken and Hoboken. Ferries and water taxis make the trip on a regular basis back and forth to Manhattan. These large, full-service marinas in New Jersey are close to dining, provisioning, transportation and waterfront events.

Directly alongside the skyscrapers of Manhattan runs the magnificent, scenic East River, twisting its way past the South Street Seaport, beautiful east-side buildings with penthouse gardens and Gracie Mansion, New York's mayoral home. The East River also leads to the cruising mecca of Long Island Sound.

Also covered in this section is the Hudson River, located west of Manhattan, connecting the Erie Canal and Lake Erie or the Champlain Canal and Lake Champlain. (Waterway Guide's *Great Lakes, Vol. 1* contains details on these routes.)

Cruising Conditions

New York Harbor is one of the world's busiest harbors. Ships and barges are always on the move in and out of the harbor, anchoring and docking at piers along the Hudson River, the East River and heading to ports in New Jersey.

You will be accompanied by tankers, freighters of all flags, cruise ships, naval vessels, a myriad of tugs and tows and recreational boat traffic, along with continual ferry service to and from Staten Island, New Jersey ports on the Hudson and through The Narrows to ports south. Full attention is required of even the most experienced skippers.

Always give big ships the right-of-way; they have limited maneuvering room. Shipping traffic monitors VHF Channel 13 and do not hesitate to contact any ship or barge if you need clarification on their intention.

New York Harbor waters are deep and well marked. In fog or rain, follow the main channel buoys closely but you can also run just outside of the channel itself in plenty of water and steer clear of big-ship traffic. Compass or GPS courses might be needed to sort out one buoy from another and take extra time at night to be certain of the lights.

Watch for debris throughout the entire New York Harbor area, especially on the outgoing tide. Because of the waterways converging in the Harbor, debris is carried in and out from many areas. Powerboats should slow down to reduce the chance of hitting such objects.

Uncertain winds generally require that sailboats use their auxiliary engines when transiting the Harbor; this is definitely the case in the East River. All vessels should monitor both VHF Channels 13 and 16 and stay alert to traffic that might be just around the corner.

CAUTION: Laws in New York prohibit the carrying of handguns on vessels in state waters without a permit. Permits must be applied for in person. Jail sentences and stiff fines are possible.

New York Area Security Zones

Source: 33CFR 165.169

All navigable waters of the Hudson River are bound by the following points:

- From the point N 40° 46.150'/W 073° 59.812' on the seawall midway between Pier 92 and 94
- Northwest to approximate position N 40° 46.233'/ W 074° 0.015' approximately 125 yards northwest of Pier 92
- Southwest to approximate position N 40° 45.945'/W 074° 0.255' approximately 150 yards west of Pier 86
- East to the seawall between Pier 84 and Pier 86 at approximate position N 40° 45.827'/W 073° 59.968' (NAD 1983)
- Northeast along the shoreline to the point of origin

The Coast Guard reports that the following security zones apply to all vessels:

- No vessels are allowed within 150 yards of Liberty Island and Ellis Island or the bridge between the two.
- No vessel is allowed within a 300-yard radius of the Indian Point Nuclear Power Station on the Hudson River at N 41° 16.207'/W 073° 57.270'. Any vessel on the Hudson River in the vicinity of Indian Point is subject to random Coast Guard boarding.
- No vessel is allowed within 25 yards of all bridge piers or abutments, overhead power cables and pier and tunnel ventilators south of the Troy, NY, locks.
- No vessel is allowed within 100 yards of all anchored or moored Coast Guard vessels or stations.

Additional restricted areas exist in Port Newark/Port Elizabeth in Newark Bay and around New York City including near heliports, cruise ships, liquified hazardous gas (LHG) vessels, marine terminals and airports. Consult the Coast Guard's *Local Notice to Mariners* for details.

When special security zones are put into place around the United Nations in the East River, vessels must go through the east channel of Roosevelt Island and under the Roosevelt Island Bridge. Vessels requiring a bridge opening (40-foot closed vertical clearance) should call the tender at 718-361-9217 or on VHF Channel 13 at least 15 minutes before you plan on passing through the lift bridge.

Check for updated security advisories in New York Harbor and the East River at www.homeport.uscg.mil/newyork or by calling 718-354-4037. Report suspicious activities at 800-424-8802, National Response Center.

■ LOWER NEW YORK HARBOR

The run from Sandy Hook across Lower New York Harbor (shown on NOAA charts as Lower Bay) to The Narrows into New York Harbor is 8 nm almost due north. On this course pass west of Romer Shoal Light to avoid the breaking seas across a shallow spot southeast of the light and the shoal itself that runs 2 nm farther on.

Leave the West Bank Light to port. Maintain a course well east of Swinburne and Hoffman Islands, which lie due west of Coney Island's Norton Point. Do not attempt to explore these small islets lying off the Staten Island shore by boat, as the water around them is extremely shallow.

Time your transit in the Lower Bay with a favorable current to shorten your cruising time. Currents in this area run up to 2 knots. Depths are good almost everywhere. If the visibility is poor, it is advisable to run GPS or compass courses. Channels are almost too well marked and the profusion of buoys, lights and lighthouses can be overwhelming at times.

Another option is to run outside the main shipping lanes where there is usually plenty of water. Stay close enough to follow the buoys but off-channel enough to stay clear of big ships. All commercial traffic monitors VHF Channel 13 in New York waters.

It is advisable to hail approaching vessels to agree on a passing strategy. The tugboat captains and pilots will respond and they usually appreciate a call from even the smallest pleasure boat. There is great security in your knowing exactly where a 1,000-foot-long car carrier is headed and that the captain acknowledges your existence!

Great Kills Harbor

Great Kills Harbor, the first storm haven on the northward route through Lower Bay before reaching The Narrows, is a harbor of refuge and a charming place to visit. Located on the east side of Staten Island about 7 nm northwest of Sandy Hook and 12 nm south of The Battery (Manhattan), it is almost completely landlocked.

Entering Great Kills Harbor immediately reminds you of a picturesque, New England harbor. Its deep water and almost completely landlocked basin is very secure, offering an ideal spot to plan your visit to New York City. The harbor is 3.5 square miles in area and is surrounded by marinas to the north, marsh to the east, beach to the west and the Gateway National Recreation Area to the south.

Gateway National Recreation Area located at the eastern end of Great Kills Harbor with a beautiful swimming beach, bathhouse and snack bar. You will also find nature trails, great fishing and multi-use paths for walking and jogging on the 523 acres. Kayak lessons and guided tours are offered during July and August at Gateway National Recreational Area (718-980-6130).

Great Kills offers excellent, efficient, public transportation to the "City," with both express buses and the Staten Island Ferry leading to the New York City subway system.

NAVIGATION: The entry into Great Kills Harbor is easy with a well-marked channel leading from the Lower Bay past Crookes Point into the harbor. A forward range is available to assist in keeping you on course. Look for the two skeleton towers with flashing white lights at the beginning of the channel and entrance into the harbor and follow the numbered buoys in between them.

The Old Orchard Shoal Lighthouse was replaced by a 12-foot-high LED light in 2014. (See more about the original lighthouse, "the first victim of Hurricane Sandy," at www.lighthousemuseum.org).

Great Kills Harbor is a port of refuge, making a good layover port for boats heading north or south and the entrance can be run in almost any weather. Keep well to the east side when entering the basin to avoid shoaling to the west outside green marker "9" and "11."

Once in the harbor, be careful of the shallow area in the middle of the mooring field. It is best to follow the channel around the perimeter of the harbor. This is a well-protected harbor with several marine facilities. We recommend you plan to take a slip here as the harbor is very crowded with moorings, leaving little room to anchor.

Dockage/Moorings: The full service Staten Island Yachts Marina & Service Center in Great Kills Harbor is mainly a sales and working yard, but they do have some transient space and accept vessels to 80 feet on floating docks with full amenities. Their team of experienced and skilled professionals can complete a full range of repairs and services. There are several restaurants within walking distance and there is a well-stocked market one-half mile away.

Great Kills Harbor, NY

GREAT KILLS		Largest Vessel	VHF	Total Slips	Approach/ Dockside Depth	Floating Docks	Gas/ Diesel	Repairs/ Haulout	Min/Max Amps	Pump-Out Station
1. Staten Island Yachts Marina & Service Center WiFi	(718) 984-7676	80			/ 10.0	F	G		30 / 50	
2. Atlantis Marina & Yacht Club-PRIVATE	(718) 966-9700	100		140	12.0 / 5.0	F		RH		P
3. Richmond County Yacht Club-PRIVATE	(718) 356-4120		9	40	12.0 / 5.0	F			30	
4. Mansion Marina	(718) 984-6611	70		217	12.0 / 5.0	F	GD	RH	30 / 200+	P
5. Great Kills Yacht Club-PRIVATE	(718) 948-9615	70		105	12.0 / 8.0	F			30	
6. Moonbeam Great Kills Marina	(718) 351-8476	150		250	15.0 / 15.0	F		H	30 / 50	

WiFi Wireless Internet Access
Visit www.waterwayguide.com for current rates, fuel prices, website addresses and other up-to-the-minute information.
(Information in the table is provided by the facilities.)

Scan here for more details:

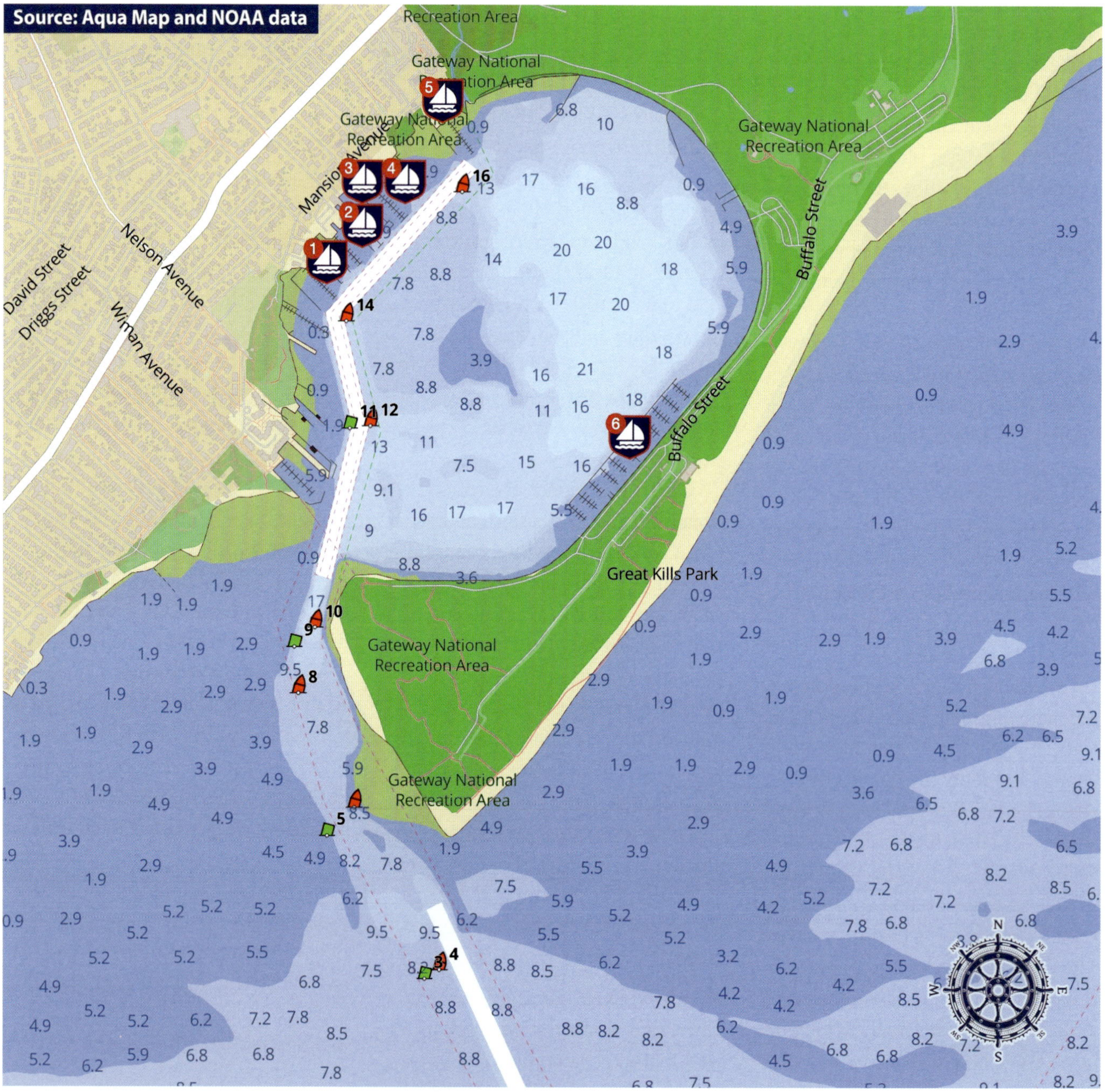

Source: Aqua Map and NOAA data

Atlantis Marina & Yacht Club is private but may have space; call ahead. The private Richmond County Yacht Club controls the majority of the moorings in the basin and offers space on a first-come, first-served basis. Call on VHF Channel 9 as you approach the harbor and follow directions to a protected mooring ball. A small service fee includes use of the launch and shoreside yacht club facilities including showers and a bar and grill. Great Kills Yacht Club is also private with limited courtesy dockage at two docks and moorings for members of reciprocal yacht clubs.

Mansion Marina is a busy, working boat yard with a lot of activity. The staff is knowledgeable and helpful and the marina can accommodate vessels to 70 feet. The floating docks of Moonbeam Great Kills Park Marina can accommodate vessels to 150 feet on the eastern side of the harbor. Follow channel markers in and turn right at the end of the fishing beach. Stay between the morning field and shore but hug the field. The marina is straight and on the right. The 250-slip facility is part of Great Kills Park and is adjacent to Great Kills Beach.

Gravesend Bay

Gravesend Bay is a good storm harbor and is directly on course from Sandy Hook to The Narrows. The harbor is located about 7 nm north of Sandy Hook and just before the high-rise Verazzano-Narrows Bridge.

Anchorage: Gravesend Bay is protected from every direction but the west. Anchor off the New York Sports Clubs Complex. The swell from the ships can be rough and, when combined with the swift current, pulling up the anchor from the mud/sand bottom may prove difficult.

Side Trip: Rockaway Inlet

Jettied Rockaway Inlet, southeast of Coney Island, is wide, easy to enter, protected from north and east weather and makes an excellent port in a storm. Its only drawback is that it is a virtual dead end. Boats bound farther east on Long Island and wishing to take the inside route on the New York waterway must bypass Rockaway Inlet and head 9 miles east along the coast for East Rockaway Inlet. (This route is described in detail in Chapter 6, "Side Trip: South Shore of Long Island".)

Once inside Rockaway Inlet, Sheepshead Bay is to port, Dead Horse Bay is farther along and to port and Jamaica Bay is dead ahead. All three offer protection from the weather and interesting sightseeing. Because many of the harbors in this area accommodate a large number of local boats, it is often difficult to find a guest mooring or transient dockage.

Long, narrow and crowded with recreational and commercial craft, Sheepshead Bay offers the closest dockage to Coney Island. Although little dockage is available for transients, there are bait and fuel barges. On the west side of Barren Island, Dead Horse Bay is a large, deep, protected bight with dockage and anchoring possibilities.

Jamaica Bay, 7 miles long and 3.5 miles wide, is the homeport for thousands of boats. It is protected from the Atlantic Ocean by barrier beaches, dotted with marshy islands and shallows and has well-marked channels with 10-foot MLW depths throughout. Once a favored hunting area, much of the bay is now included in the Gateway National Recreation Area. Jamaica Bay is surrounded by noisy John F. Kennedy International Airport as well as the more serene Jamaica Bay Wildlife Sanctuary, Rockaway Beach and Jacob Riis Beach.

NAVIGATION:

CAUTION: Increased shoaling has been observed in the vicinity of Sheepshead Bay Channel, specifically near Sheepshead Bay buoys "6" and "7." Aids marking the channel may be unreliable. All mariners are urged to use extreme caution when transiting this area.

Heading east from Rockaway Inlet, the channel passes under the **Marine Parkway (Gil Hodges Memorial) Bridge** (55-foot closed vertical clearance) and then branches north and east. The bridge monitors VHF Channels 13 and 16 and opens on signal between 8:00 a.m. and 4:00 p.m., Monday through Friday. An 8-hour notice is required at all other times. The eastern channel runs along Rockaway Beach and parallels a steel bulkhead along the south shore of the channel, south-southwest of Nova Scotia Bar.

You can make a circuit of Jamaica Bay by following the channel through the **Cross Bay Memorial Bridge** (52-foot fixed vertical clearance) and the **Beach Channel Bridge** (26-foot closed vertical clearance) along the beach. The bridge opens on signal except from 6:45 a.m. to 8:20 a.m. and 5:00 p.m. to 6:45 p.m. (commuting hours), Monday through Friday (except federal holidays).

Rockaway Inlet, NY

SHEEPSHEAD BAY		Largest Vessel	VHF	Total Slips	Approach/ Dockside Depth	Floating Docks	Gas/ Diesel	Repairs/ Haulout	Min/Max Amps	Pump-Out Station
1. Sheepshead Bay Yacht Club-PRIVATE	(718) 891-0991	50	68		45.0 / 15.0	F			30	
2. Miramar Yacht Club	(718) 646-9436		68		/					
3. Moonbeam Gateway Marina (WiFi)	(718) 252-8761	150	16	500	15.0 / 25.0	F		RH	30 / 100	P

(WiFi) Wireless Internet Access
Visit www.waterwayguide.com for current rates, fuel prices, website addresses and other up-to-the-minute information.
(Information in the table is provided by the facilities.)

Scan here for more details:

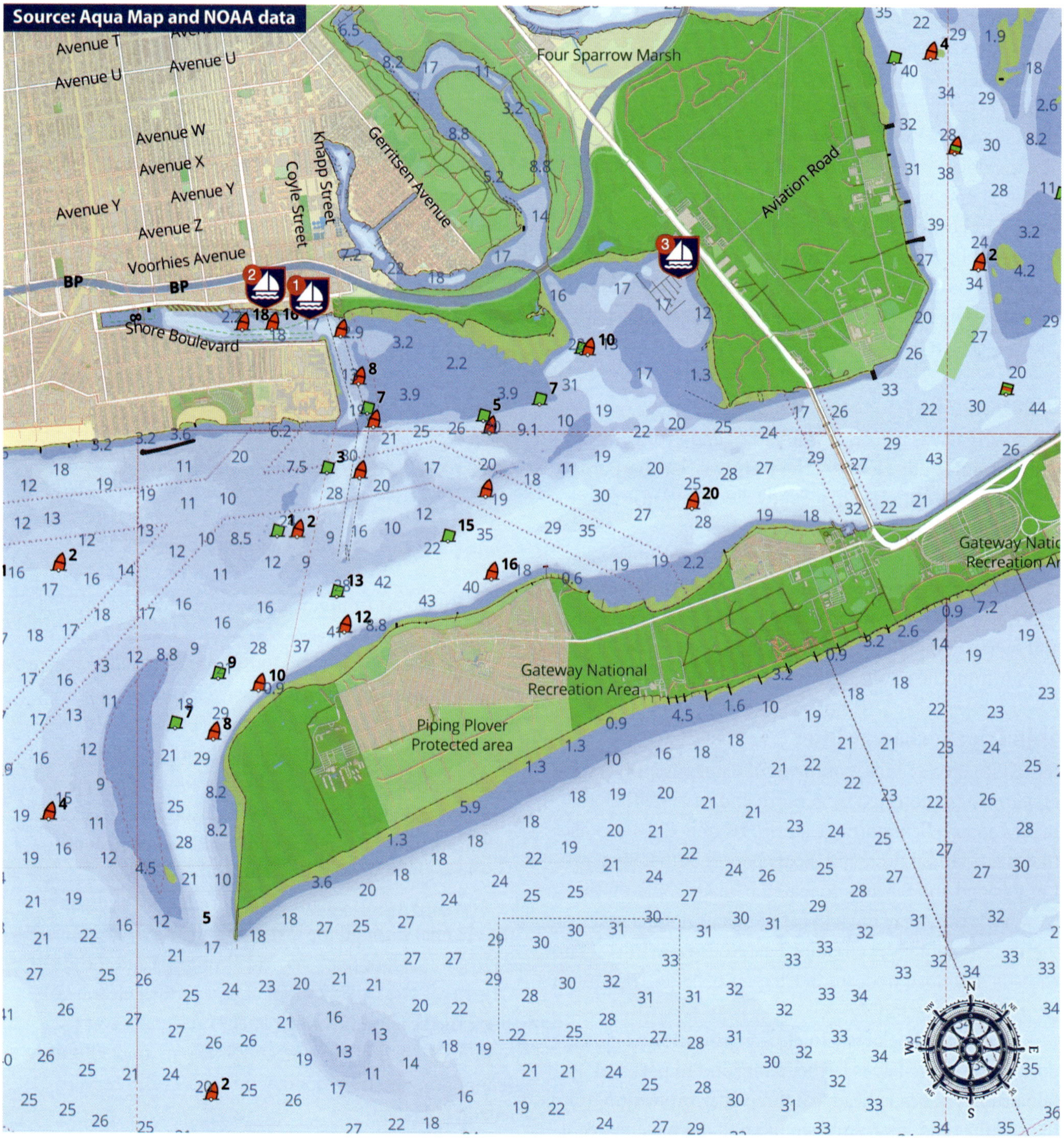

Continuing a circumnavigation of Jamaica Bay, after passing under the swing bridge, run north through Winhole Channel between the marshy islands to Grassy Bay. Submerged pilings line both sides of the channel to Howard Beach just west beyond the fixed **Railroad Bridge at Grassy Bay** (26-foot vertical clearance). Leaving Howard Beach to head back to the inlet, pass under the **North Channel Bridge** (26-foot fixed vertical clearance) and follow North Channel back to the Marine Parkway (Gil Hodges Memorial) Bridge.

Dockage/Moorings: You are welcome on the moorings at Miramar Yacht Club for a reasonable rate that includes launch service, and there is a good dinghy dock. Locked, gated security and good amenities round out the offerings. There is also shuttle service to the grocery store (one-half mile) and the train station (1 mile) or most other places you might need to go.

The private Sheepshead Bay Yacht Club offers courtesy dockage for members of reciprocal yacht clubs. Dead Horse Bay features the 560-slip Moonbeam Gateway Marina, which is part of the Gateway National Recreation Area. Call ahead on VHF Channel 6 for "Dock Assist" if you need help docking. They can also direct you when coming to dock.

Should you choose to circumnavigate Jamaica Bay, there are no anchorages but a couple of small boat facilities are located beyond the Belt Parkway Bridge (60-foot vertical clearance).

Anchorage: Sheepshead Bay has fair holding with 8- to 20-foot MLW depths in mud and is exposed south through east. Dead Horse Bay also offers an anchorage with 10- to 20-foot MLW depths with fair holding in mud. It is open and exposed from the west through the south. Choose your anchorage based on wind direction.

A good day anchorage is at Rockaway Inlet near Breezy Tower, where there is a nice (but busy) beach just outside the channel.

▉ UPPER NEW YORK HARBOR

As you pass by the northern tip of Staten Island, the entire panorama of New York City is spread before you. On the New Jersey side is a condominium complex, Port Liberté, which is reminiscent of French canals and countryside. A well-marked channel leads into the canals. Ahead, rising ever higher on the New York side, are the densely packed skyscrapers of the Lower Manhattan financial district. To the west is the Statue of Liberty, looking serene and lovely at 300-feet tall on her pedestal on Liberty Island.

> *CAUTION:* Be sure to stay at least 150 yards from both Liberty and Ellis Islands.

Ellis Island, through which millions of immigrants entered the U.S. to build new lives, lies just north of the Statue of Liberty. From a distance, its Moorish towers and minarets still have the look of a fairytale castle. There is no dockage on either island for recreational vessels. Ferry service runs to Liberty Island from The Battery in New York and from Liberty State Park in Jersey City.

Across the harbor and 0.5 mile south of The Battery is Governors Island, formerly the headquarters of the Coast Guard's Third District. Coast Guard operations specifically for New York Harbor are now headquartered in Bayonne, NJ, and Staten Island, NY. Governors Island is open to the public every Friday through Sunday and is accessible by ferry or water taxi only. (Private boats not allowed.)

The Narrows to The Battery

NAVIGATION: The **Verazzano-Narrows Bridge** (a fixed high-rise bridge with a 215-foot vertical clearance) is among the world's largest suspension bridges and is located about 8 nm north of Sandy Hook, NJ. When the bridge opened on November 21, 1962, it was the longest suspension bridge in the world.

> NOTE: The monumental 693-foot high towers of the Verazzano-Narrows Bridge are 1 5/8 inches farther apart at their tops than at their bases because the 4,260-foot distance between them made it necessary to compensate for the earth's curvature. Each tower weighs 27,000 tons and is held together with three million rivets and one million bolts.

The bridge links Staten Island to Brooklyn and serves as the dividing line between Upper Bay (Upper New York Harbor) and Lower Bay (Lower New York Harbor). Fort Wadsworth on Staten Island and Fort Hamilton in Brooklyn, both still standing, once guarded this 1-mile-wide keyhole to New York Harbor.

Beyond the Verazzano-Narrows Bridge on the Staten Island side is a quarantine station where ships anchor for clearance. The usual course into and out of the Upper Bay (New York Harbor) is either in the center of the channel or along the Brooklyn shore. Big freight terminals with ships loading and discharging are in the slips of Staten Island and Bayonne to the west and Brooklyn to the east.

CAUTION: The Staten Island ferries run almost continuously between Staten Island and terminals on the east side of The Battery in Lower Manhattan. The Staten Island Ferries are large orange vessels and these, along with a host of other ferries and sightseeing boats, create a busy marine traffic situation. Be certain of your course if you cross the bow of one of these vessels, especially when taking into account the effect of currents on your progress.

Currents in The Narrows build up to 2.5 knots on the ebb and up to 2 knots during the flood. The strongest currents in New York Harbor (up to 5 knots) are found at the northeastern end of Manhattan so skippers heading up the East River to Long Island Sound might want to base the times of their passage on Hell Gate currents. Passage through Hell Gate should be timed to carry a fair current as visible "slack water" is rare.

An optional passage to reach the East River from the Verazzano-Narrows Bridge is to hug the Brooklyn (east) shore of Upper Bay, stay east of Bay Ridge Flats through the Bay Ridge Channel and then travel east of Governors Island through the Buttermilk Channel. Currents run hard in this channel, but this route avoids the large ships, Staten Island ferries and strong currents that can be found in the Upper Bay.

Lower Hudson River

From New York Harbor to the Federal Dam at Troy, the Hudson River is measured in river miles. Mile 0 is located at the Battery at the southern tip of Manhattan Island.

NOTE: The upper Hudson River is discussed in Chapter 5 "Side Trip: The Hudson River to Troy Lock."

NAVIGATION: When you head north on the Hudson River, you will leave to the east the old commercial and cruise ship wharves, which are slowly being demolished and rebuilt. World-famous private and charter yachts are sometimes seen moored here.

The Chelsea Piers Maritime Center is part of a 30-acre sports and entertainment complex housed in historic pier buildings that includes a bowling alley, skating rink, golf driving range, day spa and a 1.2-mile-long esplanade, all overlooking the river. Many private yacht groups, dinner cruises and sightseeing tours operate out of Chelsea Piers. Nearby is the Intrepid Sea, Air & Space Museum at Pier 86 where the aircraft carrier *Intrepid* houses the museum (212-245-0072).

On the opposite side of Manhattan is the 11-block complex of Old Seaport New York, which includes a fleet of 19th-century clipper ships, four galleries, a working re-creation of a 19th-century print shop, a boatbuilding shop, a maritime craft center and museum shop. This is a great place to view the ship and pleasure traffic on the East River. Water taxis run from New Jersey and points along the Hudson to the South Street Seaport district. Ferries and water taxis to Manhattan offer

expanded nighttime services during the summer months to New York and back. The NJ Transit light-rail line (973-275-5555), located several blocks away, permits passenger service through Liberty Park and along the New Jersey shoreline to Bayonne, Hoboken and north.

Dockage: Liberty Landing Marina is located in Liberty State Park across from the lower tip of Manhattan. The family-oriented, full-service marina welcomes transient vessels up to 200 feet year-round with a 24-hour fueling facility, a fully stocked marine store, restrooms, showers, laundry and free WiFi. They have many different slip sizes available with 30-, 50-, and 100-amp electric service and a friendly, eager staff.

Liberty Harbor Marina is in the same basin with a boat storage facility and a few transient slips. This location can be a little rocky from passing traffic. Water taxis are close by to take you to the city and restaurants. Call ahead for slip availability.

Newport Marina to the north features natural protection from wakes, 400 feet of available floating dockage, ample power and water and stunning skyline views of lower Manhattan. They welcome overnight transients to 125 feet as well as offering dock and dine.

At Pier 13 in Hoboken is The Shipyard Marina, which caters to smaller boats but maintains 30 deep water slips (to 60 feet) with few on-site amenities. This facility is in dire

New York Harbor, NY

JERSEY CITY		Largest Vessel	VHF	Total Slips	Approach/ Dockside Depth	Floating Docks	Gas/ Diesel	Repairs/ Haulout	Min/Max Amps	Pump-Out Station
1. Liberty Landing Marina WiFi MM 0.46 RDB	(201) 985-8000	200	72	520	22.0 / 12.0	F	GD	RH	30 / 200+	P
2. Liberty Harbor Marina WiFi MM 0.46 RDB	(800) 646-2066	60	68	150	20.0 / 18.0	F	GD	RH	30 / 50	P
3. Newport Marina	(551) 482-3750	125	78	8	6.0 / 12.0	F			50 / 200+	
HOBOKEN										
4. The Shipyard Marina WiFi MM 3.45 RDB	(201) 232-5700		74	50	12.0 / 10.0	F			30 / 50	
MANHATTEN										
5. Chelsea Piers Marina WiFi MM 3.10 LDB	(212) 336-6600	300	68	70	19.0 / 8.0	F			30 / 100	

WiFi Wireless Internet Access
Visit www.waterwayguide.com for current rates, fuel prices, website addresses and other up-to-the-minute information. (Information in the table is provided by the facilities.)

Scan here for more details:

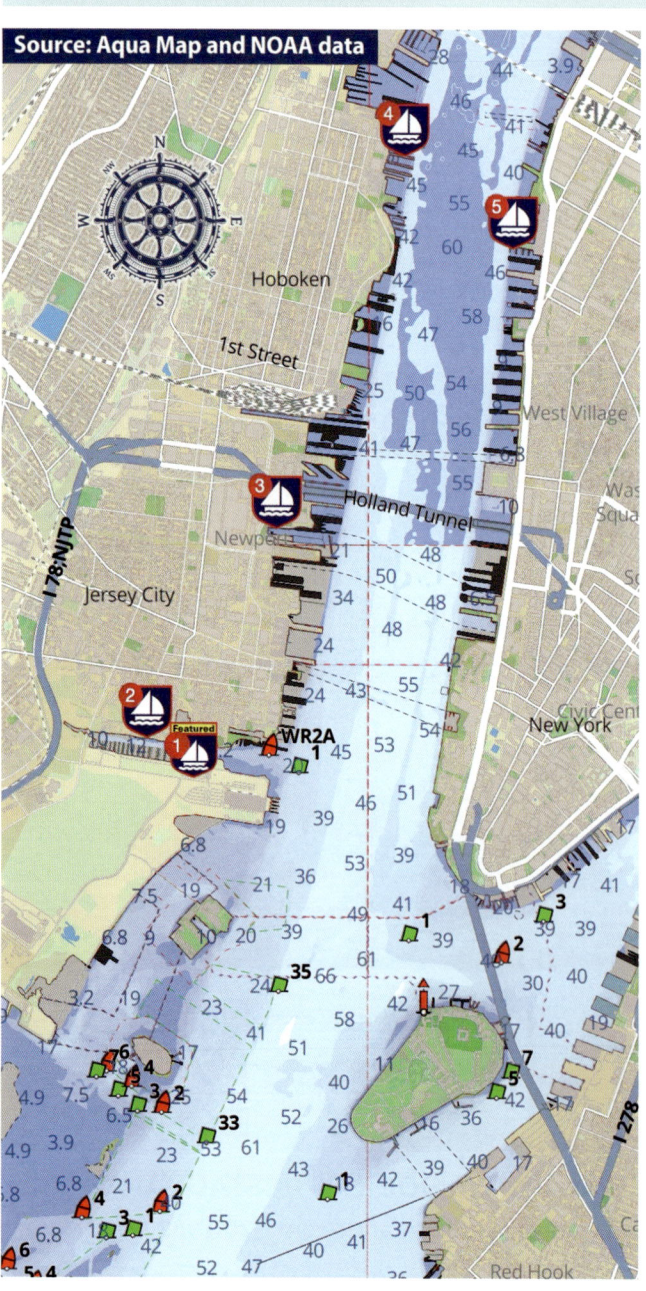

Source: Aqua Map and NOAA data

need of a breakwall and can be rolly. What it does offer are stores and restaurants within walking distance and a spectacular view of New York City.

Continuing north on the New York (east) side of the Hudson River, Marina at Chelsea Pier has 65 slips and 25 mega-berths that can accommodate vessels up to 300 feet on floating docks with a wave attenuator. Located in the Chelsea Piers Sports and Entertainment Complex, right in the heart of the Big Apple, the marina offers easy access to all the sites and attractions that New York has to offer.

> NOTE: The 79th Street Boat Basin, which houses the New York City Municipal Marina, is closed for a major re-build until 2025.

Anchorage: The "Designated Anchorages" in New York Harbor are designed for large ships and are located in the middle of the harbor. The use of these areas requires permission from the Coast Guard.

There is a well-marked pleasure boat anchorage channel at Liberty State Park with 9 to 13 feet MLW with good holding in mud. Follow the channel just south of Liberty Island at green buoy "33." Anchor close to the Liberty State Park bulkhead. Avoid the area near the breakwater on the south side of this anchorage as it is shallow. This anchorage provides sufficient protection from all but southeast winds.

The anchorage south of Lady Liberty is just to port of the green daybeacons marking the channel with room for at least 4 to 5 vessels and 9-foot MLW depths. This can be quite rolly, especially during the day, and there is lots of helicopter tour noise. Don't try to anchor behind Lady Liberty where there is a plethora of power lines.

You can try to anchor at Ellis Island, which offers good holding and 7- to 9-foot MLW depths. This will be rolly if the wind picks up and you might want to move elsewhere

Lower Hudson River, NY

MANHATTAN		Largest Vessel	VHF	Total Slips	Approach/ Dockside Depth	Floating Docks	Gas/ Diesel	Repairs/ Haulout	Min/Max Amps	Pump-Out Station
1. North Cove Marina (IGY) 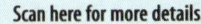 MM 0.80 LDB	(917) 677-7680	175	69	32	25.0 / 16.0	F			30 / 100	P
2. ONE°15 Brooklyn Marina	(718) 490-7136	300	71	100	39.0 / 45.0	F			30 / 200+	P

WiFi Wireless Internet Access
Visit www.waterwayguide.com for current rates, fuel prices, website addresses and other up-to-the-minute information.
(Information in the table is provided by the facilities.)

Scan here for more details:

THE EAST RIVER

The magnificent East River of New York is a 14-nm-long body of water that separates the boroughs of Manhattan and the Bronx from Brooklyn and Queens. The river passes under eight high-level bridges that are set against the spectacular backdrop of the Manhattan skyline. Each of the bridges is an architectural beauty and well worth photographing.

For a different look at the bridges, including little-known facts, visit www.frugalfrolicker.com/nyc-bridges.

Winding its way from the Battery in New York Harbor to Long Island Sound, the East River is one of only two rivers in the world with two mouths and no source, according to local lore. The other such river is the Harlem River at the north end of Manhattan, also described in this chapter. Technically, both of these "rivers" are estuaries.

Navigation Notes

The East River is heavily traveled by commercial traffic including tugs with tows, deep-draft ships, sightseeing vessels and large power boats that kick up great wakes. In its lower reaches near New York Harbor, the East River is dominated by large commercial ships heading to and from the docks on the Brooklyn shore. These ships maneuver awkwardly, hook up with tugs and are troubled by the strong current so you must stay out of their way! Ships in these waters monitor VHF Channel 13 and you should definitely contact them if you have questions or concerns about their course.

Staten Island and Governors Island ferries can also be particularly troublesome as they cross the river frequently and at high speeds. Cross their wakes just after they have crossed the channel. Do not cut close to a docked ferry. If its powerful propellers are not throwing a monstrous wash into the channel, the ferry might be about to leave its slip and enter the channel with remarkable speed. In either case, you do not want to be nearby.

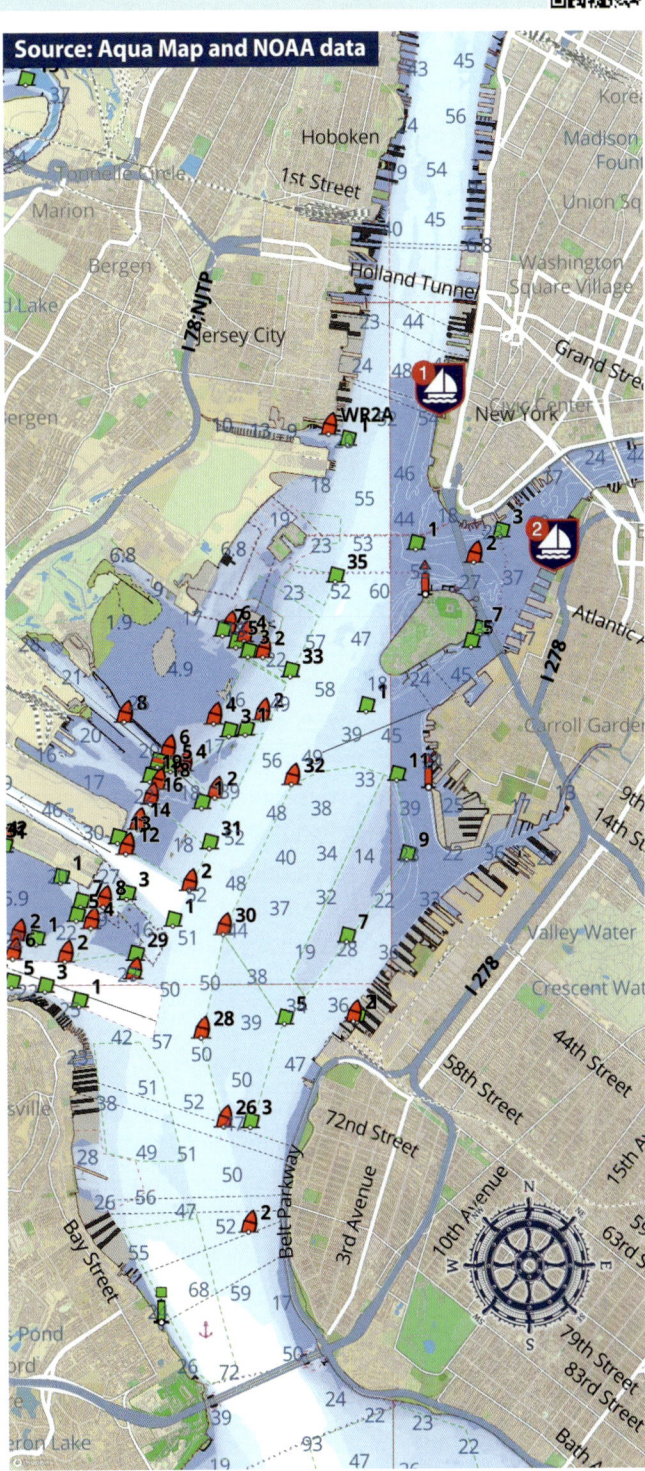

Source: Aqua Map and NOAA data

There are also many small high-speed yellow water taxis and blue ferries as well as the well-known Circle Line tourist boats to negotiate. The safest course of action is to be aware of all traffic since these commercial vessels are working on a schedule. If you wish to communicate with any commercial traffic in the East River, use VHF Channel 13. Additionally, it is important to be watchful of floating debris on the East River, especially on the outgoing tide.

> **CAUTION:** There are significant security regulations in effect on the river that are continually updated and changed by the Department of Homeland Security and the U.S. Coast Guard. Skippers should always be alert to security changes before transiting the East River. While transiting the East River and other waters of New York City, note that the marine division of the New York Police Department monitors VHF Channel 16 and is available for assistance in an emergency.

The Battery to Hell Gate

Transiting the East River from the Battery in New York City to Long Island Sound or from Long Island Sound to the Battery in New York City can be a wonderful, exciting experience. The river is deep, well marked and easy to follow. The buildings of Lower Manhattan rise to the west and Wall Street runs right down to the water below Pier 15. Fulton Ferry Landing is a wonderful park under the magnificent Brooklyn Bridge. This is the site of Bargemusic, which presents music year-round (www.bargemusic.org). There is no dockage here but the yellow ferries that run across the East River are accessible from the New York side.

NAVIGATION: The **Brooklyn Bridge**, built in 1883, has 127-foot fixed vertical clearance. Two other high-rise bridges cross the East River here: the **Manhattan Bridge** (134-foot fixed vertical clearance) and the **Williamsburg Bridge** (133-foot fixed vertical clearance). Buoyage changes above the Williamsburg Bridge, as the buoys from here count down to Long Island Sound. Thus, keep red daybeacon "18" to your port side when passing.

Roosevelt Island splits the East River at the United Nations, about 5 miles above The Battery. Boats can take either channel east or west of the island, except during security alerts, when recreational vessels must keep to the east of Roosevelt Island via East Channel. The western channel is larger with more spectacular views and fewer shoaling edges. If you have to travel the East Channel for security reasons, stay closer to the shore of Roosevelt Island as shoals extend from the Long Island side of the channel and be aware of the bridge restrictions on this route.

The **Queensboro Bridge** (also known as the 59th Streeet Bridge) crosses the East River on both sides of Roosevelt Island with 131-foot fixed vertical clearance. If passing Roosevelt Island in the East Channel, note that the **Roosevelt Island Bridge** has 40-foot closed vertical clearance. Here you have three options: (1) Call the NYC DOT Bridge Operator on VHF Channel 13, (2) call the Bridge Operations Office at 212-839-3740, or (3) call the Communications Center at 718-433-3340. The bridge will open on signal if at least 2-hour advance notice is provided. Openings may be delayed up to one-half hour. Be sure to consider the tide and current as you make arrangements for an opening.

> **CAUTION:** While the Roosevelt Island Bridge has a published open clearance of 100 feet, it does not always open fully for passage of vessels. We have received reports of boats being dismasted at this bridge. Exercise caution (or opt for the West Channel) if you need more than 40-foot vertical clearance at the bridge.

Some care must be given to avoid following navigational aids that mark some of the small rivers that empty into the East River instead of the East River markers themselves.

The key to transiting the East River, either eastward or westward, is to time the currents correctly by consulting tide and tidal current charts. Opposing currents in the river can reach over 5 knots and could seriously hinder the progress of low-powered, full displacement vessels. One cruising editor transiting the area noted the pedestrians walking along the river on the Manhattan shore were passing the boat. Wind-driven chop, a couple of standing waves, heavy traffic and inconsistent depths can further exacerbate these contrary currents. No wonder the common name for the mid-point of the East River is "Hell Gate."

Dockage: North Cove Marina (IGY) occupies a prime location in the heart of the financial district and can accommodate vessels to 175 feet on floating docks. They offer concierge service and restaurants and shopping are just steps away. With One World Trade Center as a backdrop, this marina makes for great photos to send home.

Located directly across from Manhattan on the lower East River, ONE°15 Brooklyn Marina has over 100 berths for vessels up to 250 feet. Call ahead for availability. Note we have received reports that traffic from NYC ferries sends large waves into the marina area, which can be a bit bouncy.

Alternate Route: Harlem River

One of the most amazing and under-rated routes that you can take includes the Harlem River. As much as the Hudson River, traveling up the west side of Manhattan, is remarkable, a trip up the East River is a wonderful alternative. If you are headed up the Hudson River for the second or third time, or are similarly traveling up the East River bound for Long Island Sound, consider the Harlem River as an alternative route.

> NOTE: For more information about the Harlem River, visit www.nyc.gov/html/dot/html/infrastructure/bridges-harlem.shtml.

Note that care needs to be taken to consider the tides which ebb from the East River towards the Hudson.

Traveling from the East River to the Hudson, the Harlem River, which is not heavily traveled by recreational boats, flows between the East River

Robert F. Kennedy Bridge

Hell Gate Railroad Bridge

and the Hudson River 8 miles away at the north end of Manhattan. At Wards Island, you will proceed under a graceful, arching, green Wards Island Foot Bridge (55-foot closed vertical clearance), one of the highest and longest pedestrian bridges anywhere. This end of the Harlem River is commercial with railroad switching yards and sprawling housing projects.

A series of small boathouses appear as you approach the Hudson River. These are the headquarters of rowing and sculling clubs founded more than a century ago. Columbia University's athletic field and crew house are to the east, followed by residential Inwood Hill Park and Riverdale.

NAVIGATION: Fifteen bridges cross the Harlem River. A vessel that can manage the controlling 24-foot vertical clearance will only require one bridge opening–the **Spuyten Duyvil Railroad Bridge** (5-foot closed vertical clearance), where

the Harlem River meets the Hudson River. The bridgetender can be hailed on VHF Channel 13 and, surprisingly, responds immediately to bridge opening requests when possible.

All Harlem River non-fixed bridges from **Wards Island Foot Bridge** (Mile 0) to **Henry Hudson Bridge** (Mile 6.0) open on signal if at least 4-hour advance notice is given to the New York Department of Transportation (NYCDOT) Radio Hotline (311) and the Triborough Bridge and Tunnel Authority (TBTA). The draws need not open from 6:00 a.m. to 9:00 a.m. and 5:00 p.m. to 7:00 p.m., Monday through Friday, except federal holidays, with the exception of the **Metro North (Park Ave.) Railroad Bridge**, which need not open from 5:00 a.m. to 10:00 a.m. and 4:00 p.m. to 8:00 p.m., Monday through Friday, except federal holidays. See up to date bridge schedules on Waterway Explorer (www.waterwayguide.com).

East River, NY

WESTCHESTER CREEK		Largest Vessel	VHF	Total Slips	Approach/ Dockside Depth	Floating Docks	Gas/ Diesel	Repairs/ Haulout	Min/Max Amps	Pump-Out Station
1. Metro Marine	(718) 823-0300	50		40	15.0 / 5.0	F		H	30	P

WiFi Wireless Internet Access
Visit www.waterwayguide.com for current rates, fuel prices, website addresses and other up-to-the-minute information. (Information in the table is provided by the facilities.)

Scan here for more details:

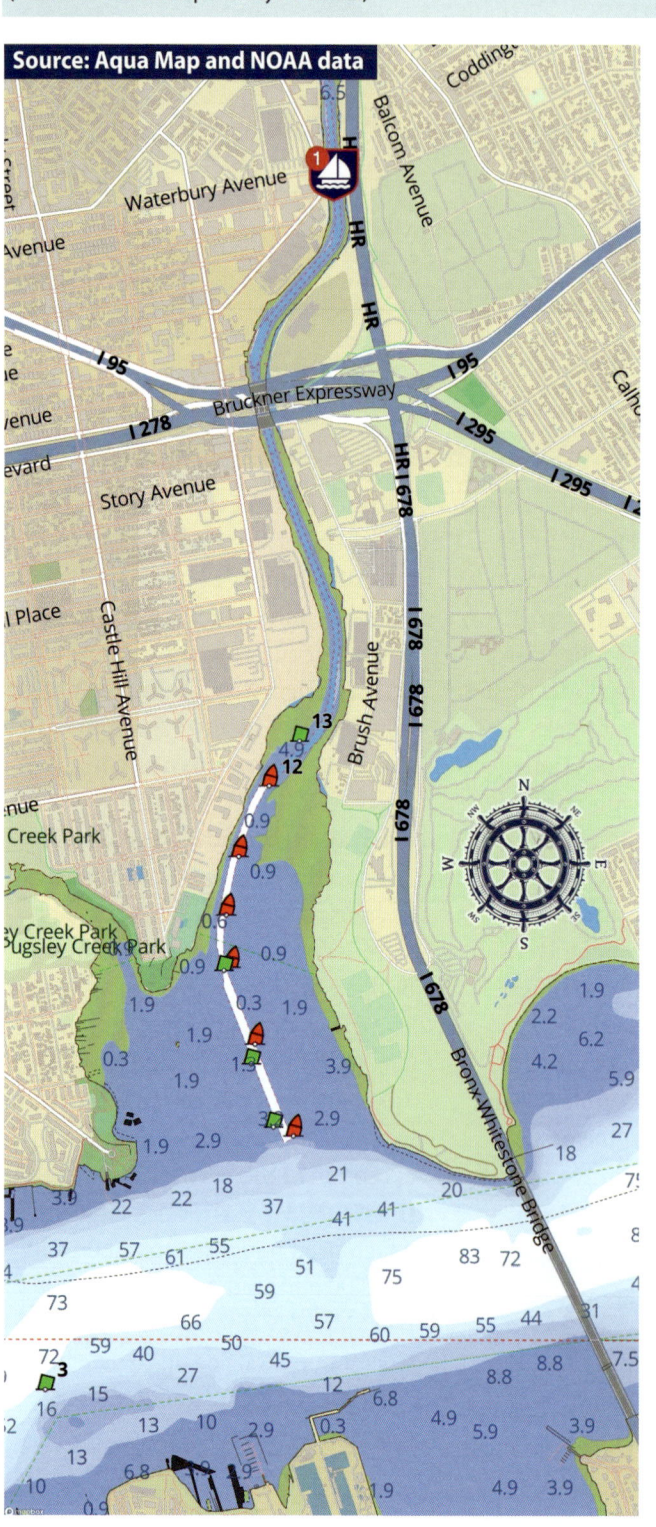

Source: Aqua Map and NOAA data

Hell Gate to Throgs Neck Bridge

Proper timing for moving eastward or westward is based on getting through Hell Gate, which is about mid-point of the 14-mile-long East River between the Battery on the southwestern tip of Manhattan and the Throgs Neck Bridge (138-foot fixed vertical clearance) on the eastern end of the river at the entrance into Long Island Sound.

The East River current is the exact opposite of Long Island Sound current in that it ebbs west and floods east, while Long Island Sound current ebbs east and floods west. The divide between these two systems is near the Throgs Neck Bridge. If timed properly, a recreational boat heading upriver can catch a good ride with the flood tide up the East River and the ebb eastward into Long Island Sound.

NAVIGATION: Upon reaching Hell Gate, stay south and east of Mill Rock and round the 33-foot flashing green daybeacon "15" at Hallets Point. This is Hell Gate proper, and the flow of water will indeed be spectacular if you arrive at maximum current. Ebb tide runs up to 5.2 knots to the southwest and floods at 4 knots to the northeast. This creates eddies and standing waves that are dangerous to small, open boats and deserve respect and a firm hand on the helm as even large boats can be shoved around.

It is much safer to transit Hell Gate at slack water, if possible, when the only real danger is meeting a large commercial vessel or tug with a barge and getting in the way. Avoid this by using VHF Channel 13 to communicate with the vessel and keeping your eyes open ahead and astern.

NOTE: Information needed to transit the East River is often incorporated in electronic charting software as tide and tidal current tables. However, NOAA Tides and Currents offers online charts, if needed, at www.tidesandcurrents.noaa.gov.

The object of the westward passage through the East River is to arrive at Hell Gate no less than 2 hours but up to 3 hours after high water at The Battery. The westward-bound recreational boat heading down the East River toward The Battery should try to pass under the Throgs Neck Bridge at or slightly before high tide at the bridge. By arriving at the bridge at this time, mariners can time their passage under the bridge to hit the current as it begins to ebb westward.

Smaller (and slower) vessels may wish to arrive at the Battery 1 hour after low tide when traveling eastward and up to 1 hour before high tide at the bridge when traveling westward. The relatively modest adverse current at the eastern end of the East River at that time should result in a slower but more subdued ride through Hell Gate.

Pass under the high-level **Robert F. Kennedy Bridge** (also known as the Triboro Bridge) with 138-foot fixed vertical clearance and the adjacent **Hell Gate Railroad Bridge** (134-foot fixed vertical clearance) then leave Wards Island and Randalls Island to port. Don't worry if your depth sounder jumps erratically at Hell Gate since the bottom ranges from 34 feet to 107 feet then to 59 feet within a few hundred yards, creating whirlpools on the surface. You have passed safely through Hell Gate when you reach Lawrence Point at green lighted buoy "13."

The main ship channel goes north of North Brother Island, but yachts can easily pass through the shorter, more direct channel between it and South Brother Island (minimum depth 25 feet MLW). Just stay clear of off-channel shoals, rocks and ledges and observe the buoys, keeping green markers to starboard, red to port, as you are now headed out to sea. Channels leading south from here have their own buoy systems so do not confuse these with those on the East River's west-east route to Long Island Sound.

Across the East River from College Point is the mouth of the commercial Bronx River, separated from the mouth of Westchester Creek by Clason Point. Westchester Creek has a dredged and marked channel with sales and repair available at the mouth and small-craft service upstream. From Old Ferry Point, the high-level

Bronx-Whitestone Bridge (130-foot fixed vertical clearance) crosses overhead.

Just to the east, the long sweep of the **Throgs Neck Bridge** (152-foot fixed vertical clearance), generally accepted as the demarcation line between the East River and Long Island Sound, runs from the peninsula to just above Willets Point. At this point, the shoreline begins to look less urban and Long Island Sound lies ahead.

On a historical note, both Throgs Neck and Willets Point are strategic locations where fortifications were built in the early 19th century to protect New York City from attack. Granite-walled Fort Totten is at Willets Point. Fort Schuyler on Throgs Neck now houses the SUNY Maritime Academy. The academy's school ship, a converted Navy transport usually berthed nearby when not underway, is where cadets learn merchant service skills.

Dockage: Metro Marine on Westchester Creek (the Bronx) has slips to 50 feet. You will have to navigate several bridges to get there including **Cross Bronx Exwy (I 295) Bridge**, **Bruckner Exwy. (I-278) Bridge** and **Cross Bronx Exwy. Bridge** (all with 52-foot fixed vertical clearance) and the bascule **Bruckner Blvd./Unionport Bridge**.

Bruckner Blvd./Unionport Bridge has 14-foot vertical clearance and opens on signal if at least a two-hour advance notice is given to the New York City Department of Transportation (NYCDOT) radio hotline, or the NYCDOT Bridge Operations Office. The draw need not be opened for vessel traffic from 7:00 a.m. to 9:00 a.m. and 4:00 p.m. to 6:00 p.m., Monday through Friday. This is close to a NY Public Library and a medical center, as well as other amenities.

Side Trip: Flushing Bay

Flushing Bay is an excellent base from which to visit the New York City or to change crews arriving or departing from New York's two major airports. The proximity of LaGuardia Airport on the west side of Flushing Bay will make itself immediately evident to boat-borne visitors and John F. Kennedy International Airport (also in the borough of Queens) is not far. A subway stop is also nearby for an inexpensive and inevitably colorful transit to Manhattan.

Closer at hand, the Flushing shopping district is a cab ride away, where a full range of shopping and restaurant possibilities are available within a few blocks. Shea Stadium, home of the Mets, is about a 15-minute walk.

East River, NY

FLUSHING BAY		Largest Vessel	VHF	Total Slips	Approach/Dockside Depth	Floating Docks	Gas/Diesel	Repairs/Haulout	Min/Max Amps	Pump-Out Station
1. Arrow Yacht Club-PRIVATE	(718) 359-9229	33	18		5.0 / 4.0	F				
2. Williamsburgh Yacht Club-PRIVATE WiFi	(718) 359-2090	39			5.0 / 5.0				30	

WiFi Wireless Internet Access
Visit www.waterwayguide.com for current rates, fuel prices, website addresses and other up-to-the-minute information.
(Information in the table is provided by the facilities.)

Scan here for more details:

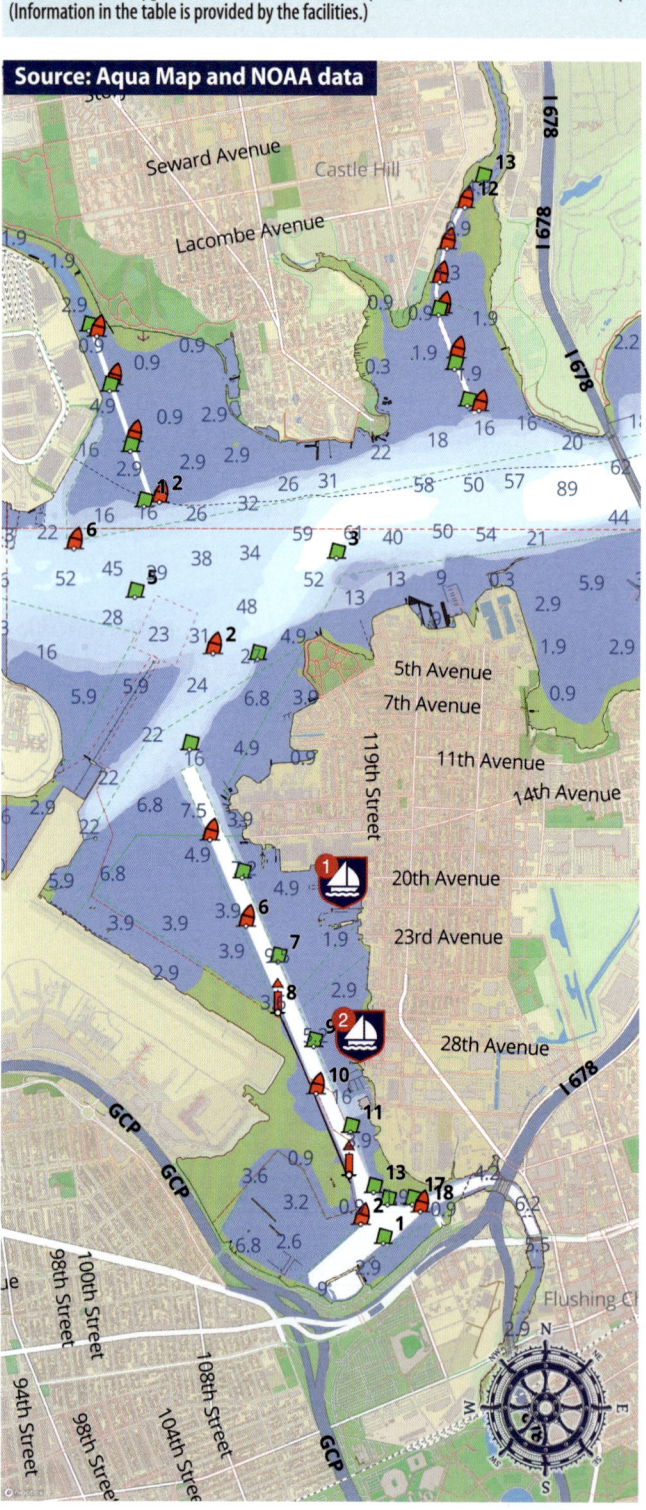

Source: Aqua Map and NOAA data

NOTE: On the way to Flushing Bay, you will pass 413.17-acre Rikers Island. The island is home to one of the world's largest correctional institutions and mental institutions and New York's most famous jail. This is an inhospitable place for those without official business so observe from a distance.

NAVIGATION: Flushing Bay offers good protection, a well-marked channel and ample anchorage room for those drawing 5 feet or less. Prevailing water depths of 4 to 5 feet MLW and a lack of marinas will discourage vessels with deeper keels. When headed south, Flushing Bay is a good place to wait out the slack tide just before the southerly flow at Hell Gate and the East River.

CAUTION: En route to Flushing Bay, you will pass LaGuardia Airport. Remember that you may not travel within 100 yards of any shore adjacent to the airport.

Dockage: There are a couple of yacht clubs in Flushing Bay, including the private Arrow Yacht Club and Williamsburg Yacht Club, which may have space for you but do call ahead.

Due to a major planned reconstruction project, Pier 1 at the World's Fair Marina is currently closed. Limited transient dockage is available for smaller recreational vessels. Please contact the Dockmasters office at 718-478-0480 or VHF Channel 71 for more information. There is no dockage available for larger vessels or commercial vessels, including passenger pick-up and drop-off. Please check back with the marina for updates.

Anchorage: You may be able to find a spot in the basin at the south end of Flushing Bay but a better bet is Big Rock Beach to the north, which offers 5-foot depths and a small beach with shore access. A gas station and bus to the city are nearby.

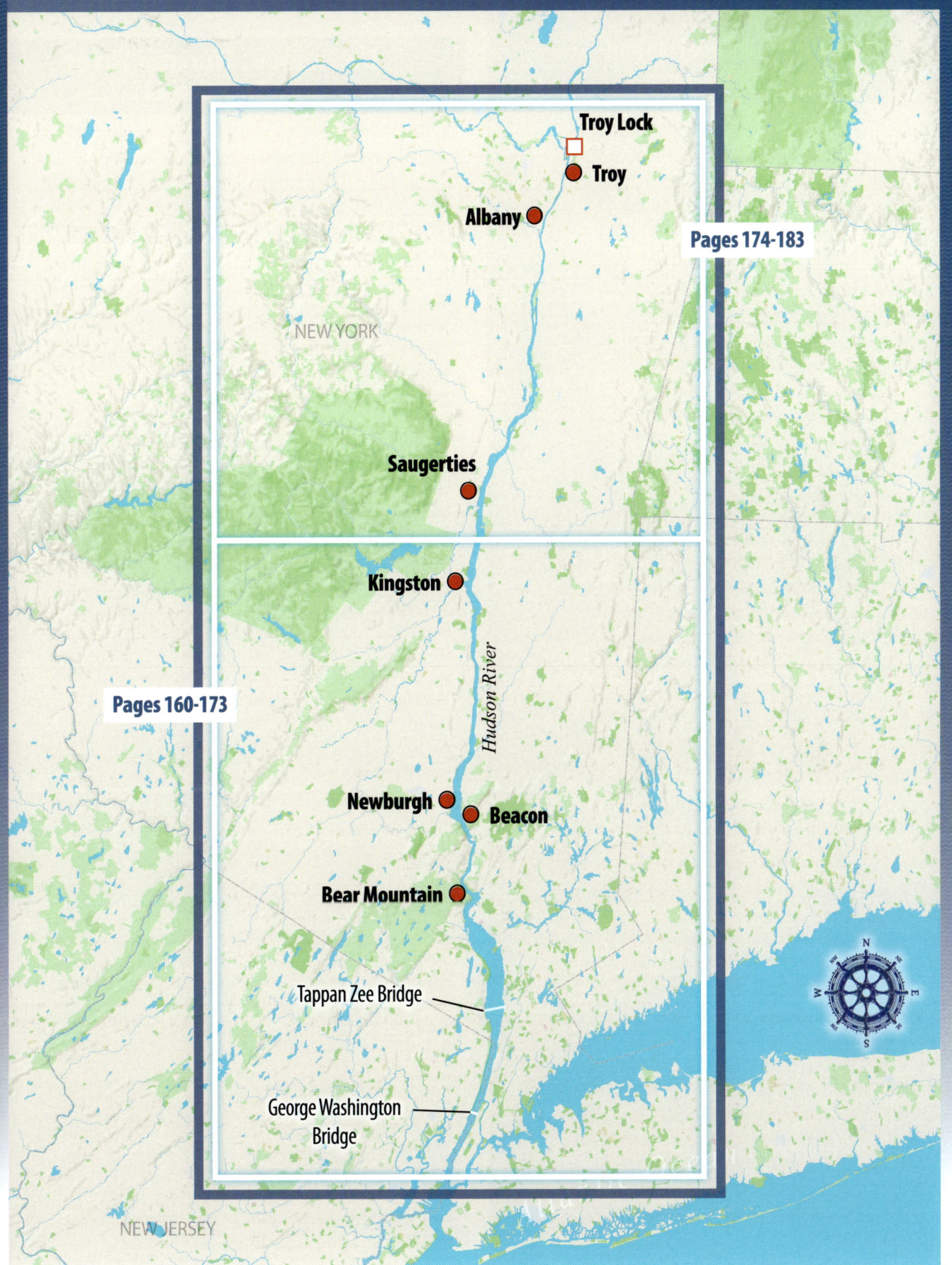

The New York Canal System Important Resources

Before starting your trip, be sure to sign up for *Canal Alerts to Mariners* for up-to-the-minute information on water levels, closures or restrictions on docking due to events at www.canals.ny.gov/boating/index.html. On the NY Canal System Corp. website you will also find:

- Hours of operation
- Tolls, passes and permits
- Canal map
- Speed limits
- Navigation information
- Lock, lift and guard gate listings
- Bridge heights
- Marinas and public docks
- Lodging options

The NY Canal Corporation recommends that boaters carry the latest edition of NOAA Chart 14786. This charts may be downloaded from NOAA (www.charts.noaa.gov/OnLineViewer/14786.shtml). There are no NOAA charts available between Mile 222 and 337 of the Erie Canal (including the Genesee River).

Along with this guide, there are two other resources we recommend you keep on hand:

1. *Cruising The New York Canal System*, a Skipper Bob publication

2. *Cruising Guide to the New York State Canal System*, published by the NY State Canal Corp. (outdated but full of useful information)

Another "must have" is the online Waterway Explorer, a free interactive web application for navigating the canal system. Specific marina and anchorage information can be found as well as details on bridges and locks. The site provides the ability to make updates, report hazards and read or write reviews on facilities. To help other boaters, please take a moment to enter a rating and add any updates when you visit a marina or anchorage. You can also sign up for weekly news and navigation updates, delivered directly to your inbox. Visit www.waterwayguide.com.

Distances: Hudson River and Erie Canal

From the Hudson River's mouth, this table gives distances as you travel north up the Hudson River and west along the Erie Canal. Table courtesy of the Village of Fairport, NY.

LOCATION	MILES	LOCATION	MILES
New York City/Piers 5 & 6	1	Lock 22	279
Yonkers	18	Sylvan Beach	284
Newburgh	61	Cleveland	293
Poughkeepsie	76	Constantia	299
Kingston	92	Brewerton	305
Albany	145	Lock 23	308
Troy	150	Three River Point	
Troy Lock	152	(Oswego Jct.)	315
Cohoes	154	Baldwinsville/Lock 24	327
Waterford/Lock 2	155	Syracuse	328
Lock 3	155.5	Cayuga/Seneca Canal Jct.	356
Lock 4	156	Lock 25	357.5
Locks 5 & 6	156.5	Lock 26	363
Crescent	159	Clyde	365.5
Lock 7	167	Lyons/Lock 27	375
Schenectady	176	Lock 28A	376.5
Lock 8	178	Lock 28B	380.5
Lock 9	183	Newark	381
Lock 10	189	Palmyra/Lock 29	390
Amsterdam	192	Macedon/Lock 30	393
Lock 11	193	Fairport	401
Lock 12	198	Pittsford	407.5
Fultonville (Fonda Terminal)	203	Lock 32	410
Lock 13	208	Lock 33	411
Canajoharie	215	Genesee River	411.5
Lock 14	215.5	Rochester	418
Fort Plain	218	Spencerport	425
Lock 15	219	Adams Basin	428
St. Johnsville	224	Brockport	433
Lock 16	225	Holley	438
Lock 17	233	Hulberton	441
Little Falls	234.5	Albion	447
Lock 18	237	Eagle Harbor	451
Herkimer	242	Knowlesville	454
Ilion	244	Medina	458
Frankfort	246	Middleport	463
Lock 19	250	Gasport	468
Utica Jct. Lock	256	Lockport/Locks 34 & 35	474
Utica Terminal	257	Pendleton	481.5
Lock 20	260	Martinsville	488
Rome	269	Tonawanda	492
New London Jct. Lock	276	Buffalo, Erie Basin	505
Lock 21	278		

NAVIGATION NOTES

The Hudson River Valley is emerging as a haven for city refugees who want the culture without the noise and crowds of the city. Many of the riverside towns are being transformed from industrial centers to New York City suburbs. On the upper river, creeks (both natural and dredged) make protected layovers.

Cruising Conditions

Cruising the Hudson River is generally straightforward. Aids to navigation are plentiful, mid-channel depths range from 15 feet to 175 feet and marinas and hospitable yacht clubs are numerous north of Manhattan. Overnight berths should be selected for maximum protection from the river's natural chop and the wake from passing recreational and commercial traffic. On the upper river, creeks (both natural and dredged) can make for good, protected layover spots.

> NOTE: It should be noted that many of the marine facilities that list or advertise themselves as "clubs" are perfectly acceptable stopovers that are not limited to members.

The route upriver is easily navigated for 91 miles to Kingston but extensive middle grounds and steep-to shoals must be given a wide berth after this point. In the lower Hudson River, rocky shoals are common off the channel and departure from the marked route must be made with caution and local knowledge. Above Kingston the bottom is mostly sandy with some mud and grass and few rocks.

The few hazards consist mainly of debris–both floating and submerged—and fish traps (in the spring). In the Albany/Troy area, just as in New York Harbor, drifting debris calls for an endless watch, particularly at a tide change and during the spring run-off.

Commercial traffic can be heavy at times with barge activity and should be given full right-of-way, especially in periods of poor visibility. It is generally best to communicate with any commercial vessels on VHF Channel 13.

Tidal Currents

Tidal water extends to Troy, where the mean tidal range varies from 3 to 5 feet and currents can be strong (an average of 1.5 knots as far north as Albany). When you are northbound, you will be going away from the tidal current change so you can hold a fair current longer than you will when southbound. The 153-mile Hudson estuary has two high and two low tides in 24 hours. With the rise and fall come changes in the direction of the flow. A rising tide is accompanied by a flood current flowing north towards Troy, and a falling tide by an ebb current flowing seaward. For this passage, skippers should have a copy of the latest tide and tidal current tables aboard. These can be downloaded from NOAA Tides & Currents (www.tidesandcurrents.noaa.gov).

In the tidal portion of the Hudson River, select your marina slip with great care. You will want to avoid slips that are in the cross current as maneuvering into or out of the slip may be difficult. You will also want to ensure that the marina is equipped with proper fendering to minimize damage to your boat.

Weather

The wind usually blows up or down the Hudson River, but near shore it tends to sweep toward the banks. Watch for summer squalls with sudden winds of up to 30 knots. Your only warning might be black clouds along the high west-bank bluffs. Get to the weather side of the river whenever you see indications of rough conditions ahead.

New York Bay / Hudson River Distances

Nautical Miles (approximate) from Sandy Hook

LOCATION	MILE
NEW YORK BAY	
Sandy Hook Channel Light "15"	0
Ambrose	8.6
Rockaway Point	5.2
Great Kills Harbor, Crookes Point	6.5
Coney Island, Norton Point	6.0
Verrazano Narrows Bridge	7.8
The Battery	14.0
HUDSON RIVER	
George Washington Bridge	24
Harlem River	26
Tarrytown	39
Grassy Point	49
EAST RIVER	
Brooklyn Bridge	14.5
Hell Gate, Hallets Point	20
Whitestone Bridge	25
Throgs Neck Bridge	26
Execution Rocks	31

Navigation

Charts might not accurately show some privately maintained markers and some markers have been discontinued, while others might not have been replaced after winter ice.

We do not recommend that you head upriver on the Hudson River without the necessary charts. Be sure to download into your navigation system the necessary Hudson River charts. Only a limited number of marinas carry charts of the river. One marina that often carries the river charts is Liberty Landing Marina in Jersey City (201-985-8000). Contact them before you leave New York Harbor or access electronic charts. Also consult the Local Notice to Mariners (www.navcen.uscg.gov) and Waterway Explorer (www.waterwayguide.com) for alerts and updates.

■ GEORGE WASHINGTON BRIDGE TO KINGSTON

From New York Harbor to the Federal Dam at Troy, the Hudson River is measured in river miles. Mile 0 is located at the Battery at the southern tip of Manhattan Island.

NOTE: The lower Hudson River is discussed in Chapter 4: "New York Harbor & the East River."

George Washington Bridge to Tappan Zee Bridge– Mile 11.5 to Mile 27

The George Washington Bridge (213-foot vertical clearance) opened in 1931 during the Great Depression. It was not until 30 years later that the lower, second deck (fondly known as the "Martha Washington Bridge") was added. To the north is Spuyten Duyvil (pronounced "spite-en die-vil"), the northern part of the Harlem River. This is on the route followed by the famous Circle Line (www.circleline.com) sightseeing boats during their scenic circumnavigations of the island of Manhattan.

George Washington Bridge

Washington Heights, NYC

Hudson River

Fort Lee Park, NJ

Hudson River, NJ

EDGEWATER		Largest Vessel	VHF	Total Slips	Approach/ Dockside Depth	Floating Docks	Gas/ Diesel	Repairs/ Haulout	Min/Max Amps	Pump-Out Station
1. Edgewater Marina 9.7 RDB	(201) 944-2628	60	16	85	20.0 / 6.0	F		RH	30 / 50	
ALPINE AREA										
2. Dyckman Marina	(212) 304-0183	150	78	22	15.0 / 15.0	F			30 / 50	
3. Alpine Marina 18.0 RDB	(201) 985-6580	300	9	125	30.0 / 22.0	F	GD		30 / 200+	P

WiFi Wireless Internet Access
Visit www.waterwayguide.com for current rates, fuel prices, website addresses and other up-to-the-minute information.
(Information in the table is provided by the facilities.)

Scan here for more details:

For those who are looking for something different, you can try going up the East River instead of the Hudson, going by the United Nations and Gracie Mansion, the residence of the Mayor of New York and turn off into the Harlem River just before Hell Gate. If you go up the East River at flood tide, you will be hit with a small penalty transiting the Harlem River and the 15 bridges you will go under. Make sure your air draft is less than 22 feet if you want to avoid any dealings with local authorities. The only opening you will need is at the **Spuyten Duyvil Railroad Bridge** as you enter the Hudson. The swing bridge operators are very responsive and will open on request as long as there is not a train coming from or going to Penn Station.

Piermont Pier, the prominent 1-mile-long point just north of the state border, was the terminus of the Erie Railroad tracks until 1850. During that era, this spot was a major rail and ship cargo transfer point. Piermont is a delightful waterfront village with a marina, waterfront restaurants and an upscale shopping plaza. Unfortunately, the shallow approach is not marked and access requires local knowledge. Pete Seegar's famous replica of a North River sloop, *Clearwater*, can frequently be spotted at the end of the pier.

NOTE: In 1966, folk music legend Pete Seeger announced plans to "build a boat to save the river." Seeger believed that a replica of the sloops that sailed the Hudson River in the 18th and 19th centuries would encourage people to preserve the integrity of the river. In 1969, the 106-foot sloop *Clearwater* was launched at Gamage Shipyard in South Bristol, Maine. On her maiden voyage she sailed to South Street Seaport in New York City and then ultimately made her home on the Hudson River, where she has made a remarkable impact in the environmental movement. Read more at www.clearwater.org.

The aura of the New York metropolis quickly dissipates beyond the **George Washington Bridge** (213-foot vertical clearance). The tall backdrop contrasts

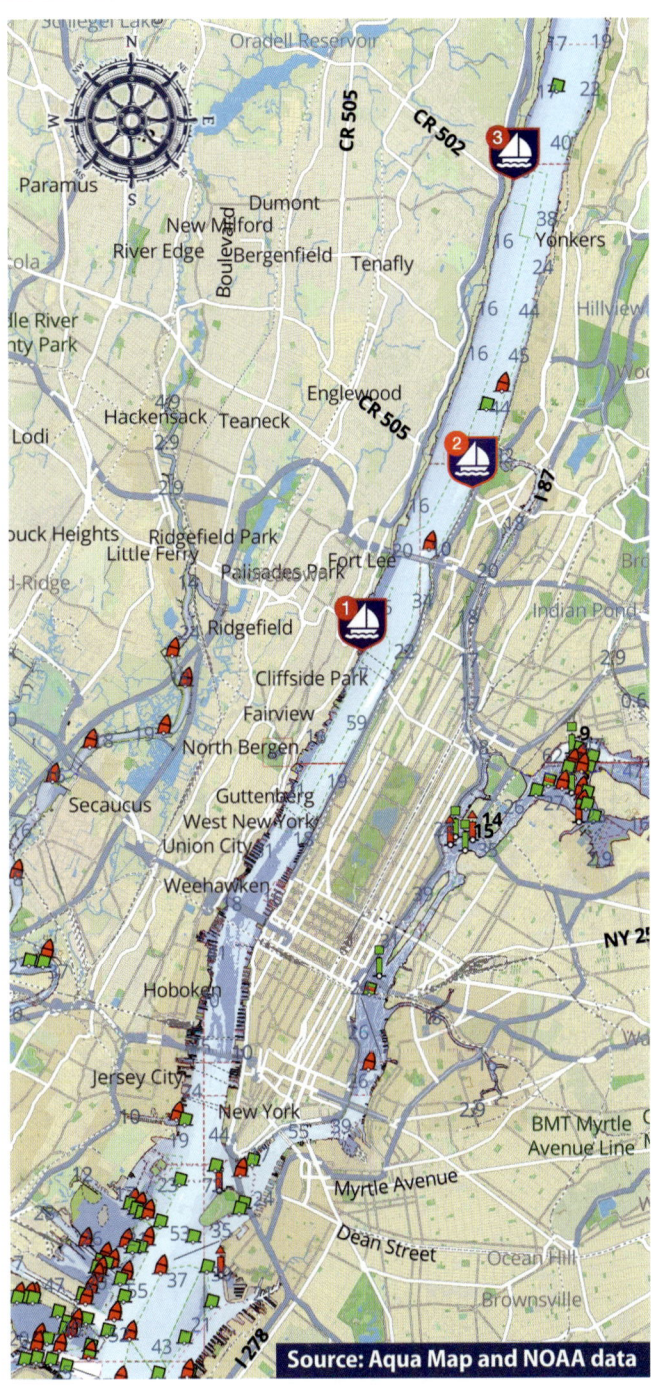

Source: Aqua Map and NOAA data

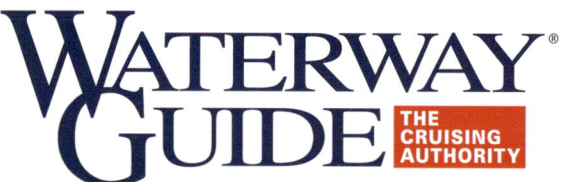
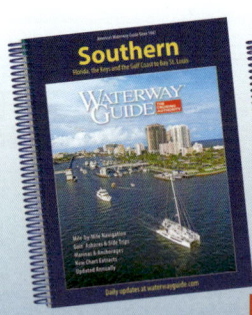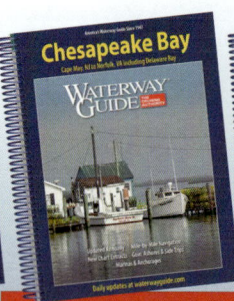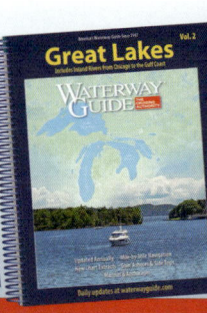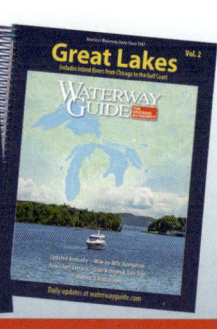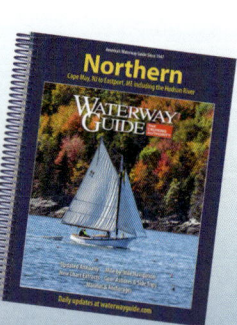
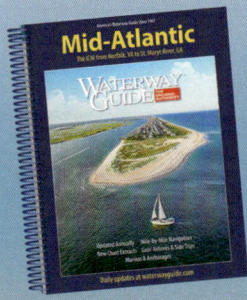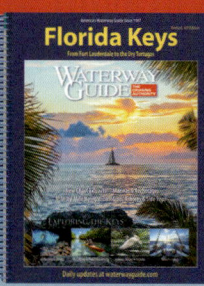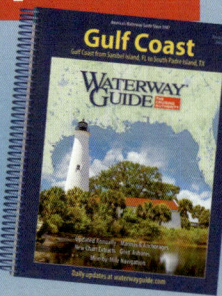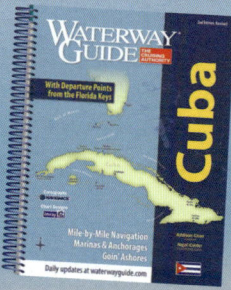
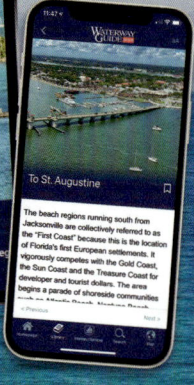

Tappan Zee Bridge

Tarrytown Lighthouse

sharply with the 300- to 500-foot thickly wooded Palisades. This striking series of cliffs (composed of columnar basalt) is named for its visual similarity to old, wooden, barrier fortifications.

Opposite Hastings-on-Hudson is the New Jersey-New York border. From this point to its headwaters in the Adirondack Mountains, the Hudson River flows entirely within New York State.

The **Tappan Zee Bridge** (139-foot vertical clearance) carries the New York State Thruway, an important interstate highway linking New York City to Albany and Buffalo.

Dockage/Moorings: Edgewater Marina, located about 2 miles south of the bridge, only has seasonal slips. A better bet is the municipal Dyckman Marina with 22 (all transient) slips and moorings to 150 feet. They have hourly and daily rates as well and offer full amenities.

Alpine Marina completed a multi-million dollar renovation in 2022 that included slip dredging and installation of new floating docks. Note that shallows and the ruins of old piers in the Hastings-on-the Hudson and Dobbs Ferry area can make parts of this shore difficult to approach closely. Any facilities you see here are likely small, local operations.

Anchorage: On the east side of the river north of George Washington Bridge at Hudson Park you will find 15 feet MLW about 200 feet from the shoreline with good holding in mud. If the wind is right, you can find a number of suitable anchorages close to shore at the base of the cliffs on the west side of the Hudson River including Hudson Palisades. You are still in New York City and you can see the skyscrapers through the central span of the bridge, but you are anchored just off cliffs several hundred feet high with no obvious human occupation. Sunset and

the city skyline in the evening are quite special.

If you anchor here, prepare to be rolled during the night by some large wakes from an occasional tow. You might want to consider lashing gear down securely before retiring for the evening. If you get ashore with your dinghy, tie to a rock. Watch for low tide as the little beach is 400 feet long and about 2 feet depth. Current is about 3 knots during high tide.

Tappan Zee Bridge to Bear Mountain–Mile 27 to Mile 46.7

NAVIGATION: Just north of the Tappan Zee Bridge on the east bank is Tarrytown. Tarrytown offers easy access and good provisioning. The quaint, pretty Main Street has emerged as a minor nightlife center. The restored Tarrytown Music Hall is a centerpiece to this activity. This area is about a 20-minute uphill walk from the water.

Bear Mountain Bridge

Across the river (west side) is labeled as Nyack on the NOAA chart but the center of town is about 1 mile away. This vibrant small town, known as the "Gem of the Hudson," is a center for the arts. In addition to its grand Victorian homes and many antiques shops, it offers a number of fine restaurants and a thriving nightlife. Groceries and one of the nation's largest malls (Palisades Center, off Hwy. 87) are only a short cab ride away.

Ossining on the eastern bank of the Hudson River was originally named Sing Sing, the same as the famous, sprawling hillside prison located here. A boycott of prison-made goods at the turn of the century led the town to change its name to Ossining so buyers could distinguish between goods made in the town from those made at the prison.

From Hook Mountain to Haverstraw, the west bank of the Hudson River rises more than 800 feet. Haverstraw Bay, northwest of Croton Point, is the widest part of the Hudson River at 3 nm across. The town of Haverstraw is nestled between the cliffs of High Tor to the west and the Hudson River.

Around the bend of the river on the east side is the Indian Point Nuclear Power Plant. (Note that dockage is not allowed here.) One mile beyond the southern part of the U-shaped channel of Peekskill is marked with buoys and a light. The National Maritime Historical Society (914-737-7878) is located next to the Charles Point Marina in Peekskill. The maritime art gallery and an extensive information center of maritime history are open daily including weekends.

Across the Hudson River is densely forested Dunderberg Mountain, which marks the southern limit of the Highland section of the river. For the next 10 miles, the river cuts through the Appalachian mountain chain and is one of the most beautiful stretches of river scenery in the country.

> NOTE: The 1,000-foot-tall Dunderberg Mountain is the legendary dwelling of the Dutch goblin held responsible for summer storms.

Between Dunderberg and Bear Mountain is Iona Island, a former Navy Depot. There is a conspicuous skeleton tower on the north side of the island. The narrow section of the river between Iona Island and the eastern shore is known as The Race. The swiftest current on the Hudson River runs here. The island was the site of a navy arsenal from 1900 until after World War II and some fences and buildings still remain. Beginning as early as March, this stretch of the river is one of the most prolific striped bass fisheries on the East Coast.

A mile or two north of Dunderberg Mountain is Bear Mountain, the site of the huge Bear Mountain State Park. All but the tour boat dock is hidden from view by the dense mountain foliage so most boaters cruising this way are unaware of the park's existence. Now that you know about it, do not pass it by.

The path from the dinghy dock leads past an immense public swimming pool nestled in a mountain gully. Farther on is a trailway museum and a zoo, home of a fine collection of Hudson Valley animals and birds. Beyond is a mountain lake with scores of rental boats. Finally, you will arrive at the wonderful old Bear Mountain Inn. This area attracts busloads of city folk on weekends.

It is here that you and your crew may first encounter the white swans, known as mute swans (an introduced species), often seen paddling leisurely around the river coves as far north as Catskill. Keeping a count of the number you have spotted can be a challenging pastime, particularly for the younger members of the crew.

The **Bear Mountain Bridge** (155-foot vertical clearance), at the time of its completion in 1924, was the world's largest suspension bridge. In addition to carrying highway traffic, it also serves as the Hudson River crossing for the famous Maine-to-Georgia Appalachian Trail.

> NOTE: During the Revolutionary War, the Americans stretched a huge chain across the Hudson River just north of the Bear Mountain Bridge site to prevent British warships from passing. Unfortunately, the British seized the chain (sending it to Gibraltar to protect their own harbor) and then sailed up the river and burned the town of Kingston.

Hudson River, NY

TAPPAN ZEE AREA		Largest Vessel	VHF	Total Slips	Approach/ Dockside Depth	Floating Docks	Gas/ Diesel	Repairs/ Haulout	Min/Max Amps	Pump-Out Station
1. Tappan Zee Marina 25.2 RDB	(845) 359-5522	35		75	/	F	G	RH	30	
2. Washington Irving Boat Club-PRIVATE 27.0 LDB	(914) 332-0517	32		100	6.0 / 3.0	F		H		
3. Tarrytown Boat & Yacht Club-PRIVATE WiFi 27.2 LDB	(914) 631-1300	70	16	100	6.0 / 4.0	F		H	30	P
4. Nyack Marina 28.8 RDB	(845) 358-3851			40	/ 3.0	F			30	
5. Nyack Boat Club - PRIVATE WiFi	(845) 353-0395	50	9		6.0 / 6.0	F				
OSSINING										
6. Westerly Marina WiFi 33.5 LDB	(914) 941-2203	100	68	180	8.0 / 6.0	F	GD	RH	30 / 50	P
7. Shattemuc Yacht Club - PRIVATE WiFi 33.5 LDB	(914) 941-8777	65	16	125	7.0 / 7.5	F		H	30 / 50	P

WiFi Wireless Internet Access
Visit www.waterwayguide.com for current rates, fuel prices, website addresses and other up-to-the-minute information.
(Information in the table is provided by the facilities.)

Scan here for more details:

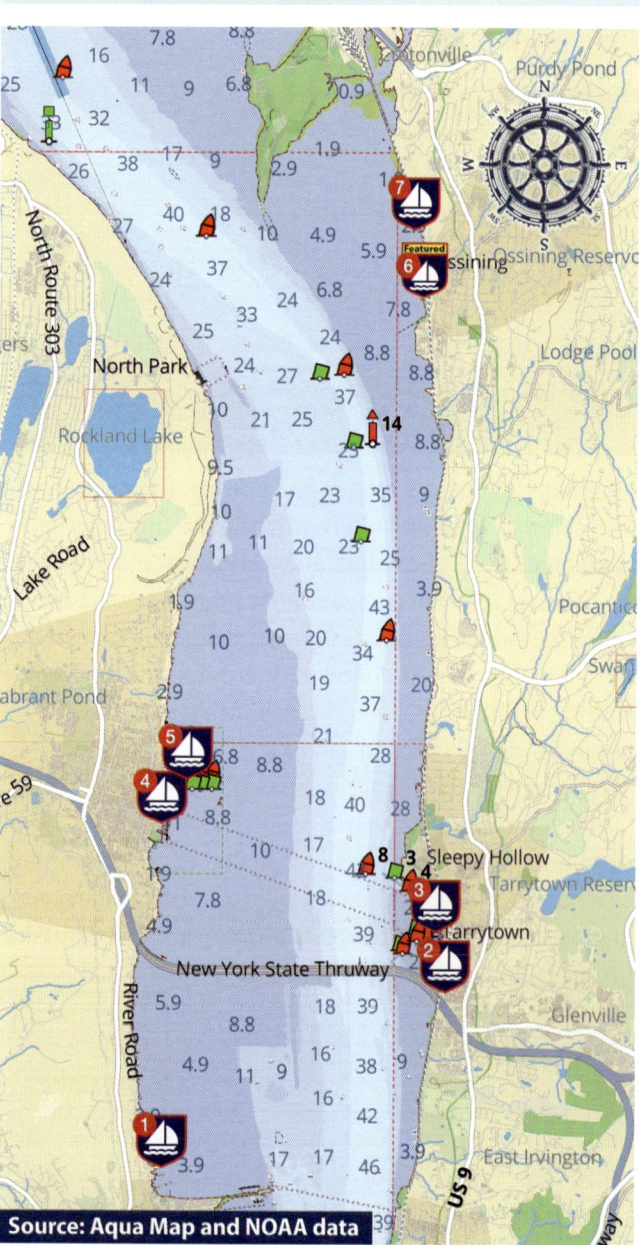

Source: Aqua Map and NOAA data

Dockage/Moorings: Tappan Zee Marina at Piermont (south of Tappan Zee Bridge) can accommodate boats to 35 feet. Call ahead for directions due to the shallow approach depths. Just north of the bridge, two private boat clubs (Washington Irving Boat Club and Tarrytown Boat & Yacht Club) are on the Tarrytown (eastern) side. The channel is well marked. Both have limited guest slips.

Across the river, the village-owned and -operated Nyack Marina can accommodate 43 small and mid-sized boats including transients. Nyack Boat Club is private but will let you take up an available mooring (with launch service) if you call ahead.

At Ossining to the north, you will find the family-oriented Westerly Marina, a boat yard with some rental slips that has been in operation since 1959. The well-respected Shattemuc Yacht Club is private but offers ample transient dockage and/or moorings. They are the oldest yacht club on the Hudson River.

The 173-slip Half Moon Bay Marina in nearby Croton-on-Hudson welcomes transients in protected transient slips with 10-foot MLW depths for vessels up to 165 feet. The adjacent Croton Point Park has a sheltered cove for swimming and sandy beaches, train service to and from Manhattan and car rentals within walking distance of the marina. This is a cruiser favorite that receives high marks for customer service. The 60-acre Safe Harbor Haverstraw is located south of Grassy Point on the western shore with slips and full amenities.

To the north at Grassy Point are a diesel fuel dock (Panco Petroleum Stony Point Terminal) and Minisceongo Yacht Club, which is private but accepts transients. Call ahead. Just to the north of Grassy Point in Stony

Hudson River, NY

CROTON-ON-HUDSON		Largest Vessel	VHF	Total Slips	Approach/ Dockside Depth	Floating Docks	Gas/ Diesel	Repairs/ Haulout	Min/Max Amps	Pump-Out Station
1. Half Moon Bay Marina WiFi 35.7 LDB	**(914) 271-5400**	165	9	173	10.0 / 10.0	F		R	30 / 50	P
STONY POINT AREA										
2. Safe Harbor Haverstraw WiFi 40.0 RDB	(845) 429-2001	110	9	900	8.0 / 8.0	F	GD	RH	30 / 50	P
3. Minisceongo Yacht Club-PRIVATE WiFi 40.8 RDB	(845) 786-8781	52	9	140	7.0 / 10.0	F		H	30 / 50	P
STONY POINT BAY										
4. Patsy's Bay Marina 41.0 RDB	(845) 786-5270	50	12	200	5.0 / 6.0	F		RH	30	
GREENS COVE										
5. Cortlandt Yacht Club WiFi 42.0 LDB	(914) 490-9796	53	16	162	7.0 / 7.0	F		H	15 / 50	P
6. Viking Boatyard WiFi 42.0 LDB	(914) 739-5090	50	9	180	5.0 / 5.0	F		RH	30	P
PEEKSKILL										
7. Charles Point Marina WiFi 44.8 LDB	(914) 736-6942	48		80	5.0 / 3.0	F		H	30 / 50	P
8. Peekskill Yacht Club-PRIVATE 45.0 LDB	(914) 737-9515	48	9	85	5.0 / 5.0			H	30	

WiFi Wireless Internet Access
Visit www.waterwayguide.com for current rates, fuel prices, website addresses and other up-to-the-minute information.
(Information in the table is provided by the facilities.)

Scan here for more details:

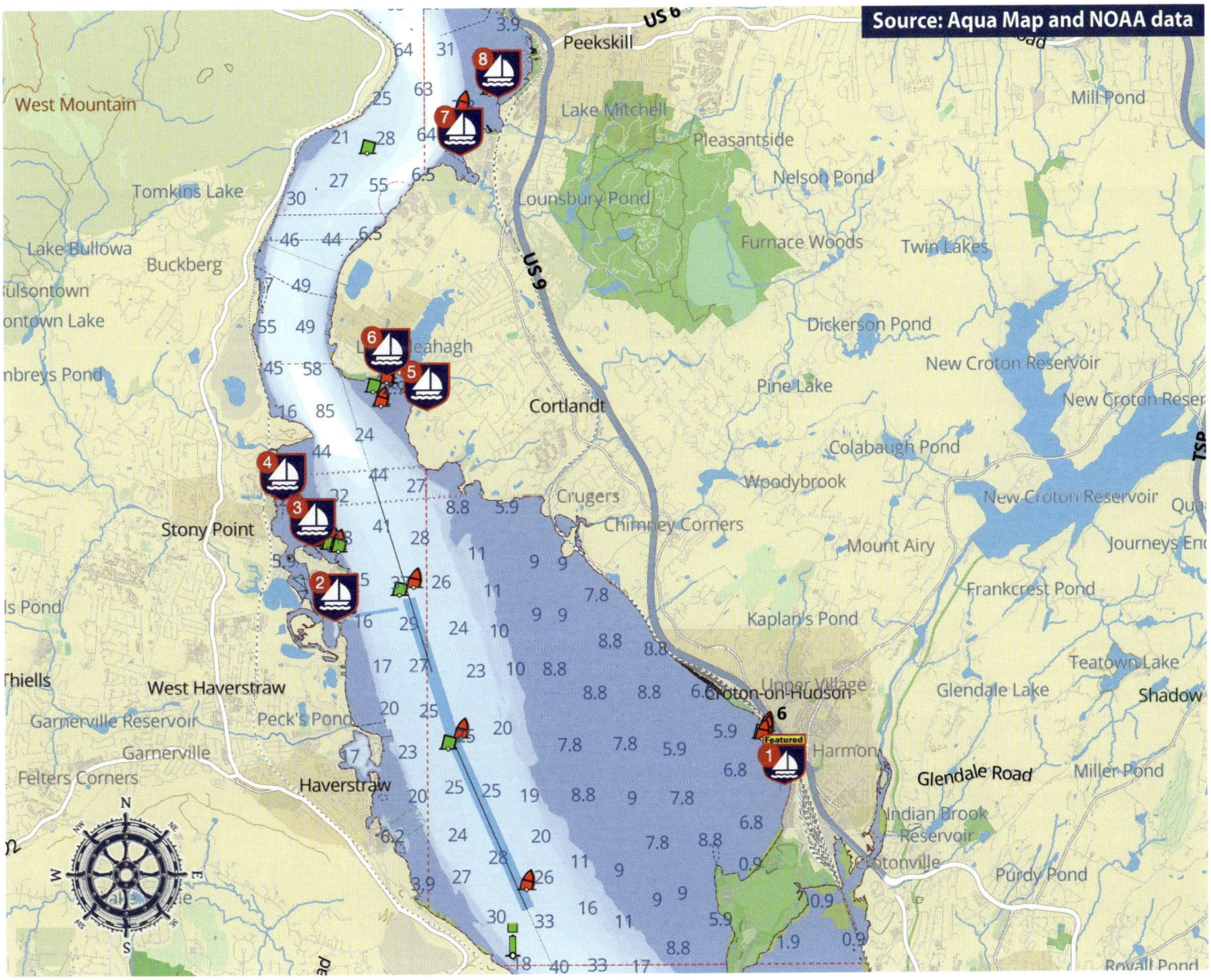

Source: Aqua Map and NOAA data

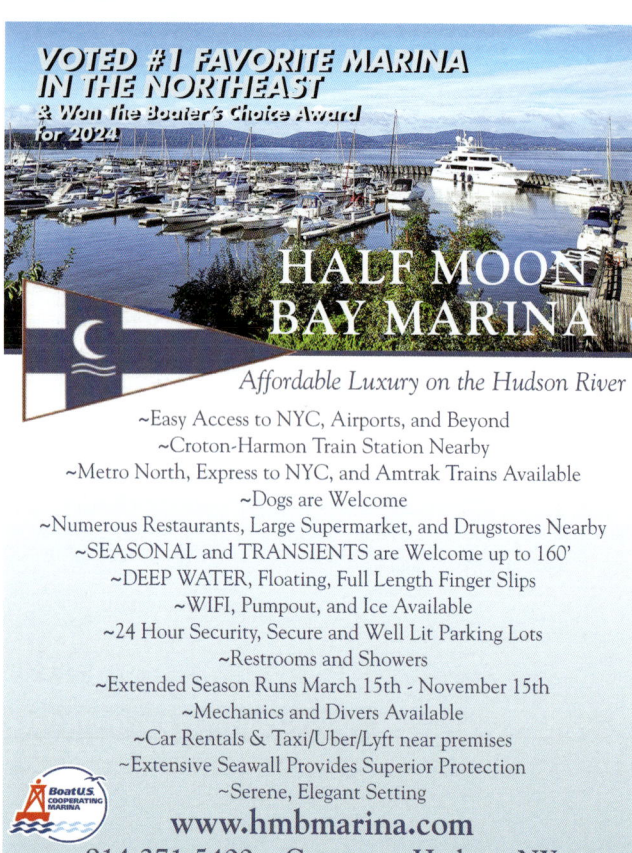
Point Bay is Patsy's Bay Marina, a boat brokerage with some transient slips.

Across the river in Green's Cove is the private Cortlandt Yacht Club, which will make room for you if needed. Viking Boatyard has slips to 50 feet and full amenities including free pump-out service.

The channel to the Charles Point Marina at Peekskill is marked but do call ahead for actual depths (reported as low as 3 feet MLW). Transient dockage is available with a restaurant and a brewery nearby. To the north at Travis Point, the private Peekskill Yacht Club offers courtesy dockage for members of reciprocal yacht clubs.

Anchorage: There is an anchorage at Nyack, northeast of the mooring field near the western shore. Here you will find 9 to 12 feet MLW and excellent holding in mud. It is open to all but the western quadrant. There is a public dock just south of the mooring field and north of a condo development. (Do not enter the private condo marina.) Shopping and restaurants are nearby. Directly across the river at Sleepy Hollow, you can anchor at Phillipse Manor Beach with protection from the west, if needed.

Peekskill, NY looking south over the Hudson River

It is possible to drop the hook off Ossining with good holding and enough water at low tide for a 6.5-foot draft vessel. This is not very protected and a ferry runs 100 feet away, but there is a dinghy dock at Westerly Marina for quick visits ashore.

Croton Point juts out into the river just north of Ossining and Croton Bay is one of the best anchorages on the river and is certainly the best between here and New York City (except in west to north winds). It has been reported that this anchorage is used by Nyack Boat Club, which offers transient moorings, limited launch service, showers and a dinghy dock. Do not shortcut the point when going in or you will find out that a shoal really does exist here.

On the north side of Croton Point there is southerly protection in front of Croton Point Park in 6 to 9 feet MLW. Although you can't take a motorized dinghy to the shore by the swimming area, you can beach the dinghy east of the area beyond the swimming signs. There is also a dinghy dock located at nearby Half Moon Bay Marina.

The anchorage across the river (west side) at Haverstraw Harbor offers 360-degree protection and is surrounded by either high hills or trees. Hug the south side of the narrow entrance channel. Some cruising boats anchor to the north of Stony Point in 14 to 19 feet MLW in south to west winds. Note that there are charted wrecks here so anchor with care.

South of Dunderburg Mountain there is an excellent anchorage in 13 to 20 feet MLW with excellent holding in mud. This provides protection from the west and north. Be certain to stay 300 yards off the Indian Point Nuclear Power Plant. Expect lots of train noise here.

To explore the striking mountainside park at Bear Mountain, anchor either in the bight between Iona Island and the tour boat dock just to the south of the Bear Mountain Bridge. Here you will find good depths and a mud bottom. The dinghy dock is behind the tour boat dock. Walk through the tunnel that passes under the railroad tracks and follow the path up the mountain. The view of your boat at anchor in the river below makes a great photo.

Hudson River, NY

STORM KING MOUNTAIN	Largest Vessel	VHF	Total Slips	Approach/ Dockside Depth	Floating Docks	Gas/ Diesel	Repairs/ Haulout	Min/Max Amps	Pump-Out Station
1. Cornwall Yacht Club - PRIVATE 📶 56.0 RDB	50	16	105	10.0 / 3.0	F		H	30 / 50	P

📶 **Wireless Internet Access**
Visit www.waterwayguide.com for current rates, fuel prices, website addresses and other up-to-the-minute information.
(Information in the table is provided by the facilities.)

Scan here for more details:

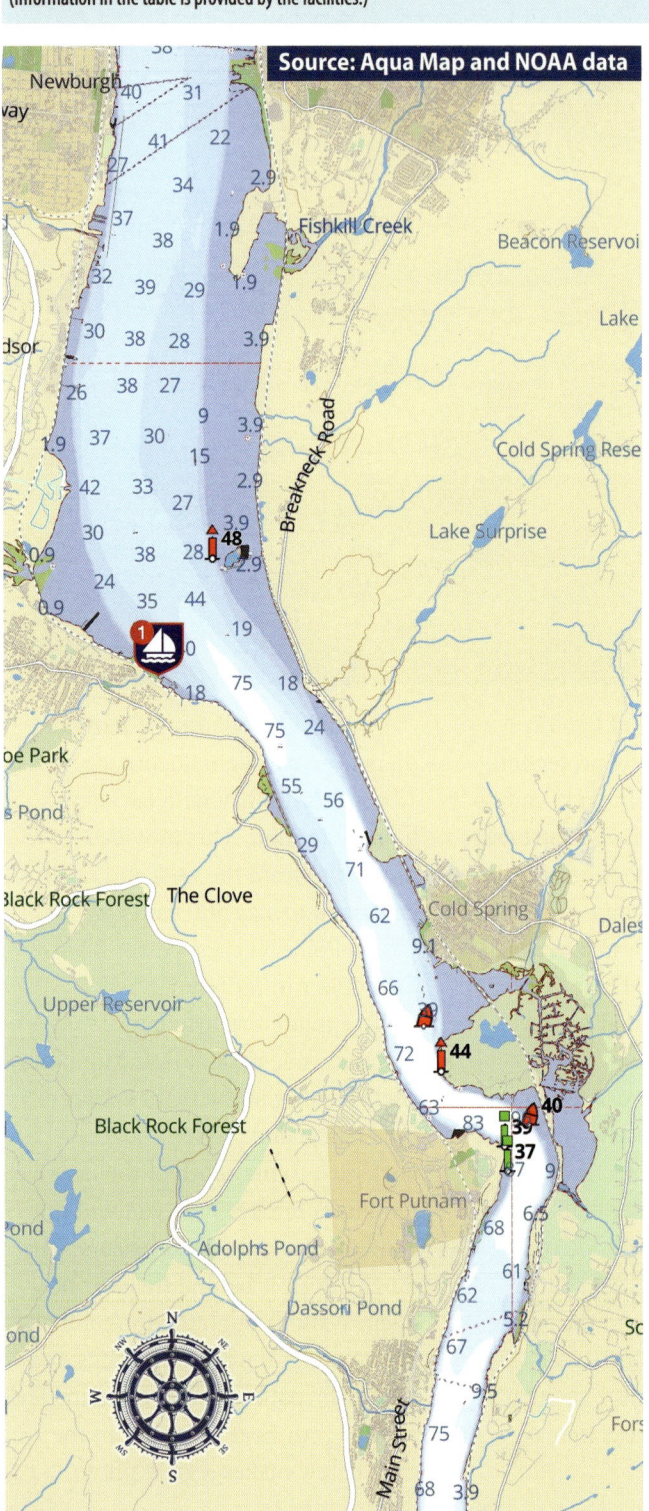

Source: Aqua Map and NOAA data

Side Trip: Visiting West Point

The historical Military Academy at West Point (circa 1802) is open for bus tours for a nominal fee. Tour hours are generally between 9:00 a.m. to 3:30 p.m. daily. The 1-hour tour makes stops at the Cadet Chapel, Trophy Point, Battle Monument and the Plain. You are off the bus approximately 50 minutes with minimal walking. Requests for tours should be made through West Point Tours.

The Frederic V. Malek West Point Visitors Center and Museum are open to the general public on a daily basis. The building is home to West Point Tours (www. westpointtours.com), the Visitors Control Center (VCC) and the Army West Point Gift Shop. All visitors need to process through the Visitors Center. See details at www. westpoint.edu/visitors or call 845-938-0390.

Dockage: Transient boaters are no longer allowed on West Point's docks due to security measures. Boaters are allowed to access South Dock for football games, where full security checks are required but dock space is limited (no overnight stays). Requests for football game dockage or passenger drop-off must be made in advance. The private Cornwall Yacht Club, approximately 5 miles away, is the closest west bank dockage. They welcome transients to 50 feet.

Anchorage: The closest anchorage is at Foundry Cove on Constitution Island on the east shore of the river. This is a quiet location with beautiful views and provides easy access to Cold Spring for provisioning.

Bear Mountain to Newburgh-Beacon Bridges— Mile 46.7 to Mile 62.1

NAVIGATION:

The narrow section of the river just north of the West Point Academy, designated as World's End, is the deepest section of the entire river (one spot charted at 175 feet deep). During the Revolutionary War, the Americans stretched another chain across the river at World's End but this was yet another vain effort.

> NOTE: Across the river is Foundry Cove, where foundries cast cannon and shot during the Civil War. This is where the first American iron warship (a revenue cutter) was built in the 1850s.

Pollepel Island, widely known as Bannerman's Island, is 4 nm north of West Point on the eastern shore. Between 1900 and 1918, munitions dealer Frank Bannerman built a replica of a medieval castle here as a summer resort and storehouse. In 1967, the state obtained the property and tours were conducted until the castle burned in 1969. Today, because of the deteriorating condition of the building, landing on the island is no longer permitted.

Four nautical miles north of Pollepel Island are the twin cities of Newburgh and Beacon. (Newburgh is on the west shore, and Beacon is on the east shore.) Despite being situated more than 60 miles inland, Newburgh was a 19th-century seaport and the home of whaling ships. George Washington's 1782 to 1783 headquarters, the Hasbrough House, still stands and is open to the public. Substantial waterfront development has sprung up in Newburgh during the last several years, mostly to accommodate local small craft.

Storm King Mountain to the south makes this a popular stop. The spectacular 1,355-foot peak rises above the western shore. The scenic highway that girds it was completed in 1940. There are several rental car agencies in Newburgh (and in West Point) should you wish to explore farther afield.

The first span of the **Newburgh-Beacon Bridges** (172-foot vertical clearance) when built replaced not only the last remaining ferry service across the Hudson River but also the oldest ferry in the U.S. It now consists of two fixed spanned highway bridges.

Dockage: Riverfront Marina Newburgh has 20 transient slips available to accommodate vessels up to 190 feet with full amenities. Dockside Boat Repairs is on site should you need them. The private Newburgh Yacht Club offers dockage for members of reciprocal yacht clubs.

Anchorage: You can find 8-foot to 11-foot MLW depths with excellent holding in mud behind Pollepel Island. Head close into shore at Breakneck Point and then carefully following the 7- to 10-foot MLW channel northward toward the island. It is somewhat exposed from the north and south but provides an interesting view of the ruins of the Bannerman Castle on Pollepel Island. (Landing on the island is not allowed.)

Newburgh-Beacon Bridges to Kingston— Mile 62.1 to Mile 91

The Hudson River continues to be deep and well marked but note that there are no cruising facilities or protected anchorages between Marlboro (Mile 84.6) and Poughkeepsie (Mile 78.1).

The **Mid-Hudson Suspension Bridge** (134-foot vertical clearance) at Mile 77.1 opened in 1930 and is one of the oldest bridges spanning the Hudson River. The massive 212-foot-high former railroad bridge has been in place for more than 100 years and once made Poughkeepsie an important railroad center. It is now a 1.28-mile pedestrian **Walkway Over The Hudson Bridge**.

The U.S. Military Academy at West Point

Hudson River, NY

NEWBURGH		Largest Vessel	VHF	Total Slips	Approach/ Dockside Depth	Floating Docks	Gas/ Diesel	Repairs/ Haulout	Min/Max Amps	Pump-Out Station
1. Riverfront Marina Newburgh (WiFi) 60.0 RDB	(845) 661-4914	200	16	120	8.0 / 7.0	F		R	50	P
2. Newburgh Yacht Club-PRIVATE (WiFi) 61.9 RDB	(845) 565-3920	60		120	5.5 / 4.0	F	GD	H	30 / 50	P
NEW HAMBURG AREA										
3. White's Hudson River Marina 68.2 LDB	(845) 297-8520	40		300	20.0 / 20.0	F	GD	RH	30	P
4. New Hamburg Yacht Club-PRIVATE 68.3 LDB	(845) 298-1707	42		86	25.0 / 60.0				20	
5. West Shore Marine 69.5 RDB	(845) 236-4486	60	16	180	12.0 / 12.0	F	GD	RH	30 / 50	
6. Marlboro Yacht Club (WiFi) 69.7 RDB	(845) 236-3932	60	68	82	20.0 / 15.0	F	G	H	30 / 50	P

(WiFi) Wireless Internet Access
Visit www.waterwayguide.com for current rates, fuel prices, website addresses and other up-to-the-minute information.
(Information in the table is provided by the facilities.)

Scan here for more details:

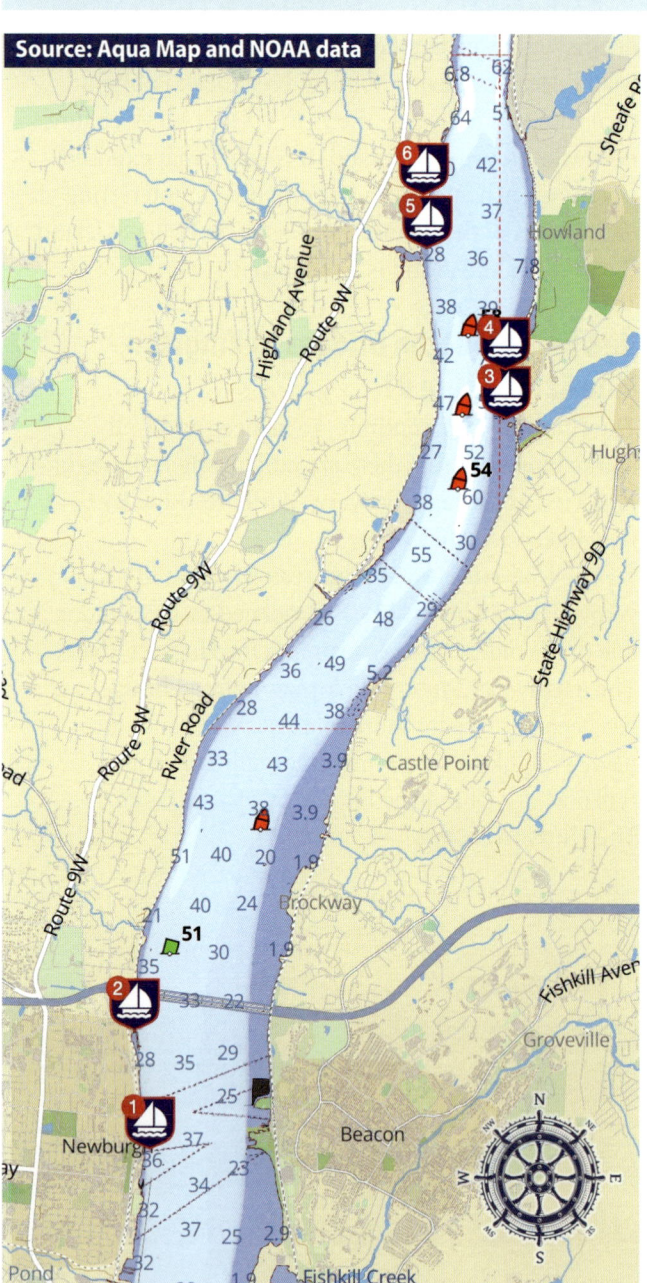

Source: Aqua Map and NOAA data

Poughkeepsie was the temporary capital of New York in 1777 and is home to Vassar College, one of the so-called "Seven Sisters" colleges (now co-ed). Historic Hyde Park, the birthplace of Franklin D. Roosevelt, is a short drive away. The house is open for tours (800-337-8474). Also located in Hyde Park on the Hudson River is the Culinary Institute of America. Several excellent restaurants are within the Institute and reservations are required well in advance so plan accordingly.

A light on the south end marks Esopus Island at Mile 84. The Esopus Lighthouse, the southernmost of several old lighthouses built along the river, marks the shoals of Esopus Meadows. This one, knocked askew by winter ice, was built in 1872. Beware of the ledge that is partly bare at low water and extends out about 300 yards from the north end.

Dockage/Moorings: Marine facilities at New Hamburg are convenient to grocery stores for provisioning. White's Hudson River Marina maintains just two transient slips and offers all types of maintenance and repairs. New Hamburg Yacht Club is private but has some transient space. (They were incorporated in 1869, by the way, and their storied history is detailed on their website.)

Across the river on the west shore at Marlboro is the full-service West Shore Marine with slips for vessels to 60 feet and the usual amenities.

Private Marlboro Yacht Club offers transient slips to 53 feet (with extra fee for electric). Reciprocal members get one night free after the first night (including electric).

Even though Poughkeepsie was once an active river port, it has few marinas. The well-regarded Shadows

Hudson River, NY

POUGHKEEPSIE AREA		Largest Vessel	VHF	Total Slips	Approach/ Dockside Depth	Floating Docks	Gas/ Diesel	Repairs/ Haulout	Min/Max Amps	Pump-Out Station
1. Shadows Marina 76.0 LDB	(845) 518-4459	100		70	12.0 / 12.0				15 / 50	
2. Hyde Park Marina (WiFi) 78.0 LDB	(845) 473-8283	150	16	150	40.0 / 11.0	F	G	R	30 / 50	
3. Rogers Point Boating Association-PRIVATE	(845) 229-2236			30	/	F	GD		30	P
4. Poughkeepsie Yacht Club-PRIVATE (WiFi) 84.0 LDB	(845) 889-4742	50		75	60.0 / 22.0	F		H	30 / 50	
5. Mills Norrie State Park Marina	(845) 889-4200		16	145	6.0 / 6.0	F			30	P

(WiFi) Wireless Internet Access
Visit www.waterwayguide.com for current rates, fuel prices, website addresses and other up-to-the-minute information. (Information in the table is provided by the facilities.)

Scan here for more details:

Marina to the south of the bridges has slips and services for vessels to 100 feet. They also have on-site water taxi service and dockside ordering from the on-site restaurant.

Transients are always welcome at Hyde Park Marina, where slips are usually available inside the protected cove and, if not, there are also outside docks (with amenities). Watch the depths at entrance. Rogers Point Boating Association is strictly private.

The private Poughkeepsie Yacht Club is not located at Poughkeepsie; it is actually 8 miles north of the city just southeast of Esopus Island. This friendly club welcomes all transient vessels on their floating dock or moorings (for free if you come from a reciprocal club).

Mills Norrie State Park Marina to the north offers reasonably priced slips with well-maintained facilities and a friendly and knowledgeable staff. The marina accommodates larger vessels with drafts over 5 feet on the outer docks. This can be a little bumpy but the marina is well protected by an island and distance from the channel.

Anchorage: We have observed boats anchored east of Esopus Island at Mile 84. The bottom is hard in 20-foot MLW depths and depths drop off fast. This, in addition to a 4-foot tide, makes this a marginal anchorage. At Mile 87.9, you can anchor at Staatsburg, also on the east side of the river. Anchor around the southern entrance to the channel at Vanderburgh Cove for best depth.

For those ready to stop for the night before exploring Rondout Creek in Kingston, an anchorage can be found along the river's west shore just south of Port Ewen. Here you will find 6 to 18 feet MLW with good holding in mud. This anchorage is exposed from the northeast through southeast so plan accordingly. Be aware of the submerged dolphins shown on the charts.

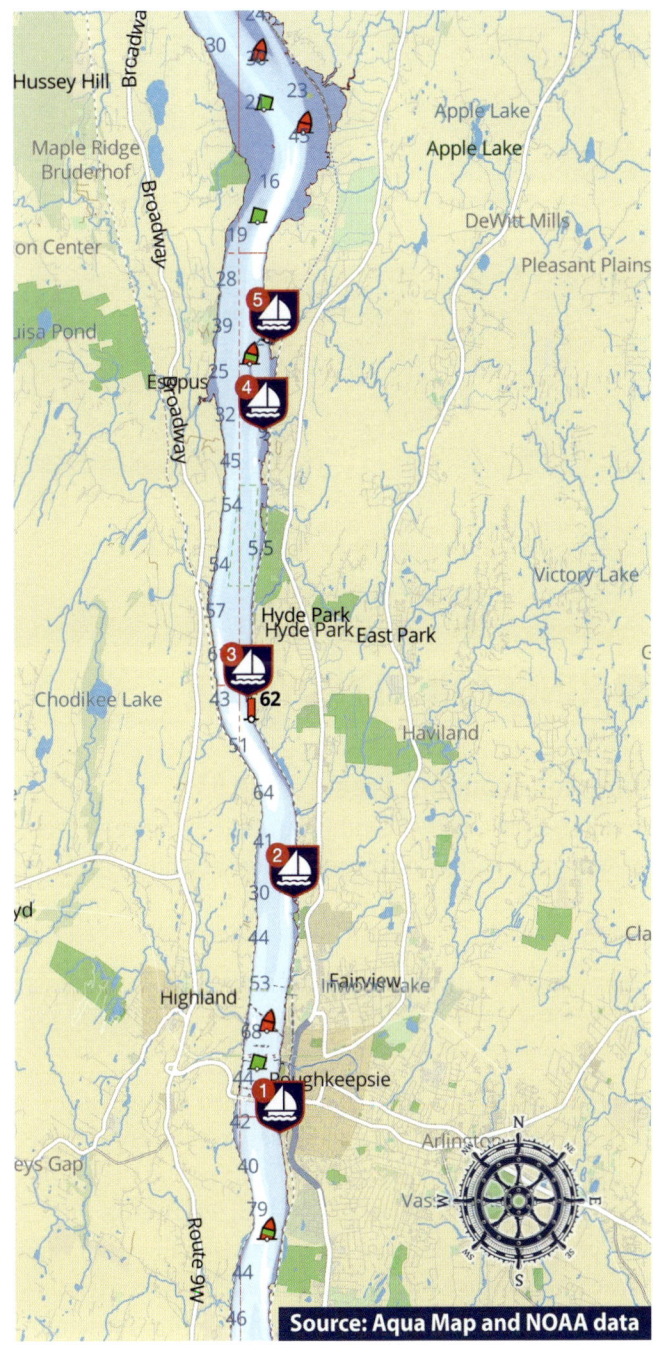

Source: Aqua Map and NOAA data

Rondout Lighthouse on the Hudson River, Kingston

■ KINGSTON TO TROY LOCK

Kingston (Rondout Creek)–Mile 93

Rondout Creek, with a lighthouse at the entrance, serves as Kingston's harbor and features more amenities than any harbor between here and New York City. The online Kingston Visitors Guide can guide you.

> NOTE: For NOAA weather reports, pay special attention to warnings for Ulster and Dutchess Counties.

NAVIGATION: Rondout Creek is entered through a dredged channel that leads between two submerged jetties marked by lights and seasonal daybeacons. On the north side of Rondout Creek just east of **U.S. 9W Bridge** (56-foot fixed vertical clearance) is the Hudson River Maritime Museum. Nowhere on the Hudson River can travelers learn more about the river's history than at this museum.

In addition to the museum, the restored historical waterfront district has an array of boutiques, craft stores and restaurants within 500 feet of the docks.

There are two other fixed high-rise bridges on the river beyond the U.S. 9W Bridge: **Old U.S. 9W (Sleightsburg) Bridge** with 86-foot vertical clearance and the **Conrail Railroad Bridge** with 144 feet of vertical clearance.

Dockage: The marina at the Hudson River Maritime Museum has full amenities and slip rental offers free admission to the museum for all passengers. Transient boaters must register online through Dockwa or by calling 845-706-8881 and must pay with credit card.

On the west side of the first bridge is the conveniently located Kingston City Marina. The dockmaster can be found in the small octagonal building at dockside. They welcome transients on their floating docks with deep water slips and can

Hudson River, NY

KINGSTON AREA		Largest Vessel	VHF	Total Slips	Approach/ Dockside Depth	Floating Docks	Gas/ Diesel	Repairs/ Haulout	Min/Max Amps	Pump-Out Station
1. Hudson River Maritime Museum **WiFi** 91.0 RDB	(845) 706-8881	250	16		30.0 / 16.0	F			30 / 50	
2. Kingston City Marina **WiFi** 91.0 RDB	(845) 331-6940	150	16	85	11.0 / 8.0	F			30 / 100	
3. Hideaway Marina 91.0 RDB	(845) 331-4565	55	16	100	7.0 / 7.0	F		RH	30	P
4. Rondout Yacht Basin **WiFi** 91.0 RDB	(845) 331-7061	72	16	150	12.0 / 12.0	F	GD	RH	30 / 50	P
5. Lou's Boat Basin **WiFi**	(845) 331-4670	42	79	50	11.0 / 10.0		G		30	

WiFi Wireless Internet Access
Visit www.waterwayguide.com for current rates, fuel prices, website addresses and other up-to-the-minute information.
(Information in the table is provided by the facilities.)

Scan here for more details:

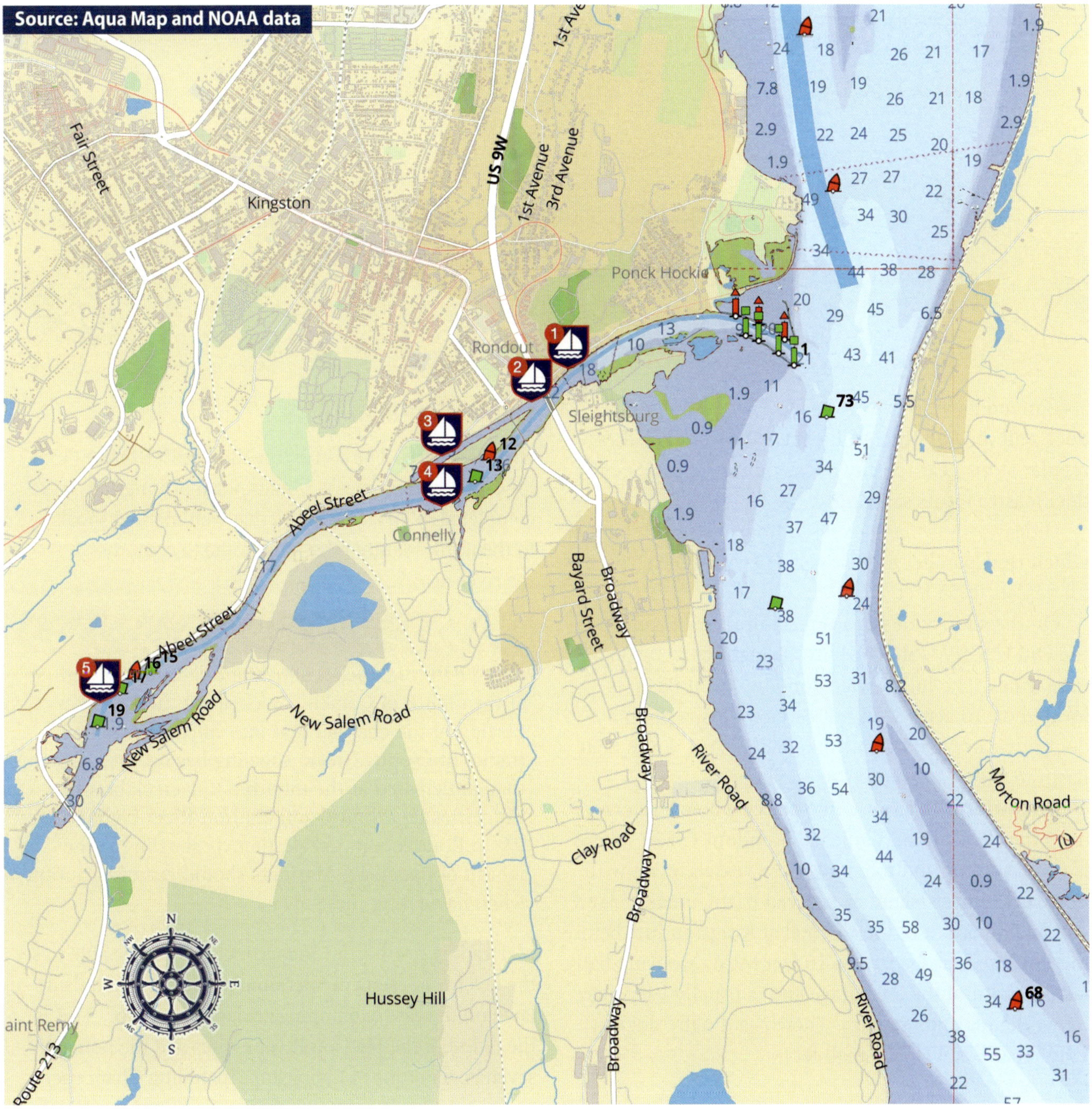

Hudson River, NY

SAUGERTIES		Largest Vessel	VHF	Total Slips	Approach/ Dockside Depth	Floating Docks	Gas/ Diesel	Repairs/ Haulout	Min/Max Amps	Pump-Out Station
1. Saugerties Marina 101.5 RDB	(845) 246-7533	65		35	15.0 / 15.0	F	GD	R	30	

WiFi Wireless Internet Access
Visit www.waterwayguide.com for current rates, fuel prices, website addresses and other up-to-the-minute information.
(Information in the table is provided by the facilities.)

Scan here for more details:

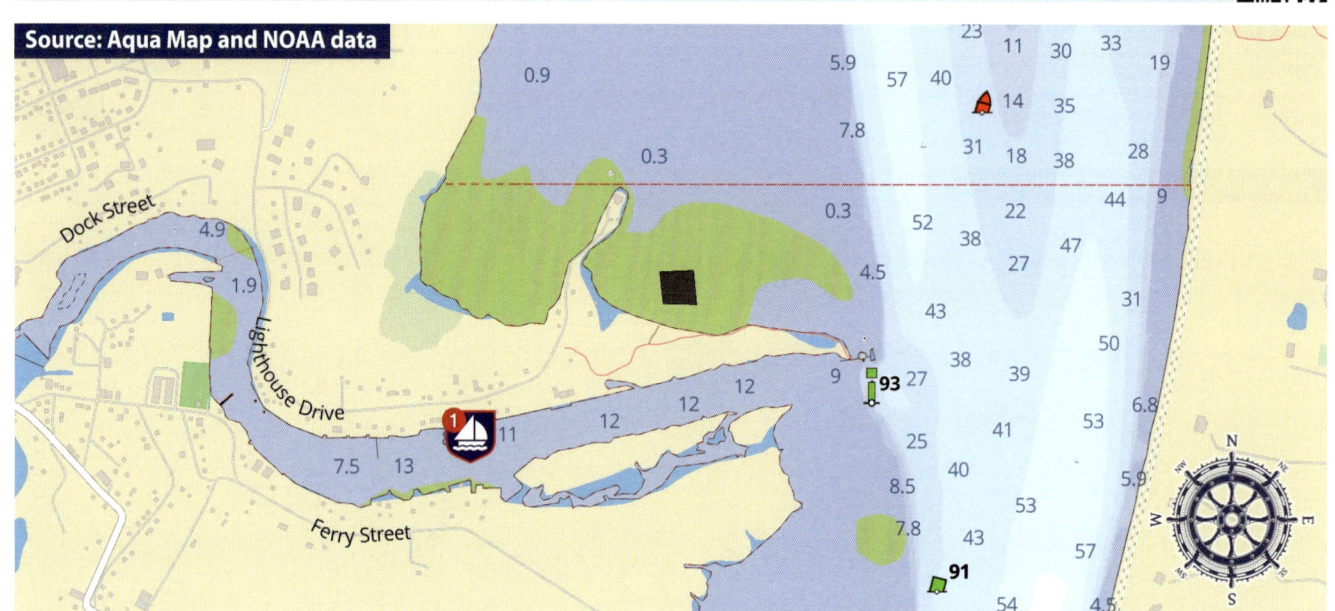

Source: Aqua Map and NOAA data

accommodate vessels to 150 feet. They also offer a dock and dine option. An inexpensive trolley makes regular stops near the city docks on weekends. See the dockmaster for its schedule.

Hideaway Marina is accessed from the same channel, which runs parallel to the river. They may have space for vessels to 55 feet.

On the south side of the creek, upriver beyond the Old U.S. 9W (Sleightsburg) Bridge are a cluster of marinas. The full-service Rondout Yacht Basin is located on 16 acres with full-service slips, a pool, a dockside eatery and a park-like picnic area. Lou's Boat Basin to the west has slips to 42 feet.

Anchorage: There are two places where you can drop the hook about 3 miles up Rondout Creek. There is good holding and room for a few vessels, even with tides, at Gumaer Island or proceed past Gumaer Island and anchor south of the channel at Kingston just before the low fixed bridge in 8 to 10 feet MLW. Mooring balls take up a lot of the anchorage and is usually very busy on weekends and holidays. There is a dinghy dock at Lou's Boat Basin (for a small fee).

Saugerties–Mile 101.8

NAVIGATION: The **Kingston-Rhinecliff Bridge** (135-foot vertical clearance), 3 miles north of Kingston, was completed in 1957. Be aware that well-marked shoals to the north require large ship traffic to crisscross the river here.

> ⚠️ *CAUTION:* Significant shoaling has been reported at the mouth of Catskill Creek along the southern portion of the channel that may impact commercial traffic. In Esopus Creek, shoaling has occurred faster than anticipated at the mouth of the creek between Saugerties Lighthouse and Hudson River Lighted Buoy 93. In Roundabout Creek, there is shoaling at the mouth of the creek. Mariners should exercise caution when navigating these areas.

Heading north from Saugerties, you may be able to see the lovely old estate of Clermont at the top of a hillside lawn on the east bank opposite daybeacon "96." This is the oldest of the Hudson River estates and the home of seven generations of Livingstons including Chancellor

Robert Livingston, the negotiator of the Louisiana Purchase as well as the co-inventor of the first practical steamboat. The British burned the original building (as well as the City of Kingston) in 1777. Clermont is now a state historic site and is open year-round until sunset. Call 518-537-6622 for details.

Dockage: Smaller than Kingston to the south or Catskill to the north, this harbor is the home of Saugerties Marina, which mostly caters to local boats (to 65 feet). Call ahead for availability.

Anchorage: The depth in Esopus Creek just past the marina is 7 to 11 feet MLW with all-around protection and good holding in mud. You can dinghy to the marina and then cross the bridge and follow the road into town (about 1.25 miles) for provisioning and amenities.

To Catskill Creek–Mile 112.2

NAVIGATION: There are several plants and factories along the river between Saugerties and the mouth of Catskill Creek. It is not unusual to find river debris (logs, tree branches, etc.) in this area, especially after a heavy rain.

⚠️ *CAUTION:* The charted Maelstrom is a dangerous whirlpool on the east side of the main channel north of Saugerties. Stay alert!

Immediately north of Catskill is the **Rip Van Winkle Bridge** (vertical clearance 142 feet), which opened in 1935. When approaching the bridge from the south cast your gaze toward the top of Church Hill (marked on the chart) to the east to see the outline of Olana, the spectacular 19th-century building that was home to Frederic Church, one of the best known of the Hudson River School landscape artists. The house, museum and property are now a state historic site.

Dockage:

⚠️ *CAUTION:* The minimum clearances of overhead structures (bridges, guard gates and utilities) range from 15.5 to 21 feet along the New York Canal System so sailors planning to exit the Hudson River and pick up the Erie Canal at Waterford need to demast prior to entering the system.

Riverview Marine Services Inc. and Hop-O-Nose Marina both have mast-stepping and storage capabilities and offer repairs. Hop-O-Nose is a full-service transient marina with pool, showers, laundry, picnic area and repairs as well as a restaurant on the premises. Hop-O-Nose recently acquired Catskill Marina so call ahead for slip details. The private Catskill Yacht Club to the north also maintains a few transient space. Call ahead.

Anchorage: Duck Cove is on the west side of the river at Mile 108.3 across from Germantown. You can anchor in 6 to 8 feet MLW below the jetty. Come in from the south below the green daymarker "109" and stay at least

Rip Van Winkle Bridge

Hudson River, NY

CATSKILL		Largest Vessel	VHF	Total Slips	Approach/ Dockside Depth	Floating Docks	Gas/ Diesel	Repairs/ Haulout	Min/Max Amps	Pump-Out Station
1. Catskill Marina **WiFi** 112.2 RDB	(518) 943-4170	130	16	85	10.0 / 10.0	F	G		30 / 50	P
2. Hop-O-Nose Marina **WiFi** 112.2 RDB	(518) 943-4640	100	16	40	10.0 / 15.0	F	G	RH	30 / 50	P
3. Catskill Yacht Club-PRIVATE **WiFi** 112.2 RDB	(518) 943-6459	40	16	40	20.0 / 10.0	F	G	R	30	P
MIDDLE GROUND FLATS										
4. Hudson Power Boat Assoc. **WiFi** 117.4 LDB	(518) 577-1798	40	16	60	30.0 / 18.0	F	G		20 / 50	P

WiFi Wireless Internet Access
Visit www.waterwayguide.com for current rates, fuel prices, website addresses and other up-to-the-minute information.
(Information in the table is provided by the facilities.)

Scan here for more details:

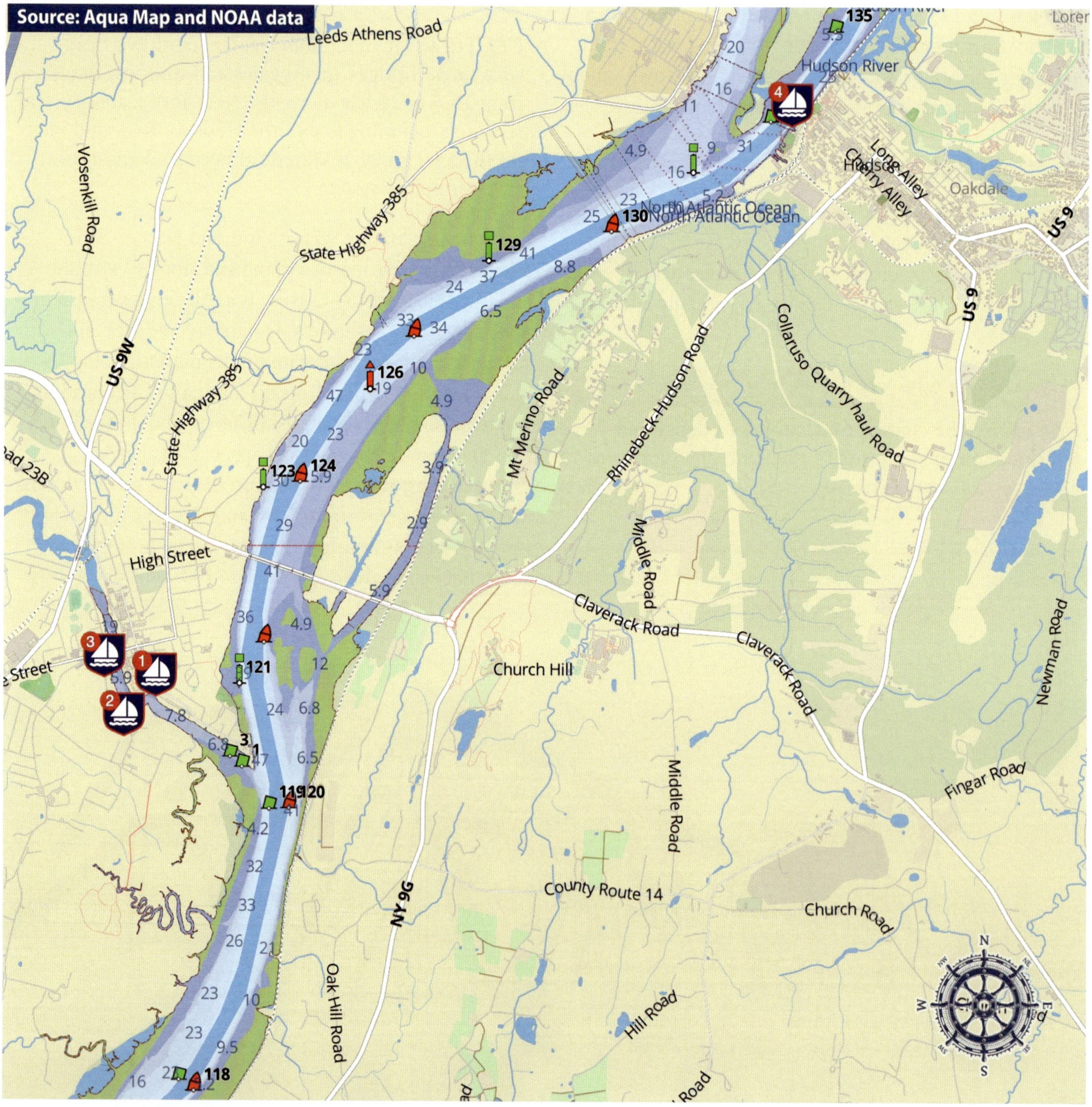

Source: Aqua Map and NOAA data

100 feet from the end of the jetty. We do not recommend anchoring in the narrow channel at Catskill Creek as it would impede the navigation of vessels coming and going.

There is a good anchorage before Hop-O-Nose Marina at Catskill Creek. It is deep (mud bottom) and with excellent wind protection. Ask at the marina about dinghy dock use.

A free dock at Catskill Point Park at the mouth of Catskill Creek is located in front of a restaurant. Do not be intimidated by the bank showing on the shore side at low tide. There is 7 feet MLW on the dock face. This is an easy stop during good weather but there are no amenities and it is posted as day use only. It is a little less than a 1 mile walk to town.

To Albany–Mile 145.5

NAVIGATION: The main ship channel passes east of Middle Ground Flats at Mile 117.5 but recreational craft frequently use the shorter route to the west, which has less current. Follow the channel to Houghtaling Island. Castleton-on-Hudson is located just north of the **Alfred H. Smith Railroad Bridge** (139-foot vertical clearance) and the high-rise **Castleton-On-Hudson Bridge** (135-foot fixed vertical clearance).

Some 10 miles to the north, you will emerge from the serenity of the upper Hudson River into the sometimes-hectic activity of seagoing ships unloading their cargoes of imported automobiles, bananas, fuel and molasses at the Port of Albany. In 1851, 15,000 Erie Canal boats and 500 sailing ships cleared this port.

> NOTE: Albany has a 4-foot to 5-foot tidal range, even though it is 144 nm from the ocean.

North of the high-rise Dunn Memorial Bridge is a restored 19th-century building that once housed the headquarters of the Delaware and Hudson Railroad and is now part of the New York State University system.

About 1 mile north of the Dunn Memorial Bridge is the **CSX Transportation Railroad Bridge** (25-foot closed vertical clearance), which opens on signal except from April 1 through December 15, from 11:00 p.m. to 7:00 a.m., when the draw will open on signal if at least 4 hours notice is given and from December 16 through March 31, when the draw will open with at least a 24-hour notice.

Dockage/Moorings: Dockage is off the main channel at Hudson, which runs to the west of Middle Ground Flats. The Hudson Power Boat Assoc. is home base for

the Columbia County Sheriff's Department, the Greenport Rescue Squad and the Hudson Fire Department. They accept transients but suggest you make a reservation ahead of time.

There is a free day dock across the river at Town of Athens (Mile 117.4) with 10-foot MLW depths that is somewhat exposed to the southwest and northeast. You can walk to town from here for limited shopping. In the summer they have live music every Friday night. No power or water.

There is another free dock at Coxsackie Riverside Park Town Dock on the west side of the river at Mile 124.3 with 12-foot approach and dockside depths. The town has invested a lot of money in upgrading the park and it shows. The two separate floating aluminum docks in front of the village Riverside Park total about 230 feet. Although the town in on the river, there is very little tidal current at the dock. There is no water or power and bathrooms are at the opposite end of the park. Overnight stays are permitted and the general ambiance of the park is positive. The dock is open to wakes from passing boats but is far enough off the channel to minimize all but the largest waves. The general store has provisioning possibilities, and there is a great tavern/restaurant nearby as well.

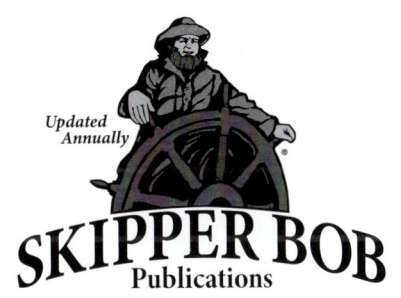
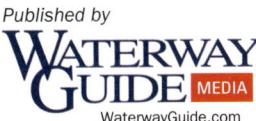

Hudson River, NY

COEYMANS AREA		Largest Vessel	VHF	Total Slips	Approach/ Dockside Depth	Floating Docks	Gas/ Diesel	Repairs/ Haulout	Min/Max Amps	Pump-Out Station
1. Donovan's Shady Harbor Marina **WiFi** 131.6 RDB	(518) 756-8001	180	16	120	15.0 / 12.0	F	GD	RH	30 / 50	P
2. Coeymans Landing Marina **WiFi** 133.3 RDB	(518) 756-6111	60	16	85	8.0 / 10.0	F	GD	RH	30 / 50	P
3. Castleton Boat Club - PRIVATE **WiFi** 136.9 LDB	(518) 732-7077	80	16	55	12.0 / 8.0	F	GD		30 / 50	P

WiFi Wireless Internet Access
Visit www.waterwayguide.com for current rates, fuel prices, website addresses and other up-to-the-minute information.
(Information in the table is provided by the facilities.)

Scan here for more details:

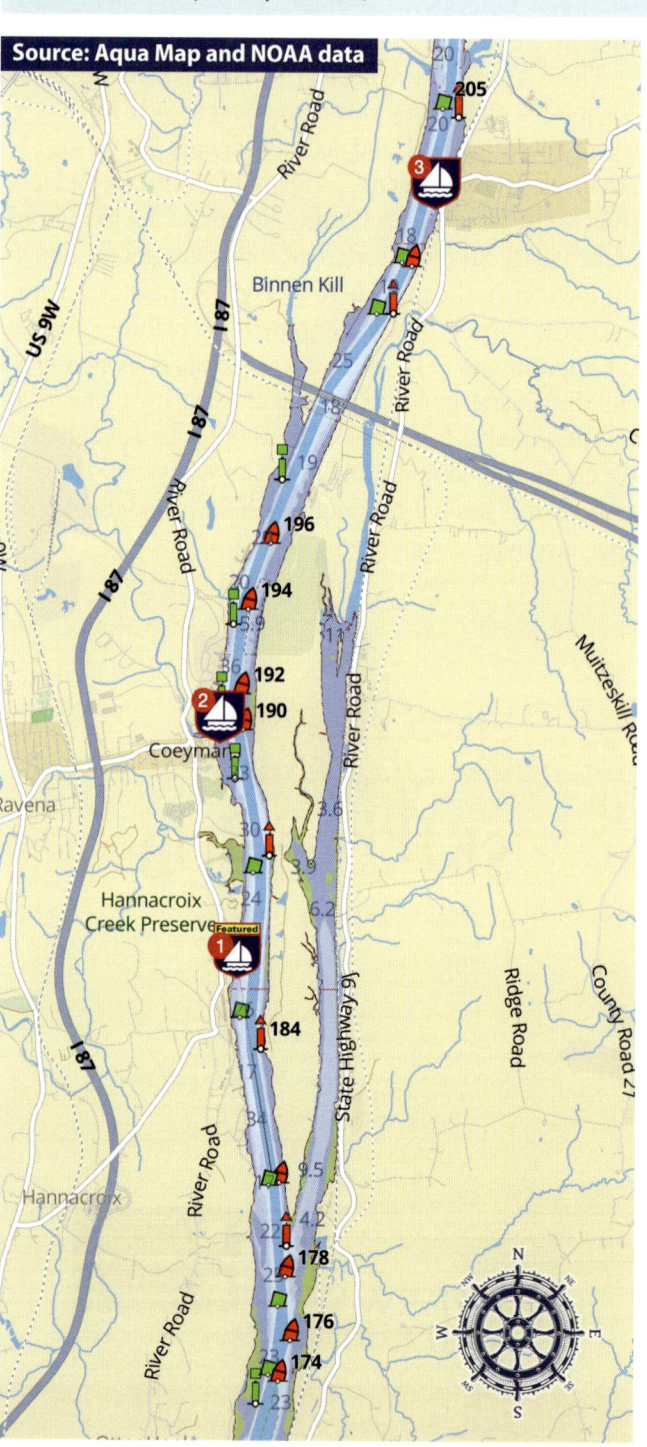

Source: Aqua Map and NOAA data

The well-regarded Donovan's Shady Harbor Marina is located in New Baltimore (Mile 187) and is an ideal transient stop for provisioning. Transient dockage reservations are available online and through Dockwa. The active marina is owned by a boating couple and hosts numerous events such as Full Moon parties and PigFest.

Transient space can also be found to the north at the full-service Coeymans Landing Marina. This popular marina welcomes transients to 60 feet with full amenities and very nice facilities. Before leaving the river channel, be sure to locate the position of the very long and very low north-south silt control dike. It may be under water with only a few warning signs visible.

The private Castleton Boat Club, located 1.5 miles north of the Castleton-On-Hudson Bridge, claims to be "the friendliest club on the river" and offers transient dockage as well as a remote-controlled gin pole for DIY mast stepping. The club's rental moorings, located across the river, include use of club facilities (showers, restrooms and bar).

Although private, Albany Yacht Club, located on the east bank just before the Dunn Memorial Bridge (Mile 135.7), will go out of their way to make room for you with slips to 180 feet. This is a fine base from which to visit the impressive Empire State Plaza & New York State Capitol (often referred to as the South Mall).

NOTE: Built in the 1960s, the South Mall complex is a magnificent showplace of modern granite architecture. In addition to the state government office buildings, the complex is home to one of the country's great modern museums and an acoustically superb bowl-shaped auditorium, affectionately called "The Egg."

Anchorage: The west side of Middle Ground Flats (Mile 118) can be used as an anchorage but take special care to stay well out of the way of passing vessels. Enter the west side of Middle Ground Flats from either the north or south. Depths are generally 15 feet MLW. From here, you can dinghy over to the town of Athens for provisioning.

Hudson River, NY

ALBANY		Largest Vessel	VHF	Total Slips	Approach/ Dockside Depth	Floating Docks	Gas/ Diesel	Repairs/ Haulout	Min/Max Amps	Pump-Out Station
1. Albany Yacht Club WiFi 145.2 LDB	(518) 445-9587	160	16	70	25.0 / 18.0	F	GD		15 / 50	P

WiFi Wireless Internet Access
Visit www.waterwayguide.com for current rates, fuel prices, website addresses and other up-to-the-minute information.
(Information in the table is provided by the facilities.)

Scan here for more details:

You will find a better anchorage behind Stockport Middle Ground above red daybeacon "150" at Mile 122. Enter from the south side of the island and follow the deep water indicated on the chart until north of Judson Point. The entrance and channel are narrower than appears on the chart and the sides shoal abruptly. Two anchors are recommended to control swinging. There is a commuter train track on the eastern shore. Depths of 7 to 10 feet MLW can be found up to and near Gays Point. A depth sounder is essential here.

Just north of the town of Coxsackie (pronounced "Cook-sacky") is another protected anchorage (Mile 125) south of Coxsackie Island. Note that it has been reported that the bar at the south end of the island extends significantly farther to the south than the chart indicates so if approaching from the south, favor the western shore. Control your wake when passing the nearby yacht club and private docks. Anchor in 10- to 15-foot MLW depths with excellent holding in mud.

Although the anchorage marked by white buoys just north of flashing red "170" is for big-ship use, recreational craft can find many attractive spots on the east side of Houghtaling Island (Mile 131.2) in Schodack Creek. Drop the hook north of 30-foot, flashing red "180" in at least 8-foot MLW depths. This is the last good anchorage when heading north. If this is too crowded, try just to the south on the creek.

To Troy Federal Lock (Lock 1)–Mile 153.9

Troy hosts an amazing Farmers' Market on Saturdays from 9:00 a.m. to 2:00 p.m. Over 200 vendors supply an overwhelming assortment of local produce, products and artisan crafts for sale. It is definitely worth planning your trip around this event.

Did You Know? In 1609 a longboat from Henry Hudson's ship, *Half Moon*, explored as far north on the Hudson River as the present city of Troy in search of a route to the Orient.

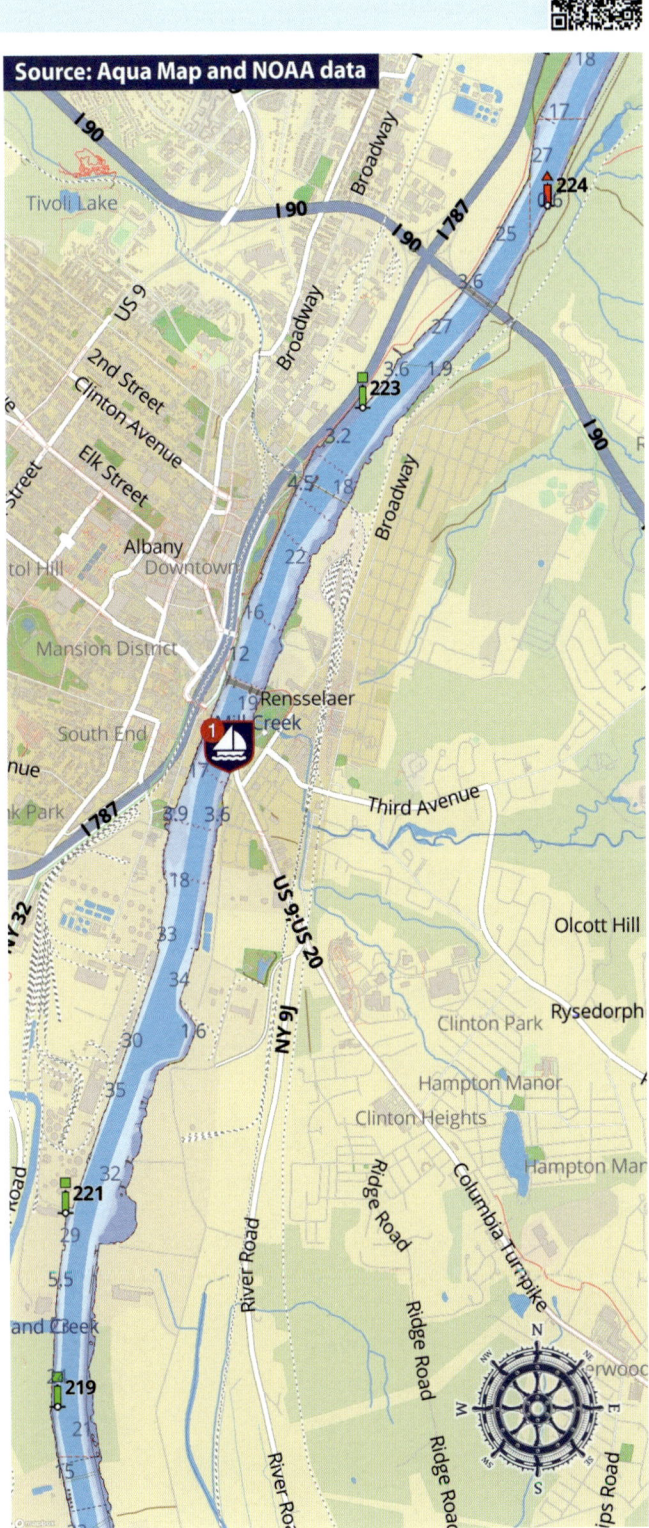

Source: Aqua Map and NOAA data

Hudson River, NY

TROY		Largest Vessel	VHF	Total Slips	Approach/ Dockside Depth	Floating Docks	Gas/ Diesel	Repairs/ Haulout	Min/Max Amps	Pump-Out Station
1. Troy Downtown Marina 152.8 LDB	**(518) 316-5535**	400	68		16.0 / 16.0	F	GD		30 / 50	P

WiFi Wireless Internet Access
Visit www.waterwayguide.com for current rates, fuel prices, website addresses and other up-to-the-minute information.
(Information in the table is provided by the facilities.)

Scan here for more details:

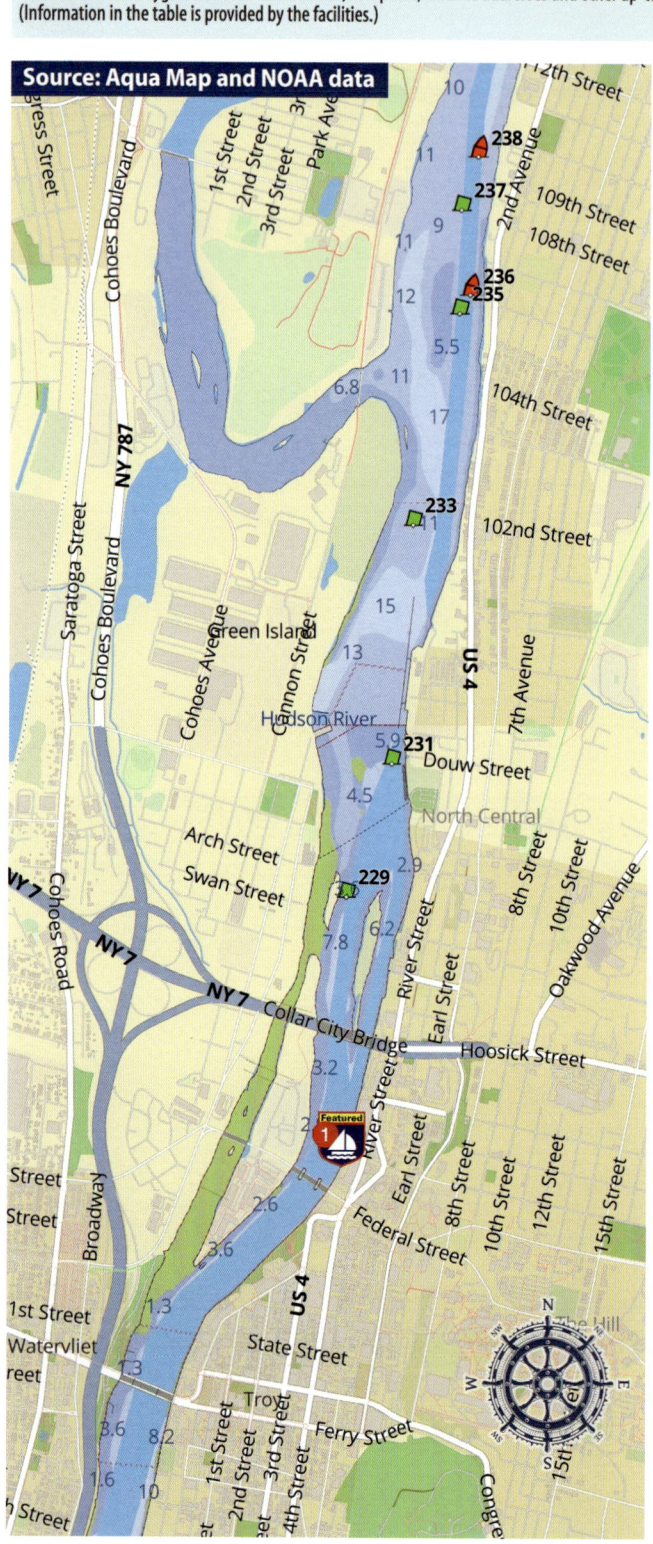

Source: Aqua Map and NOAA data

NAVIGATION: North of Albany, on the west side of the river past **Patroon Island Bridge** (60-foot fixed vertical clearance) and **Troy-Menands Bridge** (61-foot fixed vertical clearance), is the Watervliet Arsenal. Arms for U.S. military forces have been manufactured here since the arsenal's establishment in 1813.

North of Watervliet you will pass under **Congress St. Bridge** (55-foot fixed vertical clearance) and **Federal St. Bridge** (29-foot closed vertical clearance) between Troy and Green Islands.

The Federal St. Bridge is a lift bridge with a restricted schedule: From April 1 through December 15 the draw opens on signal with a 24-hour advance notice, given by calling the number posted at the bridge. From December 16 through March 31, the draw need not open for the passage of vessel traffic. The final bridge before the lock is **Collar City (NY 7) Bridge** (61-foot fixed vertical clearance) between Adams Island and Stormy Island at Mile 152.9.

Troy Federal Lock & Dam is 153 miles from The Battery in New York City. This lock is the first of a long series that can take you to Buffalo on Lake Erie, Oswego on Lake Ontario, or Whitehall on Lake Champlain. Secure your boat to the lock using the recessed pipes or cables that run from the bottom of the lock wall to the top.

The lock has a 16-foot lift and standard hours of operation are 7:00 a.m. to 5:00 p.m. daily from May 19 through October 11. (Note that the schedule varies with the season.) Vessels are required to arrive at a lock at least 15 minutes prior to closing to ensure being locked through, and at a bridge at least 5 minutes prior to ensure an opening. The lock monitors VHF Channel 13 or you can call 518-272-6442. Refer online to New York State Canal Corporation for the most up-to-date schedule.

Dockage: Troy Downtown Marina is where the (Great) Loopers meet the locals. Overnight transient docking along the city wall and two-hour complimentary docking are both available and the convenient location makes this marina a popular provisioning stop. Be sure to call ahead if you are planning to have your mast un-stepped here.

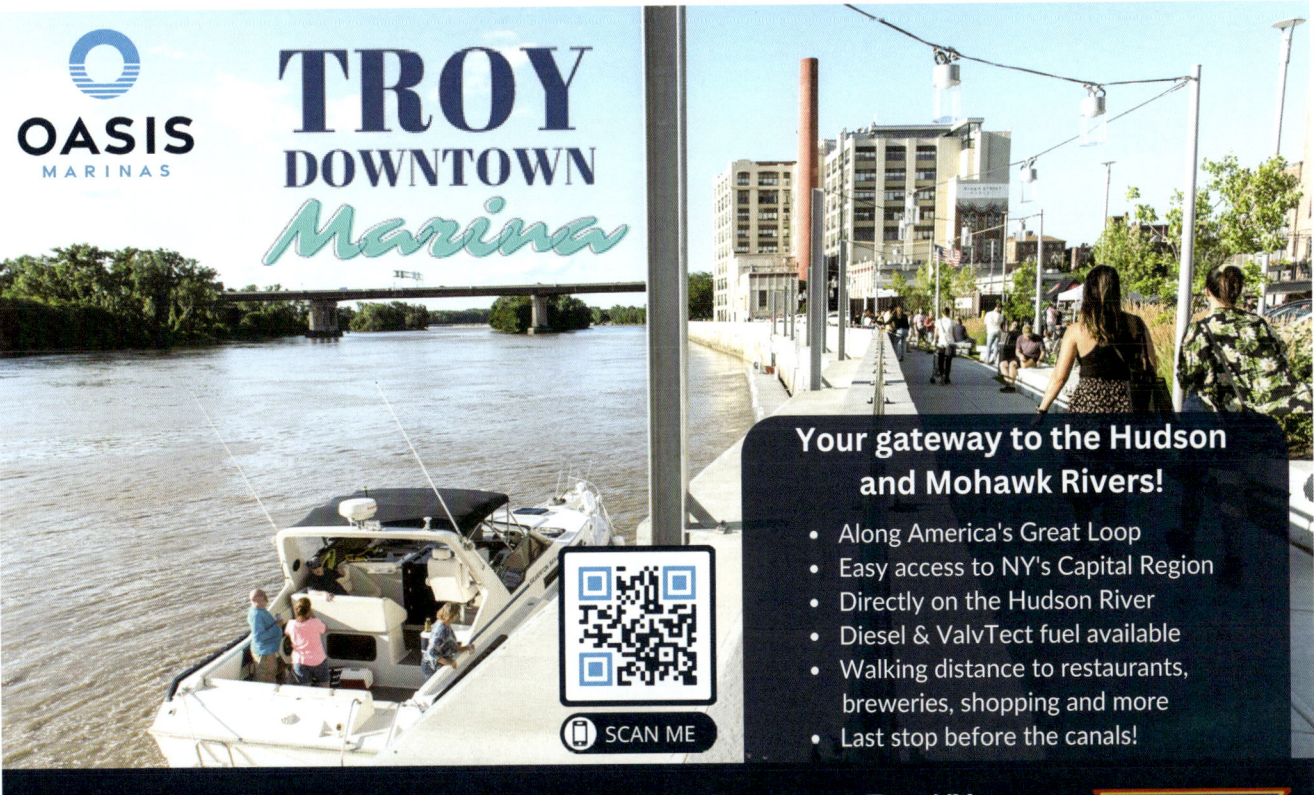
Downtown Troy, NY

Troy Federal Lock

■ NEXT STOP

After exiting the Troy Lock you enter the quiet, non-tidal waters of the Lower Champlain Canal. From here, the cruiser has several choices (all of which are detailed in the *Waterway Guide Great Lakes, Vol. 1* edition):

Option 1: Continue north up the Champlain Canal to Lake Champlain.

Option 2: Head west on the Erie Canal to Buffalo and Lake Erie.

Option 3: Head west on the Erie Canal and Oswego Canal to Oswego and Lake Ontario.

Option 4: Follow Option 3 but when returning to Troy, cross Lake Ontario and return via the St. Lawrence and Richelieu Rivers, Lake Champlain and the Champlain Canal. This route is referred to as the "Triangle Loop."

Option 5: Follow Option 4 but rather than turning into the Richelieu River at Sorel, continue on the St. Lawrence River to the Gulf of St. Lawrence, around Nova Scotia and across the Bay of Fundy, then down the New England coast and back to New York City. This is referred to as the "Down East Loop."

Regardless of what route or option you choose, you are in for an excellent adventure!

Chapter 6

Pages 201-207

Shinnecock Inlet

Shinnecock Canal

Moriches Bay

Pages 207-210

Brookhaven

Patchogue

Blue Point

Bay Shore

Babylon

Lindhurst

Great South Bay

Fire Island

Pages 199-201

Atlantic Ocean

Pages 194-199

Fire Island Inlet

Long Island Sound

CONNECTICUT

NEW YORK

Jones Beach

Jones Inlet

Pages 186-193

Long Beach

East Rockaway Inlet

■ EAST ROCKAWAY INLET TO EAST BAY

The magnificent South Shore of Long Island stretches 115 nm from Coney Island to Montauk Point. A long set of barrier islands runs between most of Long Island's mainland and the Atlantic Ocean.

Inside the barrier islands are shallow bays, islands, marshes and canals connecting numerous waterside communities. Dredged channels run from bay to bay, making a protected (albeit shallow) route similar to an inland waterway passage.

Charming bayfront villages line Long Island's South Shore. Farther east the scenery becomes more rural but summer resorts dot both mainland and barrier beaches. Those beaches closest to New York are dense with swimmers and sunbathers in the summer months, while the more remote stretches are all but deserted. There are also many parks (some with boat basins), nature trails and lots of birdwatching for enthusiasts.

Buses or trains to New York are readily available from almost any South Shore community.

The inside route of the south shore runs about 75 nm from East Rockaway Inlet to the Shinnecock Canal, where you can cross to Great Peconic Bay then to the Long Island Twin Forks cruising waters that lead to Long Island Sound.

Many of the bridges that cross the channels have restricted openings as well as limited hours of operation. The controlling vertical clearance on the inside passage is low but there are alternate channels you can take to avoid the lower fixed bridges.

CAUTION: The main channels of the inside route are well marked but the project depth for dredged channels is 5 feet MLW and the battle against shoaling is constant. At the western end depths tend to be more stable but as the route passes east, shoal spots increase and boats with more than a 3-foot draft must monitor the depth sounder continuously.

Predicted high tide occurs 10 minutes earlier than that predicted for Sandy Hook as given online by NOAA Tides and Currents.

East Atlantic Beach

Reynolds Channel

NAVIGATION: Reynolds Channel is the west to east inside route from East Rockaway Inlet for the 8 nm to Jones Inlet. This route is well buoyed with 7-foot MLW depths but shoals border the channel at its eastern end. Currents run strong near all five bridges that cross the route and at the western end of the channel near Jones Inlet. Note that some charted buoys on the East Rockaway Inlet may be missing.

You will pass under the **Atlantic Beach Bridge** (25-foot closed vertical clearance) when entering Reynolds Channel from East Rockaway Inlet. The draw opens on signal from October 1 through May 14. From May 15 through September 30 the draw will open on signal, except that it need open only on the hour and half-hour from 4:00 p.m. to 7:00 p.m. on weekdays and from 11:00 a.m. to 9:00 p.m. on Saturdays, Sundays, Memorial Day, Independence Day and Labor Day. From May 15 through September 30.

For the first 3 miles the 0.25-mile-wide Reynolds Channel is all that separates the Long Island mainland

South Shore Distances

This table gives mileage along the South Shore of Long Island. All distances are measured in approximate nautical miles.

LOCATION	BETWEEN POINTS	CUMULATIVE
VIA ATLANTIC OCEAN		
Coney Island, Norton Point	0	0
Rockaway Point	4	4
East Rockaway Inlet	8.9	13
Jones Inlet	8.3	21
Fire Island Inlet	12.6	34
Moriches Inlet	27	61
Shinnecock Inlet	13.5	74
Montauk Point	31	105
Block Island, Southwest Point	15	120
VIA INLAND WATERWAY		
East Rockaway Inlet	0	0
East Rockaway*	7	
Point Lookout	9	9
Jones Inlet	1	10
Freeport*	4	
Jones Beach	4	14
Amityville*	11	
Fire Island	12	26
Bay Shore	9	35
Patchogue	13	48
Moriches Inlet	17	65
Westhampton Beach	7	72
Shinnecock Inlet	9	81
Shinnecock Canal	3	84

*Off-waterway distance from main channel port

(with its major towns of Far Rockaway and Lawrence) from the barrier beach (with Atlantic Beach and Long Beach). Strung along the barrier strip are the seaside resorts of Long Beach, Lido Beach and Point Lookout.

The towns of Woodmere, Woodsburgh, East Rockaway and Oceanside are to the north on the mainland side and are reached via several marked passages twisting through the marshes and islands of Hempstead Bay north of Reynolds Channel.

For vessels over 30 feet, Hog Island Channel, about 4 nm east of East Rockaway Inlet and west of the Reynolds Channel Railroad Bridge, is the only entrance. Turn into Hog Island Channel between flashing green "C1" located off the tip of Simmons Hassock and flashing red buoy "C2" off the tip of Island Park (a double island). Stay well clear of a series of green cans in Hog Island Channel; the better depths are on the eastern (red) side of the channel.

Just past the junction of Hog Island Channel and Reynolds Channel are two bridges joining Island Park to Long Beach: the **Reynolds Channel Railroad Bridge** (14-foot closed vertical clearance, opens on signal) and the **Long Beach Bridges (Twin)** (20-foot closed vertical clearances). The draw of the Long Beach Bridges will open on signal from midnight to 8:00 a.m. year-round (if at least four-hour notice is given), except from 3:00 p.m. to 8:00 p.m. on Saturdays, Sundays and holidays, from May 15 through September 30, when the draw need open only on the hour and half hour.

> NOTE: About 0.75 mile east of the highway bridges on the south side of Reynolds Channel is a dock of the Long Beach Hospital, marked by a square white sign with a red cross (in case of a medical emergency).

Dockage: On Reynolds Channel you will see private docks and waterfront cottages and–except for a few full-service marinas off-channel on the mainland–most of the boat facilities are fuel and fishing stations until you reach the Hempstead Town marinas. It is inadvisable to anchor along Reynolds Channel due to the crowded conditions and the off-channel shallow water through this stretch.

A turn north into Bannister Creek just past the Atlantic Beach Bridge will bring you to Bannister Bay, home to the private Lawrence Yacht and Country Club. The club includes a 135-slip marina on Bannister Creek, a tennis complex, two pickleball courts and a clubhouse lounge with a full-service pro shop. They may recognize reciprocity but do call ahead.

East Rockaway Channel, NY

EAST ROCKAWAY CHANNEL		Largest Vessel	VHF	Total Slips	Approach/ Dockside Depth	Floating Docks	Gas/ Diesel	Repairs/ Haulout	Min/Max Amps	Pump-Out Station
1. Lawrence Yacht and Country Club-PRIVATE	(516) 239-1685			135	/	F				
2. All Island Marine	(516) 764-3300	50	68	250	8.0 / 6.0	F	GD	RH	30	
3. Crow's Nest Marina	(516) 766-2020	50		120	15.0 / 12.0	F		RH	30	P
4. Empire Point Marina **WiFi**	(516) 889-1067	60	9	65	15.0 / 8.0	F	G	RH	30 / 50	P

WiFi Wireless Internet Access
Visit www.waterwayguide.com for current rates, fuel prices, website addresses and other up-to-the-minute information.
(Information in the table is provided by the facilities.)

Scan here for more details:

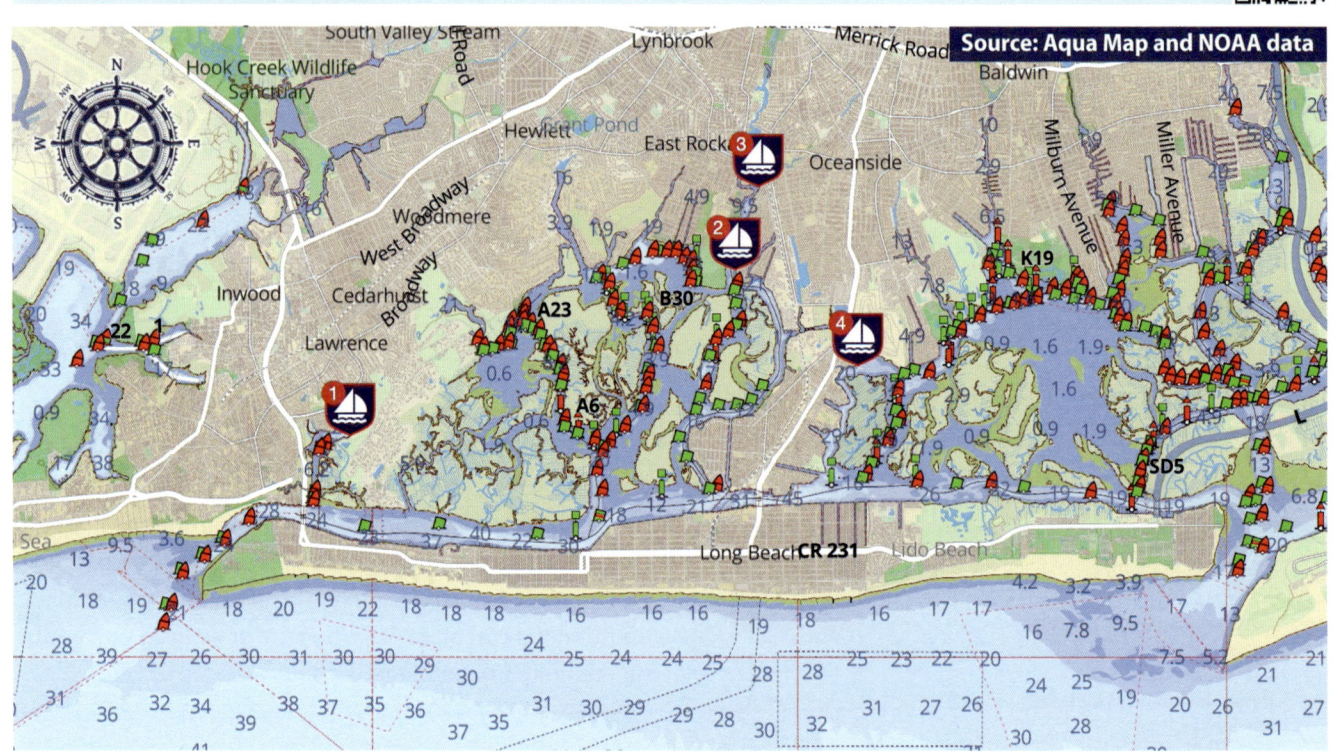

Three-quarters of a mile up Hog Island Channel, East Rockaway Channel branches off to port. Marina facilities line both sides of the channel including All Island Marine and Crow's Nest Marina. Both have some transient slips to 50 feet. Hotels, restaurants and amenities are within easy reach of the waterfront.

Small-boat marine facilities are also located on Barnum Island and Parsonage Creek to the east but these facilities are generally not set up for transients. Empire Point Marina is mainly a boatyard and brokerage but they do maintain a few transient slips to 60 feet.

The town of Freeport is reached via Long Creek or via Little Swift Creek, which cuts through Pine Marsh and Petit Marsh. There are three main waterways in Freeport: Woodcleft Canal (better known as the "Nautical Mile"), the straight and busy Hudson Channel to the east and winding Freeport Creek beyond that. Most of the service and repair yard and several waterfronts are all crowded with local and commercial boats but there are some establishments that will take care of cruising craft when possible.

On Hudson Creek, the municipal Freeport Guy Lombardo Marina has slips (to 48 feet), as does Mako Marine (to 75 feet). Mako also has a ship store with thousands of parts. Yachtsmens Cove Marina maintains some transient slips to 60 feet, while Al Grovers Marine has dockage to 50 feet. Co-owned Travelers Yacht Haven and Atlantic Yacht Haven may have space but call ahead. Several of these offer maintenance and repairs.

Anchorage: Anchoring is available on the west side of Freeport Creek, just before the abandoned Freeport Marina at Cow Meadow Park. Although the entrance is slightly shoaled, inside depths are 9 or more feet MLW with a 6-foot tidal range.

Middle Bay, NY

FREEPORT		Largest Vessel	VHF	Total Slips	Approach/ Dockside Depth	Floating Docks	Gas/ Diesel	Repairs/ Haulout	Min/Max Amps	Pump-Out Station
1. Freeport Guy Lombardo Marina	(516) 377-2372	48		252	7.0 / 5.0	F			30	P
2. Travelers Yacht Haven	(516) 377-7720	36		20	4.0 / 3.0	F		RH	30 / 50	
3. Mako Marine	(516) 378-7331	75	10	30	10.0 / 12.0	F	GD	RH	30 / 50	
4. Yachtsmens Cove Marina WiFi	(516) 546-6026	60		160	10.0 / 6.0	F		RH	30 / 50	
5. Al Grover's Marine	(516) 546-8880	50		150	6.0 / 6.0	F		RH	30 / 50	P
6. Atlantic Yacht Haven	(516) 377-7720	46		70	6.0 / 8.0	F		RH		

WiFi Wireless Internet Access
Visit www.waterwayguide.com for current rates, fuel prices, website addresses and other up-to-the-minute information.
(Information in the table is provided by the facilities.)

Scan here for more details:

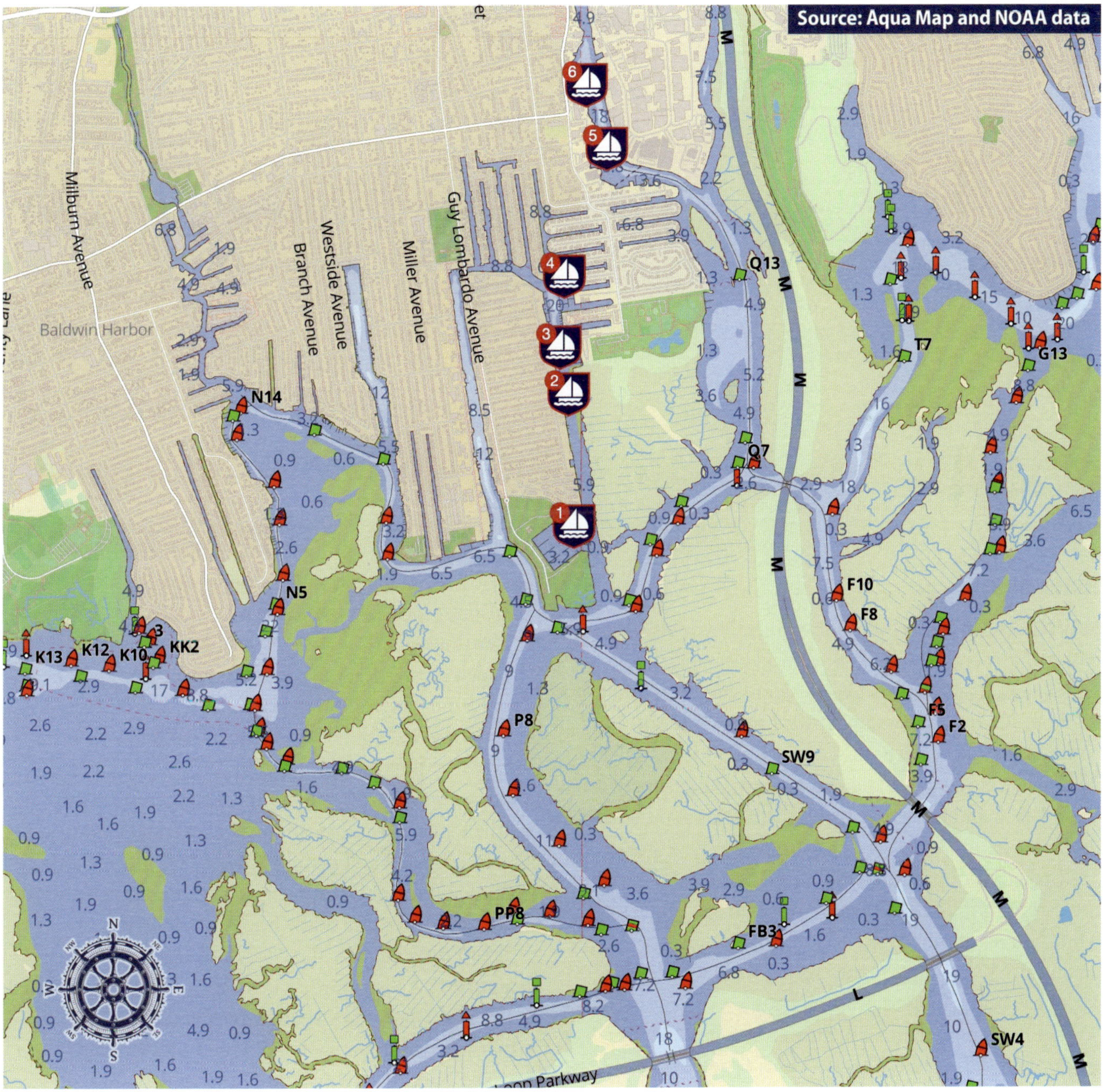

Source: Aqua Map and NOAA data

Jones Inlet, NY

POINT LOOKOUT AREA		Largest Vessel	VHF	Total Slips	Approach/ Dockside Depth	Floating Docks	Gas/ Diesel	Repairs/ Haulout	Min/Max Amps	Pump-Out Station
1. Angie M. Cullin East Marina	(516) 431-9200	50		182	10.0 / 5.0	F			30	P
2. Curtis E. Fisher West Marina	(516) 431-9200	40		152	8.0 / 6.0	F			30	

WiFi Wireless Internet Access
Visit www.waterwayguide.com for current rates, fuel prices, website addresses and other up-to-the-minute information.
(Information in the table is provided by the facilities.)

Scan here for more details:

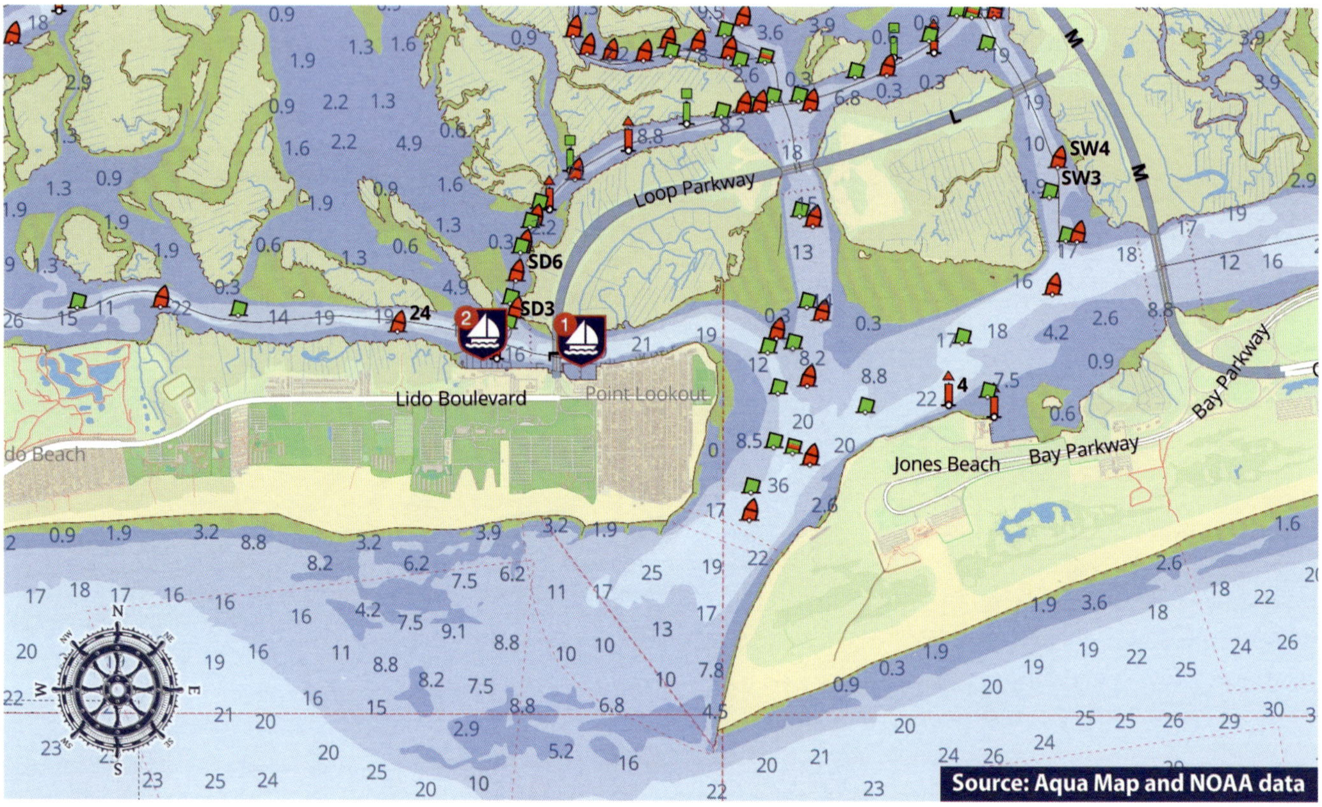

Source: Aqua Map and NOAA data

Jones Beach

NAVIGATION: Just west of Jones Inlet, Reynolds Channel passes under the 20-foot fixed vertical clearance Loop Parkway Bridge (West) between Alder Island and Point Lookout. If you can pass under the bridge, you can continue to follow Reynolds Channel, cross Jones Inlet with its strong currents and enter Sloop Channel between Short Beach and Jones Beach and the islands and marshes to the north.

If you cannot pass under the fixed bridge, an alternate route is to turn north 0.25 mile west into Sea Dog Creek, which curves around Alder Island. Swing wide around green can "SD3" entering the creek. (Shoaling to 2 feet MLW has been reported near the buoy.)

In a little more than 1 mile turn south on Long Creek, go through the **Loop Parkway–Long Creek Bridge** (21-foot closed vertical clearance) connecting Meadow Island and Alder Island and then turn east into Sloop Channel.

The draw of the **Loop Parkway-Long Creek Bridge** will open on signal every other hour on the even hour except from April 1 through October 31 on Saturdays, Sundays and federal holidays, when the draw opens on signal every three hours beginning at 3:00 a.m. Mooring platforms with flashing lights and phone numbers to call the tender for information are above and below the bascule bridge. If an opening is desired at other than a scheduled time, notice may be given from the telephone located on either side of the bridge or via VHF.

If you can negotiate the 20-foot restricted vertical clearance, there is a third route to Sloop Channel. Proceed on Sea Dog Creek, cross Long Creek and about 1 mile farther turn south on Swift Creek and pass through the fixed **Loop Parkway Bridge (East)** with 20-foot fixed vertical clearance. This is best accomplished on a rising tide as the creek is very shallow.

Running the inside length of Jones Beach (and its sister beaches beyond) to Fire Island Inlet is narrow, well-maintained State Boat Channel. The channel is marked like a street with white-capped black poles with arrows that point inward to indicate deeper water. (This is in addition to the standard green and red daybeacons.) This channel is usually swarming with fishing boats anchored in mid-channel. The channel has an enforced speed limit of 12 mph.

Dockage: Large town marinas are on both sides of Loop Parkway Bridge (West) before Point Lookout on Reynolds Channel. The Hempstead Town Marina East (officially the Angie M. Cullin East Marina) is near an oceanfront park where the swimming is good, and they welcome transients on floating docks. Hempstead Town Marina West (Curtis E. Fisher West Marina) has less transient space so call ahead.

Anchorage: South of State Boat Channel is Jones Beach, followed by a string of county and town beaches and summer colonies. West End Boat Basin is an option close to the inlet. Expect good holding and light boat traffic.

Gilgo Beach to the east presents one of the South Shore's most attractive anchorages at Gilgo Heading with at least 7-foot MLW depths. This sheltered bight almost always catches an ocean breeze across the narrow spit of land. Gilgo Beach also has a state park just as nice as Jones Beach and rarely as crowded. Both anchorages offer excellent holding in mud and sand and all-around protection.

To the east on the State Boat Channel is the Cedar Beach anchorage with 10-foot MLW depths and excellent holding and protection. Finally, the Oak Beach anchorage at the east end of Jones Beach Island offers excellent holding as well in 10 to 12 feet at MLW.

North Shore to East Bay

North of Jones Inlet, a string of interesting communities stretches east on Hampstead Bay's northern shore from Baldwin through Freeport in East Bay and then to Amityville and the beginning of Great South Bay. Interlocking secondary channels (some natural, some dredged and most well marked) twist under bridges, through marshes, sand flats and tiny islands, past manmade canals and fingers of reclaimed land.

Watch depths carefully as many channels are shoal or have silted in. With local information on prevailing depths the crew of a shallow-draft vessel can enjoy several days of leisurely cruising in the maze of canals, sloughs and waterways in this area.

The waterfront along Woodcleft Canal at Freeport has the ambiance of a seafaring village. Amenities such as seafood restaurants (many with outdoor dining and music), open-air bars, fish markets and boutiques are all a short walk from the docks.

Jones Beach

World-famous Jones Beach State Park (1 Ocean Pkwy., 516-785-1600) opened August 4, 1929, and includes 2,500 acres of the cleanest, finest ocean beaches anywhere. Miles of well-guarded swimming areas can absorb astounding throngs of people without seeming overcrowded. Jones Beach begins at Jones Inlet and extends east along the barrier beach for about 5 miles. Jones Beach has a broad 2-mile-long boardwalk, refreshment stands, restaurants, a huge swimming pool, abundant fishing and attractive anchorages. A 200-foot high red brick tower, visible for 25 miles when lit at night, serves as a striking landmark. From June through September, the Jones Beach Boardwalk Bandshell has music events every night. Nature walks are also available at the Theodore Roosevelt Nature Center (516-780-3295), which is open between Memorial Day and Labor Day, Wednesday through Sunday from 10:00 a.m. to 4:00 p.m. See details and interactive webcam at www.jonesbeach.com.

Hempstead Bay, NY

EAST BAY		Largest Vessel	VHF	Total Slips	Approach/ Dockside Depth	Floating Docks	Gas/ Diesel	Repairs/ Haulout	Min/Max Amps	Pump-Out Station
1. Blue Water Yacht Club	(516) 623-5757	55	18	270	5.0 / 5.0	F	G	RH	30	P
2. Whaleneck Harbor Marina	(516) 378-8025	55		200	5.0 / 9.0	F		RH	30	
3. Wantagh Park Marina	(516) 571-7460	45		248	6.0 / 6.0	F			30	
ISLAND CREEK										
4. Treasure Island Marina	(516) 221-7156	40		363	8.0 / 6.0	F		RH	30	P

WiFi Wireless Internet Access
Visit www.waterwayguide.com for current rates, fuel prices, website addresses and other up-to-the-minute information.
(Information in the table is provided by the facilities.)

Scan here for more details:

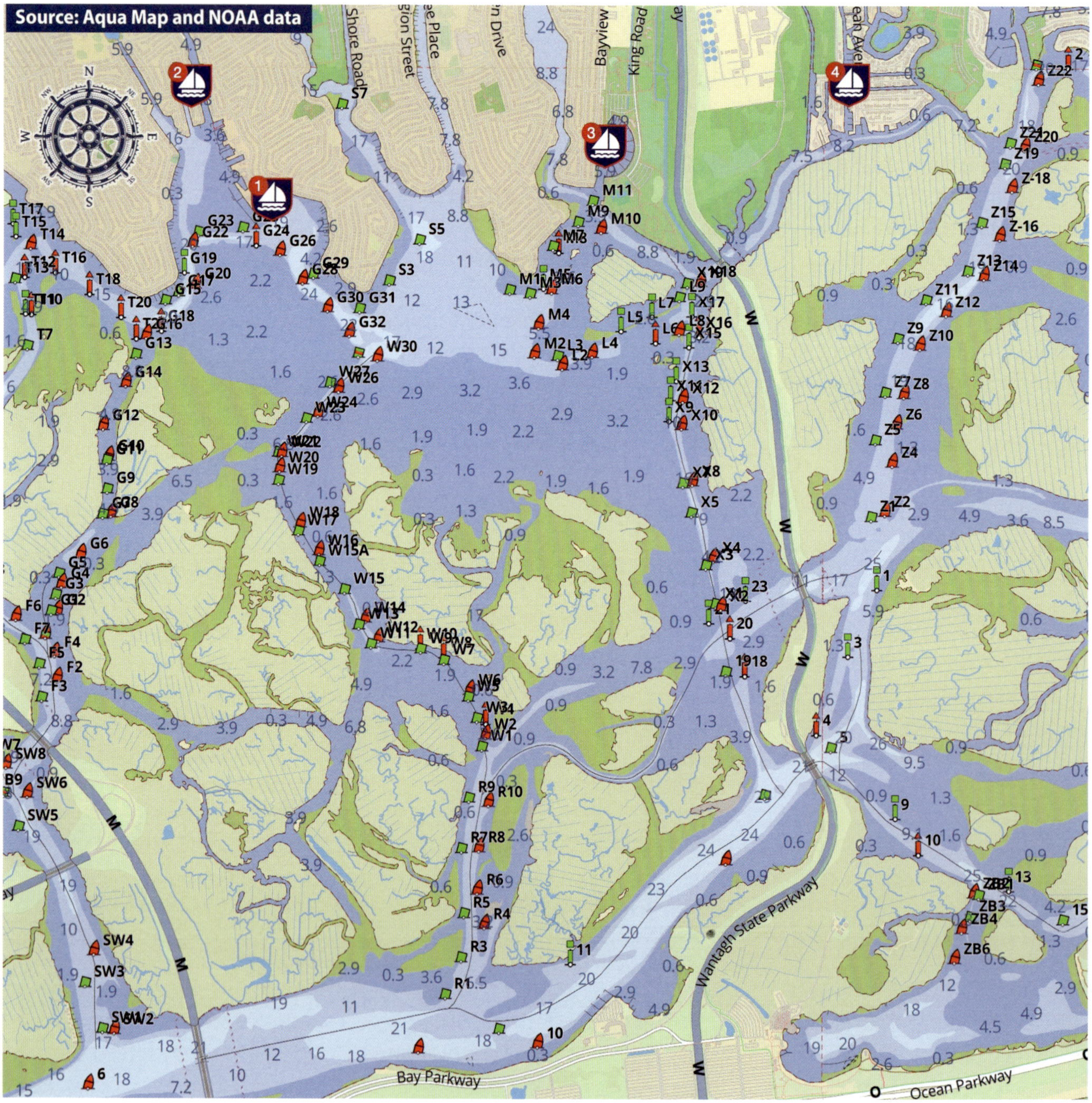

Source: Aqua Map and NOAA data

In season this area is crowded with fishers, recreational boaters, diners and sightseers.

NAVIGATION: If continuing eastward, pass through the **Meadowbrook State Parkway Bridge** (21-foot closed vertical clearance) and into Sloop Channel. The bridge opens on signal every other hour on the even hour (with 30 minute notice). From April 1 through October 31, on Saturdays, Sundays and federal holidays, the draw opens every three hours beginning at 1:30 a.m. Notice may be given from the telephone located at the moorings on each side of the bridge or by marine radio.

Abeam of the mammoth water tower, the channel veers northeast under the **Wantagh State Parkway (Sloop Channel) Bridge** (20-foot closed vertical clearance) and around a marshy area. A shortage of drawtenders makes for uncertain openings. If you absolutely must have an opening, give at least a half-hour advance notice by calling the number posted at the bridge or 631-952-6777. From 6:30 a.m. through noon and from 12:15 p.m. through 4:00 p.m., Monday through Friday, one bascule lift span may remain in the closed position. The draw will open fully between noon and 12:15 p.m. provided at least a 1-hour advance notice is given by calling the number posted at the bridge. From 7:30 a.m. through 8:30 p.m. on Saturday, Sunday and federal holidays, the draw will open on the hour and half-hour if at least a half-hour advance notice is given by calling the number posted at the bridge.

Boats that can handle 24-foot fixed vertical clearance and don't want to wait for an opening should swing north around Green Island through the fixed **Wantagh State Parkway (Goose Creek Channel) Bridge**, southeast down Stone Creek and then back to Sloop Channel.

When turning back south down Stone Creek from the bridge, give the northeastern point of Green Island a wide berth; shoals extend from this point. As you turn south, leave green daybeacon "1" to port and follow the channel. Use caution as you proceed as shoals are encroaching from both Green Island and South Line Island.

Dockage: To access marine facilities on Merrick Creek from Sloop Channel, turn north into Haunts Creek across from Jones Beach State Park and then head to the northwest along Broad Creek Channel to East Bay. Note when entering Merrick Creek that green can buoy "23" marks a large shoal area with depths of no more than 3 feet or less MLW.

On Merrick Creek you will find the large (270-slip) Blue Water Yacht Club, which can accommodate vessels up to 55 feet with full amenities. The other facilities here are primarily for dry storage (no transient slips).

Marked channels of varying depths connect the densely populated communities of Bellmore, Wantagh & Seaford, where facilities tend to be occupied by local boats. Most facilities, however, will make every effort to accommodate transients including the municipal Wantagh Park Marina, which is in a well-protected basin alongside a 111-acre park.

For cruisers, Seaford is the most important of the three communities. Its marinas are liberally sprinkled along Island Creek, Seamans Creek and Seaford Creek.

If you can't clear the 12-foot fixed vertical clearance **Wantagh State Parkway Bridge**, you'll have to go through the Wantagh State Parkway (Goose Creek Channel) Bridge (24-foot fixed vertical clearance) to access Treasure Island Marina on Island Creek, which has slips to 40 feet. (Call ahead.)

Anchorage: The wide part of East Bay between Whale Neck Point and White Point is one of the few anchorage opportunities in this area. Here you will find depths of 10 to 12 feet MLW with good holding in mud. Try to avoid anchoring in the obvious routes leading to and from the creeks.

Hempstead Bay, NY

SOUTH OYSTER BAY		Largest Vessel	VHF	Total Slips	Approach/ Dockside Depth	Floating Docks	Gas/ Diesel	Repairs/ Haulout	Min/Max Amps	Pump-Out Station
1. DelMarine Inc.	(631) 598-2946	50		40	4.0 / 6.0			RH	30	P

WiFi Wireless Internet Access
Visit www.waterwayguide.com for current rates, fuel prices, website addresses and other up-to-the-minute information. (Information in the table is provided by the facilities.)

Scan here for more details:

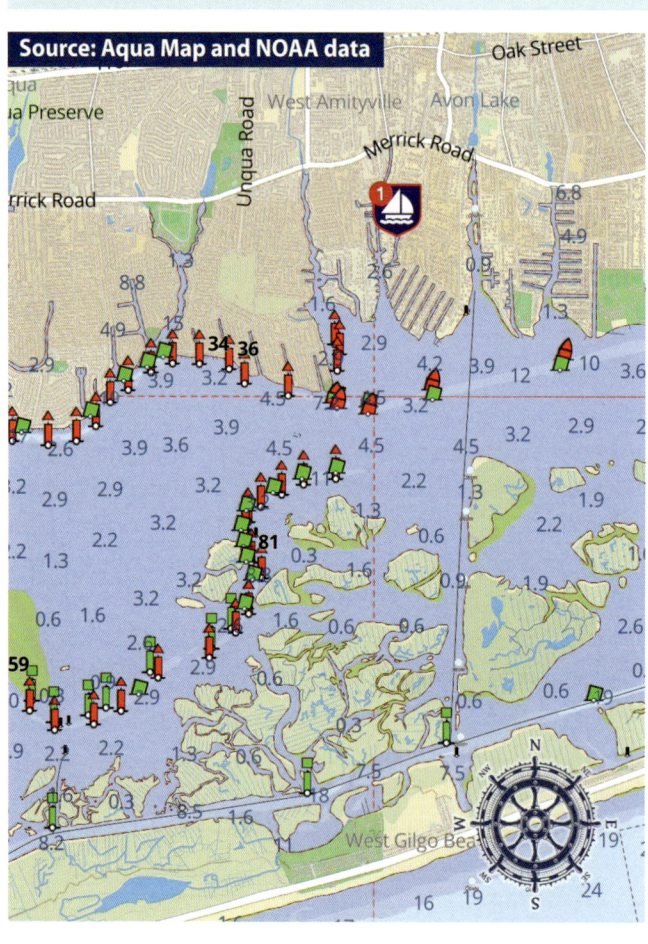

Source: Aqua Map and NOAA data

◼ GREAT SOUTH BAY

Great South Bay is 25 nm long and 5 nm at its widest point near the western end, the largest of the Long Island South Shore bays. Great South Bay begins with a narrow channel through the shoals off Amityville on the mainland and widens out to provide much of the shore's deepest water and prime sailing grounds. Mid-bay depths run from 7 to 10 feet MLW with some holes even deeper but with shallower spots as well.

To Amityville

Massapequa, Biltmore Shores and Nassau Shores to the east of Middle Bay can be reached via privately marked and maintained channels from Seaford. These towns offer some services but few are geared toward cruising boats. This area is crowded with private docks and attractive houses.

NAVIGATION: A number of creeks reach up from Great South Bay to Amityville, located about 2 nm inland. Along the creeks are marinas and boatyards, most of which are for residents. A town wharf is on the bay but it dries at low water. The area has several yacht clubs and a town beach for swimming.

Great South Bay

Great South Bay, NY

LINDENHURST		Largest Vessel	VHF	Total Slips	Approach/ Dockside Depth	Floating Docks	Gas/ Diesel	Repairs/ Haulout	Min/Max Amps	Pump-Out Station
1. Anchorage Yacht Club **WIFI**	(631) 226-2760	60	16	460	4.0 / 4.0	F	GD	RH	30	
BABYLON AREA										
2. Long Island Yacht Club-PRIVATE **WIFI**	(631) 669-3270	52	72	73	5.0 / 4.0				30 / 50	

WIFI Wireless Internet Access
Visit www.waterwayguide.com for current rates, fuel prices, website addresses and other up-to-the-minute information.
(Information in the table is provided by the facilities.)

Scan here for more details:

Source: Aqua Map and NOAA data

This route affords the opportunity to drop anchor and dinghy to shallows where you can jump out and gather clams in abundance. Scores of canals are interconnected and variously marked. Do not attempt without local knowledge.

Dockage: Your best bet for a slip is at DelMarine Inc. on Narrskatuck Creek. They have 40 slips to 50 feet but limited transient space so call ahead.

Lindenhurst & Babylon

Lindenhurst is the fourth largest incorporated village in the State of New York and dates back to a treaty signed with Native Americans in 1657, after which German immigrants settled it. Lindenhurst is a pleasant village and home to around 27,000 people. If you have a chance to go ashore here, take a walk around Feller's Pond, a shady, relaxing spot.

Babylon is the next mainland town to the east and offers many marinas along its creeks, including a municipal dock (for locals only), which is a long walk from the center of town. Nearby is Belmont Lake State Park (631-667-5055) with hiking trails, picnic tables, playing fields and a lake with boat rentals and bridle paths. All South Shore waters are teeming with fish and both sport and commercial fishing are prevalent here.

NAVIGATION: Fox Creek Channel is 2-nm long, 5-feet MLW deep and a well-marked passage that joins Lindenhurst to the State Channel farther south. There are facilities with limited transient slip space on most of the smaller creeks in this area. The 6-foot-deep Oak Island Channel connects the waterfront of Babylon with the State Channel east of Grass Island and Oak Island. Carefully observe the marked channel as you pass between Grass Island and the small, unnamed island to the east.

Great South Bay, NY

BAY SHORE AREA		Largest Vessel	VHF	Total Slips	Approach/ Dockside Depth	Floating Docks	Gas/ Diesel	Repairs/ Haulout	Min/Max Amps	Pump-Out Station
1. Bay Shore Yacht Club-PRIVATE	(631) 665-9518	50			6.0 / 6.0					
2. Seaborn Marina	(631) 665-0037	75		75	6.0 / 7.0		GD	RH	30 / 50	
3. Coastal Yachting Center & Marina	(631) 665-5144	42		60	6.0 / 6.0			RH	30	
OAKDALE										
4. The Marina - The Wharf Oakdale	(631) 567-1231	40		100	5.0 / 4.0			RH	30	
5. Oakdale Yacht Service WiFi	(631) 589-1087	100	16	290	4.0 / 4.0		GD	RH	30 / 50	

WiFi Wireless Internet Access
Visit www.waterwayguide.com for current rates, fuel prices, website addresses and other up-to-the-minute information.
(Information in the table is provided by the facilities.)

Scan here for more details:

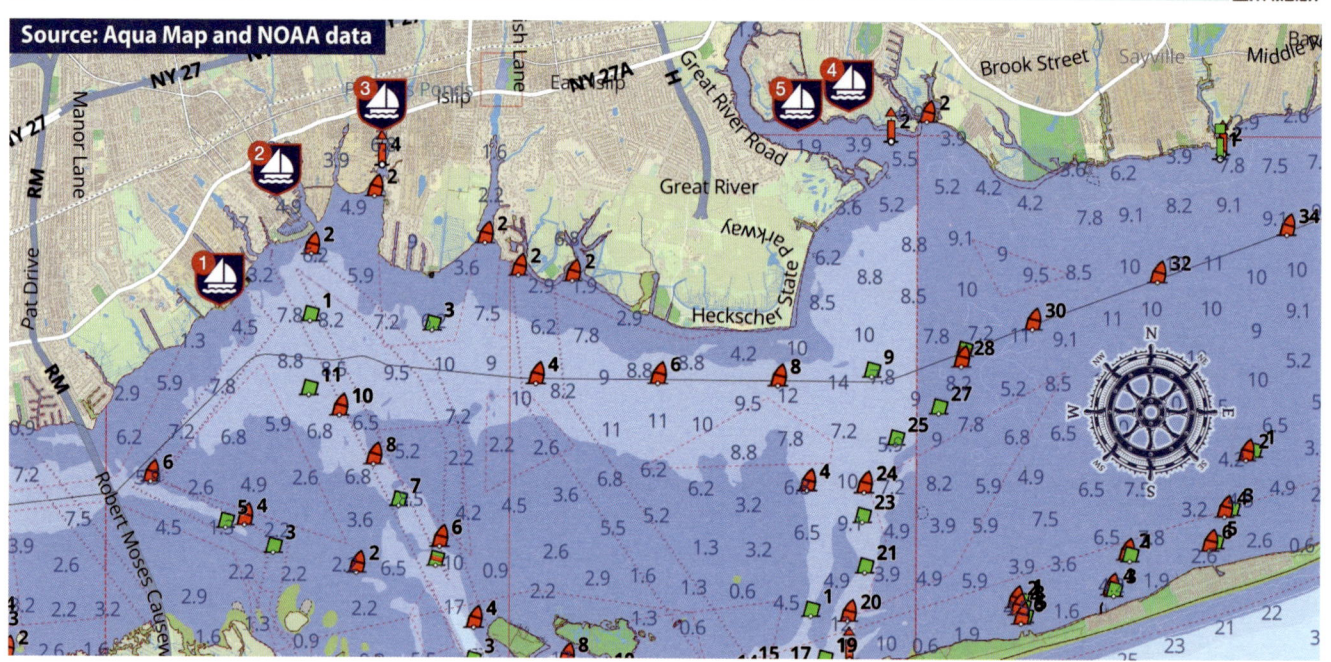

Source: Aqua Map and NOAA data

Dockage: Lindenhurst has several boatyards, yacht sales and a large ship yard (Karl Tank Shipyard), which may have supplies. Anchorage Yacht Club has privately-owned slips for rent. Some supplies are available in town, just a short walk from the docks. Slips, yard services and all fuels are available in Babylon, although facilities mostly cater to smaller vessels. Nearby Long Island Yacht Club is strictly private.

Bay Shore

On the mainland the big, bustling town of Bay Shore is the shopping and trading center for the surrounding area. It has all the necessary components of a good port of call: ample yacht services, good repair installations, a town pier, a yacht club, waterfront restaurants and hotels, and a well-stocked shopping center within walking range of the harbor.

Bay Shore's artificial canals are lined with handsome homes and two main boating areas, Watchogue Creek and Penataquit Creek, where marinas are plentiful. While not all marinas can handle transient boats, most will try. Great Cove and the surrounding creeks are well protected. Marinas on the harbor offer everything from charts to electronic repair and activity is constant, with ferries running to Fire Island, fishermen coming and going, diners tying up to restaurants and sightseers walking along shore.

NAVIGATION: One-half mile east of the entrance to Bay Shore Harbor at Brightwaters is Orowoc Creek. On the big jutting peninsula that ends at Nicoll Point is enormous Heckscher State Park (631-581-2100) with its bay beach, picnic areas, games and play areas, bridle paths and hiking trails.

With a state-operated launching ramp in a small, protected harbor, this is an ideal place of refuge and a lovely anchorage, but overnight parking and docking are prohibited. Flashing red "2" marks the entry to the creek. There is an unmarked shoal on the eastern side of the creek, so be sure to stay close to flashing red "2."

Dockage: Marine facilities, supplies and yacht sales can be found at Brightwaters, Watchogue Creek and Orowoc Creek. Your best bet for a slip is at Seaborn Marina (slips to 75 feet) or Coastal Yachting Center & Marina (slips to 42 feet). Call ahead for availability.

Anchorage: The shoreline in this section of Great South Bay has many inviting opportunities to anchor including Great Cove, which has 7 to 9 feet MLW with good holding in sand and mud and is protected from the northeast through northwest. Watch for boat traffic out of the creek to avoid wakes of numerous small boats launched at the park facility. Note that this area has many underwater cable crossings.

Oakdale

Around Nicoll and Timber Points, the Connetquot River empties into Nicoll Bay. The Connetquot River is a charming, secluded body of water with lovely wooded banks that offers good anchorage but not much in the way of depths.

NAVIGATION: Favor the eastern shore when entering. This area is the widest part of Great South Bay. Depths hold better, mid-bay shoals are fewer and sailing is deservedly popular. Fleets of centerboard sailing craft gather in various harbors. A marked channel connecting the inland route that parallels Fire Island with the route through Great South Bay runs across the bay south of Nicoll Point.

Dockage: There are several marine facilities on the east side of the Connetquot River at Oakdale, all reporting 3.5- to 4-foot dockside depths. Facilities include The Marina - The Wharf Oakdale and Oakdale Yacht Service may have space but call ahead.

Anchorage: There is an anchorage behind Nicoll Island at Timber Point with 5 to 6 feet MLW with good holding. This spot offers all-around protection.

Sayville to Blue Point

Sayville is a residential town with tree-lined streets, well-kept houses and two waterfronts: Green Harbor in West Sayville and Brown Creek, locally known as Browns River. The latter is easy to enter between the jetties at Brown Point. The blue-and-white ferryboats coming from Fire Island can be seen shuttling in and out of Brown's River and can easily be followed in.

Nearby Bayport and Blue Point are typical eastern Long Island hamlets that can accommodate cruisers in slips or at anchor.

Dockage: The dock-lined creek at Sayville has a town pier for residents only and major repair yards serving the Great South Bay fishing fleets. The full-service West Sayville Boat Basin boosts 200 feet of beachfront on 7.5 acres. They maintain transient slips to 50 feet. Land's End Motel & Marina maintains a few transient slips to 42 feet and offers a chance to get off the boat for the night.

Bay Point Marina in Bayport has slip rentals to 45 feet and full marine services. (Note that the Bayport town dock is for residents only.) Blue Point Marina on Corey Creek may have space for vessels to 40 feet but call ahead. The family-friendly marina has a restaurant on site and a beach nearby.

Patchogue

Patchogue is the shopping and industrial town for much of eastern Long Island, and the town's waterfront takes care of hundreds of boats each season. Howells Point, on the mainland about 3 nm miles east of Patchogue, marks the start of Bellport Bay.

Dockage: Deep Patchogue River is entered between breakwaters from Patchogue Bay, a bight of Great South Bay. Marinas here range from fishing stations to complete repair operations and include the friendly Island View Marina & Fuel and the large (230-slip) Leeward Cove South. (Both of these are within walking distance of Blue Point Brewing Co. by the way.)

More marine services and facilities are to the east on Swan River but few with transient slips. One notable exception is Sunset Harbour Marina, a full-service destination marina situated on 25 acres with 332 slips that can accommodate boats to 58 feet with full amenities (including a fun tiki bar). They do, however, report 3-foot dockside depths so let them know if you need more water.

Anchorage: You can anchor at Blue Point with good holding ground in 4 to 6 feet at MLW. This is well protected from all but a rare southeasterly. Only the surge of the Patchogue ferries disturbs the calm.

Great South Bay, NY

SAYVILLE		Largest Vessel	VHF	Total Slips	Approach/ Dockside Depth	Floating Docks	Gas/ Diesel	Repairs/ Haulout	Min/Max Amps	Pump-Out Station
1. West Sayville Boat Basin	(631) 589-4141	50		150	6.0 / 6.0	F	GD	RH	30 / 50	P
2. Land's End Motel & Marina	(631) 589-2040	42		38	5.0 / 5.0				30	
BAY POINT										
3. Bay Point Marina	(631) 363-6503	45		90	4.0 / 4.0		G	R	30	
BLUE POINT										
4. Blue Point Marina	(631) 419-6165	40		130	6.0 / 5.0		G	RH	30	
PATCHOGUE AREA										
5. Island View Marina & Fuel WiFi	(631) 447-1234	50		44	10.0 / 5.0		GD	RH	30	P
6. Leeward Cove South	(631) 654-3106	55		230	5.0 / 5.0	F		RH	30	P
7. Sunset Harbour Marina WiFi	(631) 289-3800	58		332	6.0 / 3.0			RH	30 / 50	P
BEAVERDAM										
8. Beaver Dam Boat Basin WiFi	(631) 286-7816	53	16	70	10.0 / 7.0	F		RH	30	

WiFi Wireless Internet Access
Visit www.waterwayguide.com for current rates, fuel prices, website addresses and other up-to-the-minute information.
(Information in the table is provided by the facilities.)

Scan here for more details:

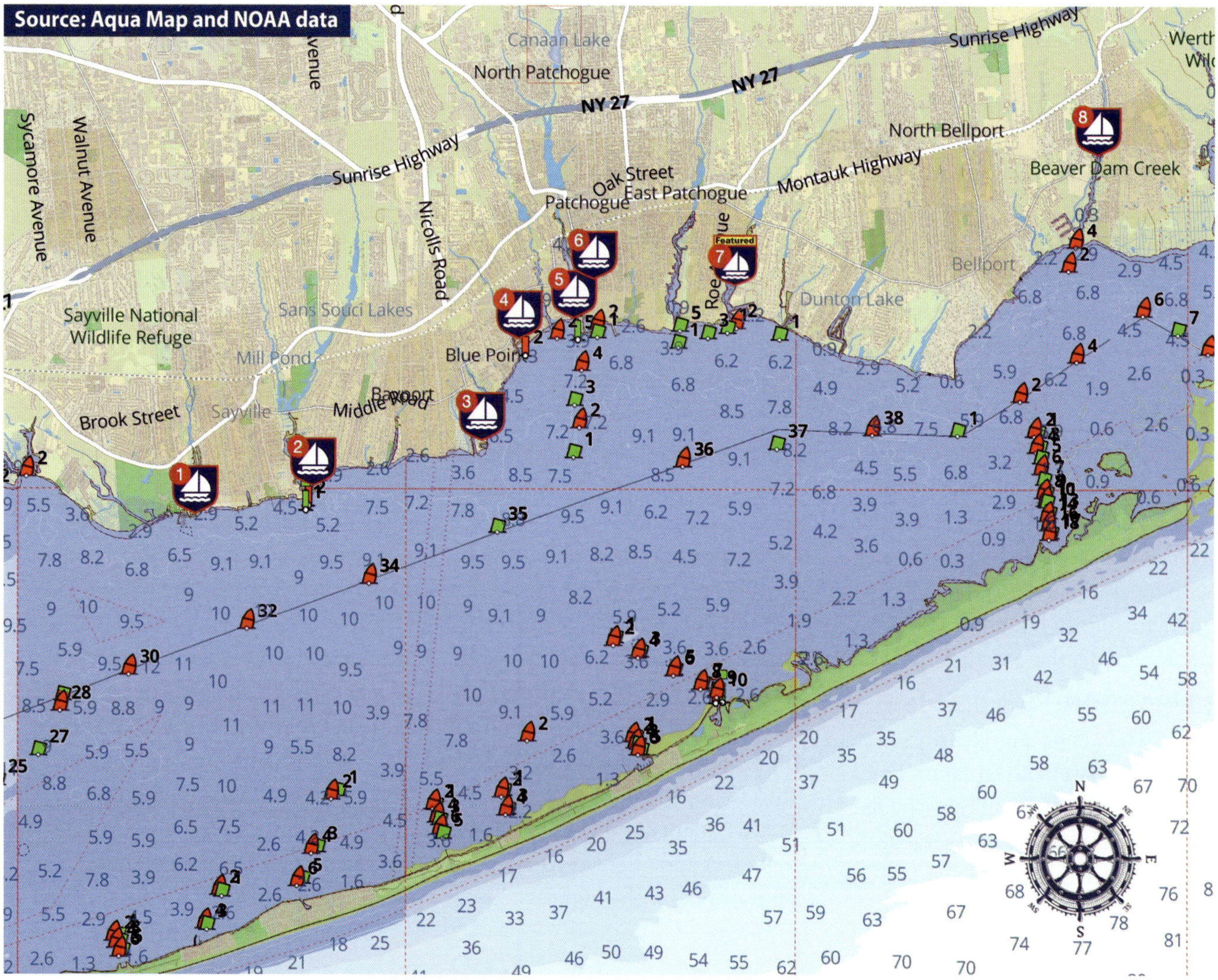

Source: Aqua Map and NOAA data

Patchogue

Bellport & Brookhaven

The villages of Bellport and Brookhaven are on its north shore, offering a scattering of marinas; however, the bay does become increasingly shallow here. Bellport Town Dock, which lies between Howells Point and Beaver Dam Creek, provides ample room for visitors to tie up on the outside for the day. (No overnight dockage.)

The town is just a 1 mile walk up a tree-shaded street, has all the charm of a New England village and boasts a chic pub and a couple of fine restaurants.

NAVIGATION:

CAUTION: Several markers have been reported missing in Bellport Bay. It is recommended you seek local knowledge and proceed with caution.

Dockage: The Village of Bellport Marina has over 150 berths with preference is given to village residents. Transient slips are available on a first-come, first-served basis if available (for a flat fee). Beaver Dam Boat Basin at Brookhaven has 70 slips to 53 feet. They can also arrange repair services, if needed.

Anchorage: There is a delightful anchorage just north of the town marina in secluded and protected Bellport. However, boats carrying a draft greater than 5 feet should approach cautiously and check the state of tide before anchoring. This area is exposed to the southwest.

■ SIDE TRIP: FIRE ISLAND

Fire Island is a beautiful, windswept barrier island, 32 nm long and connected to the mainland by a series of marked channels through the sand flats and shoals of Great South Bay. Fishing around the Fire Island Inlet is excellent and fishermen often crowd the approaches in any kind of weather.

Across Great South Bay from Babylon and connected by the Robert Moses Causeway Bridge (60-foot fixed vertical clearance) is Captree Island, a 300-acre state park devoted almost exclusively to fishing with a bird sanctuary at the eastern end. Fishing piers, fuel and bait stations along with charter and head boats for fishing are located within the park. Call 631-669-0449 for details.

The Fire Island lighthouse, originally completed in 1858, is on the western part of Fire Island National

Fire Island, NY

GREAT SOUTH BEACH		Largest Vessel	VHF	Total Slips	Approach/ Dockside Depth	Floating Docks	Gas/ Diesel	Repairs/ Haulout	Min/Max Amps	Pump-Out Station
1. Atlantique Beach & Marina	(631) 469-3868			167	9.0 / 3.0				30 / 50	P
2. Seaview Boat Basin **WiFi**	(631) 583-9380	58		53	7.0 / 7.0				30	
3. Flynn's Marina & Restaurant	(631) 583-5000	50		50	9.0 / 9.0	F			30	
4. Sailors Haven Marina	(631) 597-6014	65	9	48	8.0 / 8.0				30 / 50	P
FIRE ISLAND AREA										
5. Pines Marina Fire Island **WiFi**	(631) 597-9581	110	9	70	5.0 / 6.0				30 / 50	P
6. Davis Park Marina	(631) 597-9090	50	73	256	8.0 / 6.0	F			30	P
7. Watch Hill National Seashore Marina	(631) 597-6073	50	9	195	6.0 / 4.0				50	P

WiFi Wireless Internet Access
Visit www.waterwayguide.com for current rates, fuel prices, website addresses and other up-to-the-minute information. (Information in the table is provided by the facilities.)

Scan here for more details:

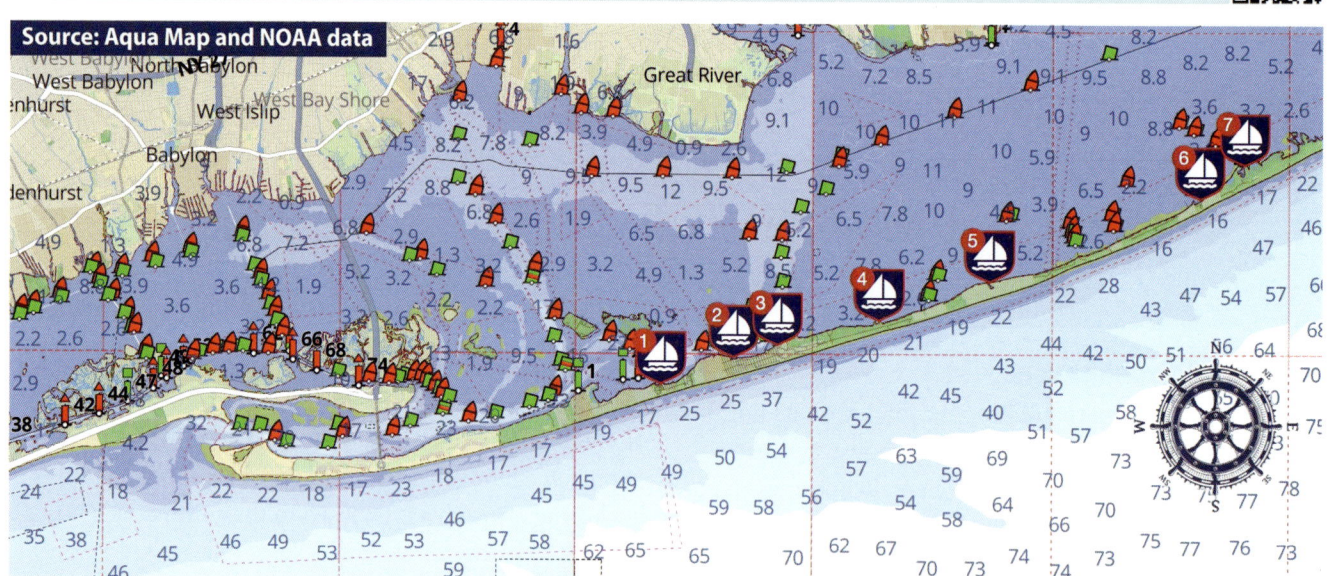

Source: Aqua Map and NOAA data

Seashore and adjacent to Robert Moses State Park. The lighthouse is 168 feet above sea level and can be seen more than 20 miles away. The lighthouse is operated by the Fire Island Lighthouse Preservation Society and offers exhibits and a nature trail. Access to the lighthouse beach is by walking, and there are no lifeguards. The lighthouse is open from May 25 through Labor Day from 9:30 a.m. to 5:30 p.m. daily. Call 631-661-4876 for details.

NAVIGATION: Reynolds Channel enters Great South Bay and passes Captree Island, Fire Island Inlet and Fire Island to the south. Channels lead to Captree State Park from east and west of the **Robert Moses Causeway**, linking it to the mainland. The State Channel cuts just south of it through the **Captree State Parkway Bridge** with 29-foot closed vertical clearance. The draw will open on signal every other hour on the even hour if at least a one-half hour advance notice is given by calling the number posted at the bridge. From April 1 through October 31, on Saturday, Sunday and federal holidays the draw opens every 3 hours beginning at 3:00 a.m.

Dockage: Captree Fuel, Bait and Tackle is a tackle shop that sells all fuels at the Fire Island Inlet. Near Ocean Beach, the municipal Atlantique Beach and Marina offers transient slips (reservations recommended). The dockmaster's office monitors VHF Channel 9 and is also available by telephone at 631-583-8610.

Nearby Seaview Boat Basin is a family-oriented community that maintains a marina, a children's playground and wading pool, six tennis courts, a ball field and a community house. They maintain 5 transient slips to 58 feet. The full-service Flynn's Marina & Restaurant (at Ocean Bay Park) offers overnight transient space as well as a day rate.

Sailors Haven Marina is a 18-slip National Seashore Park marina with 45 transient slips (to 65 feet) and a 14-day limit on stays. All slips have electric and water (extra fee charged).

Pines Marina Fire Island is an LGBTQ+ barrier island community surrounded by a national park. They can accommodate vessels to 110 feet. (Call ahead.) Davis Park Marina is a full-service town marina for residents and non-residents with available slips offered on a first-come, first-served basis. The 256-slip marina is located in an enclosed basin.

Watch Hill National Seashore Marina is another large National Seashore Park marina with slips to 50 feet. Note that none of these facilities sell fuel or offer repairs.

Anchorage: There are numerous spots to anchor in 7- to 25-foot MLW depths between Fire Island and Captree Island, either east or west of the Robert Moses Bridge. Watch for the shoal area marked with flashing red buoy "18" just east of the bridge near the Fire Island shore. Note also the cable area east of the bridge and do not anchor there.

You can also anchor in sand with good holding on either side of Atlantique Beach and Marina. This is where the ferries operate from so don't get in their way.

■ MORICHES BAY TO SHINNECOCK CANAL

Moriches Bay

Moriches Bay is about 8 nm long with central depths of 3 to 6 feet MLW with sizable shoals in its southern reaches and many coves and creeks that tend to shoal despite dredging. The towns of Moriches, East Moriches and Center Moriches rim the bay.

Seatuck Creek leads to the pretty, small village of Eastport, which has the feel of old Long Island. The main street (Montauk Highway) is lined with sunshine-bathed buildings that house shops and eateries.

NOTE: South of Remsenburg on the barrier beach is the site of Pike's Inlet for the time it existed. It was created during the Halloween 1992 nor'easter, when the ocean overran this narrow strip. Subsequent storms enlarged the breach until it was several hundred feet wide. Less than a year later the Army Corps of Engineers later put a metal wall across it and poured sand into the breach to seal it.

NAVIGATION: Continuing east the course doglegs into a dredged channel where markers must be observed. **Smith Point Bridge** (18-foot closed vertical clearance) connects mainland Shirley with eastern Fire Island. The draw opens on signal from October 1 through April 30 from 8:00 a.m. to 4:00 p.m. and from May 1 through September 30 from 6:00 a.m. to 10:00 p.m. At all other times during these periods, the draw will open as soon as possible but no more than 1 hour after a request to open is received.

The channel continues about 3 nm through Narrow Bay, past Mastic Beach into the western approach to Moriches Bay. Note that the shoal-bordered channel is only a few hundred feet wide. The shifting shoals of Moriches Bay change so rapidly that mariners often find it difficult to maneuver without running aground. The Army Corps of Engineers cautions that shoals of 1 to 5 feet MLW are located in the vicinity of Tuthill Point and 3 to 6 feet MLW in Moriches Bay. Ongoing dredging does occur; however, the area is very prone to shoaling.

Tree stakes have been reported that will guide you through the deepest sections of the bay. You are advised to leave the stakes to the south when headed east. These makeshift markers follow a zigzag pattern north to Harts Cove, east to Seatuck Cove and south to the marked channel. They are helpful for cruisers who would otherwise need to call the Coast Guard or local marinas to get information on the shoaling.

Dockage: Marinas are located on most of the creeks but they are almost exclusively for local boats and all report shallow depths. The 140-slip Atlantic Cove Marina (formerly Windswept Marina) has full-service dockage facilities (to 40 feet) including valet docking as well as hauling and launching.

Side Trip: Great Gun

Near the eastern tip of the inlet, there is a little-known park accessible only by foot or boat. Great Gun Beach is a town-run park about 0.75 mile west of the inlet. Because eastern Fire Island is a national seashore, it is nearly undeveloped. Docks, restrooms and a narrow boardwalk to the beach are all the facilities here. At night, Great Gun is nothing but the sweep of stars, the ocean and the inlet.

NAVIGATION: On the south shore of Moriches Bay, an interesting route east from Great Gun is through a small channel known locally as "Old Cut." It is a narrow, unmarked channel through the shallows running 10°

Moriches Bay, NY

EAST MORICHES	Largest Vessel	VHF	Total Slips	Approach/Dockside Depth	Floating Docks	Gas/Diesel	Repairs/Haulout	Min/Max Amps	Pump-Out Station
1. Atlantic Cove Marina (formerly Windswept Marina) (631) 878-2100	40	68	140	4.0 / 4.0	F	GD	RH	30	P

WiFi Wireless Internet Access
Visit www.waterwayguide.com for current rates, fuel prices, website addresses and other up-to-the-minute information.
(Information in the table is provided by the facilities.)

Scan here for more details:

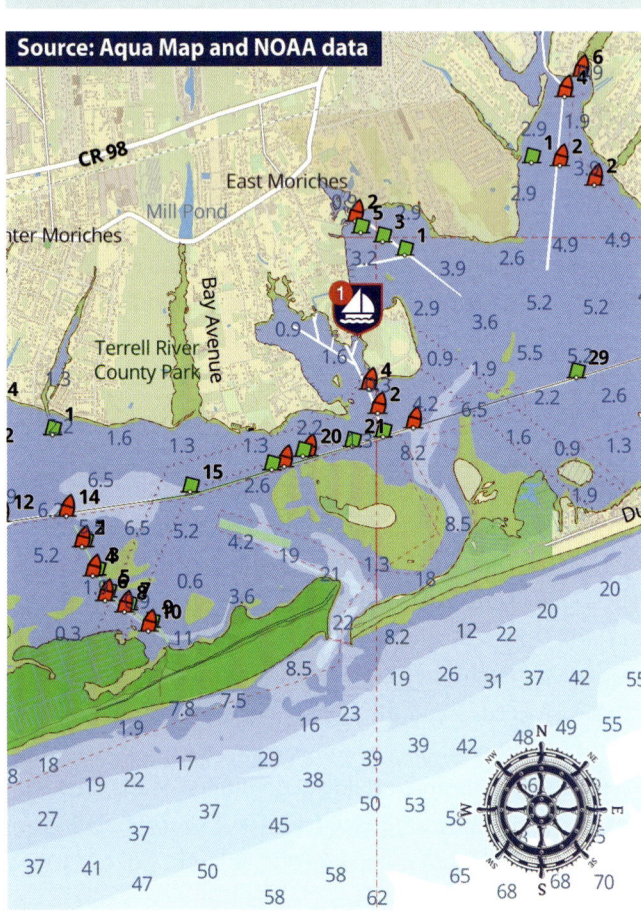

Source: Aqua Map and NOAA data

(true) from Great Gun. It intersects another channel that is dredged but not buoyed. This channel leads you into the relatively deep water just inside Moriches Inlet. These are unstable channels so slow and easy is the way.

From the inner mouth of Moriches Inlet, a curving channel leads back to the State Channel in Moriches Bay. Hug the southern and eastern banks of this channel until you are dead east (true) of the unnamed island inside the inlet, then you can move to center channel. The unnamed island has become a home to the growing seal population of the South Shore bays. You will see them basking on the beach, but will take to the safety of the water if a boat comes too close.

Anchorage: To do some basking of your own, beach the boat along the curving channel. (There is a steep

drop-off.) It is a quick walk to the ocean beach, but do not swim in the channel. Fast-moving boats hug the shore, making it dangerous.

On weekend days Great Gun attracts a small crowd of boats. It is also easy to anchor just off the docks and wade in; just allow for the tide. The restrooms are locked at about 5:00 p.m. There is more room to anchor east of the channel than west. Great Gun Beach is unmarked on the chart but you will see the buoyed channel to it through the shallows of Moriches Bay.

Westhampton Beach

NAVIGATION:

South of Speonk Point a large shoal with 2-to 3-foot MLW charted depths extends north from Gunning Point and may encroach on the channel. About 4 nm east of Moriches Inlet, transient accommodations are available along both sides of the channel at Westhampton Beach. The channel angles into Quantuck Canal in this area with two bascule bridges just 1 mile apart.

West Bay Bridge has a 10-foot closed vertical clearance and is followed by **Beach Lane Bridge** with a 14-foot closed vertical clearance. The schedule for both bridges is the same: The draw will open on signal from October 1 through April 30 from 8:00 a.m. to 4:00 p.m. and from May 1 through September 30 from 6:00 a.m. to 10:00 p.m. At all other times during these periods the draws will open as soon as possible but no more than 1 hour after a request to open is received.

Just north of this area on the mainland side is Westhampton, one of Long Island's most popular summer colonies.

The channel leaves Quantuck Canal for a straight, dredged course across Quantuck Bay and then enters Quogue (rhymes with "fog") Canal. A little more than 1 mile long, the canal bends as shoals push out from the village of Quogue, an old summer resort with big homes (but few marinas).

WESTHAMPTON BEACH		Largest Vessel	VHF	Total Slips	Approach/ Dockside Depth	Floating Docks	Gas/ Diesel	Repairs/ Haulout	Min/Max Amps	Pump-Out Station
1. Ocean Resort at Bath and Tennis WiFi	(631) 288-2500	50	9	65	9.0 / 7.0				30 / 50	P
2. Village Marina - Westhampton Beach WiFi	(631) 288-9496	55	68	125	4.0 / 4.0					P

Moriches Bay, NY

WiFi Wireless Internet Access
Visit www.waterwayguide.com for current rates, fuel prices, website addresses and other up-to-the-minute information.
(Information in the table is provided by the facilities.)

Scan here for more details:

Quogue (Post Lane) Bridge (15-foot closed vertical clearance) is near the western end of the canal. The draw follows the same schedule as the West Bay and Beach Lane Bridges. Just beyond the bridge Quogue Canal enters Shinnecock Bay.

Dockage: Ocean Resort at Bath and Tennis operates seasonally with memberships offered to those who rent a marina slip, cabana or cabin. Members have access to all of the resort amenities and services. All transient reservations must be accompanied by a deposit (minimum two nights). The well-maintained Village Marina - Westhampton Beach welcomes transients to 55 feet in a quiet, protected basin. It is conveniently located just two blocks from Main St.

Shinnecock Bay

Shinnecock Bay, last of the important South Shore bays, is a pivotal point for cruising boats. The inland passage along Long Island's South Shore ends here and to the north Shinnecock Canal gives direct access to Great Peconic Bay, the Long Island North and South Fork areas and the north shore of Long Island.

The bay is about 7 nm long and closed off north and east by the Long Island mainland and is divided by long, sandy Ponquogue Point. Access from the mainland to the barrier island is via the 55-foot fixed vertical clearance Ponquogue Bridge.

Shinnecock's port houses the second largest fishing fleet in New York State with three commercial docks. The area also provides a habitat for piping plovers, least terns and other endangered species of birds.

NAVIGATION: Shinnecock Bay starts unremarkable enough at the eastern end of narrow Quogue Canal where the channel turns north. It follows a relatively straight course through 1- to 2-foot MLW shoals past a series of private, dredged creeks (Penniman, Stone and Phillips) with attractive shores but no public marinas. Just off Phillips Point the channel crooks to the east and transient boats have a choice of marinas.

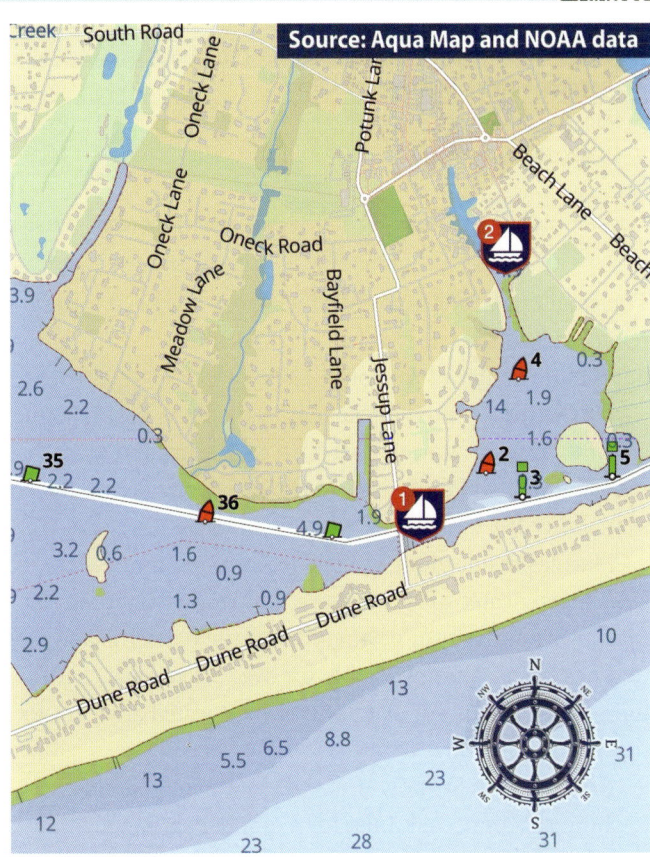

Source: Aqua Map and NOAA data

Tiana Bay lies east of Pine Neck, which is lined with several shallow finger canals. The bay is open and has fairly stable 5-foot MLW depths instead of the bars, marshes and dredged cuts of most of the eastern portion of the South Shore. According to local reports, shoals extend from Pine Neck Point nearly to the channel.

From Tiana Bay, the route passes the long finger of East Point, headland of Smith Creek, with shoals all about. Stick to the buoys. The narrow channel forks beyond the 55-foot fixed vertical clearance **Ponquogue Bridge**, where the Shinnecock Coast Guard station is located.

The southeast branch runs toward Shinnecock Inlet and the northeast branch to Shinnecock Canal. Both branches go through bars and marshes. The southeast channel toward Shinnecock Inlet passes between two of the three mud flats that are known as the Warner Islands.

Shinnecock Bay, NY

EAST QUOGUE		Largest Vessel	VHF	Total Slips	Approach/ Dockside Depth	Floating Docks	Gas/ Diesel	Repairs/ Haulout	Min/Max Amps	Pump-Out Station
1. Aldrich Boat Yard & Marina	(631) 653-5300	45		60	6.0 / 6.0	F		RH	30	
TIANA AREA										
2. Ponquogue Marina **WiFi**	(631) 728-2264	45		50	3.5 / 6.0	F		RH	30	
SHINNECOCK INLET										
3. Oakland's Restaurant & Marina	(516) 523-1435	60	68	72	5.0 / 6.0		GD		50	
SHINNECOCK CANAL										
4. Shagwong Marinas - Southampton **WiFi**	(631) 728-4220	120	68	175	8.0 / 6.0		GD	RH	50	P
5. Mariner's Cove Marine	(631) 728-0286	52		182	9.0 / 5.0	F		RH	30	P
6. Shinnecock Canal Marina	(631) 852-8291	47		50	10.0 / 6.0	F	GD		30	P

WiFi Wireless Internet Access
Visit www.waterwayguide.com for current rates, fuel prices, website addresses and other up-to-the-minute information.
(Information in the table is provided by the facilities.)

Scan here for more details:

The smallest, westernmost of the islands has been locally renamed Seal Island. This has become another seal population center of the south bays.

Dockage: Limited dockage is available at East Quogue at family-owned Aldrich Boat Yard & Marina and at well-maintained Ponquogue Marina. Call ahead for slip availability (to 45 feet).

Marinas inside along the barrier strip of Shinnecock Inlet mostly cater to sportfishers. Oakland's Restaurant & Marina is a waterfront destination on the barrier island that has been a summer staple for over 30 years with a full-service restaurant, bar and marina located adjacent to the Shinnecock Inlet.

Anchorage: Shallow-draft boats can snug in close to shore at Shinnecock Inlet for a quiet anchorage with excellent holding and easy to access to/from the ocean. It is well protected from offshore winds. Easy dinghy access to Oakland's Restaurant & Marina.

Shinnecock Canal & Lock

Shinnecock Canal is located in the northwestern corner of Shinnecock Bay above Cormorant Point. The canal is the gateway to the Peconic Bays and Long Island's north shore. West of the canal is the lively community of Hampton Bays with motels and good restaurants.

NOTE: The part of Hampton Bays along the canal was called Canoe Place until the end World War I, perpetuating the legend that a Montauk chief dug the first canal to eliminate a canoe portage. It is still charted as Canoe Place.

NAVIGATION: The 1-mile-long canal is wide and deep for the steady passage of boats in both directions. **Shinnecock Canal Railroad Bridge** has a fixed overhead clearance of 22 feet, setting the clearance restriction for the canal. The 25-foot fixed vertical clearance **CR 80 Bridge** is prior to the railroad bridge. The county maintains free, unattended, DIY ginpoles for un-stepping and re-stepping sailboat masts at each end of the canal.

The 250-foot-long and 41-foot-wide **Shinnecock Lock** with 12 feet over the sills is located about midway through the canal. The tide running southward opens the lock and parallel 27-foot tidal gates. Southbound boats usually use the tidal gates; however, larger boats are put through the lock whenever possible. Traffic lights control passage through the lock.

The lock is operated 24 hours a day and the operator controls all movement of boats through the lock by light signals. Communicate with the operator on VHF Channel 13 or by calling 631-852-8299. When approaching the lock boaters should stop at a safe distance and follow specified signals. Boaters should give three short blasts on the horn or whistle. Lock operators will reply with lights in the following manner:

Green: Lock is ready and craft may advance.

Red: Craft must wait.

No light: Craft must wait or tie up to approach wall.

Six flashes of red or green: Craft must remain stopped and await further instructions.

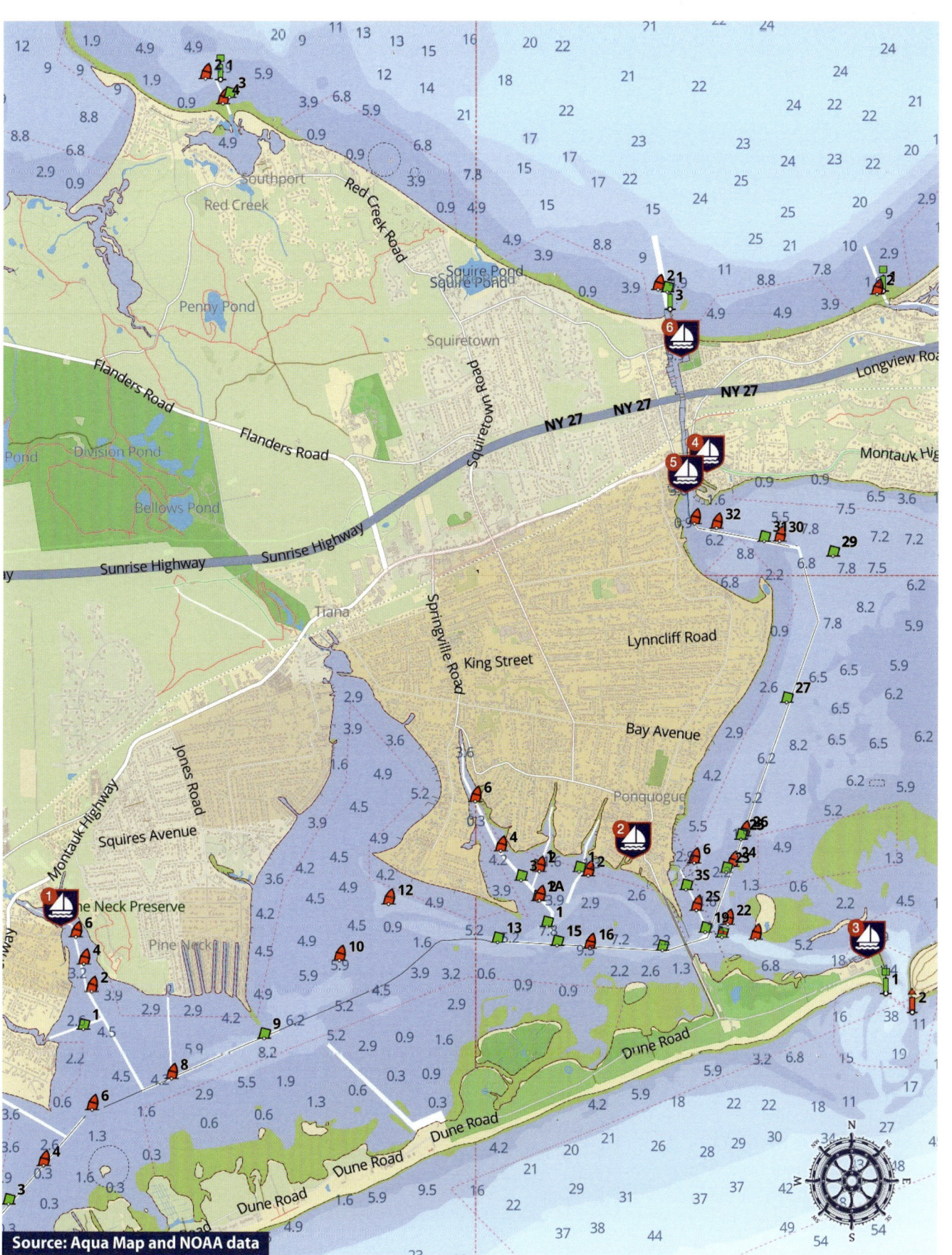

Great Peconic Bay

Shinnecock Canal

It is important to note that when the gates are open and the locks are not in use, you can pilot right through the canal. The current normally flows to the south when the gates are open (at up to 6 knots). When the gates are closed, you can still lock through. The current is relatively tame within 1 hour of the gate opening or closing. At other times it can be woolly.

Sunrise Highway (NY 27) Bridge (with 23-foot fixed vertical clearance) is located after the lock and before the marinas.

CAUTION: Avoid going south with the current when it is raging. It will be a fast ride through the narrow passage. Going north in these conditions also requires slow speed and no wake to maintain control. Northbound boats without strong engines can have a hard time and should negotiate the canal at slack water. When traveling in either direction, watch for the eddies on the south side by the bridge.

Dockage: The banks of the canal are lined with marinas, boatyards, boat brokerages and fishing stations–one after another–except near the lock. At the mouth of the Shinnecock Canal is the full-service Shagwong Marinas - Southampton offering approximately 175 wet slips that can accommodate yachts up to 120 feet. There are several boat brokerages here that maintain a few transient slips including Mariner's Cove Marine, which has transient slips to 52 feet and a wonderful beach.

Above the lock at the north end of the canal is the municipal Shinnecock

Canal Marina. This fully equipped facility includes free pump-out stations, restrooms and showers, and water and electric hookups. Meschutt Beach County Park is adjacent to the marina with lifeguard-protected swimming and a full-service concession stand.

■ OUTSIDE (OCEAN ROUTE) TO SHINNECOCK BAY

If you are in a hurry, you can run the coast of Long Island offshore. It is a pleasant trip in good weather if you have the skill and the proper boat. In bad weather, however, the outside passage can be unpleasant and potentially hazardous.

Long barrier beaches run between most of the island's mainland and the Atlantic Ocean on the south shore of Long Island. Thirty-foot depths are only 1 nm from shore for most of the outside run but there is considerable distance between inlets that are safe to enter, especially in poor conditions.

There are six inlets along the south shore. All can be shoal-prone and continually shifting. Weather systems moving along the east coast of the U.S. frequently assault the shore, sometimes creating new ingress and sometimes shoaling in existing ones. You can try to follow a local boat into one of these inlets; otherwise, you have no choice but to make the long trek around Montauk Point.

Rockaway Inlet is the first inlet along the South Shore and is 5 miles northeast of Sandy Hook. Even though the inlet does not connect with the inside waterways, there are several areas of interest within the inlet itself. The inlet enters through Dead Horse Bay into Sheepshead Bay and farther into Jamaica Bay via the **Marine Parkway (Gil Hodges Memorial) Bridg**e (55-foot vertical clearance when down, 152-foot clearance when raised).

⚠️
CAUTION: Increased shoaling has been observed in the vicinity of Sheepshead Bay Channel, specifically near Sheepshead Bay buoys "6" and "7." Aids marking the channel may be unreliable. All mariners are urged to use extreme caution when transiting this area.

There is a well-marked channel along the northern shore along Coney Island and Brighton Beach and another along the southern shore on the inside of Rockaway

Fire Island Light

Reynolds Channel

Point. Except in a dead-on west wind, this can afford a secure place to wait for weather to go around the point and continue along Long Island South Shore. (This area is discussed in more detail in Chapter 4, "New York Harbor and the East River.")

East Rockaway Inlet

NAVIGATION: The East Rockaway Inlet is the next inlet encountered proceeding along the South Shore on the outside. It is the preferable inlet to access the inside run of the South Shore because it is wide and easy to navigate. This inlet (known locally as Debs Inlet) is 10 nm from Coney Island and 13 nm from Sandy Hook. The U.S. Army Corps of Engineers tries to maintain 12-foot MLW depths in East Rockaway Inlet but as with all inlets, use caution and good common sense when you enter.

You will find the inlet easy to enter in good weather. A flashing white (every four seconds) 33-foot-high tower marks the inlet's eastern jetty extending from Silver Point. Shoaling from 1-to 5-foot MLW depths builds out from the jetty toward the west. If approaching from the east or south, give the jetty and Silver Point a wide berth.

You will pass under the **Atlantic Beach Bridge** (25-foot closed vertical clearance) when entering Reynolds Channel. The draw opens on signal from October 1 through May 14. From May 15 through September 30 the draw will open on signal, except that it need open only on the hour and half-hour from 4:00 p.m. to 7:00 p.m. on weekdays and from 11:00 a.m. to 9:00 p.m. on Saturdays, Sundays, Memorial Day, Independence Day and Labor Day. From May 15 through September 30. Once inside the inlet, you can cruise comfortably while seas build outside or you can transit the inside Reynolds Channel route and head back out at Jones Inlet.

East Rockaway inlet

Jones Inlet

NAVIGATION: Jones Inlet, almost 9 nm east of East Rockaway Inlet, is dredged periodically when bottom conditions warrant. It is well marked but the buoys are uncharted and frequently moved. The inlet has been holding at a depth of 9 feet MLW but the current chart calls for cautious navigation. The western (shoal) bar should be avoided. A VHF radio request for local knowledge is always a prudent move to avoid shoal areas that might have developed since the last buoy relocation.

Fire Island Inlet

NAVIGATION: Fire Island Inlet is the only pass between the Atlantic Ocean and Great South Bay but it should not be attempted without local knowledge. The U.S. Army Corps of Engineers dredges here periodically but also indicates that conditions will not be dependable until an extensive stabilization program is begun. Powerful storms have played havoc with the shifting shoals and submerged buoys. About 2 miles in from the mouth, the Robert Moses Bridge crosses the inlet.

> ⚠️
> *CAUTION:* Note that although the bridge is posted with 65-foot clearance, it is recommended that you pass at low tide as actual clearance seems to be closer to 60 feet.

Fire Island Inlet is about 13 nm beyond Jones Inlet. In fair weather, you can use Fire Island Inlet to get to the open waters of Great South Bay while avoiding the tediously slow and crowded channel inside from Jones Inlet. Its buoy system is excellent but not charted because of the continuously shifting shoals.

The entrance is difficult without local knowledge, even in good weather, and it is unsafe to enter when wind and tide oppose. In heavy weather, breakers bar the entrance.

Do not attempt entry in these conditions or with poor visibility. The local Coast Guard (Station Fire Island) will give information to those unfamiliar with the area.

Once inside the inlet, depths improve along the southern edge of the channel. Watch for flashing red buoy "10" and a series of green and red navigational aids, which will guide you toward the **Robert Moses Bridge** (65-foot fixed vertical clearance).

The Fire Island lighthouse, originally completed in 1858, is on the western part of Fire Island National Seashore and is adjacent to Robert Moses State Park. The lighthouse has a focal plane of 168 feet above sea level and can be seen more than 20 miles away. The light is maintained as a private aid to navigation.

The lighthouse is operated by the Fire Island Lighthouse Preservation Society and offers exhibits and a nature trail. Access to the lighthouse beach is by walking and there are no lifeguards. The lighthouse is open from May 25 through Labor Day from 9:30 a.m. to 5:30 p.m. daily. Call 631-661-4876 for details.

Shinnecock Inlet

NAVIGATION: Shinnecock Inlet was created by the great hurricane of 1938. It mostly maintains 20-foot MLW depths (with the exception of one charted 17-foot-MLW section at the entrance) and has stone breakwaters. When entering the inlet from the ocean, proceed carefully and slightly favor the west side of the channel.

Enter the inlet between the flashing green 36-foot tower "1" on the west jetty and the flashing red 36-foot tower "2" on the east jetty. Shinnecock Light (75-foot flashing red every 15 seconds) will appear to the west as you enter. Many small fishing boats use the inlet so be on the lookout during your approach.

Beyond Shinnecock Inlet are the prestigious Hamptons: Southampton, East Hampton and Bridgehampton. The Hamptons retain much of their colonial charm with trendy shops, gourmet restaurants, pleasant parks and beaches, which continue to draw the rich and famous as visitors and seasonal residents. No trip to the area would be complete without an excursion to any or all of them.

Shinnecock inlet

Section 3: Long Island Sound

Chapter 7: North Shore: To Milford Harbor, CT

Chapter 8: North Shore: New Haven, CT to Watch Hill, RI

Chapter 9: South Shore: Io Mattituck Inlet, NY

Chapter 10: Long Island Twin Forks, NY

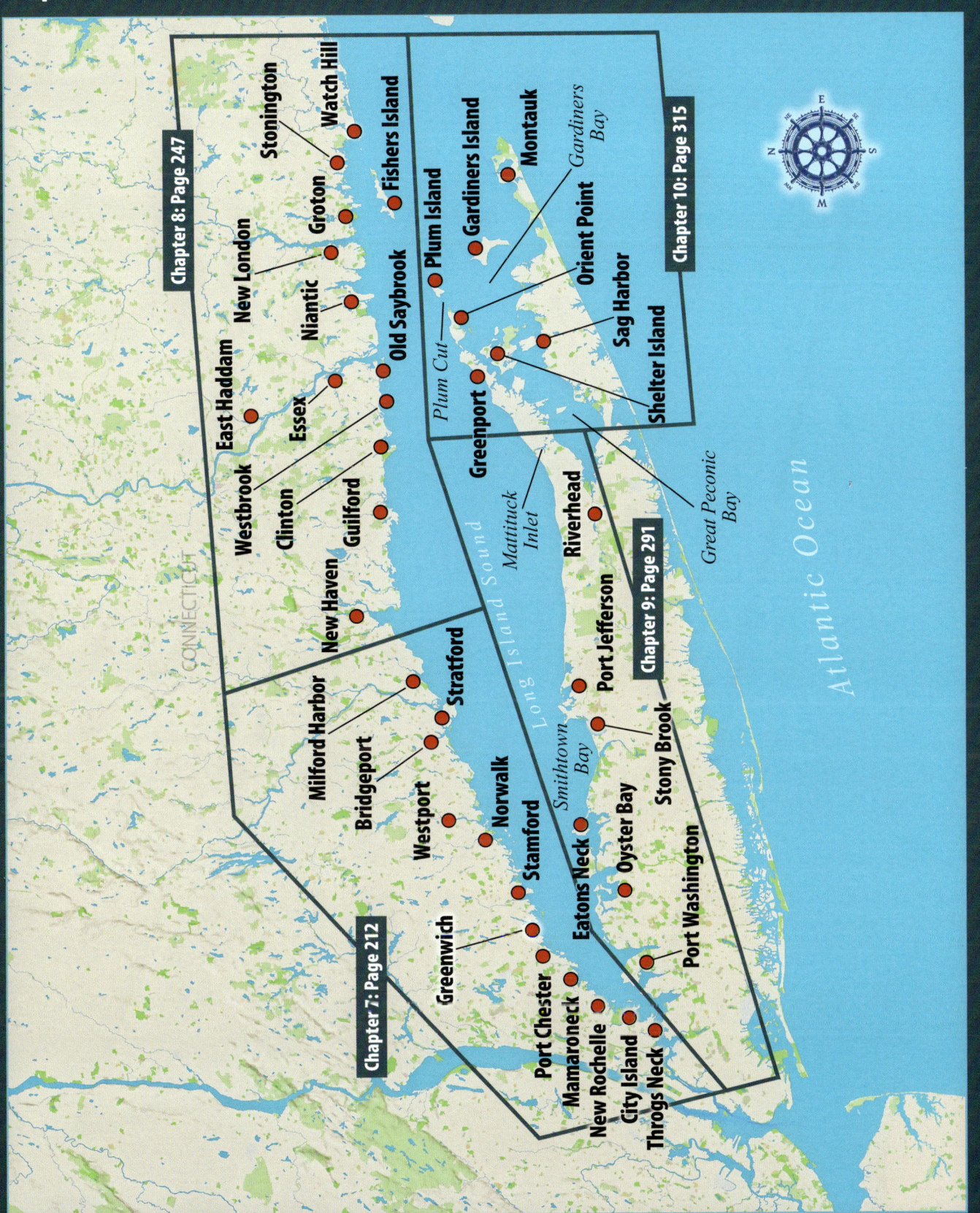

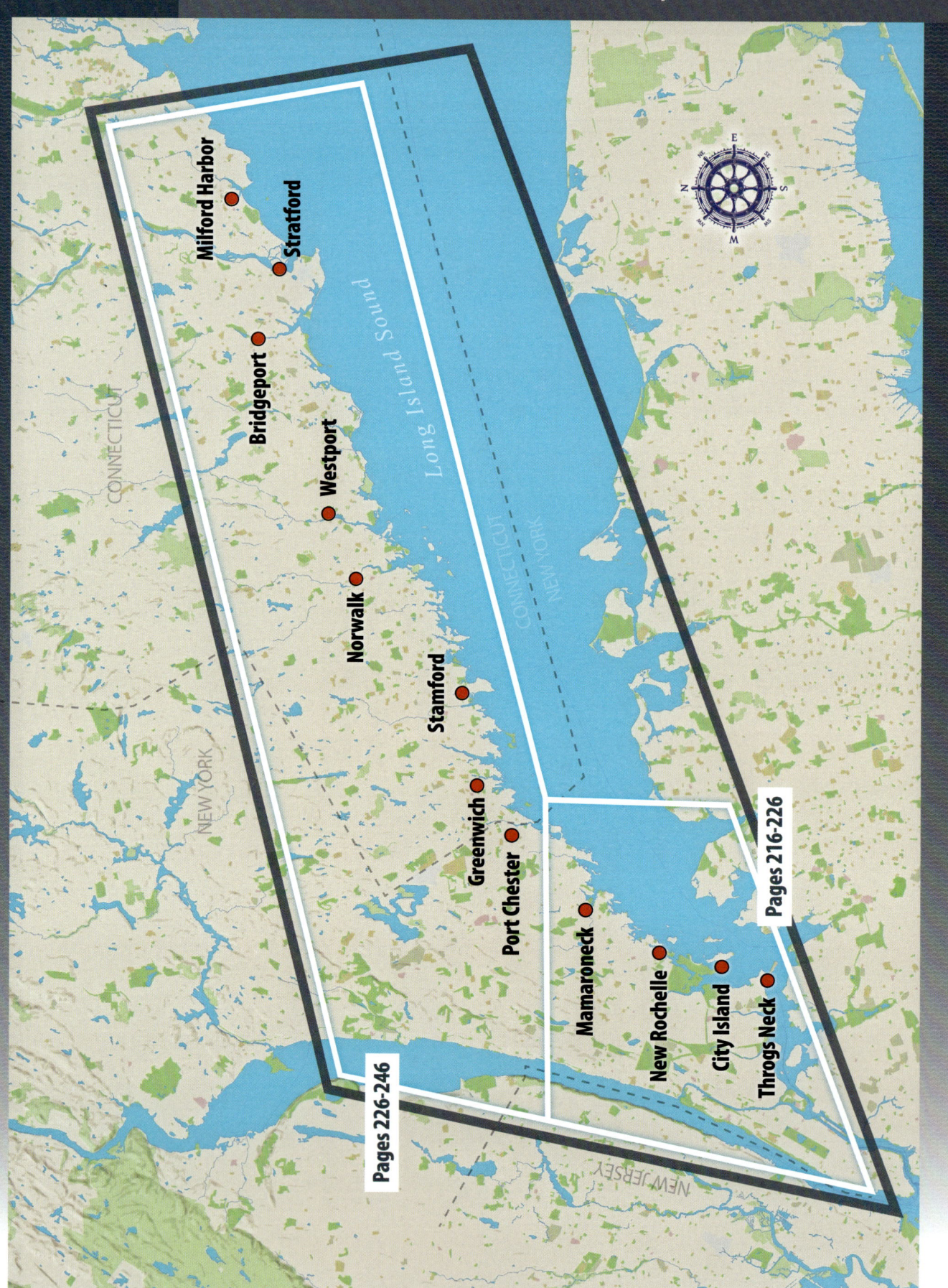

■ NAVIGATION NOTES

Long Island Sound packs history, high-tech boating and fun in an estuary that stretches 90 nm between New York City and Block Island, RI. Long and slim-looking on the chart, it is actually up to 20 nm wide in the middle.

Much as New York is just "the City," Long Island Sound requires no further name than "the Sound" in local conversation. It's a major commercial artery, an important fishing and lobstering ground and one of the famed cruising areas of the U.S.

Along the northern shore of Long Island Sound, you'll find a string of coastal cities extending from New York to Rhode Island. While many of these cities began as industrial centers because of easy access to shipping and are now populated and diverse urban centers, there are still numerous smaller towns with harbors along the shoreline.

On weekends, the Sound is a wonderland of sailboats producing a spectacular sight. In addition to the parade of cruising boats transiting the Sound, yacht clubs hold organized regattas on a regular basis. These fleets are especially common near City Island, Bridgeport, New Haven and New London under the north shore.

The local mariner need never leave the Sound from year after year. Crisscrossing between Connecticut's rocky shore and Long Island's sandy beaches, mariners cruise the summer away, anchoring in isolated coves, visiting luxurious marinas, racing under sail, fishing, taking long side trips up navigable rivers and exploring big bays.

Cruising Conditions

The weather on Long Island Sound is generally hospitable with the predictable summer thunderstorms. Thunderstorms, of course, bring strong, gusty winds. The occasional nor'easter, often lasting as long as three days, delivers winds, steep seas, low temperatures and torrents of rain. One shore or the other generally offers a lee but a nasty chop is the norm in these conditions. These seas will often continue for a couple days after the sky has cleared and while much reduced, they are still no fun to battle.

Heavy fog, which might greet the mariner several mornings a year, can be thick enough to be dangerous, even to experienced mariners. The Sound has an excellent overlapping system of fog signals and it is well charted.

> NOTE: Continuous weather reports are broadcast on VHF-FM WX-1 from New York City and New London, CT. Most commercial radio stations broadcast boating forecasts during the season.

Execution Rocks Lighthouse located on the Western end of Long Island Sound.

Cross-Sound Distances

The table below is a selection of major cruising stops on Long Island Sound and the distances between them. It is not a complete list of ports and is intended solely as a guide to cruise planning. All distances have been figured along the most direct course consistent with safe, normal navigation. All figures are approximate. Actual mileage will depend on variations of course, speed, boat, weather, currents and other cruising conditions.

FROM	MILES TO:	NAUTICAL	STATUTE
City Island (off Belden Pt.)	Stamford	17	19
	Stratford	40	46
	Clinton	64	73
	Saybrook Point	79	91
	New London	85	98
	Mystic	89	102
	Oyster Bay Harbor	17	19
	Huntington Bay	20	23
	Port Jefferson	33	38
	Mattituck Inlet	54	62
	Orient Point	75	86
Stamford (East Branch, past hurricane barrier)	City Island	17	19
	Stratford	27	31
	Clinton	54	62
	Saybrook Point	56	64
	New London	75	86
	Mystic	73	84
	Oyster Bay Harbor	9	10
	Huntington Bay	10	11
	Port Jefferson	24	28
	Mattituck Inlet	45	52
	Orient Point	61	70
Stratford (2 miles up from outer breakwater light)	City Island	40	46
	Stamford	27	31
	Clinton	31	36
	Saybrook Point	39	45
	New London	53	61
	Mystic	57	66
	Oyster Bay Harbor	30	34
	Huntington Bay	25	28
	Port Jefferson	15	17
	Mattituck Inlet	28	32
	Orient Point	42	48
Clinton (Cedar Island)	City Island	64	73
	Stamford	54	62
	Stratford	31	36
	Saybrook Point	11	13
	New London	25	29
	Mystic	30	34
	Oyster Bay Harbor	51	59
	Huntington Bay	47	54
	Port Jefferson	32	37
	Mattituck Inlet	15	17
Saybrook Point	City Island	79	91
	Stamford	56	64
	Stratford	39	45
	Clinton	11	13
	New London	17	19
	Mystic	20	23
	Oyster Bay Harbor	61	70
	Huntington Bay	56	64
	Port Jefferson	40	46
	Mattituck Inlet	20	23
	Orient Point	9	10
New London (abeam of Shaw Cove)	City Island	85	98
	Stamford	75	86
	Stratford	53	61
	Clinton	25	29
	Saybrook Point	17	19
	Mystic	12	14
	Oyster Bay Harbor	74	85
	Huntington Bay	70	81
	Port Jefferson	59	68
	Mattituck Inlet	34	39
	Orient Point	15	17

FROM	MILES TO:	NAUTICAL	STATUTE
Mystic (abeam of Shaw Cove)	City Island	89	102
	Stamford	73	84
	Stratford	57	66
	Clinton	30	34
	Saybrook Point	20	23
	New London	12	14
	Oyster Bay Harbor	78	90
	Huntington Bay	75	86
	Port Jefferson	58	67
	Mattituck Inlet	35	40
	Orient Point	16	18
Oyster Bay Harbor (off Plum Point)	City Island	17	19
	Stamford	9	10
	Stratford	30	34
	Clinton	51	59
	Saybrook Point	61	70
	New London	74	85
	Mystic	78	90
	Huntington Bay	9	10
	Port Jefferson	25	29
	Mattituck Inlet	48	55
	Orient Point	64	73
Huntington Bay (Lloyd Harbor Light)	City Island	20	23
	Stamford	10	11
	Stratford	25	29
	Clinton	47	54
	Saybrook Point	56	64
	New London	70	80
	Mystic	75	86
	Oyster Bay Harbor	9	10
	Port Jefferson	20	23
	Mattituck Inlet	41	47
	Orient Point	58	67
Port Jefferson (2 miles in from jetty light)	City Island	33	38
	Stamford	24	28
	Stratford	15	17
	Clinton	32	37
	Saybrook Point	40	46
	New London	59	68
	Mystic	58	67
	Oyster Bay Harbor	25	29
	Huntington Bay	20	23
	Mattituck Inlet	27	31
	Orient Point	44	51
Mattituck Inlet (Mattituck Creek)	City Island	54	62
	Stamford	45	52
	Stratford	28	32
	Clinton	15	17
	Saybrook Point	20	23
	New London	34	39
	Mystic	35	40
	Oyster Bay Harbor	48	55
	Huntington Bay	41	47
	Port Jefferson	27	31
	Orient Point	20	23
Orient Point (abeam of light)	City Island	75	86
	Stamford	61	70
	Stratford	42	48
	Clinton	15	17
	Saybrook Point	9	10
	New London	15	17
	Mystic	16	18
	Oyster Bay Harbor	64	73
	Huntington Bay	58	67
	Port Jefferson	44	51
	Mattituck Inlet	20	23

As a rule, in summer months winds pick up in early afternoon and get progressively stronger as the day wears on. Most powerboats wanting to make time get an early morning start or they travel at night when winds tend to die, using the chain of lights that defines a clear path down the center of the Sound. Sailboats may choose to get underway in the light winds of morning, especially if heading south from a river anchorage, before making good time under sail during the breezy afternoons.

Check the current NOAA Tide Charts and avoid situations of wind countering current if you want to avoid stiff chop.

Sailors can also set out when the wind is easing and use auxiliary power, if necessary, to run the usually placid night waters. When underway at night, stay well clear of areas where there might be lobster pots, oyster beds and fish traps; all are, at best, difficult to spot.

In addition, keep a sharp lookout for tugs with tows, which often run the Sound at night. The tows are often on very long lines and can be difficult to spot. Especially around the busy port of Bridgeport, tugs can behave rather unpredictably, circling as they bring in or let out their tows in preparation for docking. A radio call on VHF Channel 16 or 13 is advisable to clarify each vessel's intentions. It is not advisable to attempt to enter an unfamiliar harbor after dark.

Tides & Currents

At the western end of Long Island Sound, an 8-foot to 10-foot rise and fall is to be expected; mean tidal range is about 7.5 feet. The tidal range drops to less than 3 feet as you travel east.

Currents on Long Island Sound are not to be taken lightly. The currents run strongest at the narrow ends of the Sound, reaching maximum velocity (up to 4 knots) at The Race and Plum Gut on the eastern end between Fishers Island and the North Fork of Long Island. Currents taper off to 0.5 knot in mid-Sound but run hard around points and shoals. In general, the flood sets westerly and the ebb sets easterly.

Riding a fair current can improve your cruising time substantially and make the trip more comfortable, especially if you can also arrange a broad or strong following wind. It's worth an early morning to ensure the current is in your favor.

Navigation

Markers on Long Island Sound are frequent with many lighthouses, both mid-channel and ashore, offering easy-to-locate reference points. Most rocks and reefs are well charted and marked. Make sure to account for current in all courses.

For the hurried transient boater passing through the Sound, the navigation is straightforward. From the Throgs Neck Bridge at the sound's western entrance, a GPS or compass course will lead you roughly northeast past the Sound's first important aid to navigation, Stepping Stones Light (pass on the north side), near City Island. Execution Rocks Lighthouse, which appears next, can be left on either side.

At Execution Rocks, the course changes to almost due east (magnetic), straight down the Sound to the midpoint of Stratford Shoal Lighthouse about 30 nm away. The course remains due east through the widest part of the Sound, almost

20 nm across. A smooth non stop trip through the Sound to Newport will include planning for the currents mentioned above but can be done with ease.

On the other hand, there are many reasons to stop along the way. On the south side of Long Island Sound (the North Shore of Long Island), you will find large natural harbors with ample facilities and room to anchor. Hempstead Harbor, Oyster Bay and Huntington Harbor offer complete cruising grounds for small boats that never have to leave the mouth of the harbor.

On the Connecticut shore, frequent small harbors cover the coast along with numerous islands, rock outcroppings and river entrances. The harbors of the western end are more complicated to enter and more tightly packed. Marinas are ample but are normally crowded with local boats. Advance reservations are necessary for dockside space.

Many harbors are dominated by large elaborate yacht clubs such as Larchmont, Indian Harbor in Greenwich and Pequot in Southport. Docking at these clubs requires reciprocal privileges from the skipper's home club. As you continue along, the rivers get bigger and the bays at their mouths more inviting. Similarly, the facilities are a bit more spread out and tend to have more space available.

It is important to note that Special Anchorage Areas are noted on the charts in many harbors covered in this edition. When anchored in these areas, vessels 65 feet or less in length are not required to show anchor lights, day shapes or sound signals. In spite of the proliferation of mooring balls, it is possible to still find places to anchor.

When anchoring, be sure to keep an appropriate distance from mooring balls, channels, docks, boatyards, marinas and (of course) other boats. Anchoring within a Special Anchorage Area does not require permission, but permission is required for use of mooring balls within or outside the anchorage area.

■ THROGS NECK TO MAMARONECK HARBOR, NY

Throgs Neck Bridge (152-foot fixed vertical clearance) on the East River marks the entrance to Long Island Sound. After crossing under the bridge, turn sharply north around flashing red bell buoy "48" off the point of Throgs Neck.

The Stepping Stones lighthouse, a brownstone house perched on a stone foundation, is located to the northeast and is the first of the many distinctive lighthouses on the Sound. The eponymous "Stepping Stones" (jagged rocks, dry at low water) project southeast toward the Long Island shore of the sound and are marked by an unnumbered 4-second occulting green light. Leave Stepping Stones to starboard (west) and continue north.

NOTE: East Norwalk Blue Pumpout Program operates a mobile pump-out service for boaters along the North Shore of western Long Island Sound from Throgs Neck, NY to Bridgeport, CT from May to October.

Eastchester Bay

Eastchester Bay to the northwest has a few shoals and rocks, all of which are well marked. Along the western side of the bay is an almost landlocked cove and the entrance to protected Hammond Creek. To reach the cove, enter from the east under the Throgs Neck Bridge (North Span) (123-foot fixed vertical clearance) to the narrow entry, which has 5-foot MLW depths.

If traveling straight there from the East River, this means passing under the main span of the bridge (east bound), rounding SUNY Maritime College at the tip of Throgs Neck and then passing under the north span (west bound). Several marine facilities and a yacht club are here and you can anchor in the cove, if you can find depth and room. Consult your charts.

City Island, NY

City Island is only 1.5 miles long and 0.5 miles wide but its remarkable boating complexes contain the first great concentration of yachts on the trip out of the East River to Long Island Sound. City Island is part of the New York City's Bronx borough and is devoted to boating services as well as boating history. Yacht clubs, marinas, shipyards, sailmakers, electrical and electronics technicians, engine mechanics and marine supply houses abound.

City Island also boasts a long legacy of America's Cup fame. The 110-year string of 24 successful campaigns to defend the Cup began with *Magic*, completely rebuilt on City Island in 1870, and ended with *Freedom*, built on City Island in 1980. (In 1983 when City Island had no connection with the defender, America suffered her first Cup loss.) A visit to the City Island Nautical Museum is a must but it is only open on weekends (718-885-0008).

City Island is almost a self-contained community connected to the mainland by the fixed **City Island Bridge** (15-foot vertical clearance) on the northwest side of the island. The island's "nautical village" character has been preserved over the years and City Island can serve as a great stopover to refuel, time your transit through the East River and Hell Gate or stop before cruising east through Long Island Sound.

NAVIGATION: Even though most shoals and rocks are buoyed and charted, do not get too close to the dock-lined, rock-strewn shores. Even local mariners sometimes go astray on the large, menacing rock called Big Tom west of the island's southern tip. The clearly marked rock is the center of a triangle created by flashing red "2" to the south, red nun buoy "4" to the west and white and orange can "BT" to the east.

Boats staying outside the marked triangle will have no problem, but periodically someone attempts a shortcut or becomes confused by the welter of small fishing vessels obscuring the buoys and Big Tom claims yet another victim.

City Island Harbor on the island's east side between City Island and Hart Island is easily approached from the west on the main channel. Approaching from the east, the eastern side of City Island may be accessed by rounding Hart Island in either direction, although most skippers will find the route around the southern end more straightforward, especially in poor visibility.

12-Foot Fixed Bridge

MINNEFORD MARINA

City Island

The northern passage around Hart Island is generally well marked, although it has its share of obstructions. If attempting the north passage, watch carefully for Pea Island, East Nonations and Middle Reef, which are all south of David's Island and not marked. Next, proceed from flashing red bell buoy "4" to flashing green "1" without drifting south toward The Blauzes, which look like two small islands at high tide but extend a small distance all around.

Dockage/Moorings: Yacht clubs, boat yards and marinas ring City Island and a number of them can accommodate transient cruisers. On the west side of the island, Harlem Yacht Club and City Island Yacht Club both welcome transients on their moorings for a modest fee. This includes 24-hour launch service (call on VHF Channel 72) and use of the facilities. Should you need them, J.J. Burke Hardware & Marine Supply is a chandlery at 526 City Island Ave. (718-885-1559).

At the south end of the island the historic Consolidated Yachts NY Inc. is a working boat yard with few amenities but they do reserve some transient slips. PT boats were built here during WW II.

North Shore Distances
Nautical Miles (approximate)

LOCATION	BETWEEN POINTS	CUMULATIVE
Throgs Neck Bridge	0	
City Island	3	3
New Rochelle	5	8
Mamaroneck	4	12
Greenwich	8	20
Stamford	6	26
South Norwalk	11	37
Stratford	6	43
New Haven	15	58
Guilford	17	75
Connecticut River:		
Saybrook	17	92
Essex	8	100
New London	14	114
Fishers Island	5	119
Mystic	5	124

Long Island Sound, NY

CITY ISLAND		Largest Vessel	VHF	Total Slips	Approach/ Dockside Depth	Floating Docks	Gas/ Diesel	Repairs/ Haulout	Min/Max Amps	Pump-Out Station
1. Harlem Yacht Club **WiFi**	(718) 885-3078	45	72		8.0 / 4.0	F				
2. City Island Yacht Club **WiFi**	(718) 885-2487		72		9.0 / 6.0	F				
3. Consolidated Yachts NY Inc.	(718) 885-1900	150		64	14.0 / 14.0	F		RH	30 / 50	
4. South Minneford Yacht Club **WiFi**	(718) 885-3113	57	69	120	14.0 / 10.0	F		RH	30 / 50	
5. Minneford Marina **WiFi**	(718) 885-2000	125	77	164	17.0 / 10.0	F		RH	30 / 100	
6. City Island Yacht Sales & Marina **WiFi**	(718) 885-2300	70	9	45	12.0 / 8.0	F	GD	RH	30 / 50	P

WiFi Wireless Internet Access
Visit www.waterwayguide.com for current rates, fuel prices, website addresses and other up-to-the-minute information.
(Information in the table is provided by the facilities.)

Scan here for more details:

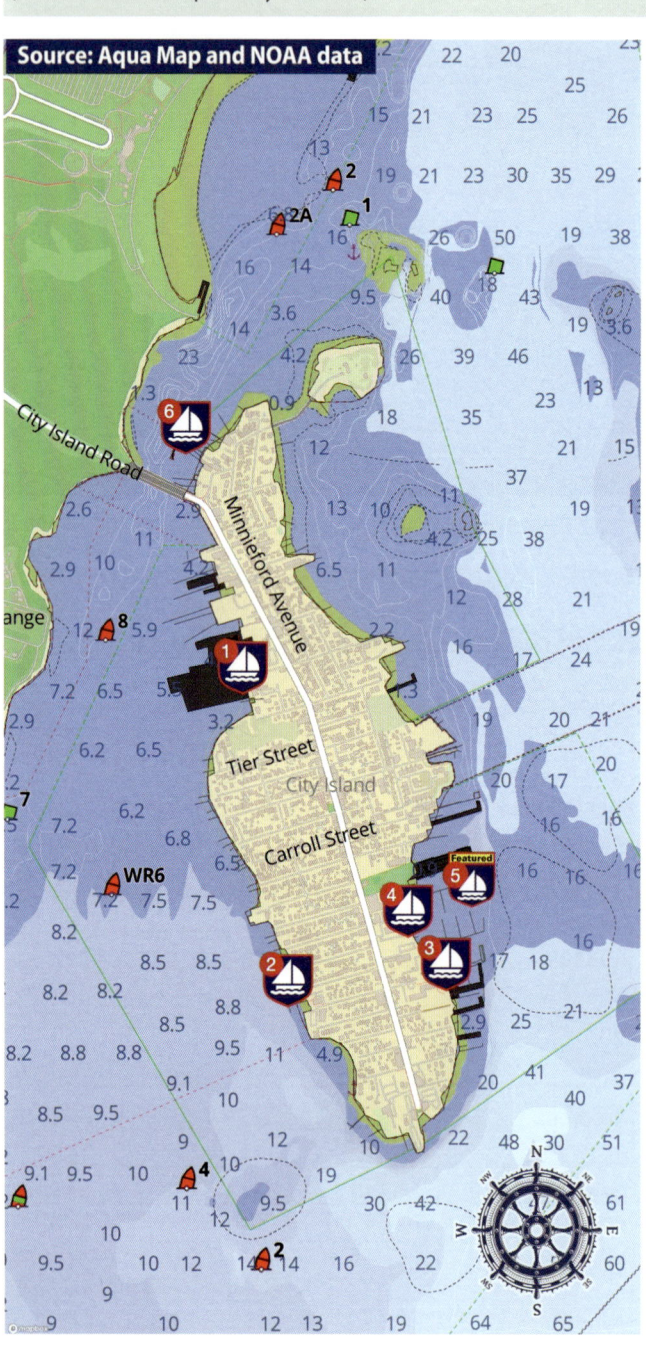

Source: Aqua Map and NOAA data

South Minneford Yacht Club is another facility with a storied past. It occupies the site of the old Minneford Shipyard, established in 1926, which produced palatial yachts for millionaires. It also built many of the great America's Cup racers including *Constellation*, *Intrepid*, *Courageous*, *Freedom* and *Enterprise* and during World War II built torpedo boats, mine sweepers and seagoing tugs. The yard was closed around 1980 and became the current marina in 1985. "Yacht Club" is a bit of a misnomer for this low key and casual facility. Slips with absentee owners are used for seasonal rentals or transients

visiting the marina. Call ahead to see if they can accommodate you.

On the southeast shore, the well-respected Minneford Marina offers slip rentals, dry rack storage, winter storage and transient dockage with full amenities on a 15-acre site. They can accommodate vessels to 125 feet.

City Island Yacht Sales & Marina at the north end of the island has 45 slips to 70 feet. Note that this facility must be approached from the east due to the fixed City Island Bridge (12-foot vertical clearance).

Anchorage: You can usually find room to anchor with acceptable depths and holding on either side of City Island with the caveat that both are exposed to the weather and frequent wakes of passing craft, some of which are tugs and barges or other serious water-moving machines. It is important to note there is no easy access ashore for dinghies as most of the yacht clubs are private. Some may allow a tie up if you dine with them or take a mooring.

The anchorage off the northwest corner of City Island between the bridge and the northerly end of a mooring field is protected from all directions but the south. There is 11 to 17 feet MLW with good holding in mud. On the east side of the island the City Island Harbor anchorage offers 14 feet MLW with good holding in mud. It is exposed northeast through southeast.

The best protection is at the island's northeastern tip in 7 to 14 feet MLW where High Island (with a tall radio transmission tower) gives shelter from the north and two small rocky outcroppings give partial protection from southerly winds across the sound. This is a designated anchorage area on the NOAA chart so boats at anchor need not turn on their anchor lights. Use a spotlight (pointed down at the water to protect the vision of other boaters) if coming in after dark. On still nights with no wind to stabilize the boat you might experience some uncomfortable wallowing.

Anchoring is prohibited north of City Island off Orchard Beach, which has been carved out of the rocky shore and filled with imported sand for beach goers.

New Rochelle Area, NY

The first city on the Westchester shore has two yacht harbors: New Rochelle Harbor and Echo Bay (formerly known as Lower Harbor and Upper Harbor, respectively). Both of New Rochelle's harbors are confined, busy and interesting for their constant activity. They are crowded with clubs, parks, marinas and moorings for thousands of widely assorted craft.

New Rochelle features more than 270 acres of parkland. Five Islands Park features pedestrian bridges linking various islands as well as fishing docks, beaches, barbecue facilities and an outdoor amphitheater. Neptune Park includes a fishing pier, bocce courts and horseshoe facilities. Glen Island Park comprises 105-acres of the parkland and offers a small, calm beach with plenty of surrounding grassland and several children's play areas.

NAVIGATION: The entry to New Rochelle from Long Island Sound can be confusing to newcomers. Those without local knowledge should arrive before dark. The approach to any of New Rochelle's three entries should be made with the chart close at hand. The westernmost approach to New Rochelle's lower harbor is the least used.

The eastbound cruiser rounding City Island can choose to approach either west (the shorter and more direct route) or east of Hart Island marked with a 23-foot-high flashing red "46" off its southern tip. A series of green can buoys mark the western edge of the deep water leading to the entrance between Davids Island and Glen Island, where the 24-foot flashing red "10" marking Aunt Phoebe Rock shows where to turn northwest for the harbor channel.

The westbound cruiser is likely to enter from the northeast between Davenport Neck and Davids Island. South of Hen and Chickens and north of Execution Rocks, turn west for the deep water between Huckleberry Island and flashing red "2" just off its northern tip (not to be confused with the flashing red "2" just south of Hen and Chickens). Pick up the channel between flashing green "5" and red nun "4" and proceed as usual, making sure not to miss green can "9," which marks Spindle Rock.

The two channels meet at quick-flashing red buoy "14," which marks the normally well-maintained channel serving New Rochelle Harbor. Controlling depth is 8 feet MLW as far as the head of the harbor, where shoals tend to develop.

Glen Island Bridge (13-foot closed vertical clearance) separates the west end of the harbor from the east and opens on signal during the day. A 2-hour advance notice is required for openings between 12 midnight and 6:00 a.m. from May 1 through October 31 by calling the

Long Island Sound, NY

NEW ROCHELLE AREA		Largest Vessel	VHF	Total Slips	Approach/ Dockside Depth	Floating Docks	Gas/ Diesel	Repairs/ Haulout	Min/Max Amps	Pump-Out Station
1. NYAC Yacht Club	(914) 738-2700	74	9	168	15.0 / 10.0	F	GD	H	30 / 50	
2. Glen Island Yacht Club / West Harbor Yacht Service - PRIVATE **WiFi**	(914) 636-1524	65		30	8.0 / 6.0	F		RH	30	
3. Huguenot Yacht Club-PRIVATE	(914) 636-6300	65	73	60	16.0 / 8.0	F		RH	30 / 50	
4. Wright Island Marina **WiFi**	(914) 235-8013	65		100	11.0 / 9.0	F	GD	RH	30 / 50	P
5. Imperial Yacht Club Inc.-PRIVATE **WiFi**	(914) 636-1122	65		100	14.0 / 7.0	F		RH	30 / 50	P
6. Castaways Yacht Club WiFi	**(914) 636-8444**	**75**		**120**	**14.0 / 9.0**	**F**	**GD**	**RH**	**30 / 50**	**P**
ECHO BAY										
7. New Rochelle Municipal Marina **WiFi**	(914) 235-6930	50	16	350	10.0 / 10.0	F	GD	RH	30 / 100	P

WiFi Wireless Internet Access
Visit www.waterwayguide.com for current rates, fuel prices, website addresses and other up-to-the-minute information.
(Information in the table is provided by the facilities.)

Scan here for more details:

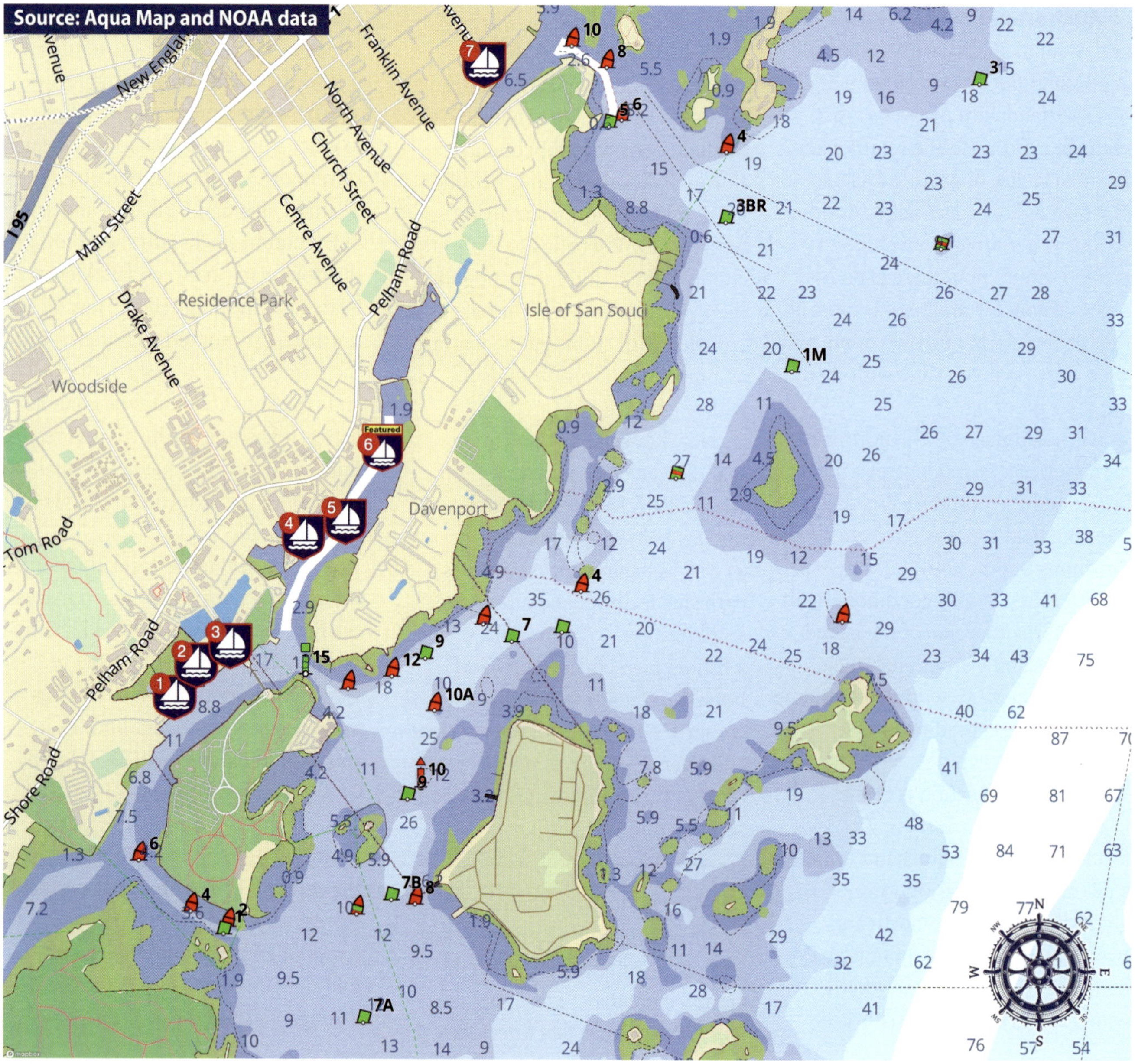

Source: Aqua Map and NOAA data

New Rochelle

CASTAWAYS YACHT CLUB

Davenport Neck

Glen Island

number posted at the bridge. A 24-hour advance notice is required for all openings from 8:00 p.m. to 8:00 a.m. from November 1 through April 30.

Crowded Echo Bay is northeast of New Rochelle Harbor. It has an outer harbor open to the southwest and an inner harbor protected from all directions. The approach to Echo Bay is north of Huckleberry Island between Middle Ground marked by green can "1M" and 6-foot MLW Hicks Ledge marked by green-over-red can buoy "HL."

During the summer, a private green light on a prominent flagstaff on the point midway between Beaufort Point and Duck Point is on a range with the green flashing buoy "3BR" for Bailey Rock. This will help you between Hicks Ledge and Middle Ground into Echo Bay.

Once in Echo Bay, pass between red nun buoy "6" to the east and green can "5" to the west at Duck Point and then proceed to Beaufort Point, where you will turn west around the point inside red nun buoy "8" and "10" to avoid the 2-foot MLW depths outside the channel. There are beaches near Duck Point and around Beaufort Point is the narrow, sheltered and slip-lined inner harbor.

Dockage/Moorings: New Rochelle Harbor is an excellent hurricane hole as it is protected by Davenport Neck and a cluster of islands. Several yacht clubs are located north of Glen Island including NYAC Yacht Club, Glen Island Yacht Club/West Harbor Yacht Service and Huguenot Yacht Club. All have some transient space and several offer repairs. Call ahead for reciprocity agreements.

In New Rochelle Harbor, the eastern branch inside Davenport Neck is crowded and narrow but well protected. While many of the marinas are restricted to local craft, several welcome transients including Wright Island Marina, which can accommodate boats to 65 feet, both power and sail, on floating docks with full services. Hauling, blocking and launching are available.

The full-service Castaways Yacht Club recognizes reciprocity with member clubs of the Yachting Club of America and offers repairs and maintenance. The private Imperial Yacht Club Inc. is set up with mostly seasonal rentals but may have room for you if you call ahead.

More options are available to the north in Echo Bay. Your best bet is New Rochelle Municipal Marina with slips to 50 feet and the usual amenities. They have 350 boat slips and 150 moorings and welcome transients. Services include launching and hauling, winter boat storage and mobile and stationary marine pump-out services.

Anchorage: The southern branch of New Rochelle Harbor below the Glen Island Bridge is cluttered with permanent moorings so there is no room to anchor. However, there is room in 14 feet at MLW just outside the harbor between the large white abandoned casino building on Glen Island's northeast corner and to the northwest of Goose Island. Turn west into the Glen Island East anchorage after passing north of green can buoy "9," taking care to stay clear of the rocky shoal on the northeast corner of Goose Island. This anchorage is protected from all but north to northeast winds.

A second option is to stay south of Glen Island and hug the shore southwest of red nun buoy "6" near the north end of Twin Island, although rocks, foul bottom and limited protection make it rarely attractive. In a storm situation anchor west of the New York Athletic Club's main clubhouse in the Olympic Rowing Lagoon with 12 feet MLW in mud.

Holding is good in Echo Bay around the two-pronged point from the marinas. This is well protected from all but northeast to southeast in 9- to 15-foot MLW depths. Pick a spot just south of the line between flashing green "3BR" and green can "5."

On hot evenings a cool, breezy (although exposed) anchorage can be found far from shore services off the northern shore of Huckleberry Island between flashing red "2" and a log house on the shore. Here you will find 22 feet MLW in excellent holding in mud. This is exposed to the northeast and is exposed to wind and waves.

Larchmont Harbor, NY

NAVIGATION: Larchmont Harbor is protected from the east by a stone breakwater but it is open to the south and southwest. To enter, pass either side of Hen and Chickens Ledge. If you pass to the north, stay south of Umbrella Rock, which is marked by green can buoy "7." You can also go between the breakwater's 26-foot-tall flashing red "2" and the string of marked rocks and reefs to the west.

Do not approach the launch dock. A marked reef lies in front of it. Skirt the shoals along Satans Toe inside the breakwater. Keep clear of North Ledge as well. It is

bare at half tide and has unmarked rocks in the center, although private navigation aids mark its north and south extremes. East of Larchmont the shore along Satans Toe and Delancey Point is rocky and shoal. Handsome estates line the shore.

Dockage/Moorings: Larchmont Harbor is a small cove with a big yacht club and ample yachting history. The private Larchmont Yacht Club is headquarters for Larchmont Race Week in mid-July, drawing hundreds of competing sailboats. Larchmont welcomes accredited members of other yacht clubs for overnight stays or for meals on its big porch overlooking the fleet. The harbor is typically crowded but guest moorings are usually available.

Anchorage: On a calm night, you can drop the hook near Horseshoe Harbor off Umbrella Point in 17 feet MLW with good holding in mud. This puts you about 1 mile from the Larchmont Yacht Club.

If you'd like to get closer so you can go ashore, you may find space on the edge of the mooring field in Larchmont Harbor behind the breakwater in 9 feet MLW with good holding in sand and mud. Both anchorages are exposed from the southeast through the west.

Long Island Sound, NY

LARCHMONT		Largest Vessel	VHF	Total Slips	Approach/ Dockside Depth	Floating Docks	Gas/ Diesel	Repairs/ Haulout	Min/Max Amps	Pump-Out Station
1. Larchmont Yacht Club - PRIVATE	(914) 834-2440	55	72		12.0 / 7.0	F		H	30 / 50	P
MAMARONECK										
2. Harbor Island Municipal Marina **WiFi**	(914) 777-7744	120	16	450	8.0 / 8.0	F				P
3. Safe Harbor Post Road **WiFi**	(914) 698-0295	55	9	50	10.0 / 8.0	F	GD	RH	30 / 50	
4. Derecktor Shipyards - Mamaroneck **WiFi**	**(914) 698-5020**	**150**			**15.0 / 15.0**	**F**	**D**	**RH**	**50 / 200+**	**P**
5. Mamaroneck Beach and Yacht Club - PRIVATE **WiFi**	(914) 698-1130	90	10	60	6.0 / 7.0	F		H	30 / 50	
MILTON HARBOR										
6. American Yacht Club-PRIVATE	(914) 967-4800				7.0 / 7.0	F	GD		30	
7. City of Rye Boat Basin	(914) 967-2011	37	16	425	6.0 / 10.0	F		R	30	P

WiFi Wireless Internet Access
Visit www.waterwayguide.com for current rates, fuel prices, website addresses and other up-to-the-minute information.
(Information in the table is provided by the facilities.)

Scan here for more details:

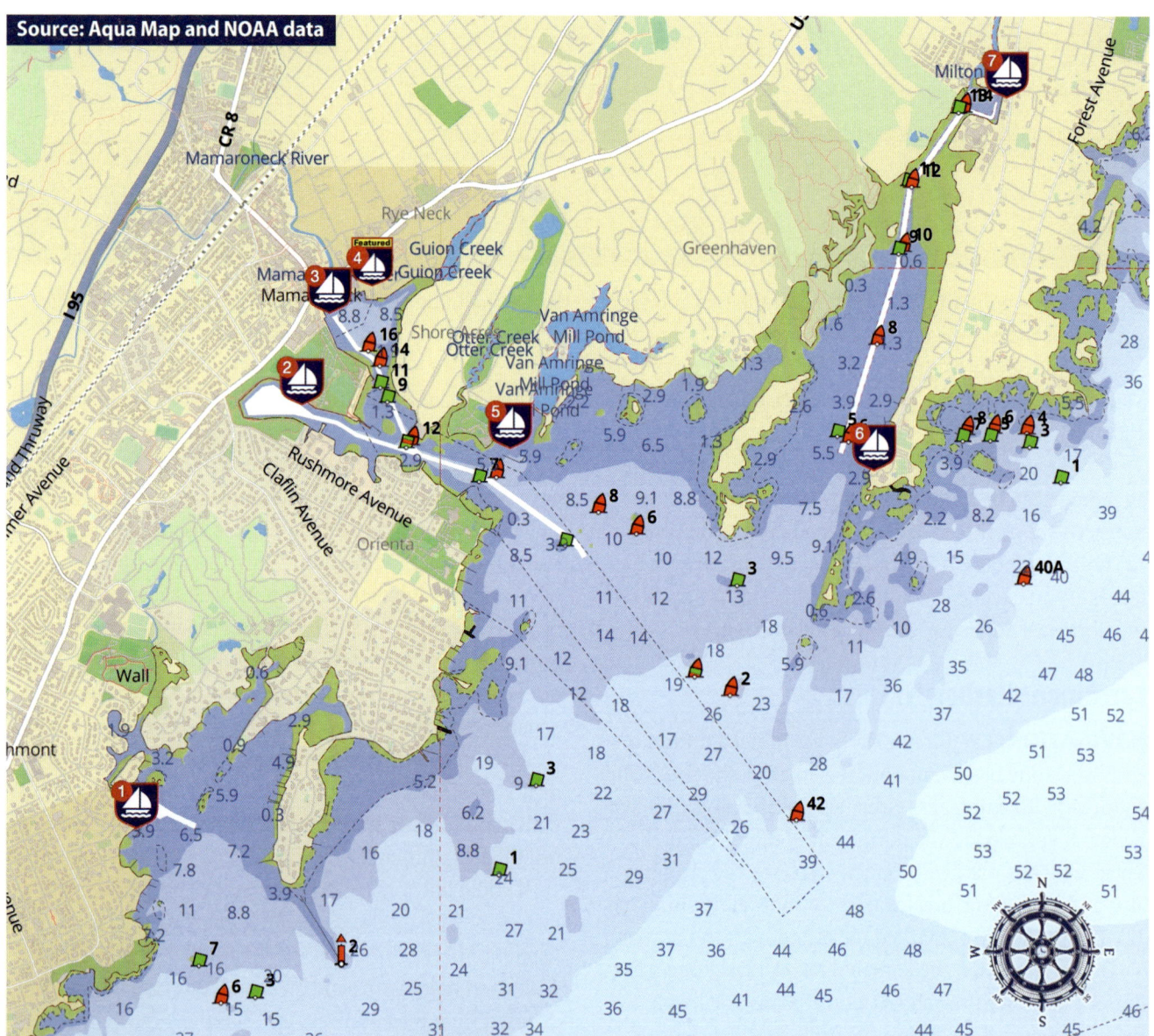

Source: Aqua Map and NOAA data

Mamaroneck & Milton Harbors, NY

Mamaroneck is a most hospitable harbor for transient boaters. In addition to the outer harbor, there are two inner basins (West Basin and East Basin) separated by a park. The busy main street in the village ends at the East Basin so services and entertainment are only a short walk away.

At the end of the East Basin close to the center of town is a long floating dock adjacent to a launching ramp. Brief tie-ups are allowed here when ramp conditions permit for a walk into town. Call the Harbormaster on VHF Channel 16 or 914-777-7744. The West Basin is more business-like and less visitor-oriented. A laundry, pharmacy and other shopping is all within walking distance. Taxi service is available should you need transportation elsewhere.

NAVIGATION: Make your entrance to Mamaroneck Harbor from Long Island Sound at flashing red bell buoy "42" (locally known as 42nd Street). Head northwest about 1 mile for flashing green "5" at Outer Steamboat Rock, leaving Ship Rock's red-flashing red-over-green buoy "MM" to the northeast. The channel to the inner harbors narrows between green can "7" and flashing red "10."

A 4-mph speed limit is strictly enforced in Mamaroneck Harbor.

At the green-over-red can junction buoy "A" channels lead to either side of Harbor Island, which is no longer an island.

Shoaling of the entrance channel has made Milton Harbor difficult to reach for most traveling boaters. The City of Rye Boat Basin confirms that there is less than 2 feet MLW in some places. The 7-foot tidal range brings the harbor within reach for those willing to come and go on a schedule.

Those with very shallow drafts or an eye on their tide charts can enter Milton Harbor by starting at the flashing red bell buoy "42," known as 42nd Street. Just east of Ship Rock marked by flashing red (2+1), red-over-green buoy "MM," head north-northeast between green can buoy "5" and red nun buoy "6," which mark the start of the harbor channel.

Leave West Rock and Scotch Caps (a line of reefs) well to the east without running west of the line created by green can buoy "3" and green can buoy "5." The harbor is exposed to the southwest.

Dockage/Moorings: Mamaroneck Harbor is located in Harbor Island Park, a sprawling 44-acre park in Mamaroneck. Mooring space is available for boats over 22 feet at Harbor Island Municipal Marina in both the East and West Basin of the harbor as well as in our outer harbor. The marina accommodates transients on moorings on a first-come, first-served basis.

The East Basin holds the full-service Safe Harbor Post Road with slips to 60 feet and marine services. Several boatyards are located in the harbor including the headquarters for Derecktor Shipyards. The famous yacht builder services, maintains and refits all types of power and sailing yachts up to 150 feet long with up to 40-foot beam. They maintain some transient slips and manage a large mooring field.

Back at the entrance to the harbor in the north shore is Mamaroneck Beach and Yacht Club, which is protected by a breakwater and surrounded by 12 acres of lush centennial trees, statues and vibrant flowers. They can accommodate vessels to 90 feet with resort amenities that include a beach, pool, tennis and fine dining.

Port Chester

At Milton Harbor to the east the private American Yacht Club on Peningo Neck has guest moorings available for members of reciprocal yacht clubs. The yacht club launch monitors VHF Channel 71.

Farther upriver the City of Rye operates the Rye City Boat Basin (officially known as George W. DePauw Municipal Boat Basin) offering 350 boat slips and stationary marine pump-out services.

Anchorage: There are 7- to 11-foot MLW depths on the west side of Hen Island outside Mamaroneck Harbor with excellent holding in mud and sand. It's a little over 1 mile from the anchorage to shore access at the Harbor Island Park.

There are places to anchor in Milton Harbor off American Yacht Club at Peningo Neck but watch your swing and the depth. (Tidal range is about 7 feet with good holding in mud.) You can dinghy to the town marina if you anchor but there may be a time limit on how long you can stay tied up.

■ PORT CHESTER, NY TO MILFORD HARBOR, CT

Port Chester, NY

Port Chester Harbor lies east of N. Manursing Island and its wildlife preserve, beach clubs and estates. The towns of Rye and Port Chester enclose the quiet harbor, which is lined with handsome homes. The downtown area boasts a restaurant row and many retailers including a hardware store, pharmacy and grocery. Most of these are more than 1 mile away up the Byram River.

Although the marinas along the river do not allow transient dinghy tie-up, if you dine at Bartaco (914-937-8226), they will usually allow a short trip to the provisioning along Westchester Ave.

The lower Byram River is tree-lined and scenic prior to the I-95 (Byram River) Bridge (60-foot fixed vertical clearance). Some of the structures at Tide Mill Yacht Basin date back to 1770 and have

been photographed and painted numerous times. It is located just under 2 miles from any shopping or the downtown area.

NAVIGATION: On approaching the harbor, watch for two large barge moorings between the Fourfoot Rocks green-over-red can buoy "F" and the Bluefish Shoal. One of the barge moorings is an easy-to-spot large white cylinder. The other is a dark-colored sphere, low in the water and hard to see with colored lines streaming from it. It is about midway between the white mooring and the Fourfoot Rocks buoy. The buoy and the moorings are not lighted so approach after sunset or at high speed is not advised without a spotlight or at high speed.

Do not cut the buoys marking Great Captain Rocks (marked by flashing red "2") and Manursing Island Reef at green can "3" just outside the breakwater.

Dockage: A privately marked channel leads south from the harbor entrance to Tide Mill Yacht Basin, a

Captain Harbor Area, NY

PORT CHESTER		Largest Vessel	VHF	Total Slips	Approach/ Dockside Depth	Floating Docks	Gas/ Diesel	Repairs/ Haulout	Min/Max Amps	Pump-Out Station
1. Tide Mill Yacht Basin	(914) 967-2995	70	68	55	7.0 / 8.0	F	GD	RH	30 / 50	

WiFi Wireless Internet Access
Visit www.waterwayguide.com for current rates, fuel prices, website addresses and other up-to-the-minute information.
(Information in the table is provided by the facilities.)

Scan here for more details:

Source: Aqua Map and NOAA data

small (55-slip), well-maintained marina and service yard. They have the only available fuel in the area but larger vessels may have difficulty accessing their fuel dock due to the narrow, tricky entrance.

Anchorage: You can anchor at the edge of the mooring field in Port Chester south of the 25-foot flashing green "5" in 7 to 8 feet MLW with good holding in mud.

Side Trip: Calf & Captain Islands, CT

The Calf Islands are just to the south of Byram Harbor. The west side of the larger Calf Island is a bird sanctuary and off-limits to visitors. Calf Island is owned by the U.S. Fish and Wildlife Service (860-399-2513) and is open throughout the year from one-half hour before sunrise to one-half hour after sunset for wildlife observation and hiking. Portions of Calf Island are also open for overnight stays by permit for those who anchor in the vicinity.

A sandbar connects the two islands that make up the Calf Islands at low tide. Little Calf Island (also known as Shell Island) is differentiated from the larger one by an imposing granite tower modeled after the Summerfield Methodist Church in Port Chester. The tower belfry is visible above the treetops of the overgrown island. It is owned by the Greenwich Land Trust and is no longer open to the public. (Warning: It is also overgrown with poison ivy.)

The three Captain Islands, originally claimed by both NY and CT, are less than 2 nm offshore south of Greenwich Harbor and mark the southern edge of Captain Harbor. They are the remnants of a glacial moraine and there are two theories on how they came by their name. Some say Captain Kidd buried treasure here at one time, while another legend identifies the namesake as Capt. Daniel Patrick, a partner in the first recorded real estate transaction and the town's first military commander.

Great Captain Island is 0.5-mile long and has a popular beach with picnic tables, grills, restrooms and showers, a couple of semi-protected anchorages and Great Captain Island light, a 19th-century restored stone lighthouse. You can anchor or grab a mooring off the beach then land by dinghy. Visitors to the beach are required to have a day pass but short visits are typically allowed.

The Greenwich Ferry serving Great Captain Island and Little Captain Island runs from June to September. The schedule is based on the tide. Wee Captain Island, the last of the three, is private.

Anchorage: Anchoring opportunities are available on both sides of Calf Island. The Calf Island East anchorage is one of the few places along this section of shoreline that are protected from winds out of the south. Base your selection on the wind and wave direction forecast and don't forget the 6- to 7-foot tidal range when choosing a spot.

Should you choose to anchor in the Captain Islands to the south, stay clear of a diamond-shaped marker over a sunken wreck 40 feet off the beach at Great Captain Island,

Greenwich, CT

Known today as one of the wealthiest towns in the U.S., the town of Greenwich was settled in 1640. A good place to start your exploration of this historical area is at the Bruce Museum in downtown Greenwich, which boasts both art and natural history exhibition space. Of special interest is the Seaside Center, dedicated to educating visitors about the ecology of Long Island Sound and features.

For many years Greenwich Point (locally termed "Tod's Point") was open only to town residents and their guests. Today all four beaches are open to the public.

NAVIGATION: Enter Greenwich Harbor from Long Island Sound via Captain Harbor. Newcomers to this area should use the eastern approach through water comparatively free of rocks and shoals. Honor both the flashing green gong buoy "1" and green can "1A" marking Hen and Chickens just northeast of Little Captain and Wee Captain islands.

Byram Harbor is the westernmost of the Greenwich harbors and offers moorings, a pretty park and beach and a municipal boat club but proof of residency is required and there are few amenities for the transient mariner.

Captain Harbor Area, CT

GREENWICH		Largest Vessel	VHF	Total Slips	Approach/ Dockside Depth	Floating Docks	Gas/ Diesel	Repairs/ Haulout	Min/Max Amps	Pump-Out Station
1. Indian Harbor Yacht Club-PRIVATE	(203) 869-2484				9.0 / 8.0	F			30	
2. Delamar Greenwich Harbor **WiFi**	(203) 733-5320	180	9	15	9.0 / 8.0	F			30 / 100	
3. Riverside Yacht Club-PRIVATE	(203) 637-1706	60		162	10.0 / 8.0	F	GD	H	30	P
4. Palmer Point Marina and Ship's Store	(203) 661-1243	55	16	140	6.0 / 6.0	F	GD	RH	30 / 50	
5. Beacon Point Marine **WiFi**	(203) 661-4033	60		250	12.0 / 2.0	F	GD	RH	30 / 50	P

WiFi Wireless Internet Access
Visit www.waterwayguide.com for current rates, fuel prices, website addresses and other up-to-the-minute information.
(Information in the table is provided by the facilities.)

Scan here for more details:

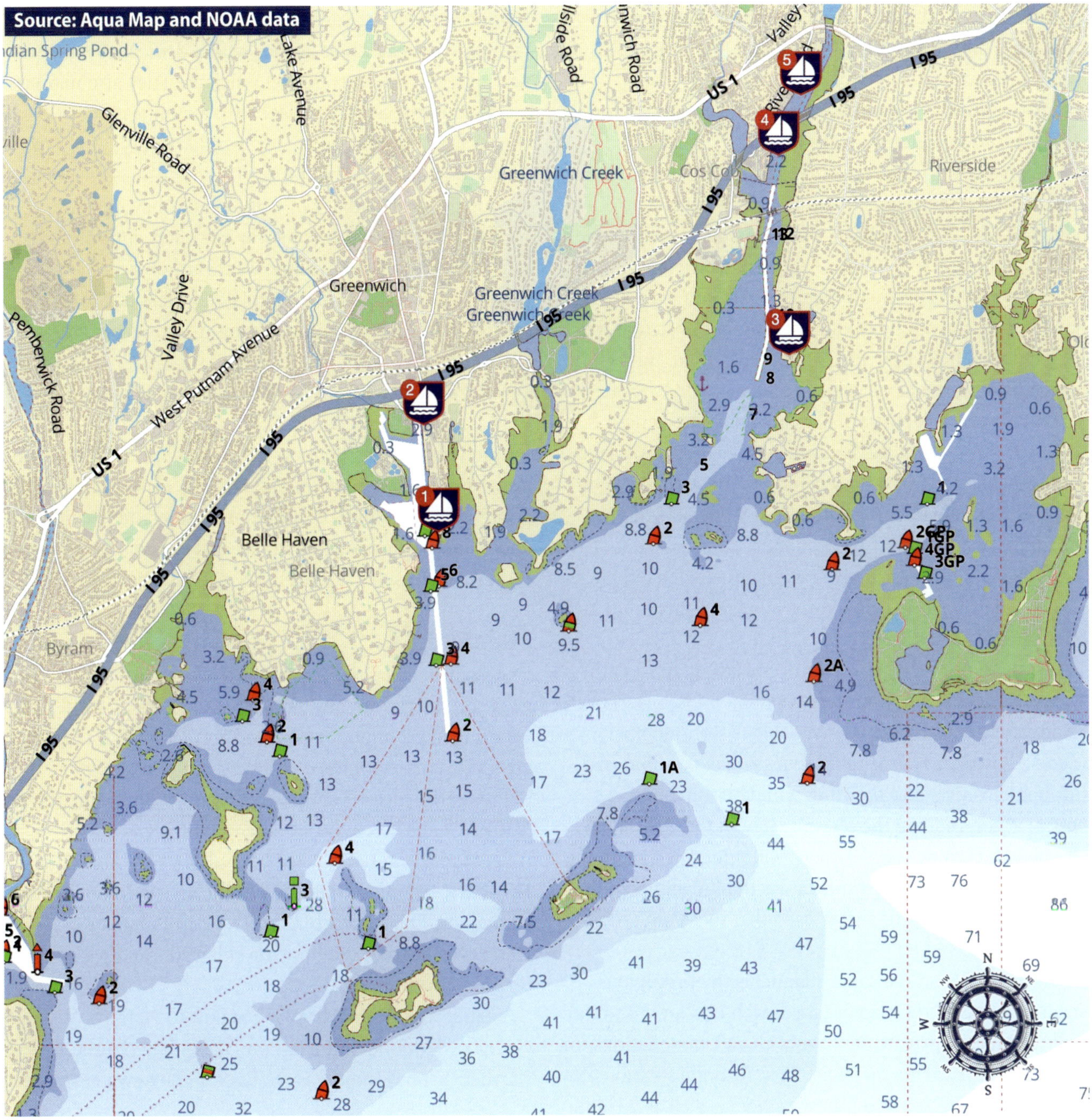

Cos Cob Harbor is the entrance to the Mianus River and is also accessed via Captain Harbor. Coming from Long Island Sound between Flat Neck Point and the Captain Islands, pass south or west of Newfoundland Reef's flashing red "4" and south or east of Red Rock's red-over-green nun buoy "R." After heading west around Hitchcock Rock's flashing red "2," turn northeast to green can buoy "3" and the dredged, marked entrance.

Keep strictly to the center of the channel to get the most depth. Six-foot depths are reported as far as the Riverside Yacht Club but careful piloting is required between it and the Metro North Bridge (Cob RR Bridge) at low tide.

Metro North Bridge (Cob RR Bridge) has a 20-foot closed vertical clearance opens on signal (as soon as practicable but no later than 20 minutes) between 5:00 a.m. to 9:00 p.m. unless a train is approaching. The draw opens on signal from April 1 through October 31, from 9:00 p.m. to 5:00 a.m. with a 4-hour advance notice and from November 1 through March 30, with at least a 24-hour notice is given by calling the number posted at the bridge. It is followed by the I-95 (Connecticut Turnpike) Bridge (45-foot fixed vertical clearance).

Dockage/Moorings: There are many moorings scattered throughout the harbors and neighboring islands, most of which are private or belong to the various yacht clubs. It is acceptable to use them for a day-stay or an overnight on a weekday but you must be prepared to leave if the owner shows up. The Town of Greenwich operates several small-boat marinas. Some allow dinghy tie-up and offer pump-out service.

On the point between Greenwich Harbor and Smith Cove, the docks and moorings at private Indian Harbor Yacht Club typically are not available to non-member yachts. However, reservation requests may be submitted through Dockwa, and the Club will determine how best to accommodate the request. Stay in the channel to Greenwich Harbor and the yacht club moorings are to the west. If you are from a reciprocal yacht club and plan to obtain a guest mooring, be advised that the dining room requires jackets.

To the north on the same channel is the prestigious Delamar Hotel and Delamar Greenwich Harbor with more than 500 feet of private dockage with accommodations for sail and motor yachts up to 180 feet. Boat guests can enjoy use of the hotel's spa and fitness center, as well as 24-hour coffee service, along with other resort amenities.

On the Mianus River to the east is Riverside Yacht Club, a private neighborhood club that welcomes guests of club members and members of yacht clubs with reciprocal privileges whenever space is available on their moorings or docks.

To the north between the bridges is the friendly Palmer Point Marina and Ship's Store, a large vessel repair facility with a well-stocked ship store and canvas repairs on site. They maintain five transient slips to 55 feet.

Above the **I-95 (Connecticut Turnpike) Bridge** (45-foot fixed vertical clearance) is Beacon Point Marine, a large power boat repair facility with a dedicated yard crew, service teams and certified technicians. They also maintain a few transient slips to 60 feet with amenities. (Note that the pool and restaurant are for members only.) A 0.5-mile walk from either marina brings you to businesses along the highway. The village of Cos Cob lies beyond.

Anchorage: Work your way in slowly and carefully pick a spot along the channel westward of Tweed Island. At the northwest end of Tweed Island there is 5 to 7 feet MLW with good holding in mud. This is open to the southwest.

Greenwich Cove, south of the Mianus River, has some deeper protected sections but these are all chock full of moored boats. Elias Point at the channel into the cove has a somewhat exposed anchorage in 9 to 13 feet MLW in good holding in mud. Be sure not to block the channel, and if anchoring fore-and-aft, stay on the channel's edge. Be sure to consider the swing room of the nearest boats.

Stamford, CT

The yachting facilities in Stamford are extensive and shore diversions are numerous, making this an ideal yachting destination for long or short layovers. Stamford History Center should be your first stop on any tour of Stamford's historic sites. The Stamford Museum and Nature Center has a kid-oriented nature center with trails, a small museum, farm animals and an otter pond. Every year Stamford offers a world-class sculpture exhibit throughout the summer months. Art in Public Place features sculptures that line the sidewalks and parks in downtown Stamford.

Stamford has three harbors: Stamford Harbor, Westcott Cove (east around Shippan Point) and Cove Harbor (farther east beyond the Cove Rocks). Breakwaters protect

Captain Harbor Area, CT

STAMFORD HARBOR		Largest Vessel	VHF	Total Slips	Approach/ Dockside Depth	Floating Docks	Gas/ Diesel	Repairs/ Haulout	Min/Max Amps	Pump-Out Station
1. Stamford Yacht Club-PRIVATE	(203) 323-3161			40	10.0 / 8.0				30	
2. TGM Anchor Point Marina	(203) 363-0733	90	68	72	12.0 / 11.0	F			30 / 50	
3. Harbor Landing Marina	(203) 355-6045	50	16	130	12.0 / 8.0	F			30 / 50	P
4. Harbor Point North Marina	(203) 965-6045	120	9	32	/	F	GD	H	30 / 100	P
5. Safe Harbor Yacht Haven **WiFi**	(203) 359-4500	118	9	366	10.0 / 13.0	F		R	30 / 50	

WiFi Wireless Internet Access
Visit www.waterwayguide.com for current rates, fuel prices, website addresses and other up-to-the-minute information.
(Information in the table is provided by the facilities.)

Scan here for more details:

Source: Aqua Map and NOAA data

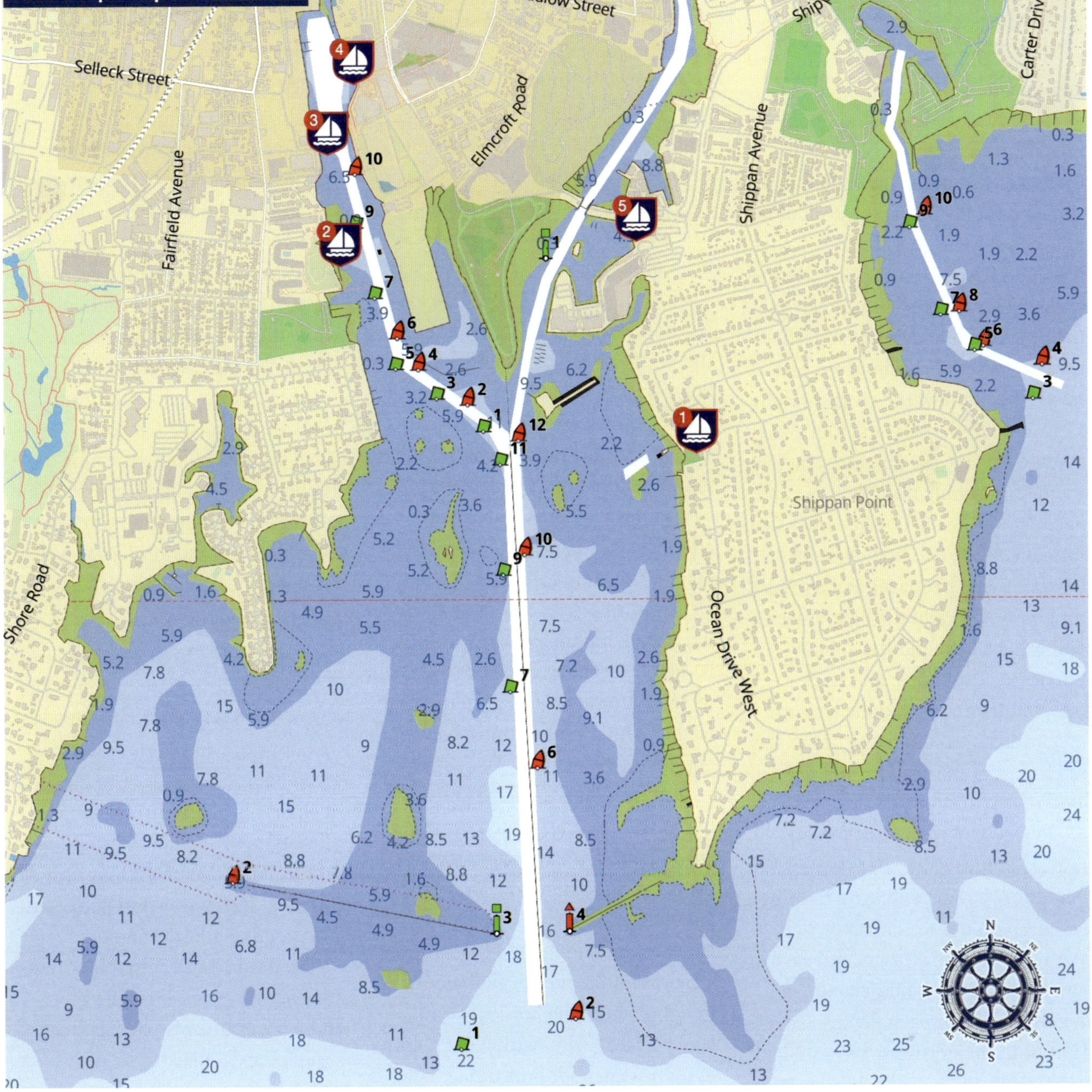

the large outer basin of Stamford Harbor and the two branches at its head: West Branch and East Branch.

NAVIGATION: Stamford Harbor is easy to enter from Long Island Sound through the two well-marked and lighted breakwaters at the entrance. The city's tall stacks and high-rise buildings are easy to spot from Long Island Sound. The 80-foot-tall lighthouse on Harbor Ledge next to the west breakwater can help a boater with the breakwater entrance, even though it's now privately owned and operated.

The entrance through the breakwater at Stamford Harbor is 0.25 mile east of the lighthouse and can be found by using the 26-foot tall quick-flashing tower and the 45-foot, 6-second flashing red marker as range lights. When approaching, keep to the west of Shippan Point and The Cows, marked by flashing red bell buoy "32." Follow the chart carefully as you proceed; rocks and foul areas abound outside the entrance channel.

If approaching from the west and heading for the anchorage rather than into one of the two branches, the line between Greenwich Point's red nun buoy "34" and the lighthouse will bring a large industrial buoy into sight. Turn north and track between that buoy and the western breakwater's red nun buoy "2" to stay safely east of the shallow rocks (3- and 5-foot MLW depths).

To reach Westcott Cove, enter around Shippan Point (east of Stamford Harbor) and leave flashing green "1" to the west on approach. Westcott Cove is pleasant and easy to enter if you stay to mid-channel for 7-foot MLW approach depths. Cove Harbor to the northeast has a difficult entry requiring local knowledge and

is devoted entirely to local boats.

Dockage/Moorings: West of the Stamford Harbor channel is a large mooring buoy used by barges along with a number of yacht club moorings. To the east of the main channel is the stately Stamford Yacht Club (established in 1890), which sponsors the famous Labor Day Weekend Vineyard Race and welcomes members of reciprocating yacht clubs. Beyond the club, the channel forks into the West and East branches.

On the West Branch, TGM Anchor Point Marina is a boutique facility with 72 slips and resort-style amenities.

Harbor Landing Marina offers best-in-class amenities, two on-site restaurants and a friendly dock staff. Their sister facility, Harbor Point North Marina, is also located on the West Branch just steps from the boardwalk with transient space and cruiser amenities.

The channel into the East Branch is straightforward. It offers 10 to 11-foot MLW depths and carries all the way to Stamford. Follow the channel north to Safe Harbor Yacht Haven, which is recognizable by the large brick buildings that surround it. Yacht Haven has 366 slips (30 reserved transient slips) in a modern facility with a family atmosphere and full amenities.

Anchorage: The large outer harbor can kick up a chop in strong winds but reasonable anchorage can be found just behind the western Stamford Breakwater. Proceed around (private) red nun buoy "2" on the west end of the breakwater and tuck in tight behind the breakwater in about 10 feet MLW with good holding in mud. Watch for protruding rocks

at low tide.

The Stamford Municipal Marina is designated for local boats only but you can tie up long enough for loading and unloading. Be aware that the security gates at each dock allow you to leave with no key but require keys to get back in.

Even though the outer cove at Westcott Cove is open to the south, a small, landlocked inner lagoon offers good depths and total protection.

Darien

Darien covers the entire area between Stamford and Fivemile River. The Gut (better known as Darien Harbor), Goodwives River and the town of Noroton lie within the western section of this area. Fivemile River is to the east. Darien on the western bank is lined with houses, while the village of Rowayton is nestled on the east side.

Along Rowayton's waterfront you will find a Post Office, a small grocery, numerous eating establishments, a hardware store and various small shops. You can buy local steamers and lobsters as well as most marine supplies here.

NAVIGATION: The entrance to Fivemile River can be seen only from the south but it is easy to enter. The channel is dredged through shoals on both sides and starts at flashing green buoy "3" located 1 mile north of Greens Ledge Light. (Note: May be off station.) Watch for lobster buoys.

Fivemile River is actually only 1 nm long. It is narrow but protected with good depths throughout.

Dockage/Moorings: Moorings are everywhere on Fivemile River and a few boatyards offer services, supplies and a place to tie up.

The westernmost Norwalk harbor is Wilson Cove just past Roton Point from Fivemile River. Although many yachts moor here permanently, it can be rough even in a moderate southwesterly wind. Rowayton Yacht Club is a private, member-owned yacht club but guest moorings with launch service for power or sailboats up to 30 feet are available on a short-term basis to visiting boaters.

The private Norwalk Yacht Club (on opposite sides of the cove at the mouth) welcomes reciprocal club boaters on guest moorings. Fee includes launch service to access club house facilities. Hail on VHF Channel 78A.

Anchorage: Just west of the mouth of Fivemile River at Butlers Island, there is a great spot for anchoring in any breeze except from the east. Depths are around 8 to 11 feet MLW with good holding. Cruisers have reported a quiet night at anchor here within 100 yards of shore while northwest winds are gusting up to 30 knots. To reach this spot, proceed on a course of 355° magnetic from Greens Ledge Light pass east of green can buoy "1" and then proceed into the unnamed cove between Contentment Island and Butlers Island. Holding here is good in thick mud.

Norwalk Area, CT

A 6-mile chain of 16 islands make up the Norwalk Islands and protect Norwalk Harbor itself. The islands were used during the Revolutionary War by Continental Army whaleboat crews who ran out into Long Island Sound to harass the British ships and then retreat to the shelter of the islands' rocks.

Nicknamed "Oyster Town," this a cruising favorite, especially for mariners zigzagging Long Island Sound and crossing over from Huntington Bay on the Long Island shore. The four primary maritime areas of Norwalk offer anything you are likely to want: good protection, marinas, repairs, yacht clubs, restaurants, beaches and good anchorage. The scenery includes hundreds of local boats, bow-to-stern weekend traffic amid the oyster stakes and crowds of people fishing, swimming, picnicking and clamming.

A short walk over the bridge in Norwalk Harbor puts the visitor in the center of SoNo, South Norwalk's sophisticated nightlife and tourism district, anchored by the Maritime Aquarium. City Market Norwalk is nearby for provisioning.

Norwalk Area, CT

WILSON COVE		Largest Vessel	VHF	Total Slips	Approach/ Dockside Depth	Floating Docks	Gas/ Diesel	Repairs/ Haulout	Min/Max Amps	Pump-Out Station
1. Rowayton Yacht Club-PRIVATE	(203) 854-0807	30	68		10.0 / 2.0					
2. Norwalk Yacht Club-PRIVATE	(203) 866-0941	50	78	130	7.0 / 8.0		GD	H		
GREGORY POINT										
3. Norwalk Cove Marina WiFi	(203) 838-5899	180	9	400	10.0 / 9.0	F	GD	RH	30 / 200+	P
NORWALK RIVER										
4. Total Marine of Norwalk	(203) 838-3210	80		90	15.0 / 9.0	F		RH	30 / 50	
5. Rex Marine Center Inc WiFi	(203) 866-5555	50		70	12.0 / 6.0	F	G	RH	30 / 50	P
6. Norwalk Visitor's Docks	(203) 866-8810	200	9	20	12.0 / 8.0	F			30 / 50	P
7. Oyster Bend Yacht Club & Marina	(203) 842-8212	36		75	6.0 / 6.0				50	
SPRITE ISLAND										
8. Sprite Island Yacht Club-PRIVATE	(203) 295-8466	33	12		8.0 / 4.5	F				
SAUGATUCK RIVER										
9. Cedar Point Yacht Club-PRIVATE WiFi	(203) 226-7411	50	78	130	10.0 / 8.0	F		H	30 / 50	
10. Saugatuck Harbor Yacht Club-PRIVATE	(203) 454-3004	53	71	160	8.0 /	F			30 / 50	

WiFi Wireless Internet Access
Visit www.waterwayguide.com for current rates, fuel prices, website addresses and other up-to-the-minute information.
(Information in the table is provided by the facilities.)

Scan here for more details:

Source: Aqua Map and NOAA data

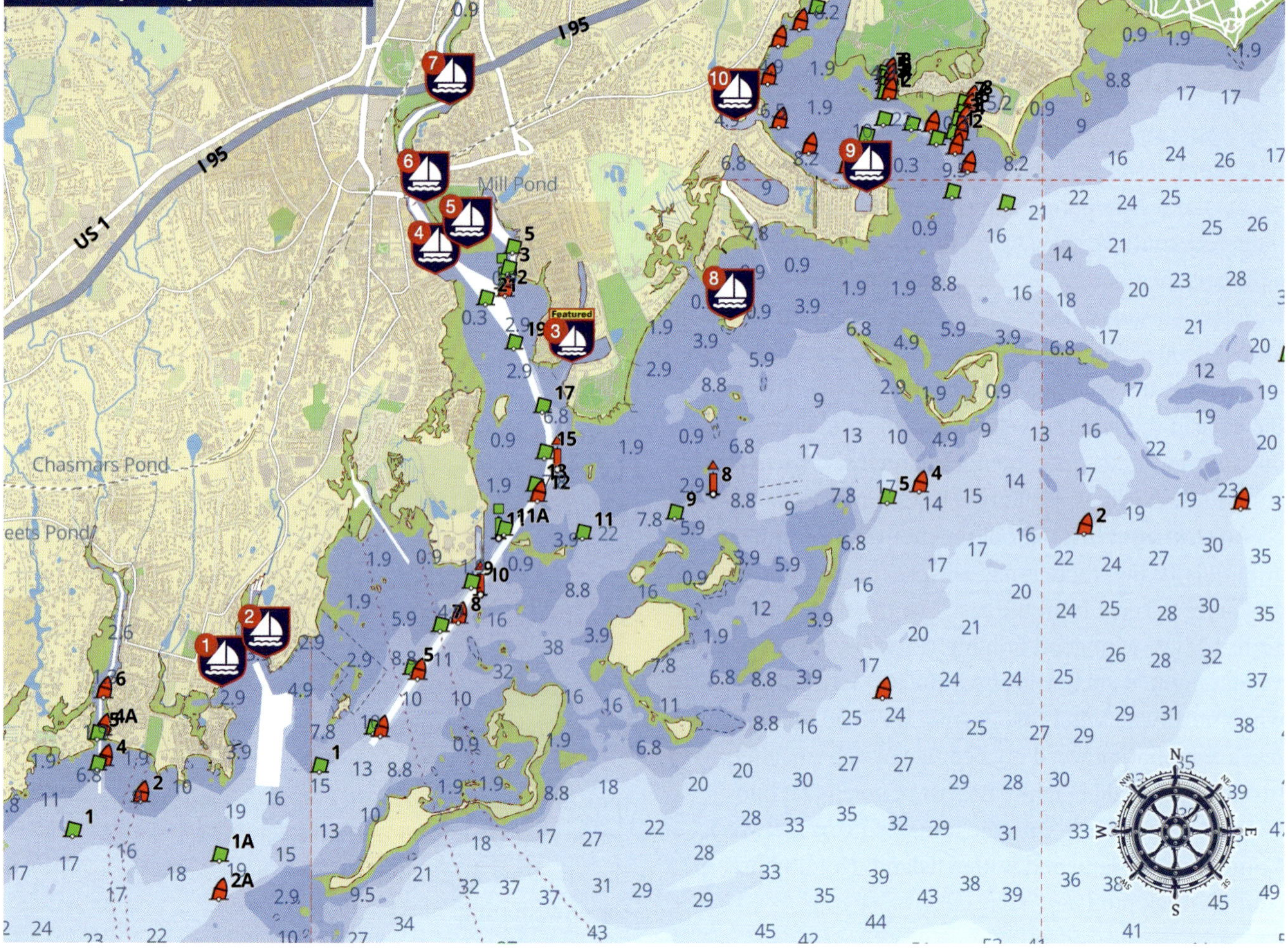

NAVIGATION: The entrance to Norwalk Harbor and Norwalk River is through Sheffield Island Harbor, north of the Norwalk Islands. The high-intensity softball field lights can be seen from as far away as Bridgeport throughout the boating season. A 350-foot-tall orange-and-white power plant stack on Manresa Island on the western side of the harbor mouth provides another landmark. Go west around Greens Ledge and give the reef west of Sheffield Island (known locally as Smith Island) a wide berth. Follow the well-marked Sheffield Island Harbor channel past Manresa Island into Norwalk Harbor.

Watch for barge traffic coming out of the power plant basin. As you move upstream, the river changes, flowing through marshes filled with waterfowl. It is worth exploring but do so in the dinghy. The channel winds through shallow flats.

Cockenoe Harbor is the eastern route to and from Norwalk Harbor. The buoyed channel (red right returning from the Sound to Norwalk Harbor) threads through islands and shoals between 61-foot Peck Ledge Lighthouse and quick flashing red "14" that marks the change between the two channels. The channel makes a hard turn around the lighthouse to keep off Cockenoe Island's southern and eastern shoals. East of Peck's Ledge, be sure pass between green can buoy "5" and red nun buoy "4," which keeps the boat from meeting the Channel Rock with 1.5-foot MLW depth.

Most boating services are located before the bridges. Anyone wanting to head through them will be stymied during rush hours. The first bridge you will encounter is **Washington Street (136) Bridge** with an 8-foot closed vertical clearance. The draw will open on signal except from 7:00 a.m. to 8:45 a.m., 11:45 a.m. to 1:15 p.m. and 4:00 p.m. to 6:00 p.m., Monday through Friday (except holidays), when the draw need not be open for the passage of vessels.

Farther upstream is the **Metro-North WALK Bridge** with a 16-foot closed vertical clearance. This bridge will open on signal from 5:00 a.m. to 9:00 p.m., except from Monday through Friday (excluding holidays), when the draw need not open from 7:00 a.m. to 8:45 a.m. and from 4:00 p.m. to 6:00 p.m., unless an emergency exists. Also, it will open only once in any 60-minute period from 5:45 a.m. to 7:00 a.m. and 6:00 p.m. to 7:45 p.m. Finally, from 9:00 p.m. to 5:00 a.m., a 4-hour notice is required for the bridge to open. (A delay of up to 20 minutes may be

GOIN' ASHORE

Norwalk, CT

ATTRACTIONS

1. Lockwood-Mathews Mansion Museum
Highlights the lives, styles and technology of the Victorian Era and regarded as one of the earliest and finest surviving Second Empire Style country houses ever built in the U.S. Tours are offered (seasonally) for a fee at 295 West Ave. (203-838-9799).

Exhibit in Lockwood-Mathews Mansion Museum

2. Mill Hill Historic Park & Museum
A collection of 19th-century buildings at 2 East Wall St. that includes a museum with antiques local history exhibits, plus a gift shop with items by area artists. Open seasonally (203-846-0525).

3. SONO Switch Tower Museum
Museum with exhibits on railroads and their switch towers in a restored switch tower from 1896 (77 Washington St., 203-246-6958).

4. Stepping Stones Museum for Children
Interactive and educational attraction geared towards younger crew members (303 West Ave., 203-899-0606).

5. The Maritime Aquarium at Norwalk
Features more than 1,000 marine animals native to Long Island Sound and its watershed in over 30 fresh and saltwater exhibits at 10 N. Water St. (203-852-0700).

SERVICES

6. Bauer Emergency Care Center / Norwalk Hospital
34 Maple St., 203-852-2160

7. Norwalk Post Office
16 Washington St. (203-854-4747)

8. SoNo Branch Library
10 Washington St. (203-899-2790)

9. VCA Emergency Veterinary Service
123 W. Cedar St. (203-854-9960)

MARINAS

10. Norwalk Visitors Dock
Seaview Ave. (203-866-8810)

11. Oyster Bend Yacht Club & Marina
23 Platt St. (203-842-8212)

12. Rex Marine Center, Inc.
144 Water St. (203-866-5555)

13. Total Marine of Norwalk
160 Water St. (203-838-3210)

Downtown Norwalk across from Veterans Memorial Park

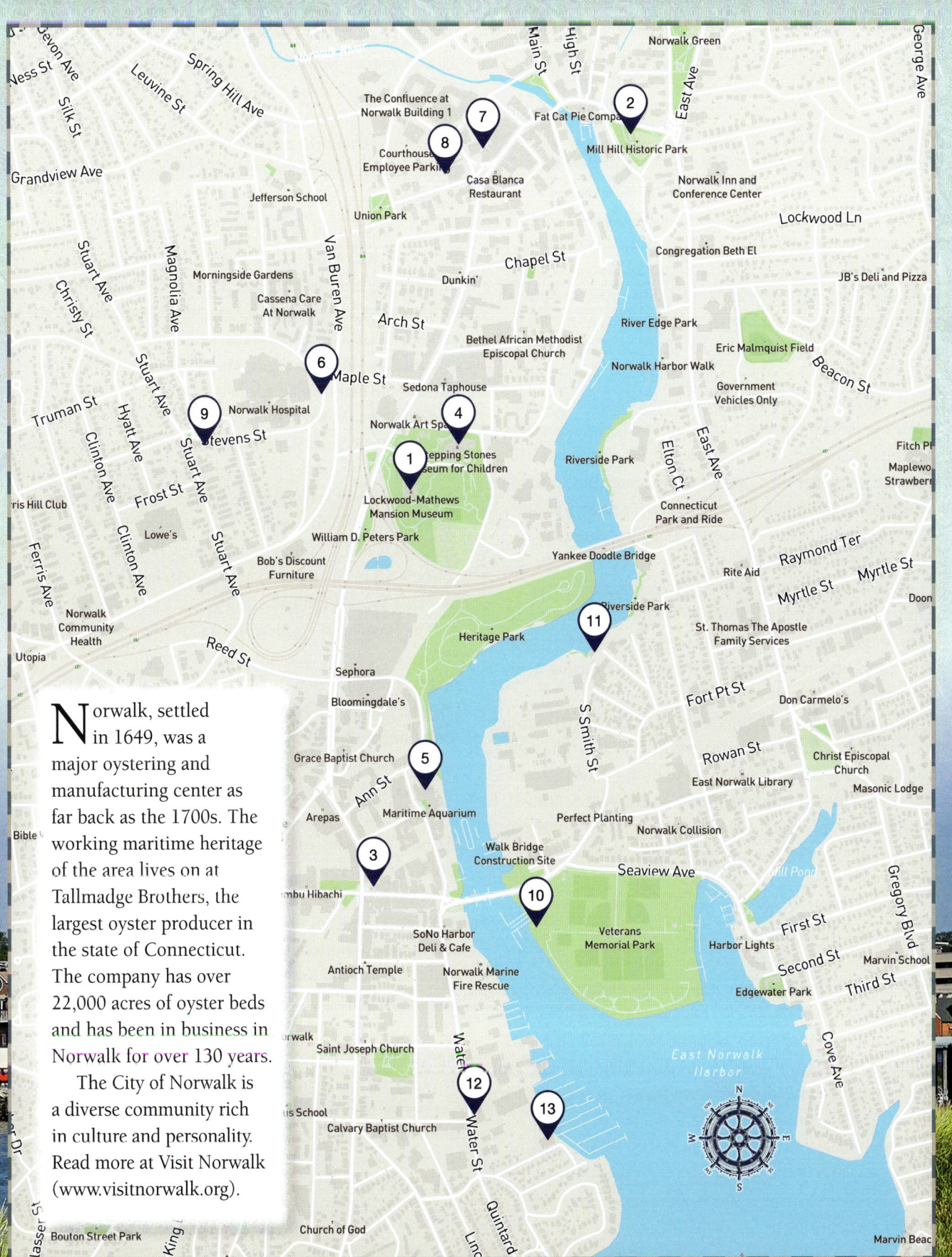

Norwalk, settled in 1649, was a major oystering and manufacturing center as far back as the 1700s. The working maritime heritage of the area lives on at Tallmadge Brothers, the largest oyster producer in the state of Connecticut. The company has over 22,000 acres of oyster beds and has been in business in Norwalk for over 130 years.

The City of Norwalk is a diverse community rich in culture and personality. Read more at Visit Norwalk (www.visitnorwalk.org).

expected if a train is approaching so closely that it may not be safely stopped.) There are more bridges farther up the Norwalk River. You can call any of the bridgetenders here on VHF Channel 13 for clarification if the above schedule leaves you mystified.

Dockage/Moorings: The 400-slip, full-service Norwalk Cove Marina is located in East Norwalk at Gregory Point and offers transient dockage plus all fuels and boat repairs. It is located inside the mouth of the Norwalk River and can accommodate vessels up to 130 feet. They have a well-stocked ship store, a popular restaurant for lunch or dinner and are pet friendly.

Several marine facilities are located up the Norwalk River with slips, moorings, repairs, and gas and diesel fuel. Total Marine of Norwalk is a full-service yachting facility featuring 90-slip marina, a large brokerage service and comprehensive boat and yacht repair. They maintain 10 reserved transient slips. Rex Marine Center Inc. is another brokerage service with floating docks for vessels to 50 feet. They boast the area's largest ship store and marine parts department.

Across the river and before the Washington Street Bridge is the municipal Norwalk Visitor's Docks with 20 slips for vessels to 200 feet (plus camp sites). Note that they charge per 8 hour stay, so it can get confusing if you are staying overnight. Ask ahead.

Oyster Bend Yacht Club & Marina has 75 boat slips for motorboats to 40 feet. The marina is located on the right bank of the Norwalk Harbor, north of the Washington Street (136) Bridge and the Metro-North WALK Bridge. It is across from Oyster Shell Park, which has waterfront pedestrian paths with educational signs, harbor views and a disc-golf course.

Anchorage: There is no place to anchor in the river. Just finding room to turn around can be a problem. (The best advice is to go to the end and turn around carefully in 6-foot MLW depths.) There is a nice anchorage with 6 feet MLW close to Norwalk Cove Marina at Calf Pasture Beach.

Many popular spots to drop the hook are available in the lee of the Norwalk Islands–in particular, the large area east of Chimon Island. Enter from the north and proceed slowly over the 6-foot MLW bar to anchor in 10-foot MLW depths just east of Chimon Rocks. Another option is Copps Island to the west. Enter from the southeast carefully; there are many shoals and rocks. There is lots of room for anchoring in 11 feet MLW.

Saugatuck River (Westport, CT)

The Saugatuck River leading to Westport is interesting to explore, but take care to factor the racing current in your plans as it can be fierce. The shores of the river are lined with attractive houses, restaurants, shops, yacht clubs, a public recreational complex and a summer theater.

NAVIGATION: Entrance to the Saugatuck River from Long Island Sound should be made east of flashing green buoy "1," which marks Georges Rock. Head northwest on either side of flashing green buoy "3" to the entrance to the marked channel in the river between Cedar Point and Seymour Rock. A well-marked channel winds up and around Bluff Point, hugging the western shore. Depths outside the markers are as shallow as 1 foot MLW.

Dockage/Mooring: Sprite Island Yacht Club is a small, private club on one of the most picturesque islands on Long Island Sound just off the shores of Norwalk and Westport. Sprite Island boasts a beach, snack bar, lawn area with grills and fire pits. The active social calendar includes weekly sailing events, happy hours and kids activities. This member-managed club may have a mooring for you but call ahead.

The hospitable Cedar Point Yacht Club at Saugatuck Shores is very popular and often crowded. They are private but will make room for transients, even at the last minute. Saugatuck Harbor Yacht Club in Duck Creek to the north welcomes members of good standing from recognized clubs. Call ahead for availability.

Anchorage: Anchorages in the vicinity of the town are extremely limited, swing room is minimal and the channel winds are tortuous. Because of one shallow spot downriver, this area is best not approached near dead-low water; however, the 7-foot tidal range will give you good water most of the time. One popular spot is by Kitts Island (south of Hendricks Point) at the mouth of the river in 11- to 15-foot MLW depths with good holding in soft mud.

The northwestern shore of Cockenoe Island is also a popular anchorage. You can go ashore to swim, hike or camp; on weekends it seems like everyone does at Cockenoe Island N. There is fair holding in rocks and thick mud with at least 7 feet MLW.

BRIDGEPORT HARBOR MARINA

Bridgeport

Bug Light

Bridgeport, CT

Bridgeport, the most populous city in Connecticut, was first settled in 1659 but not chartered as a town until 1856. Shipbuilding and whaling in the mid-19th century were made possible by the deep Black Rock Harbor.

The first bridge across the Pequannock River was financed by a lottery in 1800 and the town became known as Bridgeport. Shortly afterward, P.T. Barnum, founder of the "Greatest Show on Earth," was drawn to the area because of its rapid growth. The Barnum Museum at 820 Main St. (203-331-1104) is dedicated to the life and times of P.T. Barnum and Bridgeport's industrial heritage.

Black Rock is a pleasant neighborhood of west Bridgeport. Fairfield Avenue, a 10-minute walk from the marinas, has interesting restaurants and shops.

NAVIGATION: Black Rock Harbor, almost 2 miles west of Bridgeport, is the main harbor for recreational boats. It has a deep, well-marked channel, is easy to enter and has ample transient facilities. The harbor is sheltered to the east by Fayerweather Island, part of Bridgeport's big Seaside Park with an abandoned lighthouse at the tip.

Heading from Southport toward Black Rock Harbor, give the end of Penfield Reef a wide berth to keep clear of the numerous smaller rocks

and Black Rock itself. Be sure that the flashing light you see is at the end of the reef and then head for flashing red buoy "2" marking the Bridgeport Harbor entrance about 1.5 miles away. Do not make your turn for Black Rock Harbor until you are midway between those markers, following a course of about 330° magnetic.

Bridgeport is easy to spot because of its tall stacks, factories, oil tanks and power plants, which are all visible from Long Island Sound. The large tankers, ferries and freighters traveling its big, well-marked channel are equally evident. It has a well-marked entrance and deep water that accommodates the tremendous traffic.

Bridgeport, CT

BLACK ROCK HARBOR AREA		Largest Vessel	VHF	Total Slips	Approach/ Dockside Depth	Floating Docks	Gas/ Diesel	Repairs/ Haulout	Min/Max Amps	Pump-Out Station
1. South Benson Marina	(203) 256-3002	36		600	/		G		30	
2. Black Rock Yacht Club-PRIVATE **WiFi**	(203) 335-0587	50	14		8.0 / 5.0					
3. Fayerweather Yacht Club-PRIVATE **WiFi**	(203) 576-8860	50	14		7.0 / 5.0	F	G		30	P
4. Captain's Cove Seaport **WiFi**	(203) 335-1433	200	18	350	18.0 / 13.0	F	GD	RH	50	P
5. Cedar Marina Inc. **WiFi**	(203) 335-6262	70		140	20.0 / 7.0	F		RH	30	P
EAST BRIDGEPORT										
6. Bridgeport Harbor Marina WiFi	**(203) 330-8787**	**350**	**9**	**200**	**25.0 / 12.0**	**F**	**GD**	**RH**	**30 / 100**	
7. Bridgeport Boatworks	(860) 536-9651	350	9		/		GD	RH		
8. Miamogue Yacht Club-PRIVATE	(203) 334-9882	50		173	15.0 / 8.0	F	G		30 / 50	P
9. East End Yacht Club-PRIVATE	(203) 366-3330	40	9	200	10.0 / 10.0	F	G		30	

WiFi Wireless Internet Access
Visit www.waterwayguide.com for current rates, fuel prices, website addresses and other up-to-the-minute information.
(Information in the table is provided by the facilities.)

Scan here for more details:

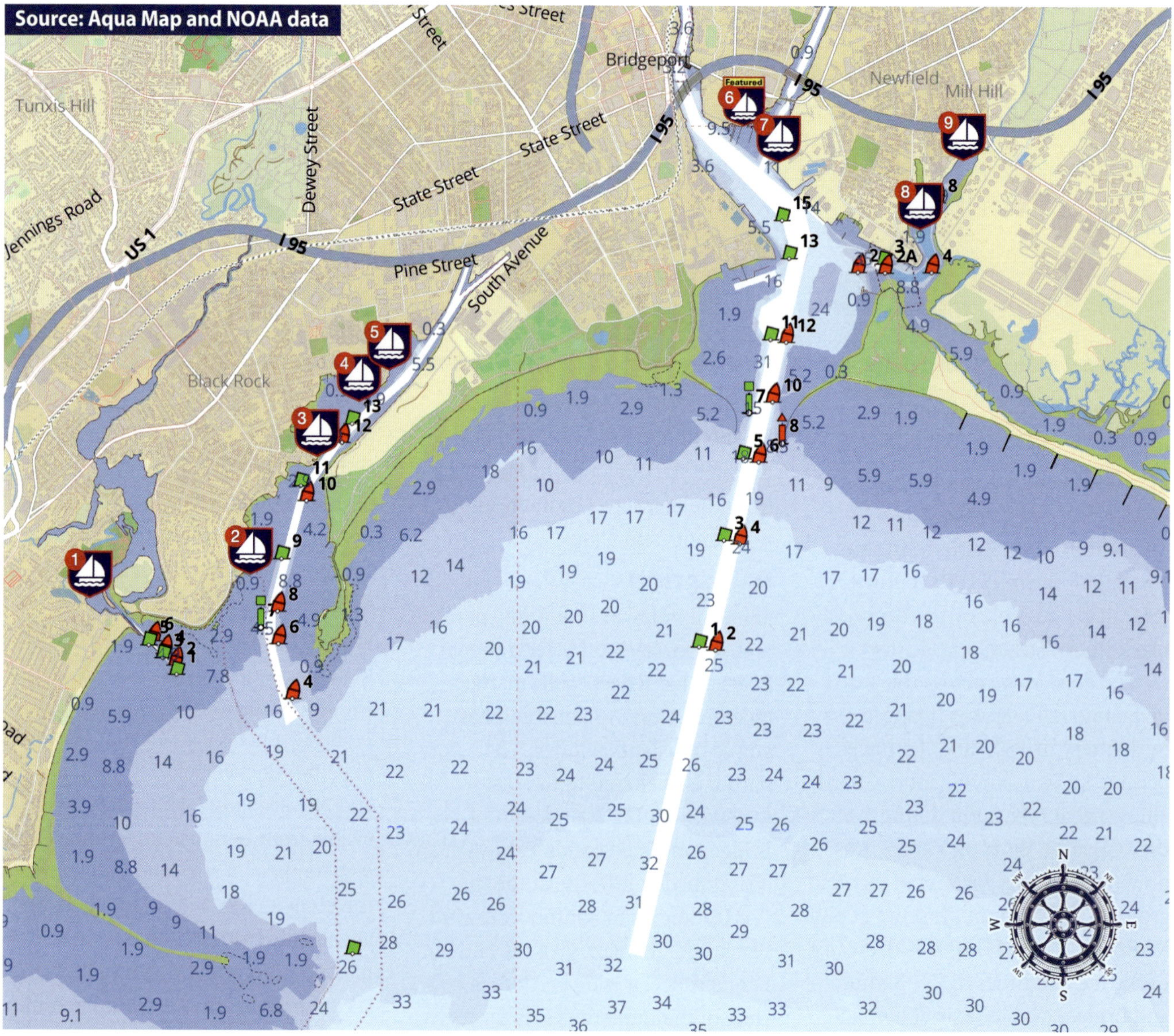

Source: Aqua Map and NOAA data

The Bridgeport-to-Port Jefferson ferry service transports passengers and vehicles across Long Island Sound several times a day. Contact ferries on VHF Channel 13 if you anticipate a close encounter. Be prepared to give way as the ferries require room to turn and maneuver.

Dockage/Moorings: South Benson Marina in Fairfield accommodates approximately 600 boats to 36 feet. The marina has a launch ramp, bathroom facilities, picnic tables, a bait shack and a fishing pier. It is adjacent to a large public beach and walking trails. Larger vessels might inquire about the guest moorings from the two yacht clubs in Black Rock Harbor, Black Rock Yacht Club and Fayerweather Yacht Club. Both monitor VHF Channel 16.

The 350-slip Captain's Cove Seaport on Cedar Creek is a family-owned and operated marina, restaurant, bar and boardwalk. Captain's Cove is home to charter fishing boats and an extensive collection of nautical memorabilia. The family-owned and -operated Cedar Marina Inc. has 140 slips with some reserved for transients (to 70 feet).

Most of the marinas at East Bridgeport that are able to handle cruising boats are located on the main channel including Bridgeport Harbor Marina. The full-service, first-class marina can accommodate vessels to 250 feet with a complete menu of marine services including dockage, vessel repairs, provisioning and winter storage. It also offers 24-hour security, concierge service and an on-site restaurant. Bridgeport Boatworks is on site providing full service work on commercial and recreational boats of any size.

Miamogue Yacht Club and East End Yacht Club are located inside Johnsons Creek, the first marked channel to the east inside the breakwaters. They are both private so call ahead.

> NOTE: All of Bridgeport's marinas are located adjacent to industrial areas. It is best to take a slip here rather than anchor, which is why we offer no anchoring recommendations.

Stratford, CT

Stratford is famous for two very diverse things: shipbuilding and helicopters. The English settled this historic city and named it for Shakespeare's Stratford-on-Avon in 1639. Shipbuilding was an important industry along the Housatonic River dating back to the 1700s. In the 1800s, large schooners were built here, most notably the 280-ton Helen Mar.

Over 100 years later, the city made a name for itself in aviation. Igor Sikorsky flew the first helicopter at his Stratford manufacturing plant in 1939 and, to this day,

Fayerweather Island Light

Long Island Sound, CT

STRATFORD		Largest Vessel	VHF	Total Slips	Approach/ Dockside Depth	Floating Docks	Gas/ Diesel	Repairs/ Haulout	Min/Max Amps	Pump-Out Station
1. Housatonic Boat Club - PRIVATE WiFi	(203) 377-9195	45	68		12.0 / 12.0	F			30	
2. Brown's Marina WiFi	(203) 377-9303	50		60	/ 6.0			R	30 / 50	
3. Safe Harbor Stratford WiFi Red 18	(203) 377-4477	85	9	200	15.0 / 12.0	F	GD	RH	30 / 100	P
4. Pootatuck Yacht Club-PRIVATE	(203) 377-9068	70	71	69	/					
5. Boardwalk Marina	(203) 378-9300	100	9	165	13.0 / 12.0	F	G	RH	30 / 50	
6. Dockside Brewery and Marina	(203) 693-3900	100		70	/				30 / 50	
MILFORD										
7. Milford Yacht Club-PRIVATE WiFi	(203) 783-0065	75	68	80	10.0 / 7.0	F		H	50	
8. Milford Harbor Mooring Field	(203) 874-1610				/					
9. Safe Harbor Port Milford WiFi	(203) 877-7802	50	9	100	8.0 / 8.0	F		RH	30	P
10. Spencer's Marina	(203) 874-4173	45	9	140	7.0 / 6.0	F	G	RH	30 / 50	P
11. Milford Boat Works WiFi	(203) 877-1475	50	68	190	9.0 / 8.0	F	GD	RH	30 / 50	P
12. Milford Lisman Landing Marina WiFi	(203) 874-1610	65	9	35	9.0 / 7.0	F			30 / 50	P

WiFi Wireless Internet Access
Visit www.waterwayguide.com for current rates, fuel prices, website addresses and other up-to-the-minute information.
(Information in the table is provided by the facilities.)

Scan here for more details:

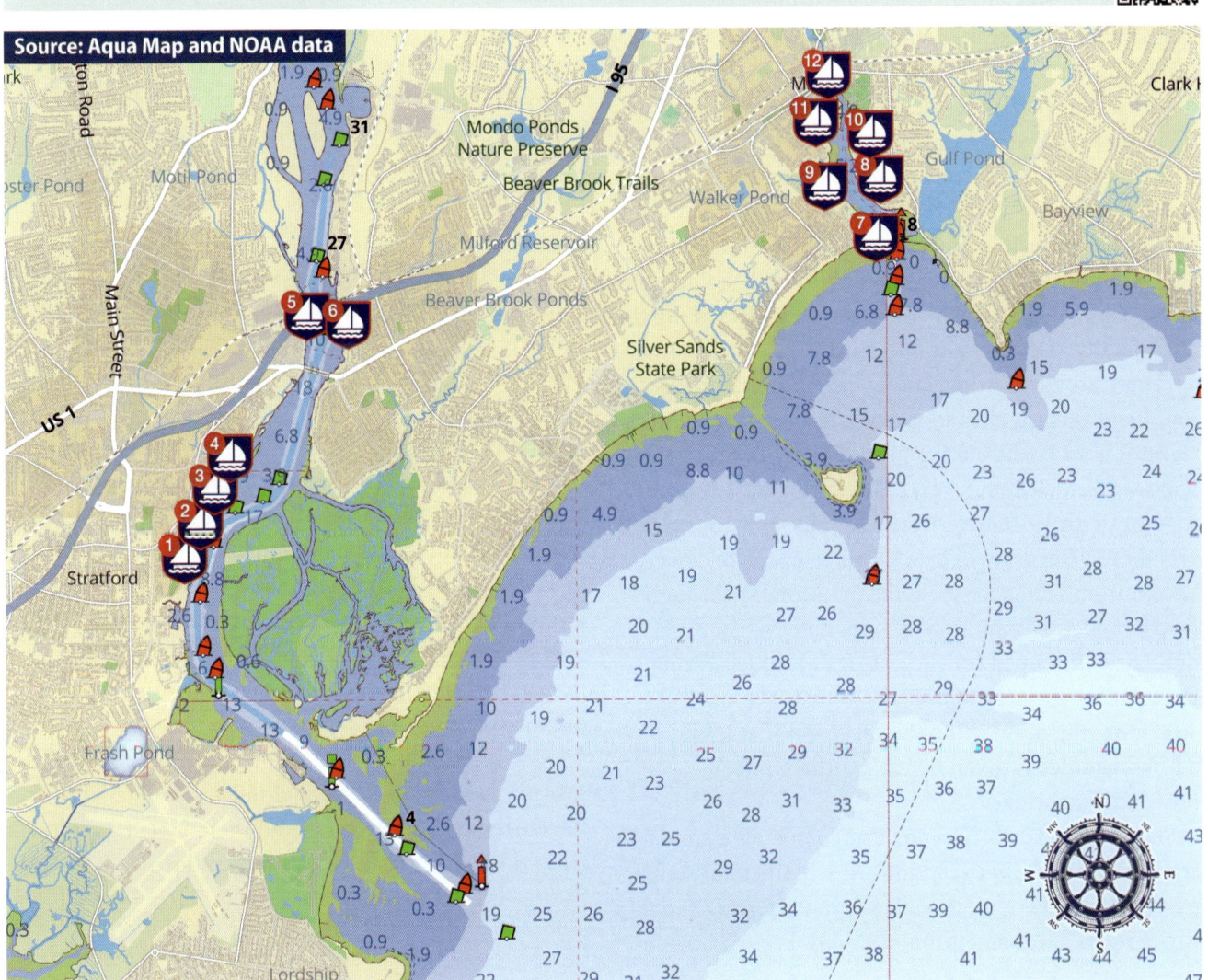

Source: Aqua Map and NOAA data

the company manufactures helicopters for both the military and civilian markets. Aeronautics buffs can visit the Connecticut Air & Space Museum (203-380-1400) and the smaller but equally interesting National Helicopter Museum (203-375-8857).

The Housatonic River's upriver stretches are scenic with green hills coming right down to the water. Devon, a small business section of Milford, is on the east bank about 2 miles north of Stratford. The river carries only 4-foot MLW depths above Devon but it is navigable and marked for 8 miles to Shelton. It is a pretty side trip for shallow-draft boats.

NAVIGATION: To reach Stratford, you can approach the Housatonic River through open, obstruction-free water. The river is about 5 miles north of Stratford Shoal Lighthouse and opposite Port Jefferson on Long Island. Tall chimneys at Devon are a good offshore landmark for the entrance between Milford Point's long, lighted breakwater (inner end submerges at three-quarter high tide) and Stratford Point. Stratford Point has shoals on all sides, an early 19th-century lighthouse and well-staked oyster beds to the east.

Currents in the narrow channel of the Housatonic River run swiftly so try to hit it at the beginning of the flood when entering. Mean tidal range at Stratford is 5.5 feet and lessens as you move upriver. The flood sets to the west and can push you toward the flats along the channel if you get caught off guard.

There are three bridges: **U.S. 1 Bridge** (with 32-foot fixed vertical clearance and a restricted schedule), **Connecticut Turnpike (I-95) Bridge** (with 68-foot fixed vertical clearance) and **Metro North (Devon) Bridge** (with 19-foot vertical clearance and a restricted schedule). The draw of U.S. 1 Bridge opens on signal except from 7:00 a.m. to 9:00 a.m., Monday through Friday, and 4:00 p.m. to 5:45 p.m. daily, when the draw need not open for the passage of vessels. From December 1 through March 31, from 8:00 p.m. to 4:00 a.m., the draw will open on signal if at least a 6-hour notice is given by calling the number posted at the bridge.

The Metro North (Devon) Bridge follows a similar schedule with a few exceptions. It will open on signal, except from 7:00 a.m. to 9:00 a.m. and from 4:00 p.m. to 5:45 p.m., Monday through Friday. From 5:30 a.m.

to 7:00 a.m. and from 5:45 p.m. to 8:15 p.m. (except Saturdays, Sundays and federal holidays), the bridge need not open more than once in any 60-minute period so it can be worthwhile to hurry a little to catch an opening. From 9:00 p.m. to 5:00 a.m., the draw will open on signal if notice is given to the chief dispatcher of the railroad before 4:00 p.m. on the day of the intended passage. A delay in opening the draw will not exceed 20 minutes for the passage of approaching trains from the time of the request.

Dockage: Full-service marinas and private yacht clubs are along the west side of the channel across from Nells Island. Housatonic Boat Club is the oldest active yacht club in Connecticut and is strictly private. Next door is Brown's Marina with seasonal and transient slips, for pleasure cruisers and recreational fishing boats to 50 feet. The family-owned facility was founded in 1956.

The friendly Safe Harbor Stratford is a popular marina so call ahead for reservations. Upscale amenities, waterfront dining and an exceptional marine service team are among their offerings. More facilities are to the north beyond the U.S. 1 Bridge including Boardwalk Marina with 10 reserved transient slips to 100 feet.

Dockside Brewery and Marina across the waterway is associated with the three-acre popular waterfront biergarten and craft brewing company, Dockside Brewery. They offer 60 slips and T-heads for boats up to 100 feet.

Anchorage: At Nells Island in the bend across from Stratford, the Housatonic River opens up with good water in the marina area. You can anchor off the northern tip of Nells Island south of green can "21" in 17 feet MLW with good holding in mud but be aware that the current is swift. Consider setting two anchors as a single anchor might break out during the current change. If you go ashore by dinghy, an outboard is a must.

A second option is to anchor on the west side of just north of the highway and railway bridges where the current is not as strong and there is still 9 to 10 feet MLW with a mud bottom at Stratford.

Milford Harbor, CT

Milford, approximately 4 miles east of Stratford, is an attractive summer resort and yachting center located at the mouth of the Wepawaug River. Milford has an easy-to-enter, well-protected but crowded harbor with good marinas that cater to transient mariners. Captain Kidd and other pirates are purported to have once roamed these waters and to have left behind buried treasure.

NAVIGATION: Entry to the Wepawaug River is through The Gulf, past low, rocky, partly wooded Charles Island. Keep the island and green can "1" to the west. The channel into Milford is well marked. It is best to stay inside the buoys as the water is very shallow on both sides as you approach the harbor. The U.S. Army Corps of Engineers tries to maintain 8- to 10-foot MLW depths throughout the channel but local tow boat companies may have the most current information.

Dockage/Moorings: In the mooring-cluttered Milford Harbor, a seemingly endless flotilla of small sailing craft is constantly on the move. Most of the facilities here cater to smaller vessels but you may be able to snag a mooring in the Milford Harbor Mooring Field.

The private Milford Yacht Club welcomes members of recognized yacht clubs and guests of MYC. Other options here include Safe Harbor Port Milford, a full-service boatyard and marina that maintains 10 reserved transient slips. Spencer's Marina across the river is a full-service marina and boatyard with the usual amenities. Call ahead for slip availability.

Milford Boat Works to the north is a family-owned and -operated marina located on Milford Harbor. They maintain transient slips to 50 feet and have a fully stocked ship store that is open year-round.

Milford Lisman Landing Marina is a very welcoming municipal marina located in town, just steps from beautiful historic downtown Milford. This is an all-transient marina with 35 slips that can accommodate vessels up to 65 feet. They have numerous amenities including trained dock staff to assist in your tie-up, free pump-out with overnight stay, a laundromat, car and bicycle rentals plus nearby tennis courts and concierge service. It is an easy bike ride to town amenities and a nice beach. There is also a walking trail in a nearby nature preserve.

Anchorage: If you crave seclusion, drop the hook behind Charles Island in 9 to 13 feet MLW. At low tide it is protected from all directions but the east and holding is good. Note that the narrow isthmus connecting the island with the mainland disappears at high tide and the swell can make the basin uncomfortable in the prevailing southwest wind. Go right up to the north side of the island for best protection. On still nights with nothing to hold your bow to the wind, you might wallow in the slight surge from the Sound.

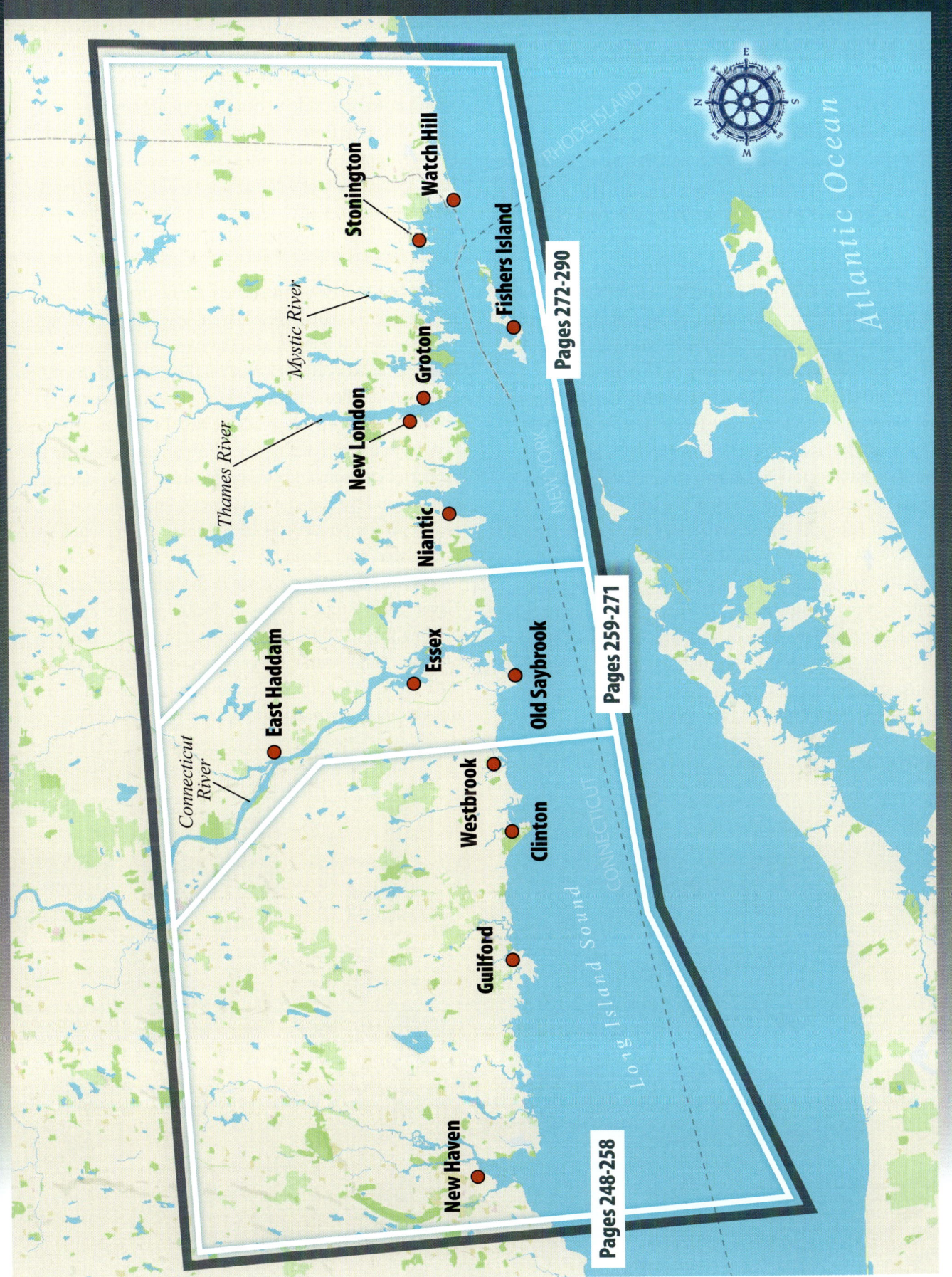

Watch Hill

Stonington

Mystic River

Fishers Island

Thames River

New London

Groton

Pages 272-290

Niantic

East Haddam

Essex

Old Saybrook

Pages 259-271

Connecticut River

Westbrook

Clinton

Guilford

Long Island Sound

New Haven

Pages 248-258

RHODE ISLAND

NEW YORK

CONNECTICUT

Atlantic Ocean

NEW HAVEN TO WESTBROOK, CT

New Haven Area, CT

New Haven, Connecticut's second largest city, is situated almost 70 nm northeast of New York City. It is the home of Yale University but, as a mostly commercial port, New Haven is one of Long Island Sound's most important harbors of refuge for commercial shipping.

The harbor is industrial and busy, but there are two marinas away from the hubbub of the inner harbor that cater to visiting yachts. Downtown New Haven is only a short taxi or bus ride away from the harbor marinas.

New Haven has all the attractions of a major American city in a small, walkable package. A stroll among Yale University's classic gargoyle halls and ivy walls, juxtaposed modern architecture, windowless secret societies and spacious college walks is worth the trip to town.

Yale's Beinecke Rare Book & Manuscript Library (203-432-2977) is one of the best of its kind in the world. You can see Portuguese charts from the Age of Exploration and an original copy of the Gutenberg Bible among other treasures. The Yale Peabody Museum of Natural History (203-432-5050) is one of the oldest and largest history museums in the country. The dinosaur collection is an impressive treat for kids under age 99 or so.

NAVIGATION: The 2-mile-wide harbor at New Haven is protected in part by breakwaters. The channel is deep, well-marked and able to handle virtually any vessel, short of a supertanker. The West River channel, west of the shipping channel after entry, is also well marked. It's narrower but deep enough to accommodate almost any recreational vessel. Outside the channels, the harbor is shoal and not navigable (with the exception of Morris Cove).

Dockage/Moorings: There are no marine facilities in the inner harbor ("New Haven Reach") for cruising yachts. About 0.5 miles into the West River channel, transient boaters are welcome on the protected moorings at the private Pequonnock Yacht Club with some amenities. Pick up any available ball. Be sure to get a pass card from the bar/yacht club. The marina offers clean and modern bathroom and shower facilities, a coin-operated laundry and two on-site restaurants. City Point Yacht Club is also private but accepts transients to 40 feet when space is available. Call ahead.

Anchorage: Morris Cove to the southeast near New Haven Yacht Club (no slips or docks) provides good holding in 8 to 10 feet MLW and an easy route in and out of Long Island Sound. However, smaller vessels may find the cove to be less than adequately protected and open to unwelcome surge and current.

New Haven

New Haven Harbor, CT

WEST RIVER		Largest Vessel	VHF	Total Slips	Approach/ Dockside Depth	Floating Docks	Gas/ Diesel	Repairs/ Haulout	Min/Max Amps	Pump-Out Station
1. Pequonnock Yacht Club - PRIVATE (WiFi)	(203) 773-9460	50	9	130	10.0 / 8.0	F		RH	30 / 50	P
2. City Point Yacht Club-PRIVATE	(203) 789-9301	40	9	182	7.0 / 6.0	F	G		30	P

(WiFi) Wireless Internet Access
Visit www.waterwayguide.com for current rates, fuel prices, website addresses and other up-to-the-minute information. (Information in the table is provided by the facilities.)

Scan here for more details:

Source: Aqua Map and NOAA data

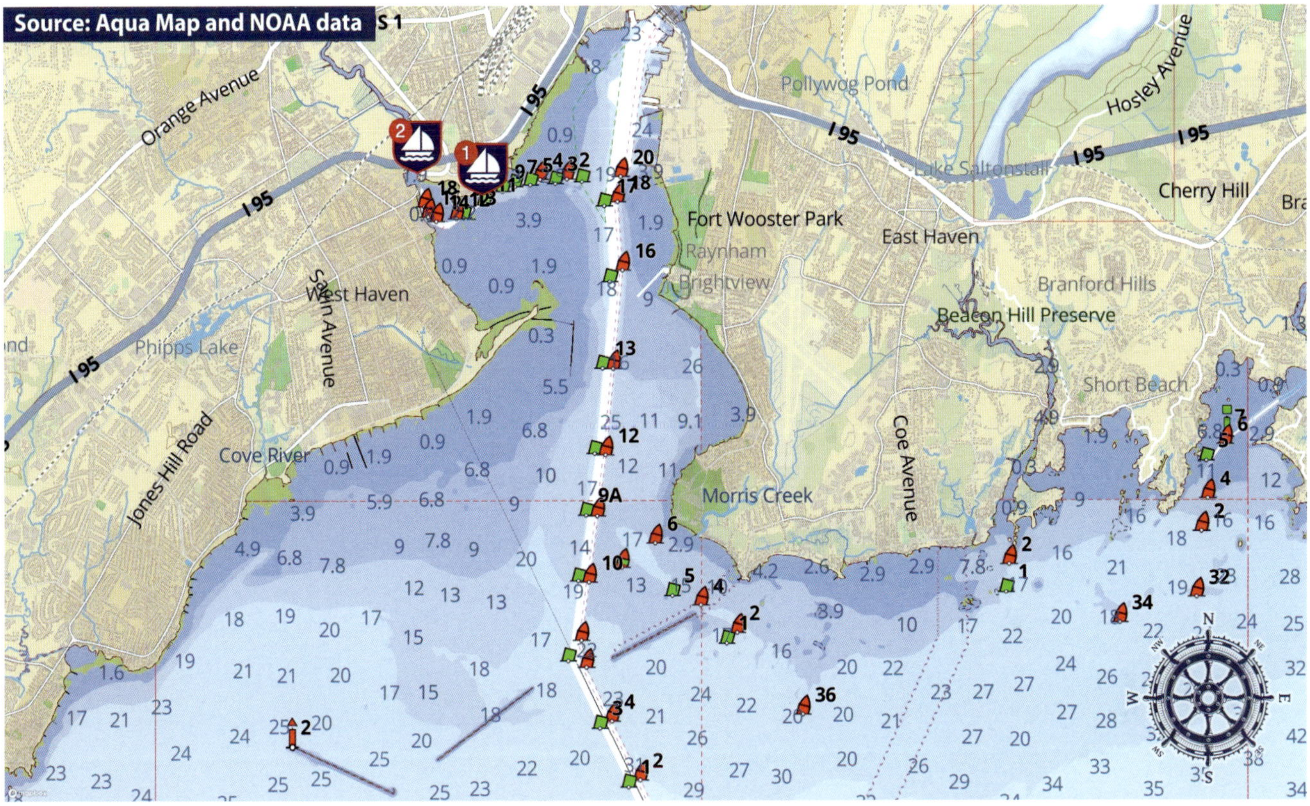

Branford, CT

Branford is the best port of refuge and easiest harbor entry in the almost 20 miles stretching between New Haven and Clinton. There are many restored homes dating from the Colonial days, when it had important salt works (meat for Revolutionary War troops was preserved in Branford salt) and granite quarries. It also was a Yankee trading center and the original home of Yale University. Today, Branford is a vibrant community of about 28,000 residents, some of whom are affiliated with Yale and other New Haven-area universities.

NAVIGATION: When entering Branford from Long Island Sound, you must thread a series of rocks guarding the entrance to the Branford River but they are well charted, buoyed and relatively easy to make out. They offer little challenge when visibility is good.

The clearest route in is to turn northward between the Cow and Calf Rocks and Five Foot Rock, traveling east of flashing red bell buoy "34" and west of red nun buoy "32." Pass west of Blyn Rock's flashing red "2" and Bird Rock's red nun buoy "4" and pick up the channel's turn slightly east at green can "5." Another slight eastward bend between Big Mermaid (marked by flashing green "7") and Little Mermaid (marked by red nun buoy "6") sends the channel through moderate shallows into the Branford River.

The Branford River, like many Long Island Sound tributaries, has strong currents. Be aware of the direction and strength of the current when docking at any of the marinas listed. Call for docking assistance if the current is running strong.

Long Island Sound, CT

BRANFORD		Largest Vessel	VHF	Total Slips	Approach/ Dockside Depth	Floating Docks	Gas/ Diesel	Repairs/ Haulout	Min/Max Amps	Pump-Out Station
1. Branford Yacht Club-PRIVATE **WiFi**	(203) 488-9798	60		253	10.0 / 10.0	F	GD	H	30 / 50	P
2. Safe Harbor Bruce & Johnsons **WiFi**	(203) 488-8329	60	9	650	7.0 / 7.5	F	GD	RH	30 / 50	P
3. Indian Neck Yacht Club	(203) 488-9276	40		90	8.0 / 8.0		G		30	
4. Branford Landing Marina **WiFi**	(203) 483-6544	55		30	8.0 / 8.0	F	GD	RH	30	

WiFi Wireless Internet Access
Visit www.waterwayguide.com for current rates, fuel prices, website addresses and other up-to-the-minute information.
(Information in the table is provided by the facilities.)

Scan here for more details:

Source: Aqua Map and NOAA data

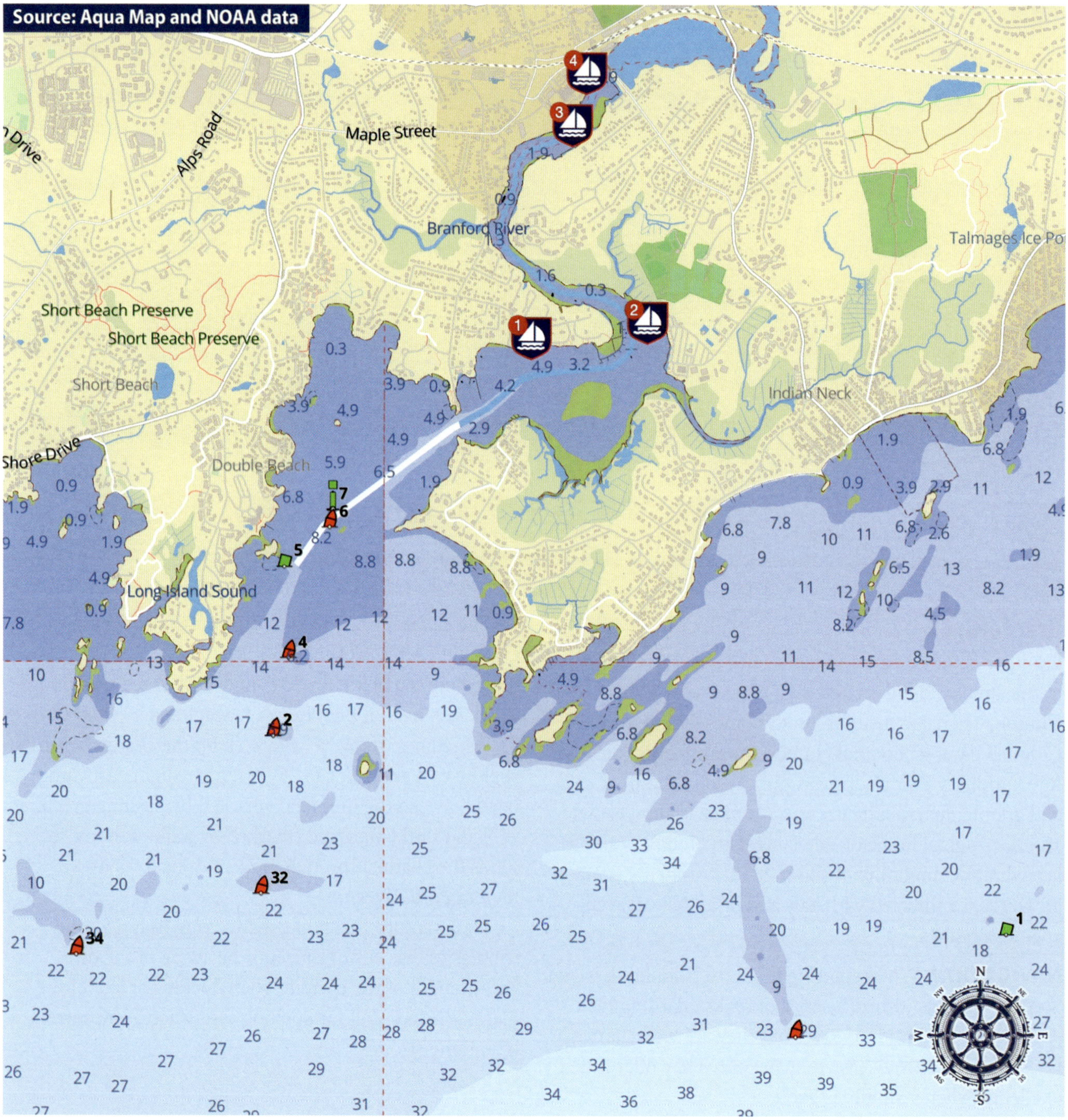

Dockage/Moorings: Note that there is no protected anchorage in Branford Harbor or the river but visiting cruisers can almost always find a berth here. Immediately to the north on entering the river, the friendly Branford Yacht Club is private but has limited provisions for transient docking that must be arranged by contacting the dockmaster at 203-488-9798.

Safe Harbor Bruce & Johnsons can likely accommodate you in one of their 650 slips. They have a large pool and on-site restaurant and can offer a full range of repairs and services supported by a comprehensive parts department and marine supply store.

Private Indian Neck Yacht Club does not typically have slips available to non-member yachts; however, guest and transient moorings are available with use of the Club launch included in the fee. Members of clubs with reciprocal privileges may dine at the yacht club.

Branford Landing Marina is a small, family-run marina with enormous inside winter storage and stellar boat maintenance and repair services. They maintain four transient slips to 55 feet with full amenities including an on-site restaurant.

The Thimbles, CT

For the next 8 miles east of Branford the intervening shore is wild, marshy and dotted with summer communities and granite quarries. It is rocky and challenging for those unfamiliar with the area. It should be approached with caution and careful study of the chart. All of the harbors here are packed with local boats and require local knowledge. Proceed with caution.

The Thimbles were created more than 10,000 years ago when glacial action exposed ancient granite bedrock. As the glacier moved, it picked up loose soil and stone and pried loose blocks of granite, leaving the islands after the glacier melted. This cluster of islands resembles the endless islands off the coast of Maine in miniature.

The Thimble Islands and nearby Stony Creek have been a popular summer community since the days of Captain Kidd, who used to hide his ships among the rocky cliffs within High Island. He may have hidden treasure here, too, although none has been found to date. (It is not a good idea to start searching on private property.)

NAVIGATION: The Thimbles consist of 25 (private) inhabited islands and hundreds of pink granite rock formations that scatter into Long Island Sound off the unique coastal village of Stony Creek. The Thimbles are the largest group of islands on Long Island Sound and are just west of Sachem Head off the Connecticut shore between Branford and Guilford. These clumps of rock form a narrow alley of deep water down the middle.

Stony Creek serves as the shore side access to the Thimbles and is well worth a dinghy ride from the anchorages. There are several dinghy docks available and a public dock for small craft. This is a busy spot occupied by a plethora of small boats, ferries, an oyster fleet and lobster and fishing vessels. Excursion boats, departing hourly May through October, run to the Thimble Islands from Stony Creek. Activity starts early and carries well into the evening.

A water taxi runs on the hour and is on-call for those wishing to get to Stony Creek. Proceed cautiously in this area. Swimmers are usually diving off the cliffs or paddling between boats. No services or facilities are available on the islands.

Anchorage: You can anchor practically anywhere with appropriate depth outside the harbor in Stony Creek, and even on crowded summer weekends you can usually find some protection and deep water. Take particular care to observe the underwater cable areas servicing the islands.

Crowded Pine Orchard to the west of Stony Creek is a summer community with fine homes, lots of rocks and a yacht club unexpectedly large and ambitious for a harbor this size. You can anchor outside in good weather when there are no winds out of the east or south.

In the Thimble Islands, private mooring buoys have erased a formerly favored anchorage between High and Pot Islands and leave far too little room for proper scope in 10 to 20 feet MLW. Some gamble on shorter scope in settled weather with decent holding in the mud. Although not recommended, some cruisers have been known to pick up one of the private moorings for a night (especially during the week) with no adverse consequences.

East of Pot Island, you will find 8 to 13 feet MLW, although rock ledges and mooring balls may push you into 15-foot MLW areas. The anchorage is approached from the south by leaving red nun buoy "2CR" to the west.

Although exposed to westerly and southwesterly winds, the area to the north of West Crib Island is a good option as well with 11 to 12 feet MLW.

Long Island Sound, CT

GUILFORD		Largest Vessel	VHF	Total Slips	Approach/ Dockside Depth	Floating Docks	Gas/ Diesel	Repairs/ Haulout	Min/Max Amps	Pump-Out Station
1. Brown's Boat Yard WiFi	(203) 453-6283	40		30	6.0 / 5.0	F	GD	RH	30	
2. Guilford Yacht Club-PRIVATE WiFi	(203) 453-0070	50	71	158	4.0 / 5.0	F			30 / 50	P
3. Guilford Town Marina WiFi	(203) 453-8092	38	9	122	4.0 / 6.0	F			30	

WiFi Wireless Internet Access
Visit www.waterwayguide.com for current rates, fuel prices, website addresses and other up-to-the-minute information.
(Information in the table is provided by the facilities.)

Scan here for more details:

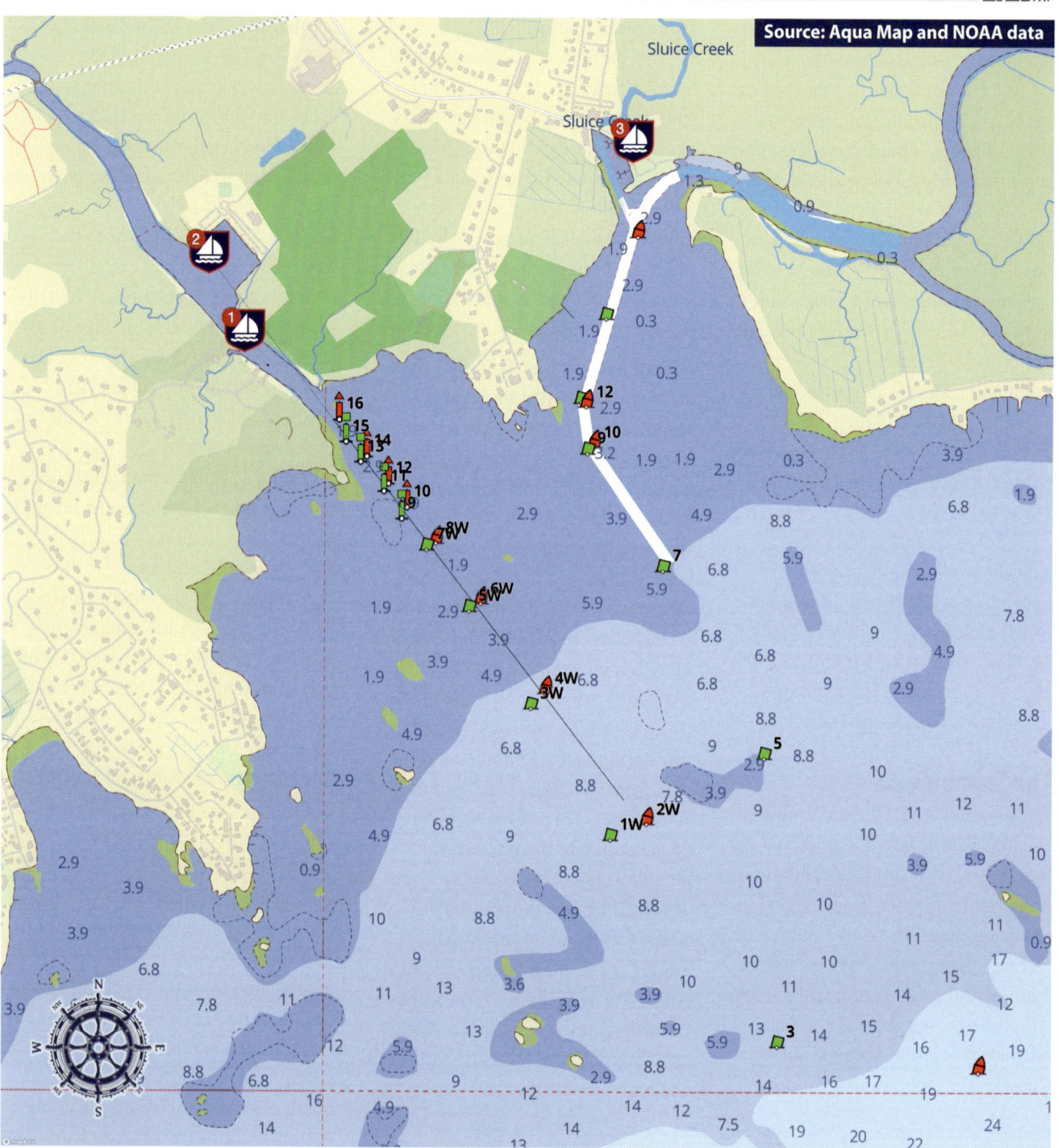

Guilford, CT

The village of Guilford provides a glimpse of New England architectural history at its best. Many structures dating back to the 17th century have survived and a walk through the harborside area is memorable.

Guilford boasts five historic house museums. The Henry Whitfield State Museum remains the oldest stone house in New England and contains many artifacts of 17th-century Guilford and the Puritan life of the period. See more at www.portal.ct.gov/ecd-henrywhitfieldstatemuseum. The shopping area and services are also available within a short walk of the harbor.

NAVIGATION: Guilford is located between the West and East Rivers about 3 miles north of uninhabited Falkner Island. Although the entrance to West River is buoyed, it is rather shallow. The East River entry is easier but requires sharp attention and good visibility for the newcomer. The entrance channel into the East River has anywhere from 3.5 to 8 feet MLW in the main channel with the shallowest part being in the approach to Guilford Point, especially between green can buoy "9" and red nun buoy "10."

Sachem Head is the harbor just west of Guilford. It is pretty, rock-lined, small and dominated by a friendly yacht club of the same name located immediately to the south upon entering. The approach is relatively straightforward. Using flashing red bell buoy "22" as a guide to avoid Goose Rocks Shoals, progress can be made in good depths to the 3-second flashing red light at the end of the harbor breakwater, which is maintained by Sachem Yacht Club from June to September.

Dockage/Moorings: About 1 mile inland of the West River entrance is Brown's Boat Yard, a full-service working yard offering marine services. A transient slip (to 40 feet) may be arranged on the yard's floating docks along the river.

A better bet for a transient slip is the 158-slip Guilford Yacht Club, a short distance farther upriver on the east side. Although a private facility, transient accommodations can be made for vessels up to 50 feet (subject to slip availability). Guilford is about 0.5 mile away and a pleasant walk (or easily-obtained ride) from the clubhouse.

Guilford Town Marina to the east at Sluice Creek has 122 slips and 14 moorings for transients to 38 feet. Transient slips are very limited. Boaters should call ahead to check availability. If you are looking for a good dinghy ride, the National Audubon Society maintains a 150-acre reserve (Guilford Salt Meadows Sanctuary) north on the East River protecting the tidal estuary and providing a panorama of scenic views.

Anchorage: In Sachem Head Harbor proper, there is 8 to 10 feet MLW with good holding in mud with protection from all but the west. The downside is that most of the space is full of moorings. Note that there are no recommended anchorages between here and Duck Island Roads, east of Clinton Harbor.

Vessels can anchor just north of Sachem Head in Joshua Cove, as long as care is taken to avoid unmarked ledges, Goose Rocks and any weather out of the south. Here you will find 7- to 9-foot MLW depths in good holding with soft mud up to the area around Foskett Island.

Clinton, CT

Clinton Harbor is a good day's run for faster boats transiting to or from ports east such as Block Island, Newport or Mystic. It is also close to the Connecticut River for cruisers on their way to Essex and slower boats that make more stops. This harbor has just about everything: ease of entry, excellent protection, accommodating marinas, eye-popping views of sea and sand and good dining and provisioning.

NAVIGATION: The approach is unencumbered south and west of Kelsey Point Breakwater, except for a shoal marked by red nun buoy "2" at the shore end of the rock jetty. Moderate currents run in the channel here on both tides. The channel is maintained to 8.5 feet MLW and 100 feet wide; however, shoaling does occur around the entrance and the channel curves so it is very important to stay in the channel.

> ⚠️ **CAUTION:** Clinton Harbor has a tight entrance at low tide when depths are lower than the charted 9-foot MLW depths. We recommend waiting for outgoing traffic to exit and favor the Cedar Island (west) side upon entering. Do not, however, cut the point of Cedar Island close as there is shoaling immediately around the point.

GOIN' ASHORE
CLINTON, CT

ATTRACTIONS

1. Adam Stanton House and General Store
Antique house museum with attached general store
(63 E. Main St., 860-669-2132).

2. Clinton Tourist Information Center
42-4 Church Rd.

3. Elisha White House
Museum within an 18th-century house (also known as
"Old Brick") containing portraits, period furniture and
domestic tools. Open for tours by appointment at
103 E. Main St. (860-669-2148).

SERVICES

4. Clinton Post Office
2 W. Main St. (860-669-4155)

5. Commonwealth Health Center
Liberty Square (114 E. Main St., 860-664-0787)

6. Henry Carter Hull Library
10 Killingworth Turnpike (860-669-2342)

7. Shoreline Animal Hospital
18 W. Main St. (860-669-9374)

MARINAS

8. Cedar Island Marina
34 Riverside Dr. (860-669-8681)

9. Clinton Yacht Haven
70 Riverside Dr. (860-669-7254)

10. Harborside Marina
131 Grove St. (860-669-1705)

11. Old Harbor Marina
79 Waterside Ln. (860-669-3500)

12. Port Clinton Marina
33 Indian Dr. (860-669-4563)

Chamard Vineyards Bistro

From the beginning, life in Clinton centered around the essentials of survival: fishing, farming and the all-important local industry of shipbuilding. Clinton became the home of the Collegiate School in 1701, with the Rev. Abraham Pierson selected to teach the first class of undergraduates. He continued teaching until his death in 1707, at which point students scattered for a period of time to other locations. Eventually, the Collegiate School was relocated to New Haven, where it became what it is today: Yale University.

Learn more about this seafaring town at the Adam Stanton House and General Store, an antique house museum at 63 E. Main St. (860-669-2132) and the Elisha White House, a museum housed in an 18th-century house (also known as "Old Brick") containing portraits, period furniture and domestic tools. Open for tours by appointment at 103 E. Main St. (860-669-2148).

A worthwhile journey is to Chamard Vineyards Bistro at 115 Cow Hill Rd. (transportation required). They serve lunch and dinner and reservations are recommended. The 40-acre property boasts 20 acres of established vines that are carefully tended by hand in the European tradition, yielding superior Cabernet Franc, Cabernet Sauvignon, Chardonnay, Merlot and Pinot Noir fruit.

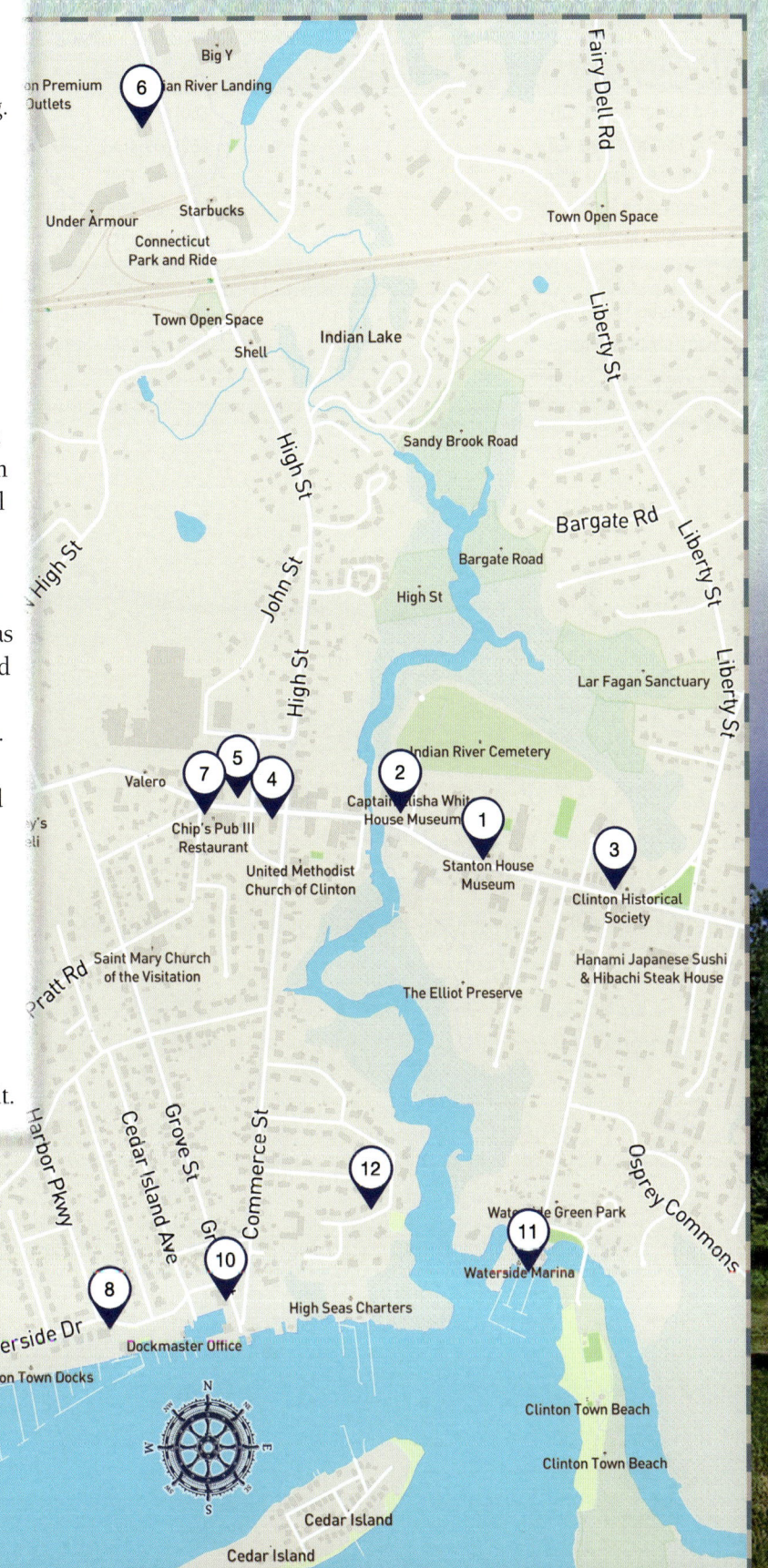

Long Island Sound, CT

CLINTON		Largest Vessel	VHF	Total Slips	Approach/ Dockside Depth	Floating Docks	Gas/ Diesel	Repairs/ Haulout	Min/Max Amps	Pump-Out Station
1. Old Harbor Marina WiFi	(860) 669-3500	45		130	7.0 / 5.0	F		RH	30 / 50	
2. Port Clinton Marina WiFi	(860) 669-4563	40	9	140	9.0 / 8.0	F		RH	30 / 50	
3. Harborside Marina WiFi	(860) 669-1705	180		75	20.0 / 9.0	F		RH	30	
4. Cedar Island Marina WiFi	(860) 669-8681	130	9	400	6.5 / 8.5	F	GD	RH	15 / 100	P
5. Clinton Yacht Haven WiFi	(860) 669-7254	50		130	5.0 / 6.0	F		RH	30 / 50	P
WESTBROOK										
6. Safe Harbor Pilots Point WiFi	(860) 399-5128	100	9	250	10.0 / 6.0	F	GD	RH	30 / 50	P
7. Harry's Marine Repair	(860) 399-6165	38		76	8.0 / 8.0	F	G	RH	30	P

WiFi Wireless Internet Access
Visit www.waterwayguide.com for current rates, fuel prices, website addresses and other up-to-the-minute information.
(Information in the table is provided by the facilities.)

Scan here for more details:

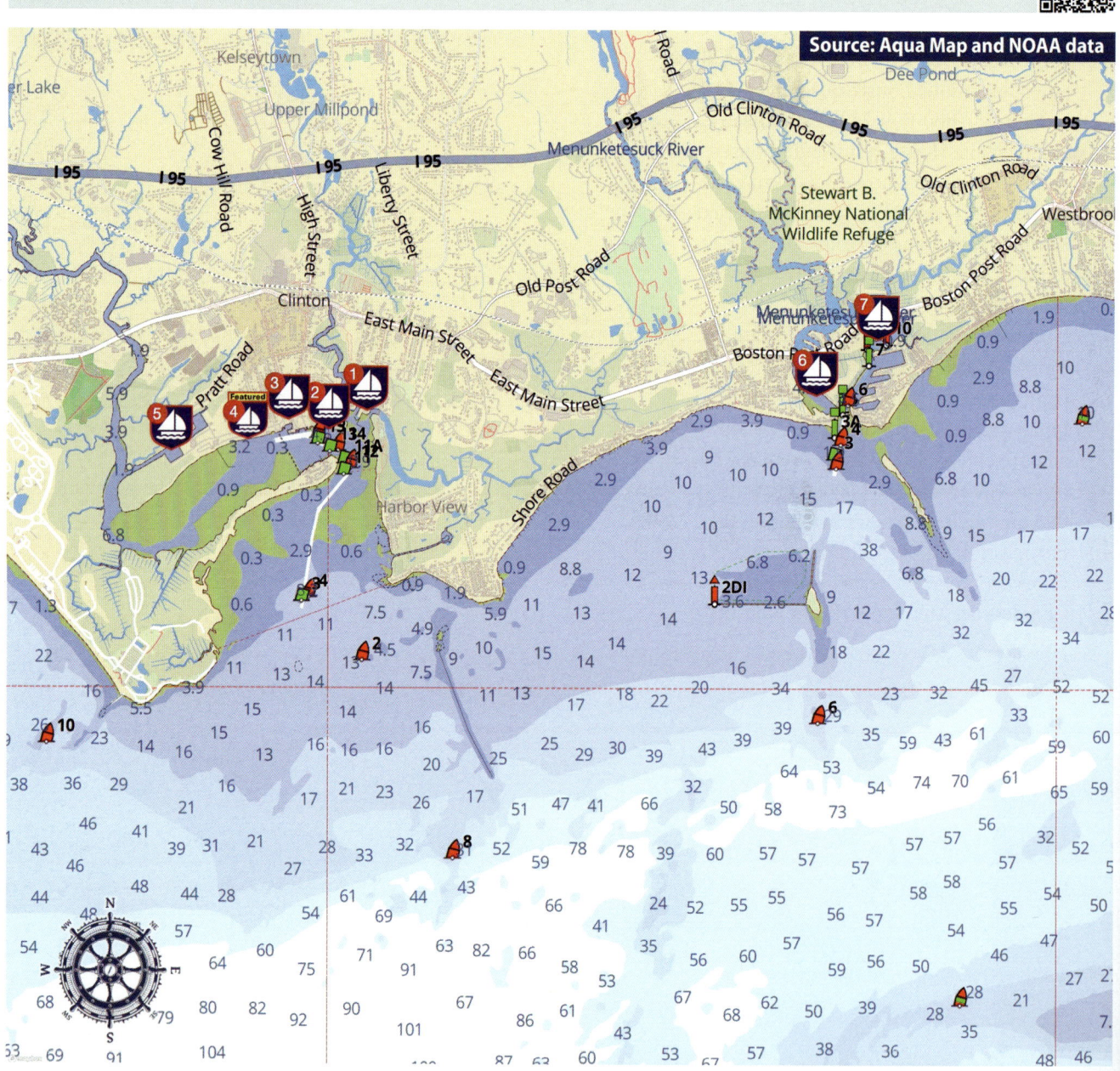

Source: Aqua Map and NOAA data

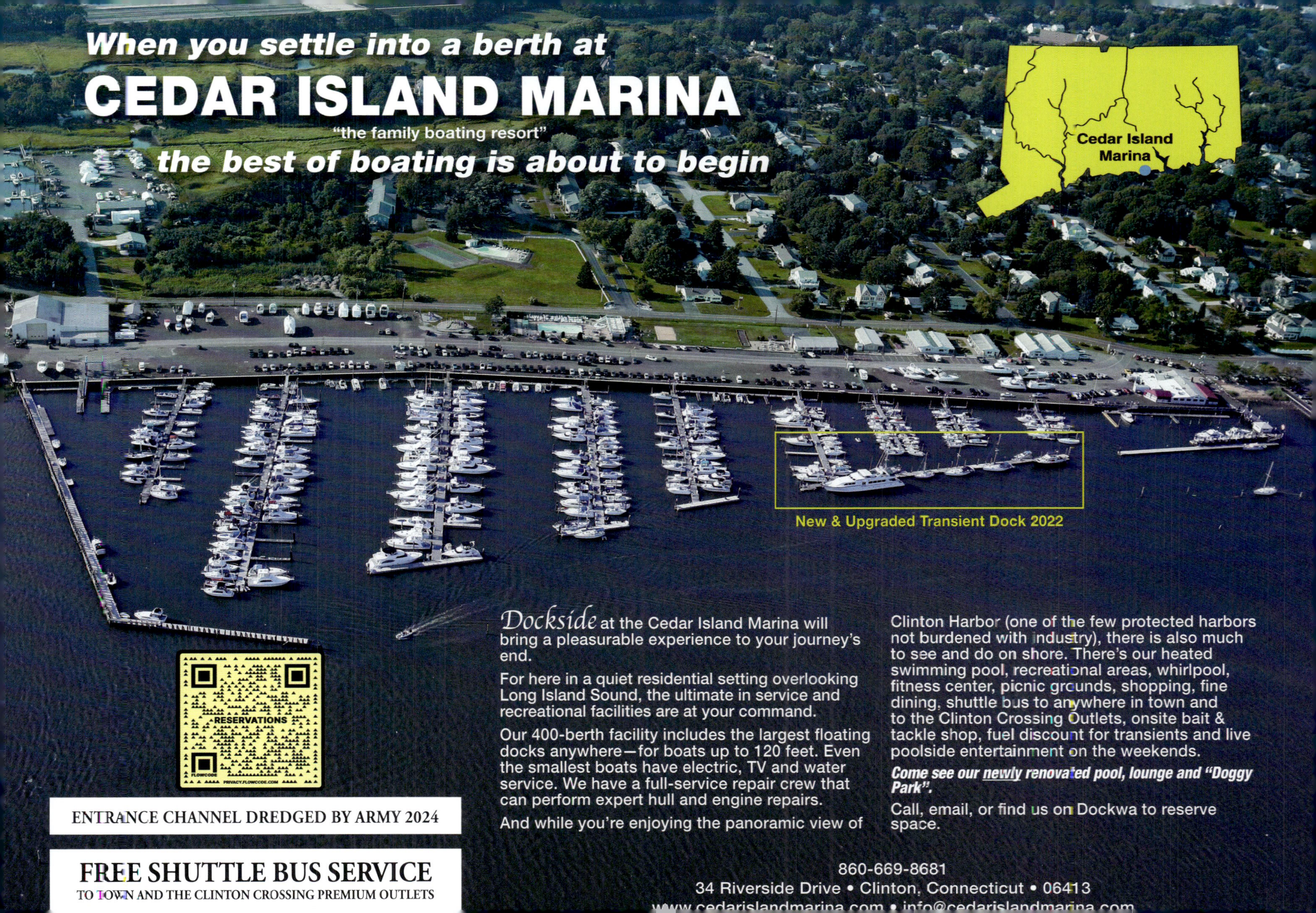

When you settle into a berth at
CEDAR ISLAND MARINA
"the family boating resort"
the best of boating is about to begin
Cedar Island Marina
New & Upgraded Transient Dock 2022
RESERVATIONS
Dockside at the Cedar Island Marina will bring a pleasurable experience to your journey's end.
For here in a quiet residential setting overlooking Long Island Sound, the ultimate in service and recreational facilities are at your command.
Our 400-berth facility includes the largest floating docks anywhere—for boats up to 120 feet. Even the smallest boats have electric, TV and water service. We have a full-service repair crew that can perform expert hull and engine repairs.
And while you're enjoying the panoramic view of Clinton Harbor (one of the few protected harbors not burdened with industry), there is also much to see and do on shore. There's our heated swimming pool, recreational areas, whirlpool, fitness center, picnic grounds, shopping, fine dining, shuttle bus to anywhere in town and to the Clinton Crossing Outlets, onsite bait & tackle shop, fuel discount for transients and live poolside entertainment on the weekends.
Come see our newly renovated pool, lounge and "Doggy Park".
Call, email, or find us on Dockwa to reserve space.
ENTRANCE CHANNEL DREDGED BY ARMY 2024
FREE SHUTTLE BUS SERVICE
TO TOWN AND THE CLINTON CROSSING PREMIUM OUTLETS
860-669-8681
34 Riverside Drive • Clinton, Connecticut • 06413
www.cedarislandmarina.com • info@cedarislandmarina.com

Upon entry into Clinton Harbor, round to the west around the moored boats and follow the channel along the northern shore to the marinas. Plan to take a slip; there is no room for anchoring here.

Dockage: Old Harbor Marina offers slips (to 45 feet) and comprehensive services for boats, including repairs, installations and maintenance by experienced technicians. Port Clinton Marina has 140 slips and offers marina service, boat commissioning, winterization, hauling and storage services. They maintain 10 transient slips to 40 feet. Continuing west, Harborside Marina is a privately owned marina and boat dealership, which may have a slip for you but do call ahead.

The 400-slip Cedar Island Marina operates a full-service, resort-type facility with pump-out service (both on the fuel dock and with a boat). It is a deep-water facility with floating docks that can accommodate large yacht clubs and vessels up to 130 feet. They have numerous amenities including a large heated pool, fitness center and on-site restaurant. A private shuttle bus transports marina patrons to Clinton and the Clinton Crossing Outlets.

Clinton Yacht Haven to the north is a dockominium with wet slips and indoor rack storage. They maintain three transient slips to 50 feet. Amenities include a pool and a playground.

Westbrook, CT

What began as a farming community and later a shipbuilding center during the American Revolution is today a fun stopover port for cruising boaters on Long Island Sound. Good protection and a full range of amenities are available just to the north of Duck Island in the waters of the Menunketesuck and Patchogue Rivers at Westbrook.

These rivers merge just before they exit into Duck Island Roads and Long Island Sound west of the Town of Westbrook. The channel is visible as you enter Duck Island Roads from the south or west.

> NOTE: Duck Island is a wildlife sanctuary and the summer home of gulls, cormorants, ducks, snowy egrets, glossy ibises, great blue herons and green and black-crowned night herons. If you are a nature lover, stay alert for this beautiful bird life but remember you are not allowed ashore.

NAVIGATION: Enter through a dredged channel beginning at flashing red buoy "2," which must be left to the east. The can and nun buoys marking this passage must be carefully observed or grounding is a near certainty. Note that green can buoy "5" is situated approximately 25 yards south of the navigable channel to the Menunketesuck River so a sharp westward turn at green can buoy "5" will provide unfortunate results. Wait and make the turn west just before green-red daybeacon "M."

In addition, the Menunketesuck River has shoaled along its western side. Deeper water is found along the dock faces located to the east. Depths here are charted at 5 feet MLW. The Patchogue River bears slightly to the east from the dredged channel and offers a 7-foot-deep MLW, 125-foot-wide alternative to the Menunketesuck. Both rivers are busy passageways but, unfortunately, anchoring is not permitted in either river.

Dockage: The sprawling Safe Harbor Pilots Point dominates the east shore of the Menunketesuck River. Together these facilities represent one of the largest (870 total slips) and best-equipped facilities on Long Island Sound. They also have a well-stocked parts department, which will match marine discount store prices.

Marine repairs are available at these and several other facilities on the Patchogue River including the 76-slip Harry's Marine Repair provides a friendly and casual setting for boaters to relax and enjoy their boats while offering all of the services expected of a working boatyard.

Anchorage: The area outside of Westbrook in Duck Island Roads just west of the breakwater and close in to Grove Beach is a wake-active anchorage that is protected from the east through north. Distant breakwaters provide some protection from other directions. This is an extremely popular anchorage in summer months.

A better location is to tuck in behind the breakwaters extending north and west from Duck Island for 5 to 7 feet MLW with good holding in sand. This is exposed to the west but the distant Kelsey Point breakwater gives some relief from any stormy seas. This is a popular spot with locals for sunset viewing. Landing on Duck Island is not permitted.

SIDE TRIP: CONNECTICUT RIVER

First-time visitors to the Connecticut River are surprised to discover the unspoiled natural beauty of the lower river, much of it seemingly unchanged since the days of the Colonial traders and boat builders. The vibrant entrance of the river quickly gives way to pastoral undulations, lined by quiet marshes and occasional intriguing coves and creeks.

The Connecticut River flows southward for 417 nm from New Hampshire near the Canadian border into Long Island Sound and is the largest and longest river in New England. The Mohegan Indians, who dominated the upper reaches around present-day Hartford, called it Quinetucket, meaning "beside the long, tidal river." It is the only major river in Connecticut with no city at its mouth due to depth restrictions from Long Sand Shoal and the entrance bar.

Today, protected and secluded anchorages are accessible via a number of inlets and off-channel backwaters. Not far up the river are marinas, restaurants, anchorages and waterside activities as well as the historic villages of Old Saybrook and Essex.

Long Sand Shoal

NAVIGATION: Two miles southeast of Duck Island Roads is the beginning of Long Sand Shoal. Well-buoyed and charted, it extends about 6 miles east to the entrance of the Connecticut River. Boats heading for the Connecticut River from Duck Island Roads should go north of the shoal. For others, the choice depends on the current, which runs up to 2 knots and is generally stronger south of the shoal.

If you are riding a fair current heading along Long Island Sound, stay to the south and get the extra lift. If you are bucking the current, stay to the north where it is weaker and be sure to keep south of the charted rocks off Cornfield Point on the Connecticut coast. Be especially conscious of Hen and Chickens, which are rocks just west of Cornfield Point. While well-charted and well-marked, it is easy to go astray in this area in poor visibility....Many have.

Connecticut River Entrance

NAVIGATION:

Two handsome lighthouses distinguish the entry into the Connecticut River from Long Island Sound. Both are on the western breakwater (Saybrook side). The Saybrook Breakwater Light, also known as the Outer Light, was first lighted on June 15, 1886. It's about 3,000 feet out from Lynde Point Light. The Lynde Point Lighthouse, sometimes called the Inner Light, was built around 1800 and abuts a gabled house. When entering the harbor be sure to head for the southernmost Saybrook Light marking the entrance along the western breakwater.

Entry between the breakwaters is easy but if wind and tide are

Connecticut River Entrance

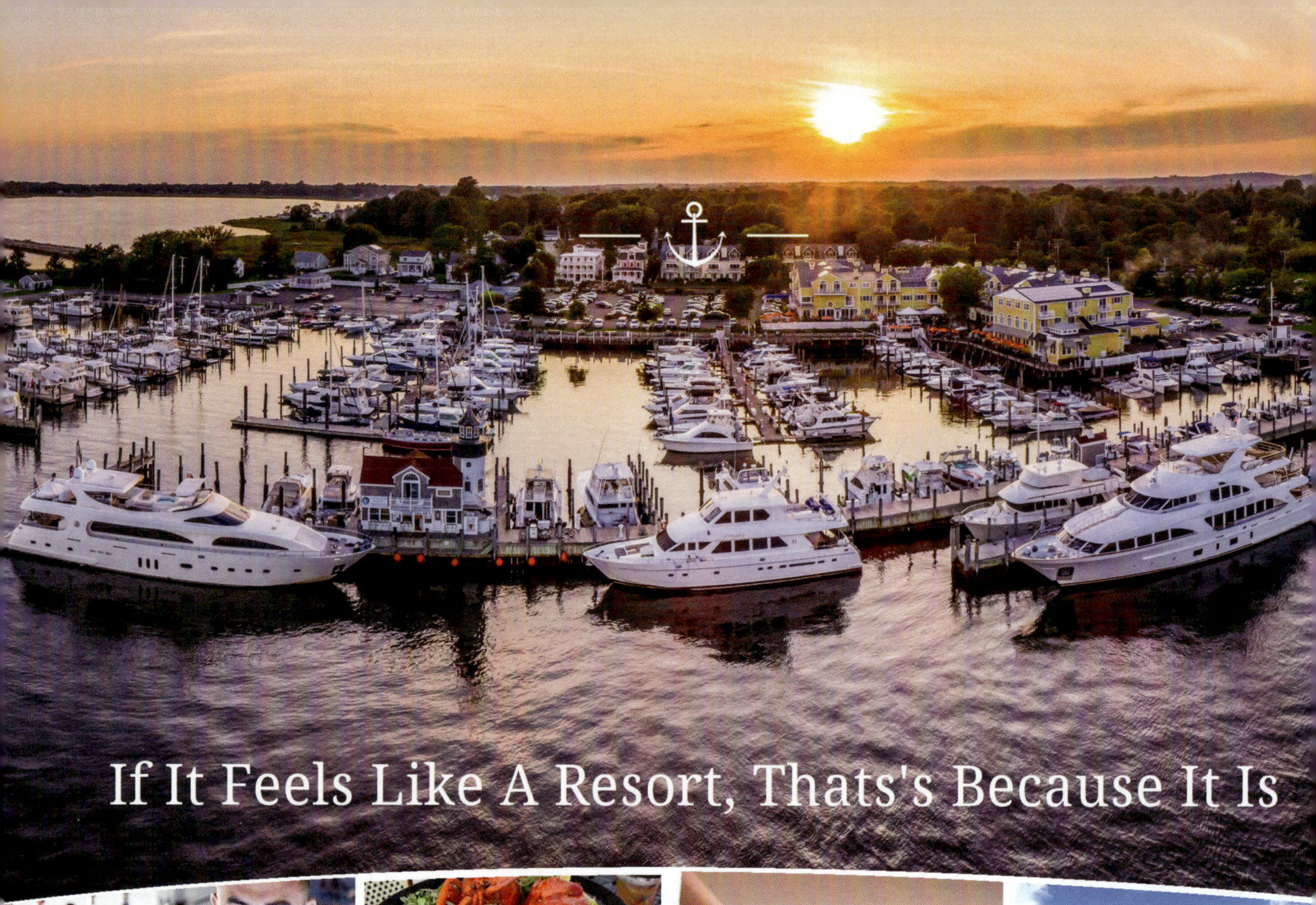

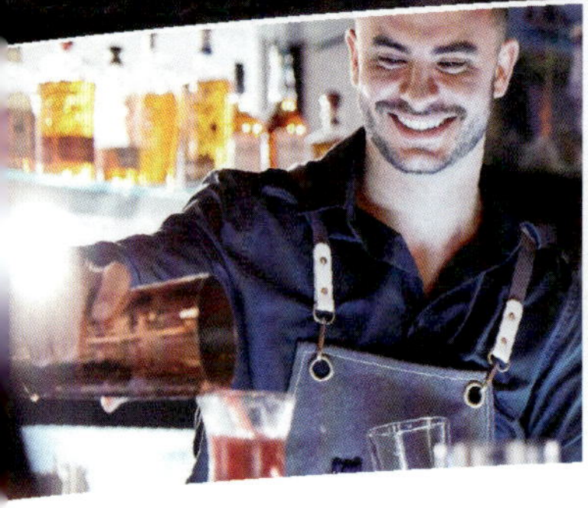

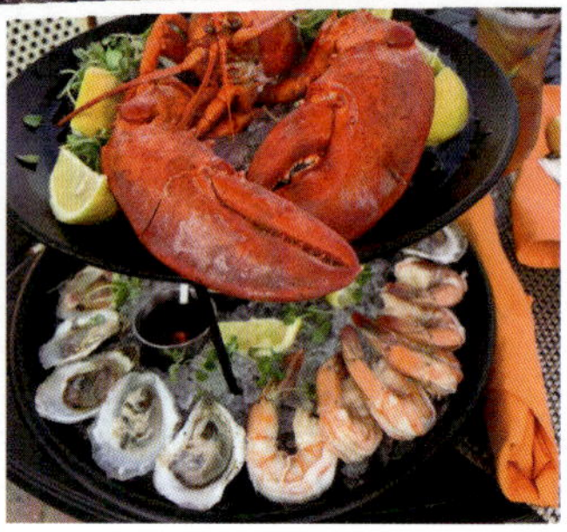

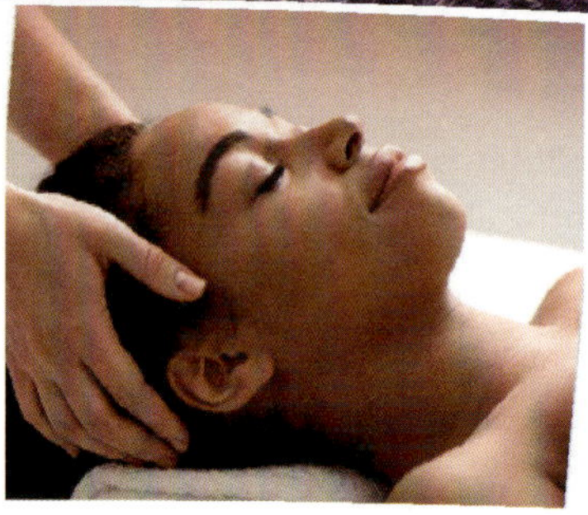

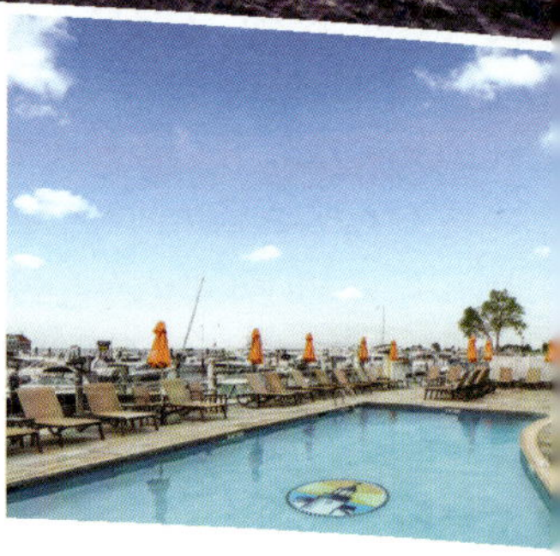

opposing, conditions can be a bit choppy. Allow for current set at all times and stay clear of off-channel shoals inside the eastern breakwater. As with any inlet, keep a sharp lookout for other vessels. Although the inlet can be busy and may feel narrow after unfettered running in Long Island Sound, ruins of old shad fishing piers make the approach east of the eastern breakwater hazardous and best for local shoal-draft vessels.

The river is well marked, deep and easy to transit; however, currents periodically run swiftly near the mouth. Farther upstream the channel narrows and demands a more vigilant watch. Large commercial vessels (including sightseeing boats) use the Connecticut River and need extra maneuvering room, particularly when currents are at their peak. (Contact these vessels on VHF Channel 13 to ascertain their intentions.)

Keep in mind that vessels going with the current have the right-of-way, unless other vessels are encumbered by draft or other circumstances. About 10 miles upstream near the town of Deep River, the salt water of the estuary changes to fresh river water.

NO WAKE ZONE

All No Wake Zones on the Connecticut River are strictly enforced by Connecticut Marine Police. Watch for the speed restriction buoys.

Old Saybrook, CT

Old Saybrook has traditionally been important for coastal trade. The existing ship captain homes in North Cove were adjacent to the warehouses and wharfs that handled the ships and their cargoes. The village of Old Saybrook is one of the earliest settlements in Connecticut. Walking tours of the town are not to be missed or you can take advantage of the free-to-borrow local bicycles. There's a local Farmers' Market (210 Main St., 860-833-0095) every Saturday and Wednesday (seasonal). Saybrook Hardware at 132 N. Main St. (860-388-3706) has nearly any (including marine) item you might need.

NAVIGATION: About 1 mile inside the entrance on the west bank of the Connecticut River is Saybrook Point. South Cove, located south of Saybrook Point, is home to beautiful wildlife but is not navigable. North Cove, north of the point, is regularly dredged and has 10 feet MLW. The entrance is straightforward with a channel marked by a series of green can buoys. In poor visibility leave flashing red buoy "14" behind to the east and then look north and west for green can buoy "15" leading the way into the cove. Don't confuse these North and South coves with the ones of the same names at Essex located farther north on the river.

Saybrook Point Resort & Marina

Connecticut River, CT

OLD SAYBROOK		Largest Vessel	VHF	Total Slips	Approach/ Dockside Depth	Floating Docks	Gas/ Diesel	Repairs/ Haulout	Min/Max Amps	Pump-Out Station
1. Harbor One Marina **WiFi**	(860) 388-9208	150	9	86	20.0 / 8.0	F	GD	R	30 / 200+	
2. Saybrook Point Resort & Marina **WiFi**	(860) 395-3080	220	9	120	10.0 / 7.0	F	GD		30 / 100	P
3. North Cove Yacht Club-PRIVATE **WiFi**	(860) 388-9132		78	4	7.0 / 7.0	F				

WiFi Wireless Internet Access
Visit www.waterwayguide.com for current rates, fuel prices, website addresses and other up-to-the-minute information.
(Information in the table is provided by the facilities.)

Scan here for more details:

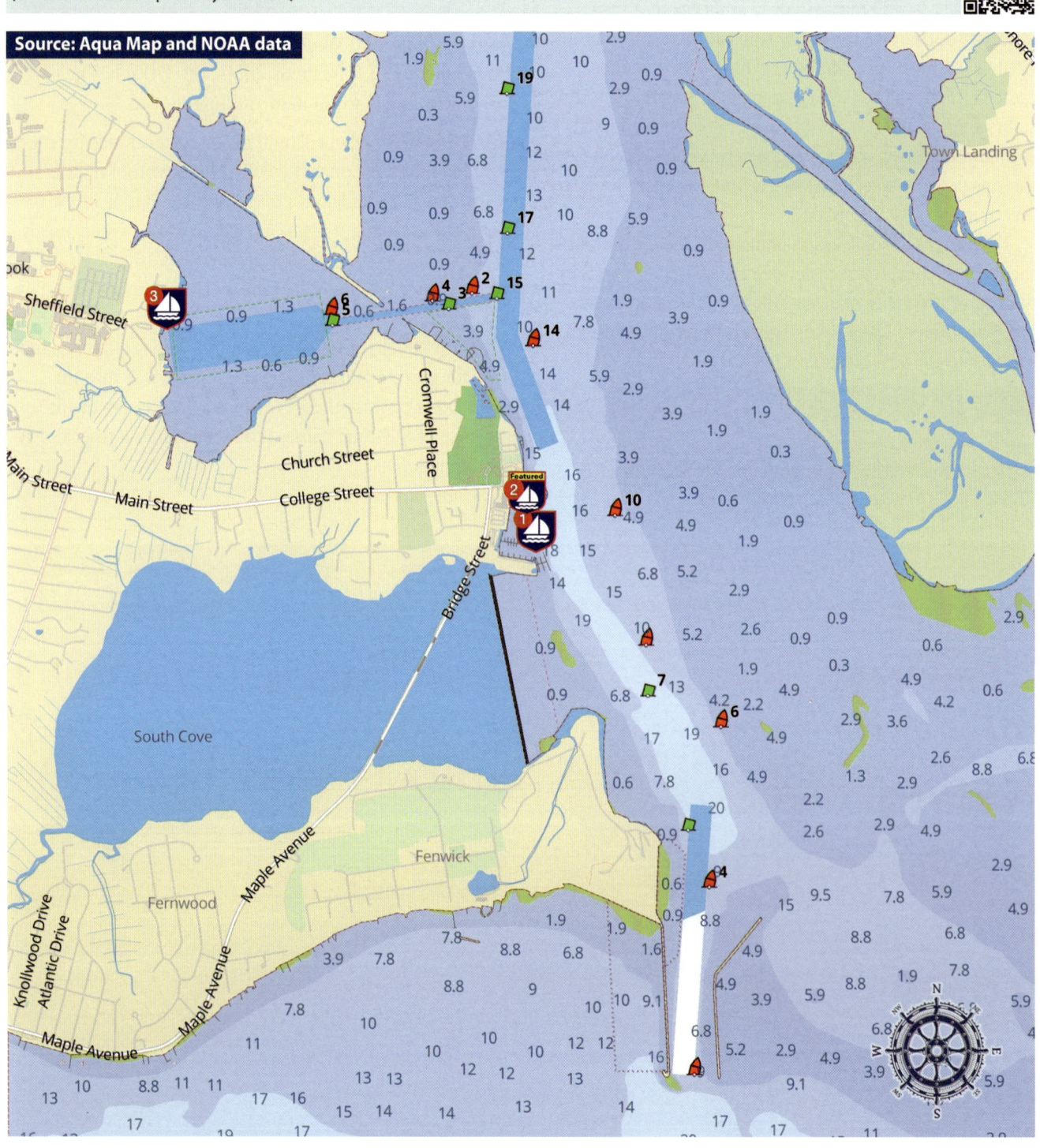

Source: Aqua Map and NOAA data

Dockage/Moorings: Saybrook Point is home to Saybrook Point Resort & Marina with world-class amenities and high-quality service for yachts of all sizes (including megayachts). On site you will find friendly concierge service, dining and an award-winning hotel and spa. The marina has 120 slips on floating docks and a fixed fuel dock with room for 220-foot boats on the breakwater wall. They also offer 480-volt power.

Also at Saybrook Point is Harbor One Marina with services and slips to 150 feet. Amenities include a waterside pool and the on-site Liv's Shack serving lunch and dinner.

North Cove is protected and attractive with an 11-foot MLW approach depth with 8- to 10-feet MLW inside. More than 100 permanent moorings have been placed here, mostly in use by locals. Three complimentary transient moorings are provided by the town of Old Saybrook at North Cove Mooring Field. You may tie up at the town dock (with 5-feet MLW) for 20 minutes to top off water. Contact the Old Saybrook Harbormaster (860-662-0385) for availability of moorings and depth information.

A transient may pick up any mooring with a yellow ribbon (indicating it's available) for up to 3 nights (72 hours). It is always possible the owner will return and ask you to vacate. Nearby North Cove Yacht Club is strictly private (members only) but you may be able to grab an empty mooring. Ask ahead.

Anchorage: In northerly or light winds, the area outside of Saybrook just west of the Saybrook Breakwater and close in to the beach is a popular swimming and picnicking anchorage for local daytrips. There are depths of 7 to 10 feet MLW with good holding in sand. This is protected from the east through north but any south or west swell will make for a lumpy night. Never anchor here in strong southerly or southwesterly winds when it becomes a dangerous lee shore. Heavy fog can develop quickly, even when the weather is clear in Old Saybrook.

Old Lyme, CT

Huntley Street, which leads directly to the shopping center on U.S. Route 1, offers a grocery store, several banks, a liquor store and a Post Office. The large, well-stocked Christiansen Hardware (860-434-7053) is at 54 Halls Road should you need them.

NAVIGATION: Almost 2 miles north of Saybrook Point, the **Old Saybrook–Old Lyme Bridge** (19-foot closed vertical clearance) is usually open but it carries the busy Amtrak line and other train traffic and closes whenever a train approaches. On the VHF radio (Channel 13) they will respond to "Old Lyme Draw." The bridgetenders communicate with their counterparts in Niantic (and the controllers in Boston) to keep the bridge open as long as possible but they will not delay a closing for an approaching boat. A countdown board that indicates the length of time until an opening cannot be trusted so be wary of tight timing on a down-current approach. **Raymond E. Baldwin Bridge** is just north with an 81-foot fixed vertical clearance.

Dockage/Moorings: Marinas and boatyards are located on both sides of the Connecticut River above the Old Saybrook–Old Lyme Bridge (19-foot closed vertical clearance). All of the facilities here are very busy and reservations are advisable.

Slips, services and repairs are available at Ragged Rock Marina, accessed by a 0.5 mile-long channel leading to the deep, virtually enclosed basin. This is one of the few boat yards in the area that allows DIY. They maintain just two reserved transient slips to 45 feet. Ferry Landing Marina is a full-service marina and boatyard offering slip rental, storage, sales and repair service.

The full-service Old Lyme Dock has the most frontage of any other local fuel dock and offers a bulk fuel discount. They also have a well-stocked ship store and room for just a couple of boats (depending on vessel size).

Beyond the high-rise Raymond E. Baldwin Bridge are more marine facilities with slips and repairs including Island Cove Marina, LLC. Your best bet for a transient slip is Safe Harbor Ferry Point with ample transient slips to 65 feet. Picnic areas, a pool and a playscape provide fun for the entire family.

The northern route to Old Lyme Marina Inc. around flashing red "22" is rocky at the entrance and shallower than the charts indicate, masking obstacles lurking in the bottom mud. Marina personnel discourage even shallow-draft runabouts from taking this route; enter from the south instead. The slips and moorings can accommodate boats up to 60 feet in a well-protected natural harbor. The marina also performs all phases of traditional and modern yacht restoration.

Connecticut River, CT

OLD LYME AREA		Largest Vessel	VHF	Total Slips	Approach/ Dockside Depth	Floating Docks	Gas/ Diesel	Repairs/ Haulout	Min/Max Amps	Pump-Out Station
1. Ragged Rock Marina WiFi	(860) 388-1049	45	9	243	5.0 / 6.0	F		H	30	P
2. Ferry Landing Marina	(860) 512-7278	120	9	300	14.0 / 7.0	F	GD	RH	30 / 50	
3. Old Lyme Dock	(860) 434-2267	200	9	25	13.0 / 13.0	F	GD		30 / 50	
4. Safe Harbor Ferry Point WiFi	(860) 388-3260	65	9	130	8.0 / 6.0	F		RH	30 / 50	
5. Old Lyme Marina Inc.	(860) 434-1272	60	9	34	15.0 / 20.0			RH	50	
ESSEX										
6. Essex Yacht Club-PRIVATE	(860) 767-8121	100	68	43	12.0 / 9.0	F			30 / 50	
7. Safe Harbor Dauntless WiFi	(860) 767-8267	60	68	40	12.0 / 10.0	F	GD		30 / 100	P
8. Essex Boat Works (EBW) WiFi	(860) 767-8276	80	9	20	10.0 / 10.0	F		RH	30 / 50	
9. Safe Harbor Essex Island WiFi	(860) 767-2483	200	9	125	9.0 / 5.0	F	GD	RH	30 / 100	P

WiFi Wireless Internet Access
Visit www.waterwayguide.com for current rates, fuel prices, website addresses and other up-to-the-minute information.
(Information in the table is provided by the facilities.)

Scan here for more details:

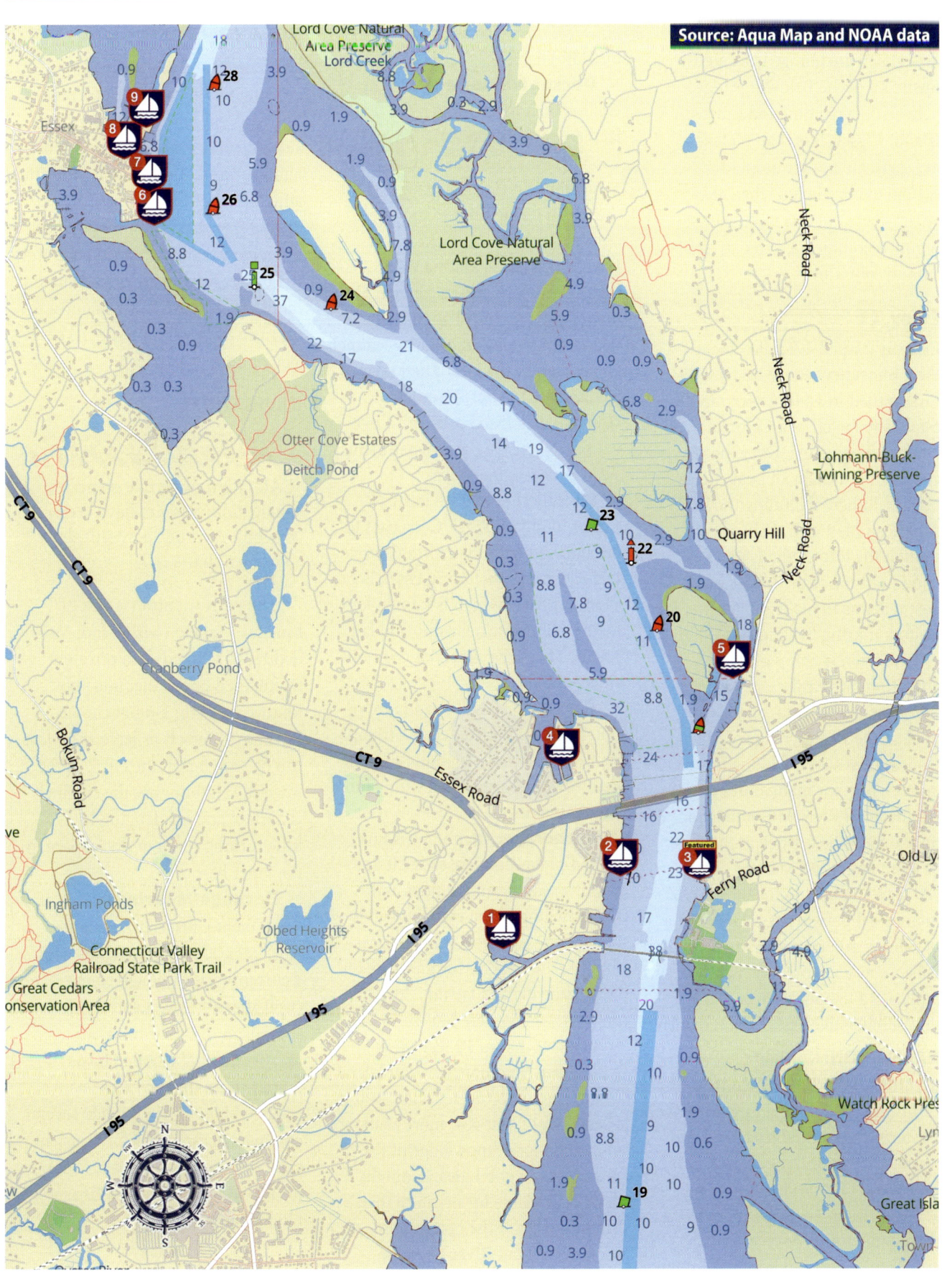

Source: Aqua Map and NOAA data

Anchorage: A Coast Guard-designated anchorage is located upstream of the Baldwin Bridge between Ferry Point and Calves Island. Vessels less than 65 feet in length are not required to exhibit anchor lights when at anchor here but it is nevertheless highly recommended due to the amount of traffic.

Essex, CT

Essex is located 2.5 miles above the Connecticut River bridges. First settled in 1648, Essex rapidly established itself as a Colonial boatbuilding center. Over the centuries hundreds of boats have been built here including the first American Man-o-War ship. Even though the lofting sheds are gone, enough flavor of the town's maritime past remains to make it a magnet for visitors touring by land and water.

The town is compact and its attractions are easily accessible by foot from the marinas and town dock at the western edge of the Connecticut River, making this a favorite port for many cruisers. The Connecticut River Museum is located on the Steamboat Dock at the foot of Main Street (67 Main St., 860-767-8269) with a rich collection of memorabilia. Exhibits rotate on the first-floor gallery and permanent collections are stored upstairs. A replica of Bushnell's Turtle, America's first submersible vessel, is on display.

NAVIGATION: North of Old Saybrook, the well-marked main Connecticut River channel skirts the western shore of Calves Island and its marshy bar and then winds gently for several miles to Essex. There are no markers for slightly more than 2 miles but the river is wide and deep. Be sure to honor red nun

buoy "24" to avoid the shoal water off Nott Island.

Dockage/Moorings: On the Connecticut River proper, the first facility you come to is the private Essex Yacht Club, which recognizes and extends reciprocal privileges for the use of its facilities to members of other yacht clubs. Next is Safe Harbor Dauntless Marina with easy-access slips and more than 50 moorings, which will are usually open to incoming transients. (Launch is included in the fee.) Their service facility, Safe Harbor Dauntless Shipyard, is located in North Cove with an extensive parts department and major repair services.

Several other marine facilities can be found in North Cove (not to be confused with the North Cove at Old Saybrook) including Essex Boat Works (EBW), which is known for their quality workmanship and fair prices. They have reserved transient slips to 80 feet.

Safe Harbor Essex Island is a top-notch marina with a helpful, friendly staff. This a family-friendly location that welcomes transients with a full list of amenities.

Anchorage: Anchorage is not a good prospect in Essex itself due to the strong reversing tides and the crowding of the mooring fields outside the channel. Many boaters drop the hook across from Essex on either side of Nott Island. Currents are quite strong here but the holding is excellent in 8 to 12 feet MLW with a firm mud bottom. Nott Island (East) is more protected than Nott Island (West) but also more shallow. Obtaining local knowledge of the mud flats is a good idea. A dinghy dock is available for no more than a 4-hour tie-up at the boat ramp next to the Connecticut River Museum.

Lyme, CT

Hamburg Cove, a favorite spot of cruising mariners, is about 1 mile upriver from Essex on the eastern side at Lyme. It is landlocked and almost round offering total protection and quiet, natural surroundings during the week. Hamburg Cove is often crowded on the weekends and frequently hot during the summer months. The cove is deep almost to its green banks and on the fresher side of upriver brackish.

NAVIGATION:

> ⚠️ *CAUTION:* Note that some navigation markers have been discontinued but may still show on older charts.

The narrow entrance east of Brockway Island (with 8-foot MLW depths) is marked with privately maintained buoys that must be followed exactly. Do not cut any of the buoys. Vessels as large as 50 feet can be seen far up the creek in the town of Hamburg but the channel is narrow and challenging with little turning room or dock space in the inner harbor.

Dockage/Moorings: Hamburg Cove Yacht Club is private and welcomes boaters from clubs with a current reciprocal agreement. (Call ahead.) Cove Landing Marine specializes in the restoration and overhaul of wooden boats but virtually any repair can be arranged here. They provide several commercial moorings for transient customers on a daily basis. (Look for the white moorings with a blue stripe.)

Connecticut River, CT

HAMBURG		Largest Vessel	VHF	Total Slips	Approach/ Dockside Depth	Floating Docks	Gas/ Diesel	Repairs/ Haulout	Min/Max Amps	Pump-Out Station
1. Hamburg Cove Yacht Club-PRIVATE	(860) 434-0215				/	F				
2. Cove Landing Marine (WiFi)	(860) 434-5240	50		60	6.0 / 8.5	F		RH	30 / 50	P

(WiFi) Wireless Internet Access
Visit www.waterwayguide.com for current rates, fuel prices, website addresses and other up-to-the-minute information.
(Information in the table is provided by the facilities.)

Scan here for more details:

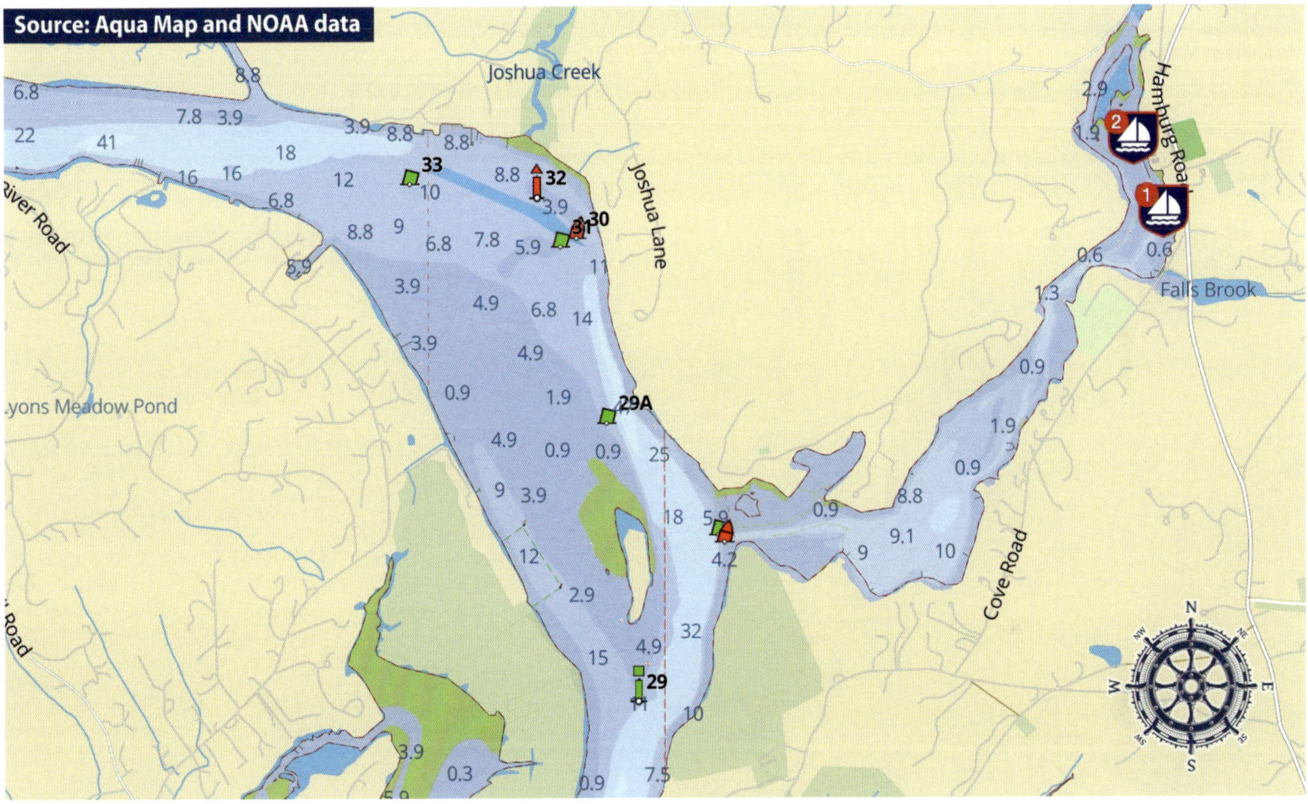

Source: Aqua Map and NOAA data

[Chart of Hamburg Cove and Connecticut River with depth soundings, showing Joshua Creek, Joshua Lane, Lyons Meadow Pond, River Road, Falls Brook, Hamburg Road, Cove Road, and marina locations 1 and 2]

Anchorage: Hamburg Cove is filled with moorings and there is no room to anchor properly. If you can find a small spot to tuck in, you will have all-around protection in 9 to 10 feet MLW with good holding in mud. It is decades-long tradition for transients to pick up any appropriate private mooring for a night or two. Should the owner appear, they will not be upset but simply politely ask you to move off. This is more likely to occur on busy summer weekends. A dinghy dock is available at Cove Landing Marine.

More room to anchor is west of Brockway Island in 13 feet MLW with good holding in sand and mud. Enter and exit only from the south as the north side is shoal. This is slightly exposed to the north and southeast.

To East Haddam, CT

It is well worth the 15 mile trip up the Connecticut River to East Haddam thanks to diverse landscapes, hills, cliffs, quarries, fields, historic towns, mansions and landmarks. Deep River is home to Pratt Cove and Selden Neck State Park, which both offer an opportunity for viewing wildlife. If you have a kayak, this is the perfect place to use it or you can take your dinghy across to the surrounding marshlands and wonderful creeks. Please be a gentle presence in these preserved areas.

In Chester's intimate and walkable village center you will find an adequate selection of shops, galleries and locally made goods. Above Chester is East Haddam, where the riverside Goodspeed Opera House performs lively, full-production Broadway musicals year-round. Check online for schedules and restrictions.

Connecticut River, CT

DEEP RIVER		Largest Vessel	VHF	Total Slips	Approach/ Dockside Depth	Floating Docks	Gas/ Diesel	Repairs/ Haulout	Min/Max Amps	Pump-Out Station
1. Safe Harbor Deep River WiFi	(860) 526-5560	65	9	283	15.0 / 5.0	F	GD	RH	30 / 50	P
2. Chester Point Marina WiFi	(860) 526-1661	60	9	135	6.0 / 6.0	F		RH	30 / 50	
3. Hays Haven Marina Inc. WiFi	(860) 526-9366	46		270	6.0 / 6.0	F	GD	RH	30	P
4. Chester Boat Basin WiFi	(860) 526-5147	45	9	141	8.0 / 6.0	F	GD	RH	30 / 50	P
5. Middlesex Yacht Club-PRIVATE WiFi	(860) 526-5634	50	79	60	10.0 / 9.0	F			30	
EAST HADDAM AREA										
6. Andrews Marina WiFi	(860) 345-2286	45	68	76	6.0 / 6.0	F		R	30 / 50	P
7. Midway Marina in Haddam WiFi	(860) 345-4330	60	13	65	12.0 / 7.0	F		RH	30	P

WiFi Wireless Internet Access
Visit www.waterwayguide.com for current rates, fuel prices, website addresses and other up-to-the-minute information.
(Information in the table is provided by the facilities.)

Scan here for more details:

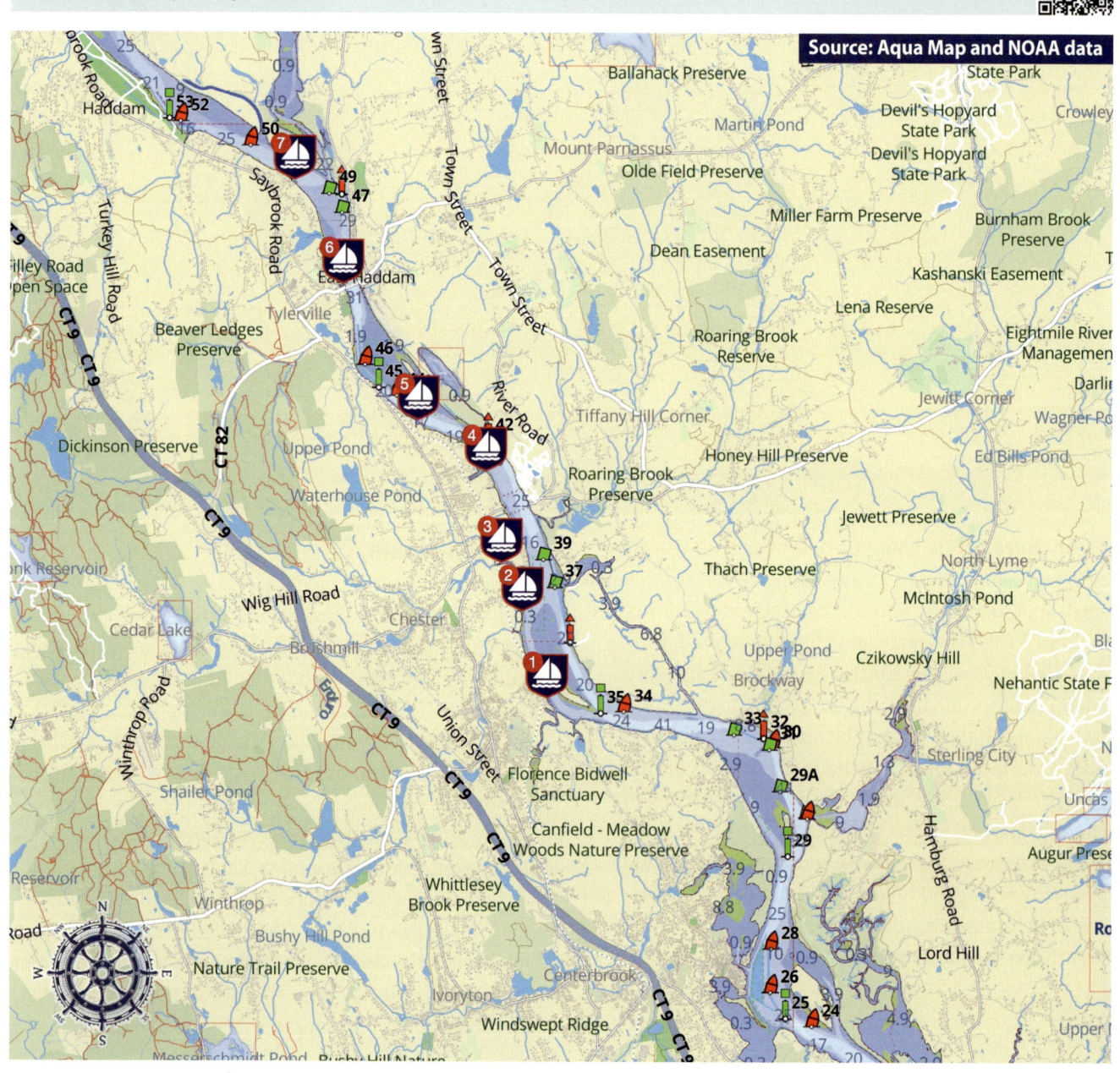

Source: Aqua Map and NOAA data

Connecticut River, CT

PORTLAND AREA		Largest Vessel	VHF	Total Slips	Approach/ Dockside Depth	Floating Docks	Gas/ Diesel	Repairs/ Haulout	Min/Max Amps	Pump-Out Station
1. Birdon Marina - Formerly Yankee Boatyard and Marina, Inc. (WiFi)	(860) 342-4735	50	68	120	20.0 / 10.0	F		RH	50	P

(WiFi) Wireless Internet Access
Visit www.waterwayguide.com for current rates, fuel prices, website addresses and other up-to-the-minute information.
(Information in the table is provided by the facilities.)

Scan here for more details:

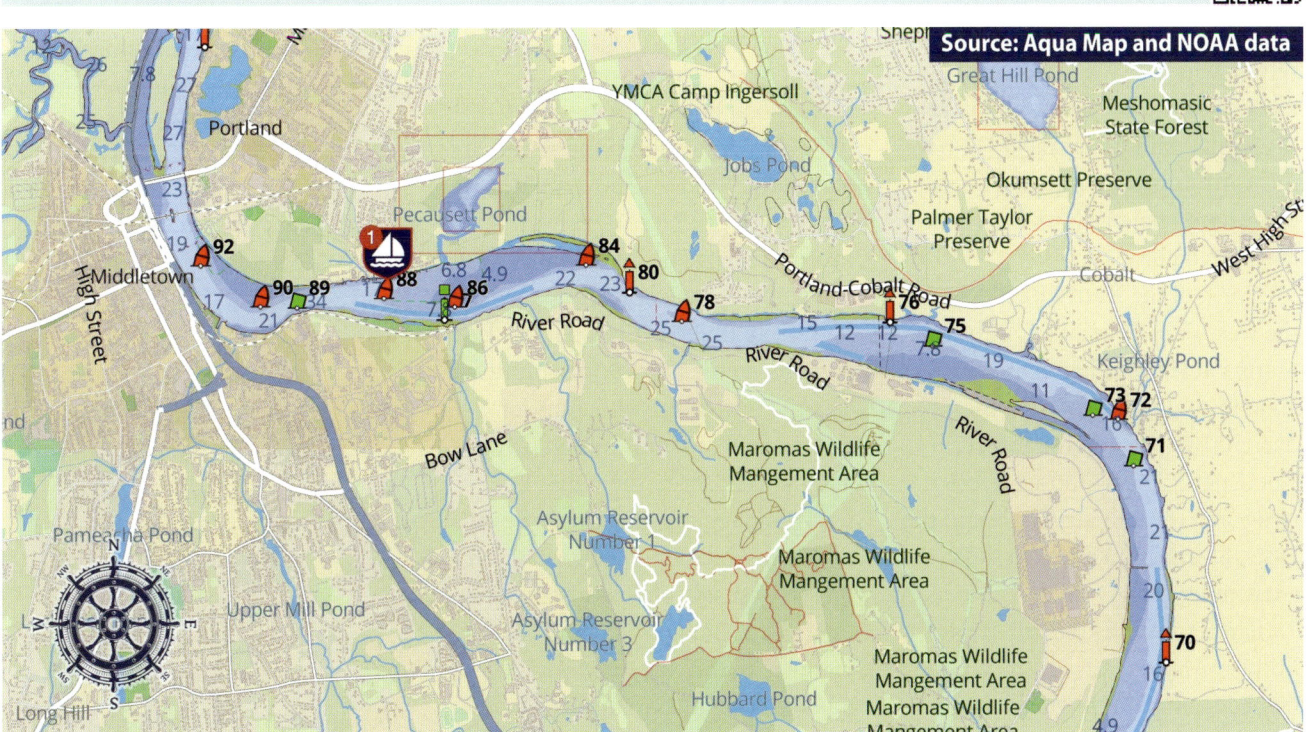

Source: Aqua Map and NOAA data

NAVIGATION: The Connecticut River gives the boater a chance to practice river navigation. Watch the charts as you go and remember that a flowing river is no place to cut corners. A river will deposit silt as the water slows on the inside of a curve and it will eat deeper channels on the outside.

At Deep River, tidal waters from Long Island Sound cease to influence the freshwater drainage from the north. Here the channel briefly divides around Eustasia Island. There are good depths to either side, although the main channel is marked to the east. If you venture into the western channel, keep an eye on your sonar readings in the area of Chester Creek Bar. The best depths are found near the eastern shore of the river.

Three miles above Chester, the village of East Haddam is unmistakably marked by the Route 82 Bridge (locally known as the East Haddam Bridge) with 22-foot closed vertical clearance. The lift bridge opens on signal open on signal except from May 1 through October 31, except

that from 6:00 a.m. to 8:00 p.m., when the draw need only open for recreational vessels on the hour.

Dockage/Moorings: For convenient dockage or ready access to the special anchorage at the north end of Chester Creek Bar, take the fork west of Eustasia Island (leave flashing green "35" on the rock pile just south of the island on the east). The floating docks of Safe Harbor Deep River visibly line the banks to the west. Transient dock space is never a problem in this protected and tranquil setting and from here it is a relatively easy dinghy ride to Selden Neck State Park (accessible only by water).

Chester Creek immediately to the north (also on the west side of the river) is home to Chester Point Marina with slips to 60 feet and amenities including a pool. Several smaller facilities with dockage for smaller vessels are nearby including the 46-slip Hays Haven Marina Inc., a safe and secure year-round marina with a family-oriented atmosphere and amenities.

About 0.5 mile above the Chester-Hadley ferry landing (beneath Fort Hill), Chester Boat Basin (formerly Chrisholm Marina) is on a deep channel cut into the west bank. They can accommodate vessels to 45 feet with full amenities. This family-friendly facility is in a park-like setting with a swing set, a small beach with a floating raft and a fire pit for the adults. Middlesex Yacht Club to the north is private but may be able to accommodate visitors from other clubs. Call ahead.

North of the **Route 82 Bridge** on the west side of the river, Andrews Marina at Harpers Landing is a great location for exploring the over 100-year-old swing bridge, Goodspeed Opera House (across the river) and the Gillette Castle and the Essex Steam Train and Riverboat, just a few miles away.

Farther north is the full-service Midway Marina in Haddam, a family-owned facility offering dockage, repairs and a yacht brokerage in a quiet, peaceful setting.

Anchorage: Beyond Brockway Island is the unmarked entrance to primitive Selden Creek. It is an excellent gunkhole where American boats hid from British raiders during the Revolutionary War. The narrow creek with a marsh-bordered entrance and no aids to navigation lies amid cliffs and high hills. Large boats have little room here. Depths, however, run from 9 to 13 feet MLW in the lower reaches and 3 to 4 feet MLW in the upper. Selden Creek runs into Selden Cove with a shallow channel back to the Connecticut River. A cruise up Selden Creek is marvelous in a dinghy or small boat. Watch out for tree stumps as you go.

Another anchoring option is north of Eustasia Island on the west side of the river between Deep River and Chester. While somewhat exposed to the north, holding is good in mud in 15-foot MLW depths.

In East Haddam you can anchor south of Goodspeeds Landing in 17 feet MLW. There is plenty of room, good holding in mud and protection from all but the north and south. Be aware, however, that the Goodspeed Airport runway is nearby and give it some serious thought when anchoring.

Just up from East Haddam is the entrance to the narrow Salmon River. The river carries good depths for about 1 mile up into Salmon Cove and then shoals considerably. Be wary of snags and give Cones Point a wide berth. Follow the deep water on the west side of Grass Island and then turn east and then north to the entrance to the cove. The cove is a quiet overnight spot for boats with moderate drafts and offers all-around protection with good holding in mud.

North on the Connecticut River

The home of Wesleyan University is in Middletown past Middle Haddam and through the scenic Straits. Across the river from Middletown is Portland, once an important quarrying and shipbuilding port. The old quarries, flooded and inactive now, produced much of the sandstone for New York City's famous brownstone houses. Dinosaur tracks were often found on the quarried slabs. Dinosaur State Park is farther north in Rocky Hill, requiring inland transportation.

If you wish to visit Hartford, it is best to dock at Wethersfield Cove and proceed into the city by taxi. (There are numerous taxi services; ask at the yacht club.) Hartford has virtually no place to tie up and anchorage, while possible, is difficult in the narrow areas outside the main channel.

NAVIGATION: North of East Haddam, a good number of boats kiss the bottom around Mouse Island Bar east of Portland, especially heading downriver, even though it is well-marked with buoys and a range. Attentiveness is necessary. At Portland you will pass under two bridges: The **Conrail Middletown-Portland Railroad Bridge** (25-foot closed vertical clearance), which is usually open unless a train is coming, and the high-rise **Arrigoni Bridge** (89-foot closed vertical clearance).

From Portland, the Connecticut River starts to meander in broad loops that are reminiscent of the Mississippi River. Even though there are quite a few ranges (mostly for downriver craft) to guide boaters through the curves and the bars, pay close attention to steerage and the depth sounder. The stretch above the bridges to Gildersleeves Island is uneventful, if you don't try to pass to the west of the island where there is a submerged dike.

Rocky Hill to the north is a quiet village with a town park with a boat launch, fishing pier and floating docks. Pull into the courtesy dock, have a hot dog and watch the Rocky Hill Ferry, the oldest continuously operating river-crossing ferry in the country. As at all ferry crossings, proceed with care.

Just past Rocky Hill, the Glastonbury Two Piers Bar Channel has an upriver range (most are downriver) marked by fixed red over flashing red (2.5 seconds). The shallows extend in a curve within the buoys so if you were to try a straight

Connecticut River, CT

WETHERSFIELD		Largest Vessel	VHF	Total Slips	Approach/ Dockside Depth	Floating Docks	Gas/ Diesel	Repairs/ Haulout	Min/Max Amps	Pump-Out Station
1. Wethersfield Cove Marina	(860) 721-2890	34		7	15.0 /					P
2. Wethersfield Cove Yacht Club	(860) 563-8780	30		32	4.0 / 15.0	F	G		30	

WiFi Wireless Internet Access
Visit www.waterwayguide.com for current rates, fuel prices, website addresses and other up-to-the-minute information.
(Information in the table is provided by the facilities.)

Scan here for more details: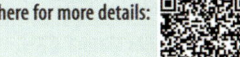

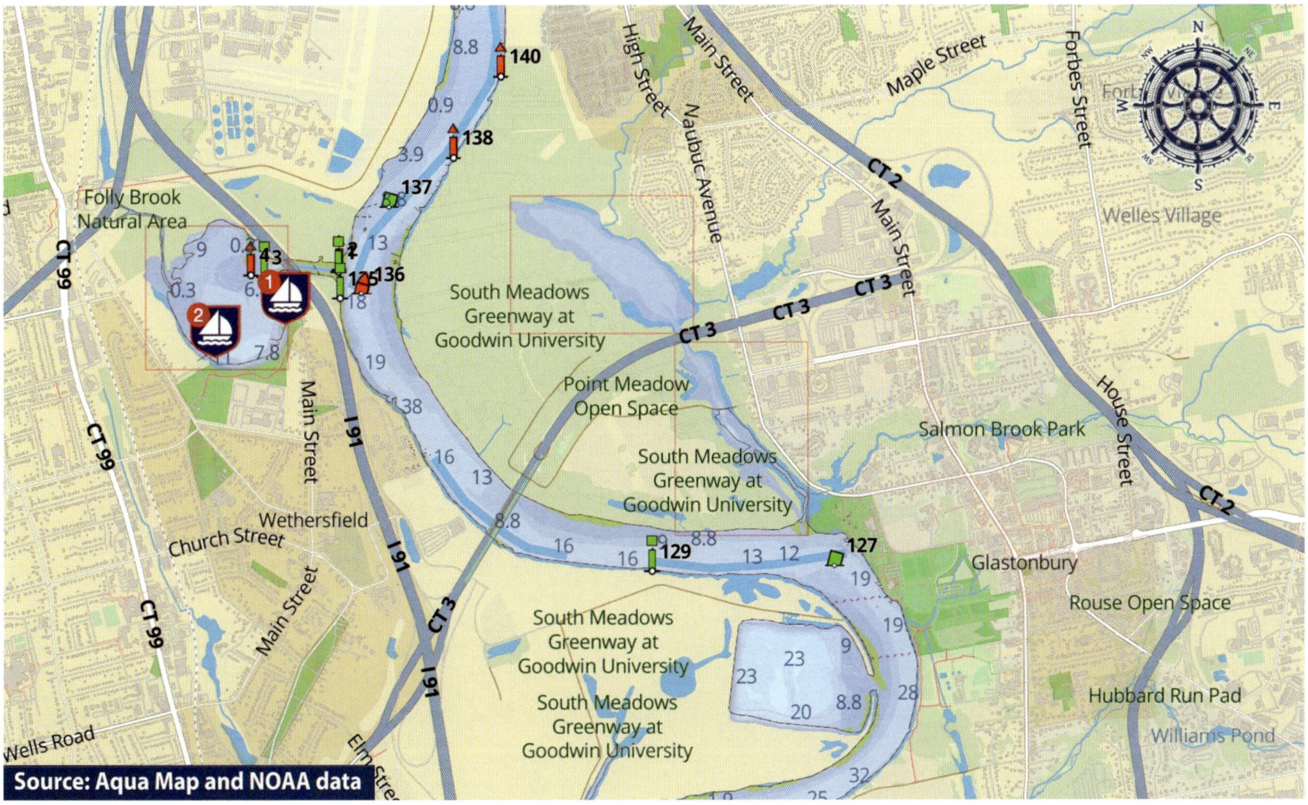

Source: Aqua Map and NOAA data

shot from inner buoy to inner buoy (especially between green cans "123" and "121"), you might go aground.

Stay to the southwestern third of the river for about 0.25 nm on either side of the **William H Putman Memorial Bridge** (80-foot fixed vertical clearance). The only hazard left is an unmarked rock off the west bank midway between the bridge and Wethersfield Cove that is almost blocked by a charted but unmarked point.

Above Hartford, the Connecticut River is unimproved and navigable only for boats with less than 3-foot drafts and 8-foot vertical clearances. The channel shifts constantly with bars and other obstructions. Local knowledge is necessary.

Dockage/Moorings: On the east bank south of Portland and east of Middletown are several services including Birdon NE (formerly Yankee Boatyard

and Marina, Inc.), a full-service boatyard that can accommodate a few transients in slips or on moorings.

South of Hartford, Wethersfield Cove is accessed via a privately marked channel. Enter slowly. There is 6 feet MLW in the basin but shoaling at the entrance. The municipal Wethersfield Cove Marina is in the basin with a boat launch ramp, 51 permanent transient boater moorings, a tender dock and 7 transient slips to 34 feet. Pump-out service is available at the dock on weekends from 6:00 a.m. to 8:00 p.m. The facility is open from Memorial Day through Columbus Day. The hospitable Wethersfield Cove Yacht Club may have room for you on their docks or moorings but do call ahead.

Anchorage: You can anchor in Wethersfield Cove in 6 feet MLW with good holding and all-around protection but you must be able to get under a 38-foot fixed vertical clearance I-91 Bridge to access the cove.

Niantic River, CT

NIANTIC		Largest Vessel	VHF	Total Slips	Approach/ Dockside Depth	Floating Docks	Gas/ Diesel	Repairs/ Haulout	Min/Max Amps	Pump-Out Station
1. Boats Incorporated **WiFi**	(860) 739-6251	36	71	175	8.0 / 6.0	F	G	RH	30	P
2. Harbor Hill Marina **WiFi**	(860) 739-0331	40		70	8.0 / 6.0	F			30	P
3. Port Niantic Inc **WiFi**	(860) 739-2155	58	13	81	8.0 / 6.0	F		RH	30 / 50	P
4. Three Belles Marina **WiFi**	(860) 739-6264	50	9	150	6.0 / 7.0	F	GD	RH	30 / 50	P

WiFi Wireless Internet Access
Visit www.waterwayguide.com for current rates, fuel prices, website addresses and other up-to-the-minute information.
(Information in the table is provided by the facilities.)

Scan here for more details:

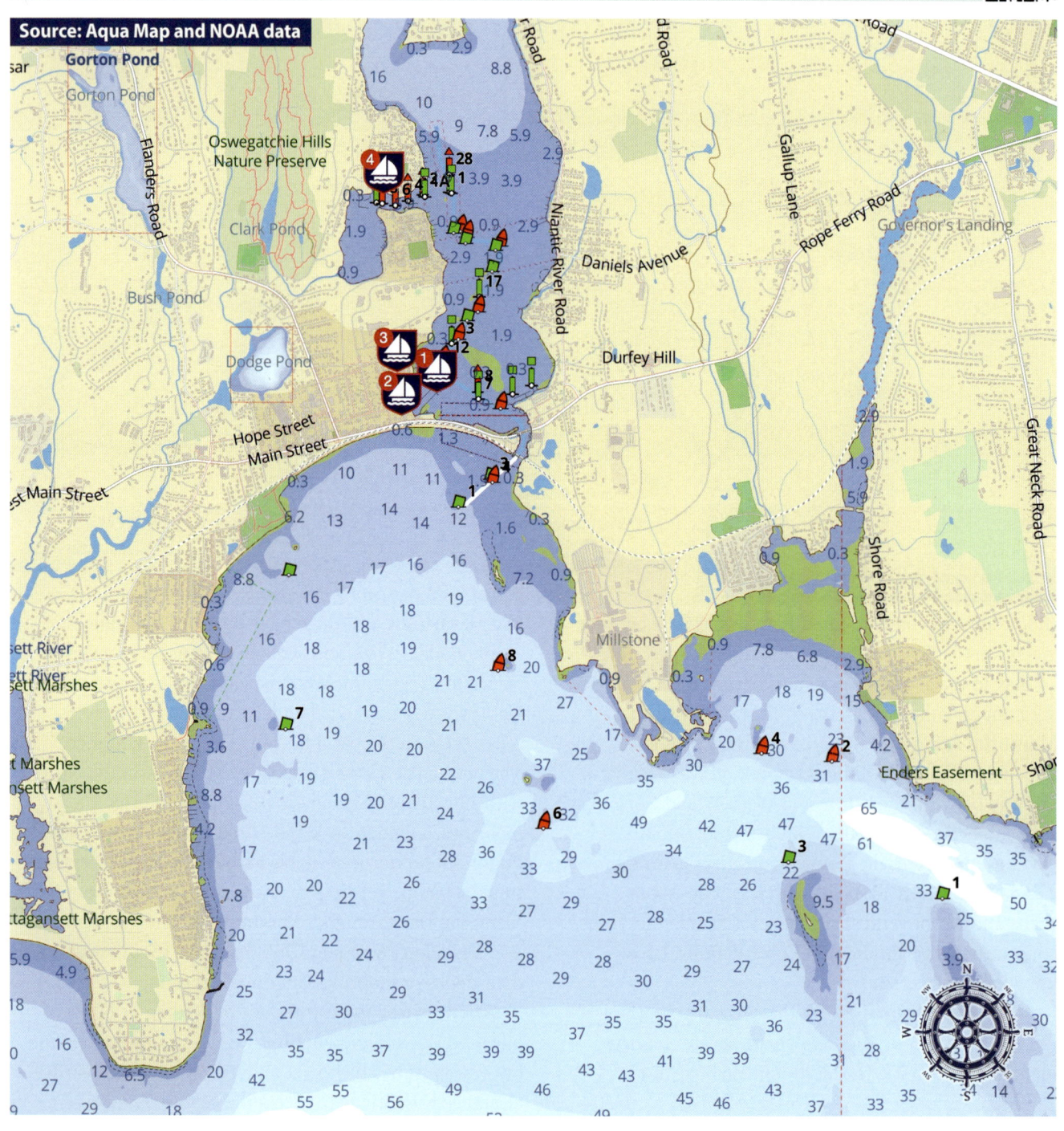

Source: Aqua Map and NOAA data

NIANTIC, CT TO WATCH HILL, RI

Niantic Area, CT

Niantic is a harbor of refuge and a commodious layover for cruisers in search of rest and provisions. Ample dock space and quiet anchorages with good holding are within walking/cycling distance of boat repairs, marine services, provisioning, restaurants, a classic movie theatre and one of the best book collections in all of New England. The Book Barn has an ever-changing collection of over 500,000 books spread out between four locations.

The history of this area dates back to the 1600s when the Dutch traders discovered this area and began to expand beyond the Hudson River. The Thomas Lee House and the Smith-Harris House are two historic sites in Niantic Village that tell much of the history of this area.

NAVIGATION: Niantic Bay, 6 nm east of the Connecticut River, is big and open with Black Point on the western headland and a prominent power plant on the eastern shore where the now abandoned chimney, noted on the chart simply as "STACK," still stands as a landmark.

The only hazard along the way is the well-marked and well-charted Hatchett Reef, and the only shelter between the Connecticut River and Niantic Bay is in the Giants Neck area in the lee of Long Rock and Griswold Island. This area should be entered with caution, the rocks are charted but numerous.

Two closely spaced bridges cross the curving entrance channel of the Niantic River. With little maneuvering room in the narrow (50-foot-wide) dogleg channel and tidal currents approaching 4 knots on either tide, full attention is recommended on this passage. The first bridge, **Amtrak (Niantic River) Railroad Bridge** (16-foot closed vertical clearance), opens on signal as long as oncoming trains are not within range. It is best to contact the bridgetender on VHF Channel 13 before you approach.

The second bridge is the **SR 156 Bridge** (32-foot closed vertical clearance), which opens on request except between 7:00 a.m. and 8:00 a.m., and between 4:00 p.m. and 5:00 p.m., Monday through Friday (except federal holidays). From November 1 through April 30, from 8:00 p.m. to 4:00 a.m., the draw opens on signal only if at least a 6-hour notice is given.

It is best to coordinate your passage with the tenders of both bridges via VHF Channel 13. It is advisable to make this passage close to slack water on either tide. For boats with high vertical clearance requirements, approach only when your signal is acknowledged.

The beauty of the Niantic River and the amenities available make this transit well worth the modest effort required. Current charts refer to all Niantic River markers as "private aids" because they are frequently moved. The channel is only 4 to 5 feet MLW with "knee-deep" water just outside the channel. Past the bridges, the channel is well marked and easy to negotiate but the numerical sequence of the buoys and daybeacons must be strictly followed.

Dockage: At the first channel bend back to north inside the river bridges is Boats Incorporated, which may have room on the seaward docks (to 36 feet) and offers storage and repairs. Harbor Hill Marina has slips to 40 feet on floating docks with modern marina amenities and a convenient on-site bed and breakfast. They maintain just two transient slips.

Port Niantic Inc. is immediately to the north with deep water slips, storage facilities, plus a full array of marine parts, repairs and installations. From the marina area it's about a 0.3 mile walk to the center of town. There is a sidewalk the whole way. It's about a 0.5-mile walk east to Cini Park and the entrance to the boardwalk and beach. The boardwalk is the pride and joy of Niantic (and rightfully so).

Upriver the well-marked, deep channel winds past the community of Pine Grove to the entrance of pretty and protected Smith Cove. Here the friendly Three Belles Marina offers just two transient slips (to 50 feet) as well as storage and some services. To enter Smith Cove, turn left into the marked channel at green and red daybeacon "SC." The town-dredged, 5-foot-MLW channel (with 2.5-foot tidal range) is reasonably well marked by daybeacons and naked poles for 0.2 mile. The village is about 1.5 miles away but a ride to town can usually be arranged.

Anchorage: In settled weather, you may be able to anchor in 10-feet MLW on the western shore of Niantic Bay at Crescent Beach. This is open and exposed to the south through east and residual swell can make it uncomfortable. This makes a better day anchorage than an overnight one. There is a dinghy dock in Niantic or you can call for a launch ride for the price of a tip to the driver.

Upriver the Niantic River widens, becomes deeper and provides some lovely anchorages with good holding and attractive surroundings. Sandy Point and Keeny Cove both have 9- to 11-foot MLW depths with good holding in mud. The scenery and quiet atmosphere are reminiscent more of a New England freshwater lake than those of a surfside recreational community.

Do not be tempted by Smith Cove behind Three Belles Marina, which is too shallow for all but the most shoal-draft vessels (2 feet MLW).

New London, CT

The seaport of New London was established in 1646. The town has a long maritime history as a ship building center and very profitable trade center. New London is located on the western side of the Thames River with its smaller sister port of Groton on the eastern side. Having emerged as a thriving whaling port that rivaled even New Bedford, MA, during the 19th century, New London is the largest and busiest commercial port in eastern Connecticut. It is also an important harbor of refuge, home to major U.S. Navy and Coast Guard facilities and in recent times a leading recreational yachting center with excellent marinas, reliable restaurants and adequate provisioning.

If time permits, stroll the Heritage Trail of 30 bronze plaques set in the downtown district sidewalks or visit the U.S. Custom House Maritime Museum to learn about the New London whaling history. Whale Row features restored 19th-century houses that are open to the public. The renovated 1888-vintage train station is not only interesting to look at, it also offers convenient Amtrak rail transportation to Boston and New York City.

Or hop aboard the water taxi to visit the Thames River Heritage Park, a collection of almost 20 national and historic sites along the shores of the Thames River. Four anchors–Fort Trumbull State Park, Fort Griswold Battlefield State Park, the Submarine Force Museum and the National Coast Guard Museum–provide visitor services.

The U.S. Coast Guard Academy (31 Mohegan Ave., 860-444-8444) dominates the bluff along the west side of the river beyond the Thames River bridges, recognizable by the Georgian brick buildings and white clock tower. The Academy Visitors Center is open from 9:00 a.m. to 4:30 p.m. daily. The public can attend movies, tours, sporting events and the occasional band concert, but dockage is not available. If you are lucky, the 295-foot fully rigged *Barque Eagle*, America's maritime ambassador, will be in port.

Race Rock Light Station

NAVIGATION: When departing Niantic Bay, eastbound mariners should give a wide berth to flashing red bell buoy "6" to avoid the rocky shoals in the vicinity of White and Little Rocks. South of Bartlett Reef (clearly marked by a 35-foot-high lattice tower with two international orange diamonds on its face), strong currents funneling through The Race (farther south) begin to make themselves evident on either tide.

Currents south of Bartlett Reef are the strongest in Long Island Sound and the waters are also the deepest (more than 300 feet in spots). Opposing winds and current can create sloppy conditions here. In a southwest breeze, an eastbound cruiser with local knowledge can stay in the lee of Two Tree Island and Bartlett Reef by running the Two Tree Island Channel to Goshen Point. Reefs and rocks are adequately marked but be aware of your location at all times because visibility can drop suddenly on the sound, and currents can set you far from your intended course. If entering New London Harbor, leave green can buoys "3," "5" and "7" to port.

CAUTION: Be on the lookout for frequent ferry crossings in this area as it bisects a major route between Orient Point and New London. Be especially cautious in reduced visibility.

The New London Harbor is located a short distance up the busy, heavily traveled Thames River. Except for water traffic, the harbor entrance is uncomplicated and well buoyed. Two distinctive lighthouses flank the entrance channel. New London Harbor Lighthouse is a classic white tower off Osprey Beach, while New London Ledge Light is a two-story, red brick building that stands on a harbor rock. Most recreational boating facilities are on the New London side of the Thames River and south of the bridges in Green Harbor and Shaw Cove.

Entry from the south is clearly marked. Pick up flashing green "1" and flashing red "2" and then follow the channel between the lighthouses into the Thames River. If entering from the east through Pine Island Channel, be aware of the many rocks in this area. While the channel is marked, don't stray to port on entry. Gaining familiarity with the area before using this short cut is a good idea.

NO WAKE ZONE

In addition to the Navy's rigorous monitoring of security zones around its ships and facilities, the U.S. Coast Guard is strict in enforcing a 6-mph speed limit within 200 feet of all docks and piers in the harbor.

Thames River, CT

NEW LONDON		Largest Vessel	VHF	Total Slips	Approach/ Dockside Depth	Floating Docks	Gas/ Diesel	Repairs/ Haulout	Min/Max Amps	Pump-Out Station
1. Thames Yacht Club-PRIVATE	(860) 383-0017	50	71		/					
2. Thamesport Marina **WiFi**	(860) 442-1151	200	9	150	20.0 / 14.0	F	GD		30 / 100	P
3. Burr's Marina **WiFi**	(860) 443-8457	120		150	12.0 / 9.0		GD	RH	30 / 50	P
4. Crocker's Boatyard Inc. **WiFi**	**(860) 443-6304**	170	9	230	12.0 / 12.0	F	GD	RH	30 / 50	P
5. New London Waterfront Park	(860) 443-3786	295	9	35	15.0 / 15.0	F				
GROTON										
6. Thames Harbor Inn and Marina	(860) 445-8111	55		20	50.0 / 50.0	F				

WiFi Wireless Internet Access
Visit www.waterwayguide.com for current rates, fuel prices, website addresses and other up-to-the-minute information.
(Information in the table is provided by the facilities.)

Scan here for more details:

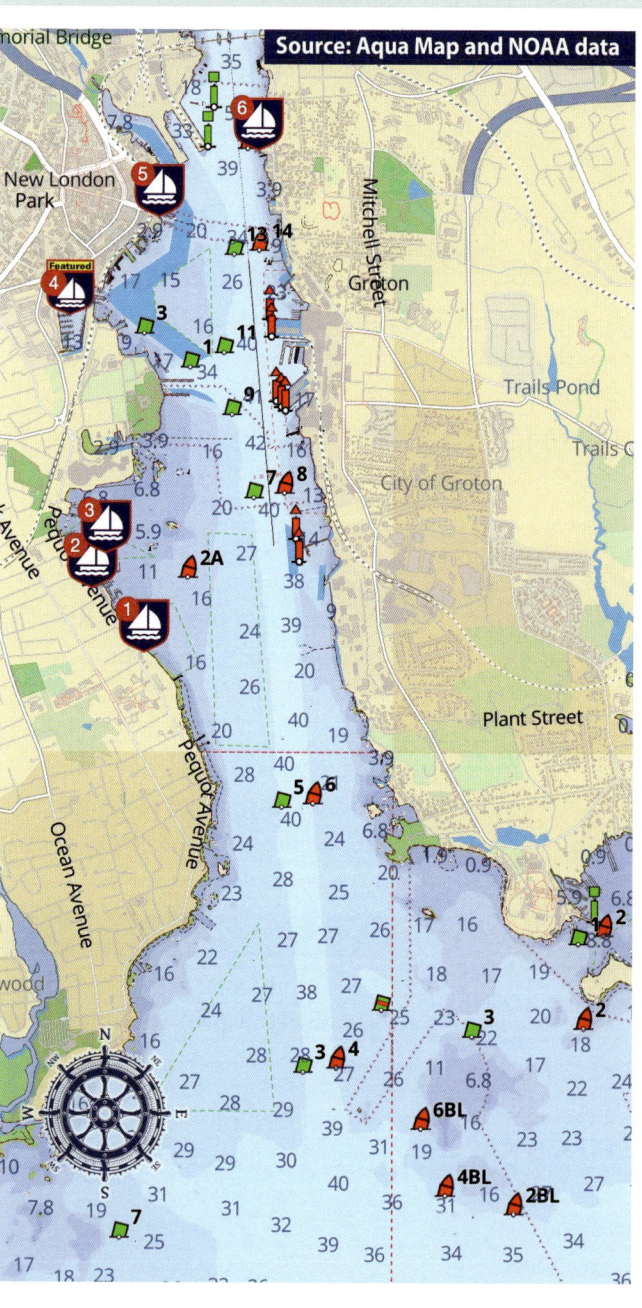

Source: Aqua Map and NOAA data

Dockage/Moorings: Excellent yachting facilities, nautical services and supplies are located in two adjacent bights on the New London side of the Thames River. Green Harbor, approximately 1 nm inside the harbor entrance, features marinas offering transient slips and services. Thames Yacht Club is private, but may be able to make room for you.

Thamesport Marina in Green's Harbor can accommodate vessels to 200 feet on floating and fixed docks with full amenities including an on-site restaurant. Next is the well-regarded Burr's Marina has slips and moorings to 120 feet. They boast a boat and tackle shop and an on-site café. It is about 3 miles to downtown New London.

Shaw Cove, just 1 nm north of Greens Harbor, at New London is totally protected and offers dockage at the full-service Crocker's Boatyard Inc., where cruisers will find deep-water slips on floating docks (for vessels up to 170 feet) and substantial repair capabilities. Nearby Breakwater Marine Services is a repair facility that may have space for you but do call ahead. A short walk up Bank St. from Shaw Cove will put you in the heart of New London shopping where there are many interesting galleries, boutiques and food markets. The **Shaw Cove Railroad Bridge** (with a vertical clearance of 6 feet MLW) opens on request (VHF Channel 13) to give access to the cove, if there is no nearby train traffic, but it is as busy as all the other Amtrak bridges in the area.

A short distance farther north is New London Waterfront Park with a 0.5-mile promenade plus five piers with slips on floating docks and seasonal moorings. Amenities include pump-out service and use of coin-operated laundry machines. Prior arrangements may also be made for electricity and water requirements. The all-transient municipal dock and moorings and the city pier are available on a first-come, first-serve basis for a reasonable flat rate; however, they are somewhat exposed to boat and ferry traffic.

Access to the free dingy dock just north of Shaw Cove and restroom/showers are included. Dockage with water and electric is available as well (for a fee). This is convenient to the bus and train station and all that downtown New London has to offer.

Anchorage: Anchoring is possible in Greens Harbor in 6 to 10 feet MLW, although it is mostly filled with moorings and is exposed to wind and waves as well as river wakes. A better choice is outside of Shaw Cove in 15-foot MLW depths. This is closer to Waterfront Park and the shore access there.

Groton, CT

Revolutionary War buffs may want to visit Fort Griswold, the site of the 1781 massacre of American defenders by British troops led by Benedict Arnold. Today, the site includes ramparts, battlements and buildings dating from the Revolution as well as a 134-foot granite monument to the defenders you can climb. Visit the Monument House

New London Harbor Lighthouse

Pequot Point Beach

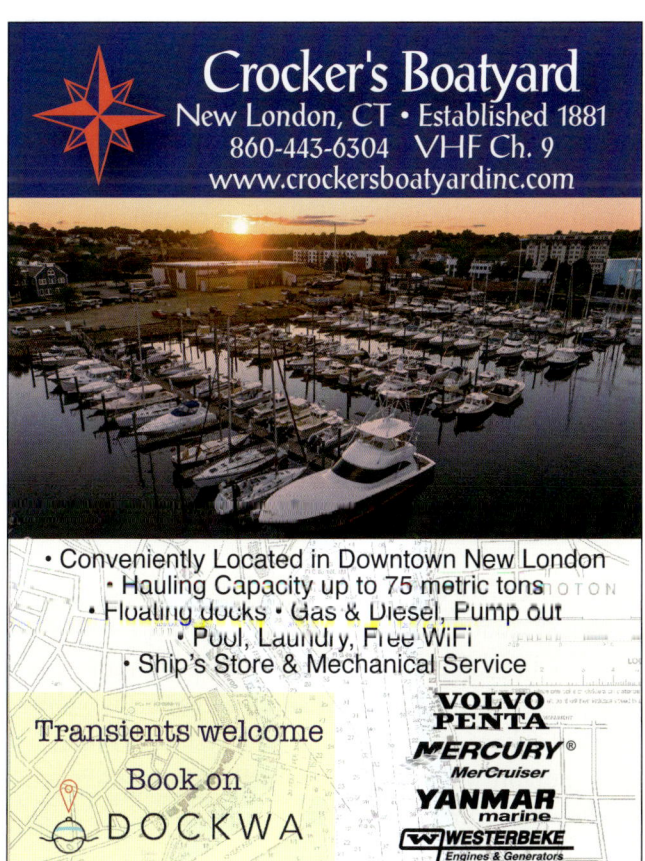

Museum located in the state park (57 Fort St., 860-449-6877) for the full story of the battle. Admission is free. The Fort is located south of the bridges in Groton.

A Navy Yard was established on the Thames River in 1868 and officially commissioned as a submarine base during World War I. Groton became known as the "Submarine Capital of the World" when the Electric Boat division of General Dynamics delivered 74 diesel submarines to the Navy in World War II. This was followed in 1954 with the launch of the U.S.S. *Nautilus*, the world's first nuclear-powered submarine now permanently berthed at Goss Cove as part of the U.S. Navy Submarine Force Museum. Located adjacent to the base, the museum is open during the summer and admission is free (800-343-0079).

About 1 mile north of the Navy Base just below Gales Ferry are the Yale (blue) and Harvard (crimson) boathouses and training quarters for the annual spring rowing regatta, the nation's oldest intercollegiate sporting

Thames River, CT

GALES FERRY		Largest Vessel	VHF	Total Slips	Approach/ Dockside Depth	Floating Docks	Gas/ Diesel	Repairs/ Haulout	Min/Max Amps	Pump-Out Station
1. Gales Ferry Marina	(860) 464-2146	38	12	85	6.0 / 5.0	F	GD	H	30	
NORWICH										
2. The Marina at American Wharf **WiFi**	(860) 222-8222	240	68	160	30.0 / 10.0	F		R	30 / 100	P

WiFi Wireless Internet Access
Visit www.waterwayguide.com for current rates, fuel prices, website addresses and other up-to-the-minute information.
(Information in the table is provided by the facilities.)

Scan here for more details:

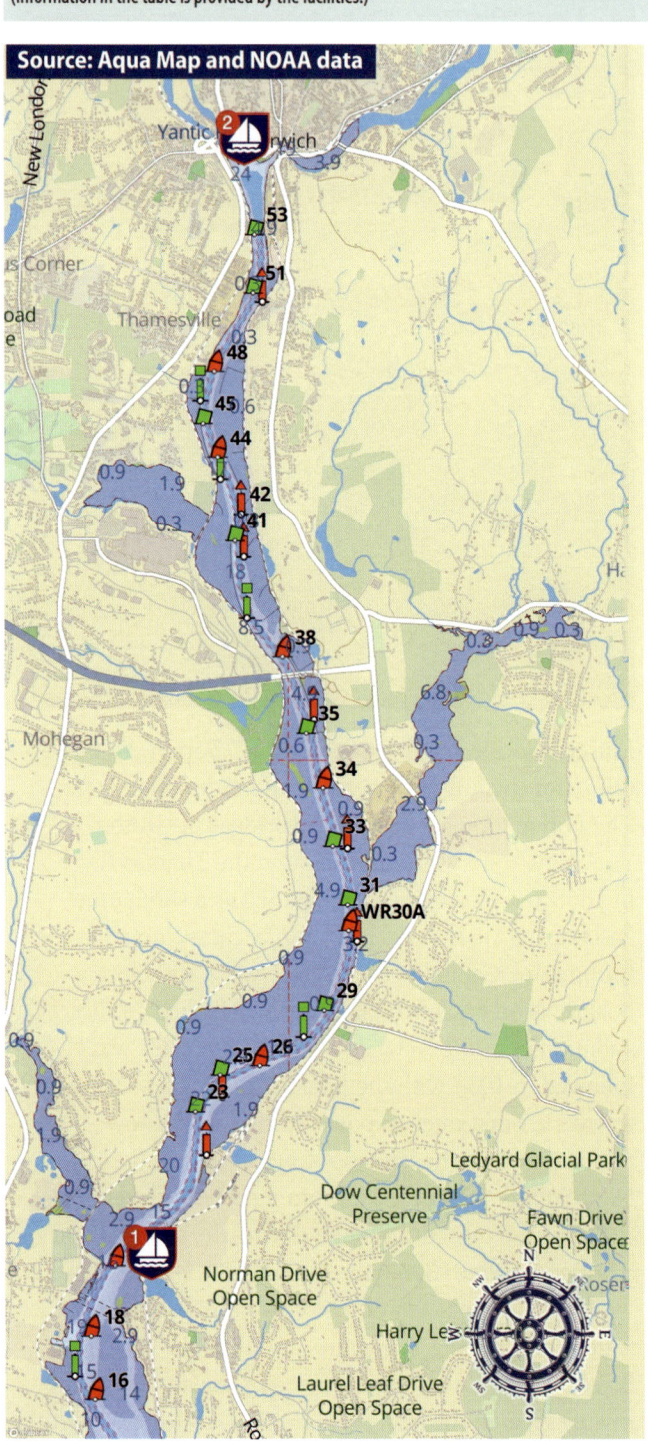

Source: Aqua Map and NOAA data

event. During Race Week, New London is like Louisville during Kentucky Derby week. Boats come in from all over the northeast and anyone expecting accommodations should make reservations well in advance. Special trains are scheduled and the shores are full of spectators and the river full of boats.

NAVIGATION: The **Amtrak Railroad Bridge** (29-foot closed vertical clearance) and the **Gold Star Memorial Bridges (I-95/U.S. 1)(Twin)** (135-foot fixed vertical clearance) cross the Thames River a little more than 3 miles north of the harbor lights. Boats requiring a clearance of over 29 feet should alert the railroad bridgetender on VHF Channel 13.

Keep in mind that railroad bridges are locked down well in advance of oncoming trains on this coastal Amtrak route. Similarly, be sure to consider the maneuverability and security requirements of large commercial and military vessels in this active port and shipping lane. The draw will open on signal to 75 feet above mean high water for all vessel traffic, unless a full bridge opening to 135.3 feet above mean high water is requested.

Dockage: Dockage in Groton can be found at Thames Harbor Inn and Marina south of the bridges. The facility features 20 boat slips and extends 100 feet to deep water, capable of harboring vessels to 55 feet. Special package deals include a shoreside room plus boat slip at a reduced rate. In addition to the usual amenities the marina offers coin-operated laundry access for boaters.

Upriver to Norwich

Norwich, about 11 miles upriver from New London, is at the head of the Thames River. The trip upriver is pleasant, river traffic is light and the channel is well marked. There are several dikes above Easter Point, most notably Mohegan Dike near the Mohegan Pequot Bridge, which are submerged at half tide.

Avery Point, CT

AVERY POINT		Largest Vessel	VHF	Total Slips	Approach/ Dockside Depth	Floating Docks	Gas/ Diesel	Repairs/ Haulout	Min/Max Amps	Pump-Out Station
1. Shennecossett Yacht Club 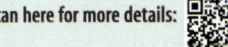	(860) 625-3180	50	68	206	7.0 / 6.0	F	GD	H	30 / 50	P
2. Pine Island Marina 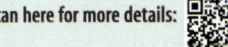	(860) 445-9729	42	68	110	7.0 / 5.0	F		RH	30	

Scan here for more details:

(WiFi) Wireless Internet Access
Visit www.waterwayguide.com for current rates, fuel prices, website addresses and other up-to-the-minute information.
(Information in the table is provided by the facilities.)

Dockage: About 4.5 miles north of the bridges is Gales Ferry Marina with slips to 38 feet and an array of maintenance and service options. At the head of the Thames River in Norwich is The Marina at American Wharf with transient slips and full amenities including a pool and restaurant.

Anchorage: You can drop the hook most anywhere north of the Navy base. Just be sure to anchor out of the channel and be mindful of the locals.

Avery Point (South Groton)

East of New London Harbor are more facilities with slips, fuel and repairs nestled between the University of Connecticut campus at Avery Point and the New London-Groton Airport.

Dockage/Moorings: The private Shennecossett Yacht Club has slips and moorings for visiting members of other yacht clubs, as well as non-members (space permitting). Pine Island Marina can accommodate power boats up to 42 feet in length in slips and up to 35-foot vessels on moorings. Launch service and dinghy storage is included for mooring transient visitors. Launch service is available 7 days a week (weather permitting).

Side Trip: Fishers Island, NY

Little 9-mile-long Fishers Island is only 2 nm off the southeastern coast of Connecticut but belongs to New York. It forms the gateways to the Connecticut. The island is very private and the entire eastern end is gated. At the western end of the island, however, there is a small village with a museum that traces the history of Fishers Island from the time of the American Indians to present day. The findings from a number of archaeological digs are also on display.

If you're looking for an exciting destination with entertainment, this is not it. However, if you seek a quiet anchorage and deserted beaches, you've come

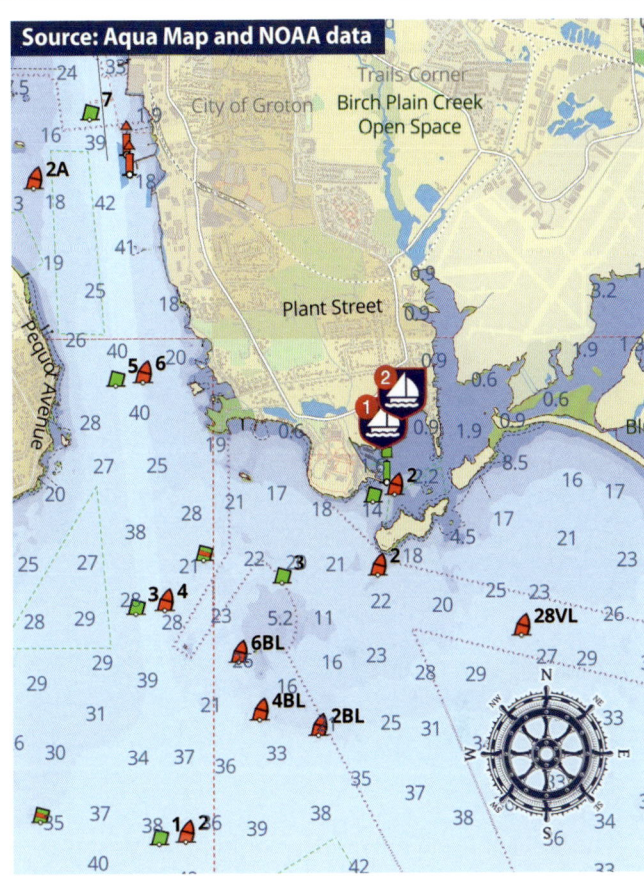

Source: Aqua Map and NOAA data

to the right spot. The east side of Flat Hammock, an island to the north of West Harbor on Fishers Island, is a pleasant afternoon spot to anchor for a swim.

NOTE: For birdwatchers, Great Gull Island to the southwest of Fisher Island has the largest nesting populations of common and roseate terns on the East Coast.

NAVIGATION: The shoreline of Fishers Island has several small harbors suitable for anchoring but only West Harbor has facilities for cruising boats. The westernmost Fishers Island harbor is Silver Eel Cove where the New London ferry docks. Visiting boats are not allowed to enter as maneuvering room for the ferry is limited. The next harbor to the east is Hay Harbor, which is shoal, rocky and crowded with sailing dinghies.

Fishers Island, NY

FISHERS ISLAND		Largest Vessel	VHF	Total Slips	Approach/ Dockside Depth	Floating Docks	Gas/ Diesel	Repairs/ Haulout	Min/Max Amps	Pump-Out Station
1. Fishers Island Yacht Club Marina - PRIVATE (WiFi)	(631) 788-7036	150	10	50	9.0 / 8.0				30 / 50	
2. Pirates Cove Marine Inc.	(631) 788-7528	45	9	15	10.0 / 6.0	F		RH	30	

(WiFi) Wireless Internet Access
Visit www.waterwayguide.com for current rates, fuel prices, website addresses and other up-to-the-minute information.
(Information in the table is provided by the facilities.)

Scan here for more details:

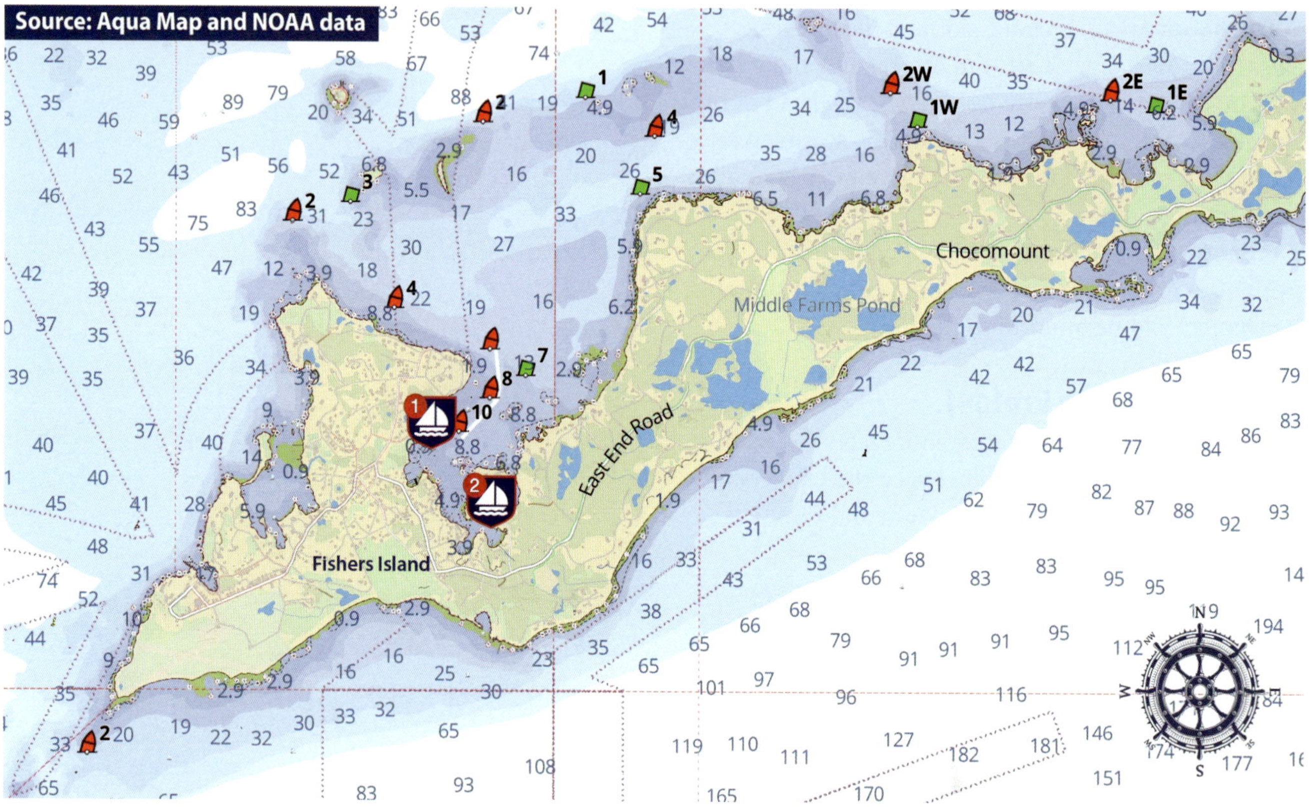

Source: Aqua Map and NOAA data

The best approach to West Harbor from the west is south of North Dumpling Lighthouse between flashing red bell buoy "2" off the tip of Fishers Island and the green can buoy "3" marking South Dumpling. Follow the red-lighted buoys along the shore to the West Harbor entrance channel. Note that the rebuilt North Dumpling Lighthouse is a private home.

Dockage/Moorings: You will find dockage, fuel and repairs in West Harbor. It is peaceful if you want to escape the heavy fog often found in the Watch Hill passage but is exposed to the north. The first-class Fishers Island Yacht Club Marina (established in 1886) is private but welcomes transients on moorings to 150 feet with launch service. Hail them on VHF Channel 10.

Pirates Cove Marine Inc., located in the almost fully enclosed hurricane-hole of an inner harbor, maintains some moorings in the outer harbor and monitors VHF Channel 9. They also have a dinghy dock but their location is a bit far from shoreside amenities.

Anchorage: West Harbor will accommodate a good number of boats at anchor. The holding ground is good in sand and it is well protected except in northerly and northeasterly winds.

Farther east beyond West Harbor you can drop the hook in Chocomount Cove in 7 to 11 feet MLW with good holding. This is very peaceful if the wind is moderate and blowing out of the south.

East Harbor also has excellent holding in 10 to 14 feet MLW. This is a great spot in any wind except those with a northerly component. Excellent swimming, paddleboarding and snorkeling (for golf balls from the course ashore) is possible here. Smaller vessels can go quite a bit further in. You can take the dinghy ashore for a pleasant walk but no services are available.

Mystic River, CT

The seafaring village of Noank, dating back to the 1820s, all but fills the small peninsula guarding the entrance to the Mystic River. Noank is quiet and noncommercial, a place for pensive walks with classic seascape vistas. The village is small and tightly knit. It is a good place to stop for a good meal out and, given the major yards in the immediate vicinity, virtually any boat part or service needed. Noank also makes a great stop for those running the sound and looking for a quick overnight mooring. From the very start of the Mystic River, there are several dock and dine opportunities (or dinghy and dine if you prefer).

To the north on the Mystic River, the village of Mystic has several faces. The east side of the river is part of Stonington, while the west side of the river is part of Groton. If you desire to soak up maritime history, Mystic is the place for you. This scenic hamlet is a family-friendly destination you may never want to leave. Within reasonable walking distance from most of the Mystic River marinas, the village is picturesque, compact and quite busy in season. This is a prime summer weekend destination for many Connecticut residents and tourists from beyond.

The village's shops and dining spots are strung out along Main Street (U.S. Rte. 1) on either side of the unique counter-weight bascule bridge at the hub of activity. West of the bridge, boutiques, galleries and gift shops with a marine theme crowd both sides of the street. There are several banks (with ATMs) and the Post Office is about one block east of the bridge. There are also small markets within a short walk of the marinas and numerous first-rate dining options. (Full provisioning requires transportation.) More restaurants can be found on the eastern side of the bridge.

Although connected to Mystic Village by a small bridge, Mason Island has long held itself somewhat apart from the mainland, largely retaining its rural-residential character. Still, there are marinas and marine services that are easily accessed from the river dotting the island's northern perimeter.

NAVIGATION: You can enter the Mystic area by proceeding south of Groton Long Point, leaving both red nun buoy "24" and red nun buoy "22" to port (north). From Groton Long Point, take a course of

Mystic Harbor

066° magnetic to Whale Rock, leaving it to the east and Mouse Island to the west. This leads past the protective breakwater into Noank's West Cove (on the west side of Noank).

Be sure to give Mouse Island's sloping western rock ledges ample room to east while staying within the green daybeacons to west. The channel is periodically dredged but expect no more than 6-foot MLW depths (and some of it is hard ledge).

> ⚠️
> *CAUTION:* If traveling straight to Mystic Harbor and skipping Noank, a safer approach is to locate green can buoy "1" and follow the channel in.

On the eastern side of the Noank peninsula, the Mystic River channel runs offshore of Morgan Point and its dormer lighthouse (private and uncharted) and then begins its winding, well-marked path just beyond flashing green daybeacon "5." The channel follows the Noank shore closely, hugging its projecting piers. The easterly side of the channel tends to shoal so give the nuns a fair berth to starboard as you pass.

Inside the harbor, the channel curves, zigzags and loops among shoals and flats in a generally northerly direction for the 1.5 miles between Ram Point (east of red nun "20") and Willow Point (west of green can "31"). Continue to follow the numbered buoys consecutively. They do not follow a straight-line course so it is easy to miss some. Be aware of current and wind affecting your course upriver so as not to be set outside the channel.

If continuing to Mystic from Willow Point, the channel doglegs right for a distance of just over 0.5 mile to Murphy Point, where it curves sharply to port (toward the northwest) to the **Amtrak Railroad Bridge**. The bridge (with 8-foot closed vertical clearance) opens on signal from April 1 to October 31 if there is no train traffic. From November 1 to March 31, the bridge opens on signal from 5:00 a.m. to 9:00 p.m. At all other times at least an 8-hour notice is required.

The next bridge to the north is the **U.S. 1 (Mystic Highway) Bridge** (with 4-foot closed vertical clearance), which opens on signal except from May 1 through October 31, from 7:40 a.m. to 6:40 p.m., when the draw need only open hourly at 20 minutes before the hour. From November 1 through April 30, from 8:00 p.m.

to 4:00 a.m., the draw will open on signal if at least a 6-hour notice is given by calling the number posted at the bridge. The wait for a closed railroad bridge can be up to 20 minutes but the scenery is pleasant, the current is moderate and there is room to maneuver.

> NOTE: Boats moving with the tide have the right-of-way when the bridge opens. Both bridges monitor VHF Channels 13.

The channel curves to starboard beyond the bridge and narrows as it deepens. Stick with the channel marked by a series of green cans. Outside the channel it is quite shallow and unsuitable for either navigation or anchorage.

Dockage/Moorings: Palmer's Cove Marina offers full service boat maintenance, boat repair and boat storage and may have transient space. Note that this facility is restricted by a low, fixed bridge (9.3-foot vertical clearance). Spicer's Noank Marina in West Cove is usually filled to capacity with seasonal rentals. Occasionally there is transient space available while local tenants are off cruising. Spicer's also maintains a large mooring field (with launch service) on both sides of the breakwater.

Limited slips and/or moorings, full-service boat maintenance, repair and storage are available at many of the other marine facilities strung along the main channel including Noank Shipyard, which may have space for you. A better bet is Noank Village Boatyard with ample slips and moorings for vessels to 125 feet with full amenities and a friendly, helpful crew.

The main transient marina on Mason's Island is Mystic River Marina on the east side of the channel and just south of Pine Point, well before the railroad swing bridge. The marina has 14-foot MLW approach depths and can accommodate vessels to 150 feet. A well-stocked ship store is among the offerings. On the north end of the island are Mason's Island Marina with a deep channel and slips and moorings (to 50 feet) and Mystic Point Marina, which can accommodate powerboats up to 40 feet on their docks.

The 270-slip Mystic Shipyard flanks both sides of the river at Willow Point. They welcome vessels to 150 feet with full amenities as well as repair, rigging and mechanical services. They also maintain 50 transient slips and will likely have room for you.

At Murphy Point on the easterly side of the river, the 242-slip Safe Harbor Mystic has extensive floating docks on the river and upscale amenities in a protected cove. They can handle virtually any repair requirement. Given its proximity to Mystic Village, this is a popular place in season so reservations are highly recommended. The well-maintained Gwenmor Marina has limited transient availability, typically for no more than two days.

Farther north between the bridges on the same side of the river are additional facilities with transient dockage including the accommodating Fort Rachel Marina, which is a short walk from town, and Seaport Marine with ample transient dockage to 150 feet and a popular restaurant.

The family-owned Mystic Downtown Marina is located in historic downtown Mystic and is close to all the village amenities. This is a 40-slip, all-transient marina with all the usual amenities. Call the Dockmaster when approaching the railroad bridge on VHF Channel 08 or by phone for slip location and docking instructions.

If you are staying in one of the facilities across the river in West Mystic, the easiest access is by dinghy to the Mystic River Park Dinghy Dock located between Seaport Marine and the drawbridge. This is smack-dab in the middle of town and gives you great access to the many restaurants and shops.

Anchorage: There may be an anchorage spot or two left outside the increasingly filled mooring field at West Cove in Noank, although this area is relatively shallow (4 to 5 feet MLW) and quite exposed to winds and wakes

from the south. Similarly, the three "Special Anchorage" areas charted east of the Noank peninsula will support drafts of no more than 5 feet MLW and are also mostly filled with local mooring floats.

A better bet is to anchor to the south at Ram Island East in depths of 7 to 11 feet MLW with good holding in firm mud. It is protected from the south through northwest. Wind or waves from the northeast through the southeast can make it uncomfortable. The island is private and the owners do not welcome uninvited guests so you may not leave the beach area.

Those with determination, experience and drafts less than 6 feet may still find anchorage possibilities to the southwest of Mason Island. The holding is good in sand and grass but there is no protection to the south. Be sure to avoid the rocks marked by red nun buoy "6" and red nun buoy "4." Swing room is in short supply due to the growing number of local moorings, which has crowded out most of the available space clear of the channel.

At Mason Island East is a beautiful anchorage with views of the Monastery on Enders Island. Like all anchorages near Mystic, it's exposed to the south but in calm conditions or any breeze out of the north, it is quite comfortable. Downtown Mystic is about a 2 mile dinghy ride from this location.

Mystic Seaport

Mystic River, CT

		Largest Vessel	VHF	Total Slips	Approach/ Dockside Depth	Floating Docks	Gas/ Diesel	Repairs/ Haulout	Min/Max Amps	Pump-Out Station
NOANK										
1. Palmer's Cove Marina	(860) 536-6207	42		100	/	F		R	30	
2. Spicer's Noank Marina (WiFi)	(860) 536-4978	52	68	444	7.0 / 7.0	F		RH	30 / 50	P
3. Noank Shipyard (WiFi)	(860) 556-2000	300	9	158	14.0 / 12.0	F	GD	RH	30 / 100	P
4. Noank Village Boatyard (WiFi)	(860) 536-1770	125	72	55	15.0 / 10.0	F		RH	30 / 100	P
MASON ISLAND										
5. Mystic River Marina (WiFi)	(860) 536-3123	150	9	145	14.0 / 14.0	F	GD	RH	30 / 200+	P
6. Mason's Island Marina (WiFi)	(860) 536-2608	50	9	120	6.0 / 5.5	F		RH	30	
7. Mystic Point Marina (WiFi)	(203) 812-9528	40		120	5.0 / 5.0	F			30	
MYSTIC										
8. Mystic Shipyard (WiFi)	(860) 536-6588	150	9	270	15.0 / 12.0			RH	30 / 50	P
9. Safe Harbor Mystic (WiFi)	(860) 536-2293	80	9	242	15.0 / 11.0	F	GD	RH	30 / 100	P
10. Gwenmor Marina (WiFi)	(860) 536-4346	48	13	110	6.0 / 6.0	F		RH	30 / 50	
11. Fort Rachel Marina (WiFi)	(860) 536-6647	60	9	110	/	F		RH	30 / 50	
12. Seaport Marine (WiFi)	(860) 536-9651	150		115	12.0 / 12.0	F		RH	30 / 100	
13. Mystic Downtown Marina (WiFi)	(860) 572-5942	55	8	29	10.0 / 8.0	F			30	P
14. Mystic Seaport Marina (WiFi)	(860) 572-5391	200	71	40	12.0 / 11.0		GD		30 / 100	

(WiFi) Wireless Internet Access
Visit www.waterwayguide.com for current rates, fuel prices, website addresses and other up-to-the-minute information.
(Information in the table is provided by the facilities.)

Scan here for more details:

Side Trip: Mystic Seaport Museum

Mystic Seaport Museum is located north of Mystic Village (860-572-0711). It is a re-created 19th-century coastal village that opens a window to America's maritime history. By re-created they mean many of the buildings were brought in from other locations in New England to preserve them but they are very authentic. Also on site is the DuPont Preservation Shipyard, where vessels are constructed or reconstructed using traditional methods of the 1800s including the *Charles W. Morgan*, the *Amistad*, the *Mayflower II* and *Sabino*.

There is so much to see and do at Mystic Seaport that it's best to dedicate more than one day to it. It is a great advantage to arrive by boat and stay at the marina docks. Admission is included in the docking fee. You may also arrive by dinghy, paying the regular admission fee per person. Visitors wander along the quays and cobbled harbor lanes, stopping at ancient houses and shops while boarding classic wooden boats including some restored to pristine condition.

Climb aboard the only remaining wooden whaling ship in the world, the *Charles W. Morgan*; one of the few remaining dory-laden Grand Banks fishing schooners,

the *L.A. Dunton*; and the training ship *Joseph Conrad*. If you are lucky, you may meet players in period costume who are steeped in their characters' lives, trades and viewpoints.

Other attractions include one of the finest nautical libraries in existence, a planetarium, masthead carvers, classic boat and model builders, chantey singers, hoop rollers, a rope-walk, a printing shop, a ship smith shop and much more. Courses and lectures on all manner of nautical subjects are offered throughout the year, and there is a veritable kaleidoscope of priceless maritime treasures on display.

The nation's last coal-fired steamer, the *Sabino*, may be available for river cruises (weather and state passenger restrictions permitting). It has converted to solar power for its shorter river cruises. Check on the current status on arrival. There are several other charters available here.

The annual Wooden Boat Show is usually the last weekend of June and is an excellent opportunity to see (or purchase) classic wooden vessels of all ages and sizes or to buy anything you might need to maintain or upgrade your own wooden gem. There are many other special events scattered throughout the year.

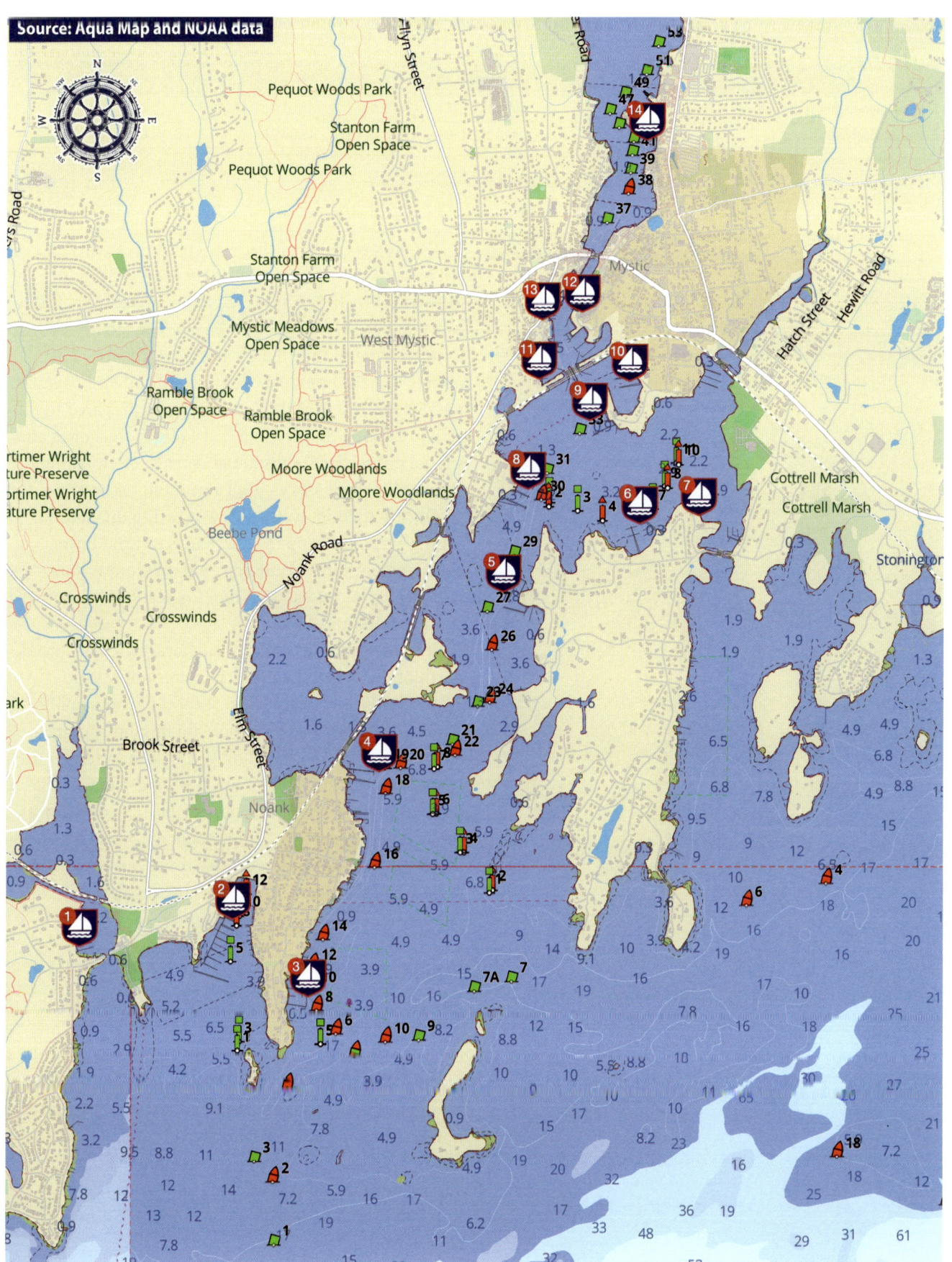

Source: Aqua Map and NOAA data

Little Narragansett Bay, CT/RI

STONINGTON, CT		Largest Vessel	VHF	Total Slips	Approach/ Dockside Depth	Floating Docks	Gas/ Diesel	Repairs/ Haulout	Min/Max Amps	Pump-Out Station
1. Stonington Harbor Yacht Club	(860) 535-0112		78		8.0 /	F			30 / 50	
2. Dodson Boatyard	(860) 535-1507	130	78	52	15.0 / 9.0	F	GD	RH	15 / 50	P

WiFi Wireless Internet Access
Visit www.waterwayguide.com for current rates, fuel prices, website addresses and other up-to-the-minute information.
(Information in the table is provided by the facilities.)

Scan here for more details:

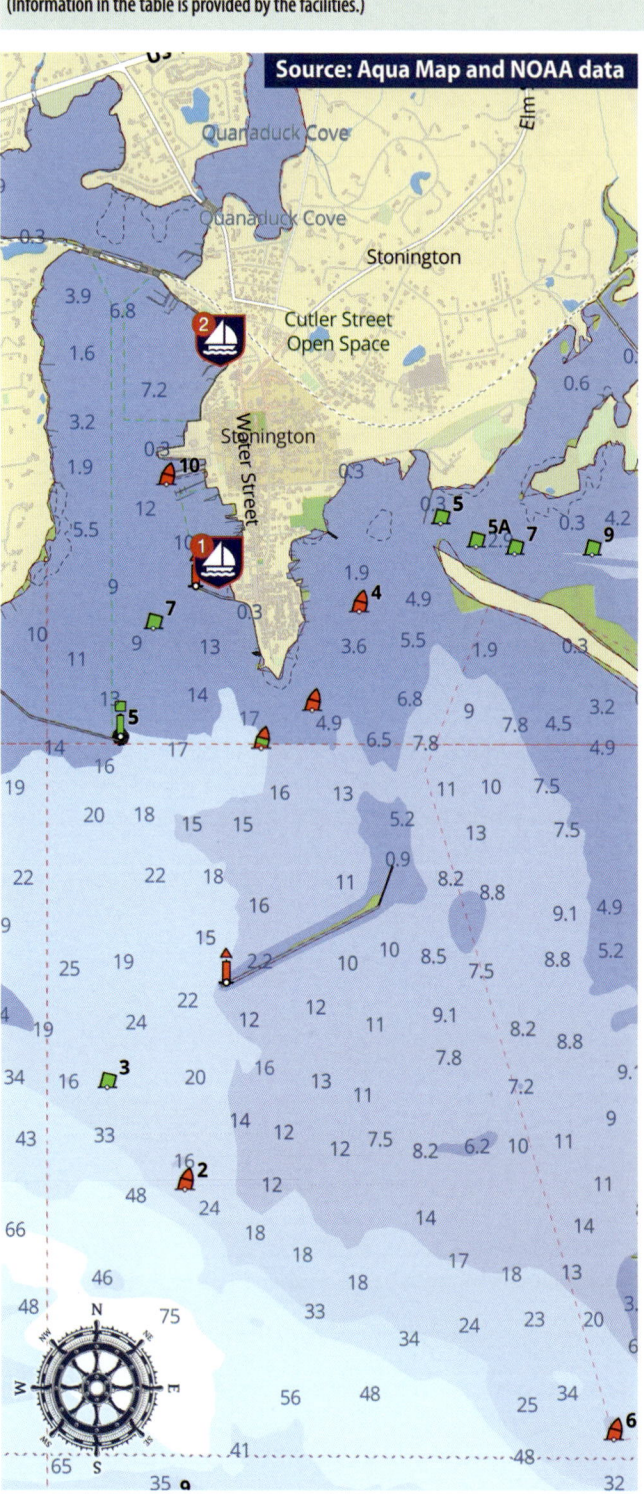

Source: Aqua Map and NOAA data

Dockage: North of the restricted U.S. 1 (Mystic Highway) Bridge, admission to the Mystic Seaport Museum is included in the fee for all aboard if you stay overnight at Mystic Seaport Marina. The facility is right in the middle of the 18-acre museum property. The marina can accommodate between 40 and 45 boats per night (more when clubs and groups are prepared to raft up) on floating docks. Note that holiday weekends and special events draw substantial crowds, often taking up all possible dock spaces. Call ahead for reservations.

Once settled in, walk to downtown to the famous Mystic Pizza and stop in at Mystic Nautical Marine Consignment for everything you didn't know you needed. It's located across from Engine Room, another good restaurant.

Anchorage: A designated anchorage area is upriver north of the federal channel, just north of Mystic Seaport Museum. The Mystic Seaport anchorage offers 8 to 9 feet MLW with good holding in sand and grass. A sign at the northern end of the museum refers to the last federal marker (green can "53") and requests that the channel beyond not be obstructed. The time limit for anchoring is 7 days. This anchorage is No-Discharge Zone. A dinghy dock is available if you wish to visit the museum grounds. (The fee is the regular cost of admission.)

Stonington, CT

Stonington is Connecticut's easternmost cruising port and the only one with some Atlantic Ocean exposure. Locals claim (with some justice) to have the most beautiful harbor on the East Coast. Stonington Borough boasts the third largest collection of historic houses and sites in CT. Many date from the mid-18th century and include former homes of notable patriots, shipwrights and ship captains. This village is also home to Connecticut's only remaining full-time, year-round fishing fleet.

NAVIGATION: Stonington is most directly approached from Mystic Harbor via the well-buoyed passage north of Ram Island and south of Mason Point and Enders Island. Continuing eastward, passage should be between the white "ER" beacon marking Ellis Reef to north and red nun buoys "6" and "4" (marking rocks) to the south. Skippers of deep-draft vessels should favor the red nun buoys to avoid the rock at 5-foot MLW depths just north of Ellis Reef.

CAUTION: Watch for the charted but unmarked White Rock, a 5-foot MLW spot south of red nun buoy "2," which marks Red Reef. A course favoring the red nun buoys should leave you well clear of White Rock. Take care in this area, which (like the rest of Fishers Island Sound) is well known for its bottom-jarring shoals. Daybeacons with the warning ROCK are to be taken at their word.

The approach to Stonington Harbor and to the Little Narragansett Bay channel leading to Watch Hill is straightforward and plainly marked by the widely spaced green-and-red four-second flashing lights situated on towers atop the ends of the two breakwaters protecting the harbor. The horn sounding from 46-foot red flashing "4" to starboard can be heard from a considerable distance.

The breakwater restricts visibility of outbound vessels from this approach, making a wide rounding of the green beacon and allowance for ample reaction time advisable in this relatively busy channel. Shallow-draft boats may also make entrance at the shore side of the breakwater just to the south of Wamphassuc Point. There are submerged rocks at the point, however, and the passage is narrow. It is best left to those with local knowledge.

Dockage/Moorings: The private Stonington Harbor Yacht Club has easy in and out and maintains reciprocity with over 75 clubs throughout the world and offers transient slips to non-members on their long face dock. Guests of the Yacht Club have access to shower facilities from 9:00 a.m. to 5:00 p.m. WiFi is available in the Clubhouse and boaters are welcome to enjoy the restaurant and bar for lunch and dinner.

Dodson Boatyard at the head of the harbor is a working boatyard offering all types of services. Transients will most will likely be directed to one of the yard's numerous rental moorings. (Hint: Ask about nightly rate before picking up a mooring.)

For launch service throughout the harbor call the Dodson Boatyard Launch on VHF Channel 78 for a pick-up (for a small fee). Free pump-out service is available with a call to Westerly Pump-Out Boat on VHF Channel 09. (Ask at Dodson's about the pump-out boat's schedule.)

Anchorage: Unfortunately, there is little anchorage room left behind Stonington Inner Breakwater (west side of the channel) as moorings have gradually filled in this traditional harbor of refuge. During all but the calmest weather, rollers sneaking around the edges of the breakwaters can turn an evening here into "a moving experience." The inner anchorages noted on the chart as "Special Anchorage" (Stonington Harbor and Stonington 2) are equally crowded with moorings.

Watch Hill, RI

Just over the Connecticut/Rhode Island State line at the Pawcatuck River is the village of Watch Hill, RI, featuring long-established seaside estates, an attractive and relatively uncrowded town beach, two sprawling clapboard-sided inns, numerous shops and boutiques oriented to the summer tourist trade. The harbor is large, protected and swim friendly.

The 61-foot lighthouse on Watch Hill has been restored and includes a well-maintained museum managed by the Watch Hill Lighthouse Keepers Assoc. The lighthouse can be accessed by foot via a private road and is open from 8:00 a.m. to sunset throughout the year.

NAVIGATION: After clearing the breakwaters protecting Stonington Harbor, the entrance to Little Narragansett Bay is marked by a red-over-green nun buoy marked "SP" located several hundred yards off Stonington Point. From there, hold a tight course to flashing red buoy "2," which marks Academy Rock (6 feet MLW). Then keep a sharp watch to stay within the nuns and cans marking the narrow channel, which has silted in spots to depths of 6 feet MLW or less.

Take particular care in rounding north of Sandy Point at the entrance to the bay and honor flashing green buoy "5," where the water runs swiftly and deep, despite how narrow the channel appears. Many local boaters find the northern shore of Sandy Point appropriately named and an appealing stop for lunch or swimming. Occasionally, you will find one of them encroaching on the channel between flashing green buoy "5" green can buoy "9."

Pawcatuck River, CT/RI

WATCH HILL		Largest Vessel	VHF	Total Slips	Approach/ Dockside Depth	Floating Docks	Gas/ Diesel	Repairs/ Haulout	Min/Max Amps	Pump-Out Station
1. Watch Hill Yacht Club-PRIVATE **WiFi**	(401) 596-4986				7.0 / 8.0	F				
2. Watch Hill Docks/Frank Hall Boat Yard **WiFi**	(401) 348-8005	100	9	23	7.0 / 8.0	F		RH	30 / 100	P
3. Watch Hill Boat Yard	(401) 348-8148	50	9	81	5.0 / 5.0	F		RH	30	
AVONDALE										
4. Avondale Boat Yard **WiFi**	(401) 348-8187	75	9	96	10.0 / 8.0	F	GD	RH	30 / 50	P
5. Greenhaven Marina	(860) 599-1049	32		65	9.0 / 6.0	F			30	
6. Frank Hall Boat Yard	(401) 348-8005	46	9	110	6.0 / 6.0	F		RH	50	P
7. Cove's Edge Marina	(401) 348-8187	30		100	/	F		RH	30	
WESTERLY										
8. Westerly Yacht Club-PRIVATE **WiFi**	(401) 596-5792	35	9	18	12.0 / 5.0	F	G		30	P
9. Norwest Marine Inc. **WiFi**	(860) 599-2442	60	68	140	7.0 / 10.0	F	G	H	30 / 50	P
10. Pier 65 Marina	(401) 348-8154	60	9	22	8.0 / 7.0	F		RH	30	

WiFi Wireless Internet Access
Visit www.waterwayguide.com for current rates, fuel prices, website addresses and other up-to-the-minute information.
(Information in the table is provided by the facilities.)

Scan here for more details:

Note that it is unsafe to cut across the bay to starboard before coming abeam of flashing green buoy "23." The entry into Watch Hill is well marked and well charted.

Watch Hill Cove should be entered only via the marked 100-foot-wide channel, which carries 6.5 feet MLW. The cove is small, attractive and noncommercial with many local boats including classic wooden tenders and motor cruisers.

Dockage/Moorings:
Immediately shoreside on entering Watch Hill Cove, the private Watch Hill Yacht Club monitors VHF Channel 10 and maintains rental moorings available on a first-come, first-served basis to members from other participating reciprocal clubs, outside of a 25-mile radius from the Club. Mooring rental includes launch service and use of the club's facilities and showers.

The slips at Watch Hill Docks/ Frank Hall Boat Yard are mostly seasonal so transient space is rarely available, but the dockmaster is accommodating and helpful.

Watch Hill Boat Yard is located in a secure harbor in a residential area. This quiet and rustic location is family oriented with numerous attractions within walking (or boating) distance. They maintain just two transient slips to 50 feet.

> NOTE: Little Narragansett Bay (like the rest of Rhode Island waters) is a No-Discharge Zone (prohibiting the discharge of any sewage even if it has been treated). This prohibition is easily honored with a call to the "Westerly Pump-Out Boat" on VHF Channel 09.

Anchorage: Just west of Watch Hill is a sheltered body of water protected to the south by Napatree Beach and Point. This anchorage, known locally as the Kitchens, has 7-foot to 9-foot MLW depths. Napatree Beach (the Kitchens) is extremely popular with locals as well as cruising boats, both power and sail. Holding is good and rafting is popular. It is not at all unusual to see 200 or more boats anchored here over a sunny summer weekend.

Watch Hill Docks/Frank Hall Boat Yard offers a free dinghy dock for those at anchor.

> NOTE: The cottages that were on Napatree were swept into Bay during the 1938 hurricane with much loss of life. The remains of the iceboxes and stoves sank into the bottom sand hence the local name "Kitchens." Don't worry, the kitchen appliances have long ago settled well beneath the reach of your anchor.

Dinghies land or anchor by the dozens on the bay side of Napatree Beach for an easy trek to the surf or to the amenities of Watch Hill ashore to the east. To the west, about a 1-mile pleasant beach walk to Napatree Point, are the still-visible remains of Fort Mansfield, a pre-World War I shore battery destroyed by the hurricane of 1938. Be very careful not to feed the large, hungry tick population here.

Source: Aqua Map and NOAA data

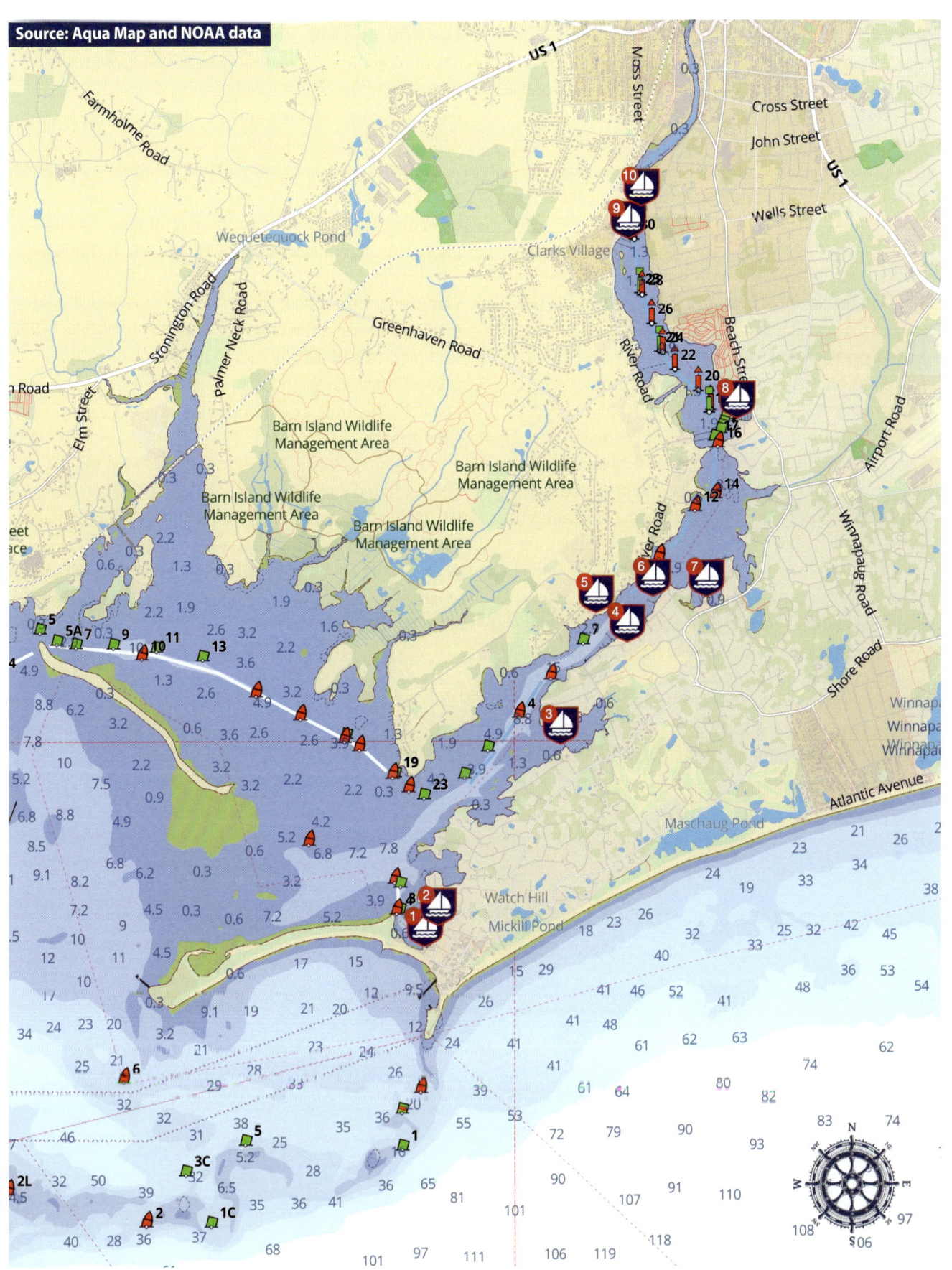

North on the Pawcatuck River

From Watch Hill, the well-buoyed Pawcatuck River wends its way northward through the towns of Avondale and Westerly (RI) to Pawcatuck (CT). Depths outside the narrow channel do not encourage anchoring and the numerous marinas, yacht clubs and boat yards on the Pawcatuck River primarily cater to the local boating community.

Dockage/Moorings: There are several marine facilities close to Avondale with slips/moorings and repairs (most for smaller, local boats) Greenhaven Marina (to 32 feet) and Cove's Edge Marina (to 30 feet).

Family-owned and -operated Avondale Boat Yard has 96 slips on floating and fixed docks with slips to 50 feet. Frank Hall Boat Yard has been family-owned and -operated for three generations in the quaint village of Avondale. They offer 110 protected slips and 18 moorings and have a ship store and personalized yacht brokerage services. They maintain a few transient slips to 46 feet. (They also manage the public docks in Watch Hill Harbor.)

Farther north is the private Westerly Yacht Club in protected Thompson Cove with excellent facilities for visitors from reciprocating clubs and member guests.

The next group of facilities is at the town of Westerly and includes Norwest Marine Inc., which welcomes transients and offers a full range of services, followed by Pier 65 Marina (with limited transient dockage). Call ahead for slip availability.

Continuing East

There is an exit from the southwestern side of Little Narragansett Bay but it is only for small vessels that are familiar with the changes that can occur after every storm. Any marks are non-standard.

It is best to retrace your path north of Sandy Point and then head south to the Napatree Point Ledge flashing red bell buoy "6." Head east past Watch Hill Point and its photogenic lighthouse and go through Watch Hill Passage.

This extremely narrow course has a swift current; if you must transit in fog or high winds, pay close attention to all markers and travel slowly. Watch Hill Passage, while well marked and usually easy to follow when visibility is good, often has many lobster buoys to watch for. It is, however, the route a newcomer should use. Be sure to keep a sharp lookout.

Alternate passages extend from the eastern tip of Fishers Island and further into the open waters of Long Island Sound but are not recommended. Wicopesset and Lord's passages are best left to very experienced cruisers or local skippers but they will get you out of an adverse current much quicker. Catumb and Sugar Reef passages are even more risky.

Watch Hill Lighthouse in Westerly, Rhode island

Pages 309-314

Mattituck Inlet

CONNECTICUT
NEW YORK

Long Island Sound

Port Jefferson

Stony Brook

Smithtown Bay

Atlantic Ocean

Pages 301-309

Eatons Neck

Huntington Harbor

Oyster Bay

Cold Spring Harbor

Port Washington

Pages 292-301

Hempstead Harbor

Manhasset Bay

Little Neck Bay

Manorhaven

Manhasset Bay

Plum Point

Long Island Sound

■ LITTLE NECK BAY TO COLD SPRING HARBOR

The North Shore of Long Island from Little Neck Bay to Plum Gut is called the "South Shore" (of Long Island Sound) by New York and Connecticut boaters. (This is not to be confused with the south shore of Long Island itself, which is discussed in another chapter.) This area of Long Island Sound is generally easy to navigate, well-marked and well charted. It has mostly deep water, extensive facilities, anchorages, convenient land transportation and a seemingly unlimited number of recreational boats.

The harbors of Manhasset Bay (Port Washington), Glen Cove, Oyster Bay, Cold Spring Harbor, Huntington Harbor and Port Jefferson are favorites among the cruising community. Because the rise and fall of the tide on portions of the western Long Island Sound's "South Shore" is substantial (6 to 8 feet), most marinas have floating docks.

The western end of the Sound is the narrow part, making it easy to crisscross back and forth between Long Island harbors and the "North Shore" harbors of New York and Connecticut. The eastern end of Long Island Sound's south shore is quite different from the Connecticut shore. The beach is mostly unbroken. There are high bluffs (sandy or rocky) and the shore is sparsely settled with only two substantial harbors in almost 60 miles.

Little Neck Bay

Little Neck Bay is the first harbor on the Long Island shore after you leave the East River. It is a large-mouthed bay with thickly settled shores and some of the best anchorages in the crowded New York City area.

The 65-acre campus of the U.S. Merchant Maritime Academy was once the estate of Walter P. Chrysler, the automobile manufacturer. He used to commute to New York City by boat. The mansion's interior is now divided into small offices but the grounds are open to the public on weekend afternoons and during Saturday morning

Little Neck Bay, NY

LITTLE NECK BAY		Largest Vessel	VHF	Total Slips	Approach/ Dockside Depth	Floating Docks	Gas/ Diesel	Repairs/ Haulout	Min/Max Amps	Pump-Out Station
1. Bayside Marina	(718) 229-0097			46	7.0 / 4.0	F			30 / 50	

(WiFi) Wireless Internet Access
Visit www.waterwayguide.com for current rates, fuel prices, website addresses and other up-to-the-minute information. (Information in the table is provided by the facilities.)

Scan here for more details:

reviews. The Academy has quite a sailing fleet at Kings Point. The American Merchant Marine Museum (516-726-6047) is located on the Academy campus in the historic Barstow House. William Barstow invented the electric meter and was also responsible for lighting the Brooklyn Bridge.

On the eastern shore at Udall's Mill Pond, just to the south of the charted dam, is the Saddle Rock Grist Mill, a 16th-century water mill that still operates, depending on the tide. It is open to the public on Sundays (1:00 p.m. to 5:00 p.m.) from May through October. You can bring the dinghy over to take a closer look but you cannot land here.

NAVIGATION: The straightforward entrance to Little Neck Bay is between Willets Point on the west and Kings Point on the east, which is marked by the 220-foot-high flagpole of the U.S. Merchant Maritime Academy.

Dockage/Moorings: Bayside Marina on the west shore of Little Neck Bay has transient moorings available with 24/7 launch service. They also offer small fishing boat rentals and a snack bar.

Anchorage: Little Bay south of Throgs Neck Bridge has 7 to 8 feet MLW in good holding in mud. It is protected from all but the north and northeast but is subject to wakes from boat traffic and noise from highway traffic. Little Neck Bay has 7- to 8-foot MLW depths down the middle with shallows along the banks and in the southeastern corner. Many boats are moored here but there are several good places to anchor unless the wind is out of the north. The cove north of Kings Point on the eastern shore has a designated special anchorage with 12 to 14 feet MLW and good holding in mud. It is, however, open and exposed to the northeast.

Manhasset Bay

Manhasset Bay is one of the most popular and most complete harbors on Long Island Sound. It has deep water throughout, good holding and is easy to enter day or night, making it an ideal stopover whether transiting east or west on Long Island Sound.

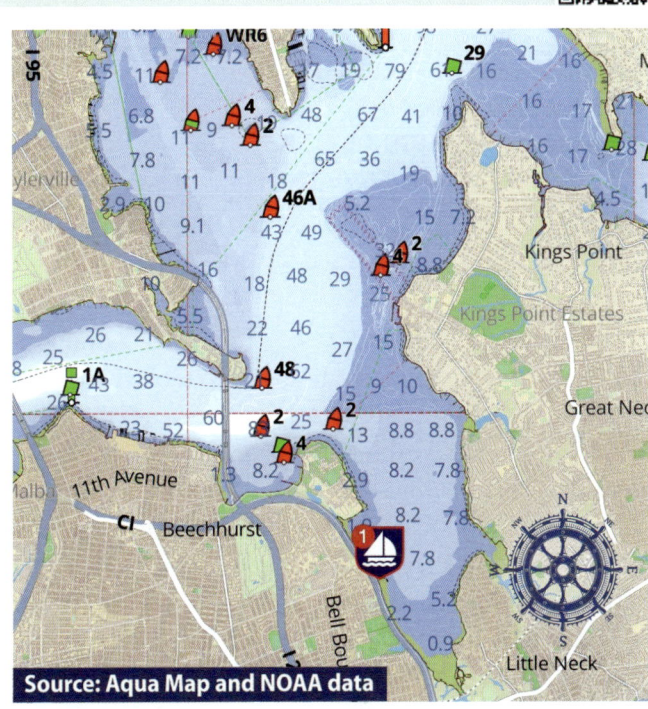

Source: Aqua Map and NOAA data

South Shore Distances
Nautical Miles (approximate)

LOCATION	BETWEEN POINTS	CUMULATIVE
Throgs Neck Bridge	0	
Little Neck Bay	1	1
Manhasset Bay	4	5
Port Washington	2	7
Hempstead Harbor	6	13
Glen Cove	1	14
Oyster Bay Harbor	11	25
Huntington Bay	6	31
Huntington Harbor	2	33
Northport Harbor	4	37
Stony Brook	14	51
Port Jefferson	8	59
Mount Sinai	5	64
Mattituck	22	86
Orient Point	18	104
Montauk Point	24	128
Block Island	13	141

Manhasset Bay, NY

MANHASSET NECK		Largest Vessel	VHF	Total Slips	Approach/ Dockside Depth	Floating Docks	Gas/ Diesel	Repairs/ Haulout	Min/Max Amps	Pump-Out Station
1. Safe Harbor Capri WiFi	(516) 883-7800	175	9	315	7.0 / 6.5	F	GD	RH	30 / 200+	P
2. North Shore Yacht Club-PRIVATE	(516) 883-9823	65	78		15.0 / 5.0	F				
3. Toms Point Marina	(516) 883-6630	36		130	5.0 / 5.0	F		RH	30 / 50	P
4. Manhasset Bay Marina WiFi	(516) 883-8411	110	9	300	8.0 / 8.0	F	GD	RH	30 / 100	P
PORT WASHINGTON										
5. Port Washington Mooring Field Manhasset Bay	(516) 767-1691				/					
6. Marina at Inspiration Wharf	(516) 883-0765	30	9	30	8.0 / 8.0	F	D	R	30 / 50	P
7. Manhasset Bay Yacht Club-PRIVATE	(516) 767-2150	100	73		7.0 / 6.0	F			30	
8. Port Washington Yacht Club-PRIVATE WiFi	(516) 767-1614	100	74		7.0 / 6.0	F		R	30	

WiFi Wireless Internet Access
Visit www.waterwayguide.com for current rates, fuel prices, website addresses and other up-to-the-minute information.
(Information in the table is provided by the facilities.)

Scan here for more details:

Activities in Manhasset Bay during the summer months are so abundant that some boats dock here in the spring and stay through the summer. Cruisers from other areas often (incorrectly) refer to the entire Manhasset Bay as Port Washington. Port Washington is actually the second largest boating center in Manhasset Bay. Other waterfront towns surrounding the Bay include Sands Point, Manorhaven, Plandome, Great Neck and Kings Point. The town of Manhasset is slightly inland and New York City is about 40 miles away by highway or railroad.

NAVIGATION: From Little Neck Bay, the preferred (and safer) route is to pass north of Stepping Stones Lighthouse, keeping it to starboard. Alternately, you can cruise along the eastern shore, keeping about midway between red nun buoys "4" and "2" on the southern edge of Stepping Stones reef and the shoreline.

The wide, unobstructed entrance to Manhasset Bay is between Hewlett Point and Barker Point. Do not cut either point coming in; both have rocks just offshore. About 1 nm inside flashing green "1" marks the crooked finger of Plum Point, which extends out from the eastern shore almost halfway across the bay and protects the inner harbor.

NO WAKE ZONE

A sizable and strictly enforced No-Wake Zone begins at Plum Point.

Dockage/Moorings: The marinas of Manhasset Bay offer complete facilities and services. The yacht clubs are friendly and offer guest moorings to other yacht club members. The shopping, provisioning and restaurants are well within reach of the marinas and anchorages including a West Marine and Ace Hardware within walking distance.

The village of Manorhaven boasts that it is the largest boating community in the State of New York. Safe Harbor Capri is located just inside the protective arm of Plum Point. Formerly separate facilities were combined to provide a complete range of integrated marine services. Amenities include all you would expect from a Safe Harbor facility including good floating docks, clean restrooms and competent dock staff. They welcome transients to 175 feet.

In between Capri's two main piers, the friendly and colorful North Shore Yacht Club is private but has several guest moorings. The mooring field is well protected, spacious and quiet. The facility maintains two launches providing a 7-day launch service schedule that accommodates early or late arrival or departure.

Other facilities are located south of Tom's Point with transient slips and boat maintenance and repairs including the well maintained, 300-slip Manhasset Bay Marina. They welcome visitors with 20 reserved transient slips and 40 moorings while also tending to the needs of hundreds of local boats. They can handle most repair or service needs and have a ship store and popular restaurant. Nearby is Toms Point Marina, a small boat facility (slips to 36 feet) and the usual amenities. This is one of the most protected marinas within the bay and a good place to be if a blow is predicted.

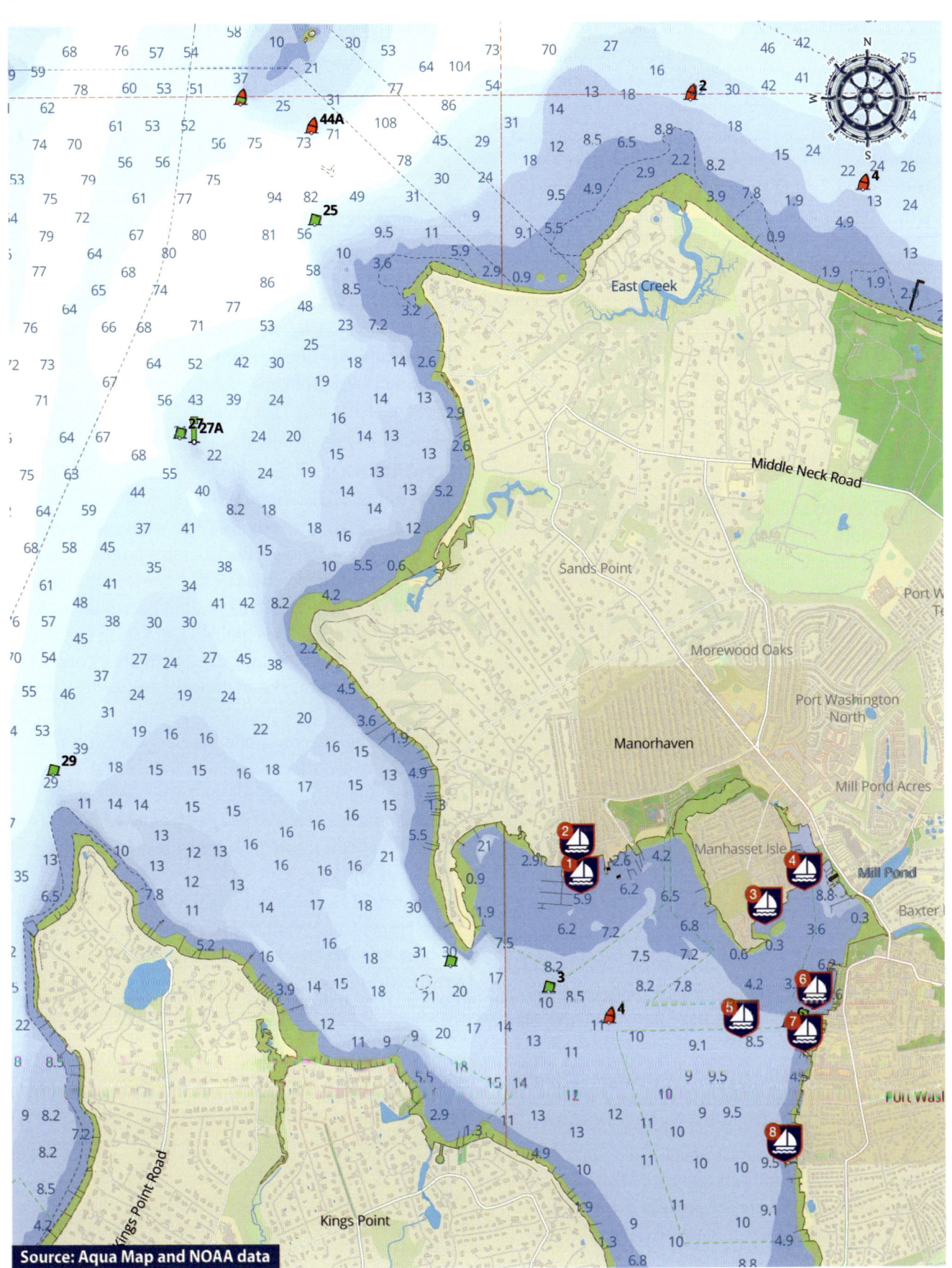

Source: Aqua Map and NOAA data

Port Washington Mooring Field has about 40 well-maintained mooring balls. These are operated by the water taxi, which charges a fee for the first night but is then free when paying for a mooring ball. The water taxi can take you to different places in the harbor including restaurants, a grocery store and a West Marine. There is a free dock, Port Washington Town Dock, adjacent to the mooring office that is suitable for dinghies. (Check posted time limit.) A second dinghy dock is at the north end of the harbor, directly across from Port Washington Stop n Shop and other shopping and provisioning options.

The 30-slip Marina at Inspiration Wharf has limited transient slips and moorings to 30 feet. Boat rentals, kayak and SUP rentals and a bait and tackle shop are on site.

Manhasset Bay Yacht Club and Port Washington Yacht Club are both private, supporting competitive racing programs and a parade of social events. Members of yacht clubs with reciprocity can usually find a mooring with launch service or a slip along with access to club amenities included in the facility fee.

> NOTE: The inner harbor is also a No-Discharge Zone. Discharge of raw or treated sewage is prohibited. The town of Port Washington offers complimentary pump-out service to boats on the hook or at moorings via its pump-out barge. (Hail on VHF Channel 09.)

Anchorage: Manhasset Bay offers protection against most winds for the entirety of its 3.5-nm length and is a snug harbor with room for numerous vessels. The first of five Coast Guard-designated anchorage areas is at Kings Point with good holding in mud with 11- to 12-foot MLW depths. Tuck in far enough to avoid swells/wake from passing traffic on Long Island Sound.

Another designated anchorage is at Toms Point but it is shallow (4 to 6 feet MLW) and open and exposed to the southwest. A better option is the designated anchorage at Port Washington with 8 to 12 feet MLW with excellent holding in mud. There is some anchoring room among the moorings and plenty around the perimeter.

In the southern end of the bay, Plandome is the most protected designated anchorage to drop the hook in 6 to 8 feet MLW with excellent holding in mud. It is exposed to the north. In the southeast corner of Manhasset Bay near Leeds Pond there is a popular anchorage used on weekends for raft-ups and swimming. This is exposed to the north.

To Hempstead Harbor

Glen Cove, surrounded by water on three sides, is a popular part of the North Shore's Gold Coast where J.P. Morgan and F.W. Woolworth had homes. Many lavish mansions and gardens remain along the 300-plus acres of nature preserves overlooking Hempstead Harbor. J.P. Morgan built the 40-acre Morgan Memorial Park in memory of his wife. The park overlooks Long Island Sound and has a picnic area, playground, concession stand, restrooms and a beach. There is also a walkway along the bluff providing panoramic views.

Just north of the creek is the 62-acre Garvies Point Museum and Preserve (516-571-8010), which documents the life and culture of Long Island, geology and Native American archaeology. The grounds include nature trails and an abundance of wildlife.

NAVIGATION: Boats eastbound from Manhasset Bay should round Barker Point passing north of Gangway Rock. Local boats often cut inside the white and orange can buoy marking Success Rock but this is not advisable unless you really know the area. Run between the lighted buoys off Sands Point to starboard and Execution Rocks to port. The grouping of the lighthouse and small buildings at Execution Rocks constitute a major landmark and one of the most important aids to navigation in western Long Island Sound.

Leave plenty of room around the ledge at Execution Rocks. The name is derived from a local belief that during the Revolutionary War British soldiers chained American patriots to the rocks at low tide and let them drown when the tide rose. This theory has been discounted but it does make a colorful story.

Hempstead Harbor, southeast across Long Island Sound from Mamaroneck and Rye, has a 4-mile-wide entrance between Prospect and Matinecock Points. The harbor is open to the northwest. Note that exiting the harbor against wind and waves from this direction can be a long motor, especially in a sailboat with light auxiliary power.

Glen Cove Creek is the deepest, best-protected, most active yachting port in Hempstead Harbor. The creek, which is north of Sea Cliff, would be almost imperceptible on first-time arrival but for yellow can buoy "A" and yellow nun buoy "B" marking the outer channel. When you are centered between the two buoys, face the creek to the east, and green entrance can buoy "1" and red

Hempstead Harbor, NY

GLEN COVE		Largest Vessel	VHF	Total Slips	Approach/ Dockside Depth	Floating Docks	Gas/ Diesel	Repairs/ Haulout	Min/Max Amps	Pump-Out Station
1. Safe Harbor Glen Cove	(516) 759-3129	70	9	550	15.0 / 6.0		GD	RH	30 / 50	P
2. Hempstead Harbour Club - PRIVATE	(516) 671-0600	50	72		8.0 / 6.0					P

WiFi Wireless Internet Access
Visit www.waterwayguide.com for current rates, fuel prices, website addresses and other up-to-the-minute information. (Information in the table is provided by the facilities.)

Scan here for more details:

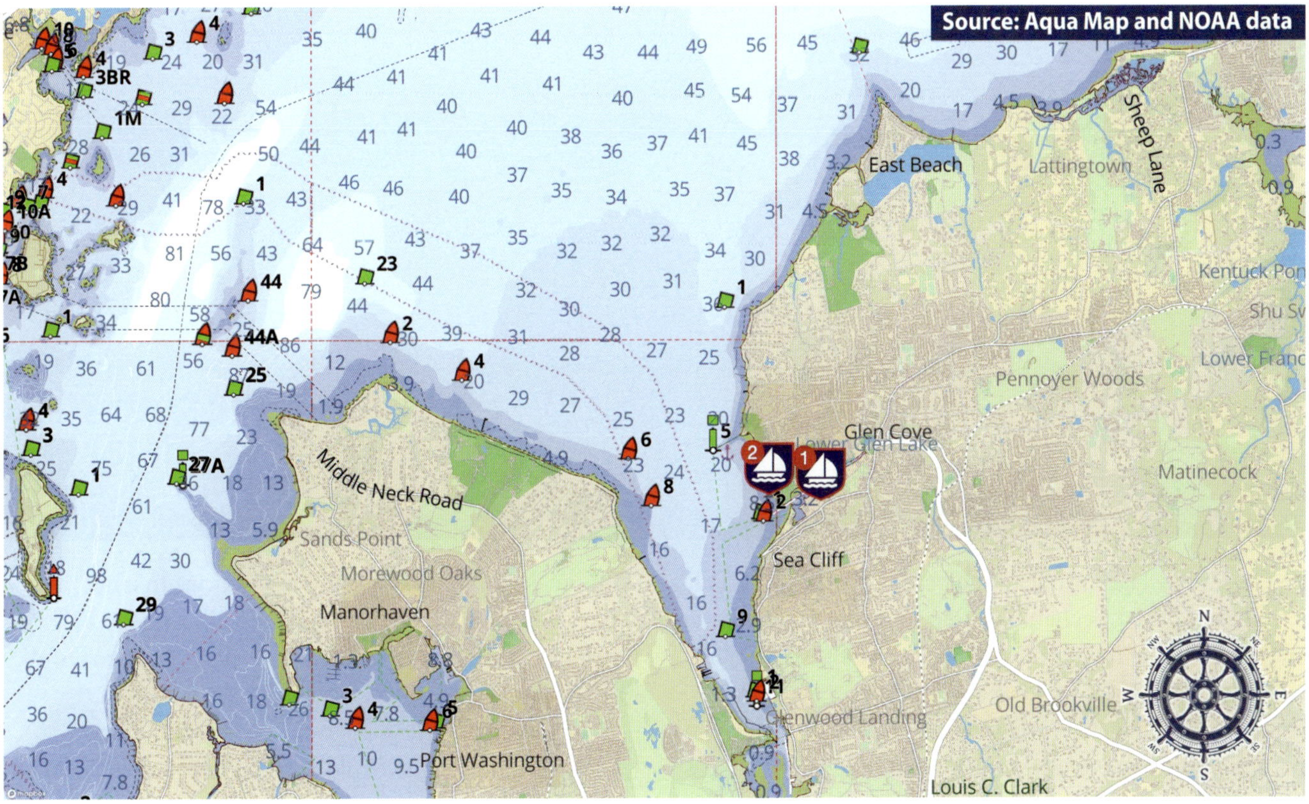

Source: Aqua Map and NOAA data

nun buoy "2" will show the way to the narrow channel between the bulkheads. At low tide, in particular, deeper-draft boats should favor the right side of the channel on entry staying closer to the collapsing bulkhead to starboard. There should be 6.5-foot MLW depths here and substantially more otherwise, given the 8-foot tidal range.

Dockage/Mooring: In an enclosed basin on the west shore is the 550-slip Safe Harbor Glen Cove with transient slips to 70 feet with resort-style amenities and an array of services. The cove is also home to the hospitable Hempstead Harbour Club. Transient vessels may be able to secure an overnight mooring at this private club but call ahead.

Anchorage: One of Long Island Sound's best beaches (unnamed on the chart, but known locally as Half Moon Beach) is the stretch of shore between Barker Point and Sands Point, west of Hempstead Harbor. Boats anchor in the bight just off the beach with excellent holding in 13- to 14-foot MLW depths.

The breakwater at Glen Cove is a protected anchorage that was used by J.P. Morgan's Corsair and other vessels of the great steam-yacht period. There is an ample anchorage area beyond the mooring fields; however, cruisers have noted that even behind the breakwater it can be uncomfortable in a northwest or westerly wind. This also applies to any anchorage farther to the south.

Oyster Bay

Oyster Bay, located east of Hempstead Harbor, has one of most attractive and unspoiled harbors on Long Island Sound. Oyster Bay Harbor is a long horseshoe with Centre Island (not really an island) in the middle and it shares an entrance (Oyster Bay) with Cold Spring Harbor.

Oyster Bay

Oyster Bay Harbor offers fine beaches, beautiful estates, a well-kept oyster fleet and a choice of generous, sheltered anchorages. The town of Oyster Bay comprises 18 small hamlet communities that collectively boast over 600 acres of park lands and pristine beaches weaving along both the north and south shores. Even though the village is small, attractions include several well-recommended restaurants and breweries.

> NOTE: Oyster Bay Harbor is the termination point of the Oyster Bay Branch of the Long Island Railroad, making it a convenient spot to tie up and head into New York City for a day trip.

On the low-lying shore of Oak Neck Point is the village of Bayville. This resort community has pretty cottages and fine public beaches, replete with the requisite hot dog stands, ice cream parlors and cocktail lounges as well as amenities for cruising boats. From here it is common to see the labor-intensive activities of Oyster Bay's colorful oyster fleet working the bottom in the traditional manner.

NAVIGATION: The route around Matinecock Point past Oak Neck and Rocky Point on Centre Island follows what was once the most elegant stretch of Long Island. The shore, lined with handsome estates, is also lined with rocks and requires careful navigation. To enter Oyster Bay from the west, round green bell buoy "17" north of Centre Island Reef and stay clear of the rocks off hilly Rocky Point.

The preferred course is southeast across the bay, leaving flashing 37-foot Cold Spring Light (where current runs strong) to starboard. Boats drawing under 7 feet usually cut through the light's red sector, running west about halfway between the light and the line from red nun buoys "2" and "4" off Plum Point. Once inside, the inner bay shoots off southeast to Cold Spring Harbor and southwest to the 4-mile U-turn around Centre Island through Oyster Bay Harbor and into West Harbor.

To reach Mill Neck Creek off West Harbor you will have to negotiate the **Bayville Bridge** (9-foot closed vertical clearance). The bridgetender can be contacted on VHF Channel 13 for an opening any day during the season (May 1 through October 31) from 7:00 a.m. to 11:00 p.m. and from November 1 through April 30 between 7:00 a.m. and 5:00 p.m., Monday through Friday. At all other times the draw will open on signal with at least a 2-hour advance notice, given by calling the number posted at the bridge.

Oyster Bay, NY

OYSTER BAY HARBOR		Largest Vessel	VHF	Total Slips	Approach/ Dockside Depth	Floating Docks	Gas/ Diesel	Repairs/ Haulout	Min/Max Amps	Pump-Out Station
1. Oyster Bay Marine Center WiFi	(516) 624-2400	160	71	32	13.0 / 22.0	F	GD	RH	30 / 50	P
2. Sagamore Yacht Club-PRIVATE	(516) 922-0555	50	78		10.0 / 7.0					
COLD SPRING HARBOR										
3. H & M Powles Marina	(631) 367-7670	31	10		20.0 / 4.0	F	GD	R		P
4. Whaler's Cove Yacht Club-PRIVATE	(631) 367-9822	44	9	50	15.0 / 25.0	F			30	

WiFi Wireless Internet Access
Visit www.waterwayguide.com for current rates, fuel prices, website addresses and other up-to-the-minute information.
(Information in the table is provided by the facilities.)

Scan here for more details:

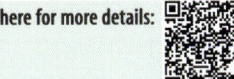

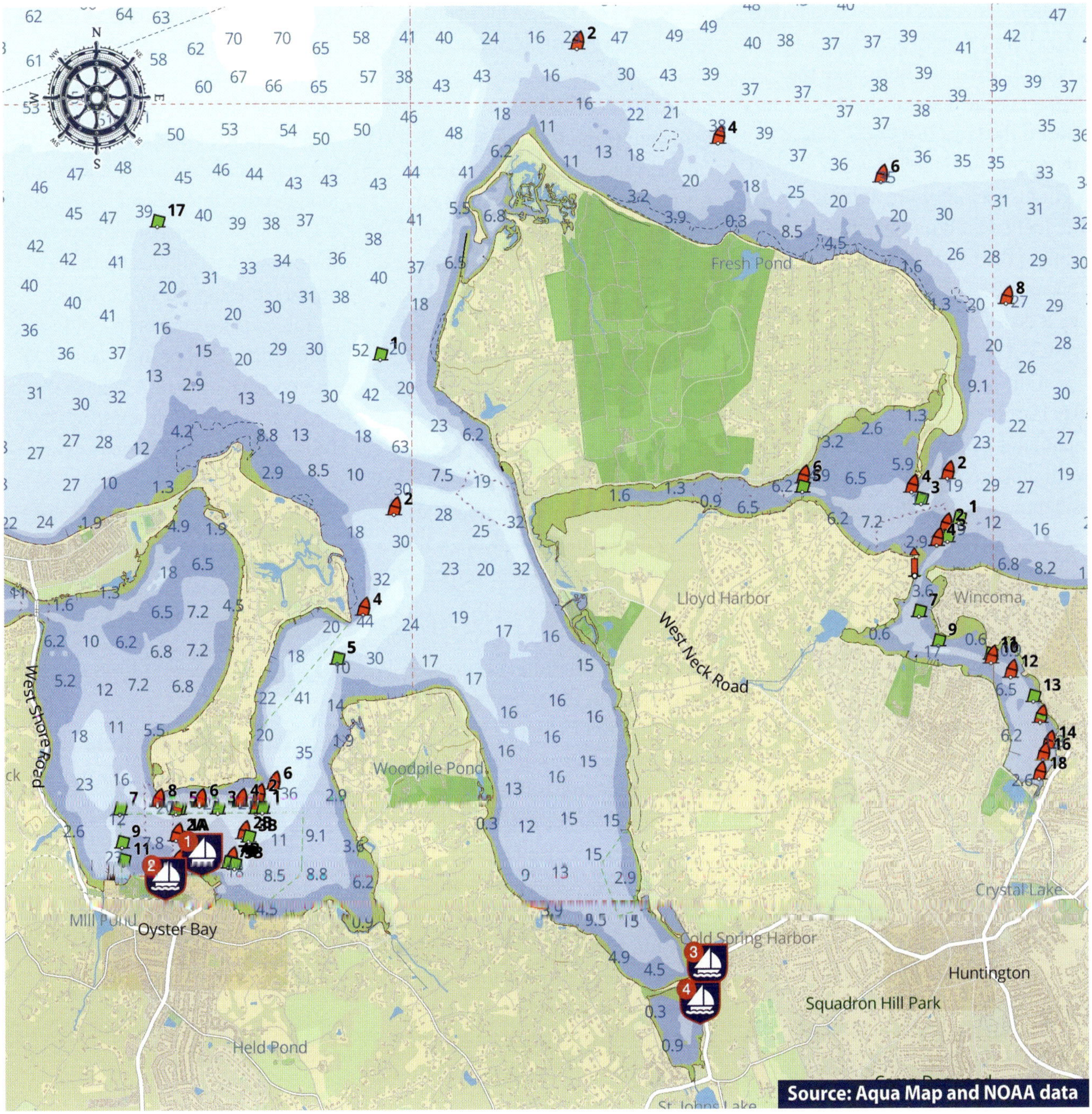

Source: Aqua Map and NOAA data

Oyster Bay is home to the famous Seawanhaka Corinthian Yacht Club. The sailing fleet here chooses two excellent harbors as home ports: Oyster Bay Harbor and Cold Spring Harbor. Deep, protected anchorages abound throughout both harbors including one of Long Island Sound's best gunkholes, the Sand Hole at Lloyds Neck.

Dockage/Mooring: Oyster Bay Marine Center has slips and moorings and offers a variety of services. To approach these facilities, take the branch of the marked channel leading toward the large fuel tanks. The branch channel then makes a hard right just before shore, leading past the fuel dock. From here it is an easy walk to the town's superb park and the amenities of the village. The town dock next to the marina does not offer transient space.

In the southwest corner of Oyster Bay Harbor, Sagamore Yacht Club maintains reciprocal relationships with most accredited yacht clubs and is happy to host visiting yachtsmen (by reservation only).

Anchorage: South of Centre Island, protection and pleasant surroundings can be found in the big cove between the town of Oyster Bay and the high wooded bluffs of Cove Neck. Two miles long and one mile wide, Oyster Cove has little current and holding is good in 8 to 9 feet MLW. It never seems to be crowded, although there might be a club raft-up or two during summer months.

A great variety of waterfowl can be seen in the marshes at the head of the cove, especially during the seasonal migrations.

A popular anchorage with good holding in 7 to 8 feet MLW is in West Harbor to the northwest of Centre Island. This is a wide, open body of water with good depth and protection all around with a few moorings and lots of beaches.

A peaceful anchorage area can be found on the southwest shore of Mill Neck Creek. This is a great place to hunker down in a blow as it provides all-around protection with 7 to 13 feet MLW with good holding in mud and grass. You will likely need to call for an opening of the Bayville Bridge (9-foot closed vertical clearance).

Cold Spring Harbor

Bordered by the 180-foot cliffs of Cooper Bluff, Cold Spring Harbor is an uncluttered bay almost 3 nm long and 1 nm wide. It has several beaches, wooded hills on the east and west sides and Cold Spring Harbor in the southeast corner. Its wooded surroundings and steep shores make this harbor seem more like a beautiful northern inland lake than a piece of Long Island Sound. Cold Spring Harbor was so named by settlers in 1653 because of the harbor's icy freshwater springs. There are actual piped cold springs where you can fill up water jugs. (Ask a local.)

The village of Cold Spring Harbor preserves the maritime history of Long Island in the Whaling Museum and Education Center (631-367-3418) located amid the cluster of 18th-century and 19th-century houses overlooking the narrow harbor. Cold Spring Harbor is also home to the DNA Learning Center (516-367-5170), the world's first Biotechnology Museum, and the Cold Spring Harbor Fish Hatchery & Aquarium (516-692-6768), which raises a variety of species of trout to stock ponds and turtles for release into the wild. It is extremely "kid friendly."

Dockage/Moorings: The harbor is filled with a local mooring field south of Cold Spring Beach. Keep to the middle of the narrow, deep channel leading in. Inside are good depths along the eastern shore, which will take you to a marine facilities along the southern shore. H & M Powles Marina may have a slip or mooring for you but call ahead before arrival. They also offers some repairs. Slips at the private Whalers Cove Yacht Club is for members only.

Anchorage: Much of the anchorage area in Cold Spring Harbor is taken up with permanent moorings. You may still be able to anchor with good depths (8 to 12 feet MLW) north of Cold Spring Beach, a skinny stretch of shore with a bulbous tip that almost closes up the inner harbor.

You can also anchor in Cold Spring Inner Harbor in 14 feet MLW with good holding near Whalers Cove Yacht Club. The approach to the inner harbor is a bit narrow so exercise caution.

NOTE: There are many beaches in the area where you can land without trespassing. When you come upon a private section, law provides that you may walk along the wet sand portion of the beach below the high tide line.

Side Trip: The Sand Hole

The Sand Hole is one of the most popular gunkholes on Long Island Sound. It offers an easy anchorage when transiting the Sound in either direction. Surrounded by a state park, it is a hike to get to by land; however, it seems as if every boat on Long Island Sound heads there on summer weekends. It can (understandably) get crowded and noisy.

The Sand Hole was originally dredged for private yachts. There is only one house overlooking it on long-established private land. The rest of the surrounding land is grassland, beach and some marshland. Should you choose to walk the shoreline be sure to stay away from the house's guarded land and take notice that parts of the barrier beach are often restricted due to nesting birds. Remember: Obey the signs, avoid the fines.

NAVIGATION: To reach The Sand Hole, steer about 50° magnetic from green gong buoy "1" at the mouth of Oyster Bay. You will see the jetty (except at high tide) and should give it a wide berth when turning in.

Anchorage: The Sand Hole has two basins. The Inner Harbor almost appears to be barred by shallow water when, in fact, depths over the bar are about 4 feet MLW. Leading just off the spit that divides the basins is a deep, narrow channel leading to the inner basin, where you will find 7- to 14-foot MLW depths.

You can opt to anchor directly behind the jetty (Outer Harbor) in 9 to 15 feet MLW. You may get some wave action from the west but will be protected from wind from all directions.

◼ HUNTINGTON BAY AREA

The eastern part of the North Shore of Long Island from Huntington Bay to Plum Gut is the widest part of Long Island Sound. The breezes freshen and the harbors become fewer in number. Huntington Bay sprawls inward from Long Island Sound. It is the largest of the Long Island harbors and marks the beginning of Suffolk County. Nassau County is to the west.

The wide entrance to Huntington Bay lays between two high, wooded headlands, each almost an island connected to the mainland by a narrow, sandy isthmus. To the west is private Lloyd Neck. To the east is the jutting headland of Eatons Neck with its famous old lighthouse and Coast Guard station.

Huntington Bay narrows as it goes south and then spreads out to the east, west and south into seven separate, sheltered, inner harbors lined by the villages of Huntington, Centerport and Northport. Boating amenities are everywhere. There are many anchorages–some crowded, some isolated–plus good beaches and fine restaurants.

Lloyd Harbor

Huntington Bay, NY

HUNTINGTON HARBOR		Largest Vessel	VHF	Total Slips	Approach/ Dockside Depth	Floating Docks	Gas/ Diesel	Repairs/ Haulout	Min/Max Amps	Pump-Out Station
1. Knutson Marine **WiFi**	(631) 549-7842	68	9	130	10.0 / 8.0	F		RH	50	P
2. Huntington Yacht Club-PRIVATE **WiFi**	(631) 427-4949	100	68	103	/ 12.0	F	GD		30 / 100	P
3. Knutson's Yacht Haven Marina Inc. **WiFi**	(631) 673-0700	100		38	20.0 / 20.0	F		RH	30 / 100	P
4. Coneys Marine	(631) 421-3366	50	9		15.0 / 12.0	F		RH	30 / 50	
5. Willis Marine Center	(631) 421-3400	80	9	120	12.0 / 10.0	F		RH	30 / 50	P
6. West Shore Marina **WiFi**	(631) 427-3444	150	9	300	15.0 / 18.0	F		RH	30 / 100	P

WiFi Wireless Internet Access

Visit www.waterwayguide.com for current rates, fuel prices, website addresses and other up-to-the-minute information. (Information in the table is provided by the facilities.)

Scan here for more details:

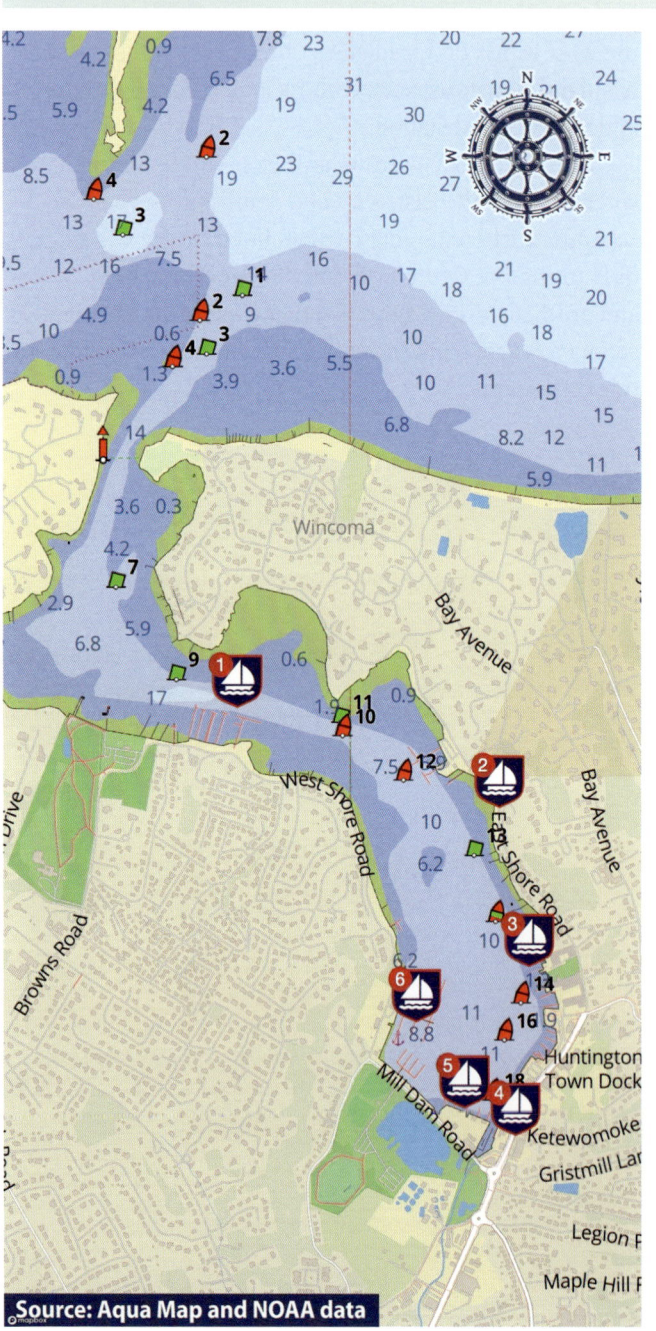

Source: Aqua Map and NOAA data

Lloyd Harbor

Lloyd Harbor is the westernmost of the Huntington Bay harbors. It has a wide outer harbor and long, narrow inner harbor. The outer harbor, almost 0.5-mile long, has a few boats at moorings, attractive houses hidden among the trees and a small summer camp but no docks or marinas. It is cool and thickly wooded but can be crowded on weekends. No motorized vessels are allowed in the narrow inner harbor.

NAVIGATION: To reach Lloyd Harbor, enter north of Huntington Harbor Lighthouse. It is a storybook graystone residence that tends to fade into the surroundings and can be difficult to spot from a distance. The narrow channel is clearly buoyed with stakes and poles marking obstructions or shoal spots. Extending westward, the inner harbor runs nearly 1.5 nm toward Oyster Bay. It provides an interesting dinghy trip (no motors allowed) and is good for windsurfing but too shallow for deep-keeled boats.

Anchorage: Anchoring and motoring is prohibited in the inner harbor at Lloyd Harbor. Several hundred feet west of Lloyd Harbor you will find spots to anchor both to the north and south near green can buoy "3" and red nun buoy "4." (Note: Not Huntington Harbor buoys.) This anchorage offers 8 to 14 feet MLW with excellent holding in mud.

The more southern anchorage area provides good protection from the prevailing southwest wind, but it is open to some surge and wakes from the constant stream of boats that use the Huntington Harbor channel. The more northern area gives protection from the north and northeast behind the spit. The speed limit is 5 knots. Stay away from the buoyed water-skiing area. Rafting is allowed but you must maintain a safe distance from other boats.

Huntington Harbor

At the southwestern end of Huntington Bay just around the lighthouse from Lloyd Harbor, a well-marked channel leads into Huntington Harbor. Although this is one of the best-protected harbors in Long Island Sound, it is also more tightly packed with boats than any eastern Long Island Sound harbor. The waters are usually crowded with racing sailboats or cruisers so proceed slowly through the fleet and be sure you do not leave a wake.

NOTE: Dominating the entrance from a hill on the southern shore is baronial Château at Coindre Hall, a 40-room, 80,000-square-foot mansion constructed in 1912 in the style of a medieval French château (open to the public).

The center of Huntington is about a 20-minute walk from the marinas on the inner harbor. The town is well worth a walking tour. Provisions and supplies are close at hand and anything the cruising mariner is likely to require is readily available. Compass Rose Marine Supply at 15 Mill Dam Rd. (631-673-4144) has a huge inventory of marine supplies and can order parts for rapid delivery (www.compassrosemarine. com). The city also offers one of the most sophisticated arts communities in the area.

NAVIGATION: The narrow but well-marked entrance to Huntington Harbor runs between a boulder reef extending out from West Neck to starboard and 1 and 2-foot MLW shallows around Wincoma Point to port upon entry. Favor the West Neck shore and allow for the 2-knot current through the narrows.

After rounding flashing green buoy "7," the channel swings east for about 1,000 yards before turning south into the harbor's lower end. Watch your wake as you navigate the channel as a 5-mph speed limit is strictly enforced. There is no room here to anchor.

Dockage/Moorings: Several marinas offer berth space in Huntington Harbor and some independent concerns rent moorings with launch service to the village. Repairs are available at several of these facilities as are gas and diesel fuel. Coneys Marine, a yacht brokerage located at the south end of the harbor, manages the mooring field at Gold Star Battalion at the north end of Huntington Harbor, which are reserved for boaters with annual leases.

Knutson Marine (which has been around since 1935) is at the head of the harbor with varied dockage and mooring options and a professional service center.

The long-established Huntington Yacht Club on the opposite side of the harbor is private but welcomes member guests and members of Yachting Club of America on their dock or moorings (swift launch service included) for a modest facility fee. Next is Knutson's Yacht Haven Marina Inc. with limited transient space.

The large and hospitable Willis Marine Center has over 120 slips and 70 moorings for vessels to 60 feet serviced by a launch. They also have a dedicated transient dock that can accommodate vessels to 110 feet with shoreside amenities.

The friendly staff at West Shore Marina welcomes transients on their floating docks and helpful dock attendants will direct you to your slip and help you tie up. Amenities at this large (300-slip) facility include grills and a pool.

The Huntington Harbor municipal floating dock offers one-hour free tie-up in the southeast corner of the harbor. This gives you enough time to visit the West Marine, located approximately one-half block away at 56 New York Ave. (631-427-4210). There is no room for anchoring here due to the proliferation of moorings.

Northport Bay

The eastern arm of Huntington Bay is Northport Bay. It is a body of water with its own complex of harbors, coves, sandy beaches, a neat town on the harbor and a colorful resident shell fishing fleet.

Long Island Lighting Company (LILCO) opened the Northport Power Station in 1967. This is the largest oil-fired electric generating station on the East coast. The four stacks are a famous landmark to boaters on the sound. They can be seen as far away as Connecticut and line up close to magnetic north.

Moving counterclockwise from the west around Northport Bay, the first harbor is Centerport Harbor on the southern shore, separated from Northport Harbor to the east by Little Neck. Duck Island Harbor is to the north, almost directly across from Centerport Harbor. Centerport Harbor is easily the quietest harbor in the area and offers some services for shoal-draft boats. You can explore the coves and marshes by dinghy but it is too narrow to anchor here with confidence.

GOIN' ASHORE

NORTHPORT, NY

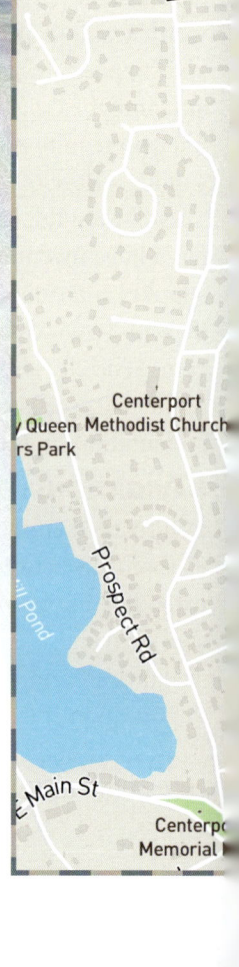

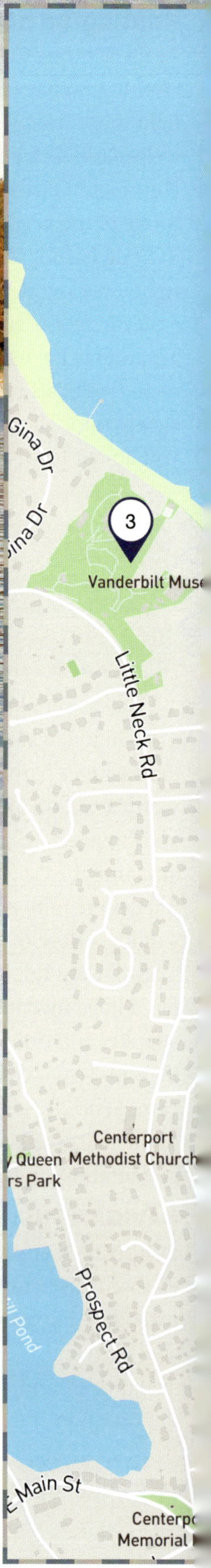

ATTRACTIONS

1. John W. Engeman Theater
Long Island's only year-round professional theater, casting its actors directly from Broadway. Featuring stadium-style seating and state-of-the-art lighting and sound at 250 Main St. (631-261-2900).

2. Northport Historical Society and Museum
Located at 215 Main St. with exhibits and a museum shop (631-757-9859).

3. Vanderbilt Museum and Planetarium
Spanish Revival mansion (built from 1910-1936) located on 43-acre watefront estate (180 Little Neck Rd., 631-854-5579). Home to the state-of-the-art Reichert Planetarium with a 60-foot dome and theater making it the largest astronomical facility on Long Island. Offers programs for all ages based on animal habitats and has large marine and natural-history collections.

SERVICES

4. CityMD Northport Urgent Care
399 Fort Salonga Rd. (631-757-5400)

5. Northport Post Office
240 Main St. (631-261-6941)

6. East Northport Public Library
151 Laurel Ave. (631-261-6930)

7. Northport Village Laundromat
20 Scudder Ave. (631-261-9274)

8. North Shore Veterinary Hospital
835 Fort Salonga Rd. (631-757-0522)

MARINAS

9. Britannia Yachting Center
81 Fort Salonga Rd. (631-261-5600)

10. Centerport Yacht Club
Beach Plum Dr. (631-697-8691)

11. Northport Village Dock
224 Main St. (631-261-7502)

12. Northport Yacht Club
11 Bluff Point Rd. (631-261-7633)

13. Seymour's Boat Yard
63 Bayview Ave. (631-261-6574)

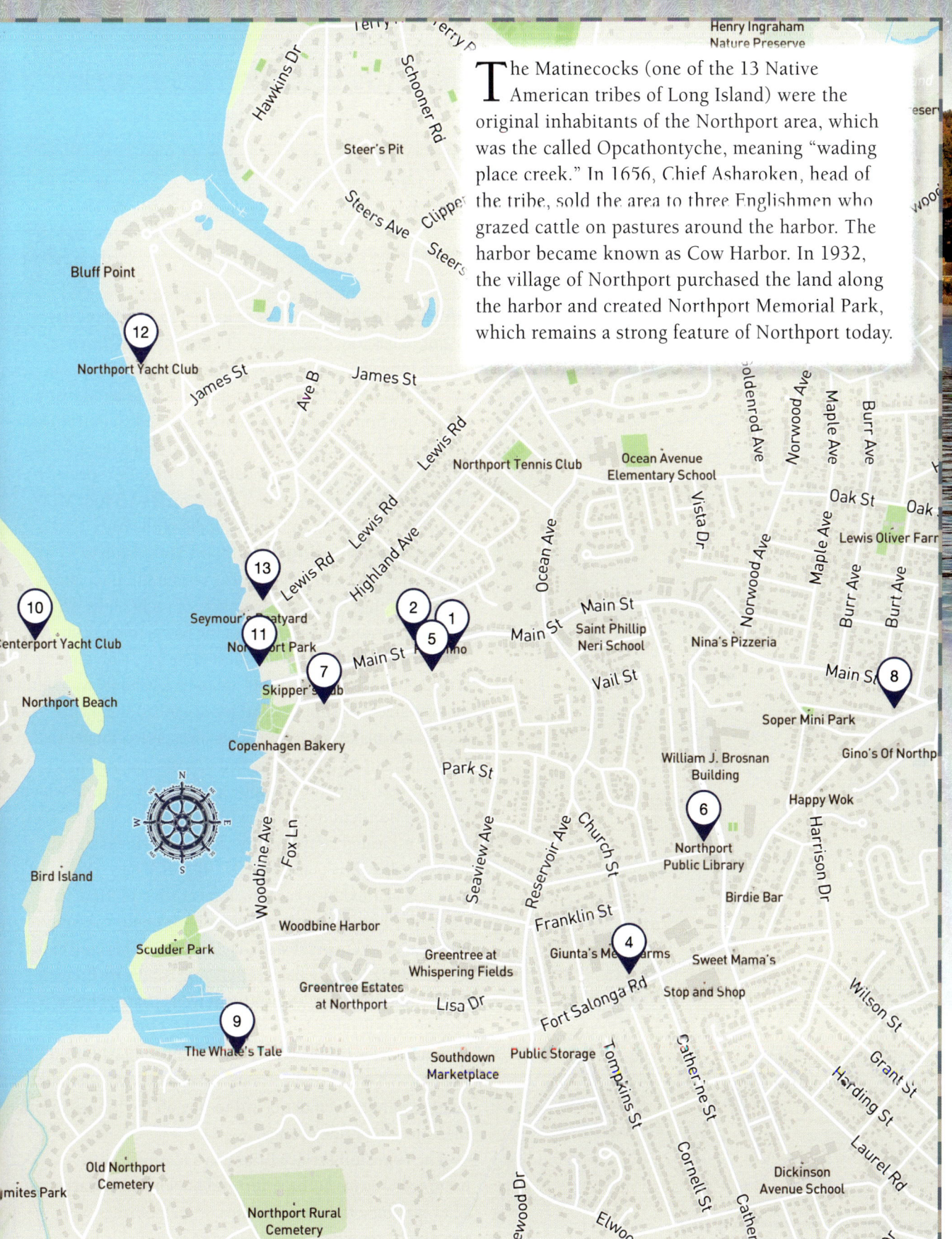

The Matinecocks (one of the 13 Native American tribes of Long Island) were the original inhabitants of the Northport area, which was the called Opcathontyche, meaning "wading place creek." In 1656, Chief Asharoken, head of the tribe, sold the area to three Englishmen who grazed cattle on pastures around the harbor. The harbor became known as Cow Harbor. In 1932, the village of Northport purchased the land along the harbor and created Northport Memorial Park, which remains a strong feature of Northport today.

Northport Harbor, NY

NORTHPORT		Largest Vessel	VHF	Total Slips	Approach/ Dockside Depth	Floating Docks	Gas/ Diesel	Repairs/ Haulout	Min/Max Amps	Pump-Out Station
1. Northport Yacht Club-PRIVATE	(631) 261-7633	50	71		7.0 / 4.0					
2. Centerport Yacht Club-PRIVATE (WiFi)	(631) 697-8691	45	68		8.0 / 6.0				30	
3. Seymour's Boat Yard (WiFi)	(631) 261-6574	60	68	12	8.0 / 7.0	F	GD	RH	30	P
4. Northport Village Dock	(631) 261-7502	120			6.0 / 6.0				30	P
5. Britannia Yachting Center (WiFi)	(631) 261-5600	45	9	310	5.0 / 9.0	F	GD	RH	30 / 100	P

(WiFi) Wireless Internet Access
Visit www.waterwayguide.com for current rates, fuel prices, website addresses and other up-to-the-minute information.
(Information in the table is provided by the facilities.)

Scan here for more details:

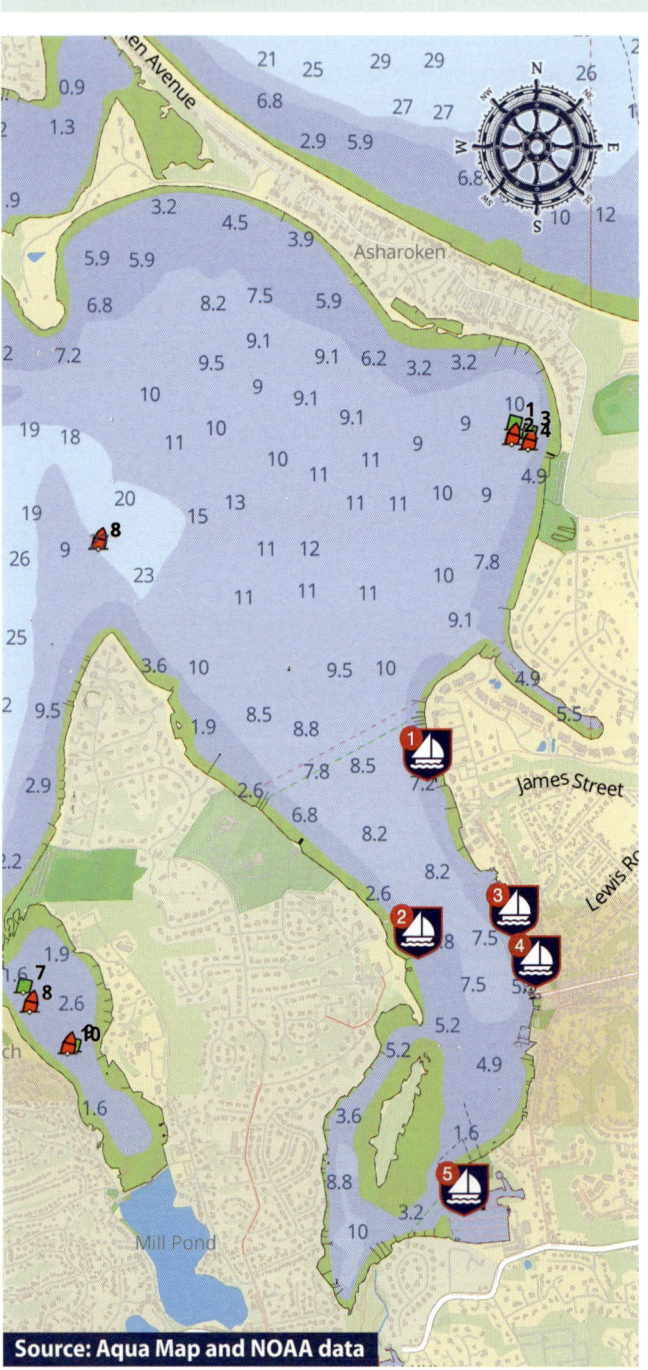

Source: Aqua Map and NOAA data

NAVIGATION: The entrance channel to Northport Bay begins at flashing green buoy "1" just off West Beach, a 1-mile-long spit extending south from Eatons Neck. Do not cut this light too closely or go inside it as a sandbar comes out from the point. The well-marked channel lines up clearly to the east. Mind the navigational aids. A 2-knot current might put you on shoals and rocks. Be especially mindful of red nun buoy "4," which marks a 3-foot MLW spot in what appears to be the middle of the bay.

Dockage/Moorings: Northport Yacht Club is private but maintain a clubhouse, restaurant, pool and guest moorings for use by members of yacht clubs with reciprocal arrangements. Across the bay is the private Centerport Yacht Club with guest moorings with launch service. Note that their docks are to be used only for taking on passengers or supplies and for disembarking. Boats should not make fast to the floats for a period longer than 15 minutes or be left unattended. (No overnight stays.)

Your best bet is the friendly Seymour's Boat Yard, which provides transient moorings with free launch service. This facility is located conveniently close to the town and all it has to offer. It is next to the Northport Village Dock, which is marked by a gazebo on its north end. Here you can take advantage of the free two-hour tie-up (possibly longer on less crowded weekdays), making this convenient for shopping in the village (or visiting Sand City Brewing Co.). After 8:00 p.m. an overnight fee is charged but a portion of it is refunded if you leave by 11:00 p.m. This accommodates people who want to come in just for the evening. No water or electricity is available and you will want to put out a fender board to stay off the pilings during the 7- to 9-foot tide change.

The large, full-service Britannia Yachting Center occupies 17 acres at the south end of Northport Harbor. They welcome transients in slips or on moorings with top-notch amenities. Launch service is available but

Northport Harbor

it is a relatively short run to the dinghy landing just inside the town dock.

Anchorage: Although an anchorage in Northport Harbor is designated on some charts, anchoring is not possible as the whole area is occupied with mooring balls. Anchorage is available, however, just outside the harbor north and northwest of Bluff Point. Holding is good in 9 to 11 feet MLW but you are exposed to north and northwest winds.

The dinghy ride to the nearest landing will require strong arms at the oars or, preferably, a motor. All spaces at the dinghy dock in Northport are rented out to locals. There is a $200 fine for violations. Check with the on-site dockmaster about where to tie up your dinghy.

Eatons Neck & Asharoken

Eatons Neck Basin is a convenient overnight spot for those transiting the sound and not wishing to enter any of the larger harbors. Known locally as Coast Guard Cove, this tiny harbor is home of the local Coast Guard station. The 144-foot white stone lighthouse on Eatons Neck is one of the oldest on Long Island. It was established in 1792 on direct orders from George Washington.

NAVIGATION: Flashing green "1" entrance buoy marks the end of a submerged breakwater at Eatons Neck and must be left to port. At low tide you are likely to see a few clam boats arrive. Note that Coast Guard rescue craft can head out at high speed and throw a heavy wake. Be certain not to anchor in the channel or anywhere that might interfere with their operations.

When heading east from Huntington Bay, give Eatons Neck Basin a wide berth. Depths are as shallow as 4 feet at MLW for almost 1 mile to the northeast.

Anchorage: Price Bend is wide open to the south with holding ground that leaves much to be desired so this is a better lunch or swimming spot than an overnight anchorage. For anchoring with better wind protection, Duck Island Harbor the best but moorings fill the harbor and it's difficult to find a spot to drop the hook. (This is partially due to a local ordinance that forbids anchoring within 50 feet of the shore.) Instead, anchor in 10 feet

America's Waterway Guide Since 1947
Southern
Chesapeake Bay
Great Lakes
Great Lakes
Northern
Mid-Atlantic
Bahamas
Florida Keys
Gulf Coast
Cuba
Skipper Bob Publications
Cruising the Gulf Coast
Marinas Along the Intracoastal Waterway
Bahamas Bound
Cruising America's Great Loop
Cruising the Trent-Severn Waterway, Georgian Bay and North Channel
Anchorages Along the Intracoastal Waterway
Cruising the Rideau & Richelieu Canals
Cruising from Chicago to Mobile
Cruising the New York Canal System
SKIPPER BOB Publications
The Mobile App from Waterway Guide
To St. Augustine
The beach regions running south from Jacksonville are collectively referred to as the "First Coast" because this is the location of Florida's first European settlements. It vigorously competes with the Gold Coast, the Sun Coast and the Treasure Coast for developer and tourist dollars. The area begins a parade of shoreside communities
Boating Destinations
Download on the App Store
GET IT ON Google Play
No Signal? No Problem!
DOWNLOAD CONTENT
The Explorer web app
waterwayguide.com
WATERWAY GUIDE MEDIA
Scan to subscribe now at www.waterwayguide.com

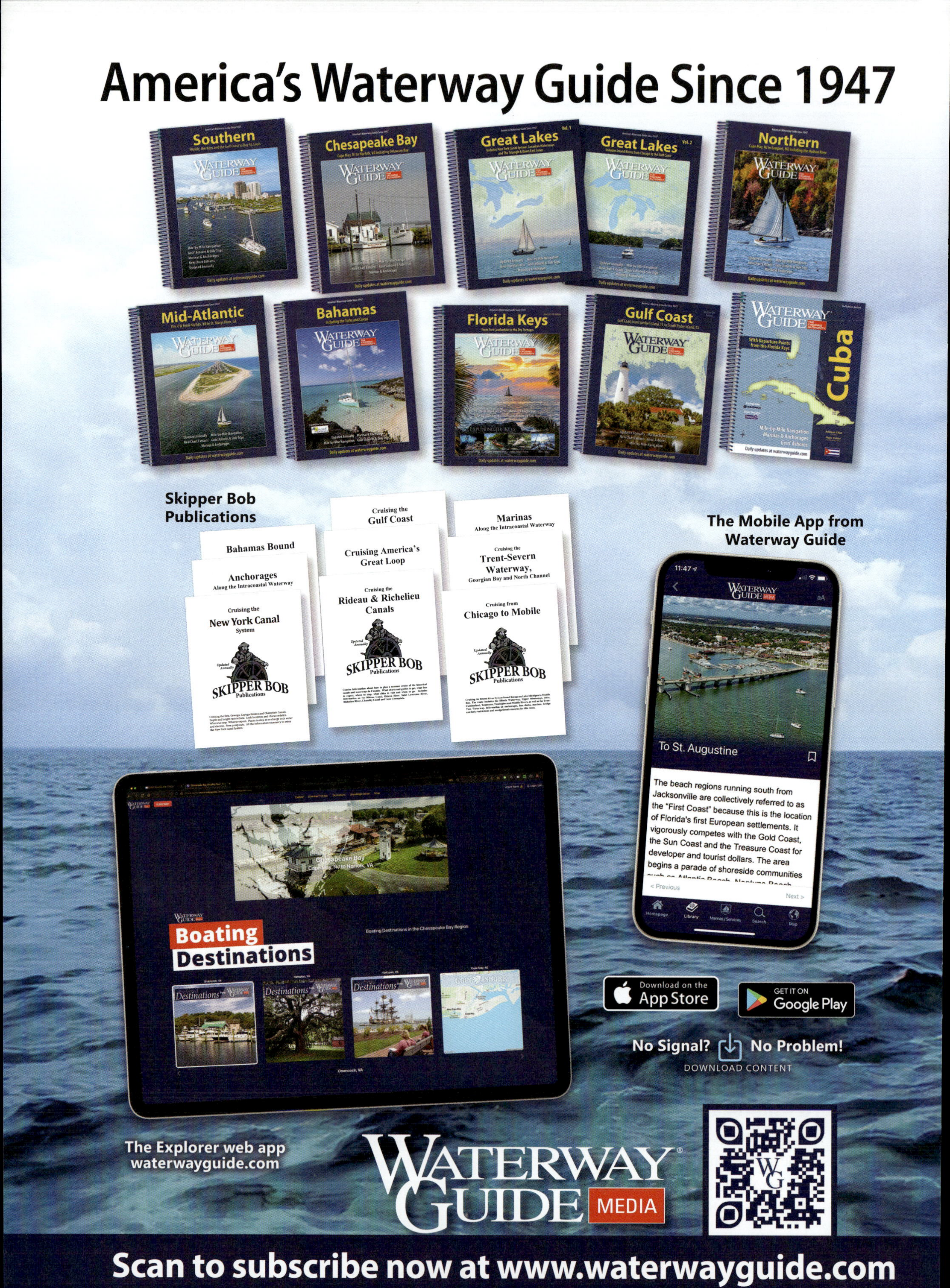

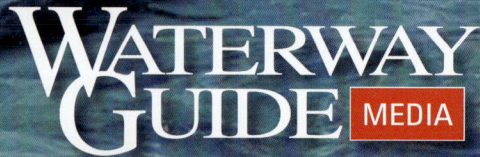

Smithtown Bay, NY

STONY BROOK		Largest Vessel	VHF	Total Slips	Approach/ Dockside Depth	Floating Docks	Gas/ Diesel	Repairs/ Haulout	Min/Max Amps	Pump-Out Station
1. Stony Brook Yacht Club-PRIVATE	(631) 751-9873	54	9	187	6.0 / 8.0				30	

WiFi) Wireless Internet Access

Visit www.waterwayguide.com for current rates, fuel prices, website addresses and other up-to-the-minute information. (Information in the table is provided by the facilities.)

Scan here for more details:

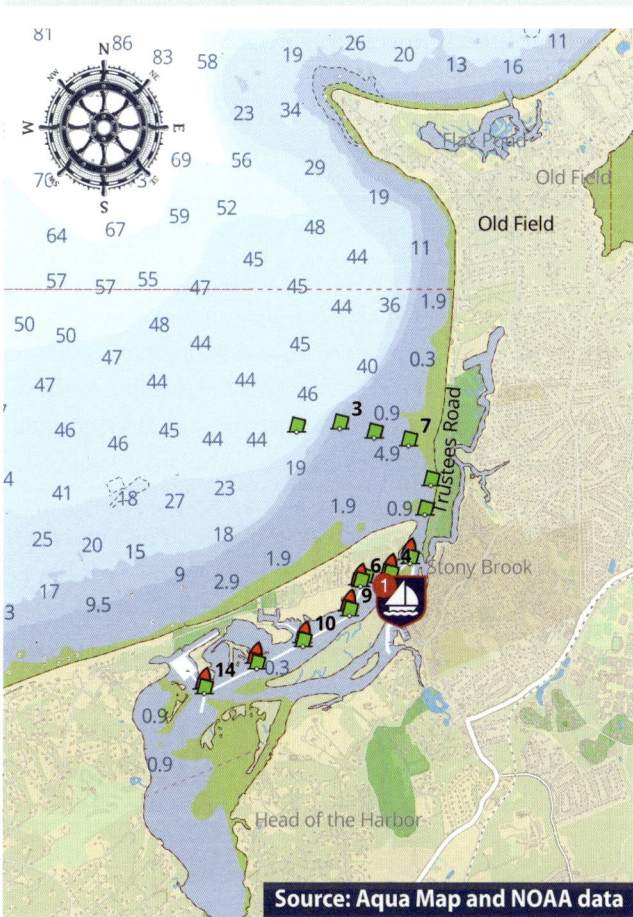

Source: Aqua Map and NOAA data

MLW with good holding in Duck Island Entrance or Asharoken Bight to the east in 7- to 9-foot MLW depths.

Eatons Neck Basin on the north end of Eatons Neck is strictly an anchorage with no amenities. The cove is exempt from the local ordinance against anchoring within 50 feet of shore. Good depths run right up to the western shore but depths become shallower and anchoring spots fewer east of the channel. Going ashore is not permitted.

NOTE: Rafting is not permitted in the town of Asharoken, which includes Asharoken Bight, Price Bend and Eatons Neck Basin. The "no rafting" law is strictly enforced by the local marine police. Local ordinances also forbid anchoring within 50 feet of the shore and require holding tanks or self-contained heads.

■ SMITHTOWN BAY TO MATTITUCK INLET

Stony Brook

Another of Long Island's appealing towns, Stony Brook lies in the southeastern corner of Smithtown Bay south of Crane Neck Point. While the harbor is crowded and difficult to enter, it is a rewarding port of call. The Stony Brook area dates back to Revolutionary times when George Washington traveled the Heritage Trail (now SR 25A). While the British Army provisioned from Stony Brook's gristmill, Washington's spy ring concurrently operated from the town.

Stony Brook Village Center is one of the first planned business centers. The Colonial-style center now houses numerous quaint shops and restaurants. The historic Stony Brook Grist Mill (circa 1751), where millers are still grinding grain, is a 5-minute walk from the Village Center and is open for tours Wednesday through Sunday, June through August (631-751-2244 or 631-689-3238). The mechanical eagle that flaps its wings on the hour while perched atop the Stony Brook Post Office (129 Main St.) is a "must see."

NAVIGATION: Most cruising boats coming from Northport Bay cut straight across the broad (about 10 miles wide) Smithtown Bay by picking up green can buoy "13" off Eatons Neck and running 100° magnetic to green gong buoy "11A" off Old Field Point (northwest of Port Jefferson), rather than taking the more direct route through Long Island Sound. When you are bucking a foul current, the trip closer to the beach and bluff-lined shore is easier and faster due to a weaker current speed.

The privately marked and maintained entrance channel leads east from the charted flashing green buoy "1." Just short of the shoreline of West Meadow Beach, the channel turns south to parallel the beach.

Strong currents speed through the narrow opening between West Meadow Beach and Long Beach, calling for cautious navigation. Inside Porpoise Cove leads southwest to Stony Brook. If your boat has a draft of greater then 2 feet, use caution when entering Smithtown Bay and Porpoise Channel. Entering at mid-high tide is recommended.

Dockage/Moorings: Stony Brook Yacht Club is a private club and has limited transient docking for boaters requiring daily or overnight docking (with a reservation). There is a strong current so care must be taken when maneuvering. There is also a small town dinghy dock available for no more than 3-hour tie-ups.

Port Jefferson

Port Jefferson, a favorite stop of cruising boats, is a deep, 2-mile-long harbor. If you are traveling east, it is the last real harbor until Mattituck some 26 miles farther on. Port Jefferson is a justly popular harbor. The village is located on the harbor and has boating amenities and beaches where you can swim and picnic.

The hilly streets in town leading to the harbor are bursting with museums, historic homes, shops, restaurants and varied architectural styles. You can take the railroad to New York City, a ferry to Bridgeport, CT, or make convenient connections by air via MacArthur Airport at Islip. Most amenities including the library and Post Office are situated on Main and East Main Streets, which run south from the waterfront.

Located on the west side of Port Jefferson Harbor, the remote little 17th-century town of Setauket offers a fascinating side trip for dinghies or small, shoal-draft boats. Setauket has a small, private marina at the head of the inlet surrounded by well-kept, Colonial-style homes.

NAVIGATION: Port Jefferson is best approached from the red and white sea buoy "PJ" Morse (A), located about 1 mile northwest of the entrance to the harbor. Coming from Connecticut, the 100-foot-high bluff of Mount Misery Point offers a prominent landmark. Once inside the entrance buoys head for the church spire in the center of town. You can see it situated between the large hospital to the east and the Port Jefferson power plant stacks to the west.

The narrow cut between Mount Misery Point and the lighted end ("flashing red "2A") of Old Field Beach can be

Smithtown Bay, NY

PORT JEFFERSON HARBOR		Largest Vessel	VHF	Total Slips	Approach/ Dockside Depth	Floating Docks	Gas/ Diesel	Repairs/ Haulout	Min/Max Amps	Pump-Out Station
1. Port Jefferson Launch Service Moorings					/					
2. Port Jefferson Yacht Club **WiFi**	(631) 473-9650	60	68		12.0 / 6.0	F			30	P
3. TPG Marinas Danfords **WiFi**	(631) 928-5200	200	9	75	25.0 / 15.0	F	GD		30 / 100	P
4. Port Jefferson Marina **WiFi**	(631) 331-3567	50	16	120	20.0 /			R	30 / 50	P
5. Murphy's Marine Service	(631) 796-4462	75	68		/					

WiFi Wireless Internet Access
Visit www.waterwayguide.com for current rates, fuel prices, website addresses and other up-to-the-minute information.
(Information in the table is provided by the facilities.)

Scan here for more details:

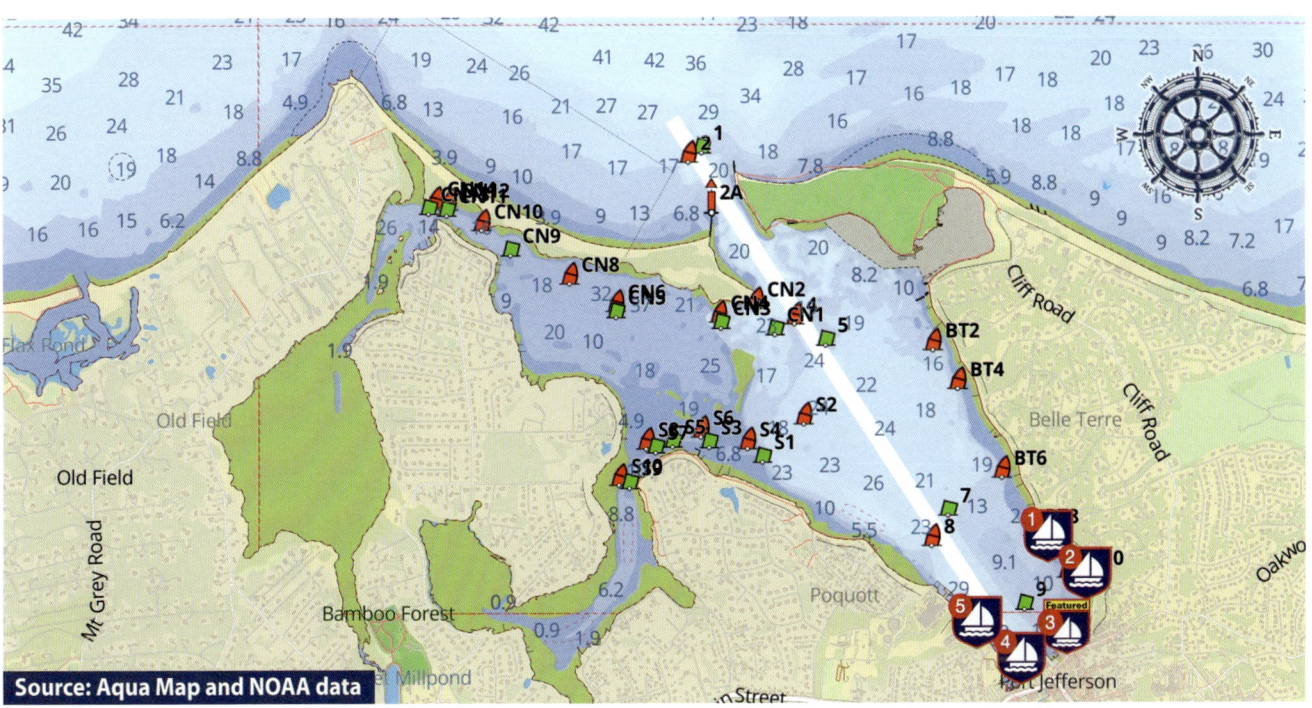

Source: Aqua Map and NOAA data

crowded with traffic, and when wind and tide are opposed it can be quite turbulent. Currents average 2.5 knots on the flood and 2 knots on the ebb. Be alert for barge and ferry traffic but otherwise there are few obstructions or dangers on the bay.

Stretching north from the head of the harbor below the high-banked eastern shore, much of Port Jefferson's recreational fleet lies tethered at moorings. The well-marked harbor channel leads directly to a hub centering on the municipal marina, ferry dock and the unmistakable power station.

Keep clear of this area to allow for the passage of commercial traffic and be aware of the frequent, swift-traveling car-carrying ferries, which back toward the power station on each return to Bridgeport. Be watchful and always be prepared to give way to the ferries.

The entrance to the Setauket Harbor is suitable for a 5-foot draft but the harbor is fully occupied with mooring balls and anchoring is not possible. There is a good dinghy dock adjacent to the private marina, which will allow you to tie up. The village center is about 1.5 mile away with a shopping center with cafés, a laundry and limited shopping.

Dockage/Moorings: Reservations for moorings managed by Port Jefferson Launch Service are made through Dockwa. Contact the launch service via VHF Channel 68 to get a ride to the harbormaster building where there are shower and laundry facilities available between 8:00 a.m. to 5:00 p.m. Water is available at the launch dock and a self-serve pump-out is available at no charge. Port Jefferson Yacht Club, also maintains guest moorings and has slips for overnight and day visitors.

Smithtown Bay, NY

MOUNT SINAI		Largest Vessel	VHF	Total Slips	Approach/ Dockside Depth	Floating Docks	Gas/ Diesel	Repairs/ Haulout	Min/Max Amps	Pump-Out Station
1. Ralph's Fishing Station & Marina	(631) 473-6655	50	67	50	15.0 / 15.0	F	GD	RH	30	
2. Mt. Sinai Yacht Club-PRIVATE	(631) 473-2993	45	9	99	17.0 / 12.0	F	GD		30 / 50	P

WiFi Wireless Internet Access
Visit www.waterwayguide.com for current rates, fuel prices, website addresses and other up-to-the-minute information.
(Information in the table is provided by the facilities.)

Scan here for more details:

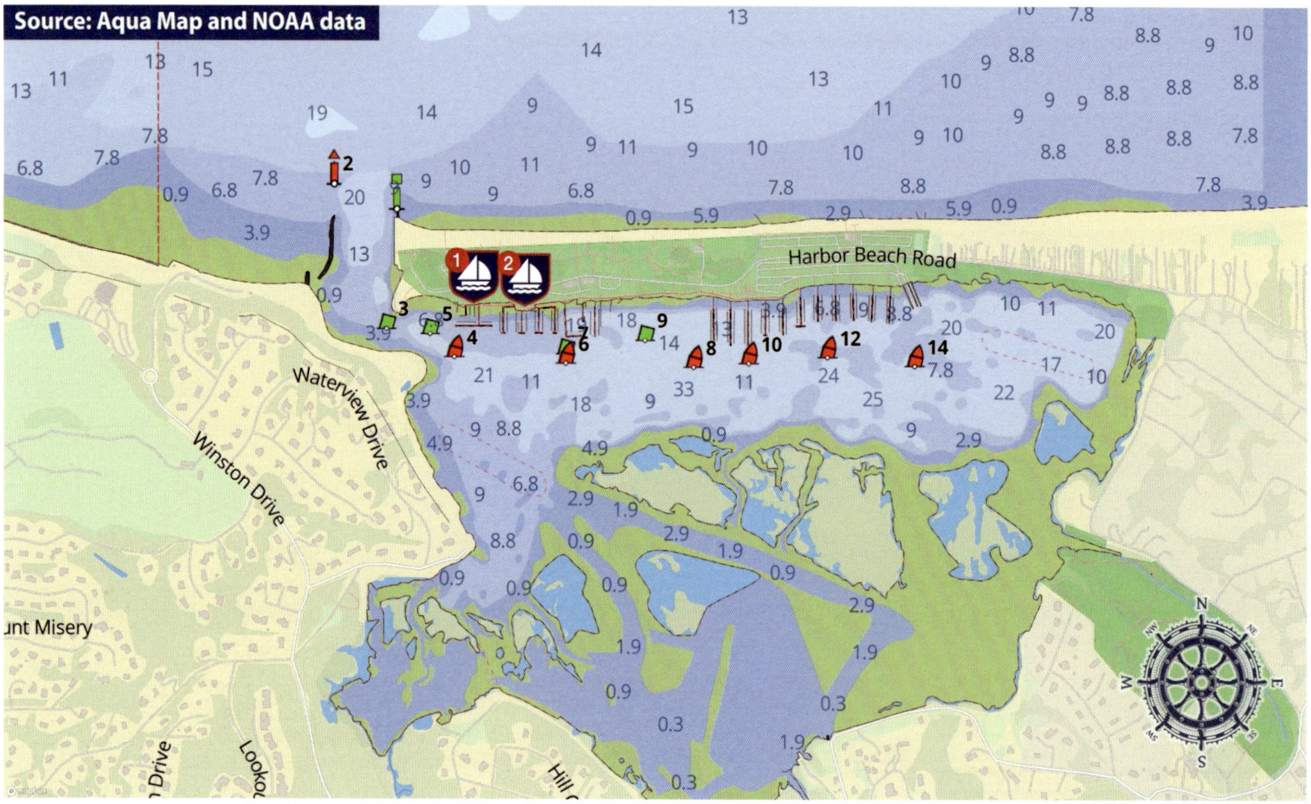

Source: Aqua Map and NOAA data

Reservations are required. It is just a short walk to the village activities, parks, shops and restaurants.

TPG Marinas Danfords just east of the ferry dock offers the protection of its wooden sea barrier and can accommodate vessels up to 200 feet in deep water (15-foot MLW) slips on floating docks. This all-transient facility also has an on-site restaurant and a spa. This is a great place to get off the boat for the night or meet up with new crew, family and friends.

The municipal Port Jefferson Marina west of the ferry landing may have transient space available on an hourly or daily basis. The marina monitors VHF Channel 09.

Murphy's Marine Service has transient moorings (bright red balls) to 75 feet and provides launch service to and from the shore. Transient facilities include bathroom, showers and coin-operated washers and dryers.

Anchorage: North of the main mooring field in Port Jefferson Harbor there is good holding and room for anchorage within a reasonable distance from shore. Call "Port Jefferson Launch" on VHF Channel 68 or you can dinghy to TPG Marinas Danfords, which has a 10-foot limit and is available for a fee.

Just to the east of the harbor entrance, Mt. Misery Cove (locally known as the Sand Pit or Pirate's Cove) is almost completely occupied by mooring balls, and room for anchorage is extremely limited. You may anchor outside the cove in at least 9-foot MLW depths but it is subject to ferry wakes. In short, there are better places to anchor.

To the west of the main channel just inside the harbor entrance, a seasonally maintained channel leads to the cove behind Old Field Beach and Conscience Bay. Several shallow spots (3- to 6-foot MLW mounds) require deep-draft vessels proceed with some care at less than half-tide.

Once inside, there are numerous private moorings here but there's still room to anchor. This is a secure and quiet anchorage with depths ranging from 10 to 14 feet MLW.

Mount Sinai Harbor

After leaving Port Jefferson, travel east for about 3 miles beyond high Mount Misery to Mount Sinai Harbor. Once an uncharted marshy gunkhole inhabited mainly by ducks and mosquitoes, the Mount Sinai Harbor was dredged and converted to a boat-packed, well-protected port with good anchorages, a fine beach (dedicated to the residents of the village of Brookhaven) and pleasant surroundings. Much of the extensive marsh area is set aside as a nature reserve and is an important nesting area for a number of birds. Ralph's Fishing Station & Marina rents sturdy two-seat kayaks for explorations of the tidal estuary.

NAVIGATION: Mount Sinai Harbor is clearly marked, first by the red Mount Sinai Harbor Breakwater Light "2," then by a private unnumbered flashing green light at the end of the east breakwater, and a flashing red light to the west. The harbor entrance hooks to port on entry but is wide enough for comfortable ingress with at least 12-foot MLW depths throughout the harbor's well-marked main channel. Locals advise that when entering the harbor, you should give a wide berth to the sandy beach (easily visible to port inside the entry jetties) when making the left turn into the harbor mooring area. The shoal extending from the beach into the channel is not marked.

Dockage/Moorings: A marina and yacht club host the immense number of boats here. When you enter the harbor, the fuel dock and facilities of Ralph's Fishing Station & Marina are immediately evident to port. They maintain transient moorings (with launch service) and offer full marine services. This is a well-protected location and is within walking distance to a beach. There is no room for anchoring here due to the proliferation of moorings. Immediately past Ralph's, the friendly Mt. Sinai Yacht Club welcomes those visiting from reciprocal clubs on their moorings for a modest facility fee.

Mattituck Inlet

The 40 miles between Mount Sinai and Plum Gut can be long ones for slow boats. Mattituck Inlet is the only stopover between the two. Mattituck is a well-protected, quiet, relaxed village typical of eastern Long Island. The entry into Mattituck Creek can be very challenging when the winds are out of the north and the water depth is a challenge at low tide. The 2-mile-long creek is winding at first then straightens with sand, marshes, trees and many lovely houses flanking its banks.

The Mattituck Creek was dammed in 1812 and a tidal gristmill turned both night and day. The old mill can still be seen on your right

Jetty at Mattituck Inlet

Mattituck Inlet, NY

MATTITUCK CREEK		Largest Vessel	VHF	Total Slips	Approach/ Dockside Depth	Floating Docks	Gas/ Diesel	Repairs/ Haulout	Min/Max Amps	Pump-Out Station
1. Strong's Yacht Center	(631) 298-4480	110		45	/ 10.0	F	GD	RH	30 / 50	
2. Strong's Water Club and Marina **WiFi**	(631) 298-4739	75	9	135	9.0 / 7.0	F	GD	RH	30 / 50	

WiFi Wireless Internet Access
Visit www.waterwayguide.com for current rates, fuel prices, website addresses and other up-to-the-minute information.
(Information in the table is provided by the facilities.)

Scan here for more details:

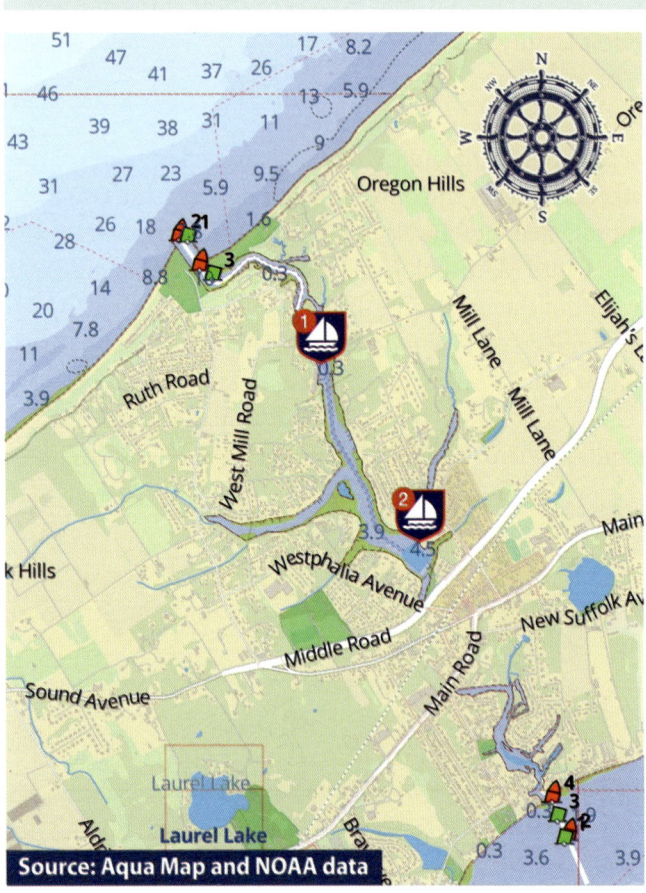

Source: Aqua Map and NOAA data

about one-third of the way into the creek. Kayaking is a popular activity in the protected waters of the Mattituck Inlet, which is home to many wading birds. It also boasts a large population of osprey nests on many of the daybeacons and the platforms set up for them.

Some of the famous Long Island vineyards in the area offer retail opportunities, tours and wine tastings. There are many "pour & pedal" tours during which you bike to from one vineyard to another throughout the course of a day. Routes, lengths and costs vary.

NAVIGATION: It is difficult to see the entry to Mattituck Inlet from offshore but the dredged and jettied channel creates a deep gap in the shoreline bluffs. The best approach is to take a compass course due south from green gong buoy "3A," 1 mile north of

the entrance, and then watch for flashing white "MI" at the end of the western jetty. The entrance channel is well marked and carries 6-foot MLW depths. If your draft is even close to 6 feet, enter on a rising tide.

A heavy sea can build up in the entrance in northerly winds blowing against an ebbing current. Once inside, the inlet and past the sharp turn to port, keep in mid-channel but favor the outside edge when the creek turns to avoid shoaling on the inside of the bends. Tidal range is more than 5 feet and currents run as much as 3 knots. Currents diminish as you travel up the creek and depths decrease somewhat.

The approach and creek at the head of the creek look almost impossible to negotiate, but it is wide enough all the way with 7 feet MLW. In the upper creek observe the very small, privately maintained channel buoys, which can appear to be fishing floats.

Dockage/Moorings: Strong's Yacht Center is a working boatyard staffed by experienced technicians and craftsmen. They also maintain some transient space for vessels to 110 feet. This location is extremely sheltered from wind and waves and has an accommodating staff and good dock service.

Strong's Water Club and Marina is at the head of the creek. This a 9-acre destination marina with transient slips to 75 feet and resort-style amenities. The town of Mattituck is a 10-minute walk away. A full-size grocery store is southwest on Hwy. 25, approximately 10 to 12 long blocks (with a bike path/sidewalk).

Anchorage: The Mattituck anchorage at the Federal Basin off Strong's Water Club and Marina is totally protected but can get very crowded on summer weekends. The holding is fair (5 to 7 feet MLW in mud) but the area offers all-around protection. Great Peconic Bay is only 1 mile overland to the south from this point. There is a town dinghy dock at the end of the basin gives access to Mattituck and famous Love Lane, a 5-minute walk.

Montauk

Three Mile Harbor

Atlantic Ocean

Pages 316-321

Pages 326-344

Gardiners Bay

Orient Point

Shelter Island

Pages 321-323

Sag Harbor

Plum Cut

Greenport

Little Peconic Bay

Southold-Bay

Long Island Sound

Great Peconic Bay

Shinnecock Canal

Pages 323-326

Riverhead

■ NORTH FORK: PLUM GUT TO SOUTHOLD BAY

Some of the finest cruising grounds can be found within the Twin Forks of Long Island, NY. The two ends of Long Island surround Great Peconic Bay and Gardiner's Bay and are known as the North and the South Forks. The eastern end of Long Island splits like two flukes of a fish tail. The deep cleft begins at the town of Riverhead. Known as the Twin Forks, the Forks or sometimes the Fish Tail, this area comprises deep bays, large islands and big jutting peninsulas that create miles of attractive cruising territory with good harbors and generally deep water. The north fork runs about 30 miles from Riverhead to Orient Point, and the south fork, 40 miles long, stretches from Riverhead to Montauk Point.

Gardiners Bay, situated below Plum Gut and inside of Orient Point, is separated from Block Island Sound and the open ocean by Gardiners Island. Gardiners Bay is the entrance to Shelter Island Sound, the Peconic Bays and an intriguing assortment of small bodies of water extending west to Riverhead. Big, irregularly shaped Shelter Island sits in the middle and nearly joins the North and South Forks.

About 8 miles east of Riverhead on the south fork, the Shinnecock Canal connects Great Peconic Bay with Shinnecock Bay and, through Shinnecock Inlet, the Atlantic Ocean.

From Gardiners Bay through Little Peconic Bay, the water depths are about 20 feet MLW in the main channels and 10 feet MLW or more through Great Peconic Bay. Project depths to the head of navigation at Riverhead are 6 feet MLW. Currents run swiftly in narrow channels but normally do not exceed 2 knots.

Marinas and anchorages are plentiful and dredging has opened many once-inaccessible side creeks and small bays to deeper draft boats. (Dredged channels have a habit of silting in so verify depths locally.)

Orient Point to Gardiners Bay

Orient Point is an excellent place to recapture the unhurried pace of what once typified small town America. Quaint, small houses date back to the 1700s and have seen Indian raids as well as a visit from George Washington. Huge exotic trees and well-loved lawns and gardens adorn the tranquil streets.

Orient Beach State Park, located at the east end of North Country Rd., offers 10 miles of beaches ideal for shelling, bird watching and nature study. Walking and shelling along the north side of Long Beach Point is a special treat. The "beach" is an expansive strand of colorful, smooth and rounded pebbles, intermixed with countless thousands of rosehips, yellow poppies and edible beach peas.

Plum Gut runs between Orient Point and Plum Island and guides you into Gardiners Bay. About 1 mile in, you will see the major docks of Orient by the Sea Marina on the western shore. The Cross Sound Ferry (New London to Orient Point) ties up here along with boats ferrying workers to the federal Plum Island Animal Disease Laboratory on Plum Island (closed to the public).

Plum Gut is one of three eastern exits from Long Island Sound and is the usual route to ports in Gardiners Bay, the inner Forks (including the Peconic Bays) and Montauk. Those with a love of fishing are advised to drop a trolling lure overboard (if licensed) at any opportunity because you are in some of the richest striped bass and bluefish grounds on earth.

NAVIGATION: Boats bound for Block Island or other New England ports usually exit Long Island Sound via The Race, off the southwestern tip of Fishers Island.

Orient Point Lighthouse

The alternative, Plum Gut, is a deep, narrow passage (less than 0.75-mile wide and 1-mile long) that acts as a funnel through which the sea surges with tremendous force during maximum current. The advantage of this route over The Race is you will be in any adverse conditions for less time.

Normal velocities are 3.5 knots on the flood and more than 4 knots on the ebb but currents can easily top 5 knots. Tidal rips are the norm and passage can be turbulent when wind and current oppose. Study the tide and current tables and try to plan your passage (whether east or west) when a fair current or slack water are expected.

Just north of Long Beach Point, Orient Harbor is open to the southwest. The village of Orient is located on its northeastern shore. Do not cut between flashing red bell buoy "2" and the restored Long Beach Bar Light at the west end of Long Beach. Instead, follow the channel between flashing red bell buoy "2" and green can "3," keeping the area immediately southwest of the lighthouse at a respectful distance. This will prevent an encounter with the shoals that creep southward.

Take care in navigating this area to avoid the additional floating nets that are sometimes stationed here. This is a relatively popular place on weekends, yet the feeling is remote and more reminiscent of Maine than Long Island.

Dockage/Moorings: Duryea's Orient Point on the south side of Orient Point is a restaurant and beach club with a market and boutique. There are slips for customers only on a first-come, first-served basis (no overnight dockage) or they may have a mooring for you. They offer few cruiser amenities but are friendly and have a great tiki bar.

Anchorage: The closest anchorage is to the southwest of Orient Point at Orient Beach State Park with good fishing and swimming. This is a fair-weather open roadstead anchorage with deep water (almost to the beach) and excellent holding in sand.

During settled weather, good anchorage can also be found in 10-foot to 20-foot MLW depths within easy reach of the shore along the north side of Long Beach Point near the two working fish weirs.

If you work your way east above the weir closest to the point, you will notice a decided drop-off from the trough-like 8- to 10-foot MLW depths paralleling the shore. Holding is excellent in the deeper trough, while a secure set in the surrounding shallower waters is typically thwarted by extensive areas of hard-packed stones. (You will encounter millions more of these on the stony beach.)

Even though Orient Harbor is open to prevailing southwesterly winds, many skippers make it their jumping-off point for Montauk or Block Island. The harbor can be crowded with sportfishers in the fall. If you can find a spot to drop the hook, you will have 7 to 20 feet MLW with good holding in mud. You can dinghy farther east to a dock that gives access to the State Park.

Greenport

Greenport, settled in 1682, remains encircled by bucolic landscapes and is a low-key and peaceful seaside village. Because of its deep and protected harbor, Greenport became a major whaling port between 1795 and 1859 when more than 20 whaling ships berthed here. The town was also a very busy shipbuilding center.

By the mid-1800s the menhaden fishing industry employed thousands of people. During the first half of the 20th century, Greenport became a huge oystering center. When the oyster industry began to shrink, Greenport turned to tourism and became a destination for global visitors. Greenport is still the annual site of a tall-ship rendezvous but now they come for fun rather than commerce.

NAVIGATION: The town of Greenport is almost 8 nm south-southwest of Orient Point across the 1-mile wide pass north of Shelter Island. Greenport Harbor is easily reached from Shelter Island Sound via a deep, well-marked channel. Flashing red 19-foot "8A" at the south end of the breakwater marks the harbor entrance. Landmarks include a water tank, white church spire and, at night, a television tower with a fixed red light.

Stirling Basin (known locally as Stirling Harbor) is the primary recreational boating center. The entrance is along the buoyed channel leading northwest from the outer harbor and roughly parallels the jetty. Favor the west shore on entry to avoid the shoal extending southwest of Youngs Point. West of the narrow cut upon entry into the nearly landlocked basin, you can see an abstract stone monument honoring sailors lost at sea. The red nun just west of the monument marks the channel's edge.

Shelter Island Sound, NY

ORIENT POINT		Largest Vessel	VHF	Total Slips	Approach/ Dockside Depth	Floating Docks	Gas/ Diesel	Repairs/ Haulout	Min/Max Amps	Pump-Out Station
1. Duryea's Orient Point (WiFi)	(631) 323-2424	100			6.0 / 10.0	F	GD	R		
GREENPORT										
2. Safe Harbor Greenport (WiFi)	(631) 477-9594	60	9	200	7.0 / 8.0	F		RH	30 / 50	P
3. Safe Harbor Stirling (WiFi)	(631) 477-0828	100	9	185	12.0 / 7.0	F	GD	RH	30 / 50	P
4. Townsend Manor Marina (WiFi)	(631) 477-2000	60	9	50	8.0 / 7.0	F			30 / 50	
5. Greenport Yacht and Ship Co.	(631) 477-2277	120		6	20.0 / 12.0			R	30	
6. Preston's Marine Supply and Docks	(631) 477-1990	65		10	20.0 / 8.0					
7. Claudio's Marina, Restaurant and Clam Bar (WiFi)	(631) 477-0355	240	9	35	45.0 / 15.0			H	30 / 100	
8. Mitchell Park Marina (WiFi)	(631) 477-2200	250	11	60	45.0 / 15.0	F			30 / 100	P
SOUTHOLD										
9. Brick Cove Marina (WiFi)	(631) 477-0830	48	16	140	6.0 / 6.0	F		RH	30 / 50	P
10. Peconic Bay Marine Basin - PRIVATE (WiFi)	(631) 407-5197	60		50	/	F				
11. Port of Egypt Marine (WiFi)	(631) 765-2445	40		150	5.0 / 5.0		GD	RH	30	P
SHELTER ISLAND										
12. Shelter Island Yacht Club-PRIVATE (WiFi)	(631) 749-0888	75	74		10.0 / 7.0					
13. Piccozzi's Dering Harbor Marina (WiFi)	(631) 749-0045	160	16	35	12.0 / 12.0		GD		15 / 100	P
14. The Pridwin Hotel & Cottages	(631) 749-0476	40		5	5.0 / 4.0				30	
15. The Island Boatyard and Marina (WiFi)	(631) 749-3333	60	9	80	6.0 / 6.0	F	GD	RH	30 / 50	P
16. Coecles Harbor Marina & Boatyard (WiFi)	(631) 749-0700	60	9	40	6.0 / 6.0	F	D	RH	30 / 50	P

(WiFi) Wireless Internet Access
Visit www.waterwayguide.com for current rates, fuel prices, website addresses and other up-to-the-minute information.
(Information in the table is provided by the facilities.)

Scan here for more details:

Dockage/Moorings: Two Safe Harbor facilities are in the harbor. Superior amenities and a distinguished yacht yard are hallmarks of Safe Harbor Greenport. This facility is popular with locals and offers full-service quality repair service and a substantial parts department plus transient dockage.

To the north is Safe Harbor Stirling, also with excellent amenities that make it a cruising destination for boating clubs as well as individual cruisers. Immaculate landscaping, poolside cabanas and community picnic areas are among the offerings. There is usually space available except for on the busiest weekends. The marina provides complimentary shuttle service to and from town, several miles distant by road from this side of the harbor and may be the best hurricane hole you will ever find anywhere.

Across the basin northwest from the basin entrance is the quiet and well-kept Townsend Manor Marina with plenty of space for transient vessels to 60 feet (with a 25-foot minimum charge). They offer resort amenities including an extra-large pool, modern showers/ restrooms and an easy walk to town. They also have an on-site hotel, on-site restaurant and a sunken bar with stunning water views.

Outside Stirling Basin in Greenport's harbor proper there are additional docking possibilities ranging from a full-service boat yard (Greenport Yacht and Ship Co.) to a municipal marina (Mitchell Park Marina) with solid floating docks protected by an extensive wave suppression system.

In addition to slips to 65 feet, Preston's Marine Supply and Docks is a chandlery with nautical gifts, decor and marine supplies. They have been in the same buildings in Greenport Harbor for over 125 years serving boats and their crews.

Next door (look for the blue roof) is Claudio's Marina, Restaurant and Clam Bar with free 2-hour dockage for diners and some overnight space. Space is limited and reservations are recommended. Upon arrival, approach the front of the wharves and stand by for further instruction. This area is not so well protected so you will want to rig fender boards for protection against wakes that bounce along unprotected bulkheads.

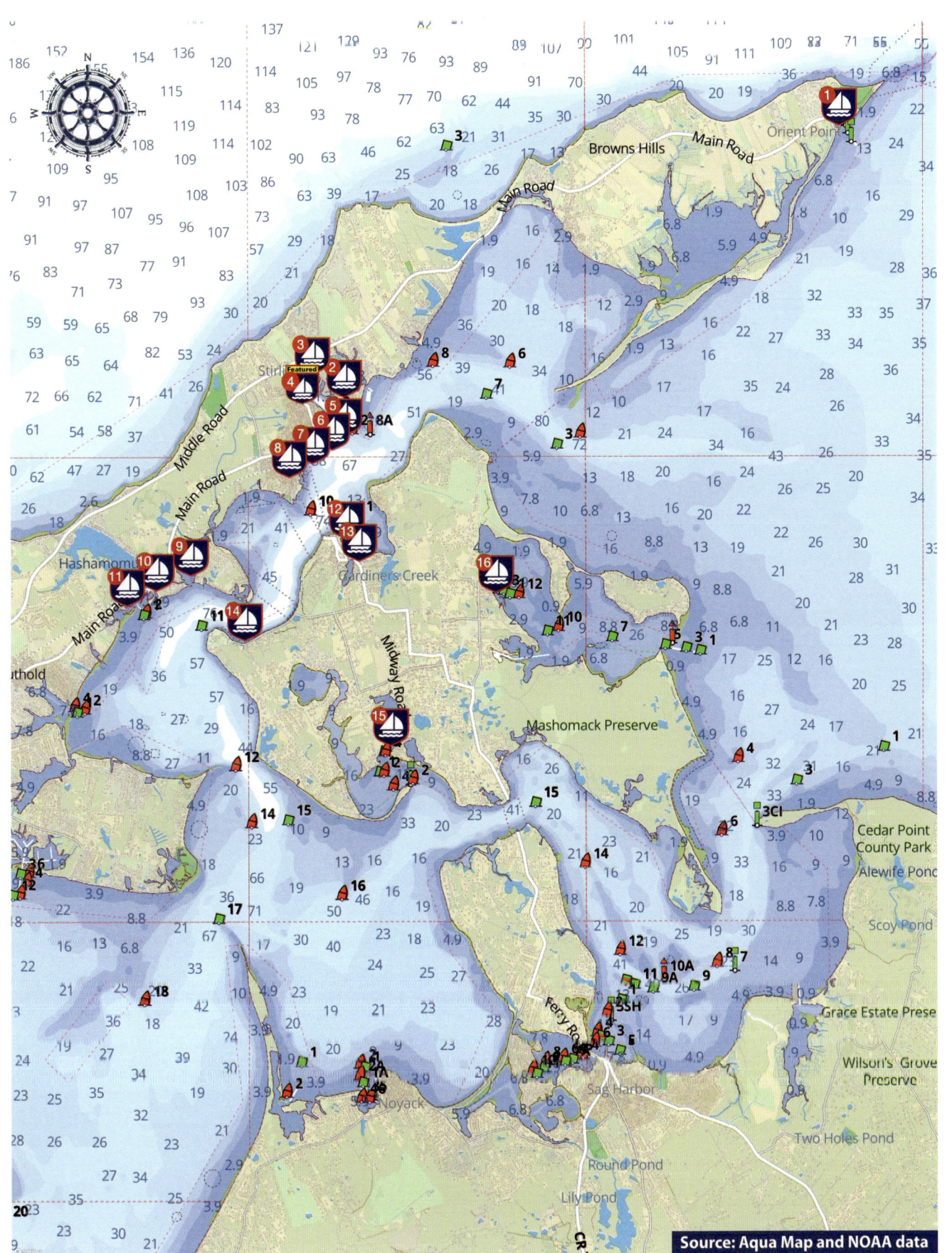

Youngs Point

TOWNSEND MANOR MARINA

Greenport

TOWNSEND MANOR MARINA

For the cruising yachtsman, Townsend Manor has one of the finest marinas in Eastern Long Island. Nestled in the protected waters of the secluded Stirling Basin, yet just a short walk from Greenport's stories and activities, are deep-water slips for transient yachts up to 60 feet and complete resort facilities for living aboard or ashore.

- 40 slips with electric & water (25 floating)
- 31-room Inn with guest suites
- Olympic swimming pool with tiki bar
- Onsite restaurant & sunken bar
- Laundry room, BBQ area
- Close to town and winery

Anchorage: You can anchor in at least 8 feet MLW inside the jetty at Greenport Harbor (allowing ample room for traffic in the marked channel to Stirling Basin) but this is a restless spot offering scant protection. Better anchorage is possible in Gull Pond/Cleaves Point located east of the breakwater. This enclosed basin has 6 to 7 feet MLW with good holding in mud and all-around protection. Greenport Town Dock can provide dinghy access to shore.

Southold Bay

Southwest of Greenport, Southold Bay has a small harbor and an attractive village. Mill Creek, the entrance to Hashamomuck Pond, has a few marinas that welcome cruising boats. Southold itself is west of Mill Creek and is a pleasant place to visit in a shoal-draft craft.

Dockage: The full-service, well-regarded Brick Cove Marina is in an enclosed basin with a 138-slip marina, offering maintenance and repairs, a pool and a private swimming beach. They also have a multi-sport court for pickleball, basketball or tennis (free to slip holders). They can accommodate vessels to 48 feet. This is an active location on the weekends in the summer when you may be treated to live music and food and beer/wine trucks.

Peconic Bay Marine Basin to the west is private but maintains some transient slips to 60 feet with full amenities. Port of Egypt Marine has a solar-heated pool, an on-site restaurant, a paddleboard shop and boutique. They also have a service center and parts department. They ask that you call ahead to check transient slip availability (to 40 feet).

■ SHELTER ISLAND

Experience a little slice of small-town New England in the midst of Shelter Island's charm and some of the most enjoyable cruising grounds on the Northeast coast. Shelter Island is an elegant summer enclave with rolling, wooded terrain, sheltered beaches, attractive homes and serpentine roads. The shoreline has protected harbors on all sides and you can circumnavigate the island in a few hours with a lunch stop at either Smith Cove or Majors Harbor.

The best way to see the island is to rent a bike from Piccozzi's Bicycle Rental and Repair at 177 N. Ferry Rd. (631-749-0045). A grocery store, book store and two hardware stores are among the offerings. Havens House Museum and Store operates (seasonally) in a historic (circa 1743) home at 16 S. Ferry Rd., (631-749-0025).

Two ferries connect Shelter Island with Long Island itself. One goes to Greenport on the North Fork, while the other goes to North Haven Peninsula and Sag Harbor on the South Fork. About 4 miles long by 5 miles wide the island is entirely surrounded by well-marked channels. Just watch for charted shoals close inshore, especially near Ram Head and Hay Beach Point.

NOTE: The town discourages the off-loading of trash on the island. Bottles, cans and paper must be separated for acceptance at each harbor's recycling center. Non-recyclable trash must be placed in Town of Shelter Island disposal bags available for purchase at each center.

Dering Harbor

Cruising counterclockwise from Greenport will bring you to Dering Harbor on the north side of the island, where a mooring in the shadow of Shelter Island Heights offers a peaceful contrast to the bustle of Greenport, 1 mile north across the channel. In fact, this is a good place for a secure mooring when the wind is up from any direction other than north. It is popular during the summer so it is best to call ahead to reserve a mooring or slip. Anchoring space is very limited and discouraged.

NAVIGATION: Entry is straightforward with 8-foot to 14-foot MLW depths into the center of the harbor, but be sure to favor Dering Point to the northeast to avoid shoals extending from the south side of the entrance. The charted "Disposal Area" (long-ago discarded oyster shells) presents no hazard to navigation.

Dockage/Moorings: The private Shelter Island Yacht Club in Dering Harbor has moorings available to members of clubs on the reciprocal list for a facility fee, which covers launch service and use of the club amenities.

Piccozzi's Dering Harbor Marina at the head of the harbor has rental moorings, dock space for vessels to 160 feet and a popular fuel dock. Piccozzi's is in close proximity to restaurants, groceries and shopping and has bicycle rentals available for exploring the island. The town dock next door permits a complimentary 2-hour tie-up.

On the northwest shore of Shelter Island, you will pass Jennings Point on the way to West Neck Harbor to the south, a favorite among cruisers. This harbor is scenic and well protected and home to The Pridwin Hotel & Cottages. This classic resort hotel has been providing guests a unique experience on Shelter Island since 1927. The nearly 10-acre site on Crescent Beach offers a few slips to 40 feet with protected waters, gentle bay breezes and breathtaking water views.

Anchorage: The mooring field at Dering Harbor occupies virtually all of the harbor anchorage space but a small boat might find a spot at the east end of the cove in 10 feet MLW with secure holding in mud.

West Neck Harbor

NAVIGATION: West Neck Harbor is on the southwest side of Shelter Island across Shelter Island Sound from Gleason Point on the North Haven Peninsula. The entry to West Neck Harbor between the bar at the end of Shell Beach and flashing red buoy "2" is daunting on review of the chart and appears challenging at your first on-site observation.

The water is actually deep here (even at low tide), allowing reliable access to knowledgeable skippers of large boats with drafts of 5 feet and more. At low tide, the deep channel is located midway between the end of Shell Beach between green Shell Beach Point Light and red buoy "2." At high tide, favor flashing red buoy "2" slightly. Thereafter, your chart shows the correct path, hugging the contour at about 100 yards off the north side of Shell Beach.

Keep an eye to the depth sounder for chart-matching numbers and avoid straying to starboard. It is best to pick a rising tide for a first attempt but the serenity beyond is well worth a little anxiety at the entrance.

Dockage: Well-protected The Island Boatyard and Marina at West Harbor has 80 slips that can accommodate power or sailboats to 60 feet with resort amenities. They also offer a free shuttle van for exploring the Islands. There is a restaurant on the premises as well as a retired twin-mast vessel once used in the Great South Bay for harvesting oysters and clams that now serves as a full bar.

Anchorage: Non-residents are limited to a 48-hour stay in West Neck Harbor and must anchor in the southern end of the harbor in the area designated by several marker buoys. There has been shoaling along the channel to West Neck Bay and, therefore, depths are somewhat less than those indicated on the chart. Nevertheless, there is good holding in mud and protection in 10 to 12 feet MLW from all but the northeast.

Smith Cove & Majors Harbor

These two unspoiled coves on the southern shore of Shelter Island are pretty, quiet and easy to enter. There are high green banks, good beaches, clean water and ample depths with good protection (except in southerly winds). Smith Cove, the westernmost of the two, is larger and deeper. The western end of the cove serves as the ferry landing to North Haven and Sag Harbor. If the strong current and an opposing wind combine, the passage from West Neck Harbor to Smith Cove can be challenging.

Anchorage: Smith Cove offers good anchorage close to a long stretch of undeveloped beach (open to the south) and is reported to have good fishing. You can drop the hook here in 15- to 20-foot MLW depths with good holding in soft mud. Majors Harbor to the southeast is an attractive bight with no services and no shore access. When entering give Majors Point and its off-lying rocks a clear berth. Inside you will find 6 to 9 feet MLW with good holding in sand.

Coecles Harbor

Continuing the circle around southern Shelter Island, Coecles (pronounced "cockles") Harbor is located on the eastern shore about 6 miles southwest of Orient Point. This large, tree-lined harbor offers an idyllic setting, excellent anchorage, a traditional full-service marina and a choice of well-regarded restaurants. It is also a delightful spot to find tiny yellow and orange cockle shells, which appear almost transparent in the sunlight.

NAVIGATION: Coecles Harbor is accessible through a marked channel just south of Ram Island. Best approach depths will be found at about 30 yards off flashing green buoy "1" and green can "3," which is followed by green lighted buoy "5" to port. Boats drawing 6 feet or more will want to wait for a rising tide (3-foot tidal range) before attempting an entry. Dredging has widened the opening between Reel Point (flashing red Coecles Harbor Entrance Light) and Sungic Point (green lighted buoy "5").

Dockage: The full-service Coecles Harbor Marina & Boatyard, located at the west end of the harbor, may be easily reached on any tide by vessels with drafts less than 5 feet. The only significant shallow spot consists of a narrow 5-foot MLW mud "hump" extending southwest of red nun buoy "10" off Little Ram Island. Otherwise, the center harbor areas carry 6- to 8-foot MLW depths with substantially better depths at high tide. The marina has slips (to 60 feet) and a pool, van service and bike rentals.

Anchorage: The designated anchorage in Coecles Harbor is just to port after entry and is clearly marked by orange and white markers. If you plan to anchor, you are required to do so here. Be sure to turn to port well before reaching green can buoy "7" and the rocks that lie just beyond that buoy. There is good holding in soft mud in 9 to 11 feet MLW. For a small fee Coecles Harbor Marina & Boatyard offers use of its dinghy dock and facilities to those at anchor.

NOTE: This area is a No-Discharge Zone and from May 15 to September 15 anchorage is limited to a 48-hour stay with a posted $250 fine and towing fees assessed against violators. This protects local shellfishing, which is available to anyone who secures a town permit.

■ LITTLE & GREAT PECONIC BAY

Little Peconic Bay

Little Peconic Bay is about 5 miles long and is full of interesting coves and creeks. It is southwest of the circumnavigation of Shelter Island and it is large and deep but can be airless in the summer. Hog Neck Bay with two pretty streams (Corey Creek and Richmond Creek) is located in the northwest corner of Little Peconic Bay. Both streams have good beaches, narrow-dredged channels and no services. Charted depth is 7 feet MLW but both creeks are better for dinghies than big boats.

Jessup Neck and Great Hog Neck mark the eastern edge of the Peconic Bays. The waters around the sand spit of Jessup Neck, a wildlife preserve with picnic grounds, provide good fishing, especially for blues and weakfish. Farther around Nassau Point is Cutchogue

Little Peconic Bay

Looking Northeast at Nassau Point

Great & Little Peconic Bays, NY

CUTCHOGUE		Largest Vessel	VHF	Total Slips	Approach/ Dockside Depth	Floating Docks	Gas/ Diesel	Repairs/ Haulout	Min/Max Amps	Pump-Out Station
1. Shagwong Marinas - Cutchogue	(631) 734-6993	60	9	120	6.0 / 9.0	F	GD	RH	30 / 50	P
2. Shagwong Marinas - New Suffolk	(631) 734-6311	40	9	60	5.0 / 6.0	F	GD	RH	30	P
MATTITUCK										
3. Strong's Marine Mattituck Bay **WiFi**	(631) 298-4770	52	68	100	4.0 / 5.0	F	GD	RH	30 / 50	P

WiFi Wireless Internet Access
Visit www.waterwayguide.com for current rates, fuel prices, website addresses and other up-to-the-minute information.
(Information in the table is provided by the facilities.)

Scan here for more details:

Source: Aqua Map and NOAA data

Harbor. Half a dozen gunkholes, fine beaches and a charming town with one of the country's oldest houses characterize this side bay.

Off Cutchogue Harbor are several dredged basins for local boats but most are shoal. All offer interesting exploration by dinghy. New Suffolk is the port for Cutchogue, 1 mile inland. The village has a commercial fishing fleet, a restaurant, rowboat rentals and bait sales. Boating amenities are on Cutchogue Harbor and up Schoolhouse Creek (unnamed on the chart). Check depths with locals.

Dockage: Two opportunities for excellent service and beautiful bay access are offered by Shawong Marinas. Shagwong Marinas - Cutchogue spans 3.82 acres and boasts well over 100 slips with deep-water access, a ship store, a fueling dock, summer dockage and winter storage capabilities for boats up to 60 feet.

Shagwong Marinas - New Suffolk is on the west side of the harbor on School House Creek is situated across 2.3 acres in the heart of Long Island's wine country with convenient proximity to pristine beaches and intimate restaurants in New Suffolk Village. Both facilities welcome transients and offer similar amenities plus yacht maintenance and repair.

Anchorage: A cove that is unnamed on the chart but known locally as Horseshoe Cove offers a protected anchorage north of Nassau Point in Cutchogue Harbor. Here you will find 9 to 11 feet MLW with good holding in mud. This is somewhat exposed to the north.

Great Peconic Bay

Dividing Little Peconic Bay and Great Peconic Bay is Robins Island, which is privately owned. The 435-acre island is home to rare animal and plant species. Landing on the island is forbidden. Two marked channels go past Robins Island. North Race is more protected but spotted with shoals. South Race is the preferred passage for deeper-draft boats and is better marked but is subject to tide rips when current and wind oppose.

Dockage: Around the harbor are a number of marinas that will accommodate small boats. On the north shore of Great Peconic Bay is the village of Mattituck (previously discussed in the Smithtown Bay to Mattituck Inlet section of this guide.)

While most of the cruising amenities are located on Mattituck Creek off the inlet from Long Island Sound, you can access the town and Strong's Marine Mattituck Bay from this side by way of James Creek. Approach depths are listed as 4 feet MLW so call ahead for exact depths. This facility offers dockage to 47 feet with full amenities plus paddleboard and kayak rentals. Strong's dockage clients also enjoy privileges at the resort-like Strong's Water Club and Marina (transportation required).

Riverhead, Flanders Bay

Flanders Bay is the gateway to the Peconic River and Riverhead. Settled in 1690, Riverhead has good shops, restaurants and an inn but few transient boat amenities. Much like the North Fork, this area is famous for farm stands and wineries. Riverhead has more than 20,000 acres involved in crops or vineyards and local produce abounds (in season). The nearby Long Island Aquarium has interactive exhibits include boat rides, shark dives, feeding stingrays and frolicking with sea lions. Another favorite stop is North Fork Brewing Co. for a Hold Me Closer Tiny Lager.

NAVIGATION: Large, full of shoals and with a twisting channel, Flanders Bay is the last link in the Peconic chain. Enter between Miamogue and Red Cedar Points, follow all aids to navigation carefully and keep a close eye on your depth sounder. The bay has nice creeks, some deep enough for larger boats, but most are more suited for dinghy navigation.

You can get to Riverhead via the Peconic River's narrow, marsh-bordered channel with 6-foot MLW depths. Buoys lead you to the head of navigation, 2 miles from Flanders Bay. The fixed **CR 105 Bridge** (25-foot vertical clearance) crosses the Peconic River about 1 mile downstream of the village so most sailboats cannot make it all the way.

Dockage: The well-regarded Great Peconic Bay Marina has slips to 65 feet with all the usual amenities plus picnic areas with barbecues, a private beach and a playground. Guests enjoy access to refueling, maintenance and repairs with certified marine service technicians. The facility is located near wonderful restaurants, breweries, nature preserves, the Long Island Aquarium and many vineyards to take the crew out on a land adventure.

Lighthouse Marina to the west has 150 slips on floating docks for vessels to 70 feet with full amenities including a solar-heated pool and waterfront bar and grill. Transients are always welcome.

Flanders Bay, NY

RIVERHEAD AREA		Largest Vessel	VHF	Total Slips	Approach/ Dockside Depth	Floating Docks	Gas/ Diesel	Repairs/ Haulout	Min/Max Amps	Pump-Out Station
1. Great Peconic Bay Marina **WiFi**	(631) 722-3565	65		175	6.0 / 6.0	F	GD	RH	30 / 50	P
2. Lighthouse Marina, Inc. **WiFi**	(631) 722-3400	70	10	150	6.0 / 8.0	F	GD	RH	30 / 50	P
3. Treasure Cove Resort Marina **WiFi**	(631) 727-8386	65	11	120	5.0 / 8.0	F	GD	RH	30 / 50	P

WiFi Wireless Internet Access
Visit www.waterwayguide.com for current rates, fuel prices, website addresses and other up-to-the-minute information.
(Information in the table is provided by the facilities.)

Scan here for more details: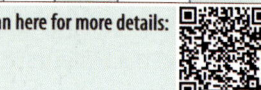

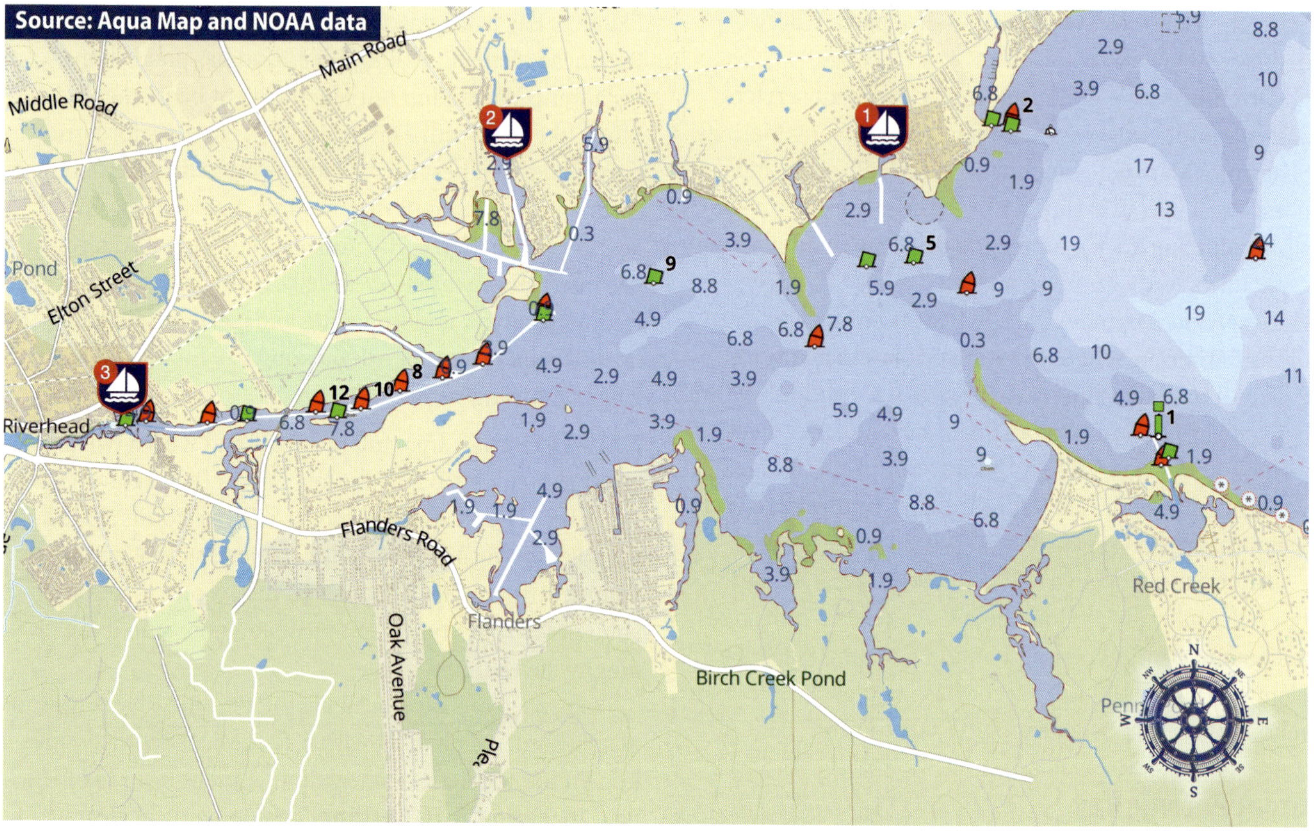

Source: Aqua Map and NOAA data

Treasure Cove Resort Marina is up the Peconic River past the fixed 25-foot clearance CR 105 Bridge with slips to 65 feet. Transient boaters receive many of the amenities enjoyed by seasonal members like laundry access, use of the indoor and outdoor pools and a fitness center. Visiting boaters may also purchase discounted tickets to the Long Island Aquarium.

East Creek Marina in Riverhead is for town residents only. Boaters are permitted to tie up at the town waterfront all day without a permit. Boaters who would like to spend an evening must come to the Recreation Department and purchase a permit. There is no room for anchoring in the Peconic River.

■ SOUTH FORK: SHINNECOCK CANAL TO LAKE MONTAUK

Shinnecock Canal

NAVIGATION: The easy-to-use Shinnecock Canal runs between Peconic and Shinnecock Bays, joining Long Island's interior waters with its southern shore. A single jetty leads into the well-marked and lighted canal entrance from Great Peconic Bay, about 8 miles east of Riverhead. Fixed bridges set controlling vertical clearance at 22 feet. The canal is regularly dredged and its banks are lined with marinas, boatyards, restaurants and fishing stations. At each end of the canal is a DIY gin pole, which you can use to un-step or step your sailboat's mast at no charge.

Noyack Bay, NY

NOYACK		Largest Vessel	VHF	Total Slips	Approach/ Dockside Depth	Floating Docks	Gas/ Diesel	Repairs/ Haulout	Min/Max Amps	Pump-Out Station
1. Mill Creek Marina	(631) 725-1351	45		145	4.0 / 4.0	F	G	RH	30	P
2. Yacht Hampton Boating Club & Marina	(631) 725-3333	40	9	56	6.0 / 6.0	F	G	R		

WiFi Wireless Internet Access
Visit www.waterwayguide.com for current rates, fuel prices, website addresses and other up-to-the-minute information.
(Information in the table is provided by the facilities.)

Scan here for more details:

Dockage: Above the lock at the north end of the canal is the municipal Shinnecock Canal Marina. This fully equipped facility includes free pump-out stations, restrooms and showers, and water and electric hookups. Meschutt Beach County Park is adjacent to the marina with lifeguard-protected swimming and a full-service concession stand. (This and other facilities on Shinnecock Canal are described in detail in Chapter 6 of this guide (Side Trip: South Shore of Long Island).

Noyack Bay

Heading east and back toward Shelter Island and North Haven Peninsula, the quiet Noyack Bay has accommodations for shallow-draft boats and a few stores and restaurants that are within walking distance of the harbor. Fishing is good in the rips off high, needle-sharp Jessup Neck, which is part of a nature preserve with paths and picnic tables.

Jessup Neck Basin is just barely navigable because of shallow depths. Boats do moor here, however, and it is quiet since it is surrounded by the nature preserve. There is a sandy beach at the south end of the bay (Long Beach) where you can rent small sailboards and other watercraft.

Dockage: Family-owned and -operated Mill Creek Marina offers transient dockage to 45 feet and is home to the popular restaurant (The Bell and Anchor) as well as kayak and SUP rentals. It is also an easy walk to Trout Pond, which is excellent for freshwater swimming. Yacht Hampton Boating Club & Marina (formerly Hidden Cove Marina Inc.) offers 32 slips for boats to 57 feet with access to resort-style amenities including a Mediterranean-inspired Beach Club equipped with loungers and games facilities.

Anchorage: North Sea Harbor is a shallow (2 to 4 feet MLW) anchorage. Pick your spot carefully, even if you see other boats nearby because locals may be sitting in shallows or on mud at low tide. The next harbor to the east, Wooley Pond, has 5- to 6-foot MLW depths. A black

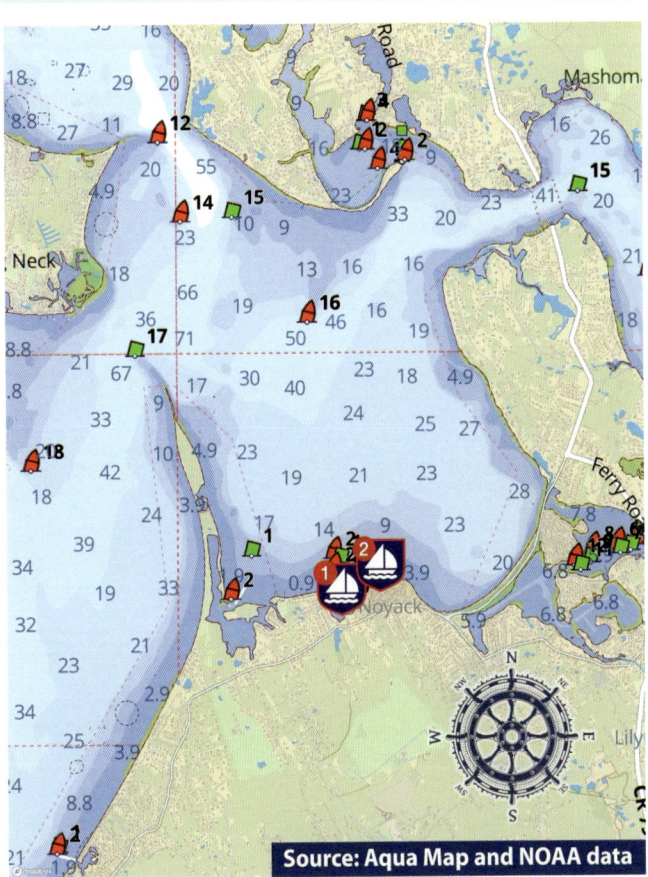

Source: Aqua Map and NOAA data

beacon and red nun "2" mark the 8-foot channel leading into this small anchorage. Peconic Marina is here with services, parts and accessories, should you need them. (They do not typically have transient slips.)

There is limited room for anchoring in the snug basin of Mill Creek at Noyak. Anchoring outside on the southern shore of Noyak Bay can be pleasant in settled weather.

Sag Harbor

Sag Harbor is one of the major cruising ports on eastern Long Island. Two important harbors provide extensive services for most any need. The town is close to both harbors and is brimming with shops, Colonial houses, restaurants and monuments to Sag Harbor's history as

Sag Harbor Bay, NY

SAG HARBOR		Largest Vessel	VHF	Total Slips	Approach/ Dockside Depth	Floating Docks	Gas/ Diesel	Repairs/ Haulout	Min/Max Amps	Pump-Out Station
1. Sag Harbor Cove Yacht Club WiFi	(631) 725-1605	80	9	160	8.0 / 7.0	F	GD		50	
2. Sag Harbor Launch & Mooring Rentals	(631) 466-8180	120	73		10.0 / 12.0			H		
3. Village of Sag Harbor Dock WiFi	(631) 725-2368	175	9	311	10.0 / 10.0	F			30 / 100	P
4. Malloy's Waterfront Marina WiFi	(631) 725-3886	210	12	75	10.0 / 10.0				30 / 200+	P
5. Sag Harbor Yacht Club-PRIVATE WiFi	(631) 725-0567	200	9	62	11.0 / 10.0		GD		30 / 200+	P
6. Sag Harbor Yacht Yard & Marina WiFi	**(631) 725-3838**	**125**	**10**	**31**	**13.0 / 10.0**	**F**		**RH**	**30 / 50**	**P**

WiFi Wireless Internet Access

Visit www.waterwayguide.com for current rates, fuel prices, website addresses and other up-to-the-minute information. (Information in the table is provided by the facilities.)

Scan here for more details:

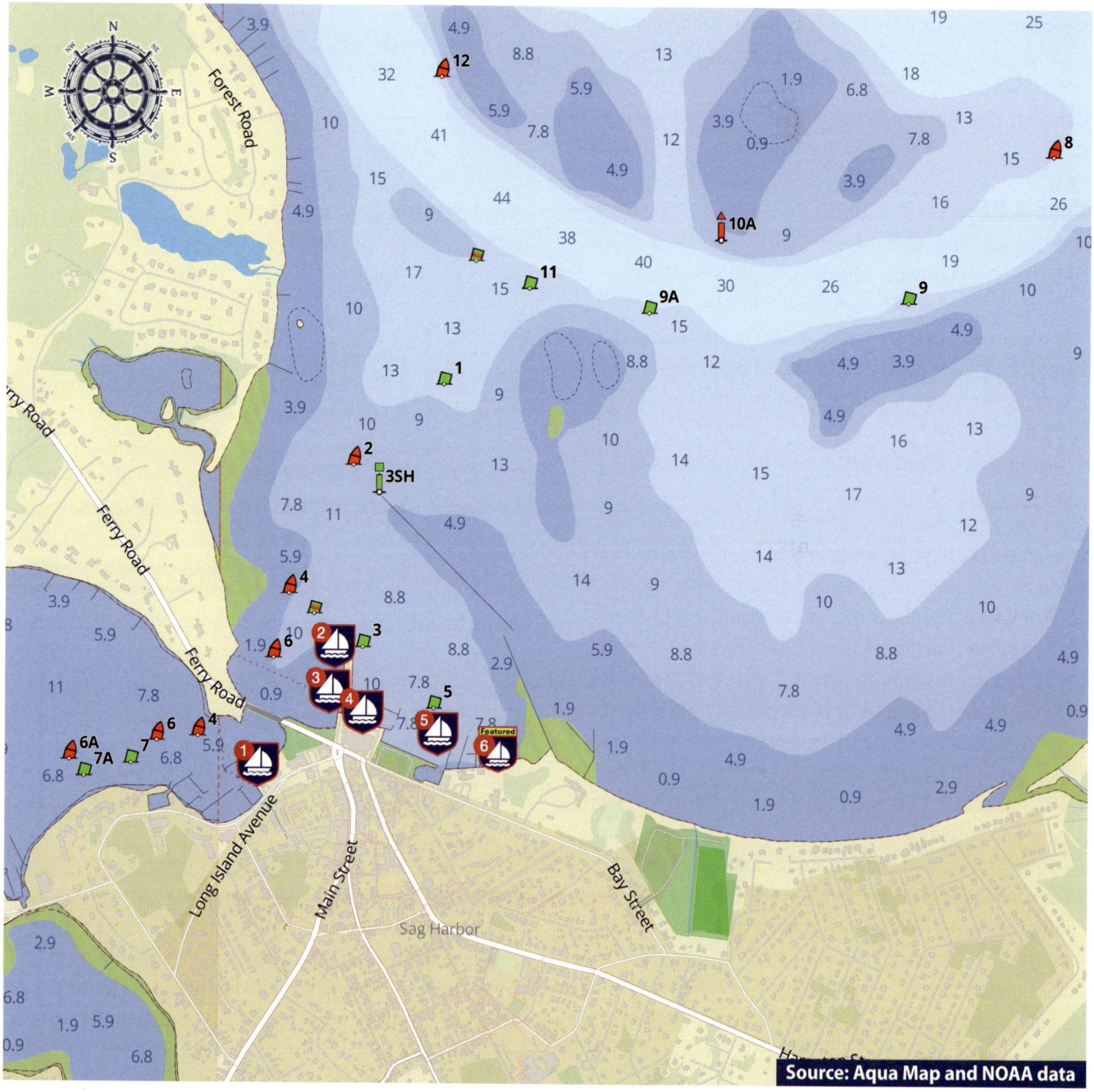

Source: Aqua Map and NOAA data

SAG HARBOR YACHT YARD & MARINA

Sag Harbor

a whaling port. There are also two hardware stores, a market, a liquor store and a bookstore within walking distance of the waterfront.

NAVIGATION: Sag Harbor is about 10 miles south of Plum Gut, 12 miles northeast of Shinnecock Canal and is easily approached from the east or west. A long breakwater extends most of the width of the harbor, but it is easy to enter the deep channel between the western end and North Haven.

If you are approaching Sag Harbor from the east, do not cut any of the buoys to avoid a large rock field. Make sure you pass very close to or west of green-and-red junction buoy "SH." Every year a good number of boats visit the rocks and some end up with serious damage.

When heading east from Sag Harbor, stick to the well-marked channel, favor the Shelter Island side and stay north of the numerous rocks marked by flashing green buoy "11."

Charted Sand Spit is a large shoal partly bare at half-tide north of the channel and marked by 10-foot tower flashing red "10A."

Dockage/Moorings: The completely protected inner harbor, Sag Harbor Cove, lies just beyond the fixed **Ferry Road Bridge** (21-foot fixed vertical clearance). These facilities are conveniently located close to Sag Harbor's Main Street (5-minute walk) plus many historic sites, vineyards, farms, mansions, scenic vistas and some of the world's best beaches. Sag Harbor Cove Yacht Club welcomes transients with slips to 80 feet and an on-site restaurant.

Some of the numerous moorings here are available to transients including those managed by Sag Harbor Launch & Mooring Rentals (25 to 120 feet). Short-term moorings are first-come, first-served and can only be assigned by contacting the launch operator on VHF Channel 73. Long or short-term tie-ups or

mooring may also be possible at the municipal Village of Sag Harbor Dock. Reservations are required.

Malloy's Waterfront Marina has 75 slips with 10 reserved transient slips to 210 feet with full amenities including docking assistance. Overnight stays are by reservation only. Dock space for day visitors is available on a first-come, first-served basis. Requests can be made on VHF Channel 12.

At the eastern end of the harbor inside the Sag Harbor breakwater are several facilities including the private Sag Harbor Yacht Club with slips and amenities (no club affiliation required). Advance reservations are recommended, especially for peak weekends.

Sag Harbor Yacht Yard & Marina has a full-service mechanic's shop that can handle engine, transmission, electrical, plumbing and welding work. They also provide rigging and mast work as well as prop and

GOIN' ASHORE

SAG HARBOR, NY

ATTRACTIONS

1. Custom House
Originally built around 1770 and best known for being the home and office of Henry Packer Dering (1763-1822), Sag Harbor's first customs master and postmaster. Currently operated by Preservation Long Island and used to educate the public about the history of Sag Harbor at 912 Main St. (631-692-4664).

2. Greening Gallery
Exhibits from curated choice of artists from international and local art scene anchored by classically trained artist Laura Grenning at 26 Main St. (631-725-8469).

3. Old Whalers Church of Sag
Egyptian revival wooden building built in 1844 at 44 Union St. Original steeple was taller and easier to see than Montauk lighthouse and served as a landmark for whaling vessels. Steeple toppled during hurricane in 1938 and has never been replaced.

4. Sag Harbor Whaling & Historical Museum
Greek-revival mansion built in 1845 for a whaling tycoon that displays exhibit artifacts of whaling and the whaling era (200 Main St., 631-725-0770).

5. The Annie Cooper Boyd House & Museum
Historic 18th century home with historic archives and exhibits at 174 Main St. (631-725-5092). In the rear of the property is the Society's interpretation of William Cooper's whale boat shop, containing an excellent small exhibit of boat building tools and videos about whaling industry.

6. World War II Memorial
Historic landmark on Bay St.

SERVICES

7. John Jermain Memorial Library
201 Main St. (631-725-0049)

8. Sag Harbor Post Office
21 Long Island Ave. (631-725-8968)

9. Sag Harbor Veterinary Clinic
28 Bridge St. (631-725-6500)

10. My Sunny Laundry
20 Main St. (631-725-7257)

11. Sag Harbor Urgent Care
34 Bay St. (631-808-3337)

12. The UPS Store
2 Main St. (631-808-3222)

MARINAS

13. Sag Harbor Cove Yacht Club
8 West Water St. (631-725-1605)

14. Sag Harbor Launch & Mooring Rentals
Long Wharf (631-466-8180)

15. Sag Harbor Yacht Club-PRIVATE
27 Bay St. (631-725-0567)

16. Village of Sag Harbor Dock
7 Bay St. (631-725-2368)

17. Malloy's Waterfront Marina
1A Bay St. (631-725-3886)

18. Sag Harbor Yacht Yard & Marina
53 Bay St. (631-725-3838)

Lance Corporal Jordan Haerter Veterans' Memorial Bridge

Windmill Beach Park

John Steinbeck Waterfront Park

Wharf St

Bay St

Bay St

Bay St

Marine Park

Bay St

Bay St

W Water St

Parking Lot A

Main St

American Hotel

Rose St

Sag Harbor Cinema

Parking Lot C

Spring St

Spring St

Garden St

Church St

Division St

Main St

Sag Harbor Fireman's Museum

Madison St

Union St

Custom House

Howard St

Sag Harbor Whaling Museum

First Presbyterian Church

Much of Sag Harbor is a National Historic Site. Its history centers heavily on its days as a whaling port, although it was inhabited well before Europeans settled here. In the mid-1800s, almost half the total population of Sag Harbor served on whaling ships. Today the town swells with vacationers in the summer drawn by the two beaches (Foster Memorial and Havens Beach), an assortment of restaurants and easy provisioning options. The Sag Harbor Yacht Club hosts a spectacular 4th of July fireworks celebration, which has become a major attraction on the East End of Long Island, annually drawing 20,000 plus spectators.

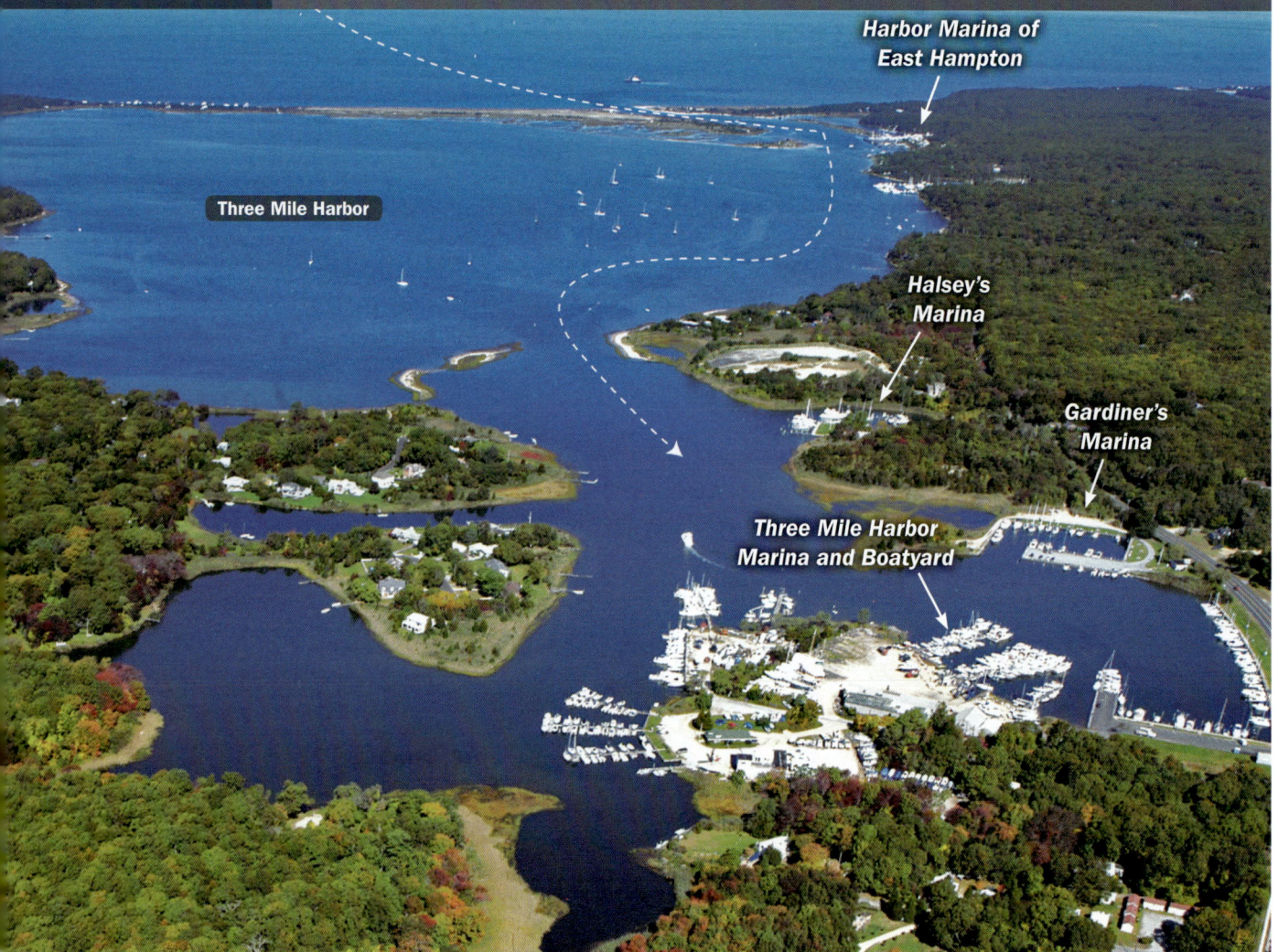

Harbor Marina of East Hampton

Three Mile Harbor

Halsey's Marina

Gardiner's Marina

Three Mile Harbor Marina and Boatyard

shaft repairs and maintain a few transient slips (to 118 feet). They have the only fully-stocked ship chandlery in the area.

Anchorage: Boats are seen anchored in 10- to 15-foot MLW depths outside the breakwater at Sag Harbor Bay to the east. Exercise extreme caution threading the shoals marked by flashing green buoy "11" and the green can "1" just west of the shoal's rocky outcrop. There is good holding in soft mud, although this anchorage is somewhat exposed to the northeast and northwest.

From here you can dinghy through the gap in the breakwater to the town dinghy dock to visit the shopping and dining district.

Ship to shore water taxi service is also available to mooring fields and anchorages.

Three Mile Harbor

Back out on the south shore of Gardiners Bay (beyond Shelter Island and Sag Harbor) is Three Mile Harbor, shown as Threemile Harbor on many charts. A short bike or taxi ride away brings you to the Historic Village of East Hampton with soft sand beaches, historical landmarks, museums, theaters, art galleries, restaurants and night clubs in the villages of East Hampton and Amagansett.

NAVIGATION: Three Mile Harbor is 15 miles west of Montauk Point,

8 miles south of Plum Gut and 6 miles east of Sag Harbor. The entrance between Sammy's Beach and Maidstone Park Beach is plainly announced by the red-and-white Morse (A) "TM" bell buoy and marked by green can "1" and red nun "2" at the beginning of the entrance channel.

Inside the breakwater-protected entrance at Three Mile Harbor, the dredged channel runs between shores for 0.5 mile before opening up to the vistas of a large and scenic harbor. The eastern shore is well developed with marinas, boatyards and restaurants. In contrast, the western side remains wild, rimmed with high green hills and dense forest along the

Three Mile Harbor, NY

THREE MILE HARBOR AREA		Largest Vessel	VHF	Total Slips	Approach/ Dockside Depth	Floating Docks	Gas/ Diesel	Repairs/ Haulout	Min/Max Amps	Pump-Out Station
1. **Harbor Marina of East Hampton** WiFi	(631) 324-5666	65	9	95	10.0 / 8.0	F	GD	RH	30 / 50	P
2. Maidstone Harbor Marina	(631) 324-2651	75		95	9.0 / 8.0	F		R	30 / 100	P
3. East Hampton Point Marina & Boatyard WiFi	(631) 324-8400	90	9	55	8.0 / 7.0		GD	RH	30 / 100	P
4. Shagwong Marinas - East Hampton	(631) 324-8400	50	9	40	7.0 / 6.0	F			30 / 100	P
5. **Halsey's Marina** WiFi	(631) 324-5666	75	9	44	10.0 / 7.5			R	30 / 50	P
6. **Gardiner's Marina** WiFi	(631) 324-5666	110	9	45	9.0 / 6.5	F		R	30 / 50	P
7. **Three Mile Harbor Marina and Boatyard** WiFi	(631) 324-1320	65	9	70	10.0 / 8.5	F		RH	30 / 50	P

WiFi Wireless Internet Access
Visit www.waterwayguide.com for current rates, fuel prices, website addresses and other up-to-the-minute information.
(Information in the table is provided by the facilities.)

Scan here for more details:

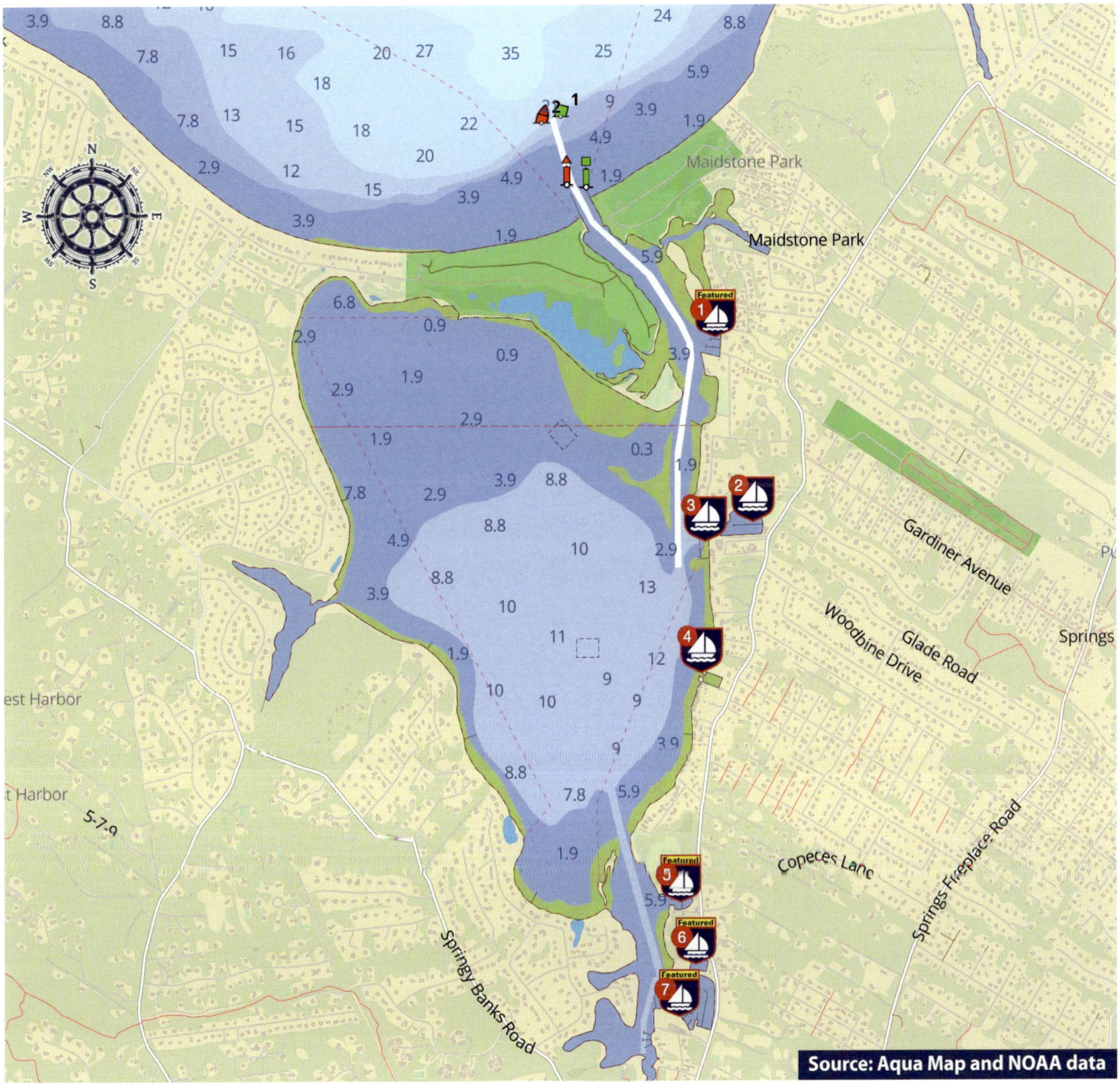

GOIN' ASHORE

EAST HAMPTON, NY

The Town of East Hampton was founded in 1648 as a farming community with ties to whaling and fishing. The governors of Connecticut Colony and New Haven Colony acquired 30,000 acres on the south fork of Long Island from the Montaukett Indians for a payment that included 100 small drill bits used to make "Wampum," a traditional shell bead of the local Indian tribes. The original settlement at the heart of the Town was incorporated as the Village of East Hampton in 1920.

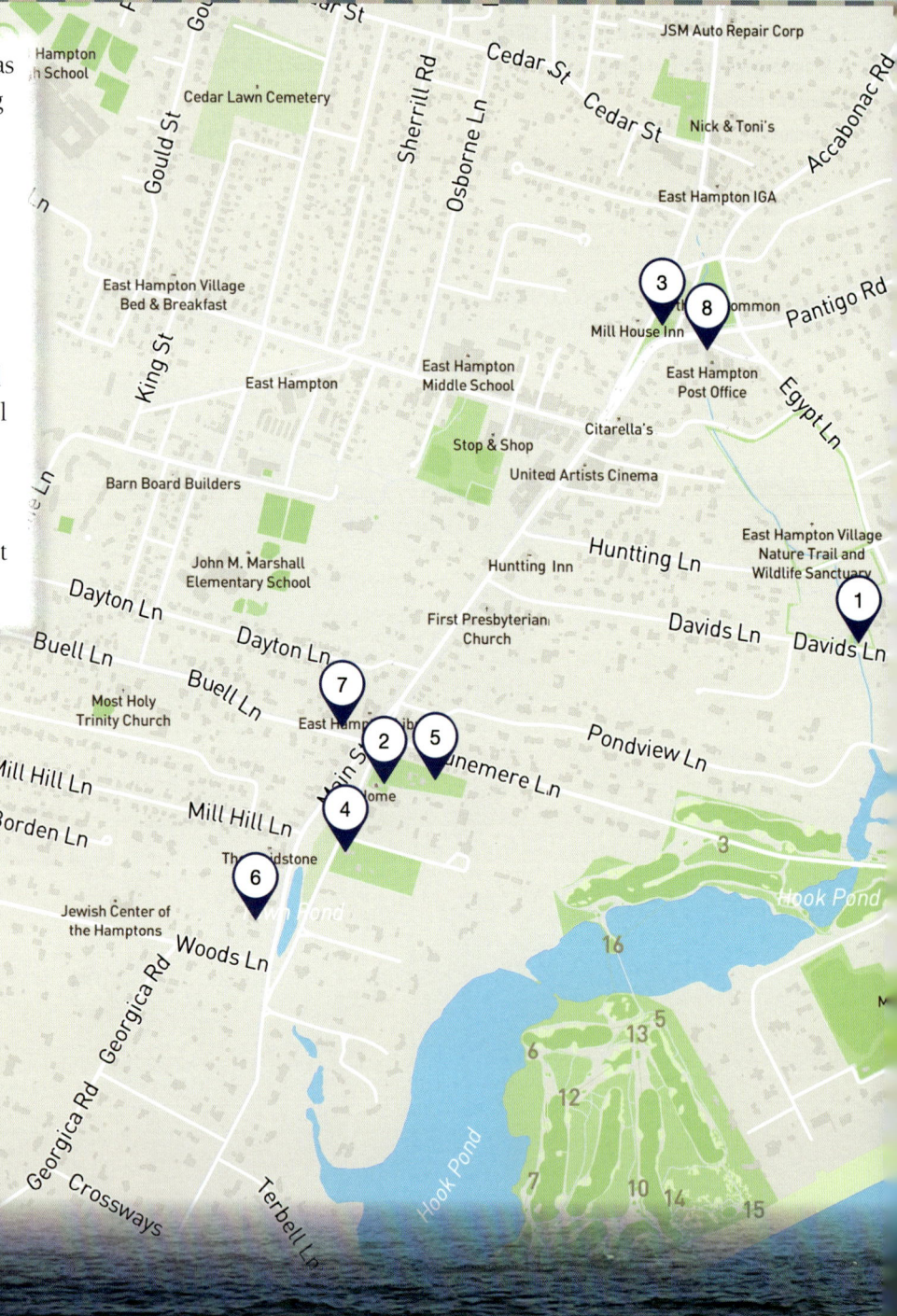

ATTRACTIONS

1. East Hampton Duck Pond
Woodsy 24-acre trail in the heart of the Village at 96 Davids Ln.

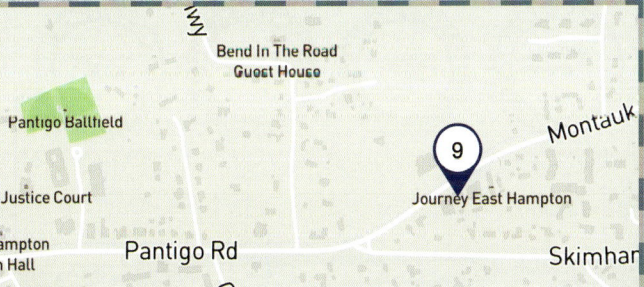

Regarded as one of the most beautiful areas in the United States, East Hampton is a world-famous, oceanside town with miles of white sandy beach located approximately 100 miles from New York City. The village of East Hampton has a rich history depicted through several historical landmarks such as those maintained by the East Hampton Historical Society, which showcase the artistic and architectural heritage. There is also a variety of shopping and dining options, including boutique shops, artisanal food markets and upscale restaurants, many of which use locally-sourced ingredients. Shopping and dining is centered along three main streets: Main Street, Newtown Lane and Park Place.

Outdoor activities usually include one of the five village beaches–Georgica, Main Beach, Wiborg Beach, Egypt Lane Beach and Two Mile Hollow. Georgica Beach, like most village beaches, is a locals beach popular with surfers that requires a vehicle parking permit. Main Beach is one of the most popular beaches in the Hamptons with lifeguards, a snack bar, restrooms and public parking.

Overall, East Hampton is a beautiful and culturally rich town that offers visitors a wide range of activities, from beach combing to cultural and historical exploration, making it a great destination for anyone looking to escape the hustle and bustle of city life.

2. Home, Sweet Home Museum
Built in the early 1700s, recognized as most distinguished lean-to or "saltbox" in the Village. Owned by relatives of John Howard Payne, composer of lyrics to popular song of the same name. Open daily May through September. October and November weekends only.

3. Hook Windmill
Landmark 200-year-old mill with all the original machinery located at 42 Main St.

4. Lion Gardiner Mill Cottage
Museum and exhibition center situated on the earliest homestead in East Hampton at 36 James Ln. (631-604-5700).

5. Mulford Farm Museum
Completely intact English Colonial farmstead built in 1680. Includes Rachel's Garden, a recreated 18th century dooryard garden, and Mulford Barn, constructed in 1721. Located at 10 James Ln. (631-324-6869).

6. Thomas & Mary Nimmo Moran Studio
Described as "a quirky, Queen Anne style-studio cottage" at 229 Main St. (631-324-6850). Built in 1884 and marking the beginning of the village as an artist's colony.

SERVICES

7. East Hampton Library
159 Main St. (631-324-0222)

8. East Hampton Post Office
12 Gay Rd. (631-324-6320)

9. East Hampton Walk-In Center
470 Montauk Hwy. (631-329-5900)

10. East Hampton Veterinary Group
22 Montauk Hwy. (631-324-0282)

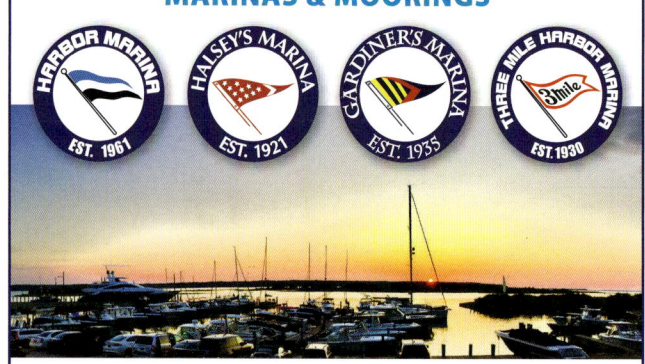

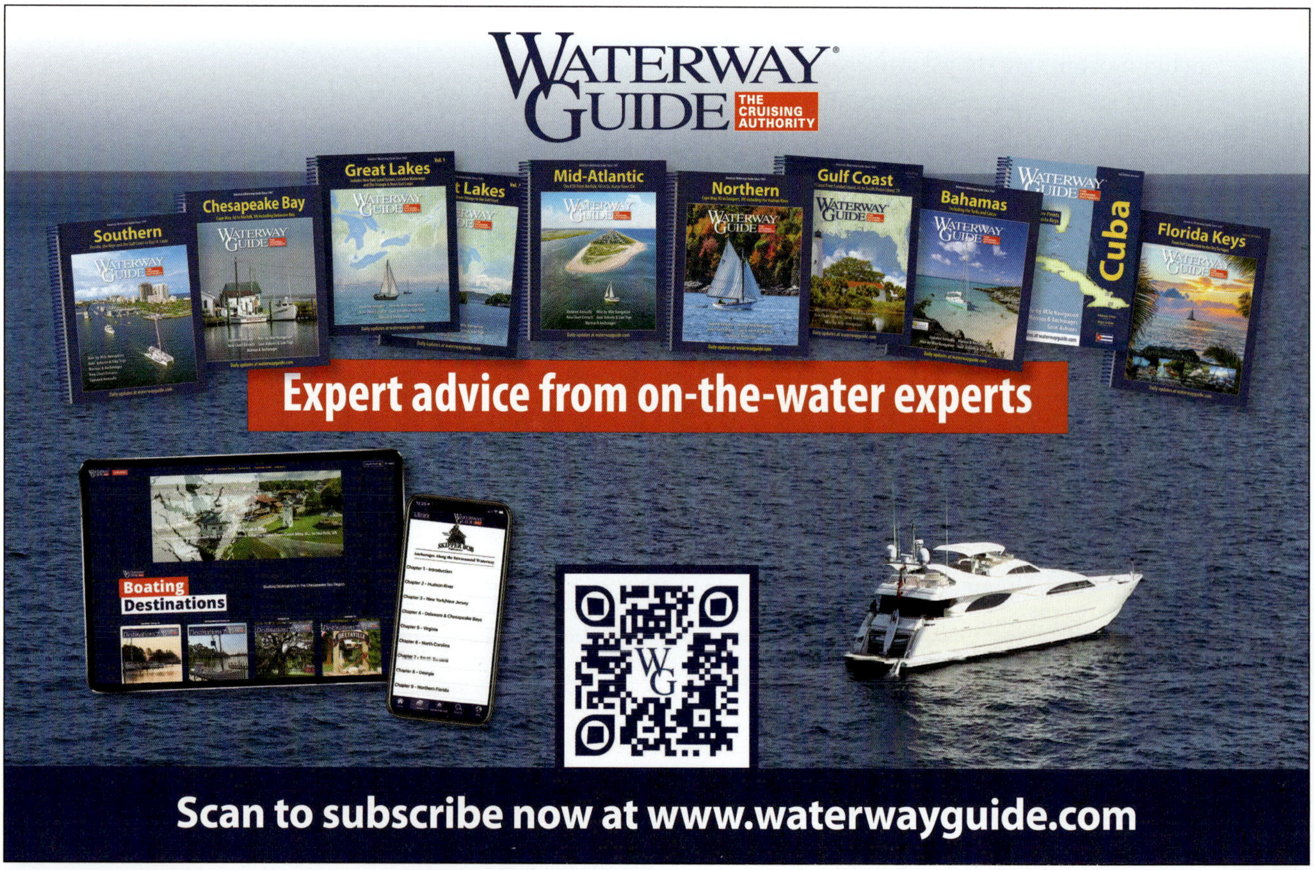

shoreline, which occasionally parts to reveal the existence of a cloistered summer home. Marsh grass and sandy patches of beach are visible off to the north.

Dockage/Moorings: Docking and marine service opportunities are extensive along the eastern shore of Three Mile Harbor. The first facility you come to is Harbor Marina of East Hampton, which is one of the four facilities here managed by Seacoast Enterprises. (The other three are at the south end of the harbor and are described below.) This full-service marina and boatyard is located on over 8 acres and features a fuel dock, fully stocked ship store, a full marine service department and a waterfront restaurant, as well as slips to 65 feet.

In a well-protected basin to the south is Maidstone Harbor Marina with slips to 75 feet and offering a wide array of amenities, services and conveniences. Nearby East Hampton Point Marina & Boatyard is a marina, hotel and restaurant (seasonal) housed in an attractive lighthouse-like structure. At its centerpiece is a classic, fully rigged Olympic racing contender. They have 58 slips to 120 feet and welcome transients.

Just to the south, the 40-slip Shagwong Marina - East Hampton can accommodate vessels to 50 feet with professional dockhands to assist incoming boaters. A well-protected location with scenic views of Three Mile Harbor and a widespread lawn are among the offerings.

Two facilities managed by Seacoast Enterprises include Halsey's Marina and Gardiner's Marina, both in well-protected basins in picturesque, park-like settings. Both maintain transient slips with full amenities. Seacoast Enterprises also operates Three Mile Harbor Marina and Boatyard, which has slips and the usual amenities. This is a full-service boatyard offering all types of repairs and maintenance. Their 3,000 square foot, well-stocked marine store has a large selection of marine parts and boating accessories, snacks, sundries, boating and local literature and nautical gifts.

For those desiring the security of a fixed mooring, Seacoast Enterprises has four (marked "T") just inside the channel. Do not pick up a pennant without a reservation. Boaters can call one number (631-324-5666) to make a reservation at any of the Seacoast Enterprise facilities or to reserve a mooring.

NOTE: The town's free pump-out service can be contacted on VHF Channel 73. (Hail "Pump-out Boat.")

Anchorage: Although the number of private moorings have been increasing in Three Mile Harbor, most of the south and west areas of the harbor are still open for excellent anchorage options in 10- to 12-foot MLW depths with excellent holding in mud. It is rarely too crowded even on busy summer weekends. There is some water skiing and tubing activity during summer weekends and evenings, but for the most part, it is a quiet area. Shore access is easy from a boat ramp at the inner harbor.

On approaching the anchorage, be sure to honor the second red marker off (and fully past) the wood barricaded docks of East Hampton Point Marina & Boatyard before turning to starboard. This will avoid a shallow but nearly invisible bar that extends along the west side of the channel.

Lake Montauk

Montauk is only 17 nm from Block Island, 14 nm from Plum Gut, 13 nm from Three Mile Harbor and 11 nm from The Race. Montauk is famous for tuna, marlin, swordfish and shark fishing in its offshore waters and for outstanding sportfishing and yachting facilities ashore. The surf around Montauk Point serves as one of the East Coast's premier striped bass fisheries and the area has become a hotbed of saltwater fly fishing.

Excellent marinas cater to sportfishing and cruising vessels of all descriptions. The place buzzes with activity during the summer yet it is easy to escape to a quiet spot with a near-empty seascape. The beaches are superb both on the Block Island Sound side and Atlantic Ocean side. The classic Montauk Lighthouse beckons and the picturesque nearby village has all the necessary amenities.

NAVIGATION: From Three Mile Harbor, the route curves around Hog Creek Point, southwest of Gardiners Island, past Acabonack Harbor, Napeague Harbor and Fort Pond Bay to Lake Montauk. Montauk Point itself is farther east. Harbors along the route tend to be shoal, wild and interesting but safer for dinghy exploration (in good weather) than for anchorages. Several of the dredged harbors are protected but prone to shoaling.

Enter Montauk Harbor, located in the northern part of Lake Montauk, via a channel protected by lighted jetties. Favor the western jetty, allow for the 2.5-knot current and keep clear of off-channel rocks inside the breakwaters. The current chart indicates 12-foot MLW depths. Along the western shore and in the bight west of Star Island

Lake Montauk, NY

MONTAUK HARBOR		Largest Vessel	VHF	Total Slips	Approach/Dockside Depth	Floating Docks	Gas/Diesel	Repairs/Haulout	Min/Max Amps	Pump-Out Station
1. Uihlein Marina and Boat Rentals	(631) 668-3799	40	14	18	9.0 / 9.0	F	G	RH	30	
2. Montauk Marine Basin WiFi	(631) 668-5900	100	19	150	7.0 / 8.0	F	GD	RH	30 / 50	
3. Diamond Cove Marina	(631) 668-6592	50		50	6.0 / 6.0	F		RH	30 / 50	
4. Westlake Marina WiFi	(631) 668-5600	50	19	100	5.0 / 5.0	F			20 / 50	
5. Snug Harbor Motel & Marina WiFi	(631) 668-2860	50	9	80	6.0 / 6.0	F			30 / 50	
6. Sam's Star Island Yacht Club and Marina WiFi	(631) 668-5052	165	9	170	10.0 / 6.0	F	GD	RH	30 / 100	P
7. Safe Harbor Montauk Yacht Club WiFi	(631) 668-7732	300	9	232	/ 12.0				30 / 200+	P
8. Montauk Anglers Club	(631) 668-3232	130	19	157	8.0 / 8.0	F	GD	RH	30 / 100	
9. Montauk Lake Club and Marina - PRIVATE WiFi	(631) 668-5705	200	12	104	9.0 / 9.0	F	GD		30 / 100	P

WiFi Wireless Internet Access
Visit www.waterwayguide.com for current rates, fuel prices, website addresses and other up-to-the-minute information.
(Information in the table is provided by the facilities.)

Scan here for more details:

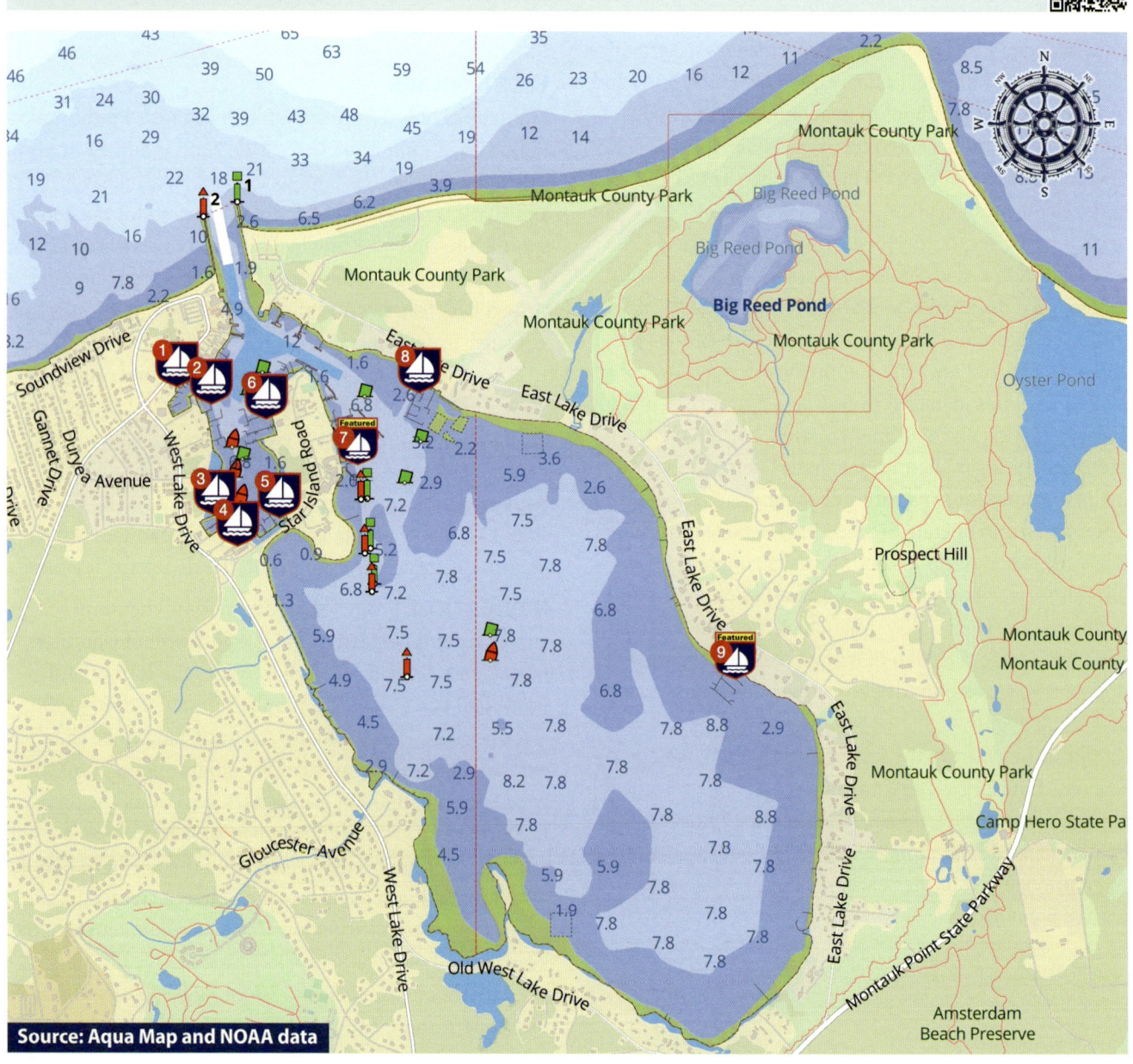

Source: Aqua Map and NOAA data

are Montauk's headquarters for charter and head boats and the ferry to Block Island. The well-marked channel to the east takes you to Lake Montauk and several opportunities for dockage and other facilities in less hectic surroundings.

If you plan to anchor, the buoys in the main channel east of Star Island must be followed carefully to clear the shoal (2- to 6-foot MLW depths) extending southwest from the eastern shore. After passing the last marina pier and pile, you must turn sharply to starboard to be sure not to miss the channel. Keep green can "5" to port then thread the needle between flashing green "7" and red "8." Missing the marks may result in a tow off the shoal.

From Montauk Point, east or south, you are in the Atlantic Ocean and your vessel should be prepared for open ocean and changes in the weather. Unexpected fog is something to be reckoned with. On Block Island Sound the famous long swells can put you to sleep but in a blow, they can be challenging. Know your weather as thoroughly as possible before starting from Montauk.

Dockage: Montauk Harbor is crowded and active. Turn to starboard on entering the channel. Dockage on the west side of the inner harbor is within easy walking distance of urban-style amenities and the Gosman's Dock complex of restaurants and shops.

Uihlein Marina and Boat Rentals has transient slips to 40 feet. Fees are based on a sliding scale depending on whether you want to stay less than 4 hours, more than 4 hours or overnight. Register at the front desk. Next is Montauk Marine Basin with slips to 100 feet (including hourly rates) plus a full-service boat yard and marine supply store.

Continuing south, Diamond Cove Marina is a café and bar offering an authentic Mexican, BBQ and seafood menu. They welcome transients to 50 feet.

Westlake Marina claims to be "Montauk's friendliest marina" and welcomes transients with dockage to 50 feet. They have a popular family-friendly seafood restaurant on site.

Snug Harbor Motel & Marina is a great place to change crew or just take a room and get off the boat for a while. The marina offers slips to 50 feet with all the usual amenities plus a pool and easy access to shopping and dining.

On the west side of Star Island, Sam's Star Island Yacht Club and Marina is a "hardcore" fishing center, where virtually all boats in their floating slips sprout outriggers. Major fishing tournaments regularly run from here and their large ship store sells bait and tackle of every type as well as marine supplies.

Montauk Point

SAFE HARBOR MONTAUK YACHT CLUB

WESTLAKE MARINA

Star Island

Lake Montauk Inlet

MONTAUK LAKE CLUB
& Marina

Guest Rooms   Spa   Bar & Restaurant   Heated Pool   Fitness Club

www.montauklakeclub.com   Latitude: 41.061255   Longitude: 71.91221   Tel: 631.668.5705   © Aerial Pros

GOIN' ASHORE

MONTAUK, NY

ATTRACTIONS

1. Bluff Lookout
Scenic overlook accessible by a small hike from Camp Hero. Use the east side entrance, which is 2 miles east of the south side route.

2. Ditch Plains Beach
A popular spot for surfing and swimming with seasonal lifeguards and scenic views. Locals say the Ditch Witch food truck serves the best beach food around (23 Ditch Plains Rd., 631-377-8270).

3. Montauk Association Historic District
A 100-acre historic district that includes seven large Shingle style homes built between 1881 and 1884 for wealthy New Yorkers as summer homes.

4. Montauk Cycle Company
For advice on the best trails and routes, trail maps, organized rides and other helpful information at 463 W. Lake Dr. (631-668-8975).

5. Montauk Point Lighthouse Museum
Completed in 1796, first lighthouse built in New York and fourth-oldest working lighthouse in nation (2000 Old Montauk Hwy., 631-668-3781).

SERVICES

6. Meeting House Lane Medical Practice
679 Montauk Hwy. (631-668-3705)

7. Montauk Laundromat
45 S. Elmwood Ave. (631-668-4349)

8. Montauk Library
871 Montauk Hwy. (631-668-3377)

9. Montauk Post Office
73 S. Euclid Ave. (631-668-7043)

10. Sandy Paws Veterinary Clinic
94 S. Euclid Ave. (631-238-5171)

MARINAS

11. Diamond Cove Marina
364 W. Lake Dr. (631-668-6592)

12. Montauk Anglers Club
467 E. Lake Dr. (631-668-3232)

13. Montauk Lake Club and Marina-PRIVATE
211 E. Lake Dr. (631-668-5705)

14. Montauk Marine Basin
126 W Lake Dr. (631-668-5900)

15. Safe Harbor Montauk Yacht Club
32 Star Island Rd. (631-668-7732)

16. Snug Harbor Motel & Marina
3 Star Island Rd. (631-668-2860)

17. Sam's Star Island Yacht Club and Marina
59 Star Island Rd. (631-668-5052)

18. Uihlein Marina and Boat Rentals
West Lake Dr. (631-668-3799)

19. Westlake Marina
352 W. Lake Dr. (631-668-5600)

The main town of Montauk is a couple of miles away from the marinas on the Atlantic Ocean side. Montauk's landmark lighthouse (1797), one of the oldest and most important on the coast, is a couple of miles in the opposite direction. Towering 168 feet over Montauk Point, the light is still serving as an active aid to navigation and can be seen 19 miles out to sea. The area around Montauk Light is considered a haven for avid birdwatchers, especially during the off-season. Tours can be arranged through the Montauk Point Lighthouse Museum & Gift Shop (2000 Montauk Hwy., 631-668-2544) near the lighthouse. There is a seasonal bus you can catch on the highway outside Ditch Plains to take you to the lighthouse or to town. Go to www.sct-bus.org for schedules and routes.

Safe Harbor Montauk Yacht Club (formerly Gurney's Star Island Resort & Marina) comes into view next. A perennial favorite among the boating community and a haven for cruisers, sportfishers and megayachts, the marina can accommodate vessels to 300 feet with resort amenities. Ocean Club Montauk restaurant is on site as well as indoor/outdoor pools with a pool club for sipping, swimming or relaxing.

All the amenities of a private yacht club are available in the comfort of a laid-back, casual atmosphere at Montauk Anglers Club on the east shore of Lake Montauk. They have ample transient slips for vessels to 50 feet plus a waterfront restaurant and a well-stocked ship store.

For those desiring a really quiet location on the lake, to the south is the private Montauk Lake Club and Marina. Visitors from reciprocal clubs are extended docking privileges (up to five days) and use of club facilities. Amenities include heated pools with poolside cabanas, an on-site restaurant, spa and fitness facility and beach access.

Anchorage: The channel to the southeast part of Lake Montauk is clearly outlined with town markers. The channel moves to red "14" and green "13" mid-lake before you turn southeast. There is plenty of anchoring room in Lake Montauk. Holding ground is fair in mud and grass so use ample scope when you drop the hook. Some cruisers use the very small beach at the Gosman's complex at the inside edge of the west entrance breakwater to pull up their dinghies. Also, the local marinas usually do not mind accommodating your dinghy and some provisions are available at most of them.

To the south there is good holding and fairly consistent depths across most of lake at 8 feet MLW. You may pull your dinghy on the sides of the beach in the southeast corner of the Lake to access basic heads or to walk to Ditch Plains or the bus stop to town (west) or Montauk Light (east).

Gardiners Point Island

In 1855 a lighthouse was constructed on Gardiners Point, which at that time was connected to Gardiner's Island. A March nor'easter in 1888 destroyed the light and changed the peninsula to an island. During the Spanish-American War, Fort Tyler was constructed on Gardiners Point Island as part of the chain of fortifications aimed at keeping the Spanish from attacking New York. Shifting sands caused the abandonment of the fort and during World War II it was used for bombing practice. Now known locally as "The Ruins," it is a serious hazard to navigation as there may be unexploded ordinance in the area. Give it a wide berth. No landing!

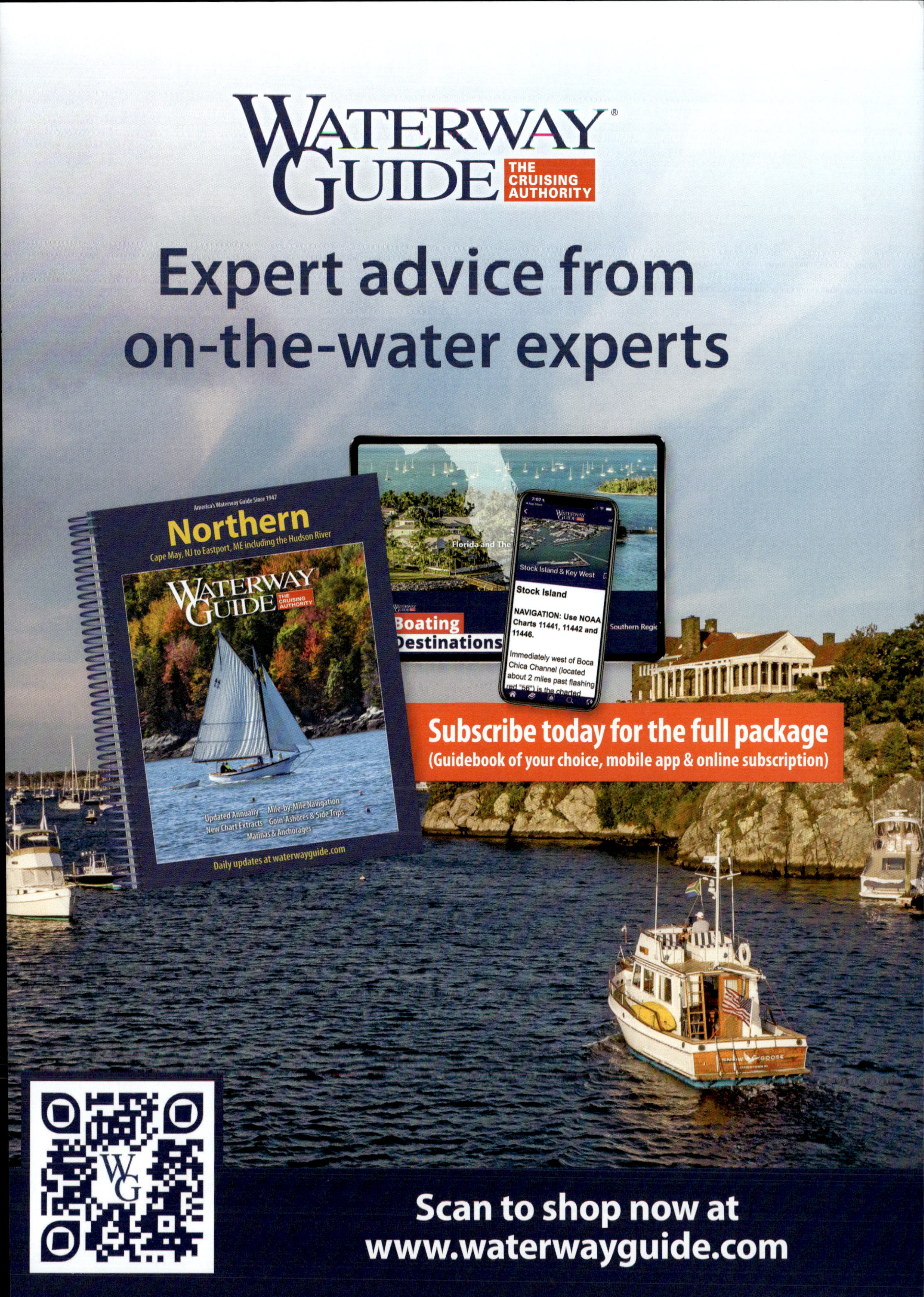
WATERWAY GUIDE
THE CRUISING AUTHORITY
Expert advice from on-the-water experts
America's Waterway Guide Since 1947
Northern
Cape May, NJ to Eastport, ME including the Hudson River
WATERWAY GUIDE
Updated Annually
Mile-by-Mile Navigation
New Chart Extracts
Goin' Ashore & Side Trips
Marinas & Anchorages
Daily updates at waterwayguide.com
Boating Destinations
Stock Island & Key West
Stock Island
NAVIGATION: Use NOAA Charts 11441, 11442 and 11446.
Subscribe today for the full package
(Guidebook of your choice, mobile app & online subscription)
Scan to shop now at
www.waterwayguide.com

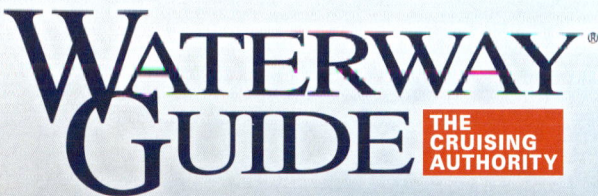

Section 4: Block Island to Nantucket Sound

Chapter 11: Page 348

Chapter 12: Page 391

Chapter 13: Page 417

Providence River

Barrington

Warren

Mount Hope Bay

Greenwich Bay

Bristol

Fairhaven

Narragansett Bay

Tiverton

New Bedford

Wickford

Sakonnet River

Conanicut Island

Buzzards Bay

Westport

Jamestown

Newport

Wakefield

Sakonnet

Rhode Island Sound

Vineyard Sound

Cuttyhunk Island

Point Judith

Atlantic Ocean

Block Island

Chapter 12: Page 391

Chapter 13: Page 417

Wareham

Onset

Cape Cod Canal

Phinneys Harbor

Marion

Pocasett

Cape Cod

Chatham

Megansett Harbor

Hyannis

Cotuit

Mattapoisett Harbor

Falmouth

Nantucket Sound

Woods Hole

Naushon Island

Martha's Vineyard

Nantucket Island

Pages 379-385

Pages 385-390

Pages 361-369

Providence River

Barrington

Warren

Mount Hope Bay

Greenwich Bay

Bristol

Tiverton

Narragansett Bay

Sakonnet River

Prudence Island

Wickford

Conanicut Island

Pages 370-379

Jamestown

Newport

Sakonnet

Wakefield

Brenton Point

Pages 356-361

Jerusalem

Rhode Island Sound

Point Judith

Pages 351-355

Atlantic Ocean

Block Island

■ NAVIGATION NOTES

After exiting the eastern end of Long Island Sound through The Race or Fishers Island Sound's Watch Hill Passage, mariners enter the exciting cruising grounds of southern New England: Block Island Sound, Rhode Island Sound and Narragansett Bay and the world-famous destination of Newport, RI.

Rhode Island waters can often be challenging. To reach Block Island is to venture into open ocean, out of sight of land on hazy days. You should review your boat's safety and navigational gear and the crew's preparedness before you set out to Block Island.

While Rhode Island has much industry, the state is completely water-oriented. Narragansett Bay, cutting 25 miles inland, gives the state a lot more shoreline than you would think, considering the state's small size.

Rhode Island's seafaring tradition dates back more than 300 years and survives today up and down the shores of Narragansett Bay. Fishermen still make a living from the sea, yachts from around the world constantly converge on Newport and visiting mariners tie up on moorings or at docks in one of the many marinas in the maze of harbors.

Our coverage continues on towards Buzzards Bay and Vineyard Sound, where small, deep water harbors, such as Falmouth on Cape Cod or Oak Bluffs on Martha's Vineyard, are thick with boats and are much different than the sprawling harbors of Nantucket and Edgartown. Cruisers will also find secluded hideaways such as Katama Bay inside the south shore of Martha's Vineyard next to Edgartown. The variety of nautical scenery is part of what draws us to Buzzards Bay, Cape Cod and the Islands.

The commercial harbors of New Bedford with a huge fishing fleet, and Woods Hole with an oceanographic fleet, contrast with the elegant yacht harbors of Quissett with its local small-boat fleet and Padanaram, on Buzzards Bay, with its traditional wooden boat fleet. There is something for every mariner and harbors for every family. There is bountiful, fresh seafood, beautiful waterfront scenery and the thrill of venturing east to Cape Cod.

Cruising Conditions

These waters are among the most beautiful on the East Coast of the United States but with a change of tide or wind they can suddenly become quite choppy and can be dangerous. A watchful eye on the chart, the compass and the weather is always necessary. NOAA Weather Radio is an essential tool and many VHF radios can notify you in case of severe weather alerts. Sudden blows are a possibility but the other major hazard is the chop set up by a current running counter to the wind.

Point Judith Light Narragansett, RI

Chop can make a skipper and their crew uncomfortable and impatient and it can also make it harder to locate buoys leading into harbors or even small boats. Constant attention and cultivated patience are necessities. Do not hesitate to stay comfortably tied up in port if weather conditions are not to your liking.

Ferry boats moving from mainland Rhode Island, Connecticut, Massachusetts and Montauk, NY, head to Block Island, Martha's Vineyard and Nantucket. They crisscross Block Island Sound, Rhode Island Sound, Vineyard Sound and both Narragansett and Buzzard's Bays constantly throughout the day. Be watchful at all times.

Tugs with barges far astern, freighters, stealthy submarines and seemingly endless, random recreational boat traffic should warn the skipper and crew to be alert and watchful at all times. You will encounter strong currents and big tidal ranges and need to keep an eye out for lobster pots, rocks and ledges.

Fog is always a possibility and can create very dangerous situations with little or no warning. From Long Island Sound along Southern New England up to Maine and beyond, many cruisers consider radar as a standard aid to navigation. From here to the north and east, boats of more than 30 feet are likely to have radar antennas mounted on a mast or atop a stern pole or pilothouse. At the very least boats in these waters should carry high-mounted radar reflectors to improve visibility to others. An AIS receiver is another helpful way to avoid larger vessels.

Dockage

There are hundreds of marinas in the area covered by this chapter but transients may not be their priority. They are often nearly full with their local customers. Finding a dockside slip for an overnight stay could prove difficult in the peak season of July and August.

Skippers accustomed to tying up every night and plugging into shore power might have a challenge finding that kind of dockage. Reserve a slip where possible but some marinas will not take reservations in advance. Their rule is generally first-come, first-served. Call the marina of your choice on VHF radio as you come within range or try calling them early in the day via cell phone if you did not get a reservation. If slips are not available, ask for a mooring of suitable size. If that fails, be prepared to anchor or, at worst, move on to the next harbor.

To avoid end-of-day disappointment, try to arrive early in the afternoon of the day you need accommodations or anchoring space. Every destination in this corner of the Eastern seaboard is well worth any effort and, fortunately, there are many places to set your anchor safely. There is nothing like a sunrise or sunset over Block Island, Nantucket, Martha's Vineyard or Cape Cod. Not much compares to this beautiful cruising area.

Anchoring & Mooring

In many, if not most harbors mentioned in this guide, designated Special Anchorage Areas are available in which vessels of less than 20 meters in length are not required to show anchor lights, day shapes or sound signals. Anchoring within a Special Anchorage Area does not require permission but permission for the use of mooring balls, within or outside of a Special Anchorage Area is required.

In spite of the proliferation of mooring balls, it is often possible to still find places to anchor, both within and outside of the Special Anchorage Areas, keeping an appropriate distance from mooring balls, channels, docks, boatyards and marinas (not to mention other boats).

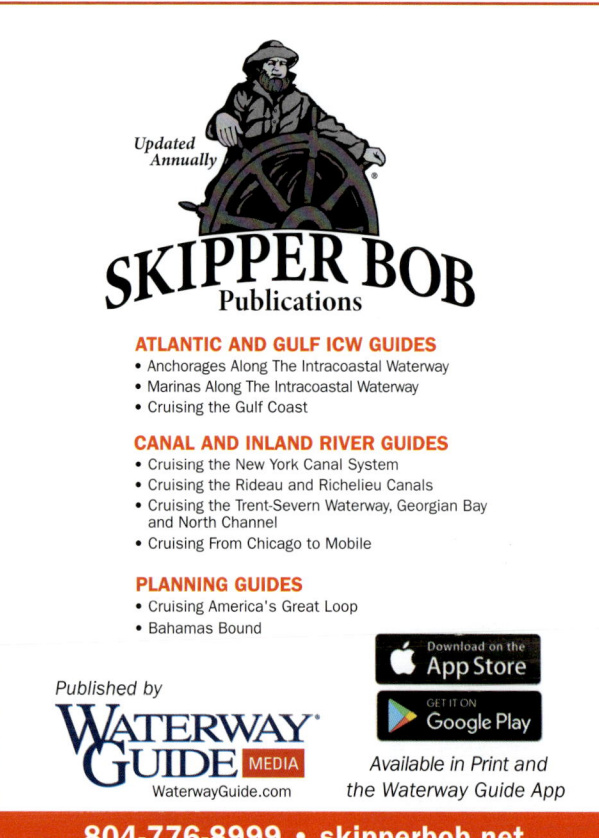

Labels on image: PAYNE'S DOCK · Block Island · TPG MARINAS CHAMPLIN'S · Great Salt Pond · Harbor Neck

■ BLOCK ISLAND

Block Island, 12 miles south of the mainland, has tall hills and bluffs that make it visible on the horizon during clear weather. It appears a tempting challenge to cruisers transiting between the Long Island Sound and the Narraganset or Buzzards Bay but offshore voyagers often greet it with happiness and sometimes with relief, since it provides a haven and a staging spot to make the most of the raging currents of those neighboring bodies of water.

Although only 6 miles long and 3 miles wide, Great Salt Pond is welcoming during rough weather on the sound. The beautiful, sun-washed beaches, cliff-side views, fresh air and island mystique draw boaters and non-boaters, young and old alike. The pork chop-shaped island has 20 miles of shoreline, high clay bluffs and lonely beaches known mainly to seabirds and the occasional seal.

Block Island is often quite crowded on high-season weekends and holidays. As many as 2,000 boats encamp here over the Fourth of July week, when a festive, carnival-like atmosphere overtakes the island, and its unique Americana parade expands contemporary understandings of patriotism. Holiday sunsets here are often celebrated with impromptu boat horn symphonies followed by revelries far into the night.

During a normal summer weekend, the island easily accommodates some 1,200 to 1,300 boats, although latecomers should expect all moorings to be taken, many with raft-ups, and shallow-depth anchorage space long gone or quite crowded. Block Island requests a nominal landing fee from every adult who arrives by private boat or ferry. The fee is collected on the honor system via collection boxes at marinas and town docks.

Cruising Conditions

While the odds are good for a trouble-free crossing, Block Island Sound should always be accorded proper respect. Easy swells can become seas in minutes. Fog is frequent, sometimes patchy and at other times all-encompassing and unnerving.

Often called the "Bermuda of the North," the temperatures on Block Island are often 10 degrees cooler than the mainland in summer and warmer than the mainland in winter. It might be foggy, cool and damp during the early morning and evening but sometimes when fog is heavy outside the breakwaters, the sun is shining on the island proper.

The island can develop its own wind, often from the southwest, which cools the island in the summer but can create problems for the anchored fleet in Great Salt Pond. At the same time, just beyond the breakwaters, calms can prevail and sailboats that reduced sail area in expectation of a rough passage to Rhode Island or Connecticut find themselves wallowing without wind in the rolling swells from the southwest. The opposite can also occur.

Navigating Block Island

Boats converge on Block Island from many directions: east from Connecticut via The Race, about 21 nm; southeast from Watch Hill Passage, about 13 nm; southwest from Newport, about 26nm; northeast from Montauk Harbor, about 17 nm; and south from Point Judith, some 10 nm across Block Island Sound.

Big ship traffic will show AIS signatures and significant radar returns but sportfishers don't stay home for a little fog and are often harder to see and avoid! Current pours through The Race and Watch Hill Passage and can significantly affect your navigation efforts in or out bound.

If you make your approach in clear weather from the west, you may think you are looking at two islands. Great Salt Pond almost bisects the island and the shore on both sides of the pond is low. The land in between will appear as you get closer with higher ground to the south.

If coming from points east or heading to Old Harbor from the west, do not cut the corner at flashing green "1BI" at the northern end of the island. That treacherous bar has caught many skippers who thought they were in deep water and the summer westerlies complicate the sailor's path. Even crossing safely north, breakers complicate the passage when ocean rollers pile up on the suddenly shallow sea bottom.

Many boats travel close to shore on the southern and western sides of the island, but unmarked rocks are all around. There is a five-turbine wind farm a little less than 4 miles southeast of Block Island. They are in deep water and the blades are above all but the very tallest vessels. Numerous small fishing boats collect near them, and prudence is advised. Currents run strong all around the island, southeasterly on the ebb and westerly on the flood.

> **CAUTION:** Stay alert! Submarines heading for New London can appear unexpectedly (especially stimulating in the fog), and ferries, freighters, naval vessels and barge traffic crisscross the waters continuously.

New Harbor (Great Salt Pond)

The Great Salt Pond is more than 1 nm long and almost as wide. New Harbor is in the southeastern corner but the whole of Great Salt Pond is often (erroneously) called New Harbor. The 11.5-foot MLW entry channel is not natural. It was cut through from Block Island Sound to the natural salt pond in 1895 after several failed attempts.

Great Salt Pond offers all the attributes of a cruising mecca: plenty of water, good marinas with repair capabilities and room to anchor, although holding varies with location. The marine facilities here also provide easy access to the island's numerous beaches, hiking trails, restaurants and lighthouses. Ferries from Point Judith and Montauk tie up regularly at marina docks in the Great Salt Pond.

NAVIGATION: The Great Salt Pond channel is well marked and easy to enter. The 49-foot-high 4-second flashing red beacon "4" will attract your attention from a distance but it is somewhat southwest of the channel itself. Red bell buoy "2" is a better place to start if you don't have local knowledge because it gets you lined up to run the channel straight ahead. It is unlighted but has a bell.

The first lighted channel markers are flashing green buoy "7" and flashing red buoy "8," both of which are stationed well within the shallow zone. Keep an eye on your set between red bell buoy "2" and the lighted buoys when the current is running. The channel heads straight past the former Coast Guard station (also on the west shore) and into Great Salt Pond itself.

Prevailing sou'westerlies and local racing traditions seem to encourage sailing vessels to enter and exit under canvas, which causes no particular difficulty. Sailing traffic with wide ranges of speed and maneuverability, along with power cruisers at various levels of skills and determination, can make the short passage interesting and colorful. In Great Salt Pond, the water is deep almost to the banks with few rocks or obstructions except at the southwestern corner.

Block Island, RI

BLOCK ISLAND		Largest Vessel	VHF	Total Slips	Approach/ Dockside Depth	Floating Docks	Gas/ Diesel	Repairs/ Haulout	Min/Max Amps	Pump-Out Station
1. TPG Marinas Champlin's WiFi	(401) 466-7777	300	11	150	25.0 / 18.0	F	GD		30 / 50	P
2. New Harbor Boat Basin	(401) 480-1429	110	9	100	14.0 / 10.0	F		R	30 / 50	P
3. Payne's Dock	(401) 466-5572	300		50	21.0 / 16.0	F	GD		30 / 50	P
4. New Harbor (Great Salt Pond) - Block Island Mooring	(401) 466-3204		12		/					P
5. Old Harbor Town Dock	(401) 466-3235		12	30	8.0 / 5.0					P

WiFi Wireless Internet Access
Visit www.waterwayguide.com for current rates, fuel prices, website addresses and other up-to-the-minute information.
(Information in the table is provided by the facilities.)

Scan here for more details:

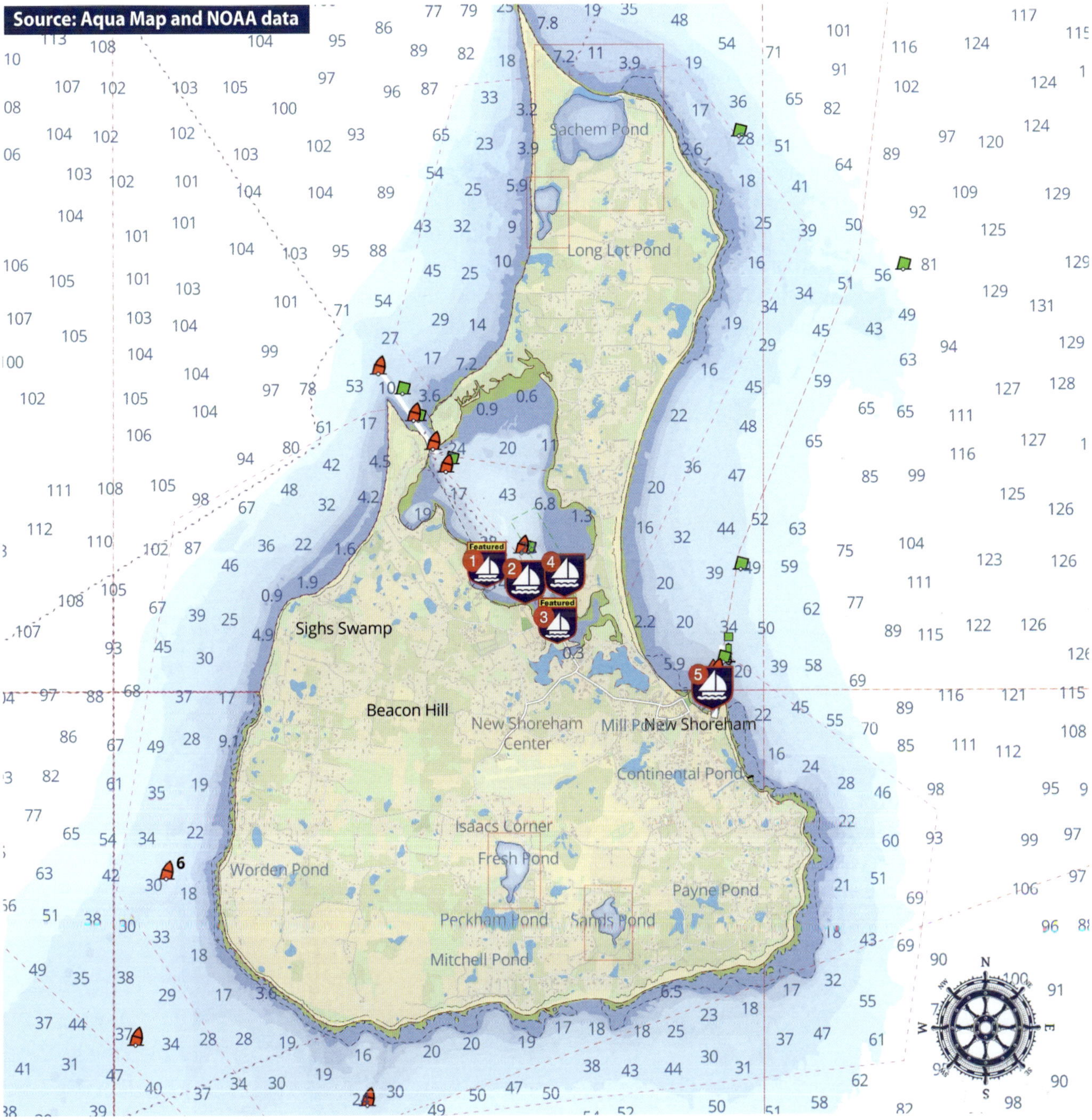

Source: Aqua Map and NOAA data

Sachem Pond

Long Lot Pond

Sighs Swamp

Beacon Hill

New Shoreham Center

Mill Pond   New Shoreham

Continental Pond

Isaacs Corner

Fresh Hond

Worden Pond

Payne Pond

Peckham Pond   Sands Pond

Mitchell Pond

Dockage/Moorings: The cost of a rental mooring when the anchorage is full is a relaxing investment in this harbor, when safety and convenience are top concerns. The town's ever-increasing New Harbor (Great Salt Pond) moorings are located along the southern edge of Great Salt Pond in front of the marinas. They are first-come, first-served. The harbormaster's launch will drop by to collect the fee, which covers trash disposal, pump-out service and two shower tokens per day (in the pavilion at Fred Benson Town Beach, described below). Rafting of up to two boats is permitted (with permission) but not required.

Early arrivals should simply pick up the pennant of an available buoy. Moorings that are light green in color with black numbers can accommodate vessels up to 45 feet, while the bright orange moorings are for vessels 46 to 55 feet in length. Other moorings are private (white with black numbers) but the harbormaster may know of ones that are available. Skippers of larger boats (40-foot lengths or more) or late arrivals who can't locate an available mooring should contact the harbormaster on VHF Channel 12 for directions to an appropriate tie-up. The town has a number of heavier moorings for larger vessels.

If you prefer a slip, several marinas line the southern shore of Great Salt Pond including the 225-slip TPG Marinas Champlin's, the first facility you will see upon entry and the largest in the harbor. Guests enjoy full access to all the resort amenities including the 42-room on-site boutique hotel, waterfront pool, two dockside restaurants, a cafe, a poolside bar and a dog park. There is also a complimentary shuttle to town.

The family-owned and -operated Payne's Dock has slips to 300 feet with full amenities and two restaurants, a bar and an ice cream parlor. This active marina is home of the fun Mahogany Shoals Bar and is close to great beaches and hiking and walking trails. New Harbor Boat Basin to the north offers 100 slips with 85 reserved for transients. Reservations are recommended.

Anchorage: Note that permitted anchorage is east of the main navigation channel in the harbor at Great Salt Pond (North). Just follow the well-marked channel and drop the anchor after turning to port on the way in by green can "11" and look for 15 to 25 feet MLW. There is almost always adequate room to anchor, although the open space is reduced by an area set aside for undisturbed shellfish beds. You can also try Great Salt Pond (South)

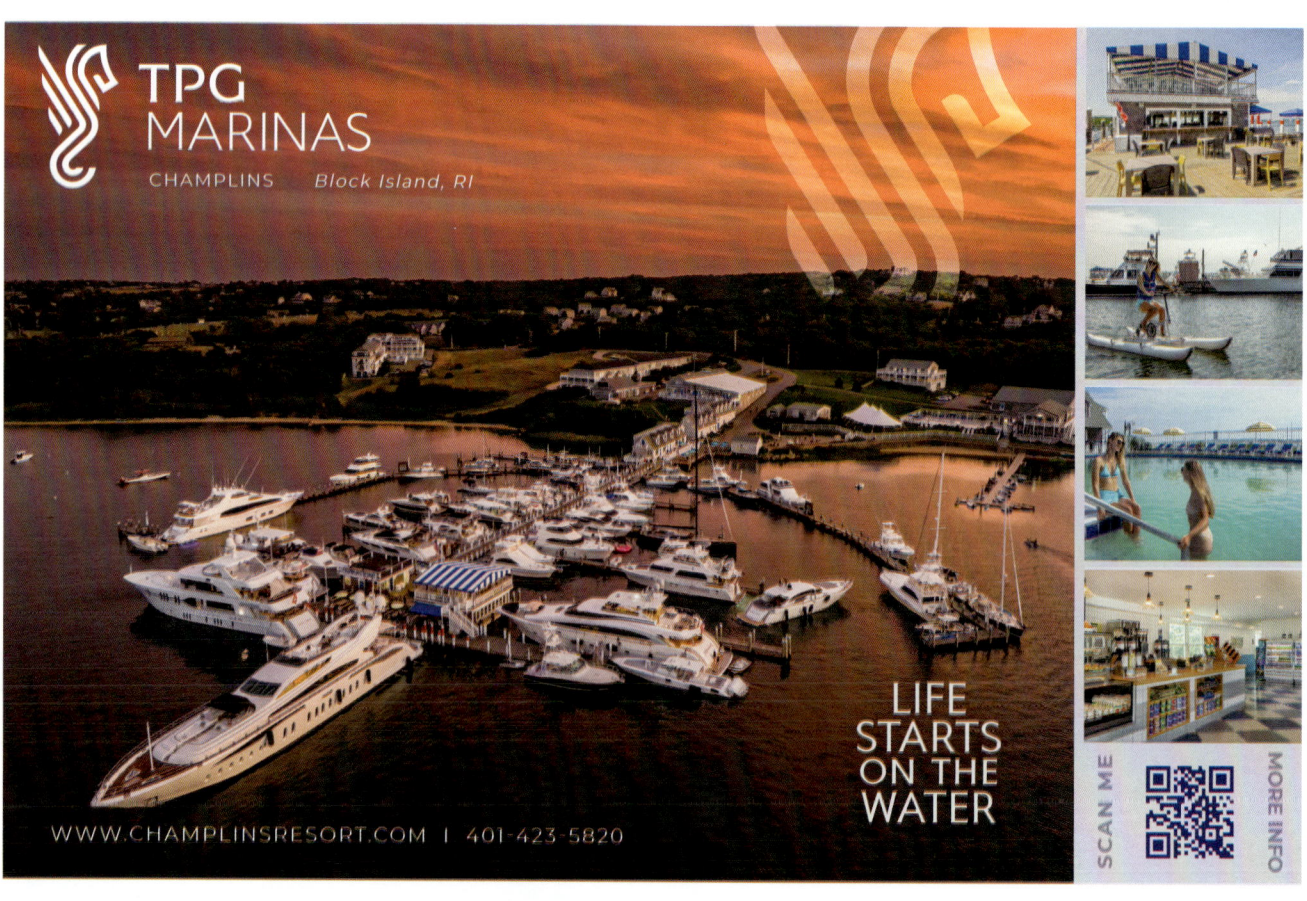

but you are not allowed to anchor in the town mooring field, within 100 feet of a commercial dock, on the west side of the harbor, within 50 feet of a residential dock private mooring or moored vessel, in the recreation area or in the navigation channels and fairways.

You must have confidence in your ground tackle to anchor anywhere in the harbor, as some boats will drag through the grassy bottom in a summer thunderstorm. Stick to the standard rules of thumb (minimum of 5:1 with chain, 7:1 on rope) and avoid the embarrassment of dragging.

Old Port Launch (VHF Channel 68) runs in most weather and late into the night. The launches are based at New Harbor Boat Basin, where there is also a dinghy dock. Dinghy dockage is also available at TPG Marinas Champlin's. Both accept separated trash and recycling. At New Harbor Boat Basin you must not tie up in the well-marked areas reserved for the launches. Your dinghy will be cut free.

The dinghy dock in New Harbor between Payne's Dock and Dead Eye Dick's was built and donated by the Wronoski family who owns the Cross Sound Ferry and Dead Eye Dick's. It is removed at the end of each season and stored in New London. There is room for about 100 dinghies (12-foot max.) If these dinghy docks are full, it's best to go to the beach between New Harbor Boat Basin and Payne's Dock. There is no overnight dockage, and vessels left for 24 hours will be removed by the Harbormaster and impounded with a $100 fine.

The Fred Benson Town Beach pavilion houses the town's showers and is reached by beaching your dinghy on the east side of the pond.

A wooden walkway over the marsh grass puts you on a busy roadway for a very short walk to the north. Turn right into the first small parking lot and head east towards the beach. From there it is a 0.5-mile trek south to the pavilion. Showers are rather expensive, as each token provides only four minutes of water. Chairs, umbrellas and windscreens may be rented at the pavilion.

> NOTE: The Great Salt Pond is a No-Discharge Zone, one of the first anywhere. Even treated effluent cannot be discharged overboard. The town of New Shoreham makes it easy to comply with The No-Discharge law by providing free pump-out service for any boat in the harbor. Simply call "Pump-out Boat" on VHF Channel 73. Although service is fast and efficient, they are busy and it is best to call early in the day to be put on the list.

Old Harbor

This small harbor of refuge, protected from the ocean by breakwaters, is on the island's eastern side (not accessible by boat from New Harbor). New Shoreham is the smallest town in the smallest state in the U.S. It was incorporated in 1672 and only encompasses Block Island, although people rarely say they are going to (or are from) New Shoreham; they say they are going to Block Island. Old Harbor is the center of town and the larger commercial ferry landing location, which means that it is the more modern, tourist-centric side of the island. New Harbor, strangely, is the more traditional, recreational port in atmosphere.

The town of New Shoreham ordinances require yachts to stand clear of the marked channel area between the harbor entrance and

the pier marked "Ferry" at the southeastern end of the harbor. Ferries leave from here for Point Judith, RI, and New London, CT, about 11 times a day in peak season (early June through Labor Day) and less frequently off season.

NAVIGATION: The straight entry to Old Harbor is easy to navigate except in strong easterlies when seas are heavy. Jetty lights and a foghorn help in bad weather. A small inner harbor in the southeastern corner has a town dock and offers excellent protection from all but extreme weather.

Dockage: The municipal Old Harbor Town Dock has 30 slips (all transient) on fixed docks with limited services. The fee covers trash disposal, pump-out service and two shower tokens per night (in the pavilion at Fred Benson Town Beach).

Anchorage: Anchoring anywhere in Old Harbor at Block Island can be a problem. It has very limited space for anchoring, which is restricted to a total of 7 days in a 14-day period. Town ordinances require yachts to stand clear of the marked channel area between the harbor entrance and the pier marked FERRY at the southeastern end of the harbor.

In addition, anchorage is not allowed within 100 feet of a commercial dock and within 50 feet of a moored vessel. Commercial boats, fishing and charter boats use Old Harbor extensively and Med-moor to walls or anchor fore-and-aft with their sterns to the breakwater. Depths are about 10 to 15 feet MLW.

There is no dinghy dockage or launch service. You can land your dinghy on the sandy beach of the outer harbor, but you wouldn't want to anchor here in the "big boat."

POINT JUDITH POND

To Point Judith Pond

In planning a transit from Block Island to the Rhode Island mainland, keep in mind that you will encounter strong currents, lots of boat traffic, frequent fog and significant shipping lanes.

When coming from Great Salt Pond around the north side of Block Island, set your course from the vicinity of flashing green bell buoy "1BI." The waters between Sandy Point and the bell buoy will show breakers in all weather and they break up the swell in a confusing fashion. From that mark it is about 7 nm to the western entrance of the Point Judith Harbor. From Old Harbor take departure from green can "5." A course of about 020° magnetic will take you to the west entrance, a little over 9 miles away.

Be alert for the strong currents flowing in or out of Rhode Island Sound and Narragansett Bay. This area can be quite choppy and confused, particularly when strong currents and winds are in opposition.

If your destination from Block Island is Narragansett Bay, chart a course to Breton Reef, well east of Point Judith. Under all conditions, keep an eye on the mouth of Narragansett Bay for departing cruise ships and other large commercial traffic. High speed ferries operate between Block Island and Point Judith. Mariners are cautioned that these craft move rapidly and at angles to the normal direction of traffic. An AIS receiver is especially helpful in such places. If a close encounter is expected, contact the ship on VHF Channel 13. Outbound ships might be headed east into the Atlantic Ocean, north to Buzzards Bay or west towards Long Island Sound.

NAVIGATION: Enter Point Judith Pond by running the strong currents between the rock jetties of the breachway in the northwest corner of the harbor. Currents at full tidal flow run 3 to 4 knots through this narrow passage where commercial and recreational traffic can be intense. Weaving, leaping and capsizing jet skiers contribute another dimension to the already turbulent waters. Consult NOAA Online Charts for the most up-to-date information. The channels, dredged out of shoal and marsh, can silt up quickly after a storm.

Point Judith Marina

Point Judith Pond

You can't count on having the full width of the channel due to large commercial fishing boats rushing to market with tackle extended. They will crowd and pass a slow boat attempting to sail or power against the current. Meanwhile, fishermen and sightseers line the jetty in all weather. Returning a friendly wave to the onlookers, although a pleasure, can be a dangerous distraction.

Once through The Breachway, the channel almost immediately divides at the prominent red and green Point junction buoy. Galilee is to the east with its big state piers berthing the commercial fishing fleet and the Block Island ferry. Jerusalem, a village of cottages, is to the west. A fair-sized area has been dredged off the docks, but the current remains strong here and larger vessels need all the maneuvering room available.

Take special care upon entering the harbor from the busier western entrance. The breakwater obscures outbound boats from the Breachway in the channel directly inside the wall. Point Judith is the home of one of the largest commercial fishing fleets on the North Atlantic seaboard and is a terminus for the Block Island Ferry so an approaching skipper who cuts close to the port side of the western opening of the refuge can get a sudden and dangerous surprise. The eastern entrance has far less traffic.

The passage into the harbor at the eastern breakwaters west of Point Judith itself are first marked by flashing red buoy "2" followed by the 39-foot flashing green "3" on the west breakwater. The western entrance of the harbor is marked on the northern breakwater by the 35-foot flashing green horn "3" and its southern neighbor, 29-foot flashing red "2." Each entrance carries 18 to 30-foot MLW depths.

CAUTION: The breakwater seawall in the Point Judith Harbor of Refuge is degraded in various areas through natural erosion to below the water line at high tide. The seawall still performs its intended function to break waves and prevent heavy seas from entering Point Judith Harbor but certain environmental conditions may cause segments of the structure to become awash and not detectable by eye or radar. Mariners are advised to maintain a safe distance from the breakwater at all times.

Anchorage: The V-shaped breakwater that protects the Point Judith Harbor provides good anchorage when sea conditions are calm. Large seas, however, will come right over the breakwater, especially at high tide and from the west where the wall is more broken down. Sand from the Pond is piling up inside the breakwater, especially on the southwestern side, forming a substantial shoal. Good holding takes work due to heavy patches of kelp that foul the bottom.

In addition to double-checking for a secure set, choose a spot well within the "V" to be clear of vessels traveling between the eastern entrance and the channel leading into Point Judith Pond. Summer evening squalls can create sudden wind shifts so avoid locations overly close to the breakwater.

There are no real accommodations for cruisers at either Galilee or Jerusalem, which flank the entrance to Point Judith Pond. Visiting boats may tie up at the state pier at Galilee for as long as 2 hours to explore or dine at several fine restaurants. Galilee's sea-oriented commerce is located along a single street paralleling Point Judith Pond. There is no shortage of fresh fish and prepared seafood to go. Those wishing a more extensive visit might do well to remain outside the pond, taking the dinghy in for shore activities or a swim.

When northerly winds interrupt the prevailing summer southwesterlies, it is best to anchor in the lee of Galilee off the beach at Sand Hill Cove, although wakes will keep the boat dancing day and night. Under these conditions, secure anchorage in sand and mud can be found in depths of 7 to 12 feet MLW.

Whatever your location in the Point Judith Harbor, the surge attending Block Island Sound's characteristic ground swells seems to find its way through the breakwater. Moderate to heavy conditions outside will provide plenty of movement inside the harbor.

NOTE: Point Judith is a No-Discharge Zone. Sealed heads, holding tanks and using a pump-out station are required.

Snug Harbor

Quiet Snug Harbor, on the western shore just north of the breachway, offers easy-access dockage, marine facilities, gas and diesel fuel and casual restaurants as well as fresh caught seafood.

NAVIGATION: You will find good protection and interesting scenery inside Point Judith Pond. Its shores

Point Judith Pond, RI

SNUG HARBOR		Largest Vessel	VHF	Total Slips	Approach/ Dockside Depth	Floating Docks	Gas/ Diesel	Repairs/ Haulout	Min/Max Amps	Pump-Out Station
1. Snug Harbor Marina Inc.	(401) 783-7766	70	9	11	6.0 / 6.0	F	GD		50	
2. Point Judith Marina **WiFi**	(401) 789-7189	110	9	185	10.0 / 12.0	F	GD	RH	30 / 100	P

WiFi Wireless Internet Access
Visit www.waterwayguide.com for current rates, fuel prices, website addresses and other up-to-the-minute information.
(Information in the table is provided by the facilities.)

Scan here for more details:

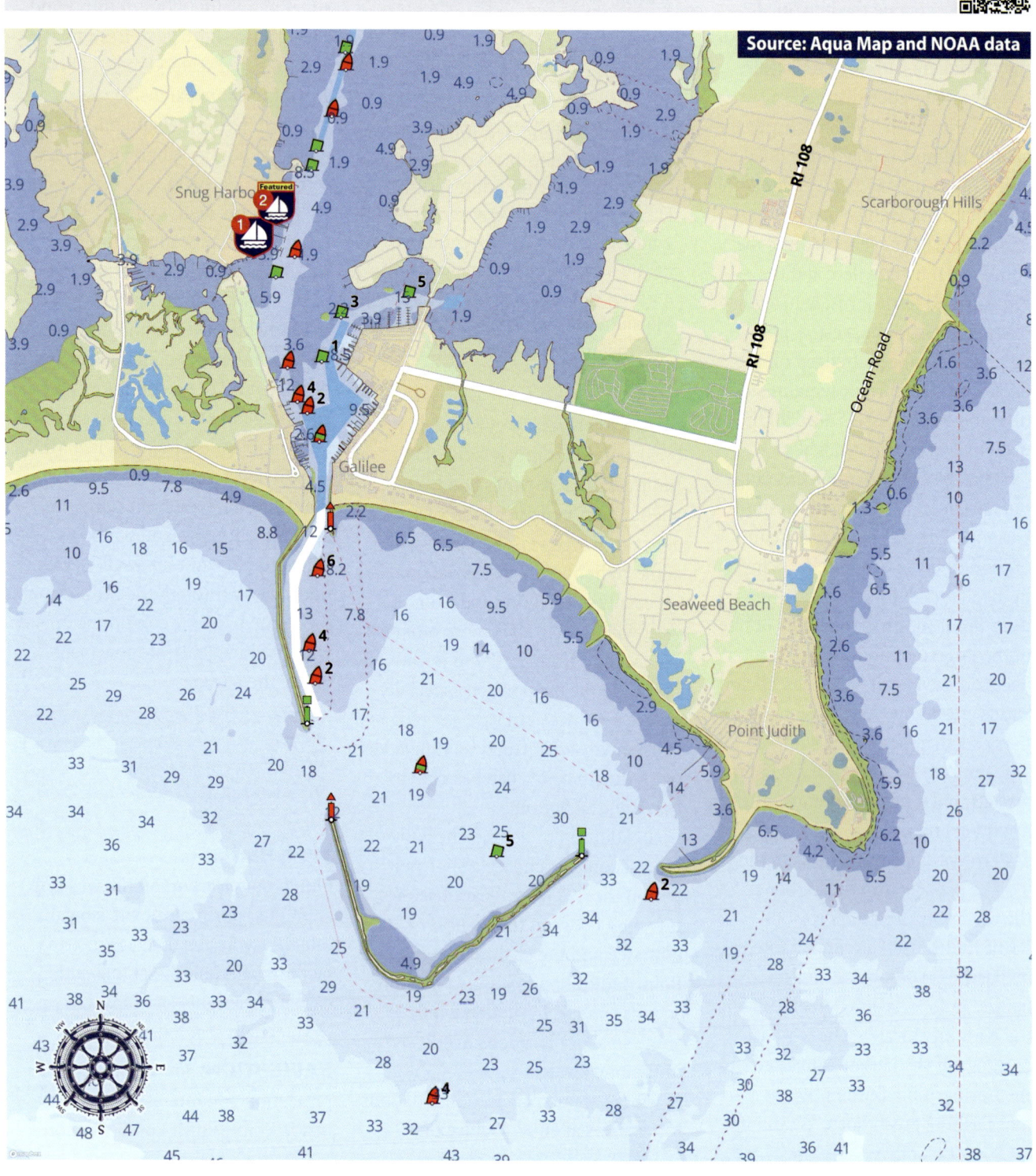

Source: Aqua Map and NOAA data

and islands are lined with fishing villages, community docks and well-equipped marinas. A marked channel carrying at least 6-foot MLW depths leads north on the west side of the pond to Snug Harbor, almost 1 mile above the entrance.

Note that there has been significant shoaling reported between red nun buoy "4" (just north of the State Pier on the Jerusalem side) and green can buoy "7." Just past the large wooden piling north of red nun buoy "6," begin to trace the westward-curving crescent of the shoreline at a distance of approximately 150 to 200 feet off the beach, leaving green can buoy "7" about 100 feet off to port. You will notice deep-draft commercial vessels taking this course, where there are 8- to 10-foot MLW depths.

Be cautious farther upstream and observe all channel markers. Boats drawing much over 5 feet may touch bottom (in soft mud) at low water, even in the center of the channel. Locals advise hugging the west side between green can buoys "17" and "19." After that depths increase to 9 feet MLW until reaching the 5- to 6-foot shoal preceding green can buoy "25" just north of the passage between Gardner Island and Beach Island.

As with all such channels try to make the passage on a rising tide if you have a deep-draft vessel. At red nun buoy "28" just north of Pine Tree Point, the channel takes a sharp turn east into The Narrows and then another turn north to head for the Upper Pond. Give the point a healthy respect.

Dockage: Snug Harbor Marina Inc. has slips to 70 feet and mostly caters to fishing vessels with a fully stocked Bait & Tackle Shop. They only maintain one transient slip so call ahead. The well-regarded Point Judith Marina has slips to 110 feet (including 7 reserved for transients) plus full amenities including a pool and laundry facilities. It is easy to arrange a rental car or call a taxi for provisioning in nearby Wakefield or inland sightseeing from here.

To Wakefield

Originally a mill town, Wakefield is centrally located close to all of Rhode Island's beaches and offers a provisioning opportunity. The interstate highway and its ramps make it a difficult walk, but a major shopping mall with a variety of stores and chain restaurants can be accessed by walking under the U.S. Rt. 1 overpass, north one long block and

Fishing boats docked at Point Judith

Upper Pond, RI

WAKEFIELD		Largest Vessel	VHF	Total Slips	Approach/ Dockside Depth	Floating Docks	Gas/ Diesel	Repairs/ Haulout	Min/Max Amps	Pump-Out Station
1. Safe Harbor Silver Spring **WiFi**	(401) 783-0783	35	7	85	5.0 / 5.0	F		RH	30 / 50	
2. Ram Point Marina **WiFi**	(401) 783-4535	53	9	180	6.0 / 6.0	F	GD	RH	30 / 50	P
3. Marina Bay Docking	(401) 789-4050	50	9	65	6.0 / 5.0	F		R	30 / 50	
4. Stone Cove Marina **WiFi**	(401) 783-8990	50		165	6.0 / 6.0	F	G		30	P

WiFi Wireless Internet Access
Visit www.waterwayguide.com for current rates, fuel prices, website addresses and other up-to-the-minute information.
(Information in the table is provided by the facilities.)

Scan here for more details:

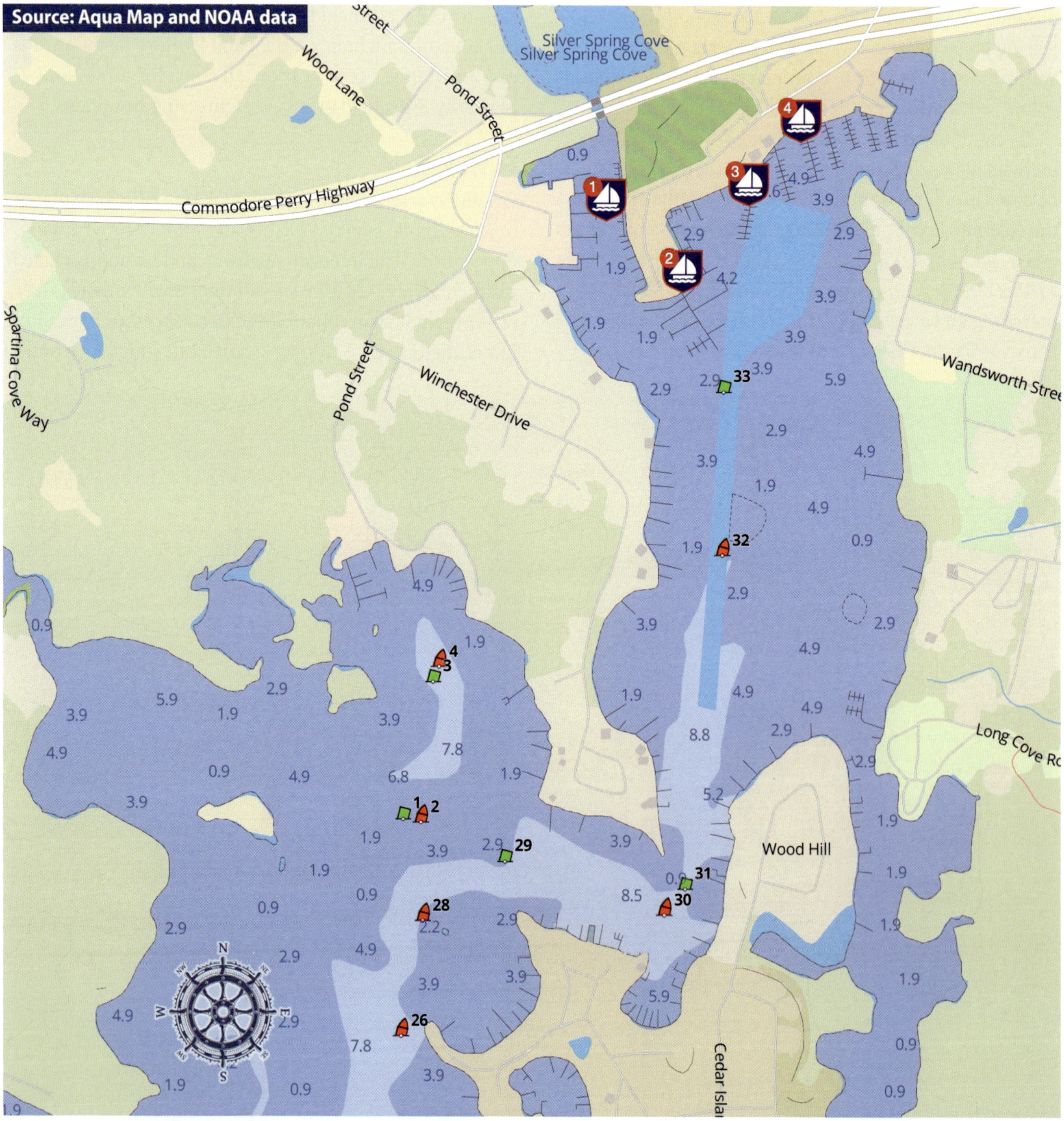

Source: Aqua Map and NOAA data

then going right about 0.2 miles to the plaza on the right. The University of Rhode Island Sailing Center is to the west of the marinas.

Dockage: Several Wakefield marinas offer slips on floating docks and repairs, mostly for smaller boats. Transient facilities in the area include the family friendly Safe Harbor Silver Spring with upscale amenities for vessels to 35 feet. Other facilities are Ram Point Marina (slips to 60 feet) and Marina Bay Docking and Stone Cove Marina, both with slips to 50 feet. All of these facilities report minimum reserved transient space so do call ahead.

Anchorage: Anchorage-intent cruisers should round Gardner Island and take the Gardner Island-Beach Island passage south (following the chart closely) to drop a hook northeast of Plato Island. Holding is excellent here in firm mud but shoaling extends from the east tip of Plato Island so check with a depth sounder to be sure you have adequate swinging room in 5 to 7 feet MLW. This is a duly-marked no wake zone but, unfortunately, enforcement is spotty at best. Plato Island is inhabited. Respect the owner's privacy.

The adjacent islands of Gardner and Beach are also private, yet you may explore with appropriate respect for their natural settings. On a summer's morning you can watch the quahog fishermen muscle their clam rakes for hours, pulling this delicacy from the now-clean pond waters. Good fishing has returned here as well. Flounder, stripers and blues are all said to be susceptible to the right rig in season.

Note the clearly marked no anchorage area in the north side of the pond. The Upper Pond is almost entirely filled with private moorings, making anchoring difficult but not impossible. You can drop the hook south of Tallow Point in Wakefield in 5 to 6 feet MLW with good holding in mud. This provides all-around protection.

■ WEST PASSAGE: NARRAGANSETT BAY TO GREENWICH BAY

Navigation Notes

Although Newport is a world-class yachting center and a high point of Narragansett Bay, the Bay has much, much more to offer. Narragansett Bay stretches 18 nm from Block Island Sound to the Providence River and was named for the original inhabitants of Rhode Island. The bay is also an estuary of national significance and a spawning ground and habitat for winter flounder, lobster, hard shell clams, seals and eel grass.

Rolling hills, green fields, woods and houses surround Narragansett Bay. It offers protected waters, well-marked waterways, sheltered coves and attractive ports of call. You can anchor nearly anywhere you find a lee or a cove and in many places you can go ashore to swim, picnic or hike.

Modern marinas, excellent marine repairs, services, suppliers, pump-out stations, restaurants, shore transportation and accommodations are easy to locate throughout the bay. However, the popularity of this "Jewel of Rhode Island" continues to outpace the availability of slip space and moorings. Those wanting the convenience of dockage or moorings should reserve them in advance.

A tour of the Narragansett from west to east could take in quite a few excellent harbors, anchorages and shore trips. Heading north up the West Passage, Dutch Harbor and its fascinating island can be followed by Wickford or Allen Harbor and then some of the pleasures of Greenwich Bay. The narrow channel between Warwick Point and Patience Island provides access to the Providence River, Warren and Bristol. These ports set up the trip south via the East Passage with very popular stops at Prudence Island, Jamestown and Newport.

Some will choose to use the less-traveled path and round Aquidneck Island's northern end in Mount Hope Bay before heading south through Tiverton (which involves a fixed bridge with 65-foot vertical clearance) and down the Sakonnet River, where Sachuest Point's Third Beach is a back door to Newport.

Villages with small, popular harbors, excellent sailing conditions and fun excursions characterize the West Passage. It is easier on this passage to anchor somewhere that feels somewhat wild while still being able to access necessities like groceries and fuel. Whether desiring a

Beavertail Point Light

hike in Goddard Memorial State Park or a ramble through the ruins on Dutch Island, visiting the village shops in Wickford or East Greenwich, or stopping at one of the full-service marinas, the West Passage will provide what you're after.

Conanicut Island's Beavertail Point Light is an easy landmark. Its 64-foot-tall tower flashes white every 10 seconds with a horn blast (radio activated) every 30 seconds in fog. The Western Passage is wide and deep at the entrance. The dangers are seaward of the point, marked by green and red bell buoy "NR," and westward where Whale Rock is marked by flashing green gong buoy "3." To head into the Bay via the West Passage, the Beavertail Point Light should be left well to the east. To head north via the East Passage it is left well to the west.

> NOTE: Beavertail Point Light, which marks the southern point of Narragansett Bay, is on the National Historic Register. The original stone base was uncovered during the hurricane of 1938. The lighthouse was built in 1749, making it the third oldest lighthouse in America. The present granite tower, built in 1856, is just north of the original light. During any significant storm hundreds of people visit Beavertail State Park to watch the waves and surf.

Dutch Harbor

The large cove of Dutch Harbor is on the west side of Conanicut Island, 2.5 miles north of Beavertail Point. It is easy to enter from either north or south. Dutch Island protects it on the west and provides excellent scenery. Northerly winds can whip up a chop. Turning and anchor room are ample with good holding in 9- to 20-foot MLW depths.

Scenic paths and abandoned bunkers make for good exploring on Dutch Island (part of the Rhode Island Park System). You must take great care exploring if you go beyond the ruins on the north end of the island. The island paths have become overgrown and even though the park system has installed fencing and rails, there are still sharp drop-offs to watch for. (All that overgrowth attracts ticks, which are a major concern for humans and pets.)

Moorings: Guest moorings are available from TPG Marinas Dutch Harbor for overnight or afternoon stopovers. Fees include launch service from the mooring field. Hail NOVA on VHF Channel 69. This is a full-service boatyard with full maintenance and service capabilities, as well as hauling and launching. From

West Passage, RI

DUTCH HARBOR		Largest Vessel	VHF	Total Slips	Approach/ Dockside Depth	Floating Docks	Gas/ Diesel	Repairs/ Haulout	Min/Max Amps	Pump-Out Station
1. TPG Marinas Dutch Harbor WiFi	(401) 423-0630	75	69		15.0 / 12.0			RH		P

WiFi Wireless Internet Access
Visit www.waterwayguide.com for current rates, fuel prices, website addresses and other up-to-the-minute information. (Information in the table is provided by the facilities.)

Scan here for more details:

Source: Aqua Map and NOAA data

this tranquil and mostly protected location, the excellent restaurants and amenities of Jamestown are an easy and pleasant 0.5-mile walk to the east.

Anchorage: Uncomplicated anchorage in mud is located just outside the mooring field at Dutch Island Harbor NE in 13- to 17-foot MLW depths. If there is a chance of a northerly wind, the small light at Dutch Island Harbor SE is an anchoring possibility.

There is no launch service available to anchored boats but there is a public dinghy dock next to the town pier (immediately south of the

boatyard dock). You can off-load your trash at the town-maintained dumpster just above the dinghy dock and use the DIY pump-out station at the town's easy-access, deep-draft dock, accommodating boats to about 40 feet. Signs limit dinghy tie-ups to 30 minutes but this is not typically enforced unless it is very crowded.

Mackerel Cove is a popular day anchorage and occasional overnight if the wind is favorable. This is very exposed to the south but offers good protection in 15- to 30-foot depths with a mostly sand bottom. This is a very scenic area and a good swimming spot.

Wickford

On the west mainland shore of the West Passage, Wickford is one of the most charming cruising destinations on Narragansett Bay. From a berth in either cove be prepared for about a 0.5-mile trek to the commercial facilities along Brown Street, running parallel to the inner harbor. It may be more convenient, particularly from a mooring or Wickford Cove dock, to take your dinghy or your boat for a short-term tie-up alongside the town dock (7-foot MLW depths) at the head of Wickford Cove. From Mill Cove it is a pleasant 0.4-mile walk to the center of Wickford's historic village.

West Passage, RI

WICKFORD		Largest Vessel	VHF	Total Slips	Approach/ Dockside Depth	Floating Docks	Gas/ Diesel	Repairs/ Haulout	Min/Max Amps	Pump-Out Station
1. Wickford Shipyard	(401) 884-1725	60		137	9.0 / 9.0	F	GD	RH	30 / 50	
2. Safe Harbor Wickford Cove WiFi	(401) 884-7014	74	9	155	9.0 / 10.0	F	GD	RH	30 / 50	P
3. Wickford Yacht Club - PRIVATE	(401) 294-9010	50	9		7.0 / 7.0				30	
4. Northwick Boatyard	(401) 932-3613	33		50	/					
5. Safe Harbor Wickford Cove North WiFi	(401) 294-8160	100	9	62	12.0 / 7.0	F			30 / 50	P

WiFi Wireless Internet Access
Visit www.waterwayguide.com for current rates, fuel prices, website addresses and other up-to-the-minute information.
(Information in the table is provided by the facilities.)

Scan here for more details:

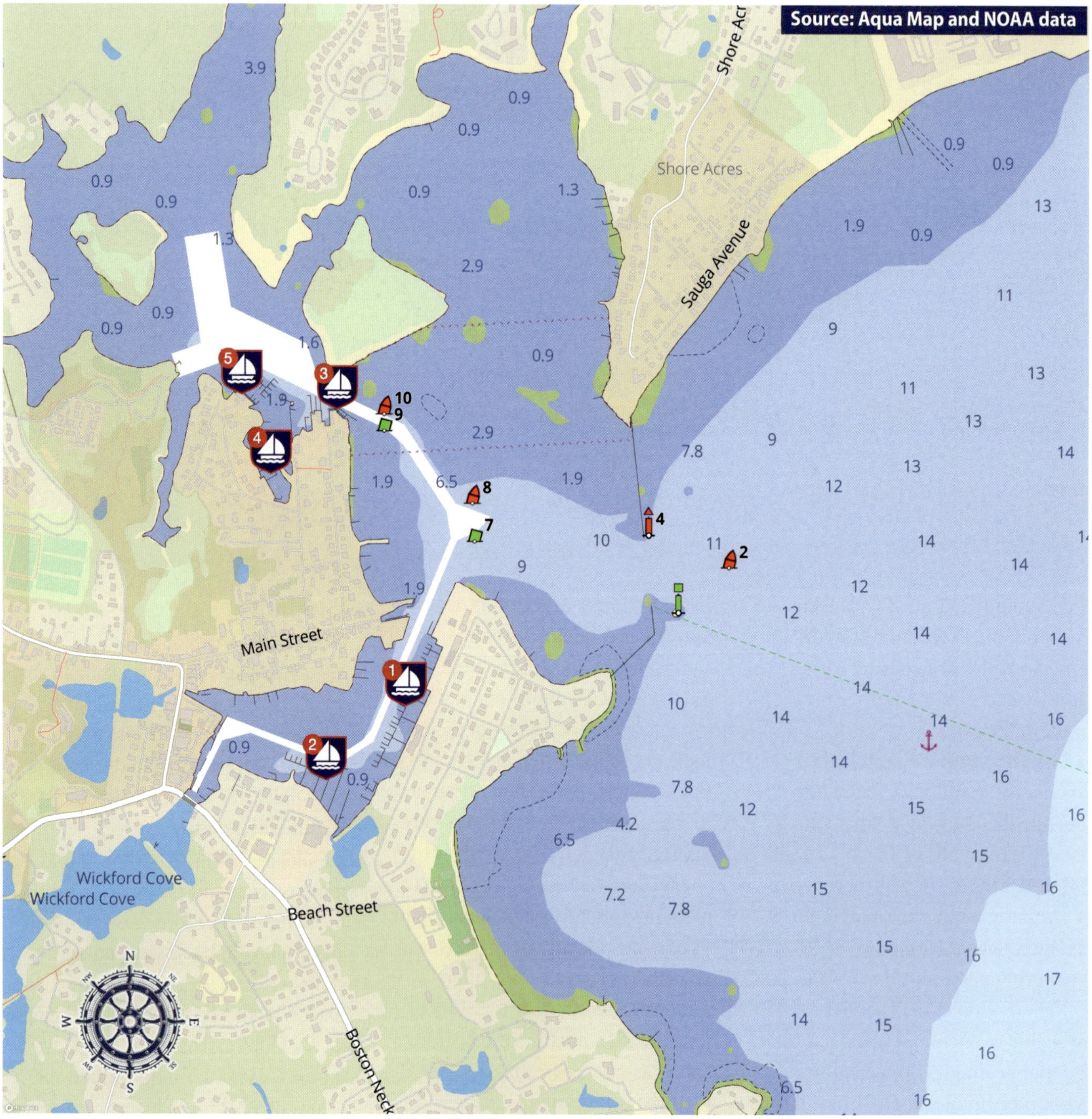

Source: Aqua Map and NOAA data

NAVIGATION: Wickford's twin harbors are located 3 nm northwest of the double-spanned **Jamestown Verrazano Bridge** (135-foot fixed vertical clearance) connecting Conanicut Island to the mainland at North Kingstown.

Fox Island forms the southeastern end of Wickford's large entrance cove. Don't let local fishing boats lead you between it and Rome Point. While there is plenty of water in this area, there are also plenty of rocks. Wickford's outer harbor is reached comfortably by continuing north past the west side of Fox Island and turning NW then continuing for 1.5 nm toward red gong buoy "2."

Enter between the well-marked, lighted ends of the jetties (flashing green 40-foot "1" and flashing red 16-foot "4") guarding the mooring field within. Green can buoy "7" identifies the split between Wickford Cove to the south and Mill Cove to the west. The channels and coves of Wickford Harbor (but not the full outer harbor) are dredged to a 7-foot MLW depth throughout. You can count on 8-foot MLW depths in Wickford Cove (despite the charted 5.5 feet) but take care to stay in the channel.

Dockage/Moorings: Wickford Cove is a tight and busy channel lined with marinas. Wickford Shipyard is to the east in Wickford Cove with slips to 60 feet. This is a working boatyard so don't expect resort amenities. What you will find is solid docks, a machine shop, a welding shop, and traditional and historic yacht rigging services. In the same cove to the south is the well-protected Safe Harbor Wickford Cove, which offers slips and moorings with free launch service and convenient dockside amenities in picturesque Wickford. Renovations made in 2023 include new seawall, docks and travel lift plus new guest facilities.

Transient pole moorings are sometimes available for sailboats only, but can be difficult to tie up to in a strong cross wind (northerly or southerly). There are also four moorings outside the Wickford Harbor seawall that might be available to transients, but are exposed in a southerly wind. Walk or dinghy into Wickford Village from here.

The complimentary Wickford Town Dock lies immediately parallel to Brown Street, which is the town's primary shopping row. There are four slips available for transients on a first-come, first-served basis with a three-night maximum. The dock is substantial in size, carries 7-foot MLW depths and is convenient for shopping and provisioning. Dinghy docks are provided in town.

Mill Cove to the north has a dredged, 7-foot (MLW) marked channel to starboard after entering the breakwater. Several marine facilities provide a variety of amenities and services here. The private Wickford Yacht Club has showers and fresh water available to transients using their moorings. There is no launch service available in the cove. Nearby Northwick Boatyard is a working yard that can accommodate smaller, shoal-draft boats (to 33 feet) in slips or on moorings.

Safe Harbor Wickford Cove North has slips to 100 feet and the usual amenities. While this is a small marina, it gets points for the well-maintained docks and helpful staff. The traditional Saturday morning donuts and coffee is a great opportunity to meet fellow boaters. A hot tub overlooking the entrance breakwater in the distance and wonderful sunsets is a bonus.

Anchorage: Anchoring is prohibited inside the harbor and a patrol boat will roust you, even if sufficient room is found. Visiting skippers frequently take advantage of settled summer weather to anchor in the bight south of the abandoned tower (preceding the port-side jetty of the harbor entrance) off town beach.

Holding off Wickford Town Beach is excellent in 7-to 8-foot MLW depths with a sand and mud bottom and protection is good from prevailing winds, although it is somewhat exposed from northeast through southeast with a long fetch. You will want both a chart and a rising tide to help you pick your way in past two shallow (2- to 3-feet at MLW) spots on the open path to the best beachside anchorage.

Additional anchoring room is north of the Wickford entrance in the Wickford Outer Harbor. Anchor on either side of the channel on the edge of the mooring balls. Holding is good in mud with depths of 6.5 feet, but it does get shallow towards the edges. It is a quick dinghy ride to the free town dock from here.

You can also drop the hook along the West Passage east of Wickford with some protection. Note, however, that fetch from prevailing southwesterly winds and front-driven northerlies can be substantial and it can get rocky here in these conditions.

Allen Harbor

Allen Harbor is 2.5 miles north of Wickford. Both Wickford Harbor and Allen Harbor, originally maintained by the Navy as part of the Seabee's training center, are now under the jurisdiction of the North Kingstown harbormaster. It's a bit tricky to identify because of the distracting industrial installations just

West Passage, RI

ALLEN HARBOR		Largest Vessel	VHF	Total Slips	Approach/ Dockside Depth	Floating Docks	Gas/ Diesel	Repairs/ Haulout	Min/Max Amps	Pump-Out Station
1. Allen Harbor Marina **WiFi**	(401) 294-1212	40		115	8.0 / 9.0	F			30	P

WiFi Wireless Internet Access
Visit www.waterwayguide.com for current rates, fuel prices, website addresses and other up-to-the-minute information.
(Information in the table is provided by the facilities.)

Scan here for more details:

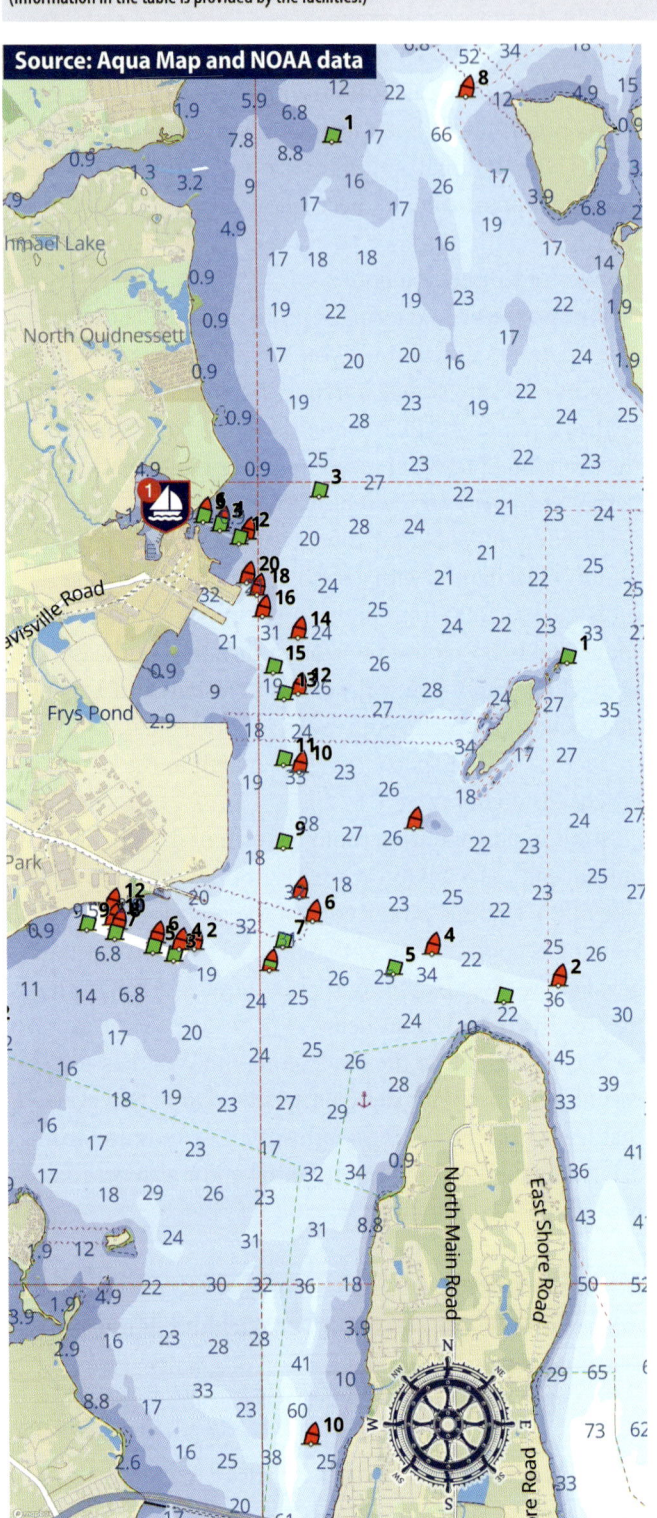

Source: Aqua Map and NOAA data

south but the masts of the recreational harbor resolve themselves as you approach.

NAVIGATION: Head northwest from flashing red buoy "14" or southwest from green can buoy "3" for the harbor entrance. Green can buoy "1" and flashing red buoy "2" provide the starting point. Aim straight down the throat and keep an eye on the depth sounder; shoals are on either side. If you draw more than 5 feet enter on a rising tide. Once inside, you will find depths of 10 to 11 feet MLW. When you continue north stay outside of green can buoy "3" marking the outer limit of Calf Pasture Point.

Dockage/Moorings: Moorings are more likely to be available than slips here. Contact the harbormaster on VHF Channel 16. The town owns and operates Allen Harbor Marina, which includes 82 moorings and 124 slips. Safe Harbor Allen Harbor is here with services and storage (but no transient slips). The town of North Kingston has a pump-out station here.

Greenwich Cove, Greenwich Bay

Greenwich Bay is a 3-mile-long arm of Narragansett Bay with three good harbors: Greenwich Cove, Apponaug Cove and Warwick Cove. Ashore are parks, beaches, amusements, transportation and boating amenities. Shoals and rocks are usually well marked, although some buoy numbers may not match older charts.

NAVIGATION: In all but the clearest weather follow at least a rough compass or specific GPS course for the entire section between Quonset Point and Warwick Point. This precaution will not only keep you clear of Calf Pasture Point but also the buoyed rocks 1 mile east of Potowomut Neck. Shoal water extends well to the east of Sandy Point. Pass well east of Round Rock off Potowomut Neck (flashing green buoy "1") and do not cut across the shoal east of Sandy Point. Follow the chart and buoys through the deep channel south of Warwick Point's lighthouse.

The long, finger-like Greenwich Cove is fully protected from all but strong northerlies. It is also one of the most popular stops on Narragansett Bay and boasts a fair mix of marine facilities and amenities along the western edge with a backdrop of unspoiled greenery on the eastern side.

Even though approach and entry to Greenwich Cove is relatively easy, this is no place to cut buoys. Stay well north of green can "5" marking Sally Rock (adjacent to a yellow URI monitoring buoy) in starting your path to green can "7." Watch the shoal west of red nun "6" but don't miss green can buoy "7" marking the shoaling north and east of Long Point.

Dockage/Moorings: There is no shortage of slips and moorings in Greenwich Cove. Some have on-site chandleries, some have restaurants and some have both. The mooring fields use all available space so don't expect good depths everywhere you see a mooring.

Greenwich Cove Marina is in a well-protected, deep-water basin and offers slips to 300 feet, launch and hauling service, a ship store and the on-site McKinley's Pub. The village of East Greenwich is a 0.25-mile walk uphill and north of the dinghy dock/boat launch on the west shore. The provisioning possibilities here are quite good.

Just to the south is the private East Greenwich Yacht Club with 125 club moorings with 10 to 15 moorings and a few slips available for transient rental (reciprocity with other yacht clubs and boating organizations).

East Greenwich Marina has 118 floating slips and can accommodate vessels to 130 feet with full amenities. They offer competitively priced transient slips and the convenience of attractions, shopping and restaurants, all within walking distance from the marina.

Anchorage: It is possible to anchor in East Greenwich but we don't recommend it as Greenwich Cove is chock full of moorings. It can be hard to anchor there without swinging into the channel. You may find a spot southwest of Chepiwanoxet Point's long shoal just outside the mooring field. The better anchorage for both swing room and scenery is off the beach between Sally Rock and Long Point in 7-feet MLW.

The trip into the East Greenwich Dinghy Dock from the anchorage is long and can be wet in a west wind. Big northerlies create big chop and a lee shore.

Goddard State Park across the cove is popular and the anchorage tends to attract day-trippers so it gets quieter at night. There is a dinghy dock at Goddard State Park that is an excellent place to begin a moderate hike. Heading north provides the opportunity to shoot a picture of your boat at anchor off the beach.

Apponaug Cove, Greenwich Bay

In the northwest corner of Greenwich Bay is Apponaug Cove with a direct, easy entrance between Arnold Neck to the west and Cedar Tree Point to the east. This cove ensures good protection from the nor'easters but is open to southeast breezes at the entrance. Shores of the cove are attractive. The pleasant little town of Apponaug is near the harbor and within easy reach are shore accommodations, provisions and beaches.

From point east head for the highly visible Safe Harbor Cowesett bulkheads before turning north for green can buoy "3." The well-buoyed, 8- to 10-foot MLW depth channel extends about 1 mile to a

fixed railroad bridge (22-foot vertical clearance). Check locally for latest depths; the edges of the channel shoal up periodically.

Dockage: Deep-water transient berths or moorings are almost certain to be at your disposal here. Safe Harbor Cowesett to the south of Apponaug Cove has 20 reserved transient slips/moorings in two basins with upscale amenities. Apponaug Harbor Marina consists of 348 concrete and wooden floating dock slips to 40 feet plus 30 moorings. There is no room for anchoring here.

Warwick Cove, Greenwich Bay

In the northeastern sector of the bay, Warwick is convenient to the T.F. Green (Providence) Airport, as is East Greenwich and other some other Narragansett Bay marinas. A major transportation center provides access to commuter trains into Boston and Amtrak trains to New York City and the Connecticut towns on the way.

Entering Greenwich Bay heading northwest then turn north after the charted flagpole without hugging Warwick Neck because of the charted rocks. If approaching from the west, don't cut green can buoy "1." Local small fishing boats can lead you astray in this area. The channel proceeds along Warwick Neck into the harbor.

When leaving Greenwich Bay, turn north between Warwick Neck and Patience Island, a state park and estuarine sanctuary. Narragansett Bay becomes the deep and well-marked Providence River at Conimicut Point. If wind and tide are in opposition, you might experience a riptide in the passage between Warwick Point and Northwest Point on Patience Island.

Greenwich Bay, RI

GREENWICH		Largest Vessel	VHF	Total Slips	Approach/ Dockside Depth	Floating Docks	Gas/ Diesel	Repairs/ Haulout	Min/Max Amps	Pump-Out Station
1. Greenwich Cove Marina (WiFi)	(401) 884-8828	300	9	186	8.0 / 10.0	F		RH	30 / 100	P
2. East Greenwich Yacht Club - PRIVATE (WiFi)	(401) 884-7700	75	9	120	12.0 / 10.0	F	GD		30 / 50	P
3. East Greenwich Marina	(401) 885-6611	130		118	10.0 / 8.0				30	
APPONAUG COVE										
4. Safe Harbor Cowesett (WiFi)	(401) 884-0544	60	9	380	12.0 / 6.0	F	GD	RH	30 / 200+	P
5. Apponaug Harbor Marina (Dickerson's Marina Inc.) (WiFi)	(401) 739-5005	40		348	8.0 / 6.0	F	D	RH	30	P
WARWICK COVE										
6. Harbor Lights Marina (WiFi)	(401) 737-6353	50	9	225	8.0 / 6.0	F	GD	RH	50	P
7. Fairwinds Marina (formerly Warwick Cove Marina)	(401) 921-1955	45	71	90	7.0 / 6.0	F		R	30	
8. Safe Harbor Greenwich Bay (WiFi)	(401) 884-1810	60	9	600	10.0 / 7.0	F	GD	RH	30 / 50	P
9. Bay Marina Inc. (WiFi)	(401) 739-6435	50		200	6.0 / 6.0	F		RH	30 / 50	

(WiFi) Wireless Internet Access
Visit www.waterwayguide.com for current rates, fuel prices, website addresses and other up-to-the-minute information.
(Information in the table is provided by the facilities.)

Scan here for more details:

Source: Aqua Map and NOAA data

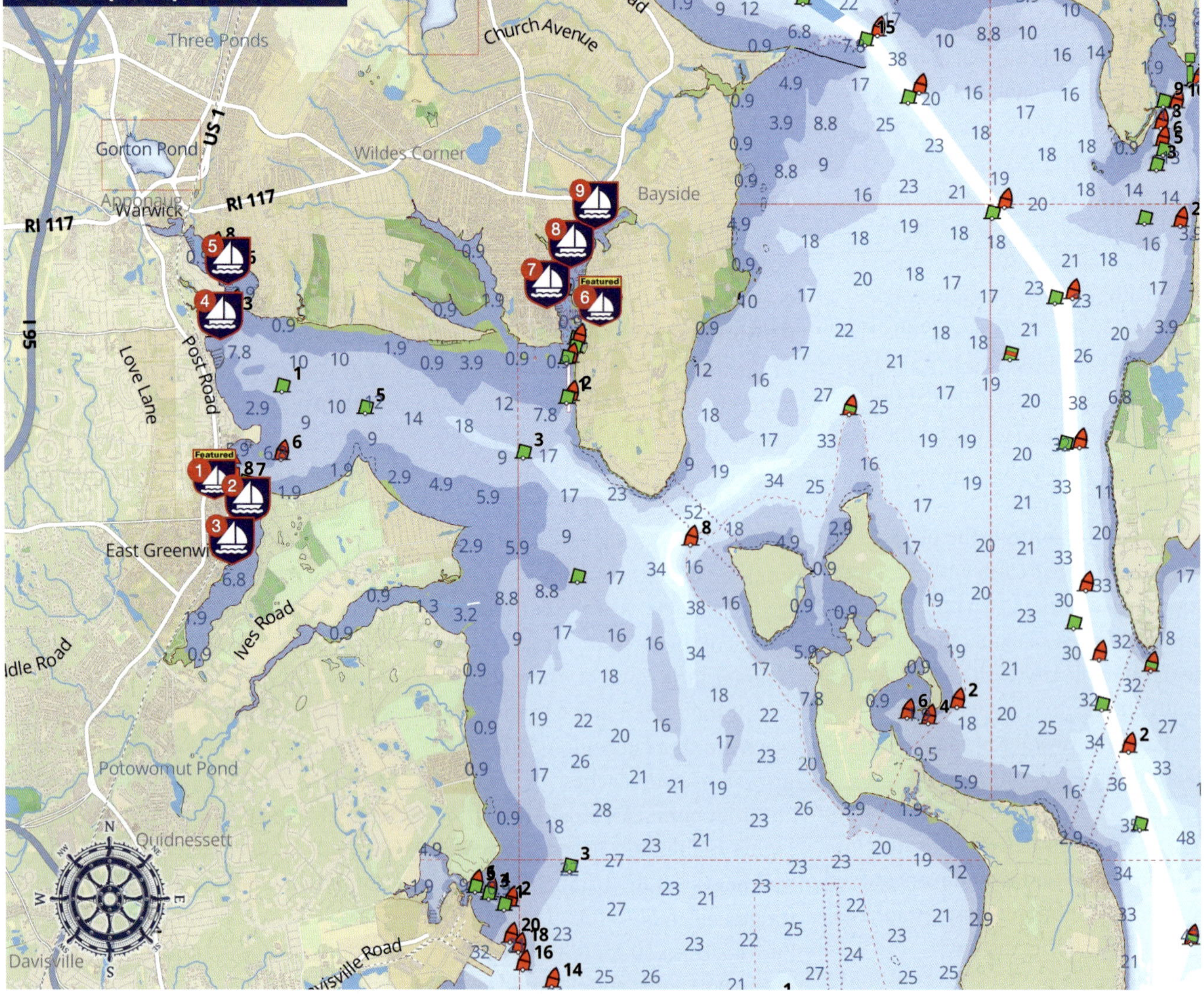

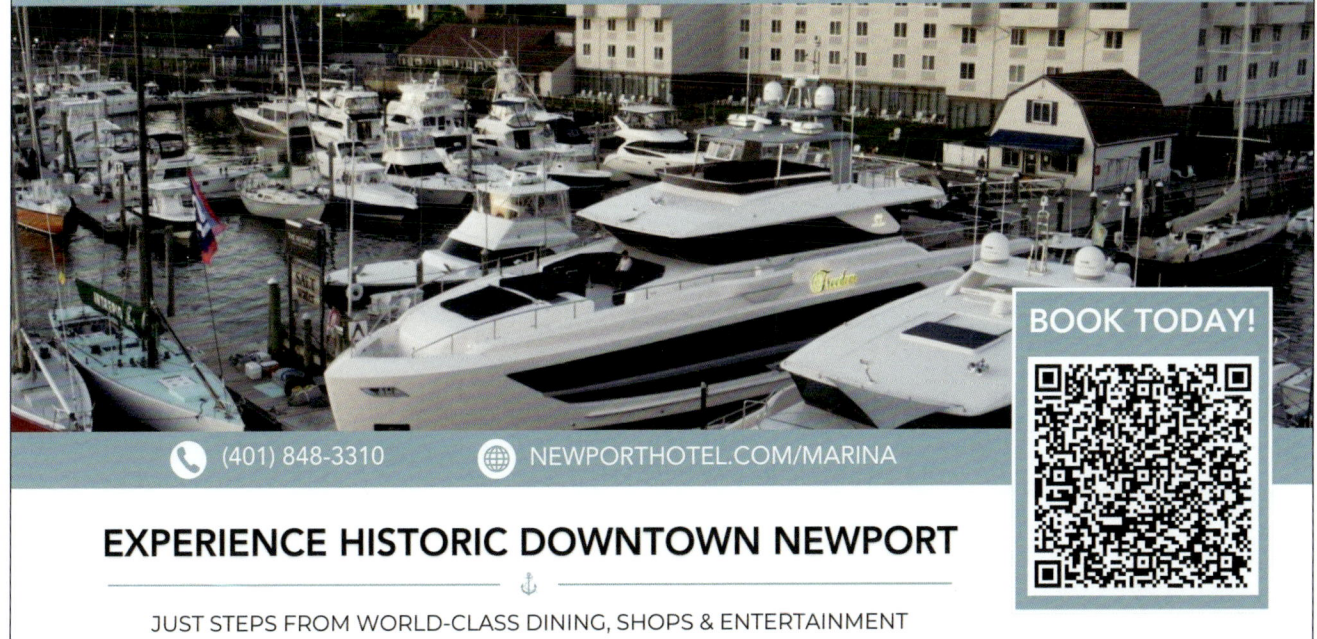
Dockage: Busy Warwick Cove is loaded with fishing stations and marinas but most of these facilities cater to smaller vessels and may be filled to capacity with local boats. Fairwinds Marina (formerly Warwick Cove Marina) has slips to 45 feet and competitive rates but call ahead for transient slip availability.

Safe Harbor Greenwich Bay offers seasonal and transient boats to 60 feet dockage in a family-oriented atmosphere with resort amenities like a swimming pool and community picnic and barbecue areas. Grocery stores, chandleries and fine dining are all nearby. Family-oriented Bay Marina Inc. to the north has slips to 50 feet (including reserved transient slips).

Back at the entrance to the cove on the east shore is Harbor Lights Marina with slips to 50 feet and resort amenities including an infinity pool and a tiki bar. Have clubs on board? There is also a golf club and several eateries on site.

Anchorage: The narrow, dredged entrance to Warwick Cove is well marked around a shoal that is exposed at low water off the southeastern end of Horse Neck. Between here and the harbor head are moorings and the Warwick Cove Harbor anchorage basin. Make contact with the harbormaster through Warwick Town Hall who direct you to a mooring or a spot to anchor for the night. There are a number of small areas to anchor and locals use the upper reaches to seek protection from serious storms.

HARBOR LIGHTS MARINA

Warwick Cove

WARWICK NECK

■ NEWPORT AREA

To Newport Harbor

Cruisers focused on visiting Newport or Jamestown and moving on will use the East Passage. The trip past Newport Neck often feels like accidentally joining a parade. Keep a camera handy because whatever your taste in boats, you'll most likely see one or more of your favorites underway here in season.

When bound for Newport, enter the deep, well-buoyed passage between Beavertail Point and the 40-foot-tall Castle Hill Lighthouse. You'll pass magnificent waterfront estates including the 28-room Hammersmith Farm, the childhood home of Jackie Kennedy Onassis. If entering from the east, honor quick flashing red whistle buoy "2" off Brenton Reef, the 20-foot MLW depths are less important than the fishing gear that comes all the way up to the surface during some seasons. Red gong buoy "4" and red bell buoy "6" mark the last two significant reefs.

The pre-Civil War Fort Adams, at the northern tip of Newport Neck, marks the entrance to Newport Harbor where the water is deep right up to its banks.

Brenton Cove

Tucked inside the protective arm dominated by Fort Adams, Brenton Cove is filled with private and rental moorings. This spot is removed from the churn of activity in the center harbor and, as such, it is a quieter place to review the ongoing passing spectacle.

Forget the prospect of serenity during mid-June of every even-numbered year, however, when the cove becomes a rendezvous center for the finest and best equipped ocean-racing yachts in the world, making last-moment preparations for the biennial Newport-to-Bermuda race. At that time you will spend more time waiting for and riding the launch to town.

The shore of Brenton Cove is home to Harbor Court, the Newport base of the New York Yacht Club (NYYC). This impressive structure was previously the home of John Nicholas Brown of Brown University fame and was purchased and converted by the NYYC in the 1990s.

Dockage/Moorings: You can rent a transient mooring from Brenton Cove Moorings that includes launch service (VHF Channel 09). They have a unique floating dock system with fore and aft helix moorings attached to 30-foot docks that can accommodate vessels

to 60 feet. Rafting is possible. Launch service, pump-out service and toilet and shower facilities are available. The private Ida Lewis Yacht Club will accept visitors from recognized reciprocal clubs if space is available. Call on VHF Channel 78A.

Anchorage: Anchoring is not permitted in Brenton Cove proper, where moorings have triumphed fully in the battle for available space. You can anchor to the east in the area fanning out north of Ida Lewis Yacht Club (conspicuous on the rocky island of the same name) and the long pier from shore just a bit more to the east (Breton Cove East). The holding is good in mud with 18 to 23 feet MLW, but you will need substantial swing room with the ebb and flood of the tidal currents.

Skippers are warned to stay to the shore side of the cable area marked on the harbor chart and delineated with buoys in the water. You may not leave your vessel unattended overnight. The harbormaster maintains tight control of the anchorage and mooring fields to insure compliance with local regulations. Anchoring is limited to 14 days with at least 4 days between visits according to Newport ordinance.

NOTE: Cannons are fired from the lawn at Ida Lewis Yacht Club at 8:00 a.m. and at sundown, alerting crews to raise and lower the standards of many nations throughout the harbor.

It is also possible to drop the hook off Fort Adams. This is a tight but popular day anchorage in deeper water. You will see up to 20 boats squeeze in here for events at Fort Adams like the Newport Jazz and Folk festivals and fireworks, but it is not a good overnight spot. Observe signs that warn of an underwater cable to the south.

The east side of the pier east of Ida Lewis Rock (and Yacht Club) provides short-term dinghy access as does Fort Adams. Launch service is available from Oldport Marine Services (VHF Channel 68) but be prepared to wait because it takes time for launches to circumnavigate the harbor and make frequent stops.

Newport

Newport is a world-class yachting center. Just about every boat traveling the coast or coming from international ports makes a stop at Newport. Big yachts, sail and power, lay over at one of several major yards, putting in for crew changes, provisioning or refurbishing. Yachts and tourists

Newport Harbor, RI

BRENTON COVE		Largest Vessel	VHF	Total Slips	Approach/ Dockside Depth	Floating Docks	Gas/ Diesel	Repairs/ Haulout	Min/Max Amps	Pump-Out Station
1. Brenton Cove Moorings	(401) 474-6061	60	9		14.0 /	F	GD		50	P
2. Ida Lewis Yacht Club-PRIVATE	(401) 846-1969	50			12.0 / 8.0	F			30 / 50	P
NEWPORT										
3. West Wind Marina WiFi	(401) 849-4300	200	9	60	/ 13.0	F			30 / 100	P
4. Casey's Marina WiFi	(401) 849-0281	200	9	35	16.0 / 12.0	F	D	RH	30 / 100	P
5. Newport Marina WiFi	(401) 849-2293	140	9	45	17.0 / 12.0	F			30 / 200+	P
6. Newport On-Shore Marina WiFi	(401) 849-0480	100	9	65	12.0 / 5.0	F			30 / 100	
7. City of Newport Maritime Center WiFi	(401) 845-5870	40			11.0 / 4.0					P
8. Forty 1 North WiFi	(401) 848-7950	250	9	29	12.0 / 12.0	F			30 / 200+	P
9. Newport Yachting Center WiFi	(800) 653-3625	180	9	200	22.0 / 18.0	F	GD	R	30 / 100	P
10. Bannister's Wharf Marina WiFi	(401) 846-4556	280	9	30	20.0 / 16.0	F	GD		30 / 100	P
11. Bowen's Wharf WiFi	(401) 324-4108	105	9		20.0 /	F			30 / 100	P
12. Newport Harbor Hotel & Marina WiFi	**(401) 848-3310**	150	9	60	17.0 / 8.0	F			30 / 100	P
13. Newport Yacht Club-PRIVATE WiFi	(401) 846-9410	140	78	64	20.0 / 15.0				30 / 50	P
14. Newport Mooring Service	(401) 846-7535		9		/					
15. Newport Harbormaster Moorings	(401) 845-5815		16		/					P
16. Safe Harbor Newport Shipyard WiFi	(401) 846-6000	315	9	60	20.0 / 20.0	F	D	RH	20 / 100	P
GOAT ISLAND										
17. Newport Harbor Island Resort WiFi	**(401) 851-3350**	220	9	22	20.0 / 20.0	F			30 / 200+	P
18. Goat Island Marina WiFi	**(401) 849-5655**	250	9	175	19.0 / 17.0	F	GD		30 / 100	P

WiFi Wireless Internet Access
Visit www.waterwayguide.com for current rates, fuel prices, website addresses and other up-to-the-minute information.
(Information in the table is provided by the facilities.)

Scan here for more details:

stop in Newport for the spectacle of the incredible collection of vessels from all over the world and the interesting people who travel on them.

This is possibly the most sophisticated yachting center in the U.S. and maybe the world. Varnish work, fiberglass and wood hull repairs, onboard catering, custom rigging services, new keel designs, maritime history, fine dining and galleries... Newport is where to find it all.

NAVIGATION: Although wide at the mouth, Newport Harbor is well protected, easy to enter and deep throughout. The only cautionary advice for first-time skippers rounding the 32-foot-tall flashing red "2" and red nun "4" off the point north of Fort Adams is to be aware that large, unusual and otherwise distracting

vessels ply these busy waters in profusion. They are often under full sail and occasionally at speeds that mock known safety limits. Take more than ordinary caution and concentrate on the navigational and tie-up tasks at hand.

Moorings: Despite Newport's popularity, transient space on floating docks or at moorings are usually available. Note, however, that dockage limited to 14 days with at least 4 days between visits according to Newport City ordinance. Moorings for visiting boaters are available from a variety of public and private operators, including Oldport Marine Services, Newport Mooring Service and the Newport Harbormaster's office.

The Newport Harbormaster Moorings located off Ann Street Pier

and Perrotti Park are available on a first-come, first-served basis and arrival before 11:00 a.m. (especially on a weekend) is the only way to secure a spot. Mariners can inquire to availability by hailing the Newport Harbormaster on VHF Channel 16.

The harbormaster also manages the City of Newport Maritime Center located at Ann Street Pier. The former armory, built in 1894, offers coin-operated showers, laundry and ice and vending machines for boaters. The social area is an excellent place to meet fellow-boaters and the building's history is on display there. Step back and face the water, then look up. The room was used for target practice and the heavy beams retain the scarring from many a bad aim.

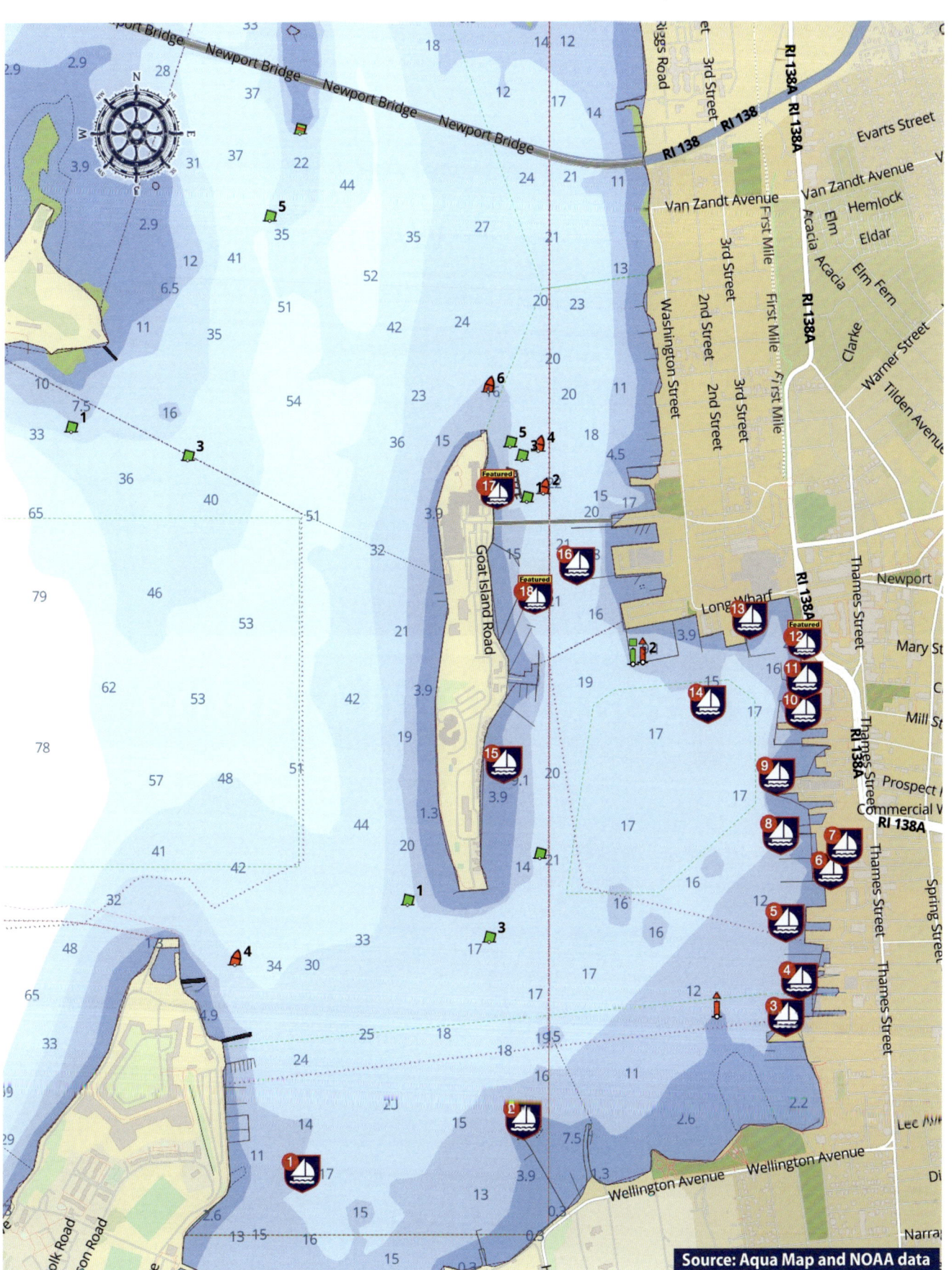

Source: Aqua Map and NOAA data

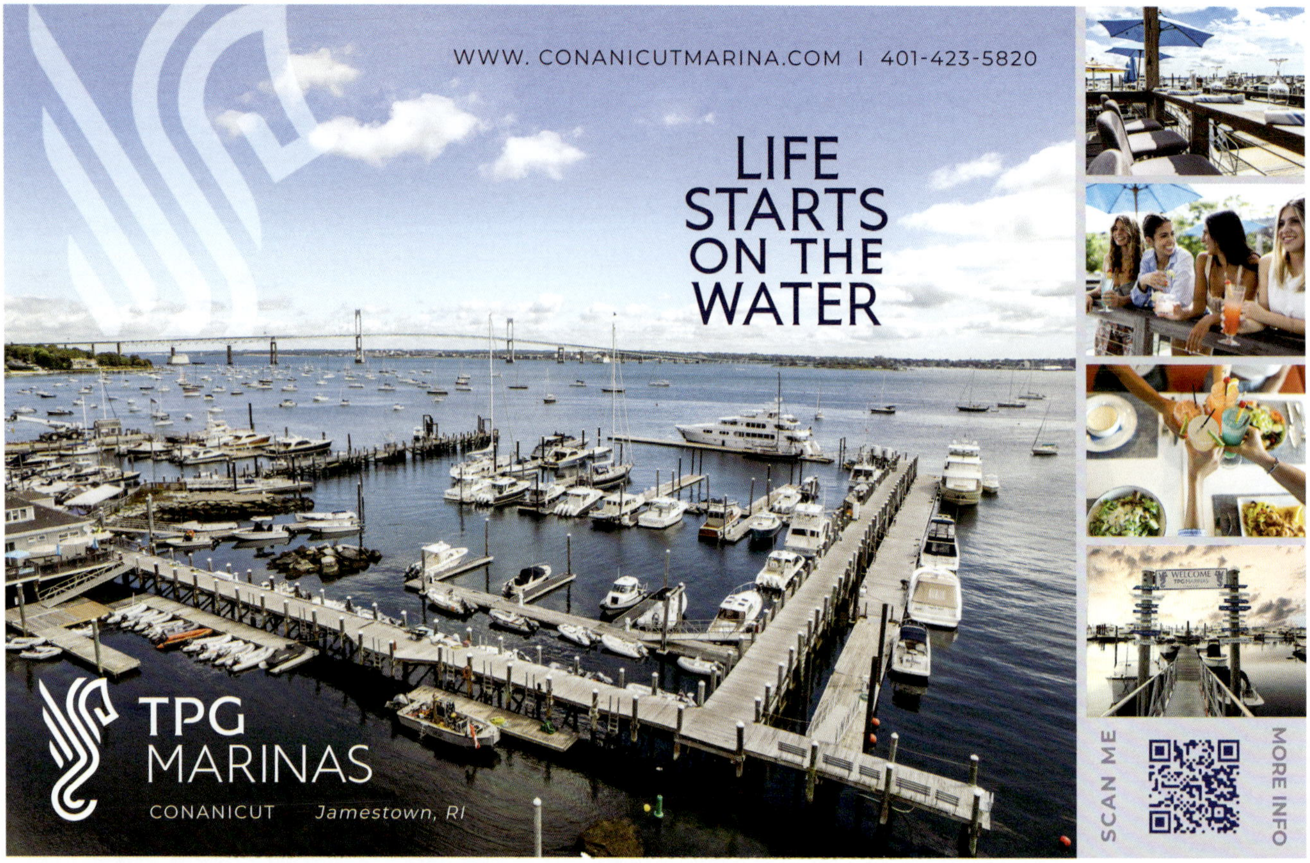
WWW. CONANICUTMARINA.COM | 401-423-5820
LIFE STARTS ON THE WATER
TPG MARINAS
CONANICUT Jamestown, RI
SCAN ME
MORE INFO

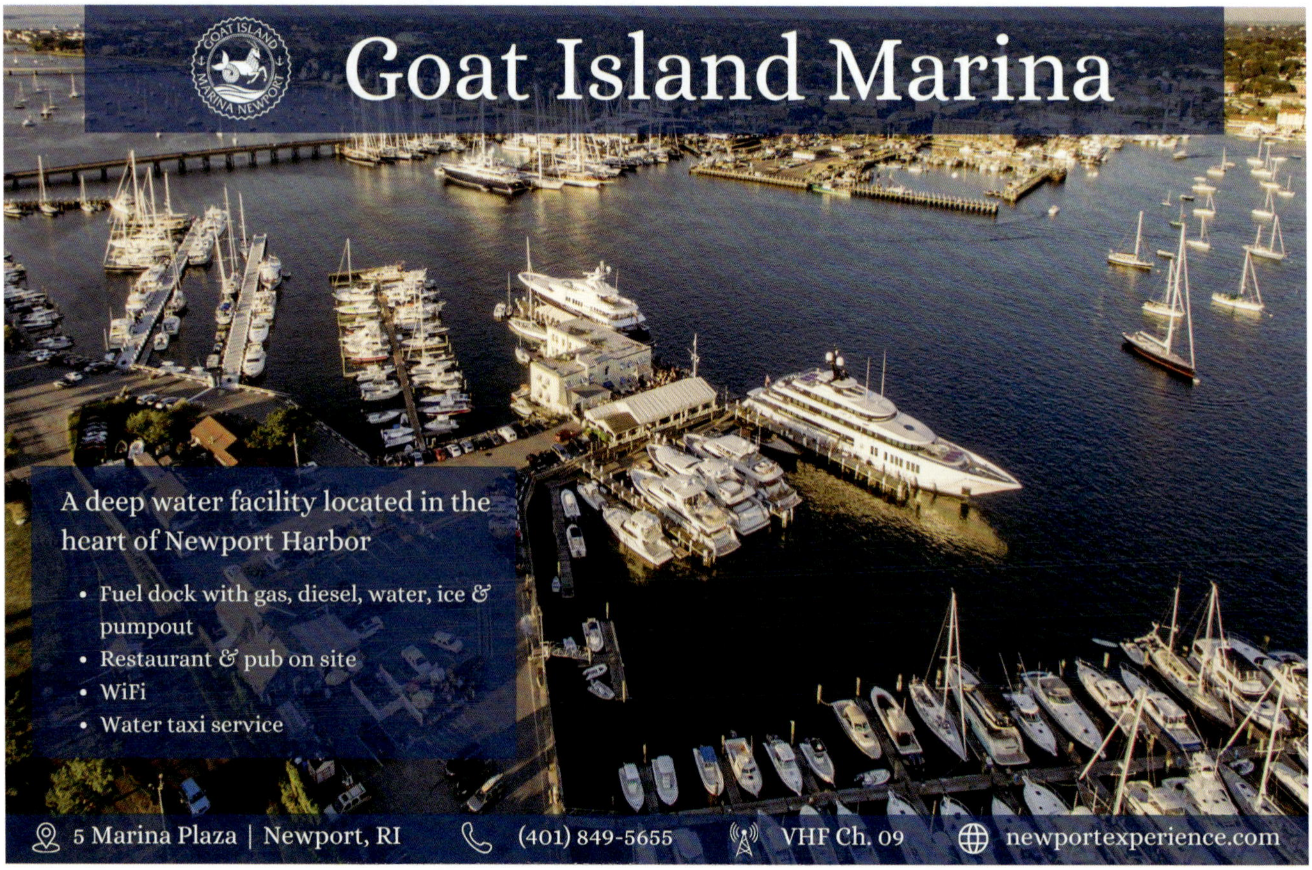
GOAT ISLAND MARINA NEWPORT
Goat Island Marina
A deep water facility located in the heart of Newport Harbor
• Fuel dock with gas, diesel, water, ice & pumpout
• Restaurant & pub on site
• WiFi
• Water taxi service
5 Marina Plaza | Newport, RI
(401) 849-5655
VHF Ch. 09
newportexperience.com

The friendly staff at Oldport Marine Services can also assist with finding a mooring. Many moorings are seasonal but rented when the owners are away. They also offer launch service throughout the harbor (call on VHF Channel 68) but be prepared to wait due to the time it takes to circumnavigate the harbor and make frequent stops. The large harbor can make the launch a good option for anyone uncomfortable negotiating heavy traffic in a dinghy.

Two blocks north of Oldport Marine's launch dock is the Seaman's Church Institute where you will find clean showers with soap and fresh towels for a small fee from 7:00 a.m. to 9:00 a.m. The Institute also has coin-operated laundry machines. This venerable institution has been looking out for the special needs of seafarers for generations and deserves the kind words and donations it receives from the yachting community.

Dockage: West Wind Marina is Newport's only family-owned and -operated marina. They cater to seasonal and transient boaters of all types, from mega-yachts to sailboats to sportfishing vessels. They also have an on-site restaurant and nightclub. Casey's Marina is a working boatyard with slips to 200 feet on floating docks and some transient space.

Newport Marina to the north welcomes transients to 140 feet in a convenient location with full amenities, including a heated pool. Note that The Marina at Brown & Howard Wharf will allow you to dock for dinner, lunch or shopping (on a space available basis) but does not offer overnight transient slips. Continuing north, Newport On-Shore Marina has a limited number of transient slips (to 100 feet). Reservations are recommended.

Upscale dockage to 250 feet and resort amenities are available at Forty 1 North. They have ample transient space and a courteous, attentive staff will assist you with dockage

Newport Yachting Center, home of the annual Newport International Boat Show in September, is easy to spot on entering Center Harbor. With over 2,500 feet of available transient dockage, they can accommodate yachts up to 180 feet with full services and amenities. The deck on top of the dock house is a great place to watch all the activity in Newport Harbor.

Bannister's Wharf Marina is a 30-slip, deep-water marina with floating docks as well as a 280-foot fixed pier and ample transient space. This was once the home port

for some of the world's most famous yachts including *Endeavour*, *Shamrock V*, *Ticonderoga* and Dennis Connor's *Stars and Stripes*. The facility also has guest rooms and is home to the venerable Clarke Cooke House Restaurant.

Nest door is Bowen's Wharf with deep water dockage accommodating yachts up to 105 feet. The marina is conveniently located amidst bustling Bowen's Wharf with an array of shoreside activities and world-class restaurants. They accept transient and day dockage as well as winter seasonal dockage. Reservations are highly recommended.

A bit farther north the Newport Harbor Hotel & Marina is a prime location with resort amenities. The family-friendly facility has 60 (all transient) slips, a heated saltwater pool and an on-site restaurant. A fire pit, lawn games and hammocks round out the offerings. This is also home to four classic 12-Meter America's Cup Yachts that have been meticulously restored and maintained.

Visiting members listed in the Register of American Yacht Clubs may visit the private Newport Yacht Club with up to three guests, four times per year. Amenities include a full bar and pub and Sunday brunch (seasonal). Call ahead on VHF Channel 09.

Located in the heart of Newport, Safe Harbor Newport Shipyard is surrounded by Colonial captains' homes, cozy eateries and seaside boutiques. Slips are well-protected from wind and surge and the marina offers an array of on-shore amenities for the visiting boater.

Across the harbor on Goat Island is Newport Harbor Island Resort (formerly Gurney's Newport Resort & Marina) with ample amenities including a spa, fitness center, indoor and outdoor pool and complimentary launch service to town. They have 22 (all transient) slips for vessels to 250 feet. They also offer sunset cruises and water sports.

Goat Island Marina is a full-service operation that can accommodate vessels to 250 feet. Here you can enjoy breathtaking harbor views while relaxing at your slip or take a quick shuttle ride into town to experience Newport's revered shopping and exciting nightlife.

Anchorage: Due to the proliferation of moorings, the preferred anchorage is at Breton Cove East (described above). There are eight dinghy docks in the harbor including one on the Ann Street Pier with direct access to City of Newport Maritime Center.

GOIN' ASHORE

NEWPORT, RI

Newport abounds in maxi-yachts, 70-knot powerboats, cruise ships, round-the-world racers and luxurious cruising palaces. These waters are a terminus for many of the world's great races, such as the Cruising Club of America's Newport-to-Bermuda Race on even years and the OSTAR single-handed race, as well as the Maxi Series. The Classic Yacht Regatta, Admiral's Cup trials, the New York Yacht Club Cruise and the Volvo Ocean Race and other special events with some regularity. The America's Cup trials and races dominated Newport for many decades and the legacy of those events is evident everywhere. At moorings around the harbor you will see many 12-meter racers from the classic period of the America's Cup. These refurbished racers are used for day charters and occasional regattas.

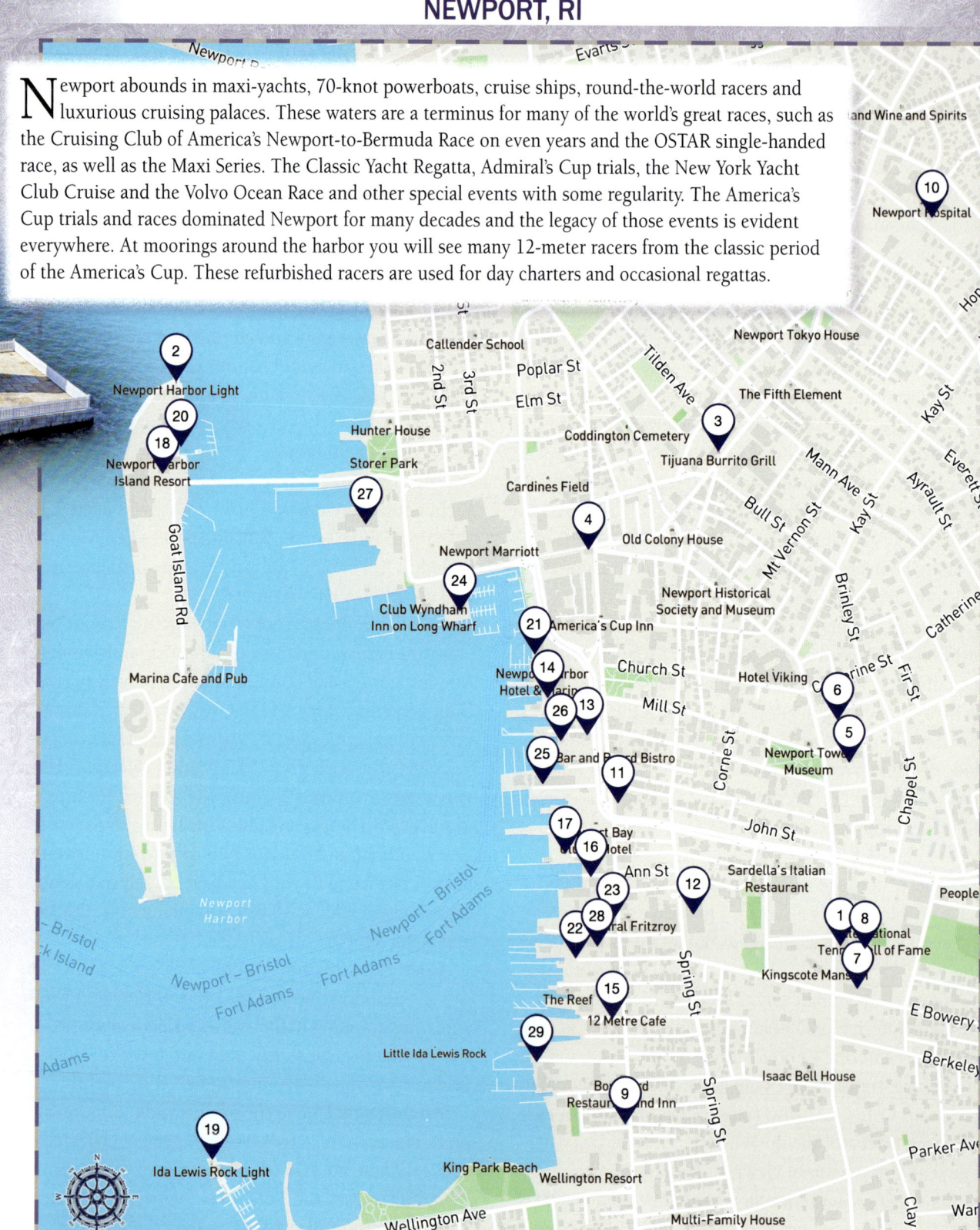

ATTRACTIONS

1. Audrain Auto Museum
With a goal to acquire and preserve automobiles with historical significance to Newport, this unique museum houses cars and motorcycles ranging from pre-war cars to supercars of the 2000s. The Audrain Building represents Gilded Age architecture style inspired by the Florentine Renaissance and defined by broad arched windows and a terra cotta roof crowned with lion finials at 222 Bellevue Ave. (401-856-4420).

2. Goat Island Light
Small (20-foot) lighthouse at the tip of Goat Island activated in 1824. (Also called Newport Harbor Light.) Walkway leads from deck at rear of Gurney's Newport Resort to lighthouse. Gorgeous views.

3. Newport Historic District
Well-preserved district with meticulously and beautifully maintained buildings, churchs and houses (most of which are inhabited and private).

4. Museum of Newport History
Relive maritime and social history of the region in this classic 1772 Brick Market building at 127 Thames St. (401-841-8770).

5. Newport Art Museum
Multi-building campus housing regional 19th-century to contemporary works at 76 Bellevue Ave. (401-848-8200).

6. Redwood Library and Athenaeum
Oldest lending library in America and the oldest library building in continuous use in the country, with beautiful books and superb exhibits at 50 Bellevue Ave. (401-841-5680).

SERVICES

7. Micki's Laundromat
272 Bellevue Ave. (401-847-5972)

8. Newport Ace Hardware
Chain hardware store with tools and home supplies at 1 Casino Terrace (401-849-9442).

9. Newport Animal Clinic
541 Thames St. (401-849-3401)

10. Newport Hospital Emergency Hospital
20 Powel Ave. (401-846-6400)

11. Newport Post Office
320 Thames St., Ste. 1 (401-847-9835)

12. Newport Public Library
300 Spring St. (401-847-8720)

MARINAS

13. Bannister's Wharf Marina
1 Bannister's Wharf (401-846-4500)

14. Bowen's Wharf
Bowen's Wharf (401-849-2243)

15. Casey's Marina
10 Spring Wharf (401-849-0281)

16. City of Newport Maritime Center
365 Thames St. (401-845-5870)

17. Forty 1 North
351 Thames St. (401-846-8018)

18. Goat Island Marina
5 Marina Plaza (401-849-5655)

19. Ida Lewis Yacht Club-PRIVATE
170 Wellington Ave. (401-846-1969)

20. Newport Harbor Island Resort
1 Goat Island (401-849-2600)

21. Newport Harbor Hotel & Marina
49 America's Cup Ave. (401-847-9000)

22. Newport Marina
26 Lee's Wharf (401-849-2293)

23. Newport On-Shore Marina
405 Thames St. (401-849-0480)

24. Newport Yacht Club-PRIVATE
110 Long Wharf Ave. (401-846-9410)

25. Newport Yachting Center
20 Commercial Wharf (800-653-3625)

26. Oldport Marine Services
1 Sayers Wharf (401-847-9109)

27. Safe Harbor Newport Shipyard
1 Washington St. (401-846-6000)

28. The Marina at Brown & Howard Wharf
21 Brown & Howard Wharf (401-751-0700)

29. West Wind Marina
26 Waites Wharf (401-849-4300)

East Passage, RI

JAMESTOWN		Largest Vessel	VHF	Total Slips	Approach/ Dockside Depth	Floating Docks	Gas/ Diesel	Repairs/ Haulout	Min/Max Amps	Pump-Out Station
1. Safe Harbor Jamestown Boatyard	(401) 423-0600	70	72		12.0 / 7.0			RH	50	
2. Clark Boat Yard & Marine Works, LLC WiFi	(401) 423-3625	65	69		/			RH	30	P
3. TPG Marinas Conanicut WiFi	(401) 423-7157	210	71	100	35.0 / 15.0	F	GD	RH	30 / 100	P
4. TPG Marinas Taylor Point WiFi	(401) 423-5820	175	71	100	35.0 / 15.0	F	GD	RH	30 / 100	P

WiFi Wireless Internet Access
Visit www.waterwayguide.com for current rates, fuel prices, website addresses and other up-to-the-minute information.
(Information in the table is provided by the facilities.)

Scan here for more details:

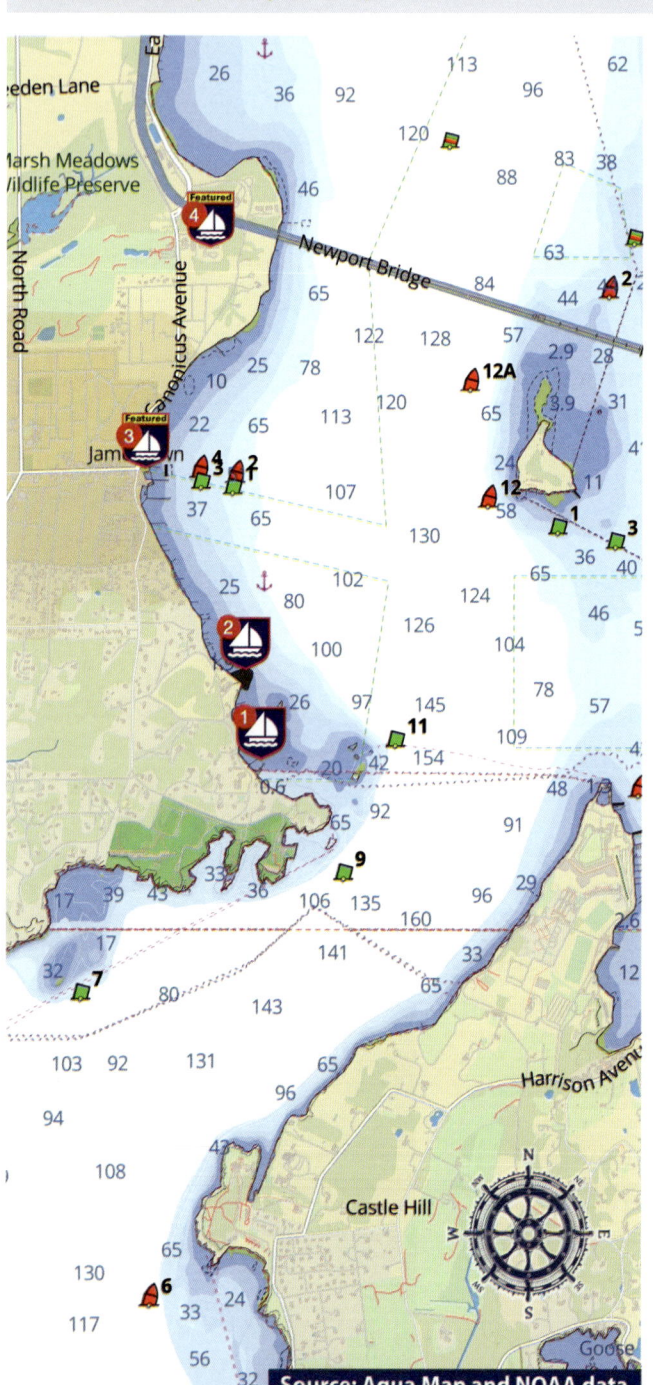

Source: Aqua Map and NOAA data

A tighter dinghy dock at the foot of Extension St. is slightly closer to the anchorage area but the same distance from groceries and other supplies, all of which are uphill from the waterfront. Some of the marinas near the bridge to Goat Island provide short-term dinghy access.

> NOTE: A mobile pump-out boat services the entire harbor (including Jamestown). Simply call "pump-out boat" on VHF Channel 09 or give them a call at 401-855-7539. They will also pick up and dispose of your trash for a small fee.

Jamestown, Conanicut Island

Two miles across East Passage from Newport on Conanicut Island is the summer resort and residential town of Jamestown, a popular stop for the cruising boater. There are excellent restaurants and shops in an idyllic village setting, full-service marine facilities and good places to walk or cycle amid vistas of crashing surf, sheer cliffs, rolling pastures and woodlands.

The view across The Dumplings toward Newport is glorious, and nearby Fort Wetherill State Park is great for walks, picnics and exploration of the World War II fortifications. The Fort area is also a popular diving spot.

The Jamestown-Newport Ferry leaves from Conanicut Marine Services Inc. and takes passengers and bicycles to Newport and back with stops at Rose Island, Fort Adams, Waites Wharf, Bowens Wharf and Perrotti Park. It runs Memorial Day to Labor Day with a reduced schedule in September.

Dockage/Moorings: On entering East Passage from Block Island Sound, Safe Harbor Jamestown Boat Yard is the first yacht facility you will encounter. They offer dockage and moorings with launch service and first-class amenities to 70 feet. It is sheltered from prevailing southerlies by Bull Point at the southeastern tip of Conanicut Island. Clark Boat Yard & Marine Works, LLC to the north offers moorings to 65 feet. All mooring rentals include launch service, unlimited holding tank pump-out service, shower/head and WiFi.

TPG Marinas Conanicut (VHF Channel 71) operates the recreational waterfront at the village center, supervising seasonal and transient moorings. They have over 4,500 linear feet of dockage for boats up to 225 feet in length plus 150 moorings. The launch service to the mooring field is fast and the drivers are deserving of a gratuity for their careful and courteous work. All fuels are available (including propane and compressed natural gas) and kayaks can be rented here.

TPG Marinas Taylor Point is a 10-acre inland facility that provides secure and safe inside and outside storage for more than 200 vessels.

■ EAST PASSAGE: NARRAGANSETT BAY TO PROVIDENCE

Melville

NAVIGATION: Less than 2 miles wide at most points, Narragansett Bay runs deep to the Providence River to the north and lies between the bay's three large islands: Conanicut Island and Prudence Island on the west and 12-mile-long Aquidneck Island on the east.

Melville is 7 miles north of Newport on the east side of East Passage just above Dyer Island. If you want to avoid the hubbub of Newport and Jamestown but still take advantage of the area's many attractions, Melville is a great alternative. During World War II Melville was the site of a PT boat officer training center. Among the officers trained there was future U.S. President John F. Kennedy.

Dockage: The 15-acre Hinckley Yacht Services Portsmouth is a boatyard and home to an array of top-flight specialty marine shops and fabricators. They maintain some transient slips as well.

Safe Harbor New England Boatworks in a protected basin to the north. The marina's world-renowned team has built successful Round the World racers and America's Cup contenders. Their famed reputation is complemented with a complete array of premium shoreside amenities and a friendly, family-centric atmosphere.

Prudence Island

Near the north end of Prudence Island, Potter Cove (not to be confused with the Potter Cove charted just north of the Newport Bridge on Conanicut Island) offers good shelter but no amenities. This natural basin is almost landlocked by the elbow of the curving sand spit.

The entrance is well buoyed, although it will not look that way on approach from the main channel. You must locate and honor all three nun buoys: red nuns "2," "4" and "6" to starboard or you will snare your keel on the shoals off Gull Point. Note that the cove runs shallow to the north, punctuated by minuscule Shell Island, just visible at low tide, and a wreck marked by a Coast Guard buoy. The beach is a popular place for gatherings and will sometimes have a dozen dinghies pulled up nice and high.

Moorings/Anchorage: There are a large number of private moorings in Potter Cove but no public ones. Anchoring is allowed outside Potter Cove where you can set a hook in 10 to 11 feet MLW off the pebbled beach running to the southeast between the cove and Mount Tom Rock. Note that frequent swells from boat traffic in the channel will find their way into this anchorage.

From here you can dinghy in for exploration of the Narragansett Bay Estuarine Sanctuary surrounding the cove. On the west side of the island you can anchor at Coggeshall Cove, which is well protected from east and north winds. This is a good anchorage for shallow-draft boats. Note the rocks close to shore.

Bristol Harbor

Cupped securely between the arms of Popasquash and Bristol Necks, Bristol Harbor is one of Narragansett Bay's most important for recreational boating history and maritime scenery. The Herreshoff Marine Museum is here and houses the America's Cup Hall of Fame. For museum information, admission and hours, call 401-253-5000. There is also a great park to walk to with wildlife, bike trails, tennis courts, baseball fields and a beach. Although considered an excellent stop for the boating culture, note that there is no fuel in the harbor so plan ahead.

East Passage, RI

MELVILLE		Largest Vessel	VHF	Total Slips	Approach/ Dockside Depth	Floating Docks	Gas/ Diesel	Repairs/ Haulout	Min/Max Amps	Pump-Out Station
1. Hinckley Yacht Services Portsmouth **WiFi**	(401) 683-7100	220	9	101	20.0 / 15.0	F	GD	RH	30 / 200+	P
2. Safe Harbor New England Boatworks	(401) 683-4000	150	9	360	15.0 / 15.0	F	GD	RH	30 / 100	P

WiFi Wireless Internet Access
Visit www.waterwayguide.com for current rates, fuel prices, website addresses and other up-to-the-minute information.
(Information in the table is provided by the facilities.)

Scan here for more details:

NAVIGATION: Bristol Harbor is 2 miles long and over 1 mile wide. Although open to the south except where Hog Island breaks up the wind and waves, it is protected to the north, east and west. The well-marked channels on either side of Hog Island make for a painless entry. Nonetheless, take care to honor the channel buoys marking the shoal extending northward of Hog Island and the rocky ledge on the southeast of Popasquash Neck.

Dockage/Moorings: The Herreshoff Marine Museum has moorings and dockside slips available for transients to 200 feet. Reservations are recommended. They do not provide launch service but dinghy docks are available throughout town.

The Town of Bristol Marina and Maritime Center has 23 all-transient slips to 90 feet. They also have moorings. Call for current rates and availability or reserve on Dockwa. (Please note: The water supply on the dock is not potable.) The town docks are a short walk from countless historic shops and restaurants in the heart of Bristol.

Bristol Yacht Club is private but rents moorings to visiting cruising club members as well as individual cruisers. The facilities fee includes launch service, access to the club's dinghy dock and use of the facilities in the clubhouse annex. Bristol Marine has slips and moorings with launch service, bathrooms and showers. There is a great park within walking distance with lots of wildlife, bike trails, tennis courts, baseball fields and a beach. It is a pleasant 1-mile walk to town, although you can often find a ride.

Anchorage: Bristol Harbor is big enough and generally deep enough to accommodate a large local fleet with anchorage room to spare. It would be advisable for cruisers to call the Bristol Harbormaster (401-253-1700) for suggestions on anchoring. When the prevailing southwesterlies stiffen up, the harbor can develop a noticeable chop. In most other conditions, it is pleasant and comfortable. It is a bit of a pull into town from the

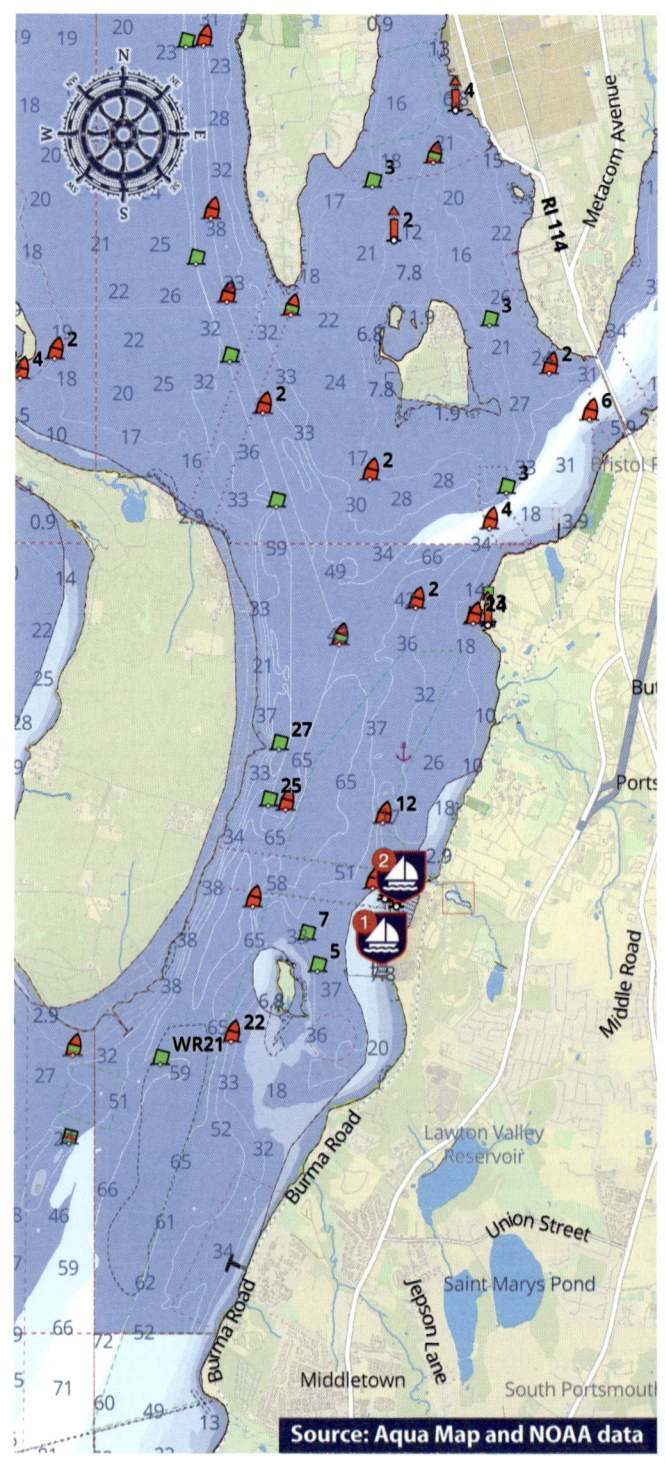

Source: Aqua Map and NOAA data

Providence River, RI

BRISTOL		Largest Vessel	VHF	Total Slips	Approach/ Dockside Depth	Floating Docks	Gas/ Diesel	Repairs/ Haulout	Min/Max Amps	Pump-Out Station
1. Herreshoff Marine Museum WiFi	(401) 253-5000	200	72	12	16.0 / 10.0	F			30 / 100	
2. Town of Bristol Marina and Maritime Center WiFi	(401) 253-1700	150	16	23	/	F	GD		30 / 50	P
3. Bristol Yacht Club - PRIVATE	(401) 253-2922	55	68		12.0 / 6.0	F				
4. Bristol Marine WiFi	(401) 253-2200	100	69	20	12.0 / 8.0	F		RH	50	P
BARRINGTON										
5. Barrington Yacht Club - PRIVATE WiFi	(401) 245-1181	43	68		/ 7.5		GD		30 / 50	P
6. Stanley's Boat Yard Inc.	(401) 245-5090	55	16	130	10.0 / 5.0	F		RH	30 / 50	P

WiFi Wireless Internet Access
Visit www.waterwayguide.com for current rates, fuel prices, website addresses and other up-to-the-minute information.
(Information in the table is provided by the facilities.)

Scan here for more details:

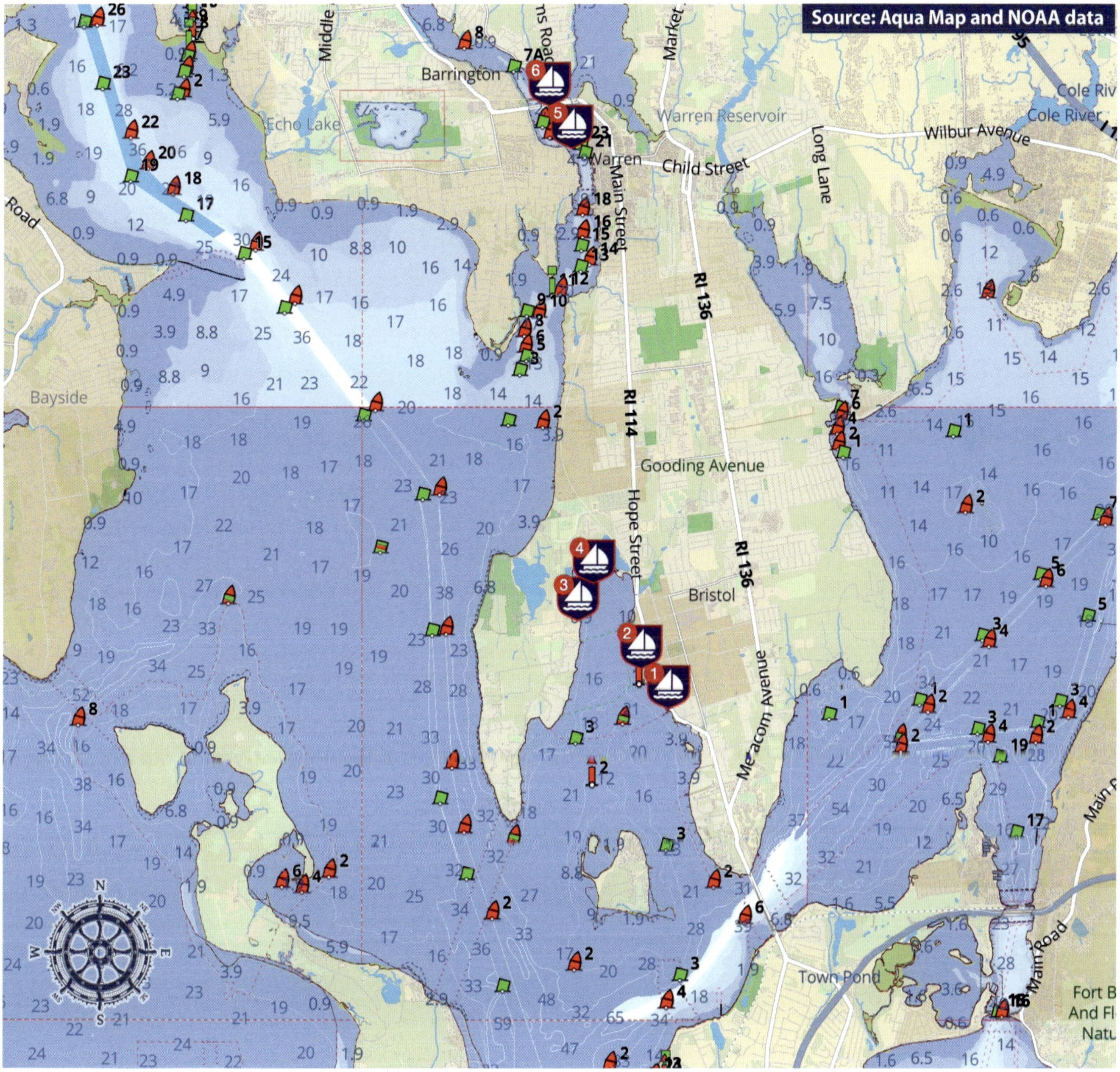

Source: Aqua Map and NOAA data

anchorage. You can tie up your dinghy just north of the old stone armory in front of Rockwell Park.

The Bristol Maritime Center located in the historic naval reserve armory building on the east side of Bristol's harbor offers services for boaters that include restrooms and showers, laundry facilities and an area to relax and meet with other visiting boaters. Contact the Bristol Harbor Master's Office at 401-253-1700 for more information.

Cruisers who are not visiting the town can anchor east of Hog Island south of Bristol Harbor proper. Good holding in mud can be found north of green can "3" in 17- to 25-foot MLW depths.

Warren & Barrington

Barrington was originally a part of Warren, which was famous for the fine vessels launched from its yards in the middle of the 19th century. These vessels engaged in whaling, merchant service and the West India trade. Three notable ships were built in Warren by Chase & Davis: the 1853 clipper *Lookout*, the 1853 clipper bark *Gem of the Sea* and the 1854 clipper bark *Mary Ogden*. Today it is the homeport of a (relatively) small cruise liner that travels to New England, Canada, Florida and the Bahamas.

NAVIGATION: A bit before the start of the Providence River at the most northern part of Narragansett Bay, a narrow channel winds its way north on the Warren River, eastward of Rumstick Neck. The channel threads through shoals with ample aids to navigation.

At Tyler Point, about 2 miles upstream, the Barrington River flows in from the northwest. To the east is the industrial boatbuilding town of Warren. To the west is Barrington, the main recreational boat center for the area. Fixed bridges with 10- and 5-foot vertical clearances, respectively, will restrict many boats from traveling upriver.

Dockage/Moorings: Barrington Harbor has extremely strong currents but protection from all winds. The Harbormaster in Barrington makes a real effort to assign moorings by making efficient use of the space available in this popular harbor. (Call 401-437-3930, police dispatch, for a mooring assignment.) Moorings are for 40-foot maximum length vessels with no on-shore amenities. There are two pump-out stations in the area as well as all fuels. It would be difficult to find a place to anchor here due to the proliferation of moorings.

The private Barrington Yacht Club offers a bar, clubhouse, pool and dockage to reciprocal members. Dockage is offered based on availability on the transient dock. Guests arriving by boat should display reciprocal club burgee. Stanley's Boat Yard Inc. has slips and moorings including a few for transients and offers an array of services. They have been in business since 1938.

Anchorage: The closest anchorage is Smith Cove on the Barrington side of the lower Warren River. The anchorage offers good holding ground and protection from westerly winds but is exposed to easterlies.

Providence River

West of Warren at Conimicut Point, Narragansett Bay becomes the deep and well-marked Providence River. The other point on the 1-mile-wide mouth is Nayatt Point on the eastern shore. A 58-foot-high, rip-rap lined lighthouse 0.5 mile off Conimicut Point leads traffic (mostly oceangoing and other commercial craft) into the river. The Nayatt Point Lighthouse opposite Conimicut Point at Barrington also guides vessels along the Providence River. Nyatt Point Lighthouse was built in 1856 but is now a private residence and is on the National Register of Historic Places but is not open to the public.

A concentration of marinas stands between the northern end of Pawtuxet Neck and Fields Point on the outskirts of the City of Providence. These are on the river itself but well off the main channel. Close by are shore accommodations and transportation. Less than 1 mile to the west is Roger Williams Park Zoo, which houses over 100 species from around the world.

The Seekonk River is a tidal extension of the Providence River that flows 5 miles from Providence and East Providence to the Blackstone River and Pawtucket Falls. The river is home to the Brown University rowing team as well as the Narragansett Boat Club (the oldest rowing club in the country).

NAVIGATION: Nearly landlocked Bullock Cove on the eastern shore is the first harbor heading north on the Providence River. A well-marked channel from Bullock Point leads into Bullock Cove beginning at flashing green buoy "1." At mean high water

Providence River, RI

BULLOCK COVE		Largest Vessel	VHF	Total Slips	Approach/ Dockside Depth	Floating Docks	Gas/ Diesel	Repairs/ Haulout	Min/Max Amps	Pump-Out Station
1. East Providence Harbor Master	(401) 639-8437		9		9.0 / 9.0					P
2. Safe Harbor Cove Haven WiFi	(401) 246-1600	100	9	348	13.0 / 12.0	F	GD	RH	30 / 50	P
PAWTUXET AREA										
3. Rhode Island Yacht Club-PRIVATE	(401) 941-0220	70	78	90	8.0 / 6.0	F		H	50	P
EDGEWOOD AREA										
4. Edgewood Yacht Club-PRIVATE	(401) 781-9626	50	14	55	6.0 / 5.0	F			20 / 30	P
PROVIDENCE										
5. Providence Marina WiFi	(401) 369-7547	70		56	/	F			30	P

WiFi Wireless Internet Access
Visit www.waterwayguide.com for current rates, fuel prices, website addresses and other up-to-the-minute information.
(Information in the table is provided by the facilities.)

Scan here for more details:

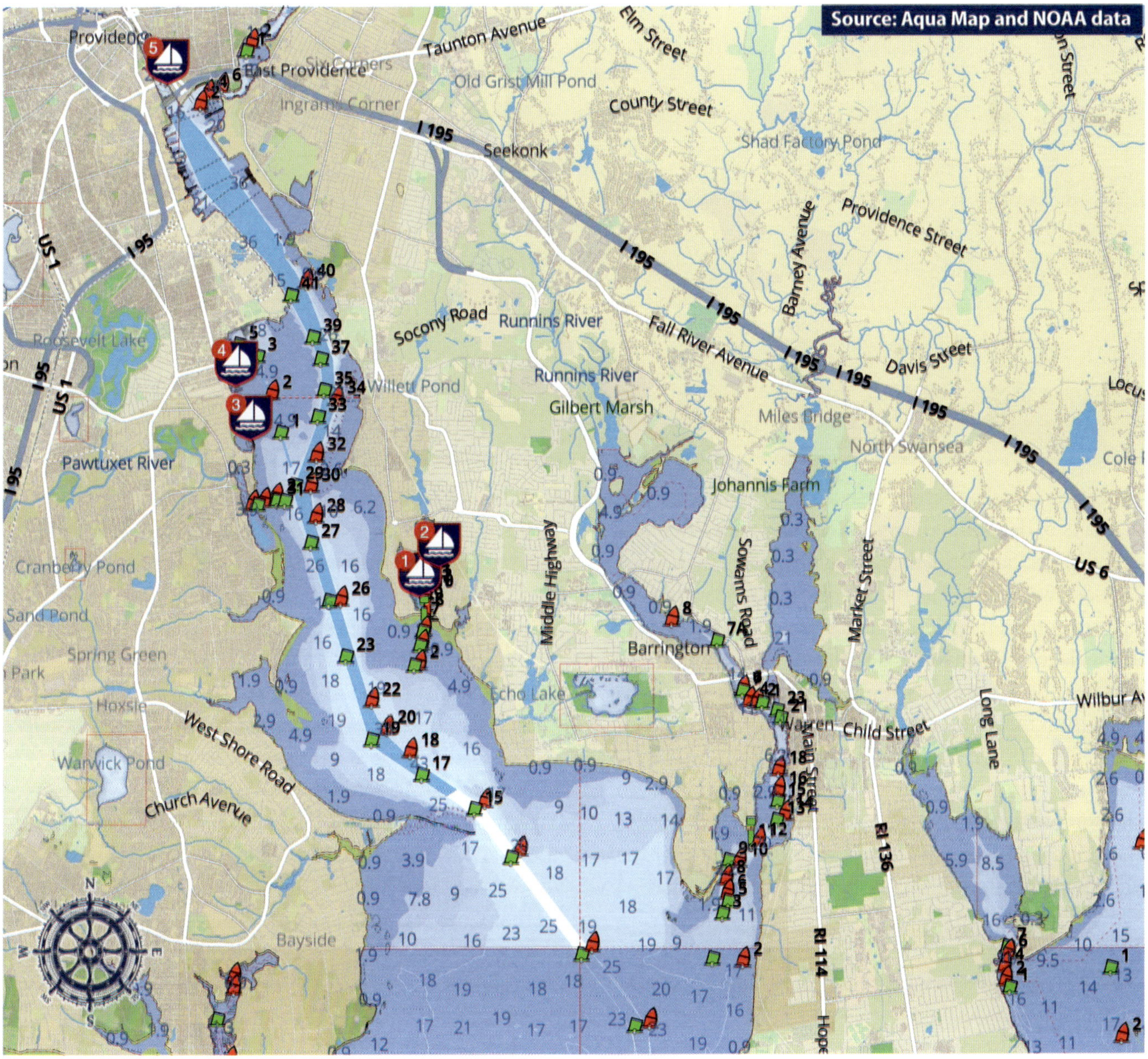

Source: Aqua Map and NOAA data

Mount Hope Bay

expect 10-foot depths, but with a 6-foot tidal range skippers of deep-draft boats will want to check the local tide table or call ahead to the marina before entering.

Narrow, dredged Pawtuxet Cove is a little farther upriver and on the western shore behind Pawtuxet Neck. The village of Pawtuxet was founded in 1638 and is an interesting historic location to visit. Enter Pawtuxet Cove from the main river channel through a straight cut lined by rocks and shoals. Private range lights may be visible to help guide you through the opening between the point and the end of the dike. At the opening, turn north for the harbor and marinas but turn south for the anchorage. In recent years, the entrance channel has shoaled to less than 6 feet MLW. Refer to the Waterway Explorer (www.waterwayguide.com) and NOAA online charts (www.nauticalcharts.noaa.gov) for the most up-to-date information.

Edgewood is as close to Providence as most boats get. A hurricane barrier just past the **IWAY(I-95) Bridge** (35-foot fixed vertical clearance) followed by the Fox Point hurricane barrier (21-foot fixed vertical clearance and is 20 feet wide) blocks navigation farther up the Providence River. Only a short ride from the center of town, Edgewood makes an ideal layover spot from which to visit the historic city. The river from here north is heavily commercial and the waterborne traffic is fearsome.

Dockage/Moorings: The East Providence Harbor Master on Bullock Cove maintains rental moorings in the relatively narrow harbor. Call on VHF Channel 09 (or 401-639-8437) for availability. The full-service Safe Harbor Cove Haven dominates the eastern shore with its floating dock complex. The marina features updated docks and a diversity of upscale amenities and is a major repair center with and on-site marine metal fabrication and a canvas shop. This is also home to an impressive collection of America's Cup vessels. There is a dinghy landing at the town dock but there is no room to anchor in Bullock Cove.

The private Rhode Island Yacht Club at Pawtuxet Village has 90 slips and manages a large mooring field. Non-members may request an available or mooring for transient/temporary periods through Dockwa. Also nearby is the private Edgewood Yacht Club, which accommodates members of other yacht clubs with reciprocity rights to 50 feet in slips or on moorings. They provide launch service and full amenities.

Providence Marina is the only marina in downtown Providence. Seasonal and transient slip holders enjoy full access to outstanding amenities including three on-site restaurants.

Anchorage: The only anchorage basin on this part of the Providence River is in a diked area south of the entrance to Pawtucket Cove. Here you will find 6 to 8 feet MLW with good holding in mud.

■ MOUNT HOPE BAY TO SAKONNET

Mount Hope Bay

The Rhode Island/Massachusetts border divides Mount Hope Bay. Mount Hope itself is high on Bristol Neck. The bay is easy to reach from busier nearby waters and offers safe and scenic cruising. Its upper eastern shore is the waterfront for Fall River, a mill town with heavy commercial boat traffic plying well-marked channels.

At Fall River you can visit the famous battleship *Massachusetts* ("Big Mamie"), the star attraction of Battleship Cove and Maritime Museum (508-678-1100). You can also explore the submarine *Lionfish*, the destroyer *Joseph P. Kennedy Jr.* plus a helicopter, gunboats and P.T. Boats. The on-site maritime museum has nautical history exhibits. Numerous other area attractions including the Vietnam Veteran's Memorial Wall are within easy walking distance.

NAVIGATION: Mount Hope Bay can be accessed by proceeding east from Providence River and passing under the high-level **Mount Hope Bridge**. It can also be reached from the Sakonnet River to the south as described below.

It is 6.5 miles to the high-rise **Charles M. Braga Jr. Bridge**. Next is the restricted **Brightman Street Bridge** (27-foot-closed vertical clearance). The draw opens on signal between 5:00 a.m. and 9:00 p.m. daily. Between 9:00 p.m. and 5 a.m. the draw will open on signal after at least a one-hour advance notice is given by calling the number posted at the bridge. From June 1 through August 31, the draw need not open for the passage of pleasure craft from 7:00 a.m. to 9:30 a.m. and from 4:00 p.m. to 6:30 p.m., Monday through Friday, except holidays.

Dockage/Moorings: The 300-slip Borden Light Marina, Inc. at Fall River welcomes transients to 65 feet on their docks. More marine facilities are located across the Bay and up the Taunton River. Some of these are boat brokerages that maintain a few slips. You will have to navigate two bridge (60-foot closed vertical clearance) to reach Bristol Marine, Somerset, a working yard that maintains transient slips and/or moorings.

Farther north, the private Taunton Yacht Club may have space for you but call ahead. Shaw's Boat Yard Inc. is a year-round yard serving New England boaters for over 60 years. They offer a wide range of services including dockage to 60 feet.

Anchorage: Coves at the entrance to each of three small rivers along the northern shore of Mount Hope Bay offer potential anchorages and opportunities for dinghy exploration beyond navigable depths. During most summer weather, there is good anchorage along the western shore of a cove at the mouth of the Cole River–West in 9 to 12 feet MLW with good holding in mud. It is also possible to anchor off Swansea Marina (no transient slips) at Ocean Grove Beach just beyond the mooring field in 9-to 14-foot MLW depths. This is somewhat exposed to the south.

The Cole River itself is not navigable beyond the cove (despite the several deep-footed vessels that have somehow found the way to a protected berth beyond the breakwater). However, it is a good place to explore by dinghy. The best time to enter is at slack water just before the ebb. Otherwise, an unfavorable current can present quite a challenge.

The Lee River to the east has no amenities but it also presents no obstructions and is closest to the marked channel to Fall River. In a pinch, you can drop the hook in Fox Hill Cove in soft mud with 8 to 11 feet MLW in the shadow of a massive electric plant.

Mount Hope Bay, MA

COLE RIVER		Largest Vessel	VHF	Total Slips	Approach/ Dockside Depth	Floating Docks	Gas/ Diesel	Repairs/ Haulout	Min/Max Amps	Pump-Out Station
1. Borden Light Marina, Inc. **WiFi**	(508) 678-7547	65		300	/	F	GD	RH	30 / 50	P

WiFi Wireless Internet Access
Visit www.waterwayguide.com for current rates, fuel prices, website addresses and other up-to-the-minute information.
(Information in the table is provided by the facilities.)

Scan here for more details:

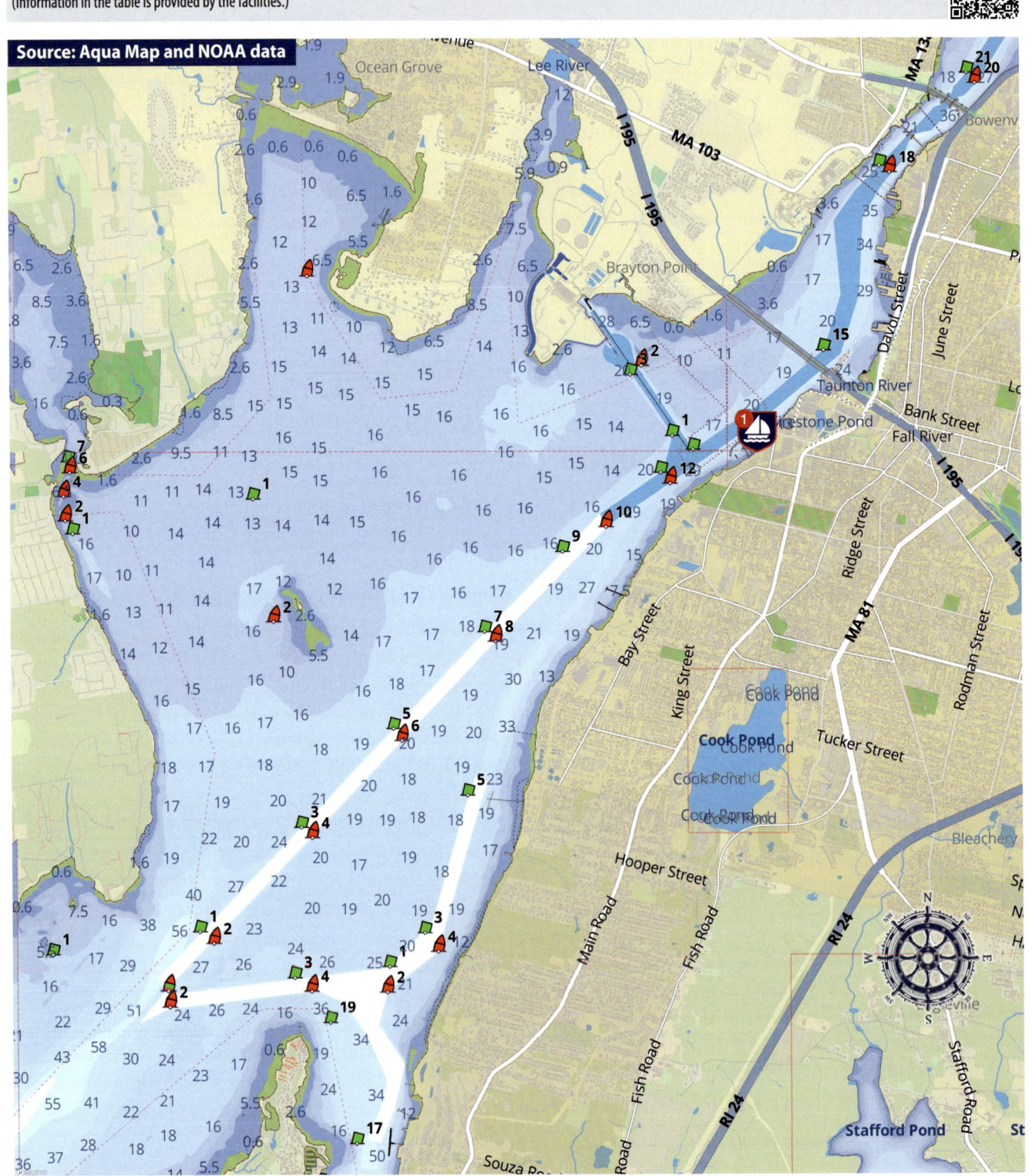

Source: Aqua Map and NOAA data

Taunton River, MA

TAUNTON RIVER (SOUTH)		Largest Vessel	VHF	Total Slips	Approach/ Dockside Depth	Floating Docks	Gas/ Diesel	Repairs/ Haulout	Min/Max Amps	Pump-Out Station
1. Bristol Marine, Somerset **WiFi**	(508) 678-1234	100		25	21.0 / 6.0			RH	30 / 50	P
TAUNTON RIVER (NORTH)										
2. Taunton Yacht Club-PRIVATE	(508) 669-6007	40	68	40	5.0 / 8.0		GD			
3. Shaw's Boat Yard Inc.	(508) 669-5714	60		60	7.0 / 6.0	F		RH	30 / 50	

WiFi Wireless Internet Access
Visit www.waterwayguide.com for current rates, fuel prices, website addresses and other up-to-the-minute information.
(Information in the table is provided by the facilities.)

Scan here for more details:

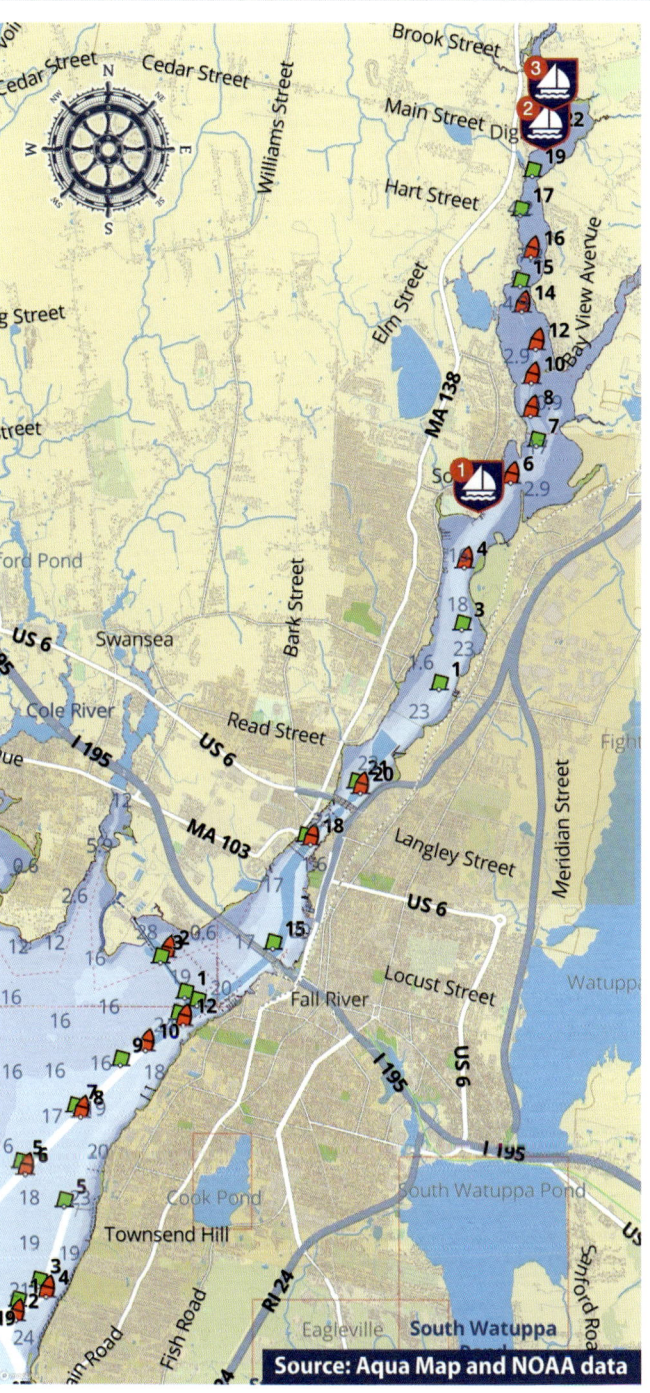

Source: Aqua Map and NOAA data

The Sakonnet River (Tiverton)

The Sakonnet River, lying between Aquidneck Island and the mainland, is easternmost of the Narragansett north-south waterways. Many fishermen and recreational boats use the 13-mile-long river named Saughkonet by the Wampanoag people for "black goose place." Its waters and anchorages seem dramatically quiet, particularly in comparison to the crowded waters of Newport, located not far to the west.

The Sakonnet Passage is deep, the main channel is close to midstream and all shoals and obstructions are clearly marked. A scattering of towns and harbors along the river offer recreational boating amenities. Tiverton is just south of Mount Hope Bay and north of small, wooded Gould Island, which sits dead center in the Sakonnet River.

During the Revolutionary War, Tiverton gained acclaim for a particularly daring act by one of its parishioners, Col. William Barton, who led a raiding party to capture a British general. Today, only a tower remains of the historic Fort Barton and there is little else around to attract tourists. For boaters, however, it is a protected and attractive spot with ample facilities on both sides of the river.

NAVIGATION: Enter the river from Mount Hope Bay by going eastward around Common Fence Point, Aquidneck's northernmost tip. Continuing south, pass between the bare pilings that formerly supported a swing bridge and under the 65-foot fixed vertical clearance **Rt 24/138 Bridge**. This marks where the river narrows into picturesque Tiverton Basin, the Sakonnet's most active boating center.

Be prepared for swift currents at the bridge, except at slack water. At the bottom of the pinch, the rustic remains of the 1810 stone bridge that linked Tiverton to Aquidneck for 150 years restricts the flow of water in an already tight passage. Expect swift currents on either tide.

Sakonnet River, RI

TIVERTON AREA		Largest Vessel	VHF	Total Slips	Approach/ Dockside Depth	Floating Docks	Gas/ Diesel	Repairs/ Haulout	Min/Max Amps	Pump-Out Station
1. Safe Harbor Sakonnet **WiFi**	(401) 683-3551	50	9	314	6.0 / 10.0	F	GD	RH	30 / 50	P
2. Tiverton Yacht Club-PRIVATE	(401) 816-0811			21	35.0 / 8.0	F				
3. Standish Boat Yard	(401) 624-4075	70	16	24	35.0 / 10.0	F	GD	RH	30 / 50	P
4. Safe Harbor Island Park **WiFi**	(401) 683-3030	70	9	76	25.0 / 7.0	F		RH	30 / 50	P

WiFi Wireless Internet Access
Visit www.waterwayguide.com for current rates, fuel prices, website addresses and other up-to-the-minute information.
(Information in the table is provided by the facilities.)

Scan here for more details:

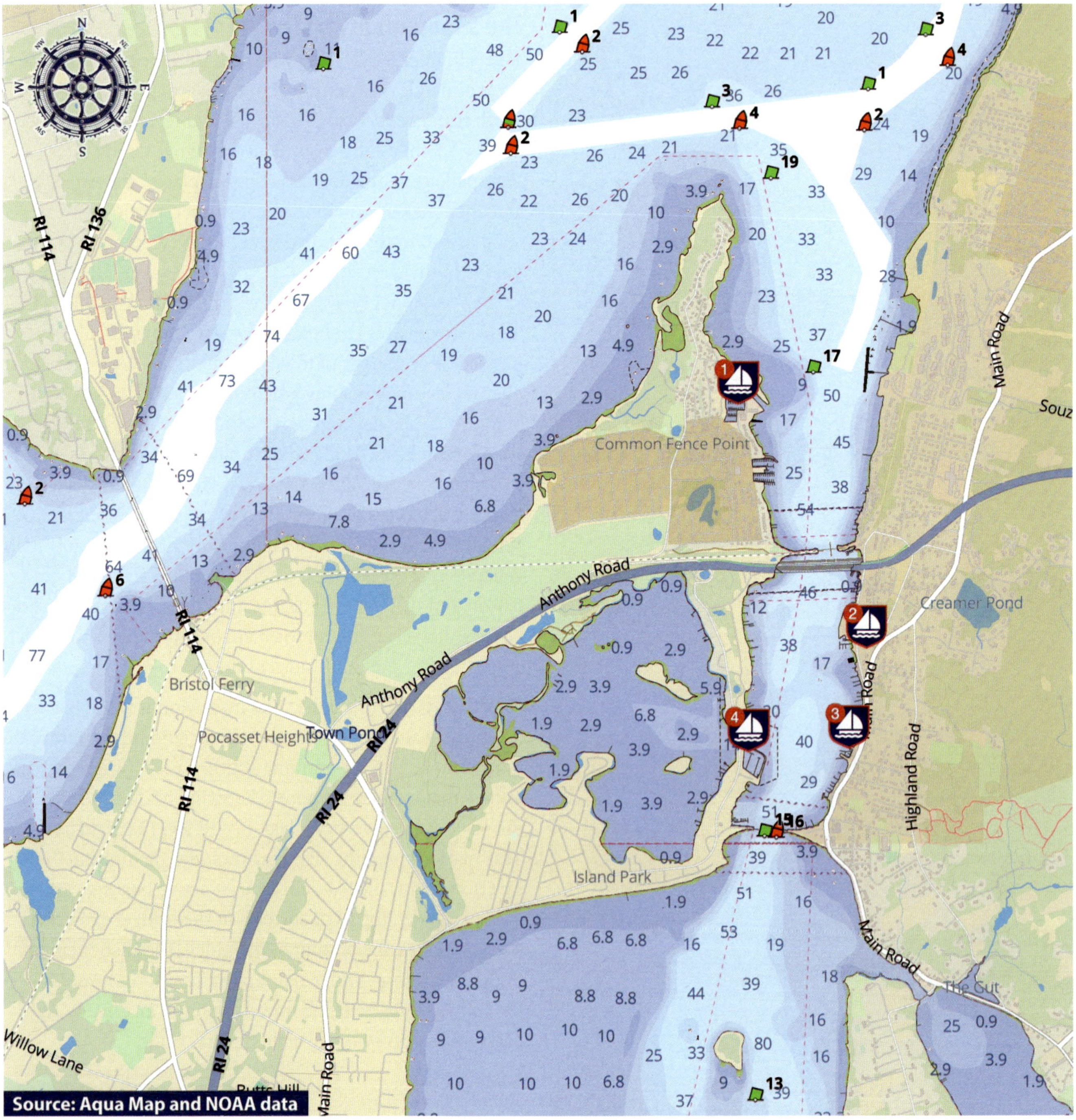

Source: Aqua Map and NOAA data

Sakonnet River, RI

SAKONNET		Largest Vessel	VHF	Total Slips	Approach/ Dockside Depth	Floating Docks	Gas/ Diesel	Repairs/ Haulout	Min/Max Amps	Pump-Out Station
1. Sakonnet Point Club-PRIVATE 	(401) 635-4753	75	6	31	8.0 / 8.0	F			30 / 50	
2. Sakonnet Yacht Club-PRIVATE	(508) 994-2075				8.0 / 6.5					
3. Sakonnet Harbor Moorings	(401) 835-4474	40	6		/					

 Wireless Internet Access
Visit www.waterwayguide.com for current rates, fuel prices, website addresses and other up-to-the-minute information.
(Information in the table is provided by the facilities.)

Scan here for more details:

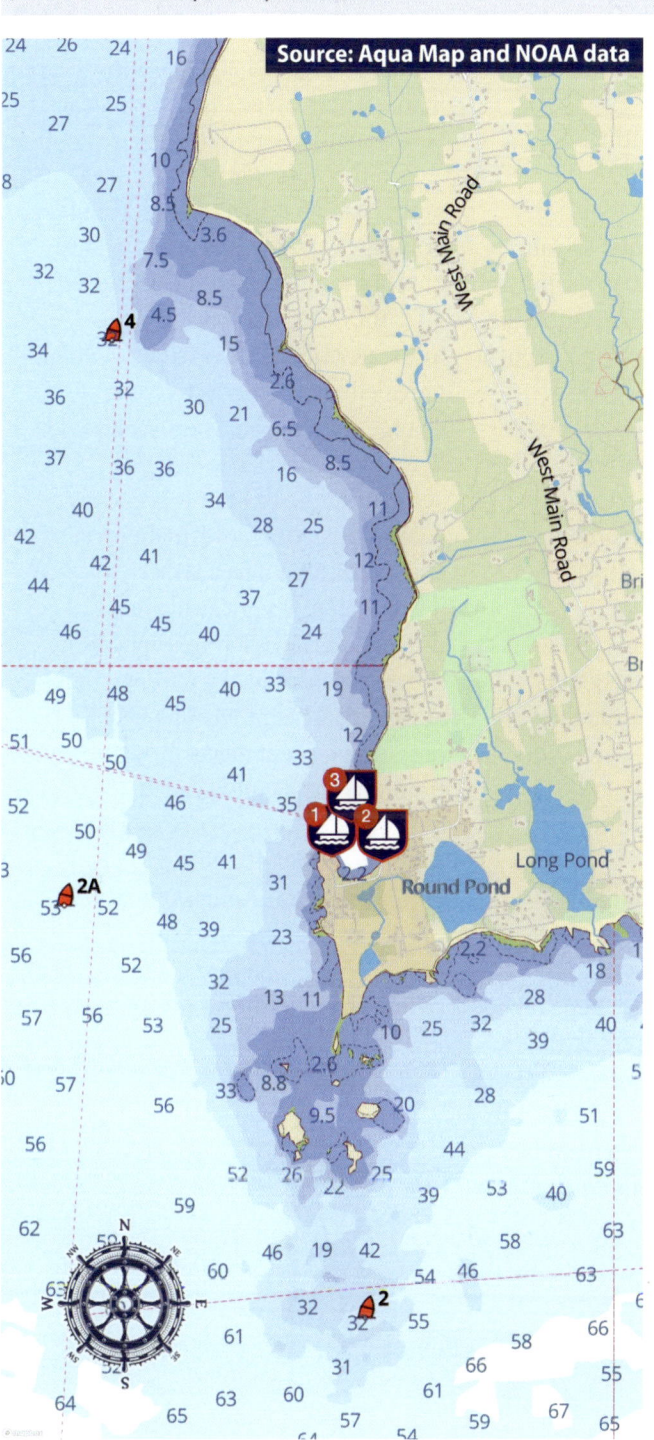

Source: Aqua Map and NOAA data

Dockage/Moorings: About 0.5 mile south of Common Fence Point just south and west of green can "17," head west to Cedar Island Pond to starboard to reach the well-protected Safe Harbor Sakonnet, which has limited transient space (and is actually located in Tiverton not Sakonet). What they do have is a spacious 6-acre spread between the North and South Yards to offer plenty of service accommodations and storage space.

Just south of the bridges on the eastern shore, the private Tiverton Yacht Club will accommodate a transient boat on their outer dock if space is available. A small grocery store is located near the clubhouse.

Standish Boat Yard to the south at Tiverton has limited transient options for dockage and moorings and requests that guests book well in advance if possible. Services include mast un-stepping and storage. Safe Harbor Island Park has 25 reserved transient slips and/or moorings to 70 feet and offers all types of maintenance and repairs.

Anchorage: Significant depths, swift currents and commercial traffic make anchoring unwise at Tiverton. It is far better to locate a mooring or slip. For boats drawing 4 feet or less and having vertical clearance requirements of less than 25 feet (due to a fixed bridge), The Cove located west of Tiverton Basin at Hummock Point is a favorite gunkholing spot. Most cruisers will have to reserve this spot for dinghy exploration.

To Sakonnet Harbor

On the eastern side of the Sakonnet River near its mouth, Sakonnet Harbor is well protected from the south and east behind Sakonnet Point and from the west by an 800-foot breakwater extending northward from Breakwater Point. This is the boating center for the resort area of Little Compton, located 3 miles inland.

Quite a few mariners on the trek between Cape Cod Canal or the Islands and Newport are forced to take an unintended turn into the river when conditions in the sound deteriorate. Once inside, they are amazed to find that the angry 10-foot waves, powered by 35- to 40-knot gusts outside, fall away almost immediately to placid waters and gentle breezes in the protection of the river's banks.

> NOTE: Sakonnet Vineyard, about 5 miles from the harbor, produces about 10,000 cases of wine a year in its solar-heated winery. They named a wine after the state bird, which is a chicken called the Rhode Island Red.

NAVIGATION: It is easy to exit the river between Sakonnet and Sachuest Points but be alert for often-inconspicuous floating fishnets, traps, weirs and lobster buoys. Stay close to the navigation buoys. Rocks, reefs and islets surround the prominent lighthouse off Sakonnet Point. The same precautions apply when entering the river, although even in poor visibility these impediments may be far less daunting than the boisterous seas that can squall up suddenly in Rhode Island Sound to the south.

The Sakonnet River is an excellent refuge to keep in mind when planning an outside passage south of Narragansett Bay. If coming in from the Rhode Island Sound, you can identify the entrance to Sakonnet Harbor by the 4-second flashing red light "2" at the breakwater's end. After the first week of June, the best route of entry is that used by the fishing boats–upriver from the south, below the numerous fish traps, standing off the breakwater at about 50 yards

then turning abruptly southeast at the entrance.

Before early June, the fish-trap line is strung at right angles from the breakwater, making the southern approach impossible. Barrels and high-standing radar reflectors at each end mark the traps but spotting them can be quite difficult in fog or when the wind is up. Additional traps, similarly marked, are to the southwest of red bell buoy "2A" near the center of the river.

Dockage/Moorings: Private Sakonnet Point Club has reciprocal club affiliations with The University Club Providence, The Hope Club in Providence and Bay Club at Mattapoisett. Nearby Sakonnet Yacht Club is strictly private.

Your best bet is to pick up one of the two town-owned guest moorings from Sakonnet Harbor Moorings. Call the Sakonnet Harbormaster at 401-835-4474. A breakwater provides adequate protection throughout much of the year and a nearby beach offers good swimming. This harbor is quite small and there is no room for anchoring.

Anchorage: About halfway down the river from Tiverton, Fogland Point juts out from the eastern shore to create a large bight. Fogland Point anchorage is easy to enter, roomy and has good holding in 11 feet MLW but is wide open to the north. Plenty of water can be found at the mouth but don't go too far in as depths tend to shoal.

Below High Hill Point on the eastern side of the river is an unnamed cove, which has been known to serve as a good anchorage. Here you will find 9 to 15 feet MLW with good holding in mud and shell. This is somewhat exposed from the northwest through the southwest. Watch for the large spread of aquaculture floats, where oysters for Newport's best restaurants are grown.

On the west side of the mouth of the Sakonnet River behind Flint Point is Sachuest Cove. Give plenty of room to unmarked rocks charted off Flint Point. The cove is open to the northeast but is seldom crowded and makes a welcome change from the Newport scene. You might experience a slight surge from the bay but it is usually comfortable for an overnight stay and has at least 8 feet MLW.

No amenities are available directly off the beach (except when the ice cream truck is present), but Second Beach and Easton's Beach provide excellent views. Accessible from the north end of the anchorage is the 325-acre Norman Bird Sanctuary (401-846-2577) with a museum, 7 miles of marked hiking trails and a nice bathing beach, which offers excellent swimming with lifeguards on duty.

Tiverton, RI

Sakonnet River

Pages 392-407

Pages 407-413

Pages 413-416

Wareham

Onset

Cape Cod Canal

Phinneys Harbor

Pocasett

Marion

Megansett Harbor

Matapoisett Harbor

Fairhaven

New Bedford

Appanagansett Bay

Woods Hole

Buzzards Bay

Westport

Naushon Island

Cuttyhunk Island

Atlantic Ocean

N E S W

■ WESTERN SHORE TO CAPE COD CANAL

Navigation Notes

Had the colonists known their birds, this body of water might have been called Osprey Bay. Instead, Buzzards Bay is one of many examples of home-spun naming by early colonists. Even though rocks, reefs and shoals extend from the shorelines, the bay runs broad and open almost 30 miles northeasterly. It bulges in the middle then bends and narrows at the top, a funnel for the western entrance to the Cape Cod Canal.

Gooseberry Neck's Hen and Chickens islands are nearly 5 miles from Cuttyhunk Island's Sow and Pigs Reef at the bay's western mouth, which begins just east of the border between Rhode Island and Massachusetts.

Prevailing southwesterly winds blow 15 to 20 knots on summer afternoons. The winds funnel up the narrowing bay to create short, steep seas. A 4- to 5-foot sea state is not unusual, especially on an ebb tide, which opposes the southwesterly winds creating the characteristic Buzzards Bay chop.

Riding the end of the flood north provides the most settled conditions in a southwesterly wind but take care not to get caught in the turnaround: Heading into the Cape Cod Canal against the current is a difficult proposition for slow boats. Lucky for cruisers, both sides of the bay have multiple excellent stops where boaters can wait out the tide and enjoy a waterfront small town at the same time.

The ship channel is busy enough that smaller boats do well to run outside of it. Most will be able to stay north of the channel and cut the corner heading around Sconticut Neck and West Island (south of Fairhaven) but study the chart for hazardous ledges and rocks. Refer to the Waterway Explorer (www.waterwayguide.com) for the most up-to-date information.

The fog on Buzzards Bay tends to burn off by late morning but a haze might linger. Despite its reputation as a rough body of water, the bay provides fine sailing and snug, picturesque harbors. Many sailors, especially racers, consider Buzzards Bay to be some of the finest sailing in New England with reliable winds and charming natural harbors on both shores.

The complex shoreline of Buzzards Bay and most of New England is due to the rise in sea level after the last ice age. The remnants of this can still be seen along Buzzards Bay Moraine, which runs north to south in Bourne and Falmouth, then curves to become the Elizabeth Islands. Also left behind were a sandy ridge on the eastern shore of the bay and a slowly rising shoreline to the west.

Westport Harbor

Westport

Westport was originally formed as part of Old Dartmouth and was incorporated in 1878. The one-time whaling center of Westport Point is now a recreational boating and commercial fishing port.

Virtually landlocked behind the overlapping points of The Knubble with its lighthouse on a granite mound and Horseneck Point, Westport Harbor is well protected in all but near-hurricane conditions. Despite the formidable approach shown on the chart, sailboats routinely traverse the relatively shallow entrance and flats-strewn channel to the amenities within.

The low-lying but lush scenery is characteristic of what was once typical in southern New England harbors with their low stone walls girding narrow fields leading to the sea, rushing streams, green marshes and sandy beaches, all prefacing the weathered-shingle houses and 19th-century commercial structures of a picturesque uphill village, crowded with active watermen and recreational boaters.

On the surf side of the access road to Tripp's, the town's parking lot shows the way to the sandy beach path across gorgeous, wind-swept dunes to unspoiled Horseneck Beach (popular with surfers because of its open-ocean frontage) and to the Cherry and Webb Conservation Area on Horseneck Point.

Several miles from the harbor the 100-acre Westport Rivers Vineyard and Winery (508-636-3423) welcomes visitors to its award-winning winery for free 20-minute tours, wine tasting and review of the vineyard's art gallery. The well-preserved 19th-century homes in this unspoiled fishing village are, alone, worth a launch or dinghy ride across the river but there is so much more to see.

NAVIGATION: The narrow entry at the mouth of the Westport River between The Knubble and Horseneck Point is visible only from close inshore. The shallow bar at the entrance (controlling depth of 6 feet MLW) is dynamic and constricted currents from the estuary's two branches can reach 4 knots at full ebb. Those who know the area advise not to try the entrance during poor visibility or in a southerly blow.

From flashing green bell buoy "1" near Two Mile Rock, head toward the 35-foot (flashing green every 6 seconds) beacon at the eastern tip of The Knubble, being sure to honor green daybeacon "3" marking Two Mile Rock itself on approach. When the green can buoy "5" (marking Dogfish Ledge) is abeam to the southwest, red

nun buoy "6" will be northeast. The channel then jogs to the northeast, marked by green can buoys "5A" and "5B" off Halfmile Rock. Red nun buoy "8" marks the northeast side of the channel off Horseneck Point. The opening into the harbor should be visible.

After rounding The Knubble, follow the channel buoys carefully around Horseneck Point and into Westport Harbor along the northeast shore of Acoaxet and the Lions Tongue into the snug cove about 1 mile west of the village of Westport Point.

> ⚠️ **CAUTION:** Westport Channel has experienced increased shoaling, with considerable narrowing of the channel. Mariners are advised that shoaling has been identified and extends the entire width of the channel, affecting both commercial and recreational vessels. Favor the green side of the channel. Mariners should proceed with caution while transiting the area.

When you leave Westport, stand well offshore and clear south of the cluster of ledges at Hen and Chickens, Old Cock and The Wildcat, the last marked by green can buoy "1" and a prominent wreck marked by a slanting pipe that sticks 20 or more feet out of the water.

The next harbor east of Slocums Neck leads to Little and Slocum Rivers (between Barneys Joy and Mishaum Points), which is too shoal for transit but could provide anchorage between red nun "2" and the bar.

Dockage/Moorings: To the south on entry into Westport Harbor less than 0.5 mile west of the village landing, F.L. Tripp & Sons Inc. usually has transient moorings available as well as a few slips with full amenities. Rental moorings are marked with a small yellow float. Hail the launch service on VHF Channel 09 and ask their hours.

The Westport Yacht Club's unpretentious, weathered clubhouse next door matches the friendly attitude of its members. The private club cannot offer dock space but may have a mooring for visitors from other clubs.

Anchorage: You can anchor overnight at Westport Harbor but be aware that the swift current scours the bottom and holding is poor in 6 to 13 feet MLW in a rocky bottom. If you plan ahead, you will find better protection up the East Branch of the Westport River through the Westport Point Bridge (21-foot closed vertical clearance),

Westport Harbor, MA

WESTPORT		Largest Vessel	VHF	Total Slips	Approach/ Dockside Depth	Floating Docks	Gas/ Diesel	Repairs/ Haulout	Min/Max Amps	Pump-Out Station
1. F.L.Tripp & Sons Inc. WiFi	(508) 636-4058	65	9	178	10.0 / 12.0		GD	RH	30 / 50	P
2. Westport Yacht Club-PRIVATE WiFi	(508) 636-8885	60			8.0 / 12.0					

WiFi Wireless Internet Access
Visit www.waterwayguide.com for current rates, fuel prices, website addresses and other up-to-the-minute information. (Information in the table is provided by the facilities.)

Scan here for more details:

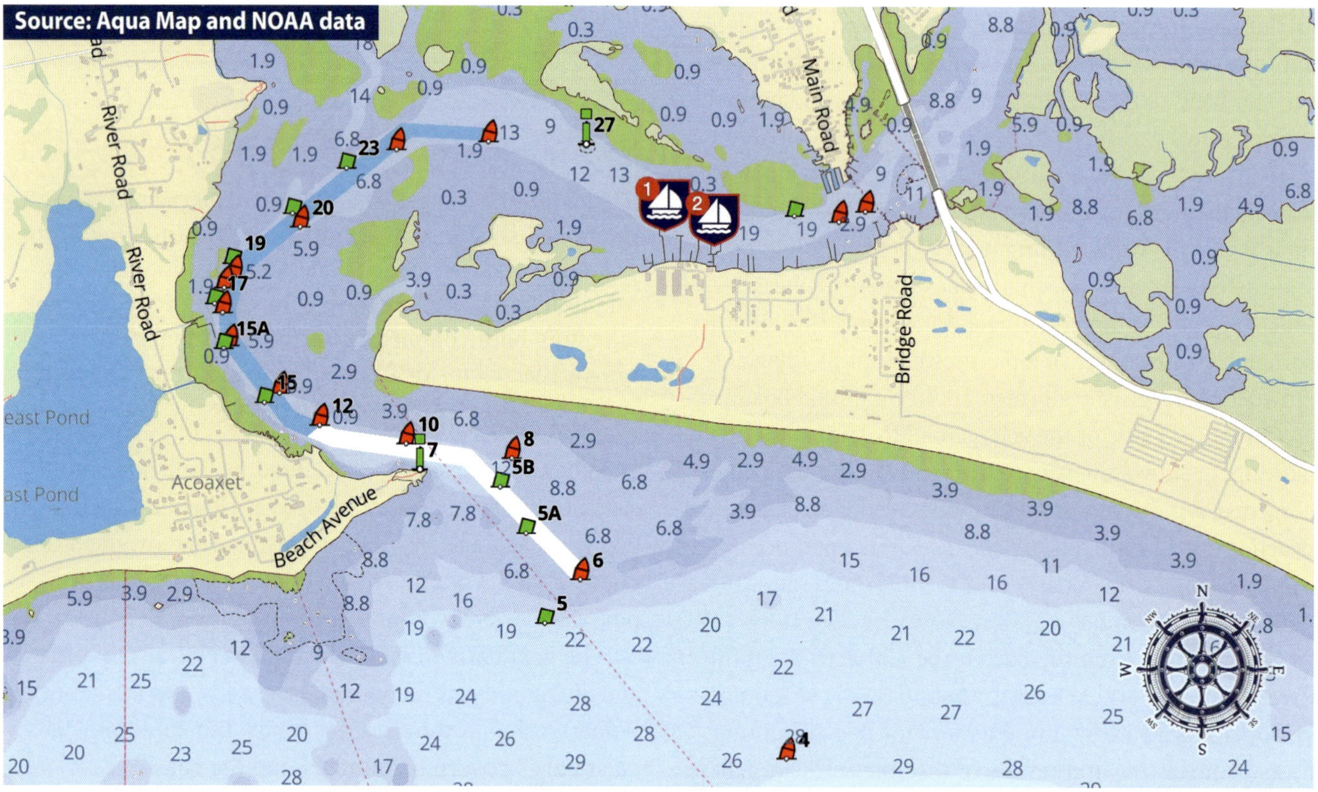

[Chart: Source: Aqua Map and NOAA data]

which opens on signal with a 24-hour notice. Here you will find good protection east of Great Island in 6- to 12-foot MLW depths with good holding in mud. Watch for Sunk Rock, which is charted but unmarked, in the center of the channel upriver from the bridge.

The privately marked East Branch of Westport River makes a worthwhile dinghy trip. On a rising tide you can explore all the way to the fixed (7-foot vertical clearance) **Hix Bridge** but note that this trip in depths of 1 to 2 feet MLW requires a very shallow-draft boat. The shores are lovely and rolling hills with summer cottages are sprinkled among the working farms with fields that stretch down to the water's edge. The islands in the river are privately owned.

NOTE: Westport Harbor and the east and west branches of the Westport River are No-Discharge Zones. Pump-out service is available at F.L.Tripp & Sons Inc.

Apponagansett Bay

Beyond Mishaum Point off Smith Neck and north 2 miles beyond Round Hill Point, Apponagansett Bay forms an open harbor that has been famous to sailors for generations. Invariably known as Padanaram (pronounced "pay-dan-air-am") despite its designation as "South Dartmouth" on the charts, this is the home of the large and active New Bedford Yacht Club and the South Wharf Yacht Yard (known locally as Concordia Yard), once builders of the graceful wooden yawl of the same name.

This busy and colorful harbor is the mooring ground and point of departure for thousands of Buzzards Bay cruisers and racers. It is a favorite destination port for many others. Contact the Dartmouth Natural Resources Trust (508-991-2289) for a guide to walking trails around the village. You will find many lovely shops and galleries

Buzzards Bay, MA

APPONAGANSETT BAY		Largest Vessel	VHF	Total Slips	Approach/ Dockside Depth	Floating Docks	Gas/ Diesel	Repairs/ Haulout	Min/Max Amps	Pump-Out Station
1. New Bedford Yacht Club-PRIVATE **WiFi**	(508) 997-0762	70	68	100	10.0 / 9.0		GD		30	P
2. South Wharf Yacht Yard **WiFi**	(508) 990-1011	135	9	101	10.0 / 15.0	F		RH	30 / 100	P

WiFi Wireless Internet Access
Visit www.waterwayguide.com for current rates, fuel prices, website addresses and other up-to-the-minute information.
(Information in the table is provided by the facilities.)

Scan here for more details:

along Elm St. and Bridge St. This compact village is a good place to enjoy the nautical ambiance, poke in the shops, dine and restock the lockers.

Immediately across Bridge St. is Sail Loft (774-328-9871) directly on the harbor, which is a favorite dining spot with the cruising community, as is Little Moss (508-994-1162). Nearby Farm and Coast Market (7 Bridge St., 774-992-7093) has both a deli-grocery and a café. They sell beer and wine, meats, produce and breads and cheeses and have an excellent breakfast.

NAVIGATION: The harbor approach is rock-strewn but straightforward once you are on course. Enter the passage north of Dumpling Rocks slowly until you sort out the buoys. Refer to Waterway Explorer (www.waterwayguide.com) and NOAA online charts (www.nauticalcharts.noaa.gov) for the most up-to-date information.

Honoring green gong buoy "5" and 52-foot flashing green "7" marking Dumpling Rocks, take a course of 031 degrees magnetic to flashing red (2+1) red-over-green gong buoy "AB" and then take a course of 331 degrees magnetic to avoid Hussey Rock on the western shore. The entrance to Apponagansett Bay is marked by the 25-foot-tall flashing red "8" at the western end of the breakwater on Ricketsons Point.

Dockage/Mooring: The red-roofed New Bedford Yacht Club (NBYC) and its vast mooring field dominate Padanaram and Apponagansett Bay. Even though dock space is in very short supply at the private club, a nightly use fee allows visitors use of a member mooring (if available), the club launch, facilities and dining room. Call ahead.

South of the charted swing bridge (usually open) is South Wharf Yacht Yard, which welcomes transients to 135 feet on its docks and is capable of addressing almost any marine repair or modification. They are well known for their prompt and friendly service.

New Bedford Harbor

Anchorage: On the way to Apponagansett Bay, you will pass Slocums Ledge, where you can duck in for 8 to 12 feet MLW. Leave red nun "2" to starboard and proceed cautiously. Do not go east of a line from red nun "2" to the fixed bridge across the Little River and watch for the charted 6-foot spot to the west of that line.

You will find plenty of anchorage space in Apponagansett Bay beyond the mooring field outside the harbor channel and southwest of red nun buoy "10." There is good holding here in 10- to 12-foot MLW depths quite close to the west shore of the bay. This area, however, is exposed to the east and southeast and boats on moorings will chase away those who anchor close enough to make them nervous. Clarks Cove to the east has no services but good holding and provides excellent protection in a fall northerly.

New Bedford/Fairhaven

New Bedford at the mouth of the Acushnet River is busy, commercial, colorful and imbued with a historic seafaring flavor. Two towns line the harbor head and river–New Bedford on the west and Fairhaven to the east–connected by Route 6, which makes both accessible to the area's major recreational boating center on Popes Island.

New Bedford was once the hub of the American whaling industry, and it retains many a reminder of the days when its fleet was larger than all others combined. The harbor is an active commercial and fishing port, still boasting a fleet of trawlers, draggers, scallopers and lobster boats. Ferries to Cuttyhunk, Martha's Vineyard and Nantucket are all available from New Bedford. The New Bedford Whaling Museum (508-997-0046) and the Seamen's Bethel, a church with the pew once occupied by *Moby Dick* author Herman Melville, are both easy to visit on foot.

Fairhaven and Popes Island are increasingly important bases for repairs and supplies with marine specialists for engines, machinery and fabrication, rigging, propellers, electronics, canvas and sails. Standard Marine Outfitters (508-990-7917) across the street from the Pope's Island Marina has a full selection of marine hardware and clothing plus a parts department and commercial fishing counter in the building behind. West Marine (508-994-1122) is about 1 mile from Pope's Island and 1.5 miles from the Fairhaven Shipyard locations.

NAVIGATION: A massive stone hurricane barrier has made New Bedford/Fairhaven a snug harbor of refuge. The near 1-mile-long barrier encloses the harbor except for a 150-foot channel passage. If a major storm threatens, gates are closed across the opening. From the Buzzards Bay fairway buoy "BB" to the hurricane barrier (approximately 8 nm) the New Bedford Channel is clearly

Buzzards Bay, MA

FAIRHAVEN AREA		Largest Vessel	VHF	Total Slips	Approach/ Dockside Depth	Floating Docks	Gas/ Diesel	Repairs/ Haulout	Min/Max Amps	Pump Out Station
1. Fairhaven Shipyard Companies South Yard (WiFi)	(508) 999-1600	200	9	165	18.0 / 18.0	F	GD	RH	30 / 100	
2. Seaport Inn & Marina (WiFi)	(508) 997-1281	85		104	7.5 /	F	GD		30 / 50	P
3. Pope's Island Marina (WiFi)	(508) 979-1456	150	9	204	10.0 / 10.0	F			30 / 100	P
4. Breakwater Marinas - Fairhaven (WiFi)	(508) 994-1133			69	/	F		RH	30 / 50	

(WiFi) Wireless Internet Access
Visit www.waterwayguide.com for current rates, fuel prices, website addresses and other up-to-the-minute information.
(Information in the table is provided by the facilities.)

Scan here for more details:

marked with few obstructions. All but a couple of the channel buoys now carry flashing lights. Current through the narrow barrier opening runs up to 2.5 knots, with a slight easterly set.

Dockage/Moorings: Fairhaven Shipyard Companies South and Fairhaven Shipyard Companies North are first on entry to the harbor on the eastern shore in a cluster of nautical support companies. The south facility has deep-water floating and fixed slips for vessels to 200 feet. Both facilities offer a full-range of shipyard services with a large team of skilled workers. They can handle any repair, large or small.

The well-regarded Pope's Island Marina can accommodate most recreational boats entering the harbor. The marina manages all moorings in New Bedford Harbor and keeps 35 to 40 available for transient boaters. Nearby is Seaport Inn & Marina with slips to 85 feet and hotel rooms, should you want to get off the boat.

Breakwater Marinas-Fairhaven to the north welcomes transients on their floating docks or on a mooring with the usual amenities. They also offer marine services and sell some groceries.

On the western shore of the river at New Bedford is Sea Fuels Marine, which operates a 250-foot fuel dock with wholesale fuel pricing and marine supplies. They also supply barge service for any size vessel in the harbor and have a fully stocked marine supply warehouse.

Anchorage: Anchoring is restricted to 14 days at a time but you are not likely to find room here for even a one-day stay. Nevertheless, there are ample dinghy docks including those at Pope's Island Marina, the Gifford Street boat ramp, south of the State Pier next to the schooner Ernestina, and at Tonneson Park next to the NBPA Visitors Center.

There is launch service between New Bedford and Fairhaven (seasonal). To schedule a pickup, call on VHF Channel 09 or 508-989-1328.

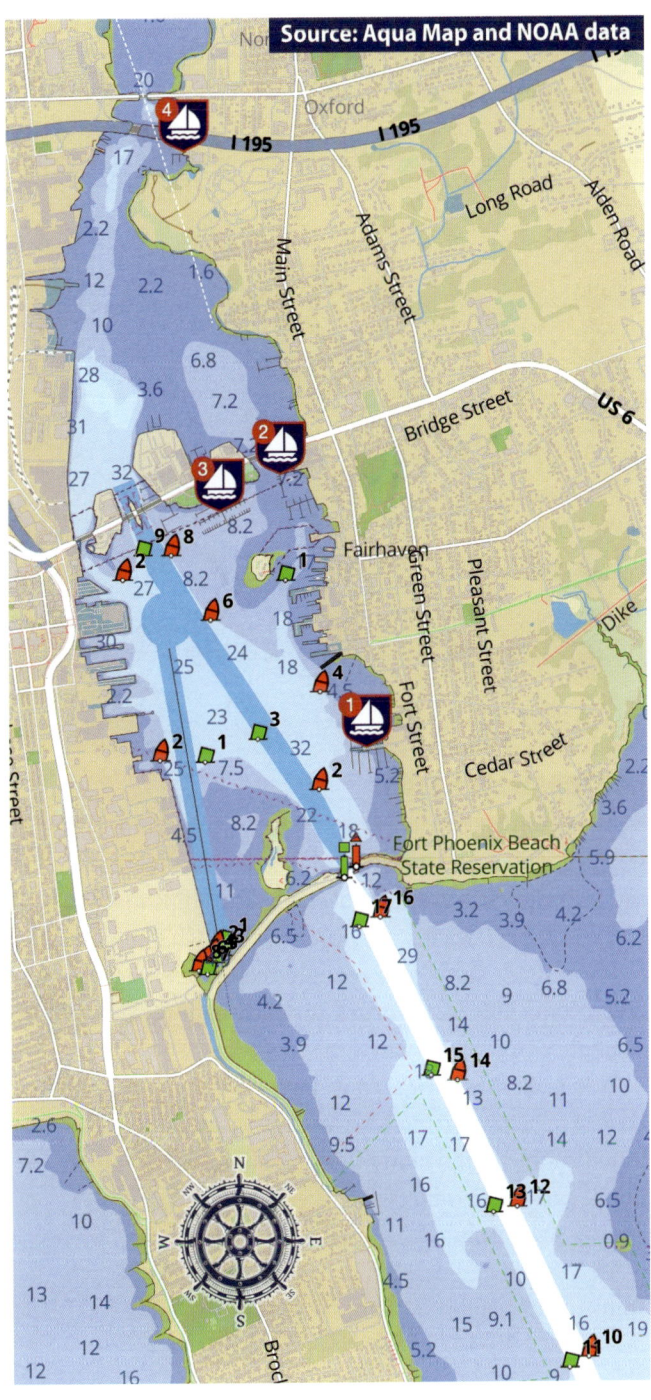

Source: Aqua Map and NOAA data

Buzzards Bay, MA

WEST ISLAND			Largest Vessel	VHF	Total Slips	Approach/ Dockside Depth	Floating Docks	Gas/ Diesel	Repairs/ Haulout	Min/Max Amps	Pump-Out Station
1. West Island Marina WiFi		(508) 993-0008	50	18	115	4.5 / 4.5	F	GD	RH	30	P
MATTAPOISETT											
2. Brandt Cove Marina WiFi		(508) 758-3812	45	68	75	/	F		R	30 / 50	P

WiFi Wireless Internet Access
Visit www.waterwayguide.com for current rates, fuel prices, website addresses and other up-to-the-minute information.
(Information in the table is provided by the facilities.)

Scan here for more details:

Source: Aqua Map and NOAA data

Mattapoisett Harbor

Mattapoisett Harbor is beautiful and easy to enter. The village is postcard New England–clapboard, picturesque and historic. Some of the finest whaling ships in the world were built here during the heyday of the whaling industry. Shipyard Park at the village center commemorates a time when some 400 men worked the yards and the bowsprits of mighty vessels shrouded the roadways.

You can't miss Ned's Point Lighthouse at Mattapoisett Harbor. The unique 35-foot tower was constructed of beach rubble found along the very shoreline it stands upon, and the entrance is marked by 35 rough-cut granite steps from a local quarry. The lighthouse has guided sailors in Buzzards Bay for over 175 years. Tours are available.

The excellent Inn on Shipyard Park (508-758-4922) is the first restaurant off the boat and offers both a bar and sit-down dining with a raw bar, shareable plates, burgers and seafood. Open seasonally. County Rd. curves in a mirror of the shoreline and puts many fine shops less than 1 mile from Shipyard Park.

NAVIGATION: Although the approach is straightforward, numerous submerged obstructions lie adjacent to the buoys marking the generous channel access. Snow Rock, for example, will find the bottom of a 5-foot-draft vessel straying beyond the channel marked by red nun buoys "6" and "8." It is best to remain carefully within the channel buoys until well past red nun buoy "8."

Note that the harbor is an inverted "U" from the southeast, funneling in the prevailing southerlies and is quite pleasant on a hot, light air day but is rolly when the wind pipes up across the diagonal-width fetch of Buzzards Bay.

Dockage/Moorings: On the way to Mattapoisett, you will pass Nasketucket Bay and West Island Marina, a full-service marina with transient services (slips and moorings), an on-site restaurant and exceptional views of Buzzards Bay. They also have a fuel dock and offer a variety of services.

Brandt Cove Marina is located in an extremely well-protected cove just to the southwest of Mattapoisett Harbor. The family-oriented, 75-slip marina welcomes transients to 45 feet. Full marine service is provided by Mattapoisett Boatyard located in the harbor.

Also in Mattapoisett Harbor are several substantial town piers that provide space for transient tie-ups, but fender your vessel thoroughly against damage from the rough timbers and pilings. There is a self-service pump-out facility at the Mattapoisett Town Wharf, open 24 hours a day and the harbormaster (508-758-4191) operates a pump-out boat Sunday through Thursday.

Anchorage: There may be limited anchorage space near the town piers in the two designated Mattapoisett Harbor anchorage areas. Avoid blocking the roundabout channel circling the harbor's center mooring area. You will find at least 8 feet MLW and protection from all but the southeast.

Additional anchorage room is along the north side of the substantial bight just inside Ned Point where you can drop the hook in at least 12-foot MLW depths. As in many New England harbors, there are more moorings and fewer anchorage areas each year. Plan accordingly.

Sippican Harbor (Marion)

Sippican Harbor, the route to the beautiful town of Marion, is tranquil and easy to enter. Tradition has it that as many as 87 ship captains lived in Marion in the mid-1800s. Of the beautiful captain's homes, many were bought by "summer people" once tourism brought visitors in the late 1800s and some of those historic homes remain today.

The town has ancient trees shading narrow, cottage-lined streets and the harbor offers protected moorings, marinas and shops that offer all you are likely to need, making this a favorite layover port for cruising boats. Virtually all shopping is within two blocks (to the left) of Island Wharf on Front St. Marion General Store (140 Front St., 508-748-0340) has basic provisions, cheeses, wine and beer, ice and baked goods made on the premises.

The town also has a natural history museum, a historic society, art center and the Tabor Academy, an independent secondary school, easily recognized by its extensive red roofs. Tabor Academy understandably includes sailing in its curriculum and maintains a fleet of launches, day sailors, rowing shells and the 92-foot schooner *Tabor Boy*.

NAVIGATION: Bird Island to the east recognizable by its lighthouse and Converse Point to the west with a flagpole and large summerhouse, clearly mark the entry to Marion. Keep clear of the Converse Point rocks by leaving flashing green buoy "3" and green can buoy "5" to the west and then laying a course for red nun buoy "6." Simply follow the well-marked, 6-foot MLW channel to the harbor head. Even though the channel is dredged periodically, it

Sippican Harbor

Sippican Harbor, MA

MARION		Largest Vessel	VHF	Total Slips	Approach/ Dockside Depth	Floating Docks	Gas/ Diesel	Repairs/ Haulout	Min/Max Amps	Pump-Out Station
1. Beverly Yacht Club-PRIVATE WiFi	(508) 748-0540	50	68		/ 7.0					P
2. Burr Bros. Boats Inc. WiFi	(508) 748-0541	69	68	43	6.0 / 7.5	F	GD	RH	30 / 50	P

WiFi Wireless Internet Access
Visit www.waterwayguide.com for current rates, fuel prices, website addresses and other up-to-the-minute information.
(Information in the table is provided by the facilities.)

Scan here for more details:

Source: Aqua Map and NOAA data

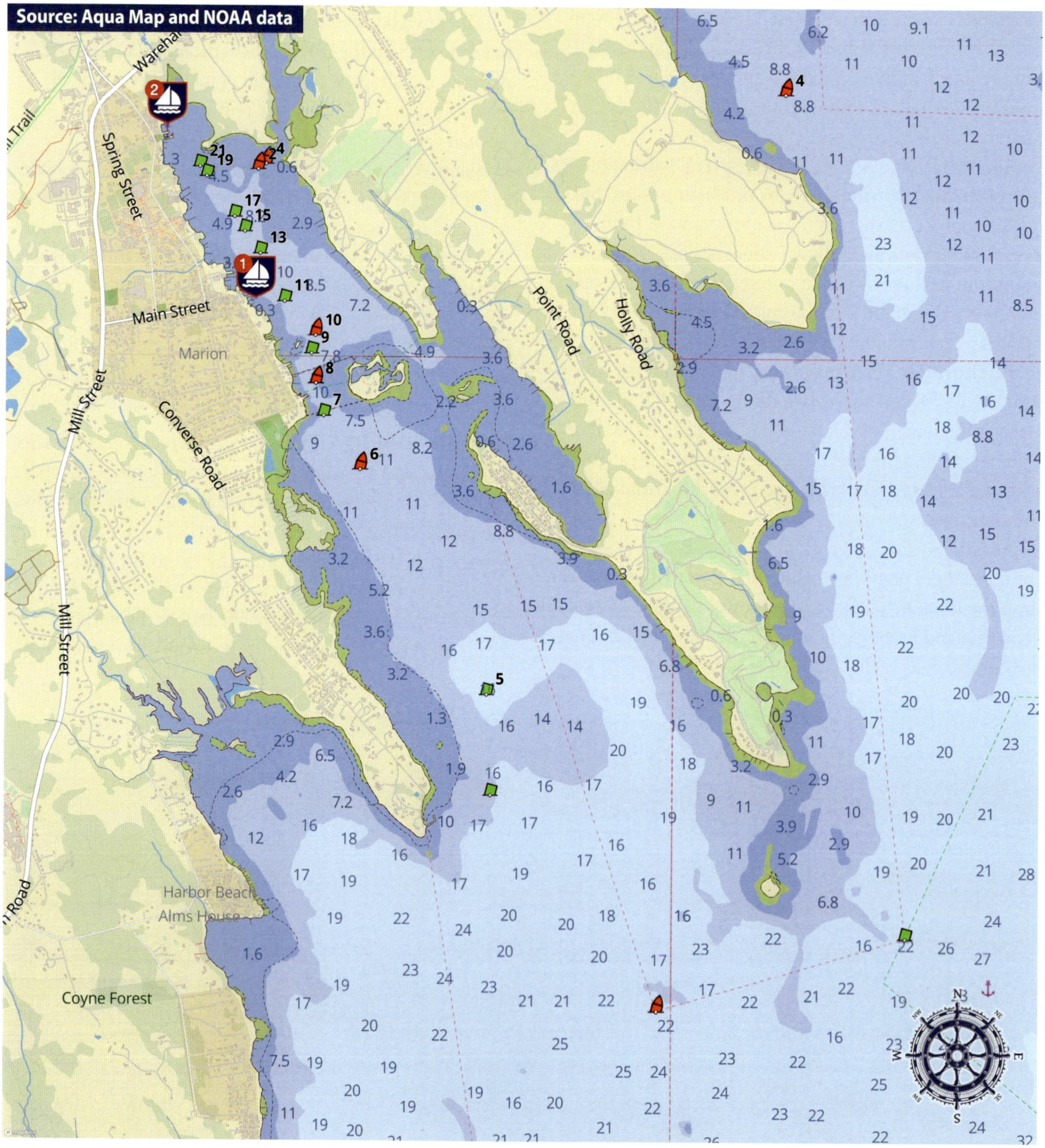

Wareham River, MA

WAREHAM		Largest Vessel	VHF	Total Slips	Approach/ Dockside Depth	Floating Docks	Gas/ Diesel	Repairs/ Haulout	Min/Max Amps	Pump-Out Station
1. Zecco Marina	(508) 295-0022	55	16	120	8.0 / 6.0	F	GD	RH	30	P

WiFi Wireless Internet Access
Visit www.waterwayguide.com for current rates, fuel prices, website addresses and other up-to-the-minute information. (Information in the table is provided by the facilities.)

Scan here for more details:

Source: Aqua Map and NOAA data

shoals quickly beyond the buoys and turning room can be at a premium during the busy summer season.

Dockage/Moorings: The distinguished (and private) Beverly Yacht Club becomes visible to the northwest as you pass green can buoy "9." Members of other recognized clubs may be able to secure a mooring for a facility fee. They strongly recommend that you call the office at least 24 hours prior to your arrival.

Next door, Marion Town Landing has dock space to accommodate tie-ups to take on drinking water or to use the town's free mobile pump-out service. Call the Marion harbormaster

on VHF Channel 09 or by phone (508-748-3535) for this service. There is a dinghy dock at nearby Barden's Boat Yard Inc. and gas and diesel fuel but no slips.

At the head of the harbor, Burr Bros. Boats Inc. offers docking, rental moorings, a well-stocked store and launch service (on weekends). They also offer mechanical services.

Anchorage: Although there is no anchorage in Marion proper, boats can anchor in outer Sippican Harbor in settled weather in 9 to 11 feet MLW in sand. This is open and exposed to the southeast.

Wareham River

Wareham is about 2 nm up the Wareham River and 5 nm from Cleveland Ledge Channel. This resort territory offers good beaches, busy protected coves, crowded anchorages and wonderful scenery and makes an attractive base for exploring.

NAVIGATION: The Wareham River channel is winding but well marked with a depth of 8 feet MLW. Shallow water lies outside the channel on either side; watch buoys carefully to stay in deep water. Near Wareham the river narrows and currents of up to 3 knots can be expected. When a

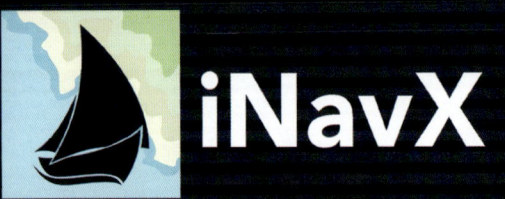 
 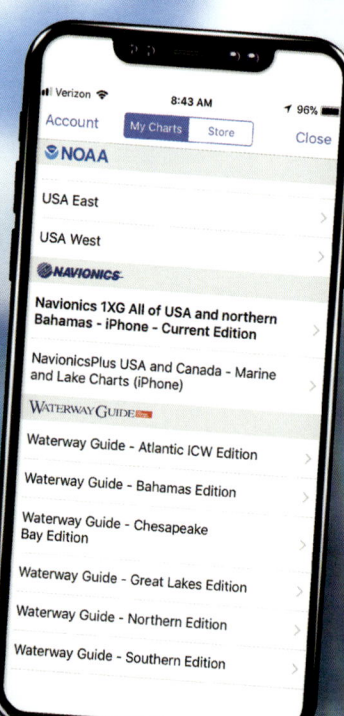

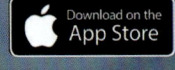 

southwester meets a strong current flowing westward out of the canal, the head of Buzzards Bay can become rough with short, steep seas. The eastbound skipper should lay over at Marion under these circumstances. The westbound skipper, anticipating these conditions, can seek the shelter of Onset Harbor (described below) to wait for more favorable weather.

Dockage/Moorings: Zecco Marina on Wareham Neck has 120 floating slips plus moorings and a dinghy dock. They has a complete parts department and maintains some transient space. Full boat maintenance and repairs are offered on site (year-round) by Dick's Marine.

The complimentary Wareham Town Dock is located right downtown for boats up to 45 feet. We have been told overnight access is available if approved by the harbormaster but do ask permission.

Anchorage: A popular anchorage is north of Long Beach Point in 7 to 9 feet MLW with good holding in sand. (Note that Long Beach Point might be completely submerged at high tide.) Anchor west of the line between red nun buoy "12" and green can buoy "13." This offers good access to restaurants, shopping and such. Tie up the dinghy at the Wareham Town Dock.

Onset

Whatever the weather, Onset makes an attractive cruising stop and a good place to await favorable wind and tide for a trip across the bay or north through the Cape Cod Canal. This Victorian seaside village offers protection from most winds, has attractive white sand beaches, easy accessible facilities and a sizable anchorage area not carpeted with moorings.

Onset Village is just uphill from the town docks. The Onset Village Market (231 Onset Ave., 508-291-1440) combines a grocery and meat market with a substantial liquor store and will provide return-trip transportation and/or grocery delivery for a small fee. The Onset Scenic Trail is a relaxing route for pedestrians, bicyclists and motorists.

Wickets Island in Onset Bay is a city park and a great spot for walking your four-legged crew members. The shores are lined with small boats on busy weekends. You can land a dinghy on the beach on the north side or on the floating dock on the west side.

NAVIGATION: Examine the chart carefully so that the course is clearly fixed in your mind before making the sharp turn to Onset from Hog Island Channel. The

Buzzards Bay, Onset, MA

Cape Cod Canal (West), MA

ONSET		Largest Vessel	VHF	Total Slips	Approach/Dockside Depth	Floating Docks	Gas/Diesel	Repairs/Haulout	Min/Max Amps	Pump-Out Station
1. Safe Harbor Onset Bay WiFi	(508) 295-0338	120	9	100	8.0 / 6.0	F	GD	RH	30 / 50	P
2. Point Independence Yacht Club WiFi	(508) 295-3972	70	9	65	8.0 / 7.0	F	GD		30 / 50	P
3. Stonebridge Marina WiFi	(508) 295-8003	45	9	60	8.0 / 7.0	F	GD	R	30	P
4. Wareham Harbormaster / Onset Town Pier	(508) 291-3100	100	9	6	12.0 / 7.0	F				P
COHASSET NARROWS										
5. Taylor's Point Marina WiFi	(508) 759-2512	50	9	148	6.0 / 9.0	F	GD		30 / 50	P
PHINNEYS HARBOR										
6. Monument Beach Marina	(508) 759-3105	40	16	61	9.0 / 6.0		G		30	

WiFi **Wireless Internet Access**
Visit www.waterwayguide.com for current rates, fuel prices, website addresses and other up-to-the-minute information.
(Information in the table is provided by the facilities.)

Scan here for more details:

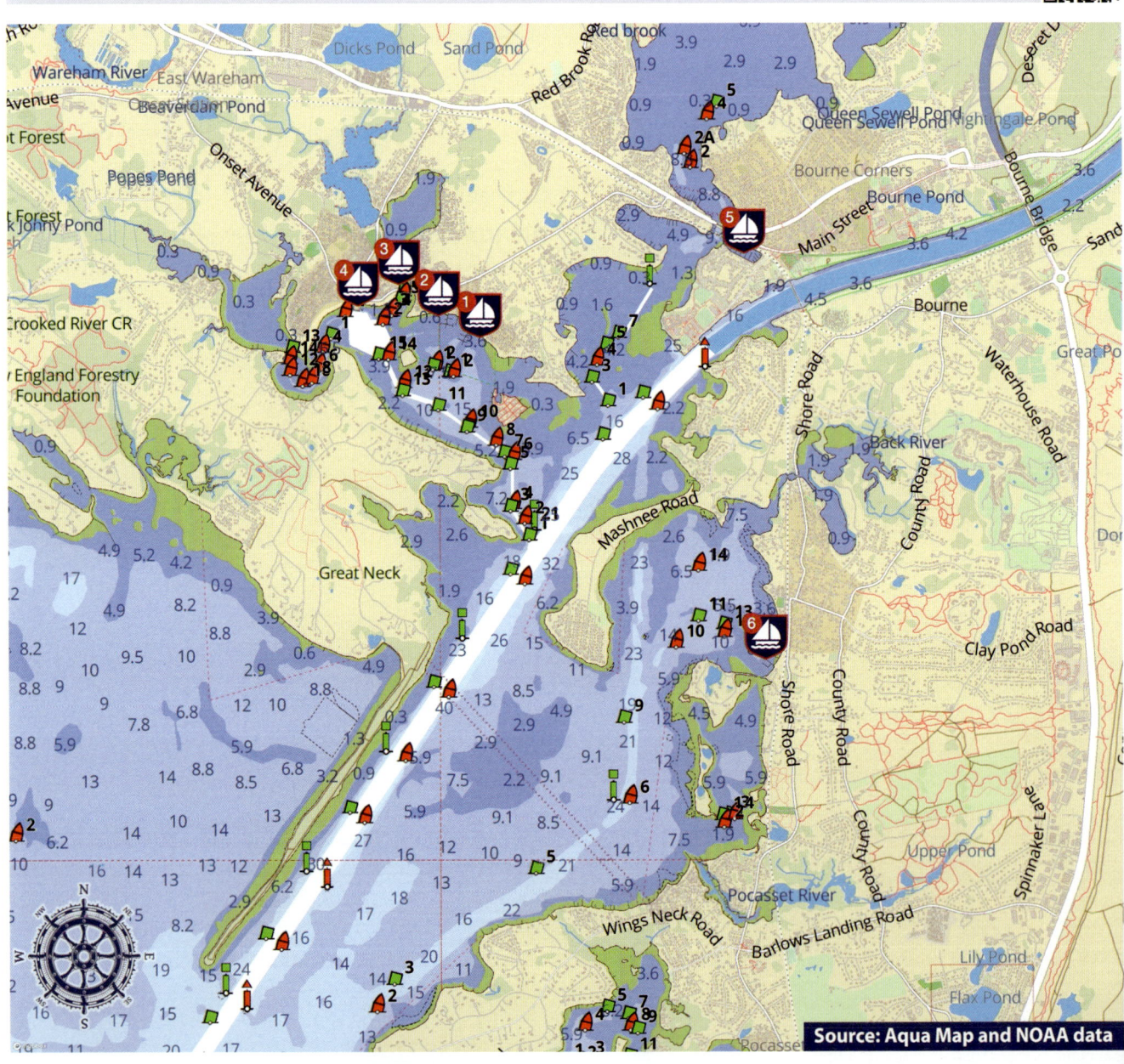

Source: Aqua Map and NOAA data

turning point for the channel leading to Onset Bay off Hog Island Channel is just south of the 35-foot tower presenting quick flashing green "21," which marks the canal channel, not the Onset Channel. Green can buoy "1" immediately east of Hog Neck begins the sequential marks of the Onset Channel.

While it may feel strange to pass between two green markers, red nun buoy "2" follows closely after to confirm the northeast side of the Onset channel. Allow for swift current, which may attempt to push your boat into a buoy out of the channel. The current diminishes beyond Burgess Point. Be wary of possible shoaling on the west side between green can buoys "5" and "7."

Dockage/Mooring: Once you have passed red nun "10" on the Onset Channel, turn north toward the small private aids (green can buoy "1" and red nun buoy "2") to approach Safe Harbor Onset Bay, which maintains a large mooring field and substantial transient dockage (to 120 feet). The well-protected marina has convenient dockside amenities and is well known for its preeminent refinishing and fiberglass shop.

The friendly Point Independence Yacht Club will rent slips to visiting boaters for a reasonable facility fee. Even though the club is oriented primarily to powerboats, its floating face dock with 8-foot MLW dockside depths can accommodate almost any recreational vessel. The club has a lovely sand beach and is surrounded by a quiet, residential community with quick access to the historic Onset village. Nearby Stonebridge Marina has slips and moorings, as well as a beach, laundry facilities and an on-site bar and grill.

Back in the Onset Channel, continue west then north around Wickets Island to reach the docks at Onset Town Pier, which provides plenty of dinghy space and a few slips with easy access to shops and restaurants. The town also rents transient moorings with launch service (Onset Town Moorings). You can reach the friendly and accommodating Warham Harbormaster on VHF Channel 09. The restrooms are public and only open during hours of operation (no showers). Dumpsters in the parking area will accommodate your trash and single-stream recycling.

Anchorage: There is a designated anchorage between Wickets Island and Long Neck at Onset Bay with good holding in at least 8 foot MLW depths. There is plenty of room to anchor outside of the mooring fields and channels. The dinghy ride to the Onset Town Pier is a pleasant ride in most weather. The dinghy dock covers the entire back side of the floating portion of the dock and is often packed. Leave plenty of slack in your painter so others can approach the dock or get out around you.

For skippers of boats drawing 6 feet or less there is also space with good holding in dense mud west of the Onset Channel between Burgess Point/Hog Neck. Be alert for swirling currents in this location.

Cape Cod Canal

The Cape Cod Canal cuts across the neck of Cape Cod to points north and east, saving boats from the long, tricky trip through Nantucket Shoals and around Cape Cod to reach Boston or Maine. The Canal is heavily traveled, well marked and offers an attractive trip. In some seasons schooners traverse the canal heading to and from various festivals, giving other boaters close-up views of historic ships.

When the canal opened in 1914 it was 15 feet deep and 100 feet wide. During both World Wars the canal was heavily used to avoid attack by German U-boats, which lurked in offshore waters. The modern day version is the world's widest sea-level canal with a channel width of 540 feet and average depth of 32 feet. Recreational vessels use the canal extensively and service roads on either side provide trails for skateboarding, bicycling and hiking along with access for fishing.

Anyone who transits the Cape Cod Canal will likely recognize the campus of the Massachusetts Maritime Academy on Taylor Point. The 540-foot training ship of the Academy, *USTS Kennedy*, dominates the west end of the canal. Both the academy and ship are available for tours at no charge (508-830-5000).

NAVIGATION: The canal is able to handle vessels up to 825 feet long but all vessels larger than 65 feet must contact the Marine Traffic Controller on VHF Channel 13 before entering the canal. The 7-mile-long land cut can be almost clear of fog when both Buzzards and Cape Cod bays are thick with it.

> *CAUTION:* Mariners are advised that all vessels 65 feet and over should not enter the Cape Cod Canal until clearance has been obtained from the Marine Traffic Controller by radio. Vessels shall request clearance at least 15 minutes prior to entering the Cape Cod Canal at any point.

Sagamore Bridge on Cape Cod Canal

The Cape Cod Canal (including approaches) extends from 1.6 miles seaward of the Cape Cod Canal Breakwater Light canal's east entrance in Cape Cod Bay, through the land cut to Cleveland East Ledge Light in Buzzards Bay, to approximately 4 miles southwest of Wings Neck.

Vessels should contact Cape Cod Canal Marine Traffic Control on VHF Channel 13. All vessels are required to maintain a radio guard on VHF Channel 13 during the entire passage. Speed limit is 10 mph.

Despite the width and depth of the canal, tidal range conflict between the Cape Cod Bay end (9 feet) and the Buzzards Bay side (4 feet) remains fierce creating currents of about 3.5 knots on the eastward-setting flood and 4 knots to 6 knots on the ebb. Give careful attention to the tide and tidal current charts and make a very conservative estimate of the time you will need to pass both through the canal and beyond in order to allow for the effects of a foul-setting tide.

A westbound cruiser who chooses to power through against the flood will be sad to see that struggle continue down Buzzards Bay, whereas heading into the canal early in the ebb provides a boost all the way down the bay. The flood provides the eastbound cruiser a quick trip through the canal but turns foul on the other side. This is less problematic than in Buzzards Bay since the current is not as concentrated in Cape Cod Bay and many post-canal destinations don't require heading straight into it.

Even though commercial traffic is heavy on the canal, you should have no difficulties if you pick tide and weather carefully, proceed cautiously and stick to the right side of the channel (as if driving on a highway).

NO WAKE ZONE

The U.S. Army Corps of Engineers cautions that the canal is a No-Wake Zone; boaters must observe a 10-mph speed limit, yet complete their transit within 2.5 hours. If you are unable to complete the transit in that time, you may be required to hire a helper tug at your expense. This last requirement makes it particularly important to calculate your speed-versus-tide requirements with some care.

All boats must be under power. Sailing through the canal is not permitted; neither are turning around, fishing or anchoring. Finally, monitor VHF Channel 13 as you transit the canal for communications from the Army Corps of Engineers and be ready to alert them to emergency situations.

The **ConRail Railroad Bridge** crossing the canal is usually open except during the occasional passage of a train to or from Cape Cod. Closed vertical clearance is a mere 7 feet so very few vessels will clear the bridge during a closure. Monitor VHF Channel 13 for alerts to any closings. If running with a strong, favorable current, look well ahead to assure passage under the bridge as turning at the last minute may not be an option. The bridge operator sounds two long blasts before lowering the bridge. It takes approximately 2.5 minutes to raise or lower it. If the bridge is lowered during periods of decreased visibility, the bridge operator will signal five short blasts every two minutes.

Two highway bridges cross the canal beyond the railroad bridge–the **Bourne Bridge** and the **Sagamore Bridge**–both with 135-foot fixed vertical clearances.

Dockage: A good place to spend the night before embarking on the canal is at the municipal Taylor's Point Marina on Cohasset Narrows, north of the canal. They have just a few reserved transient slips to 50 feet. The marina includes 148 slips, a fuel dock and pump-out station, private bathrooms and showers and a marine store. The facility is conveniently located off Main St. and just around the corner from the Massachusetts Maritime Academy at the west end of the Cape Cod Canal.

Anchorage: You can drop the hook north of Hog Island near the south end of the Cape Cod Canal in 10 to 20 feet MLW with good holding in sand and mud at Hog Island. There is plenty of room to anchor just off the channel with easy in and out. This is a pleasant location to wait for a favorable current to transit east on the Cape Cod Canal.

Phinneys Harbor

South of the Cape Cod Canal on the eastern shore is big, open and shoal-dotted Phinneys Harbor with a marked entrance and the town of Monument Beach on its eastern shore. Mashnee Island forms its western boundary and Tobys Island forms its eastern boundary. It is 0.70 mile to the village of Monument Beach from the marina, where you will find a Post Office, limited groceries and wholesale seafood.

NAVIGATION: A marked channel leads into Phinneys Harbor, branching off from Hog Island Channel at green lighted buoy "1" due west of Wings Neck Light. A westbound boat may be tempted to cut the corner towards Phinneys Harbor, but in doing so be aware of the shoals extending south from Mashnee Island and watch your depth carefully. Also be wary of ledges close to the southern end of Mashnee Island. The route to an anchorage and small marina at Monument Beach is well marked to the east, north of Tobys Island. Keep a mid-channel course to avoid rocks to the east and south of the channel.

Dockage/Moorings: The municipal Monument Beach Marina is located in a beautiful setting with a fine public beach to either side of its main pier. It includes a dock with 61 slips (to 40 feet), 35 moorings and private bathrooms and showers.

Anchorage: The conspicuous rock pile off the eastern side of Mashnee Island serves as a guide to the deepwater gully that leads to a secure anchorage protected from the north but open to the south. Here you will find 7 to 14 feet MLW with good holding in sand.

The most protected anchorage in the area lies in the northeastern corner of Phinneys Harbor near the entrance to Back River, which is very shoal; do not venture upstream. Here you can drop the hook in 9 to 11 feet MLW with good holding in sand and mud. To the south you can anchor right off Monument Beach in 12 to 14 feet MLW with good holding in hard sand.

◼ EASTERN SHORE TO WOODS HOLE

The eastern shore of Buzzards Bay is generally high and handsome with fine old trees and houses. Water is comparatively deep close to the banks and the shore is indented by wide, open bays and protected harbors.

Pocasset & Red Brook Harbors

Three-pronged Bassetts Island subdivides the water here. Most of Bassetts Island is privately owned; however, the town owns the south end of the island and it is open to the public. It is a 0.5-mile walk up a gentle grade from Barlows Landing to the village where you will find a hardware store, a market and restaurants.

Large, well-protected Red Brook Harbor is to the southeast at the village of Cataumet. Ample boating amenities, good anchorage and pleasant surroundings define this active harbor. The Chart Room (508-563-5350) has been feeding people aboard a converted barge since 1966 and offers live, nightly entertainment at the piano bar as well as seafood entrées and sandwiches. The seasonal restaurant recommends dinner reservations.

The final harbor in this big semicircle of harbors is Hospital Cove at Cataumet. The shores of this handsome and scenic harbor are dotted with greenery and pleasant houses.

NAVIGATION: You can enter Bassetts Island through either of two narrow, twisting, shoal-prone passages. The northern one inside Wings Neck is a little deeper and more popular but is unmanageable when the tide

Upper Buzzards Bay, MA

RED BROOK		Largest Vessel	VHF	Total Slips	Approach/ Dockside Depth	Floating Docks	Gas/ Diesel	Repairs/ Haulout	Min/Max Amps	Pump-Out Station
1. Kingman Yacht Center WiFi	(508) 563-7136	120	71	235	8.0 / 10.0	F	GD	RH	30 / 50	P
2. Parker's Boatyard Inc. WiFi	(508) 563-9366	50	69	9	6.0 / 8.0	F	GD	RH	30	P
MEGANSETT HARBOR										
3. Safe Harbor Fiddler's Cove WiFi	(508) 564-6327	65	9	130	7.0 / 7.0	F	GD	RH	30 / 50	P

WiFi Wireless Internet Access
Visit www.waterwayguide.com for current rates, fuel prices, website addresses and other up-to-the-minute information.
(Information in the table is provided by the facilities.)

Scan here for more details:

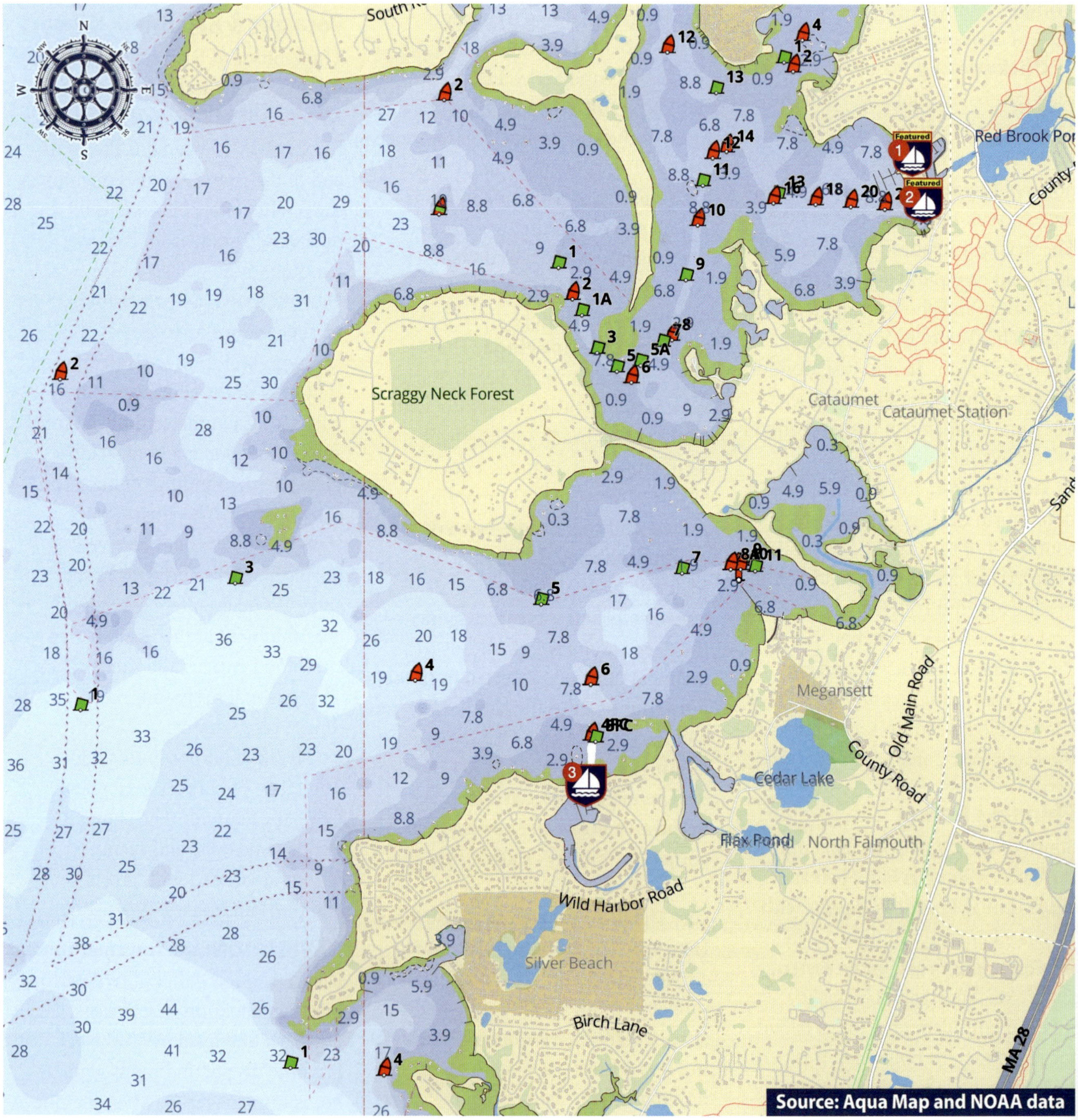

Source: Aqua Map and NOAA data

![Aerial view of Red Brook Harbor with labels: Kingman Yacht Center, Parker's Boatyard Inc., Red Brook Harbor]

ebbs against a southwester. The southern entrance along Scraggy Neck has 6.5-foot MLW charted depths. You can reach Hospital Cove either from Red Brook Harbor or via the southern entrance around Scraggy Neck from Buzzards Bay.

When exiting this circuit of harbors, give full respect to the buoys marking charted hazards. To the north of Scraggy Neck watch for Eustis Rock exposed at high water and marked by red and green nun buoy "ER." A forbidding area of rocks also lies to the west of Scraggy Neck, marked by Southwest Ledge red nun buoy "2."

Dockage/Moorings: Well-regarded Kingman Yacht Center in Red Brook Harbor has an extensive dock complex and massive sheds. This is Cape Cod's largest full-service marina and boatyard with 10-foot MLW dockside depths, 235 slips and 130 moorings with launch service and use of the dinghy dock. They can accommodate vessels to 120 feet with full cruiser amenities. A white sand beach, miles of hiking trails and spectacular sunsets round out the offerings. They also complete marine repairs and maintenance and a fully stocked chandlery.

Family-owned Parker's Boatyard Inc. is a classic New England facility rich in history. This full-service yard offers 130 moorings with launch service and a dinghy dock plus dockside accommodations for boats to 50 feet. They sell gas and diesel fuel and provide all types of maintenance and repairs. Provisioning is available from this location within a short driving distance.

Anchorage: Around the western point of Bassets Island there is a secure anchorage in 9 to 14 feet MLW in the sweeping bight along the northern side of the island. Holding is good in soft mud but it is somewhat exposed

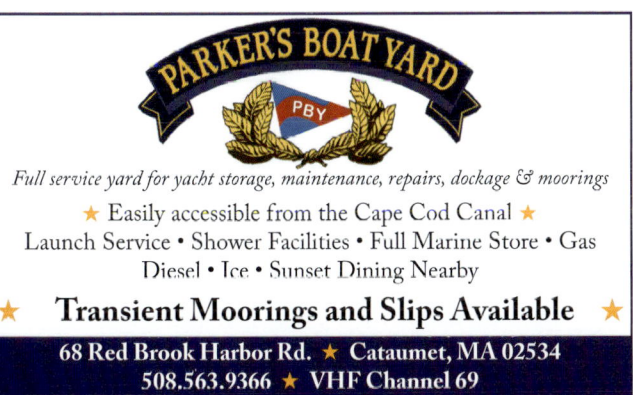

to the northeast. Barlows Landing north of the island's northern arm permits dinghy tie-ups at the floating dock in front of the small pier next to the town beach.

You can drop the hook behind Long Point in Red Brook Harbor in 8 feet MLW with good holding in sand and rock. This is somewhat exposed to the north.

While Hospital Cove provides good holding in a relatively secluded spot, the gradual increase of moorings here has limited the anchorage to a comparatively small area near the channel. Make allowance for swing room both in relation to the channel and to the moored boats toward land. There are no public landings and no marinas, just peace and quiet, except in strong northwesterly winds. Piping southwesterlies can also be quite noticeable here because they blow across the narrow isthmus leading from Cataumet to Scraggy Neck but, fortunately, the short fetch prevents significant wave action from building.

Megansett Harbor

Megansett Harbor to the south lies between Scraggy Neck and Nyes Neck and is wide open to the west. It has three well-protected inner harbors and a large bight (protected only from the north) in the outer harbor east of the bulge of Scraggy Neck.

Dockage: On the southern side of outer Megansett Harbor and southeast of Cataumet Rock (at red nun buoy "4"), the 9-foot MLW channel to Fiddlers Cove is dredged frequently and well marked. Inside this virtual hurricane hole of protection is Safe Harbor Fiddler's Cove. A courteous staff tends to floating docks and mechanics are on call 7 days a week. A true waterfront resort, the lavish clubhouse provides a library, lounge, pool table and fireplace. They have limited reserved transient space so call ahead.

Anchorage: Inner Megansett Harbor has a narrow, marked entry with a bar that shoots out from the breakwater. Beyond are a launching ramp, hospitable yacht club and town dock. It is possible to anchor here in 5- to 7-foot MLW depths.

At its eastern end around a projecting point of land is Squeteague Harbor, a cove with less than 3-foot MLW depths at its difficult entry but 6 feet MLW once inside. There is very limited space to drop the hook as moorings take up most of the available space. It is well worth exploring, if only by dinghy or shoal-draft boat.

South of Nyes Neck you may find secure anchorage and protection from a northerly in Wild Harbor. The entry is marked by flashing green buoy "1" and red nun buoy "4" and has adequate depth for most cruisers (9 to 12 feet MLW). Avoid this harbor if there is a prediction of wind shift to the prevailing southwest as it is completely exposed.

Quissett Harbor

Quissett Harbor

NAVIGATION: The well-marked entrance to Quissett Harbor is located between The Knob, a prominent hillock on the northern point, and Gansett Point. Follow the channel carefully to avoid the rocks beyond its confines. A course outside red nun buoys "4," "6" or "8" or green "3," "5," and "7" could result in contact with a very hard bottom, depending on your draft.

According to Quissett Harbor Boatyard, Inc. personnel, the large rock charted between "4" and "6" is not accurate. Call ahead if you have concerns or want additional local knowledge.

Moorings: Quissett Harbor Boatyard, Inc. usually has an open rental mooring on a first-come-first-served basis in the outer harbor just past nun "6." Rental moorings are white with a blue stripe and marked "QBY." They will come to you in the early evening to collect the mooring fee. (Note: They do not process credit cards.) Occasionally they are able to offer moorings in the inner harbor. They are best known, however, for their excellent boat restoration and repairs.

The dinghy dock is on the north side of their pier. There is no launch service but a pump-out boat will respond to a hoisted orange flag (the locally understood signal) or a request of the yard's launch driver or dockmaster. From here you can take the trolley into Woods Hole.

Anchorage: The proliferation of local boats and moorings has greatly reduced swing room in both the inner and outer harbors at Quissett Harbor. Nevertheless, if you can find space, this is a beautiful spot. Make sure you are aware of a few shallow spots (marked on the charts but not by buoys) as they are rocky.

Woods Hole

The village of Woods Hole is the most important oceanographic center on the east coast. Major research facilities firmly settled here are NOAA's NorthEast Fisheries Center, the Marine Biological Laboratory (whose summer labs have produced more than 50 Nobel Laureates) and the Woods Hole Oceanographic Institution. It was researchers from Woods Hole who discovered the *Titanic* in 1985. The Ocean Science Discovery Center at Woods Hole (508-289-2663) is open daily from Memorial Day to Labor Day and on a more limited schedule beyond those dates.

About 2 miles north of Woods Hole, Quissett Harbor has generally deep water, high, wooded shores with handsome houses, good protection and easy entrance but no provisions. The small peninsula enclosing the northern side of the harbor is now a nature preserve that is well worth a trip ashore for a walking tour. During the summer season the WHOOSH Trolley (800-352-7155) stops here with service to Woods Hole and Falmouth.

NAVIGATION: Woods Hole marks the difficult and sometimes dangerous passage between Buzzards Bay and Vineyard Sound at the southwestern tip of Cape Cod. Woods Hole consists of three unique harbors: Great Harbor, wide, deep and open to the south; Eel Pond, a hurricane hole in the center of the village; and Little Harbor, given over to U.S. Coast Guard government operations.

Nobska Light is an active aid to navigation located at the division between Buzzards Bay and Vineyard Sound in Woods Hole, on the southernmost tip of the Cape Cod land mass before it devolves into a string of islands. You will pass it as you exit Woods Hole and travel to Martha's Vineyard.

Tidal currents of 5 knots or more make Woods Hole Passage a strait to be entered with respect if the current is running at its maximum. Even with your boat under control, the short distance is inevitably an interesting piloting experience. A less taxing approach is to plan for the passage at slack tide just as it is turning in your favor. Consult your tide tables and be sure to study a large-scale chart before you enter the passage.

It's important to note that buoy numbers run from east to west, starting in Vineyard Sound (between Nonamesset Shoal's green gong buoy "1" and Great Ledge's flashing red bell buoy "2"). Although the numbers reset at Woods Hole Passage, the proper orientation of your course to the reds and greens does not change. In the language of "red-right-return," you are "returning" to Buzzards Bay throughout the passage. Red Ledge is a shoal area just off the northeastern tip of Nonamesset Island (Mink Point).

Note the critical green and red lighted junction buoy "SB" at Red Ledge, marking the intersection of the two major channels leading through Woods Hole Passage. Whether you are heading directly through Woods Hole Passage or making a detour into Great Harbor, the recommended tracks are well charted and marked.

Woods Hole Area, MA

QUISETT HARBOR		Largest Vessel	VHF	Total Slips	Approach/ Dockside Depth	Floating Docks	Gas/ Diesel	Repairs/ Haulout	Min/Max Amps	Pump-Out Station
1. Quissett Harbor Boatyard, Inc.	(508) 548-0506	70			11.0 / 16.0	F		RH		P
WOODS HOLE										
2. Woods Hole Yacht Club-PRIVATE	(508) 548-9205	65			6.0 / 6.0					
3. Woods Hole Marine	(508) 540-2402	50	9	26	7.0 / 15.0				30	

WiFi Wireless Internet Access
Visit www.waterwayguide.com for current rates, fuel prices, website addresses and other up-to-the-minute information.
(Information in the table is provided by the facilities.)

Scan here for more details:

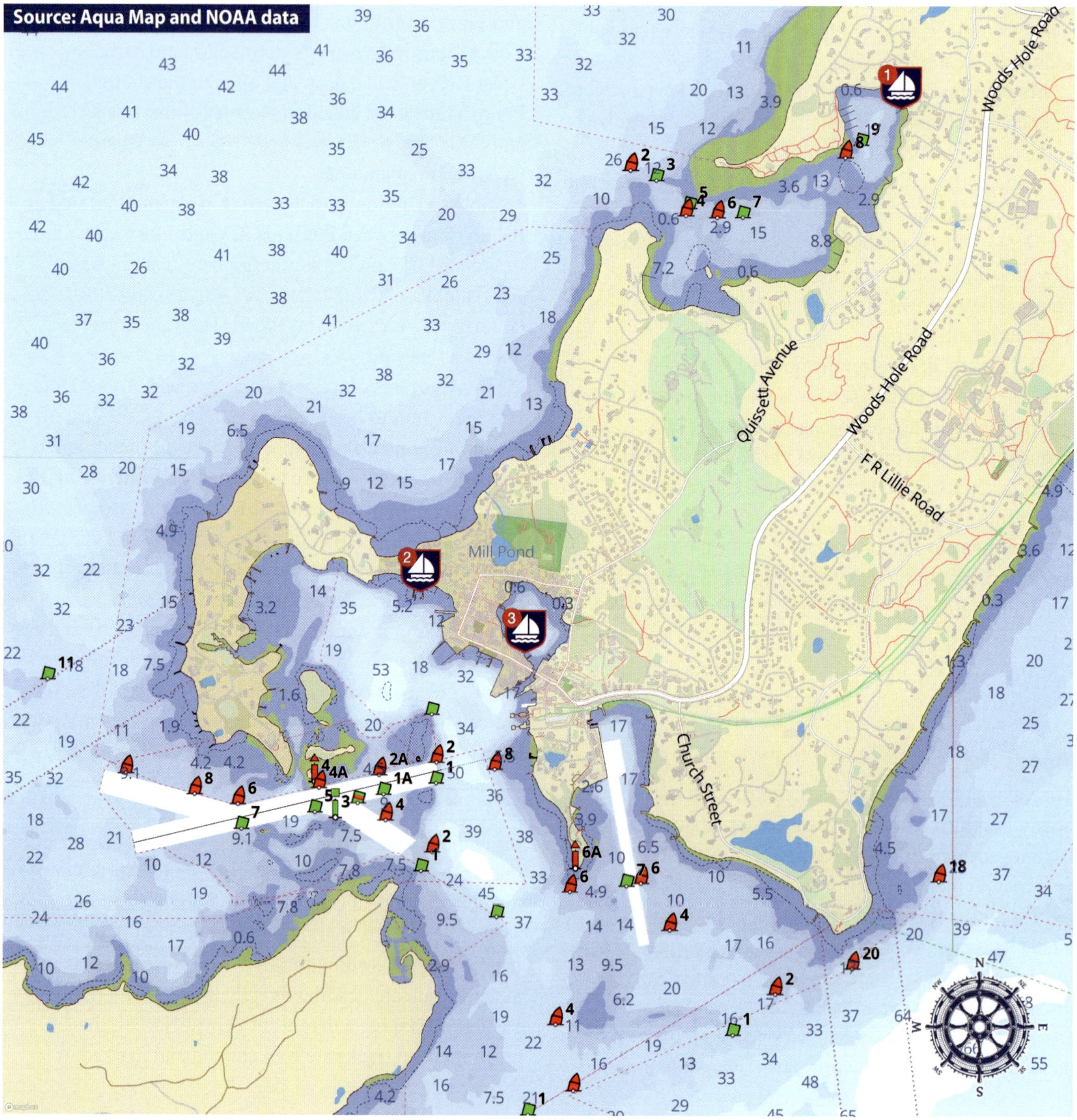

Source: Aqua Map and NOAA data

The current rarely drags under the oversized buoys so laying a course is relatively simple. Keep in mind, however, that the current does not exactly follow the channel. At full flow you may find yourself pushed off course and straining to correct in an underpowered vessel. Except at slack water you will also encounter tidal swirls that require a firm hand at the helm to stay in mid-channel. Unless you have radar avoid this passage when visibility is poor.

If passing from Buzzards Bay to Vineyard Sound in a strong favorable current, be very aware of red nun buoy "2" (just off Mink Point), which marks the edge of the shoals extending from Red Ledge. It is not unusual to see vessels pushed east toward these shoals. The exit from Woods Hole to Vineyard Sound is wide and clearly marked. Great Ledge lays almost dead center, is well marked and you can pass it on either side. The route west of Great Ledge, however, between green gong buoy "1" and flashing red bell buoy "2" is less confined and easier to follow.

Dockage/Moorings: To the west in Great Harbor the friendly Woods Hole Yacht Club is private but offers reciprocity to members registered under US Sailing. Visitors must check-in with the steward. This area is exposed to the south with a considerable fetch for wave buildup.

The most secure transient berth is at Woods Hole Marine in Eel Pond. They have seasonal moorings and dock space with an occasional transient slip. Given the diminutive size of this facility (26 slips) and the limits to maneuverability in this pinched harbor, you should make a reservation and ask for specific directions. A trolley bus leaves from out front for Falmouth every 30 minutes.

Enter the pond through the channel leading under the Eel Pond (Water Street) Bridge (5-foot closed vertical clearance) in the center of the village. The bridge will open on signal from May 15 through June 14 and from September 16 through October 14, from 7:00 a.m. to 7:00 p.m. and from June 15 through September 15, from 6:00 a.m. to 9:00 p.m. on the hour and half-hour. The marina docks are immediately to the west past the bridge.

Anchorage: You can drop the hook north of Woods Hole with open space for several boats. This offers excellent protection from the west, south and east but is open to the north. It is perfect for hiding out from a southerly. There is no shore access.

▪ THE ELIZABETH ISLANDS

The Elizabeth Islands are a chain of small islands extending about 14 nm off the southwestern end of Cape Cod and separating Vineyard Sound from Buzzards Bay. The islands are of varying sizes and–with the exception of Cuttyhunk and Penikese–are privately owned by the Forbes family. Mariners are permitted to land in certain areas if they observe the rules: leave dogs aboard, build fires only below the high-water mark, keep to the trails, do not try to bushwhack and clean up after your visit.

Four passages from Buzzards Bay into Vineyard Sound are located between the Elizabeth Islands: Woods Hole, Robinsons Hole, Quicks Hole and Canapitsit Channel. Woods Hole and Quicks Hole are the safest, deepest and best-marked passages. Canapitsit Channel and Robinsons Hole can be used in calm weather with caution. Otherwise, uncharted rocks and strong currents can make these areas unsafe for all but local mariners.

Naushon Island

Naushon Trust owns Naushon Island and most of the land is clearly posted against trespassing but cruising boats are welcome in peaceful Hadley Harbor, a totally protected natural refuge, easily accessible from Buzzards Bay and located directly across from Woods Hole.

NAVIGATION: To reach Hadley Harbor from the Vineyard Sound side, eschew the open-looking but unmarked northern side for the narrow passage just off the northwestern corner of Nonamesset Island. The red nun buoy "2" and green can buoy "3" lead you well south of the privately maintained white-and-brown daybeacon marking an uncovering shoal. Follow Nonamesset Island as it curves south through the pinch as it passes eastward of Bull Island. The Inner Harbor widens as it turns west, then south, around Goats Neck.

Anchorage/Moorings: The far end of Hadley Harbor is crowded with moorings (complimentary of a first-come, first-served basis) but an excellent anchorage is available north of the private landing and boathouses between Bull Island and Goats Neck. This is a beautiful spot to get away from it all or wait out a blow. Holding is very good in soft mud and at least 11 feet MLW. Some shoals and rocks are located close to the shore so skippers should feel their way cautiously and make anchoring allowances for shifting winds during the evening.

Public access is permitted on tiny Bull Island where picnic grounds are maintained during the season. Take your dinghy to the small landing on the southeast corner of the island. Dogs should be kept on leashes and barbecue fires tended responsibly. Signs warn of ticks and danger of Lyme disease; be sure to apply your insect repellent liberally.

> NOTE: Anchorage should be avoided in any place where the channel is constricted. The Naushon Ferry bringing freight and passengers from Woods Hole needs plenty of room to maneuver.

On the Buzzards Bay side of Naushon Island, Kettle Cove makes a good daytime stop should you need it. It is open to wind from the west through the north but on a fine day with a southwesterly breeze, you can drop the hook, have lunch and swim from the beach. Here you will find 7 to 12 feet MLW with good holding in sand.

If you are cruising on the Vineyard Sound side of Naushon Island, you can stop in Tarpaulin Cove if weather permits. The cove has wooded shores and a fine beach but it is open to the south and east. The best protection is in the southwestern corner due north of the 78-foot-high lighthouse in about 11 feet MLW (about 150 to 200 yards south-southwest of green can buoy "1").

The cove can easily accommodate 75 large boats without crowding and is often used by rallies and associations traveling together. The scene ashore is reminiscent of 18th-century America–a classic seaside farmhouse with various outbuildings, rambling stonewalls and deserted beaches.

Cuttyhunk Island

Westernmost of the island chain is Cuttyhunk, located within easy reach of South Shore and Cape Cod ports and offering a particularly attractive stopover en route to Martha's Vineyard and Nantucket heading east or Newport heading west. Nashawena Island is located between Cuttyhunk Island (to the west) and Quicks Hole (to the east).

Cuttyhunk Island is 2 miles long and less than 0.5 mile wide. There are about 50 official residents but most of them aren't year-round. Summer visitors are served by a population swollen to maybe 400. There are a few

Cuttyhunk Harbor, MA

CUTTYHUNK POND		Largest Vessel	VHF	Total Slips	Approach/ Dockside Depth	Floating Docks	Gas/ Diesel	Repairs/ Haulout	Min/Max Amps	Pump-Out Station
1. Cuttyhunk Marina	(508) 990-7578	110	9	85	10.0 / 8.0		GD		30 / 50	

WiFi Wireless Internet Access
Visit www.waterwayguide.com for current rates, fuel prices, website addresses and other up-to-the-minute information.
(Information in the table is provided by the facilities.)

Scan here for more details:

Source: Aqua Map and NOAA data

trucks for hauling but most people walk or ride golf carts. Walking along the paved road west leads to a dead end at the island's highest point with spectacular views of this eastward-running archipelago, its surrounding waters and the distinctive cliffs of Martha's Vineyard to the southeast.

Cuttyhunk Fishing Club (508-997-0858), which was founded in 1894, is almost exactly as it was when William Howard Taft accompanied President Theodore Roosevelt for a fishing trip here. Breakfast on the porch (or inside) comes with breathtaking views of the Elizabeth Islands to the east and Martha's Vineyard to the southeast. Another worthy stop is the Cuttyhunk Historical Society and Museum (508-984-4611) combines historical exhibits with displays of local art. Most of the island's other amenities are found in the weathered shacks along Fisherman's Dock.

M/V Cuttyhunk, the island's dependable ferry to and from New Bedford, is run by Cuttyhunk Ferry Company (508-992-0200) and is the lifeblood of the island. The Cuttyhunk Water Taxi *Seahorse* (508-789-3250) also runs between New Bedford and Cuttyhunk. All trips are scheduled by appointment.

NAVIGATION: The Middle Ground red-and-green nun buoy "MG" marks the entrance to Cuttyhunk Harbor from the west. Leave red nun buoys well to your west on approach to avoid Edwards Rock, marked by red nun "2W"; Whale Rock, marked by a white-and-orange obstruction buoy; and Pease Ledge, southwest of red nun buoy "4." Red bell buoy "6" is posted to the northeast of the entrance to the inner harbor channel jetty, which is marked by a 29-foot-high tower with a red flashing "8" to the north and green can buoy "9" to the south.

The approach to Cuttyhunk Harbor from the east begins at red-and-white Morse (A) bell buoy "CH." On entering the outer harbor from the east leave red nun buoy "2E" to the north to avoid shoals that extend southward from Gull Island and leave green can buoy "1E" to the south to avoid the shoal working out from Knox Point. The channel into Cuttyhunk Pond is occasionally dredged to alleviate the encroaching shallows on each side. If both your keel and your fear of shoaling run deep, phone or radio ahead to the Cuttyhunk Harbormaster (VHF Channel 09, 508-990-7578) for specific advice.

Dockage/Moorings: Cuttyhunk Marina has 50 transient slips and 50 closely spaced rental moorings (marked "Town of Gosnold") available on a first-come, first-served basis. You must supply your own bridle and chafing gear. An agile hand forward will be required to thread the eye of the unusual stand-up pennant on these moorings. A relatively short tether is advised in view of the limited swing room. (No more than two boats are permitted to raft.) Be aware that there is no protection from north-northwest.

The town launch will come by early in the evening to collect the mooring fee. The mooring field is likely to be filled to capacity on summer weekends and holidays. Public restrooms next to the recycling trailers are available 24/7 but there are no shower facilities. Cuttyhunk's fuel facility (both gasoline and diesel) is next to the abandoned red-roofed Coast Guard building.

> NOTE: Cuttyhunk's recycling center accepts separated clear, green and brown glass, plastics, aluminum and other metals. Mixed trash can also be deposited here for a small fee.

Anchorage: Just inside Cuttyhunk Pond, it may be possible to anchor north of the town moorings, although a thin grass cover makes holding less than ideal. Nevertheless, it does provide all-around protection in 7 to 10 feet MLW. Be aware that the area outside the white buoys is not dredged and shallows rapidly. The dinghy landing in the marina gets crowded so be prepared to clamber from dinghy to dinghy holding your long painter.

The Cuttyhunk Harbor north of the jetty is less crowded with potentially good holding in a hard sand and mud mix with 12 to 17 feet MLW. Patches of grass can frustrate a clean anchor set in this area. Also, considering Buzzards Bay's well-earned reputation for strong onshore afternoon winds, be certain you are firmly secured before going ashore or retiring below. Anchoring throughout the outer harbor is possible but be aware that current becomes an issue closer to the Canapitsit Channel.

If you want to get away from the crowds at Cuttyhunk, it is possible to anchor on the northeast side of Nashawena Island adjacent to Quicks Hole Passage. Here you will find at least 8 feet MLW with excellent holding in sand. This is open to the north and southeast and should only be attempted in settled weather. There are no services here.

Woods Hole

Cape Cod

Chatham

Chatham Roads

Hyannis

Cotuit

Falmouth

Buzzards Bay

Nantucket Sound

Nantucket Island

Martha's Vineyard

Atlantic Ocean

Pages 439-444

Pages 418-429

Pages 430-439

Falmouth Harbor

■ FALMOUTH TO STAGE HARBOR

Nantucket Sound is an exciting and tempestuous body of water due to its well-marked shoals and it is a fabulous destination that can be traveled as though it's a very, very large bay. A circular voyage through its ports and anchorages begins with the natural beauty of the Elizabeth Islands, continues along Cape Cod's south shore harbors with plenty of marinas and turns for Nantucket at Hyannis Port, the last of the deep-draft harbors on the southern coast. Heading farther east is for shoal-draft boats only.

The prevailing southwesterlies give a close reach from Hyannis Port to the fabulous island of Nantucket and then a beam reach back northwest to Martha's Vineyard. These islands are a favored cruising grounds for thousands of recreational boaters. The best-known harbors grow ever more congested each season, while lesser-known ports are continually being "discovered" by those who seek refuge from the crowds. The discovery of hidden coves and harbors is one of the many joys of cruising these waters.

Falmouth

Falmouth is not only a good base for cruising the islands, it also has one of Cape Cod's best harbors with at least 8-foot MLW depths and every conceivable amenity. It is thoroughly protected and easy to enter. At the head of the harbor on the eastern side, the Island Queen passenger ferry will take you to Oak Bluffs on Martha's Vineyard. Band concerts in Falmouth are on the western side of the marine park and provide entertainment on Thursday evenings during the summer.

In town, the seasonal bustle of a seaside resort village awaits you. Houses built by ship owners and sea captains in the 18th and 19th centuries surround the traditional village green. Accommodations and dining possibilities are almost unlimited.

Although the town of Falmouth is located about 1 mile away, most of the essentials for provisioning and reviving water-weary crews are close to the marinas. A market, West Marine and liquor store are all on the west side of Scranton Ave. across from the Falmouth Town Marina harbormaster's office. A self-service laundry is a 5-minute

Falmouth Harbor, MA

FALMOUTH		Largest Vessel	VHF	Total Slips	Approach/ Dockside Depth	Floating Docks	Gas/ Diesel	Repairs/ Haulout	Min/Max Amps	Pump-Out Station
1. Falmouth Marine & Yachting Center	(508) 548-4600	70	9	23	10.0 / 10.0	F	GD	RH	30 / 50	P
2. MacDougalls' Cape Cod Marine Service ⓌⒾⒻⒾ	(508) 548-3146	120	9	110	10.0 / 10.0	F	GD	RH	30 / 100	P
3. Falmouth Town Marina	(508) 457-2550	200	16	100	9.0 / 6.0	F			30 / 100	P

ⓌⒾⒻⒾ Wireless Internet Access
Visit www.waterwayguide.com for current rates, fuel prices, website addresses and other up-to-the-minute information.
(Information in the table is provided by the facilities.)

Scan here for more details:

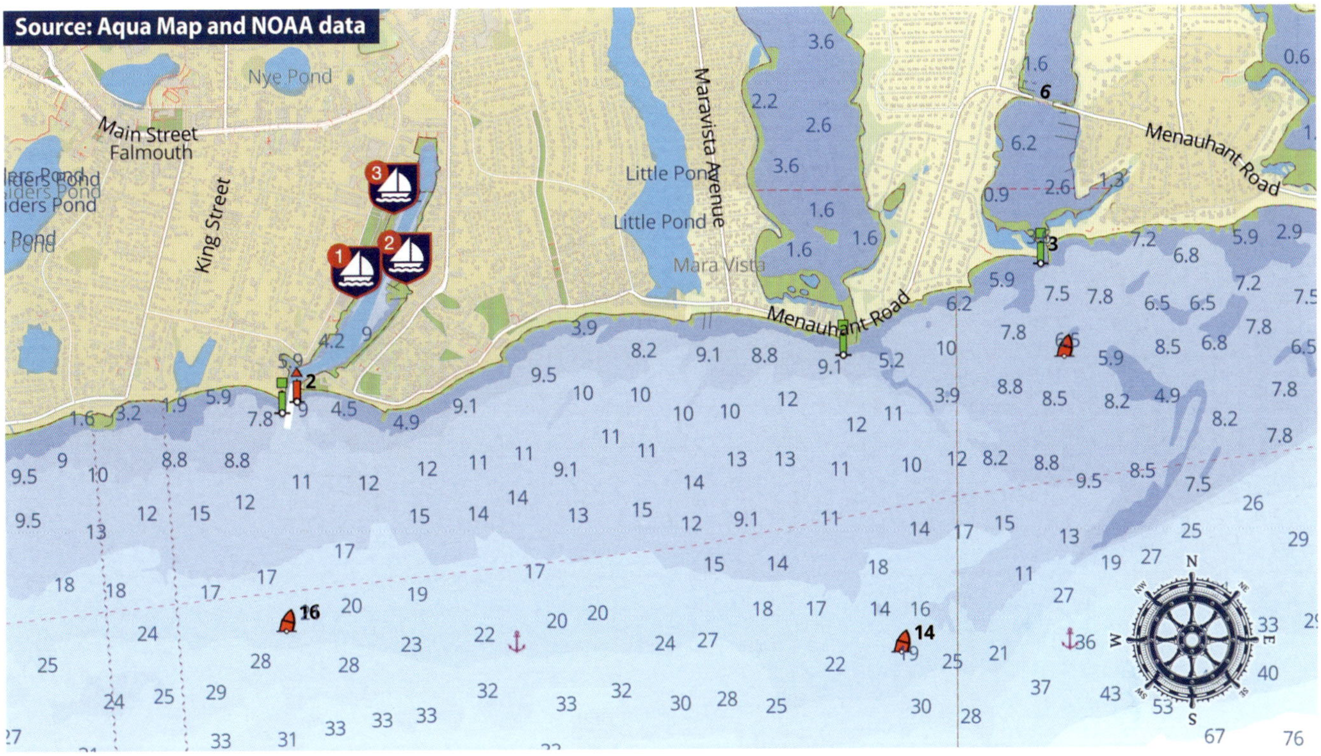

Source: Aqua Map and NOAA data

[Navigation chart of Falmouth Harbor showing marinas 1, 2, 3, depth soundings, Menauhant Road, King Street, Maravista Avenue, Little Pond, Nye Pond, Main Street Falmouth, and compass rose]

walk north. Farther along at the end of Scranton Ave. and to the right, a fair-sized mall boasts chain stores and fast-food restaurants.

NAVIGATION: Flashing red bell buoy "16" about 0.50 mile offshore marks the approach to the breakwater entrance. The entrance is straightforward, although narrow with 6-foot MLW depths that are relatively consistent in the channel and throughout the dredged harbor. Past the entrance, the harbor broadens slightly and both banks are lined with marine facilities and amenities.

> This is a No-Discharge Zone and a pump-out station is located at the town dock. There is no room for anchoring here.

Dockage/Moorings: Marine facilities line the Falmouth Inner Harbor with slips and moorings. Falmouth Marine & Yachting Center offers 15 slips and 15 moorings and offers maintenance, repairs, hauling

and storage. You can land a dinghy at the free Falmouth Harbor Dock (day use only).

Falmouth Town Marina has consists of 100 slips, the Tide's Bulkhead, the Davis Bulkhead, and four slips in Green Pond. Use the online form to request a slip reservation. The Flying Bridge Restaurant (508-548-2700) has an easy-access fuel dock (at the Mobil sign) and several small finger piers for restaurant patrons. Pier 37 will also allow you to dock while you dine.

MacDougalls' Cape Cod Marine Service on the western shore of the harbor has extensive marine amenities. They offer both moorings and slips (to 120 feet) and have a large on-site chandlery and retail supply store as well as specialty shops for installations, custom fabrications, sailmaking and canvas repairs. They rebuild and re-power gas and diesel engines and have the largest paint booth facility on Cape Cod.

Falmouth Harbor, MA

COTUIT		Largest Vessel	VHF	Total Slips	Approach/ Dockside Depth	Floating Docks	Gas/ Diesel	Repairs/ Haulout	Min/Max Amps	Pump-Out Station
1. Cotuit Bay Moorings	(508) 790-6273		68		/					P
2. Crosby Yacht Yard Inc. (WiFi)	(508) 428-6900	65	9	125	6.0 / 5.0	F	GD	RH	30 / 50	P

(WiFi) Wireless Internet Access
Visit www.waterwayguide.com for current rates, fuel prices, website addresses and other up-to-the-minute information.
(Information in the table is provided by the facilities.)

Scan here for more details:

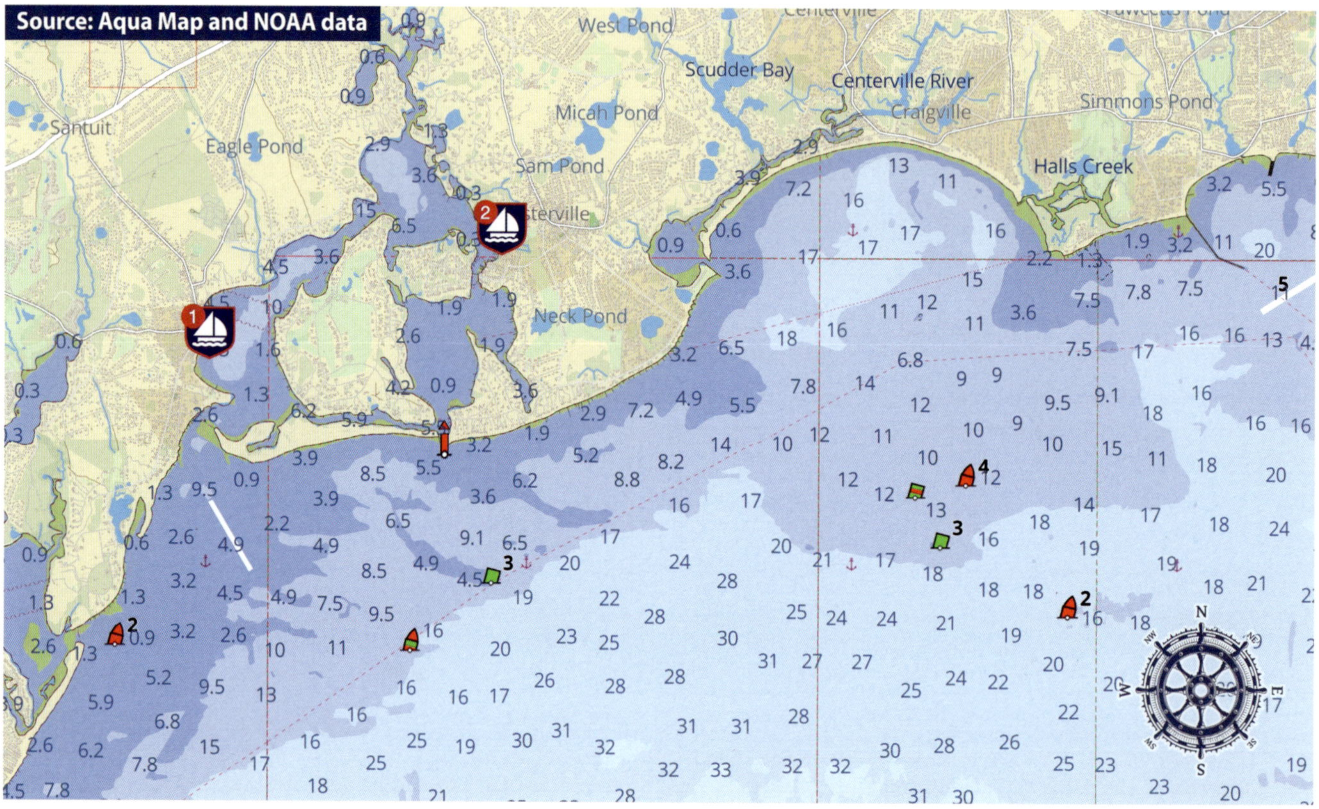

Source: Aqua Map and NOAA data

Cotuit & Osterville

Less than 20 nm away is the next popular cruiser destination, the Village of Cotuit. The east side of Cotuit Bay is all Osterville Grand Island. Inside Cotuit Bay is a big, almost circular area with a well-buoyed, continuous waterway leading through three bays and a narrow river. Each offers coves and creeks for gunkholing, good beaches, fine anchorages, ample yacht amenities and charming towns.

The complete landlocked circuit can be made without leaving sheltered water, although a boat drawing 5 feet or less has a better chance of a successful circuit of Osterville Island. The Eel River in the southeastern corner of West Bay is also worth a dinghy trip but it shoals at the entrance. Most of the West Bay activity is around the bridge providing easy provisioning, a library, shopping and restaurants. Cotuit Town Dock has a dinghy landing.

NAVIGATION: Between Popponesset Beach and Wianno Beach on Nantucket Sound, two buoyed channels lead inland to one of the most beautiful harbor complexes on the south shore. Westernmost is the 4-foot MLW channel to Cotuit and Cotuit Bay.

To reach Cotuit follow the long, dredged channel that leads for more than 1 mile through 1- and 2-foot MLW shoals that encroach closely on either side. The channel makes an S-curve around the pointing finger of Sampsons Island and then around Bluff Point. Stay well off the point. The narrow channel lies close to the shore of Sampsons Island and is somewhat parallel to it until the small black buoy (privately maintained). Most vessels will need to enter Cotuit on a rising tide.

North Bay is the connecting link between Cotuit and West Bays and the entrance to delightful Prince Cove. From Cotuit Bay, follow the buoyed passage from the deeper northern end (7 to 10 feet MLW) that leads past Point Isabella into North Bay. According to local authorities, this channel is good for 5 feet MLW.

From North Bay, pass through the **West Bay Bridge** (15-foot closed vertical clearance), which connects Osterville on the east shore with Little Island and Osterville. The bridge opens on signal from May 1 through June 15 and from October 1 through October 31, from 8:00 a.m. to 6:00 p.m.; and from June 16 through September 30, from 7:00 a.m. to 9:00 p.m. At all other times from May 1 through October 31, the draw shall open on signal if at least a 24-hour advance notice is given by calling the number posted at the bridge.

The final link in the Cotuit–North–West Bays circuit is Seapuit River, west of the entrance to West Bay from Nantucket Sound. From West Bay it leads between the dunes of Dead Neck (landing is prohibited) and the southern shore of Osterville Grand Island. The NOAA chart shows a shoal area for quite a distance behind Dead Neck but locals claim that the controlling depth is 4 feet MLW.

An alternate route into this area is through West Bay. The narrow, dredged approach to West Bay from Nantucket Sound is deep, well-marked and has a breakwater on both sides. Once inside, the first opening to the west leads to Cotuit Bay via Seapuit River and the main 6-foot MLW channel runs northward up West Bay between shoals.

Dockage/Moorings: Marinas, fuel docks and boat yards are clustered north of the West Bay Bridge between Oysterville and Little Island including Nauticus Marina, home to *America 3*, winner of the 1992 America's Cup. (No transient slips.)

Cotuit Bay Moorings are managed by the Town of Barnstable. The mooring balls have an orange stripe for an easy visual upon approach. The mooring has a pick-up buoy. The usage of this mooring is by reservation only. Cotuit Launch is a privately run service and a fee is required for usage. Call on VHF Channel 68 (operational hours depend on the day). There is a pump-out boat in this area if you need assistance

The well-regarded Crosby Yacht Yard Inc. has been in business since 1850 and offer a full range of boat and marine services as well as seasonal and transient dockage and moorings, repairs, restoration and maintenance. Call ahead.

Anchorage: You can drop the hook in the northeastern corner of West Bay at Osterville in at least 8 feet MLW with good holding in mud and all-around

protection. One of the best anchorages around is in North Bay at Little Island where you will find 7 to 10 feet MLW with excellent holding in mud and all-around protection. (Prince Cove is best investigated by dinghy due to its narrow, hard-to-negotiate entry.)

At the Cotuit Bay entrance, tuck behind Sampsons Island in at least 7 feet MLW with good holding in sand and mud. This is somewhat exposed to the northeast. This puts you close to Cotuit Town Dock for dinghy dockage.

Hyannis

Hyannis was settled by a handful of Puritans well over 400 years ago and their surnames still figure prominently in the town's grand list. But not all of the area's famous residents came early. The Kennedys are an example, having arrived in 1926.

Hyannis Harbor is one of the most popular areas with boaters on Cape Cod. The harbor is deep and easy to enter with summer traffic of all sorts–yachts under sail, commercial vessels, charter fishing and "head boats," ferries from Martha's Vineyard and Nantucket, as well as recreational boats of all kinds.

Hyannis acts as the hub of Cape Cod offering cruisers a wide range of services from health (Cape Cod Hospital) and retail (Cape Cod Mall) to cultural (Cape Cod Maritime Museum) and transportation (Barnstable Municipal Airport, Cape Cod Regional Transit Authority and ferry service to the islands). For cruisers, the town's attractions are close at hand just a little more than 1 mile away from the waterfront. (Guests in a hurry can use the Hyannis Marina courtesy vans or ride the Cape Cod Trolley.) Ocean Street Market (774-552-3912) has limited groceries and provisions.

NAVIGATION: The most straightforward approach to Hyannis from the west is through the buoyed channel, being sure to respect the buoys marking numerous rocks and ledges on approach from east or west. Following the lead of the red and white Morse (A) "HH" bell buoy, head north toward the Hyannis breakwater. Once inside, you can see the Kennedy compound, which faces the harbor and Nantucket Sound. From the breakwater east, the marked channel begins its long sweep through Lewis Bay toward Harbor Bluff.

On approach, the channel angles northeast on a direct course to Hyannis' busy inner harbor, where access to marine services and town amenities is assured. This harbor routinely services large megayachts with drafts exceeding 10 feet.

GOIN' ASHORE

HYANNIS, MA

ATTRACTIONS

1. Cape Cod Maritime Museum
Open mid-March to mid-December with displays and programs for "celebrating, preserving and interpreting Cape Cod's maritime past, present and future" at 135 South St. (508-775-1723).

2. John F. Kennedy Hyannis Museum
Showcases the life of John F. Kennedy with a focus on his time spent in the Hyannis area at 397 Main St. (508-790-3077).

SERVICES

3. Cape Cod Hospital
27 Park St. (508-771-1800)

4. Clothesline Laundry Inc.
71 Barnstable Rd. (508-778-1976)

5. Hyannis Post Office
385 Main St. (508-775-7344)

6. Hyannis Public Library
401 Main St. (508-775-2280)

MARINAS

7. Bismore Park Marina
1189 Phinney Ln. (508-790-6273)

8. Dockside Marina
145 School St. (508-680-3293)

9. Hyannis Marina
1 Willow St. (508-790-4000)

10. Hyannis Yacht Club-PRIVATE
490 Ocean St. (508-775-9331)

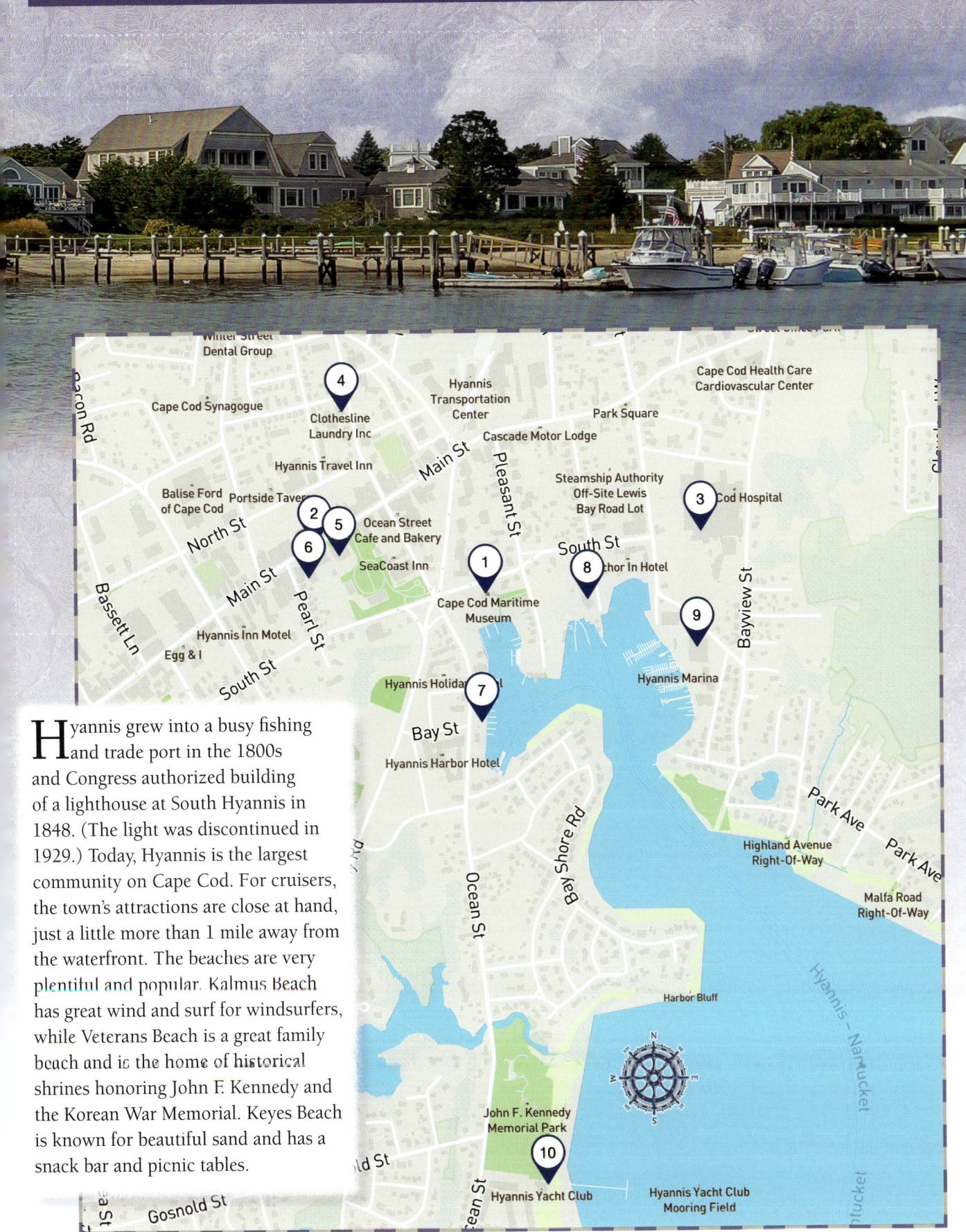

Hyannis grew into a busy fishing and trade port in the 1800s and Congress authorized building of a lighthouse at South Hyannis in 1848. (The light was discontinued in 1929.) Today, Hyannis is the largest community on Cape Cod. For cruisers, the town's attractions are close at hand, just a little more than 1 mile away from the waterfront. The beaches are very plentiful and popular. Kalmus Beach has great wind and surf for windsurfers, while Veterans Beach is a great family beach and is the home of historical shrines honoring John F. Kennedy and the Korean War Memorial. Keyes Beach is known for beautiful sand and has a snack bar and picnic tables.

Lewis Bay, MA

HYANNIS		Largest Vessel	VHF	Total Slips	Approach/Dockside Depth	Floating Docks	Gas/Diesel	Repairs/Haulout	Min/Max Amps	Pump-Out Station
1. Hyannis Yacht Club-PRIVATE	(508) 778-6100	140	69	24	10.0 / 8.0				30	
2. Hyannis Transient Moorings	(508) 790-6273		9		/					
3. Bismore Park Marina	(508) 790-6273	75	16	24	12.0 / 8.0				30 / 50	P
4. Dockside Marina WiFi	(508) 790-4000	150	9	29	15.0 / 14.0	F		H	30 / 50	
5. Hyannis Marina WiFi	(508) 790-4000	200	9	180	16.0 / 16.0	F	GD	RH	30 / 100	P

WiFi Wireless Internet Access

Visit www.waterwayguide.com for current rates, fuel prices, website addresses and other up-to-the-minute information. (Information in the table is provided by the facilities.)

Scan here for more details:

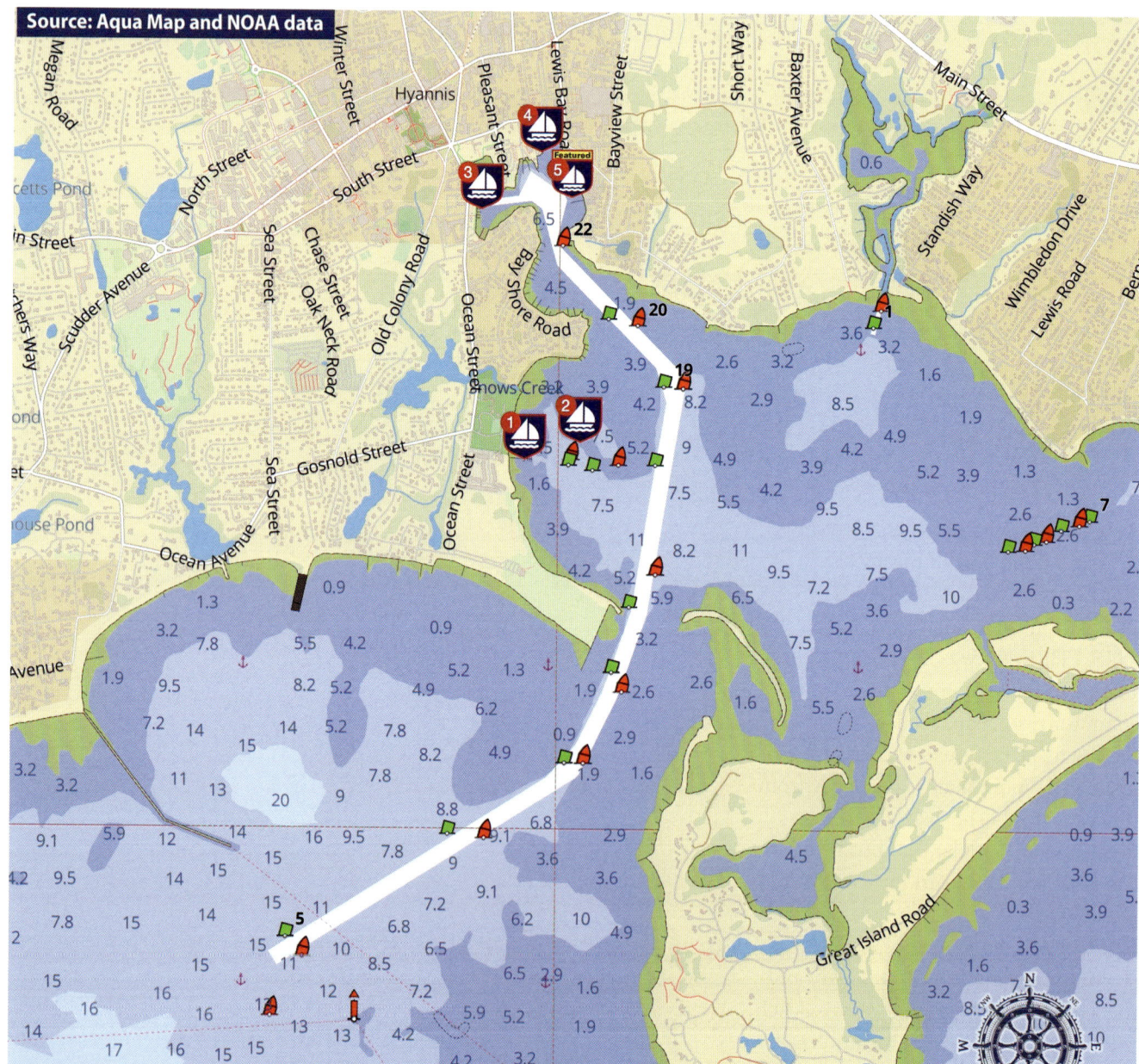

Source: Aqua Map and NOAA data

Experience

HYANNIS MARINA

CAPE COD'S FINEST RESORT MARINA

- 16'+ MLW approach & dockside depth
- Exclusive harborside pool and tiki bar
- 2 full menu restaurants onsite
- Private showers & bathrooms
- High speed fuel, volume discounts
- Laundromat on site
- Courtesy cars
- Ships store • Parts • Service
- Airport within 3 miles
- Dockside high speed WiFi

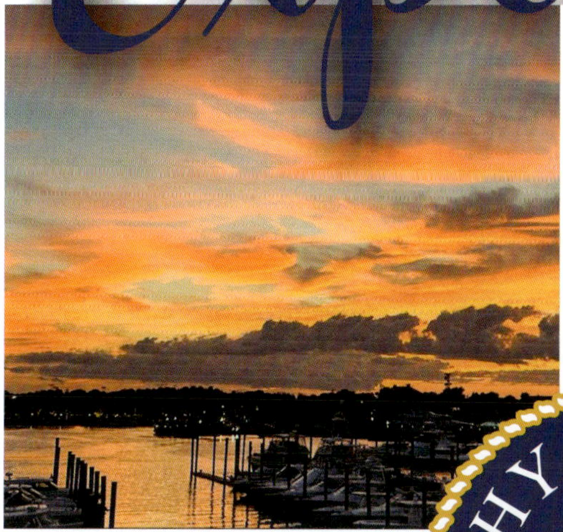

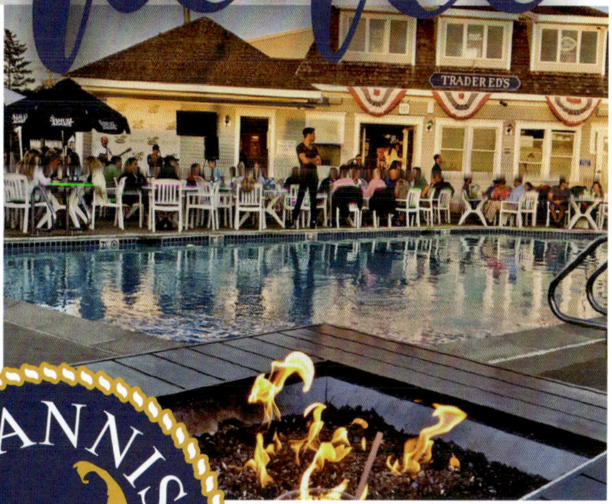

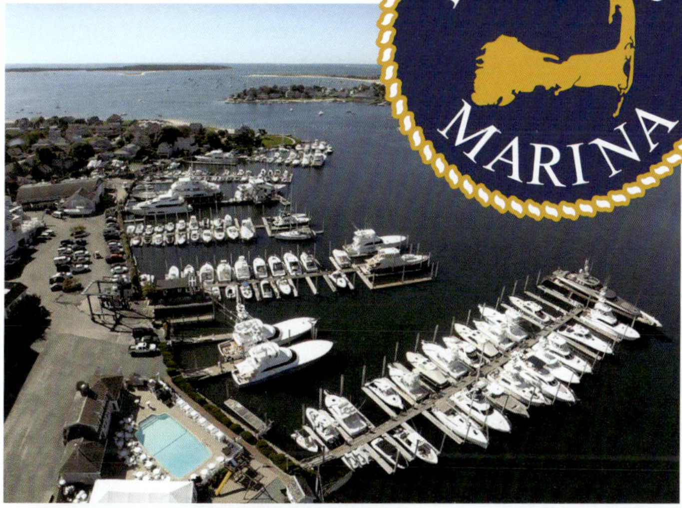

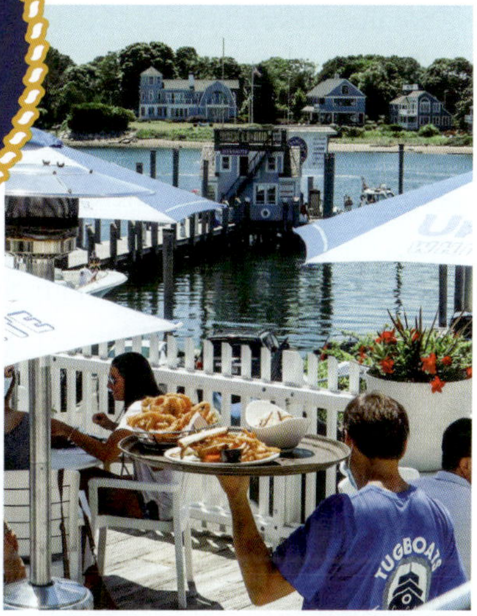

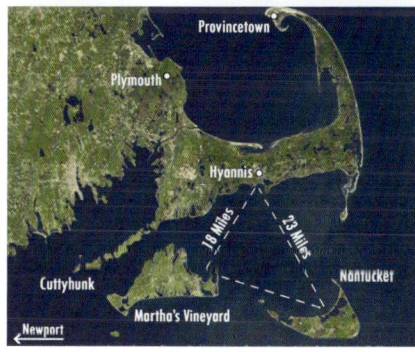

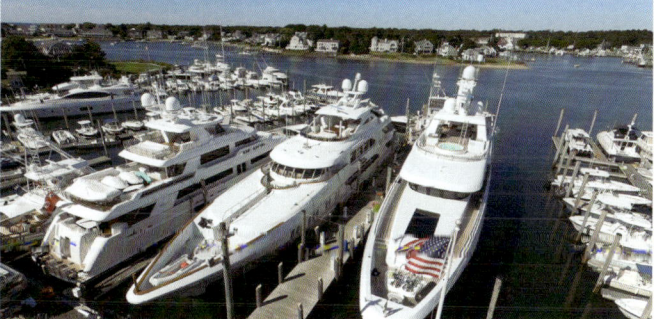

Dockage: On entering Lewis Bay, you will first see the Hyannis Yacht Club west of the channel behind Dunbar Point. They may be able to accommodate members of other yacht clubs and guests of members. Call ahead.

The Hyannis Transient Moorings are spread throughout the Hyannis waterways but are in close proximity to the Federal Channel. The small Fish Hills mooring field is the inner-most near Hyannis Inner Harbor. Lewis Bay Moorings are located in Lewis Bay off Hyannis Yacht Club, while Hyannis Port Moorings is near Hyannis Port Yacht Club. Private launch (not associated with the town) is available for the last two.

At the inner harbor and within the protection of Harbor Bluff is the municipal Bismore Park Marina with slips to 75 feet and two (seasonal) pump-out stations. The marina has a bathroom open during operational hours; however, there are no shower facilities. They may also have a mooring available, if you prefer. Dockside Marina is to the north with slips to 150 feet and a variety of vessels including commercial work boats, draggers, scallopers, dredges, barges, commercial fishing boats, charter boats and pleasure boats.

Your best bet for a slip is at the large and modern Hyannis Marina, which can accommodate everything from small motorboats to deep-draft sailboats and megayachts up to 200 feet in length. The marina is in a club-like setting with a full-capability service and repair yard. There are floating docks with all the usual amenities, a harborside pool (with a poolside cabana), a full-menu restaurant and a marine store and gift shop.

Anchorage: Cruisers that prefer anchoring will find 7 to 8 feet MLW with good holding in mud northeast of crescent-shaped Egg Island in Lewis Bay. The remainder of Lewis Bay is suitable in settled weather but open to the southwest. This isn't on the "main drag" but provides protection and its quiet.

South Yarmouth/West Dennis

One of Cape Cod's prettiest rivers and a popular cruising area for small boats, the long, winding Bass River loops lazily inland toward the towns of South Yarmouth and West Dennis. Attractive houses, old windmills, several restaurants, hotels, motels, good-looking yachts and fine marinas are above and below the fixed 15-foot bridge between South Yarmouth and West Dennis.

NAVIGATION: If you plan to stop in the Bass River, flashing red buoy "2" marks the beginning of the approach. The approach to the jettied entrance across Dogfish Bar is narrow and depths fluctuate from about 7 to 3.5 feet MLW, depending on when it was last dredged and the amount of silting since. Enter only on a rising tide.

CAUTION: Severe shoaling has been reported between Bass River Channel Buoys "2" and "9" and there is a severe decrease in the channel's width. Mariners should proceed with caution while transiting the area.

Harbor Bluff

Hyannis Marina

Hyannis

Harwich Port Area, MA

BASS RIVER		Largest Vessel	VHF	Total Slips	Approach/ Dockside Depth	Floating Docks	Gas/ Diesel	Repairs/ Haulout	Min/Max Amps	Pump-Out Station
1. Bass River Marina WiFi	(508) 394-8341	40	71	160	10.0 / 10.0	F	G	RH	30 / 50	P
ALLEN HARBOR										
2. Allen Harbor Marine Service, Inc.	(508) 430-6008	50	68	52	6.0 / 6.0	F	GD	RH	30 / 50	P
3. Allen Harbor Yacht Club-PRIVATE	(508) 432-9774	55	9		6.0 / 4.0	F	GD			P
SAQUATUCKET HARBOR										
4. Saquatucket Municipal Marina	(508) 430-7532	55	68	195	6.0 / 8.0	F	GD		30 / 50	P

WiFi Wireless Internet Access
Visit www.waterwayguide.com for current rates, fuel prices, website addresses and other up-to-the-minute information.
(Information in the table is provided by the facilities.)

Scan here for more details:

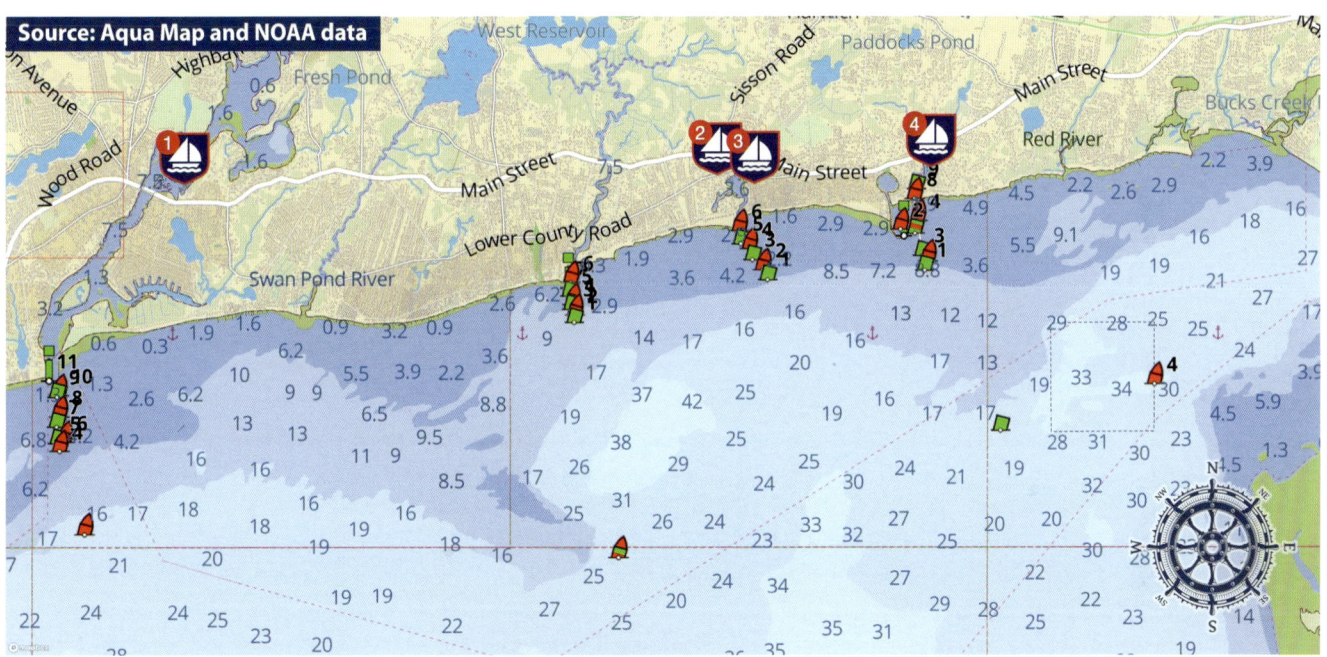

Source: Aqua Map and NOAA data

The 15-foot fixed vertical clearance **Bass River (MA 28) Bridge** connects West Dennis and South Yarmouth north of red nun "22A."

Dockage: Gas and diesel fuel, transient slips and repairs can be found on the Bass River, at Allen Harbor and at Saquatucket Harbor, which shares a common entrance with Wychmere Harbor. Bass River Marina specializes in boat sales and storage and has 160 slips that can handle powerboats to 40 feet. In addition to slip rentals, the marina offers access to a comprehensive service department and a fully stocked chandlery.

To Chatham Roads (Stage Harbor)

Continuing east, Harwich Port has a colorful 300-year history as a shipbuilding, whaling and cod fishing center. The three good harbors (Allen, Wychmere and Saquatucket) are maintained to 6 feet MLW. Fine beaches remain and have been joined by good restaurants and full service amenities.

Large, protected Stage Harbor is the last port on the south side of Cape Cod and the logical starting point for boats making the outside run around the hook to Provincetown.

As much a fishing port as a yacht harbor, Stage Harbor has appealing creeks and coves and good boating amenities and anchorages.

NAVIGATION: Allen Harbor to the west of Harwich Port is so well protected that the entrance is hard to find, and you will not see the harbor until the last turn of Doanes Creek. Numbered buoys lead you to the 20-foot tall, quick-flashing green Allen Harbor Entrance Breakwater Light on the west side of the entrance and into Doanes Creek, which has 6-foot MLW depths.

Chatham Harbor, MA

CHATHAM		Largest Vessel	VHF	Total Slips	Approach/ Dockside Depth	Floating Docks	Gas/ Diesel	Repairs/ Haulout	Min/Max Amps	Pump-Out Station
1. Oyster River Boat Yard	(508) 945-0736	34	9	26	3.0 / 5.0	F	G	R	30	
2. Stage Harbor Marine	(508) 945-1860	114	9	30	10.0 / 6.0	F	GD	RH	30	P
3. Outermost Harbor Marine	(508) 945-2030	53	80	100	3.0 / 3.0	F	G	RH	30	
4. Ryders Cove Boat Yard	(508) 945-1064	30	9	32	4.0 / 4.0	F	G	RH		

WiFi Wireless Internet Access
Visit www.waterwayguide.com for current rates, fuel prices, website addresses and other up-to-the-minute information.
(Information in the table is provided by the facilities.)

Scan here for more details:

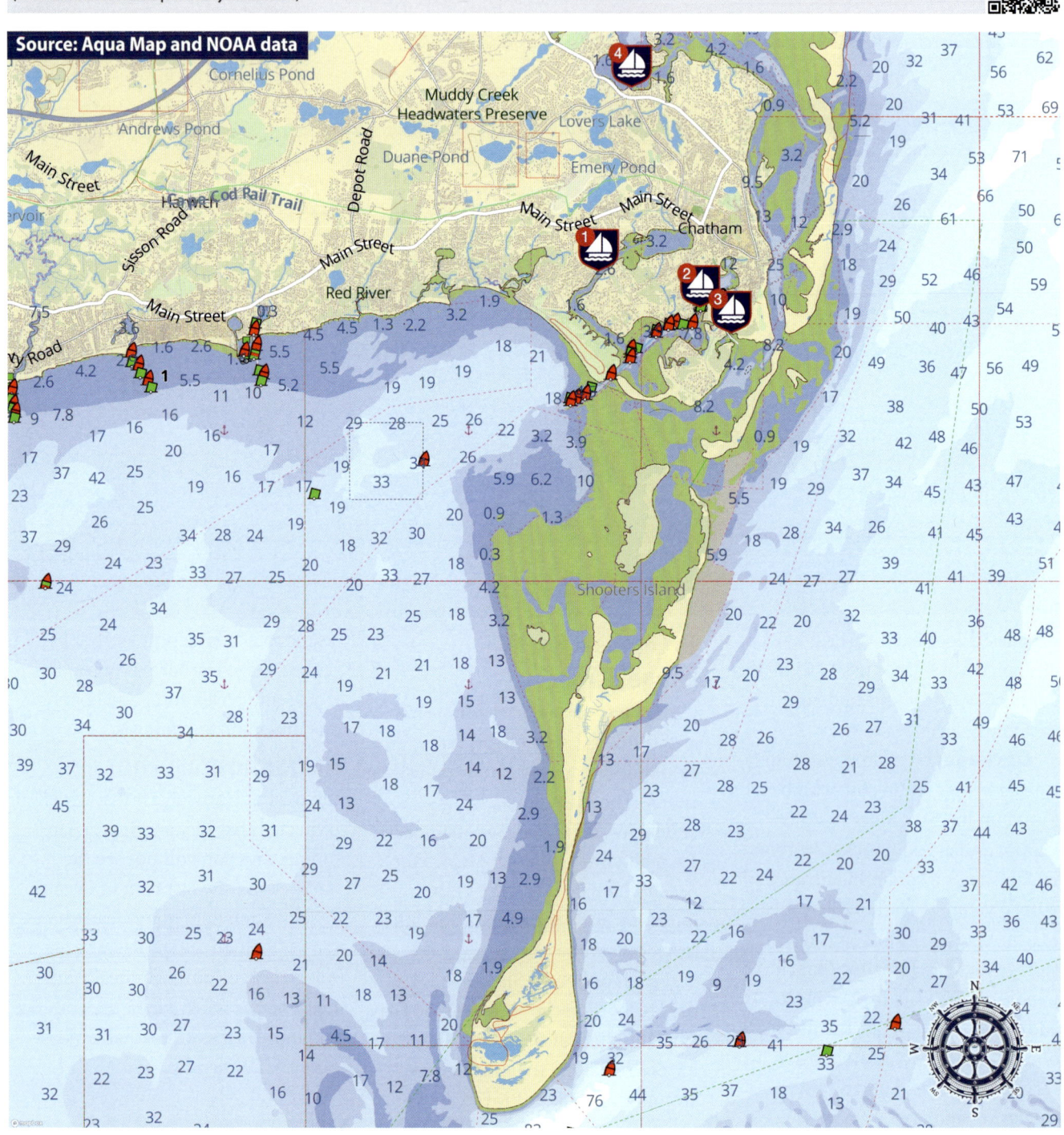

Source: Aqua Map and NOAA data

When approaching Chatham Roads, watch for fish weirs on the northwestern side and along the edge of shallows on the Martha's Vineyard side of Monomoy Island. Very shoal-draft boats, aided by local knowledge, use the cut between Morris Island and Monomoy Island to reach Chatham Harbor. Otherwise, you must circumnavigate Monomoy Island to reach this shoaling passage inside the barrier beach. Even this route, however, calls for caution and local knowledge of the shoals.

You can reach Stage Harbor via a land cut through Harding Beach. Follow the main channel buoys to reach the inner harbor. The **Chatham Highway Bridge** (8-foot closed vertical clearance) will open on signal from May 1 to October 31 from 8:00 a.m. to 5:00 p.m. if at least a 1-hour notice is given by calling the Town of Chatham Harbormasters Department (508-945-1213). From 5:00 p.m. to 8:00 a.m., the draw will open on signal if at least a 12-hour notice is given. At all other times, the bridge will only open with a 24-hour advance notice. Local boats mostly occupy the area above the bridge.

Dockage/Moorings: The full-service, family-owned Allen Harbor Marine Service, Inc. is a boatyard and marina with a few reserved transient slips to 50 feet. Nearby is the private Allen Harbor Yacht Club, which welcomes visiting yachtsmen of recognized yacht clubs based on slip or mooring availability. This includes privileges to their club. Slip rentals must be paid in advance. There is no room for anchoring in Allen Harbor.

The Saquatucket waterfront has been redeveloped in recent years and slips added to the town marina. Call the friendly Saquatucket Municipal Marina on VHF Channel 16 or 68. They have ample slips for transients to 55 feet. Harwich Port's stores, restaurants and art gallery are 1 mile from Allen Harbor and 2 miles from Saquatucket.

The round, nearly landlocked Wychmere Harbor just to the west shares a channel with Saquatucket, and while it may look inviting, it is jammed with moorings. The crowded harbor does not have transient dockage but if you ask at the town dock, someone might be able to point out an available mooring or slip. There is no room for anchoring here.

A bit off the beaten path, Oyster River Boat Yard on Oyster Pond River north of Stage Harbor has just 26 slips to 34 feet.

Stage Harbor Marine at the foot of the Chatham Highway Bridge is the closest to amenities but has just one reserved transient slip so call ahead. Outermost Harbor Marine, accessed via a channel between Morris Island and Nauset Beach, has slips (to 53 feet) and moorings (to 35 feet) and marine parts and services can be found here. Note that the marina reports 3-foot MLW approach depths so call ahead for exact depths and directions.

To the north of Chatham, Ryders Cove Boat Yard has 33 slips and 73 moorings (to 30 feet) with 4-foot MLW approach depths. They maintain some transient space but call ahead.

Anchorage: You can anchor behind Harding Beach Point south-southeast of red nun "10" in 12 to 15 feet MLW with excellent holding in sand. Note that the channel and shoals around Harding Beach are constantly shifting. Do not rely on charts for this area. Eyeball navigation is recommended and best left to small or shoal-draft boats. Nevertheless, it is a beautiful spot and amazing sandy beaches. Expect company on the weekends.

Deeper-draft vessels can drop the hook just off the channel in Stage Harbor northeast of green can "13" in 13 feet MLW with good holding in mud and grass. If you and your dinghy are up to it, there are public landings on both the Oyster River and the Mitchell River, close to Main Street.

SIDE TRIP: MARTHA'S VINEYARD

A distance of less than 4 nm divides Martha's Vineyard from the southern shore of Cape Cod. The Vineyard is a relaxed summer resort with four distinctively different harbors (Menemsha, Vineyard Haven, Oak Bluffs and Edgartown), high land, wooded bluffs, historic towns and handsome houses. The southern and western shores consist of ocean beach, salt marsh and the multicolored cliffs of Gay Head towering high above the sea. Colored veins of earth-hued clay (white, yellow, tan, sienna, rust, brown) make the cliffs a muted rainbow.

Remember that many of the towns on The Vineyard are "dry" so bring your own (brown bagging) is the rule when it comes to alcohol. This method is permitted at most restaurants. Martha's Bike Rentals (833-362-7842) will deliver and pick up bikes anywhere on the island.

Edgartown Harbor

Edgartown is one of the world's great yachting centers. This is a wonderful walking town with lovely boutiques, small cafés and galleries. Many impressive yachts are moored here in season. Particularly striking are the classic wooden power vessels kept in peak condition by ever-polishing, multi-member crews.

Elegant, historic New England houses–all meticulously restored–line the streets ashore. With the help of prevailing sea breezes, grand shade trees provide natural air-conditioning and flowers abound.

Katama Bay continues to be a naturalist's delight. Ospreys, terns, whippoorwills and a variety of gulls all seem to thrive here. Near-deserted South Beach, one of the most unspoiled and beautiful in the islands, is a relatively easy motorized dinghy ride from almost any spot in the bay.

NAVIGATION: Entry to Edgartown Harbor is relatively simple; however, the rocks and shallows known as the Middle Flats are marked by red nuns at roughly 1-mile increments, west of safe water. A few green cans along the eastern side of the entrance make sure you don't stray too close to the Cape Poge Elbow.

Although the inner harbor is deep and well-marked, currents of several knots at the height of the tidal flow are further complicated by frequent and rapid cross-channel transits by the Chappaquiddick ferry, *On Time*.

When entering the inner basin, it's safest to round green can buoy "9," even though the mooring field beyond it gives the illusion of safe passage. The sandbar between the green can buoy "9" and Chappaquiddick Point has snagged many a keel.

Dockage/Moorings: Edgartown Harbor controls some 700 moorings in the harbor, about 100 of which are reserved for transients on a first-come, first-served basis. Launch service is available; call the Harbormaster on VHF Channel 68 or 401-847-9109.

Although moorings in Edgartown Harbor are numerous, actual dockage is in short supply. Mad Max Marina (home of a popular catamaran charter) and the private Edgartown

Yacht Club (for members of reciprocal clubs) may be options.

> NOTE: Edgartown is in a no-discharge zone; boats are forbidden to discharge sewage of any kind (even treated) into harbor waters. A free pump-out station operates from 9:00 a.m. to 5:00 p.m. and is stationed on Memorial Wharf (next to the ferry landing). Additionally, a town pump-out boat is on call (VHF Channel 74) with free service to all those anchored or on moorings.

Anchorage: Anchoring is not permitted in the crowded mooring field inside the harbor. However, shortly before entering the Edgartown inner harbor, you will find ample anchorage space (increasingly popular with large charter vessels and schooners) off Sturgeon Flats on the northerly side of Chappaquiddick Island in deep water (17 to 20 feet MLW) with good holding in mud. This area is exposed to the north, however, and likely will challenge your comfort levels in all but the calmest weather.

The town of Edgartown does not permit overnight anchorage in Cape Poge Bay; however, it is a nice day anchorage or dinghy exploration area. The narrow passage into the bay is marked by green can buoy 7 located about a thousand yards due west of the entry.

Shoaling restricts the passage of deep-draft boats much beyond North Neck and cautious skippers might choose to anchor before reaching the inner shallows preceding the 9- to 10-foot MLW depths. The approximately 2-foot tidal range here should discourage boats of more than a 4-foot draft from attempting passage to the inner bay, even on a rising tide.

Martha's Vineyard, MA

EDGARTOWN HARBOR		Largest Vessel	VHF	Total Slips	Approach/ Dockside Depth	Floating Docks	Gas/ Diesel	Repairs/ Haulout	Min/Max Amps	Pump-Out Station
1. Edgartown Harbor	(508) 627-4746	90	74	3	20.0 / 25.0	F	GD	R	50	P
2. Mad Max Marina	(508) 627-7400	165	71	8	15.0 / 15.0				30 / 100	
3. Edgartown Yacht Club-PRIVATE	(508) 627-4746		72		/	F				
OAK BLUFFS HARBOR										
4. Dockside Marina WiFi	(508) 693-3392	70	9	8	12.0 / 7.0		GD		30 / 50	P
5. Oak Bluffs Marina WiFi	(508) 693-4355	110	71	81	9.0 / 11.0		GD		30 / 50	P
VINEYARD HAVEN HARBOR										
6. Tisbury Wharf Company WiFi	(508) 693-9300	300	9	15	17.0 / 14.0		GD		30 / 100	P
7. Vineyard Haven Marina WiFi	(508) 693-0720	200	9	52	12.0 / 12.0				50 / 200+	P
8. The Black Dog Wharf WiFi	(508) 693-3854	190	72	15	14.0 / 11.0				30 / 100	P
9. Town Dock at Owen Park WiFi	(508) 696-4249	60	9		7.0 / 6.0					P
LAGOON POND										
10. Safe Harbor Vineyard Haven	(508) 693-4174	38	68	55	4.0 / 6.0	F	G	RH	15 / 30	P
MENEMSHA										
11. Menemsha Harbor, Town of Chilmark	(508) 645-2846	70	16		8.0 / 10.0	F	GD	R	30 / 50	P

WiFi Wireless Internet Access
Visit www.waterwayguide.com for current rates, fuel prices, website addresses and other up-to-the-minute information.
(Information in the table is provided by the facilities.)

Scan here for more details:

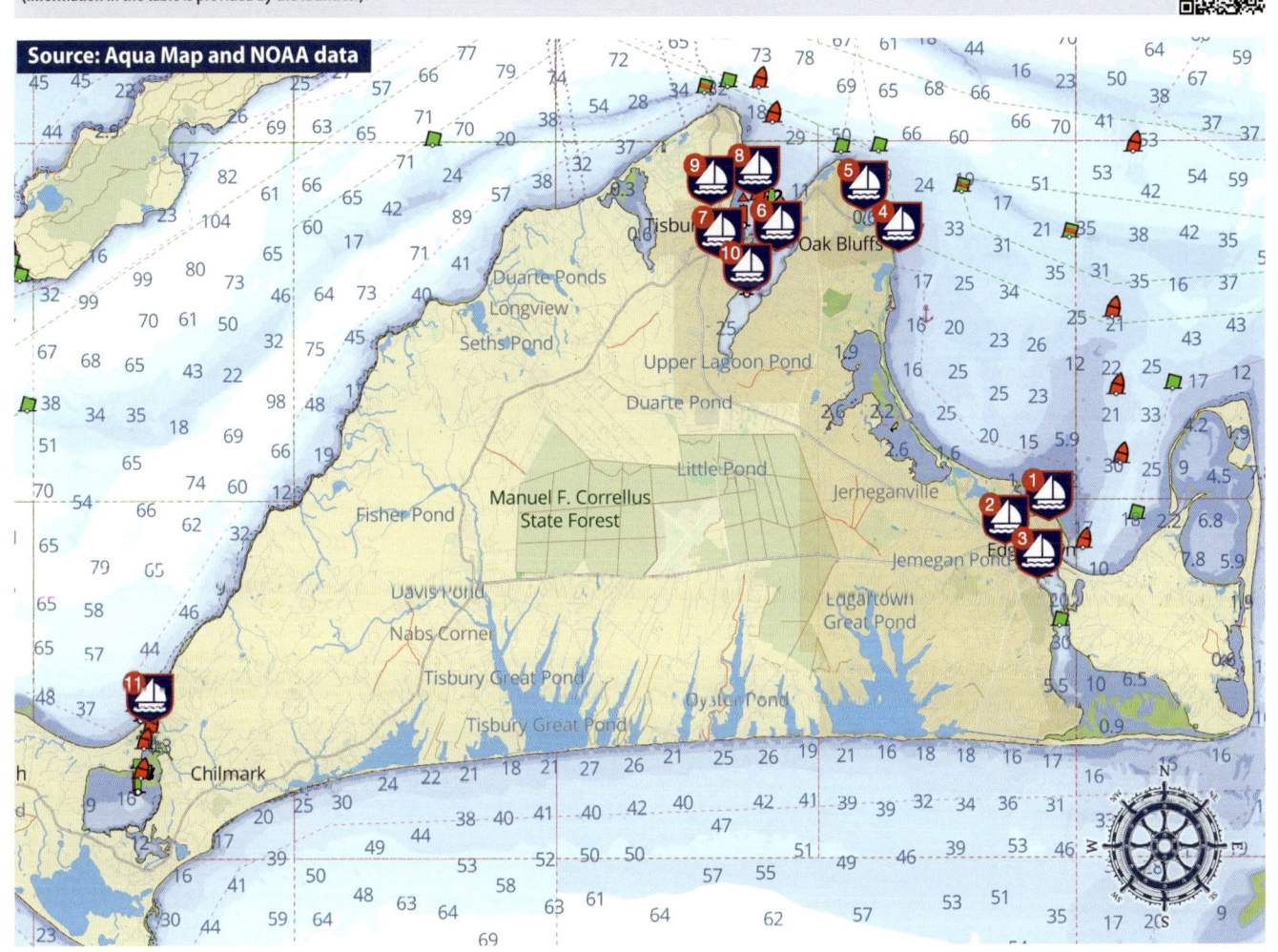

Source: Aqua Map and NOAA data

GOIN' ASHORE

EDGARTOWN, MA

ATTRACTIONS

1. Edgartown Art Gallery
Home to curated collection of oil paintings, watercolors, and pastels in a diversity of styles and subject matter at 27 S. Summer St. (508-627-5991).

2. Edgartown Harbor Light
One of five lighthouses on the island. Open seasonally (121 N. Water St., 508-627-4441).

3. Old Whaling Church
Funded by mariners and those dedicated to seafaring trades and quite literally built by them, too. Regarded as one of the finest examples of Greek Revival architecture in New England (89 Main St., 508-627-4442).

4. The Carnegie Heritage Center
Free museum and heritage center detailing local history. Located in the heart of Edgartown at 58 N. Water St. (774-549-9107).

5. Vincent House Museum & Gardens
Built in 1672, this modest home was constructed using traditional techniques of medieval England. The island's oldest surviving residence on the island, it was continuously owned by the Vincent family until 1940 (99 Main St., 508-627-8017).

SERVICES

6. Edgartown Post Office
29 Church St. (508-627-6029)

7. Edgartown Public Library
26 Edgartown-West Tisbury Rd. (508-627-4221)

8. Island Health Care
245 Edgartown-Vineyard Haven Rd. (508-939-9358)

9. Vineyard Veterinary Clinic
276 Edgartown-Vineyard Haven Rd. (508-627-5292)

MARINAS

10. Edgartown Harbor Master
1 Morse St. (508-627-4746)

11. Edgartown Yacht Club–PRIVATE
1 Dock St. (508-627-4361)

12. Mad Max Marina
25 Dock St. (508-627-7500)

The seaport village of Edgartown was the first colonial settlement on Martha's Vineyard and has been the county seat since 1642. In the late 1700s, Martha's Vineyard developed a booming whaling industry and by the 1800s, more than 100 Edgartown men were captains of whaling ships. Between Nantucket and Martha's Vineyard together, they owned one-quarter of America's whaling fleet. By the beginning of the 20th century, the influence of Edgartown in the whaling industry began to decline. Today, Edgartown is known more for summer tourism.

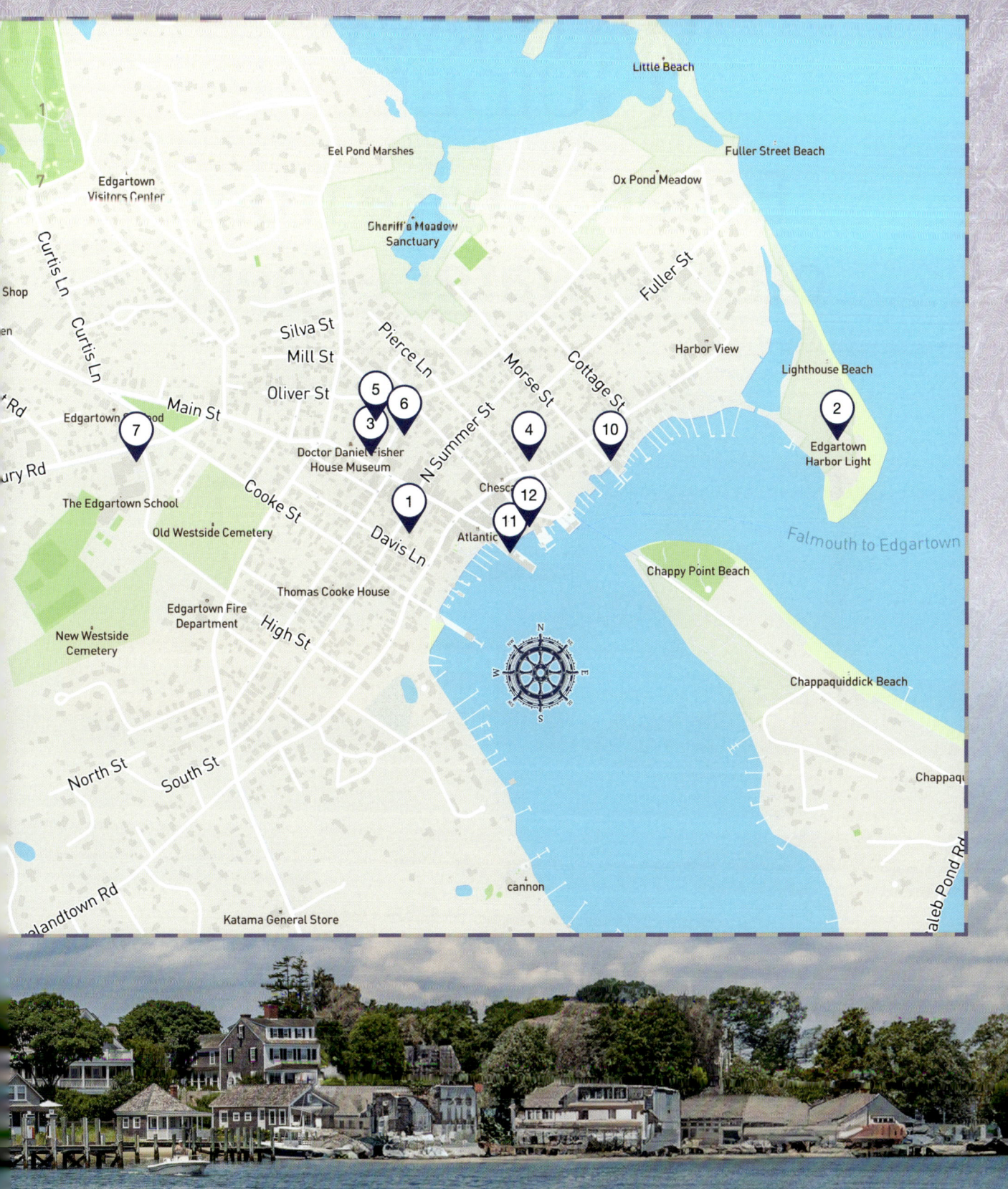

Little Beach

Eel Pond Marshes

Fuller Street Beach

Ox Pond Meadow

Edgartown
Visitors Center

Sheriff's Meadow
Sanctuary

Curtis Ln

Curtis Ln

Shop

Silva St

Mill St

Oliver St

Pierce Ln

Fuller St

Harbor View

Cottage St

Morse St

Lighthouse Beach

Rd

Main St

Edgartown Seafood

N Summer St

⑤

③

⑥

④

⑩

② Edgartown
Harbor Light

ury Rd

7

Doctor Daniel Fisher
House Museum

Cooke St

①

Chesc

⑫

Falmouth to Edgartown

The Edgartown School

Davis Ln

Atlantic

⑪

Chappy Point Beach

Old Westside Cemetery

Thomas Cooke House

N

Chappaquiddick Beach

New Westside
Cemetery

Edgartown Fire
Department

High St

W   E

S

Chappaqu

North St

South St

Caleb Pond Rd

Chappaqu

landtown Rd

cannon

Katama General Store

Edgartown, viewed from Chappaquiddick Island

Oak Bluffs

Photo courtesy of Oak Bluffs Division of Tourism

Oak Bluffs Harbor

Just to the south of the high bluffs of East Chop lies Oak Bluffs, known in the 19th century as "Cottage City." Tiny houses gaily painted and festooned with gingerbread and scrollwork can still be seen here at the Martha's Vineyard Camp Meeting Grounds, a Methodist camp that dates back to 1835. Today, Oak Bluffs is the resort harbor of Martha's Vineyard.

The harbor is crowded and hectic and there is much to enjoy here. Some skippers will actually pass on Oak Bluffs Harbor because it always looks full. In fact, because of the careful organization of this harbor, far more mooring and slip space is available than in either Vineyard Haven or Edgartown (but there's no room for anchoring).

NAVIGATION: The landlocked harbor has a dredged breakwater entry good for 7-foot MLW depths.

Access is straightforward, marked by a red 4-second flashing light atop a 30-foot-high tower at the end of the breakwater to the north. Be careful during the arrival or departure of the passenger ferry. Sharing space in the harbor channel with this vessel is not advisable.

Dockage/Moorings: Oak Bluffs Marina is the largest marina on Martha's Vineyard with 81 berths and 45 moorings. Their unusual, pear-shaped floats are marked "Town of Oak Bluffs." You will need your own bridle. Moorings are first-come, first-served; no reservations so be prepared to raft up (up to four boats per mooring). The marina offers launch service, a pump-out facility and easy access to nearby amenities. Note that it is not possible to take on water while refueling. To replenish water tanks you will need to contact the marina manager.

Another option is Dockside Marina, where dockage is against a sea wall with a ladder for low tide and pilings to keep you in place. Bags of ice are available at the fast-food stand at the head of the harbor. There's good eating along Circuit Ave. Just stroll up and back until the right scent hits you.

Vineyard Haven

In 1845 most coastal shipping traveled through Vineyard Sound with 13,814 vessels counted in that year alone. This was due to Vineyard Haven's premiere location on the sailing routes. The island's chief port, Vineyard Haven, still has a busy harbor that serves as the primary ferry terminal and the foremost commercial and recreational marine center.

The harbor is wide and open to the northeast but a rock breakwater protects the inner harbor beach and recreational beach from all but the worst of the incoming swells.

The beach is the big attraction on the Vineyard and many beaches can easily be reached from the marinas by bike. Beyond the numerous marine facilities, Vineyard Haven has just about any recreational and provisioning opportunity you might want set in the ambiance of an old New England village.

NAVIGATION: Enter Vineyard Haven Harbor between the lighthouses on the headlands of West Chop and East Chop. The harbor mouth is more than 1 mile wide at its outermost extremity, narrowing gradually upon approaching the inner harbor breakwater and the ferry wharf at harbor's head. Buoys on entry are gauged to deep-draft vessels; however, due respect must be paid the rocky ledges along the eastern shore of West Chop, which begin at Allegheny Rock, marked by green can "25" and west of red nun buoy "4."

One of the least known pleasures of Martha's Vineyard is the beautiful, ample and well-protected harbor of Lagoon Pond just southeast of Vineyard Haven Harbor and securely nestled beneath the bluffs of East Chop. The **Lagoon Pond Bridge** (closed vertical clearance of 15 feet) is a replacement for the 1935 original, which left only a small gap for masts to pass through. From May 15 through September 15, the draw opens on signal from 8:15 a.m. to 8:45 a.m., from 10:15 a.m. to 11:00 a.m., from 3:15 p.m. to 4:00 p.m., from 5:00 p.m. to 5:45 p.m. and from 7:30 p.m. to 8:00 p.m. At all other times the draw will open for the passage of vessels if at least a 4-hour advance notice is given by calling the number posted at the bridge. From September 16 through May 14 the draw will only open on signal if at least a 24-hour advance notice is given by calling the number posted at the bridge.

Dockage/Moorings: The conveniently located Tisbury Wharf Company accepts megayachts (to 300 feet) on one of three piers. Take advantage of the convenient shops and eateries across the street from Tisbury Wharf or explore the rest of the Island via the adjacent MV *Transit Authority*, which offers transportation to every island town and points of interest.

Nearby Vineyard Haven Marina is a "premiere boutique" facility that can accommodate megayachts (to

Harbour Houses on Nantucket Island

200 feet) and offers a private beach, on-site restaurant and other resort amenities. Family owned and -operated The Black Dog Wharf to the north has been a fixture here since 1964 and offers hourly tie-ups and long-term transient slips.

The Town Dock at Owen Park offers protected tie-ups (tucked behind the breakwater), whether hitched to the pier or tethered to a town mooring. Short-term tie ups are possible in 8- to 10-foot MLW depths alongside the municipal pier and an overnight stay may be arranged as well. The harbormaster's office also has free hot showers. Call the Harbormaster (VHF Channel 09) for availability and directions. A dinghy dock is available on the north side of the pier.

Safe Harbor Vineyard Haven maintains the rental moorings (to 45 feet) along the western side of Lagoon Pond. Lagoon Pond is navigable (controlling depth 6.5 feet MLW) and well-marked throughout its 1.75-mile length. Be sure to go south around the white private buoy at Robbins Rock about 1 mile past the restricted Lagoon Pond Bridge (closed vertical clearance of 15 feet).

> NOTE: The free town pump-out boat serves boats at marinas, on moorings or anchored. Call on VHF Channel 09.

Anchorage: Substantial anchorage room is still available outside the mooring field along the easterly side of West Chop- south of the rocky outcrop marked by a warning buoy and inside a line between red nun buoys "4" and "6." Holding is good with a firm bottom in 7 to 15 feet MLW but the area is fully exposed to the northeast and to the wakes of frequently arriving and departing ferries.

There is good holding at the Vineyard Haven anchorage. There is wind protection from all directions except north-northeast. Expect some ferry and other boat wakes. There is good access by dinghy to the town ferry dock. Public washrooms are available in the park. Provisioning options are a short walk from the dinghy dock, and there is a West Marine Express within walking distance.

Powerful blows from the northeast can easily be ridden out beneath the highest of the tan-and-white cliffs on the eastern shore of Lagoon Pond, where you will find 7 to 9 feet MLW. There is a three-day anchoring limit. A dinghy dock is available at the boat ramp just north of Cedar Neck.

Vineyard Hiking & Biking

Martha's Vineyard is home to dozens of hiking trails through the woods, along the oceanfront and high over the bluffs. A few of the very accessible trails include:

• Great Rock Bight–located off North Road in Chilmark with a few miles of easy hiking and views of Vineyard Sound. Trails are dog friendly.

• Long Point Wildlife Refuge–offers miles of trails with broad vistas and lots of island vegetation on the south shore. Trail leads right to the beach.

• Caroline Tuthill Preserve–easy to access off of Edgartown-Vineyard Haven Road and leads over hills and through the woods. Water views are of Sengekontacket Pond. Trail is dog friendly.

• Menemsha Hills–a 211-acre preserve where you can climb the second-highest point on Martha's Vineyard for awesome ocean views. Three miles of trails transit wetlands, woodland groves, coastal plains and a rocky ocean edge. Dogs are not allowed.

• John Presbury Norton Farm to Womesket Preserve– easy hiking trails that eventually lead to Blackwater Pond. Trail is dog friendly.

• Chappaquiddick Island–offers several trails.

Trail maps for most of these hikes are available at www.thetrustees.org.

It is possible to anchor in 6 to 10 feet MLW with good holding in sand and mud in Lake Tashmoo on the north side of Martha's Vineyard. There is a well-marked channel leading into this protected anchorage and a dinghy dock at the foot of Lake Street. There is a three-day anchoring limit here as well.

Note that the entrance channel to Lake Tashmoo has shoaled again after winter storms and there are places in the entrance channel showing 4-5 feet MLW. Approach the red buoy at the entrance on a course of 220° M, aiming between the stone jetties. Once between the jetties stay left of center until you reach the end of the stone jetty on the right side then swing right to hug the right side of the channel until about halfway to the first red buoy inside the harbor. Then you should move a little closer to center channel until past the first red buoy. After this follow the red and green buoys into the main harbor.

Watch out for a couple of large sandbanks on the right farther into the harbor. The sands in the channel are constantly shifting so enter with caution and be prepared for changes in the best course.

Menemsha

Consciously quaint Menemsha, about 3 nm east of Aquinnah (Gay Head) on the Vineyard Sound side, is a fishing port working at staying unspoiled. You can hike along vacant dunes, watch the long liners unload, socialize with local artists and get a well-prepared meal or deli sandwich here.

The Menemsha Basin is homeport to lobster boats, trawlers, sportfishers and charter and party boats. Shanties used by fishers line the picturesque but crowded harbor head. A couple of fish markets, several fine restaurants, a market and a wide variety of shops can be found in this picturesque town. Fish markets will cook your purchase if requested and you can go behind the market and eat at one of their picnic tables.

Menemsha is the closest harbor to Aquinnah, the westernmost town on Martha's Vineyard, which is not easily accessible by boat. The Wampanoag Tribe runs the Aquinnah Cultural Center (508-645-7900) and gift shop. Other gift and craft shops as well as restaurants and snack shops are nearby. You can also walk to Gay Head Light (circa 1844), which was moved 129 feet back from the

Menemsha Harbor

eroding cliff in 2015 and offers a magnificent view of the Elizabeth Islands.

> NOTE: While many long-time residents and visitors will still refer to Aquinnah as "Gay Head," all road signs have been changed.

NAVIGATION: Access to the Menemsha Basin is straightforward and can handle commercial drafts of up to 18 feet. The entrance is marked by green lighted bell buoy "1," which is located approximately 300 yards off the channel's mouth. The 25-foot-high, 4-second flashing green "3" indicates the end of the seawall to the northeast and a 43-foot, 4-second flashing red "2" indicates the stone jetty prominent to the southwest. The currents in this passage are straightforward and swift. It is best to pick a slack tide for entry.

Just past the entrance to Menemsha Harbor, the channel continues up to Menemsha Pond. This pond is shallow and overnight stays are not allowed even if you have a shallow draft boat. There is, however, good clam and mussel digging in the pond. Be sure to get a shellfish license if you decide to dinghy in and dig around. The town publishes a brochure detailing this area at Menesha Pond.

Dockage/Moorings: Transients can be accommodated at Menemsha Harbor, Town of Chilmark with slips and a 120-foot linear transient dock on the east side of the harbor. There is space for larger vessels (up to 85 feet) on the west side of the harbor. The docks cater to powerboats and there are moorings for sailboats.

Two heavy town moorings are offered in the inner harbor but expect to raft up (50-foot maximum boat length). There are six additional moorings in the outer harbor. Only use these moorings in a prevailing southerly. They can be extremely uncomfortable otherwise. There are showers but few other amenities and no launch service. Contact the Chilmark Harbormaster on VHF Channel 16. Fuel can be acquired from the town dock or Menemsha Texaco Service, which also sells ice (no slips).

> NOTE: Menemsha is a No-Discharge Zone with $1,000 cash fine for violators (treated effluent included). A pump-out station is available.

Anchorage: There is plenty of room to anchor in Menemsha Bight with protection from the east-southeast. There is easy beach and harbor access by dinghy. Exploring the inner pond by dingy is fun and sunsets are an "event" here.

■ SIDE TRIP: NANTUCKET ISLAND

Nantucket, one of the most beautiful islands on the east coast, is 14 miles long, 3.5 miles wide and 27 miles out to sea. It is by far one of the most popular vacation spots for cruisers. When you first step ashore, you will be overwhelmed by the feeling you are stepping back in history when whaling ships filled the port and sea captains walked the gas-lit cobblestone streets.

The entire island of Nantucket is a historic district designated as a National Historic Landmark. Don't miss an opportunity to visit and spend time on this island out of time; your experience will be memorable.

NAVIGATION: A passage to Nantucket crosses some 30 miles of open water and may call for navigation in fog. The journey to Nantucket from the west is between shoals: south of Horseshoe Shoal; north of Hawes, Norton and Cross Rip shoals; and then east of Tuckernuck Shoal. The closer to the shoals your course, the more noticeable the tidal rips.

Aids to navigation are widely spaced. Frequent dead reckoning and GPS fixes should be considered mandatory as is a keen lookout (with radar if possible) for other recreational boats, fishing vessels and ferries that frequent these much-traveled waters. If the sky is clear and the water sparkling, the island stands out in spectacular fashion, even though its highest point is only 108 feet above sea level.

The red-and-white Morse (A) bell buoy "NB" marks the entrance to the buoyed 1.5-mile channel leading to Brant Point. Semi-submerged breakwaters to either side reveal the danger of straying beyond the channel's confines. A navigational range (two towers: the first a quick-flashing light and the second a constant light) will come into view directly down the center of the channel just west of the Brant Point Lighthouse. Follow the channel buoys while turning slightly to port in order to round the 26-foot occulting red 4-second Brant Point Lighthouse. Keep a watchful eye for ferryboats and other vessels that must also negotiate this relatively narrow passage.

Once beyond Brant Point, Nantucket Boat Basin becomes immediately evident ahead, and just to the south of the boat basin enclosure, the town pier usually has a raft of fishing vessels tied to its T-shaped end. To the east of the wide inner-harbor channel upon entry, a large mooring field also should be visible.

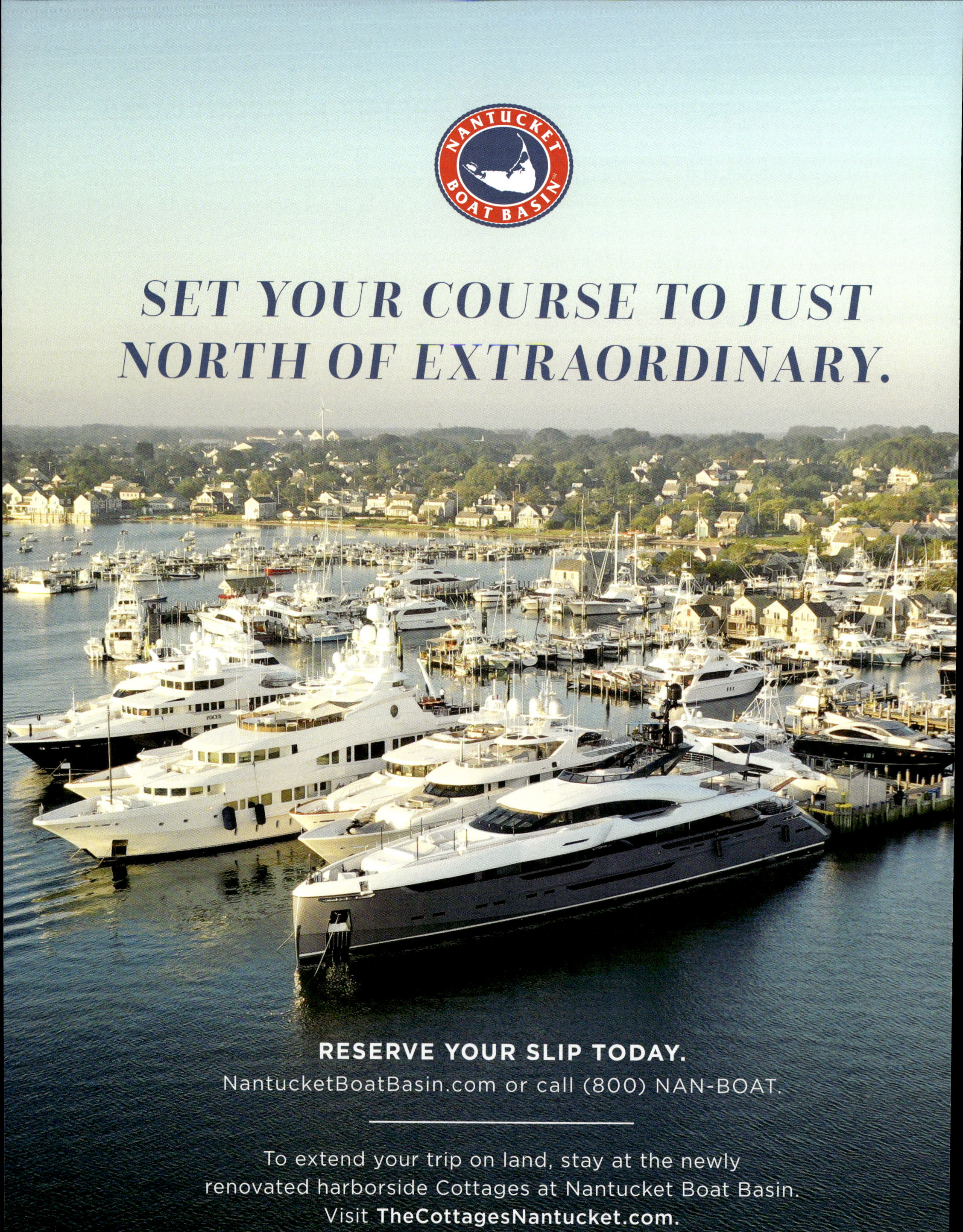

SET YOUR COURSE TO JUST NORTH OF EXTRAORDINARY.

RESERVE YOUR SLIP TODAY.

NantucketBoatBasin.com or call (800) NAN-BOAT.

To extend your trip on land, stay at the newly
renovated harborside Cottages at Nantucket Boat Basin.
Visit **TheCottagesNantucket.com.**

Nantucket Harbor, MA

NANTUCKET		Largest Vessel	VHF	Total Slips	Approach/ Dockside Depth	Floating Docks	Gas/ Diesel	Repairs/ Haulout	Min/Max Amps	Pump-Out Station
1. Nantucket Yacht Club-PRIVATE	(508) 228-1400	110			15.0 / 15.0			H		
2. Nantucket Boat Basin WiFi	(508) 325-1350	200	9	240	12.0 / 12.0		GD		30 / 200+	P
3. Nantucket Moorings	(508) 228-4472	85	68		11.0 /					P

WiFi Wireless Internet Access
Visit www.waterwayguide.com for current rates, fuel prices, website addresses and other up-to-the-minute information.
(Information in the table is provided by the facilities.)

Scan here for more details: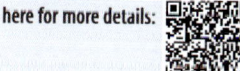

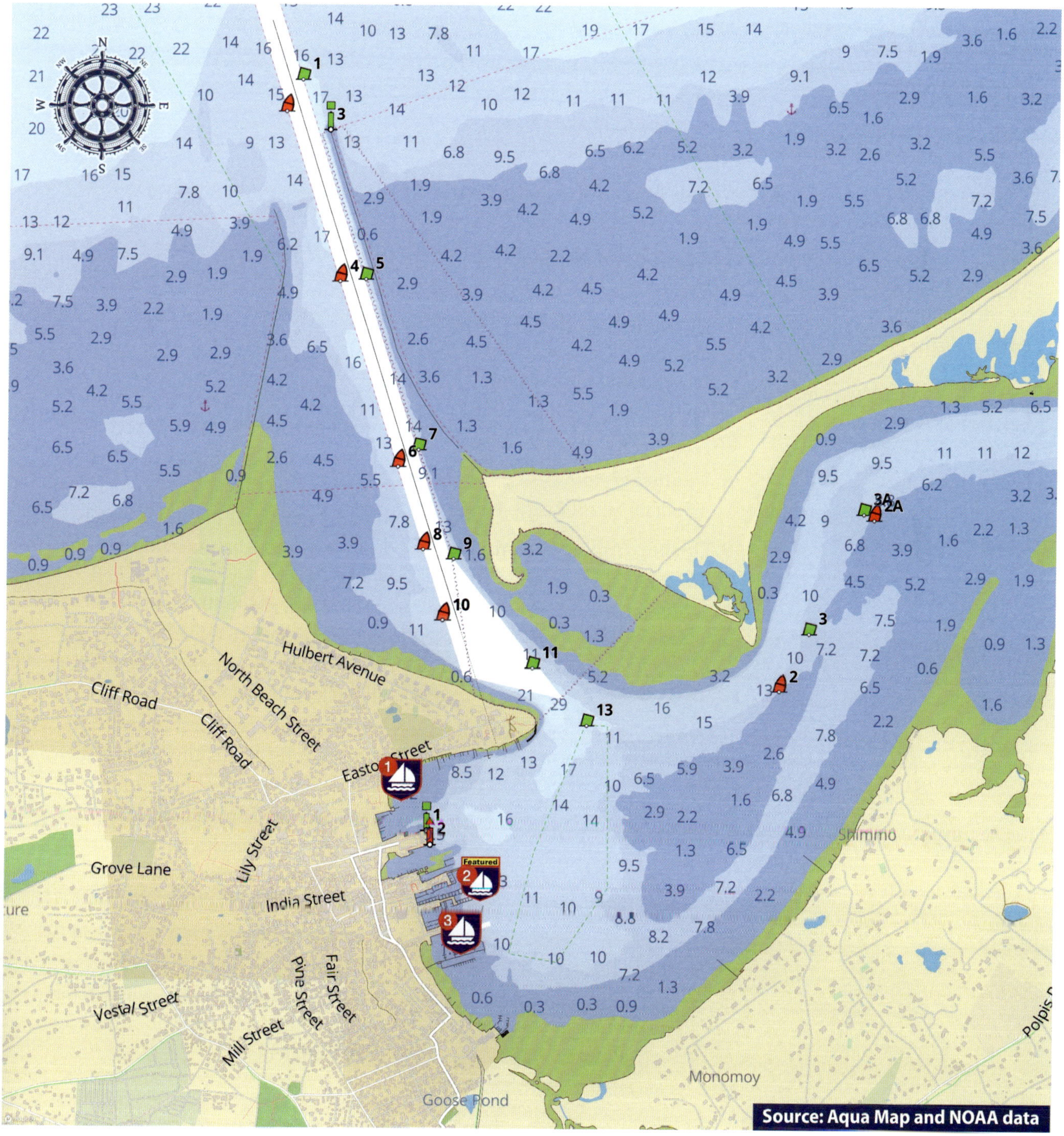

Source: Aqua Map and NOAA data

GOIN' ASHORE

NANTUCKET, MA

ATTRACTIONS

1. Brant Point Lighthouse
Scenic 26-foot tall, cylindrical, wood tower was built as a replacement in 1901 and is the ninth light station built at this historic site on Easton St. since colonial times.

2. Nantucket Whaling Museum
World-class collection of whaling artifacts, exhibits and tours at 13 Broad St. (508-228-1894). A "must see" is a fully reconstructed 46-foot-long sperm whale skeleton that is now on display at the museum.

3. Natural Science Museum
Learn about the plants, animals, and birds of Nantucket at this cross between a history museum, zoo and science center (7 Milk St., 508-228-0898).

4. Jethro Coffin House
Saltbox home built in 1686, well-known as the oldest house on Nantucket. Tours are available at 16 Sunset Hill Ln. (508-228-1894).

5. The Old Mill
Built in 1746, this is believed to be the oldest American windmill in continuous operation.

SERVICES

6. Nantucket Cottage Hospital
57 Prospect St. (508-825-8165)

7. Nantucket Atheneum
Worth a visit on architectural merit alone but you will also find current newspapers and periodicals, as well as some solitude in this literary oasis (1 India St., 508-228-1110).

8. Nantucket Post Office
5 Federal St. (508-228-4477)

9. Offshore Animal Hospital
11 Crooked Ln. (508-228-1491)

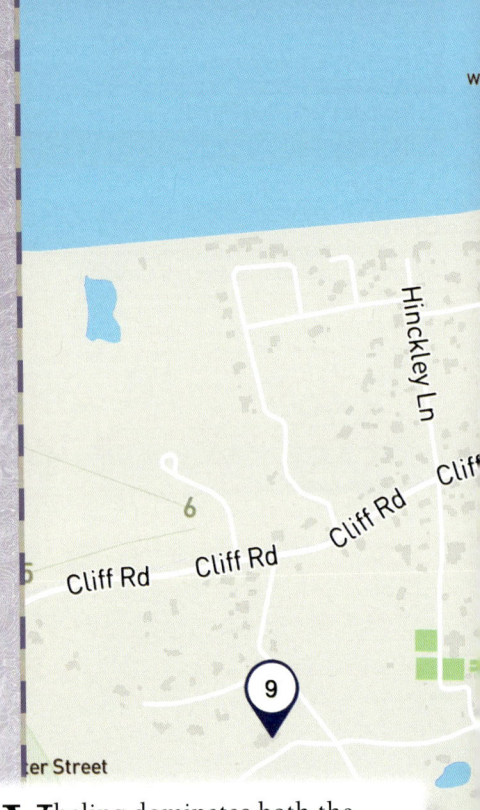

Whaling dominates both the history and current mystique of this far-flung and naturally barren sea island of Nantucket. From as far back as the 1700s Nantucket was known as the whaling capitol of the world. *Moby Dick* was published in 1851 after Melville came to Nantucket before the whaling boom in 1830. Hundreds of people from all walks of life worked the rope walks, candle factories, chandleries and sail lofts of this tiny Industrial island. The last whaling ship left Nantucket in 1869. Local author Nathanial Philbrick's *In the Heart of the Sea* summed up the history and intensity of the whaling industry quite poetically and is a must read. It didn't take long for tourism to thrive on this wind-swept island where today it is the principal source of income for island residents.

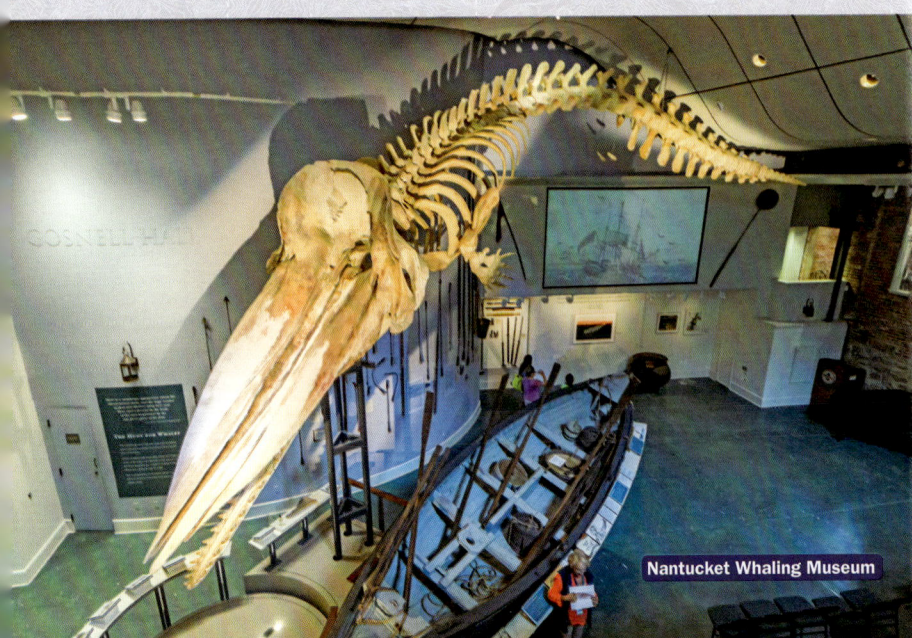

Nantucket Whaling Museum

MARINAS

10. Nantucket Boat Basin
Swains Wharf (508-325-1350)

11. Nantucket Moorings
34 Washington St.
(508-228-7261)

12. Nantucket Yacht Club
1 S. Beach St. (508-228-1400)

Brant Point Light Station

Dockage/Moorings: Nantucket Boat Basin sets an industry standard for service for transients. You will find slips to accommodate boats to 200 feet as well as dockside electricity, water, all fuels, propane refills and individualized pump-out stations designed to reach virtually every slip. Ashore are restroom and shower facilities, a large 24-hour coin-operated laundry, rental cottages and lofts along the wharves and even a pet-friendly park.

The concierge, located on the fuel dock, will arrange restaurant reservations, sightseeing trips, car rentals and such. The management recommends early reservations (before March) for this popular, end-destination marina; many peak-season weekends are booked as much as a year in advance.

Nantucket Moorings holds the exclusive town franchise for 125 transient moorings and maintains a field of round white floats secured by heavy tackle. Expect to pay daily rates for these (without other services) that are among the highest in New England. Even at this premium, the popularity of this destination harbor is such that an advance reservation is highly recommended. Nantucket Yacht Club at the head of the harbor is strictly private (members and guests only).

Harbor Launch (hail on VHF Channel 68) will provide reliable service and their dock personnel will dispose of your trash for an extra fee.

Anchorage: The space shown as "General Anchorage" on some charts is almost completely filled with moorings. Some limited anchor room still remains in Nantucket Harbor North and Nantucket Harbor East in 15 to 20 feet MLW with excellent holding. If you do not mind a considerable dinghy ride to town, there is plenty of swing room and 10- to 12-foot MLW depths in the harbor behind Coatue. Holding is spotty (due to grass) but the scenery is splendid.

Wherever you anchor in Nantucket Harbor, the protection afforded by a nearby "landmass" identified on the chart as Coatue is deceptive: Low-lying dunes do not block the wind.

The fetch is considerable, particularly from the east and northwest, portending wet dinghy (even launch) rides and rock-and-roll evenings during all but the most settled weather.

A dinghy dock is just inside the southern side of the town's T-shaped pier. Water is available at the T-end of the town pier where you will also find a free pump-out station. A second, larger dinghy float complex is on the north side of the pier closer to shore.

Restrooms and showers are located at the head of the dock just behind the Harbormaster's office. Recycling bins and a dumpster are located on the right side of the Harbormaster's office and bags of cube ice are available for purchase inside. The center of town is a pleasant two-block walk to the right from here.

In addition to the town's pump-out station, Nantucket Boat Basin offers courtesy pump-out service at its fuel dock, immediately north of the municipal pier. For boats on moorings or at anchor, the town operates a free pump-out boat: call "Headhunter" (get it?) on VHF Channel 09 or contact the Nantucket Harbormaster (also VHF Channel 09 or 508-228-7260) for pump-out boat hours and availability.

NOTE: Nantucket is a federal No-Discharge Zone: no dumping of sewage—treated or untreated—is permitted, holding tanks must be used and heads must be sealed.

Section 5: Above Cape Cod

Chapter 14: Cape Cod Bay to Salem Sound, MA

Chapter 15: Gloucester, MA to Cape Elizabeth, ME

Chapter 16: Casco Bay & the Mid-Coast of Maine

Chapter 17: Penobscot Bay & Down East Maine

Eastport

Sorrento

Castine

Frenchman Bay

Mount Desert Island

Deer Island

Penobscot Bay

Rockport

Island Au Haut

Rockland

Vinalhaven Island

Kennebec River

Bath

Boothbay Harbor

Freeport

Casco Bay

Monhegan Island

Portland

Cape Elizabeth

Kennebunkport

Portsmouth

Atlantic Ocean

Newburyport

Gloucester

Salem Sound

Marblehead

Boston

Boston Harbor

Scituate

Provincetown

Plymouth

Cape Cod Bay

Chapter 17: Page 561

Chapter 16: Page 519

Chapter 15: Page 491

Chapter 14: Page 446

Salem Sound

Pages 479-490

Salem

Marblehead

Pages 467-479

Boston

Boston Harbor

Massachusetts Bay

Atlantic Ocean

Cohasset

Scituate

Green Harbor River

Duxbury

Provincetown

Plymouth

Wellfleet

Pages 460-466

Cape Cod Bay

Sesuit

Barnstable

Pages 449-459

Distances — Down East

This table provides point-to-point mileage for the Maine coast. All distances are given in approximate nautical miles.

LOCATION	MILES
SAND COAST	
Kittery	0
York Harbor	11
Wells Harbor	14
Kennebunk River	5
Cape Porpoise Harbor	5
Biddeford/Saco	15
CASCO BAY	
Portland Head Light	19
Falmouth Foreside	7
Yarmouth	8
South Freeport	8
Potts Harbor, Harpswell Neck (from Portland Light)	11
Mackerel Cove, Bailey Island	6
SEGUIN ISLAND TO MUSCONGUS BAY	
Seguin Island	15
Bath, Kennebec River	12
Ebencock Harbor, Sheepscot River (from Seguin Island)	8
Boothbay Harbor (from Seguin Island)	10
Christmas Cove, Damariscotta River	6
Pemaquid Point	4
Monhegan Island	9
Friendship (from Pemaquid Point)	12
PENOBSCOT BAY	
Rockland (from Pemaquid Point)	31
Rockport	6
Camden	5
Dark Harbor, Isleboro Island	7
Belfast	11
Castine (from Rockland)	22
Stonington, Deer Isle (from Rockland)	20
Carvers Harbor, Vinalhaven (from Rockland)	13
Isle au Haut	11
MOUNT DESERT/FRENCHMAN BAY	
Southwest/Northeast Harbors	28
Bar Harbor	12
Winter Harbor	6
EAST OF SCHOODIC POINT	
Petit Manan Island (from Bar Harbor)	17
Jonesport	17
Machiasport	20
Cutler	13
West Quoddy Head	15
Lubec	3
Eastport	3

Distances — MA Waters

This table provides both point-to-point and cumulative distances from the Cape Cod Canal and from Boston. All measurements are given in approximate nautical miles.

LOCATION	BETWEEN POINTS	CUMULATIVE
EAST FROM CAPE COD CANAL		
Cape Cod Canal	0	0
Barnstable	10	10
Sesuit Harbor	7	17
Wellfleet	12	29
Provincetown	25	54
NORTH FROM CAPE COD CANAL		
Cape Cod Canal	0	0
Plymouth	20	20
Duxbury	2	22
Scituate	18	40
Cohasset	6	46
Boston	15	61
NORTH FROM BOSTON		
Boston	0	0
Marblehead	19	19
Salem	5	24
Beverly	1	25
Manchester	6	31
Gloucester	5	36
Rockport	1	753
Essex	8	61
Newburyport	16	77
Rye	15	92
Portsmouth	6	98
Isles of Shoals (offshore)	7	105

■ NAVIGATION NOTES

The cold waters north and east of Cape Cod are the birthplace of much of America's maritime heritage. Every harbor and almost every ledge carries a piece of American history or a legend of the sea. Cruising these waters gives the modern-day sailor a strong feeling of sea tradition.

The fastest traditional sailing ships the world has ever known sailed out of these ports including the great clipper ships Flying Cloud, Sovereign of the Seas and Lightning, among others. Often considered the most seaworthy and able sailing vessels ever built, the huge Gloucester fishing schooners made their fame and fortune fishing the Grand Banks in the dead of winter. They were designed and built along the river banks near Cape Ann.

Cruising Conditions

Cape Cod is shaped like a great sandy arm–the upper arm extending easterly 31 miles from the mainland, the forearm heading 25 miles northward and then the fist angling 7 miles back west. Most boats make the leisurely cruise up the coast to explore the historical ports from Plymouth to Boston, Marblehead, Salem and Gloucester and then on to Portsmouth, Kittery and the beginning of the Down East coast.

For others, the eastern end of Cape Cod Canal is the jumping-off point for a short offshore run to Gloucester on Cape Ann then another run for Portland Harbor's large navigational buoy (which replaced an old lightship), from which all of Casco Bay, the Mid-Coast and Penobscot Bay are easily accessible. Others bide a while in Provincetown before the long offshore run directly to Isle au Haut or Mount Desert Island and Acadia National Park. These routes take you through Stellwagen Bank, a prolific whale-watching area.

A voyage in these waters warrants considerable preparation and flexibility. A journey from one harbor to another will probably involve a stretch of open water so skipper, crew and vessel must be prepared for the challenge. The water is markedly colder than the water below the Cape and the vessel's water supply and hull will feel much cooler as a result. Most locals and cruising boats that tackle this area have a heating source to warm up the cabin on cool mornings. Swimming is a more venturesome exercise than in more southern climes, and an accidental swim must be considered a matter of life or death because hypothermia is a risk, even in the summer.

Fog can be a factor on any day (especially in June and July), although it might burn off by mid-morning and leave a clear, warm day. A wind from a southerly or easterly direction may bring in unannounced fog at any time. The skipper making his way through "a pea-souper" for the first time is likely to take his navigational skills more seriously thereafter. Fog is usually accompanied by calm waters and light winds but beware the "smoky sou'wester." During this condition a stiff breeze builds up rough seas that

PROVINCETOWN MARINA

Provincetown, Massachusetts

break on the ledges and obscure the sounds of bells and gongs. And if the fog remains heavy, obscuring islands, buoys and other boats, it is advisable to stay put in the harbor.

The rise and fall of the tide is an important factor in each day's plans, especially as you voyage farther east Tides of 10 to 13 feet are not unusual in these parts. Keep in mind that many harbors are available to even the deepest-draft vessels at high tide, but that same tide can put you high and dry where hours earlier there was plenty of water underneath the keel. Conversely, anchoring for low-tide depths will be dangerously short scope at high water.

Furthermore, that ledge at the mouth of the harbor that is clearly visible as you enter at low water might be submerged and dangerous when you leave. Tidal currents are less predictable than they are below Cape Cod and may unexpectedly flow even after predicted high and low tides.

Navigation

The charted Pollack Rip Channel leads from Nantucket Sound and across the Monomoy Shoal to the ship channel off Cape Cod. The east entrance to Pollock Rip Channel continues to have severe shoaling east of flashing red "4." When transiting the channel, mariners are urged to transit at their slowest safe speed and proceed with extreme caution.

The passage through or around the crooked elbow of Cape Cod may not win you an earring like crossing the equator, but it marks a major step for most coastal cruising plans and the entrance into an endless mariner's paradise. To cruise "above

the Cape" is to venture farther away from civilization and the recreational boating crowds. Self-sufficiency and competent seamanship become more important.

The water is colder, weather changes quickly, the fog is thicker and the ledges are crueler in the swells of the open ocean. The sea here can be less forgiving to carelessness and inexperience than any other waters we cover. There are no barrier islands offering an "inside passage" and protection from the sweep of the sea, except in small cross-cuts between rivers and deep in the bigger bays.

Anchoring & Mooring

In many, if not most harbors mentioned in this guide, designated Special Anchorage Areas are available in which vessels of less than 20 meters in length are not required to show anchor lights, day shapes or sound signals. Anchoring within a Special Anchorage Area does not require permission but permission for the use of mooring balls within or outside of a Special Anchorage Area is required.

In spite of the proliferation of mooring balls, it is often possible to still find places to anchor, both within and outside of the Special Anchorage Areas, keeping an appropriate distance from mooring balls, channels, docks, boatyards and marinas (not to mention other boats).

Also, as previously mentioned, "yacht club" here doesn't necessarily mean private, as it does farther south. Many private clubs welcome transients and not necessarily from reciprocal yacht clubs. Call ahead for details.

■ PROVINCETOWN TO CAPE COD CANAL

In contrast to the resort atmosphere on the south side of the Cape Cod arm, the ambiance inside the curve of Cape Cod Bay is quiet and relaxed. Even the weather cooperates. The boisterous southwester that creates heavy seas in Buzzards Bay can become a pleasant offshore breeze on Cape Cod Bay.

Beyond Plymouth, flats, shoals, ledges and rocks appear, big headlands and capes thrust outward and harbors are spaced far apart. Yet, inside the welcoming harbors of Provincetown and Wellfleet, sand dunes and sea grass mark your way and make for relaxed beachcombing.

Provincetown

Located at the extreme northern tip of Cape Cod, Provincetown has one of the most popular large harbors on the Atlantic coast. The marinas and some moorings are tucked behind an extended seawall and all of the anchorages are lovely and give access either to the highly entertaining town or the beaches wrapping around to protect the harbor against ocean surge.

In Provincetown (affectionately called "P-town") makes a wonderful stop because of its vibrant arts scene, performance street artists, a variety of restaurants and the delightful nightlife. Much like Key West, it has a salty edge of the world feel. If the busy town overwhelms, rent a bicycle, horse, car or beach buggy to get away to the fine beaches. Far Land Provisions is a deli/bakery offering sandwiches and light fare plus specialty grocery items within

GOIN' ASHORE

PROVINCETOWN, MA

ATTRACTIONS

1. Pilgrim Monument

The 252-foot monument is the tallest all-granite structure in the country and commemorates the Mayflower Pilgrims' first landing in the New World in Provincetown in November 1620. Access from downtown is via an inclined elevator on Bradford St. adjacent to Town Hall. Tickets are available and a quick ride in the glass enclosed cabin brings you to the base of the monument. The walk to the top includes 116 steps and 60 ramps and takes about 10 minutes at a leisurely pace. Provides great views of the harbor.

2. Provincetown Art Association and Museum

Permanent collection and special exhibitions in six gallery spaces, plus three landscaped sculpture gardens at 460 Commercial St. (508-487-1750).

3. Provincetown Museum

Local museum highlighting the town's rich maritime and cultural stories, early days of modern American theater, building of the monument and an interactive multimedia presentation that illustrates the early history of the Wampanoag Nation on Cape Cod, up to and including the arrival of the Mayflower in 1620. Located at (1 High Pole Hill Rd., 508-487-1310).

4. SEA SPACE Marine Discovery Center

Family friendly exhibits and hands-on activities offered daily at 237 Commercial St. (508-487-3623). Admission is free.

5. Shark Center Provincetown

Offers visitors in-depth look at great white sharks through interactive exhibits, videos and displays at historic MacMillan Wharf. Shark ecotourism trip available on 25-foot vessel. (Reservations must be made in advance.)

SERVICES

6. Lands' End Marine Supply

Chain hardware store with home tools and some boat supplies (337 Commercial St., 508-487-0784).

7. Outer Cafe Health Services

49 Harry Kemp Way (508-487-9395)

8. Provincetown Laundromat

68 Shank Painter Rd. (508-487-9835)

9. Provincetown Post Office

219 Commercial St. (508-487-0368)

10. Provincetown Public Library

Town library in an airy former church built in 1860 with a half-scale model of a 1905 schooner at 356 Commercial St. (508-487-7094).

11. Veterinary Wellness Center of Provincetown

43 Race Point Rd. (508-909-4800)

THE FIRST LANDING PLACE OF THE PILGRIMS, NOV. 11, 1620, O.S. THE MAP IN MOURT'S RELATION SHOWS THAT NEAR THIS SPOT THE PILGRIMS FIRST TOUCHED FOOT ON AMERICAN SOIL. ERECTED BY THE RESEARCH CLUB OF PROVINCETOWN 1917

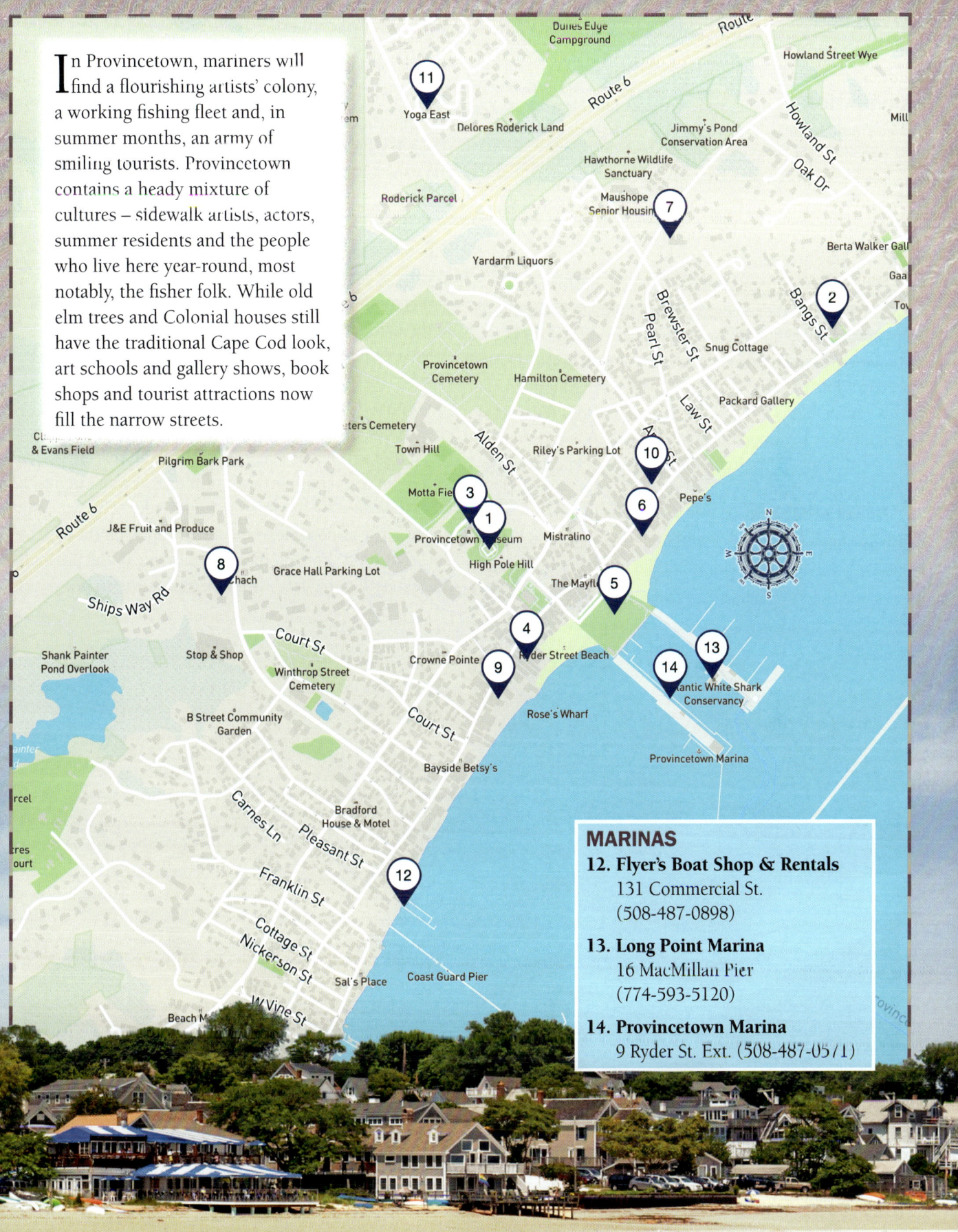

In Provincetown, mariners will find a flourishing artists' colony, a working fishing fleet and, in summer months, an army of smiling tourists. Provincetown contains a heady mixture of cultures – sidewalk artists, actors, summer residents and the people who live here year-round, most notably, the fisher folk. While old elm trees and Colonial houses still have the traditional Cape Cod look, art schools and gallery shows, book shops and tourist attractions now fill the narrow streets.

MARINAS

12. Flyer's Boat Shop & Rentals
131 Commercial St.
(508-487-0898)

13. Long Point Marina
16 MacMillan Pier
(774-593-5120)

14. Provincetown Marina
9 Ryder St. Ext. (508-487-0571)

walking distance (150 Bradford St., 508-487-0045). Should you need boat supplies, Lands' End Marine Supply is at 337 Commercial St. (508-487-0784).

NAVIGATION: The big, wide Provincetown Harbor is over 1 mile from Long Point to the town dock and is easy to enter under almost any condition. Situational awareness is important, nonetheless. Quite a few schooners, whale-watching tours and fishing charter boats operate in the area and it's a popular place to show off one's tacking prowess.

Whether coming in from offshore, the Boston area or the canal, the rounded edges of Race Point and Wood End can be approached very closely unless weather dictates otherwise. Race Point's 41-foot flashing light is also a radio beacon while 45-foot Wood End Light is a flashing red with a horn that is quite useful in seasonal fog. The end of Long Point is less approachable. Make for quick-flashing green bell buoy "3" rather than for the 36-foot occulting green light on shore.

Dockage/Moorings: A cluster of facilities on Provincetown Harbor offer slips and moorings. Long Point Marina is situated just seaward of the town landing with

a few transient slips and a mooring field. Note that while they have water and electricity, they do not offer showers.

Provincetown Marina has a 650-foot wave attenuator dock that provides a calm boat basin for its 100 slips and 100 moorings. They allow boaters to fill their water tanks or wash their boats for a fixed fee. Amenities include showers, lockers, laundry and an outdoor Captain's Lounge with large-screen TVs and fire pits. Just a short walk down the pier is the downtown and Commercial St. with an incredible array of restaurants and shops. Reserve as early as March if looking to visit on peak weekends.

Flyer's Boat Shop & Rentals also maintains moorings in the harbor. Fees include unlimited daytime launch service. Call for details. The Provincetown Harbormaster may be reached at 508-487-7030 and VHF Channel 12 is monitored for pump-out service.

Anchorage: The mooring field now completely fills previously acceptable anchoring areas. You may be able to find room to anchor northeast of the breakwater in 6 to 12 feet MLW, keeping in mind the 9-foot tides. This area puts you as close as possible to the dinghy dock on the first dock out from shore on the northeast side of the pier but it is exposed to big fetch from the east to the south.

Cape Cod Bay, MA

PROVINCETOWN		Largest Vessel	VHF	Total Slips	Approach/ Dockside Depth	Floating Docks	Gas/ Diesel	Repairs/ Haulout	Min/Max Amps	Pump-Out Station
1. Long Point Marina WiFi	(774) 593-5120	140	14	14	20.0 / 11.0	F	D	R	30 / 100	
2. Provincetown Marina WiFi	(508) 487-0571	250	9	100	13.0 / 13.0	F	GD		30 / 200+	P
3. Flyer's Boat Shop & Rentals WiFi	(508) 487-0898	95	11		25.0 / 12.0	F		RH		P
WELLFLEET										
4. Town of Wellfleet Marina	(508) 349-0320	55	16	200	10.0 / 6.0	F	GD		30	P

WiFi Wireless Internet Access
Visit www.waterwayguide.com for current rates, fuel prices, website addresses and other up-to-the-minute information.
(Information in the table is provided by the facilities.)

Scan here for more details:

Source: Aqua Map and NOAA data

The anchorage 1 mile south of the Provincetown breakwall has better protection from the prevailing southwesterly winds but it is reportedly more shallow than the north anchorage. Get as close to the ledge as your draft permits and be cautious of a sunken fishing boat marked with a small red buoy located towards the east side of the anchorage. Chop can create a long, wet ride back from town in any real southwesterly.

Anchoring is prohibited around the piers and between the breakwall and the mooring field on the southwest side.

Wellfleet Harbor

The next viable harbor for shallow draft boats is Wellfleet Harbor. Once second only to Gloucester as a cod and mackerel fishing port, Wellfleet is a quiet summer resort nestled among dunes, ocean and moors. Located about halfway down the "hook," the town has high green hills, sleepy rural streets, lovely old houses and a tidy village straight out of Colonial America. It was here that Marconi built his first wireless station in 1901 and sent the first trans-Atlantic telegram in 1903.

Wellfleet is adjacent to the Cape Cod National Seashore, which offers excellent birding, hiking, swimming and surfing. Groceries, restaurants and shopping range up Commercial Street. Fresh seafood is available from a number of markets in this seaside town.

NAVIGATION: The protected harbor about 26 miles east of the Cape Cod Canal has a 5-mile-long, shoal-littered entry east of Billingsgate Shoal and Island. The latter qualifies as an island only at low water. The channel and harbor have been partially dredged to 10 feet MLW and more dredging is scheduled. Updates can be obtained from the Wellfleet Dredging Task Force (508-349-0300).

Flashing green buoy "3" sets up the boater for the turn north. Lieutenant Island Bar is well marked with red buoys but Smalley Bar (on the west side of the channel) has no greens. A straight line between flashing red buoys "8" and "10" is safe, and a ribbon of deep water leads past green can buoy "11" to the narrow, dredged channel that begins with red nun buoy "12."

Looking toward Wellfleet Harbor you will see a couple of church spires and the fire lookout tower located in South Wellfleet. The Wellfleet Harbor breakwater light, flashing red "14," sits upon a skeleton-like tower to the east as you enter.

Dockage/Moorings: The Town of Wellfleet Marina and mooring basin is located behind Shirttail Point. There are patches of 1 to 2 feet MLW and an average of 2 to 3 feet MLW in the mooring field, making this a "no go" for deep-draft boats. The Wellfleet Harbormaster may be reached at 508-349-0320 for exact depths and updates on whether any dredging has been completed. On the public wharf is a well-placed launching ramp. VHF Channels 09 and 16 are monitored for pump-out service.

Anchorage: If your draft permits (and there is space), you can drop the hook in Wellfleet's Inner Harbor off the town wharf in 4 to 7 feet MLW. Pay attention in the channel between the inner and outer harbors as it can get narrow in spots. There are shoals on both sides so keep an eye on the buoys.

In settled weather there is good mud bottom north of Smalley Bar. Watch for the shoal marked by green can buoy "11" and keep the 10-foot tidal range in mind. The depths will range from 7 to 10 feet MLW. The anchorage is open to the southwest and you can get some fetch.

To the south of Billingsgate Island is a good anchorage in 8 to 13 feet MLW. The shoal serves as a natural breakwater from north winds and seas.

Sesuit Harbor

Sesuit Harbor has the easiest entry on Cape Cod Bay's southern shore. The breakwater-protected entry channel is short and comparatively straight but does have a tendency to shoal. It is periodically dredged to 6-foot MLW depth but exercise proper caution and watch the depth sounder. This is a good place to seek local knowledge before entering. Note that there is a 4-mph speed limit and anchoring is not allowed in the harbor.

Dockage: Sesuit Harbor is home to Northside Marina with dockage for 120 boats up to 65 feet in length plus rack storage, a fuel dock, engine repairs, a ship store and a waterfront restaurant offering breakfast, lunch and dinner. This is an excellent base from which to do some sightseeing in the nearby villages. The town of East Dennis provides provisioning possibilities, restaurants and other services.

Dennis Municipal Marina is nearby with slips (to 60 feet). Note that they cater mostly to local boats are not really geared towards cruising vessels. Nearby Dennis Yacht Club is strictly private.

NOTE: The Sesuit Harbormaster may be reached on VHF Channel 09 for pump-out service.

Cape Cod Bay, MA

SESUIT HARBOR		Largest Vessel	VHF	Total Slips	Approach/ Dockside Depth	Floating Docks	Gas/ Diesel	Repairs/ Haulout	Min/Max Amps	Pump-Out Station
1. Dennis Yacht Club-PRIVATE	(508) 385-3741	30			5.0 / 5.0					
2. Northside Marina	(508) 385-3936	85		120	6.0 / 6.0	F	GD	RH	30	P
3. Dennis Municipal Marina	(508) 385-5555	60	9	268	6.0 / 8.0	F			30	

Wi Fi) Wireless Internet Access
Visit www.waterwayguide.com for current rates, fuel prices, website addresses and other up-to-the-minute information.
(Information in the table is provided by the facilities.)

Scan here for more details:

Source: Aqua Map and NOAA data

Barnstable

Barnstable is the largest community on Cape Cod. It is made up of seven villages: Barnstable, Centerville, Cotuit, Hyannis (including Hyannis Port), Marston Mills, Osterville and West Barnstable. The town was named after a village in Devon, England. The first settlers were farmers but fishing and salt soon became major industries. Before the arrival of the railroads towards the end of the 1800s there were as many as 800 ships harbored there.

Barnstable is about 70 miles southeast of Boston, which made it a popular summer location for prominent 19th-century Bostonians. Some of the most famous people to have summered in Barnstable included Presidents Ulysses S. Grant, Grover Cleveland and, of course, the Kennedys. Given its location, beaches and wide variety of shops, it is no wonder that tourists come in droves to the Barnstable area.

NAVIGATION: Entry to Barnstable Harbor should not be attempted in periods of high winds or seas. The constantly shifting channel is tricky and the prevailing currents tend to set a vessel outside the channel. From a distance you will be able to see a lighted radio tower in Barnstable, the tower of a former lighthouse on the south side of Beach Point and, farther in the distance, a spire from a Yarmouth church.

So much of the entrance is marsh that the surroundings change completely between high and low tide. Followed the buoyed channel from red-and-white bell buoy "BH" to just south of Beach Point and take care to pass north of Horseshoe Shoal by leaving green can buoy "9" and flashing green buoy "11" to the south.

Once west of green can buoy "13," the channel west to the yacht club is buoyed with green cans and red nuns and shouldn't be mistaken for the buoys marking the

Barnstable Harbor Lighthouse

NOTE: The entire Nantucket Sound is designated as a No-Discharge Zone so it's helpful to take full advantage of Barnstable's pump-out stations before traveling on.

channel south to Maraspin Creek after flashing green buoy "1." The harbor is small and charts indicate an approach depth of 7 feet MLW but lows as shallow as 5 feet have been seen.

> ⚠️ *CAUTION:* Be advised that shoaling exists in the Barnstable Harbor Entrance channel approximately 200 feet into the channel north of red lighted daybeacon "6." Depth is estimated to be 2 feet MLW. Use caution while transiting the area. Contact the Harbormaster for the most up-to-date information.

Anchorage: This is a very small harbor, although the large Whale Watcher boat docks at Millway Marina. Gas, diesel and water is available at the marina, as well as public restrooms and a small dock for loading/unloading with a 15-minute limit. There are, however, no transient slips.

There are other facilities here with seasonal slips and moorings but availability is always an issue in the summer months as there are long waiting lists to use the marinas and moorings. This is a place where it is best to plan to anchor. Even then, this harbor is best suited to shallow-draft boats.

The channel approaching Barnstable Harbor widens after rounding flashing red buoy "8" and good holding can be found south of the channel in at least 7 feet MLW. Be aware of the shoal between the channel and the anchorage and follow the channel markers, which are frequently moved to reflect shifting channels. Anchoring farther up in the harbor is discouraged due to strong currents.

If you anchor north of Horseshoe Shoal at Beach Point, be aware of the tide status and your swinging radius and remember that the mean tide range is 9.5 feet. Tides flood southward and ebb northward at an average of 1.3 knots. Get as far out of the channel as possible and be prepared for close encounters with fishing and whale-watching boats speeding through. If you poke in south of Horseshoe Shoal, watch out for the charted cable area extending southward from Beach Point. This is badly exposed to the northeast at high tide.

Cape Cod Canal (East End)

Heavily traveled, well marked and attractive, the Cape Cod Canal passage cuts across the neck of Cape Cod from Buzzards Bay to Cape Cod Bay, saving boats from the 135-mile trip through Nantucket Shoals and around Cape Cod to reach Boston or Maine. Over 14,000 commercial and recreational vessels transit the 17.5-mile waterway each year.

Sandwich is the site of the Cape Cod Bay entrance to the Cape Cod Canal. Sandwich, established in 1637, is the oldest town on Cape Cod and is rich in history and New England charm. It is surrounded by beautiful walking and biking trails, bird sanctuaries, saltwater estuaries, fresh water ponds and the seashore to tempt cruisers into a longer stay. The Sandwich Boardwalk is a favorite for visitors and residents alike. The Cape Cod Canal Visitor Center in Sandwich (508-833-9678) lays out the current features and operation of the Cape Cod Canal as well as providing historical objects and stories.

NAVIGATION:

CAUTION: All vessels greater than 65 feet must contact the Marine Traffic Controller on VHF Channel 13 before entering the canal. Request clearance at least 15 minutes prior to entering the Cape Cod Canal at any point. Any delay on your part requires a second clearance to continue.

Other restrictions include:

- Vessels must be adequately powered, properly equipped and seaworthy.

- Sailboats must use auxiliary power during canal passage. Use of sails while motoring is permitted; however, large course changes and/or tacking are strictly prohibited in the land cut and approach channels.

- All vessels are required to maintain a radio guard on VHF Channel 13 during the entire passage.

- A 10-mph speed limit and "no excessive wake" is in effect for Cleveland Ledge and Hog Island channels and the land cut of the canal. The wake restrictions and speed limit are strictly enforced.

- Stopping, anchoring, fishing, unnecessarily idling at a low speed or otherwise obstructing navigation within the limits of the canal is prohibited. Low-powered vessels not making adequate headway are an obstruction to navigation. Vessels must stay to the right-hand side of the channel while transiting.

- Personal watercraft, kayaks, canoes, windsurfers or other non-motorized craft are not permitted to operate within or pass through the canal.

The canal is able to handle vessels up to 825 feet long and has a 32-foot MLW controlling depth. Despite the width and depth of the canal, the current within the canal can reach a velocity of 6 knots. Vessels of low power should not attempt to transit the canal against the current. Give careful attention to the tide and tidal current charts and make a very

conservative estimate of the time you will need to pass both through the canal and beyond in order to allow for the effects of a foul-setting tide.

The Army Corps of Engineers also cautions that boaters must complete their transit within 2.5 hours. If you are unable to complete the transit in that time, you may be required to hire a helper tug at your expense. This last requirement makes it particularly important to calculate your speed-versus-tide requirements with some care.

Prominent on the east end of the canal is the 500-foot stack from the power plant on the southern bank near the boat basin where larger vessels must wait for permission to transit the canal. Boats over 65 feet long must obey the two traffic lights– one on the eastward approach from Cape Cod Bay and the other at Wing's Neck on the westward approach from Buzzard's Bay. The red-amber-green configuration of these lights will indicate if any traffic emergencies have occurred in the canal potentially affecting your passage. The 7-mile-long land cut can be almost clear of fog when both Buzzards and Cape Cod Bays are thick with it.

Two highway bridges cross the canal before the low railroad bridge (the **Bourne Bridge** and **Sagamore Bridge**), both with 135-foot fixed vertical clearances. The **ConRail Railroad Bridge** is normally open except during the very rare passage of a train to or from Cape Cod. If the draw is not in the fully open position, the opening signal is one prolonged and one short blast. Closed vertical clearance is a mere 7 feet so very few vessels will clear the bridge during a closure. Monitor VHF Channel 13 for alerts to any closings.

Cape Cod Bay, MA

CAPE COD CANAL (EAST)		Largest Vessel	VHF	Total Slips	Approach/ Dockside Depth	Floating Docks	Gas/ Diesel	Repairs/ Haulout	Min/Max Amps	Pump-Out Station
1. Sandwich Marina/East Boat Basin **WiFi**	(508) 833-0808	160	9	198	11.0 / 11.0	F	GD		30 / 100	P

WiFi Wireless Internet Access
Visit www.waterwayguide.com for current rates, fuel prices, website addresses and other up-to-the-minute information.
(Information in the table is provided by the facilities.)

Scan here for more details:

Source: Aqua Map and NOAA data

Sandwich Boardwalk

If running with a strong, favorable current, look well ahead to assure passage under the lift span as turning at the last minute may not be an option. The bridge operator sounds two long blasts before lowering the bridge. It takes approximately 2.5 minutes to raise or lower it. If the bridge is lowered during periods of decreased visibility, the bridge operator will signal five short blasts every 2 minutes.

Even though commercial traffic is heavy on the canal, you should have no difficulties if you pick tide and weather carefully, proceed cautiously and stick to the right side of the channel as if driving on a highway.

Dockage: Sandwich Marina/East Boat Basin, operated by the Town of Sandwich, has floating piers throughout the harbor with 24 transient slips and clean facilities. Reservations are strongly recommended. Arrange in advance to rent slip space from the marina if you wish to lie over at the eastern end of the canal. They offer slips for 2- to 4-hour stays as well as overnight. (Do not tie up at the fuel dock where USCG and pilot boats moor.) Friendly dockhands will likely help you dock. The Sandwich Harbormaster's office monitors VHF Channels 08 and 09 for pump-out service. There is no room for anchoring in this tiny harbor of refuge.

The charted commercial pilings opposite the entrance to the harbor of refuge are reserved for barge traffic, which can arrive at any time and recreational boats are banned from using these pilings. Video monitors will pick you up immediately and a Coast Guard boat will arrive quickly to ask you, in no uncertain terms, to move along.

CAPE COD CANAL RESOURCES

- An online telecam is updated every 30 minutes from sunrise to sunset at: www.telecamsystems.com/capecodcanal

- Weather for the canal: 508-759-5991 or www.weather.gov/forecasts/graphical/sectors/massachusetts.php#tabs

- Navigational Regulations at: www.nae.usace.army.mil/recreati/ccc/navigation/navreg.htm

■ PLYMOUTH TO COHASSET HARBOR

Plymouth

About 20 miles northwest from the east end of the Cape Cod Canal is the historic town of Plymouth, nestled deep behind Plymouth Beach. In the northern segment, the Cowyard leads to Duxbury Bay.

Plymouth, known as "America's Hometown," was the site of the first enduring colony in New England, founded in 1620 by the passengers of the *Mayflower*, establishing New England. In the Plymouth Village Historic District you will find many restored 18th-century houses including half a dozen you may visit. The Pilgrim Hall Museum (508-746-1620) is one of the very oldest in the country and contains an impressive collection of Pilgrim lore and possessions including Miles Standish's swords.

Plimoth Plantation (508-746-1622) is a re-enactment town demonstrating the colonists' 17th-century lifestyle and the ship that brought them, although the spelling is changed to differentiate it from the town and original locations. Inside the plantation's 1622 fort, costumed interpreters reenact the daily lives of their original counterparts as they tend gardens, cook food over open fires and make their own furniture, baskets and pottery. The reproduction *Mayflower II*, which was built in Plymouth, England, using 17th century tools and sailed to Plymouth, MA, in 1957 to great acclaim. After receiving a four-year, 11-million-dollar Mystic Seaport "spa treatment," the ship is back in Plymouth.

NAVIGATION: Entry to the bays between Plymouth and Duxbury begins inside the long finger of Gurnet Point's high, bare cliff with its white, 102-foot-tall lighthouse, the oldest freestanding wooden lighthouse in the country and home of America's first female lighthouse keeper. From the outset you will have to navigate around lobster buoys and fishers in skiffs.

The navigational aids down the wide channel keep cruisers off Browns Bank and a generous distance from Saquish Head. However, the outgoing tidal rip across the channel can present quite a challenge to inbound craft under sail. Duxbury Pier Light (locally known as "Bug Light" as are so many squat lighthouses) sits at the confluence of the Plymouth channel and the Cowyard, which leads north to Duxbury. The light was turned over to a non-profit in 2019 with the understanding that they would care for it in perpetuity so it will remain a photogenic staple of every visit.

The flashing green bell buoy "9" and red-over-green "Nummet Channel" buoy "NC" located southwest of Duxbury Pier mark the entrance to Plymouth Harbor Channel. The red-over-green buoy "NC" denotes that the southerly channel to Plymouth is primary while the westerly channel into Kingston Bay is secondary.

The Plymouth Harbor channel parallels the beach in a southeasterly direction for about 1 mile between two 16-foot flashing lights: quick-flashing red "12" and flashing green "17." There the channel takes a sharp turn southwest for another well-marked run past the breakwater to the inner harbor. Anchoring is prohibited in the Plymouth inner harbor, which is filled with commercial craft and private moorings.

Dockage/Moorings: The Greek Revival monument protecting what remains of Plymouth Rock lies dead ahead upon entering the inner harbor. The private Plymouth Yacht Club welcomes visiting boaters to their moorings and is prominently located on the knoll south of green can buoy "23." The yacht club is followed immediately by the extensive facilities of Safe Harbor Plymouth, a full-service boatyard and marina with deep-draft transient slips. The yard has complete repair and fabrication shops and easy access to both gasoline and diesel fuel.

The Plymouth Town Wharf is located at the end of the buoyed channel with just three moorings and a convenient dinghy dock. Call the helpful Plymouth Harbormaster for a mooring (with water taxi service) at 508-830-4182. Shoreside restrooms and showers are available. VHF Channels 09 and 16 are monitored for pump-out service.

Anchorage: At the elbow of the dredged channel, behind Plymouth Beach, is a narrow anchorage. Follow depth contours carefully to anchor in 7 to 10 feet MLW at the Plymouth anchorage. It is remote from the bustle of town and harbor, but not from the traffic in and out. There is serious wake in the morning when the whale watching boats depart.

Duxbury

Miles Standish founded the Colonial town of Duxbury early in Massachusetts' history. Even though traditional clapboard housing stock of the period remains, today Duxbury bustles with summer resort and tourist traffic flocking to the contemporary shops and restaurants. The harbor is well protected and visiting cruisers are welcomed but available space is tight.

Duxbury Bay Area, MA

PLYMOUTH		Largest Vessel	VHF	Total Slips	Approach/ Dockside Depth	Floating Docks	Gas/ Diesel	Repairs/ Haulout	Min/Max Amps	Pump-Out Station
1. Plymouth Yacht Club-PRIVATE	(508) 747-0473	45	8		12.0 / 12.0					
2. Safe Harbor Plymouth **WiFi**	(508) 746-4500	150	9	105	10.0 / 8.0	F	GD	RH	30 / 50	P
3. Plymouth Town Wharf	(508) 830-4182	110	16		7.0 / 11.0		GD			
DUXBURY										
4. Duxbury Town Pier	(781) 934-2866	50	16		8.0 / 8.0			R		P
GREEN HARBOR RIVER										
5. Taylor Marine	(781) 837-9617	45		130	6.0 / 6.0	F	GD	H	30	P
6. Safe Harbor Green Harbor	(781) 837-1181	60	65	180	8.0 / 8.0	F	GD	R	30 / 50	

WiFi Wireless Internet Access

Visit www.waterwayguide.com for current rates, fuel prices, website addresses and other up-to-the-minute information.
(Information in the table is provided by the facilities.)

Scan here for more details:

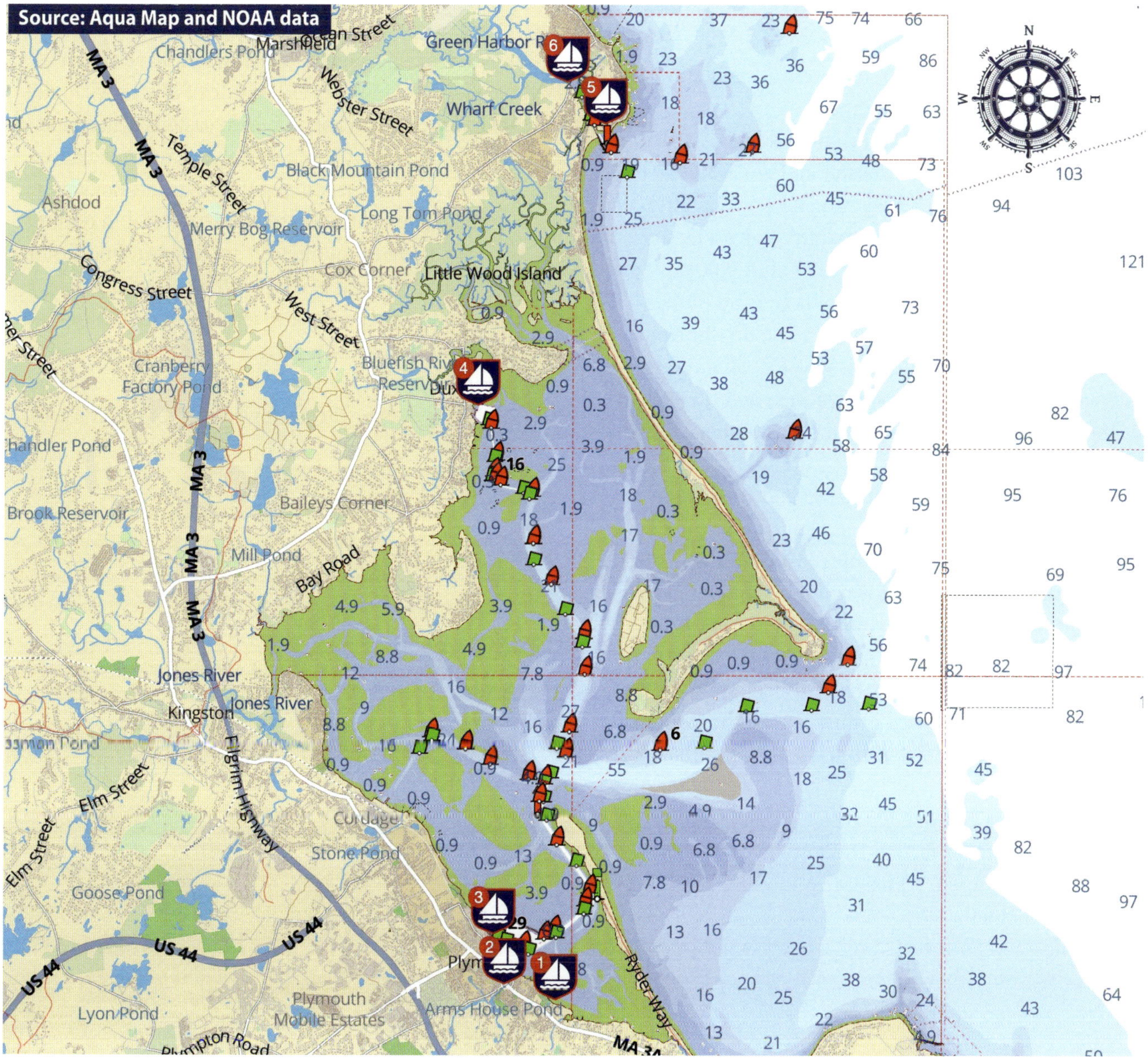

Source: Aqua Map and NOAA data

NAVIGATION: Duxbury Bay is a big, shallow body of water. After rounding Duxbury Pier Lighthouse, a 35-foot tall flashing red, mind the buoys and watch the chart while the Cowyard is to the east and the eroded remains of Saquish Head's long point stretch to the west. The channel divides west of privately owned Clarks Island. The privately marked eastern branch follows the west side of Clarks Island to a fixed bridge (5-foot vertical clearance) 3 miles north, which connects Duxbury to Powder Point. The main channel turns to the northwest and leads into Duxbury Harbor.

The Duxbury channel and harbor are shoal-prone, reducing the optimal depth significantly between dredging projects. Call ahead or check with locals for current depths. Privately maintained channel buoys mark the encroaching shoal at the southern tip of the Cowyard's long bar and 0.5 mile west at the mouth of the Jones River north of The Nummet.

Dockage/Moorings: Transient and guest moorings are managed by the harbormaster and are available on a first-come, first-served basis. To check availability, call the Harbormaster at the Duxbury Town Pier at 781-934-2866 (or VHF Channel 16) after 9:00 a.m. on the day you plan to arrive. While there is no pump-out service offered by boat, you can use the shoreside pump-out station, which monitors VHF Channel 16. You may land your dinghy at the town pier, and there is a bakery, fish market, wine store and Post Office all within walking distance.

Anchorage: Red nun buoys "4" and "6" lead to an anchorage off Goose Point in Kingston Bay in 10 to 15 feet MLW with some protection from the north. Duxbury's harbormaster allows dinghy landing at their dock but it's a long trip from here. Farther north in Duxbury Bay you can drop the hook to the west of Clarks Island at Cowyard in 10 to 18 feet MLW, where the Pilgrims first anchored or just north of it for some protection from the north through south. Depths are highly variable in the Cowyard. Check specific locations carefully against charted depths and actual soundings.

The closest anchorage to Duxbury is north of red nun buoy "12" in 9 to 13 feet MLW. Be sure to stay out of the channel.

> NOTE: The current is strong here so swim with care (and maybe a line).

Green Harbor River

Just 5 miles north of Gurnet Point, Green Harbor River is home to many charter and recreational fishing boats. Green Harbor Lobster Pound (781-834-4571) is on the western shore at Marshfield with lobsters, clams, scallops, fish and shrimp and is open daily from Memorial Day to Labor Day.

NAVIGATION: Flashing green buoy "3" has been set 600 yards southeast of the jettied entrance at the north end of long curving Duxbury Beach. The Army Corps of Engineers dredges here most years to maintain project depths of 6 feet MLW but shoaling is swift since a jetty breach worsened the situation. Be prepared for decreasing depths and a narrowing of the 100-foot nominal channel over time, exercise caution and obtain local knowledge.

Many local fishermen do not enter or leave Green Harbor within 90 minutes either side of low tide. Do not attempt to enter on an ebb tide with easterly winds and be cautious of submerged boulders on the south side of the channel. On the way in watch out for Bartlett Rock and pick up the channel at red nun buoy "2GH" if in doubt.

After leaving red nun buoy "6" to the east, find flashing red "8" sited on the end of a jetty off Blackmans Point. Center up between the western jetty and the flashing red "8" then head straight along the western jetty (without straying toward it). Center up between that jetty and the point as you enter the narrowest part of the channel.

Watch for moored boats that may make this narrow passage even smaller.

Dockage: Taylor Marine offers slips and supplies and an excellent beach is a short walk away. To the north and across the harbor is the 180-slip Safe Harbor Green Harbor, which welcomes transients with reserved slips, and has a restaurant with an outdoor deck overlooking the marina, a bait shop and a marine safety school. The facility is also located within walking distance to shops and groceries. There is no room for anchoring in this tiny harbor.

Scituate Harbor

Scituate (pronounced "SIT-you-it" from the Wampanoag word satuit or "cold brook") rings a small, snug harbor, one of the most accommodating on the East Coast for recreational boats. The town harbor surrounds Scituate and offers a variety of fine restaurants to satisfy any appetite, a supermarket, hardware stores and a theater company/playhouse.

Although it is a crowded harbor and anchoring is prohibited, the harbor and town are well worth a stop for a day or two. The Scituate Lighthouse, built in 1810, provides a good view of the harbor and surrounding areas. Other sites of historical interest are the Cudworth House, Lawson Tower and the Stockbridge Mill, which are all easily visited. A seasonal Coast Guard station is located inside the channel entrance.

NO WAKE ZONE

Speed limit in the harbor is 6 mph and is strictly enforced, as is the No-Discharge law.

NAVIGATION: Scituate Harbor is easily entered between Cedar Point to the north, marked by the old Scituate Light, and First Cliff to the south. From the red-and-white Morse (A) gong buoy "SA" follow a course of 289° magnetic to the mouth of the channel. A breakwater protects the well-marked basin and its many lobster buoys. Scituate Harbor's entrance channel is well marked but stay to the center until well past the jetties.

If unfamiliar with this port, do not attempt the approach after dark. Channel depth is charted at 10 to 12 feet MLW but shoals are present on the outside edges.

Dockage/Moorings: Private marinas, yacht clubs and a town-operated marina may have slips available by reservation or on a first-come, first-served basis. The Scituate Harbor Yacht Club is private but welcomes visiting yachtsmen from other recognized yacht clubs on their transient moorings (with launch service). Visitors can enjoy use of the on-site café.

Satuit Boat Club is a favorite stop among cruisers looking for transient moorings with launch service to local restaurants and pet-friendly access to the beach. The club

Scituate Lighthouse

Scituate Harbor, MA

SCITUATE		Largest Vessel	VHF	Total Slips	Approach/ Dockside Depth	Floating Docks	Gas/ Diesel	Repairs/ Haulout	Min/Max Amps	Pump-Out Station
1. Scituate Harbor Yacht Club-PRIVATE **WiFi**	(781) 545-0372	38	9	97	10.0 / 10.0	F	GD		50	
2. Satuit Boat Club-PRIVATE **WiFi**	(781) 545-9752	58	9		8.0 / 8.0	F	GD	RH		P
3. TPG Marinas Scituate Harbor **WiFi**	(781) 545-2165	75	9	85	11.0 / 9.0	F	GD		30 / 50	
4. TPG Marinas Mill Wharf **WiFi**	(781) 545-3333	55	9	89	11.0 / 8.0	F	GD		30 / 50	
5. Cole Parkway Marina	(781) 545-2130	50	16	180	10.0 / 8.0				30 / 50	P
6. Scituate Launch/Waterline Moorings **WiFi**	(781) 545-4154	50	9		10.0 / 8.0			RH		P
7. Scituate Marine Park & Maritime Center	(781) 545-8724	45		78	12.0 / 10.0	F		RH		

WiFi Wireless Internet Access
Visit www.waterwayguide.com for current rates, fuel prices, website addresses and other up-to-the-minute information.
(Information in the table is provided by the facilities.)

Scan here for more details:

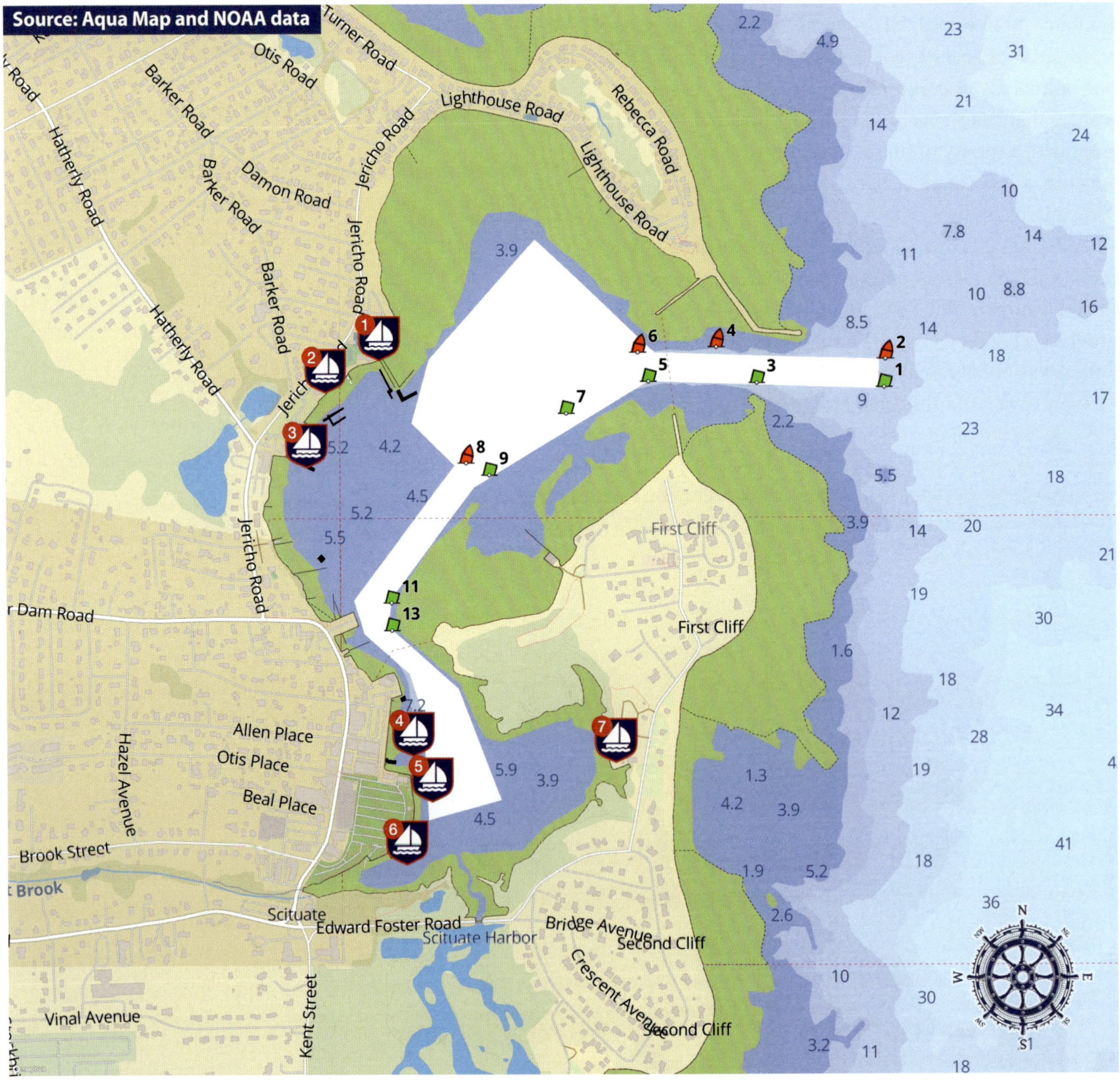

Source: Aqua Map and NOAA data

is private but can arrange use of a member's vacant mooring. The flat fee includes launch service and the use of the club's facilities. Reservations are not necessary but you can reserve a mooring by calling 781-545-9752.

Both TPG Marinas Scituate Harbor and TPG Marinas Mill Wharf (to the south) maintain a few transient slips and offer services and full amenities. The municipal Cole Parkway Marina is managed by the Town of Scituate's Harbormaster and maintains 10 transient slips.

Scituate Launch/Waterline Moorings supervises a large number of rental moorings and can often accommodate transients. Rental includes showers and launch service into town or to the many restaurants on the harbor. Call the launch on VHF Channel 09 for hours of operation and pump-out boat status.

The Scituate Marine Park & Maritime Center has slips (to 45 feet), a public kayak ramp and public bathrooms and showers. There is a walking trail around the perimeter of the park as well as two historical buildings preserving Scituate's maritime history.

Cohasset Harbor

Cohasset is a popular, crowded harbor on the fringes of Boston with a large local fleet and good anchorage. Ashore you will find plenty of restaurants and beaches. This quiet location offers boaters the flavor of a quintessential New England coastal town.

NAVIGATION: The entrance channel to Cohasset Harbor is charted as 7 feet MLW and most of the cove has 6 to 9 feet MLW. It shallows badly deeper in and there are barely shoal-draft depths to and past the town landing. Contact the Cohasset Harbormaster on VHF Channel 10 for approach depths.

Dockage/Moorings: The hospitable Cohasset Yacht Club is private but may have a space for you. Call ahead. Cohasset Harbor Marina has 75 (all transient) slips or contact the Cohasset Harbormaster on VHF Channel 10 for slip, mooring and pump-out service requests. What used to be an anchorage is filled with mooring balls. The cove no longer has space for anchoring, even in incredibly shallow Bailey Creek.

Scituate Harbor

Cohasset Harbor, MA

COHASSET COVE		Largest Vessel	VHF	Total Slips	Approach/ Dockside Depth	Floating Docks	Gas/ Diesel	Repairs/ Haulout	Min/Max Amps	Pump-Out Station
1. Cohasset Yacht Club-PRIVATE	(781) 383-9633	45	10		6.0 / 6.0				30	
2. Cohasset Harbormaster	(781) 383-0863	55	9		/			RH		P
3. Cohasset Harbor Marina	(781) 383-1504	42		75	7.0 / 6.0	F		R	20 / 50	P

WiFi Wireless Internet Access
Visit www.waterwayguide.com for current rates, fuel prices, website addresses and other up-to-the-minute information.
(Information in the table is provided by the facilities.)

Scan here for more details:

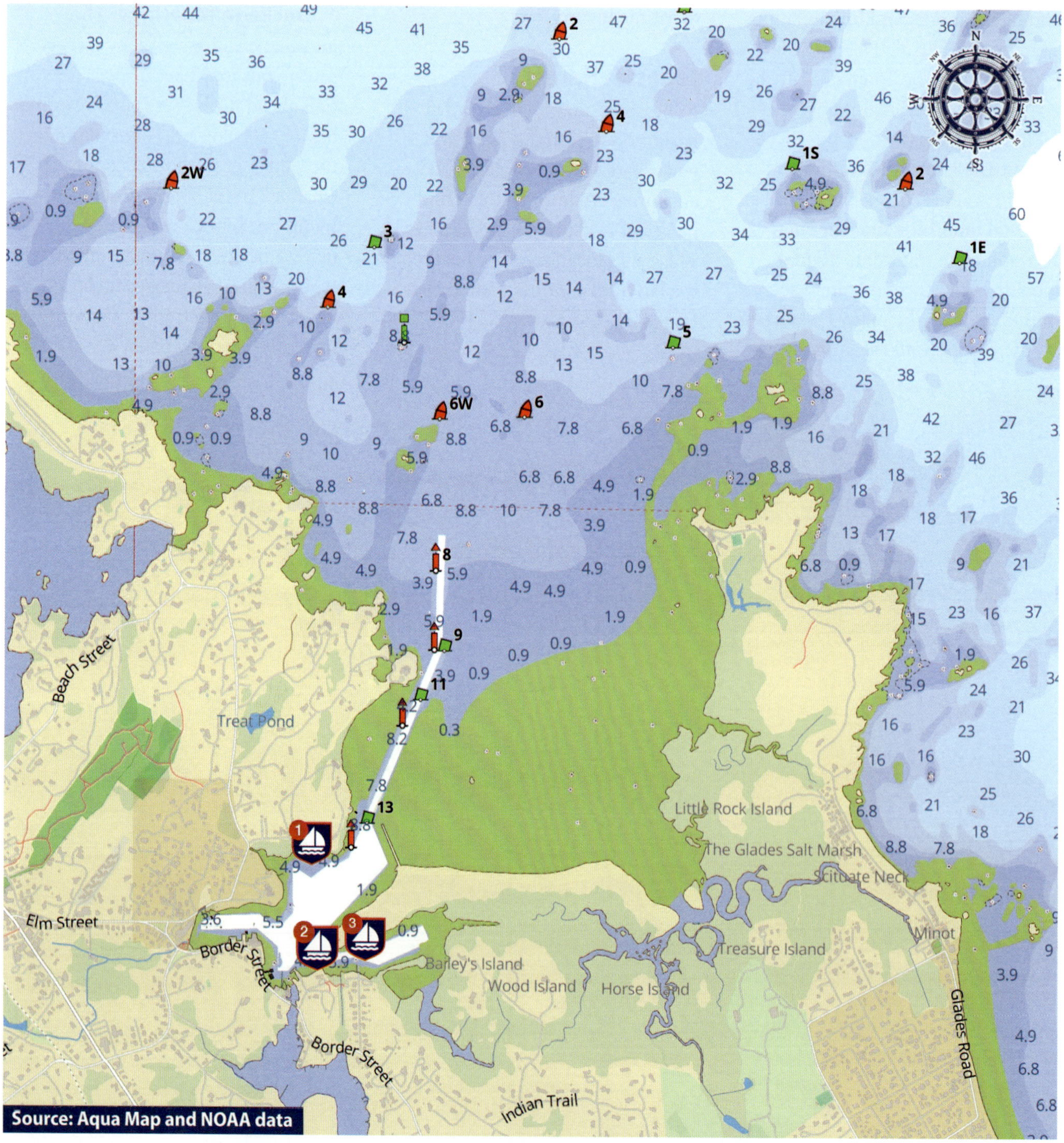

Source: Aqua Map and NOAA data

■ BOSTON HARBOR AREA

Boston's attractions, historic landmarks and amenities are so numerous that they deserve a guidebook of their own. Fortunately, several are widely available in tourist shops around the harbor. Boston and its environs offer dozens of friendly yacht clubs, protected marinas, secluded anchorages, boatyards and facilities for recreational craft, many of which welcome cruising boats.

Fascinating sightseeing is within easy distance of almost anywhere you dock. Nearby are historic towns and notable shore resorts to visit as well as dozens of islands to investigate by dinghy.

Entering Boston Harbor

Like all big-city harbors, Boston is crowded with commercial and recreational boats of all types. Freighters, tankers, cruise ships, high-speed ferries and excursion boats vie with pleasure craft of all descriptions. The Harbor hums with activity and nautical history.

NAVIGATION: Red-and-white Morse (A) buoy "B," located 8 miles east-northeast of Deer Island, guides you into Boston Harbor. Note that the Coast Guard has received reports of periodic GPS reception problems near buoy "B" and ask that mariners use caution in this area and report any reception issues by calling 703-313-5900 or emailing tis-pf-nisws@uscg.mil.

The Deer Island Light fog signal has been changed to a Mariner Radio Activated Sound Signal (MRASS). During times of reduced visibility, mariners are requested to turn to VHF Channel 83A/157.175Mhz and key their microphone 5 times consecutively to activate the fog signal for 60 minutes.

Boston Harbor requires an attentive navigator. Hazards include crisscrossing wakes and ferry routes, numerous buoys and channels, shipping traffic, and unmarked shoals, rocks and ledges in apparently good water. Many side waters, notably Quincy and Dorchester Bays, are relatively unmarked. Even the numerous islands rarely look as you would expect from the charts. The plethora of lights and buoys can be confusing. Be sure to keep them sorted out in your mind and on your chart.

Also keep an eye astern for two reasons: ferries traveling up to and over 30 knots for one, and for another the currents, which can run to 2.5 knots or more and set you off course into very shallow, dangerously rocky waters.

Marking the entry on Massachusetts Bay is the 85-foot Minots Ledge Light, famous up and down the coast as the "I Love You Light" for its "one-four-three" flashing light pattern. From here the approach is via any of three natural channels: Eastern Channel, The Gangway and Western Channel. All are marked and well charted, threading between outlying rocks and ledges. These passages, like those found in Maine and on the northern shore of Long Island Sound, are somewhat difficult but present no problem in clear weather.

Local boaters like the wider Gangway Channel despite its unmarked rocks. The Coast Pilot prefers the narrower but deeper and clearer Eastern Channel. The Western Channel between Brush Ledge and Chittenden Rock is the shallowest with depths less than 6 feet MLW and all agree that the best time to enter, especially if you draw more than 5 feet, is on a rising tide.

Both main entrances to the harbor have numerous, well-marked side channels feeding off in all directions. If entering the harbor from the south, the more southerly and frequently used by recreational craft is Nantasket Roads, giving direct access to a vast circle of bays, anchorages and rivers in the harbor's southern sector. The other entrance, President Roads, is the main ship channel leading to the inner harbor and to northern parts of the outer harbor. Connecting the two are The Narrows and Nubble Channel.

With all its smaller bays and rivers the Boston area has many viable anchorages. Only a small handful will be noted in the text below. You must keep the tidal range in mind when setting an anchor. The average rise and fall in the Boston Harbor area is 9.5 feet and some high tides can be almost 12 feet MLW. An anchor rode of 50 feet in 10 feet of water (5:1 scope) is woefully inadequate at high tide of 20 or 21 feet. Do not fail to consult the Boston tide tables when setting the anchor.

Nantasket Roads

Wide Hull Bay is perhaps the easiest of any Boston harbor to enter from Massachusetts Bay. The buoyed channel of the Weir River to the south passes around Worlds End, a 251-acre park maintained by The Trustees of the Reservation with sweeping views of Boston and 4.5 miles of carriage paths and footpaths, perfect for moderate hiking. The channel then leads to Nantasket Beach, a favorite Boston retreat with over 1 mile of fine beaches. To the west a channel leads past Crow Point's range lights into Hingham Harbor.

Continuing in a clockwise direction, the long, deep Weymouth Back River is midway between Hingham Harbor and Weymouth Fore River. Wide and open to Germantown Point, the Weymouth Fore River has protected reaches that extend to East Braintree and Weymouth on the south.

Big and generally shallow Quincy Bay has a number of yacht clubs along its shores. The town of Quincy (pronounced "KWIN-zee") is the birthplace of U.S. presidents John Adams and John Quincy Adams, a story that is well documented at the fascinating Adams National Historic Park, which is accessible by conducted van tour only. Information and tickets may be found at the National Park Service Visitor Center (617-770-1175). The United States Naval Shipbuilding Museum is housed in the *U.S.S. Salem*, a heavy cruiser docked at the former Fore River Shipyard. Call 617-479-7900 for more information on tours and times.

NAVIGATION: Enter Nantasket Roads between Point Allerton at the northern end of Nantasket Beach and Little Brewster Island, the site of the 102-foot-tall Boston Lighthouse. A short 2 miles west, turn south into Hull Gut (with a 2- to 3-knot current) to pass between Windmill Point and Peddocks Island into Hingham Bay with its various arms and islands.

Well-marked Hingham Bay has few obstructions all the way to the Weymouth Back and Fore Rivers. Upriver from the deep-draft channel on the Weymouth Fore River, depths

are uncertain. The **SR3A (Fore River) Bridge** (with 60-foot closed vertical clearance) opens on signal except from 6:30 a.m. to 9:00 a.m. and from 4:30 p.m. to 6:30 p.m., Monday through Friday, excluding holidays. In a bit of excellent charity, a portion of the old temporary bridge here is now a short bridge over a formerly dangerous river in Perches, Haiti.

Dockage/Moorings: The Hingham Harbormaster manages three moorings located on the east side of Worlds End and two moorings at Langlee Island in Hingham Harbor (available with online reservation at Dockwa).

The private Hull Yacht Club welcomes transient boats on moorings in Allerton Harbor in the northeast corner of Hull Bay. They offer cruising guests the usual amenities plus launch service, pump-out arrangements and use of all club facilities. Moorings are provided on an availability basis, free of charge, for boats from reciprocating clubs.

The friendly Safe Harbor Sunset Bay has slips to 80 feet and is a good location for exploring Boston Harbor and the islands. Steamboat Wharf Marina to the south has 120 feet of guest dockage at the west end of Nantasket Pier. Space is limited and this facility fills up fast so plan to make reservations ahead of time by calling the marina or using the online reservation request form.

The private Hingham Yacht Club at Crow Point on Hingham Harbor has a limited number of moorings (to 30 feet). Call ahead. The public landing has pump-out service.

The Weymouth Back River offers both protection and a range of marine and other facilities including Hingham Shipyard Marinas with

moorings and Tern Harbor Marina with slips and moorings. These facilities are conveniently adjacent to the commuter ferry to downtown Boston as well as a ferry to the Boston Harbor Islands. A dozen restaurants are within easy walking distance of Stodders Neck in the big strolling outdoor mall, which also has a movie theater and shopping. The Weymouth Harbormaster may be reached at 781-682-6109 and VHF Channel 9 is monitored for pump-out service.

If Weymouth Fore River is your destination, turn northwest at Germantown Point and follow the entrance channel into Town River Bay. Captain's Cove Marina is located up the river past Hole Point in a protected inlet in which boaters often take shelter during storms. They offer 180 slips for power and sailing vessels up to 55 feet.

Nearby MarineMax Boston is located on 11 acres and has slips to 70 feet. The popular Bay Pointe Waterfront Restaurant is on site serving delicious seafood and beautiful waterfront views. Grocery stores and other provisioning options are nearby.

Anchorage: Directly off Nantasket Roads to the south is Perty Cove on the northwest side of Peddocks Island. This has fair holding in 11 to 16 feet MLW with mud and rock and is open and exposed from north through southwest. There is plenty of room to anchor despite a plethora of mooring balls. Can be rolly in a strong westerly wind.

Hull Bay has several good anchorages protected from all but westerlies. Designated anchorage areas are located at Spinnaker Island (which protects Allerton Harbor) and at Bumkin Island in 6 to 10 feet MLW.

Nantasket Roads Area, MA

HULL BAY		Largest Vessel	VHF	Total Slips	Approach/ Dockside Depth	Floating Docks	Gas/ Diesel	Repairs/ Haulout	Min/Max Amps	Pump-Out Station
1. Hull Yacht Club-PRIVATE **WiFi**	(781) 925-9739	45	71		6.0 / 9.0			H		
2. Safe Harbor Sunset Bay **WiFi**	(781) 925-2828	80	7	170	12.0 / 12.0	F	G	RH	30 / 50	P
3. Steamboat Wharf Marina **WiFi**	(781) 925-0044	120	7	87	14.0 / 12.0	F		R	30 / 50	
4. Hingham Yacht Club-PRIVATE	(781) 749-3806	30	71		15.0 / 9.0		GD			P
WEYMOUTH BACK RIVER										
5. Hingham Shipyard Marinas **WiFi**	(781) 749-2222	135	9	500	15.0 / 12.0		GD	R	30 / 100	P
6. Tern Harbor Marina **WiFi**	(781) 337-1964	110	9	150	15.0 / 10.0	F		RH	15 / 50	P
WEYMOUTH FORE RIVER										
7. MarineMax Boston **WiFi**	(617) 288-1000	70	9	255	45.0 / 8.0	F	GD	RH	30 / 50	P
8. Captain's Cove Marina **WiFi**	(617) 328-3331	60	69	180	40.0 / 20.0	F			30 / 50	P

WiFi Wireless Internet Access
Visit www.waterwayguide.com for current rates, fuel prices, website addresses and other up-to-the-minute information.
(Information in the table is provided by the facilities.)

Scan here for more details:

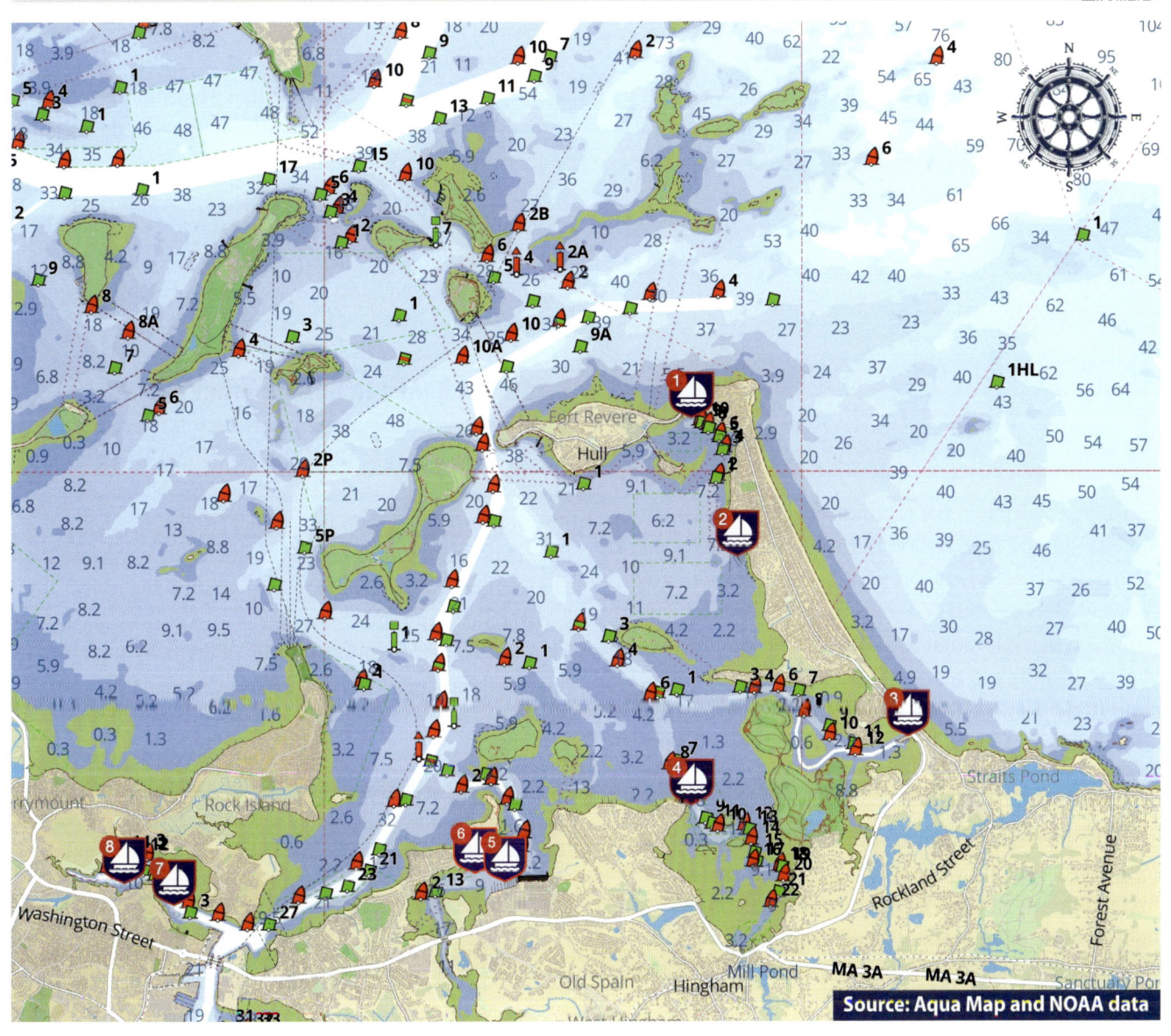

Source: Aqua Map and NOAA data

On approach to Bumkin Island take care to avoid the submerged rock that's 2 feet below the surface at low tide. It is marked by a red barrel used as a privately maintained buoy and located about 400 yards north-northeast of the western tip of the island.

Slim anchorage is available at Worlds End to the southeast, where you will find 7 to 9 feet MLW with excellent holding in mud and all-around protection.

Good holding can be found on the east side of the entrance channel of the Weymouth Back River after making the turn south (past Grape Island) but the ferry and other traffic keep the waters roiling. Anchor anywhere out of the channel to the east of flashing red buoy "4" and north of green can buoy "7" in 16 to 19 feet MLW. Farther up the river beyond the fixed 36-foot vertical clearance 3A Hwy. Bridge is Beal Cove with 10 feet MLW.

Boston Harbor Islands National Park

The islands of outer Boston Harbor have long been a wonderful cruising ground. These islands offer history, hiking and geocaching, picnic trails and camping, all within a stone's throw of downtown Boston (also accessible by ferry). The ferry docks are mostly reserved for off-loading people and supplies with limited space to land a dinghy; however, the beach area on most islands is ample and fair game.

NOTE: Private boaters may not land on Thompson, Moon, Long, or Gallops Islands. Pets are restricted from specific islands. All the National Parks have a carry in, carry out policy when it comes to trash. See details at Boston Harbor Islands State Park.

Georges Island on the northern edge of Nantasket Roads is a hub of the Boston Harbor Islands. Historic Fort Warren, a Civil War-era fort known for its graceful granite archways and reputed ghost "the Lady in Black," offers an afternoon of exploration and a panoramic view of Boston Harbor. Visitors can take a guided tour of the fort or explore the island on their own. Restrooms, picnic areas with grills and a snack bar are here. In addition, Georges Island is a frequent stop for the island ferries and a jump off point to other islands.

Little Brewster Island east of Nantasket Roads is home to the Boston Light, which is located on the site of the first lighthouse in the U.S. Although boaters can view the light from offshore, it is not recommended to attempt a landing on the dock. Tours of the island and light begin at Fan Pier in South Boston and include a narrated history of Boston harbor and its lights as well as viewing of two other lighthouses.

Dockage/Moorings: Public moorings are available on Spectacle, Peddocks, Georges and Gallops Islands (with no island access at Gallops), and Spectacle Island Marina is on Spectacle Island. The calmest, most sheltered moorings are found on the west side of Peddocks Island (71 total moorings). Moorings and slips are available for reservation via Dockwa. Additionally, the Hingham Harbormaster manages four moorings located on the east side of Worlds End, as well as two moorings at Langlee Island in Hingham Harbor.

Three complimentary moorings are located off Thompson Island on a first-come, first-served basis (Thompson Island Moorings). Note that there is no public access to Thompson Island from these moorings.

Anchorage: The best anchorage at Georges Island is north of the dock, but substantial weekend traffic and eddying currents through and around the islands keep the waters disturbed. The superb view of the Boston skyline at sunset makes a little rocking well worthwhile. The south side of nearby Gallups Island is another option. The east side of Long Island with 8- to 12-foot MLW depths doesn't have a skyline view but the lighthouses are spectacular from here.

President Roads to Boston Inner Harbor

President Roads leads into Boston Harbor to the north and Dorchester Bay to the south. The inner coves of Dorchester Bay and tidal reaches of the Neponset River are home to a number of yacht clubs as well as large, full-service marinas. Winthrop to the northeast of President Roads has numerous beaches due to its geographic location.

As you enter the Inner Harbor, downtown Boston's historical buildings and skyscrapers dominate the view to port. The huge and distinctive federal courthouse on the northeast elbow of South Boston serves as a sentinel beacon to the first of several excellent marinas that will take your lines for a berth in the center of the city's historic district. You will sure to notice the planes taking off and landing at Logan Airport as you approach.

Boston skyline seen from Piers Park, MA

NO WAKE ZONE

Mariners are advised that a No Wake speed limit is enforced in Boston Inner Harbor commencing at the northwest corner of Logan International Airport southwesterly across the harbor to Pier 7 next to the Fish Pier. Increased commercial and recreational traffic within the enforceable zone poses significant hazards. Mariners are advised that you are responsible for the wake your vessel produces and any damages to facilities or other vessels that may occur. Mariners are advised to proceed at slowest speed possible to minimize wake.

From the Inner Harbor just beyond the Coast Guard base a turn west takes you into the mouth of the Charles River. The adjacent water shuttle leaves every 15 minutes for Faneuil Hall Marketplace and downtown.

Immediately east of the marina of the same name, the *U.S.S. Constitution* ("Old Ironsides") has found its final berth in the Charlestown Navy Yard (also known as Boston Navy Yard and Boston Naval Shipyard). The famed frigate of the War of 1812 is maintained as a historic site by the National Park Service (617-426-1812 or 617-242-5601). The yard is also home to the *U.S.S. Cassin Young*,

The Boston Harborwalk

A near-continuous, 43-mile linear park along Boston's shoreline, the Harborwalk connects Boston's eight waterfront neighborhoods to Boston Harbor and each other. It stretches from the Neponset River in lower Dorchester to Constitution Beach in East Boston via Charlestown, the North End, Downtown, Seaport, South Boston and Dorchester. Part of the richness of the Harborwalk is its variety, reflecting the various activities and urban textures of adjacent land. In places, the Harborwalk extends into maritime industrial areas, allowing visitors to observe at close range working port operations. In others, Harborwalkers can enjoy a swim, go fishing, visit over forty parks and a dozen museums, or sample the latest foodie destination restaurant.

The Harborwalk connects to a number of inland trails and parks, including the Emerald Necklace, Charles River Esplanade, Rose Kennedy Greenway, Freedom Trail, South Bay Trail and East Boston Greenway. Please note that, with the exception of wheelchairs, the Harborwalk is a non-motorized pathway. Bicycles are welcome on the portion of the Harborwalk from the Neponset River Greenway to Castle Island State Park. North of Castle Island, however, pedestrian traffic becomes heavier and bicyclists should move to bike lanes. See a full map online at Boston Harborwalk (www.bostonharborwalk.org).

a 250-foot long destroyer commissioned in 1902 and serving the Navy until the mid-1950s.

Getting around is not a problem. Boston Water Taxi (617-227-4320) can transport you and your guests on a short trip across the harbor to Logan International Airport, among other destinations. Train stations are easy walks from marinas and the historical downtown is a pleasure to walk.

Dockage/Moorings Safe Harbor Marina Bay is more of a self-contained yachting community than a marina. It is one of the largest marinas in the northeast with 686 berths. Transient slips are usually available and easily approached in at least 13-foot MLW depths. In addition to coin-operated laundry machines and ice, you can access ATM and express mailing services from the marina. Restaurants and a supermarket are nearby, or call a cab (Marina Bay Taxi, 617-472-4111) for rapid access to a pharmacy and complete provisioning possibilities in downtown Boston, a 15-minute ride.

There are a number of mooring possibilities west of Squantum Point on the Neponset River as well as several private yacht clubs including Savin Hill Yacht Club, Dorchester Yacht Club and Old Colony Yacht Club. Call ahead if you plan to stay at any of these clubs as they have varying requirements. Columbia Yacht Club and South Boston Yacht Club in Old Harbor to the northeast are both strictly private.

At Winthrop (east of Logan Airport) Crystal Cove Marina has 10 reserved transient slips to 70 feet. Nearby Atlantis Marina is part of a condominium complex. Call ahead for slip availability. The well-regarded Belle Isle Seafood is nearby (617-567-1619). Note they are a cash only operation.

On the west side of Logan Airport are more slips and repairs at Boston Harbor Shipyard and Marina where amenities include a fitness center, boaters' lounge, laundry facilities, 24-hour security and a restaurant. This is home to a wide range of support services including water taxi pick-up, boat repair services, a bait & tackle shop, Boston Scuba and Seatow. Nearby Harbor Fuels Boston has the lowest fuel prices in Boston Harbor.

> NOTE: A large fleet of daysailers may be out and about here. They belong to the Boston Harbor Sailing Club, a major organization that promotes interest in boating.

Boston Harbor Area, MA

BOSTON HARBOR ISLANDS NATIONAL PARK		Largest Vessel	VHF	Total Slips	Approach/ Dockside Depth	Floating Docks	Gas/ Diesel	Repairs/ Haulout	Min/Max Amps	Pump-Out Station
1. Spectacle Island Marina	(857) 452-7221	60		40	12.0 / 10.0	F				
PRESIDENT ROADS										
2. Safe Harbor Marina Bay (WiFi)	**(617) 847-1800**	**300**	**10**	**686**	**14.0 / 13.0**	**F**	**GD**	**RH**	**30 / 100**	**P**
3. Savin Hill Yacht Club-PRIVATE	(617) 288-9293				/		G			
4. Dorchester Yacht Club-PRIVATE (WiFi)	(617) 436-1002	40			6.0 / 6.0	F	G			P
5. Old Colony Yacht Club-PRIVATE	(617) 436-0513	46			6.0 / 4.0					
6. Columbia Yacht Club-PRIVATE	(617) 268-2790		9		7.0 / 4.0	F	G	H		
7. South Boston Yacht Club-PRIVATE	(617) 268-6132	30			6.0 / 6.0	F	G			

(WiFi) Wireless Internet Access
Visit www.waterwayguide.com for current rates, fuel prices, website addresses and other up-to-the-minute information.
(Information in the table is provided by the facilities.)

Scan here for more details:

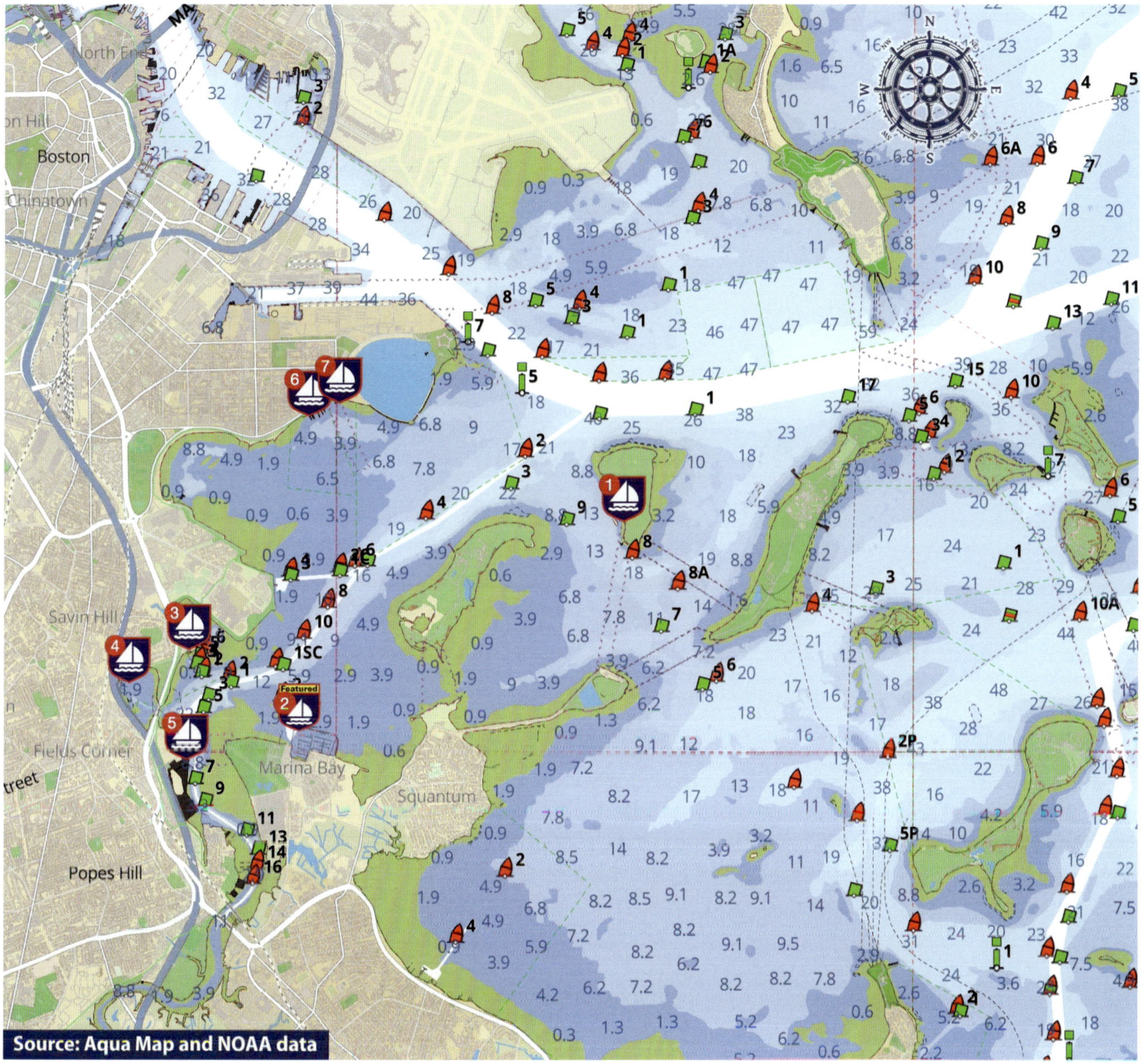

(Chart: Boston Harbor Area showing marina locations 1–7)

Source: Aqua Map and NOAA data

Boston Harbor Area, MA

WINTHROP AREA		Largest Vessel	VHF	Total Slips	Approach/ Dockside Depth	Floating Docks	Gas/ Diesel	Repairs/ Haulout	Min/Max Amps	Pump-Out Station
1. Crystal Cove Marina **WiFi**	(617) 846-7245	70	10	118	6.0 / 6.0	F	GD	RH	30	P
2. Atlantis Marina	(617) 846-5262	120	9	130	25.0 / 30.0	F		R	30 / 100	P

WiFi Wireless Internet Access
Visit www.waterwayguide.com for current rates, fuel prices, website addresses and other up-to-the-minute information.
(Information in the table is provided by the facilities.)

Scan here for more details:

Source: Aqua Map and NOAA data

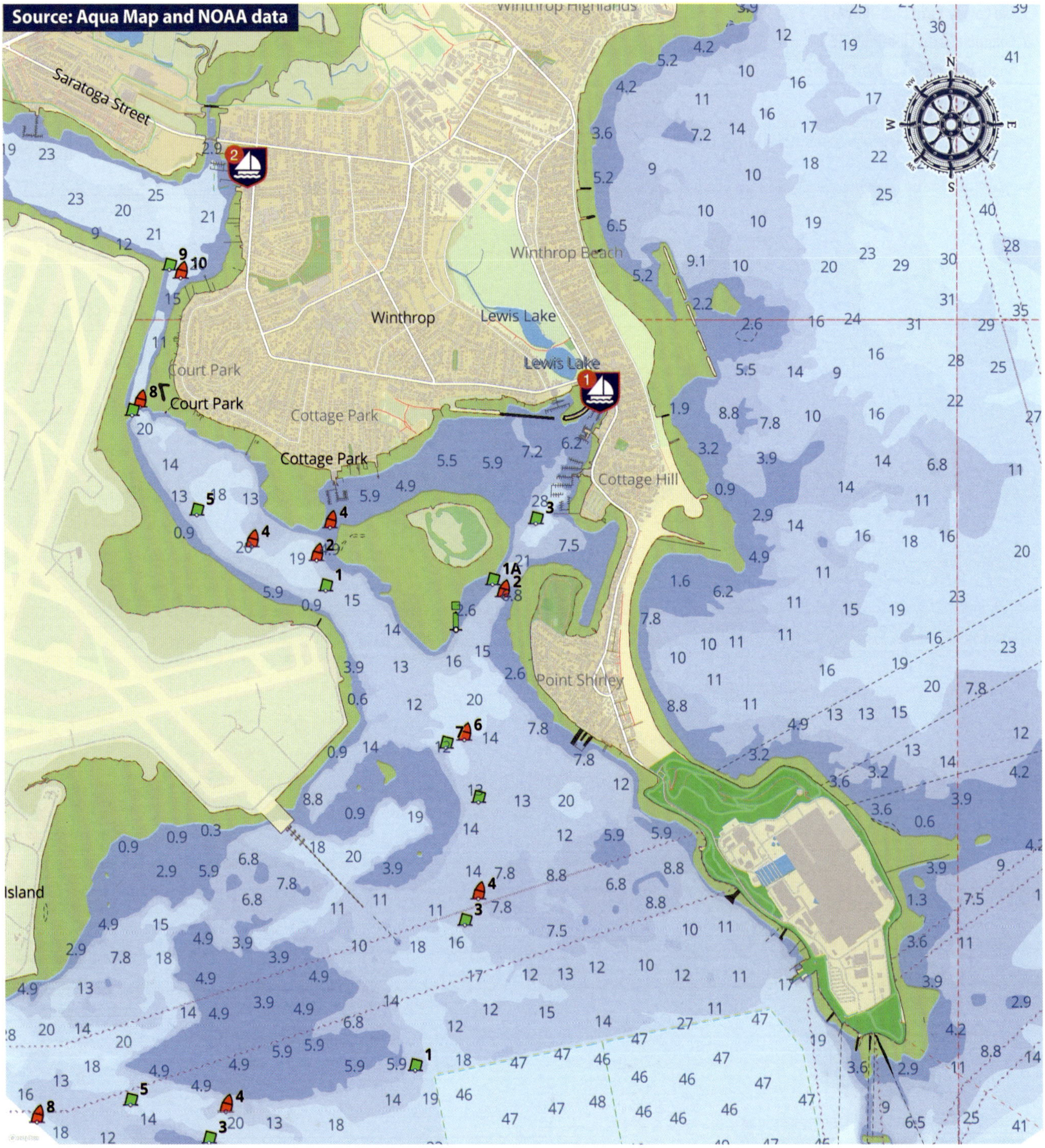

Fan Pier Marina Boston is the only marina in the Seaport District, a lively neighborhood of restaurants, shopping and entertainment. With 100 slips and a 600-foot attenuator breakwater, this marina can accommodate vessels to 500 feet. Make your reservations early as weekends sell out. Just past the distinctive New England Aquarium on Central Wharf, Faneuil Hall Marketplace, Quincy Market and the best Italian food on this continent await you on the North End, easily accessible from several marine facilities.

Facilities with ample transient space include Marina at Rowes Wharf and Boston Waterboat Marina, tucked behind the north side of Long Wharf. Along with dockage and moorings, Boston Waterboat Marina offer a protected dinghy landing as well as on-site marine supply and maintenance. The marina traces its heritage to the days when Boston's actual waterboat, which was tasked to tend oceangoing vessels moored in the harbor, once berthed here. It is the city's oldest continually operating yachting facility and has been family owned for over 150 years.

On the next wharf is Boston Yacht Haven Inn & Marina. This marina offers slips that can accommodate vessels up to 400 feet with dockside electricity, water and in-slip, pump-out stations. On shore the 10-room boutique hotel has amenities for both yacht owners and crew in addition to the usual marina amenities. The concierge will assist you in making reservations for dinner, attending the theater or touring around Boston. Make your reservations as early as March if planning a visit on peak weekends.

On the north side of the Charles River, Constitution Marina offers protected floating berths in the scenic outer harbor. It is located right on the Freedom Trail in the Charlestown neighborhood of Boston and has a year-round liveaboard community. There is usually ample transient space, although reservations are advised. Laundry facilities and a heated swimming pool are available at the marina's main building and restaurants are within easy walking distance.

With a full range of dockside services, Charlestown Marina offers 350 single and doubled-sided slips on both Piers 6 and 8 with 300- and 600-foot wave attenuators creating a calm boat basin. The Pier 6 attenuator is rated for a Cat 5 hurricane. They also have a floating amenities barge with restrooms, showers and laundry facilities

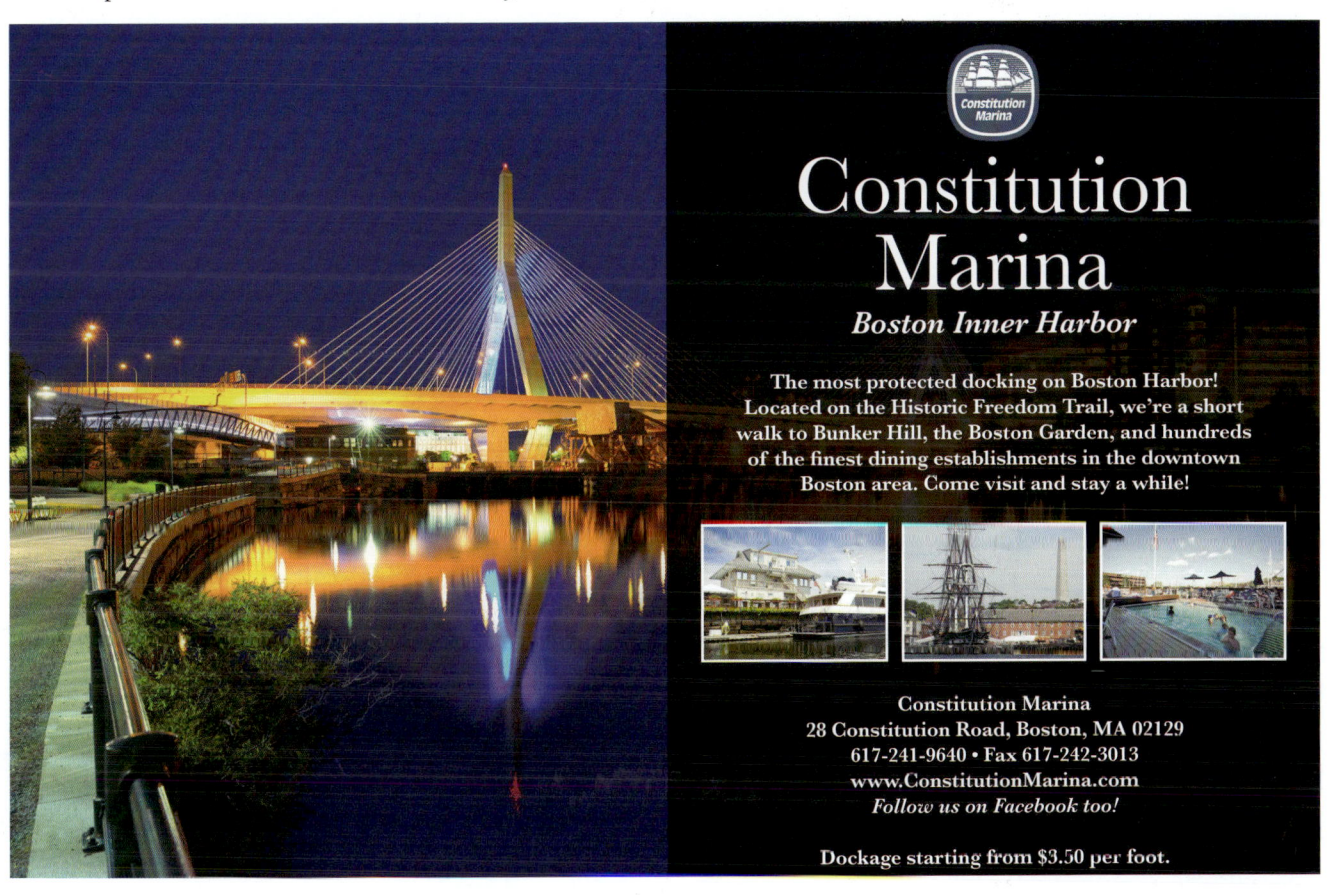

Boston Harbor Area, MA

BOSTON'S INNER HARBOR		Largest Vessel	VHF	Total Slips	Approach/ Dockside Depth	Floating Docks	Gas/ Diesel	Repairs/ Haulout	Min/Max Amps	Pump-Out Station
1. Boston Harbor Shipyard and Marina WiFi	(617) 561-1400	125	9	180	25.0 / 25.0	F	GD	RH	30 / 50	P
2. Fan Pier Marina Boston WiFi	**(617) 865-5757**	**500**	**9**	**100**	**25.0 / 25.0**	**F**	**GD**		**30 / 100**	**P**
3. Marina at Rowes Wharf WiFi	(617) 748-5013	200	9	38	30.0 / 25.0	F		H	30 / 100	P
4. Boston Waterboat Marina WiFi	**(617) 523-1027**	**200**	**9**	**45**	**15.0 / 14.0**	**F**	**D**		**30 / 100**	**P**
5. Boston Yacht Haven Inn & Marina WiFi	**(617) 367-5050**	**400**	**9**	**100**	**25.0 / 25.0**	**F**	**GD**		**30 / 200+**	**P**
6. Constitution Marina WiFi	**(617) 241-9640**	**145**	**69**	**300**	**35.0 / 10.8**	**F**		**R**	**30 / 200+**	**P**
7. Charlestown Marina WiFi	**(617) 242-2020**	**500**	**71**	**371**	**45.0 / 35.0**	**F**	**GD**		**30 / 200+**	**P**
MYSTIC RIVER										
8. Marina at Admirals Hill WiFi	(617) 889-4002	60	9	136	6.0 / 6.0	F		RH	30 / 50	P
9. The Mystic Wellington Yacht Club Inc.-PRIVATE	(781) 396-2367			128	/				30	

WiFi Wireless Internet Access
Visit www.waterwayguide.com for current rates, fuel prices, website addresses and other up-to-the-minute information.
(Information in the table is provided by the facilities.)

Scan here for more details:

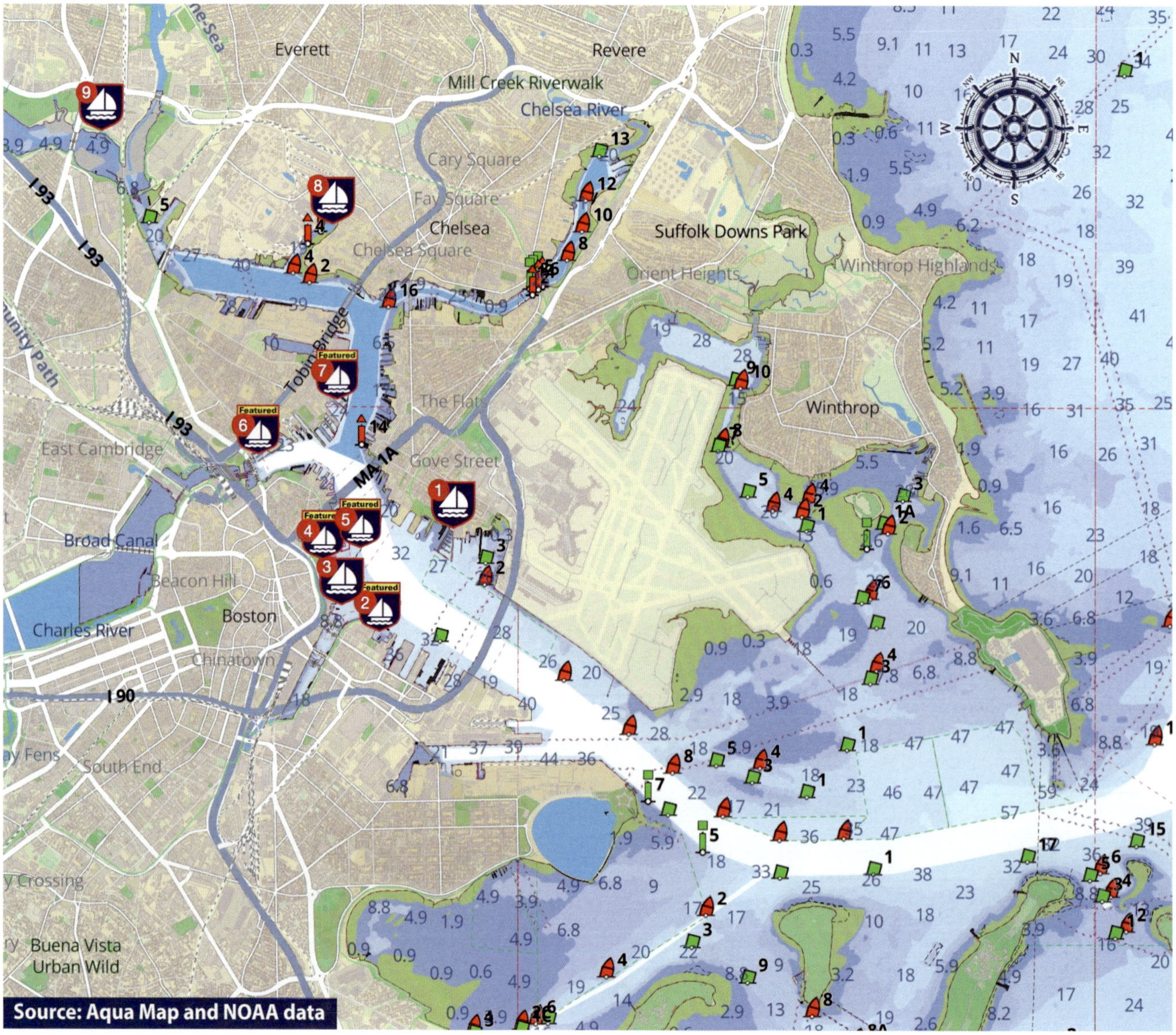

Source: Aqua Map and NOAA data

BOSTON YACHT HAVEN INN & MARINA

BOSTON WATERBOAT MARINA

CONSTITUTION MARINA

CHARLESTOWN MARINA

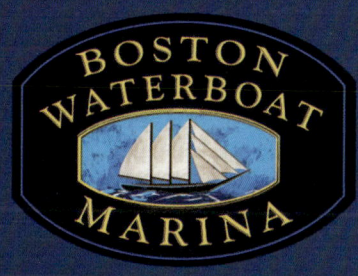

CONSTITUTION MARINA

Charles River

Chelsea is across the Mystic and Chelsea Rivers from Boston, straight ahead while heading up the harbor. It is the second most densely populated city in Massachusetts and the smallest by area. Marina at Admirals Hill is past the high-rise bridge and a park then north up a side channel with slips (to 60 feet) and repairs. Parks, trails, restaurants and more are within walking distance. The Mystic Wellington Yacht Club Inc. to the north is strictly private.

NAVIGATION: North Channel (preferred) and South Channel both lead from President Roads into big Broad Sound. Wide North Channel, marked by large, lighted sea buoys, is the primary thoroughfare for both big ships and recreational craft. South Channel is narrower, aids are smaller and ledges encroach. From Finns Ledge at the northern end of North Channel, it is 3 miles to Bass Point on the southwestern tip of Nahant. Beyond Nahant are two narrow channels—one leading to Lynn Harbor and the other to Point of Pines and Pines River.

Dockage: Point of Pines Yacht Club on the Pines River has been a fixture there for over 100 years, while Lynn Yacht Club in Lynn Harbor has been around for over 150 years. They are among the oldest clubs in the area. (They are also strictly private.) Fortunately, the municipal Seaport Landing Marina in Lynn Harbor offers transient dockage to single boats or club fleets and is capable of accommodating vessels up to 65 feet in length with full amenities.

Anchorage: Nahant Harbor off Broad Sound has 17 to 23 feet MLW with good holding in sand. It is protected from the northeast through northwest.

■ SALEM SOUND

Four historic harbors—Marblehead, Salem, Beverly and Manchester—line Salem Sound, a 4-mile-wide break in the shore located to the northeast of Boston Harbor's entrance. Although all four began as commercial fishing villages, they have evolved into popular recreational harbors with dockage, moorings, marine suppliers and a wealth of shoreside attractions.

Broad Sound, MA

PINES RIVER		Largest Vessel	VHF	Total Slips	Approach/ Dockside Depth	Floating Docks	Gas/ Diesel	Repairs/ Haulout	Min/Max Amps	Pump-Out Station
1. Point of Pines Yacht Club-PRIVATE WiFi	(781) 284-9717	50		70	20.0 / 15.0	F	G		30	
LYNN HARBOR										
2. Lynn Yacht Club-PRIVATE	(781) 595-9825	50	9	50	12.0 / 8.0	F		H	30	
3. Seaport Landing Marina	(781) 592-5821	65	16	165	20.0 / 15.0	F	GD	RH	50	P

WiFi Wireless Internet Access
Visit www.waterwayguide.com for current rates, fuel prices, website addresses and other up-to-the-minute information.
(Information in the table is provided by the facilities.)

Scan here for more details:

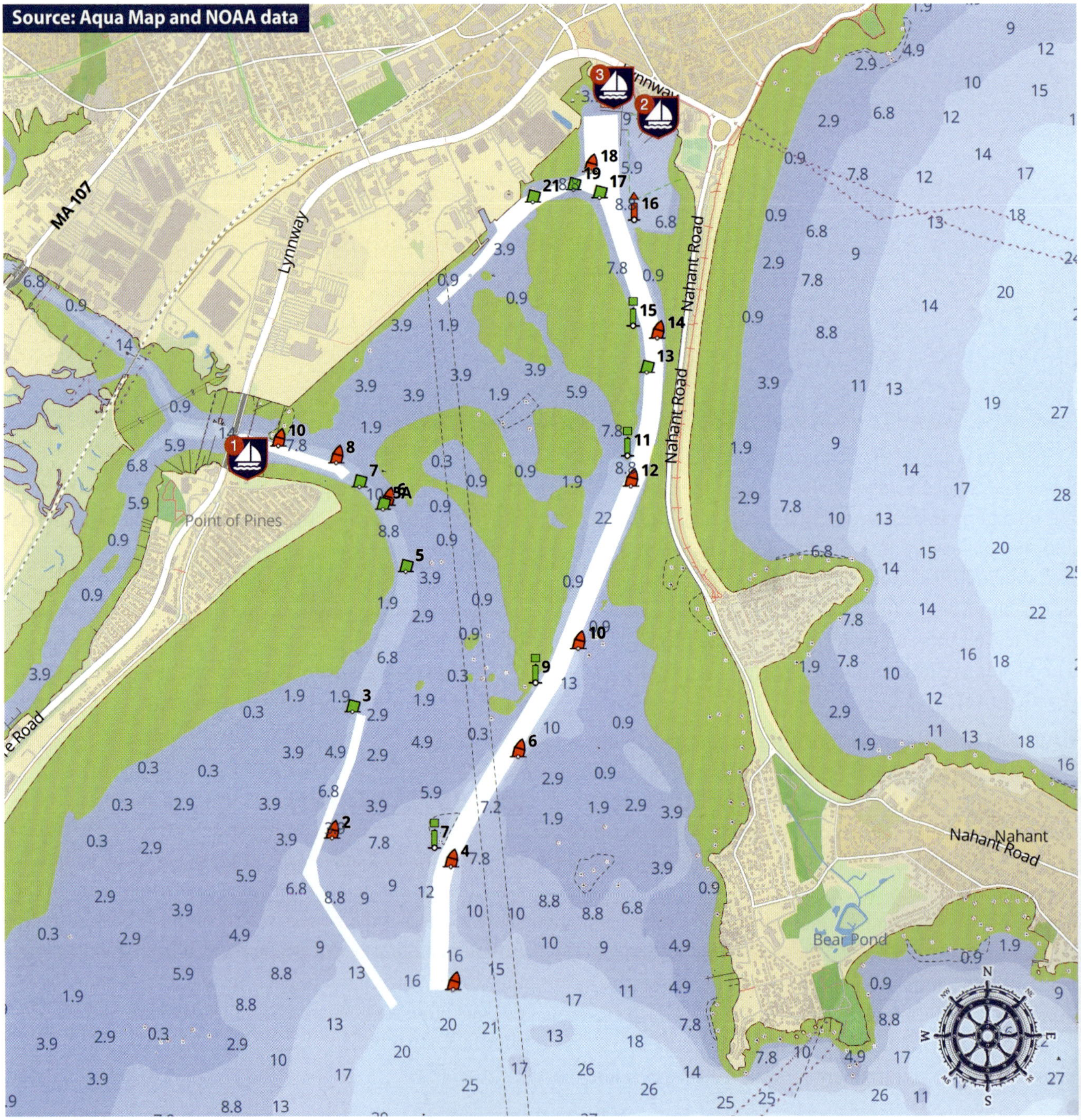

Salem Sound's mouth is littered with islands, rocks and ledges with three main channels threading through them. Strangers should be wary of trying to enter or leave in heavy weather or poor visibility, but keep the camera handy on a clear day. Good landmarks are on both sides of the sound including the tall lights on Bakers Island and Marblehead Neck, the looming red brick steeple of Abbot Hall, the three stacks of Salem's power plant and the observation tower on Gales Point.

The historical tendency here was to go easy on boats by leaving them on moorings rather than beating them up on rough piers. That trend has been carried to the extreme and every bit of water that's not actively set aside as a channel has been filled with moorings. In high summer, the carpet of boats swinging together on their pennants is quite the sight to behold.

Marblehead

Famous throughout the yachting world as the "Yachting Capital of America," Marblehead was historically a fishing village. Even today, the harbor maintains a small fleet of lobster and fishing vessels. But now more than ever, this is a key layover port for cruising and racing boats from the world's most serious yachting circles.

NAVIGATION: Salem Channel is the northernmost entrance to Salem Sound and deep-draft passage used by commercial craft heading for Salem's terminals. It runs between Bakers Island and Great Misery Island, through Salem Sound and then turns to the southeast to Salem Harbor. In the middle of Salem Sound is Children's Island Channel, which leads between Children's Island and Eagle Island. Marblehead Channel to the west runs between Children's Island and Marblehead Neck then along the peninsula past mid-sound rocks and shoals to

Salem Harbor

Marblehead Harbor

Marblehead Harbor, MA

MARBLEHEAD		Largest Vessel	VHF	Total Slips	Approach/ Dockside Depth	Floating Docks	Gas/ Diesel	Repairs/ Haulout	Min/Max Amps	Pump-Out Station
1. Corinthian Yacht Club-PRIVATE WiFi	(781) 631-0005	100	9		10.0 / 7.0					
2. Eastern Yacht Club-PRIVATE	(781) 631-4059				/			H		
3. Marblehead Yacht Club-PRIVATE	(781) 631-9771				8.0 / 6.0	F			30	P
4. Dolphin Yacht Club-PRIVATE	(781) 631-8000		68		20.0 / 8.0					
5. Boston Yacht Club-PRIVATE	(781) 631-3100	80	68		20.0 / 20.0	F	GD			P
6. Marblehead Harbormaster	(781) 631-2386	100	16		22.0 / 15.0	F			30 / 100	P
7. The Landing Restaurant & Marina WiFi	(781) 639-1266	60		12	25.0 / 15.0				30	
8. Marblehead Trading Co.	(781) 639-0029	100		4	30.0 / 17.0	F	GD	RH	30 / 100	

WiFi Wireless Internet Access
Visit www.waterwayguide.com for current rates, fuel prices, website addresses and other up-to-the-minute information.
(Information in the table is provided by the facilities.)

Scan here for more details:

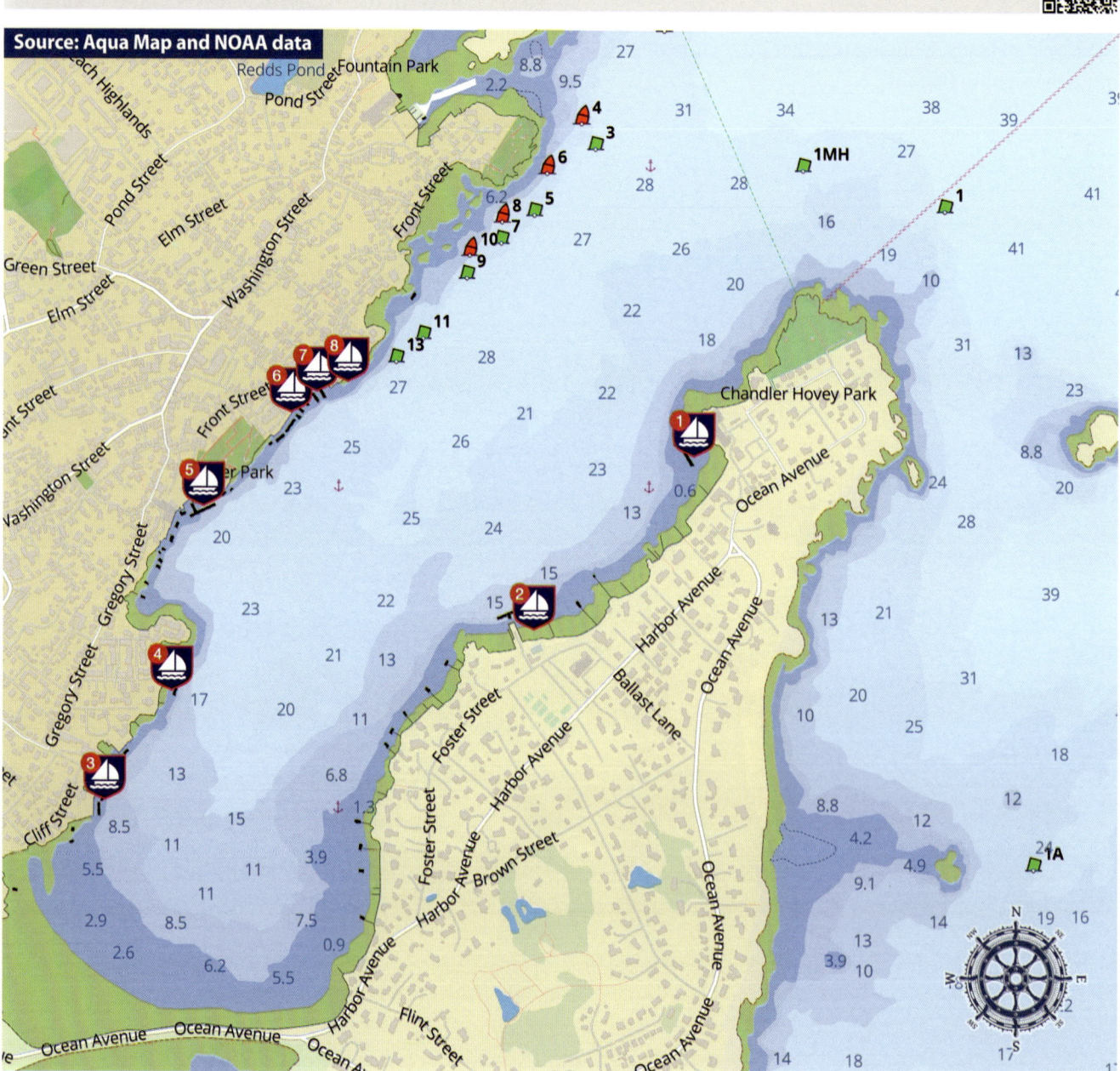

Source: Aqua Map and NOAA data

Salem Harbor. Tidal range here averages 9 feet but the tidal current has little force except in Beverly Harbor, in the northwest of Salem Sound, where it sets across the channel in several places.

The Marblehead Harbor is well protected in all directions except the northeast. Indeed, many vessels have fetched up on the causeway beach at the head of the harbor during a three-day nor'easter. If the wind veers toward that direction, seek shelter on the Beverly side.

Dockage/Moorings: While anchoring in this busy harbor is not an option, several yacht clubs and the town of Marblehead are likely to have moorings available to visitors. Most of the 2,300 or so moorings in the harbor are privately owned (with a 15-year waiting list to get one), and you must call ahead to one of the several listed facilities to arrange for a mooring, based upon availability. Hansen Marine Engineering (32 Tioga Way, 781-631-3282) is a thoroughly outfitted marine engine parts supply, should a DIY project beckon you.

One of the several private yacht clubs here may be able to arrange a guest mooring and most offer launch service. Corinthian Yacht Club offers transient moorings for a nightly fee. The fee includes launch service to and from the club where showers and a laundry facility are available. Eastern Yacht Club offers launch service to their private club (for an extra fee), as do Marblehead Yacht Club and Dolphin Yacht Club.

The private Boston Yacht Club is as elegant as it is famous. Members of recognized yacht clubs and their guests may request a rental mooring on a first-come, first-served basis (includes launch service) but be sure to pack a blazer for dinner.

Contact the Marblehead Harbormaster (VHF Channel 16) for availability of a mooring and for assistance on your approach. Washrooms, showers and laundry facilities are available at the Marblehead Town Landing. There is a large dinghy dock and additional docks for loading and unloading (30-minute limit).

The Marblehead Trading Co., the first facility on the northern shore, is a compact but complete boatyard with major lift capacity and a marine supply store, The Forepeak Ship's Chandlery (781-631-7184). They maintain just 4 transient slips to 100 feet. This is a working boatyard so don't expect resort amenities. The Landing Restaurant & Marina is just next door with a globally inspired menu and a few slips to 60 feet. Ask ahead about staying overnight.

Salem

Salem Harbor is homeport to a multi-million-dollar replica of the 171-foot *Friendship of Salem*, a world-ranging square-rigged trading ship originally launched in 1797 on which daily tours are given. Peabody Essex Museum and numerous other intriguing points of interest, restaurants and boating amenities are all within easy walking distance of this premier harbor. Visit Salem during the month-long Haunted Happenings celebration in October and you'll see an entirely different side of the original "witch" city.

NAVIGATION: From Marblehead, follow the South Channel (Marblehead Channel), leaving Grays Rock to the northeast and pass directly between green Kettle Bottom Ledge daybeacon "1" and red nun buoy "2." As you continue, pass between green can buoy "3" and red nun buoy "4" marking the Endeavors Rocks to the north and south. Next, leave red nun buoy "6" and the submerged Aquavitae rocks to the north. Enter Salem Channel between Baker and Great Misery Island and then follow the well-marked, deep-water ship channel into Salem Harbor. The lighted stacks or chimneys of the Salem Harbor power plant on Salem Neck can be seen for many miles out to sea.

> NOTE: Salem is the U.S. Customs Port of Entry for the region and Customs maintains a dock for incoming vessels. The Salem Harbormaster (978-741-0098 or VHF Channel 09) can assist with mooring requests.

Dockage/Moorings: Fred J. Dion Yacht Yard Inc. at the head of the harbor can handle virtually any yacht refitting or rebuilding requirement and has a substantial stock room. The yard is a third-generation family business with a tradition of quality service since 1914. Call on VHF Channel 09 for availability and directions. Palmer's Cove Yacht Club to the north is private (no transients).

Located inside the ample protection of Derby Wharf is Pickering Wharf Marina, which is central to an array of shops and restaurants in the mini-mall on Pickering Wharf. Because of its convenient access and central location, a berth here is in high demand during the summer; advance reservations are recommended. They can accommodate sailboats and powerboats to 120 feet with full amenities.

GOIN' ASHORE

SALEM, MA

ATTRACTIONS

1. New England Pirate Museum
Historic presentations on pirates with wax figures, some artifacts and a souvenir shop (274 Derby St., 978-741-2800).

2. Peabody Essex Museum
Modern museum featuring regional American/Asian art and artifacts plus an atrium and garden restaurant (161 Essex St., 978-745-9500).

3. Salem Maritime National Historic Site
Historic buildings, wharves and a tall ship on a 9-acre park exploring the age of sailing ships (160 Derby St., 978-740-1650).

4. Salem Witch Museum
Life-size stage sets, exhibits and tours exploring the 1692 Salem witch trials through modern-day witchcraft at 19 1/2 N. Washington Square (978-744-1692).

5. The House of the Seven Gables
Tours of the restored 1668 home that inspired Hawthorne's novel plus verdant seaside gardens at 15 Derby St.(978-744-0991)

SERVICES

6. Feline Hospital
81 Webb St. (978-744-8020)

7. Derby Street Laundry
82 Derby St. (978-887-6912)

8. Hawthorne Animal Health Care
120 Canal St. (978-741-2300)

9. J & W Marine Service Inc
Boat and outboard brokerage with some limited marine supplies at 56 Bridge St. (978-744-7717).

10. Lafayette Laundry
114 Lafayette St. (978-962-9618)

11. Salem Family Health Center
47 Congress St. (978-744-8388)

12. Salem Public Library
370 Essex St. (978-744-0860)

13. Salem Post Office
2 Margin St. (978-744-4671)

MARINAS

14. Palmer's Cove Yacht Club
74 Leavitt St. (978-744-9722)

15. Pickering Wharf Marina
23 Congress St. (978-744-2727)

16. Safe Harbor Hawthorne Cove
10 White St. (978-740-9890)

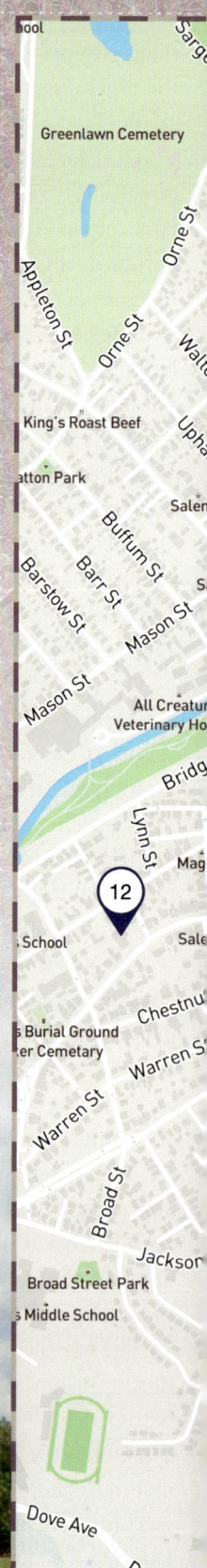

For a period of 20 years around the turn of the 18th century during the "Golden Age of Sail," Salem was truly America's trading capital and crossroads of the world. Daring sea captains and undaunted investors launched voyages that would open up the lucrative eastern trade to New England. Vessels laden with cod, rum, molasses, shingles and other products plied angry waters around Cape Horn and Cape of Good Hope to exchange their goods for exotic spices and other luxuries, returning to reap vast profits. By 1800, Salem was the sixth largest city in America and the richest per capita. Although those days are gone, the aura of that time persists in the grand homes and government houses that marked the era and, in a few remaining wharves, memorializing the many that once stretched their arms toward returning ships from the Orient.

Salem Harbor Area, MA

SALEM		Largest Vessel	VHF	Total Slips	Approach/ Dockside Depth	Floating Docks	Gas/ Diesel	Repairs/ Haulout	Min/Max Amps	Pump-Out Station
1. Fred J Dion Yacht Yard Inc.	**(978) 744-0844**	100	9	20	10.0 / 8.0	F		RH	30	
2. Palmer's Cove Yacht Club-PRIVATE WiFi	(978) 223-7527	40	78	162	/			H	30	
3. Pickering Wharf Marina	(978) 744-2727	55	9	100	8.0 / 8.0	F			30 / 50	
4. Safe Harbor Hawthorne Cove WiFi	(978) 740-9890	65	8	110	15.0 / 6.0	F		RH	30 / 50	
BEVERLY										
5. Jubilee Yacht Club-PRIVATE	(978) 922-9611	50	78		35.0 / 7.0	F	GD			
6. Tuck Point Marina	(978) 922-4631	35	7	53	35.0 / 25.0			H	30 / 50	
7. Beverly Port Marina Inc. WiFi	(978) 232-3300	200	79	350	28.0 / 28.0	F	GD	RH	30 / 100	
DANVERS RIVER										
8. Liberty Marina	(978) 774-5105	50	9	180	12.0 / 8.0	F		RH	30 / 50	
9. Danversport Marina WiFi	(978) 774-8644	55	9	304	8.0 / 8.0	F	G	RH	50	P

WiFi Wireless Internet Access
Visit www.waterwayguide.com for current rates, fuel prices, website addresses and other up-to-the-minute information.
(Information in the table is provided by the facilities.)

Scan here for more details:

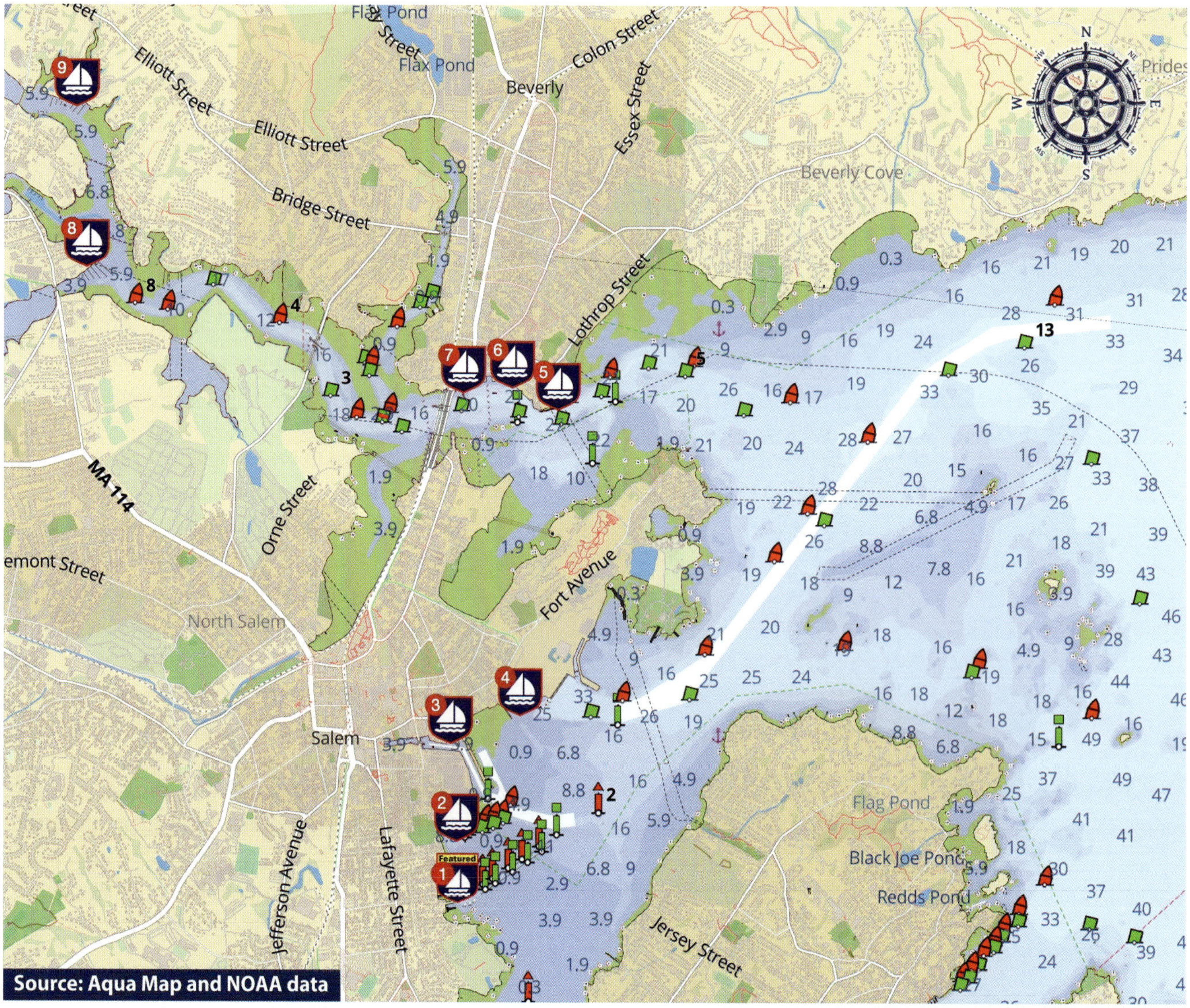

Source: Aqua Map and NOAA data

Salem Historic City Center

Safe Harbor Hawthorne Cove has the first transient docks encountered on entry to the northwest just past the power plant's huge stacks. The marina offers 110 slips to 65 feet and 270 moorings for seasonal customers and transient boaters. They also offer repairs. The marina is conveniently located next to the famed House of Seven Gables and in close proximity to some of the most historic and reportedly haunted sites in the U.S.

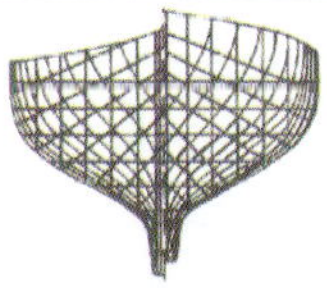

Be sure to call the marina on VHF Channel 78 for approach instructions to their private channel. If all else fails, the Salem Harbormaster is very helpful and overnight tie-up can usually be arranged.

NOTE: The town of Salem requires a closed head (No-Discharge Zone) and offers free pump-out services only on weekends. Call Salem Pump-out on VHF Channel 09.

Anchorage: A few boats can anchor outside the Salem Harbor mooring area to the south of flashing green "23" in 7 to 17 feet MLW. Holding is good in mud and grass, although it is exposed to the north-northeast. Most boats honor the no-wake buoy by inches so it is best to be south of it.

Beverly Harbor

There are three free docks here for typing up your dinghy: Dinghy Dock-Central Wharf and Dinghy Dock-South River Harborwalk are in Salem and West Town Landing is on the Marblehead side of the harbor.

Beverly Harbor

Although dubbed "Birthplace of the American Navy" in honor of the schooner *Hannah*, the first ship commissioned for the Continental Navy by Gen. George Washington, Beverly's harbor area today has only a few reminders of its historic past including Hospital Point Lighthouse (circa 1801).

NAVIGATION: Entrance into Beverly Harbor is easily made at Tuck Point by keeping Hospital Point Range Front Light to the north and following the deep, well-marked channel up the Danvers River. Be mindful of the rocks to the southwest of green can "13," which depending on the tide may or may not be exposed.

Watch for shoaling near **Veterans Memorial Bridge** (49-foot fixed vertical clearance) that crosses the Danvers River between Beverly and Salem. Just beyond that is a

MBTA/AMTRAK Railroad Bridge with a closed 3-foot vertical clearance (usually open). The swing bridge opens on signal from 5:00 a.m. to midnight daily. On Christmas Day and New Years Day, the draw will open as soon as possible but not more than 1 hour after notice is given by calling the number posted at the bridge. You can contact the Beverly Harbormaster for more details at 978-921-6059.

Beyond the bridge, the Bass River (carrying depths to 5 feet MLW) branches off to the north. Severe shoaling has been reported on the Bass River from the **Hall Whitaker Bridge** (5-foot closed vertical clearance) to Bass Haven Yacht Club. The draw for the bridge will open on signal if at least a 24-hour notice is given. Mariners are advised to use caution while transiting the area.

The Danvers River continues to the west with good depths beyond the **Kernwood Avenue Bridge** (8-foot closed vertical clearance). The draw will open on signal from May 1 through September 30, midnight to 5:00 a.m., and from October 1 through April 30, from 7:00 p.m. to 5:00 a.m., only after at least a 1-hour advance notice is given by calling the number posted at the bridge.

Farther travel up the Danvers River is somewhat problematic for deep-drafted vessels as the channel is winding and sometimes narrow. You are well advised to keep an eye on the depth sounder.

NO WAKE ZONE

The entire Danvers River is a No-Wake Zone.

Dockage/Moorings: Private Jubilee Yacht Club has limited rental moorings and also maintains a launch service. Family-oriented Tuck Point Marina has 53 slips and welcomes transients (to 35 feet). Beverly Port Marina Inc. to the west has 50 transient slips to 200 feet as well as a well-stocked ship store, laundry facilities and a comprehensive service department. A good selection of fine restaurants and a movie theatre are within a healthy walking distance up Cabot Street.

Liberty Marina is located farther upriver where the Danvers River splits and the Crone River branches to the west. They offer a family-friendly environment with slips to 50 feet plus a full menu of maintenance and repair services. Danversport Marina is located where the Danvers becomes the Porter River with some reserved transient space with full amenities including a pool and sundeck.

Side Trip: Great Misery & Little Misery Islands

These islands were originally inhabited by the Masconomet people and named by the European arrivals for the three miserable winter days that shipbuilder Captain Robert Moulton spent here in the 1620s. Located at the mouth of Manchester Bay, these nearly joined scenic gems offer quiet refuge from the crowded harbors of the Salem Sound area, although weekend day-trippers are numerous. These islands are maintained by the Trustees of the Reservation and offer 2.5 miles of moderate hiking trails but no services.

Anchorage/Mooring: The City of Beverly maintains moorings between Great & Little Misery Islands. A number of private or local yacht club moorings are often available at Cocktail Cove, the small bight on the north side of Great Misery Island. You can drop the hook at Little Misery Island in the tiny bay leading to the unnavigable cut between the two islands. The islands are largely open and their accessible beaches invite exploration by dinghy.

Manchester

Beautifully kept clapboard homes quietly line the narrow, shaded streets in the well-known New England village of Manchester. Commercial establishments are sprinkled along the road tracing the head of the harbor. Crosby's Marketplace (978-526-4444) is stocked with all the supermarket basics and many specialty items. There is a laundromat, a sizable hardware store, gift shops and restaurants. The large Manchester City Library is just up the hill overlooking the harbor. Visitors can use the Internet access at the library one time for up to 1 hour. Singing Beach, an excellent swimming spot, is just a 1-mile walk from the boatyards.

NAVIGATION: When cruising the 6 miles from Beverly to Manchester, you will find good water close to shore for a waterside view of the elegant estate and summer homes of Boston's Gold Coast. The entrance to Manchester is crowded but the unhurried harbor is graced by the Manchester Yacht Club's beautiful Victorian gazebo perched on a promontory near the entrance in front of its refined clubhouse. The channel is straight and well marked but a bit shallow. Boats drawing more than 5 feet are advised to arrive on a rising tide.

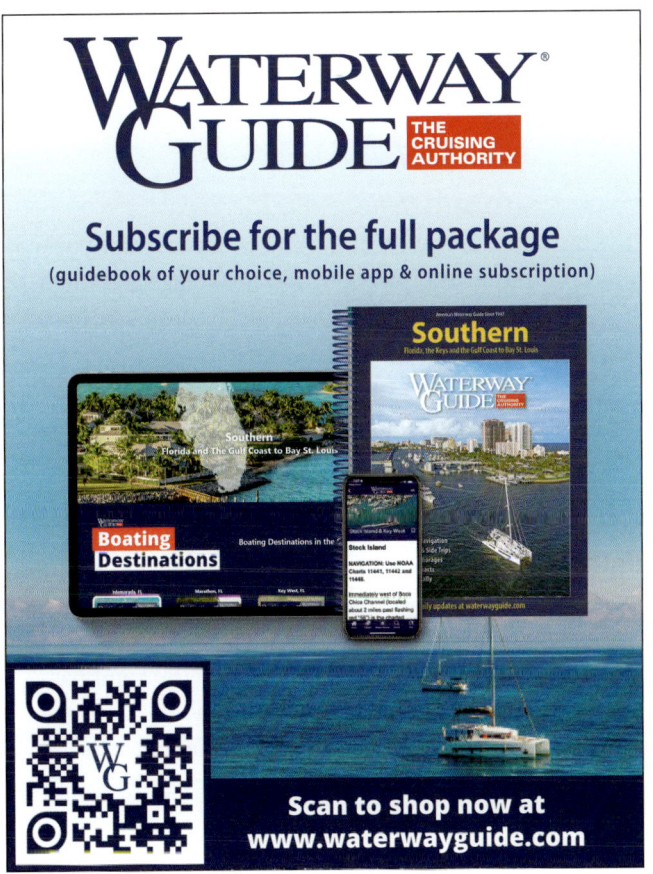

Manchester Harbor, MA

MANCHESTER		Largest Vessel	VHF	Total Slips	Approach/ Dockside Depth	Floating Docks	Gas/ Diesel	Repairs/ Haulout	Min/Max Amps	Pump-Out Station
1. Manchester Yacht Club-PRIVATE	(978) 526-4595		78		/					
2. Crocker's Boat Yard	(978) 526-1971	60	78	16	7.0 / 7.0	F		RH	30	
3. Manchester Marine Corp. (WiFi)	(978) 526-7911	45	72	40	9.0 / 7.0	F	GD	RH	30 / 50	P

(WiFi) Wireless Internet Access
Visit www.waterwayguide.com for current rates, fuel prices, website addresses and other up-to-the-minute information.
(Information in the table is provided by the facilities.)

Scan here for more details:

Source: Aqua Map and NOAA data

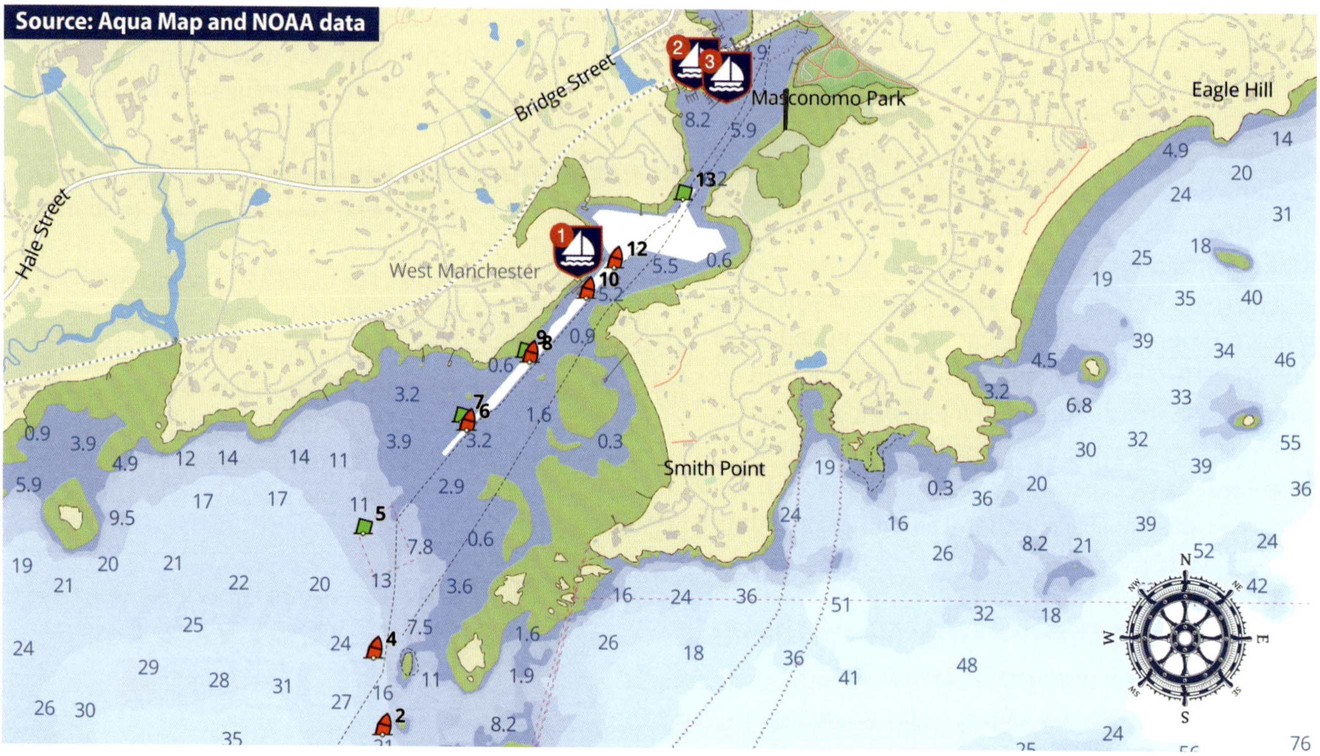

The harbor above Proctor Point is virtually landlocked affording excellent protection, and the village, although small and picturesque, is surprisingly accommodating to cruising visitors.

Dockage: The private Manchester Yacht Club does not have transient space, but Crocker's Boat Yard has some limited dockage space in the inner harbor at the top of the bight north of green can buoy "13." The family-owned and -operated working yard has a long history of maintaining wooden boats and have the staff and facilities for most any job-wood, fiberglass, power or sail.

Manchester Marine Corp. next door is another working yard that has been around since 1892 and has an in-house staff of craftsmen, technicians and customer service professionals. They maintain some transient floating dock space as well as guest moorings.

Anchorage: There is room to anchor in the inner basins of Manchester Harbor in 6 feet MLW; however, anchoring is restricted to vessels 45 feet and under and is strictly enforced. Reed Park at the northeastern end of the harbor allows short-time tie-ups (15 minutes) and a local launch is available through Manchester Harbor Launch Service (978-770-9911).

Cape Elizabeth

Saco

Biddeford

Pages 505-518

Kennebunkport

Gulf of Maine

Kittery

York Harbor

Portsmouth

Island of
Shoals

Atlantic Ocean

*Plum
Island Sound*

Newburyport

Rockport

Pages 492-505

Essex

Gloucester

Gloucester Waterfront

■ GLOUCESTER TO NEWBURYPORT

Sandy beaches, culturally vibrant villages and boat-loads of history await between the Queen's capes. Cape Ann to Cape Elizabeth can be taken in a leap, but that discounts temptations like the offshore Isles of Shoals and rewarding river towns like Newburyport, Portsmouth, Kittery and Kennebunkport.

The ambiance north from Gloucester reflects a growing distance from the more recreational-focused ports farther south and cruisers feel a shift in the balance of services. Working waterfronts slot maritime businesses and visitors' pleasures neatly together to the benefit of both.

Gloucester

The name Gloucester has been synonymous with fishermen and their boats for three centuries. The remaining fishing fleet has been joined by busy schooner cruise business and both of those are wonderful foreground against the green hills dotted with wind towers, lighthouses and the old town's spires. Photographers will rejoice.

On the western shore near the entrance of Gloucester is Normans Woe Rock of Longfellow's famous poem "Wreck of the Hesperus." Poems and memorials aside, Gloucester is also a highly practical stop. The harbor offers different anchorages for whichever wind threatens plus repairs for any size boat, restaurants with docks and an active summer community. Grocery stores are short walks from either side of the inner harbor and marine hardware can be obtained at the end of the harbor.

NAVIGATION: Serious ledges litter the coast between Manchester and Magnolia Harbor. Stay at least 1 mile offshore to avoid the navigational difficulty. Do not be tempted to follow the lobster boats working closer inshore; they work the ledges in ways that would be unsafe for most recreational boats.

Approaching Gloucester Harbor is made easier by a pair of large, bright lights. The Eastern Point Lighthouse flashes its big white light every 5 seconds from a height of 57 feet. It's rated as visible to 20 nm so use it to get near enough to find the Dog Bar Breakwater Light but don't approach too close to the ledges just south of the lighthouse. (As an aside, the Eastern Point Lighthouse was the 1880 home of painter Winslow Homer.)

Dog Bar Breakwater Light is a tower on a platform anchored to the rock of the breakwater and is charted as the Gloucester Breakwater Light. It is 45 feet tall and has a 4-second occulting red light (i.e., it is regularly lighted and clicks off briefly every 4 seconds as opposed to the more usual flashing light that is regularly off and clicks on briefly). Most recreational boats can take advantage of the full width of the Gloucester Harbor entrance rather than squeezing between green can buoy "1DB" and red nun buoy "2DB." Round Rock Shoal is marked by red and green flashing buoy "RR" but only shallows to 15 feet MLW and is, therefore, of little danger to most cruising vessels.

Dockage/Moorings: For a harbor of the size and historic seafaring renown of Gloucester, surprisingly few marine facilities are open to cruising visitors. The town maintains 28 transient moorings for vessels to 60 feet in three areas. The Gloucester Inner Harbor Mooring Field is well protected and close to shore. The western harbor moorings at Tenpound Island Mooring Field provide protection from the west through northeast and excellent views of the town.

The Gloucester Southeast Harbor Mooring Field is farthest from shore access and the most exposed to wake and wind chop but don't discount the entertainment value of watching the informal sunset schooner parade against a fiery sky. Launch service is complimentary if you are renting a town mooring. Contact the Gloucester Harbormaster for details.

The private Eastern Point Yacht Club at the mouth of the river provide moorings through Dockwa. They also have several rooms for rent should you choose to get off the boat for awhile. Rental moorings include launch service to and from the restaurant and bar at the cove's edge. The town launch also serves this area.

Ocean Alliance is known for their over 50 years of whale conservation but they also offer transient dockage with the fees directly supporting ocean research and conservation. (Note there is a minimum LOA of 38 feet due to the wake in the harbor.) Ocean Alliance Docks–Gloucester is located at the head of Gloucester Harbor away from the hustle of industrial harbor activities. The facility is housed in a historic Paint Factory and is within walking distance to the Rocky Neck Cultural District with restaurants, shops, galleries and parks.

Facilities to the south include North Shore Sport Fishing Dock and Beacon Marine Basin Inc. They may have space for you on their floating docks but call ahead. Brown's Yacht Yard to the southeast is a full-service boatyard with six transient slips and three transient moorings. There is no launch service but dinghy tie-ups are permitted at the yard's full-service dock.

Pier 7 Marina welcomes transients at their dock or on a mooring with full amenities. They do not offer launch service; however, you may contact Gloucester Launch directly on VHF Channel 72 or call 978-726-0155. It is a short walk to waterfront restaurants, live theater, art galleries, beaches and nightlife destinations. The large Cruiseport Gloucester Marine Terminal is west of the state fishing pier. They have diesel and cater to large, commercial vessels.

Anchorage: There are no viable anchorages in the Gloucester Inner Harbor and why would you with all those moorings to choose from? If you are set on anchoring, there is plenty of deep water in the outer harbor. The harbor's considerable fetch and openness to prevailing southwesterlies makes a spot behind the breakwater at Eastern Point the most chop-protected choice in summer. Even so, you are almost certain to roll with the wrap-around ocean surge in this otherwise attractive location.

In a shoulder-season nor'easter, snugging up close to the few moorings in Wonson Cove provides the most protection outside the inner harbor in 14 to 22 feet MLW with a mud bottom. (Don't forget the 9-foot tidal range and the scope that goes along with high tides.)

A dinghy dock is in the inner harbor's North Channel behind the water taxi stop. Tie up between the floating dock and the rock wall on either side of the docks.

Side Trip: Blynman Canal, Annisquam River

Blynman Canal leads from the northwestern end of the Gloucester outer harbor into the Annisquam River and makes a good foul-weather (and picturesque fair-weather) alternative to the offshore run around Cape Ann. It is an easy run for small, maneuverable boats but offers a tricky blind curve that can create trouble for full-keel sailboats and others that don't back well.

GOIN' ASHORE

GLOUCESTER, MA

ATTRACTIONS

1. Cape Ann Museum

Houses collections celebrating the rich history of Cape Ann's evolving artistic and cultural history. The fine arts collection spans the full range of art created on and about Cape Ann (27 Pleasant St., 978-283-0455).

2. Gloucester Fisherman's Memorial

A natural destination for any mariner, the 8-foot-tall statue looks out to sea just east of the entrance to Blynman Canal on Stacy Blvd. Each Memorial Day wreaths and flowers are thrown from the base of the statue in honor of the fishermen who never returned. The 94-year-old memorial was added to the National Register of Historic Places in 1996.

3. Gloucester Harborwalk

A total of 42 granite story posts define this self-guided walking tour, each highlighting an aspect of Gloucester's history as a seaport, the rich culture and people, and how the town has evolved in response to a modern, sustainable fishing industry.

4. Gloucester Visitor Center

Located at Stage Fork Park at 24 Hough Ave. (978-281-8865). Walking trails, picnic areas, play equipment, a dog park and beautiful views are offered in addition to exhibits and tourist information. Also the location of the Gloucester Farmers Market held on Thursdays from 3:00 p.m. to 6:00 p.m.

5. Maritime Gloucester

Restored industrial harbor buildings with education and visitor centers, aquariums and exhibitions (23 Harbor Loop, 978-281-0470).

6. Ten Pound Island Lighthouse

Active lighthouse built of cast iron and brick in 1881 to guide boats into the town's inner harbor. The island allegedly received its name from the amount of money the early settlers paid the local American Indian tribe for it or for the number of sheep pens (pounds) that it could hold.

SERVICES

7. Gloucester Post Office
15 Dale Ave. (978-283-2361)

8. Isabel Babson Memorial Library
69 Main St. (978-283-5624)

9. Lahey Health Urgent Care
305 Gloucester Crossing Rd. (978-381-7700)

10. SeaPort Veterinary Hospital
100 Eastern Ave. (978-283-8883)

MARINAS

11. Beacon Marine Basin
211 E. Main St. #19 (978-283-2380)

12. Brown's Yacht Yard
139 E. Main St. (978-281-3200)

13. Gloucester Harbormaster
19 Harbor Loop (978-282-3012)

14. North Shore Sport Fishing Dock
211 E. Main St. (978-283-6880)

15. Ocean Alliance Docks–Gloucester
32 Horton St. (978-281-2814)

16. Pier 7 Marina
6 Cripple Cove Ln. (781-858-5279)

From the shelter of the Inner Harbor marinas, there is plenty to see and do in Gloucester. The area's history is long for an American town: Gloucester was first settled only 3 years after the pilgrims landed in Plymouth. Gloucester is best known, however, for the Georges and Grand Banks fisheries. The largest and best-known seafood business (Gorton's) gave us the iconic fisherman image of a man in slickers and a sou'wester hat. Gloucester was one of the land-based settings for Sebastian Junger's book *The Perfect Storm* about the sad demise of a local fishing boat, the *Andrea Gail*. While you're in town, tip a cold one at the Crow's Nest (334 Main St., 978-281-2965) in honor of the crew.

NOAA Fisheries

Harrison Avenue Conservation Area

9 Starbucks

Harbor 9 Golf & Sports Bar

10

Marshalls

Market Basket

Dodge St

Perkins St

East Veterans School

Eastern Ave

Elizabeth Road Playground

Hartz St

Fishermans Memorial Park

Taylor St

Fair St

Russell's Florist

Taylor St

Friend Street Playground

Bass Ave

Lee's

7-Eleven

E Main St

Sayward St

Taylor St

Destino's

Crows Nest

Main St

16

Massachusetts Environmental Police

Dunkin'

Jim's Bagel and Bake Shoppe

Shaw's

Governor's Park

Prospect Street Cemetery

7 3 1

Gorton's Seafood

E Main St

Beacon St

High Street Cemetery

Cape Ann Museum

Traverse S

Haskell St

8

Two Sisters

Sargent House Museum

Main St

4

Topside Bistro

13

Brown's Mar

12

Mount Pleasa Cemetery

Gang Nam Gloucester

5

East Gloucester Elementary School

2

Captain Sol Jacobs Pa

Schooner Adventure

Inner Harbor

Gloucester Community Church

Calder

Beauport Hotel Gloucester

Cape Pond Ice

Harbor Cove

14

11

Plum St

Fort Point

Gloucester Marine Railways

15

The Studio

Beacon Hill

Babson Ledge

Black Rock

Oakes Cove

E Main St

Marble St

Swinsons Farm Park

Marb Conserv

Rocky Neck Beach

Atwater Reservation

6

Green Rock

Wonson Cove

Orchard Rd

U.S. Coast Guard

Grapevin

Gloucester Harbor, MA

GLOUCESTER		Largest Vessel	VHF	Total Slips	Approach/ Dockside Depth	Floating Docks	Gas/ Diesel	Repairs/ Haulout	Min/Max Amps	Pump-Out Station
1. Eastern Point Yacht Club-PRIVATE (WiFi)	(978) 283-3520				25.0 / 6.0	F				
2. Gloucester Southeast Harbor Mooring Field	(978) 325-5750				/					
3. Ocean Alliance Docks - Gloucester (WiFi)	(978) 281-2814	150			/ 8.0	F			30 / 50	
4. North Shore Sport Fishing Dock	(978) 283-6880	46	16		12.0 / 8.0	F	GD		30	
5. Beacon Marine Basin Inc.	(978) 283-2380	100		50	15.0 / 15.0	F	GD	R	30	
6. Brown's Yacht Yard (WiFi)	(978) 281-3200	70	9	20	12.0 / 12.0	F	GD	RH	30 / 50	
7. Pier 7 Marina (WiFi)	(781) 858-5279	70	7	30	25.0 / 15.0	F			30 / 100	
8. Gloucester Harbormaster	(978) 325-5750		16		/					
BLYNMAN CANAL										
9. Cape Ann's Marina Resort (WiFi) MM 1.0	(978) 283-2116	150	10	278	10.0 / 8.0	F	GD	RH	30 / 100	P
10. Gloucester Marina	(978) 283-2828	40		100	10.0 / 20.0	F		RH	30	
11. Annisquam Yacht Club-PRIVATE	(978) 283-4507	40	68		6.0 / 6.0					

(WiFi) Wireless Internet Access
Visit www.waterwayguide.com for current rates, fuel prices, website addresses and other up-to-the-minute information.
(Information in the table is provided by the facilities.)

Scan here for more details:

The route is frequently narrow and lined with boats on moorings. This can be helpful as it forms a sort of curb to drifting outside the channel. Regardless, boats with drafts deeper than 5 feet will do well to pass when the 8-foot tide is at or near high due to shoaling.

NAVIGATION: If entering from Gloucester Harbor, the canal's entrance at the fast-operating **Blynman (SR 127) Bridge** (8-foot closed vertical clearance) is all but invisible until you are lined up with it. The bridge opens on signal except from noon to 6:00 p.m. on Thanksgiving Day, 6:00 p.m. on December 24 to midnight on December 25 and from 6:00 p.m. on December 31 to midnight on January 1, when the draw will open on signal if at least a 2-hour advance notice is given by calling the number posted at the bridge. It is not uncommon to wait up to 10 minutes after signaling for an opening. Be sure to stand well off until you are sure the opening is clear.

The current runs fast, as do the commercial fishing boats you'll share this passage with, and the narrow confines of the draw provide no room for passing. Boats leaving the canal are provided the courtesy of going first.

The route turns north beyond the bridge at green can buoy "49" and is straight for 0.3 mile to the **MBTA Railroad Bridge** with a 16-foot closed vertical clearance (opens on signal and usually open unless a train is approaching). A 90-degree turn in the channel just north of the bridge creates a serious traffic hazard. It

is impossible for southbound boats to see northbound boats until they are within 50 feet of the very narrow bridge. The southbound cruiser should swing wide to the north at this point for as much advance warning as possible and proceed at steerage speed until the opening is confirmed to be clear.

One-half mile farther the channel turns sharply north and goes under the **SR 128 (Yankee Division) Bridge** (65-foot fixed vertical clearance) into the Annisquam River. The surveyed depth is 6 feet MLW from Western Harbor to the railroad bridge. The remainder of the river carries 7 feet or better MLW.

⚠️ *CAUTION:* Severe shoaling has been reported in the Annisquam River. Channel buoy "24" has been relocated to mark the best water. Mariners should proceed with caution while transiting the area.

The northern end's heavy shoaling and narrow channel create difficult circumstances in a heavy sea but the route is well buoyed. Avoiding bad weather off Cape Ann is one reason to take this route but consider carefully how you will power into open water beyond the long western shoal.

Dockage: Between the bridges on the Blynman Canal lies Cape Ann's Marina Resort, a 265-slip marina with a fantastic on-site restaurant. They have been hosting

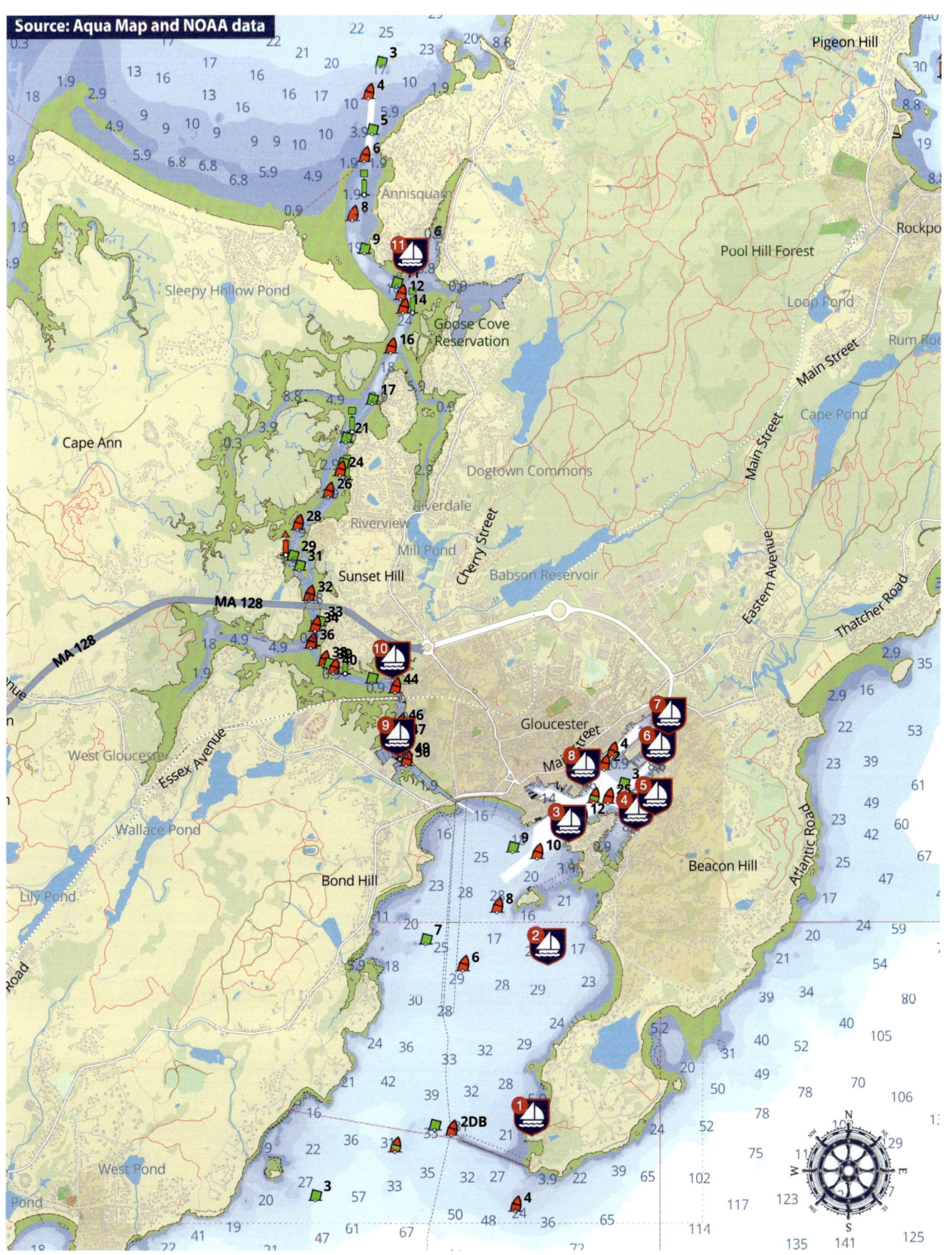

Source: Aqua Map and NOAA data

recreational boaters for over 50 years and invite you to dock and dine or stay the night, the weekend or the season It is a mile to town for shopping and additional restaurants. Nearby Gloucester Marina has very limited transient space. Call ahead.

Private Annisquam Yacht Club at the north end of the canal has a limited number of guest moorings and can accommodate visiting boats up to 50 feet. Launch service is available. Bird watching and picnicking at beautiful Wingaersheek Beach is a short dinghy ride away.

Anchorage: You can drop the hook near green can buoy "11" in at least 9 feet MLW in Annisquam near the yacht club.

Rockport Harbor

Several small harbors break the coastline of Cape Ann but Rockport at the southwestern end of Sandy Bay stands out as one of the foremost art centers on the East Coast. The fisherman's shack here has been the subject of so many paintings that it is known throughout the art world as "Motif No. 1." The lobster buoys that adorn the shack honor local lobstermen who have passed away.

Wander out on Bearskin Neck and you will find restaurants, a fish market, craft and gift shops and historic sites. Cruise up Main St. and in addition to a great selection of art studios you will find the Rockport Art Association (978-546-6604), home base to some of the best-known professional artists in the

country who live, work and teach in Rockport. Art courses of a few days to several weeks are offered all summer and there are open studios on designated weekends.

History buffs will enjoy a visit to the Sandy Bay Historical Society (978-546-9533) for an overview of North Shore history and to hear the colorful tale as to how Rockport became a "dry" town. Be sure to call ahead for their limited hours. It's a bit of a hike to Halibut Point State Park (16 Garfield Ave., 978-546-2997) at the tip of Cape Ann but well worth the trip when you see the breathtaking views of the ocean from this former Babson Farm granite quarry.

Thacher Island (south of Rockport) affords a unique view of lighthouse history. The north and south towers on Thacher Island

Rockport Harbor

Gloucester Harbor, MA

ROCKPORT		Largest Vessel	VHF	Total Slips	Approach/ Dockside Depth	Floating Docks	Gas/ Diesel	Repairs/ Haulout	Min/Max Amps	Pump-Out Station
1. Sandy Bay Yacht Club-PRIVATE (WiFi)	(978) 546-9433		9		6.5 / 6.5	F				P
2. Rockport Harbormaster	(978) 546-9589	143	9		6.5 / 6.5	F				P

(WiFi) Wireless Internet Access
Visit www.waterwayguide.com for current rates, fuel prices, website addresses and other up-to-the-minute information.
(Information in the table is provided by the facilities.)

Scan here for more details:

Source: Aqua Map and NOAA data

are the only operating twin lighthouses in America. The Thacher Island Association maintains three moorings for visiting boats. Call the keeper in advance at 508-284-0144.

Once moored you may row ashore to the ramp but expect a small per-person landing fee. You can climb the North Tower for views from Maine to Boston, hike and explore the trails covering the 50-acre island and visit the various buildings of the light station. However, there are no amenities or services on the island.

NAVIGATION: Rockport is protected by two outer and two inner breakwaters but is still open to strong northeasterly and easterly winds. The bay's southern entrance between Straitsmouth Island and Avery Ledge is narrow and rocky but the northern entrance is wide, deep and easy to navigate. Rockport Harbor itself consists of

an outer basin and two inner basins divided by the town wharf. Controlling depth is 7 feet MLW. Larger boats stop at Gloucester and visit overland.

> NOTE: If the wind is blowing strong from the east or northeast, the anchorage and tie-up spaces are uncomfortable or even dangerous here. In that case, it is best to continue on to Essex or Newburyport, if possible.

Dockage/Moorings: Rockport has no fuel docks, marine stores, or shipyards at this time, so plan accordingly. Also, Rockport Harbor is not large and only a few moorings are available by reservation. All transient vessel tie-ups in Rockport Harbor are under the direction of the Rockport Harbormaster (VHF Channel 09). It is recommended you call ahead for reservations (especially on summer weekends) at 978-546-9589.

Because of the tides and harbor depth, the maximum draft accommodated is 6.5 feet.

Private Sandy Bay Yacht Club is nearby with launch service and has space for a few vessels to tie up alongside the pilings. They also have shower facilities, a snack bar and a friendly staff to assist you with your lines.

Anchorage: When you contact the harbormaster you will likely be directed outside to an anchorage off the church (charted as "CH SP") in the cove north of town and south of Sandy Bay Ledge (Rockport Harbor). Here you will find 11- to 22-foot MLW depths with good holding in mud and rock. In less than ideal conditions it is not the most comfortable anchorage but you can easily dinghy ashore to visit the town.

Essex

The Annisquam River enters Ipswich Bay north of Cape Ann. The bay and surrounding areas are famous for their clam beds. You will encounter a few attractive harbors along this sandy coast but enter all of them carefully as shoals constantly change the channels. Again, note that using the canal and river as a "short cut" south to Gloucester Harbor in lieu of going around Cape Ann is not advisable.

In the southwest corner of Ipswich Bay is the entrance to Colonial Essex with well-preserved houses, excellent seafood restaurants (many dockside) and facilities for shallow-draft boats up to 40 feet. The village is a short walk from the waterfront.

Many of the great Gloucester schooners were built here and the Story Shipyard that built them still stands at the head of the shallow, winding river. Essex Shipbuilding Museum (978-768-7541) is located in an old schoolhouse and contains photographs and artifacts from the great days of Essex shipbuilding. The extensive history includes the circa 1927 Evelina M. Goulart now on display at the museum.

NAVIGATION: The entrance from Ipswich Bay shifts constantly and the aids to navigation (not charted) shift to match. In heavy weather seas across the bar might make the entry impassable. Entry and passage of Essex River are best made at half-tide or better. The mean tidal range is about 9 feet. Controlling depth to the town, which is about 4 narrow, shallow, meandering miles upriver, is 4 feet MLW and the river bottom is all (forgiving) mud.

Dockage: The small boat marinas here can only be accessed by shallow (less than 4-foot draft) boats. The 80-slip Essex Marina accepts vessels to 34 feet but do call ahead before making the trip to be sure they can accommodate you and for exact depths. Perkins Marine and Pike Marine are here with marine repair and services, should you need them.

Anchorage: If conditions for leaving Essex Bay are bad, head for the protected anchorage in the lee of Castle Neck Island. While there are no amenities, this is a comfortable place to wait out the weather before crossing the bar back into Ipswich Bay. Be careful as depths shallow quickly (ranging from 3 to 7 feet MLW) as you move west into the anchorage.

Side Trip: Plum Island Sound

Plum Island Sound is the juncture for the gentle rivers and streams flowing from the west and north between Castle Neck and Newburyport creating a superb kayaking area. It lies behind Plum Island's barrier strip, home to the Parker Island National Wildlife Refuge, where you might see native and migrating wildfowl. This area is a beachcomber's paradise, favored by shell collectors who seek whelks, periwinkles, slipper shells and blue mussels along the narrow sandy beach.

The sound and its northern extension, Plum Island River, make a 10-mile link between Ipswich and Newburyport but the river is suitable only for dinghies.

Newburyport

Newburyport on the Merrimack River is the smallest city in the state and one of the oldest (founded in 1635). The city boasts some finest examples of Colonial and Federal-era architecture in the nation, reminders of the days when its ships sailed around the world. Some of the most famous clipper ships in history were built here.

This classic New England coastal village offers historical interest, shopping and dining adventures. The Custom House Maritime Museum (978-462-8681) and the Cushing House Museum of Old Newbury (978-462-2681) are both well worth an afternoon visit.

NAVIGATION: Newburyport Harbor has a well marked and jettied inlet entrance via the Merrimack River, well known for its strong currents and regular shoaling. Call the Coast Guard for the latest information as you approach the Merrimack River

Merrimack River, MA

NEWBURYPORT		Largest Vessel	VHF	Total Slips	Approach/ Dockside Depth	Floating Docks	Gas/ Diesel	Repairs/ Haulout	Min/Max Amps	Pump-Out Station
1. Newburyport Harbor Marina **WiFi**	(978) 462-3990	125	74	70	12.0 / 12.0	F	GD	RH	30 / 100	P
2. Newburyport Central Waterfront Park	(978) 462-3746	140	12		12.0 / 22.0	F			30 / 50	P
3. Hilton's Marina **WiFi**	(978) 462-3990	100	74	65	12.0 / 12.0	F		RH	30 / 50	P
4. Windward Yacht Yard **WiFi**	(978) 462-6500	80	74	160	15.0 / 15.0	F		RH	30 / 50	P
5. Cove Marina **WiFi** 3	(978) 462-4998	60	10	142	15.0 / 15.0	F		RH	30 / 50	
6. Newburyport Yacht Club PRIVATE **WiFi**	(978) 463-9911	55	71	192	30.0 / 10.0	F		H	30	P
7. Newburyport Boat Basin **WiFi**	(978) 465-9110	60	74	225	12.0 / 12.0	F		RH	30 / 50	P
8. Merri-Mar Yacht Basin Inc. **WiFi**	(978) 465-3022	100	16	50	20.0 / 15.0	F		RH	30 / 50	P
9. Yankee Landing Marina	(978) 463-0805	80		60	20.0 / 15.0	F		H	30	

WiFi Wireless Internet Access
Visit www.waterwayguide.com for current rates, fuel prices, website addresses and other up-to-the-minute information.
(Information in the table is provided by the facilities.)

Scan here for more details:

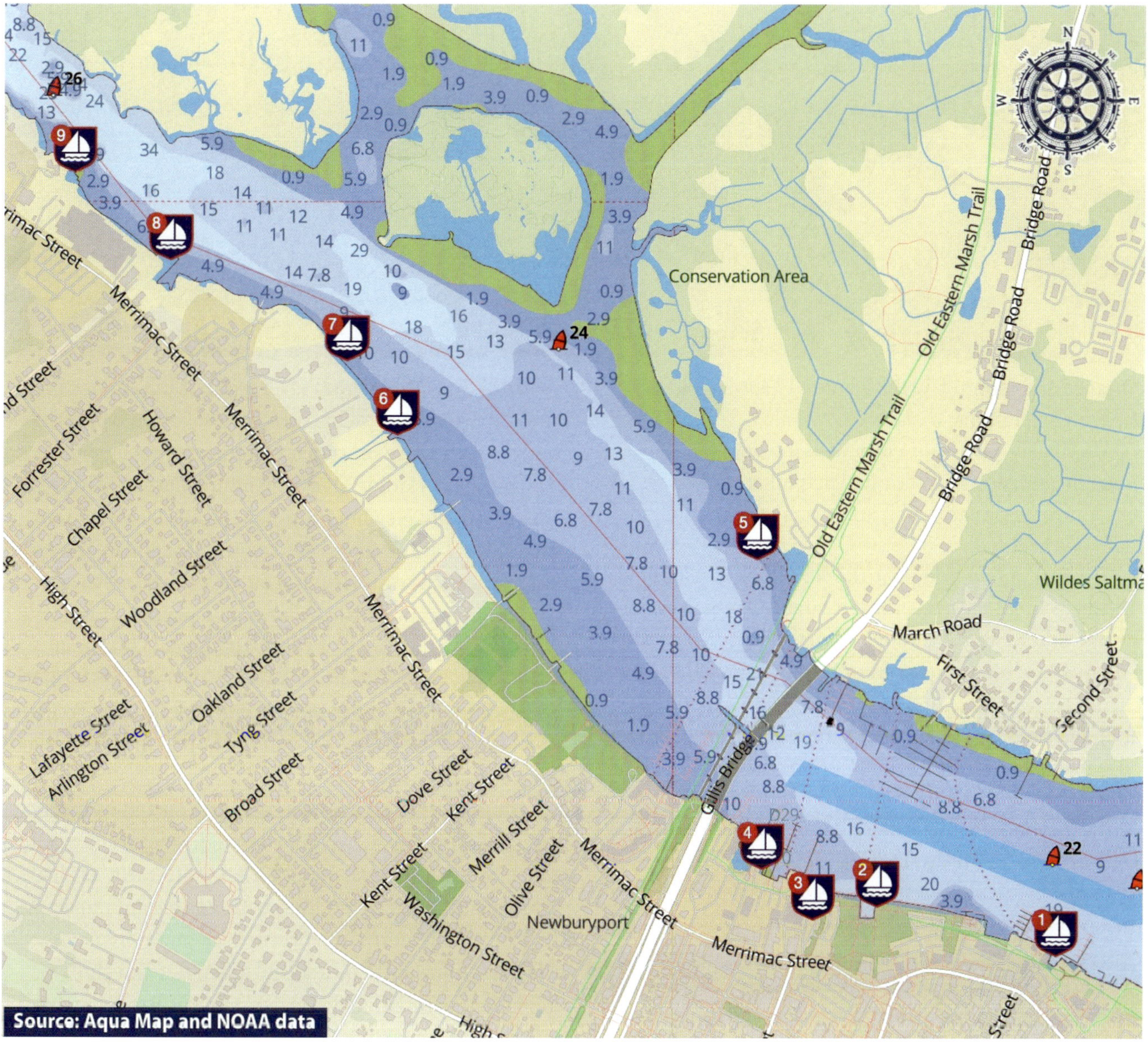

Source: Aqua Map and NOAA data

Gillis Memorial Bridge

Merrimack River

Salisbury

Newburyport

entrance and monitor VHF Channel 13 for ongoing dredging operations.

Alternately, plan your entry with the tide, which is significant enough to be quite helpful at roughly 9 feet. Currents run around 2 knots on the ebb and 3 or more on the flood.

The first of two bridges is the **Newburyport (U.S. 1) Bridge** (35-foot closed vertical clearance), which opens on signal from May 1 through November 15, from 6:00 a.m. to 10:00 p.m., except from Memorial Day through Labor Day, when the draw opens on signal only on the hour and half-hour. At all other times the draw will open on signal after at least a 1-hour advance notice is given by calling the number posted at the bridge.

Just beyond the highway bridge is the **Boston and Maine Railroad Bridge** with 13-foot closed vertical clearance. It opens on signal but is usually left in the open position.

NO WAKE ZONE

No-Wake speed limits are strictly enforced here.

Dockage/Moorings: Over a dozen full-service boat yards, marinas and yacht clubs are above and below the bridges with space for transients and varying amenities. Newburyport Harbor Marina, Hilton's Marina, Windward Yacht Yard and Newburyport Boat Basin (located above the bridges) are all under the same management and have ample transient slips with full amenities and services.

The city's municipal harbor is an amenable host to both cruising boats and a sportfishing fleet. Transient vessels may tie up for an afternoon or overnight (for a fee) at Newburyport Central Waterfront Park for easy access to downtown restaurants, museums, shops and galleries and even a local theatre.

Transients (to 60 feet) are welcome on a mooring at the family-friendly Cove Marina where guests enjoy a full range of amenities and are pet-friendly. (Nearby Bridge Marina and Rings Island Marina do not accept transients.)

Continuing north, the private Newburyport Yacht Club has transient slips and full amenities (no club affiliation required) and Merri-Mar Yacht Basin Inc. has

transient dockage with basic amenities and offers marine repair and services.

Yankee Landing Marina offers 27 moorings with essential amenities including bathrooms and shower facilities as well as boat servicing.

If you want to get away from the crowds, Hampton River Marina to the north of Newburyport is located in a snug harbor just over the Massachusetts/New Hampshire state line. Guests enjoy easy walking access to Hampton Beach Village attractions including restaurants, shopping and entertainment. They have limited space so call ahead.

To access Hampton River Marina, you will need to negotiate the 18-foot closed vertical clearance NH1A (Ocean Blvd.) Bridge. Vessels that can pass under the closed draw with a clearance of 1 foot or more should not signal for an opening. However, if the drawtender is uncertain as to whether the vessel can safely pass, the draw will open. For all others, the draw opens on signal from April 1 through October 31 during daylight hours from 3 hours before to 3 hours after each high tide. (High

tide occurs one-half hour later than the time of published high tide for Portland, ME.)

Anchorage: You can drop the hook north of red nun buoy "20" in 10 to 12 feet MLW in Newburyport but be aware of the charted cable area.

Side Trip: Isles of Shoals

The Isles of Shoals straddle the state line between New Hampshire and Maine well out into Bigelow Bight. Capt. John Smith charted this group of islets and ledges in 1614. Taken by their wind-swept beauty, he also attempted to name them in his honor, but the earlier name given the isles by itinerant fishermen is the one that stuck.

There are currently nine islands included in the Isles of Shoals: Appledore Island, Star Island, Seavey Island, Malaga Island, Cedar Island, Smuttynose Island, Lunging Island, White Island and Duck Island. Despite their popularity with weekenders out of Portsmouth and distance cruisers stopping over during the trek to or from Maine, all of them are privately owned and only one,

Hampton Harbor, NH

HAMPTON BEACH		Largest Vessel	VHF	Total Slips	Approach/Dockside Depth	Floating Docks	Gas/Diesel	Repairs/Haulout	Min/Max Amps	Pump-Out Station
1. Hampton River Marina (WiFi)	(603) 929-1422	65	11	134	11.0 /	F		H	30 / 50	

(WiFi) Wireless Internet Access
Visit www.waterwayguide.com for current rates, fuel prices, website addresses and other up-to-the-minute information.
(Information in the table is provided by the facilities.)

Scan here for more details:

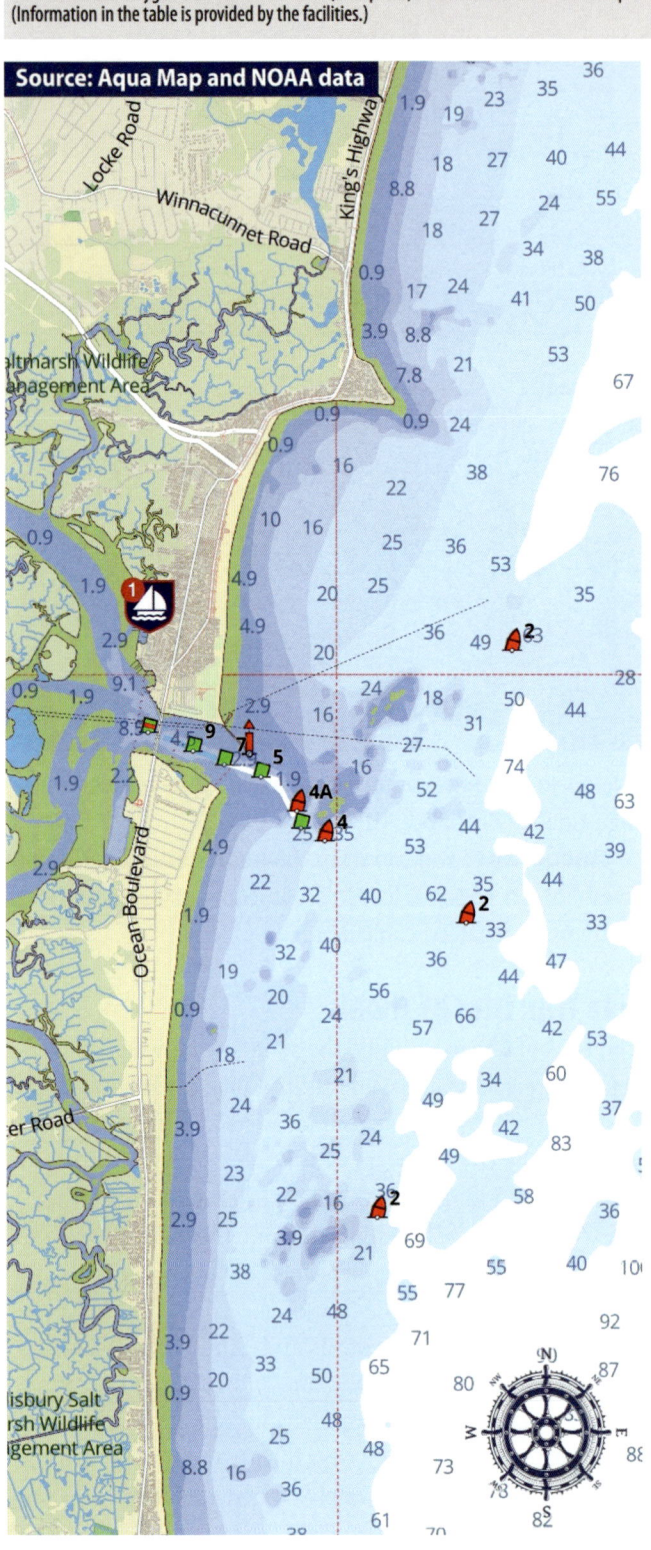

Source: Aqua Map and NOAA data

Smuttynose Island (technically across the Maine line), is open to visitors.

To visit Smuttynose Island, negotiate dinghy passage into Haley Cove and land on an obliging rock adjacent to the island's two evident fishing cottages. During the summer months you will likely be met by a volunteer "ranger" who will lend you a booklet describing a self-guided walking tour of this pleasant and historic spot. The views are gorgeous on a clear day from almost every aspect of this easily traversed ocean jewel.

At less than high tide Smuttynose Island is connected to tiny Malaga Island, the one place around where seagoing pets can find a relief station. Smuttynose Island is also connected via a rock breakwater to barren Cedar Island immediately to the south.

Star Island on the south (New Hampshire) side of Gosport Harbor provides the green but treeless setting for what was once the Star Island Hotel. Now owned by the non-profit Star Island Corporation (603-430-6272), the island hosts conferences and retreats. They offer a complimentary tender service rather than allowing dinghies to land on their docks so cruisers can access the island for self-guided tours, a snack bar and family-style meals with reservations. Check in at the reception desk for a copy of the corporation's map and guidelines.

Appledore Island (north of Smuttynose Island) also tolerates visits from the general public (no pets), although most of the island's acres (also Duck Island farther north) have been designated Critical Natural Areas of the State of Maine and are off-limits. This includes all buildings.

NAVIGATION: When approaching Isles of Shoals from the south, red nun buoy "2" south of Anderson Ledge provides the first guidance. Steer between it and Isles of Shoals Light, an 82-foot lighthouse with a 15-second white light located on the eastern end of White Island. In any difficult weather or visibility, stay west of red nun buoy "4" and use red-and-white bell buoy "IS" as the safe vector for entering Gosport Harbor.

Portsmouth Harbor

From the north stay well to the west of Duck Island and its surrounding rocks and ledges. A course from red nun buoy "2" off the western side of Appledore Island to red-and-white bell buoy "IS" provides safe entry to the harbor. From the Piscataqua a heading of 140 degrees will bring you to the red-and-white bell buoy "IS." On the chart it will look as though you are following the New Hampshire/Maine line.

Moorings/Anchorage: Gosport Harbor has served visiting mariners for almost 400 years but it has done so with a sustained reputation for poor holding and scant protection. To offset this difficulty, private parties from the mainland have established moorings of convenience here. Local tradition has it that they are yours for the taking on a first-come, first-served basis. There are no guarantees on their condition and if the owner shows up, you will be asked to vacate the mooring. There are plenty of moorings, except on peak summer weekends.

If the wind is up from the northwest, Gosport Harbor is not the place to be. If this is the case, cruisers either avoid the Isles of Shoals altogether or take shelter in the cove formed by the southwestern side of Smuttynose Island and the causeway leading from there to Cedar Island. Here you can drop the hook in at least 7 feet MLW with good holding and some protection from all but the east.

■ PORTSMOUTH, NH TO CAPE ELIZABETH, ME

Portsmouth, NH

New Hampshire meets Maine on the Piscataqua (pronounced "pis-KA-tuh-quah") River. The Abenaki name was used by Capt. John Smith in 1614 but the spelling wasn't regularized until 1623, the same year that the very first colonial saw mill was completed on this river's banks. History didn't leave this area alone and World War II saw four captured German submarines towed to the Portsmouth Naval Shipyard for study. The biggest prize contained a disassembled Messerschmitt Me 262 jet fighter and a top secret bonus: 1,232 pounds of uranium oxide. That nuclear material was provided to the Manhattan Project and became part of the atomic bomb dropped on Hiroshima.

The border between the states is a matter of much history as well, and what may or may not be the final word was laid down by the U.S. Supreme Court in 2002 giving Seavey Island to Maine. Cruisers won't need to worry about borders. The Portsmouth/New Castle and Kittery sides are certainly different but an enjoyable walk across the Memorial (U.S. 1) Bridge and Badger Island brings the two together. Portsmouth is a lovely old town

Little Harbor

with lots to do and see, while Kittery's charms are quieter and more spread out.

Among New England seaports, Portsmouth probably has more of its historic architecture intact than any other. Dozens of 17th-, 18th- and 19th-century homes, churches, shops and pubs were spared the city fire of 1813 and the wrecking crews of more recent times. The town is laced with historic houses inviting inspection. There is a collection of more than 30 such structures saved from urban renewal in the Puddle Dock area and recreated in their exact look and feel during specific periods of the past four centuries.

Named after the earliest Portsmouth settlement, the Strawberry Banke Museum (603-433-1100) sits on 9.5 acres of museum grounds with each building showing a slice of living history from a bygone era along with serious archaeological and crafts work that continues by staff and artisans. The museum office is located just

west of the waterfront behind Prescott Park and the Public Gardens. A visit to the *U.S.S. Albacore* (603-436-3860) provides a fascinating self-guided tour of the 1953 retired submarine.

Within a few blocks' walk from the waterfront, you will encounter several banks, a supermarket, multiple bookstores and lots of interesting shops. A dozen different dining out options may be found within an 8-block area of the waterfront, along Market, Ceres and Congress Streets.

NAVIGATION: The well-marked, deep-water entry to Portsmouth Harbor was designed and is maintained for the passage of large naval ships, making it easy for smaller vessels to navigate under the right conditions. Whaleback Light provides a dramatic welcome on entry and should be left well to the east. The main channel turns west at flashing green buoy "5" to head south of Seavey Island, which cannot be circumnavigated due to

New Castle Island

low fixed bridges on the Kittery side. If continuing up the Piscataqua, stay south of Seavey Island.

The Piscataqua River leaves Portsmouth Harbor west of New Castle Island to start its winding northward course up into rural New Hampshire. Pleasant communities with considerable yachting activity line the banks.

This is where you get your first taste of Down East tides. The tidal range of 10 feet creates currents that drag buoys under. Locals profess that theirs are the most brutal currents on this stretch of coast. To minimize excitement, check the tide and current tables to coordinate comings and goings with slack water and minimal flows. It's best to time your arrival for slack water about 1.5 hours behind the turnaround of the tide to avoid the 3-knot currents through tricky stretches of navigation.

The river develops fierce currents at full flow, whistling along under the **Memorial (U.S. 1) Bridge** (3 miles upriver) at 3 to 4 knots on an average tide. The bridge (21-foot closed vertical clearance) opens on signal except from May 15 through October 31, from 7:00 a.m. to 7:00 p.m., when the draw need open only on the hour and half hour for recreational vessels.

Next is the 56-foot closed vertical clearance **Sarah M. Long Bridge**, followed by the fixed high-rise (134-foot vertical clearance) **I-95 Bridge**. The main channel draw of the Sarah M. Long bridge opens on signal except from May 15 through October 31 between 7:00 a.m. to 7:00 p.m., when the draw need only open at quarter of and quarter after the hour. The secondary draw remains in the fully open position from May 15 through October 31 except when a train is crossing of a train. Trains are controlled so that any delay in opening should not exceed 5 minutes.

Portsmouth Harbor, NH

NEW CASTLE ISLAND		Largest Vessel	VHF	Total Slips	Approach/ Dockside Depth	Floating Docks	Gas/ Diesel	Repairs/ Haulout	Min/Max Amps	Pump-Out Station
1. Safe Harbor Wentworth by the Sea WiFi	(603) 433-5050	250	16	170	10.0 / 10.0	F	GD		30 / 200+	P
2. Portsmouth Yacht Club - Public Fuel Dock	(603) 436-9877	50	9		20.0 / 15.0		GD			
PISCATAQUA RIVER										
3. Prescott Park Municipal Dock	(603) 498-6816	55	9	10	40.0 / 18.0	F			30	
4. Marina at Harbour Place WiFi	(888) 802-5871	175	13		35.0 / 18.0	F			30 / 100	
5. Piscataqua Marina WiFi	(207) 439-3810	125		34	65.0 / 6.0	F		RH	30 / 50	P
NEWINGTON										
6. Great Bay Marine Inc. WiFi	(603) 436-5299	70	68	128	30.0 / 8.0	F	GD	RH	30 / 100	P
KITTERY POINT AREA										
7. Safe Harbor Kittery Point WiFi	(207) 439-9582	60	71	10	35.0 / 22.0	F		RH	30 / 50	P
8. Pepperell Cove WiFi	(207) 451-0829	90	16	6	15.0 / 11.0	F			30 / 50	

WiFi Wireless Internet Access
Visit www.waterwayguide.com for current rates, fuel prices, website addresses and other up-to-the-minute information. (Information in the table is provided by the facilities.)

Scan here for more details:

About 5 miles upstream **Little Bay Bridge** (46-foot fixed vertical clearance), which is actually three bridges, crosses from Dover Point to Newington Station. The river forks here and fixed bridges (46-foot vertical clearance) cross from Dover Point to Newington Station. On the western branch, Little Bay and its tributary streams, including scenic Great Bay, offer good anchorages and fascinating exploration.

Dockage/Moorings: Safe Harbor Wentworth by the Sea Marina is a resort property offering full amenities surrounding its floating docks in Little Harbor (south of New Castle Island). The marina provides impeccable service and the ultimate in convenience for guests arriving by sea. Transients have access to the marina's heated pool, tennis courts and concierge services in addition to laundry facilities, fuel and on-site restaurants. Some additional amenities include courtesy vehicles and trolley service to historic Portsmouth.

Numerous state moorings are also maintained in Little Harbor for lease to local residents. At any given time, half a dozen of these moorings are likely to be vacant and may be picked up by overnight visitors but with the caveat that an uninvited guest should be prepared to leave if the rightful lease-holder returns.

Portsmouth Yacht Club on the north end of New Castle Island is private but welcomes transients at their guest moorings located in front of our docks and in Pepperell Cove diagonally across the harbor. The fee includes access to the club's showers and restrooms and launch service will bring you to the yacht club or the Pepperell Cove docks. Hail on VHF Channel 78 or call 603-436-9877 to request a mooring. The club also has a dinghy landing. A ride or taxi will be needed for a trip to town.

Portsmouth operates Prescott Park Municipal Dock south of the Memorial Bridge. Reservations are recommended. The dockmasters monitor VHF Channel 09 and request notice of arrivals. Transient stays

are limited to 72 hours. The swift currents and high wakes require careful approach and tie-up but the location in the heart of downtown is a true pleasure.

Marina at Harbour Place on the north side of the restricted Memorial (U.S. 1) Bridge (21-foot closed vertical clearance) offers deep-water transient dockage for yachts to 175 feet and is located in the heart of downtown Portsmouth. As previously noted, the current is strong here. If you are able, plan to arrive during slack tide. Call ahead for approach advice. The friendly and knowledgeable staff can assist with dockage.

Also above the bridge with some transient space is Piscataqua Marina at Badger Island. This is convenient to Kittery's "Gourmet Alley" located about one-half mile away with vendors offering meats, produce, cheese, pasta, breads, sweets, craft beer and wine and more. Nearby Badgers Island Marina does not accept transients.

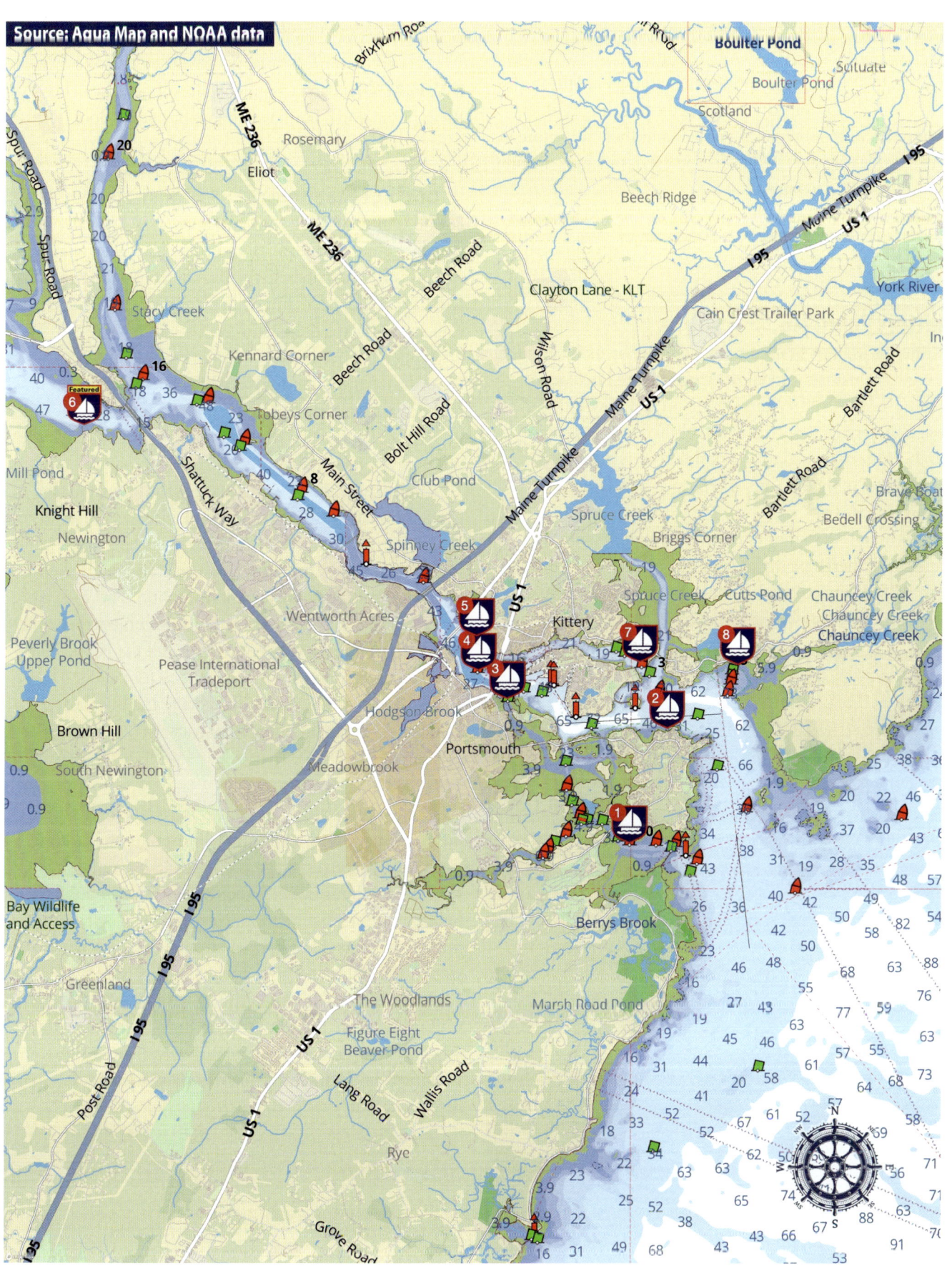

Source: Aqua Map and NOAA data

Six miles upriver at Newington is Great Bay Marine Inc. welcomes transients with 128 slips accommodating vessels to 70 feet, 84 moorings (including 4 at Hilton Park for tall rig sailboats) and a dedicated dinghy dock. They also offer all types of services and their ship store is geared towards the DIY boater and carries paints, cleaning supplies and hardware.

We don't recommend anchoring on the Piscataqua River (except as noted below) due to the fast flow and large tidal range.

Kittery Point, ME

Kittery is Maine's first port and you may be lucky enough to see the historic gundalow (cargo barge) *Piscataqua* plying a 21st-century cargo trade up and down its namesake river. Settled and established as a fishery in 1623, Kittery turned to boatbuilding early. *Ranger*, the first vessel to fly the Stars and Stripes, was launched from here in 1777.

Although Portsmouth receives a lot of deserved attention, there's plenty to explore on the Maine side of the river. Many colonial homes are open to the public, old Fort McClary (now a memorial park) makes a great stop

and the Portsmouth Naval Shipyard and several friendly marinas bring a rich maritime history into the present.

NAVIGATION: Back Channel splits off the Piscataqua River to the north but has two low bridges (7-foot controlling vertical clearance) connecting Kittery to the Portsmouth Naval Shipyard on Seavey Island.

Dockage/Moorings: Safe Harbor Kittery Point at the entrance of the Back Channel is a working boatyard with a few docks and a handful of mooring balls (with plans for expansion). They operate the Back Channel mooring field and have a shoreside dinghy dock and pump-out service. Call ahead for space availability.

Pepperell Cove is the first mooring field and is northeast on Portsmouth Harbor. The helpful harbormaster is willing to pick up transients on moorings in his workboat, and a restaurant and general store at the dock are open seasonally.

Anchorage: The Piscataqua River is known for its fast flow. Boaters are advised to find a location just outside the mooring field in Pepperell Cove between nun "4" and the western shore. You may find a spot among the lobster buoys west of the mooring field in front of Fort McClary in 7 to 14 feet MLW. This is comfortable unless the wind pipes up from the south. Feel free to call the Pepperell Cove harbormaster on VHF Channel 9 for details. The Kittery Point dinghy docks are usually full but those at anchor can use them, if there is space.

York Harbor, ME

York is a secure harbor and noted hurricane hole with a busy summer resort community. Museums of Old York is a Maine Colonial village (207-363-4974) and home to Old Gaol, built in 1719 and the last English public building in the infant nation. Near the Old Gaol is the Emerson-Wilcox House, used alternately as a general store, Post Office and tavern where Post Road travelers stopped for rest, food and drink. These are within easy walking distance to York Village shops, restaurants and art galleries plus a convenience store and laundromat. A walking tour through the historic district leads a 17-acre nature preserve.

NOTE: Be sure to arrive with enough room in your holding tank for the duration as there is no pump-out service in the harbor.

York Harbor Entrance

NAVIGATION: It is about 6 miles north from Kitts Rock outside Portsmouth Harbor to popular, landlocked York Harbor. Currents run strong in the narrow, winding channel, causing surges and boils. It's inadvisable to enter at night or in fog without local knowledge.

From the south, lighted red-and-white bell buoy "YH" is farther offshore than any shallow ledges but green can buoy "3" is quite close to depths as low as 5 feet MLW off Argo and Western Points. Splitting the difference can be efficient while staying safe. Coming from the north, the position of red nun buoy "2" incorporates a healthy safety margin for rounding East Point.

Enter at slack or against the ebb for best steerage. If entering on the flood, the turn slightly south after green can buoy "7" is where the current becomes a problem. A heading at or even just south of red nun buoy "8" may not accommodate the sweep toward Stage Neck. Stay south of the straight line between those two buoys until abeam of red nun buoy "8" then take care not to be swept too close to green daybeacon "9." The current eases in the inner harbor. The river is crossed above Bragdon Island by the fixed **Lilac Lane Bridge** with a 15-foot vertical clearance.

Dockage/Moorings: The York Harbor-Town of York dock located next to the bridge has five transient moorings and also manages other vacant moorings for visitors on a first-come, first-served basis. The moorings have controlling depths of about 9 feet and can accommodate boats to 50 feet. In addition to transient moorings, the town has two town docks, the first by the bridge over the York River and the second along the causeway to Harris Island. There is no water or trash disposal.

> ⚠️ **CAUTION:** The tide swirls around in the harbor, so boats go every which way. If there is a large boat on a mooring nearby, you might be wise to check the distance.

Donnell's Marina to the north maintains four transient slips and can accommodate large boats, with 10-foot MLW alongside depths. Nearby Agamenticus Yacht Club allows a two-hour dinghy tie-up and water at their floats. York Harbor Marine Service is also here, should you need them.

Note that anchoring is prohibited in York Harbor due to the expansion of the mooring field above and below Bragdon Island.

York Harbor, ME

YORK RIVER		Largest Vessel	VHF	Total Slips	Approach/ Dockside Depth	Floating Docks	Gas/ Diesel	Repairs/ Haulout	Min/Max Amps	Pump-Out Station
1. York Harbor-Town of York	(207) 363-0433				8.0 / 8.0					
2. Donnell's Marina	(207) 363-4308	80		6	10.0 / 10.0	F			30 / 100	

WiFi Wireless Internet Access
Visit www.waterwayguide.com for current rates, fuel prices, website addresses and other up-to-the-minute information.
(Information in the table is provided by the facilities.)

Scan here for more details:

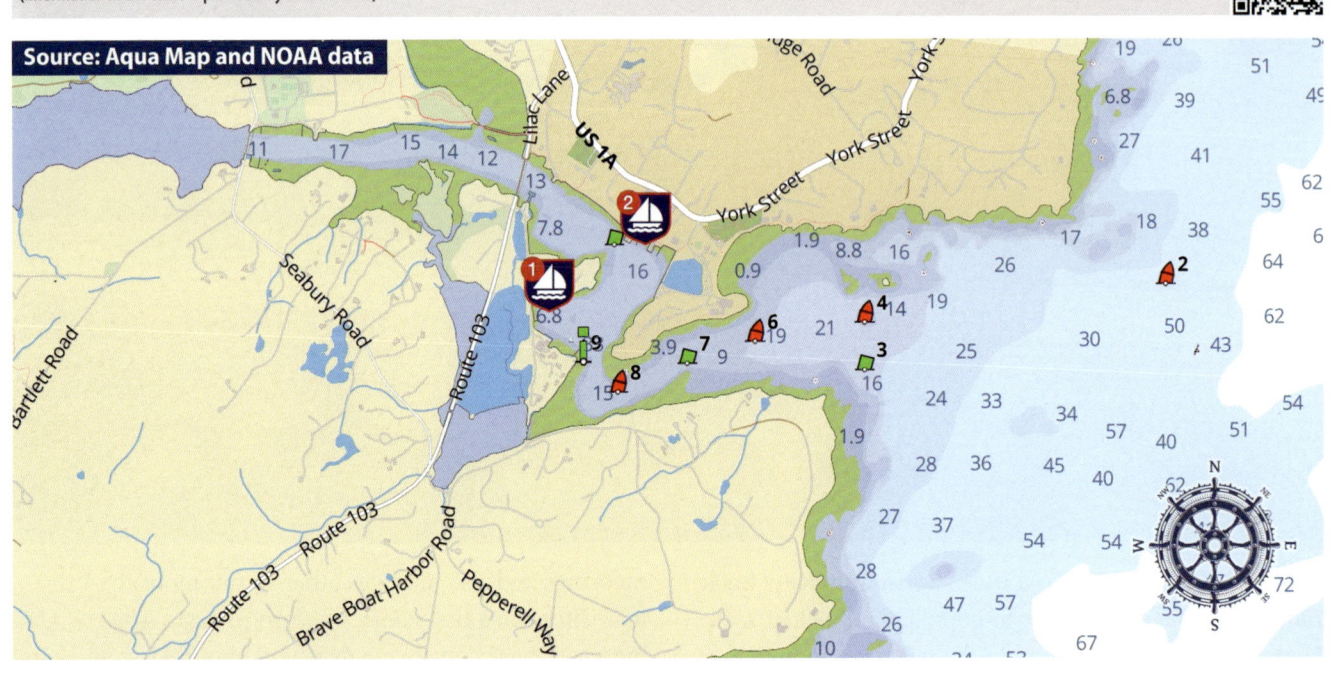

Source: Aqua Map and NOAA data

Cape Neddick Light

Cape Neddick, ME

Cape Neddick is best known for the very picturesque Nubble Light (officially the Cape Neddick Light), which was built in 1879 and has a beacon that reaches 13 miles offshore. The small Cape Neddick Harbor offers emergency shelter for small boats.

NAVIGATION: If approaching from the south, pass the light and continue 0.75 mile to the unnamed cove south of Barn Point or a bit more than 1 mile into Cape Neddick Harbor at the entrance of the Cape Neddick River. Barn Point has shoals leading both north and south with unmarked but charted rocks.

Anchorage: In settled weather deep-water anchorage can be made long enough to enjoy the view in the bight just north of the Cape Neddick Light. In a prevailing southwesterly seek shelter in the unnamed cove between Cape Neddick proper and Barn Point. Just north of Barn Point is Cape Neddick Harbor with depths of 10 to 12 feet MLW well into the cove and fair holding in rock and sand. Watch the chart carefully through the area as there are rocks and shoals but no aids to navigation.

Wells Harbor, ME

WEBHANNET RIVER		Largest Vessel	VHF	Total Slips	Approach/ Dockside Depth	Floating Docks	Gas/ Diesel	Repairs/ Haulout	Min/Max Amps	Pump-Out Station
1. Wells Harbor Town Dock	(207) 646-3236	44	9		5.0 / 7.0	F				

WIFI Wireless Internet Access
Visit www.waterwayguide.com for current rates, fuel prices, website addresses and other up-to-the-minute information.
(Information in the table is provided by the facilities.)

Scan here for more details:

Source: Aqua Map and NOAA data

Wells Harbor, ME

Ten miles north of Cape Neddick is Wells Harbor, a less-traveled road for cruisers. The Rachel Carson Wildlife Refuge offers nature hikes, photography and bird watching several miles away for those willing to rent a car (207-646-9226).

NAVIGATION: Two jetties marked by lights protect Wells Harbor's entrance. Favor the south jetty on the way in then proceed straight in 8-foot MLW depths around green can buoy "5." The channel shallows to 4 feet MLW from here to the town landing.

Dockage: There are limited dockage options for transient boats to 44 feet with shoal draft at the Wells Harbor Town Dock. Call ahead for actual depths. The mooring field is completely silted in and there is no place to anchor.

Kennebunkport, ME

Kennebunkport has become one of Maine's most popular tourist magnets. Its maritime heritage and extraordinary 19th-century architecture, a veritable treasure trove of Colonial- and Federal-era sea captain's homes, are worth the short journey up the Kennebunk River.

The amazingly ornate and intricate Wedding Cake House (104 Summer St.) was built in 1825 and is one of the most photographed Gothic Revival Style buildings in the U.S. White Columns (8 Main St.) sports its original furnishings and decor. No visit to Kennebunkport is complete without stopping at the Seashore Trolley Museum (207-967-2712) dating from 1939 and currently the largest railroad museum in the world.

Kennebunkport is an excellent place to provision. The Dock Square area just east of the Hwy. 9 Swing Bridge and about 0.5 mile north of the marinas has a general market, gourmet shop, pharmacy, well-stocked bookstore and several interesting galleries.

Kennebunk River, ME

KENNEBUNKPORT		Largest Vessel	VHF	Total Slips	Approach/ Dockside Depth	Floating Docks	Gas/ Diesel	Repairs/ Haulout	Min/Max Amps	Pump-Out Station
1. Chicks Marina (WiFi)	(207) 967-2782	165	9	40	7.0 / 7.0	F	GD		30 / 100	
2. Kennebunkport Marina-PRIVATE	(207) 967-3411	80	9	96	6.0 / 6.0	F		R	30 / 50	
3. Yachtsman Hotel + Marina Club	(207) 967-2511	120	9	64	7.0 / 7.0	F			30 / 100	
4. Arundel Yacht Club - PRIVATE (WiFi)	(207) 967-3060		9		/				30	
5. DiMillo's Kennebunk Marina (WiFi)	(207) 318-0628	85	9	28	8.0 / 8.0	F			30 / 50	

(WiFi) Wireless Internet Access
Visit www.waterwayguide.com for current rates, fuel prices, website addresses and other up-to-the-minute information.
(Information in the table is provided by the facilities.)

Scan here for more details:

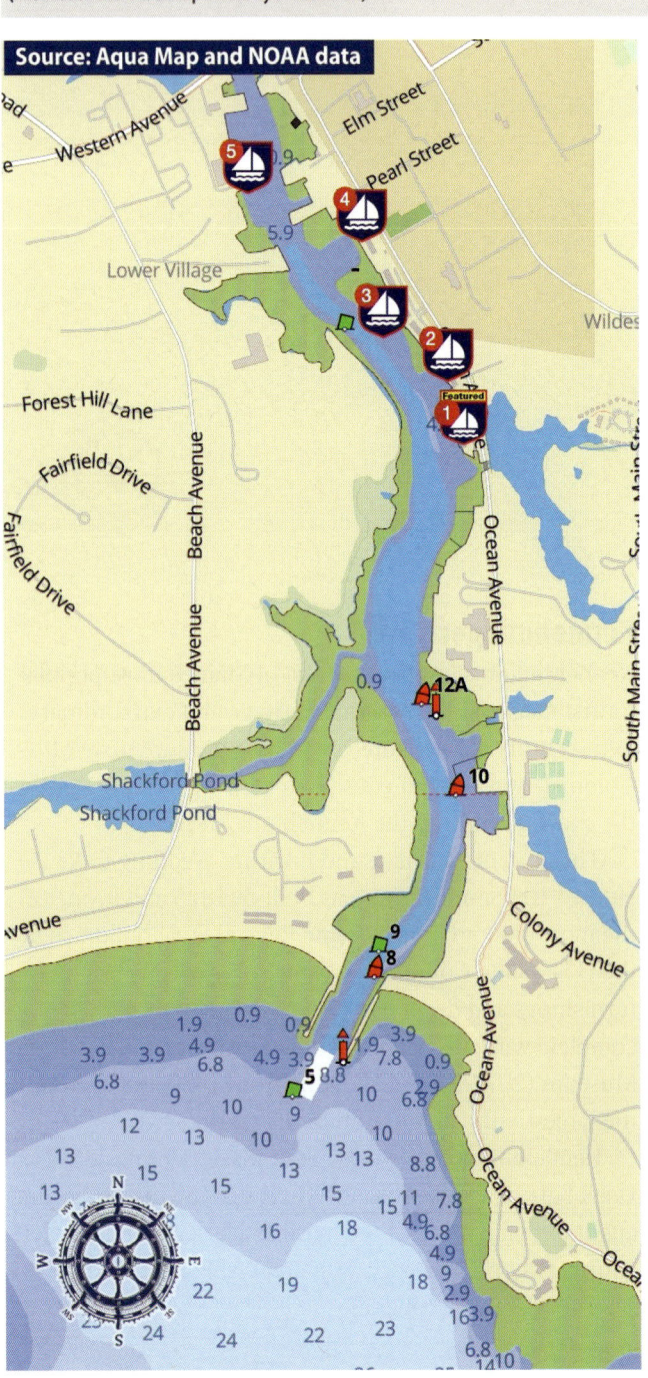

Source: Aqua Map and NOAA data

NAVIGATION: The entrance to Kennebunk River is well protected by substantial breakwaters and the east one is lighted. The preferred approach is east of flashing green bell buoy "1" and green can buoy "3" then favor the eastern jetty.

An approach can also be made from the southwest between black-and-white "F" and green-and-white "O" located approximately in the middle of the fairly extensive rocky ledge charted as Fishing Rock.

The river is best negotiated just after low tide so the mud flats are revealed and wave action over the bar at the mouth is subdued. Entrance during peak ebb can be downright nasty when the river's tidal current meets ocean swells driven by prevailing southwesterlies, all to the tune of powerful craft of all descriptions muscling their way out before being trapped by low water.

At dead low water, particularly when there is a less than average tide, several spots upstream will challenge keels of over 3 feet. The river is well marked but moored boats may obscure buoys. New visitors should stay to mid-channel, especially giving room to red nun buoy "8." If your vessel is large, a security call on VHF Channels 16 and 13 is recommended prior to entering the channel. Navigate river bends carefully to avoid being swept outside the channel.

Even though it still stands on its 1896 granite abutments, the Hwy. 9 Swing Bridge (5-foot closed vertical clearance) is structurally deficient and does not open for boat traffic.

When leaving Kennebunkport to proceed east, be aware of the large security area off Walkers Point, which is closed to navigation.

Dockage: Slips are plentiful in Kennebunkport. Chicks Marina, a full-service facility with a hospitable welcome for visiting yachts, has dockage to 165 feet and

Kennebunk River

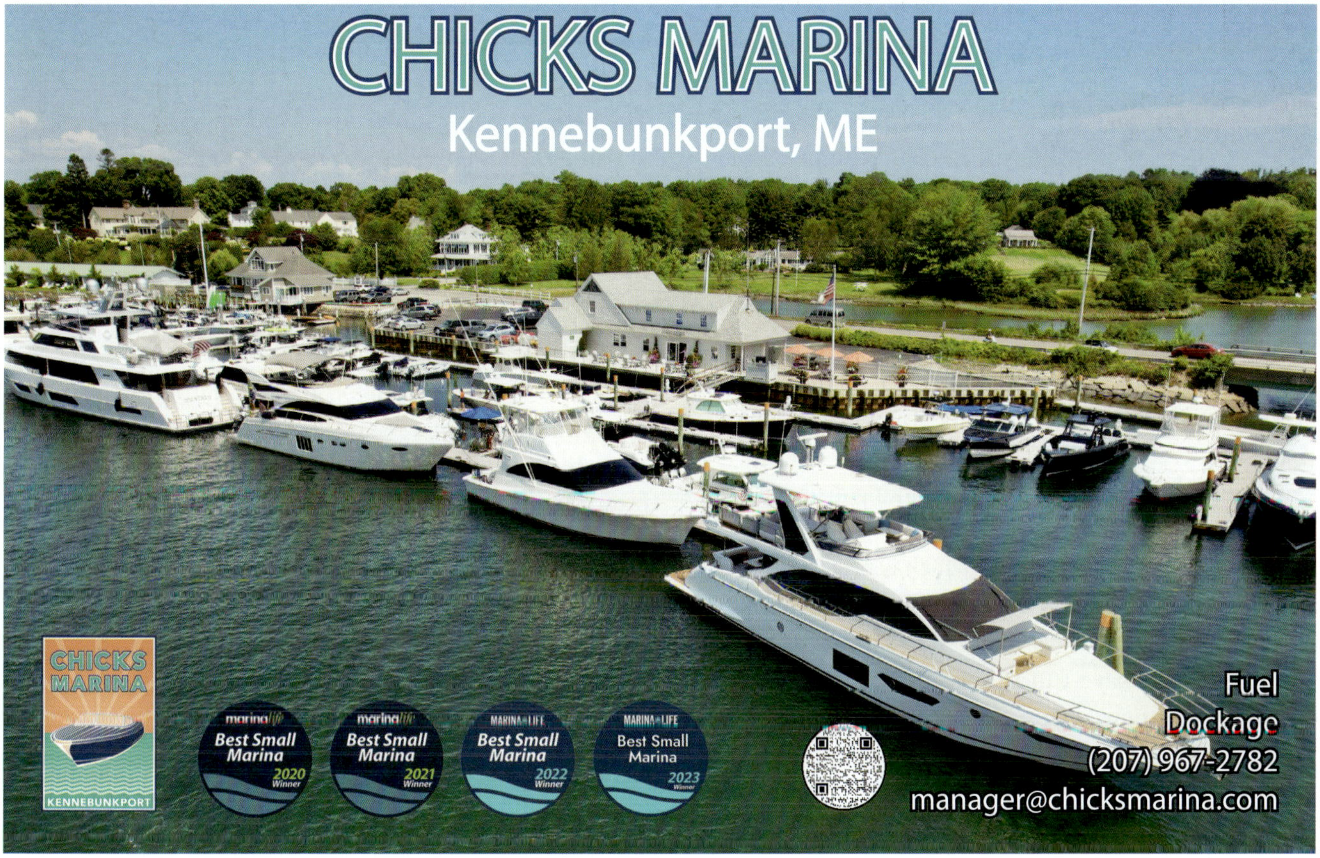

Chicks Marina

CHICKS MARINA
Kennebunkport, ME

CHICKS MARINA
KENNEBUNKPORT

marinalife **Best Small Marina** 2020 Winner

marinalife **Best Small Marina** 2021 Winner

MARINA*LIFE* **Best Small Marina** 2022 Winner

MARINA*LIFE* **Best Small Marina** 2023 Winner

Fuel
Dockage
(207) 967-2782
manager@chicksmarina.com

Saco River

offers concierge service including restaurant reservations, car rentals, boat washing, repairs, general maintenance and diving work. Other amenities include a sundeck, coffee and fresh baked goods each morning, and a 6-person electric shuttle for shopping and dining. The same family has operated the marina for over 25 years.

The private Kennebunkport Marina is open year-round with 96 slips and 70 feet of dock space, mechanical and engine services, a ship store and kayak rentals. Call ahead for slip availability.

Yachtsman Hotel + Marina Club has a unique floating barge pool and nice rooms, should you wish to change out crew or just get off the boat for a night or two. Both facilities are within easy walking distance to Kennebunkport's famed Dock Square.

Next is Arundel Yacht Club, which is private but accepts transient requests from both AYC Members and visiting sailors on Dockwa. The waitlist option works best as they only have 1 to 2 transient slips and can only confirm reservations about 24 hours in advance for non-members due to club rules. This is a "last minute" option for stays of 1 or 2 nights, not for visiting sailors who need a confirmed slip further in advance.

The gated DiMillo's Marina & Yacht Sales has slips for vessels to 85 feet with all the usual amenities in a secure, quiet setting. They also have a popular on-site restaurant. The helpful dock staff will assist you on VHF Channel 71 or call 207-318-0628. This is the closest transient marina to the sites of Kennebunkport.

> NOTE: Anchoring is not permitted anywhere on the river.

Cape Porpoise Harbor, ME

A deep-water commercial lobster boat harbor with an easy, straight entrance, Cape Porpoise is seldom visited by recreational boats, even though it offers the only full protection between Portsmouth and Portland for boats drawing up to 8 feet and makes a reasonable midway stop.

Few services are available here and those that are cater to the lobster fleet. However, if you allow the working folk first crack at fuel and loading at the town dock, tie your dinghy with a long line and observe other working harbor etiquette, you may find it to be a wonderful stop.

NAVIGATION: Old Prince bell buoy "2" and 38-foot flashing white Goat Island Light make the harbor easy to

Saco River, ME

BIDDEFORD POOL		Largest Vessel	VHF	Total Slips	Approach/ Dockside Depth	Floating Docks	Gas/ Diesel	Repairs/ Haulout	Min/Max Amps	Pump-Out Station
1. Biddeford Pool Yacht Club-PRIVATE (WiFi)	(207) 282-0485		68		8.0 /		GD			
BIDDEFORD										
2. Marston's Marina (WiFi)	(207) 283-3727			120	/	F	G		30	P

(WiFi) Wireless Internet Access
Visit www.waterwayguide.com for current rates, fuel prices, website addresses and other up-to-the-minute information.
(Information in the table is provided by the facilities.)

Scan here for more details:

Source: Aqua Map and NOAA data

find, even in fog. The drying ledges on each side of the entrance channel should not be crossed without local knowledge. If the seas are breaking on the outer ledges, reconsider stopping.

Dockage/Moorings: The free public dock on Bickford Island offers dinghy floats, a phone, a dumpster and a take-out chowder house where you can get ice. Water, gasoline and diesel fuel are available but tie-ups at the dock can be difficult and require fender boards or resignation to grimy pilings.

Biddeford & Saco, ME

About 8 nm from Cape Porpoise Harbor is Wood Island Harbor just north of Biddeford Pool. This is a pretty spot with ample space to walk along rock-bound coastal scenery and to watch the tidal workings of the pool.

The twin towns of Biddeford and Saco (which were curiously ignored during southern Maine's coastal revival of the 1980s) lie on either side of the Saco River about 4 miles upstream.

NAVIGATION: If you require more than 5-foot MLW depths, call ahead for local information before attempting passage upriver. The current runs swiftly the entire length of the Saco River and causes significant shoaling. Look for a smooth sea and rising tide before entering the river.

The entrance jetties are covered for their first 0.5 mile at high water so heed the channel markers inside the jetties.

Dockage/Moorings: The private Biddeford Pool Yacht Club has a few transient moorings available to visiting boaters. The moorings are located in the outer harbor, just inside Stage Island and between the island and Half Tide Rocks. The mooring rate includes showers, two round-trip launch rides and WiFi.

Marston's Marina is a small boat marina that caters to local sportfishers with 120 slips for boats to 28 feet and 15 moorings for boats in the 30-foot range. The town of Saco to the north has a few private moorings that may be available (if empty) but do ask first.

Anchorage: Wood Island Harbor is protected by Wood Island and surrounding ledges in most weather conditions but its grassy bottom makes for poor holding. The anchorage is best approached from the north, leaving both Wood Island and green can buoy "1" (marking the entrance to the Saco River) to the south and passing between the westernmost ledge of Wood Island and the distinctive stone monument on Stage Island. Watching your depths, skirt the large mooring field while looking for anchorage in 8 to 15 feet MLW.

Biddeford Pool Yacht Club has a launch service available for anchored boaters. (Note that the pool itself is almost entirely landlocked and tiny at low water and not an anchorage option.)

There is room for several boats to anchor on the north side of the channel northwest of Chandler Point in 5 to 8 feet MLW. Note that the current runs swift here.

Cape Elizabeth, ME

A breakwater connecting Cape Elizabeth and Richmond Island creates two anchorages. The western one is Richmond Island Harbor with protection from the northwest through the southeast. Here you will find 11 to 15 feet MLW with good holding in sand.

During summer's prevailing southwesterlies, go around to Seal Cove on the eastern side of the breakwater. Note that there are charted but unmarked rocks in Seal Cove that require you stay close to Richmond Island upon entry. You can drop the hook in 9 to 14 feet MLW with good holding in sand. Expect some surge, as the breakwater doesn't provide much protection.

Portland Head Lighthouse, Cape Elizabeth

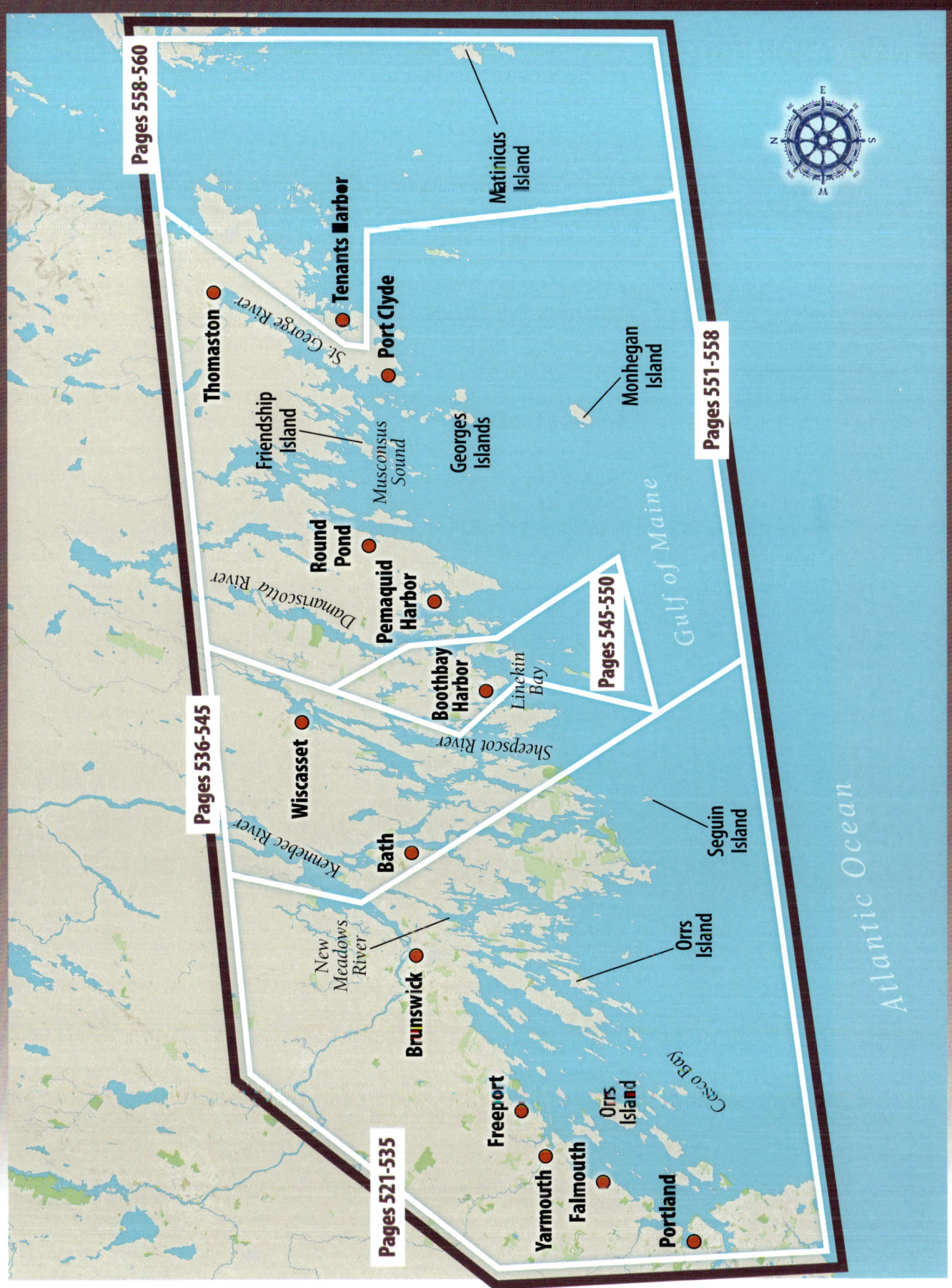

Pages 558-560

Matinicus Island

Tenants Harbor

Thomaston

St. George River

Port Clyde

Friendship Island

Musconsus Sound

Georges Islands

Monhegan Island

Pages 551-558

Round Pond

Pemaquid Harbor

Damariscotta River

Pages 545-550

Boothbay Harbor

Linckin Bay

Gulf of Maine

Wiscasset

Pages 536-545

Sheepscot River

Kennebec River

Bath

Seguin Island

New Meadows River

Orrs Island

Brunswick

Atlantic Ocean

Freeport

Orrs Island

Casco Bay

Yarmouth

Falmouth

Pages 521-535

Portland

■ NAVIGATION NOTES

Maine stands in glorious company as a fabled summer cruising ground featuring dramatic tides and currents, underwater rocks, isolated anchorages surrounded by thick green wooded hills and small seaports bustling with industries that respect traditions going back hundreds of years.

The Gulf of Maine measures 250 miles across between Kittery and Eastport, which is the easternmost town in the U.S. By land, it's a 293-mile trip. The space between them, though, is crenellated by 4,568 miles of breath-taking coastline. Added to that, there's another 2,000-plus miles inscribing island after beautiful island, a stunning 4,627 of them.

Adventurers heading "Down East" (as it's called due to those aforementioned winds and the northeastern slope of the continent) often choose a zigzag path that allows them to explore the thousands of islands, many navigable rivers, tributaries, inlets, bights and bays.

Of the many wonderful and picturesque lighthouses in Maine, two are worth an extra mention. The highest lighthouse in the country at an elevation of 186 feet is on Seguin Island. And Casco Bay's Great Diamond Island has Pocohontas Light, the smallest lighthouse registered with the U.S. Coast Guard at 6 feet tall.

Cruising Conditions

The cruising ambiance shifts heading north as the sweeping beaches become rare and the shoreline becomes rocky. Areas near mudflats can offer great holding but tide- and sea-scoured rock bottoms can be treacherous, even with modern ground tackle. The 10- to 15-foot tidal range often doubles the low-water safe scope while creating currents that put a dangerous strain on under-scoped ground tackle. While the rule of thumb is 7-to-1 scope, 10-to-1 dramatically increases the chances of a good night's sleep, even in the many deep-water harbors.

No matter where you go in Maine, the name of the game is "Dodge the Lobster Buoy." Those lucky (or well-prepared) people with their prop in an aperture or protected by a cable from keel to skeg may not worry much but any unprotected prop can easily pick up a line. If you suspect you've run over a buoy line, put your engine in neutral immediately. In areas with greater tide heights, an additional float (called a leader and usually white) is attached on a fairly short line that can trip up everyone but those with prop cages such as the lobster boats are fitted with.

Casco Bay's urban/rural divide allows boaters to get all the city they want in Portland while keeping quiet islands within a short day trip. An entire summer could be filled

Bailey Island

Mackerel Cove

investigating the necks jutting south into Casco Bay, but the 17 miles of coastline between Cape Small and Pemaquid Point epitomize the rugged scenery that has made Maine famous.

Traveling east through the Mid-Coast, there are five big waterways: the Kennebec River, the Sheepscot Bay and River, Boothbay Harbor, the Damariscotta River and Johns Bay. Two basic itineraries recommend themselves for cruising this section of Maine: running the outer shores and islands for a fast trip or exploring the deep bays and rivers that wind in a more north/south direction and using the inside passages to make your way east. Changing your mind is as simple as heading in (or out) at the next river or bay opening.

Muscongus Bay is an unfinished jigsaw puzzle of islands, ledges, rocks and river banks. The spaces between provide a myriad of passages between copious safe harbors. Some boaters sail directly to the famed cruising of Penobscot Bay to avoid the careful navigation required but the small towns are pure Maine, focused on going about their business rather than serving cruisers, an atmosphere with its own rewards.

> NOTE: If you plan to stay awhile, Maine has some strenuous registration and tax laws pertaining to watercraft of all sorts. Go to Maine Dept. of Inland Fisheries (www.maine.gov/ifw/fishing-boating) or check with a local marina for details.

■ CASCO BAY & THE CALENDAR ISLANDS

Casco Bay is the beginning of the famously rocky coast of Maine. Long necks (as peninsulas are known hereabouts) divide the 12-mile width of the bay in generally northeast-to-southwest directions with cross cuts breaking the 20-mile length into islands. Rock ledges require careful navigation at all times, but the water is deep enough in most of the channels and the ledges are well-enough marked that it's easy to stay out of trouble with some attention. Charted but unmarked hazards are fairly common so take navigation seriously. Shallows around the islands provide a wealth of unofficial anchorages for the weather-savvy.

The islands of this area were once known as the Calendar Islands, one for every day of the year. In reality, there are 785 islands and exposed ledges in Casco Bay.

We don't have room here to describe them all but we do highlight a few favorites. Visit Waterway Explorer (www.waterwayguide.com) for more details.

Two ferry services provide transportation to the island. The Chebeague Transportation Company makes the 15 minute run from Cousins Island, which is connected by the fixed **Drinkwater Point Bridge** (25-foot vertical clearance) to Yarmouth. Casco Bay Lines provides year-round service for six islands–Peaks Island, Little Diamond Island, Great Diamond Island, Long Island, Chebeague Island and Cliff Island.

Portland

Portland has a long, colorful history and is still an active seaport for oceangoing vessels. As Maine's largest city it is also a major port of call for cruising yachts with well-appointed marinas and pretty much anything you need before continuing Down East. A walk along Commercial St. (the waterfront boulevard), through the preserved and restored downtown grid, reveals interesting shops, pubs and restaurants. The Public Market House is a historic building re-purposed to hold a variety of vendors selling cheeses from Maine farms, fresh cut flowers, sandwiches on fresh baked breads and beer from several microbreweries in a historic location.

A large portion of the waterfront, formerly occupied by Bath Iron Works, has facilities for cruise ships and ferries that ply the Casco Bay. The town looks dramatically different if you arrive when one of the giant cruise ships are in port and the streets and restaurants are full.

NAVIGATION: Portland is announced well to seaward by the red-and-white "P" lighted whistle buoy (5 miles east-southeast of Cape Elizabeth) with a sound signal and RACON (- -) and the ship channel leading into the harbor is clearly marked. Nevertheless, monitor a continuous position as keel-grinding obstructions abound outside the channel, which first slants north and then hooks sharply east. Keep a sharp lookout for commercial traffic in this busy channel.

Portland Harbor can be easily visualized in a clockwise circle that begins in South Portland. Spring Point Ledge light, a 54-foot, 6-second flashing white light with a fog signal (MRASS), the end of the jetty extending from Spring Point in South Portland. Most of Portland's amenities are on the Fore River, where flashing green buoy "5" marks the turn southeast.

Docks and moorings make it very easy to stay in deep water as far as the **Casco Bay Bridge** (55-foot closed vertical clearance, opens on signal) but above the bridge it becomes important to stay to the center of the channel or keep an eye on the depth sounder.

> **CAUTION:** Shoaling has been reported in the inner harbor of Casco Bay's federal channel, which could impede the approach of larger vessels and significantly reduces the available channel where large passenger ships regularly maneuver on and off berths in Portland. Deep draft vessels are advised to use caution when transiting the area.

Dockage/Moorings: Just inside a jetty in a well-protected harbor is the well-regarded Spring Point Marina, which has dockage for vessels up to 200 feet. Leave the mooring field to the south and call VHF Channel 09 for docking instructions. The marina has a well-stocked marine store and service department and an on-site brokerage and boat rentals. The marina is located in a largely residential area with two lighthouses a short walk away. Breakwater Marina is in the same basin and may have space (to 45 feet) but call ahead.

Beyond Spring Point the Fore River divides South Portland from Portland proper. Past the abandoned lighthouse tower (Bug Light), the family-owned and -operated Sunset Marina has 10 slips reserved for transients and can accommodate vessels to 250 feet with full amenities and an on-site restaurant. They also offer some repairs and services. Private Centerboard Yacht Club will accommodate visiting yachts to 36 feet on moorings with launch service to the club and across the harbor to downtown Portland. This is a member-maintained facility.

Continuing south, South Port Marine has 30 transient slips for boats up to 160 feet and with 8-foot draft. They are also a brokerage, sell marine supplies and offer repairs from re-powers to complete refurbishing and including 24-hour emergency hauling.

Thomas Knight Park & Knightville Landing just past the Casco Bay Bridge is a town dock that was originally conceived to be a paid dock with an honor system (signs and rusted cash box are present as evidence), but it clearly has not been anything but "free" for as long as most people remember. Expect no services (and you might be pleasantly surprised if the water is on). Across the river on the Portland side there are several service large boatyards should you need them (no transient slips).

DiMillo's on the Water (207-772-2216) makes DiMillo's Marina & Yacht Sales to the north easy to spot. The restaurant is a huge and handsomely re-outfitted ferryboat, which serves well-prepared food at moderate prices. The friendly marina can accommodate yachts to 250 feet in their deep-water slips with full amenities and they maintain on-site service technicians. They also offer a well-stocked ship store, provisioning service and a rental car. Note that ferries and water taxis create significant wakes in this area and the fairways are relatively small.

To the north is Fore Points Marina, which was designed with megayachts in mind but welcomes boats of all sizes (no restrictions) with full-service amenities and modern utilities. A full-service concierge and professional dock staff and hi-speed, in-slip fueling round out the offerings. The scenic and well-protected harbor is convenient to Old Port for shopping and dining.

The full-service Maine Yacht Center is located behind a floating concrete breakwater in Back Cove near Edward Payson Park. They have 80 slips and 400 feet of "alongside" tie-up and can accommodate yachts up to 150 feet. Amenities include clean bathrooms and showers, laundry facilities and a comfortable lounge with wonderful views of Casco Bay. Call ahead for slip availability.

Anchorage: Because this is a deep-water port with 10- to 12-foot tides and a lot of moorings, anchoring requires quite a bit of rode and some ingenuity. You can also anchor off Fort Preble at the east end of the harbor in deep water with full protection from the west.

The free Portland Dinghy Dock is a good place to leave the dinghy for a jaunt around town but being considerate to others. Fore Points Marina and DiMillo's Marina & Yacht Sales each offer dinghy dockage for a fee.

The most scenic anchorage is a little over 1 mile north in the mouth of the Presumpscot River, although the currents can be strong. Feel your way in north of red nun buoy "6" for 10 to 15 feet MLW in mud and sand.

Peaks & Great Diamond Islands

Peaks Island is the most populated island in Casco Bay with numbers that swell to 4,000 in the summer months. It is part of the City of Portland and is served by Casco Bay Lines. It has its own elementary school, library and police station. Due to its size, it is the only island in Casco Bay that allows cars.

Great Diamond Island is also part of Portland and is on the ferry route. The island was used as a military base starting in the late 19th century and continuing through World War II. After the base was decommissioned, the bunkers and residences were left idle for over 30 years before being developed and sold to private citizens. Most of the island is private. The primary modes of transportation are golf carts and bicycles.

Dockage: Transient slips and moorings are available at Peaks Island Marina. They recommend making a reservation prior to your arrival to guarantee space. Hourly slip and mooring rentals are on a first-come, first-served basis. There is no launch service but they have a dinghy dock that puts you right downtown for access to shops and restaurants.

Great Diamond Island to the north is home to Diamond's Edge Restaurant and Marina with 43 slips and full amenities. They welcome boaters to dock and dine at the restaurant featuring fresh, local New England favorites. If arriving by boat to dine, book online via Dockwa.

Anchorage: You may find space outside the mooring field at Peaks Island in deep water but this area is exposed to the ferry and small boat wakes, which can make for a lot of rolling. It quiets down at night. Dinghy to Peaks Island Marina for shore access.

At Cow Island north of Great Diamond Island, there is room for anchoring on the west side outside the mooring field with good holding. (The moorings are private.) The 26-acre Cow Island is part of Long Island to the east.

Falmouth Area

Falmouth is located just north of Portland along the coast and covers approximately 32 square miles from the coastline to rural areas farther inland. Attractions in indoor and outdoor ice skating facilities, specialty shops, high-end boutiques and an array of fine restaurants. A couple of miles from the waterfront a market and hardware store are among the provisioning possibilities.

Falmouth also has many parks and recreational areas including Mackworth Island trails along Casco Bay and Gilsland Farm Center, headquarters for the Maine Audubon Society. The center offers two miles of trails along the

Portland Harbor, ME

PORTLAND AREA		Largest Vessel	VHF	Total Slips	Approach/ Dockside Depth	Floating Docks	Gas/ Diesel	Repairs/ Haulout	Min/Max Amps	Pump-Out Station
1. Spring Point Marina WiFi	(207) 767-3213	200	9	275	10.0 / 8.0	F	GD	RH	30 / 100	P
2. Breakwater Marina WiFi	(207) 799-2817	45	9	125	7.0 / 7.0	F	GD	R	30 / 50	P
3. Sunset Marina WiFi	(207) 767-4729	250	9	160	30.0 / 15.0	F	GD	R	30 / 50	P
4. Centerboard Yacht Club-PRIVATE WiFi	(207) 799-7084	36			8.0 / 4.0	F				
5. South Port Marine WiFi	(207) 799-8191	160	16	170	8.0 / 13.0	F	GD	RH	30 / 200+	P
6. Thomas Knight Park & Knightville Landing	(207) 767-7650	35	13	3	8.0 / 6.0	F				P
7. DiMillo's Marina & Yacht Sales WiFi	(207) 773-7632	250	9	125	40.0 / 35.0	F	GD	R	30 / 100	P
8. Fore Points Marina WiFi	(207) 517-4860	630	10	150	24.0 / 24.0	F	GD		30 / 200+	P
9. Maine Yacht Center WiFi	(207) 842-9000	150	16	80	12.0 / 16.0	F	GD	RH	30 / 100	P
PEAKS ISLAND										
10. Peaks Island Marina	(207) 415-7642	65		35	/	F				
11. Diamond's Edge Restaurant and Marina WiFi	(207) 766-5694	109	9	43	/	F			30	
FALMOUTH FORESIDE										
12. Handy Boat Service WiFi	(207) 781-5110	65	9		20.0 / 10.0	F	GD	RH	30 / 50	P
13. Portland Yacht Club-PRIVATE WiFi	(207) 781-9820	64	68		25.0 / 8.0	F			20	

WiFi Wireless Internet Access
Visit www.waterwayguide.com for current rates, fuel prices, website addresses and other up-to-the-minute information.
(Information in the table is provided by the facilities.)

Scan here for more details:

Presumpscot River estuary through the hills, forest and salt marsh of Falmouth.

Sailing visitors arriving in mid-August can see or participate in the Monhegan Island Race, which has been run annually for most of the 20th century.

NAVIGATION: About 5 miles north of Portland, the suburb of Falmouth Foreside is the yachting center of Casco Bay, even though Clapboard Island to the east provides the only protection and the south chop can get fierce. Falmouth Foreside is easily accessible from Bigelow Bight via the well-marked channel through Hussey Sound or north from Portland through a wide, unobstructed passage. The thicket of masts between Clapboard Island and the mainland guides the way.

Moorings: Falmouth Town Landing hosts the largest recreational anchorage/mooring field north of Marblehead. All moorings are privately owned and unlikely to be available to transients. As you approach their mooring field, Handy Boat Service can guide you to an affordable mooring (with launch service) and take care of your fuel needs and repair work. They have over 50 transient mooring to 65 feet plus dock space and a full service boatyard, on-site convenience store and The Dockside Grill restaurant.

The private Portland Yacht Club next door is the second oldest yacht club in the U.S. They maintain 10 moorings of various sizes for visiting yachts and offer coin-operated laundry, showers and launch service. If you plan to stay overnight or longer, call the club a few days ahead to reserve a mooring (207-781-9820). The hailing frequency (VHF Channel 68) is monitored during launch service hours.

Anchorage: Squeezing in on the shore side of the moorings isn't a good idea due to shoaling and seriously packed-in moorings, plus the whole area is exposed from northeast through south. If dedicated to going ashore here, your best bet may be anchoring just past the northernmost moorings in Falmouth Foreside. The southern end of the mooring field is better protected and more peaceful but it's a long ride to the marina dock. Dinghy tie-ups are not permitted under the pier at the town landing and folks on moorings for the season have assigned spaces.

Another option is to anchor off the western shore of Clapboard Island in 7 to 11 feet MLW. It is a 1-mile dinghy ride from here to the harbor. There is a quiet, well-sheltered anchorage at Sturdivant Island that is protected in most winds. This is "off the beaten path" so there are not a lot of boat wakes. This is a nice option when the bay is busy and you want a little peace and quiet.

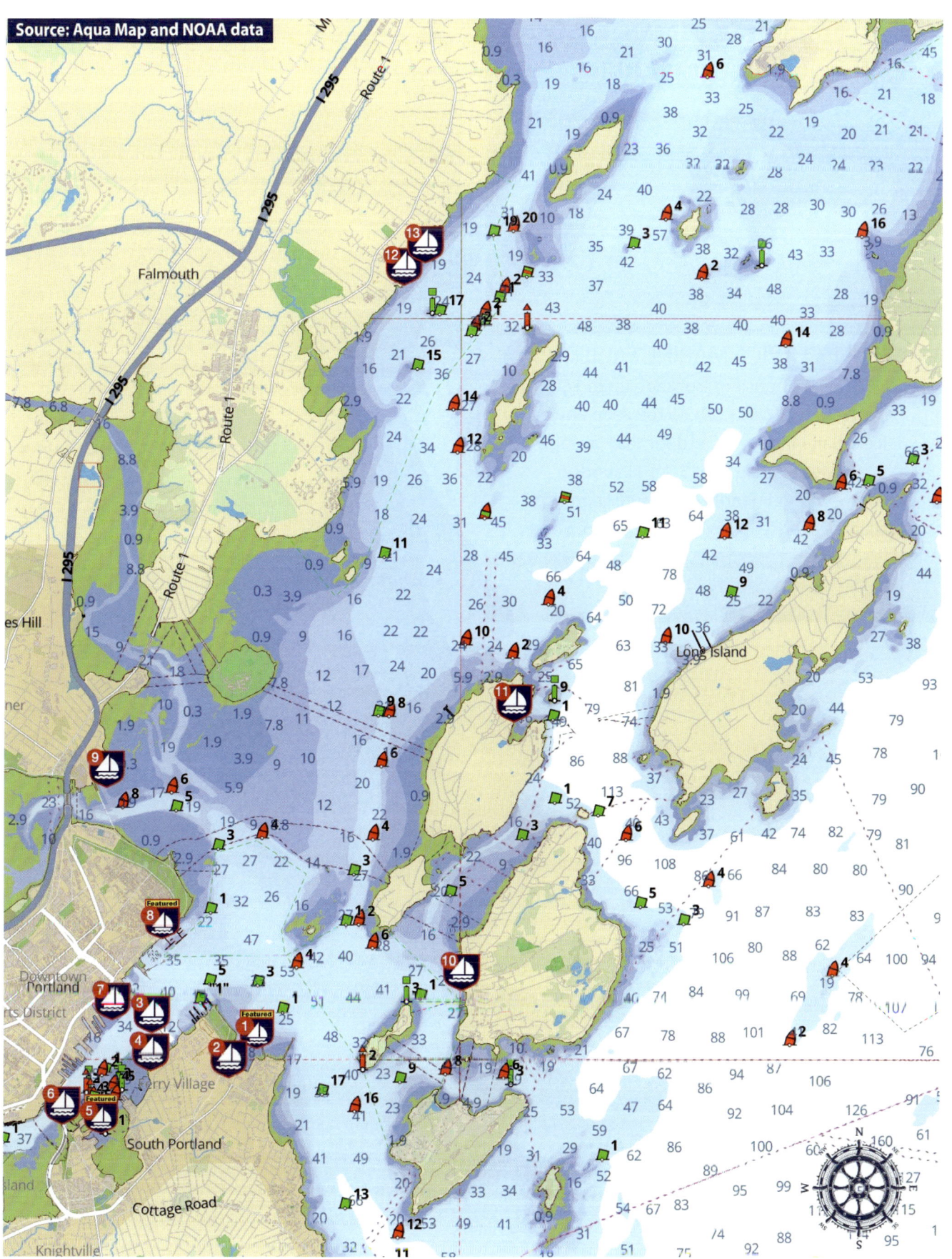

Source: Aqua Map and NOAA data

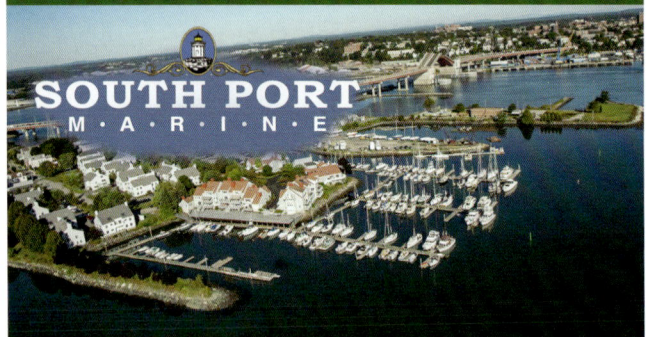

Sparhawk Mill in Yarmouth

Yarmouth

A side trip up the Royal River to Yarmouth is well worth the 2-mile dogleg passage through the tidal flats to visit the fishing village at the head of navigation. In the age of sail, wooden boat-building shipyards lined the river and many of the historic homes belonged to ship captains or owners. The town comes alive for the Yarmouth Clam Festival in mid-July where all vendors are volunteer organizations raising funds. Landing Boat Supply (207-846-3777), a well-stocked chandlery in an old sardine cannery, lies between Yarmouth Boat Yard and Yankee Marina and Boatyard. The nearest supermarket and a hardware store are 1 mile away

NAVIGATION: The channel is typically less than 50 feet wide and shoals fast enough that the buoys are less trustworthy than your depth sounder. It is routinely dredged and carries 7 foot MLW depths. Unlike much of Maine, the Royal River has a forgiving mud bottom. A dinghy ride under the fixed bridge at the head reveals an old mill and the falls that powered it (at Grist Mill Park).

Dockage: There are is no room for anchoring and just a few transient slips available here so call ahead. On the southerly side of the river within walking distance of the village is Royal River Boat with fully serviced berths. Amenities include pump-out service, shower and laundry facilities and access to a courtesy vehicle. They also offer a wide range of services (year-round).

The family-owned, full service Yankee Marina and Boatyard has just a few reserved transient slips to 65 feet with the usual amenities. It is located on 6 acres and also offers storage and marine services. The 100-slip Yarmouth Boat Yard has a few reserved transient slips to 46 feet. Their factory-certified technicians can assist you with repair, maintenance and specialty service needs.

South Freeport

One of the most accommodating yacht harbors in Maine, South Freeport on the Harraseeket River is large, completely protected and relatively easy to enter. For most, going ashore at South Freeport means a courtesy car ride to the outlet shopping and other temptations of Freeport proper, several miles away. De rigueur in this harbor is a tour of L.L. Bean's flagship store (877-755-2326) and a photo with the giant boot. The L.L. Bean Outlet (207-552-7772) is just a few blocks away at Freeport Village Station.

The remains of a grand hotel that was built in 1903 and burned to the ground in 1914 is located above Harraseeket Yacht Club in South Freeport Harbor. The tower of Casco Castle was built from local stone and is all that survived the fire. It stands out as the most prominent village landmark visible from far offshore and is featured on the Harraseeket Yacht Club burgee.

NAVIGATION:
Given the number of small islands, rock outcrops and ledges in upper Casco Bay, the best approach for first-timers to the harbor is via Broad Sound, east of Jewell Island beginning at red and white striped Broad Sound Entrance bell buoy "BS." From the west end of Whaleboat Island, keeping Whaleboat Island Light to starboard, follow the series of nun and can buoys leading to the opening of the Harraseeket River. In poor visibility check your depths to maintain 25 feet MLW so as to skirt the east edge of Crab Ledge and Crab Island on approach.

The harbor entry is made between Bowman Island and Stockbridge Point

Casco Bay, ME

ROYAL RIVER		Largest Vessel	VHF	Total Slips	Approach/Dockside Depth	Floating Docks	Gas/Diesel	Repairs/Haulout	Min/Max Amps	Pump-Out Station
1. Royal River Boat **WiFi**	(207) 846-9577		9	75	7.0 / 7.0	F	GD	RH	30	P
2. Yankee Marina and Boatyard **WiFi**	(207) 846-4326	65		100	8.0 / 8.0	F		RH	30 / 50	P
3. Yarmouth Boat Yard **WiFi**	(207) 846-9050	46	73	125	6.0 / 6.0	F	G	R	30 / 50	
HARRASEEKET RIVER										
4. Harraseeket Yacht Club-PRIVATE	(207) 865-4949	30			20.0 / 10.0					
5. Strouts Point Wharf Company **WiFi**	(207) 865-3899	135	16	120	20.0 / 18.0	F	GD	RH	30 / 200+	P
6. Brewer South Freeport Marine **WiFi**	(207) 865-3181	150	9	110	16.0 / 14.0	F	GD	RH	30 / 50	P

WiFi Wireless Internet Access
Visit www.waterwayguide.com for current rates, fuel prices, website addresses and other up-to-the-minute information.
(Information in the table is provided by the facilities.)

Scan here for more details:

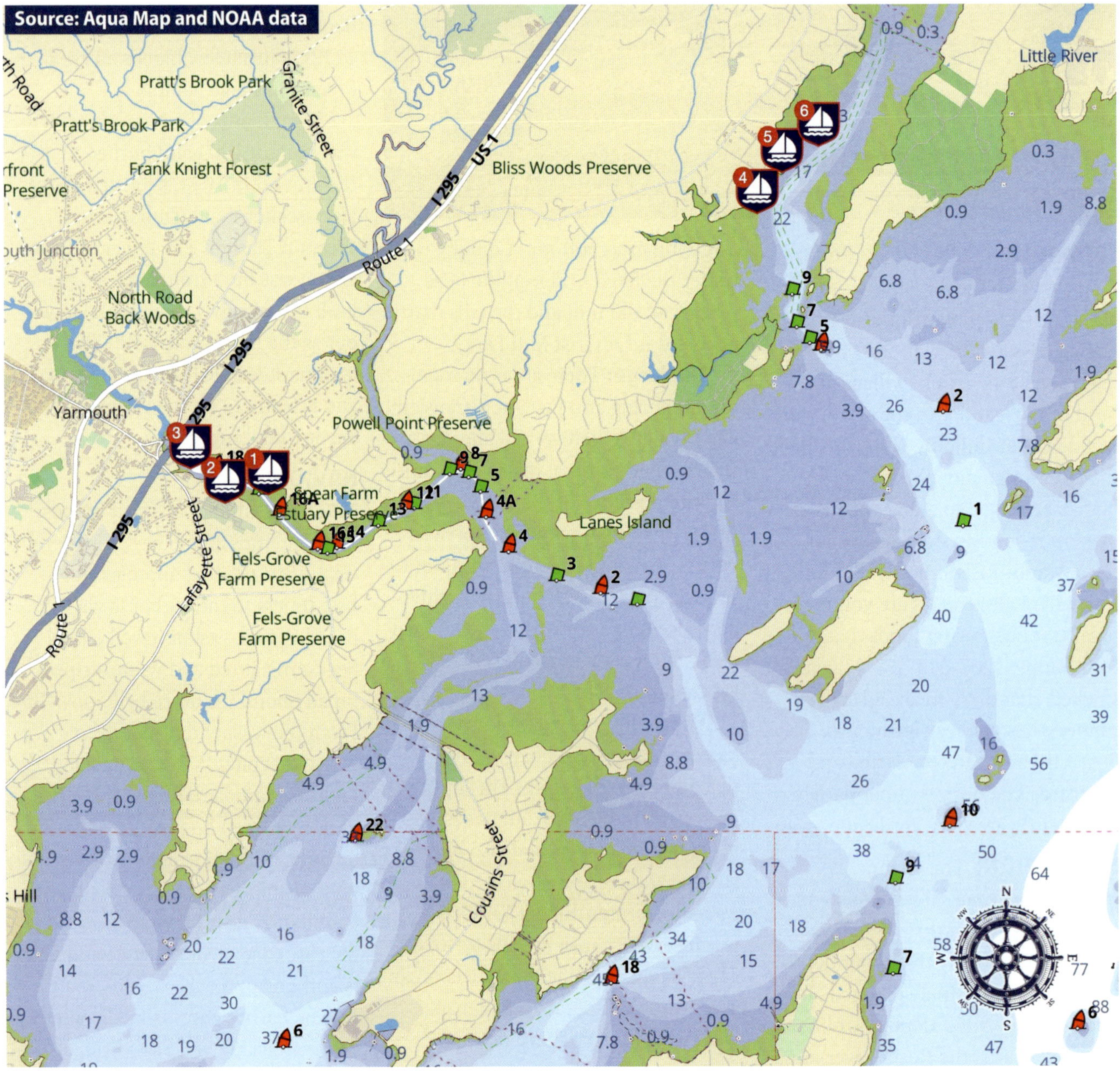

Source: Aqua Map and NOAA data

to the west of the channel and Pound of Tea Island, the islet southwest of Moore Point to the east. Depths drop quickly north of green can buoy "7" so it is best to keep the can relatively close on the west side while rounding Pound of Tea Island into the deep harbor beyond.

Moorings: Anchoring is not permitted in the harbor, but moorings can be arranged through Strouts Point Wharf Co., which specializes in year-round yacht repair and restoration from year round boat repair and maintenance, seasonal dockage and moorings with shower accommodations.

Brewer South Freeport Marine, which also has the capability to handle nearly any marine repair need, maintains some transient slips and first-class amenities. Yacht brokerage, sail loft services and a ship store are also on site.

The private Harraseeket Yacht Club in South Freeport Harbor has just one guest mooring with capacity for a vessel of not more than 30 feet. On busy weekends when accommodations are tight, you may want to call the Freeport harbormaster for assistance on VHF Channel 09 or 16 or 207-865-4546.

Great Chebeague Island

Ten miles northeast of Portland is Great Chebeague Island, the biggest of the Calendar Islands, which has a population of just over 360 year-round residents. Chebeague Island has a storied history of sailing, notably among the stone sloopers, who carried ballast for the sailing ships of the 19th century America and later granite for many of the country's most spectacular buildings, including the Washington Monument. The many lovely Greek Revival homes on the island were built by the sloopers.

NAVIGATION: If transiting the northwest side of Great Chebeague Island, keep well over toward Littlejohn Island leaving flashing red buoy "18" to the southeast before turning toward Great Chebeague. You can use the big, yellow Chebeague Island Inn building as a range. Simply head right for it. On the southeast side of the island, depths are good but the slots between Great Chebeague and Hope and Rogues Islands are carpeted with lobster buoys.

If arriving from the south, rounding Crow Island's green can buoy "5" is a safer bet than following the locals in between Crow and Chebeague Islands.

Moorings: Chebeague Island Inn has 8 moorings that are typically used by guests staying at the Inn or eating at the restaurant. They do, however, allow transient boaters to stay when moorings are available on a first-come, first-served basis (for a fee). Once secured to a mooring, call the main line at the Inn (207-846-5155) to inform them of your plans, make payment and schedule a launch pick-up if needed.

Anchorage: The best anchorage is in Chandler Cove on the south side of the island off the stone pier in about 10 feet MLW. Keep outside the moorings because it gets shallow as you get close to the pier. Holding is good in mud. You can dinghy to the ferry float and tie up there to go into town. Getting there means transiting the narrow hooked channel created by Long Island's north point poking up between Little and Great Chebeague. If there's even a hint of fog outside, this channel will be thick with it.

Jewell Island

Deserted except by boaters and maintained by Maine State Parks, Jewell Island is a prime example of what mariners hope to find in Maine. The island was a World War II outpost for submarine spotting. The tower is open for climbing and offers a breathtaking view of the Gulf of Maine. Local tales put both Captain Kidd and bootleggers ashore with their different treasures.

NAVIGATION: When approaching from the west use red bell buoy "6" off of the southwestern tip of Cliff Island as a target. Follow the western contour of Jewell Island and avoid the ledges to the south of the old wharf. Continue until north of red nun buoy "4" as you leave it south so that you can look straight into the protected harbor between Jewell Island and Little Jewell Island before starting in.

When approaching from the east head south of red nun buoy "2" off Drunkers Ledges then west toward West Brown Cow. Leave red-and-white bell buoy "BS" well to the north and keep Cliff Island dead ahead until you are abeam the northern tip of Jewell Island.

Anchorage: A secure anchorage on the western side of Jewell Island, affectionately known as Cocktail Cove, provides a lovely spot to stay aboard and a safe spot to leave the boat while going ashore. If you plan to stay overnight, get in by early afternoon because the harbor is always popular, especially on weekends. This encourages

WATERWAY GUIDE®
THE CRUISING AUTHORITY

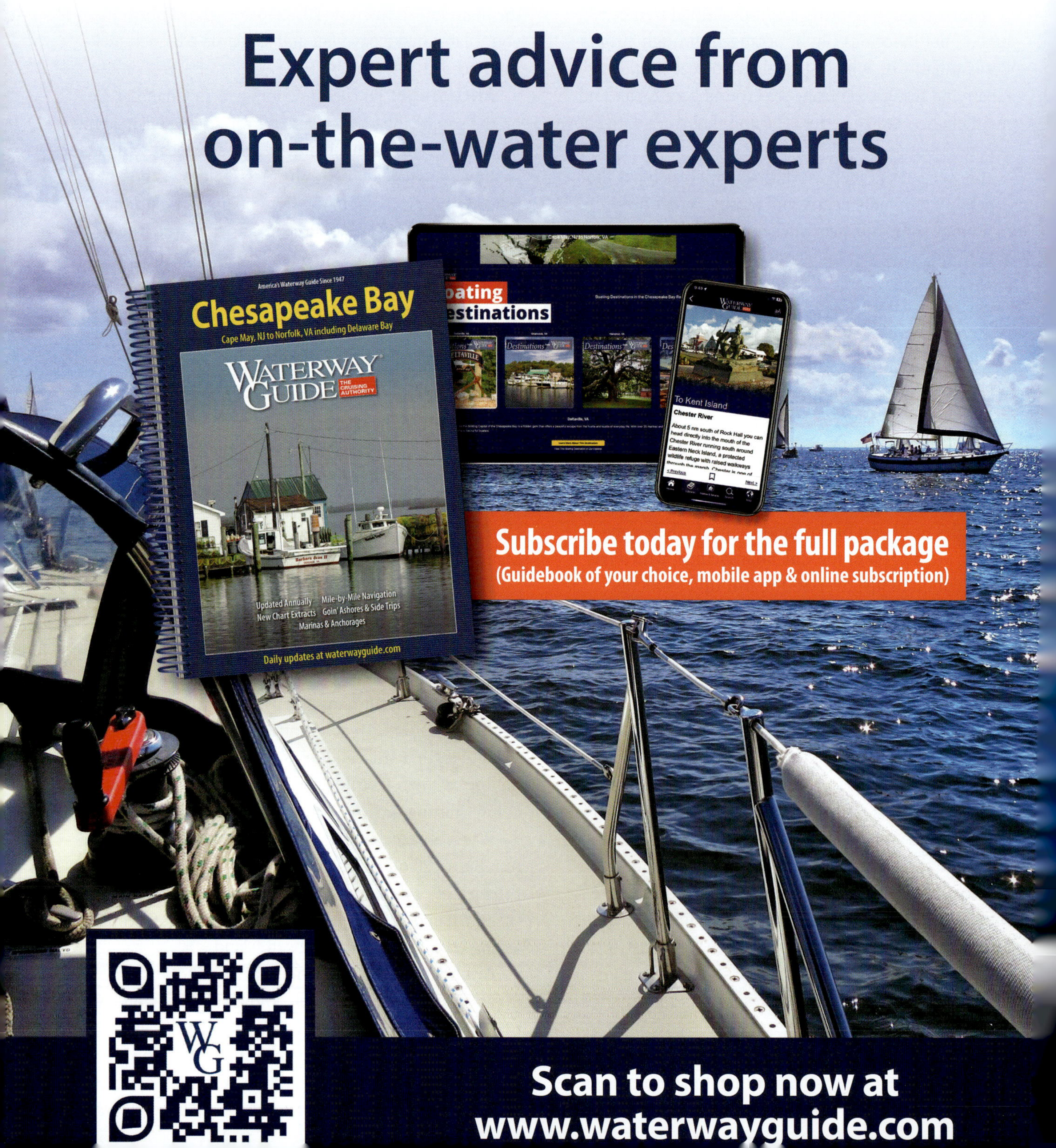

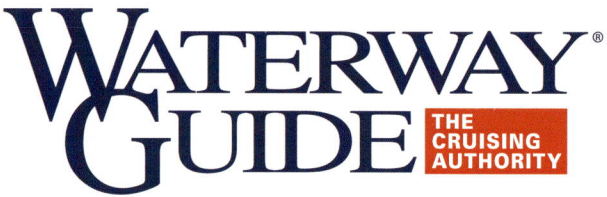

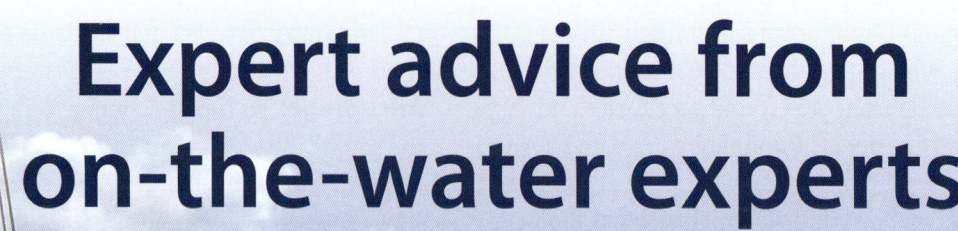

Harpswell Neck

Potts Harbor

short scope so be friendly and ask nearby boaters how much chain/rode they have out. Favor Jewell Island's western shore slightly with an eye to needed swinging room with the turn of the tide.

If Cocktail Cove is full or you'd rather have more space, you can also drop the hook in the north or south coves at nearby Cliff Island in 8 to 16 feet MLW with good holding. There is a charted ledge that runs north to south in the cove. Anchoring is excellent on either side of this ledge. The northern cove is protected from all winds with a southerly component. At times a swell from the ocean somehow sneaks in through the entrance channel from the southeast. If this is the case, anchoring on the eastern side of this cove would be less rolly. There is beach access by dinghy to explore or for pet duties.

Eagle Island

Admiral Robert Peary, who led the sometimes-disputed first expedition to the North Pole, retired on Eagle Island with his wife and two children. Eventually, the 17-acre island was gifted to the State of Maine and their house is now a National Historic Landmark. In a wonderful private/public partnership, the State maintains the house and grounds with help from and improvements funded by the Friends of Peary's Eagle Island.

A video at the Welcome Center and audio wands for self-guided tours help visitors get to know this amazing family. The player piano that accompanied Peary's sea-voyage to Greenland is in the parlor and the knowledgeable and welcoming docents are happy to allow visitors to work the pedals after donning protective booties.

Moorings: Complimentary moorings maintained by Maine State Parks are first-come, first served on Eagle Island. The 2-hour limit is flexible if they are not full, and the island is a nice spot for a picnic lunch.

Potts Harbor

Located in a bight at the south end of Harpswell Neck, Potts Harbor has long been favored by cruising skippers but its history goes back farther. In the 1830s at the dawn of the lobster craze, "smacks" (wooden sailboats with holes drilled through the hull to circulate seawater through built-in tanks) made regular trips from the fishing hamlets at the end of Harpswell all the way to New York City with live lobsters.

Both Bar Island and Potts Point are part of the Maine Island Trail and are available for public landing. (This includes your four-legged crew members.) At Potts Point, you can walk through a quiet residential

Casco Bay, ME

MEREPOINT BAY		Largest Vessel	VHF	Total Slips	Approach/ Dockside Depth	Floating Docks	Gas/ Diesel	Repairs/ Haulout	Min/Max Amps	Pump-Out Station
1. Chebeague Island Inn - Mooring Field	(207) 846-5155	125			/					
2. Paul's Marina	(207) 729-3067	40	9		6.0 / 6.0		GD	RH	30	P
POTTS HARBOR										
3. Dolphin Marina & Restaurant WiFi	(207) 833-5343	200	9	40	40.0 / 12.0	F	GD	RH	30 / 50	P
ORR'S ISLAND AREA										
4. Orr's Bailey Yacht Club-PRIVATE	(207) 833-7312	47			9.0 / 9.0	F	G			
5. Safe Harbor Great Island WiFi	(207) 729-1639	70	9	57	12.0 / 10.0	F	GD	RH	30 / 50	P
NEW MEADOWS RIVER										
6. Sebasco Harbor Resort	(800) 225-3819	90	9	35	20.0 / 6.0	F	G			P
7. Cundy's Harbor Town Moorings	(207) 833-5771				/					
8. New Meadows Marina WiFi	(207) 443-6277	40		60	7.0 / 6.0	F	G	RH	30	

WiFi Wireless Internet Access
Visit www.waterwayguide.com for current rates, fuel prices, website addresses and other up-to-the-minute information.
(Information in the table is provided by the facilities.)

Scan here for more details:

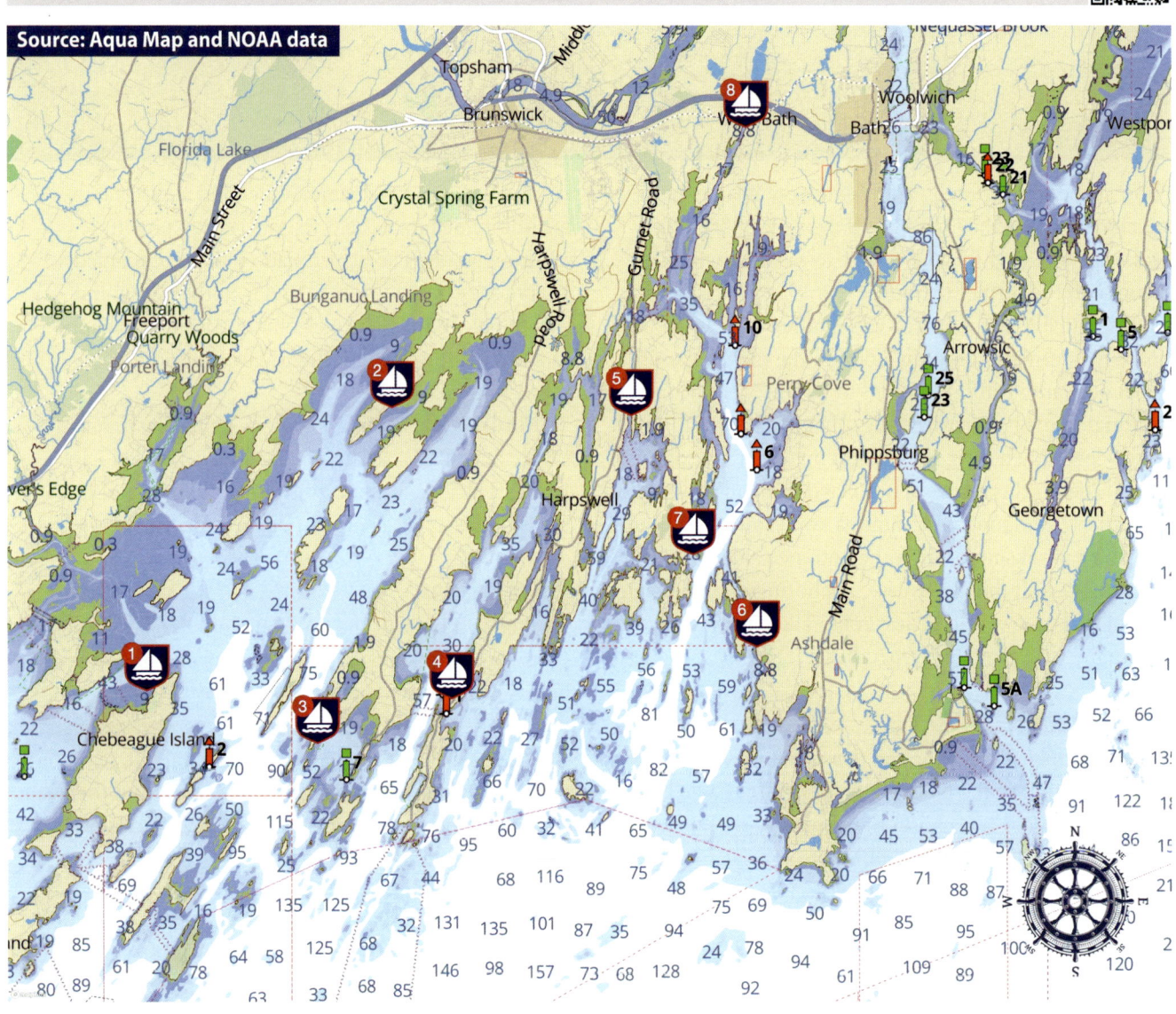

Source: Aqua Map and NOAA data

neighborhood and down to Potts Point Preserve, which has pretty views and pebble beaches.

NAVIGATION: The preferred approach to Potts Harbor is from the southwest through Broad Sound, taking the north side of red nun buoy "4" to negotiate the channel between Upper Flag Island and Horse Island. In good light the crooked, although well-marked channel leading in from Merriconeag Sound is also usable and, for some sailors, an enjoyable challenge with its sharp turn between Haskell Island and Potts Point.

From whichever direction you enter, keep an eye on the seaweed covering edges of Thrumcap Island and proceed north past green can buoy "13" before turning to pass the tiny island.

Dockage/Moorings: The family-friendly Paul's Marina is on Merepoint Bay with moorings and a fun General Store with a rainbow selection of loose candies in jars. They also have a takeout menu of sandwiches and wraps.

Dolphin Marina & Restaurant on Potts Harbor to the south offers transient slips and moorings with launch service. The launch comes by every morning and offers up complimentary fresh blueberry muffins and coffee. There are no other services nearby. Provisioning is possible in Brunswick but the distance is greater (about 20 minutes by car) than may appear on your chart.

Anchorage: Potts Harbor is somewhat protected by surrounding islets and ledges yet offers matchless long-distance views of Casco Bay's archipelago scattered to the southwest. The designated anchorage basin is full of moorings, but there is

room to anchor just south in 16 to 22 feet MLW in good holding. It is not as protected as it looks and can get uncomfortably rolly. Dolphin Marina & Restaurant has a dinghy landing if you want to visit their restaurant.

Tiny Bar Island to the north is a better option. There is room to anchor outside of the lobster fleet moorings just to the west of Bar Island. There is good holding in thick mud with shell in 15 to 18 feet MLW. This is very protected from all directions except south-southwest, but there are still several small islands to break up waves and swell. The town of Harpswell also has a town dock that can be used for quick shore visits. (Time limit is posted.)

Basin Cove is farther from the marina but has less traffic and also offers 16 to 22 feet MLW in mud. The entrance requires crossing a "reversing falls" and an old dam that is uncovered at low tide. It is best to seek local knowledge and check out the area in your dinghy before attempting for the first time due to currents and rocks at the entrance.

Stover Cove at West Harpswell is a nice, well-sheltered anchorage. Give the few moorings a wide berth. This is a popular day anchorage with locals, but clears out in the evening. It is a short dinghy ride to the fantastic Cook's Lobster & Ale House.

Orrs Island Area

Orrs Island is at the convergence of Merriconeag and Harpswell Sounds north of Bailey Island. The fixed Bailey Island Bridge (13-foot vertical clearance), the only granite cribstone bridge in the world, is a national landmark. Many of the inhabitants are long-timers and can tell a

mighty fine sea story if you find one in a chatty mood.

Snow and Little Snow Island add wooded beauty to the head of Quahog Bay, while also completing the protection from all directions. The flatness of the bottom is unusual in this glacier-scoured region and provides copious amount of room for spreading out. This ordinarily peaceful spot occasionally brings noisier visitors on jet skis, but the bay is big enough that the more courteous ones stay away. Snow Island is private.

NAVIGATION: Keep an eye on the many ledges running more or less north and south when headed from Orr's Island to Orr's Cove to the north. Leave Yarmouth Island to the east and Pole Island to the west with Center Island ahead on entry. There is room between Pole Island's North Ledge and the rocks off Center Island to allow passage between them if looking to anchor south or southeast of Snow Island.

It is simpler to leave Center Island to the east if heading up to Orrs Cove or looking to anchor north of Snow Island. Orrs Cove is easy to navigate as far as the marina because the central channel is bordered thickly with boats on moorings.

Dockage/Moorings: The private Orr's Bailey Yacht Club on the southwestern end of Orrs Island has several guest moorings available on a first come, first-served basis for use by visiting yachts of no more than 40 feet with a 2-night limit. A donation of $25 per night is suggested (on an honor system) and allows for use of the facilities during your visit. Water is available at the float and there is a dumpster for trash disposal.

At the upper reaches of Quahog Bay, Safe Harbor Great Island is a tidy, full-service marina and boatyard in Orrs Cove. They offer some services and repairs in addition to transient slips and moorings (leaving no room for anchoring in the cove). The mooring field is exposed to the south and can get pretty choppy but otherwise offers great protection from the west and some protection from north through east. We are told Walmart in Brunswick will deliver provisions to the marina... That's a plus for sure!

Anchorage: Long Cove to the north is a beautiful, sheltered spot to anchor for the night or wait out the weather. This is way off the beaten path, meaning you will likely have the place to yourself!

For peace and quiet, turn to the east before Center Island and you will still be in 14-foot MLW depths and ready to drop the hook in well-protected peace south of Snow Island. Pick your spot based on draft and forecast winds for best protection. Holding is excellent in mud. There are several spots to anchor between Snow and Little Snow, south of Little Snow and southeast of Bens Island. Little Snow Island is a MITA camping site so you can land there to explore and walk the dog.

NOTE: A free, on-demand pump-out boat is available thanks to the Quahog Bay Conservancy on Snow Island. Call or text 207-522-1105 for details.

New Meadows River

Easternmost of Casco Bay's long inlets, New Meadows River offers a choice of well-equipped harbors and some of the bay's best anchorages. Go ashore at Cundys Harbor to visit Watson's General Store (207-725-7794) or catch a bite to eat at Holbrook's Wharf Grill.

NAVIGATION: The first possible stop after heading west around Cape Small (or the last one if heading east) is the Small Point Harbor. A broad entrance between Wood Island and Hermit Island make entering a breeze but beware the well-named Middle Ledge. It's marked with unlighted green can buoy "3" so take care if traversing the harbor at night.

The next harbor north is Sebasco Harbor east of Harbor Island. Stay midway between the buoys to avoid rocky ledges on either side. Note that flashing red buoy "8" marks the New Meadows River. It can be used to line up with green can buoy "1" to the east but it will be left to

the north when entering Sebasco Harbor. The Dry Ledges will be to the south.

Dockage/Moorings: At the south end of the river at Cape Small, the Sebasco Harbor Resort offers dockage and full resort amenities including on-site suites, upscale dining, golf and tennis. The CUP symbol on current charts is the cupola on the top of the resort hotel. Hail on VHF Channel 09 for docking assistance or mooring assignment.

The quintessential Maine fishing village of Cundy's Harbor (Cundy Harbor on the NOAA chart) is within the town of Harpswell. The town manages Cundy's Harbor Town Moorings. Call 207-833-2771 for details and reservations.

North on New Meadows River beyond Sebascodegan Island is New Meadows Marina, a fully outfitted marina with dockage, a fully stocked marine store, hauling and launching and full service repairs.

Anchorage: An idyllic hurricane hole called The Basin is a favored anchorage of many Casco Bay cruisers and will be crowded when severe weather is forecast. To get inside, head northward up the New Meadows River about 2 miles beyond Sebasco Harbor. Watch for the house on the northern shore and head for it once it is in view. Stay in mid-channel until you are inside the basin. As you round the southern tip of the peninsula you may encounter 7-foot MLW depths. It can be a little challenging to enter and exit due to the proliferation of lobster pots and a strong current. Holding is fantastic in thick mud and shell.

You can anchor to the south near Sebasco Harbor Resort in 5 to 25 feet MLW with good holding in mud. Sebasco Harbor is somewhat exposed to the southwest.

Goose Rock at Small Point Harbor does good duty as an anchorage in sand in 12 to 15 feet MLW (just be sure to avoid the charted rock). This is open to the south but protected from northwest to east winds.

Side Trip: Seguin Island

Seguin Island Light shines steadily, day and night, 180 feet above the water, and is the highest focal point of all the operational lighthouses in Maine. This unmistakable light beams from a 53-foot tower set atop a 145-foot hill.

Yachts heading east and westbound craft returning from Down East are usually glad to see the turtle shape of Seguin Island on the horizon. The island defines the two

Seguin Island

approaches to the Kennebec River, and the strong tidal currents plus an opposing wind can help a thoughtful skipper decide which direction to take or whether to wait out the chop by visiting Seguin Island.

George Washington commissioned the Seguin Island Light in 1795. It was originally built with a wooden tower but the constant battering required a granite brick tower to be built in 1857. This provided an opportunity to install a First Order Fresnel lens, the largest and brightest class of lens. The lighthouse was automated in 1985 and, even though the Coast Guard still maintains the condition of the light and foghorn, the property was transferred outright to the non-profit group, Friends of Seguin Light.

The maintenance and major construction work on the island is mostly done by volunteers with Friends of Seguin Light and during the summer months the lighthouse is tended by a volunteer Keeper Couple. The Lighthouse Keepers maintain the residence and the immediate lighthouse grounds, tell stories, give tours and give the place that warm lived-in feeling.

NAVIGATION: A south approach to Seguin Island is safest for cruisers since the only ledge in that direction has depths of 20 feet MLW, while the north side presents numerous hazards. Ellingwood Rock creates

a local magnetic disturbance of up to 8° for a 1-mile radius. If fixing your position with GPS, this is not as much of an issue but be aware and pay close attention to possible differences between GPS readings and a magnetic compass.

The Sequin Island Light's horn will help your dead reckoning, especially in fog. Once east and barely north of the island point your bow at the northern tip until the house at the head of the bight is clearly in view. Turn south and favor the western shore as you enter.

Moorings: One large metal Coast Guard mooring might be available at Seguin Island but it will beat your boat in any surge. Six small mooring floats are available of all shapes and sizes compliments of the Friends of Seguin Island. No one monitors use and they are first-come, first-served. Be prepared to turn and head back out if all the moorings are taken. Midday is the best time to attempt to pick one up, after boaters have taken a morning walk on the island and before the rest of the travelers arrive.

Anchoring is prohibited due to the power cable for the island, which runs right up the sand and pebble beach where you can leave your dinghy while walking the island's trails or climbing the lighthouse tower. This spot is a dangerous one if the winds kick up from the east.

Kennebec River, ME

BATH		Largest Vessel	VHF	Total Slips	Approach/ Dockside Depth	Floating Docks	Gas/ Diesel	Repairs/ Haulout	Min/Max Amps	Pump-Out Station
1. Maine Maritime Museum WiFi	(207) 443-1316	300		10	25.0 / 14.0	F				
2. Kennebec Tavern & Marina WiFi	(207) 442-9636	32		65	40.0 / 40.0	F	G		30	

WiFi Wireless Internet Access
Visit www.waterwayguide.com for current rates, fuel prices, website addresses and other up-to-the-minute information.
(Information in the table is provided by the facilities.)

Scan here for more details:

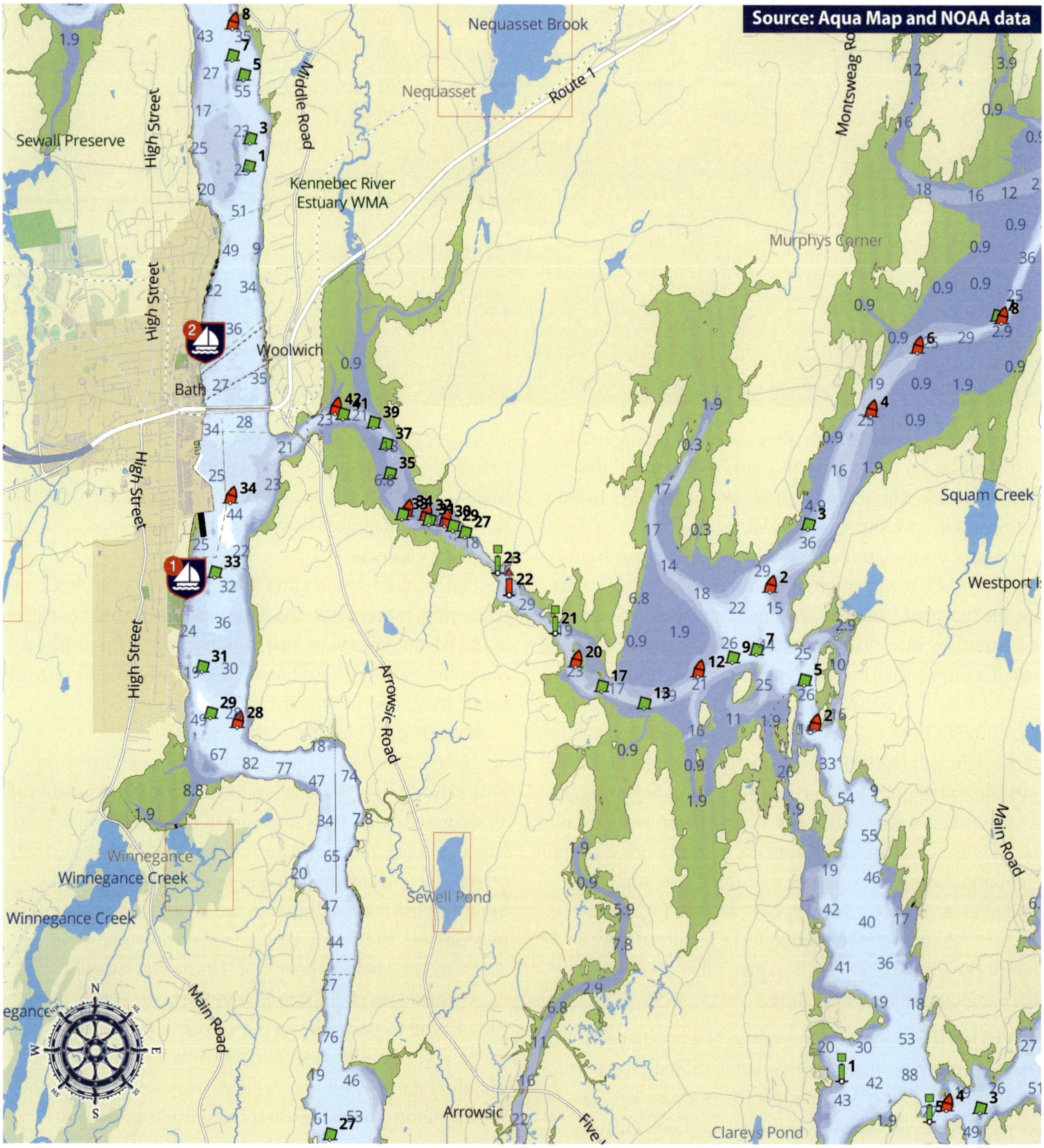

Source: Aqua Map and NOAA data

KENNEBEC & SHEEPSCOT RIVERS

Kennebec River

The very first attempt at planting an English colony in New England took place at Fort Popham in 1607, only a few months after Jamestown, VA, was settled. Though loss of life wasn't nearly as devastating as that experienced down south, leadership problems plagued the settlement, which was originally named Sagadahoc. The first leader died in the middle of a power struggle and the next one inherited a title and estate in Devon, providing him with strong reasons to give up on the infant settlement. The most successful project undertaken by the erstwhile colonists was the demonstration that the trees in the New World could be used for shipbuilding. They constructed the pinnace *Virginia of Sagadahoc* and promptly sailed her back to England, abandoning the settlement.

Deserted Fort Popham on Hunnewell Point at Atkins Bay is a semi-circular granite fort built in 1861 and used during the Civil War, the Spanish-American War and World War I. Popham Beach State Park provides an excellent recreational swimming area for an energetic crew. From Popham, yachts often follow a fair tide past the hills on the Phippsburg side to the west and the salt marshes to the east. If you have a line with lure or bait on board, you might find it worthwhile to try for a bluefish. These lonely marshes and grassy meadows supplied salt hay used by early settlers. The expanse of waving meadow grass gives the impression that little has changed ecologically for several centuries.

As the Kennebec River twists north, groups of houses introduce signs of civilization. North of Lee Island the river narrows but beyond the dogleg at Winnegance Creek, the channel widens again as you approach Bath. Depending on wind and tide, you may see boats anchored in the creek.

The upper Kennebec River is more placid than at its mouth and provides ample opportunity for explorations; however, currents run swiftly its entire length. It is navigable for 40 miles to Maine's capital, Augusta. Bath, one of the country's leading shipbuilding centers, is 10

JAMES RICHARD JEWETT BUILDING

267

Display at the Maine Maritime Museum

miles up the river. If entering the Kennebec heading north to Bath, enter on the slack before the flood and ride the current up.

Bath is an energetic "big town, small city" kind of place. The famous Bath Iron Works builds commercial ships and state-of-the-art naval vessels. Back in 1938, Bath Iron Works turned out the America's Cup defender *Ranger*, still considered the fastest sloop ever built. Wooden shipbuilding lives on as well at the Maine Maritime Museum (207-443-1316). The museum offers an active wooden boatbuilding shop, vintage boat collection, seven major exhibits as well as tours of the Bath Iron Works and lighthouse river cruises in season with reservations.

A replica of the pinnace *Virginia of Sagadahoc* (which was the first ship built in what became the U.S.) was built by the organization Maine's First Ship. *Virginia* left her wharf for the first time under her own power in December 2022. Work on the interior is progressing. This huge undertaking is a volunteer effort and visitors can take part in the work.

Waterfront Park (Commercial St.) is the focal point for visiting boaters and a complimentary transient dock is the park's centerpiece. Leave the inside of the northern section free for the harbormaster's patrol vessel. A public launch ramp is at the northern end of the town near Waterfront Park.

NAVIGATION: The mouth of the Kennebec River is 1 long mile north of Seguin Island and invites you to explore the lower reaches of this historically famous and splendid waterway. A strong southwesterly wind against an ebbing tide might produce confused sea conditions as

you approach the mouth of the river but with sufficient power, careful navigation will soon bring the well-found yacht into calmer water off Fort Popham. As usual, the best time to enter the river is at slack water or on a rising tide.

Pass east of Pond Island and west of Jack Rock. Although there is good depth east of Jack Rock and it is marked with green daybeacon "5A," the tidal rips make the main channel (using green can buoy "5" and red nun buoy "6") the safer bet. A long shoal south of Perkins Island pushes the deep water channel far to the west at red nun buoy "12" though locals rarely bother to round that red. Just west of Perkins Island's lighthouse green can buoy "13" marks a sudden 5-foot MLW spot. Goat Island and the Pettis Rocks (off Lee Island) should be passed on the east. North of those the mid-river islands, rocks and ledges disappear and navigation is straightforward as far as Bath.

Note that the **Carlton Bridge** crossing the Kennebec River between Bath and Woolwich (10-foot closed vertical clearance) opens on signal during the day but from May 15 through September 30, you must call the phone number posted on the bridge 2 hours prior to a requested opening between 5:00 p.m. and 8:00 a.m. A 24-hour notice is required outside that season. The span is usually often left in the raised position, making it possible to pass without signaling for an opening. Downtown Bath is north beyond the adjacent fixed **Carlton (U.S. 1) Bridge** (70-foot vertical clearance).

Dockage/Moorings: Dockage is usually available at the Maine Maritime Museum to the south of the bridges. From late-May to

mid-October, the museum offers 10 moorings and floating dock space for vessels to 300 feet. To ensure availability of suitable accommodations for your vessel, advanced reservations are highly recommended.

Kennebec Tavern & Marina offers free dockage for diners and you may be able to arrange an overnight slip (34 feet) for a fee. The food, by the way, is amazing. You will have to negotiate the restricted 10-foot closed vertical clearance Carleton Bridge. From May 15 through September 30 the draw opens on signal except from 5:00 p.m. to 8:00 a.m., when the draw opens on signal if a two-hour notice is given by calling the number posted at the bridge.

The City of Bath provides free dockage at Linwood E. Temple Waterfront Park for a limited (3-hour) stay on the long concrete dock running parallel to the city park. Overnight boaters and boaters that would like to exceed the 3-hour maximum limit require permission from the Harbormaster. Tie up where available and call to check in (207-443-5563). Open seasonally.

Anchorage: Tuck into Atkins Bay at the south end of the Kennebec River in 7 to 10 feet MLW with good holding in mud. This is somewhat exposed from the northeast and southwest.

Just to the north is a nice small bay below Bluff Head at Fisher Eddy where you can pull in out of the current and river traffic. Expect 28 feet at high tide and be sure to use (at least) 7:1 scope. Two miles south of Bath and on the west side of the river, Winnegance Creek offers good holding in mud at 8 to 16 feet

MLW, and because it is situated in a bend in the river, the north and slight east exposure is less important than the protection from the fierce currents.

Inside Passage: Bath to Boothbay Harbor

The inside passage between Bath and Boothbay Harbor is truly the wilds of Maine. When Champlain explored the Sasanoa River his boats had to be pulled up the river from Boothbay to Bath. That's not one of the "delights" in store for modern cruisers but the seaweed-strewn rocks and wooded shores provide excitement and scenery in abundance.

To run this 11-mile winding passage is a delight for boats drawing less than 7 feet and able to negotiate the fixed **Wilder Memorial Bridge** (51-foot vertical clearance) over the Sasanoa River. However, several important cautions should be kept in mind:

- Before you pass under the Wilder Memorial Bridge refer to Waterway Explorer (www.waterwayguide.com) and NOAA online charts (www.charts.noaa.gov) for the most up-to-date information.

- While the state of the tide is not easily predicted, plan to start an eastward trip when the tide at Boothbay is at low water and a westward trip on the Boothbay high water.

- On the westward trip, Hockomock Bay between Phipps Point and Hockomock Head, out of the main current, is a good place to anchor in 12 to 14 feet MLW to wait on the tide if a sailboat's auxiliary isn't powerful enough to buck the current.

- Keep close watch on the series of channel buoys south along the main body of Hockomock Bay between Mill Point and Castle Island to avoid being swept into the shallows.

- Upper Hell Gate (south of Money Point) and—even more so—Lower Hell Gate (between Westport Island and Beal Island) require motoring hard if a boater misjudges the tides.

- Expect strong currents and swirling rips through Lower Hell Gate regardless of the state of the tide. A strong hand on the tiller or wheel is necessary. Three knots on the flood and 3.5 knots on the ebb are common in this area but up to 9 knots have been observed at The Boilers east of red nun buoy "2."

- An alternate route for the side trip-enthused cruiser stretches north from Hockomock Bay, through idyllic Montsweag Bay's camps and nature preserves to the Cowseagan Narrows fixed bridge (48-foot vertical clearance) and then to the Sheepscot River at charming Wiscasset. This semi-circumnavigation of Westport Island has the scenic pleasure of the inside route in extended format.

NAVIGATION: The channel between Bath and Knubble Bay is marked from southeast to northwest so the numbers will descend if beginning the trip in Bath. Past the Wilder Memorial Bridge (51-foot fixed vertical clearance), the buoys lead a curved path around the mudflats of Hanson Bay and down to Upper Hell Gate at green daybeacon "23."

Upper Hell Gate is followed immediately by a large rock, which appears in the middle of the river. Red daybeacon "22" shows the straight-line safe course east of the rock. The route west of this rock is wider and deeper but the curves are more difficult to handle when the Sasanoa Rover is in full flow. Between Tibbett and Swett Points at green daybeacon "21" the river narrows dramatically again but without the swirls and rips of the Hell Gates.

The wide open space of Hockomock Bay will allow time for a deep and relaxing breath, but watch the boat's motion because the current can pull you out of the channel. Diving south at green can buoy "5" you will be back on the narrow rocky way and the waters near red nun buoy "2" rarely stop roiling (thus known as The Boilers).

Knubble Bay brings you to Robinhood Cove, a good place to bide a while, or to Goose Rock Passage and the remainder of the trip to Boothbay Harbor. Heading east, pass MacMahan Island and cross the Sheepscot River to find the buoys that lead to Ebenecook Harbor and on to Townsend Gut and Boothbay.

Sheepscot River

Big, easy-to-enter Sheepscot Bay leads into the Sheepscot River with deep channels, tree-lined shores, craggy rocks and small towns. Cape Harbor at the eastern entrance to the bay between Cape Island and Cape Newagen is attractive, convenient to open water and easily entered from the west via a marked channel. You can approach from the east but the passage is shallow and calls for local knowledge.

Accessible either through the Little Sheepscot River (easiest from Five Islands) or from the east through Goose Rock Passage, Robinhood Cove is both a perfectly sheltered retreat from the elements and part of an intricate connective system between the Sheepscot and Kennebec Rivers. In this area many large land masses are actually islands created by the interweaving rivers.

The driving distances between points can be significant, which has allowed much of the land here to remain less-settled than many more easily-accessed parts of the Maine coast. Robinhood Cove is a good example of a type; there are no services down in the cove but excellent food and services at an easily accessed waterway crossing.

South of Robinhood Cove on the east side of the Sheepscot River is large Ebenecook Harbor on the northwestern shoulder of Southport Island. Ebenecook Harbor is large, protected and easy to enter in any weather. Many local small-boat sailors enjoy their time tacking between the islands, and the open area west of Cameron Point is frequently an energizing scene.

Three coves at the south end offer lovely scenery and protected stops. The Southport General Store at 443 Hendricks Hill Rd. (207-633-6666) is well stocked and has a popular deli.

NAVIGATION: Easiest and safest transit into Robinhood Cove is made during slack water to avoid the considerable effects of ripping tidal currents. Goose Rock Passage's trickiest turn is marked by red nun "4," which seems impossibly far south at high tide but is crucial to honor. The current gets tricky in the vicinity of Riggs Cove and the Derecktor Robinhood mooring field and then reverses in the narrowing just south. No navigation aids mark the cove because it is deep and open down the middle with no hazards except at the edges.

To get to Ebenecook Harbor approaching Southport Island from the south turn east at the top of Dogfish Head and proceed south to the marina or anchorage areas. For a trickier but less-trafficked route from the north turn northeast once south of Ram Island and make for green day beacon "1." Continue on the northeasterly course until Spectacle Island is visible 0.5 mile southeast. Follow Isle of Springs and leave Spectacle Island to the west. A 4-foot MLW spot makes it important not to bend your course toward Sawyer Island but it is deep quite close to Indiantown Island.

DERECKTOR ROBINHOOD

Riggs Cove

Sheepscot River, ME

SHEEPSCOT RIVER		Largest Vessel	VHF	Total Slips	Approach/ Dockside Depth	Floating Docks	Gas/ Diesel	Repairs/ Haulout	Min/Max Amps	Pump-Out Station
1. Derecktor Robinhood **WiFi**	(207) 371-2525	110	9	115	70.0 / 20.0	F	GD	RH	30 / 50	P
EBENECOOK HARBOR										
2. Hodgdon Yacht Services - Southport Boatyard **WiFi**	(207) 633-2970	80	9	40	15.0 / 8.0	F	GD	RH	30 / 50	P

WiFi Wireless Internet Access
Visit www.waterwayguide.com for current rates, fuel prices, website addresses and other up-to-the-minute information.
(Information in the table is provided by the facilities.)

Scan here for more details:

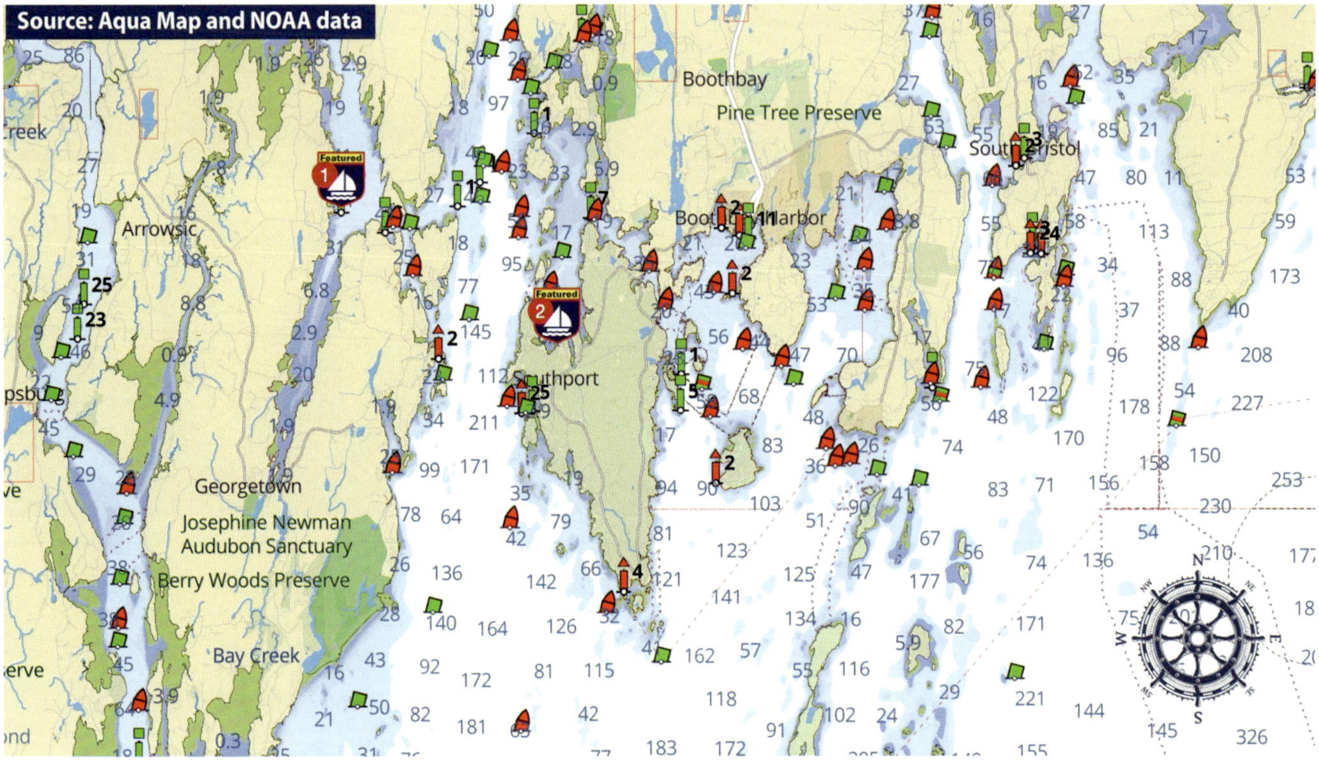

Source: Aqua Map and NOAA data

Once between Spectacle and Indiantown Islands, green can buoy "3" shows the way to the southern coves. Red nun buoy "2" marks the north end of the shoals separating Maddock Cove and Pierce Cove. The three coves have no aids to navigation so go carefully to avoid the rocks and shoals. Love Cove's entrance is also bordered by rocks submerged through most of the tide and can be difficult to line up properly without a chartplotter.

Dockage/Moorings: As you reach the western mouth of Goose Rock Passage or coming around the Nubble, Derecktor Robinhood will be visible immediately ahead. At this full-service facility you will find ample slips and moorings for transients as well as a fully capable shipyard. A courtesy car is available should you need more supplies. The Brunswick sprawl starts with Bath on the west side of the Kennebec.

Hodgdon Yacht Services–Southport Boatyard located at the southwest corner of Ebenecook Harbor has been building boats for 200 years and is the nation's oldest boat builders. Hodgdon can accommodate varying scopes of work to meet boaters' needs with easily accessible facilities and in-house expertise in specialty trades. They also offer a complete range of waterfront facilities including slips, moorings, fuel dock and provisioning options. This is one of their three locations in Maine.

Anchorage: Moorings fill Riggs Cove but travel farther south into Robinhood Cove for 7 to 15 feet MLW and good holding in mud and rock. The center of the cove is very deep and the entrance is thick with lobster buoys, but there is quite a bit of space along the sides on the north end for easier access to shore via Derecktor Robinhood. If you prefer to be farther from the

HODGDON MARINA

TUGBOAT INN & MARINA

BROWN'S WHARF INN & MARINA

Ebenecook Harbor

crowds, the south end is a gorgeous combination of rock outcroppings and forested hills. (If you prefer to be even farther removed, just keep heading south.)

Campbell Cove to the north is quiet with a few cottages hidden in the woodland shore. There are few lobster pots and plenty of room for several boats with 6 foot MLW depths (with 10-foot tide). Farther north you can anchor between Phipps Point and Hockomock Head out of the main current to wait if a sailboat's auxiliary isn't powerful enough to buck the current in Lower Hell Gate.

Ebenecook Harbor on the eastern shore of the Sheepscot River offers good anchorage options in a choice of sheltered coves. You can drop the hook east of Dogfish Head in 15 feet at MLW but watch your depth, be aware of the tide state and check the chart for cable crossing areas before setting the anchor.

Pierce Cove and Love Cove to the east on Ebencook Harbor are good anchorages with many moorings. In either of these, you will find at least 7 feet MLW, excellent holding in mud and protection from all but the north. The large quantity of unoccupied moorings makes this a popular spot to borrow one as long as you remain ready to move if the owner appears.

To Wiscasset (Sheepscot River)

Wiscasset, a major port of entry for goods from England until the War of 1812, is still a thriving village that today is more given to tourism than trade. Buildings and gardens from the town's heyday are now major attractions for history buffs. Locals refer to Wiscasset as the prettiest village in Maine, where you can take a delightful, self-guided walking tour of several historic buildings including Castle Tucker (circa 1807), an authentic Victorian house containing no reproductions; Wiscasset Academy (circa 1807), now home to the Maine Art Gallery; and The Customs House (circa 1869-1870). A variety of classic gardens are open to the public as well as many of the town's private homes, which have been well restored.

Sheepscot River, ME

WISCASSET		Largest Vessel	VHF	Total Slips	Approach/ Dockside Depth	Floating Docks	Gas/ Diesel	Repairs/ Haulout	Min/Max Amps	Pump-Out Station
1. Wiscasset Yacht Club-PRIVATE	(207) 687-8035	30			20.0 / 6.0					
2. Wiscasset Town Dock (WiFi)	(207) 691-7006	250	9	3	20.0 / 20.0	F		H		

(WiFi) Wireless Internet Access
Visit www.waterwayguide.com for current rates, fuel prices, website addresses and other up-to-the-minute information.
(Information in the table is provided by the facilities.)

Scan here for more details:

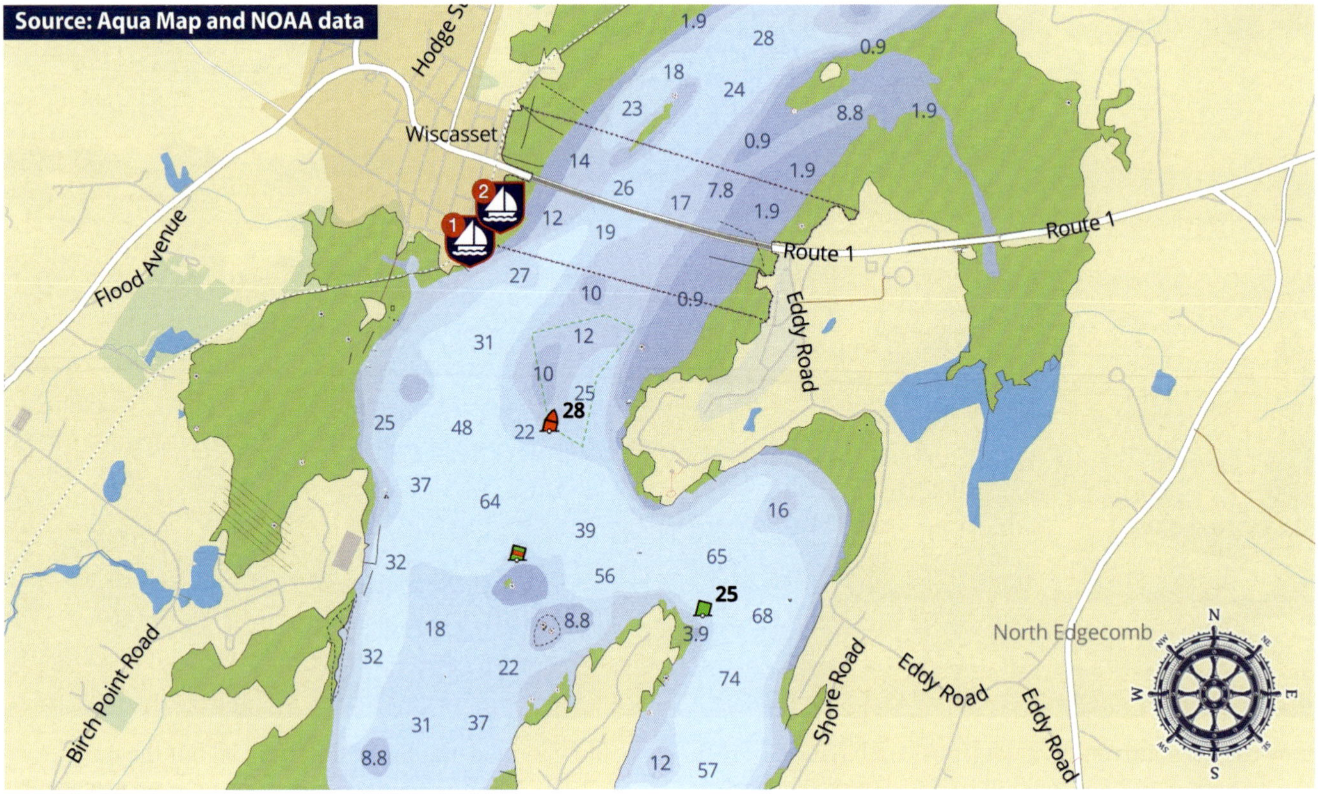

Source: Aqua Map and NOAA data

NAVIGATION: For the 9 island-studded miles to the **U.S. 1 Bridge** at Wiscasset (4 miles south of the limit to navigation at Sheepscot), the Sheepscot River is deep, well marked and attractive with lobster buoys covering every square foot of water. Look for the measured mile with shore ranges on the eastern bank at Barters Island to the east.

Dockage/Moorings: Friendly Wiscasset Yacht Club just south of the Town Landing has two guest moorings, while the Wiscasset Town Dock has three moorings and limited slip space available on a first-come, first-served basis. Overnight tie-up to the town moorings requires harbormaster permission and payment. Water is available and there are restrooms on the wharf that are open during the day. These facilities are a short walk from historic Wiscasset.

Anchorage: On the way to Wiscasset you will pass an anchorage opportunity at Indiantown Island on the eastern shore of the Sheepscot River. This is a nice anchorage for visiting the trails and nature preserve on Indiantown Island. One free guest mooring in about 6 feet MLW is first-come, first-served. Dinghy ashore to the Indiantown Island dinghy dock to take a nice hike around the island.

Even though slips and moorings are few in number at Wiscasset, there is ample anchorage in 12 to 20 feet MLW with secure holding east of the town's mooring field near Davis Island. Tidal currents run swiftly on both ebb and flow, which should encourage setting a secure hook (tested in both directions) with adequate scope.

Note that vessels anchoring in Wiscasset waters for more than 7 days must obtain permission from the Harbormaster and will be limited to 14 days in a calendar year.

Boothbay Harbor

Townsend Gut

Take the lovely channel called Townsend Gut to avoid going the long way around Southport Island between the Sheepscot River and Boothbay Harbor. This is also the continuation of the inside passage from Bath.

NAVIGATION: Head north from Ebenecook Harbor and pass 24-foot flashing green "7" on Cameron Point, leaving room for the rocks that are awash at low tide. Turn toward and then favor red nun buoy "6" marking Indiantown Island Ledge, one of the tightest squeezes on the cruise. Stay in the middle to pass through the next narrowing.

Hodgdon Cove opens up to the north and is good hangout area while waiting for the bridge opening. The fast-operating **Southport (SR27) Bridge** (also known as Townsend Gut Bridge) with 10-foot closed vertical clearance opens on signal except from April 29 through September 30, between 6:00 a.m. and 6:00 p.m., when the draw will open on the hour and half hour only.

Currents run swiftly through here. Hug the bold western shore and stay south of red nun buoy "2." Leaving Townsend Gut heading east, Boothbay Harbor is northeast and Mouse and Burnt Islands are southwest.

■ BOOTHBAY HARBOR TO LINEKIN BAY

Boothbay Harbor

Boothbay (pronounced "BOOTH-bay") Harbor is a summer resort with natural beauty, an easy entrance and many shore attractions. There's also ample yachting amenities on all but the busiest of holiday weekends when the harbor can be crowded both on the water and ashore. An unusual wooden pedestrian footbridge built in 1900 spans the inner harbor, saving visitors and residents from the long walk around. It is occasionally washed out by ice but is always rebuilt, and it protects a small-boat area that is heavily used by kayaks, dinghies and other low-profile vessels.

This easily approached and scenic bay has a well-documented maritime history dating from the 15th century. During the summer, sloops and a host of other classic hulls and rigs add interest to a harbor already bursting with boating color.

Although the center of activity is Boothbay Harbor, all the significant islands protecting this classic bay

Boothbay Harbor, ME

BOOTHBAY HARBOR AREA		Largest Vessel	VHF	Total Slips	Approach/ Dockside Depth	Floating Docks	Gas/ Diesel	Repairs/ Haulout	Min/Max Amps	Pump-Out Station
1. Boothbay Harbor Yacht Club-PRIVATE **WiFi**	(207) 633-5750	60	9		20.0 / 14.0	F				
2. Hodgdon Marina **WiFi**	(207) 633-2970	200	9	30	16.0 / 16.0	F	GD	RH	30 / 100	
3. Signal Point Marina	(207) 633-6920	60	9	48	25.0 / 15.0	F			30 / 50	P
4. Bristol Marine - The Boothbay Harbor Yard **WiFi**	(207) 633-3171	200	16	8	25.0 / 9.0	F		RH	30 / 50	
5. Tugboat Inn & Marina **WiFi**	(207) 633-4434	100	9	30	15.0 / 10.0	F			30 / 50	P
6. Boothbay Harbor Marina **WiFi**	(207) 633-6003	130	9	40	20.0 / 14.0	F			30 / 50	P
7. Oceanside Marina-Boothbay Harbor Oceanside Golf Resort **WiFi**	(207) 633-4455	80	9	15	18.0 / 8.0	F			50	P
8. Brown's Wharf Inn & Marina **WiFi**	(207) 633-5440	170	9	40	25.0 / 25.0	F			30 / 50	P
9. Carousel Marina **WiFi**	(207) 633-2922	180	9	50	30.0 / 22.0	F	GD	R	30 / 100	P

WiFi Wireless Internet Access
Visit www.waterwayguide.com for current rates, fuel prices, website addresses and other up-to-the-minute information.
(Information in the table is provided by the facilities.)

Scan here for more details:

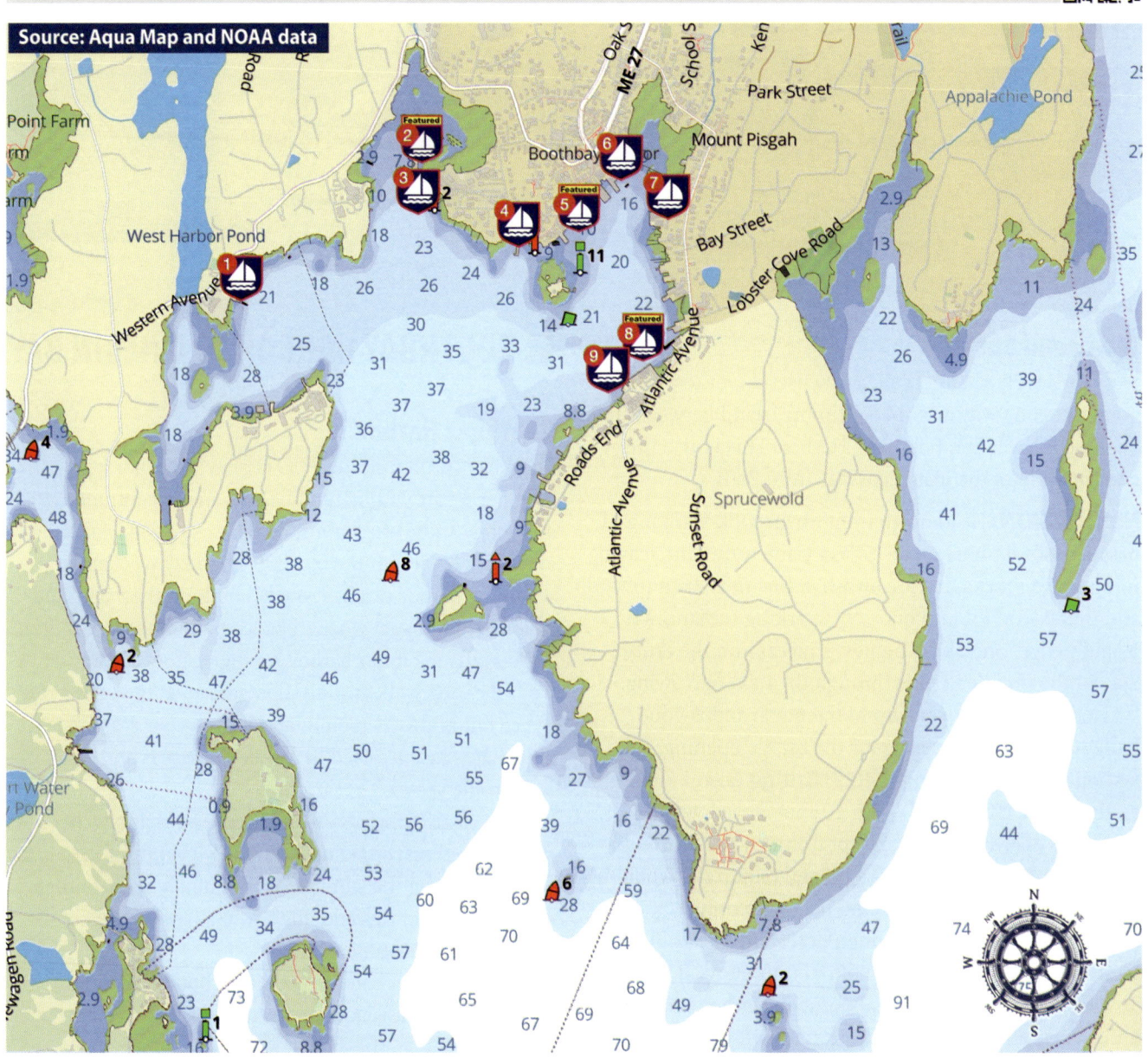

Source: Aqua Map and NOAA data

are populated during the summer months. This has been an enduring truth since 1837, when legions of "invalids" breathed the pure air and bathed in the clear water, resources hard to come by in densely populated Boston and New York. Visit the Boothbay Harbor Information Center (17 Commercial St.) for more information.

NAVIGATION: Boothbay Harbor is deep and access is easy from any direction in any weather. The popular entrances are protected Townsend Gut from the west and the somewhat-protected Fisherman Island Passage from the east. From Fisherman Island Passage head from Dictator Ledge's red nun "6" across Linekin Bay's mouth for Spruce Point.

Coming from offshore, Damariscove Island is the first protection from eastern swells, and the Cuckolds' 59-foot-tall lighthouse's flashing white light and horn simplify entrance in thick weather or at night. Head west of Squirrel Island and east of Burnt Island, then to flashing red buoy "8," which shows the safe water west of Tumbler Island. From there the harbor blooms before you and your heading will depend on your plans.

The easiest access to shoreside fun in this resort town is found in the northeastern cove (or inner harbor) of Boothbay Harbor. Excellent full-service marinas crowd along the eastern and western edges of the inner harbor. Most offer both moorings and transient slips but it is best to call ahead (VHF Channel 09) for a reservation.

Dockage/Moorings: Boothbay Harbor Yacht Club west of Mill Cove is private but welcomes visiting yachts (to 60 feet) on their guest moorings. The mooring fee entitles visitors to use of the launch service and amenities including laundry, tennis and bar and dining room. The club is identifiable by the BHYC sign on its roof.

West of McFarland Island in Mill Cove is Hodgdon Marina, which caters to boat of all types including megayachts. This is one of three locations in Maine. This facility provides dockside depths from 8 to 18 feet MLW, 750-linear feet of dock space, plus 500 linear feet of face dock, moorings and full marina amenities. Hodgdon is located on the quiet side of the harbor, yet still within walking distance of downtown's restaurants, galleries and shops. Don't feel like walking? They also offer complimentary bicycle use.

Signal Point Marina is located in the same basin and is part of a "dockominium," a condominium complex that maintains some transient slips to 60 feet. This is located on a peninsula between the harbor and Mill Cove, a few minutes walk from the village center.

Bristol Marine - The Boothbay Harbor Yard maintains 23 moorings and a dock for seasonal and transient visitors. Originally founded in 1869, the yard specializes in the maritime skills and trades that made New England famous and has shipwrights and service professionals on site to meet all your needs.

Snugly protected between two wharves, the Tugboat Inn & Marina provides sheltered dockage for boats of all kinds. Slips and moorings (no launch service) are available for short or long term stays. They also have waterfront rooms and suites, making this is a great place for a crew change or to just get off the boat for a while.

The conveniently located Boothbay Harbor Marina has slips with full amenities at the head of the harbor. They publish nightly as well as hourly rates. The nearby footbridge connects the west side to the east side of the harbor and makes for a pleasant evening stroll.

Across the water is Oceanside Marina-Boothbay Harbor Oceanside Golf Resort with waterfront accommodations and an 18-hole championship golf course. Call ahead for overnight slip availability (to 100 feet). Docks are also available for hourly use as well by those dining at their on-site (5-star) restaurant, Coastal Prime.

Continuing south, the family-run Brown's Wharf Inn & Marina has been in business for more than 70 years. Brown's has 6 transient moorings, 40 slips (15 reserved for transients) and alongside dockage for vessels to 170 feet. Two shopping trolleys leave from this location on a regular basis.

Nearby Carousel Marina welcomes transients in slips or on moorings with full amenities. Facilities include an on-site restaurant (Whale's Tale), a clubhouse, easily accessible fuel dock and overnight rooms available for the use of transient boaters or their guests. It's a pleasant walk into town.

Anchorage: Mill Cove between Farland Point and Railway Point offers a designated anchorage with good holding in 15 to 25 feet MLW outside the mooring field. The shallows north of McKown Point are a long dinghy ride from town but have 17- to 26-feet MLW depths and good holding in mud and rock.

Boothbay Harbor, ME

LINEKIN BAY		Largest Vessel	VHF	Total Slips	Approach/ Dockside Depth	Floating Docks	Gas/ Diesel	Repairs/ Haulout	Min/Max Amps	Pump-Out Station
1. Linekin Bay Resort **WiFi**	(207) 607-6134		9		32.0 / 18.0	F				

WiFi Wireless Internet Access
Visit www.waterwayguide.com for current rates, fuel prices, website addresses and other up-to-the-minute information. (Information in the table is provided by the facilities.)

Scan here for more details:

Linekin Bay

In contrast to Boothbay Harbor, Linekin Bay just east of Spruce Point is quiet, non-commercial and nearly deserted. The original Scotch-Irish settlers and their descendants fought development so obstinately that even the man it's named after, Benjamin Linekin, couldn't have his way without a fight. The Montgomery clan had been farming the neck for decades when the newcomer Linekin arrived and built a house, causing friction. When he retreated to Boston for the harsh winter, they disassembled Linekin's house and carried it and his possessions away completely. (Linekin took the Montgomerys to court but a sympathetic jury found them not guilty.)

The highlight of Linekin Bay, in addition to excellent protection in an easterly or southeasterly blow, is the renowned P.E. Luke Yard (207-633-4971) on the southeastern coast. Marine engineering buffs will relish a free tour of Luke's private museum of the company's colorful history in the world of traditional boatbuilding and ocean yacht racing. Luke's has an extensive repair trade and manufactures heavy three-piece storm anchors and ingenious automatic feathering props.

NAVIGATION: If continuing east from Boothbay, note that the best course in good weather is to pass well to the east of Squirrel Island then continue through the Fisherman Island Passage to the red-and-white Morse (A) bell buoy "HL" off the mouth of the Damariscotta River. Entrance to Linekin Bay is an easy matter through the wide, deep passage between bold and wooded Negro Island (off the west side of Ocean Point) and green can buoy "1."

Dockage/Moorings: The 20-acre Linekin Bay Resort dominates the northern edge of the cove, and the remainder of the shore is dotted by homes. The resort offers mooring rental that includes launch service during operating hours and access to the resort's amenities (based on availability). They also have a dock and dine option.

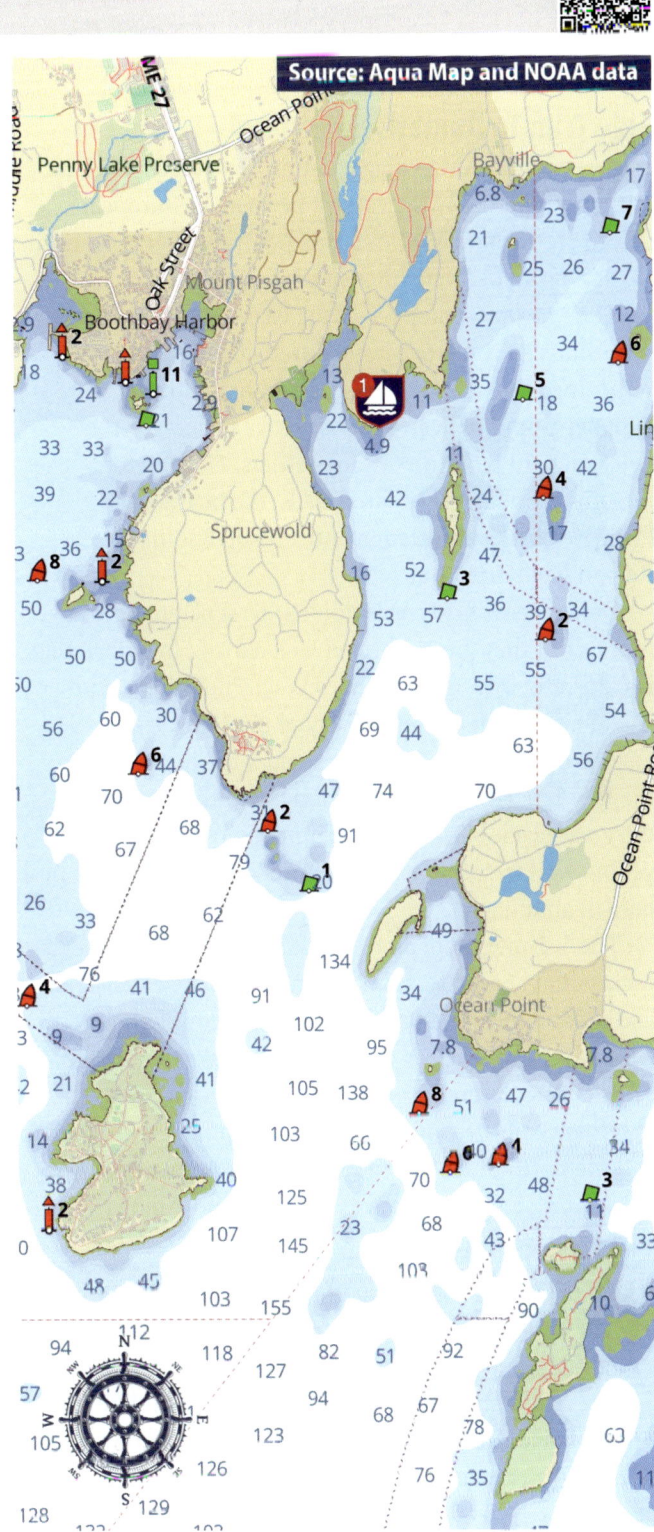

Source: Aqua Map and NOAA data

Anchorage: An often-overlooked anchorage is Lewis Cove on the western side of Linekin Bay. There is excellent holding and good protection in 14 to 22 feet MLW with excellent holding in mud outside the mooring field. Dinghies may be left on the inside of either the Main Dock or East Dock at Linekin Bay Resort. If you are unsure of the best spot for your dinghy, please ask the dockmaster on duty.

Side Trip: To Damariscove Island

If year-round fishing villages count, Damariscove Island was unquestionably the earliest permanent European colony in the New World. It was permanent, that is, until the last resident family moved to the mainland in 1939.

The *Mayflower* stopped at the island to barter for provisions en route to Massachusetts Bay in 1620, returning early the following year to beg additional supplies from the hearty Damariscove fishers for the beleaguered Plymouth Colony settlers. Now all that remains are abandoned farmsteads, the boarded-up former Coast Guard station and a rustic Boothbay Region Land Trust hut.

Damariscove's 209 acres look to be separated into two islands but they are connected by a narrow, low neck that is 0.25-mile wide and 1.7 miles long. This windswept island echoes the austere beauty of the Hebrides and of lost Viking outposts. The largest eider duck colonies in the U.S. reportedly nest here along with their nemesis, the great black-backed gull. Common yellow throats, yellow warblers, catbirds and Savannah sparrows also nest here in abundance.

The 1.5-mile walk along the Pond Loop Trail traverses rocky shore, coastal tundra, salt marsh, freshwater pond and upland meadow. Passage here during mid-summer's wildflower profusion is certain to leave a lasting memory. The delicate natural beauty of the island argues for strict observance of the Conservancy's rules: no fires or camping and the northern end of the island is off limits for the protection of nesting eider ducks until mid-August. Pets are not allowed at any time.

NAVIGATION: South of Boothbay Harbor in Booth Bay, the approach to Damariscove Island is more straightforward than it might appear, especially when you look at waves broken by the reef known as The Motions. The reef is located to the west of an entrance barely revealed by the sharp cliffs cascading into the narrow slot of a harbor. Several warnings are in order:

- Stay well inside Bantam Rock, which is actually a cluster of rocks extending toward the island from red lighted buoy "2BR" located about 1 mile to the south-southwest of the harbor entrance.

- When passing east of red-and-white gong buoy "TM" (The Motions) set a course for the center of the harbor opening and maintain enough speed to retain steerageway in following seas.

- Once abeam of the western tip of the harbor entrance, correct your course to favor that side slightly as there is a submerged boulder off the eastern shore very nearly even with the tip of the western point.

Moorings/Anchorage: On the way south to Damariscove Island, the two complimentary Ram Island Moorings can provide great lunch stop or even an overnight so long as the swell and wind isn't too bad. Dinghy ashore to Ram Island to visit the stubby circa 1883 light tower linked to the island by a long walkway.

The Boothbay Region Land Trust maintains two complimentary moorings available for 24 hours in Damariscove Island Harbor. There is even a small rowboat on the stone pier for use by visitors who pick up a mooring. If both moorings are taken, you can anchor in soft mud just past the abandoned Coast Guard Station (now privately owned) at the south end of the Damariscove Island Harbor. In this long, narrow bight, fore and aft anchors will allow adequate scope for the 10-foot tides while preventing grounding at low tide.

It is also possible for a boat or two to set a careful hook in the inner harbor beyond the channel's choke point and abeam of the Nature Conservancy's hut, also to the west. Since swing room is quite limited and there is almost always a lobster car and boat nearby, nighttime fenders are in order.

During settled weather, it is possible to anchor at the north end of Damariscove Island at Bar Cove Beach then row in for a landing on the pebbled beach below the island's freshwater pond. The cove is sheltered from the surge produced by prevailing southwesterlies but is open to the northeast.

> NOTE: Wherever you anchor, the Boothbay Region Land Trust asks that you check in with them before hiking ashore.

Damariscotta River

■ DAMARISCOTTA RIVER TO GEORGES ISLAND

Damariscotta River

Around Linekin Neck from Boothbay Harbor via the well-marked Fisherman Island Passage, the Damariscotta River is about a century removed from its more active neighbor to the west. It is one of Maine's most beautiful rivers and flows past 15 miles of wooded islands, hidden coves, jagged rock outcroppings and high, green bluffs.

Once plied by commercial schooners, the Damariscotta River's lazily winding channel is easy to navigate. You will pass harbors with sophisticated attractions, good food and two small but important shipbuilding villages. At the head of the river are two Colonial cities that once served as ports of entry. The tidal range here is 9 feet so it is advisable to travel on a fair tide.

Two blocks south of the harbor on the road to Ocean Point is East Boothbay General Store (207-633-7800) serving fresh pastries, newspapers and coffee that draw an early bird crowd. The store also stocks some dry goods, dairy and deli items and a limited variety of sodas, beers and wines.

NAVIGATION: Close to the river entrance about 1 mile north of thickly wooded Inner Heron Island, Christmas Cove at Rutherford Island has an easy entrance, perfect protection, a handsome shoreline and magnificent views. While the rocks that form an informal breakwater look intimidating upon entry, careful navigation will provide safe entry.

After passing red nun buoy "4" north of Inner Heron Island, head for the center of the harbor entrance leaving Foster Point (and red-over-green nun buoy "FP") to the north. Inside the outer harbor look for red daybeacon "2," which is on rocks and then green daybeacon "3" farther in and pass between them without getting close to either.

Johns Bay, ME

DAMARISCOTTA RIVER		Largest Vessel	VHF	Total Slips	Approach/ Dockside Depth	Floating Docks	Gas/ Diesel	Repairs/ Haulout	Min/Max Amps	Pump-Out Station
1. Coveside Marina & Restaurant	(207) 644-8282	60		12	10.0 / 10.0	F			30	
2. Gamage Shipyard	(207) 644-8181	100	9	44	10.0 / 10.0	F		RH	50	P
3. Ocean Point Marina (WiFi)	(207) 633-0773	150	16	70	35.0 / 15.0	F	GD	RH	30 / 50	P

WiFi Wireless Internet Access
Visit www.waterwayguide.com for current rates, fuel prices, website addresses and other up-to-the-minute information.
(Information in the table is provided by the facilities.)

Scan here for more details:

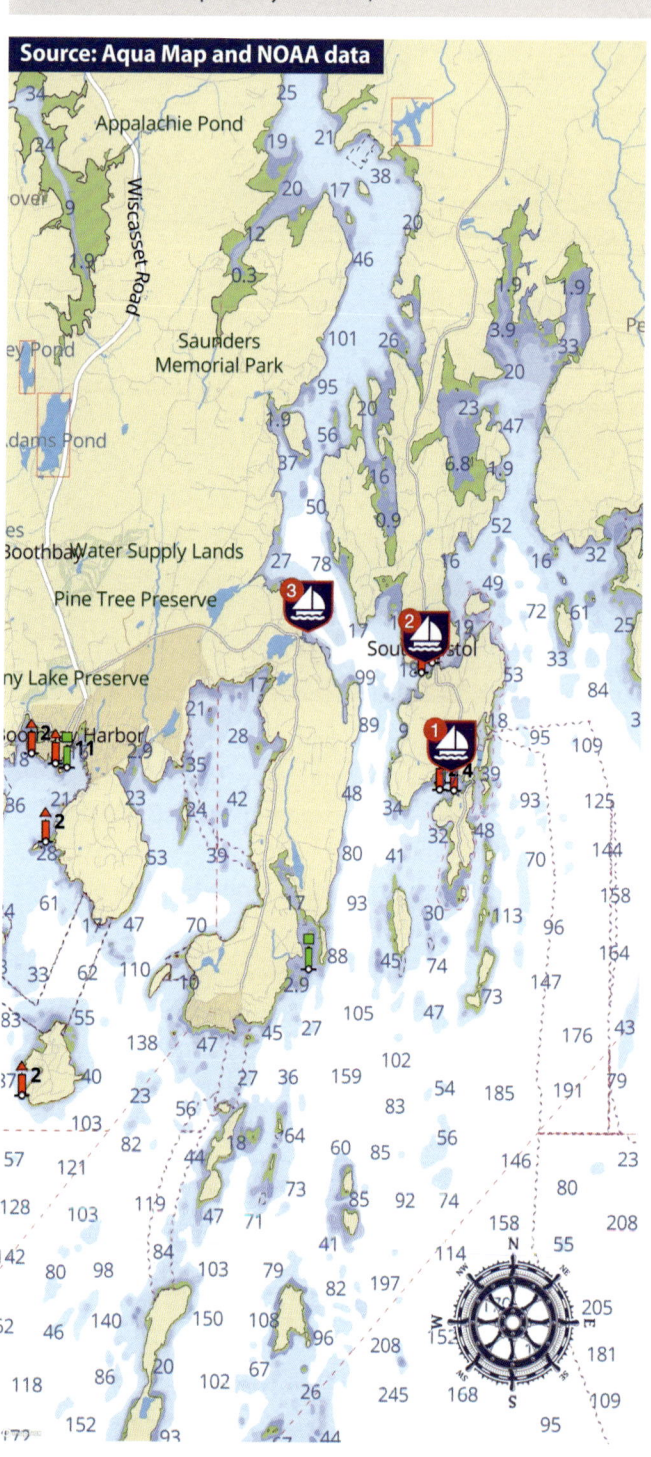

Source: Aqua Map and NOAA data

Until the river reaches the twin villages of Damariscotta and Newcastle, 13 miles from the open ocean, it offers only beautiful scenery and an unlimited choice of peaceful anchorages. River currents run rapidly (up to 5 knots on the ebb) and the upper 2 miles of the river are winding and narrow, although reasonably well marked. Those with limited cruising experience in such waters should seek local knowledge before making the trip. Cruising upriver to Damariscotta is a nice day trip when fog on the outside limits your options.

Dockage/Moorings: There is no room for anchoring in Christmas Cove due to the proliferation of moorings but a mooring or dock space is usually available from Coveside Marina & Restaurant at the south end of Rutherford. Book through Dockwa. Enjoy the varied menu of the well-regarded restaurant with spectacular views of the Cove or visit the relaxed Burgee Bar, a sailor's delight with ragged, yet colorful burgees, brought in from all over the world, hanging from the rafters.

At the north end of Rutherford Island, the historic Gamage Shipyard is located on the west side of The Gut Bridge (4-foot closed vertical clearance), which opens on signal. The shipyard has 44 slips for boats to 100 feet and 12 rental moorings (to 60 feet). They also offer vessel refit and restoration among other services.

The small boatbuilding village of East Boothbay is located on the west side of the Damariscotta River with a mooring-filled cove. Ocean Point Marina is easily spotted because of its prominent sheds and long fuel dock paralleling the river's western shore. This is a full-service boatyard with transient and seasonal dockage and moorings plus a fully-stocked ship store, an on-site café and a full-service restaurant. They also rent kayaks.

You can also ask the Newcastle and Damariscotta volunteer harbormaster if a mooring is available (207-563-3398), if you plan to travel that far upriver.

Anchorage: The inner portion of Christmas Cove is too tight with moorings for anchoring but there is plenty of room on the opposite side of Christmas Cove outside a few more moorings. It is a short ride to the dinghy dock at the Coveside Marina & Restaurant.

Once past Fort Island, there is a small anchorage with excellent protection in Seal Cove on the east side of the river. The bar going into the anchorage carries 5 feet MLW with 12 to 17 feet MLW once inside the inner basin. Anchoring outside of the bar provides plenty of swing room and good protection with excellent holding in 20 feet MLW. This is a quiet spot where the seals (and those who come to see them) are the noisiest things around.

Another option is Long Cove, approximately 0.5 mile north. Here you will find at least 10 feet MLW and good holding with good protection from all but the northwest. Watch for the charted rocks on your way in. This is adjacent to the Plummer Point Preserve with 1.5 miles of trails and beautiful views of the river. It is better to go around the unnamed island and approach from the north at MLW. The rocks between the anchorage and the Preserve are tricky, even in a dinghy!

NOTE: Hodgsons Island, Plummer Point Preserve, and Seal Cove Preserve all offer hiking trails.

Once past Miller Island, there is a good anchorage to the west in Pleasant Cove with 13 to 16 feet MLW and good holding in sand and mud.

It is possible to anchor in front of the town dock (out of the intense current) at Newcastle at the north end of the river in 10 to 11 feet MLW. Floats off the town dock are reserved for short-term, courtesy dockage (up to 2 hours) and there is an ample dinghy dock. The current is pushed to high velocity here due to the restriction of the channel just south of the bridge, making docking a challenge. Damariscotta on the west shore offers a range of services on Main St., half a block off the harbor front. There is a full-service grocery store 1 mile east of the town dock.

Pemaquid Harbor

Circular Pemaquid Harbor is a pleasant stopover 3 miles up Johns Bay on the eastern shore. Visit the reconstructed Colonial Pemaquid State Historic Site of Fort William Henry (207-677-2423) and gaze at a splendid view of the bay, Pemaquid River and Johns Island from its parapets. On a warm day, the swimming is excellent on crescent-shaped Pemaquid Beach. Limited day dockage may be available.

NAVIGATION: A number of routes lead into deep and open Johns Bay. You can sail around Thrumcap Island, then to the north between it and Pemaquid Point; or you can follow the deep, narrow Thread of Life, a fascinating buoyed thoroughfare northwest of Thrumcap Island, which runs between Thread of Life ledges and Turnip Island.

For perhaps the most interesting route of all, travel The Gut, a shortcut from the Damariscotta River, running through the lift bridge at South Bristol (4-foot closed vertical clearance, opens on signal). The wooded, rocky shores make this an especially beautiful trip. Keep a sharp eye for lobster buoys here.

Anchorage: Northwest of Witch Island you can drop the hook in 21 to 28 feet MLW with good holding in mud. This is somewhat exposed to the north. Watch for possible lobster buoys when you swing with the tide. You can also anchor across the river in Pemaquid Harbor to the north in 10 to 18 feet MLW with excellent holding in soft mud and all-around protection. If you are craving a lobster dinner, there is a Fisherman's Co-op a short dinghy ride away. Pemaquid Harbor is a quintessential Maine small town and delightful to explore. While not very well known, it is definitely worth a stop.

Round Pond (Muscongus Sound)

Once an active shipbuilding, quarrying and cargo port, Round Pond on Muscongus Sound is now most active in the lobster trade and home to a considerable number of cruising vessels. The Post Office is about 0.5 mile south of the village center. Muscongus Bay Lobster (207-529-5528) has fresh lobsters at the head of the dock. You may also be able to get gasoline and diesel fuel here.

NAVIGATION: When heading north in Muscongus Sound, honor the marks precisely. On approaching Round Pond, strictly observe green can buoy "9" southeast of Poland North Ledge (just awash at low tide). Look for the small red house as a landmark for the Round Pond entry channel. Lobster pots are thickly placed throughout this area in both the harbor channel and the sound itself.

Muscongus Sound, ME

ROUND POND		Largest Vessel	VHF	Total Slips	Approach/ Dockside Depth	Floating Docks	Gas/ Diesel	Repairs/ Haulout	Min/Max Amps	Pump-Out Station
1. Padebco Full Service Boatyard & Custom Boat Builders	(207) 529-5106	50			9.0 / 3.0	F	GD	RH		
HOCKOMOCK CHANNEL										
2. Broad Cove Marine Service (WIFI)	(207) 529-5186	42	9	16	6.0 / 6.0	F	GD	R		P

(WIFI) Wireless Internet Access
Visit www.waterwayguide.com for current rates, fuel prices, website addresses and other up-to-the-minute information.
(Information in the table is provided by the facilities.)

Scan here for more details:

Source: Aqua Map and NOAA data

Dockage/Moorings: There are many private mooring balls in Round Pond's harbor. Contact the Round Pond harbormaster for assistance in locating a vacant mooring (207-529-5123). The town dock with some dinghy space is just to the right of the paved boat ramp. Use a long painter and tie up loosely so others can maneuver around you.

Padebco Full Service Boatyard & Custom Boat Builders is located at the floating wharf farthest north of the town dock and offers rental moorings and a wide range of services from repairs, re-powers, refits, refurbishing to hauling, launching and storage. They are also helpful with acquiring supplies. Their transient moorings are marked with their name and a flag on the pickup stick. (If the flag contains a boat name or last name, assume the mooring is not available for use.)

Just 1.5 miles north of Muscongus Harbor on the west side of Hockomock Channel is Broad Cove Marine Service, an old-time Maine lobster dock with wholesale and retail live lobster and picnic-style dining on the wharf (seasonal). A transient mooring is usually available and can be reserved on VHF Channel 09.

Anchorage: There is room for anchoring in Round Pond in 9 to 17 feet MLW with all-around protection. You can also anchor behind Oar Island on Hockomock Channel in 8 to 14 feet MLW with good holding in mud and rock. This is somewhat exposed to the southeast.

Friendship Island

About midway across Muscongus Bay on the Meduncook River is Friendship Island, birthplace of the Friendship sloop. Originally designed for fishing and lobstering, these elegant sailboats are now in demand as a recreational craft on the U.S. East and West Coasts among wooden boat aficionados. Friendship is a busy fishing and lobstering town and appreciates cruisers who respect the work being done.

Round Pond

NAVIGATION: The entrance to Friendship Harbor is north of Friendship Long Island and south of Hatchet Cove. It has a good, easy-to-enter harbor that is protected in all but southwesterly winds. The center is deep but don't stray toward Friendship Long Island while approaching green daybeacon "9." The town dock is north of green can "7."

Anchorage: After passing through Friendship Harbor, turn due south after green can buoy "7" (but be ready for locals to cut it thereby cutting you off). Next, proceed through the channel between Friendship Long Island and Garrison Island. Turn west after red nun buoy "6" and anchor in 7 to 12 feet MLW in mud and sand. This is well protected from all directions but the southeast and you're likely to be alone here except for the lobster boats zooming by all day. It's the anchorage closest to the town dock, which has a dinghy dock that is an education on how to tie up properly when sharing space with many other boats.

Walk straight uphill then turn right on the first major road for supplies at Wallace's Market & Italian Deli (207-832-2200), which stocks an impressive array of canned and boxed goods for such a small store. Their real strengths are produce, meats, cheeses, deli salads and sandwiches.

Hatchet Cove is northwest of Friendship and has at least 11 feet MLW but it's a long row to get to the dinghy dock. Anchoring is also possible a little farther south among boats in the cove lying between Friendship Island and Cranberry Island. Expect 9 to 14 feet MLW with good holding in mud and rock.

Harbor Island to the south is private property but you can anchor in the cove in at least 7 feet MLW with good holding in mud and grass. The owners may even welcome you ashore on the beach in the southwest corner of the anchorage. From here there are lovely trails to the wild western shore. But be respectful and do not approach the house.

Working outward from Friendship, you will discover several secure anchorages and a number of picturesque offshore island communities seldom visited except by the boats that come to pick up herring and lobsters. These remote and peaceful spots have few visitors and nothing set up for cruisers to do or buy.

St. George River

Several easy, attractive miles upriver at the head of navigation on the St. George River is historic Thomaston where large, beautiful vessels are still built, as they have been for decades. The major tourist attraction at Thomaston is the restored Montpelier, home of Gen. Henry Knox, fellow campaigner of George Washington and the nation's first Secretary of War. The General Henry Knox Museum (207-354-8062) offers a window

St. George River, ME

THOMASTON		Largest Vessel	VHF	Total Slips	Approach/ Dockside Depth	Floating Docks	Gas/ Diesel	Repairs/ Haulout	Min/Max Amps	Pump-Out Station
1. Lyman-Morse Boatbuilding	(207) 354-6904	150	16	10	12.0 / 10.0	F	GD	RH	30 / 100	P
2. Thomaston Harbormaster	(207) 706-6980	70			7.0 / 8.0					

WiFi Wireless Internet Access

Visit www.waterwayguide.com for current rates, fuel prices, website addresses and other up-to-the-minute information. (Information in the table is provided by the facilities.)

Scan here for more details:

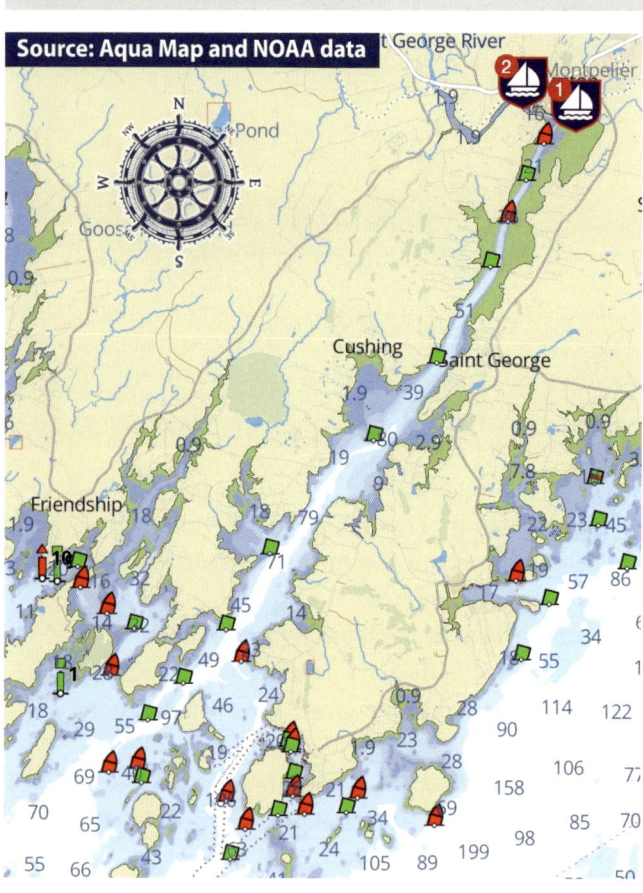

Source: Aqua Map and NOAA data

into real lives of the past. Within a few blocks are several churches, banks and a public library. Epifanes North America (207-354-0804) has a beautiful office here with a spectacular view and welcomes visitors curious about these high-quality paints and varnishes.

NAVIGATION: Heading east from Friendship starting south of Garrison Island, honor red nun buoy "4" and turn east to miss the long shoal extending northeast from Morse Island. Make a 290° turn around green can buoy "3" and head southwest for red nun buoy "2" off the western end of Gay Island, favoring Morse Island to the northeast.

Continue past Gay Island, leave the southern tip well to the north and then look for green can buoy "1" marking Goose Rock Ledge. Steer northeast leaving that mark well to your north and then work your way up the St. George River.

>>>>>>>>>>>>> ⚠ >>>>>>>>>>>>>

CAUTION: Heavy shoaling to less than 2 feet MLW has been observed in the St. George River in the vicinity of Thomaston Harbor. Mariners are advised to use caution when transiting St. George River north of red nun "16" to the 40-foot fixed vertical clearance **Brooklyn Heights Road Bridge.**

Discussing lobster buoys can become monotonous in Maine, but this passage contains an incredible concentration of them with the additional complication of secondary buoys on short lines in case the primaries are dragged under by the mix of extreme tides and currents.

Dockage/Moorings: Up the river at Thomaston you will find several established boat yards and a few transient slips or moorings. Lyman-Morse Boatbuilding specializes in service and refits but they maintain some transient dockage along their face docks (to 150 feet), in slips at the head of the harbor (when available) and on harbor floats in the inner harbor.

The Thomaston Harbormaster assigns moorings on a first-come, first-served basis (with the first day free of charge). Call 207-706-6980 to check availability.

Anchorage: Maple Juice Cove about halfway up on the west side of the river is in a predominantly residential area and has excellent protection and good holding in mud with 8 to 14 feet MLW. Turkey Cove on the east side of the river is more exposed and can be bumpy in southwest winds. Both provide protection and easy entrance but have no nearby amenities. Pleasant Point Gut to the south has 12 to 16 feet MLW and good holding. It is somewhat exposed to the east.

Port Clyde

Once called Herring Gut, Port Clyde lies between Marshall Point and Hupper Island, close to the west-east route, east of the entrance to the St. George River. It is the home port of the Monhegan Boat Line passenger ferry and is widely used by locals as a harbor of refuge and is always busy with lobster boats. Port Clyde General Store and the adjoining restaurant closed in 2023 so the closest provisioning is in Tenants Harbor or Rockland.

NAVIGATION: Port Clyde's northern entrance between Hupper Island and a ledge off Hupper Point is tricky and the chart shows 5- to 6-foot MLW depths at points. Reports of 8-foot MLW depths where the chart calls for 2 feet MLW might tempt a boater but ease in unless the tide is high. The southern entrance is easier, well marked and wide open.

Anchorage: There is a deep-water anchorage with protection from the southern rollers north of Hupper Island. It is open to the northwest but the holding is deep mud in 21 feet MLW. The anchorage right off Port Clyde Harbor is even deeper at 25 feet MLW and is both open to southern weather and somewhat rolly.

> NOTE: Low water depths here can mean 30 to 40 feet at high tide. Use appropriate scope for your tackle and the weather.

Side Trip: Georges Islands

You will feel like you have truly arrived Down East in this seemingly remote fishing outpost. The few structures are ramshackle but businesslike and the docks are mounted on stripped fir tree poles at an impressive height. The tidal currents are fierce.

Allen Island is privately owned and is developed only to the extent of an attractive house, barn and outbuilding complex for an experimental sheep ranching operation. Dogs are not allowed on Allen Island. Lobstering activity starts well before dawn on Benner Island with "harrumphing" engines joining the bleating of the lambs in this otherwise idyllic setting.

Burnt Island to the east has a scallop shaped harbor fashioned by Burnt Island's northern beach and Little Burnt Island to the northwest.

Anchorage: You can anchor between Benner and Allen Islands in the protected Georges Harbor, following the tradition set by English explorer George Waymouth

in 1605 aboard the *Archangel*. There is at least 7 feet MLW with good holding in sand and rock.

Burnt Island provides good protection from the prevailing southwesterlies. The holding is good in at least 7 feet MLW with a sand bottom but this location is quite exposed to winds shifting east and north.

Side Trip: Monhegan Island

Long a favorite retreat for artists and writers, Monhegan Island is far enough off the beaten path to remain relatively undisturbed by tourism and commercial development.

Even though it is only 9 miles southwest of the ferry landing in Port Clyde and little more than a dozen miles from the moorings at Tenants Harbor, the island never seems to attract more than a few sailors and a scattering of rough-clad day hikers who quickly blend in with the island's fishers and summer resident painters. They disappear along the island's 17 miles of mapped trails to imposing outlooks and quiet glens or they are off to visit the rustic studios of some 20 professional artists who regularly display their works here.

The Monhegan Associates Trail Map, available for a small charge at the inns and most shops, is invaluable for those hoping to sort out the island's maze of marked and highly scenic trails. If you decide to use the online version, download it to your phone so you don't lose it along with your signal.

> NOTE: If you happen to be making the trip in June, stop by Eastern Egg Rock to (respectfully) see the Atlantic Puffins who breed there on the west side.

NAVIGATION: The island is easily approached from any direction with relatively few obstructions. Monhegan's powerful light (flashing every 15 seconds, 178 feet above sea level) is visible for many miles at sea and is an important landmark for those making overnight crossings from southern New England or farther south.

Monhegan Light will guide you directly into the open entrance of Monhegan Harbor. Care must be taken from Sheepscot Bay to the west or from Muscongus Bay to the north to avoid the shallow ledges surrounding Duck Rocks (south of flashing green bell buoy "5"). Harbor entry can be made from the south between Monhegan and Manana Islands.

Dockage/Moorings: Tie-ups are possible for up to 30 minutes at the town dock but your vessel must remain attended. Stand clear for the arrival or departure of the daily ferries. (They typically arrive late morning and depart in the afternoon.) When landing your dinghy remember the 10-foot tidal change and plan accordingly.

For an overnight stay it is best to arrange for a mooring from the Monhegan harbormaster, who is usually available at the fish shack next to Fish Beach (second beach down from the town dock). You can hail him on VHF Channel 19A or call 207-594-9342.

One of the limited private moorings off the town beach may be available without charge or at a small fee. Otherwise, after the ferryboats have left for the day, visitors may tie up on any of their four heavy-tackle mooring balls (north of the town dock) until the next day's ferry arrivals.

Anchorage: Anchoring is not recommended in the harbor's deceptive mix of sand and rocks. It looks secure but is not. Anchored boats regularly are dragged away by swift tidal currents. In settled weather locals suggest that a hook can be set securely in Deadman Cove. This location requires deep water scope and a strong pulling arm for the dinghy, but it offers fair holding in grass and rock. When landing your dinghy remember the 10 foot tide change in tide and plan accordingly.

It is possible to tether a dinghy to the town pier next to the vertical ladder but the rapid rise and fall of a substantial tide makes landing here undesirable for a visit of more than a few minutes. The better alternative is at Fish Beach. Even here, a long dinghy tether secured to a location above the high-water mark will be required.

■ TENANTS HARBOR & MATINICUS

North and east of Monhegan Island, the mouth of Penobscot Bay welcomes waterborne pilgrims to this sailor's mecca. Although exposed to an easterly blow, Tenants Harbor is the first of several fine shelters on the course ascending the bay. Much as pleasure-boaters enjoy the area, it's also crucial to the commercial fishing industry. Give a friendly wave to the folks feeding us all.

Muscle Ridge Channel located northeast of Tenants Harbor offers an inside passage to Rockland. Protected from the open sea by a string of outlying islands, it is studded with well-marked rocks and ledges that should present no problem in good visibility and numerous bights and coves provide shelter when needed.

Tenants Harbor

Although privately owned and not open to the public, Tenants Harbor Lighthouse at the east end of Southern Island is noteworthy. The light, built in 1857, marks the entrance to Tenants Harbor. The light is owned by Jamie Wyeth (Andrew's son) and is beautifully maintained. This quaint town doesn't have a ton of amenities but Tenants Harbor General Store (207-372-6311) is a provisioning opportunity.

At the top of the gentle rise above the public landing, turn right on Tenants Harbor's Main Street for a 1-block walk the this old-fashioned country store. They offer a good selection of fresh fruits, veggies and meats, general groceries, ice, beer, wine, fresh lobster rolls and seafood. The Post Office and a laundry are just up the street.

NAVIGATION: About 4 miles up the coast Tenants Harbor is a good refuge in fog or heavy weather and its approach is well marked and unobstructed. The unusual-looking Tenants Harbor Lighthouse and attendant buildings mark the approach at the end of Southern Island. If approaching after dark, look for the illuminated flag on the tall flagpole. The nearby flashing green bell buoy "1" should be left to the south as you enter the wide mouth of the harbor.

The harbor entrance is deep with no obstructions on the straight course down the center of the harbor channel. Nevertheless, watch carefully to negotiate the minefield of brightly colored and closely spaced lobster buoys and toggles throughout the channel.

Muscle Ridge Channel begins with Whitehead Light, a gray tower with a green occulting light (4 seconds on and a blink off) but take care with South Breaker, which is marked with bell buoy "SB." After green can buoy "3," turn west if visiting the large, well-marked Seal Harbor between Whitehead Island and Sprucehead Island. The green-red-green Burnt Island Ledge buoy shows green for the main channel (Muscle Ridge) and red for the Seal Harbor entrance. The channel is well provided with reds and greens but two sets stand out that require extra care.

South of Ash Island, an un-numbered red-green-red nun marks the Upper Gangway Ledge, while green can buoy "15" shows rocks off Ash Island. Grindstone Ledge is marked by green can buoy "21" and red nun buoy "22" to keep cruisers off shallow rocks to either side.

Penobscot Bay, ME

TENANTS HARBOR		Largest Vessel	VHF	Total Slips	Approach/ Dockside Depth	Floating Docks	Gas/ Diesel	Repairs/ Haulout	Min/Max Amps	Pump-Out Station
1. Tenants Harbor Boat Yard (WiFi)	(207) 372-8063	170	9		7.0 / 7.0	F	GD	RH	30 / 50	P
2. Tenants Harbor Town Dock	(207) 372-6363	40	16		15.0 / 3.0					

(WiFi) Wireless Internet Access
Visit www.waterwayguide.com for current rates, fuel prices, website addresses and other up-to-the-minute information.
(Information in the table is provided by the facilities.)

Scan here for more details: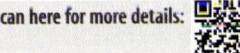

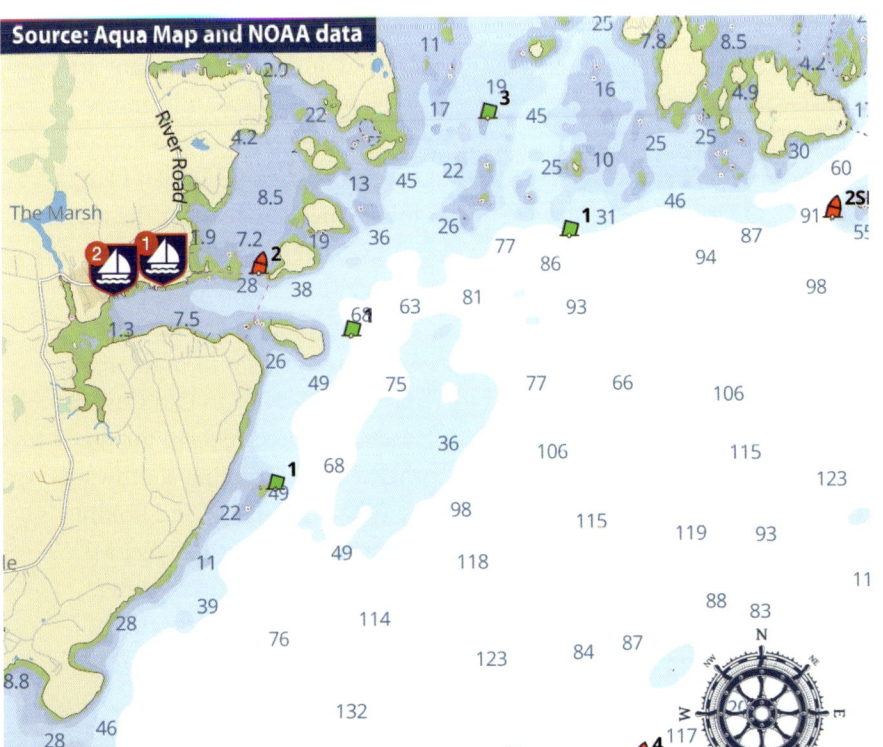

Source: Aqua Map and NOAA data

Dockage/Moorings: Tenants Harbor Boat Yard has transient tie-up spaces available as well as moorings but with few amenities. The actual rental moorings may be difficult to distinguish from lobster buoys. Colors change somewhat with the seasons so look closely to distinguish the rental moorings from the lobster buoys. They also sell gas and diesel fuel (year round) and offer all manner of boat repair and maintenance. (Note that they also have a daily dinghy dockage fee.)

Tenants Harbor Town Dock & Moorings is a U-shaped affair with plenty of dinghy room inside, leaving the face dock for larger vessels. Expect 3 feet MLW here with a 9-foot tidal range. The town moorings in the inner harbor are round and white with a blue band marked "Rental" (in Sharpie). The public landing and dinghy dock are at the head of the harbor to the north. Ice and other supplies are available adjacent to the public wharf and a motel and restaurants are right nearby. The town services trash barrels placed at the head of the dock ramp.

Anchorage: Anchoring is no longer allowed in Tenants Harbor. Boats may anchor in Tenants Outer Harbor, on the south side, inshore from Southern Island. Or anchor near Spectacles in Long Cove to the north. Nearly all areas of Long Cove can be used for anchoring. There are a few scattered moorings in the southwest and southeast corners to avoid and some workboat moorings along the western shore. Other than that, pick your spot based on wind conditions. Holding is good in gravel and mud.

Dix and High Islands on the eastern side of Muscle Ridge Channel (across from Sprucehead) are the largest of a group of islands providing good anchorage and shelter. The entrance going east is straightforward. Stay well north of red nun buoy "10" and well south of red daybeacon "12." Pilot a center course between Oak Island to the south and Little Green Island to the north. Snug up to a windward shoreline to find protection from all but northwesterly winds. The anchorage has 8- to 20-foot MLW depths but be mindful of the charted 3-foot MLW shoal between High and Little Green Islands.

High Island is an MCHT site with a nice hiking trail circling the island and a few group camping sites. It makes a great place to stretch your legs and walk the dog.

NOTE: In the late 19th century as many as 2,000 quarrymen worked at Dix Island. Today their houses are gone. The private association that now owns Dix Island permits cruising visitors ashore but prohibits littering, fires or camping and swimming in the quarries.

Side Trip: Matinicus Island

Remote Matinicus Island is accessible by ferry from Rockland, located 20 miles away. Matinicus shares with Vinalhaven some of the richest lobstering bottom in the world and has been taking full advantage of them for ages. In the mid-1800s there were 15 families living on the island and 22 individual lobster boat owners.

Matinicus Island is a quintessential offshore Maine fishing and farming community and is not well organized for tourists and visiting cruisers. It is perhaps because of this that the island is such a special place to visit. The stylistic Down East tall-timbered waterfront here is matched by classic New England farmsteads, some still delivering summer produce to the semi-weekly Farmers' Markets. (Check signs ashore for times and locations.) On a clear day a leisurely walk around the island's level roadways offers 19th-century vistas and profound seascapes at every turn.

NAVIGATION: Matinicus Harbor is best approached in fair weather and good visibility due to the numerous islets and ledges surrounding the entrance. From the north, stay east of Zephyr Rock marked by flashing green buoy "5," followed by No Mans Land (an island), The Barrel (just awash and charted but not marked by a navigational aid) and Harbor Ledge (immediately north of the red-and-green entrance bell buoy).

From the south, leave Ragged Island and its surrounding islets to the west, making passage toward the entrance bell just west of West Black Ledge. Leave the south end of Wheaton Island well to west to avoid the submerged rocks there. When entering the harbor simply keep to the Matinicus shore to avoid the shallows on the Wheaton side and the center harbor reef.

Moorings/Anchorage: Limited anchorage (room for only a few boats) is located just inside the lee of Wheaton Island to the south in 10 to 20 feet MLW. The moorings situated farther to the south in the area between Wheaton Island and Matinicus Island are attached to the bottom via a series of underwater cables, which will foul an anchor. One or two of these moorings may be available for overnight rental; ask around at the wharf. Do not attempt to claim the apparently empty area in the center of the harbor. It's empty because Indian Ledge looms menacingly near the surface at low water.

Additional anchorage (in calm weather) is available in Old Cove just south of the main harbor. Entrance to Old Cove is unencumbered (except for the rocky ledge stringing southward of Wheaton Island) and holding is secure in sand with 15 feet MLW. Enter the cove at dead center, making certain to clear the cut between Wheaton and Matinicus Islands with enough distance to accommodate adequate rode scope without blocking the channel.

Intrepid (and substantial) lobster boats blast through the narrow and not altogether deep passage between the main harbor and Old Cove frequently, often at night, on any tide. This and the ocean swells will make certain that you are rocked asleep (or awake). Nevertheless, the cut is convenient for a dinghy trip to the town wharf inside the main harbor.

Tie the dinghy to the side of the steel ladder on the town wharf, allowing enough painter length for the 9-foot tidal range and space for transport boats that also make the ladder their destination.

Matinicus Rock Lighthouse

Eastport

Cutler

Pages 607-612

Gulf of Maine

Jonesport

Pages 605-607

Winter Harbor

Schoodic Point

Sorrento

Frenchman Bay

Pages 602-605

Bar Harbor

Mount Desert Island

Atlantic Ocean

Long Island

Pages 594-602

Swans Island

Isle Au Haut

Pages 587-594

Blue Hill

Deer Island

Eggemoggin Reach

Searsport

Castine

Penobscot Bay

N Haven Island

Vinalhaven Island

Pages 532-587

Belfast

Islesboro

Camden

Rockport

Rockland

Pages 562-581

ROCKLAND HARBOR TO CASTINE

Fifteen miles south of Vinalhaven Island, the imposing 90-foot lighthouse on Matinicus Rock guides offshore mariners into Penobscot Bay. Penobscot Bay is 20 miles wide and nearly 30 miles long and is the largest of Maine's coastal indentations. This watery basin of flooded mountain range is rimmed by Camden Hills and Mount Battie to the west and Blue Hill and Cadillac Mountain to the east.

Large and small islands–dominated by Islesboro to the north with North Haven Island and Vinalhaven Island to the south–separates East and West Penobscot Bays, and those two bays are subdivided into a welter of smaller bodies of water with their own characters. Deer Isle and Isle au Haut mark Penobscot Bay's eastern boundary. Justifiably, Penobscot Bay is the most popular cruising destination in Maine.

West Penobscot Bay, lying between the mainland and the islands, has few offshore rocks and ledges and is easy to navigate in the absence of fog. As fog descends bring to bear all your navigational skills and equipment: GPS, radar, AIS, compass, charts, fog horn and bell. Navigation must be precise and buoys must be strictly followed but shoaling isn't a serious factor and charts change slowly. Sand- and mud-accustomed mariners will find the stakes of a grounding higher than in southern cruising grounds, while visitors from the Puget Sound or northeastern Europe will find themselves right at home.

Rockland Harbor

Rockland's large, open, easy-access harbor is ringed by all the services you would expect from a major recreational boating center including marinas with slips and moorings. Still, if there is a serious blow rolling in, cruisers and any nearby commercial vessels head for more protected waters at the northern end of the bay or out to the numerous island coves and harbors. Superb views of the Camden Hills to the north are guaranteed in the absence of fog.

Rockland is famous for having a wonderful selection of fine restaurants representing a globally eclectic array of choices within a walk of the dinghy dock. Hamilton Marine is the largest marine retailer north of Boston with an extensive selection of hardware at 20 Park Dr. (207-594-8181). Stock includes some iconic Mainer items you may have begun to envy on your travels such as a canvas gunwale guard for your dinghy.

Small Owls Head Harbor south of Rockland is home to a substantial lobstering fleet. Owls Head Lighthouse, an active aid to navigation at the entrance of Rockland Harbor, is worth a visit.

NAVIGATION: Muscle Ridge Channel jogs east after it passes between Ash Island and Fisherman Island. If your destination is Owls Head, the northern route begins at the green-red-green can over Emery Ledge. There is no need to deflect west toward green daybeacon "1" if continuing. Red nun buoy "4" is the better navigational aid to aim for.

Around the bold, jutting headland of Owls Head and its picturesque lighthouse is Rockland Harbor. Easily approached from any direction, the harbor is protected from northeasterly weather by a 4,346-foot granite breakwater. The end of the breakwater, which is marked by a 5-second flashing light with a fog signal (MRASS) mounted on a 39-foot tower, should be left to the north. Fully 0.5 mile to the south, green can buoy "1" marks Spears Rock off the north tip of Battery Point.

Dockage/Moorings: The private, gated facility of Safe Harbor Rockland offers friendly service and full amenities for boats to 250 feet. This facility offers a comprehensive experience from brokerage to restorations and customizations, full yard services and an ever-expanding marina. From here you can enjoy a few leisurely hours at a private sandy beach or take an easy stroll along the boardwalk to downtown Rockland, where you will find a plethora of shops, galleries, restaurants and museums. Courtesy vehicles are available for touring nearby Rockport and Camden.

Town moorings (to 50 feet) and transient slips (to 100 feet) on floating docks are available at the Rockland Public Landing. Call the Rockland Harbormaster on VHF Channel 09 or 16. The harbormaster's office is at the end of the pier left of the Coast Guard station. Showers (with tokens) and laundry facilities are available. Dinghies can be tie up free if you're on a town mooring.

Landings Restaurant & Marina just east of the public landing has seasonal and transient slips and a gas and diesel fuel barge with high-speed pumps. Several dinghy docks are available for the convenience of

Rockland Harbor, ME

ROCKLAND		Largest Vessel	VHF	Total Slips	Approach/ Dockside Depth	Floating Docks	Gas/ Diesel	Repairs/ Haulout	Min/Max Amps	Pump-Out Station
1. Safe Harbor Rockland WiFi	(207) 596-0082	200	16	34	12.0 / 12.0	F		R	15 / 50	P
2. Rockland Public Landing WiFi	(207) 594-0312	95	16	15	12.0 / 10.0	F			50	P
3. Landings Restaurant & Marina WiFi	(207) 596-6573	200	9	72	25.0 / 12.0	F	GD		30 / 100	P
4. Journey's End Marina WiFi	(207) 594-0400	275	16	85	20.0 / 14.0		GD	RH	30 / 100	P
5. Knight Marine Service WiFi	(207) 594-4068	82	9	10	12.0 / 12.0	F	GD	RH	30	

WiFi Wireless Internet Access
Visit www.waterwayguide.com for current rates, fuel prices, website addresses and other up-to-the-minute information.
(Information in the table is provided by the facilities.)

Scan here for more details:

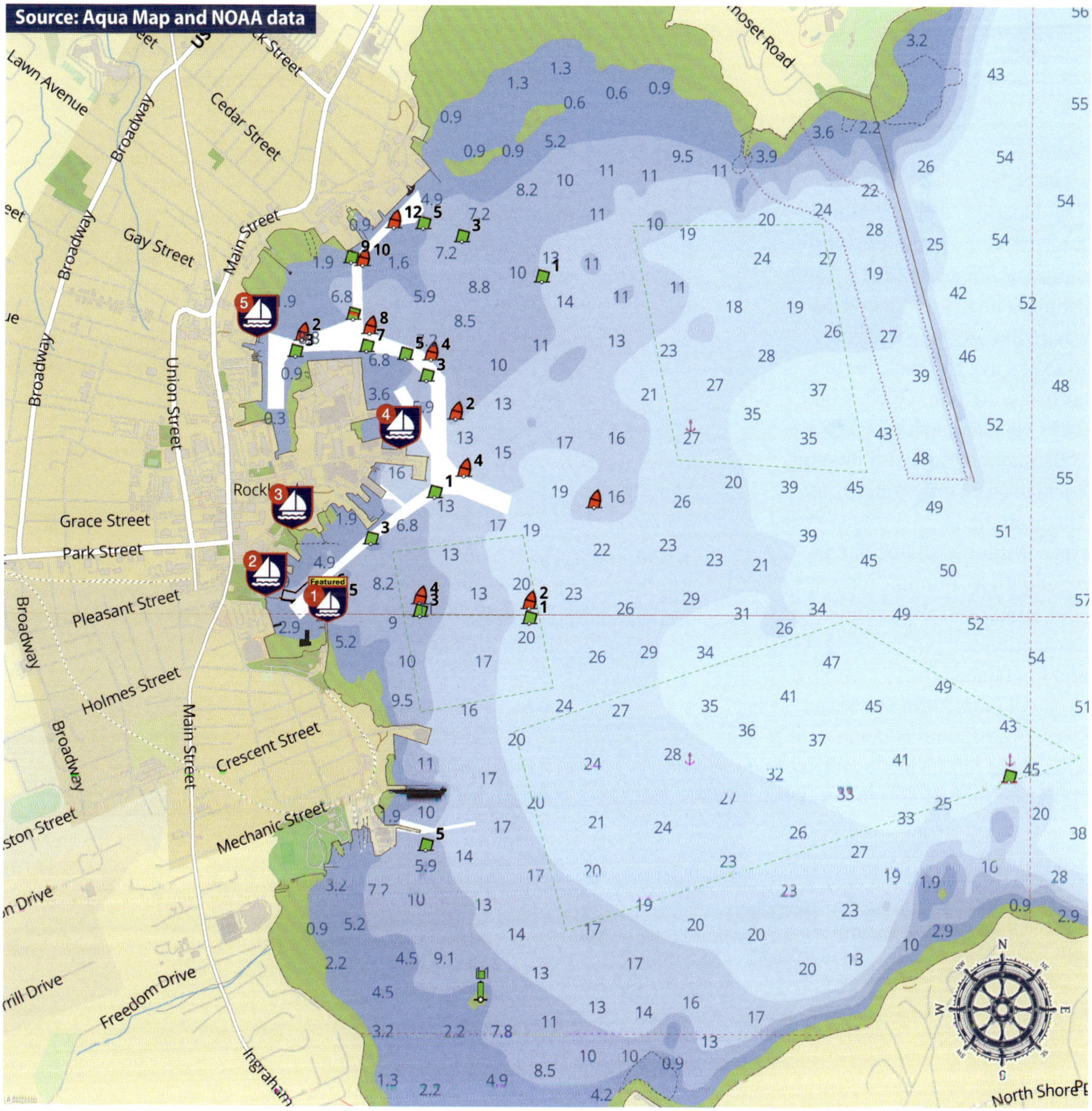

Source: Aqua Map and NOAA data

GOIN' ASHORE
ROCKLAND, ME

Owls Head Lighthouse

ATTRACTIONS

1. Center for Maine Contemporary Art
Exhibitions of paintinngs, photography and other artwork by Maine-based artists at 21 Winter St. (207-701-5005).

2. Farnsworth Art Museum
Paintings and sculptures by renowned American artists with Maine connections, most notably the Wyeths at 16 Museum St. (207-596-6457).

3. Maine Lighthouse Museum
Home to the largest collection of Fresnel lighthouse lenses in the U.S., among other fascinating artifacts (1 Park Dr., 207-594-3301).

4. Project Puffin Visitor Center
Fun and educational spot at 311 Main St. (207-596-5566). Be sure to check out the QR codes where you can get the sounds of all types of native birds.

5. Rockland Harbor Trail
Trailhead for a 5-mile walking trail extending from the Rockland Breakwater begins at 5 Laurel St.

SERVICES

6. Hamilton Marine
Largest marine retailer north of Boston with an extensive selection of hardware at 20 Park Dr. (207-594-8181). Stock includes some iconic Mainer items you may have begun to envy on your travels, such as a canvas gunwale guard for your dinghy.

7. Knox County Health Clinic
22 White St. # 201 (207-301-6996)

8. Park Street Laundromat
117 Park St. (207-594-9393)

9. Penobscot Bay Regional Chamber of Commerce
25 Park St. (207-596-0376)

10. Rockland Post Office
21 Limerock St., Ste. 9998 (207-596-6461)

11. Rockland Public Library
80 Union St. #2925 (207-594-0310)

Rockland is a classic Maine coastal town and the lobster capital of the world. The lobster fishing industry and its working waterfront are supported by an expansive and picturesque multi-use harbor, which is best scene via a jaunt along Harbor Walk, a public footpath hugging Rockland's historic waterfront. The prominence of a robust visual arts contributes to Rockland's reputation as a unique, creative community and the premier destination for experiencing visual arts in Maine.

Small Owls Head Harbor south of Rockland is home to a substantial lobstering fleet. Owls Head Lighthouse, an active aid to navigation at the entrance of Rockland Harbor, is worth a visit.

MARINAS

12. Journey's End Marina
120 Tillson Ave. #100
(207-594-0400)

13. Knight Marine Service
525 Main St.
(207-594-4068)

14 Landings Restaurant & Marina
5 Park Dr.
(207-594-4899)

15. Rockland Public Landing
75 Mechanic St.
(207-594-0312)

16. Safe Harbor Rockland
60 Ocean St.
(207-596-0082)

Rockport Harbor

mooring tenants and visitors. Be sure to stop in the office when you make landfall.

Journey's End Marina is a year-round, full service marina with slips and moorings to 275 feet. The small (10 slip) Knight Marine Service to the north offers dockage, moorings and a completely equipped boat yard with boat hauling and storage. This is one of the few yards in the area that still allows DIY. There is a small lunch take-out with tables on the dock.

Anchorage: As in many popular harbors, the number of moorings has increased dramatically over the past decade but ample anchorage room and depth is generally available outside the mooring field in Rockland Harbor.

Note that there is a cable area immediately behind the breakwater. Avoid anchoring in this area and be mindful that portions of the breakwater may be submerged at high tide. Watch for shallows and always consider the 10-foot tides in your scoping equations.

The most secure anchorages for heavy weather (especially from the east) are located in the extreme northern and southern ends of the harbor. The southern location provides the best protection from prevailing southerlies and is very popular with visiting cruisers. Anchor just east of the outer moorings between green daybeacon "3" and the boat ramp. Holding is good in thick, sandy mud. These areas put the boater a healthy row from the town pier's dinghy dock where there is a $5 per day fee to tie up. Pay at the harbormaster's office.

Anchoring is possible outside the mooring field at Owls Head Harbor to the south in 13 to 23 feet MLW with good holding and protection.

Rockport Harbor

Built on the hills surrounding this harbor 5 miles north of Rockland, protected yet commodious Rockport was once a working harbor, but today is dotted with pleasure boats and is a cruiser favorite. The harbor is protected by all but southerly winds and has a full-service marina, public landing and an attractive and busy restaurant serving all your Maine favorites.

Rockport & Camden Harbors, ME

ROCKPORT		Largest Vessel	VHF	Total Slips	Approach/ Dockside Depth	Floating Docks	Gas/ Diesel	Repairs/ Haulout	Min/Max Amps	Pump-Out Station
1. Rockport Marine Inc. WiFi	(207) 236-9651	105		5	20.0 / 10.0	F	GD	RH	50	
CAMDEN										
2. Camden Yacht Club-PRIVATE	(207) 236-3014	42	68	3	12.0 / 9.0					
3. Camden Harbormaster	(207) 236-7969	160	16		10.0 / 10.0	F			30 / 100	
4. Lyman-Morse at Wayfarer WiFi	(207) 236-4378	200	71	37	12.0 / 14.0	F	GD	RH	30 / 100	P

WiFi Wireless Internet Access
Visit www.waterwayguide.com for current rates, fuel prices, website addresses and other up-to-the-minute information.
(Information in the table is provided by the facilities.)

Scan here for more details:

Source: Aqua Map and NOAA data

It is difficult not to notice the lime kilns that were commercially critical to the area a century ago. You may also see the diminutive wood-fired locomotive that hauled lime and cordwood to the kilns.

NAVIGATION: Rockport Harbor is easy to enter, deep almost to the shore and free of ledges and boulders. The exception is Porterfield Ledge at the center of the entrance, marked by a great pillar of granite blocks topped by a green-and-white daybeacon.

When entering from the north and east take care not to cut corners when rounding Indian Island. A submerged reef extends to the south of the island. Leave the 25-foot-high, flashing red 6-second light "2" at Lowell Rock well to the north.

Dockage/Moorings: Rockport Marine Inc. specializes in custom wooden boatbuilding and yacht restoration. They maintain few slips and moorings for transients. The marina does not monitor the radio or provide launch service so pick up a mooring pennant from one of the numbered white buoys then dinghy in to complete your arrangements. The team of craftsmen here design, build, and restore some of the world's most renowned wooden yachts.

The Rockport Marine Park on the northwestern side of the inner harbor just west of the boat club has two large floats with 6 feet MLW to accommodate crew changes, trips to replenish the larder and refilling of water tanks. If space permits, overnight tie-ups are sometimes possible. Contact the Rockport Harbormaster on VHF Channel 16 for availability.

Camden Harbor

Anchorage: You can anchor in 17 to 25 feet MLW in Rockport Outer Harbor if space is available but this location will require long dinghy rides ashore. The Rockport inner harbor has 9 to 11 feet MLW with good holding in mud, if you can find a space. There is a dinghy tie-up behind the fuel dock in the harbor.

Camden Harbor

Located at the foot of Mount Battie, Camden is one of Maine's busiest and best-equipped harbors. The harbor is full of boats including the largest coastal schooner fleet in the country offering week-long and hourly cruises of the spectacular Maine coast. Camden is where the 3-mile-long Megunticook River drops approximately 142 feet and ends in a 25-foot waterfall, which may be rushing or not, depending on the water in the river. The fall can best be seen from Harbor Park or the Camden Public Landing.

A visit to nearby Curtis Island to see the lighthouse and walk the island is possible by docking your dinghy on the small beach located on the eastern side of the island; mid-tide is the best time to visit.

NAVIGATION: As you approach from the south, The Graves is marked on its eastern edge by flashing green gong buoy "13" and may be left to either side. If taking the shore side, however, stay well away from the buoy. Camden Harbor is marked by red bell buoy "2" located about 600 yards from the accessible southeastern entrance. Leave Curtis Island, identified by an occulting 53-foot-high green light, to the south and west while honoring the straight line between red nun buoys "4" and "6."

The northeastern approach is far narrower, although quite well marked by the red-and-white bell buoy "CH" located just less than 0.5 mile east-northeast off Northeast Point, then by a 20-foot-high flashing red "2" on the point. The channel's south edge, created by the Northeast Ledge, is marked by green can buoy "1" then green daybeacon "3."

Islesboro Island, ME

GILKEY HARBOR		Largest Vessel	VHF	Total Slips	Approach/ Dockside Depth	Floating Docks	Gas/ Diesel	Repairs/ Haulout	Min/Max Amps	Pump-Out Station
1. Dark Harbor Boat Yard	(207) 734-2246	100	9		14.0 / 6.0		GD	RH		

WiFi Wireless Internet Access
Visit www.waterwayguide.com for current rates, fuel prices, website addresses and other up-to-the-minute information.
(Information in the table is provided by the facilities.)

Scan here for more details:

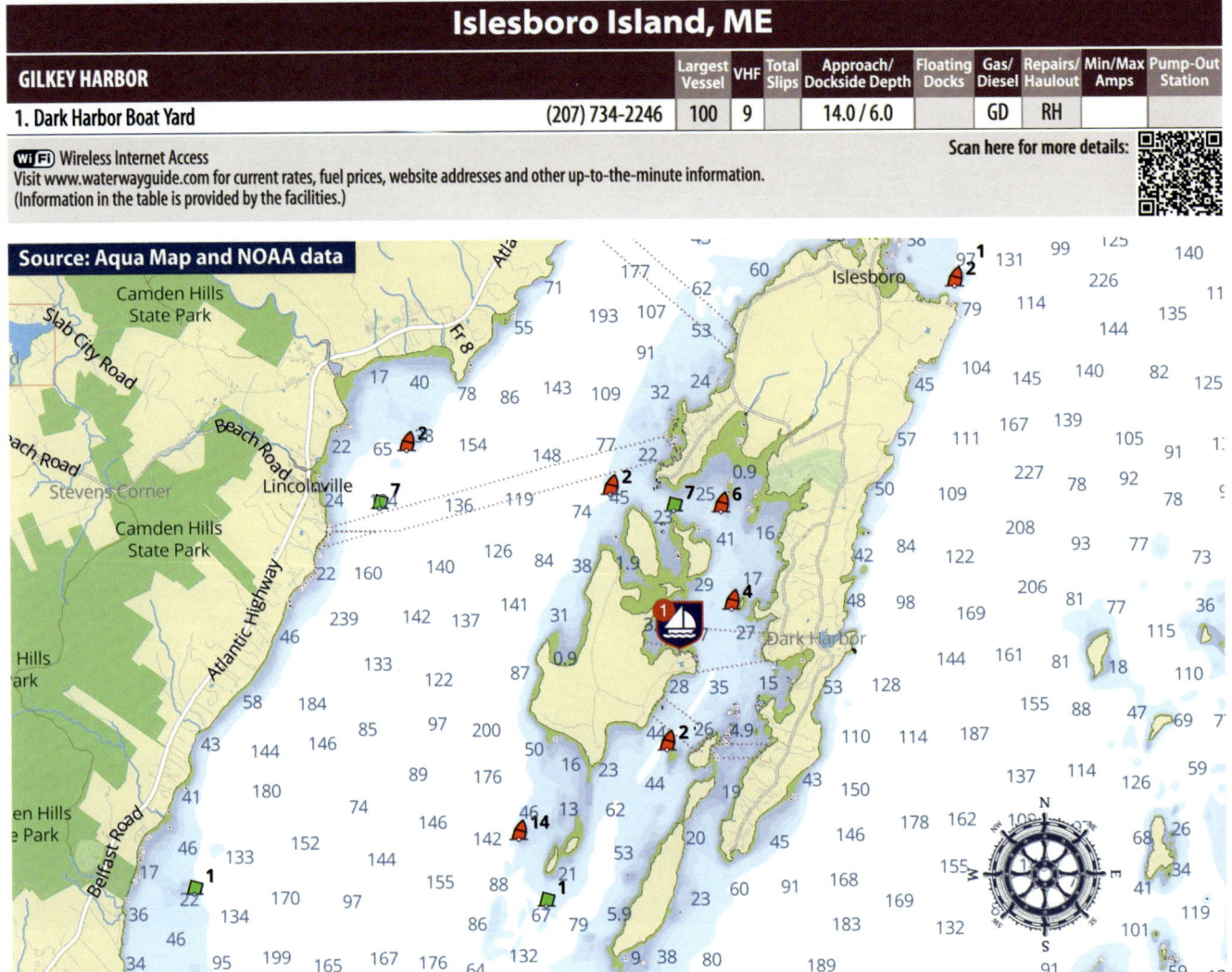

Source: Aqua Map and NOAA data

Dockage/Moorings: The Camden Harbormaster can help you find a slip or pump-out service in this busy harbor. The office is at the head of the harbor. The Camden Town Dock at Steamboat Landing on Eaton Point has 10-foot MLW dockside depths. This is a good place to land the dinghy if you are staying on a mooring in the southern part of the harbor.

Transients are welcome at the dock of the Camden Yacht Club for short (20-minute) tie-ups for crew changes and to take on water or drop off trash. Visiting captains with recognized reciprocity may stay overnight on an inner harbor float or mooring with launch service (when capacity allows).

Lyman-Morse at Wayfarer's complex on Camden's inner harbor has been entirely rebuilt with state of-the-art systems and infrastructure making this a one-stop destination for cruisers. They offer transient dockage along face docks, in slips at the head of the harbor (when available), and on harbor floats in the inner harbor. The marina also manages moorings in the outer harbor with launch service. These are somewhat exposed and will be rolly with any east component wind or swell, when the moorings on the south side near Curtis Island are better.

The Lyman-Morse complex offers two noteworthy restaurants–Salt Wharf with a popular rooftop bar and Barren's Distillery, which features a full menu along with local spirits.

Anchorage: Anchoring in Camden is tricky. Only one small area is outside the mooring field and inside the Inner Ledges. It's deep (20-30 feet MLW), and you'll likely share the anchorage with large yachts. This is in the outermost area of the harbor and is very exposed. The ledges do not protect from seas or wind at high water.

Side Trip: Islesboro

The large Islesboro is the heart of a group of islands cutting across Penobscot at mid-bay. This fashionable resort with grand old estates (at Dark Harbor) has a busy yachting community and regular ferry service to Lincolnville on the mainland north of Camden. A convenient launching ramp is adjacent to the ferry dock.

NAVIGATION: Gilkey Harbor is easily approached from either north or south. The lovely town of Dark Harbor on the northeastern side of Seven Hundred Acre Island is the hub of the most scenic route to northern Penobscot Bay–a rocky through-passage along Islesboro's southern half.

CAUTION: Two navigational cautions: (1) Note that the nuns and cans switch sides after Spruce Island and (2) do not attempt Bracketts Channel, a privately marked southeastern channel between Islesboro and Job Island. The ledges and current make this narrow channel hazardous unless you know it well.

Moorings: Moorings are available from Dark Harbor Boat Yard off the east side of Seven Hundred Acre Island in Cradle Cove. The boat yard has a public restroom, pay showers and laundry and offers a full line of services.

At the northern end of the through-passage opposite Grindel Point, a mariner's park encompasses all of wild, remote Warren Island. Accessible only by boat, uncrowded and a regular port of call for cruising schooners, Warren Island State Park has 10 free moorings for cruising boats. The inner moorings are 150-pound mushrooms, while the two outermost are 1-ton blocks. A dock and float with 4-foot MLW depths and picnic tables are available.

Anchorage: On entry into Cradle Cove, mind the private stakes marking the ledges on either side of the wide channel. There is still plenty of room to turn and maneuver. Shielded by northerly necks of Seven Hundred Acre Island, this anchorage affords excellent protection and good holding in 9- to 16-foot MLW depths. Large yachts will anchor alongside small travelers, making for an amusing lineup at

times. To the north you will find 8 to 24 feet MLW between Warren Island and Spruce Island.

Ames Cove is home to the Tarratine Yacht Club. Moorings may be available here but if not, there is good holding in the cove and the nearly 100-year-old clubhouse offers a pleasant view from the anchorage. Pendleton Yacht Yard in Ames Cove (Dark Harbor) has a dinghy dock that is available for 2 hours on either side of high tide.

Good anchorage in 17- to 28-foot MLW depths may be had to the north in the cove just above Thrumcap Island with good holding in mud. This is somewhat exposed to the north.

Sabbathday Harbor on the east side of Islesboro has good holding in 10 to 15 feet MLW with protection from all directions but south.

Belfast

Belfast Harbor spans the river from bank to bank before the Belfast Foot Bridge. A mile-long paved walkway follows the shoreline along the city's harbor, starting at the boathouse at the south end and ending on the opposite side of the harbor.

Belfast Harbor

GOIN' ASHORE

BELFAST, ME

ATTRACTIONS

1. Belfast Farmers Market
Farm fresh produce, meats, honey and syrup, plants and cut flowers, and much more. Operates year-round on Fridays from 9:00 a.m. to 1:00 p.m. at 256 High St. (207-450-8282).

2. Belfast Historical Society and Museum
Dedicated to the collection and preservation of artifacts relevant to Belfast history. Features vintage photographs, maps, postcard collections and interpretive displays at 10 Market St. (207-338-9229).

3. Belfast Rail Trail
Crushed stone and tree-lined trail begins at Armistice Footbridge and runs northwest parallel to the river, ending at the Belfast & Moosehead Lake Railroad City Point station (2.3 miles). Train still operates on weekends throughout summer.

4. Marshall Brewing Company
Locally owned and operated Beer Garden offering over 30 craft beers, small bites and seafood. Check out the Sail Pumper Sour Brown Ale with cherries. Also offers a full slate of events including live music on the waterfront at 36 Marshall Wharf (207-338-2700).

SERVICES

5. Belfast Post Office
1 Franklin St. (207-338-1820)

6. Belfast Free Library
106 High St. (207-338-3884)

7. Belfast Veterinary Hospital
193 Northport Ave. (207-338-3260)

8. ConvenientMD Urgent Care
18 Belmont Ave. (207-607-5270)

9. Survival At Sea
Primarily mail-order marine supply store specializing in life rafts and safety equipment at 101 Front St. (207-363-0220).

10. Waldo County General Hospital
118 Northport Ave. (207-338-2500)

MARINAS

11. Belfast City Landing
25 Front St. (207-338-1142)

12. Belfast Marina
15 Front St. (207-323-9040)

13. Front Street Shipyard
101 Front St. (207-930-3740)

Experience the Belfast waterfront by foot and stroll along the harbor along the Harbor Walk, resting at the comfy Adirondack chairs before continuing over the Belfast Harbor Footbridge. The best way to see it all is to take one of the walking tours of Belfast's historic district or the self-guided Museum in the Streets. This heritage-discovery tour features 2 large maps and 30 panels of photographs and interpretive text describing historic houses, the downtown, the waterfront and a few of the town's best-known residents.

Be sure to visit the eclectic collection of galleries and artist studios in Belfast's historic downtown. Work up an appetite? Locals are all abuzz about Satori, a 32-seat restaurant located in the historic "Gothic Building." With hand-rolled sushi and a variety of Japanese kitchen foods, they are also on top with a craft cocktail program created by an award-winning bartender.

Penobscot Bay, ME

BELFAST		Largest Vessel	VHF	Total Slips	Approach/ Dockside Depth	Floating Docks	Gas/ Diesel	Repairs/ Haulout	Min/Max Amps	Pump-Out Station
1. Belfast City Landing **WiFi**	(207) 338-1142	200	16	25	15.0 / 13.0	F	GD		30 / 100	P
2. Belfast Marina	(207) 323-9040	120	19	52	10.0 / 8.0	F			30 / 50	
3. Front Street Shipyard **WiFi**	(207) 930-3740	200	9	68	20.0 / 14.0	F		RH	30 / 100	P

WiFi Wireless Internet Access
Visit www.waterwayguide.com for current rates, fuel prices, website addresses and other up-to-the-minute information.
(Information in the table is provided by the facilities.)

Scan here for more details:

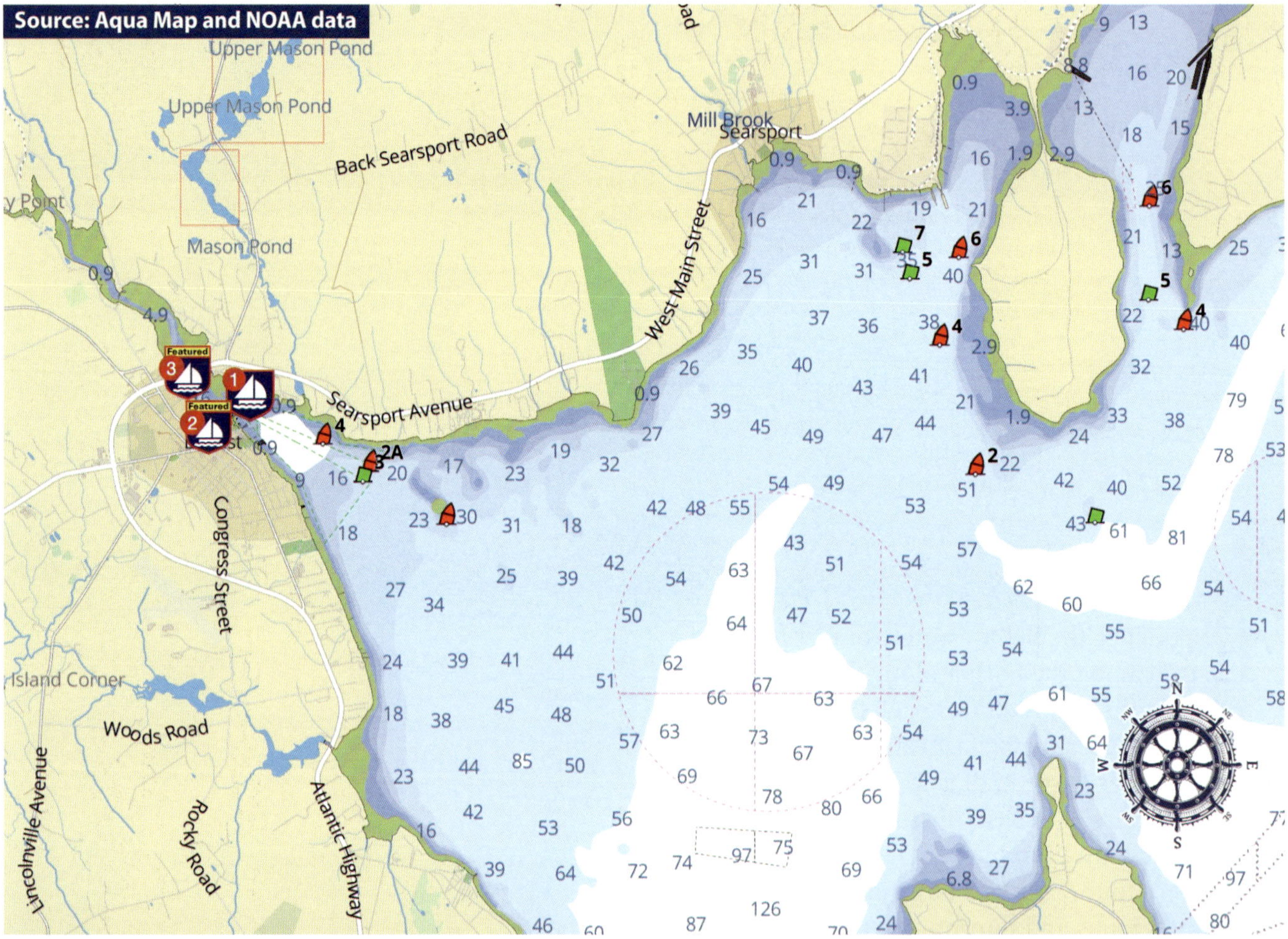

Custom boat builder French & Webb (21 Front St., 207-338-6706), known for their precision joinery, welcomes visitors to their shop bordering the waterfront park. An art-deco Colonial Theatre, art galleries, antiques shops, renowned book stores and the largest, year-round Maine Farmers' Market are part of the draw here. It is also home to several well-known Maine festivals.

NAVIGATION: The steep shore is broken by few harbors north of Camden. Heading north along the coast, the entrance to the Passagassawakcag River is a broad-mouthed funnel. The entrance is marked by Steels Ledge Monument Light, which makes a good radar target. Be aware that Steels Ledge shoals to the northwest, easily avoided by staying south of red lighted bell buoy "2."

Dockage/Moorings: Belfast City Landing offers slips for transients as well as rental moorings with all the usual amenities on shore. Contact the harbormaster on VHF Channel 09 for a slip or mooring assignment. Reservations are strongly recommended (207-338-1142). They also offer short-term dockage for lunch or a visit to town. Vessels should not pick up vacant rental moorings or slips without notifying the Harbor Office.

Belfast Marina has 10 reserved transient slips to 120 feet with the usual amenities. Their wave attenuating docks ensure peaceful dockage. This facility is adjacent to the town harbor walk and one block from Main St. amenities.

Nearby is Front Street Shipyard, which builds custom boats and is capable of handling megayachts. They maintain slips, moorings and floats for seasonal and transient boaters and offer free dinghy dockage, WiFi, shower facilities and a lounge area. A courtesy car occasionally can be made available for short provisioning trips. Even boaters who don't stay with Front Street Shipyard should take the short walk down the waterfront to see the enormous lift and the equally enormous boats that require so much hauling power.

Anchorage: Ironically, moorings fill the inner portion of the harbor at Belfast, which means "good anchorage". You can anchor off the entrance to the river west of Steels Ledge in 11- to 21-foot MLW depths with good holding in mud and rock. Be sure to leave the main channel open for the small cruise ships that dock in town. You can also anchor to the south at Belfast Dam (Browns Head) in 7 to 23 feet MLW.

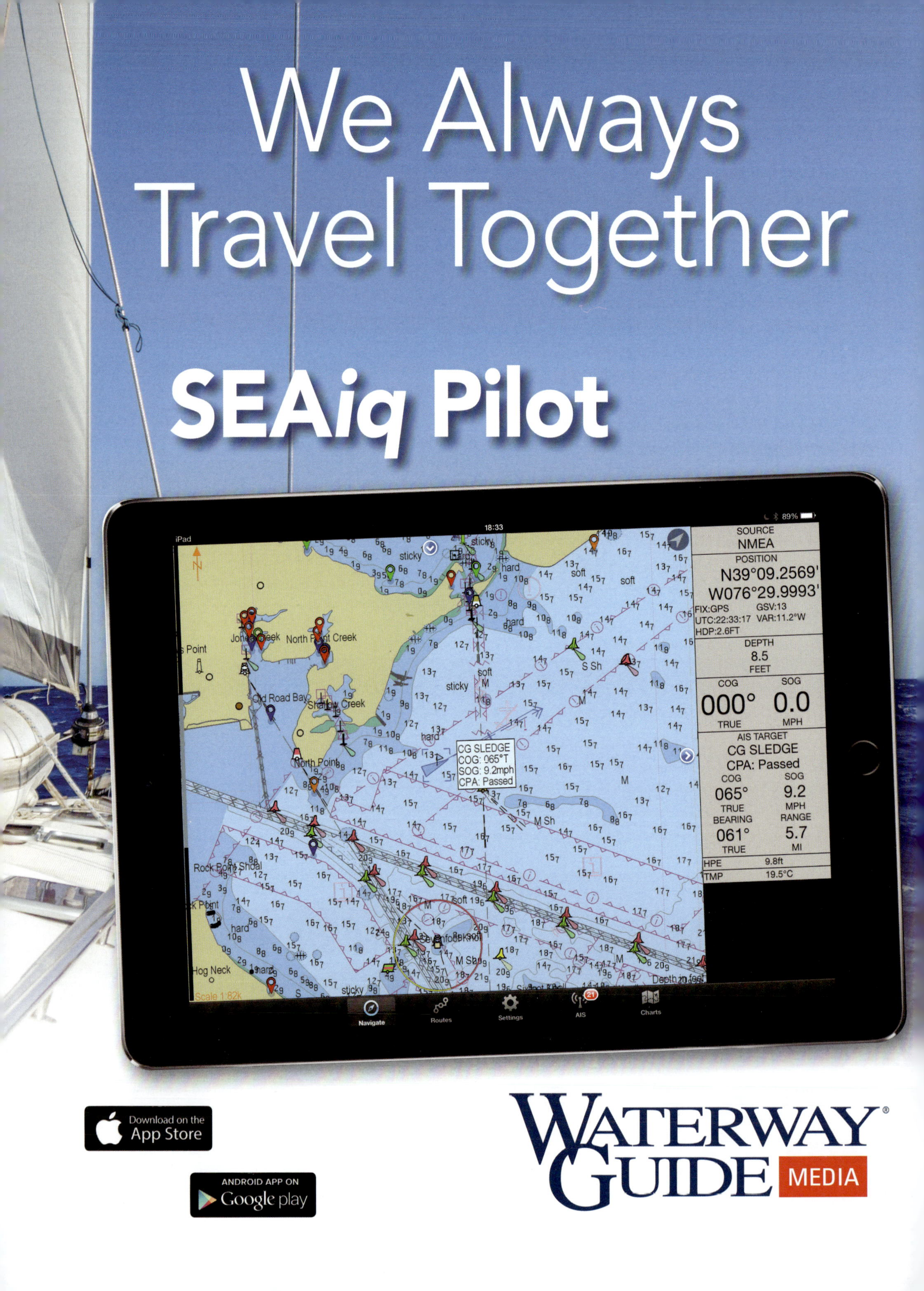

We Always Travel Together

SEAiq Pilot

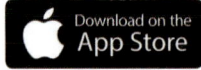

WATERWAY GUIDE MEDIA

Searsport Harbor

This ancient home to ship captains and flourishing maritime industries is today dominated by a recreational small boat fleet including some very serious anglers. Searsport's Main St. (U.S. Route 1) is about 0.25 mile due north from the docks. Within a few blocks you'll see a Post Office, a grocery store and a couple of banks.

The Penobscot Marine Museum (207-548-2529), where "Maine and the Sea Make History" is farther along to the east at the end of the business district. The museum's evolving collection of marine paintings, treasures brought home from abroad by local ships years ago, restored 19th-century buildings and re-creations of Searsport life in a bygone era are almost certain to appeal to your crew. Hamilton Marine, the largest marine supplier north of Boston, has a store in Searsport with marine supplies, gear, equipment, books and charts. This large, family-run operation will special-order parts for rapid delivery but their local-pro selection is vast and worth a look (207-548-6302).

NAVIGATION: Four miles northeast of Belfast the expansive, wide-open harbor of Searsport offers no obstructions on approach and easy shore access.

Moorings/Anchorages: The anchorage and mooring field for recreational boats is to the northwest on approaching the wide, scalloped harbor at Searsport. As you approach the recreational fleet, check in with the Searsport Harbormaster (monitoring VHF Channels 09, 10, 71 and 78A) to inquire about the availability of a mooring or for current anchoring instructions. The

town mooring (#1, attached to a large granite block) may be available or possibly the museum's large mooring ball (#55, hooked to a 10-ton block) will be unclaimed.

You will most likely be anchoring outside the mooring field in Searsport Harbor in 23- to 32-foot MLW depths with a 9-foot tidal range. Prevailing southwesterlies are tempered by Islesboro Island, yet it is often quite breezy in the afternoon. The accompanying seesaw action of waves over a long fetch regularly sends boats on insufficient scope drifting into the mooring field even though the holding is good. Make sure your anchor is well set and consider being generous with the scope, remembering to factor in the additional depth at high tide.

The Searsport Public Landing complex (periodically dredged to 4.5 feet MLW) makes it possible for smaller vessels and those working with the tide to tie up for 2- to 4-hour periods on one of the inner docks. For most visitors it will be more convenient to pull a tender up to one of the floating dinghy landings inside the L-shaped outer dock for the walk to town. (Be sure to note signs with rules for each dock.) Oil tankers, potato reefers and other large commercial ships dominate the more protected Long Cove beyond Mack Point east of the village.

North on the Penobscot River

If you made it this far Down East, you'll be rewarded with some of the most remarkable scenery and cruising grounds a boater may experience. Slow down and savor every moment; few get to experience the treasures offered by this incredibly diverse bio-region.

Bucksport's harbor is about 1-nm long, and provides breathtaking views of Fort Knox and the Penobscot Narrows Bridge and Observatory. Across from Bucksport is Fort Knox Park, a granite fortress with picnic grounds. Fort Knox was built in the 1840s to defend against a feared third British invasion (following the Revolutionary War and the War of 1812), which never occurred.

The Penobscot Narrows Observatory (207-469-6553) in the western tower of the high-rise highway bridge near Fort Knox is the highest bridge observatory in the world and offers a tremendous view of Penobscot Bay and the surrounding area. For boaters this will involve anchoring or mooring in Bucksport and walking or getting a taxi to the bridge. A combined trip to the bridge and Fort Knox Park makes a great outing.

Shops are handy in downtown Bucksport and the old railroad station has been converted into a historical museum. The neighboring towns of Bangor and Hampden worked together to develop 11 acres as a boating center with a marina, restaurant, motel and chandlery. Bangor is perhaps best known by the general public as the home of best-selling American author Stephen King.

NAVIGATION: The Penobscot River is navigable for 25 miles to Bangor but the current flows swiftly at its mouth and must be entered on a rising tide. Expect significant currents. Past Fort Point Cove, the river narrows over the 4 miles to Bucksport (past the high-rise **Penobscot Narrows Bridge**) and then widens out at Frankfort Flats, another 2 miles up the river. Heavy

Penobscot River, ME

BUCKSPORT		Largest Vessel	VHF	Total Slips	Approach/ Dockside Depth	Floating Docks	Gas/ Diesel	Repairs/ Haulout	Min/Max Amps	Pump-Out Station
1. Bucksport Public Dock / Municipal Marina (WiFi)	(207) 469-5902	300	9	52	16.0 / 15.0	F	GD		30 / 50	P

(WiFi) Wireless Internet Access
Visit www.waterwayguide.com for current rates, fuel prices, website addresses and other up-to-the-minute information.
(Information in the table is provided by the facilities.)

Scan here for more details:

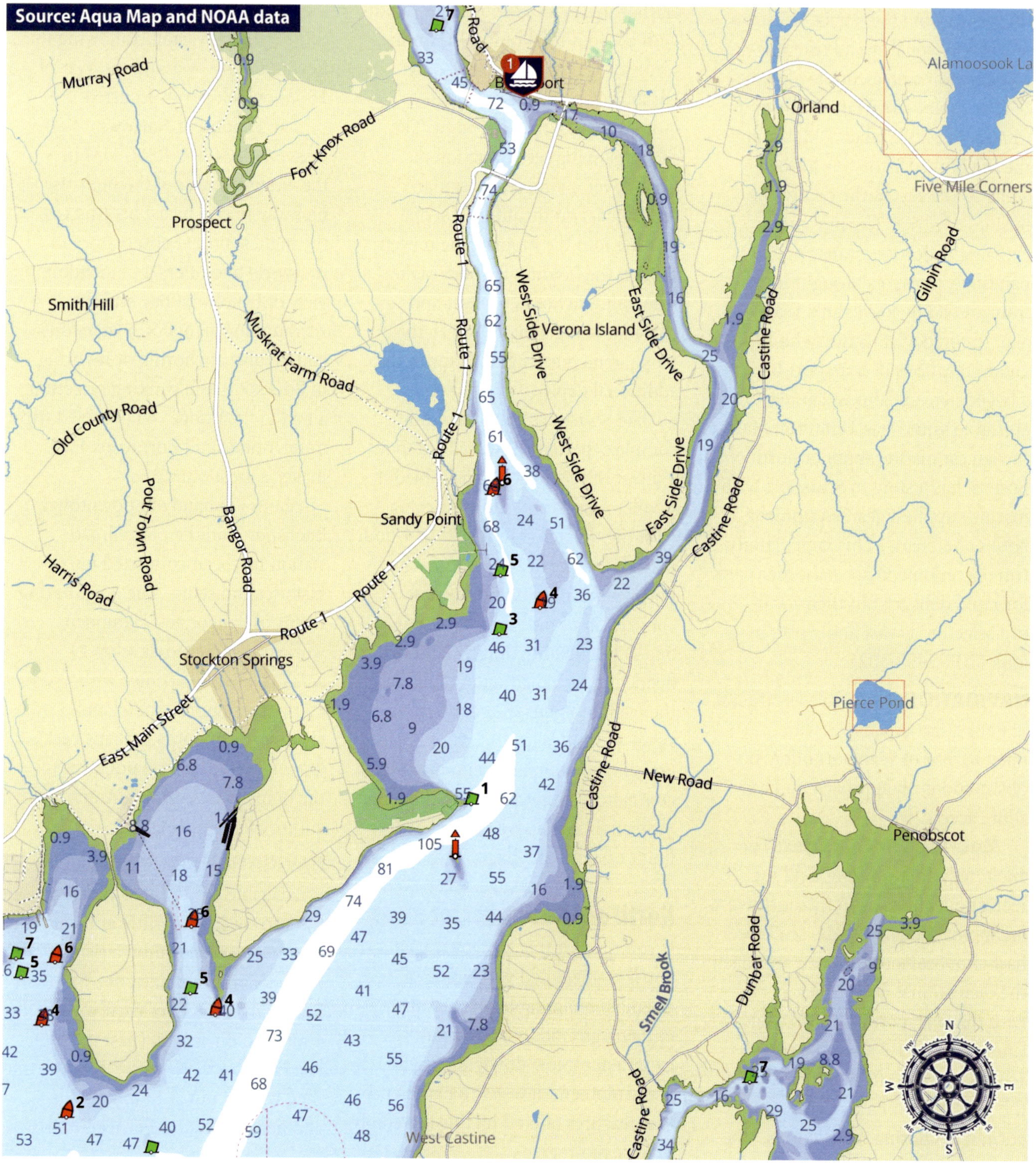

Source: Aqua Map and NOAA data

Penobscot River, ME

BANGOR		Largest Vessel	VHF	Total Slips	Approach/ Dockside Depth	Floating Docks	Gas/ Diesel	Repairs/ Haulout	Min/Max Amps	Pump-Out Station
1. Hamlin's Marina	(207) 907-4385	55	9	20	30.0 / 8.0	F		RH		P
2. Bangor Landing Waterfront Park	(207) 992-4490	165	16	30	16.0 / 15.0				50	P

WiFi Wireless Internet Access
Visit www.waterwayguide.com for current rates, fuel prices, website addresses and other up-to-the-minute information.
(Information in the table is provided by the facilities.)

Scan here for more details:

commercial traffic makes night running tricky. Bangor is about 12 miles upstream from Winterport.

Dockage: Whether visiting for the day or longer, the city can accommodate you at one of their two facilities (Bucksport Public Dock/Municipal Marina). The 315-foot public floating dock has a few slips, while the marina has 50 slips to 50 feet with all the usual amenities plus a courtesy shuttle for trips to town.

There are more facilities farther north. Dock rental is limited and reserved for customers who purchase boats at Hamlin's Marina but mooring facilities are available to the general public, as is a dockside restaurant. The 30-slip Bangor Landing Waterfront Park offers 210 feet of guest dockage with electricity and pump-out service near the village center. Restrooms are public.

Anchorage: Anchoring north of Fort Point State Park provides protection from the south and west in at least 7 feet MLW. Riverside picnic sites, hiking and bicycling trails, fishing and paddling are among the offerings. Interpretive signs describe Fort Point's history as a military, maritime, and tourist center. Bicyclists can ride to the lighthouse or take the 7-mile loop around Cape Jellison. If you anchor at Bucksport, make sure you are solidly hooked as the current runs swift. Much of the bottom is covered with sawdust from lumbering days and offers poor holding. There is no room for anchoring at Bangor.

Castine

Castine is one of the oldest towns in New England, pre-dating the colonial settlement at Plymouth by 7 years. It was originally a fur trading post and remains well worth a visit. During its highly contested early colonialist days, Castine changed hands 25 times among the English, French, Dutch, Spanish and American colonists. The town is rich with reminders of its exciting past. Paul Revere ruined his military career in an ill-fated attempt to capture Fort George from the British in 1779. The fort is

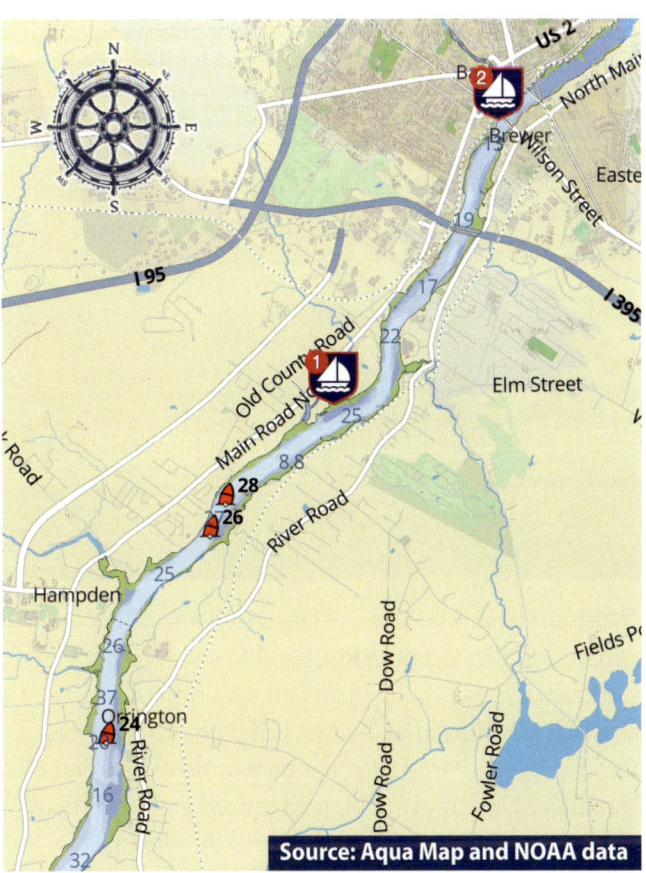

Source: Aqua Map and NOAA data

open to the public but the entire town is on the National Historic Register.

Castine is an active summer resort, although it is more reserved and far less hectic than Camden. Your best bet is to pick up a copy of *A Walking Tour of Castine* from any local merchant. The Castine Historical Society (207-326-4118) houses a permanent exhibit on the ill-fated Penobscot expedition of 1779 and seasonal exhibits on various aspects of Castine's rich history. Admission is free. Dominating the harbor is the *State of Maine*, the 13,000-ton, 500-foot-long training ship of the Maine Maritime Academy, which offers undergraduate and graduate degrees in engineering, transportation and management. Both the vessel and the Academy are open to visitors (800-464-6565).

Castine Harbor

NAVIGATION: The bluffs of Dice Head guard the entrance to the Bagaduce River and Castine Harbor at the head of East Penobscot Bay off the northern end of Islesboro. The red-and-white bell buoy "CH" assists those entering during a fog but there is no red marker off Nautilus Island. If in doubt, tend toward green can buoy "1" then stay toward the north side of the channel.

Dockage/Moorings: Overnight dockage is permitted at the Castine Town Dock. If you want to come alongside or are inquiring about a mooring, reach out to the harbormaster (207 266-7711). Fees apply after 5:00 p.m. and include use of restrooms, free WiFi and pump-out service. Trash disposal is also available for $2/bag. Short-term tie-ups are limited to 2 hours between 9:00 a.m. and 5:00 p.m. It should be noted that the current around the docks can be "squirrelly" so be prepared. The town dock does have room to tie up your dinghy on the backside of the floats.

Eaton's Boat Yard on the waterfront on the center of historic Castine is more likely to have space for an overnight stay alongside their docks or on a rental mooring. This iconic working yard is worth a visit, even if you choose to stay elsewhere.

Holbrook Island is a state park with hiking trails. There are several first-come, first-serve orange guest moorings for visiting the park. One is off the island's dock, and three are in the Tom Cod Cove mooring field. Land your dinghy at the floating docks, one on the island and one in the cove on the mainland. Park maps can be found at either location. Both areas have hiking options.

Anchorage: The holding ground is poor off Castine, where depths of the Bagaduce River run to 72 feet (12 fathoms) and swift tidal currents scour the bottom. A secure anchorage can be found, however, to the south. The closest anchorage to town and out of the main current is the area just south of Hosmer Ledge off Hospital Island.

Indian Bar in Smith Cove has a small mooring field and anchorage with 15 to 25 feet MLW. There's a rocky beach area nearby to land a dinghy near picnic benches and trails. The residence to the north of the beach area has clearly posted privacy signage. It is within a reasonable distance to dinghy to the town of Castine.

The most attractive gunkhole in Castine is well inside the protection of Smith Cove to the southeast of Sheep Island. When heading for this anchorage be careful of

East Penobscot Bay, ME

CASTINE HARBOR		Largest Vessel	VHF	Total Slips	Approach/ Dockside Depth	Floating Docks	Gas/ Diesel	Repairs/ Haulout	Min/Max Amps	Pump-Out Station
1. Castine Town Dock	(207) 266-7711	80	9	3	60.0 / 25.0	F			30 / 100	P
2. Eaton's Boat Yard	(207) 326-8579	200	9	8	12.0 / 11.0	F	GD	RH	30 / 100	

WiFi Wireless Internet Access
Visit www.waterwayguide.com for current rates, fuel prices, website addresses and other up-to-the-minute information.
(Information in the table is provided by the facilities.)

Scan here for more details:

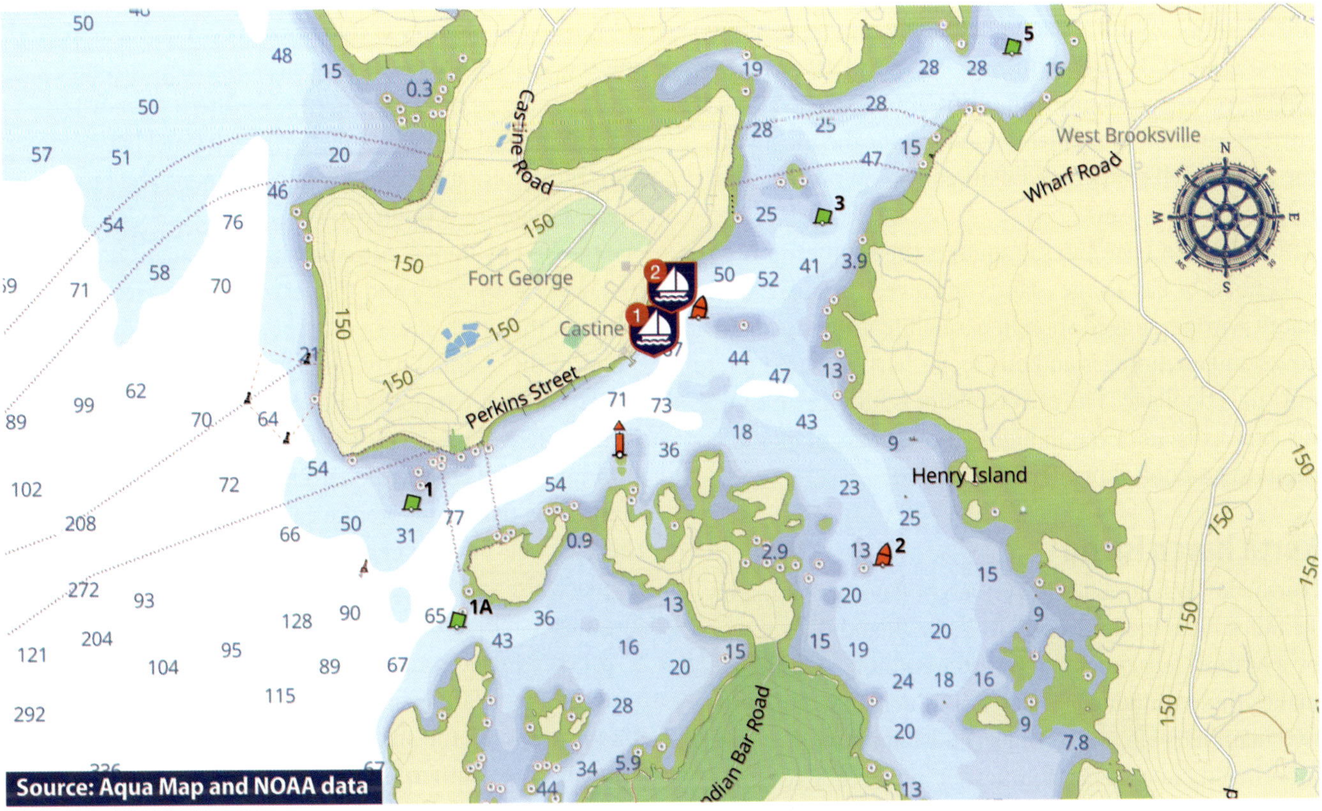

Source: Aqua Map and NOAA data

the buoyed Middle Ground rock in mid-harbor to the west of Sheep Island. It comes clear out of the water with spring tides.

One of the most interesting of Castine's anchorages is entered from East Penobscot Bay. Stay clear of the buoyed mid-channel rock in the entrance marked by green can buoy "1A." An alternate entrance to Holbrook Harbor is between Cape Rosier on the south and Holbrook and Ram Island (known locally as "Rain") on the north side. When anchoring between Holbrook and Ram Island, use the center of the channel or risk ending up on the copious rocks and ledges to either side. A larger anchorage extends throughout the rest of the harbor with weather perhaps determining which shore would be most comfortable to huddle behind. Another popular anchorage spot is east of Ram Island, along the beachy isthmus on the mainland.

Side Trip: The Barred Islands

Approximately 4 nm south of Cape Rosier, the Barred Islands combine to form an anchorage surrounded by unspoiled, spruce-capped islets between Great Spruce Head Island to the west and Butter Island to the east. If you are entering the lagoon-like bay formed by these islands for the first time, it is best to enter from the northwest at below half-tide after running southeasterly past green can buoy "3" off Great Spruce Head Island. Favor the northernmost of Peak Island since it is bold, while a reef extends to the north from Little Barred Island on the southern side of the harbor entrance. The anchorage to the southeast of Barred Island affords good holding with protection offered by a sandbar and rocks that block the prevailing southwesterlies. This anchorage has outstanding scenery and ospreys provide constant entertainment as they fish for dinner.

NORTH HAVEN & VINALHAVEN ISLANDS

The northern cap of the archipelago is known as the Fox Islands (for the abundant silver foxes seen by the first European explorers here). North Haven Island with its various channels, coves and islets offers exciting and scenic cruising for the rugged-at-heart. Excellent, uncluttered harbors are abundant and a non-stop variety of "one-off" and classic cruising boats ply these waters. No doubt you will contend with obstructions, dense fog, swift currents and extreme tidal ranges, but for the most part the area is well charted and marked and no problem for the seasoned cruiser.

Vinalhaven Island to the south is the southernmost of Penobscot Bay's large islands and a very popular local haunt with its rugged shoreline, satellite islands, scores of coves and anchorages and one major harbor with a remote but rugged village. The eastern shore is full of gunkholes for exploring and even in high season there's plenty of room to go hook-down for days on end.

North Haven Island

North Haven Island lies in Penobscot Bay approximately 12 miles from the midcoast city of Rockland. It is served by a Maine Department of Transportation ferry, which makes three round trips a day from Rockland. There are two main harbors on North Haven Island that offer good mooring/anchorage possibilities—Pulpit Harbor (on the northern side of the island) and Southern Harbor.

Even though North Haven Island has long been a favored summer getaway for some of the country's wealthiest and most influential families, you will find no mansions here, just farmhouses and "Cabotville," a cluster of funky cottages near Pulpit Harbor named for the Cabot family who were early pioneers in the area. North Haven Inn and Market is nearby with essentials plus local produce.

The quiet village of North Haven is about halfway through Fox Islands Thorofare on North Haven Island and is centered on the ferry landing. The village and surrounding island countryside have long been a summer refuge for families from among the leading names of American industry, law and politics. The North Haven village store has been reborn as Waterman's Community Center (207-867-2100) with a coffee shop and activities for all ages including plays and films. There is also a first-class art gallery, a small brewery and a family-run boatyard founded in 1888.

NAVIGATION: On the northwestern shore of North Haven Island guarded by pointed Pulpit Rock is popular Pulpit Harbor. Do not be dismayed if you see a line of boats ahead of you turning in; there is plenty of room. Narrow coves fanning outward from the entrance provide abundant space. Entry is easy; enter between the rock and the western shore. During clear weather, entrance to the nearly 2-mile-long bight of Southern Harbor is straightforward in the relatively wide channel between Amesbury Point and the Dumpling Islands. The Fox Island Thorofare is the narrower opening but also the one marked by buoys. After passing the Sugar Loaves (red daybeacon "22") and Calderwood Rock (red nun "20") on the north side steer a course straight down the center of the channel between Amesbury Point and the westernmost outcropping of the Dumpling Islands. The northwestern shore has fewer dangerous rocks for the first third but don't favor it too hard as Seal Ledge provides an invisible danger before the easy-to-see Lobster Island. There's a well-marked channel into North Haven and (like anyplace else in Maine) you have to watch the tides and currents. Windjammers go through here regularly.

If Perry Creek is your destination, proceed south from the Fox Island Thorofare, enter at the center of the channel between the small island off the tip of Hopkins Point and the southern shore. At high tide submerged ledges extending from both north and south will not be visible; centering on the channel is critical. Once fully past the small island at the entrance, turn west and favor the southern shore, heading at the first small point inside to avoid a 4-foot MLW spot.

While it is possible to anchor outside the mooring field adjacent to the village waterfront at North Haven, it is not recommended because of uncertain holding and rapid, bi-directional currents that scour this area. This is also the ferry approach.

Dockage/Moorings: Fortunately, vacant rental moorings are almost always available at a competitive fee. Two moorings to 50 feet are available from Thayer's Y-Knot Boatyard in Southern Harbor, which reports 4-foot MLW approach and dockside depths with a 10-foot tidal range. This is a full-service boatyard facility.

Penobscot Bay Islands, ME

SOUTHERN HARBOR		Largest Vessel	VHF	Total Slips	Approach/ Dockside Depth	Floating Docks	Gas/ Diesel	Repairs/ Haulout	Min/Max Amps	Pump-Out Station
1. Thayer's Y-Knot Boatyard	(207) 867-4701	50	16		4.0 / 4.0			RH		
NORTH HAVEN										
2. Browns Boatyard (WiFi)	(207) 867-4621	60	16		15.0 / 5.0	F	GD	RH	30	

(WiFi) Wireless Internet Access
Visit www.waterwayguide.com for current rates, fuel prices, website addresses and other up-to-the-minute information.
(Information in the table is provided by the facilities.)

Scan here for more details:

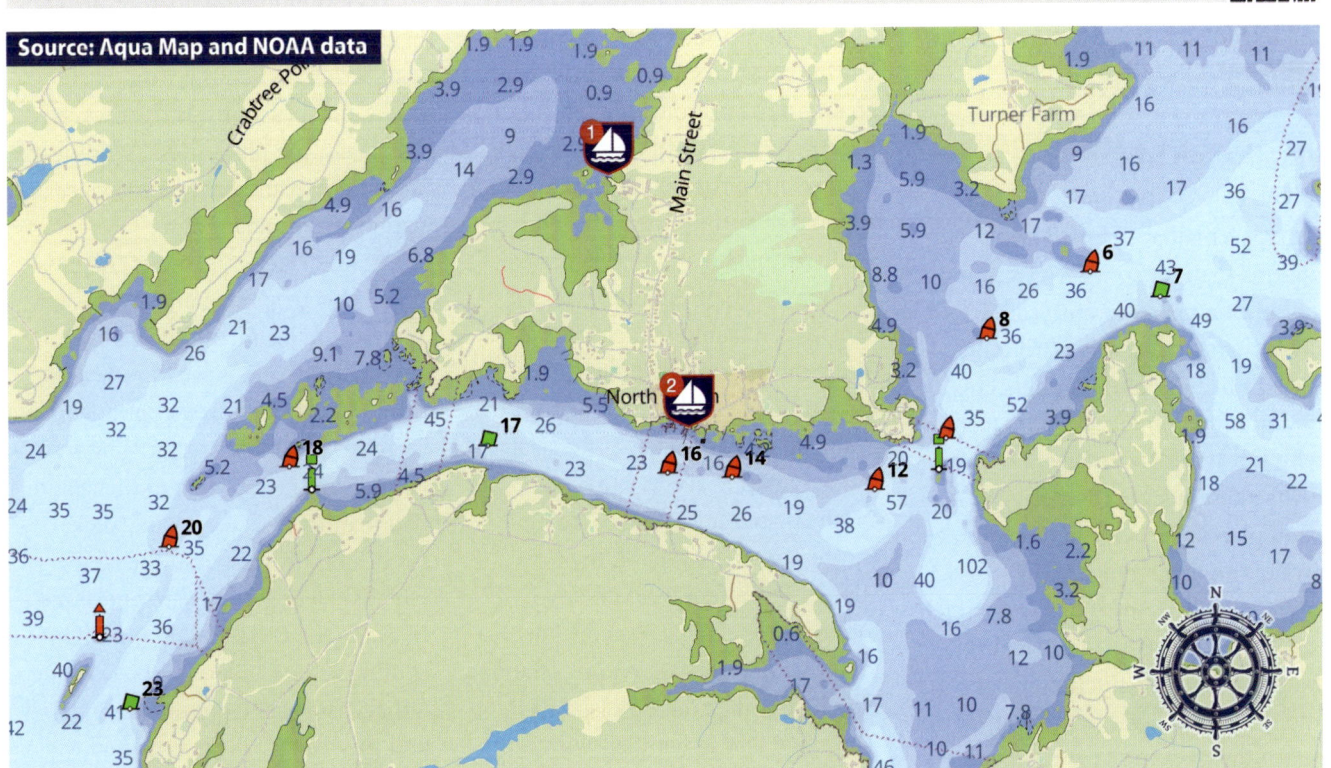

Source: Aqua Map and NOAA data

Browns Boatyard (rental buoys marked "JOB") owns all moorings east of the ferry landing at North Haven. Moorings are suitable for boats up to 60 feet. In addition to moorings, there is dock space with 5-foot MLW dockside depths. They do not take reservations and ask that you call 867-4621 or contact them via VHF Channel 16 when you arrive. This is a full-service yard that has been serving this community since 1888 providing repair and maintenance of wood and fiberglass boats and small engine work.

The town dock is easily accessible from the mooring field (and is where you catch the passenger ferry to Vinalhaven). The dock has generous dinghy space and allows 2-hour tie-ups for larger boats. Note that you cannot dispose of trash here or anywhere else on the island.

Anchorage: You can anchor in 9- to 15-foot MLW depths with relatively secure holding in a soft mud bottom directly in Southern Harbor. This anchorage is exposed to the prevailing southwesterlies, which can kick up some wave action at times.

It is a pleasant walk to town from the anchorage at Pulpit Harbor. A proliferation of moorings means you'll be in the more open outer harbor in more than 20 feet MLW. At the eastern end of the harbor, a public float provides a (usually crowded) dinghy dock. Exploring the upper reaches of the channel past the dock with a dinghy is a rewarding pastime.

Kent Cove at Fox Island Thorofare is located in the northeastern bight of the cove between Indian Point and the island off the western shore. It is fully exposed to the south but is easily accessible and secure. There is good protection from nearly all directions at Stimpson-Little

Thorofare. There is good holding in 12 to 14 feet MLW. You may find a schooner or two anchored here.

CAUTION: Note the Cable Area to the west. Signs on shore indicate the exact location. Because of this you must enter the Little Thorofare from the east.

Vinalhaven Island

As the largest of Maine's offshore islands, Vinalhaven has more options than most, from swimming and hiking to eating out. Island life centers on Carvers Harbor on the south shore of the island. This important commercial port is teeming with lobster boats, draggers, seiners, floats and tenders. The village is a good place to provision, dine out or arrange an emergency repair.

This is also a great place to stretch the legs. The classic municipal watering troughs, hitching posts and other remnants of the granite quarrying days of old are evident. A visit to the Nature Conservancy preserve on Lane Island at the southernmost head of the harbor is a good way to walk off the sea-legs on a cool summer morning.

The seasonal Vinalhaven Historical Society (207-863-4410) up the hill from the central village is well worth a visit. Across Main Street from the town landing, Carver's Harbor Market (207-863-4319) has fresh locally grown vegetables, fruits, meats, live lobsters, beer, wine and all kinds of dry goods. They also have an ATM and the Post Office is right next door.

NAVIGATION: Fox Islands Thorofare runs between North Haven Island and Vinalhaven Island and is the most popular passage across Penobscot Bay. It is about 7 miles long and is well marked with all obstructions clearly charted and buoyed. Note that the buoys are numbered from east to west. It has several snug anchorages, although holding can be poor with a thin layer of mud over a slick layer of Maine's world-famous granite. A little extra chain on the bottom is helpful in staying put. You will find excellent harbors for a rustic but secure anchorage both to the north and south of this breathtaking channel.

Our coverage circumnavigates Vinalhaven Island in a clockwise direction to be sure to cover the multitude of good anchorages available on every side of the island, starting with Seal Cove, which is southeast of the Village of North Haven and is directly off the Fox Islands Thorofare. Carver Cove to the east is easily entered from either west or east of Widow Island, which straddles the Fox Islands Thorofare and is popular with the windjammer fleet.

Dockage/Anchorage: Seal and Carver Cove are easily accessed from Fox Islands Thorofare. For the anchorage at Seal Cove, just to the south, enter from East Penobscot Bay on the same course as taken to Winter Harbor. Steer center channel just past the westernmost of the two Hen Islands and then take an abrupt turn to the southeast along the bold shore of the western Hen Island. Pick a spot southwest of the cable area indicated on the chart in Seal Cove and north of the small island located near the western shore of the cove. Obstructions along the eastern end of Penobscot Island will not be visible at high water. On a clear day you can work your way around the east end of Penobscot and Davids Islands then around to the north of Hay Island.

The best anchorage at Carver Cove is found at the mouth of the cove's extension at its south end in 8- to 13-foot MLW depths. Holding is good in mud with good protection from the prevailing summer southerlies. When the wind backs to the northeast or north, however, this is not the place to be. Wildlife–of the aquatic, land based and aviary variety–is abundant here.

Winter Harbor is one of the most rustic and unspoiled anchorages on Vinalhaven Island and is relatively easy to enter and is well protected from every direction except northeast. To reach the anchorage at Winter Harbor on the east side of the island, enter south of Calderwood Neck, north of Bluff Head and the Hen Islands. Steer a center channel course to avoid the entrance's 2-foot MLW spot near the Calderwood Neck side. Otherwise, passage is unencumbered and the scenery is unsurpassed. Winter Haven is the smaller and more western of the two Winter Harbors of the State of Maine, the other being the town on the Schoodic Peninsula and part of Acadia National Park. During the height of the summer cruising season, there are likely to be several boats anchored in the center of this beautiful sea finger, yet anchorage is less than certain here.

More secure holding is reported on the Penobscot Island side of the harbor in 8 to 10 feet MLW just northeast of the two small islets and immediately across from the unmistakable 163-foot sheer rock bluff on the Calderwood Neck side of the harbor. The harbor is passable

Penobscot Bay Islands, ME

VINALHAVEN		Largest Vessel	VHF	Total Slips	Approach/ Dockside Depth	Floating Docks	Gas/ Diesel	Repairs/ Haulout	Min/Max Amps	Pump-Out Station
1. Hopkins Boat Yard	(207) 863-2551				16.0 / 8.0			RH	30 / 100	

WiFi Wireless Internet Access
Visit www.waterwayguide.com for current rates, fuel prices, website addresses and other up-to-the-minute information.
(Information in the table is provided by the facilities.)

Scan here for more details:

Source: Aqua Map and NOAA data

by small boat for almost 2 miles into the interior of Vinalhaven where it becomes the Mill River.

To some cruisers, the anchorages of Seal Bay to the east surpass even those of Winter Harbor in their unspoiled dramatic beauty and silent seclusion. If you are seeking an anchorage to ride out severe weather, there is none better. The best holding is between the northern ends of Burnt Island and Hay Island in 7 to 10 feet MLW. There is also good holding past Burnt Island in 6 to 10 feet MLW.

Additional good anchoring can be found in about 10 feet MLW at the southeast end of Seal Bay (Seal Bay SE) near Coombs Neck. Approach on a mid-tide or better to avoid several low spots reported on the path to this location. Thick-blooded locals favor the sandy beach on Hay Island for swimming and sunbathing (but southern cruisers should be advised that the water is cold year-round).

Carvers Harbor at the south end of the island may be approached via marked channels from either south or west. Both channels enter the south end of Carvers Harbor Inlet. The southern approach is marked by 19-foot-high flashing red "2." The western approached is via The Reach from Hurricane Sound north of Greens Island by entering the northeastern end of The Reach between green can buoy "11" and red nun buoy "10." Despite well-placed navigation aids, these winding, rock- and ledge-strewn passages are no place to be in dense fog. There may be anchorage space in the southeastern end of Carvers Harbor in 9 to 18 feet MLW but swing room will be at a premium.

Hopkins Boat Yard in Carvers Harbor may have a slip but note they only take cash. They are also a good contact for emergency repairs. There will likely be a few moorings available for visiting cruisers in the harbor but they are

Carvers Harbor

hard to spot. It is best to call Hopkins for availability and location. The town-maintained dock at the extreme head of the harbor has ample space for a dinghy tie-up (2-hour limit). Trash barrels are located just above the landing at the town's breakwater.

Continuing our clockwise route around the island, Long Cove is at the northeastern end of Hurricane Sound due east of Leadbetter Island. The entrance is marked by a great pile of granite tailings on the hill to the right of the channel and visible for some distance from the west. Enter the channel just north of Fiddlehead Island. The channel then turns left and narrows as it enters the inner anchorage, which will most likely be overcrowded on a summer weekend. Long Cove forms a remote mini-fjord stretching for the better part of 1 mile into the interior of Vinalhaven Island.

> NOTE: American eagles nest here and their aerial presence offers a rare treat, but ospreys are in abundance as well and the two species constantly battle for fishing rights. Their acrobatics at the far end of the inner cove are a daily event for cruisers from all over the globe.

Long Cove is filled with private moorings. Still, there is usually room to set a hook with good holding by proceeding east to somewhat deeper water (25- to 30-foot MLW depths). Near the top of a rising tide, it is possible to cross the reef that cuts off access to the far reaches of Inner Long Cove during low tide. The water deepens appreciably beyond the reef with numerous pools of 20 to 30 feet MLW, making good anchorage spots amid rustic surroundings as well as being a perfect hurricane hole. If it's too crowded in the inner cove, Outer Long Cove has good holding in 16 to 25 feet MLW with fewer mosquitoes.

Side Trip:
Hurricane Sound Islands

Southwest of Vinalhaven, parallel strings of classic Maine islands form a delightful passage with remote harbors and scenic vistas. Hurricane Island was once the site of a thriving granite quarry business with a local population in excess of 1,000. The industry had a short life, lasting only from the mid-1870s until 1915, but in its heyday island granite was used in the bridges and buildings of major cities throughout the country including the Metropolitan Museum of Art in New York City.

The 2.5-mile path around the island winds through woods loaded with raspberry and blueberry bushes and field-pea vines to an ocean side granite ledge offering a magnificent view of island-dotted seascapes. The path continues past a summerhouse, cantilevered from a sheer cliff over a breathtaking view of the southern approach to Penobscot Bay. Smoking and campfires are strictly prohibited.

NAVIGATION: The Hurricane Island floating dock and mooring field are located on the island's east side. If approaching from the north, be careful to avoid the ledge encircling the island's aquaculture research site on the north end of the island. Coming from the south and southeast, be careful to avoid an unmarked ledge running north to south between the mooring field and the rest of Hurricane Sound. The best approach is from the northeast.

Moorings/Anchorage: The Hurricane Island Foundation welcomes visiting mariners on one of their four moorings on the island's east side. On approach look out for the spindle-marked ledge fronting the east side of the island, which will block a straightforward run at the moorings. The moorings are marked by bright orange floats with pick-up toggles and are located on the east side of the island on a first-come, first-served basis (donations encouraged). They ask that you notify them ahead of time (207-867-6050) if you wish to reserve a mooring as they fill up for events and weekends. Moorings are available for a recommended donation of $25 (overnight) and $15 for day use.

There is plenty of space on the main pier for visitors to tie up a dinghy, and you will likely be greeted ashore by a friendly staff member who can direct you to the many trails to explore and answer any questions. Time alongside the floating dock is restricted due to the frequent island traffic, especially during the peak of summer visitors and summer programming.

You can anchor at nearby White Islands in at least 10 feet MLW. Approach and entry to this snug anchorage is straightforward. Coming from the west across West Penobscot Bay, round Big White Island and head up the narrow, deep passage between Big White Island and Little White Island. If approaching from the Hurricane Sound area along Vinalhaven, proceed westward, leaving Hurricane Island to port and giving berth to the ledges off the north end of Hurricane. Then, turn up into the passage between Big and Little White Islands.

The small White Islands anchorage can only accommodate four to five boats. The holding ground is good with mud in most locations. Some areas are narrow yet still carry good depths. Among the most protected spots is alongside Big White Island toward the north end of Little White; in this spot you will feel little effect from seas at high tide. The other option is to proceed a little farther into the archipelago just north of Big White Island and to the west of Little Green Island in the deep areas. At high tide this area can feel a bit more exposed as high tide arrives and the ledges disappear. However, it is a delightful spot.

■ TO DEER ISLE & ISLE AU HAUT

Eggemoggin Reach

The broad and well-marked Eggemoggin Reach route is northernmost of the sheltered inside passages that join Penobscot Bay to Jericho Bay. It runs southeast between the mainland and the Deer Isles.

The passage offers dozens of enticing islets and coves, some with yacht facilities and boatbuilding establishments. It is called a reach because the prevailing southwesterlies usually blow across the length of the channel allowing wind-driven vessels to sail on a reach, whether eastbound or westbound. The **SR 15 Highway Bridge** (also called the Deer Island Bridge) has a vertical clearance of 85 feet.

> NOTE: Not to be missed is a tidal float trip by dinghy up the winding, 2-mile "river" that makes up this cove to the shallow tidal basin at its head. The trip should begin with the tapering of the flood about 1 hour before slack tide. Returning on the ebb and waiting for the tide change will come more slowly than your ascent on the rapids of the flood so count on needing at least 3 hours for this worthwhile adventure.

Bucks Harbor at the western mouth of Eggemoggin Reach and protected by tiny Harbor Island has been a special favorite of cruisers for many years. An active yacht club, marina and other facilities welcome visiting yachts. Provisions can be obtained at the top of the rise from the yacht club at Buck's Harbor Market (207-326-8683), stocking all the basics and fresh baked breads, specialty meats, gourmet cheeses, fine wines, beer and local produce.

Center Harbor (self-proclaimed "wooden boat capital of the world") is farther down Eggemoggin Reach and tucked in behind Chatto Island. The harbor is dominated by Brooklin Boat Yard at its eastern end, specializing in the construction and reconstruction of wooden boats of all sizes. In 1998 the yard launched the traditional 76-foot W-class cutter *Wild Horses*, designed by the late Joel White.

Eggemoggin Reach, ME

BUCKS HARBOR AREA				Largest Vessel	VHF	Total Slips	Approach/ Dockside Depth	Floating Docks	Gas/ Diesel	Repairs/ Haulout	Min/Max Amps	Pump-Out Station
1. Bucks Harbor Yacht Club-PRIVATE			(207) 326-0556				28.0 / 20.0	F				

WiFi Wireless Internet Access
Visit www.waterwayguide.com for current rates, fuel prices, website addresses and other up-to-the-minute information.
(Information in the table is provided by the facilities.)

Scan here for more details:

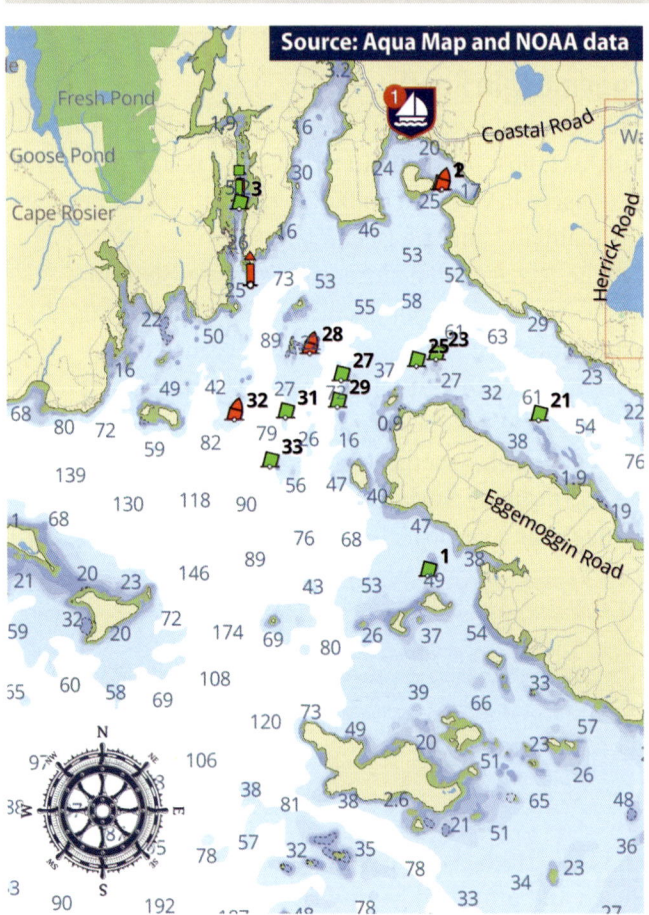

Source: Aqua Map and NOAA data

Because of this wooden boat orientation and the specialized maintenance services provided here, many owners of traditional boats make Center Harbor their homeport. Classic lines, shapes and styles (flawlessly restored) encourage a stop for closer review. *WoodenBoat Magazine* and its associated boat school are headquartered in Brooklin.

NAVIGATION: If Horseshoe Cove is your destination, a critical find is privately maintained red daybeacon "2" northwest of Thrumcap Island about 0.25 mile off the point marked "Horseshoe Cove" on the chart. It marks the end of a shoal extending from the point. Do not cut it or you may end up at low water on the exposed ledges with the seals. Follow a course centering between the red daybeacon to the northeast and the small island off the shore to the southwest.

Immediately after entry into Horseshoe Cove, a slight turn north will align your passage directly down the center of the relatively narrow channel ahead. About 0.5 miles from the entrance, two closely spaced green markers (can "3" and daybeacon "5") indicate an otherwise tricky twist in the channel. Favor these buoys and leave them close to the west. Shortly after, small red daybeacon "6" indicates a rounded rock exposed at low tide.

The inner harbor at Bucks Harbor can be easily approached on either side of Harbor Island from red-and-white Morse (A) bell buoy "EG" at the mouth of Eggemoggin Reach to the south. The inner harbor is unobstructed (save for submerged Harbor Ledge, marked by a white and orange lighted "DANGER" buoy).

In a pastoral stretch of green fields, gently rolling land, tiny towns and awesome "pine orchards," Benjamin River enters the Eggemoggin Reach from the north at the village of West Brooklin. Entry is easiest at low tide when it is possible to see the channel ledge extending from the eastern shore and all but blocking access to the inner harbor of the Benjamin River. Incoming yachts must heed red nun buoy "4" and favor the western shore as it curves to the northwest until reaching the 50-foot MLW pool inside.

Moorings/Anchorage: Horseshoe Cove at the western entrance to Eggemoggin Reach may be a little difficult to find and enter but it's well worth a night on a mooring. There is no swing room available in the mooring area but anchorage is possible south of the green can buoys "3" and "5" in more than 20 feet MLW. This is well protected and absolutely beautiful.

Orcutt Harbor, over Long Mountain directly to the east of Horseshoe Cove, is easy to enter and reasonably well protected at its far reaches. Its character is somewhat suburban with many well-trimmed lawns reaching its edges. Favor the eastern shore upon entry to avoid a 5-foot MLW spot off the western shore. Another 5-foot-

Eggemoggin Reach, ME

BENJAMIN RIVER		Largest Vessel	VHF	Total Slips	Approach/ Dockside Depth	Floating Docks	Gas/ Diesel	Repairs/ Haulout	Min/Max Amps	Pump-Out Station
1. Benjamin River Marine	(207) 359-2244				/					
CENTER HARBOR										
2. Brooklin Boat Yard	(207) 359-2236	120			7.0 / 5.0	F		RH		

WiFi Wireless Internet Access
Visit www.waterwayguide.com for current rates, fuel prices, website addresses and other up-to-the-minute information.
(Information in the table is provided by the facilities.)

Scan here for more details:

Source: Aqua Map and NOAA data

deep rock about two-thirds of the way along the bight is identified on the chart. There are no shoreside amenities for 7 miles. There is good holding in mud in 7 to 20 feet MLW in upper Orcutt Harbor.

It is possible to anchor in Bucks Harbor in 23-foot MLW depths with secure holding at the eastern end (outside the mooring fields), making it a favorite spot for touring schooners.

Buck's Harbor Marine in South Brooksville closed for the 2023 season in June with no anticipated reopening date, and their moorings are no longer being maintained. (Use at your own risk.) Bucks Harbor Yacht Club maintains two guest moorings (marked BHYC) available on a first-come, first-served basis (cannot be reserved). Check with the dock attendant for availability. Due to demand, there is a 24-hour limit. Three additional

moorings are offered only to transient boaters with a dinner reservation at the upscale Buck's Restaurant. Diners may tie their dinghy at the yacht club float after 5:00 pm. It is possible to tie up briefly (no more than 30 minutes) at the club's floating dock in 12-foot MLW depths.

Benjamin River Marine at Brooklin may have a vacant mooring but do call ahead. This is a private and scenic location. Anchoring is possible along the eastern side of the Benjamin River in mud with 7 to 18 feet MLW. Fuel is not available and services are very limited.

As previously mentioned, Brooklin Boat Yard dominates Center Harbor with lobster-buoy-shaped moorings and a full-service yard. Call ahead for mooring availability. You can tie up a dinghy behind the marina's float for a walk to town. It is also possible to dock briefly here (with 4 to 5 feet MLW) to take on water or off-load trash. There is not room for anchoring in this harbor. The Village of Brooklin is about 0.2 mile up the rise from the docks to the main road, then to the right about 1 mile farther.

Near the eastern end of Eggemoggin Reach, Naskeag Harbor provides adequate protection in most conditions. Best anchorage is found close to the north of Hog Island, avoiding The Triangles, a rocky ledge halfway between the island and Naskeag Harbor. Here you will find 14 to 16 feet MLW in thick mud.

Stonington (Deer Isle)

The working waterfront town of Stonington sits on the side of a hill sloping down to the harbor on the south shore of Deer Isle. The inhabitants of Stonington once depended on granite quarries and sardine canneries but now derive their living mainly from lobster pounds and summer visitors. Proclaimed the lobster capital of Maine (measured by shear poundage of lobster meat delivered to the world from this port), draggers, fishing smacks, yachts, an excursion boat, a ferry and fishers all make Stonington their home port, giving harbor and town an appealing blend of these diverse elements.

The Stonington Chamber of Commerce offers a downtown walking trail map that features pictures of the buildings from far back in their histories. The free Deer Isle Granite Museum (207-367-6331) features a working model of the local granite quarry as it was operated in the early 1900s when it supplied granite for such enduring works as the Kennedy Memorial, the Brooklyn Bridge and the Rockefeller Center. Open seasonally.

NAVIGATION: The large summer resort island of Deer Isle is the southern edge of Eggemoggin Reach. The SR 15 Highway Bridge (also called the Deer Island Bridge) has a vertical clearance and joins Little Deer Island to the mainland. Bridge lovers will seriously enjoy passing under this 85-foot vertical clearance bridge.

At the southern end of Deer Island, the narrow but well-marked Deer Island Thorofare threads between rocky outcroppings and tiny islands and past protected coves and scenic anchorages. Consider carefully before entering in fog and use sound signals to communicate your presence to the professional mariners who use the area in all weather. When traveling through the Thorofare, expect to encounter very dense concentrations of lobster buoys.

Crotch Island on the western end of the Deer Island Thorofare is home to an active granite quarry. Look for the gantry used to lift granite blocks for loading on a barge.

Dockage/Moorings: A town dock and a dinghy dock sit between the commercial fishing piers in Stonington. The town also has floats and a shoreside walkway. Nearly 1 mile west of the village center, full-service Billings Diesel & Marine on Moose Island has well-equipped shops dedicated to every phase of boat maintenance along with three marine railways, a lift and a crane. They also have alongside dockage for boats up to 75 feet and 11 massive granite block moorings for boats to 50 feet. Dockage and moorings are available on a first-come, first-served basis.

Stonington

Deer Isle, ME

STONINGTON		Largest Vessel	VHF	Total Slips	Approach/ Dockside Depth	Floating Docks	Gas/ Diesel	Repairs/ Haulout	Min/Max Amps	Pump-Out Station
1. Billings Diesel & Marine **WiFi**	(207) 367-2328	75	16	25	20.0 / 10.0	F	GD	RH	30 / 200+	P

WiFi Wireless Internet Access
Visit www.waterwayguide.com for current rates, fuel prices, website addresses and other up-to-the-minute information.
(Information in the table is provided by the facilities.)

Scan here for more details:

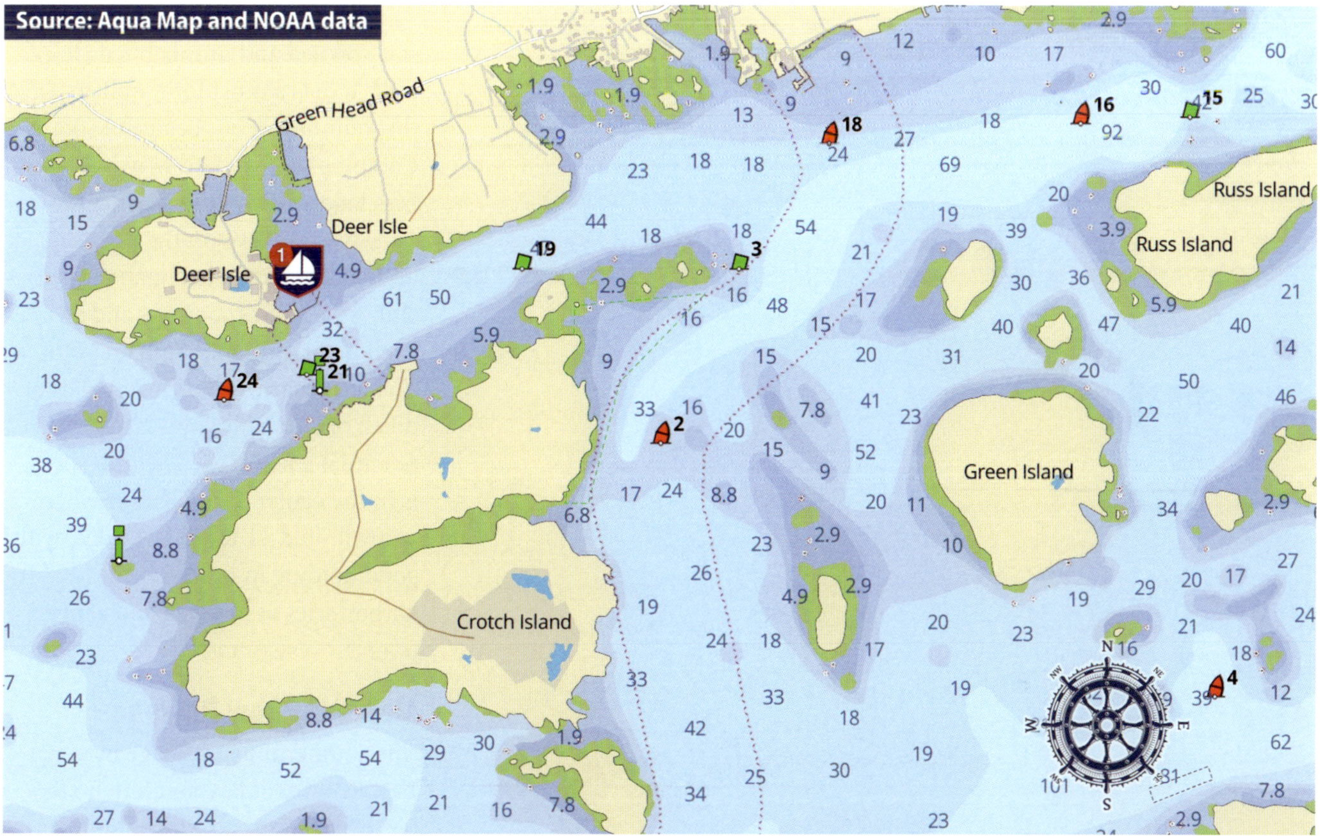

Source: Aqua Map and NOAA data

Penobscot Bay Islands, ME

ISLE AU HAUT	Largest Vessel	VHF	Total Slips	Approach/ Dockside Depth	Floating Docks	Gas/ Diesel	Repairs/ Haulout	Min/Max Amps	Pump-Out Station
1. Isle au Haut Thorofare Moorings				/					

WiFi Wireless Internet Access

Scan here for more details:

Visit www.waterwayguide.com for current rates, fuel prices, website addresses and other up-to-the-minute information. (Information in the table is provided by the facilities.)

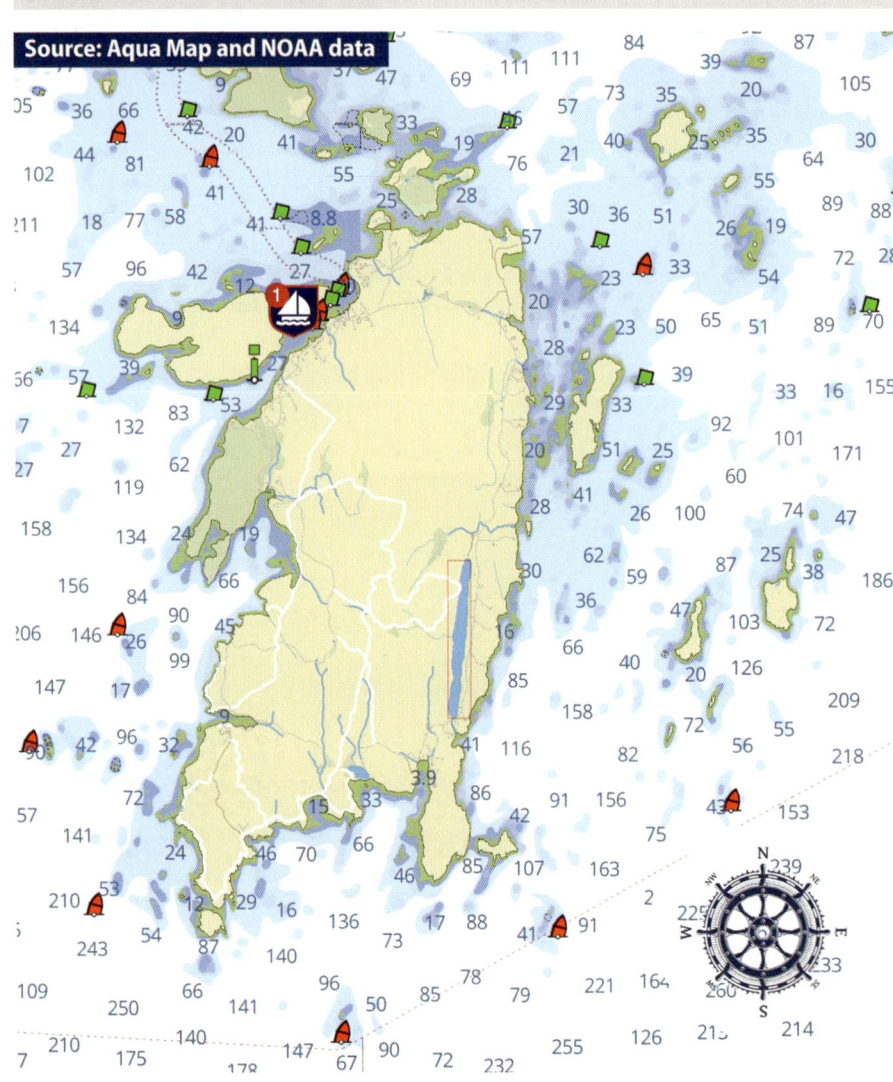

Source: Aqua Map and NOAA data

11 to 22 feet MLW. A dinghy trip to state-owned and uninhabited Hell's Half Acre is a must for a walk around this diminutive but beautiful spot. Camping is permitted here but build fires below the high-water mark.

Sylvester Cove on the west side of the island has a hospitable yacht club with guest moorings and an anchorage south of Dunham Point. The long, narrow Northwest Harbor north of Dunham Point is another potential anchorage. The best spot is in the center of the harbor where you will find 11 to 15 feet MLW with good holding in mud. The head of the harbor dries at low tide and is open to northwest winds.

Merchant Row Passage

The southernmost passage between East Penobscot Bay and Jericho Bay lies between the south end of Deer Island (Stonington area) and Isle au Haut. Merchant Row Passage is wider and deeper than Deer Island Thorofare, easy to navigate (with all major obstructions buoyed) and hemmed in by islands ranging in size from a single big rock to 1-mile-long Merchant Island.

Merchant Row consists of protected, uninhabited islands providing many anchorages. Opportunities abound to go ashore for beachcombing or blueberry picking and it is never too crowded to find a private anchorage.

Anchorage: McGlathery Island is a particularly favored spot. Best

(Reservations not accepted.) They offer full amenities and have a fully stocked marine store.

Anchorage: You can anchor out of the channel of the Deer Island Thorofare to the south of Deer Island in 15 to 24 feet MLW north of On the western shore of Deer Isle is Crotch Island. This only provides protection from the north; try to anchor out of the fast-moving current.

There are several scenic summer anchorages south of the Deer Island Thorofare. One fine anchorage is due east of the northern end of Camp Island in 11 to 17 feet MLW and another is west of the southwestern end of Bold Island next door.

The lengthy slot east of Hells Half Acre between Bold Island and Devil Island is also a gorgeous anchorage with good holding in depths from anchorages are in the cove on the north side of the island in 21-foot MLW depths or in the slot between McGlathery and Round Island just to the west in 8 to 10 feet MLW. McGlathery Island is a nature preserve and its beaches, cliffs and woods beg to be explored. On Wreck Island just west of McGlathery you may see evidence of grazing sheep brought to the island from the mainland for the summer season.

Isle au Haut

This heavily wooded Isle au Haut (pronounced "eye-la-HO") Island, so named in 1604 by Samuel de Champlain, is 550-feet high and is part of Acadia National Park with miles of trails to explore. There is one main road in town and the only connection to the outside world is the privately run Stonington mail/passenger boat and private vessels. The 71 year-round residents, however, generously share the island with a considerable number of summer people.

The Village of Isle au Haut opposite Kimball Island (on the west side of the island) has a store, small school, church, community center and town wharf. At the northern end of the Isle Au Haut Thorofare is the summer community of Point Lookout.

NAVIGATION: Navigation markers at Isle au Haut are well positioned and easy to find. There is a spot to watch in the Thorofare Channel where there is less than 6 feet MLW. It's best to pass through here on a rising tide and beware of the several rocks just outside the narrow channel. Stick close to the channel markers.

Moorings: There are three mooring balls marked "RENTAL" in the Isle au Haut Thorofare Moorings on the west side of the island off Point Lookout Landing (also known as Laundry Cove). Payment is on the honor system and you are asked to place your donation in a soda bottle attached to the mooring. When choosing a mooring be sure to watch out for the charted rock, awash at low tide, near Kimball Island.

You can drop passengers off at the town landing, but you may not leave your boat there for any length of time as it serves as the ferry landing and the working dock for the local fishing boats. It's a short walk to The Island Store (3 Main St., 207-335-5211), which features fish and produce, beer, wine and ice, as well as a Post Office and library.

Guest moorings are also available off Point Lookout to the north (where the view toward the Camden Hills from behind Flake Island is unbeatable). The dock at Point Lookout is private, but it's an easy dinghy ride through the Thorofare to the town dock. The town also owns three rental guest moorings just off the town dock, but it's much busier here than off Point Lookout.

Anchorage: The anchorage in Marsh Cove at the west end of the Thorofare is an attractive option

Isle Au Haut Light

in settled weather. Moores Harbor on the western shore and Head Harbor on the southern both look inviting on the chart but are wide open to the prevailing southwesterly winds.

Duck Harbor on the southwest shore of the island and north of Duck Harbor Mountain is a gunkhole for one or two boats, more if all agree to anchor fore-and-aft. A bold rock outcropping marks the northern side of the entry at Duck Harbor. Note the many marked and unmarked ledges outside the entrance in Isle au Haut Bay. If the wind is more south than west, it is a protected spot with good holding in 8 to 10 feet MLW but it shoals quickly beyond the ferry dock.

Getting ashore via dinghy is easy at the prominent float and jetty. Only dinghies can be tied to the inside of the float. Your reward for hiking the challenging Duck Mountain Trail is a great view of your boat 300 feet below and even the outer islands on a clear day.

■ TO MOUNT DESERT ISLAND

Blue Hill Bay

Blue Hill Bay has few obstructions, numerous coves, wooded islands and dramatic scenery on all sides. About 14 miles long, this mostly uninhabited area derives its name from the rounded mountain that towers over it to the northwest. The evergreen trees on the mountain take on a bluish cast from a distance.

To the north on the western shore is Blue Hill Harbor. The harbor is nestled in a rustic setting and is fully protected against winds from any quarter, yet convenient to provisioning, shopping and good restaurants. In short, Blue Hill Harbor is everything a cruising destination should be.

Cruising sailors seldom use Union River Bay because its narrow north–south orientation makes sailing difficult in the prevailing summer southerlies but this spot is very inviting for travelers who value their privacy. Ellsworth, north on the Union River, has a delightful Main Street that is accessible by dinghy at low tide. Be aware of possible strong currents, especially in rainy weather. A dam above Ellsworth controls the river current and level.

NAVIGATION: Blue Hill's inner harbor is most easily approached on a due-north course from a position off Sand Point on Blue Hill Neck (across Blue Hill Bay from

a second Long Island). Shallow ledges guard the entrance making it necessary to carefully observe the entrance buoys. The flagpole (west of Sculpin Point and identified on the Blue Hill Harbor chart) will be visible long before the channel cans come into view and should be used for a bearing on approach.

Entry into the harbor is safest by leaving both green cans "1" and "3" to port, then green can "5" to port and red nun "2 " to starboard, rounding Sculpin Point, which can be submerged at high tide.

Moorings: On the east side of the inner harbor moorings are usually available for a modest facilities fee from the private Kollegewidgwok Yacht Club (pronounced "College-widge'-wok"). Moorings are first come, first served. (They do not accept mooring reservations.) Look for KYC markings on the floats or call the club's launch tender (VHF Channel 09) for assistance. The club provides tie-up space for your dinghy and a comfortable clubhouse with a harbor view. They also offer pump-out service via their electric boat, Clearwater. It is a scenic 1.7-mile walk to the village from the yacht club.

Anchorage: Blue Hill Harbor West has plenty of anchorage space in 10 to 20 feet MLW. If setting the hook, it is best to wait for low tide when the limits to safe anchorage will be more apparent. There is good holding here in a mud bottom.

Above half-tide you can take your dinghy across the inner harbor to the town dock at the harbor's northwestern head, just across from the Blue Hill Memorial Hospital. Below half-tide, the dock is left high and dry for some distance. The inner harbor's combination of an 11-foot-plus tidal range and a densely packed mooring field makes an attempt to anchor on the easterly side of the harbor ill advised.

There are two well-protected anchorages to the north: Mill Cove (8- to 13-foot MLW depths) and Patten Bay (14- to 20-foot MLW depths). The latter is within walking distance of the grocery store in Surry.

Mount Desert Island

Samuel de Champlain named this large magnificent island L'Isle de Monts Desert when he visited in 1604. Even though some visitors pronounce the name like "dessert," locals place the accent on the first syllable for the bare, "desert-like" mountaintops. Cadillac Mountain, 1,530 feet high, is the highest point on Mt. Desert Island and on the East Coast. On a clear day, the mountain is visible from 35 to 45 miles seaward.

East Penobscot Bay, ME

BLUE HILL HARBOR		Largest Vessel	VHF	Total Slips	Approach/ Dockside Depth	Floating Docks	Gas/ Diesel	Repairs/ Haulout	Min/Max Amps	Pump-Out Station
1. Kollegewidgwok Yacht Club-PRIVATE **WiFi**	(207) 374-5581	50	9	20.0 / 12.0	F	GD		30	P

WiFi Wireless Internet Access
Visit www.waterwayguide.com for current rates, fuel prices, website addresses and other up-to-the-minute information.
(Information in the table is provided by the facilities.)

Scan here for more details: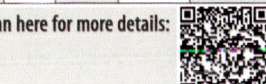

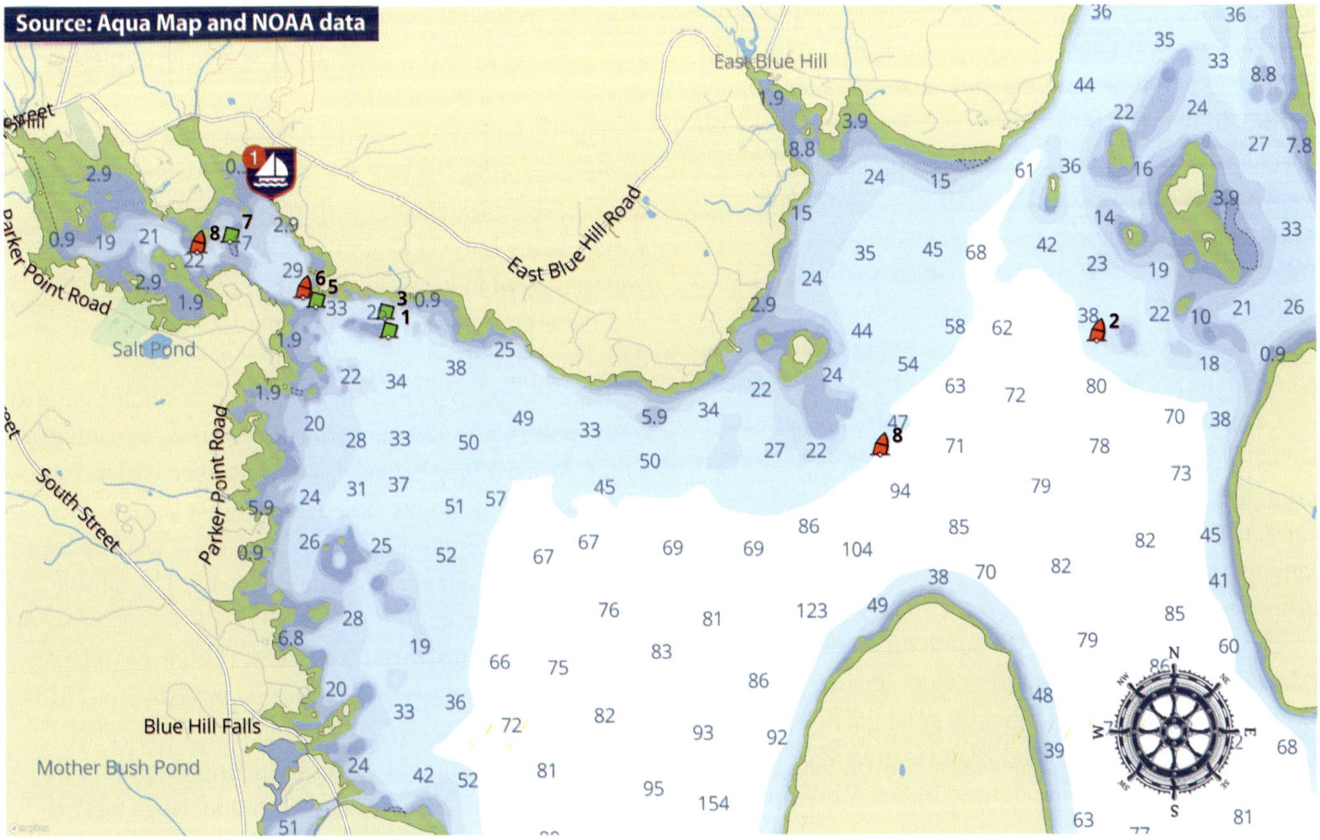

Source: Aqua Map and NOAA data

The free, propane-powered *Island Explorer* shuttle bus service (seasonal) is sponsored by Friends of Acadia and L.L. Bean and connects all the Acadia National Park destinations, villages and cruising harbors of Mount Desert: Bar Harbor, Northeast Harbor, Somes Sound, Southwest Harbor and Bass Harbor as well as the airport. It's a great way to explore the entire island.

The shallow Mount Desert Narrows and a fixed 25-foot vertical clearance bridge on the northwest side of the island connecting it to the mainland prevent the circumnavigation of Mount Desert.

Our coverage of the island moves counterclockwise from the bridge.

To Bass Harbor

Bass Harbor in the southwestern corner of the island just off Blue Hill Bay is southernmost of the fabulous isle's yacht harbors. A lovely port in the shadow of Mount Desert's hills, Bass Harbor has a substantial lobster fleet, a ferry to Swans Island and facilities in the inner and outer harbors.

In recent years Bass Harbor has become popular with cruisers seeking serenity and scenery. Restaurants and bed and breakfasts dot the shore of

the harbor, which is flanked by the cozy communities of Bass Harbor on the east and Bernard on the west.

NAVIGATION: The entrance to Bass Harbor is easy. Pass either side of Weaver Ledge (marked by two buoys) into the outer harbor (open to the south). On the eastern shore are the ferry slips, a full-service boatyard, the town dock and the village of Bass Harbor.

When approaching the innermost area of the harbor be alert for red nun buoy "6," which can be obscured by moored boats and is deceptively close to the shore. Leave it to the east on entering the inner harbor and then turn into the mooring pool.

There is a fuel dock (and wholesale seafood) near the entry to the well-buoyed inner harbor at F.W. Thurston Co. (207-244-3320). The Tremont Harbormaster (207-244-4564) oversees all activities in the harbor. On the western shore is the charming old community of Bernard where the yellow roof of Thurston's Lobster Pound (207-244-7600) is prominent. Thurston's has short-term tie-ups (two boats at a time) and is a great place for a real Maine lobster dinner. The inner harbor is completely filled with private moorings making anchoring impossible.

Anchorage: Western Bay on the northwest side of Mount Desert Island has two good anchorages: Northwest Cove with 7 to 10 feet MLW and Goose Cove with 7 to 13 feet MLW (which is actually across Mount Dessert Narrows in Trenton). Both experience surge when southwesterlies are blowing.

Great Cove to the south is a nice anchorage with a small beach off the northeast side of Bartlett Island. There is good protection from the southerlies and nice views of the "quiet side" of Mt. Desert Island. There is a municipal landing at Bartlett Narrows but there are no services ashore except for a trash dumpster.

Pretty Marsh Harbor to the south on Mount Desert Island's western shore is easy to enter. The harbor is well protected and scenic and provides good holding in 8 to 13 feet MLW. Nearby Hardwood Island is privately owned. Seal Cove to the south has at least 14 feet MLW but is open to westerlies.

Bass Harbor at the southwest end of Mount Desert Island offers almost all-around protection (except directly from the south) in 7 to 9 feet MLW.

Southwest Harbor

Southwest Harbor is a good stop for provisioning and playing "tourist." There are hiking possibilities (including Flying Mountain Hiking Trail and Wonderland Trail) and birders and wood carvers will want to visit the Wendell Gilley Museum (207-244-7555) with a distinctive collection of bird and waterfowl carvings, demonstrations and workshops on wooden decoy carving.

Hamilton Marine Dive & Fishing Supply Southwest Harbor (207-244-7870) has an extensive marine parts selection and is located on the north side of the harbor. A West Marine (207-244-0300) is located on the south side

of the harbor. In the village at the harbor head you will find Sawyer's Specialties, a purveyor of fine wines, beer, liquor and other delicacies. Ask about delivery. The Food Mart IGA (207-244-5601) is a supermarket 1 mile up the road with reasonable prices for a destination island.

NAVIGATION: If approaching from the west, the pinch between the Bass Harbor Head Lighthouse and Great Gott Island creates a confluence of forces that must be respected. Most of the water between those landmasses washes over an 8-foot ledge.

The 14-foot MLW channel between gong buoy "WB" to the west and gong buoy "EB" to the east rushes with fast currents and whistles with compressed and directed winds. Gong buoy "EB" periodically comes off station so you may need to keep checking the bearing to "WB" as you pass through the channel if you don't have an up-to-date chartplotter.

If sailing, keep an eye on other boats to catch a glimpse of the wind sheer and plan your sheet-easing accordingly. Enter Western Way between Great Cranberry Island and the mainland of Mount Desert. Southwest Harbor opens up to the west and is a busy port frequently used by large commercial vessels and recreational boats. The lobster boat traffic is constant.

Dockage/Moorings: Southwest Harbor has a large mooring field; contact the Harbormaster (207-244-7913 or VHF Channel 09) to reserve a mooring. The town maintains public dinghy docks on the north and south sides of the harbor. There are 6 guest moorings located mid-harbor, just north of the town dock available on a first-come, first-serve basis. They are bright yellow on top, and white and red on the bottom. Pay online or at the harbormaster's office.

The Hinckley Company's well-known yacht yard and ship store are on the south shore at Manset. What began in 1928 as a small service yard today ranks as a world-class builder of power and sailing yachts. Hinckley Yacht Services Southwest Harbor has 70 moorings and can accommodate vessels to 150 feet with basic amenities.

Dysart's Great Harbor Marina at the head of the harbor has 135 floating slips with 50 reserved for transients behind a breakwater and numerous amenities including a West Marine, a sail loft, bakery, provisioning service and a restaurant. Their friendly staff will help you dock and arrange shoreside accommodations should you need to get off the boat or pick up crew.

Beal's Lobster Pier next to the Coast Guard station invites you to dock at their pier while you visit the restaurant. Slips at the Claremont Hotel around the corner are for registered guests arriving by boat.

Anchorage: Anchoring is no longer allowed in Southwest Harbor. Good holding can be found between the Southwest Harbor shore and Greening Island north of the harbor proper and east of the Coast Guard station. Holding is best closer to Greening Island in 12 to 17 feet MLW. This does, however, create a lengthy dinghy ride to shore access at the town dock. Use caution to avoid the charted cable area.

The closest dock to town in the Upper Town Dock located in the northwest corner of the harbor. It is the first large floating dock ahead to starboard after the second green can. Trash may not be left here. Lower Town Dock is on the northeast shore, just north of Beal's Lobster Pier. Tie-up times are posted and enforced at both docks.

Somes Sound

Considered the only true fjord on the North American east coast, Somes Sound begins its dramatic 6-mile cleavage into the heart of Mount Desert Island at the busy channel off Clark Point, the tip of the peninsula that separates Southwest Harbor from the sound. Throughout most of the sound's length, 600 to 800-foot hills ease down to the water's edge and beyond. Mountains of substantially greater size add grandeur to an awe-inspiring landscape and seascape.

Outside the prevailing southwesterly winds, those under sail will find the sound reminiscent of lake sailing–whistling winds abating almost instantly to a dead calm, rapid wind shifts and reversals of 180 degrees. Part way along, Valley Cove attracts adventuresome crews with the promise of accessible paths to the summits of the sheer cliffs above for stunning views. The water is deep in the cove (up to 90 feet) within a short distance of the shore.

A short walk from the landing is the Village of Somesville, the oldest settlement on Mount Desert Island. The town's white-washed clapboard houses and vintage public buildings are bordered by garlands of brilliant flowers, encouraging visitors to stretch their legs in search of the perfect photo from the head of the harbor.

Bass Harbor Lighthouse

Mount Desert Island, ME

SOUTHWEST HARBOR		Largest Vessel	VHF	Total Slips	Approach/ Dockside Depth	Floating Docks	Gas/ Diesel	Repairs/ Haulout	Min/Max Amps	Pump-Out Station
1. Hinckley Yacht Services Southwest Harbor	(207) 300-2010	150	10		30.0 / 25.0		D	RH		P
2. Dysart's Great Harbor Marina **WiFi**	(207) 244-0117	220	9	135	15.0 / 15.0	F	GD	R	30 / 200+	P
NORTHEAST HARBOR										
3. Northeast Harbor Marina - City **WiFi**	(207) 276-5737	180	9	60	12.0 / 12.0	F			30 / 100	P
4. Hinckley Northeast Harbor **WiFi**	(207) 401-2646	60		18	6.0 / 6.0	F		RH	30 / 50	
BAR HARBOR										
5. Bar Harbor Municipal Pier **WiFi**	(207) 288-5571	185	9	8	16.0 / 11.0	F			30 / 100	P
6. Harborside Hotel, Spa & Marina **WiFi**	(207) 801-3904	200	1	8	7.0 / 8.0	F	D		30 / 200+	P
7. Bar Harbor Regency Oceanfront Resort & Marina	(207) 801-3904	150			15.0 / 12.0	F	GD		30 / 100	

WiFi Wireless Internet Access
Visit www.waterwayguide.com for current rates, fuel prices, website addresses and other up-to-the-minute information.
(Information in the table is provided by the facilities.)

Scan here for more details:

The Mount Desert Historical Society Museum (207-276-9323) is tucked behind a flower-ringed pond crossed by the Thaddeus Shepley Somes Bow Bridge, which fairly begs to be photographed. It crosses a lake created by a dam that was originally built by the island's first permanent settler, Abraham Somes. The museum offers year-round entertaining and informative educational programs.

Turn north on the highway from the harbor road then cross the street to use the sidewalk for less than a 1-mile walk to basic commercial amenities. On the Run (207-244-5504), also known as Circle K, stocks some groceries and various deli items and prepared sandwiches among other sundries. You can have your propane tank filled here and there are FedEx and UPS drop stations. The Mount Desert Post Office is right across the street.

NAVIGATION: Somes Harbor, the very northwest tip of Somes Sound, is entered west of Myrtle Ledge through the deep but narrow passage between green can buoy "7" and Bar Island (owned by the State of Maine and open for exploration).

Moorings/Anchorage: Several moorings are likely to be vacant in Somes Harbor, although no one manages their use while their owners are away. The boatyards here may also have vacant moorings but ask before attaching. Should you choose not to grab a vacant mooring, there is plenty of room to anchor in Somes Harbor. At the head of the sound to the east of Squatum Point is another nice anchorage (unless the wind is out of the south) with 6-foot MLW depths.

Sargent Cove northeast of Mason Point has 15-foot MLW depths and good holding. On the west side of the harbor, Somesville Landing Corp. maintains a substantial floating dock and ramp to accommodate dinghies (transients to the south, locals to the north). They request donations for upkeep.

To the south, Valley Cove on the southwestern side of Somes Sound is a good anchorage. Make sure you have sufficient scope for 30- to 40-foot MLW depths.

Northeast Harbor

As in Southwest Harbor, the streets of Northeast Harbor are thronged by visitors who enjoy a meal off the boat and finding hidden treasures in small shops. A gift and wine specialties shop, bookstore, coin-operated laundry, newspaper and stationery store and several attractive galleries and boutiques line Main Street. The Great Harbor Maritime Museum is also located on Main Street in a former town fire station. The well-stocked F.T. Brown Hardware and Marine (207-276-3329) is a fifth-generation, family-run business stocked with some foul-weather clothing and fishing gear. They also carry basic marine supplies in a shed behind the store. Island Bike Rental is just beyond that.

Morris Service Northeast Harbor is home to Morris Yachts, which has been building sailboats by hand, one at a time, since 1972. Stop by to see the artistry of some of Maine's finest craftsmen. (Note: They do not offer transient slips.)

NAVIGATION: Northeast Harbor is a landlocked bight that is easily entered from the south. Its only obstruction

is a rock located about 500 yards directly off the center of the harbor's mouth marked by green can buoy "1" to the east and red bell buoy "2" to the west. The rock may be passed on either side, but if you opt for the eastern passage, take care to observe the red-right-returning rule west of Bear Island and heed red nun buoys "2A" and "4."

The inner harbor is deep (at least 11 feet MLW) right up to Clifton Dock and the Town Marina, with exception of one 6-foot ledge that is marked on the charts. Northeast Harbor is well-organized but always seemingly filled to capacity and hosts nearly every conceivable type of recreational vessel. Anchoring is not permitted in the harbor.

Dockage/Moorings: The municipal Northeast Harbor Marina dominates the western cove of the harbor to the north with slips and moorings (with launch service). Some are two-point moorings and cruisers traveling in company can request both sides of the same float. In any event, the moorings are a relatively easy ride by tender from the ample dinghy dock at the municipal pier.

The Yachtsmen's Building on the waterfront provides top-notch amenities including a reading room to those in slips or on moorings. They also maintain a complimentary 2-hour-max floating dock with water and power just south of the looming concrete municipal pier. The dock is in high demand.

Bar Harbor

Located on the east side of Mount Desert under the imposing summits of Cadillac, Dorr and Champlain Mountains, Bar Harbor attracts throngs of hikers, climbers and kayakers as well as sedentary vacationers and motorists. Surprisingly few arrive by water. An exception to this rule is the recent increase in visits by cruise ships. Be aware that you might share the harbor and channel with a 1,000-foot cruise liner or two and the town may be inundated with their several thousand passengers. But don't let that dismay you from visiting as the town and surrounding area are spectacular.

NAVIGATION: Bar Harbor is easily approached from the south on either side of Egg Rock, identified by a red 5-second flashing light and fog signal (MRASS) on a 64-foot tower. The harbor is open to the east and can be entered through any of the deep channels between the Porcupine Islands. A breakwater extends to the west from Bald Porcupine Island, marked by a quick flashing 20-foot light at its western end. The breakwater will be submerged at high water but do not attempt to cross it.

Dockage/Moorings: Bar Harbor Harbormaster can help you find a mooring in the Bar Harbor Municipal Pier Mooring Field. (Call on VHF Channel 9.) The office is located in the Port Security Building on the Town Pier. The town's large dinghy dock is located on the western side of the pier. Tour boats run through the morning field to access the dock to pick up and disembark passengers. Expect noise from their tour speeches and some wakes.

While overnight dockage is unlikely to be available, it might be possible to tie up for a brief period at the floats on the eastern side of the Bar Harbor Municipal Pier while you provision, change crews or replenish your water supply.

Both Harborside Hotel, Spa & Marina and Bar Harbor Regency Oceanfront Resort & Marina to the north offer transient dockage that includes access to resort amenities. (Access to the village center from the latter will require about a 1-mile walk or taxi ride.)

Anchorage: While it is possible to anchor outside the mooring area just east of the municipal pier in Bar Harbor,

Mount Desert Island

Bar Harbor

the holding ground is poor in sand and grass and the relatively open harbor can become quite rough. Leaving an anchored boat unattended here is not recommended.

Side Trip: Great & Little Cranberry Islands

Just 2 to 3 miles southwest of Mt. Desert's Southwest Harbor, the Cranberry Islands seem remote yet accessible and familiar. Combining a mix of working lobstermen, long-term summer residents, artists and artisans, these islands are both interesting and friendly places to visit. Even though the namesake cranberry bogs have long been drained, these islands still excel for pleasant walks with seascape backdrops of Mount Desert.

The Town of Cranberry Isles comprises five islands that form part of the Great Harbor of Mt. Desert boundary: Great Cranberry Island, Little Cranberry Island (aka "Islesford"), Sutton Island, Bear Island (at the mouth of Northeast Harbor) and Baker Island.

Great Cranberry Island, the largest of the group, is home to some 40 year-round residents and a much expanded summer population. Great Cranberry Island Historical Society (207-244-7800) details the history and sense of community of the islands in its arts center. Behind the museum is a lovely public trail (about 1 mile) through the woods to Whistlers Cove on the Western Way. Cranberry Road is lined with views of water on both sides and lovely old ship captains' homes.

Little Cranberry Island is smaller, yet attracts a greater number of visitors by boat. Perhaps this is because the number of shoreside attractions is greater and the woodsy walks, although just as appealing, are shorter. The vibrant community of Islesford–some 400 in the summer, although it pares down to about 70 in the winter– seems to instill those who visit with a yen to return for years to come.

The Islesford Dock is a local gathering place and something of a destination point for locals "in the know" from Mount Desert. Just inland of the dock and to the left, the National Park Service maintains the tiny but fascinating Islesford Museum, which displays well-presented artifacts and pictures of traditional Maine island life. The Neighborhood House and Library has a remarkable children's collection and houses Julia's Garden, a sculpted cedar fencing enclosing a must-see collection of local mosses, plants and flowers.

Islesford Dock Restaurant is a hopping destination that can provide small plates and drinks or full meals with equal ease. Keep your eyes peeled for the seafood stew in a copper tureen and consider how hungry you really are. The Lobstermen's Co-op sells fresh live lobsters to the left of the ferry dock.

NAVIGATION: The approach to Spurling Cove on the north side of Great Cranberry Island is open and straightforward. The few outlying obstructions are well marked. Little Cranberry Island is as easily accessed as its sister island to the west. Simply steer north of red bell buoy "2" marking Spurling Rock and an unnamed 6-foot MLW hump and enter Hadlock Cove, west and then south of green can buoys "1" and "3."

Moorings/Anchorage: Although wide open to the north and northwest, anchorage is possible outside the mooring field in Spurling Cove in 10- to 15-foot MLW depths and there is a dinghy float at the (west) public dock. If weather conditions preclude anchoring off Great Cranberry, consider taking a mooring in Northeast Harbor and

riding one of the regular ferries to the island.

The Town of Cranberry Isles maintains several guest moorings available on a first-come, first-served basis. The moorings are free and available for up to three days. They are marked by large white balls, each with a blue horizontal stripe, and have "Town Guest" painted on them. At Little Cranberry, there are also private moorings marked as being for rent with phone numbers on them.

Anchoring is possible outside the mooring area in Hadlock Cove but the bottom here is covered with thick grass and often kelp. (Even more so toward the head of the harbor.) Setting a hook securely enough to handle relatively swift currents of reversing tides may require several tries.

Tie up loosely at the crowded dinghy dock alongside the ferry landing so each dinghy can make its way to the dock for loading and unloading. Stay clear of the face dock, which is regularly taken over by the inter-island ferry from Northeast Harbor.

SWANS ISLAND & LONG ISLAND

Swans Island

Remote Swans Island lies directly in the path of the Eggemoggin Reach southwest of Mount Desert Island. A year-round ferry serves the year-round population of about 325 from Bass Harbor. There are three villages: Atlantic in Mackerel Cove on the north coast and Swans Island and Minturn in Burnt Coat Harbor to the south.

A tour of the island paths is a must from Buckle Harbor on the northwest side of the island. Wild strawberries growing atop granite boulders, seascape cameos through mossy vistas, the door of a long-vanished cabin framing a nearly hidden pathway in the mist, the scolding of an invisible squirrel or a doe venturing out to a seaside meadow as your dinghy departs.... You get the picture.

There is no public transportation on the island but locals will often offer a ride and the Island Market & Supply (207-526-4043) sells groceries and take-out and may deliver. There is no alcohol on this dry island; even brown bags are out of bounds at the restaurant.

You can have a freshwater swim at Quarry Pond at Minturn. If a sandy, secluded ocean beach is your preference, ask for directions. Three are within walking distance of the main harbor.

NAVIGATION:

> ⚠ *CAUTION:* Midway between the tip of Roderick Head and green can "3" (off the ferry landing), an enormous ledge presents a considerable hazard to navigation since it is submerged at high tide. During high water give this visible ledge a very wide berth at slow speed, watching the depth sounder.

Burnt Coat Harbor on the southwest side of the island is long, narrow and well protected and serves as home port for the small villages of Swans Island and Minturn. Enter south of green

Penobscot Bay, ME

SWANS ISLAND		Largest Vessel	VHF	Total Slips	Approach/ Dockside Depth	Floating Docks	Gas/ Diesel	Repairs/ Haulout	Min/Max Amps	Pump-Out Station
1. Swans Island Moorings	(207) 266-1937				/					

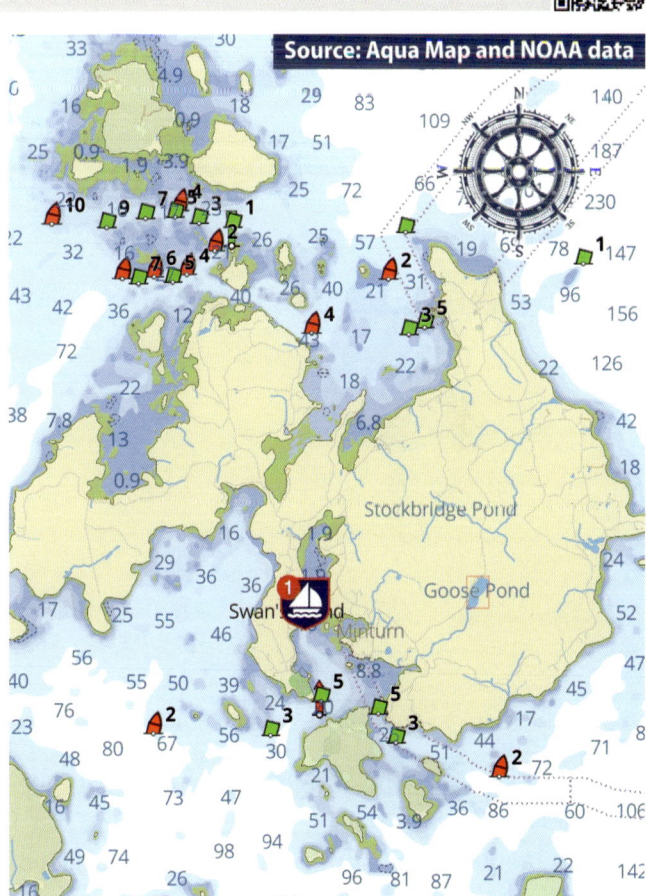

WiFi Wireless Internet Access
Visit www.waterwayguide.com for current rates, fuel prices, website addresses and other up-to-the-minute information. (Information in the table is provided by the facilities.)

Scan here for more details:

can buoy "3" off Gooseberry Island Ledge and pass between green gong buoy "5" off the tip of Hockamock Head (also marked by the 75-foot Burnt Coat Harbor Light) and red daybeacon "4" north of Harbor Island. Although not recommended, vessels do enter and exit through the narrow but well-marked channel between Harbor Island and Stanley Point. Follow a local boat with similar underwater characteristics for greater peace of mind. The last 100 yards after green can buoy "5" are nerve-wracking without local knowledge.

Moorings/Anchorage: An anchorage is located between Swans Island and Buckle Harbor just south of York Narrows. Enter Buckle Harbor, noting the charted 6-foot MLW spot between green can buoys "7" and "5" in the York Narrows Channel. This is a secure anchorage that can accommodate a dozen boats with good holding in 7 to 10 feet MLW.

Mackerel Cove is large enough to accommodate a Spanish armada. It is easily entered from York Narrows between Orono and Round Islands to the north and Swans Island shore on the south. Two favored anchorage spots are on either side of Roderick Head (Roderick Head East and Roderick Head West) in 8 to 15 feet MLW. Protection from the prevailing southwesterlies is excellent.

The only improved landing in Mackerel Cove is found near the ferry dock on the east side of the cove. Should you choose to set a hook here, stay well south of the ferry's comings and goings from Bass Harbor on Mount Desert Island. There are private moorings in Mackerel Cove and it is possible to pick up a vacant one, but be prepared to move should the owner appear. The views of Mt. Desert Island are impressive from this well-protected anchorage.

Heavy-tackle rental Swans Island Moorings (brightly painted lobster floats) are available from the Fishermens Cooperative (382 Harbor Road, 207-526-4327), along with diesel fuel and engine

oil. (Recreational boats are asked to fuel up before 1:00 p.m. to make room for returning lobster boats.) Approximately 0.5 mile north of the Fishermen's Co-Op, the harbor shallows appreciably, making even a grocery run by dinghy tide dependent.

Turn north for anchorage outside the mooring field at Swans Island in 20 to 35 feet MLW. The amount of scope necessary and the lobster boats passing in the early morning restrict the number of boats that can safely anchor here. Anchorage is also possible on the north side of Harbor Island in Long Cove but can be uncomfortable due to its greater vulnerability to ocean swells and constant traffic from lobster boats using the narrow channel just south.

Penobscot Bay, ME

LONG ISLAND			Largest Vessel	VHF	Total Slips	Approach/ Dockside Depth	Floating Docks	Gas/ Diesel	Repairs/ Haulout	Min/Max Amps	Pump-Out Station
1. Lunt's Dockside Deli Moorings		(207) 334-2902				/					

WiFi Wireless Internet Access

Visit www.waterwayguide.com for current rates, fuel prices, website addresses and other up-to-the-minute information. (Information in the table is provided by the facilities.)

Scan here for more details:

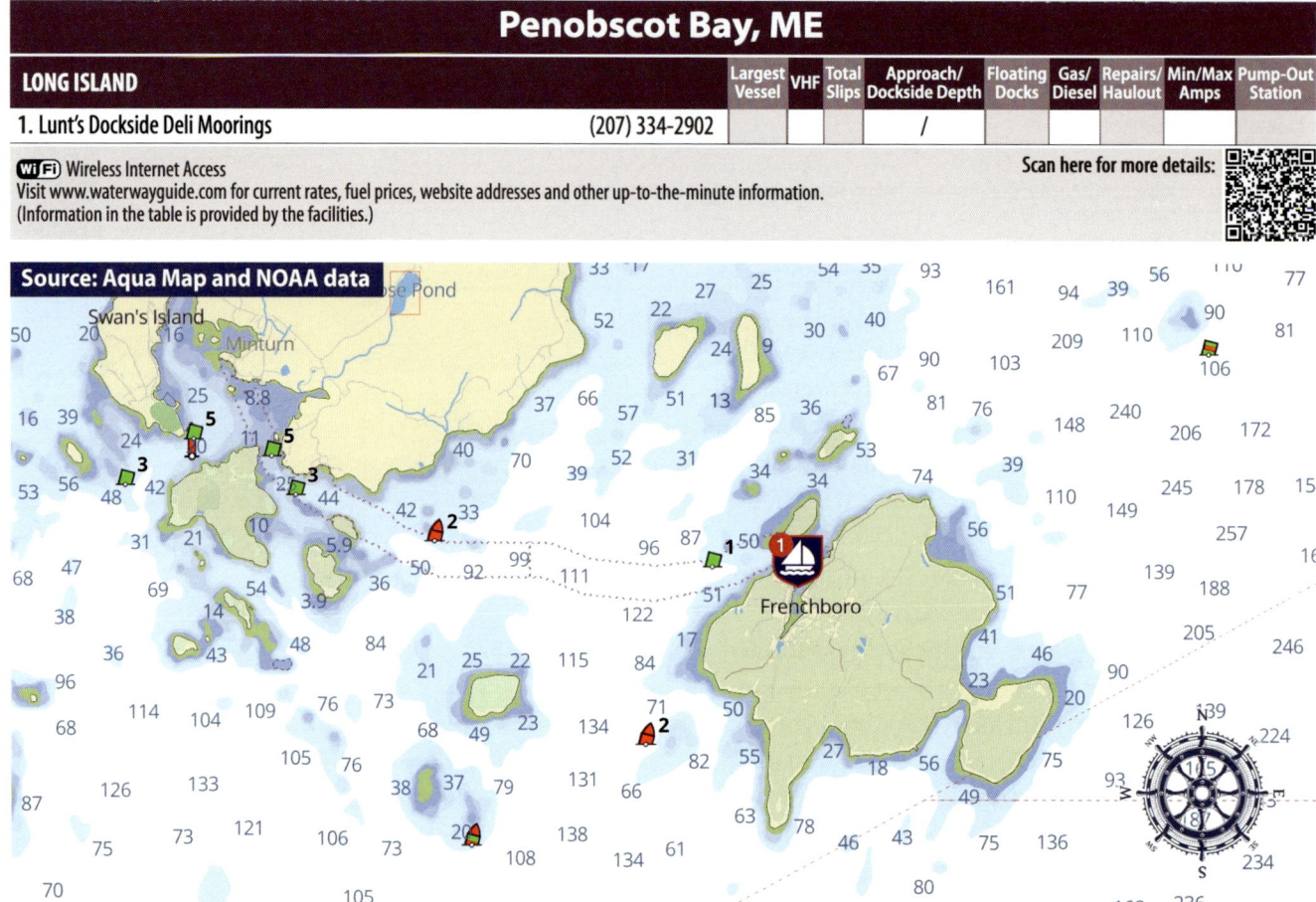

Source: Aqua Map and NOAA data

Long Island

Southeast of Swans Island is the former pirate's hideout of Long Island, which is high, wooded and round and not "long" at all. Long Island is popular both as an end-of-the-line stop and as a great place to work out some of those cruising kinks on a trip farther east.

Roads on both sides of the harbor are paved but intriguing dirt roads and trails lead off in several directions and can be picked up from the harbor or by beaching a dinghy in Eastern Cove. One interesting walk begins at the head of the harbor where a narrow dirt road departs the pavement southward, undulating pleasantly to the granite-bound south shore. A walk east along the rocks picks up a well-worn path with a circle back through an ancient fir-fringed bog, where orchids bloom every July and white-winged crossbills trill throughout the summer. Before exploring you should wisely invest in an island trail map at the museum.

Perched on a side hill at the head of the harbor (beyond a variety of precarious lobstering sheds and docks), the island's small museum captures the spirit of a seafaring past. It is run by the Frenchboro Historical Society (207-334-2924). The attached lending library will loan books to visitors on the promise to mail them back. There is also a tiny Frenchboro Post Office attached to a local lobsterman's house. The Long Island Store that was part of the community for 100 years was sold in 2020 and is now Byers & Sons Long Island Bakehouse and serves pizza, sandwiches and sweets. (Be sure to thank them for being here.)

NAVIGATION: Frenchboro, the tiny hamlet at Lunt Harbor, is the vision of what a classic out-island Maine fishing village should look like. The harbor is fortified against all winds but the strongest northeasterlies, and even those are partially blocked by Harbor Island at its mouth. Lunt Harbor is easily accessible and may be approached from the west using green bell buoy "1" as a guide to the channel between Harbor Island and the northwestern shoulder of Long Island. About one-third of the way along Harbor Island, a hard turn to the south will take you into the open mouth of the harbor. From the east the red-and-white Morse (A) gong buoy "LI" aids the passage south-southwest below Crow Island and Harbor Island for an almost straight course into the harbor.

Moorings: Pick up one of Lunt's Dockside Deli Moorings in the outer harbor and row in for a tie-up behind the face dock and pay the fee at the deli take-out window (207-334-2902). Rental moorings available on a first-come, first-served basis and are marked with large white mooring balls with white pickup buoys.

Anchorage: Eastern Cove on the east side of Long Island is as remote and unspoiled as it is beautiful. The cove is protected from the south and east by Richs Head and the main island to the north and west. Holding is good and exploration of the long-abandoned farmsteads ashore is well worthwhile, although the rubble on the beach can be hard on a dinghy. A couple of mile walk through the woods will bring you to the small Lunt Harbor on the other side of the island. Southwest Point provides the dramatic feeling of being at land's end when staring south over open water.

■ FRENCHMAN BAY

Frenchman Bay offers a few harbors on its eastern side but most of the services (and they are significant) are offered in the well-established and visitor-centric harbors of Mount Desert Island. Frenchman Bay is 4 miles wide, 10 miles long and easy to navigate, and it offers dramatic views of Mount Desert and the bluffs of the Schoodic Peninsula to the east. A group of islands with deep channels between them cuts across the bay about halfway up, creating shelter for the upper bay.

It is a spectacular run up the bay along sea-washed cliffs past Thunder Hole (where you can hear the surf crashing against the rocks at the right tidal stage), Sand Beach (behind Old Soaker) and great inland mountains.

Sorrento

Sorrento is at the tip of Waukeeg Neck and resembles its namesake, Sorrento, Italy, which is another city by the sea with spectacular mountain vistas. Onshore you will find a Post Office and a gorgeous historic library and not much else.

Anchorage: Protection is excellent throughout the Sorrento Harbor in at least 8-foot MLW depths. Both Sorrento and Hancock Point have town docks.

Sorrento Harbor

Winter Harbor, ME

SAND COVE			Largest Vessel	VHF	Total Slips	Approach/ Dockside Depth	Floating Docks	Gas/ Diesel	Repairs/ Haulout	Min/Max Amps	Pump-Out Station
1. Winter Harbor Yacht Club		(207) 963-2346	55	9		50.0 / 20.0					

WiFi Wireless Internet Access
Visit www.waterwayguide.com for current rates, fuel prices, website addresses and other up-to-the-minute information.
(Information in the table is provided by the facilities.)

Scan here for more details:

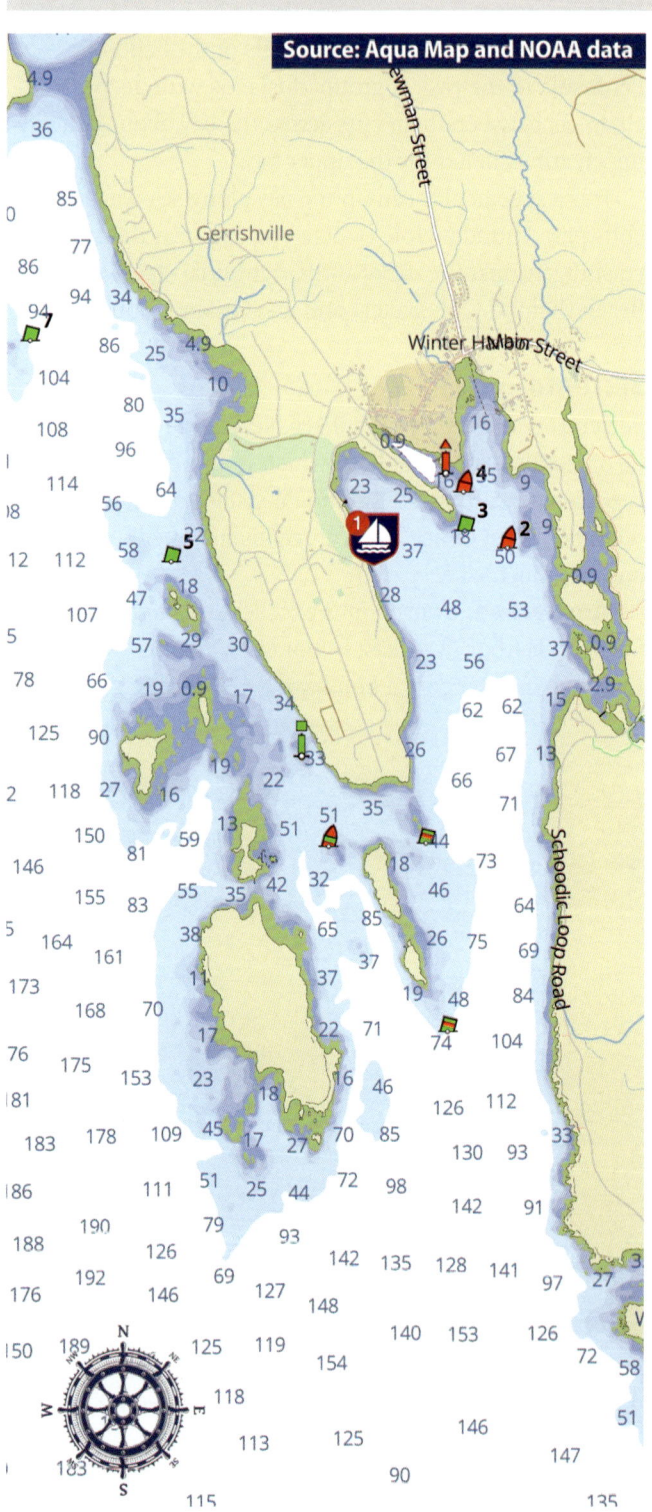

Source: Aqua Map and NOAA data

Winter Harbor

The head of Winter Harbor has three separate coves. Sand Cove, bordered by Grindstone Neck, is home to the Winter Harbor Yacht Club and its colorful fleet of racing sloops and classic yachts. The inner harbor is reserved for lobster boats. Henry Cove is the harbor for the village with fishing boats and small outboard vessels. The ferry from Bar Harbor is also in Henry Cove. Each harbor has a landing with a floating dock but ease of access to the village varies.

Henry Cove is closest to provisioning options and amenities. The Post Office is about 0.5 mile east on Main Street and a small grocery store, Winter Harbor Provisions, is nearby at 254 Main St. (207-963-2256). Want fresh lobster straight off the boat? Try Winter Harbor Lobster Co-Op at 23 Pendleton Rd. on the inner harbor. Every purchase goes directly to the local independent fishers and the communities they live in.

The Channing Chapel (207-963-7556), home to an excellent public library, was built of beach and field stones in 1888. The owner established a free library of the classics in the upper rooms and that tradition was continued except for a long period after the chapel was sold in 1958. The library returned in 1996 under the auspices of the Channing Chapel Preservation Society.

NAVIGATION: From the north the option to head around the islands off the Grindstone Neck may seem troublesome compared to cutting between Spectacle and Turtle Islands, but the ledges between the island are unmarked and are better attempted with local knowledge. Taking the route south of Turtle and Mark Islands has the additional benefit of providing a good view of an abandoned lighthouse on Mark Island's hillside.

Continuing due north from the green-over-red gong buoy "MI," the wooded shores of Grindstone Neck will eventually retreat west and reveal the distinctive clubhouse of the Winter Harbor Yacht Club on the west shore of Sand Cove. Harbor Point will be directly ahead with Inner Winter Harbor and Henry Cove north and east, respectively.

Dockage/Moorings: Most visiting yachts prefer the Sand Cove area for its ambiance and decent protection. Your boat may pitch a bit here when the wind is up but the Winter Harbor Yacht Club moorings are up to the task. Visiting yachts using guest moorings may be accommodated for up to one full week (seven consecutive days) with a maximum of 7 days total for the season. Launch and trash disposal services, showers and use of the pool are included with the mooring fee. Moorings are available for short-term stays (until 3:00 pm) for a flat fee (or free if you eat at their snack bar).

There are no other facilities on Sand Cove and the village is about a 1-mile walk north. Another mile or so trek on the dirt road east from the clubhouse will take you to pleasant outlooks over the pink granite shore at the southern tip of Grindstone Neck.

Local fishing vessels have wisely claimed virtually the entire Inner Harbor, which offers the harbor's overall best protection. There is no room to anchor but it may be possible to secure a vacant mooring; ask a lobsterman.

Winter Harbor Lobster Co-Op in the inner harbor has a dock and float with both gasoline and diesel fuel (207-963-5857). It may be possible to rent dock space with electricity here. The village is just a few blocks away from the landing.

Anchorage: There is plenty of deep water and anchorage room in 23 to 35 feet MLW with excellent holding in mud on either end of the Sand Cove mooring field in the outer harbor. Continuing past the mooring field to the end of the cove might reveal room to anchor off the pebble beach in 7 to 10 feet MLW, cutting out a good deal of the walk into town after beaching the dinghy.

Henry Cove, a straight shot in from the outer harbor, is the most exposed of the three coves but is relatively convenient to groceries and restaurants. Henry Cove offers in 17 to 22 feet MLW with excellent holding in mud but more exposure to the south.

Winter Harbor Yacht Club offers launch, showers and trash disposal service to anchored boats (for a fee).

■ EAST FROM SCHOODIC POINT

Beyond Mount Desert and Schoodic Point lies a green, lonesome land of ragged islands, rocky reaches, swift Bay of Fundy currents and ever-increasing tidal stages. An exciting, even dangerous coast, this is an area for the experienced captain or the wary neophyte, not the afternoon sailor in a small powerboat or low-powered auxiliary. The currents along this stretch of coast often create strong "whirlpool" eddies, which the prudent navigator should avoid, especially during peak ebb flow.

From Schoodic Point east, tidal range increases rapidly. Sixteen feet is normal for U.S. waters (easterly storms add a fathom) and in the Bay of Fundy, the tidal difference reaches 60 feet. Obviously, such tidal changes produce powerful currents of widely varying set. No graphs or sets of tables help much and current predictions are impossible.

For the last swath of Maine coast the best guidebook is experience and vigilance. You will need excellent planning and routing skills, practical navigational know-how, a thorough oceangoing knowledge of your boat and how she responds under all weather conditions and enough mechanical ability to make repairs as needed.

Between Winter Harbor and Eastport, more than 60 miles away, there are no lifts and few mechanics. All vessels should be equipped with a depth sounder, a VHF radio, GPS, radar and a stable dinghy. A cabin heater is often welcome to dry out during foggy spells and to warm up on chilly evenings. The best time for cruising extends from mid-July to late August, although some cruisers enjoy the clear, cool weather of early September.

Also, a few dozen islands and ports where gas and diesel fuel is available lie between Schoodic Point and the U.S./Canadian border (which bisects Quoddy Roads). These are working ports, not yachting centers but cruising folks are welcomed with a smile. Most Down East towns have no facilities other than small lobster boat docks so be prepared to make touch-and-go dockside stops, if any at all, and get out on a mooring or anchor for the night.

Few of these ports have fresh water in abundance; fewer still have dockside amenities but most offer mechanical services. In general, fuel ports lie well up the reaches so allow for a fairly lengthy in-shore run when fuel gets low. The exception is Eastport, which is described later in this section.

Despite such daunting observations, the ragged island outposts to the east bear silent witness to an increasing parade of recreational craft under sail and power each summer, as intrepid voyagers seek the solitude and pleasure of a near-wilderness experience.

Inshore or Offshore Route?

The 39-foot fixed vertical clearance Bridge Street (Beals Island) Bridge on Moosabec Reach usually dictates the choice between going offshore or running the coast. (The bridge was refurbished in 2021, increasing the width of the navigation opening while keeping the same vertical clearance.)

The cruiser who runs outside the islands and headlands and works the sea buoys has a comparatively easy but less interesting run than the vessel cruising the reaches and thoroughfares. The former faces the usual blue water sea and weather problems, while the latter follows stretches of coast where carpets of lobster buoys intermingle with small islands and ledges crowded with sunbathing seals. The route has hazards that make piloting a challenge even to the experienced cruising mariner, but the payoff of breathtaking scenery makes the adventure well worth the effort.

When Schoodic Head and the island disappear into the fog astern, some harbors of a different stripe lie ahead. As long as the wind is fair and seas are moderate, do not let fog interfere with your cruising plans. Fog is simply a fact of life here so having the proper tools to deal with it is essential.

Jonesport

This small fishing village of Jonesport has a state pier, launching ramp, ice and some provisions (at a small convenience store). Jonesport Pizza Shop (187 Main St., 207-497-2187) is the town's breakfast spot in addition to selling pizza, beer and some groceries. There is also a Post Office and a library.

NAVIGATION: If you can handle the 39-foot fixed vertical clearance **Bridge Street (Beals Island) Bridge**, sail through Moosabec Reach to Jonesport. Otherwise, you must use the eastern approach around Head Harbor Island. The tidal range at Jonesport is impressive as is the speed of ebb and flood currents.

Moorings: Jonesport Shipyard is located here with four breakwater-protected moorings. Their floating dinghy dock is available for those needing water. Note that depth at the dinghy dock at high tide is approximately 8 to 10 feet. The shipyard provides expert wood and fiberglass repair and restoration as well as DIY space. Do not try to dock at the Look Lobster Wharf.

Anchorage: East of Petit Manan on the way to Jonesport are many islands in Narraguagus Bay and Pleasant Bay that are highly regarded as secure anchorages. In Narraguagus Bay, anchor north of Trafton Island in 8 to 14 feet MLW with fair holding in soft mud and rock. This is exposed to the north. From here you can pass through deep Flint Island Narrows to an anchorage northeast of Flint Island, where you will find at least 22 feet MLW with good holding in sand and rock. This is exposed to the north.

If you need protection from the north, Eastern Harbor behind Moose Neck has at least 7 feet MLW and good holding in mud and rock. There are also good anchorages scattered throughout the islands of Western Bay. Just pick through the islands carefully and watch for ledges and uncharted rocks.

Eastern Bay

This island-studded Eastern Bay lies partly enclosed between Great Wass Island on the west side and Head Harbor Island and Steele Harbor Island on the east. In clear weather Eastern Bay is an intricate but generally well-buoyed puzzle. In fog it becomes a worrisome place when landmarks and navigational aids are obscured. Fortunately, a reliable foghorn is mounted on the lighthouse (flashing 30-second light at 72 feet in elevation) at what is known as Moose Peak, showing the way into the deep passage of Main Channel Way east of Mistake and Knight Islands.

Most of Great Wass Island is owned by the Nature Conservancy, which maintains hiking trails. Park your dinghy at a likely landing spot on the south side of Mud Hole (keeping in mind the 10-foot tidal range when tying off the painter) and scramble up the bank for about 50 yards to reach the unmistakable trail above.

In a 2-hour summer walk through the spruce forests, along the boreal bogs and out to the granite beaches you will undoubtedly observe dozens of types of mosses and lichens, a variety of mushrooms, bell flowers, beach irises and possibly unusual plants such as the baked-apple berry and dragon's mouth orchid. American eagles are frequent visitors as are numerous songbirds including the palm warbler, which nests here.

A short dinghy ride into the cut between Knight and Mistake Islands will bring you to an abandoned Coast Guard boathouse and ramp. A wooden boardwalk leads

Moosabec Reach, ME

JONESPORT		Largest Vessel	VHF	Total Slips	Approach/ Dockside Depth	Floating Docks	Gas/ Diesel	Repairs/ Haulout	Min/Max Amps	Pump-Out Station
1. Jonesport Shipyard	(207) 497-2701	45	9		6.0 / 6.0	F		RH		

WiFi Wireless Internet Access
Visit www.waterwayguide.com for current rates, fuel prices, website addresses and other up-to-the-minute information.
(Information in the table is provided by the facilities.)

Scan here for more details:

Source: Aqua Map and NOAA data

through the scrub and the abundant blueberry and raspberry bushes on the way to the lighthouse on Moose Peak. (Be ready for a piercing blast from the foghorn if light conditions weaken.) The lightkeeper's house is long gone but the scenery and views on a clear day make the trip well worth the effort.

> **CAUTION:** Do not attempt to enter the false channel between these two islands in a cruising vessel. While high tide gives the appearance of a channel here, a barely submerged rock ledge bars the way.

Anchorage: Having entered Main Channel Way, west of Steel Harbor Island, make a turn south around the northern end of Knight Island, which will lead to a well-protected anchorage between Mistake-Water Islands in 10 to 15 feet MLW. There is room for half a dozen boats here but be wary of kelp that can foul your anchor and of shoaling that occurs on the western side of Mistake Island.

Eastern Bay has numerous other anchorages, particularly along the east and north shores of Great Wass Island. The best of these in terms of beauty of

surroundings and hurricane hole protection is Mud Hole-Inner Harbor. This 1-mile-long cleft in the east side of Great Wass Island is northwest of the northern tip of Knight Island.

Entry and departure are most safely made on a rising tide (half tide or higher), skirting the south side of the harbor entrance to avoid a grass-covered shoal that blocks the north side. Reports are that the submerged remains of an old weir obstruct the area about 0.125 mile outside the entrance to the south (on entry). You will want to skirt that location before heading toward the south side of the harbor entry to work your way inside, where you will find depths of 16 feet MLW and excellent holding in mud.

In settled weather good anchorage can be made outside at Mud Hole Point in at least 14 feet MLW to permit exploration by dinghy.

Roque Island

Privately owned Roque Island has a large outer harbor with a deservedly famous beach. The entire island is posted as a wildlife stronghold and a sign prominently posted by the Roque Island Gardner Homestead Corp. denies access beyond the beach itself except to those with written permission from the island's owners. The owners request that you do not enter the southern half of the 1-mile-long beach, which is reserved for the Gardner family. Despite these restrictions, the area is worth a stop because of its extraordinary beauty. Bald eagles are almost inevitably sighted here and Seal Ledge on the eastern side of the harbor is still appropriately named.

Anchorage: Pick your spot at Roque Island according to wind. It is exposed from the south so expect some rollers. Secure anchorage is easy in sand or mud and located only a short ride from a dinghy landing on the beach.

Lakeman Harbor, formed by Marsh, Bar and Lakeman Islands at the southeastern end of Rogue Island, offers a protected inner harbor with secure holding in 7 to 8 feet MLW. Chandler Bay to the north in Roque Harbor has 10 to 15 feet MLW and excellent holding in hard sand.

On the northern side of Roque Island, Shorey Cove is protected from the prevailing southwesterlies and offers good holding in 7 to 11 feet MLW with pleasant views of the Gardner houses, barns and docks. Public use of the dock is prohibited. The rock "Rep" in the center of the channel west of Great Spruce Island is reportedly not to be found by either depth sounder or keel.

Cutler

Beyond Cross Island and northwest of Grand Manan Channel is Cutler, marked by the 56-foot Little River Island light and horn. Cutler is closer to open water than many of the villages along this coast, yet is a secure anchorage except in a piping nor'easter.

Cutler is the last good harbor on the Maine Coast before the Canadian border, making it a good point of departure for the Canadian Maritime Provinces and a gathering place for club cruises rallying for an international passage. The harbor is well protected, and even though you can see right out to the ocean on either side of Little River Island, very little surge enters.

This is a lovely, busy fishing village with well-maintained houses, fishing boats, and working piers. The scenery is picturesque, and the inhabitants are helpful and friendly. Cutler has little to offer in the way of amenities but there is WiFi available at the town library. Cutler is the home of the U.S. Navy's very low frequency (VLF) transmitter station, which provides one-way communication to U.S. strategic submarine forces.

NAVIGATION:

>>>>>>> ⚠️ >>>>>>>

CAUTION: The tidal range in Cutler is the greatest along the Downeast Coast, from plus 15.5 to minus 0.9 feet. Take this into consideration when putting out anchor rode and when approaching a floating dock/wharf.

Moorings/Anchorage: There are many moorings in Cutler but most are occupied. We have heard of cruisers picking up an empty mooring and calling the phone number on the mooring and getting permission to hook up. Most boats anchor in soft mud outside the mooring field in

Mermaid at Eastport, Moose Harbor

Friar Roads, ME

LUBEC		Largest Vessel	VHF	Total Slips	Approach/ Dockside Depth	Floating Docks	Gas/ Diesel	Repairs/ Haulout	Min/Max Amps	Pump-Out Station
1. Lubec Municipal Marina	(207) 733-8999		9	10	/	F	D	H	30 / 50	
EASTPORT										
2. Eastport Breakwater/City Dock	(207) 853-4614	180	16	50	40.0 / 8.0	F	GD	H		

WiFi Wireless Internet Access
Visit www.waterwayguide.com for current rates, fuel prices, website addresses and other up-to-the-minute information.
(Information in the table is provided by the facilities.)

Scan here for more details:

Cutler. Dragging anchor is commonplace in a blow. You can land a dinghy on the dark beach in front of the village's cluster of houses, although you should make provision for the 13-foot tides (influenced by the Bay of Fundy).

> NOTE: Downeast cruisers need to pay attention to the measurement unit for depths along this part of the coast. On certain charts, they are recorded in meters.

You can also make landing farther down the harbor at the float at the end of the Little River Lobster Co. dock (207- 259-7704). Just tie your dinghy to the dock and carefully climb the wooden ladder marked with a sign that says, "Pass at Your Own Risk."

Lubec Narrows

A day's sail east of Cutler will bring you to West Quoddy Head, the easternmost point of land in the United States. Around the corner from the barber-pole lighthouse, Lubec Channel leads to the town of Lubec and eventually to Eastport. Lubec is located on the narrows of the same name, separating Maine from Canada.

The town of Lubec is located beyond the fixed **FDR International Memorial Bridge** at the narrows (with a vertical clearance of 47 feet). If you are determined to

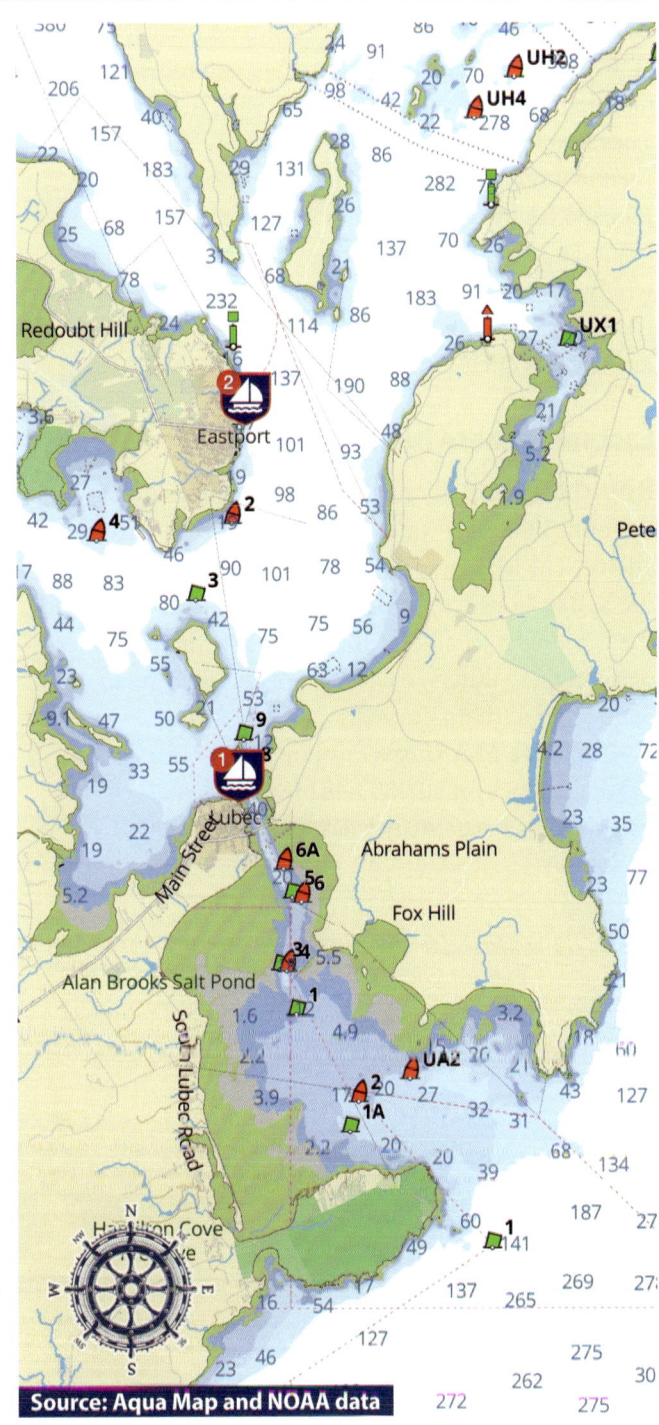

Source: Aqua Map and NOAA data

take this route, plan to reach the bridge at low slack water (which lasts 5 to 15 minutes) or at the early stage of the flood. Incoming currents become swift here (up to 6 knots) and the outgoing even more so (as swiftly as 8 knots).

The passage is quite narrow and long-tethered Coast Guard buoys might appear to be off-station at low water. (As a result, many locals advise in favor of the longer passage around East Quoddy Head on Campobello Island through Head Harbor Passage and Friar Roads.)

Mooring/Anchorage: There are two transient moorings available at Lubec Municipal Marina. They also have a floating dock for short-term tie-ups (maximum of 2 hours). Should you choose to anchor, Johnson Bay in Lubec has 9 foot MLW and good holding in mud and rock. This is open to the north so choose wisely. You can take an Uber from here to Campobello Island where the former home of Franklin and Eleanor Roosevelt is open to the public.

Eastport, Moose Island

NAVIGATION: Forty miles by highway from Lubec but only 3 miles by water, Eastport is a better layover choice. The large gray stone building just to the left of the harbor houses the Post Office on the upper level and the U.S. Customs office below. (This is by far the easiest place in these waters to check back into the United States after a trip to Canada.)

Dockage/Moorings: Eastport's Harbormaster (VHF Channel 16, 207-853-4614) assigns space at the Eastport Breakwater/City Dock and on moorings with

price breaks for week- and month-long stays. The ship store for Moose Island Marine is located immediately at the end of the short road leading from the breakwater to Water Street. An impressive array of parts and supplies is available and specialty items can be ordered quickly. Waco Diner (207-853-9226) has a pier with floats and offers transient dockage that is complimentary for stays of less than 24 hours.

■ NEXT STOP

At the Canadian border mariners may choose to continue north for superb cruising opportunities or retrace steps homeward. An adventuresome side trip before heading back south is to see firsthand the extraordinary riptides creating 6-foot dancing waters and dinghy-sized whirlpools in Passamaquoddy Bay and up the lower reaches of the St. Croix River. (As a bonus, this is along the international border so there is no need to check in and out of Canada.)

Finally, if you wish to hop over to Nova Scotia, the closest point is from Mt. Desert Island to Yarmouth, requiring about crossing approximately 100 nm of open water in the Gulf of Maine. However, apart from weather conditions, there is nothing to block a straight course across and the trip is long enough to even out the current so no timing is required. (Note that you will need to check in with the Canadian Customs authorities upon arrival.)

Whatever direction you choose, it's bound to be full of adventure and discovery.

Campobello Island, Canada

FDR International Memorial Bridge

Lubec Narrows

Lubec, ME

Marina/Sponsor Index

Sponsors are listed in **BOLD** and are highlighted in yellow in marina tables.

Sponsors are listed in **BOLD** and are highlighted in yellow in marina tables.

Sponsors are listed in **BOLD** and are <mark>highlighted in yellow</mark> in marina tables.

Sponsors are listed in **BOLD** and are <mark>highlighted in yellow</mark> in marina tables.

Sponsors are listed in **BOLD** and are <mark>highlighted in yellow</mark> in marina tables.

Subject Index

Most relevant pages are listed in **BOLD**

Most relevant pages are listed in **BOLD**

Goin' Ashore Index